UNIX POWER TOOLS

NUTSHELL HANDBOOKS

RANDOM HOUSE ELECTRONIC PUBLISHING

AN O'REILLY & ASSOCIATES/RANDOM HOUSE BOOK

UNIX POWER TOOLS®

Jerry Peek, Tim O'Reilly, Mike Loukides,
and other authors of the Nutshell Handbooks, including
Linda Mui, Dale Dougherty, Larry Wall, and Randal Schwartz, plus
Usenet contributors including Chris Torek, Jonathan Kamens,
Bruce Barnett, and Tom Christiansen

O'REILLY & ASSOCIATES, INC.

103A MORRIS STREET • SEBASTOPOL CA 95472

RANDOM HOUSE
ELECTRONIC PUBLISHING

New York

UNIX Power Tools®

by Jerry Peek, Tim O'Reilly, Mike Loukides, and other contributors
(See the Preface for a complete list of contributors.)

Published in the United States by O'Reilly & Associates, Inc., Sebastopol, CA, and Random House, Inc., New York, and simultaneously in Canada by Random House of Canada, Limited.

Manufactured in the United States of America

0 9 8 7 6 5 4 3

ISBN 0-679-79073-X

Editor: Tim O'Reilly

Printing History:

March 1993	First Edition.
May 1993	Minor corrections.
October 1993	Minor corrections.

O'Reilly & Associates, Inc.: Sebastopol   Cambridge   Bonn

Random House: New York   Toronto   London   Sydney   Auckland

Table of Contents

Part 1: Making Yourself at Home

Chapter 2: *Logging In*   **41**

Chapter 3: *Logging Out*   **59**

Chapter 19: Linking, Renaming, and Copying Files — 323

Chapter 20: Creating and Reading Archives — 343

Chapter 25: *Other Ways to Get Disk Space* 433

How to Use this Book

Article Number

The first two digits indicate what chapter the article is in, the last two digits indicate the number of the article within that chapter. The article number is used to refer to this article in all cross references throughout the book.

Dictionary-style Headers

As in a dictionary, we show you the entry that starts and ends each page, in case the article heading isn't visible. On a left-hand page, the number of the first article on that page (which may be continued from a previous page) is shown in the upper-left corner. On a right-hand page, the number of the last article on that page is shown in the upper-right corner.

Cross-reference in a Sentence

If you want to know more about the topic in blue type, read the article whose number appears between the parentheses immediately following the terms in blue.

Summary Box

You'll see summary boxes all through the book. They summarize a topic and point you to articles with examples and explanation.

Screw Icon

Be careful with this feature, or you might get screwed.

31.18 Setting vi Options Automatically for Individual Files

The *.exrc* file *(5.09)* can set *vi* options for all files—or for files in a certain directory *(31.06)*. The articles listed below show other ways to set your *vi* setup.

- A controversial feature because of security problems, modelines *(31.19)* are still handy if you use them carefully. They let you store setup commands for each file, in the file itself.

- Instead of modelines, you can make separate setup files for each file you want to edit. These don't have the security problems of modelines because you can make the setup files read-only. See article 31.21.

- Article 31.20 lets you choose any one of a number of setups by typing a setup-choosing command from the shell prompt. All *vi* commands you start afterwards will use that setup. You can start a new setup any time.

-JP

31.19 Modelines: Bug or Feature?

Some versions of *vi* and *ex* have a *modeline* or *modelines* option. When that option is set in your *.exrc* files *(5.09)*, you can store setup commands at the top or bottom of any file you edit. When you start the editor, it will read the setup commands and run them. This is a lot like having a separate *.exrc* for each file you edit.

> Modelines can be a security problem. If any troublemakers should edit your files and change your modelines, think about the difficulties they can cause you.
>
> Most newer version of *vi* disable modelines by default.

Here's a sample file—a shell script *(48.01)* with a modeline on the second line:

```
#! /bin/sh
# vi:set number wrapmargin=0 autoindent showmatch:

while read line
do
        . . .
```

The mode line has #, the shell's comment character, at the start of it—so, the shell will ignore the line but *vi* will still read it. This is only necessary in a shell script, but it demonstrates that the modeline need not start in column 1. The modeline itself consists of a space or tab, the string *vi:* or *ex:*, the commands to be executed, and a closing colon. The space or tab before the modeline and the closing colon are both important—they tell the editor where the modeline

---

Footer

The chapter title appears in the footer near the inside margin of the right-hand page, so you can always see the general topic of the chapter.

Bomb

If you see a bomb icon in the margin, read the article whose number is listed underneath it. That article gives an explanation of trouble you might have using the tip or script in the current article. (You can think of a bomb as a cross-referenced screw.)

Author's Initials

The author's full name is listed in the Preface.

CD-ROM

If you don't want to type this script into a file yourself, or if we're talking about a C program that isn't shown, you can install it from the CD-ROM that comes with this book. Give the install program the name listed under the icon. See article 54.05 for complete installation instructions.

Cross-reference in a Code Example

Cross-reference in Example Code: When a cross reference occurs in an example, the cross-referenced text and the article number appear in the margin.

10.18

long . . . I started a Bourne shell, which lets you pipe to the input of a loop (47.22). The shell prints secondary prompts (10.11) until you finish entering the loop:

```
% sh
$ find . -type f -mtime -1 -print |
> fmt -1000
> while read files
> do pr -n $files
> done | lpr
$ exit
%
```

read (10.20)

The shell put each line of filenames from *fmt -1000* into the files shell variable, ran *pr* with those filenames, and piped the output of all the *pr*s to the standard input of *lpr*. The *lpr* command didn't know that it was being fed by lots of *pr* commands—all it saw was a series of 66-line pages that the *pr*s output.

If you have *xargs* on your system, you can do the same thing this way:

```
% find . -type f -mtime -1 -print | xargs pr -n | lpr
```

(10.20)

xargs reads text from its standard input, collects a reasonable amount, then runs the command line pr -n `path/file path/file . . . .` Then *xargs* reads more text and runs *pr* again, over and over, until it's read all the text. The output of the *xargs* command (which is actually the output of all those *pr*s) is fed to a single *lpr* command.

Parting shot (by ML): there's really no excuse for *xargs* or any of these other tricks; they're just a patch for design error. UNIX should be able to handle arbitrarily long command lines; maybe in some future version, it will.

—*JP*

10.19 Handle Too-long Command Lines with xargs

xargs is one of those UNIX utilities that seems pretty useless when you first hear

---

35.03

testsed

testsed

The shell script *testsed* automates the process of saving the output of *sed* in a temporary file. It expects to find the script file, *sedscr*, in the current directory and applies these instructions to the input file names on the command line. The output is placed in a temporary file.

```
for x
do
        sed -f sedscr $x > tmp.$x
done
```

The name of a file must be specified on the command line. As a result, this shell script saves the output in a temporary file with the prefix *tmp.*. You can examine the temporary file to determine if your edits were made correctly. If you approve of the results, you could then use *mv* to overwrite the original file with the temporary.

You might also incorporate the *diff* command into the shell script. (Add the line diff $x tmp.$x after the sed command line.)

If you find that your script did not produce the results you expected, remember that the easiest "fix" is usually to perfect the editing script and run it again on the original input file. Don't write a new script to "undo" or improve upon changes made in the temporary file.

runsed

runsed

The shell script *runsed* was developed to make changes to an input file permanently. In other words, it is used in cases when you would want the input file and the output file to be the same. Like *testsed*, it creates a temporary file, but then it takes the next step: copying the file over the original.

```
temp=/tmp/runsed$$
for x
do
        echo "editing $x: \c"
        if test "$x" = sedscr; then
            echo "not editing sedscript!"
        elif test -s $x; then
            sed -f sedscr $x > $temp
            if test -s $temp; then
                if cmp -s $x $temp; then
                    echo "file not changed: /c"
                else
                    cp $temp $x
                fi
                echo "done"
            else
                echo "sed produced an empty file - check your sedscript."
            fi
        else
            echo "original file is empty."
        fi
done
```

\c 9.04
if 46.08
test 46.19

cmp 29.10

Preface

A Book for Browsing

Technical books can be boring. But this is not an ordinary technical book! This book is like an almanac, a news magazine, and a hypertext database rolled into one. Instead of trying to put the topics in perfect order—and expecting you to start at the beginning, then read through to the end—we hope that you'll browse. Start anywhere. Read what you want. (That's not quite true. First, you should read this Preface and the pages before it titled *How to Use this Book*. They will help you get the most out of your time with this book. Next, skim through the UNIX Fundamentals in Chapter 1. *Then* read what you want.)

Like an Almanac

The book is full of practical information. The main purpose isn't to teach you concepts (though they're in here). We've picked a lot of common problems and we'll show you how to solve them.

Even though it's not designed to be read in strict order, the book is organized into chapters with related subject matter. If you want to find a specific subject, the table of contents is still a good place to start. In addition, many of the chapters contain **shaded boxes**. These are like small tables of contents on a particular subject, which might be even more limited than the scope of the chapter itself. Use the **Index** when you're trying to find a specific piece of information instead of a general group of articles about a topic.

Like a News Magazine

This book has **short articles**. Most show a problem and a solution—in one page or less. The articles are numbered within each chapter.

Not all articles are "how-to" tips. Some articles have background information and concepts.

Like a Hypertext Database

Each article doesn't define all the concepts and words used. Instead, it gives you "links" that let you get more information *if you need it*. It's easy to get more information when you need it but skip the link if you don't. UNIX Power Tools® uses two kinds of links. For examples, see the pages before this Preface titled *How to Use this Book*.

Programs on the CD-ROM

someprog

The book describes scripts and freely available programs that are available on an accompanying CD-ROM disk. An article about a program or file that's on the CD-ROM will have a CD icon next to it, like this. To get one of these programs, use our *install* script *(54.05)*. And that cross reference (article 54.05) means that the install script is described in article 5 in Chapter 54.

About UNIX Versions

There are lots of similarities between different versions of UNIX. But it's almost impossible to write a book that covers every detail of every version correctly. Where we know there might be big differences or problems, we'll print a note in the text. Other places, we're forced to use "weasel words" like "Some versions of xxxxxx will do..." without telling you exactly *which* versions. When you see those weasel words, what can you do?

- If the command or feature won't destroy anything when it doesn't work, try it! For instance, don't experiment with *rm*, the command that removes files. But *cat*, a command that shows files, most likely won't hurt anything if some feature we tell you about doesn't work with your version.

- Look at the *online* manual *(52.01)* or check your *vendor's* latest printed manuals. Even these can be wrong. For instance, your system administrator may have installed a local version of a command that works differently—but not updated the online documentation. (The *which* *(52.07)* and *whereiz* *(5.10)* commands, along with some knowledge about the organization of your filesystem *(15.08)*, can help you find this out yourself.)

  Be careful with "generic" manuals, the kind you buy at a bookstore; there are a lot of versions of UNIX and the manual may not match your version too closely.

- Ask your system administrator or another "guru" for help before you use a command that might be dangerous.

Cross-References

If a cross-reference is to a single word, for example, a command name like this: *tar* *(20.05)*, the cross reference is probably to an article that introduces that command. Cross references to phrases, like this: writes the verbose information to its standard output *(20.08)* are to an article that explains more about the concept or problem highlighted in blue.

Cross references don't necessarily give a complete list of all articles about a topic. We've tried to pick one or a few articles that give the best information. For a more complete list, use the Index.

Typefaces and Other Conventions

Italic is used for the names of all UNIX utilities, switches, directories, and filenames and to emphasize new terms and concepts when they are first introduced. It's also used in programs and examples to explain what's happening or what's been left out at the . . . marks.

Bold is used occasionally within text to make words easy to find—just like movie stars' names in the People section of your local newspaper.

`Constant Width` is used for sample code fragments and examples. A reference in text to a word or item used in an example or code fragment is also shown in constant width font.

`Constant Bold` is used in examples to show commands or text that would be typed in literally by the user.

`Constant Italic`, **`Constant Bold Italic`** are used in code fragments and examples to show variables for which a context-specific substitution should be made. (The variable *`filename`*, for example, would be replaced by some actual filename.)

function(n) is a reference to a manual page in Section *n* of the UNIX programmer's manual. For example, *getopt*(3) refers to a page called *getopt* in Section 3.

% is the C shell prompt.

$ is the Bourne shell prompt.

:-) is a "smiley face" that means "don't take this seriously." The idea started on Usenet *(1.33)* and it spread *(53.12)*.

. . . stands for text (usually computer output) that's been omitted for clarity or to save space.

CTRL starts a control character. To create CTRL-d, for example, hold down the "control" key and press the "d" key. Control characters are not case sensitive; "d" refers to both the uppercase and lowercase letter. The notation ^D also means CTRL-d. Also, you'll sometimes see the key sequence in a box (for example, CTRL-d) when we want to make it clear exactly what you should type.

□ is used in some examples to represent a space character.

TAB is used in some examples to represent a TAB character.

The Authors

This book had three main authors: Jerry Peek, Tim O'Reilly, and Mike Loukides. But we had material from a host of contributors—either people who originally posted a good tip to Usenet, authors of Nutshell Handbooks who let us take material from their books, or authors of software packages who let us take a few paragraphs from README files or other documentation.

The author is identified by his or her initials at the end of the article. Here's a list of names that the initials correspond to:

AD	Angus Duggan
AF	AEleen Frisch
AN	Adrian Nye
BA	Brandon S. Allbery
BB	Bruce Barnett
BR	Bill Rosenblatt
CT	Chris Torek
DC	Debra Cameron
DD	Dale Dougherty
DG	Daniel Gilly
DH	Dave Hitz
DR	Daniel Romike
DS	Daniel Smith
EP	Eric Pearce
EK	Eileen Kramer
GS	Gene Spafford
HS	Henry Spencer
JIK	Jonathan I. Kamens
JM	Jeff Moskow
JP	Jerry Peek
JS	John Strang
LK	Lar Kaufman
LL	Linda Lamb
LM	Linda Mui
LW	Larry Wall
MAL	Maarten Litmaath
ML	Mike Loukides
MS	Mike Stansbery
RS	Randal Schwartz
SG	Simson Garfinkel
SW	Sun Wu
TC	Tom Christiansen
TM	Tony Mason
TOR	Tim O'Reilly
UM	Udi Manber

The Fine Print

Where we show an article from an author on Usenet, that person may not have thought of the idea originally, but may just be passing on something he or she learned. We attribute everything we can.

Request for Comments

Please tell us about any errors you find in this book or ways you think it could be improved. Our U.S. mail address, phone numbers, and electronic mail addresses are:

O'Reilly & Associates, Inc.
103 Morris Street, Suite A
Sebastopol, CA 95472
in U.S. and Canada 1-800-998-9938
international +1-707-829-0515
FAX 1-707-829-0104

Internet: *bookquestions@ora.com*   UUCP: *uunet!ora.com!bookquestions*

Acknowledgements

This book wouldn't exist without Ron Petrusha. As the technical book buyer at Golden-Lee, a major book distributor, he discovered us soon after we started publishing Nutshell Handbooks in the mid-80's. He was one of our early boosters, and we owed him one. So when he became an editor at Bantam, we took him seriously when he started asking if there was anything we could do together.

At first nothing seemed to fit, since by that time we were doing pretty well as a publisher. We needed to find something that we could do together that might sell better than something that either company might do alone. Eventually, Ron suggested that we co-publish a UNIX book for Bantam's "Power Tools" series. This made sense for both of us. It gave Bantam access to our UNIX expertise and reputation, and gave us a chance to learn from Bantam about the mass market bookstore trade, as well as build on their already-successful "Power Tools" series.

But what would the book contain? There were two features of Bantam's original *DOS Power Tools* that we decided to emulate: its in-depth treatment of under-documented system features, and its large collection of freely available scripts and utilities. However, we didn't want to write yet another book that duplicated the format of many others on the market, in which chapters on each of the major UNIX tools follow each other in predictable succession. Our goal was certainly to provide essential technical information on UNIX utilities, but more importantly, to show how the utilities can be combined and used to solve common (and uncommon) problems.

Similarly, because we were weary of the multitude of endlessly tutorial books about UNIX utilities, we wanted to keep the tone brisk and to the point. The solution I came up with, a kind of "hypertext in print," actually owes a lot to

Dale Dougherty. Dale has been working for several years on hypertext and online information delivery, and I was trying to get him to work with me on this project. So I tried to imagine the kind of book that he might like to create. (We have a kind of friendly rivalry, in which we try to leapfrog each other with ideas for new and better books!) Dale's involvement never went far beyond the early brainstorming stage, but the book still bears his indirect stamp. In some of the first books he wrote for me, he introduced the idea that sidebars—asides that illuminate and expand on the topic under discussion—could be used effectively in a technical book. Well, Dale, here's a book that's nothing but sidebars!

Dale, Mike Loukides, and I worked out the basic outline for the book in a week or two of brainstorming and mail exchanges. We thought we should be able to throw it together pretty quickly by mining many of our existing books for the tips and tricks buried in them. Unfortunately, none of us was ever able to find enough time, and the book looked to be dying a slow death. (Mike was the only one who got any writing done.) Steve Talbott rescued the project by insisting that it was just too good an idea to let go; he recruited Jerry Peek, who had just joined the company as a writer and UNIX consultant/tools developer for our production department.

Production lost the resulting tug of war, and Jerry plunged in. Jerry has forgotten more UNIX tips and tricks than Mike, Dale, or I ever knew; he fleshed out our outline and spent a solid year writing and collecting the bulk of the book. I sat back in amazement and delight as Jerry made my ideas take shape. Finally, though, Jerry had had enough. The book was just too big and he'd never signed on to do it all alone! (It was about 1000 pages at that point, and only half done.) Jerry, Mike and I spent a week locked up in our conference room, refining the outline, writing and cutting articles, and generally trying to make Jerry feel a little less like Sisyphus.

From that point on, Jerry continued to carry the ball, but not quite alone, with Mike and I playing "tag team," writing and editing to fill in gaps. I'm especially grateful to Mike for pitching in, since he had many other books to edit and this was supposed to be "my" project. I am continually amazed by the breadth of Mike's knowledge and his knack for putting important concepts in perspective.

Towards the end of the project, Linda Mui finished up another book she was working on and joined the project, documenting many of the freely available utilities that we'd planned to include but hadn't gotten around to writing up. Linda, you really saved us at the end!

Thanks also to all the other authors, who allowed us to use (and sometimes abuse!) their material. In particular, we're grateful to Bruce Barnett, who let us use so much of what he's written, even though we haven't yet published his book, and Chris Torek, who let us use many of the gems he's posted to the net over the years. (Chris didn't keep copies of most of these articles; they were saved and sent in by Usenet readers, including Dan Duval, Kurt J. Lidl, and Jarkko Hietaniemi.)

Jonathan Kamens and Tom Christiansen not only contributed articles but read parts of the book with learned and critical eyes. They saved us from many a "power goof." If we'd been able to give them enough time to read the whole thing, we wouldn't have to issue the standard disclaimer that any errors that remain are our own. H. Milton Peek provided technical review and proofreading of parts of the book. Four sharp-eyed Usenet readers helped with debugging: Casper Dik of the University of Amsterdam, Byron Ratzikis of Network Appliance Corporation, Dave Barr of the Population Research Institute, and Duncan Sinclair.

In addition to all the acknowledged contributors, there are many unacknowledged ones—people who have posted questions or answers to the net over the years, and who have helped to build the rich texture of the UNIX culture that we've tried to reflect in this book. Jerry also singles out one major contributor to his own mastery of UNIX. He says: "Daniel Romike of Tektronix, Inc. (who wrote articles 12.07 and 12.08 around ten years ago, by the way) led the first UNIX workshop I attended. He took the time to answer a ton of questions as I taught myself UNIX in the early 1980s. I'm sure some of the insights and neat tricks that I thought I've figured out myself actually came from Dan instead."

James Revell and Bryan Buus scoured "the net" for useful and interesting free software that we weren't aware of. Bryan also compiled most of the software he collected so we could try it out and gradually winnow down the list.

Thanks also to all of the authors of the software packages we wrote about and included on the disk! Without their efforts, we wouldn't have had anything to write about; without their generosity in making their software free in the first place, we wouldn't be able to distribute hundreds of megabytes of software for the price of a book.

Jeff Moskow of Ready-to-Run Software solved the problem we had been putting off to the end, of packaging up all the software for the disk, porting it to the major UNIX platforms, and making it easy to install. This was a much bigger job than we'd anticipated, and we could never have done it without Jeff and the RTR staff. We might have been able to distribute source code and binaries for a few platforms, but without their porting expertise, we could never have ported all these programs to every supported platform. Eric Pearce worked with RTR to pre-master the software for CD-ROM duplication, wrote the installation instructions, and made sure that everything came together at the end! (Eric, thanks for pitching in at the last minute. You were right that there were a lot of details that might fall through the cracks.)

Edie Freedman worked with us to design the format of the book—quite an achievement considering everything we wanted the format to do! She met the challenge of presenting thousands of inline cross-references without distracting the reader or creating a visual monstrosity. What she created is as attractive as it is useful—a real breakthrough in technical book design, and one that we plan to use again and again!

Lenny Muellner was given the frightful task of implementing all of our ideas in *troff*—no mean feat, and one that added to his store of grey hair.

Eileen Kramer was the copyeditor, proofreader, and critic who made sure that everything came together. For a thousand-plus page book with multiple authors, it's hard to imagine just how much work that was.

Ellie Cutler wrote the index; Chris Reilley created the illustrations.

Additional administrative support was provided by Bonnie Hyland, Donna Woonteiler, and Jane Appleyard.

—*Tim O'Reilly*

1

Introduction

1.01   *What's Special about UNIX?*

If we were writing about any other operating system, "power tools" might mean "nifty add-on utilities to extend the power of your operating system."

That sounds suspiciously like a definition of UNIX: an operating system loaded with nearly 20 years' worth of nifty add-on utilities.

UNIX is unique in that it wasn't designed as a commercial operating system meant to run application programs, but as a hacker's toolset, by and for programmers. In fact, an early release of the operating system went by the name PWB (Programmer's Work Bench).

When Ken Thompson and Dennis Ritchie first wrote UNIX at AT&T Bell Labs, it was for their own use, and for their friends and co-workers. Utility programs were added by various people as they had problems to solve. Because Bell Labs wasn't in the computer business, source code was given out to universities for a nominal fee. Brilliant researchers wrote their own software and added it to UNIX in a spree of creative anarchy that hasn't been equalled since, except perhaps in the recent introduction of the X Window System *(1.31)*.

Unlike most other operating systems, where free software remains an unsupported add-on, UNIX has taken as its own the work of thousands of independent programmers. During the commercialization of UNIX within the past ten years, this incorporation of outside software has slowed down, but not stopped entirely, especially in the university environment.

A book on UNIX Power Tools® therefore inevitably *has* to focus not just on add-on utilities (though we do include many of those) but on how to use clever features of the many utilities that have been made part of UNIX over the years.

It's also essential that this book teach you some of the underlying principles that make UNIX such a tinkerer's paradise.

In the body of this book, we assume that you are already moderately familiar with UNIX—a journeyman hacker wanting to become a master. But at the same time, we don't want to leave beginners entirely at sea, so in this chapter, we include some fundamental concepts. We've tried to intersperse some simple tips and tricks to keep things interesting, but the ratio of concept articles to tips is much higher than in any other part of the book. The concepts covered are also much more basic. If you aren't a beginner, you can safely skip this chapter, though we may bounce you back here if you don't understand something later in the book.

Don't expect a complete introduction to UNIX—if you need that, buy an introductory book. What you'll find here is a selection of key concepts that you'll need to understand to progress beyond the beginner stage, and answers to frequently asked questions and problems. In some ways, consider this introduction a teaser. If you are a beginner, we want to show you enough of UNIX to whet your appetite for more.

Also, don't expect everything to be in order. Because we don't want you to get in the habit of reading through each chapter from beginning to end, as in most books, the articles in this chapter are in loose order. We've tried not to make you jump around too much, but we've also avoided a lot of the transitional material that makes reading most books a chore.

—*TOR*

1.02 *Who Listens to What You Type?*

Probably the single most important concept for would-be power users to grasp is that you don't talk to UNIX directly. Instead, you talk to a program called the *shell*. The shell protects UNIX from the user (and the user from UNIX).

The UNIX operating system proper is referred to as the kernel *(1.14)*. Usually, only programs talk to the kernel (through system calls *(55.01)*). Users talk to the shell, which interprets their commands and either executes them directly or passes them on to other programs. These programs in turn request lower-level services from the kernel.

For example, when you type a command to display files whose four-character filenames start with the letter "m":

??? 1.16   % **cat m???**

it is the shell that finds the filenames, makes a complete list of them, and calls the *cat (26.02)* command to ask it to print the expanded list. The *cat* command calls on the kernel to find each file on the disk and print its contents as a stream of characters on the display.

Why is this important? First of all, you can choose between several different shells *(1.08)*, each of which may have different rules for interpreting command lines.

Second, the shell has to interpret the command line you type and package it up for the command you are calling. Because the shell reads the command line first, it's important to understand just how the shell changes what it reads.

For example, one basic rule is that the shell uses "white space" (spaces or tabs) to separate each "argument" of a command. But sometimes, you want the shell to interpret its arguments differently. For example, if you are calling *grep (28.01)*, a program for searching through files for a matching line of text, you might want to supply an entire phrase as a single argument. The shell lets you do this by quoting *(9.10)* arguments. For example:

```
% grep "UNIX Power Tools" articles/*
```

Understanding how the shell interprets the command line, and when to keep it from doing so, can be very important in a lot of special cases, especially when dealing with wildcards *(1.16)* like the * (asterisk) above. Article 9.03 explains more about how the shell interprets what you type.

You can think of the relationship of the kernel, the shell, and various UNIX utilities and applications as looking like Figure 1-1.

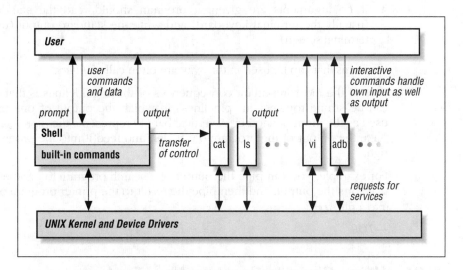

Figure 1-1. Relationship of Kernel, Shell, Utilities, and Applications

Note that there are some interactive commands that take input directly from the user, without intervention from the shell. The shell's only job is to start them up. A text editor, a mail program, or almost any application program (desktop publishing, spreadsheet) includes its own command interpreter with its own rules.

—TOR

1.03 Programs are Designed to Work Together

As pointed out by Kernighan and Pike in their classic book, *The UNIX Programming Environment*, there are a number of principles that distinguish the UNIX environment. One key concept is that programs are tools. And like all good tools, they should be specific in function, but usable for many different purposes.

In order for programs to become general-purpose tools, they must be data-independent. This means three things:

1. Within limits, the output of any program should be usable as the input to another.

2. All of the information needed by a program should either be contained in the data stream passed to it or specified on the command line. A program should not prompt for input or do unnecessary formatting of output. In most cases, this means that UNIX programs work with plain text files that don't contain "non-printable" or "control" characters.

3. If no arguments are given, a program should read the standard input (usually the terminal keyboard) and write the standard output (usually the terminal screen).

Programs that can be used in this way are often called *filters*.

One of the most important consequences of these guidelines is that programs can be strung together in "pipelines" in which the output of one program is used as the input of another. A vertical bar (|) represents the pipe *(1.04)*: it means "take the output of the program on the left and feed it into the program on the right."

For example, you can pipe the output of a search program to another program that sorts the output, and then pipe the result to the printer program or redirect it to a file *(14.01)*.

—*TOR*

1.04 Using Pipes to Create a New Tool

It's easy enough to imagine a trivial use of pipes *(1.03)*. For example, whenever the output of a command is longer than will fit on a single screen, you might want to pipe to a pager program such as *more (26.03)*, which shows the output a screenful at a time, and waits for you to press a key before it shows the next screen. If you were a writer like me, and wanted to check each "which" that you wrote to find out if any of them should have been "that," you might use the search program *grep (28.01)* and type:

[Ww] *27.04*

```
% grep '[Ww]hich' chapter1 | more
```

(Article 14.01 has more about pipes.) *more* lets you see the output a screenful at a time.

However, if you want to see how pipes can be really useful, you need to be a little more ambitious, or maybe just have a more specialized problem.

For example, the *troff (45.14)* formatting package (used in our office for typesetting some of our books) includes an indexing feature that allows the user to enter indexing commands of the following form:

```
.XX "topic, subtopic"
```

When the document is printed, the formatting package collects these entries, adds page numbers, and assembles the index. It is important that all entries be consistent. For example, if at one point the user makes the entry:

```
.XX "Indexing, introduction to"
```

and at another point:

```
.XX "Index, introduction to"
```

the program will generate two separate entries rather than merging them into one entry with two page references.

In order to check the consistency of index entries, one could enter the following command:

```
% cat files | grep .XX | sort -u | more
```

In this command, *files* is a list of the files to be checked. *grep* searches through that text for a specified string or pattern. *sort* −*u (37.06)* puts the lines selected by *grep* in alphabetical order and removes duplicate lines.

The pipeline is started with the *cat (26.02)* command, which simply types the contents of a file so that the input to the pipeline will be a single, continuous stream of text. (Otherwise *grep* will print the name of the file in which the string is found, which will keep the lines from being sorted correctly. In some versions of *grep*, the −*h* option can be used to suppress filenames. To see if this works on your UNIX system, type grep -h .XX files, omitting *cat* and the pipe.)

This is a very specific—and normally very tedious—job that needs to be done. And because UNIX provides general-purpose tools and an easy way of using them together in a kind of assembly line, you are provided a relatively simple way to get the job done.

But . . .

"Ugh!" you say, "That's just what I hate about UNIX. All these long filenames and options I can't remember. Who wants to type all that stuff!"

Precisely. That's why UNIX makes it so easy to create custom commands, in the form of aliases *(11.02)* and shell scripts *(1.05)*

—TOR

1.05 Anyone Can Program the Shell

One of the really wonderful things about the shell is that it doesn't just read and execute the commands you type at a prompt. The shell is a complete programming language.

The ease of shell programming is one of the real highlights of UNIX for novices. A shell program need be no more than a single complex command line saved in a file—or a series of commands.

For example, let's say that you occasionally need to convert a Macintosh Microsoft Word file for use on your UNIX system. Word lets you save the file in ASCII format. But there's a catch: the Macintosh uses a carriage return (ASCII character 015 *(53.03)*) to mark the end of each line, while UNIX uses a linefeed (ASCII 012). As a result, with UNIX, the file looks like one long paragraph, with no end in sight.

That's easy to fix: the UNIX *tr (36.09)* command can convert every occurrence of one character in a file to another:

```
% tr '\015' '\012' < file.mac > file.unix
```

But you're a novice, and you don't want to remember this particular piece of magic. Fine. Save the first part of this command line in a file called *mac2unix* in your personal *bin* directory *(5.02)*:

```
tr '\015' '\012'
```

Make the file executable with *chmod (23.07)*:

```
% chmod +x mac2unix
```

Now you can say:

```
% mac2unix < file.mac > file.unix
```

But say, why settle for that? What if you want to convert a bunch of files at once? Easy. The shell includes a general way of referring to arguments passed to a script, and a number of looping constructs. The script:

for *46.15*

$x *7.08*

```
for x
do
    echo "Converting $x"
    tr '\015' '\012' < "$x" > "tmp.$x"
    mv "tmp.$x" "$x"
done
```

will convert any number of files with one command, replacing each original with the converted version:

```
% mac2unix file1 file2 flle3 ...
```

As you become more familiar with UNIX, it quickly becomes apparent that doing just a little homework can save hours of tedium. This script incorporates only two simple programming constructs: the *for* loop and variable substitution *(7.08, 7.01)*. As a new user, with no programming experience, I learned these two constructs by example: I saved a skeleton *for* loop in a file and simply filled in the blanks with whatever commands I wanted to repeat.

Simple shell programs like this did more for my feeling that computers could automate my work than anything since my first introduction to word processing. It made real sense of the line, "Let the computer do the dirty work."

In short, UNIX is sometimes difficult because it is so rich and complex. The user who doesn't want to learn the complexity doesn't have to—the basic housekeeping commands are as simple as MS-DOS on the IBM PC. But the user who wants to take the time to investigate the possibilities can uncover a wealth of useful tools.

—TOR

1.06 *Power Tools for Editing*

My wife won't let me buy a power saw. She is afraid of an accident if I use one. So I rely on a hand saw for a variety of weekend projects like building shelves. However, if I made my living as a carpenter, I would have to use a power saw. The speed and efficiency provided by power tools would be essential to being productive.

For people who create and modify text files, *sed (35.24)* and *awk (38.18)* are power tools for editing. Most of the things that you can do with these programs can be done interactively with a text editor. However, using *sed* and *awk* can save many hours of repetitive work in achieving the same result.

sed and *awk* are peculiar and it takes time to learn them, but the capabilities they provide can repay the learning many times over, especially if text editing is a normal part of your trade.

Both of these programs let you write editing scripts to do many of the things that you might otherwise do laboriously with repeated commands in an editor like *vi (31.02)*.

Even more important, they let you do edits on data that is streaming through UNIX pipes *(45.23, 19.10, 18.17)*—data that may never be written back into a file.

However, the primary motivation for learning *sed* and *awk* is that they are useful for devising general solutions to text editing problems. For some people, myself included, the satisfaction of solving a problem is the difference between work and drudgery. Given the choice of using *vi* or *sed* to make a series of repeated edits over a number of files, I will choose *sed,* simply because it makes the problem more interesting to me. I am refining a solution instead of repeating a series of keystrokes. Besides, once I accomplish my task, I congratulate myself on being clever. I feel like I have done a little bit of magic and spared myself some dull labor.

Initially, using *sed* and *awk* will seem like the long way to accomplish a task. After several attempts you may conclude that the task would have been easier to do manually. Be patient. You not only have to learn how to use *sed* and *awk* but you also need to learn to recognize situations where using them pays off. As you become more proficient, you will not only solve problems more quickly, you will solve a broader range of problems.

—*DD* from the Nutshell Handbook *sed & awk*

1.07 *Power Grows on You*

It has been said that UNIX is not an operating system as much as it is a way of thinking. In *The UNIX Programming Environment*, Kernighan and Pike write that at the heart of the UNIX philosophy "is the idea that the power of a system comes more from the relationships among programs than from the programs themselves."

Almost all of the utility programs that run under UNIX share the same user interface—a minimal interface to be sure—but one that allows them to be strung together in pipelines to do jobs that no single program could do alone.

There are many operating systems with features UNIX can't match—better performance, better documentation, more ease of use. But none of them are so powerful or so exciting to use once you get the hang of pipes and filters, and the programming power of the shell.

A new user starts by stringing together simple pipelines and, when they get long enough, saving them into a file *(1.05)* for later execution. Gradually, if he has the right temperament, the user gets the idea that the computer can do more of the boring part of many jobs. Perhaps he starts out with a *for* loop *(10.10)* to apply the same editing script to a series of files. Conditions and cases soon follow and before long, he finds himself programming.

On most systems, you need to learn consciously how to program. You must take up the study of one or more programming languages and spend a fair amount of concentrated effort before you can do anything productive. UNIX, on the other hand, teaches programming imperceptibly—it is a slow but steady extension of the work you do simply in interacting with the computer.

Before long, you can step outside the bounds of the tools that have already been provided by the designers of the system, and solve problems that don't quite fit the mold. This is sometimes called hacking; in other contexts, it is called "engineering." In essence, it is the ability to build a tool when the right one is not already on hand.

Dale Dougherty compares UNIX to the Volkswagen beetle, that unique automobile of the '60s and '70s. Its simple design was in part what made it popular; the "bug" was hand-maintainable. VW owners (users) could tinker with their cars, performing such tasks as changing spark plugs by hand. They scoffed at owners of other cars who depended upon auto mechanics. It is perhaps this same feeling of independence (let me do it myself) that the UNIX environment fosters in its users. There are many other, quite capable software environments that are packaged to keep users out, like a television set.

In some ways, the secret of UNIX is that its working parts are visible. The UNIX environment, like the VW beetle, is designed so that users can take it apart and put it back together. UNIX provides general-purpose tools, all of which are designed to work together.

No single program, however well thought out, will solve every problem. There is always a special case, a special need, a situation that runs counter to the expected. But UNIX is not a single program. It is a collection of hundreds of them, and with these basic tools, a clever or dedicated person can meet just about any computing problem.

Like the fruits of any advanced system, these capabilities don't fall unbidden into the hands of new users. But they are there for the reaching. And over time, even those users who want a system they don't have to think about will gradually reach out for these capabilities. Faced with a choice between an hour spent on a boring, repetitive task and an hour putting together a tool that will do the task in a flash, most of us will choose the latter.

—TOR

1.08 *There are Many Shells*

With most operating systems, the command intepreter is built in; it is an integral part of the operating system. With UNIX, your command interpreter is just another program. Traditionally, a command interpreter is called a "shell," perhaps because it protects you from the underlying kernel—or because it protects the kernel from you!

Several different shells are available: you are free to choose the one that best suits your interests or your application. The most common ones are:

sh   The Bourne shell (named after its creator, Steve Bourne). This is the oldest of the current UNIX shells and is available on all UNIX systems. It is a bit primitive and lacks job control features (the ability to move jobs from the foreground to the background). Most UNIX users consider the Bourne shell superior for shell programming or writing command files.

csh   The C shell. It was developed at Berkeley as part of their UNIX implementation and has been by far the most popular shell for interactive use. You will occasionally find a System V UNIX where the C shell isn't available, but this is very rare. It has a lot of nice features that aren't available in the Bourne shell, including job control *(13.08)* and history *(12.02)* (the ability to repeat commands that you have already given). However, while you won't have trouble with normal usage, it isn't hard for a shell programmer to push the C shell to its limits *(49.02)*. There are a lot of hidden bugs.

jsh   A new version of the Bourne shell that adds job control. You will only see this with UNIX System V Release 4.

ksh The Korn shell (also named after its creator, David Korn). The Korn shell is compatible with the Bourne shell, but has most of the C shell's features plus some completely new features, like history editing *(12.14):* the ability to recall old commands and edit them before executing them. It is also more reliable than *csh*. The Korn shell is a standard part of UNIX System V Release 4; it has also been included in some other UNIX implementions.

bash

bash The "Bourne-again" shell developed by the Free Software Foundation *(55.01).* This shell is not a standard part of any UNIX system, but you can get it from the Power Tools disk. *bash* is fairly similar to the Korn shell. It has all of the C shell's features, plus history editing and a built-in help command.

tcsh

You may run into some extended versions of the C shell like *tcsh*. There are also a few third-party shells that serve special purposes, like emulating the VAX/VMS command language (DCL). I don't know if there is a DOS-lookalike shell available, but there probably is. Why you would want it is another question: all of the standard UNIX shells do a lot more than the DOS command interpreter. Furthermore, I like to discourage UNIX users from pretending that UNIX is something else. You are going to be spending a lot of time using UNIX: you will be better off learning it properly than trying to make it look like some other operating system.

In this book, we'll stick to the C shell for interactive use and the Bourne shell for shell programming. Once you are thoroughly grounded in *csh* and *sh*, you should have no trouble picking up *ksh* and *bash*.

—*ML*

1.09 Which Shell am I Running?

You can usually tell which shell you are running by the prompt it displays. The Bourne shell usually uses $ as a prompt. The C shell uses %.

It's possible to customize the prompt *(8.01)* so that it displays additional information, but most users and system administrators will keep the convention of ending the prompt with the original prompt character.

To be certain, type one of these commands (the second is for systems that use NIS, Sun's Network Information Service, to manage network-wide files):

```
% grep yourloginname /etc/passwd
% ypcat passwd | grep yourloginname
```

You should get back the contents of your entry in the system password file.*
For example:

```
tim::23:10:Tim O'Reilly:/usr/tim:/bin/csh
```

---

*That may match more than one entry. Searching for *tim* could also find a user named *timothy* or *fatima*. A more accurate regular expression *(27.01)* is `'^yourloginname:'`.

The fields are separated by colons. The last field should show the shell you are using. */bin/csh* (or */usr/bin/csh*) is the C shell, */bin/sh* is the Bourne shell (or Korn shell), and so forth. An empty last field defaults to the Bourne shell.

In case you're interested in the rest of the line, the first field shows your login name. The second stores your encrypted password, if any; this may be kept in a separate "shadow password" file. The third and fourth fields show your user ID or UID *(40.03)* and group ID or GID *(40.03)*, respectively. The fifth field often contains information about you, and the sixth your home directory.

—TOR

1.10 Internal and External Commands

Some commands that you type are *internal, built into* the shell. For example, the *cd* command is built-in. That is, the shell interprets that command and changes your current directory *(1.21)* for you. The *ls* command, on the other hand, is an *external* program stored in the file */bin/ls*.

The shell doesn't start a separate process to run internal commands. External commands require the shell to *fork* and *exec (1.11)* a new subprocess *(40.03)*; this takes some time, especially on a busy system. (Article 8.04 shows an example where extra speed can be important.)

When you type the name of a command, the shell first checks to see if it is a built-in command and, if so, executes it. If the command name is an absolute pathname *(1.21)* beginning with /, like */bin/ls*, there is no problem: the command is likewise executed. If the command is neither built-in, nor specified with an absolute pathname, the shell looks in its search path *(9.05)* for an executable program or script with the given name.

The search path is exactly what its name implies: a list of directories that the shell should look through for a command whose name matches what is typed.

The search path isn't built into the shell; it's something you specify in your shell setup files *(2.02)*.

By tradition *(22.04)*, UNIX system programs are kept in directories called */bin* and */usr/bin*, with additional programs usually used only by system administrators in */etc* and */usr/etc*. Many versions of UNIX also have programs stored in */usr/ucb* (named after the University of California at Berkeley, where many UNIX programs were written). There may be other directories containing programs. For example, the programs that make up the X Window System *(1.31)* are stored in */usr/bin/X11*. Users or sites often also have their own directories where custom commands and scripts are kept, such as */usr/local/bin*.

The search path is stored in an environment variable *(7.01)* called *PATH (7.04)*. A typical *PATH* setting might look something like this:

```
PATH=/bin:/usr/bin:/usr/bin/X11:/usr/ucb:/home/tim/bin:
```

The path is searched in order, so if there are two commands with the same name, the one that is found first in the path will be executed.

You can add new directories to your search path *(9.05)* on the fly, but the path is usually set in shell setup files.

—TOR

1.11 How the Shell Executes Other Commands

When the shell executes an external command *(1.10)*, what happens?

UNIX programs are executed through a combination of two system calls (low-level requests to the operating system) called *fork* and *exec*.

The *exec* system call tells the kernel to execute another program. However, the kernel replaces the calling program with the new one being called. This doesn't work too well if you want to return to the original program after the second one has done its job.

To get around this problem, programs that want to stick around first copy themselves with the *fork* system call. Then the copied program *exec*s the new program, terminating itself in the process.

You don't really need to know this little tidbit about what goes on behind the scenes, but it sure helps to know about *fork* and *exec* when reading some UNIX manuals. Article 40.02 has more information.

—TOR

1.12 What Makes a Shell Script?

A shell script is just an ASCII file *(55.01)* containing a saved sequence of commands.

If you were to store a list of commands in a file for one-time use, you could execute it by typing:

```
% sh mycommands
```

where *mycommands* is the name of the file containing the list of commands. This would tell the shell to treat the file as a list of commands to be executed.

But there's a better way to tell the shell to execute the contents of a file, and that is to make the file executable with the *chmod (23.07)* command:

```
% chmod +x mycommands
```

Then, all you have to do to execute the script is type its name. (To make it even easier to use, you should store it in a personal *bin* directory and add it to your search path *(9.05)*.)

Of course, in either case, all of the lines in the file need to be meaningful to the shell! If you accidentally made a letter to your mother executable, and tried to run it as a shell script, you'd get error messages like this, containing the first word of each line in the letter:

```
letter: Dear: not found
```

The shell would try to interpret that word as a command, and report back that it doesn't know any command by that name.

Also, to really make good use of shell scripts, you need to understand how to pass arguments to a script *(46.14)* and how to use some simple programming constructs *(1.05)*.

—TOR

1.13 Why Fundamentals are Important

Yes, we know. Fundamentals, principles, and all of that is boring. You bought a book called *UNIX Power Tools* and expected to read about all sorts of clever tricks. You didn't want the book to start with a bunch of lectures.

Well, this book contains plenty of tricks. We promise. But there's something else you ought to know. For UNIX, the biggest difference between a power user and a duffer is that a power user knows what he's doing and why he's doing it. The duffer may know as many commands and have his own army of tricks—but he won't know when to use them, or why he's using them. Many of the tricks aren't really tricks at all: they're really fairly obvious solutions to common problems, once you've learned how to think about the problem correctly. Our goal is to help you to become "creative" about UNIX: to get you to the point where you can analyze your own problems and come up with your own solution for them. A grab-bag is really no good unless you know how to give yourself your own presents.

—ML

1.14 The Kernel and Daemons

If you have arrived at UNIX via DOS or some other personal computer operating system, you will notice some big differences. UNIX is, was, and always will be a multi-user operating system. It is a multi-user operating system even when you're the only person using it. It is a multi-user operating system even when it is running on a PC with a single keyboard. And this fact has important ramifications for everything that you do.

Why does this make a difference? Well, for one thing, you're never the only one using the system, even when you think you are. Don't bother to look under your desk to see if there's an extra terminal hidden down there. There isn't. But UNIX is always doing things "behind your back," running programs of its own, whether or not you are aware of it. The most important of these programs, the *kernel*, is the heart of the UNIX operating system itself. The kernel assigns memory to each of the programs that are running, partitions time fairly so that each program can get its job done, handles all I/O (input/output) operations, and so on. Another important group of programs, called *daemons*, are the system's "helpers." They run from time to time performing small but important tasks like handing mail, running network communications, feeding data to your printer, keeping track of the time, and so on.

You can use UNIX for a long time without being aware of the kernel or any of the daemons. If you suddenly see a "panic" message on your terminal and your system stops in its tracks (crashes), you've just had a run-in with the kernel. Something has gotten the kernel confused, and it has decided to give up rather than risk doing something foolish. And there's not much you can do to remedy a panic; the problem usually isn't your fault. But you should know where they're coming from. Similarly, daemons may occasionally bombard you with messages. And when you give the *ps* command (see below), there may be some names that you don't recognize. These are probably the names of daemons that happen to be doing something benevolent at the moment. Right now, we won't worry about them. But you should know that they are there.

Not only are you sharing the computer with the kernel and some mysterious daemons, you're also sharing it with yourself. I am currently using a Sun 3 workstation. If I give the command *ps* (40.05), which lists all the programs I am running, I get the report below:

```
PID TT STAT   TIME COMMAND
1449 co IW    0:01 sunview
1453 co S     0:27 clock -Wp 497 32 -WP 704 0 -Wi -Wh 1
1451 p0 IW    0:04 shelltool
1452 p0 IW    0:00 -bin/csh (csh)
1454 p1 R     2:52 shelltool
1455 p1 S     0:01 -bin/csh (csh)
2217 p1 R     0:00 ps
1504 p2 S     1:54 shelltool
1505 p2 IW    0:01 -bin/csh (csh)
1884 p2 S     1:32 emacs princip3.otl
```

I may think that I'm only running the editor Emacs, but the computer is actually doing a lot more for me. I'm also running *sunview*, which keeps track of Sun's display, and I'm running a program that displays a little clock in one corner of my screen. I'm running several "command tools," which are windows (or areas of the screen) that act like separate terminals. Each command tool has a *shell* (*csh*), which is a command interpreter that deciphers everything I type at the keyboard. And I'm running the *ps* command. And, waiting patiently somewhere, my lonely Emacs editor is waiting for me to type some more.

If you are running the X window system or if you're using some 386-based computer with the System V *layers* facility, you will see something different. But we guarantee that you're running at least two programs, and quite likely many more. If you want to see everything that's running, including the daemons, type the command ps -aux (for BSD) or ps -el (for 386/IX or XENIX). You'll be impressed.

Because there is so much going on at once, you have to get used to a different way of thinking about UNIX. The UNIX kernel is a traffic cop that mediates different demands for time, for memory, for disks, and so on. Not only does the kernel need to run your programs, but it also needs to run the daemons, any programs that other users might want to start, or any programs that you may have scheduled to run automatically *(42.01)*. When it runs a program, the kernel allocates a small slice of time—up to a second—and lets the program run until that slice is used up, or the program decides to take a rest of its own accord (this is called "sleeping"). At this point, whether or not the program is finished, the kernel finds some other program to run. The UNIX kernel never takes a vacation. It is always watching over the system.

Once you understand that the kernel is a manager that schedules many different kinds of activity, you understand a lot about how UNIX works. For example, if you have used any computer system previously, you know that it's a bad idea to turn the computer off while it is writing something on the disk. You will probably destroy the disk, and could conceivably damage the disk drive. The same is true for UNIX—but with an important complication. Any of the programs that are running can start doing something to the disk at any time. One of the daemons makes a point of accessing the disk drive every 30 seconds or so, just to stay in touch. Therefore, you can't just turn a UNIX computer off. You might do all sorts of damage to the system's files—and not just your own, but conceivably files belonging to many other users. To turn a UNIX system off, you must first run a program called *shutdown*, which kicks everyone off the system and makes sure that a daemon won't try to play with a disk drive when you aren't looking. Then you run a program named *sync*, which makes sure that the disks have finished doing everything. Only then is it safe to pull the switch. When you start up a UNIX system, it automatically runs a program called *fsck*, which stands for "filesystem check"—its job is to find out if you shut down the system correctly and fix any damage that might have happened if you didn't.

In this book, we will avoid administrative issues like *shutdown*, *sync*, and *fsck*. But they provide good examples of how UNIX differs from simpler operating systems. If you understand why these programs are needed, you are on your way to becoming a power user.

—*ML*

1.15 Filenames

Like all operating systems, UNIX files have names: words (sequences of characters, whatever) that let you identify a file. Older versions of UNIX had some restrictions on the length of a filename (14 characters), but modern versions have removed these restrictions for all practical purposes. Sooner or later you will run into a limit, but if so, you are probably being unnecessarily verbose.

Technically, a filename can be made from almost any group of characters (including non-printing characters) except a slash (/). However, you should avoid filenames containing most punctuation marks and all non-printing characters. These will usually be a pain. To be safe, limit your filenames to the following characters:

- **Uppercase and lowercase characters**. UNIX is *always* case-sensitive. That is, uppercase and lowercase letters are always different (unlike DOS and

VAX/VMS, which consider uppercase and lowercase letters the same). Therefore, *myfile* and *Myfile* are different files. It is usually a bad idea to have files whose names differ only in their capitalization, but that's your decision.

- **Underscores (_).** Underscores are handy for separating "words" in a filename to make them more readable. For example, *my_long_filename* is easier to read than *mylongfilename*.

- **Periods (.).** Periods are used by some programs (such as the C compiler) to separate filenames from filename extensions *(1.17)*. Extensions are used by these programs to recognize the type of file to be processed, but they are not treated specially by the shell, the kernel, or other UNIX programs.

  Filenames that begin with a period are treated specially by the shell: wildcards won't match *(1.16)* them unless you include the period (like .*). The *ls* command, which lists your files, ignores files whose names begin with a period unless you give it a special option (*ls* -*a (17.12)*). Special configuration files are often "hidden" in directories by beginning their names with a period.

- **Certain other punctuation.** About the only other punctuation mark that is always safe is the comma (,)—although it isn't part of the POSIX-portable character set. The other punctuation marks may have special meanings in one situation or another. Stay away from them, or you will create filenames that are inconvenient to work with.

I'm so dead-set against using weird, non-printing characters in filenames that I won't even tell you how to do it. I will give you some special techniques for deleting files with weird names *(24.10)*, in case you create some by accident.

Some things to be aware of:

- UNIX does not have any concept of a file *version*. There are some revision control programs *(21.12)* that implement their own notion of a version, but there is nothing analogous to VAX/VMS's version number. If you are editing a file, don't count on UNIX to save your previous versions—you can make scripts to do this *(46.11)* though, if you want to; the GNU Emacs editor also makes backups *(33.04)*

- Once you delete a file in UNIX, it is gone forever *(24.02)*. You can't get it back without restoring it from a tape. Be careful when you delete files. Later, we'll show you programs *(24.07, 24.08)* that will give you a "grace period" between the time you delete a file and the time it actually disappears.

Article 5.06 has more tips for naming files.

—*ML*

1.16 Wildcards

The shells provide a number of *wildcards* that you can use to abbreviate filenames or refer to groups of files. For example, let's say you want to delete all filenames in the current directory *(1.21)* ending in *.txt*. You could delete these files one by one, but that would be boring if there were only five and *very* boring if there were a hundred. Instead, you can use a wildcarded name to say "I want all files whose names end with *.txt*, regardless of what the first part is." The wildcard is the "regardless" part. Like a wildcard in a poker game, a wildcard in a filename can have any value.

The wildcard you see most often is * (asterisk), but we'll start with something simpler: ? (question mark). When it appears in a filename, the ? matches any single character. For example, letter? refers to any filename that begins with *letter* and has one character after that. This would include *letterA*, *letter1*, as well as filenames with a non-printing character as their last letter, like *letter^C*.

The * wildcard matches any character or group of zero or more characters. For example, *.txt matches all files whose names end with *.txt*, *.c matches all files whose names end with *.c* (by convention, source code for programs in the C language), and so on.

The * and ? wildcards are sufficient for 90 percent of the situations that you will find. However, there are some situations that they can't handle. For example, you may want to list files whose names end with *.txt*, *mail*, or *let*. There's no way to do this with a single *; it won't let you exclude the files you don't want. In this situation, use a separate * with each filename ending:

    *.txt *mail *let

Sometimes you need to match a particular group of characters. For example, you may want to list all filenames that begin with digits, or all filenames that begin with uppercase letters. Let's assume that you want to work with the files program.*n*, where *n* is a single-digit number. Use the filename:

    program.[0123456789]

In other words, the wildcard [*character-list*] matches any single character that appears in the list. The character list can be any group of ASCII characters; however, if they are consecutive (e.g., A-Z, a-z, 0-9, or 3-5, for that matter), you can use a hyphen as shorthand for the range. For example, [a-zA-Z] means any alphabetic character.

There is one exception to these wildcarding rules. Wildcards never match /, which is both the name of the filesystem root *(1.19)* and the character used to separate directory names in a path *(1.21)*.

If you are new to computers, you probably will catch on to UNIX wildcarding quickly. If you have used any other computer system, you have to watch out for one very important detail. Virtually all computer systems except for UNIX consider a period (.) a special character within a filename. Many operating systems even require a filename to have a period in it. With these operating systems, a * does not match a period; you have to say *.*. Therefore, the equivalent of rm * does virtually nothing on most operating systems. Under UNIX, it is very dangerous: it means "delete all the files in the current directory, regardless of their name." You only want to give this command when you really mean it.

But here's the exception to the exception. The shells and the *ls* command consider a . special if it is the first character of a filename. This is often used to hide initialization files and other files that you aren't normally concerned with; the *ls* command doesn't show these files unless you ask *(17.12)* for them. If a file's name begins with ., you always have to type the . explicitly. For example, .*rc matches all files whose names begin with . and end with *rc*. This is a common convention for the names of UNIX initialization files.

Table 1-1 has a summary of the different sorts of wildcards available.

Table 1-1. Shell Wildcards

Wildcard	Matches
?	Any single character.
*	Any group of zero or more characters.
[ab]	Either a or b.
[a-z]	Any character between a and z, inclusive.

Wildcards can be used at any point or points within a path. Remember, wildcards only match names that already exist. You can't use them to create new files *(10.04)*—though some shells have curly braces ({ }) *(10.05, 16.03)* for doing that. Article 1.18 has more about how wildcards are handled.

—ML

1.17 *Filename Extensions*

In DOS and some other file systems, filenames often have the form *name.extension*. For example, Lotus 1-2-3 files have extensions such as *.wk1*. The operating system treats the extension as separate from the filename and has rules about how long it must be, and so forth.

UNIX doesn't have any special rules about extensions. The dot has no special meaning as a separator, and extensions can be any length. However, a number of programs (especially compilers *(54.08)*) do make use of one-character extensions to recognize some of the different types of files they work with. In addition, there are a number of conventions that users have sometimes adopted to make clear the contents of their files. (For example, you might name a text file containing some design notes *notes.txt*.)

Table 1-2 lists some of the extensions you might see to filenames, and a brief description of the programs that recognize them.

Table 1-2. Filename Extensions that Programs Expect

Extension	Description
.a	Archive file (library)
.c	C program source file
.h	C program header file
.f	FORTRAN program source file
.F	FORTRAN program source file to preprocess
.o	Object file (compiled and assembled code)
.s	Assembly language code
.z	Packed file
.Z	Compressed file *(25.06)*
.1 to .8	Online manual source file

In Table 1-3 are some extensions that are often used by users to signal the contents of a file, but that are not actually recognized by the programs themselves.

Table 1-3. Filename Extensions for User's Benefit

Extension	Description
.txt	ASCII text file
.tar	*tar* archive *(20.05)*
.shar	Shell archive *(20.02)*
.sh	Bourne shell script *(1.05)*
.csh	C shell script *(49.02)*
.mm	Text file containing *troff*'s *mm* macros *(45.15)*
.ms	Text file containing *troff*'s *ms* macros *(45.15)*
.ps	PostScript source file

—ML, TOR

1.18 Who Handles Wildcards?

Wildcards *(1.16)* are actually defined by the UNIX shells, rather than the UNIX filesystem. In theory, a new shell could define new wildcards, and consequently, we should discuss wildcarding when we discuss the shell. In practice, all UNIX shells (including *ksh, bash,* and other variants *(1.08)*) honor the same wildcard conventions, and we don't expect to see anyone change the rules. (However, different shells do different things when a wildcard doesn't match *(16.05)*.)

You may see different wildcarding if you buy a special-purpose shell that emulates another operating system (for example, a shell that looks like DEC's DCL)—in this case, your shell will obey the other operating system's wildcard rules. But even in this case, operating system designers stick to a reasonably similar set of wildcard rules.

The fact that the shell defines wildcards, rather than the filesystem itself or the program you're running, has some important implications for a few commands. Most of the time, a program never sees wildcards. For example, typing:

```
% lpr *
```

is exactly the same as typing:

```
% lpr file1 file2 file3 file4 file5
```

In this case everything works as expected. But there are other situations in which wildcards don't work at all. Assume you want to read some files from a tape, which requires the command *tar x (21.04)*, so you type the command `tar x *.txt`. Will you be happy or disappointed?

You'll be disappointed—unless older versions of the files you want are already in your current directory *(1.21)*. The shell expands the wildcard `*.txt`, according to what's in the current directory, *before it hands the completed command line over to tar for execution.* All *tar* gets is a list of files. But you're probably not interested in the current directory; you probably want the wildcard `*` to be expanded on the tape, retrieving any `*.txt` files that the tape has.

There's a way to pass wildcards to programs, without having them interpreted by the shell. Simply put `*.txt` in quotes *(9.10)*. The quotes prevent the UNIX shell from expanding the wildcard, passing it to the command unchanged. Programs that can be used in this way (like *uucp* and *rcp (1.33)*) know how to handle wildcards, obeying the same rules as the shell (in fact, these programs usually start a shell to interpret their arguments). You only need to make sure that the programs see the wildcards, that they aren't stripped by the shell before it passes the command line to the program. As a more general rule, you should be aware of when and why a wildcard gets expanded, and you should know how to make sure that wildcards are expanded at an appropriate time.

Note: If your shell understands the { } characters *(10.05)*, you can use them because they can generate any string—not just filenames that already exist. You have to type the unique part of each name, but you only have to type the common part once. For example, to extract the files called

---

project/wk9/summary, project/wk14/summary, and *project/wk15/summary* from a *tar* tape, you might use:

```
% tar xv project/wk{9,14,15}/summary
x project/wk9/summary, 3161 bytes, 7 tape blocks
x project/wk14/summary, 878 bytes, 2 tape blocks
x project/wk15/summary, 2268 bytes, 5 tape blocks
```

Some versions of *tar* understand wildcards, but many don't. There is a clever workaround *(21.09)*

—ML

1.19 *The Tree Structure of the Filesystem*

A multi-user system needs a way to let different users have different files with the same name. It also needs a way to keep files in logical groups. With thousands of system files and hundreds of files per user, it would be disastrous to have all of the files in one big heap. Even single-user operating systems have found it necessary to go beyond "flat" filesystem structures.

Almost every operating system solved this problem by implementing a tree-structured, or *hierarchical,* filesystem. UNIX is no exception. A hierarchical filesystem is not much different from a set of filing cabinets at the office. Your set of cabinets consists of many individual cabinets. Each individual cabinet has several drawers; each drawer may have several partitions in it; each partition may have several hanging (Pendaflex) folders; and each hanging folder may have several files. You can specify an individual file by naming the filing cabinet, the drawer, the partition, the group of folders, and the individual folder. For example, you might say to someone: "Get me the 'meeting of July 9' file from the Kaiser folder in the Medical Insurance Plans partition in the Benefits drawer of the Personnel file cabinet." This is backwards from the way you'd specify a filename, because it starts with the most specific part, but the idea is essentially the same.

You could give a complete path like this to any file in any of your cabinets, as shown in Figure 1-2. The concept of a "path" lets you distinguish your July 9 meeting with Kaiser from your July 9 interview with a job applicant or your July 9 policy planning meeting. It also lets you keep related topics together: it's easy to browse through the "Medical Insurance" section of one drawer or to scan all your literature and notes about the Kaiser plan. The UNIX filesystem works in exactly the same way (as do most other hierarchical filesystems). Rather than having a heap of assorted files, files are organized into *directories.* A directory is really nothing more than a special kind of file that lists a bunch of other files (see article 19.02). A directory can contain any number of files (although for performance reasons, it's a good idea to keep the number of files in one directory relatively small—under 100, when you can). A directory can also contain other directories. Because a directory is nothing more than a special kind of file, directories also have names. At the top (the filesystem "tree" is really upside down) is a directory called the "root," which has the special name / (pronounced "slash," but never spelled out).

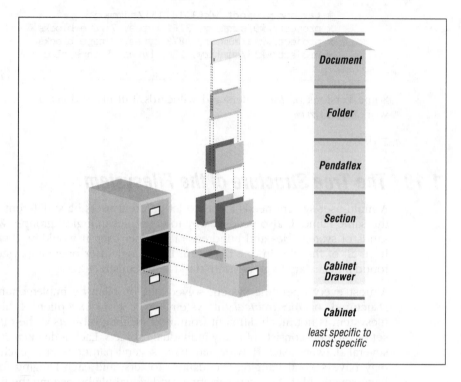

Figure 1-2. A Hierarchical Filesystem

To locate any file, we can give a sequence of names, starting from the filesystem's root, that shows its exact position in the filesystem: we start with the root and then list the directories you go through to find the file, separating them by slashes. This is called a *path*. For examples, let's look at the the simple filesystem represented by Figure 1-3. The names */home/mkl/mystuff/stuff* and */home/hun/publick/stuff* both refer to files named *stuff*. However, these files are in different directories so they are different files. The names *home*, *hun*, and so on are all names of directories. The complete paths like the two we gave above are called "absolute paths." There are shorter ways to refer to a file called relative paths *(1.21)*.

—*ML*

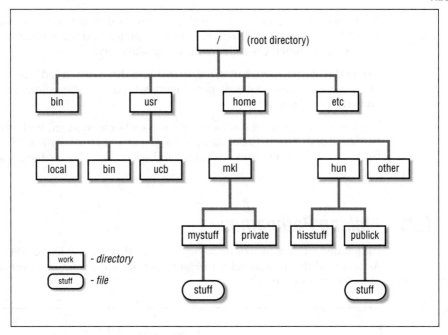

Figure 1-3. A UNIX Filesystem Tree

1.20 Your Home Directory

In recent years, DOS and the Macintosh have added hierarchical filesystems (1.19) much like those in UNIX and other large systems. But there is an important difference.

On many DOS and Macintosh systems, you start right at the "root" of the filesystem tree. In effect, you start with a blank slate, and create subdirectories to organize your files.

A UNIX system comes with an enormous filesystem tree already developed. When you log in, you start somewhere down in that tree, in a directory created for you by the system administrator (who may even be yourself, if you are administering your own system).

This directory, the one place in the filesystem that is your very own, to store your files (especially the shell setup files *(2.02)* that you use to customize the rest of your environment) is called your *home directory*.

Home directories were originally stored in a directory called */usr* (and still are on some systems), but are now often stored in other directories, perhaps named */u* or */home*.

To change your current directory *(1.21)* to your home, type cd with no pathname; the shell will assume you mean your home directory. Article 15.12 explains "nicknames" for your home directory and other users' home directories.

—*TOR*

1.21 Making Pathnames

Pathnames locate a file (or directory, or any other object) in the UNIX filesystem. As you read this article, refer to Figure 1-4. It's a diagram of a (very) small part of a UNIX filesystem.

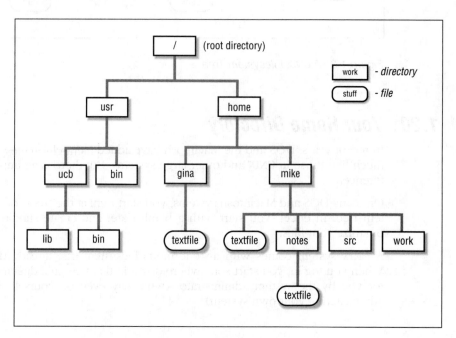

Figure 1-4. Part of a UNIX Filesystem Tree

Whenever you are using UNIX, you have a *current directory*. By default, UNIX looks for any files or directories that you mention within the current directory. That is, if you don't give a full pathname (starting from the root, */*), UNIX tries to look up files *relative* to the current directory. When you first log in, your current directory is your home directory *(1.20)*, which the system administrator will assign to you. It typically has a name like */usr/mike* or */home/mike*. You can change your current directory by giving the *cd* command, followed by the name of a new directory (for example, `cd /usr/bin`). You can find out your current directory by giving the *pwd* ("print working directory") command.

If your current directory is */home/mike*, and you give the command *cat textfile*, you are asking UNIX to locate the file *textfile* within the directory */home/mike*. This is equivalent to the absolute path */home/mike/textfile*. If you give the command *cat notes/textfile*, you are asking UNIX to locate the file *textfile* within the directory *notes*, within the current directory */home/mike*.

A number of abbreviations help you to form relative pathnames more conveniently. You can use the abbreviation **.** (dot) to refer to the current working directory. You can use **..** (dot dot) to refer to the parent of the current working directory. For example, if your current directory is */home/mike*, *./textfile* is the same as *textfile*, which is the same as */home/mike/textfile*. The relative path *../gina/textfile* is the same as */home/gina/textfile*; **..** moves one level from */home/mike* (to */home*), and then searches for the directory *gina* and the file *textfile*.

In the C shell and Korn shell, you can use the abbreviation ~ (tilde) to refer to your home directory. *~name* refers to the home directory of the user *name*. See article 15.12.

Here's a summary of the rules that UNIX uses to interpret paths:

If the pathname begins with /
> It is an absolute path, starting from the root.

If the pathname begins with ~ or with *~name*
> The C shell and Korn shell turn it into an absolute pathname starting at your home directory (~), or at the home directory of the user *name* (*~name*).

If the pathname does not begin with a /
> The pathname is relative to the current directory. Two relative special cases use entries that are in every UNIX directory:

> 1. If the pathname begins with **./**—the path is relative to the current directory; for example, *./textfile*.

> 2. If the pathname begins with **../**—the path is relative to the parent of the current directory. For example, if your current directory is */home/mike/work*, then *../src* means */home/mike/src*.

Article 19.02 explains where **.** and **..** come from.

Note: The **.** and **..** may appear at any point within a path. They mean "the current directory at this point in the path" and "the parent of the current directory at this point in the path." You commonly see paths starting with **../../** (or more) to refer to the grandparent or great-grandparent of the current directory. However, they can appear at other places in a pathname as well. For example, */usr/ucb/./bin* is the same as */usr/ucb/bin*; and */usr/ucb/bin/../lib* is the same as */usr/ucb/lib.* Placing **.** or **..** in the middle of a path may be helpful in building paths within shell scripts, but I have never seen them used in any other useful way.

—ML, JP

1.22 How UNIX Keeps Track of Files: Inodes

The ability to mumble about *inodes* is the key to social success at a UNIX gurus' cocktail party. This may not seem attractive to you, but sooner or later you will need to know what an inode is.

Seriously, inodes are an important part of the UNIX filesystem. You don't need to worry about them most of the time, but it does help to know what they are.

An inode is a data structure on the disk that describes a file. It holds most of the important information about the file, including the on-disk address of the file's data blocks (the part of the file that you care about). Each inode has its own identifying number, called an *i-number.* You really don't care about where a file is physically located on a disk. You usually don't care about the i-number—unless you're trying to find the links *(19.03, 18.23)* to a file. But you do care about the following information, all of which is stored in a file's inode:

- The file's ownership: the user and the group *(23.14)* that own the file.

- The file's access mode *(1.23, 23.02)* : whether or not various users and groups are allowed to read, write, or execute the file.

- The file's timestamp *(22.05, 22.06)* : when the file itself was last modified, when the file was last accessed, and when the inode was last modified.

- The file's type: whether the file is a regular file, a special file, or some other kind of abstraction masquerading *(1.29)* as a file.

Each filesystem has a set number of inodes that are created when the filesystem is first created (usually when the disk is first initialized). This number is therefore the maximum number of files that the filesystem can hold. It cannot be changed without reinitializing the filesystem, which destroys all the data that the filesystem holds. It is possible, though rare, for a filesystem to run out of inodes, just like it is possible to run out of storage space—this can happen on filesystems with many, many small files.

The *ls -l (23.02)* command shows much of this information. The *ls -i* option shows a file's i-number. The *stat (22.13)* command lists almost everything in an inode.

—ML

1.23 File Access Permissions

Under UNIX, access to files is based on the concept of users and groups.

Every "user" on a system has a unique account with a unique login name and a unique UID *(40.03)* (user ID number). It is possible, and sometimes convenient, to create accounts that are shared by groups of people. For example, in a transaction processing application, all of the order-entry personnel might be assigned a common login name (as far as UNIX is concerned, they only count as one user). In a research and development environment, certain administrative operations might be easier if members of a team shared the same account, in addition to their own accounts. However, in most situations each person using the system has one and only one user ID, and vice versa.

Every user may be a member of one or more "groups."* The user's entry in the master password file (*/etc/passwd (37.03)*) defines his "primary group membership." The */etc/group (23.14)* file defines the groups that are available and can also assign other users to these groups as needed. For example, I am a member of three groups: *staff, editors,* and *research.* My primary group is *staff*; the *group* file says that I am also a member of the *editors* and *research* groups. We call *editors* and *research* my "secondary groups." The system administrator is responsible for maintaining the *group* and *passwd* files. You don't need to worry about them unless you're administering your own system.

Every file belongs to one user and one group. When a file is first created, its owner is the user who created it; its group is the user's primary group or the group of the directory it's created in *(23.05, 23.14)*. For example, all files I create are owned by the user *mikel* and the group *staff.* As the file's owner, I am allowed to use the *chgrp* command to change the file's group. On filesystems that don't have quotas *(25.17)* , I can also use the *chown* command to change the file's owner. (To change ownership on systems with quotas, see article 23.22.) For example, to change the file *data* so that it is owned by the user *george* and the group *others,* I give the commands:

```
% chgrp others data
% chown george data
```

If you need to change both owner and group, change the group first! You won't have permission to change the group after you aren't the owner. Some versions of *chown* can change both owner and group at the same time:

```
% chown george.others data
```

File access is based on a file's user and group ownership and a set of access bits (commonly called the *mode bits*). When you try to access a file, you are put into one of three classes. You are either the file's owner, a member of the file's

---

*In Berkeley and other newer UNIX systems, users have the access privileges of all groups they belong to, all at the same time. In other UNIX systems, you use a command like *newgrp* to change the group you currently belong to.

group, or an "other." Three bits then determine whether you are allowed to read, write, or execute the file. So, as Figure 1-5 shows, there are a total of nine mode bits (three for each class) that set the basic access permissions:

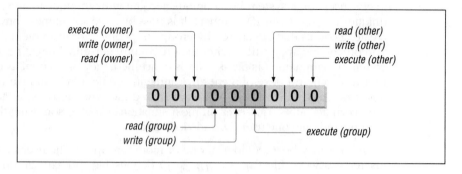

Figure 1-5. Filesystem Permission Bits

It is common to see these nine basic mode bits interpreted as an octal (base-8) number, in which each digit specifies the access permitted for one class. Each three bits makes one octal digit. Figure 1-6 shows how to do it.

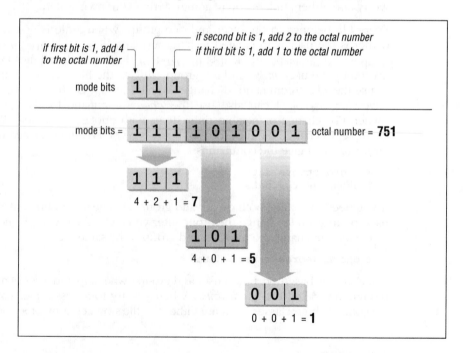

Figure 1-6. Changing Permission Bits to an Octal Number

Let's turn the mode bits 111101001 into an octal number. Break it into chunks of three bits: 111 101 001. The first group, 111, is 4+2+1 or 7. The second group,

101, is 4+0+1 or 5. The third group, 001, is 0+0+1 or 1. So those mode bits can be written as the octal number 751.

To tie this together, look at Figure 1-5 again—and work out these examples yourself. For example, if the owner of a file has read and write access, but no one else is allowed to touch the file, we say that it has the access mode 600. A file that is readable, writable, and executable by everyone has access mode 777. A file that is readable and writable by everyone (i.e., a public text file) has mode 666.

It is also common to see the mode bits expressed as a sequence of ten alphabetic characters (look at the listing from *ls –l (23.02)*). The first character tells you the file's type. For a plain file, this character is a -. For a directory, it's a d. The next three bits report the owner's access, the middle three bits report group access, and the final three bits report access for others. An r indicates that read access is allowed, w indicates that write access is allowed, and x indicates that execute access is allowed. For example:

```
-rw-------        is mode 600
-rwxrwxrwx        is mode 777
-rw-rw-rw-        is mode 666
```

You can change a string like rw-rw-rw- into an octal number with the technique in Figure 1-6. Split it into three-bit chunks. For example, rw- would have the value 4+2+0—that's 6. Therefore, rw-rw-rw- is 666 octal.

If the file is executable, a few other bits come into play. One is the "sticky bit," which tells UNIX to leave the executable in memory after the program has finished running. In theory, leaving the executable around reduces the program's startup time for subsequent users. The sticky bit was an interesting idea a long time ago, but it is obsolete now: modern virtual memory techniques like demand paging have made it unnecessary. Many UNIX users and UNIX books still believe that the sticky bit does something important, so you will hear it mentioned from time to time.

More important are the "set user ID" and "set group ID" (SUID and SGID) bits. If you execute an SUID file, your user ID is set to the user ID of the file's owner. Therefore, if you execute an SUID file that is owned by root, you are the superuser—for the duration of the program. Likewise, executing an SGID file sets your group ID to the file's group while the file is executing. SUID and SGID files can be security holes, but they really exist to enhance security. For example, you might want to allow any user to create a backup tape, but you shouldn't give every user the root password. Therefore, you can create a special version of the *dump* utility that is owned by root and that has the SUID bit set. When a user invokes this utility, he or she will be able to back up the entire filesystem because the *dump* command will run as if it were executed by root. But the user can't do anything else: he doesn't know the superuser password and can't do anything that *dump* won't let him do. Used carefully, SUID programs can be a powerful administrative tool.

Note: SUID and SGID programs are such major security holes that many conscientious administrators refuse to add new SUID utilities. Some versions of UNIX ignore the SUID and SGID bits for shell scripts (command files)—on those versions, only compiled programs can be SUID or SGID. SUID and SGID programs always lose their special properties when they are copied. However, making SUID and SGID programs completely safe is very difficult (or maybe impossible). For better or for worse, a lot of standard UNIX utilities (*uucp* and *lpr*, for example) are SUID.

Article 23.01 introduces other information about file access permissions.

—ML

1.24 The Superuser (Root)

In general, a *process (40.01)* is a program that's running: a shell, the *ls* command, the *vi* editor, and so on. In order to kill a process *(40.10)*, change its priority *(41.09)*, or manipulate it in any other way, you have to be the process' owner (i.e., the user who started it). In order to delete a job from a print queue *(45.01)*, you must be the user who started it.

As you might guess, there needs to be a way to circumvent all of this security. Someone has to be able to kill runaway programs, modify the system's files, and so on. Under UNIX, a special user known as *root* (and commonly called the "superuser") is allowed to do anything.

On any system, the root user should always have a password. The system administrator should be very careful about giving out the superuser password and can't be blamed if he won't give the superuser password to anyone. Historically, UNIX systems have tended to be very lax: at many sites, all the users know the superuser password and don't hesitate to use it whenever they have the slightest problem.

Common as it may be, this is a very bad practice—systems where everyone knows the superuser password have no security whatsoever. People can read each other's mail, trample all over each other's files, scribble on disks by accident, or mail all of the company's proprietary documentation to a competitor (and delete the log files so there's no record that they did it). Worse, even if every user is an angel, being superuser makes it easy for someone to cause big problems accidentally—for instance, typing `rm *` in an important directory when you thought you were somewhere else. Wise system administrators don't use their superuser status except when they have to *(23.23)*.

In this book, we'll assume that you don't have the superuser password. Almost all of what we describe can be done without becoming superuser.

—ML

1.25 *Access to Directories*

UNIX uses the same mode bits *(1.23)* for directories as for files, but they are interpreted differently. This interpretation will make sense if you remember that a directory is nothing more than a list of files. Creating a file in a directory, renaming a file or deleting a file from a directory requires changing this list: therefore, you need write access to the directory to create or delete a file. Modifying a file's contents does not require you to change the directory; therefore, you can modify files even if you don't have write access to the directory (providing that you have write access to the file).

Reading a directory is relatively straightforward: you need read access to be able to list the contents of a directory (find out what files it contains, etc.). If you don't have read access, you can't list the contents of the directory. However (surprise!) you can still access files in the directory, provided that you already know their names.

Execute access for a directory has no meaning per se, so the designers of UNIX have reassigned this bit. It is called the *search bit.* Search access is needed to perform any operation within a directory and its subdirectories. In other words, if you deny execute access to a directory, you are effectively denying access to the directory and everything beneath it in the directory tree.

The SUID bit is meaningless for directories. However, recent UNIX versions have added a new meaning to the SGID bit *(23.05)* and sticky bit *(23.06).*

The exception is that the superuser *(1.24)* can do absolutely anything at any time.

Article 23.01 introduces other articles about file and directory access.

—ML

1.26 *What a Multi-user System Can Do for You*

Even if you are the only user, a multi-user system can do a lot of things for you that a simpler operating system can't. For one thing, you can run several programs at the same time: you don't have to wait for one program to finish before you start the next. Even if you don't have a fancy windowing terminal or a workstation *(1.31),* you can still run jobs in the *background (1.27).* Instead of waiting until the program finishes, UNIX lets you give another command immediately. It then runs both programs at the same time, along with the other programs that are running. You are time sharing with yourself.

Running a job in the background is a good way to take advantage of the time the system spends running long jobs. For example, assume that you have just gotten a huge C program from a friend and want to compile and run it *(54.08).* But you don't want to sit while you're waiting for the compiler to do its work; you'd like to write a letter to your friend. So you can start the compilation in the background and start your editing session in the foreground.

```
% cc -O bigprogram.c &
[1] 2236
% vi letter.txt
```

The & means "run the job in the background." The next line is information the shell prints out to make it easier for you to work with your background processes. [1] is a job number, which you'll only see on shells with job control *(13.01)*. The 2236 is a process ID *(40.03)*.

—*ML*

1.27 How Background Processing Works

Remember that the shell sits there listening to what you type, and calling other programs to do jobs that it doesn't have built-in commands to do.

Normally, when the shell calls another program, it waits for the other program to finish. All the ampersand (&) at the end of a command line does is tell the shell not to wait.

Both the Bourne shell and the C shell allow background processing. But, on UNIX systems that have job control *(13.01)*, the C shell and Korn shell give you a lot of extra capabilities for manipulating background processes.

Here's the tip of the iceberg:

- If you forget to put a job into the background, you can stop it on the fly with a suspend signal *(40.01)* by typing CTRL-z. Then use the *bg* command to put it into the background and restart it:

```
% find /usr -name tim -print > mine
CTRL-z
Stopped
% bg
[1]     find /usr -name tim -print > mine &
```

- You can bring the current background job *(13.03)* into the foreground with the *fg* command. This is handy when UNIX stops the background job that needs input from your keyboard (you can't type to jobs running in the background).

- If you have a lot of background processes running, you can use the *jobs* command to list them all, and then bring a selected job into the foreground by job number. You can also kill jobs by job number rather than by process ID.

—*TOR*

1.28 Some Gotchas with Background Processing

1. If you're using the Bourne shell, you have to watch out for putting a series of commands separated by semicolons *(9.03)* into the background. The Bourne shell puts only the last command on the line into the background, but waits for the first.

   An easy way to test this is with the following command line, which waits for 15 seconds, then does an *ls*:

   ```
   $ sleep 15; ls &
   ```

   In the Bourne shell, you won't get your prompt back until the *sleep (42.02)* command has finished.

   The proper way to put a series of Bourne shell commands into the background is to group them with parentheses:

   () 14.07
   ```
   $ (sleep 15; ls )&
   ```

   This may strike you as a defect, but in fact, it's a sign of the greater precision of Bourne shell syntax, which makes it somewhat exasperating for interactive use, but much better for programming.

2. It doesn't make any sense to run an interactive program such as an editor in the background. For example, if you type this from the C shell:

   ```
   % vi &
   [1] 3071
   ```

   you'll get a message like the following:

   ```
   [1]   + Stopped (tty output) vi
   ```

   vi can only be active in the foreground. However, it does make sense to have *vi* stopped *(13.08)* in the background.

   If you are running *vi* or any other interactive program, you can quickly get back to the shell by typing CTRL-z to stop the program. This will automatically bring the shell back into the foreground.

   Stopping *vi (13.04)* is more efficient than using its shell escape mechanism *(31.26)*, since it lets you go back to your original shell rather than starting a new one. Simply type fg to get back to where you were in editing.

3. We have shared a system with new users who were overenthusiastic users of background processes, rather like the man who loved loving so much he sought many lovers. Because each background process is competing for the same resources, running many of them can be a drain on the system. This means that everything takes longer for everyone. We used to have people who thought that if they ran three *troff (45.14)* processes at once, they'd get their three files formatted faster than if they did them one after another. Boy, were they mistaken.

4. If you use the Bourne shell, any background processes you have running will normally be terminated when you log out. To avoid this, use the *nohup (40.18)* command.

5. Not all processes are created equal. UNIX maintains a queue of processes ordered by priority. Foreground processes, such as a user typing a command at a prompt, often receive higher priority than background processes. However, you may want to run background processes at an even lower priority, by using *nice (41.09)* This is a relatively painless way of being kind to other users—and making your foreground job run faster—though it will make your background tasks take a little longer.

—TOR, DD

1.29 When is a File Not a File?

UNIX differs from most operating systems in that it is file-oriented. The designers of UNIX decided that they could make the operating system much simpler if they treated everything as if it were a file. As far as UNIX is concerned, disk drives, terminals, modems, network connections, etc. are all just files. Some recent versions of UNIX (such as System V Release 4) have gone further: even processes *(40.01)* are files. Like waves and particles in quantum physics, the boundary between files and the rest of the world can be extremely fine: whether you consider a disk a piece of hardware or a special kind of file depends primarily on your perspective and what you want to do with it.

Therefore, to understand UNIX, you have to understand what files are. A file is nothing more than a stream of bytes—that is, an arbitrarily long string of bytes with no special structure. There are no special file structures, and only a few special file types (for keeping track of disks and a few other purposes). The structure of any file is defined by the programs that use it, and not by the UNIX operating system.* You may hear users talk about file headers and so on, but these are defined by the applications that use the files, and not by the UNIX filesystem itself.

UNIX programs do abide by one convention, however. Text files use a single newline character (linefeed) between lines of text, rather than the carriage return–linefeed combination used in DOS or the carriage returns used in the Macintosh. This difference may cause problems when you bring files from other operating systems over to UNIX. DOS files will often be littered with carriage returns (CTRL-m) which are necessary for that operating system but are superfluous for UNIX. These carriage returns will look ugly if you try to edit or print the file and may confuse some UNIX programs. Mac text files will appear to be one long line with no breaks. Of course, you can use UNIX utilities to convert DOS and Mac files for UNIX—see article 1.05.

—ML

---

*Many executable files—programs—begin with a *magic number*. This is a special two-byte-long sequence that tells the kernel how to execute the file.

1.30   Redirecting Input and Output

When you run most UNIX programs, their output goes to your terminal. If the programs prompt you for input, they read it from your terminal. You can tell the shell to redirect that output and input from places besides your terminal. For instance, you can save the output of a program in a file, or tell a program to read data from a file instead of the keyboard. The shell handles the redirection of input and output. Article 14.01 explains the syntax you use to control redirection.

A program can also take its input from the output of another program. This kind of redirection is called a *pipe (1.03)* Most UNIX utilities are designed to work with data coming from a pipe; a program that transforms that data in some way is called a *filter.*

To understand the nitty-gritty details of redirection, you need to understand *open files* and *file descriptors.* See article 47.20.

—JP, TOR

1.31   The X Window System

In 1988, an organization called the MIT (Massachusetts Institute of Technology) X Consortium was formed to promote and develop a vendor-neutral windowing system called the X Window System. (It was called "X" because it was a follow-on to a window system called "W" that was developed at Stanford University.)

A window system is a way of dividing up the large screen of a workstation into multiple virtual terminals, or windows. Each window can contain a separate application program. While the "big win" is to have applications with point-and-click mouse-driven user interfaces, one of the most common applications at this point is still a simple terminal emulator (*xterm*). X thus allows a workstation to display multiple simultaneous terminal sessions. This makes many of the standard UNIX multi-tasking features such as job control less important, since programs can all be running in the foreground in separate windows. [The X Window System has also brought about a display terminal called an *X terminal.* An X terminal gives users access to X without buying a complete workstation.—*JP*]

Not everyone has X though, and it's a whole separate can of worms, so we don't cover X or any other window system in this book. If you like this book, twist our arms, and maybe you'll see *X Window System Power Tools* this time next year   :−) *(53.12)*

—TOR

1.32 One Big Hole

Another big hole in this book is that we don't cover any of UNIX's communications and networking utilities—things like electronic mail, netnews, UUCP, *rlogin, rcp, rsh, telnet, ftp, archie,* WAIS...and all the wonderful Internet resources that are really the "killer applications" for UNIX.

Why do we leave out this most central of UNIX technologies? There's only one good reason: space. The book was heading up towards 1500 pages, and something had to go. We looked for discrete areas that we could cut and save for another book. This isn't a promise, but if this book goes over well, look for *UNIX Networking Power Tools* next year—or look at some of the Nutshell Handbooks we do have available now, like *The Whole Internet User's Guide and Catalog* by Ed Krol, *TCP/IP Network Administration* by Craig Hunt, and *Managing uucp and Usenet* by Tim O'Reilly and Grace Todino.

You'll see other holes as well—the X window system, and utilities for hardcore programmers. We hope you agree, though, that it was better to go for more depth in what we did cover than to try to shoehorn in more superficial material just to say we cover everything.

Article 1.33 has an overview of UNIX networking. And because we didn't want to cut out some good material that fit pretty well with other existing articles, we did leave in a few other networking tips. We just didn't provide as much background or cross-referencing for all of the commands and concepts.

—TOR

1.33 UNIX Networking and Communications

Generally speaking, a network lets two or more computers communicate and work together. Partly because of its open design, UNIX has been one of the operating systems where a lot of networking development is done. Just as there are different versions of UNIX, there are different ways and programs to use networks from UNIX.

We don't cover networking in this book (1.32). This article has a summary of some common UNIX networking and communications utilities.

The Internet

    A worldwide network of computers. Internet users can transfer files, log into other computers, and use a wide range of programs and services.

mail

    A UNIX program that's been around for years, long before networking was common, is *mail.* It sends electronic memos, usually called *e-mail messages,* between a user and one or more other users. When you send e-mail, your message waits for the other user(s) to start their own mail program. The people who get your message can file it, print it, reply to it, forward it to other people, and much more. System programs can send you mail to tell you about problems or give you information. You can send mail to programs, to ask them for information. World-wide mailing lists connect users into discussion groups. There's more, of course.

There are zillions of mail programs for UNIX—some standard, some from vendors, and many freely-available. The more common e-mail programs include *mail, Mail, mailx, mush, elm,* and MH (a package made up of many utilties including *comp, inc, show,* and so on). Find one that's right for you and use it!

ftp The *ftp* program is one way to transfer files between your computer and another computer with TCP/IP, often over the Internet network. *ftp* requires a username and password on the remote computer.

Anonymous ftp (54.07) uses the *ftp* program and a special restricted account named *anonymous* on the remote computer. It's usually used for transferring freely-available files and programs from central sites to users at many other computers.

UUCP UNIX-to-UNIX Copy is a family of programs (*uucp (54.07), uux, uulog,* and others) for transferring files and e-mail between computers. UUCP is usually used with modems over telephone lines.

Usenet Usenet isn't exactly a network. It's a collection of thousands of computers worldwide that exchange files called *news articles.* This "net news" system has hundreds of interactive discussion groups, electronic bulletin boards, for discussing everything from technical topics to erotic art.

telnet This utility logs you into a remote computer over a network (such as the Internet) using TCP/IP. You can work on the remote computer as if it were your local computer. The *telnet* program is available on many operating systems; *telnet* can log you into other operating systems from your UNIX host and vice versa. A special version of *telnet* called *tn3270* will log into IBM mainframes.

rlogin Similar to *telnet* but mostly used between UNIX systems. *rlogin* passes the *TERM* variable *(6.11)* setting and window size between hosts. Special setups, including a file named *.rhosts* in your remote home directory, let you log into the remote computer without typing your password.

rcp A "*remote cp*" program for copying files between computers. It has the same command-line syntax as *cp* except that hostnames are added to the remote pathnames.

rsh Starts a "*remote shell*" to run a command on a remote system without needing to log in interactively.

NFS NFS isn't a user utility. The Network FileSystem and related packages like NIS (the Network Information Service) let your system administrator mount remote computers' filesystems onto your local computer. You can use the remote filesystem as easily as if it were on your local computer.

write	Sends messsages to another user's screen. Two users can have a discussion with *write*.
talk	A more sophisticated program than *write*, *talk* splits the screen into two pieces and lets users type at the same time if they want to. *talk* can be used over networks, though not all versions of *talk* can talk to each other.

If you'd like more information, there are quite a few books about networking. Some Nutshell Handbooks on networking and communications include *The Whole Internet User's Guide and Catalog* (e-mail, Usenet, *ftp*, *telnet*, and more); *Using UUCP and Usenet*; *!%@:: The Directory of Electronic Mail Addressing & Networks*; and many more advanced books for programming and administration.

—*JP*

1.34 What's Wrong with UNIX

Unfortunately, the same thing that's special about UNIX is also the source of most of what's wrong.

An operating system burdened with 20 years' worth of nifty add-on programs *(1.01)* is bound to have an awful lot of inconsistencies and overlapping functions.

This can be awfully confusing even for experienced users. All you have to do is watch the "flame wars" (arguments) on Usenet *(1.33)* to realize how little understanding and agreement there is among self-styled experts about exactly how things work.

UNIX's checkered heritage shows up most clearly in programs with overlapping functions that seem to do almost the same thing. What's the logic behind the way both *tset (6.12)* and *stty (43.03)* can be used to set serial line characteristics?

There isn't any. These two programs represent independent efforts to solve related problems. The overlap is entirely unintentional, and in a managed development effort, would have been resolved in favor of a single program with a unified interface.

No one said it would be easy. But no other operating system that I know about is as much fun.

—*TOR*

## Part One

Making Yourself at Home

Do us a favor. Don't keep reading.

Instead, start browsing. Flip through the book till you see something interesting. Read the articles around it till an interesting cross-reference takes you somewhere else.

Keep it fun. Try to learn something new each day. Browse through the book until you find something that makes you smile. Then set the book aside until the next time you need a break.

If you do insist on reading straight through, you'll find stuff in the next four chapters about logging in and out, about passwords, about organizing your home directory, and about setting up your terminal.

—TOR

2

Logging In

2.01 Customizing the Shell

You probably know that shells can be customized to work the way you want them to with shell and environment variables *(7.08, 7.01)*, command aliases, shell functions *(11.01)*, and so on.

You can set variables and create aliases by hand at any time, but the shell will "forget" your settings when you log out. To use the same settings every time you log in, put the commands in special shell setup files *(2.02)* in your home directory. These files aren't just for setting things like shell variables. Shells can run any UNIX command when you log in and log out. All of this can save time and make your login session do more for you.

—JP

2.02 Shell Setup Files—Which, Where, and Why

The original Bourne shell has one file that it reads when you log in: it's called *.profile* and is in your home directory. Put all your setup commands there.

The Bourne shell doesn't read *.profile* when you start a subshell *(40.04, 14.07)*, though. Subshell setup information has to come from environment variables *(7.01)* that were set in *.profile* when you first logged in or from commands you typed since.

In the Korn shell, if the *ENV (7.03)* environment variable is set to the pathname of a file, any Korn shell (including a subshell) will read that file as it starts up, before it runs other commands. Next, a login Korn shell *(2.08)* will read the *.profile*.

C shell users can have three shell setup files:

- The *.login* file is read when you start a login shell—usually, that's when you log in, but not always *(53.09, 2.07)*!

- The *.cshrc* file is read any time a C shell starts—that includes shell escapes and shell scripts.*

- The shell reads *.logout* when you end a login shell. But when you log out, you aren't always ending a login shell *(2.07)* Hmmmm.

Let's make some sense of this *csh* setup file mess!

When you log in to a UNIX system, the *login* program usually starts a shell for you. (Logins for programs like *ftp* and *uucp* don't start one though.) When a C shell starts, it reads a file named *.cshrc* in your home directory. That's the place to put commands that should run every time you start a shell. For instance, shell variables like *cdpath* *(15.05)* and *prompt* *(8.01)* should be set here. Aliases *(11.02)* should, too. Those things aren't passed to subshells through the environment, so they belong in *.cshrc*.

If your *csh* is a login shell, it reads the *.login* file next. (Unfortunately, window systems, the *rsh* *(1.33)* command, and others don't always start login shells *(53.09, 2.08)*) Here's where you should set:

- Environment variables *(7.01)* (which UNIX will pass to subshells automatically),

- Commands like *tset* *(6.03)* and *stty* *(6.09, 43.03)*

- Commands you want to run every time you log in—checking for mail and news *(1.33)* running *fortune* *(3.03)* checking your calendar for the day, etc.

—*JP*

2.03 *What Goes in Shell Startup Files?*

Shell startup files like *.login* and *.profile* typically do at least the following things:

- Set the search path *(9.05)*

- Set the terminal type *(6.03)* and make various terminal settings *(6.09, 43.03)*

- Set environment variables *(7.01)* that might be needed by programs or scripts that you typically run.

- Run one or more commands that you want to run whenever you log in. For example, if your system *login* program doesn't show the message of the day *(2.14)* your startup file can. Many people also like to print an amusing or instructive fortune *(3.03)*

You might want to run *who* *(53.04)* or *uptime* *(41.07)* for information about the system.

---

*If you write a *csh* script, you should probably use the –*f* option to keep C shell scripts from reading *.cshrc*. Of course, even better, you probably shouldn't use *csh* for scripts *(49.02)*

In the C shell, the *.cshrc* file is used to establish settings that will apply to every instance of the C shell, not just the login shell *(53.09)* For example, you typically want aliases *(11.02)* to be available in every interactive shell you run.

Even novices can write simple *.profile* or *.login* and *.cshrc* files. The real trick is to make these startup scripts really work for you. Here are some of the things you might want to try:

- Creating a custom prompt (article 8.01).

- Coordinating custom setup files on different machines (article 2.13).

- Making different terminal settings depending on which terminal you're using (article 2.12).

- Seeing the message of the day only when it changes (article 2.14).

- Doing all of the above without making your login take forever (article 2.05).

—TOR

2.04 Tip for Changing Account Setup: Keep a Shell Ready

The shell is your interface to UNIX. If you make a bad mistake when you change your *.cshrc, .login* or *.profile* file *(2.02)* or your password, it can be tough to log in and fix things.

Before you change your setup, it's a good idea to start a login session to the same account from somewhere else. Use that session for making your changes. Log in again elsewhere to test your changes.

Don't have a terminal with multiple windows or another terminal close to your desk? You can get the same result by using *rlogin* or *telnet (1.33)* to log in to your host again from the same terminal. What I mean is:

```
somehost% vi .cshrc
      ...Make edits to the file...
somehost% rlogin localhost
      ...Logs you in to your same account...
An error message
somehost% logout
Connection closed.
somehost% vi .cshrc
      ...Edit to fix mistake...
```

If you don't have *rlogin* or *telnet*, the command su - *username (23.23)* where *username* is your username, will do about the same thing.

—JP

2.05 Tips for Speeding up Slow C Shell Logins

When I first started using the C shell in the early 1980s, I made incredible *.cshrc* and *.login* files with all kinds of nice customizations. Aliases, commands to check my mail, calendar systems, shell scripts in the background to watch things for me ... boy, was this great! Great except when I tried to log in, that is. I was working on an overloaded VAX 11/750. Logging in could take a few minutes, from the time I got the ;login: prompt until I finally got my shell prompt % (... well, it was really a much fancier prompt, but that's another story :-)).

The C shell seems (to me) to be pretty slow at reading long *.cshrc* and *.login* files—especially at setting aliases. So, I learned some ways to get logged in faster. They were especially nice when I was at someone else's terminal and needed to log in for something quick. You might not want to use these exact techniques, but I hope they'll give you some ideas if your logins take too long.

Quick Login

Add a "quick login" setup to the top of your *.cshrc*. As soon as the C shell starts and sets a few essentials, this setup asks whether you want a prompt right away. If you answer yes, it starts another C shell with the –f option (important: this makes the subshell (40.04) skip your *.cshrc* so you don't get a loop):

```
login: jerry
Password:
Last login: Tue Jan 21 12:34:56 PST 1985
      ...
Answer y for quick login or RETURN for standard: y
For a standard login, type 'exit 77'.
% mail bigboss
Subject: I'm on my way
Carol, I'm leaving for the meeting now. See you by 10:00.
.
% CTRL-d

login:
```

From there, I can run a few quick commands. Typing CTRL-d or exit quits the quick subshell and kills my original login shell, too. If I want to stay logged in on that terminal, I type exit 77. That makes the quick subshell return an exit status (46.07) of 77; the test in the *.cshrc* notices this and continues logging me in, reading the rest of the *.cshrc* and *.login*.

Here's the top of the *.cshrc* file to set that up:

```
                 # only do stuff below if this is an interactive shell
if 49.03          if (! $?prompt) goto cshrc_end
! $? 49.04

                 # QUICK LOGIN:
                 if (! $?LOGGEDIN) then
{} 10.05             set path = (/bin /usr/ucb /usr/local/{bin,mh} {/usr,~}/bin .)
                     echo -n "Answer y for quick login or RETURN for standard: "
```

```
                 if ("$<" =~ y*) then
$< =~  49.04           echo "For a standard login, type 'exit 77'."
                       csh -f
                       # PLAIN "exit" JUST EXITS .cshrc... THIS IS BRUTAL BUT IT WORKS:
kill 40.10             if ($status != 77) kill -9 $$
$$ 9.15          endif
                 endif

setenv 7.01      setenv LOGGEDIN yes

                     ...Rest of .cshrc...

                 cshrc_end:
```

> Be sure to use an `if ($?prompt)` test *(2.09)* first to keep this command from being read by noninteractive shells. If you don't, noninteractive shells for jobs like *at* may hang, waiting for an answer to the "quick login" question—or just be confused and not work.

A Second Alias and Command File

Maybe you have a set of aliases or setup commands that you use only for certain projects. If you don't need that setup every time you log in, you can put the setup commands in a separate file. Make an alias named something like *setup* that reads the file into your setup shell. Only type `setup` when you need the extra setup done.

Here's the alias:

~ 15.12
```
alias setup 'if (! $?setup) source ~/lib/cshrc2'
```

and the start of the `~/lib/cshrc2` file:

```
set setup  # variable to stop re-sourcing

alias foo bar
    ...
```

The first line in the *cshrc2* file sets a shell variable that keeps the *setup* alias from re-reading the file into this shell. This saves time if you forget that you've already run *setup*.

Once-a-day Setup

Maybe there are some commands that you want to run only once a day, the first time you log in. For example, I had a reminder system that showed my calendar for the day, reminded me of birthdays, etc. A test like this in *.login* handles that:

$date[n] 49.05
set 7.08
`..` 10.14
```
# Put day name in $date[1], month in $date[2], date in $date[3], etc:
set date=(`date`)
# if today's daily setup file doesn't exist, make it and do stuff:
```

```
       if (! -e ~/tmp/,setup.$date[3]) then
-e 49.04       touch ~/tmp/,setup.$date[3]
touch 22.07    do_calendar
                 ...Other once-a-day setup...
       endif
unset 7.08  unset date
```

That test uses *csh* arrays *(49.05)* to get today's date and make an empty file in my *tmp* directory with a name like *,setup.23*. Once a file is created (say, on June 23), then the setup commands won't run again that day. I have a program that periodically removes files named with a comma (,) *(24.19, 24.21)* so *,setup.23* will be long gone by the next month's twenty-third day. That could also be done from the *.logout* file *(3.01, 3.02)*.

—*JP*

2.06 Use Absolute Pathnames in Shell Setup Files

One common mistake in shell setup files *(2.02)* is lines like these:

```
           source .aliases
`..` 10.14  echo "Logged in at `date`" >> login.log
```

What's wrong with those lines? Both use relative pathnames *(1.21)* for the files (*.aliases, login.log*), assuming that the files are in the home directory. Those lines won't work when you start a subshell *(40.04)* from somewhere besides your home directory. That's because your files *.cshrc* or *ENV* (like *.kshrc*) are read whenever a shell starts. If you ever use the *source* or . commands *(46.22)* to read the *.profile* and *.login* from outside your home directory, you'll have the same problem.

Use absolute pathnames instead. As article 15.12 explains, the pathname of your home directory is in the tilde (~) operator or the $HOME or $LOGDIR environment variable:

```
source ~/.aliases
echo "Logged in at `date`" >> ~/login.log
```

—*JP*

2.07 C Shell Setup Files aren't Read when You Want them to Be?

The C shell reads its *.cshrc, .login,* and *.logout* setup files at particular times *(2.02)*. Only "login" C shells *(2.08)* will read the *.login* and *.logout* files. Back when *csh* was designed, this restriction worked fine. The shell that started as you logged in was flagged as a login shell, and it read all three files. You started other shells (shell escapes, shell scripts, etc.) from that login shell, and they would read only *.cshrc*.

Now, UNIX has interactive shells started by window systems (like *xterm (1.31)*), remote shells (like *rsh (1.33)*), and other shells that might need some things set from the *.login* or *.logout* files. Depending on how these shells are invoked, these might not be login shells—so they might read only *.cshrc*. How can you handle that? Putting all your setup commands in *.cshrc* isn't good because all subshells *(40.04)* read it . . . you definitely don't want to run terminal-setting commands like *tset* during shell escapes!

To handle problems at login time, put almost all of your setup commands in *.cshrc* instead of *.login*. After the "login-only" commands have been read from *.cshrc*, set the *ENV_SET* environment variable as a flag. (There's nothing special about this name. You can pick any name you want.)

The shell will copy the "flag" variable to subshells and the *.cshrc* can test for it—if the variable exists, the login-only commands are skipped. That'll keep the commands from being read again in a shell escape.

Here are parts of a *.cshrc* that show the idea:

```
        . . . Normal .cshrc stuff . . .
    if ($?prompt && ! $?ENV_SET) then
        # Do commands that used to go in .login file:
        setenv EDITOR /usr/ucb/vi
        tset
            . . .
        setenv ENV_SET done
    endif
```

if *49.03*
$? *49.04*

You should probably put a comment in the *.login* file to explain what you've done.

The *.logout* file should probably be read only once—when your last ("top-level") shell exits. If your top-level shell isn't a login shell, you can make it read *.logout* anyway. Here's how. First, along with the previous fixes to your *.cshrc* file, add an alias that will read your *.logout* file when you use the *exit* command. Also set the *ignoreeof* variable *(3.05)* to force you to use the *logout* command when you log out. Now the chunk of your *.cshrc* will look like:

```
    if ($?prompt && ! $?ENV_SET) then
            . . .
        # Make all top-level interactive shells read .logout file:
        set ignoreeof
        alias exit 'source ~/.logout; ""exit'
            . . .
    endif
```

"" exit *11.06*

—*JP*

2.08 *Identifying Login Shells*

When you first log in to a UNIX system from a terminal, the system usually starts a *login shell*. This is where you want to do general setup—initialize your terminal, set environment variables, and so on. The C shell reads your *.login* file here.

Other shells are either subshells *(40.04)* (started from the login shell) or separate shells started by *at (42.03)*, *rsh (1.33)*, and so on. These C shells don't read *.login*.

To make it possible to find out which you've got, add the following line to the top of your *.login* file. The line sets a shell variable *(7.08)* named *loginshell*:

```
set loginshell=yes
```

Now wherever you need to know the type of shell, use a test like:

if *49.03*
$? *49.04*

```
if ($?loginshell)
```

This works because only login shells read *.login*.

If you use the Bourne or Korn shells, you can add a line to your *.profile*:

```
loginshell=yes
```

The *loginshell* variable will only be defined in login shells.

—JP

2.09 *Speeding Up Your C Shell with set prompt Test*

Every time you start a C shell—in a shell escape *(31.26)*, the *su (23.23)* command, a shell script, an *at* job *(42.01)*, etc.—the *csh* reads the *.cshrc* file in your home directory. Some of those shells are "noninteractive," which means the shell is running a single command or reading from a script file *(1.05)*—you won't be typing any commands yourself. If your *.cshrc* has commands like *alias (11.02)*, *set cdpath (15.05)*, and others that are only useful in interactive shells, it wastes time to make noninteractive shells read them.

You can tell the shell to skip commands that will only be used in interactive shells. Set up your *.cshrc* this way:

```
# COMMANDS FOR ALL C SHELLS:
set path = (...whatever...)
    ...
```

if *49.03*
! $? *49.04*

```
if (! $?prompt) goto cshrc_end

# COMMANDS FOR INTERACTIVE SHELLS ONLY:
alias foo bar
    ...
set cdpath = (~ ~joe/project)

cshrc_end:
```

(2.10)

The ! $?prompt succeeds only on noninteractive shells, when the shell hasn't set the *prompt* variable. On noninteractive shells, the command goto cshrc_end makes the shell skip to the line at the end of the file labeled cshrc_end:.

Of course, if you set your own prompt *(8.01)*, be sure to do it on some line below the ! $?prompt test. Otherwise, the test will always succeed!

Note: Some books tell you to use a test like this instead:

```
if (! $?prompt) exit

# commands for interactive shells only:
   ...
```

But some C shells will log out when they see the *exit* command in a *.cshrc* file. Using goto cshrc_end is more portable.

Article 8.03 explains another problem that this $?prompt test solves.

—JP

2.10 *Gotchas in set prompt Test*

Lots of users add an if (! $?prompt) exit test *(2.09)* to their *.cshrc* files. It's gotten so common that some vendors add a workaround to defeat the test. For instance, some versions of the *which* command *(52.07)* set the *prompt* variable so that it can see your aliases "hidden" inside the $?prompt test. I've also seen a version of *at* that starts an interactive shell to run jobs.

If you've buried commands after if (! $?prompt) that should only be run on interactive shells or at login time, then you may have trouble.

There are workarounds. What you'll need depends on the problem you're trying to work around.

- The version of *which* on the Power Tools disk works without reading your *.cshrc* file, so there's no problem there.

- Here's a way to stop the standard *which* from reading parts of your *.cshrc* that you don't want it to read. The first time you log in, this scheme sets a *CSHRC_READ* environment variable *(7.01)*. The variable will be copied into all subshells *(40.04)* (like the one that *which* starts). In subshells, the test if ($?CSHRC_READ) will branch to the end of your *.cshrc* file:

```
if (! $?prompt) goto cshrc_end

# COMMANDS BELOW HERE ARE READ ONLY BY INTERACTIVE SHELLS:
alias foo bar
   ...

if ($?CSHRC_READ) goto cshrc_end
```

```
# COMMANDS BELOW HERE ARE READ ONLY AT LOGIN TIME:
setenv CSHRC_READ yes
   ...
```

```
cshrc_end:
```

- If you have a buggy version of *at (42.03)* that runs jobs from interactive shells, make your own front-end to *at (11.01)* that sets an environment variable named *AT* temporarily before it submits the *at* job. Add a test to your *.cshrc* that quits if *AT* is set:

```
# at JOBS RUN INTERACTIVE SHELLS ON MY BUGGY VERSION OF UNIX.
# WORKAROUND IS HERE AND IN THE at ALIAS BELOW:
if ($?AT) goto cshrc_end
```

() *14.07*
\at *11.06*

```
    ...
alias at '( setenv AT yes; \at  \!* )'
    ...
```

```
cshrc_end:
```

Most modern versions of *at* save a copy of your environment and restore it, later, when the *at* job is run. At that time, the *AT* environment variable will be set; the C shell will skip the parts of your *.cshrc* that you want it to. It's ugly, but it works.

Those workarounds probably won't solve all the problems on your version of UNIX, but I hope they'll give you some ideas.

—JP

2.11 Faster Korn Shell Startup with $– Test

Do you use the Korn shell—and does your account have an *"ENV* file" *(2.02)* (a startup file named in the *ENV* environment variable)? You might have the same problem *(2.09)* that C shell users have with *.cshrc*: noninteractive shells read aliases and other lines that you want to be read only by interactive shells. Speed up your file by adding a test like this:

case *46.06*

```
case $- in
  *i*);;
  *) return 0;;
esac
# COMMANDS BELOW THIS LINE WILL ONLY BE RUN BY INTERACTIVE SHELLS:
   ...
```

The test checks to see if the shell's *–i* option is set. If it isn't, the `return 0` quits the file.

—JP

2.12 Automatic Setups for Different Terminals

If you work at several kinds of terminals, terminal setup can be tough. For instance, my X terminal sends a backspace character when I push the upper-right key, but the same key on another terminal sends a delete character—I want *stty erase (6.09)* to set the right erase character automatically. Maybe you want a full set of calendar programs started when you log in to the terminal at your desk, but not when you make a quickie login (2.05) from somewhere else.

Here are some ideas for changing your login sequence automatically. Most of the examples are for the C shell and use that shell's *switch (49.06)* and *if (49.03)* . If your login shell is *sh* or *ksh*, just convert the examples to use *case (46.05)* and *if (46.08)* . The third example here shows both kinds of shells.

- If all you want to do is initialize your terminal (set the *TERM* variable *(6.11)* , set your erase character, and so on), the *tset (6.03)* command may be all you need.

- If your *TERM* environment variable is set differently on each terminal, you can add a test like this to your *.login* file:

```
switch ($TERM)
case vt100:
    ...do commands for vt100
    breaksw
case xxx:
    ...do commands for xxx
    breaksw
default:
    ...do commands for other terminals
    breaksw
endsw
```

and so on.

- If you log in from other hosts (1.33) or from hosts running the X window system (1.31) , the *who* command will probably show a hostname and/or window information in parentheses:

```
% who
barbie    ttyq9    Aug 27 11:16    (ncd5.foo.com:0.0)
ken       ttyqb    Aug 27 13:12    (macsnack.foo.com)
```

(Long hostnames may be truncated. Check yours before you write this test.) If this will help, add commands like these to your *.login* file:

```
tty 3.08
\(..\) \1 35.10
```

```
set tty="`tty`"
switch (`who | sed -n "/ $tty:t /s/.*\(( .*) )/\1 /p"`)
case *0.0:
    ...do commands for X display 0
case macsnack*:
    ...do commands for the host macsnack.foo.com
```

That uses the C shell's *:t* modifier *(12.08)* to get a port name like *ttyq9*, then uses *sed (35.24)* to search for that line and give the text between the

parentheses for that port name to the switch. This `case *0.0:` matches
lines ending with `0.0`, and the `case macsnack*:` matches lines that start
with `macsnack`.

To do the same thing in the Bourne and Korn shells, use a *case* structure
(46.06):

basename 47.18

```
basetty=`basename \`tty\``
case "`who | sed -n \"/ $basetty /s/.*(\(.*\))/\1/p\"`" in
*0.0)
    ...do commands for X display 0
macsnack*)
    ...do commands for the host macsnack.foo.com
```

- If you know that certain port numbers are used for certain kinds of logins,
  you can test that. For example, many systems use *ttyp0*, *ttyq1*, etc. as network ports for *rlogin* and *telnet (1.33)*. This test will branch on the port name:

```
switch ("`tty`")
case /dev/tty[pqrs]?:
    # rlogin, telnet:
    ...
case /dev/tty02:
    # terminal on my desk:
    ...
```

- Certain systems set certain environment variables. For example, the X Window System sets a *DISPLAY* environment variable. (If you aren't sure about
  your system, use the *env* or *printenv* command *(7.01)* to look for changes in
  your environment at different systems.) You can test that:

if 49.03
$? 49.04

```
if ($?DISPLAY) then
    # on X window system
    ...
else if ($?WIN_PARENT) then
    # on SunView system
    ...
else
    ...
endif
```

- Finally, your system may have a */etc/ttytab* or */etc/ttys* file that lists the type
  of each terminal port. Lines in the file look something like this:

```
console "/usr/etc/getty std.9600"   vt100       on  local
tty00   "/usr/etc/getty std.9600"   dialup      off local
tty01   "/usr/etc/getty std.9600"   plugboard   off local
    ...
ttyp0   none                        network     off
    ...
```

(For example, port *ttyp0* is *network*, the type used by *xterm (1.31)*, *telnet (1.33)*,
and so on.)

I made a little shell script named *ttykind (6.10)* that searches for a port in the first column of */etc/ttys*. It outputs the port type from the third column. In that case, the test in my *.login* file would use:

```
set tty="`tty`"
switch ("`ttykind $tty`")
case dialup:
    ...
case network:
    ...
```

- You can also deal with many of these cases using the venerable but obscure *tset (6.03)* program to select and initialize the correct terminal type. Another program you can use to set the terminal type is *qterm (6.05)*, available on the Power Tools disk.

—JP

2.13 A .cshrc.$HOST File for per Host Setup

I work with different types of machines every day. It is often necessary to set things up differently for, say, a DEC 3000, than a SPARCStation 2. Going beyond that, you may want to set things up differently on a per-host basis.

I have this test in my *.cshrc* file:

setenv 7.01
if 49.03
~ 15.12

```
setenv HOST "`hostname`"
if (-e ~/lib/cshrc.hosts/cshrc.$HOST) then
    source ~/lib/cshrc.hosts/cshrc.$HOST
endif
```

So, if I log in to a machine named *(52.06)* bosco, and I have a file called *~/lib/cshrc.hosts/cshrc.bosco*, I can *source (46.22)* it to customize my environment for that one machine. Examples of things you would put in a *.cshrc.$HOST* file:

- Search path *(9.05)*: some machines have a */usr/local/bin*, and some have a */usr/lbin*. The same goes for *cdpath (15.05)*.

- Terminal settings *(6.09)*: I always like to reach for the upper-right part of a keyboard to erase characters. Sometimes this is the location for the BACK-SPACE key, and sometimes it is the DELETE key. I set things up so that I can consistently get "erase" behavior from whatever key is there.

- Other shell variables *(7.08)* and environment variables *(7.01)* may be different. You may run a package on a certain machine that relies on a few environment variables. No need to always set them and use up a little bit of memory if you only use them in one place!

In general, this idea allows you to group together whatever exceptions you want for a machine, rather than having to write a series of *switch (49.06)* or *if* statements *(49.03)* throughout your *.cshrc* and *.login* files.

—DS

2.14 Handling the System Message-of-the-Day

Many systems show a message at login time. The message can be long and scroll off so fast you can't read it. If you log in often, the *motd* will probably have announcements that you've read over and over again. Here are some ways to deal with that problem:

- Article 2.16 is a script that shows the whole *motd* only if it's been changed since the last time you logged in. This nice trick uses the *make* utility *(29.12)*.

- Article 17.06 shows another way to do the same thing as the previous article using *ls −t (17.02)*.

- My favorite way, the *motd.diff* script, shows only the new or changed lines in the message (see article 2.15).

—*JP*

2.15 motd.diff: Show New Lines in Login Messages

One UNIX system I worked on had a really longgggggggg login message that scrolled across my screen. It had a lot of old stuff that I'd seen for the last three weeks. For a while, I started ignoring it. But I knew that some day the system manager would put a shutdown notice in there that I wouldn't see . . .

This script solved the problem. I run it from my *.login* file. Each time I log in, the script compares the new *motd* file to the one on my previous login. If lines were added, I see them; the script pauses to give me time to read:

```
login: jpeek
Password:

Additions to system message-of-the-day:
===== 9/5/91 =====
The system will be down for maintenance from 9 to 11 tonight.
Hit RETURN to continue:
```

If there are no new lines, my login is nice and quiet.

motd.diff

This works best on systems that look for a file named *.hushlogin* in your home directory and don't print login messages if the file exists.* Install the program from the Power Tools disk, then add the command *motd.diff* on a line in your *.login* or *.profile*.

---

*That also shuts off the message You have mail. But I *always* have mail, so I don't need that. :-) If you do, and you use a command like Berkeley *mail* or *mailx*, add this line to your *.login* file:

```
if { mail -e } echo You have mail.
```

Those curly brace ({ }) operators *(49.04)* work with the *if (49.03)*, to test the exit status *(46.07)* of *mail −e*. If *mail −e* returns zero ("success"), *echo (9.04)* prints You have mail..

motd.diff uses *diff (29.01)* to compare the system's current *motd* to the *motd* at your last login on that host (stored in a file named *.last.motd.hostname* in your home directory). The script finds whether lines have been added by *grep*ping for the character > at the start of each line of *diff* output:

```
diff $lastmotd /etc/motd > $temp
   ...
if grep "^>" $temp >/dev/null     # diff USES > TO MARK NEW LINES
then
       ...show lines...
```

The *comm (29.11)* command also shows lines that have been added to a file. But *comm* only handles sorted files; this trick works on unsorted files. The i f *(46.08)* tests *grep*'s exit status *(46.07)* (*grep* returns a zero status when it finds matching lines). *grep*'s output is "thrown away" into */dev/null (14.14)*—some versions of grep have a *−s* ("silent") option to do the same thing.

This script is designed to work on networked filesystems where my same home directory is mounted on more than one computer. If your home directory isn't shared between computers, or if all systems have the same system messages, you can edit the script to delete the *hostname* variable and command.

—JP

2.16 Unclutter Logins: Show Login Messages Just Once

I used to work on a system with a huge message-of-the-day (login message). After a while, I started ignoring the *motd* when I was busy. I missed some important announcements.

.hushlogin

If you're ignoring your *motd*, too, you might want to try this. When many UNIX systems see a *.hushlogin* file in a user's home directory, they don't print the *motd*. The setup below makes the *.hushlogin* do triple duty: it's the file read by *make (29.12)*, it shows the *motd* if it's been changed, and it holds the timestamp from the last time *motd* was shown. Be sure that the two command lines (starting with @) are indented with TAB characters, not spaces:

```
# This is read by "make" at login time, shows motd when it changes
.hushlogin: /etc/motd
        @cat /etc/motd > /dev/tty
        @touch .hushlogin
```

/dev/tty *47.20*

touch *22.07*

As you'll see below, the standard output of *make* is discarded. So, the makefile redirects the stamdard output of *cat (26.02)* to show *motd* directly on */dev/tty*, your terminal.

Put the line below in your *.login* or *.profile*. Redirecting *make*'s standard output to */dev/null (14.14)* gets rid of the message `.hushlogin' is up to date when *motd* hasn't changed:

```
(cd; make -f .hushlogin .hushlogin > /dev/null)      # show motd if modified
```

The *cd* command and subshell operators *(14.07)* make sure that this always runs in your home directory—even if you use the *source* or *. (46.22)* commands from another directory.

—*JP, TC* adapted from *comp.unix.questions* on Usenet, *16 October 1988*

2.17 *Approved Shells; Using Unapproved Login Shell*

Since 4.2BSD, Berkeley UNIX systems have restricted *chsh* (or a command like it) to change your login shell only to a shell that's listed in the file */etc/shells*. That's partly a safety feature, like requiring you to type your old password before you can change to a new one: it keeps other people from giving you a strange login shell as a joke. It's also for security—a way for the system administrator to give a list of shells that are robust enough to run peoples' accounts.

The usual "approved" shells are the Bourne and C shells. If you want to use another shell as your login shell and your system has */etc/shells*, ask the system administrator to add your shell. The shell will need to be moved to a secure system directory so system crackers can't corrupt the shell.

If the system administrator won't approve your login shell, here's a work-around. It lets you log in with an approved shell, then automatically replace the shell with whatever you want:

1. If your login shell isn't C shell, use *chsh* or a command like it to change it to the C shell.

2. In your home directory, make a hard or symbolic link *(19.04)* to your shell. Use a name starting with a minus sign (–); this makes the shell act like a login shell *(53.09)*. For example, to make a symbolic link in your home directory named *–ksh* to the shell */usr/local/bin/ksh*, type this command:

   ./ 24.13
   ```
   % ln -s /usr/local/bin/ksh ./-ksh
   ```

3. Add lines to the top of the *.cshrc (2.02)* file that replace the *csh* process with your login shell. (The *exec (47.07)* command replaces a process.)

   • If you use a Bourne-type shell that reads the *.profile* file at login time, use lines like these:

   TERM *6.11*
   su *23.23*
   if *49.03*
   $? *49.04*
   ```
   # OVERRIDE DEFAULT LOGIN C SHELL TO USE ksh.
   setenv SHELL /usr/local/bin/ksh
   # IF $TERM SET (BY login OR rlogin), START LOGIN SHELL.
   # UNFORTUNATELY, THIS MAKES su USE A LOGIN SHELL TOO.
   if ($?TERM) then
       cd
       exec -ksh   # USE "LOGIN SHELL" SYMLINK IN $HOME
   else
       exec $SHELL
   endif
   echo "******** WARNING: exec ksh FAILED ********"
   ```

- If your new login shell is a *csh*-type shell that also reads *.cshrc*, you need to add a test to *.cshrc* that prevents an infinite loop. This test uses the *SH_EXECD* environment variable as a flag:

```
# OVERRIDE DEFAULT LOGIN C SHELL TO USE tcsh.
if (! $?SH_EXECD) then
    setenv SH_EXECD yes
    setenv SHELL /usr/local/bin/tcsh
    # IF $TERM SET (BY login OR rlogin), START LOGIN SHELL.
    # USE switch, NOT if, DUE TO csh BUG WITH IMBEDDED else.
    # UNFORTUNATELY, THIS MAKES su USE A LOGIN SHELL TOO.
    switch ($?TERM)
    case 1:
        cd
        exec -tcsh     # USE "LOGIN SHELL" SYMLINK IN $HOME
        breaksw
    default:
        exec $SHELL     # USE NON-LOGIN SHELL
        breaksw
    endsw
    echo "******** WARNING: exec tcsh FAILED ********"
endif
```

4. Test your new setup:

    - Try commands that start subshells *(40.04)*, like *su, rsh*, and so on *(2.07)*, to be sure that they start your new shell.

    - Put the *csh* command *set echo (9.13)* at the top of your *.cshrc* file to be sure your commands there are working.

    - Type a command that will work only in your new shell (not in a C shell).

    - Use the *ps (40.05)* command ps $$ (on System V, ps -f -p $$) to look at your new shell process ($$ is your shell's process ID number *(40.03)*).

    - Before you log out of this shell, try logging in from somewhere else *(2.04)* to be sure your new shell startup files work.

5. You're set to go.

If your login shell isn't listed in */etc/shells*, the *ftp (1.33)* program may refuse to transfer files to your account. That's partly to stop *ftp* access to your system through special accounts that don't have passwords, like *sync, who, finger*, and so on. If you use the workaround steps above, though, that shouldn't be a problem; you'll have an approved shell listed in */etc/passwd* and *ftp* usually doesn't run your login shell, anyway.

—JP

3

Logging Out

3.01 Running Commands When You Log Out

Is there something you want to do every time you log out: run a program that deletes temporary files, asks you a question, or prints a fortune to your screen? If you use the C shell, make a file named *.logout* *(2.02)* in your home directory and put the commands there. Before a login C shell exits, it'll read that file. But not all shells are login C shells; you might want these shells to read your logout-type file, too. Articles 2.07 and 2.08 have some suggestions.

Some ideas for your *.logout* are:

- A command like *fortune* *(3.03)* can give you something fun to think about when you log out.

- A background command to clean up temporary files, as in article 3.04.

- A command to list a "reminder" file—for example, work to take home.

- A script that prompts you for the hours you've worked on projects so you can make a timesheet later.

- The command *clear(23.19)* to erase your screen. This keeps the next user from reading what you did.* It also helps to stop "burn-in" damage to terminals caused by characters left over from your login session. (Some UNIXes clear the screen before printing the `login:` prompt. Of course, this won't help users who connect with a data switch *(55.01)* or port manager because the connection will be broken before the next login prompt.)

If you connect to this host over a network, with a slow modem or on a data switch—and you don't see all the *.logout* commands run before your connection closes—try putting the command `sleep 2` *(42.02)* at the end of the file. That

---

*Some terminals and windows have "scroll back" memory of previous screens. *clear* usually doesn't erase all of that.

makes the shell wait two seconds before it exits, which gives output more time to get to your screen.

—JP

3.02 *Running Commands at Bourne/Korn Shell Logout*

The C shell has a setup file named *.logout (2.02)*. Commands in *.logout* are run when you log out. The Bourne and Korn shells don't have a logout file, though. Here's how to make one:

1. In your *.profile* file, add the line:

trap *46.12*
. *46.22*

```
trap '. $HOME/.sh_logout; exit' 0
```

(Some systems may need $LOGDIR instead of $HOME.)

2. Make a file in your home directory named *.sh_logout*. Put in the commands you want to be run when you log out. For example:

if *46.08*
[–f *46.19*

```
clear
if [ -f $HOME/todo.tomorrow ]
then
     echo "=========== STUFF TO DO TOMORROW: ============"
     cat $HOME/todo.tomorrow
fi
```

The *trap* will read the *.sh_logout* file when the shell exits.

—JP

3.03 *Electronic Fortune Cookies*

```
It's a damn poor mind that can only think of one way to spell a word.
               -- Andrew Jackson
Too much of a good thing is WONDERFUL.
               -- Mae West
Democracy is a form of government that substitutes election by the
incompetent many for appointment by the corrupt few.
               -- G. B. Shaw
Research is what I'm doing when I don't know what I'm doing.
               -- Wernher von Braun
I do not feel obliged to believe that same God who endowed us with
sense, reason, and intellect had intended for us to forgo their use.
               -- Galileo
Computers are useless; they can only give answers.
               -- Picasso
Dyslexics of the world, untie!
```

These messages come from a program named *fortune*—usually in the */usr/games* directory. Every time you run *fortune* you'll get a message like one of these. Most users run *fortune* from their *.profile* or *.logout* files. If the directory */usr/games* isn't in your search path *(9.05)*, use the command */usr/games/fortune* instead.

Every time someone runs *fortune*, the program has to write to its *fortunes.dat* file. Computers with networked filesystems might put that file on a "read-only" filesystem that most users can't write to. If you get that error and your system is set up to run *rsh (1.33)* without needing a password, ask your system administrator which computer has the filesystem mounted writable. Then run:

```
% rsh that-machine /usr/games/fortune
```

Some other versions use another way to keep track of fortunes; their files don't need to be writable.

—JP

3.04 *Automatic File Cleanup*

If you use a system to make temporary files *(22.03)*, your *.logout* file can clean up the temporary files. The exact cleanup command you'll use depends on how you create the files, of course. The overall setup looks something like this in *.logout*:

~ *15.12*
```
(set nonomatch; cd ~/temp && rm -f *) &
```

The parentheses runs the commands in a subshell *(14.07)* so the *cd* command won't change the current shell's working directory. The set nonomatch *(16.05)* tells the C shell to be quiet if there aren't any temp files to clean up. The && *(46.09)* means that rm won't run unless the cd succeeds. Using cd ~/temp first, instead of just rm ~/temp/*, helps to keep *rm*'s command-line arguments from getting too long *(16.07)* if there are lots of temporary files to remove.

If you could be logged in more than once, be careful not to remove temp files that other login sessions might still be using. One way to do this is with the *find* *(18.02)* command—only remove files that haven't been modified in the last day:

xargs *10.19*
```
find ~/temp -type f -mtime +1 | xargs rm -f &
```

—JP

3.05 *Stop Accidental C Shell Logouts*

Do you occasionally type CTRL-d by mistake and find out that you're suddenly logged off the system? If you do, you should know about the *ignoreeof* shell variable. CTRL-d is the end-of-file character; when a shell sees it, it thinks that no more input is coming, so it quits. If you're in your login shell *(53.09)*, you're suddenly logged out. If you're not in your login shell, you may still be in trouble: a window may have disappeared, or your environment may have suddenly changed because you dropped from a subshell *(40.04)* into the parent shell.

If you're a C shell user, you can solve this problem by setting the *ignoreeof* shell variable:

```
set ignoreeof        # prevent accidental shell termination
```

(Most users set this in their *.cshrc* or *.login* files.) Now typing CTRL-d won't terminate the shell. Instead, you'll get a polite message: Use `logout' to logout or perhaps Use `exit' to leave csh.

In the Korn shell, use set -o ignoreeof instead. If you use the Bourne shell, article 3.06 has a workaround for the problem.

If you're like me, you won't use this feature; I happen to find CTRL-d a convenient shorthand for the *logout* or *exit* commands. But my taste is certainly disputable, and even I will admit that my fingers sometimes err.

—ML

3.06 *Stop Accidental Bourne Shell Logouts*

It's pretty easy to type one too many CTRL-d characters and log out of a Bourne shell without meaning to. The C shell has an *ignoreeof* shell variable *(3.05)* that won't let you log out with CTRL-d. So does the Korn shell; use set -o ignoreeof.

Here's a different sort of solution for the Bourne shell. When you end the shell, it asks if you're sure. If you don't answer yes, a new shell is started to replace your old one.

First, make a file like the C shell's *.logout* that will be read when your Bourne shell exits *(3.02)*. Save your tty *(3.08)* name in an environment variable *(7.01)*, too—you'll need it later:

trap 46.12
```
TTY=`tty`; export TTY
trap '. $HOME/.sh_logout; exit' 0
```

(48.10)

(Your system may need $LOGDIR instead of $HOME.) Put the following lines in your new *.sh_logout* file:

exec < 47.20

case 46.06

exec 40.02
–sh 53.09
```
exec < $TTY
echo "Do you really want to log out? \c"
read ans
case "$ans" in
[Yy]*) ;;
*)   exec $HOME/bin/-sh ;;
esac
```

The last line is some trickery to start a new login shell *(53.09)*. The shell closes your tty *(47.20)* before reading your *.sh_logout* file; the exec < $TTY reconnects the shell's standard input to your terminal.

Note that if your system is *very* slow, you may not get the reminder message for a couple of seconds—you might forget that it's coming and walk away. That hasn't been a problem where I've tested this. If it is for you though, replace the read ans with a program like *grabchars* *(47.31)* that times out and gives a default answer after a while. There may be some Bourne shells that need other tricks—and others that don't need these tricks—but this should give you an idea of what to do.

—JP

3.07 Detaching a Session with screen

screen

If your system supports ptys *(43.08)*, there's a really useful program you should have. *screen (13.09)* lets you start a process—like a shell (*csh*, *sh*, etc.), a news-reading program, or whatever—then whenever you want, detach the whole process and log out. You can then log in someplace later and resume where you left off—or have *screen* keep running whatever you started after you log out. You can start many windows, even on a non-windowing terminal, and switch between them.

Normally, you can exit *screen* by exiting each shell individually, or by using CTRL-a CTRL-\ to kill all sessions. And if you want to end a *screen* session but pick it up later on, you can exit using CTRL-a CTRL-d.

Instead of a `screen is terminating` message, you'll get one that says `[detached]` —followed by a prompt:

```
[detached]
%
```

To reattach the session later on, start *screen* with the *–r* option. You'll be placed in exactly the same *screen* session that you were in before. All your processes are still running—for example, if you were in the middle of editing a file in one of your *screen* sessions, the editing session is still active. You can just continue where you were.

This is great because it means that not only can you keep active sessions all the time (even if you log out), you can also resume them from different terminals. So for example, I could go home, log in from there and pick up exactly where I left off.

—LM, JP

3.08 What tty am I On?

Each login session has its own *tty (40.06)*—a UNIX device file that handles input and output for your terminal, window, etc. Each tty has its own filename. If you're logged on more than once and other users want to *write* or *talk (1.33)* to you, they need to know which tty to use. If you have processes running on several ttys, you can tell which process is where.

To do that, run the *tty* command at a shell prompt in the window:

```
% tty
/dev/tty07
```

You can tell other users to type `write` *your-username* `tty07`.

Some systems have different kinds of ttys: a few dialup terminals, some network ports for *rlogin* and *telnet,* etc. *(1.33).* You or your system administrator can look in a system file like */etc/ttys (6.10)* to find out which ttys are used for what. You can use this to make your login setup more automatic. For example, most network terminals on our computer have names like /dev/ttyp*x* or /dev/ttyq*x*, where *x* is a single digit or letter. I have a test in my *.logout* file *(3.01)* that clears the screen and prints a fortune *(3.03)* on all ttys except network:

```
# Clear screen and print fortune on non-network ttys:
if ("`tty`" !~ /dev/tty[pq]*) then
    clear
    fortune
endif
```

`` 10.14
!~ 49.04

—*JP*

4

Passwords

4.01 The Care and Feeding of Passwords

Although passwords are the most important element of computer security, users often receive only cursory instructions about selecting them. If you are a user, be aware that by picking a bad password—or by revealing your password to an untrustworthy individual—you are potentially compromising your entire computer's security. If you are a system administrator, be sure that all of your users are familiar with the issues raised in this chapter.

—SG, GS from the Nutshell Handbook *Practical UNIX Security*

4.02 Passwords: How and Why

When the *login* program asks your password, it needs some way of knowing that the password you type is the correct one. Many early computer systems (and quite a few still around today!) kept all of the passwords for all of their users unencrypted and plainly visible in a single file which could be accessed only by privileged users and operating system utilities. The problem with this approach is that the contents of the password file almost invariably—through accident, programming error, or deliberate act—becomes available to unprivileged users.

The real danger posed by such systems is that people can make copies of the password file and expropriate them without the knowledge of the system administrator. For example, if the password file is saved on backup tapes, then those backups must be kept in a physically secure place. If a backup tape is stolen, then *everybody's* password must be changed.

UNIX avoids this problem by not keeping actual passwords anywhere on the system. Instead, UNIX stores a value that is generated by using the password to encrypt a block of zeros with a one-way function called *crypt*(3); the result of the calculation is (usually) stored in the file */etc/passwd* (37.03). When you try to log in, the program */bin/login* does not decrypt your password stored in the file. Instead, */bin/login* takes the password that you typed, uses it to transform another block of zeros, and compares the newly transformed block with the block stored in the */etc/passwd* file. If the two encrypted passwords match, the system lets you in.

The security of this approach rests upon the strength of the encryption algorithm and the difficulty of guessing the user's password. To date, the *crypt* algorithm has proven highly resistant to attacks.

Note: Don't confuse the *crypt*(3) algorithm with the *crypt (23.18)* encryption program. *crypt* uses a different encryption system from *crypt*(3) and is very easy to break.

The crypt(3) Algorithm

The algorithm that *crypt*(3) uses is based on the Data Encryption Standard (DES) of the National Institute of Standards and Technology (NIST). In normal operation, DES uses a 56-bit key (eight 7-bit ASCII *(53.03)* characters, for instance) to encrypt blocks of original text, or *clear text*, that are 64 bits in length. The resulting 64-bit blocks of encrypted text, or *ciphertext*, cannot easily be decrypted to the original clear text without knowing the original 56-bit key. There is no published or known method to easily decrypt the encrypted text without knowing the key.*

The UNIX *crypt*(3) function takes the user's password as the encryption key and uses it to encrypt a 64-bit block of zeros. The resulting 64-bit block of cipher text is then encrypted again with the user's password; the process is repeated a total of 25 times. The final 64 bits are unpacked into a string of 11 printable characters that are stored in the */etc/passwd* file.

Although the source code to *crypt*(3) is readily available, no technique has been discovered (or publicized) to translate the encrypted password back into the original password. The only known way to defeat UNIX password security is to guess passwords from a dictionary, encrypt them, and compare the results with the encrypted passwords stored in */etc/passwd*. This approach to breaking a cryptographic cipher is often called a *key search* or a *dictionary attack*.

Robert Morris and Ken Thompson designed *crypt*(3) to make a key search computationally expensive. Software implementations of DES are usually slow; iterating the encryption process 25 times makes the process of encrypting a single password 25 times slower still. On the original PDP-11 processors, upon which UNIX was designed, nearly a full second of computer time was required to encrypt a single password. To eliminate the possibility of using DES hardware encryption chips, which are a thousand times faster than software running on a

---

* "Easily" has a different meaning for cryptographers than for mere mortals. To decrypt something encrypted with DES is computationally very expensive; even using the fastest known machines might take hundreds of thousands or even millions of years.

PDP-11, Morris and Thompson modified the DES tables used by their software implementation, rendering the two incompatible. In addition, to prevent a bad guy from simply encrypting an entire dictionary, they added a bit of salt.

What is Salt?

Just as table salt adds zest to popcorn, the salt that Morris and Thompson sprinkled into the DES algorithm added a little more spice and variety. The DES salt is a 12-bit number, between 0 and 4095, which slightly changes the result of the DES function. Each of the 4096 different salts makes a password encrypt a different way.

When you change your password, the */bin/passwd* program selects a salt based on the time of day. The salt is converted into a two-character string and stored in the */etc/passwd* file along with the encrypted password. This way, when you type in your password at login, the same salt is used again. UNIX stores the salt as the first two characters of the encrypted password.

Table 4-1 shows how a few different passwords encrypt with different salts.

Table 4-1. Passwords and Salts

Password	Salt	Encrypted Password
nutmeg	Mi	MiqkFWCm1fNJI
ellen1	ri	ri79KNd7V6.Sk
Sharon	./	./2aN7ysff3qM
norahs	am	amfIADT2iqjAf
norahs	7a	7azfT5tIdyhOI

Notice that the last password, *norahs*, was encrypted two different ways with two different salts.

Having a salt means that the same password can encrypt in 4096 different ways. Although the salt doesn't increase the amount of time to search for a single password, it forces a bad guy to search for each user's password individually, because different users' passwords will be encrypted with different salts. As a side effect, the salt makes it possible for a user to have the same password on a number of different computers and to keep this fact a secret, even from somebody who has access to the */etc/passwd* files on all of those computers.

—*SG, GS* from the Nutshell Handbook *Practical UNIX Security*

4.03 Bad Passwords: Open Doors

A bad password is any password that is easily guessed.

In the movie *Real Genius*, a computer recluse named Lazlo Hollyfeld breaks into a top-secret military computer over the telephone by guessing passwords. Lazlo starts by typing the password *AAAAAA*, then trying *AAAAAB*, then *AAAAAC*, and so on, until he finally finds the password that matches.

Real-life computer crackers are far more sophisticated. Instead of typing each password by hand, crackers use personal computers that make the phone calls and try the passwords, automatically redialing when they become disconnected. Instead of trying every combination of letters, starting with *AAAAAA* (or whatever), crackers use *hit lists* of common passwords such as *wizard* or *demo*. Even a modest home computer with a good password guessing program can try thousands of passwords in less than a day's time. Some hit lists used by crackers are a few hundred thousand words in length. Therefore, any password that *anybody* might guess to be a password is probably a bad choice.

What's a popular password? Your name. Your spouse's name or your parents' names. Other bad passwords are these names backward or followed by a single digit. Short passwords are also bad, because there are fewer of them: they are, therefore, more easily guessed. Especially bad are "magic words" from computer games, such as *xyzzy*. Other bad choices include phone numbers, characters from your favorite movies or books, local landmark names, favorite drinks, or famous computer scientists (see the list below for still more bad choices).

Many versions of UNIX make a minimal attempt to prevent users from picking bad passwords. For example, under Berkeley UNIX, if you attempt to pick a password with fewer than six letters that are all of the same case, the *passwd* program will ask the user to "Please use a longer password." After three tries, however, the password program relents and lets the user pick a short one. (Different versions of System V have different restrictions on the kinds of passwords that you can choose.)

Long passwords alone are not a refuge. To be secure, a password should not be any of the following:

* Your name, spouse's name, parent's name, pet's name, child's name.

* Names of close friends or co-workers, favorite fantasy characters, boss' name, *anybody's* name.

* The name of the operating system you're using, hostname of your computer, your phone number, your license plate number.

* Any part of your social security number, anybody's birth date, other information that is easily obtained about you.

* Words such as *wizard, guru, gandalf,* and so on.

* Any username on the computer in any form (as is, capitalized, doubled, etc.).

- A word in the English dictionary or in a foreign dictionary. A place. A proper noun.

- Passwords of all the same letter. Simple patterns of letters on the keyboard, like *qwerty*.

- Any of the above spelled backward.

- Any of the above followed or prepended by a single digit.

Surprisingly, experts believe that a significant percent of all computers contain at least one account where the username and the password are the same. Such accounts are often called "Joes." Joe accounts are easy for crackers to find and trivial to penetrate. Most computer crackers can find an entry point into almost any system simply by checking every account to see if it is a Joe account. This is one reason why it is dangerous for your computer to make a list of all of the valid usernames available to the outside world.

—*SG, GS* from the Nutshell Handbook *Practical UNIX Security*

4.04 Good Passwords: Locked Doors

Good passwords are passwords that are difficult to guess. In general, good passwords:

- Have both uppercase and lowercase letters.

- Have digits and/or punctuation characters as well as letters.

- Are easy to remember, so they do not have to be written down.

- Are seven or eight characters long.

- Can be typed quickly, so somebody cannot follow what you type by looking over your shoulder.

It's easy to pick a good password. Here are some suggestions:

- Take two short words and combine them with a special character or a number, like *robot4my* or *eye-con*.

- Put together an acronym that's special to you, like *Notfsw* (None Of This Fancy Stuff Works) or *AUPEGC* (All UNIX programmers eat green cheese).

(Of course, *robot4my*, *eye-con*, *Notfsw*, and *AUPEGC* are now all *bad* passwords because they've been printed here.)

—*SG, GS* from the Nutshell Handbook *Practical UNIX Security*

4.05 Two Characters You Shouldn't Use in a Password

You probably know that UNIX accepts almost any character in a password. That's good for security. There are two characters that you probably shouldn't use, though: # (hash mark) and @ (at sign).

That's because old UNIX systems used them for erasing characters and lines (some still do), and the *login* program on some UNIXes still makes that assumption. (Unfortunately, the *passwd* program will let you use those characters when you set a password. But then you can't log in!)

—JP

4.06 Changing Your Password

You can change your password with the UNIX *passwd* command. *passwd* first asks you to type your old password, then asks for a new one. By asking you to type your old password first, *passwd* prevents somebody from walking up to a terminal that you left yourself logged into and then changing your password without your knowledge.

UNIX makes you type the password twice when you change it:

```
% passwd
Changing password for sarah.
Old password: tuna4fis
New password: nosmis32
Retype new password: nosmis32
%
```

(For security, *passwd* won't display the password as you type it.) If the two passwords you type don't match, your password remains unchanged. This is a safety precaution: if you made a mistake typing the password the first time, the chances are that you will not make the same mistake the second time. If UNIX asked you for your new password only once, you might inadvertently change it to something other than what you intended, and then you'd be stuck.

Note: On systems that use Sun Microsystems' NIS, you may need to use the command *yppasswd* to change your password. Except for having a different name, *yppasswd* works the same way as *passwd*, but updates your password in the network database.

(4.05)

Even though passwords are not echoed when they are printed, the DELETE key (or whatever key you have bound *(6.09)* to the "erase" function) will still delete the last character typed, so if you make a mistake, you can correct it.

After you have changed your password, your old password is no good. *Do not forget your new password!* If you do forget your new password, you will need to have the system administrator set it to something you can use to log in and try again. If the system administrator sets your password for you, immediately change it to something else that only you know!

—*SG, GS from the Nutshell Handbook* Practical UNIX Security

4.07 *Checking Out Your New Password*

After you have changed your password, try logging in to your account with the new password to make sure that you've entered the new password properly. Ideally, you should do this without logging out *(2.04)*, so you will have some recourse if you did not change your password properly. This is especially crucial if you are logged in as *root (1.24)* and you have just changed the *root* password.

—*SG, GS from the Nutshell Handbook* Practical UNIX Security

4.08 *Passwords on Multiple Machines*

If you have several computer accounts, you may wish to have the same password on every machine, so you have less you need to remember. However, if you have the same password on many machines and one of those machines is compromised, all of your accounts are compromised. One common approach used by people with accounts on many machines is to have a base password that can be modified slightly for each different machine. For example, your base password might be *kxyzzy* followed by the first letter of the name of the computer you're using. On a computer named *athena* your password would be *kxyzzya*, while on a computer named *ems* your password would be *kxyzzye*. (Don't, of course, use exactly this method of varying your passwords.)

—*SG, GS from the Nutshell Handbook* Practical UNIX Security

4.09 *Writing Down Passwords*

Users are admonished to "never write down a password." Of course, you should not write your password on your desk calendar or on a Post-it label attached to your terminal.

A password that you memorize is more secure than the same password written down, simply because there is less opportunity for other people to learn your memorized password. But a password that must be written down in order to be remembered is quite likely a password that is not going to be guessed easily. If you write your password in your wallet, the chances of somebody who steals your wallet using the password to break into your computer account are remote indeed.*

---

*Unless, of course, you are an extremely important person and your wallet is stolen as part of an elaborate plot.

If you must write down your password, follow a few precautions:

- Do not identify your password as being a password.

- Do not include the name of the account or the phone number of the computer on the same piece of paper.

- Do not attach the password to your terminal, keyboard, or any part of your computer.

- Mix in some "noise" characters or scramble the written version of the password in a way that you remember, but make the written version different from the real password.

Never record a password online. Likewise, *never send a password to another user via electronic mail.* In *The Cuckoo's Egg*, Cliff Stoll tells of how a single intruder broke into system after system by searching for the word "password" in text files and mail messages. With this simple trick, the intruder learned of the passwords of many accounts on many different computers across the country.

—*SG, GS* from the Nutshell Handbook *Practical UNIX Security*

5

Organizing Your Home Directory

5.01 What? Me Organized?

Computers and offices have one thing in common: it's easy to lose things. If you walk into my office, you'll see stacks of paper on top of other stacks of paper, with a few magazines and business cards scattered in. I can often find things, but I'd be lying if I said that I could *always* find that article I was reading the other day!

When you look at a new computer user's home directory, you often see something that's similar to my office. You see a huge number of unrelated files, with obscure names. He or she hasn't created any subdirectories, aside from those the system administrator told him he needed; and those probably aren't even being used. His home directory probably contains programs for several different projects, personal mail, notes from meetings, a few data files, some half-finished documentation, a spreadsheet for something he started last month but has now forgotten, etc.

Remember that a computer's filesystem isn't that much different from any other filing system. If you threw all of your papers into one giant filing cabinet without sorting them into different topics and subtopics, the filing cabinet wouldn't do you any good at all: it would just be a mess. On a computer, the solution to this problem is to sort your files into *directories*, which are analogous to the filing cabinets and drawers.

The UNIX filesystem *(1.19)* can help you keep all of your material neatly sorted. Your directories are like filing cabinets, with dividers and folders inside them. In this chapter, we'll give some hints for organizing your computer "office." Of course, things occasionally get misplaced even in the most efficient offices. Articles 18.21 and 18.22 show some scripts that use the *find* and *grep* commands to help you find files that are misplaced.

—ML

5.02 A bin Directory for Your Programs and Scripts

If you compile programs *(54.08)* or write shell scripts *(1.05)*, it's good to put them in one directory. This can be a subdirectory of your home directory. Or, if several people want to use these programs, you could pick any other directory—as long as you have write access to it. Usually, the directory's name is something like *bin*—though I name mine *.bin* (with a leading dot) *(1.15)* to keep it from cluttering my *ls* listings.

1. For instance, to make a *bin* under your home directory, type:

   ```
   % cd
   % mkdir bin
   ```

2. Once you have a directory for storing programs, be sure that the shell can find the programs in it. Type the command echo $PATH and look for the directory's pathname. For instance, if your directory is called */u/walt/bin*, you should see:

   ```
   % echo $PATH
   ...:/u/walt/bin:...
   ```

   If the directory isn't in your *PATH*, add it *(9.05)*.

3. Finally, if other people are sharing the directory, use a command like *chmod go+rx bin (23.07)* to give them access.

When you add a new program to your *bin* directory, if you use the C shell, you need to use the shell's *rehash* command. That's because the C shell doesn't search your path directly but instead uses a hash table to find the commands more quickly.

—*JP from the Nutshell Handbook* MH & xmh: E-Mail for Users & Programmers

5.03 Organizing Nonexecutable Scripts

Most UNIX users put their own shell scripts and compiled binary programs in a subdirectory called *bin (5.02)*, within their home directory. But what about other kinds of scripts, which aren't executable, but which might be handy to re-use?

For example, I use *sed (35.24)* for many complex editing tasks. I could run *sed* from a shell script to make the whole command executable, but more often than not, I just use the *runsed (35.03)* script, which looks for a file in the current directory called *sedscr*.

I keep my various *sed* scripts in a subdirectory of my home directory called *sedlib*, and then simply copy or link *(19.03)* them to *sedscr* whenever I want to use them with *runsed*.

—*TOR*

5.04 Directories for Emacs Hacks

If you use any Emacs *(33.01)* editor (GNU Emacs or any of the commercial alternatives), you may have written lots of handy LISP programs for use while you're editing. It's convenient to create a separate directory for these; a good name for this directory is (obviously) *emacs*; it's usually located in your home directory.

If you use GNU Emacs, you should put the following line in the *.emacs* file:

```
(setq load-path (append load-path '("your-emacs-directory")))
```

This tells Emacs that it should look in your personal Emacs directory to find your programs. (It's similar to the *PATH(7.04)* environment variable.)

—*ML*

5.05 Private (Personal) Directories

You might want to create a private directory for your personal files: love letters, financial data, complaints about your boss, off-color jokes, or whatever you want to keep there. Call it anything you want, but *private* is a good name. [I usually give my private directories names that *don't* imply they're private.—*JP*] Once you've created a private directory, you should set its file access mode *(23.02)* to 700; this means that you're the only person allowed to read, write, or even list the files that are in the directory. Here's how:

```
% mkdir private
% chmod 700 private
```

On any UNIX system, anyone who knows the root password can become superuser and read any files he or she wants. So a private personal directory doesn't give you complete protection by any means—especially since, on many UNIX systems, most users know the root password. But it does keep prying eyes away. If you really need security, you can always encrypt *(23.18)* your files.

—*ML*

5.06 Naming Files

Let's think about a filing cabinet again. If the files in your filing cabinet were called *letter1, letter2, letter3,* and so on, you'd never be able to find anything.

The same is true on your computer. You should come up with a descriptive name for each file to create. UNIX systems let you have very long filenames. A few systems have a 14-character limit, but most allow names that are 256 characters long—certainly longer than you will ever need.

I can't tell you how to make a filename descriptive, except to suggest that rather than using names like *letter,* you make a filename that describes what the letter is about. In the case of a letter, using the recipient's name may help—assuming that you can easily make a connection between *john_shmoe* and "that's the letter about trends in gold prices" (though I'd suggest that the name *gold_price_trends_oct* is an even better name than *john_shmoe*). Bruce Barnett has suggested that, by using long filenames, you can create a simple "relational database." For example, you could find out everything you've recorded about the price of gold with a command like `more *gold*price*`. Of course, this doesn't provide the fancy features that a commercial database would have—but you may not need those features and, if so, why spend good money to buy them?

Similarly, if you're a programmer, the name of each file in your program should describe what the code does. If the code diagonalizes matrices, the file should be called something like *diag_mat.c*. If the code reads input from bank tellers, it should be called something like *teller_input.c*.

Another way to distinguish between different kinds of files is by using suffixes or filename extensions *(1.17)*.

—*ML*

5.07 *Make More Directories!*

Creating many directories has several advantages:

- First, it is easier to find any particular file if your home directory is well-sorted. Imagine a rack of filing cabinets that isn't sorted; people just insert files wherever they fit. You may as well throw your data out; when you need something, you'll never be able to find it.

- Second, UNIX can access files much faster when directories are relatively small. Ideally, directories should have at most 60 (or so) files in them.

- Third, directories are an important part of UNIX file protection *(23.01)*. You can use directories to help protect certain files against access by others.

Make directories liberally! Make a new directory for every new project you start; make subdirectories within these directories for subtopics. Your home directory should ideally contain *nothing* but subdirectories. Here are some recommended conventions:

- If you're a programmer, create a new directory for each project. For example, create a directory called *src* for source files, a directory called *doc* or *man* for documentation, a directory called *obj* for object files, a directory called *rel* for the current working version (or almost-working version) of the program, a directory called *test* for test files and results, and so on. If the program is large, your *src* directory (and your *obj* directory) should also be split into different subdirectories, each containing different parts of the project.

- It's a good idea to put all personal files (as opposed to work files) in a directory which can be protected against snoopers. See article 5.05.

- Many users save all of their mail *(1.33)* in one directory (often called *Mail*), which is then divided into subdirectories by topic. I use a variation of this scheme; I keep general mail in my *Mail* directory, but I save correspondence about particular projects with the project itself. For example, my Power Tools mail is shelved with the source code for this article.

Article 5.08 shows some quick ways to make directories.

—*ML*

5.08 *Making Directories Made Easier*

In article 5.07, we told you that you should have lots of directories. Experienced UNIX users are creating new directories all the time. How do you make a directory?

It's easy. Use the *mkdir* command, followed by the name of your new directory:

```
% mkdir directory
```

This creates the new directory you want. It doesn't necessarily have to be in your current directory. For example:

```
% cd /home/los/mikel
% mkdir /src/books/power/articles/files
```

The only requirements are:

* The parent of the directory you want to create must exist (in this case, */src/books/power/articles*).

* You must have write access to the parent directory.

What if the parent directory doesn't already exist? Assume, for example, that */src/books* already exists, but the *power* and *articles* directories don't. You can make these "by hand," or (on many UNIX systems) you can add the −*p* (parent) option:

```
% mkdir -p /src/books/power/articles/files
```

This tells *mkdir* to create all the intermediate directories that are needed. So the above command creates three directories:

1. */src/books/power*

2. */src/books/power/articles*

3. */src/books/power/articles/files*

[If your *mkdir* doesn't have −*p*, you can use C shell history (12.02):

```
% mkdir /src/books/power
% !!/articles
mkdir /src/books/power/articles
% !!/files
mkdir /src/books/power/articles/files
```

That's almost as quick. —*JP*]

If you are using System V, you can also supply the "file protection mode" to be assigned to the directory. (By default, the file protection mode is derived from your *umask(23.04).*) To do so, use the *–m* option. For example:

```
% mkdir -m 755 /src/books/power/articles/files
```

This creates the directory with access mode 755, which allows the owner to do anything with the directory. Note that this must be a numeric mode; see article 23.01 for an introduction to file and directory protection.

—ML

5.09 *Setting Up vi with the .exrc File*

You can store commands and settings that you want executed any time you start the *vi* or *ex* editors *(31.02)* in a file called *.exrc* in your home directory. You can modify the *.exrc* file with the *vi* editor, just as you can any other text file.

If you don't yet have an *.exrc* file, simply use *vi* to create one. Enter into this file the *set, ab(31.31),* and *map(32.02)* commands that you want to have in effect whenever you use *vi* or *ex.* A sample *.exrc* file looks like this:

```
set nowrapscan wrapmargin=7
set sections=SeAhBhChDh nomesg
map q :w^M:n^M
" To swap two words, put cursor at start of first word and type v:
map v dwElp
ab ORA O'Reilly & Associates, Inc.
```

The ^M characters are RETURNs. Make them by pressing CTRL-v, then RETURN *(32.05)*. Lines that start with a double quote (") are comments. Since the file is actually read by *ex* before it enters *vi,* commands in *.exrc* should not have a preceding colon.

In addition to reading the *.exrc* file in your home directory, *vi* will read a file called *.exrc* in the current directory. This allows you to set options that are appropriate to a particular project *(31.06)*.

If your *.exrc* file doesn't seem to be working, watch carefully for error messages just as *vi* starts, before it clears your screen. If you can't read them quickly enough, try the tricks in article 44.08.

—TOR from the Nutshell Handbook *Learning the vi Editor*

5.10 Find All Command Versions with whereiz

Use *which* *(52.07)* to get the full pathname of a command. But *which* only shows the first directory in your *PATH* *(7.04)* with that command. If you want to find other commands with the same name in other directories, the standard *which* won't show them to you. (The *which* on the Power Tools disk will—if you use its *−a* option.) *whereiz* will:

```
% which grep
/usr/bin/grep
% whereiz grep
/usr/bin/grep /usr/5bin/grep
```

On my system, the */usr/bin* directory holds a Berkeley-like version of a command. The */usr/5bin* directory holds System V versions. */usr/bin* is first in my path, but it's good to know if there's also a System V version. *whereiz* also lets you see if there are both local and system versions of the same command in your path.

Here's the script. The name ends in a *z* because many UNIX versions already have a *whereis* *(52.05)* command.

whereiz

```
#! /bin/sh

# COMMAND THAT TESTS FOR EXECUTABLE FILES... SYSTEM-DEPENDENT:
testx="test -x"

# REPLACE NULL FIELD IN $PATH WITH A .
fixpath="`echo $PATH | sed \
    -e 's/^:/.:/' \
    -e 's/::/:.:/g' \
    -e 's/:$/:./'`"

IFS=":  "          # SET $IFS (COLON, SPACE, TAB) FOR PARSING $PATH
for command
do
        where=""                # ZERO OUT $where

        # IF DIRECTORY HAS EXECUTABLE FILE, ADD IT TO LIST:
        for direc in $fixpath
        do $testx $direc/$command && where="$where $direc/$command"
        done

        case "$where" in
        ?*) echo $where ;;  # IF CONTAINS SOMETHING, OUTPUT IT
        esac
done
```

&& *46.09*

The *sed* *(35.24)* command "fixes" your *PATH*. It replaces a null directory name (`::` in the middle of the *PATH* or a single `:` at the start or end of the *PATH*), which stands for the current directory. The null member is changed to the relative pathname for the current directory, a dot *(1.21)*, so the *direc* shell variable in the loop won't be empty. In line 12, the double quotes (`" "`) have colon, space, and tab characters between them. This sets the *IFS* *(36.19)* variable to split the "fixed" search path, at the colon characters, into separate directories during the *for* loop *(46.15)*. That's a useful way to handle any colon-separated list.

—*JP*

6

Setting Up Your Terminal

6.01 There's a Lot to Know about Terminals

This is one of three chapters about terminal setup. It covers most of what you need to know to set up your terminal from your shell setup files *(2.02)*.

Chapter 43, *Terminal and Serial Line Settings*, goes into terminals in a little more depth, giving background concepts and some more specialized tips.

Chapter 44, *Problems with Terminals*, deals with the many problems that can occur—many of them seeming inexplicable to the novice—and gives some hints about what to do about them.

—*TOR*

6.02 The Idea of a Terminal Database

Terminals differ. Manufacturers produce a variety of terminals, each one including a particular set of features for a certain price. There are new terminals and old, smart terminals and dumb ones, terminals with big screens and terminals with small screens, printing terminals and video displays, and terminals with all sorts of special features.

Differences between terminals do not matter much to programs like *cat (26.02)* or *who (53.04)* that use the terminal screen as a sort of typewriter with an endless scroll of paper. These programs produce sequential output and do not make use of the terminal's special features; they do not need to know much to do their job. Only programs such as screen editors, which make use of screen-handling features, need to know about differences between terminals.

In the late 1970s, Bill Joy created the *vi (31.02)* text editor at U.C. Berkeley. Like all screen-oriented editors, *vi* uses the terminal screen non-sequentially. A program performing non-sequential output does not just print character after character, but must manipulate the text that was sent before, scroll the page, move the cursor, delete lines, insert characters, and more. While it would be possible to keep redrawing the screen in its entirety, many features are provided in hardware or firmware by the terminal itself, and save too much time and trouble to be ignored.

The first version of *vi* was written specifically for Lear Siegler ADM3a terminals. *vi* was such an improvement over line-oriented editors that there was great demand to port *vi* to other brands of terminals. The problem was that each terminal had different features and used different control codes to manipulate the features that they did have in common.

Rather than write separate terminal drivers *(44.01)* for each terminal type, Bill Joy did something very clever, which all UNIX users now take for granted. He wrote a version of *vi* with generic commands to manipulate the screen instead of hardcoding the control codes and dimensions for a particular terminal.

The generic terminal-handling mechanism Joy came up with had two parts: a database describing the capabilities of each of the terminals to be supported, and a subroutine library that allows programs to query that database and to make use of the capability values it contains. Both the library and the database were given the name *termcap*, which is short for *term*inal *cap*abilities.

At this point, users take for granted the fact that you can use just about any terminal with a UNIX system and use screen-oriented programs like *vi* without any problem. But it is really quite remarkable!

The *termcap* database is contained in a single text file, which grew quite large over the years to include descriptions of hundreds of different terminals. To improve performance, AT&T later introduced a database called *terminfo*, which stores terminal descriptions, in compiled form, in a separate file for each terminal.

If a program is designed to use *termcap* or *terminfo*, it queries an environment variable called *TERM (6.11)* to determine the terminal type, then looks up the entry for that terminal in the terminal database, and reads the definition of any capabilities it plans to use into external variables. Programs that use *termcap* or *terminfo* range from screen editors like *vi* and *emacs (33.01)*, which use the complete terminal description, to a program like *clear (23.19)*, which needs to know only one capability (the escape sequence to clear the screen). Other programs include *more (26.03)*, *pg*, *rogue*, *tset (6.03)*, *ul*, and *nroff (45.14)*.

—*JS* from the Nutshell Handbook *termcap & terminfo*

6.03 *Setting the Terminal Type When You Log In*

If you always work at the same terminal, there's no problem with setting the terminal type explicitly in your *.login* file *(2.02)*:

setenv *7.01*
```
setenv TERM vt100
```

or in your *.profile(2.02)*:

export *7.01*
```
TERM=vt100; export TERM
```

But if, like many UNIX users, you might log in from time to time at different terminals, from home, or on different systems over a network, you need some more intelligent method for setting the terminal type.

It's possible to set up various kinds of tests *(2.12)* in your shell setup files to do this. But you can also do a surprising amount of terminal type testing with *tset*, even though it was nominally designed for initializing the terminal *(6.12)*:

- If no arguments *(1.02)* are specified and *TERM* is already set, *tset* uses the value of *TERM* to determine the terminal type.

- If no arguments are specified and *TERM* is *not* set, then *tset* uses the value specified in */etc/ttytype* or */etc/ttys(6.10)* (BSD 4.3 and derivatives only).

- If a terminal type is specified as an argument, that argument is used as the terminal type, regardless of the value of *TERM*.

- The −*m* (map) option allows a fine degree of control in cases where the terminal type may be ambiguous. For example, if you sometimes log in on a dialup line, sometimes over a local area network, and sometimes on a hardwired line, the −*m* option can be specified to determine which login is currently being used, and the terminal type can be set accordingly.

In the Bourne shell, *tset* can be used to set the value of *TERM* as follows:

```
TERM=`tset - -Q options`; export TERM
```

(Given the − option, *tset* prints the value that it determines for the terminal type to standard output *(14.01)*. Otherwise, it initializes the terminal *(6.12)*, but keeps the terminal type to itself. The −*Q* (quiet) option causes *tset* to suppress printing of a message it normally prints regarding the values to which it has set the erase and kill characters—a job it does in its alternate role as terminal initializer. The backquotes *(10.14)* surrounding the *tset* command cause its output to be interpolated into the command line.)

In the C shell, you should use the *eval (9.08)* command to capture the output of *tset*; this will also allow you to set the *TERMCAP* variable *(6.04)*. (You must also issue the command set noglob, as explained in article 16.04.)

To see what *tset* can do, consider a case where the terminal's serial line is connected to a dialup modem, through which several different users might be connected, each using a different type of terminal. Accordingly, the default terminal type in *etc/ttytype* should be set to *dialup*. The *tset* command could then be used in the *.profile* or in the *.login* file as follows, with the appropriate terminal type set for each user:

```
set noglob
eval `tset -s -Q -m 'dialup:vt100'`
```

This means that if *ttytype* says *dialup*, use *vt100* as the terminal type. A colon separates the *ttytype* value and the value to which it is to be mapped. If a user wants to be prompted to be sure, place a question mark after the colon and before the mapped terminal type:

```
set noglob
eval `tset -s -Q -m 'dialup:?vt100'`
```

The prompt will look like this:

```
TERM = (vt100)
```

If the user presses RETURN, the preferred terminal type will be used. Alternatively, another terminal type could be entered at that time.

You can cause *tset* to prompt for a terminal type even without testing a generic entry like *dialup*. Just specify the desired terminal type, preceded by a question mark, after the *–m* option. For example:

```
set noglob
eval `tset -s -Q -m '?vt100'`
```

It is also possible to specify different terminal types for different line speeds. Say, for example, that you normally used a Wyse-50 with a 9600-bps modem when dialing in from home, but used a portable PC with a VT100 terminal emulator and 2400-bps modem when you were on the road. You might then use a *tset* command like this:

```
set noglob
eval `tset -s -Q -m 'dialup@2400:vt100' wy50`
```

Assuming that the type is set in *ttytype* as *dialup*, *tset* will use the type *vt100* if at 2400 bps and, if not, will use the type *wy50*.

[Watch out for the linespeed switches. They don't work on a lot of networked systems—usually, the line speed at the computer's port is higher than the speed at the terminal. The same problem occurs, these days, with dialup modems that use data compression.—*JP*] Various symbols can be used for line-speed calculations:

    `@speed`   Means at the specified speed.

    `<speed`   Means less than the specified speed.

    `>speed`   Means greater than the specified speed.

An exclamation point can precede the operator to reverse the sense of the comparison. (For example, `!@1200` would mean at any speed other than 1200 bps. In the C shell, you have to type `\!@1200` *(12.02)* instead.)

Multiple −*m* options can be specified; the first map to be satisfied will be used. If no match is found, a final value specified on the line without a −*m* option (as in the above example) will be used. If no value is specified, the type in */etc/ttytype* will be used.

These changes may not always work; article 44.03 explains why. Article 43.09 has aliases for adjusting your terminal.

—*TOR* from the Nutshell Handbook *termcap & terminfo*

6.04 *Setting the TERMCAP Variable with tset*

(41.08)

For C shell users, *tset (6.03)* has an even more powerful function. The −*s* option causes it to send to standard output a series of C shell commands not only to set *TERM*, but also to set the *TERMCAP* variable to the actual contents of the *termcap* entry. This speeds up launch time for programs that use *termcap*: they no longer need to search through the */etc/termcap* file until they find the relevant entry; it is already at hand.

Invoke *tset* as follows:

eval *9.08*
```
set noglob
eval `tset -Q -s other-options-here`
```

In order to understand what *tset* is doing, let's take a moment to send its output to the screen (i.e., issue the command without evaluating it):

```
% tset -Q -s wy50
set noglob;
setenv TERM wy50 ;
setenv TERMCAP 'n9|wy50:li#24:co#80:am:bs:bw:ul:\
:cm=\E=%+\040%+\040:nd=^L:up=^K:do=^J:ho=^^:bt=\EI:\
:cl=^Z:ce=\ET:cd=\EY:al=\EE:dl=\ER:ic=\EQ:dc=\EW:\
:so=\EG4:se=\EGO:sg#1:ue=\EGO:us=\EG8:ug#1\040:\
:me=\E(EGO:mb=\EG2:mp=\E):mh=\EGp:mr=\EG4:mk=\EG1:\
:kl=^H:kr=^L:ku=^K:kd=^J:kh=^^:k1=^A@^M:k2=^AA^M:\
:k3=^AB^M:k4=^AC^M:k5=^AD^M:k6=^AE^M:k7=^AF^M:k8=^AG^M:\
:k9=^AH^M:k0=^AI^M';
unset noglob;
```

(Article 43.11 explains the format of *termcap* entries.) The set noglob command *(16.04)* causes the shell to suspend interpretation of special characters; otherwise the presence of these characters in the *termcap* entry could cause problems. After execution, the shell is reset to its normal state.

Article 44.03 explains a situation where these changes won't work.

—*TOR* from the Nutshell Handbook *termcap & terminfo*

6.05 Querying Your Terminal Type: qterm

tset (6.03) is a powerful tool to use if you often log in at different terminals. You can use *tset* to prompt you with a default terminal type, giving you the opportunity to specify a new terminal type when you log in:

    TERM = (vt100)

A problem with *tset*, however, is that it requires you to know your terminal type. You might log in at a new terminal and have no idea what to set the terminal type to. Or your terminal might be configured to emulate another terminal type, without your knowledge. New users in particular tend to be confused by the *tset* prompt.

qterm

As an alternative, try Michael Cooper's *qterm* program on our Power Tools disk. *qterm* sends the terminal a test string and determines what sort of terminal you're using based on how the terminal responds. Using *qterm*, you can make sure you always use the correct terminal type by placing the following line in your *.login*:

`. .` 10.14

    setenv TERM `qterm`

or in *.profile*:

    TERM=`qterm`;export TERM

The advantage of *qterm* is that it sets the terminal type without your intervention. You don't need to know what your terminal type is, it just gets set automatically.

qterm works by sending the terminal a query string and returning the terminal type depending on the terminal's response. *qterm* is configured using a listing of responses and the terminals they correspond to. By default, *qterm* looks for the listings in a systemwide location, such as */usr/usc/lib/qtermtab* or */usr/local/lib/qtermtab*. In addition, you can call *qterm* with the *+usrtab* option, so that it will look for a file called *.qtermtab* in your home directory.

The string used to query the terminal is usually ESC Z. The sample *qtermtab* file distributed with *qterm* defines the responses several different terminals give for that string:

```
#
# QtermTab - Query terminal table for qterm.
#
#SendStr ReceiveStr      TermName       FullTermName
#
^[Z      ^[[?1;0c        vt100          Base vt100
^[Z      ^[[?1;1c        vt100          vt100 with STP
^[Z      ^[[?1;2c        vt100          ANSI/VT100 Clone
          ...
^[Z      ^[/K            h29            Zenith z29 in zenith mode
^[Z      ^[/Z            vt52           Generic vt52
^[Z      ^[[0n           vt100          AT&T Unix PC 7300
```

If your terminal isn't listed here, you can just add it. To find out your terminal's response to the query string, just echo ESC Z to your terminal and see what the response is. For example, I logged in from my Macintosh terminal emulator at home and found that *qterm* didn't recognize my terminal type:

```
% qterm
Terminal NOT recognized - defaults to "vt100".
vt100
```

qterm defaults to the right terminal description, but I'd still rather define my own entry. I find out my terminal's response to the ESC Z string:

echo 9.04

```
% echo "^[Z"
^[[E;Y|
```

(Note that the ESC prints as ^[.) Then I add the entry to my *qterm* description file:

```
^[Z        ^[[E;Y|       vt100       Macintosh terminal emulator
```

Now when I run *qterm*, the terminal is recognized:

```
% qterm
Terminal recognized as vt100 (Macintosh terminal emulator)
vt100
```

The string `Terminal recognized as . . .` is sent to standard error *(14.01)*; only the terminal type itself is sent to standard output *(14.01)*. So if you use the following command line:

```
% setenv TERM `qterm`
Terminal recognized as vt100 (Macintosh terminal emulator)
```

the TERM variable is set correctly:

```
% echo $TERM
vt100
```

Now for the caveat: *qterm*'s results are only as accurate as the *qtermtab* file. Not all terminals respond to the ESC Z string, and you may not be able to find a string that it does respond uniquely to. And some terminals do uncanny imitations of others. For example, I'm currently using an *xterm* *(1.31)* window, but *qterm* thinks I'm using a *vt100*:

```
% echo $TERM
xterm
% qterm
Terminal recognized as vt100 (ANSI/VT100 Clone)
vt100
```

As a hack, you can just edit your *.qtermtab* file. For example, I could edit my *.qtermtab* so the ^[[?1;2c response is mapped to *xterm*:

```
#^[Z       ^[[?1;2c       vt100       ANSI/VT100 Clone
^[Z        ^[[?1;2c       xterm       xterm window
```

And then call *qterm* with the *+usrtab* command-line option:

```
setenv TERM `qterm +usrtab`
```

—*LM*

6.06 Checklist: Terminal Hangs When I Log In

If your terminal seems to "hang" (freeze, lock up) when you log in, here are some things to try:

✓ Have an experienced user look at your account's setup files (*.profile*, or *.cshrc* and *.login*). There could be some obvious mistakes that you didn't catch.

✓ Log in to another account and use the *su stucklogin (23.23)* command (if the stuck account uses the Bourne shell) or the *su –f stucklogin* command (if the stuck account uses C shell). Change (*cd*) to the home directory. Rename the account's setup files (*.profile*, or *.cshrc* and *.login*) so the shell won't see them as you log in.

If you can log in after that, you know that the problem is with the account's setup files.

✓ Set shell debugging *(9.13)*. From another account or as the superuser, start an editor and put the following line at the top of the *.profile*. It'll tell you whether the *.profile* is being read at all and where it hangs:

```
set -xv
```

You'll see each line read from the *.profile* and the commands executed on the screen. If you don't see anything, then the shell probably didn't read the *.profile*. C shell users should put this command at the top of *.cshrc* instead:

```
set echo verbose
```

Note that on many UNIX systems, the shell won't read its startup files if the files aren't owned by you. You might use *ls –l (23.02)* to check.

✓ Look at the entry in the */etc/passwd* file *(37.03)* for this user. Be sure it has the correct number of fields (separated by `:`). Also, see if there's another user with the same login name. (If your system has the commands *vipw*(8) and *pwck*(8), your system administrator should be using them to edit and check the *passwd* file. They avoid many of these problems.)

✓ Does your account use any directories remotely-mounted (by NFS) *(1.33)*? If the remote host or network is down, and any command in your startup files (especially *set path*) tries to access those directories, the shell may hang there.

To fix that problem, *su* to the account as explained above and take the command or directory name out of your startup file. Or, if this problem happens a lot, the system administrator can mount an NFS filesystem "soft" (instead of the default, "hard") and limit the number of retrys.

✓ What looks like a "hang" might also be that you just aren't getting any output to the terminal, for some very weird reason. Then the *set* *–xv* wouldn't help you. In that case, try adding this line to the start of the *.profile*:

```
exec > /tmp/sh.out.$$ 2>&1
```

If the Bourne shell starts reading the *.profile*, it'll make a file in */tmp* *(22.03)* called sh.out.*nnn* with output from the commands and the shell's *set* *–xv*.

There's no command like that for the C shell.

—JP

6.07 *What termcap and terminfo Do and Don't Control*

One important point to realize about *termcap* and *terminfo* is that many programs do not use them at all, and that there are several other mechanisms that may also affect terminal operation.

The operation of the serial interface is controlled by several system files (*/etc/ttys* and */etc/gettytab* on BSD and other non-AT&T systems, and */etc/inittab* and */etc/gettydefs* in System V). Users can affect serial-line parameters with the *stty* *(6.09, 43.03, 43.02)* command. In addition to normal communications parameters such as data rate, start and stop bits, parity, and so on, these parameters include such things as the translation of the carriage returns generated by most terminals into the linefeeds expected by most UNIX programs, division of input into lines, and definition of special control characters for erasing a character that has been typed, killing a line of typed input, and interrupting a running process.

One other area that *termcap* and *terminfo* do not control is terminal tab setting. This is done by the *tabs* command. For more information, see the manual pages on *stty*(4) and *termio*(7) (System V).

termcap and *terminfo*, by contrast, tend to control visual attributes of the terminal. The terminal capabilities defined for a terminal tell a screen-oriented program how big the screen is (for screen-by-screen paging and cursor movement), how to move to any point on the screen, how to refresh the screen, how to enter and exit any special display modes (such as inverse video, blinking, or underlining), and so on. [The screen size may be set in other ways, too. See article 44.05. —*JP*]

But there is some overlap. For example, a terminal can be unusable because a program has left either the serial line modes or the terminal itself in an unexpected state. For this reason, terminal initialization *(6.12)*, as performed by the *tset* and *tput* programs, initializes both the terminal and the serial line interface.

—TOR from the Nutshell Handbook *termcap & terminfo*

6.08 Terminal Escape Sequences

Most terminals use special character strings called *escape sequences* to control their operation. These strings begin with the escape character (ASCII character 033) *(53.03)*.

This character can be generated alone by the ESC key found on most keyboards, or by typing the left bracket character while holding down the CONTROL key (often shown as ^[). But it's also generated by many of the special keys on your keyboard. For example, an UP ARROW key might generate an escape sequence like ^[OA. When the terminal sees this sequence of characters, it knows to move the cursor up one line.

The special escape sequences used by your terminal are stored in the terminal's termcap or terminfo entry *(43.11, 6.02)*, which allows programs to respond appropriately to all of the special keys on the keyboard. Programs themselves issue escape sequences to do such things as move around the screen, highlight text, and so on.

However, there are cases where it's useful to issue escape sequences manually—or in an alias or shell script that you write. For example, you can highlight your prompt *(8.08)* or write an alias to switch your terminal display to inverse video *(43.09)*.

Most of our examples use escape sequences for the common DEC VT100 series of terminals (which are also recognized by almost all terminal emulation programs).

How do you find out what escape sequences your terminal uses? After all, it is quite hardware-specific. If you have a terminal manual, they should be listed there. Otherwise, you can look at the termcap or terminfo listing itself *(6.11)*, and with the help of the manual page, or a book such as the Nutshell Handbook, *termcap & terminfo*, decipher the obscure language used there. Or, use a program like *tcap* or *tput(43.10)*; it will find those sequences for you.

To actually type an escape sequence into a file, use your editor's "quote next character command" (CTRL-v in *vi(32.05)*) before pressing the ESC key. To use an escape character in an alias, try the technique shown in article 43.09.

Don't be confused if you see an escape sequence that looks like this:

    ^[[1m

Some terminals use a real left bracket at the start of their escape sequence; it will follow the escape character itself (represented as ^[). Even though they look the same on the screen, they are really different characters (CTRL-[or ESC is different from [, just like CTRL-c is different from C).

—*TOR*

6.09 Setting your Erase, Kill, and Interrupt Characters

Have you ever sat down at a terminal where the "erase" key (the character that deletes the last thing you typed) wasn't where you thought it would be? If you have, you know how disorienting this can be! The *stty (43.03)* command gives you a way of changing the erase character (along with several others) so you can restore some order to your world.

stty takes two kinds of input. If you want to give the command interactively, type `stty erase` *char*, where *char* is the key you normally use for erase—BACKSPACE, DELETE, whatever—followed by RETURN. This will do the trick, provided that the character you type isn't already used for something. If the character is in use, or if you're putting *stty* commands into your *.login* or *.profile* file, it's better to "spell these characters out." "Control" characters in *.login* are allowed, but they aren't a great idea. If you like to use the BACKSPACE key as the erase key, add the line below:

```
stty erase ^h
```

If you want to use the DELETE key, quote the ? character so the shell won't treat it as a wildcard *(1.16)*:

```
stty erase ^\?
```

That is: *stty* lets you represent a control key with the two-character combination ^*x*, where ^ is the literal key ^ (caret) and *x* is any single character. You may need to put a \ before the *x* to prevent the shell from interpreting it as a wildcard [and a \ before the ^ to prevent some Bourne shells from interpreting it as a pipe!—*JP*].

Of course, you're not limited to the BACKSPACE or DELETE keys; you can choose any other key you want. If you want to use "Z" as your Delete key, type `stty erase` Z. Just make sure you never want to type a real Z!

Table 6-1 lists functions that *stty* can change.

Table 6-1. Keys to Set with stty

Character	Function	Good Setting		See Article
erase	Erases the previous character.	^\?	(DELETE)	6.09
kill	Erases the entire line.	^u	(CTRL-u)	10.02
werase	Erases the previous word.	^w	(CTRL-w)	10.02
intr	Terminates the current job.	^c	(CTRL-c)	40.09
quit	Terminates the current job, makes a core file.	^\\	(CTRL-\)	40.09
susp	Stops the current job (so you can put it in the background).	^z	(CTRL-z)	13.01
rprnt	Redisplays the current line.	^r	(CTRL-r)	10.03

The command *stty everything* (for BSD UNIX) or *stty −a* (for System V) shows all your current terminal settings. The *werase* and *rprnt* characters aren't implemented on many System V versions.

As a historical note: the erase character was originally #, and the kill character was originally @. These assignments go back to the olden days *(43.02)*, when terminals printed with real ink on real paper and made lots of noise. However, I'm told that there are some modern systems on which these settings are still the default.

Note: Terminal emulators, editors, and other programs can fool around with all of this stuff. They *should* be well-behaved and reset your terminal when you leave them, but that's often not true. So: don't expect your settings to work within a terminal emulator; they may, or they may not. And don't expect your settings to be correct after you exit from your terminal emulator. Again, they may, or they may not.

The *tset* program also fools around *(6.12)* with key settings. Therefore, in your shell setup files *(2.02)*, put *stty* after *tset*.

—*ML*

6.10 Find Port Type with ttykind

The *TERM (6.11)* environment variable usually holds the type of terminal or window you're using: *vt100, xterm,* and so on. Your shell setup files can test *TERM* to configure your login session *(2.12)*.

But the information in *TERM* might not be enough. For instance, your VT100 terminal could be connected over a dialup line, from a data switch, over a network from a remote host, and so on. Sometimes you may want certain things to be done differently, depending on whether you're dialing in from home, connected from your desk, using a remote login from another building, and so on.

Your system may have a */etc/ttytab* or */etc/ttys* file that lists the type of each terminal port. Lines in the file look something like this:

```
console  "/usr/etc/getty std.9600"   dw3        on   local
tty00    "/usr/etc/getty std.9600"   dialup     off  local
tty01    "/usr/etc/getty std.9600"   plugboard  off  local
    ...
ttyp0    none                        network    off
    ...
```

(For example, port *ttyp0* is *network,* the type used by *xterm, telnet,* and so on.)

On BSD-derived systems, *tset (6.03)* can be used to query these files. If that doesn't work, or you want something that you can tweak yourself, here's a script called *ttykind.* It reads */etc/ttys* and finds a tty name *(3.08)* in the first column. It outputs the port type from the third column. This can then be used as the basis for a test in your *.login* file.

ttykind

basename *47.18*

```
#! /bin/sh

# Strip off any /dev/ in tty number.
tty=`basename $1`

case "$tty" in
"") echo "`basename $0`: Problem with tty number '$1'." 1>&2; exit 1 ;;
*)  # Use eval so any quoted fields in ttys (like
    # "/etc/getty std.9600") will be set as just one word.
    # Output fourth argument, the port type:
    eval set x `grep "^$tty[ TAB ]" /etc/ttytab`
    test -n "$4" && echo $4
    ;;
esac
```

x *36.19*

The script works with an argument like /dev/*ttyxx* (typical output from the *tty* command in backquotes *(10.14)*) or the plain tty name without /dev/. It uses *grep* to search for a line starting with the port name and a space or tab. The line that *grep* finds is set *(46.18)* into the shell's command-line parameters (with an **x** first to be sure there's at least one argument)—but before the parameters are set, that line is passed to *eval (9.08)* so any quoted fields in the line (like "/etc/getty std.9600") will be set as just one word. Without *eval*, the quotes wouldn't be effective and the second field would be set in two separate parameters. If the third field ($4, counting the first **x**) isn't empty, the script outputs it. For example:

```
% ttykind tty00
dialup
```

—*JP*

6.11 *Finding what Terminal Names you Can Use*

A program that wants to make use of the terminal capability database selects an entry according to the value of the *TERM* environment variable *(7.01)*. This variable is typically set when a user logs in. A second variable, either *TERMCAP (6.04)* or *TERMINFO*, may also be set, if it is desirable to point to a terminal description that is not in the standard location.

It's easy enough to find out what terminal type the system thinks you are currently using. Simply type:

```
$ echo $TERM
```

If nothing is printed, *TERM* has not been set. (In the C shell, the message `TERM: Undefined variable` will be printed.)

It's also easy enough to set the terminal type. This is typically done when the user logs in but can be done from the command line as follows:

```
$ TERM=wy50; export TERM
% setenv TERM wy50
```

But what if you sit down at a strange terminal and want to set the terminal type? How do you know what terminal name to use as the value of *TERM*?

The terminal names to which *TERM* can legitimately be set can be determined by searching through */etc/termcap* or by listing the names of files in the */usr/lib/terminfo* directory hierarchy.

The *termcap* terminal database is stored in the single file */etc/termcap*. It is an ASCII file: all the information it contains is readable, if not immediately comprehensible. Each entry consists of a list of names for the terminal, followed by a list of the terminal's capabilities.

The first line of each entry shows several different names, or aliases, for the terminal. At least one of the names will usually reflect the manufacturer's shorthand name for the terminal, but a long name is usually included as well, so you can simply search for the manufacturer's name to get started. For example, if you were using a Wyse Technologies Wyse-50, you could check to make sure that a terminal description for that terminal existed in the *termcap* database by typing:

```
% grep Wyse /etc/termcap
n9|wy50|Wyse Technology WY-50:\
```

One or more lines like the one shown in the example above should be printed (if any matching entries are found). Each line will show several names for the terminal, separated by vertical bars (|). The second name, wy50, is the one most commonly used as the value of *TERM*.

The compiled *terminfo* database is stored in a directory hierarchy under */usr/lib/terminfo*. Each terminal entry is compiled (by a program called *tic*) and stored in a separate file. All terminals whose names begin with the letter "a" are stored in the directory */usr/lib/terminfo/a*, and so on through the alphabet.* Links *(19.03)* are used so that the terminal description can be accessed with any one of several names. [The *ls −R (17.04)* command will list all the descriptions at once. A command like *find −name '*xxx*' −print (18.04)* will find descriptions with a certain brand or model *xxx* in the name.—*JP*]

So, on a system supporting *terminfo*, you would look for the entry with the *ls* command:

```
$ ls /usr/lib/terminfo/w
wy-50
wy100
wy50
wyse-50
wyse50
```

You should use the name of the appropriate file for the value of *TERM*.

---

*The source is sometimes provided by some systems in */usr/lib/terminfo.ti*. Entries can be decompiled or displayed with a program called *infocmp*.

If it is not obvious from the name of the file which entry to use, you can use the following command to print out the long name of the terminal:

```
$ tput -Tname longname
```

For example:

```
$ tput -Twy50 longname
Wyse Technologies Wy-50
```

You should be aware that for a terminal with configurable options (such as a terminal with an 80- or 132-column mode), there may be several *termcap* or *terminfo* entries. Until you know enough about the terminal database to compare the entries and find out how they differ, you will simply need to take your chances. Experiment with each of the entries and see which works best. Article 43.11 explains more about the format of *termcap* and *terminfo* entries. [If none of them seem to work, setting *TERM* to a name like *dumb* or *unknown* will give you a basic setup while you check other entries. The *vi* editor will use its open mode *(31.36)* and pagers like *less (26.04)* will complain a little, but you should be able to get by. —*JP*]

—*TOR* from the Nutshell Handbook *termcap & terminfo*

6.12 *Initializing the Terminal with tset*

As you log in, especially if you're using a terminal that's shared with other users, it's a good idea to initialize your terminal (reset it to its default state). If your system has *termcap*, use *tset (6.03)*. On systems with *terminfo*, use *tput (6.13)*.

In fact, despite its role in terminal type setting, you might say that the "proper" function of *tset* is to initialize the terminal. It outputs an initialization string (if one is defined in the terminal's *termcap* entry), which should set the terminal to a reasonable state. In this role, it overlaps somewhat with *stty (43.03, 6.09)*, setting the erase and kill characters to CTRL-h and CTRL-x. (Options allow the user to specify alternate values for these characters, as well as for the interrupt character.) When done, it prints the following message:

```
Erase is control-H
Kill is control-X
```

(or whatever else you have set these characters to). This message can be suppressed by adding the −*Q* (quiet) option.

A special form of the *tset* command, called *reset*, is found on some systems. In addition to *tset*'s normal processing, it sets various *stty* modes to what it considers a "reasonable" state *(44.04, 44.02)*. It can thus be used to reset both the terminal and the serial line control parameters in cases where a bombing program or user bungling has left the terminal in an unusable state.

There are some cases in which normal end-of-line processing has been disabled, and the system will no longer perform the carriage return to linefeed translation UNIX requires to work with most terminals. In these cases, you may need to type:

CTRL-j reset CTRL-j

to get *reset* to work.

—*TOR* from the Nutshell Handbook *termcap & terminfo*

6.13 Initializing the Terminal with tput

The *tput* program used with *terminfo* is somewhat equivalent to *tset* (6.03, 6.12), but does not have the ability that *tset* has to determine the terminal type. On the other hand, it allows you to pick out particular terminal capabilities and print out their values or store them into shell variables. [The *tcap* (43.10) program does the same kind of thing for *termcap.—JP*] This allows shell programs to make use of terminal capabilities (43.10) such as inverse video or underlining.

By default, *tput* assumes that you are using the terminal type specified by the *TERM* (6.11) variable. If you want to override the value of *TERM*, you can specify another terminal type with the *–T* option. For example:

```
$ tput -Twy50 ...
```

In System V Release 3, *tput* has a keyword option that allows you to reset the terminal by outputting the initialization strings (there are several) from a *terminfo* description:

```
$ tput init
```

The command:

```
$ tput reset
```

issues the reset strings from the *terminfo* entry. If no reset strings are defined, the initialization strings are issued instead, and the command acts exactly like *tput init.*

In earlier releases of System V, these keywords are not supported, and you must issue multiple *tput* commands to output each of the initialization or reset strings by name.

The following shell program, contributed by Tony Hansen of AT&T, will do the trick:

tputinit

```
:
# Evaluate and output the iprog capability
eval `tput iprog`
# output the is1 and is2 initialization strings
tput is1
tput is2

# if the terminal supports tabs, set them
# otherwise, disable them
if [ -n "`tput ht`" ]
then stty tabs; tabs -8
```

```
        else stty -tabs
        fi
        # output contents of the initialization file, if present
-s 26.10 cat -s "`tput if`"
        # output the is3 initialization string
        tput is3
```

See your system manuals, or the Nutshell Handbook *termcap & terminfo*, for a description of the various initialization capabilities used in this script.

—*TOR* from the Nutshell Handbook *termcap & terminfo*

7

Shell and Environment Variables

7.01 What Environment Variables are Good For

Many UNIX utilities, including the shell, need information about you and what you're doing in order to do a reasonable job.

What kinds of information? Well, to start with, a lot of programs (particularly editors) need to know what kind of terminal you're using. The shell needs to know where any commands you want to use are likely to be found. Lots of UNIX programs (like mail programs) include a command to start an editor as a subprocess; they like to know your favorite editor. And so on.

Of course, one could always write programs that made you put all this information on the command line. For example, you might have to type commands like:

```
% mail -editor vi -term aardvark48 -favoritecolor blue_no_red
```

But your favorite editor probably doesn't change every day. (Nor will your favorite color.) The terminal you use may change frequently, but it certainly won't change from the time you log in until the time you log out. And you certainly wouldn't want to type something like this whenever you want to send mail.

Rather than forcing you to type this information with every command, UNIX uses *environment variables* to store information that you'd rather not worry about. For example, the *TERM (6.11)* environment variable tells programs what kind of terminal you're using. Any programs that care about your terminal type know (or ought to know) that they can read this variable, find out your terminal type, and act accordingly.

Similarly, the directories that store the commands you want to execute are listed in the *PATH (7.04)* variable. When you type a command, your shell looks through each directory in your *PATH* variable to find that command. Presumably, UNIX wouldn't need a *PATH* variable if all commands were located in the same directory; but you'll soon be writing your own commands (if you aren't already), and storing them in your own "private" command directories *(5.02)*, and you'll need to tell the shell how to find them *(9.05)*.

Environment variables are managed by your shell. The difference between environment variables and regular shell variables *(7.08)* is that a shell variable is local to a particular instance of the shell (such as a shell script), while environment variables are "inherited" by any program you start, including another shell *(40.04)*. That is, the new process gets its own copy of these variables, which it can read, modify, and pass on in turn to its own children. In fact, every UNIX process (not just the shell) passes its environment variables to its child processes.

(7.02)

You can set environment variables with a command like this:

```
% setenv NAME value          C shell
$ NAME=value; export NAME    Bourne or Korn shell
```

; 9.03

There's nothing particularly special about the *NAME*; you can create environment variables with any names you want. Of course, these don't necessarily do anything for you; variables like *PATH* and *TERM* are important because lots of programs have "agreed" *(7.03)* that these names are important. But if you want to create an environment variable that holds the name of your lover, that's your business:

```
% setenv LOVER Judy
```

If you're so inclined, you could write a program called *valentine* that reads the *LOVER* environment variable and generates an appropriate message. If you like short-term relationships or tend to forget names, this might even be convenient!

By convention, the names of environment variables use all uppercase letters. There's nothing to enforce this convention—if you're making your own names, you can use any capitalization you please. But there's no advantage to violating the convention, either. The environment variables that are used by standard UNIX programs all have uppercase names. [I usually make my shell variable names lowercase so it's easy to tell the difference. —*JP*]

If you want the C shell to forget that an environment variable ever existed, use the command *unsetenv NAME*. (Some Bourne shells, but not all, have a similar command: *unset NAME*.)

If you want to list all of your environment variables, use the command *printenv* (on BSD systems) or *env* (on System V). The *printenv* command also lets you ask about a particular variable. Here's a typical report:

```
% printenv EDITOR
EDITOR=/usr/local/bin/emacs
% printenv
HOME=/home/los/mikel
SHELL=/bin/csh
TERM=sun
USER=mikel
PATH=/usr/local/bin:/usr/ucb:/bin:/usr/bin:.:/home/los/mikel/bin
LOGNAME=mikel
```

```
PWD=/home/los/mikel/power/articles
PRINTER=ps
EDITOR=/usr/local/bin/emacs
```

The *set (7.08)* command provides a similar listing of shell variables.

You can also use the *echo (9.04)* command to show the value of a particular variable, preceding the variable name with a dollar sign (which tells the shell to substitute the value of the variable):

```
% echo $TERM
xterm
```

—ML

7.02 *Parent-Child Relationships*

No, this is not about the pop psychology of computing. It's just a quick reminder of one important point.

In the environment variable overview *(7.01)* we said that each process gets its own copy of its parent's environment variables. We chose those words carefully, and if you think about them, you won't make one common mistake.

Sooner or later, almost everyone writes a shell script that gathers some information, sets a few environment variables, and quits. The writer then wonders why there's no trace of the "new" environment variables to be found. The problem is simple. A UNIX process *(40.03)* cannot change its parent's environment; a UNIX process gets its *own* copy of the parent's environment, and any changes it makes it keeps to itself. A process can make changes and pass them to its children, but there's no way of going in reverse.

(You can't teach an old dog new tricks.)

—ML

7.03 *Predefined Environment Variables*

We've said that environment variables are used to store information that you'd rather not worry about, and that there are a number of standard environment variables that many UNIX programs use. These are often called "predefined" environment variables—not because their values are predefined, but because their names and uses are predefined. Here are the most important ones:

- *PATH (7.04)* contains your command search path *(9.05)*. This is a list of directories in which the shell looks to find commands. It's usually set in one of your shell setup files *(2.02)*.

- *EDITOR* can be loaded with the name of your favorite editor. It's usually set in one of your shell initialization files. Some programs distinguish between *EDITOR* (usually set to a line editor *(34.01)* such as *ed*) and *VISUAL* (set to a full-screen editor like *vi*). Many people don't follow that convention; they set both to the same editor. (The Korn shell checks *VISUAL* and *EDITOR*, in that order, to determine your command editing mode *(12.14)*.)

- *PRINTER (45.04)* can be loaded with the name of your default printer. It's quite useful at a site with many printers—you don't need to tell lpr *(45.02)* which printer to use. This variable is usually set in one of your shell setup files.

- *PWD* contains the absolute pathname of your current directory. It's set automatically by the *cd* command in some UNIX shells. *PWD* may be fooled *(15.14)* by *cd*ing through symbolic links.

- *HOME (15.12)* (called *LOGDIR* on some systems) contains the absolute pathname of your home directory. It's set automatically when you log in.

- *SHELL* contains the absolute pathname of your login shell. It's set automatically whenever you log in.

- *USER* (called *LOGNAME* on some systems) contains your username. It's set automatically when you log in, and doesn't change.

- *TERM (6.11)* contains the name of your terminal type in the *termcap* or *terminfo* database. It's usually set in a shell setup file.

- *TERMCAP (6.04)* can be loaded with the complete *termcap* database entry for the terminal you are using. This may make some programs start up more quickly, but it's not necessary. Set (under some conditions) by the *tset* command, which is usually run in your shell setup file.

- *OLDPWD* contains the name of your previous working directory. Set by the *cd* command. Korn shell only.

- *ENV* contains the name of an initialization file to be executed whenever a new Korn shell is started. (See article 2.02.) Korn shell only.

- *PAGER* can be set to the name of your favorite page-by-page screen display program like *more (26.03)* or *less (26.04)*. (Programs like *man (52.01)* use *PAGER* to determine which paging program to use if their output is longer than a single screen.)

- *EXINIT (31.06, 7.10)* stores setup options for the *vi* editor (and the *ex* editor, where *EXINIT* got its name).

- *PS1* contains the primary prompt (i.e., interactive command prompt) for Bourne and Korn shells. (The C shell doesn't store the prompt in an environment variable. It uses a shell variable called *prompt* because the *.cshrc* file *(2.02)* is read to set up each instance of the shell. See article 8.02.)

- *PS2 (10.11)* contains the secondary prompt (used within compound commands like *while* and *for*) for Bourne and Korn shells.

- *MANPATH (52.09)*, if your *man (52.01)* command supports it, is a colon-separated list of directories to search for manual pages.

- *TZ (7.06)* contains the time zone. This is a name of a file in */usr/lib/zoneinfo* that provides time zone information for your locality. It is read by commands like *date (53.10, 7.07)*.

- *DISPLAY* is used by the X Window System *(1.31)* to identify the display server (keyboard and screen handling program) that will be used for input and output by X applications.

Because the Bourne and Korn shells don't make as strict a distinction between environment variables and shell variables as the C shell does, we've included a few things here that might not be on other people's lists.

We may have implied that environment variables are relatively constant (like your favorite editor). That's not true. For example, in a windowing environment, the current length of your window might be kept in an environment variable. That can change as often as you resize your window. What is true (fortunately) is exactly what we've said: environment variables store information that you'd rather not have to worry about.

—ML

7.04 *The PATH Environment Variable*

Of all the environment variables, the *PATH* and *TERM (6.11)* variables are the most important. The others are often great conveniences; but *PATH* and *TERM* can make your life miserable if they get screwed up.

The *PATH* variable is just a list of directories, separated by colon (:) characters. The shell searches through these directories in order whenever it needs to find a command. So, if you want to execute commands in */bin, /usr/bin, /usr/local,* the current directory, and your personal *bin* directory, you would put a line like the one below in your *.login* file. The empty entry :: means "the current directory."

$HOME/bin *5.02*   `setenv PATH /bin:/usr/bin:/usr/local::$HOME/bin`

Article 9.05 explains more about setting the path.

The most common problem with *PATH* is that, somehow, it gets deleted. This usually happens if you try to change *PATH* and do so incorrectly. When *PATH* is deleted, your shell can only find its built-in commands *(1.10)* and commands for which you give the complete pathnname. Here's a demonstration:

```
% setenv PATH          Set PATH to null accidentally
% ls
ls: Command not found.
```

Needless to say, this can be very frustrating—especially if you can't figure out what's going on. There are a couple of easy fixes. The easiest is just to log out and log back in again. (*logout* is a built-in C shell command, so you won't have trouble finding it. If you get an error message like "Not login shell," try *exit* instead.) Another fix is to read *(46.22)* whichever initialization file defined your *PATH* variable, usually *.login* for C shell users or *.profile* for Bourne shell users:

```
% source ~/.login
$ . .profile
```

This will almost certainly give you *some* of your path back; the problem is that a lot of initialization files merely add a few "private" directories to a system-wide default path. In this case, just execute the system-wide initialization files first (if your system has them). Their pathnames vary:

```
% source /usr/lib/Cshrc
% source /usr/lib/Login
% source ~/.login
```

The other common *PATH* problem is that users sometimes can't find the commands they want. This happens most often when someone writes a new shell script with the same name as a standard UNIX command—say, *true*. He or she tries to execute it and can't; in fact, all that happens is:

```
% true
%
```

After staring at the script for a long time, the user sometimes gets the right idea: the script is fine, it's the path that's wrong. The *PATH* variable will look something like this:

```
% printenv PATH
/bin:/usr/local:/usr/ucb:/usr/bin::/home/mkl/bin
```

The shell searches the *PATH* in order; therefore, it finds the system's standard *true* command before seeing the new one. The new command never gets a chance. You *could* fix this problem by putting the current directory and *$HOME/bin* at the head of the search path, in which case, commands in the current directory and your private *bin* directory will override the standard commands. However, that's *not* recommended; it's a well-known security hole.

So what is recommended? Nothing much, except: if you write shell scripts or other programs, give them names that are different from the standard UNIX utilities *(46.20)*. If you really need an overlapping name, you can use a relative pathname *(1.21)* to specify "the program called *true* in the current directory":

```
% ./true
```

Here are some related articles. You can search your *PATH* for a command with *which (52.07)*, *findcmd (17.11)*, and *whereiz (5.10)*. Article 7.05 explains the C shell's *path* variable.

—*ML*

7.05 PATH and path

For the C shell, it's slightly incorrect to say that *PATH* contains the search list for commands. It's a bit more complicated. The *PATH* environment variable is used to set the *path* shell variable; that is, whenever you *setenv PATH (7.04)*, the C shell modifies *path* accordingly. For example:

```
setenv PATH /bin:/usr/bin:/usr/local::$HOME/bin
```

In *PATH*, an empty entry (`::`) stands for the current directory. The C shell's *path* shell variable *(7.08, 7.09)* is the actual search list. Its syntax is slightly different; the list of directories is enclosed in parentheses *(49.05)*, and the directories are separated by spaces. For example:

~ *15.12*
```
set path=( /bin /usr/bin /usr/local . ~/bin )
```

If you set the *path* shell variable, the C shell will automatically set the *PATH* environment variable. You don't need to set both. Many people use a *set path* command instead of *setenv PATH.*

—*ML*

7.06 The TZ Environment Variable

The *TZ* environment variable is a little obscure, but it can be very useful. It tells UNIX what time zone you're in. The default time zone was set when your system was first installed (and we'll assume it was done correctly). However, there are lots of times when you want to change your time zone temporarily. For example, you might be connected via a communications program to a UNIX system in another time zone; its notion of the correct time is right for its location, but not for your location. Or you may move your system to another location; you need to change the time zone, but you don't want to reinstall the software (which can be painful). Article 7.07 shows how to use *TZ* to check the time in another zone.

To set *TZ*, give a command like:

```
% setenv TZ timezone
```

This setting takes effect immediately; if you give the *date (53.10)* command, you'll see the current time in your new zone.

The time zones are, basically, files in the directory */usr/lib/zoneinfo*, or its subdirectories. You'll have to look through there to see what's available—but a lot is available, including all the time zones in the US, Canada, Australia, most of Europe, and a lot of Asia, Africa, and South America. A lot of "oddball" time zones are included: for example, the state of Indiana, for which large parts observe Daylight Savings Time, and Michigan, for reasons that are completely unclear to me.

So, let's say you want to set the current time so that it's correct in Wyoming. You look in */usr/lib/zoneinfo* and see a directory named *US*. You then look in the *US* directory, and see a file named *Mountain*. So your time zone setting is *US/Mountain*:

```
% setenv TZ US/Mountain
% date
Wed Mar  4 19:34:53 MST 1992
```

You don't have to worry about the difference between daylight and standard time, or the fact that Daylight Savings Time rules aren't the same everywhere. That information is all encoded in the *zonefiles* database.

—ML

7.07 What Time is it in Japan?

csh_init

The *TZ (7.06)* environment variable has some convenient uses, particularly if you do business with people scattered all over the globe. Let's say you want to call your trading partner in Japan to find out how the stock exchange is doing. But you want to know, first, whether or not the market has opened (or whether your partner is even awake!). You can (quickly) set *TZ* to "Japan," print the date, and reset *TZ*. Or you can write an alias *(11.02)* that does this for you:

( ) *14.07*
```
% alias tm '(setenv TZ \!$ ; date )'
% tm Japan
Thu Mar  5 10:48:07 Japan 1992
% date
Wed Mar  4 20:48:58 EST 1992
```

It's 10 AM over there; should be a good time to call. Of course, the argument to *TZ* has to be one of the time zone files in */usr/lib/zoneinfo*. One "gotcha": all the "useful" files in this directory begin with uppercase letters. If you type `tm japan`, you'll get the Greenwich mean time—which is only about nine hours off!

[Another problem you may have is figuring out just what time zone is right for some parts of the world. For example, unless you know your geography fairly well, you might have trouble figuring out that the appropriate *TZ* setting for Sydney, Australia is *Australia/NSW* (New South Wales), while Melbourne is *Australia/Victoria.— TOR*]

Note: *tm* uses a subshell *(14.07, 40.04)* so I don't have to worry about resetting the time zone correctly. Using a subshell is inefficient, but easy.

—ML

7.08 Shell Variables

Shell variables are really just the "general case" of environment variables *(7.01)*. If you're a programmer, remember that a UNIX shell really runs an interpreted programming language. Shell variables belong to the shell; you can set them, print them, and work with them much as you can in a C program (or a FORTRAN program or a BASIC program). If you're not a programmer, just remember that shell variables are pigeonholes that store information for you or your shell to use.

If you've read the section on environment variables, you realize that we defined them in exactly the same way. How are shell variables different from environment variables? Whenever you start a new shell or a UNIX program, it inherits all of its parent's environment variables. However, it does *not* inherit any shell variables; it starts with a clean slate. If you're a programmer, you can think of environment variables as "global" variables, while shell variables are "local" variables. By convention, shell variables have lowercase names.

Just as some programs use certain environment variables, the shell expects to use certain shell variables. For example, the C shell uses the *history (12.01)* variable to determine how many of your previous commands to remember; if the *noclobber (14.06)* variable is defined, the C shell prevents you from damaging files by making mistakes with standard output. Most users insert code into their *.cshrc* files *(2.02)* to define these important variables appropriately.

To set a shell variable, use one of these commands:

```
% set name=value          C shell
$ name=value              Bourne or Korn shell
```

As a special case, if you omit *value*, the shell variable is set to a "null" value. For example, the following commands are valid:

```
% set name                C shell
$ name=                   Bourne or Korn shell
```

This is important: giving a variable a null value is not the same as deleting the value. Some programs look at variables to see whether or not they exist; they don't care what the actual value is, and an empty value is as good as anything else. If you want to make the shell forget that a variable ever existed, use the *unset* command. Unfortunately, older Bourne shells don't have a command like *unset*:

```
% unset name              C shell
$ unset name              Korn, newer Bourne shells
```

If you want to list all of your environment variables, use the command *printenv* (Berkeley UNIX) or *env* (System V).* If you want to list all of your Bourne or C shell variables, just type set. Here's a typical report in the C shell:

```
% set
argv    ()
cwd     /home/los/mikel/power/articles
```

---

* *printenv* and *env* are external *(1.10)* commands; they work with any shell.

```
history 40
home    /home/los/mikel
noclobber
path    (/home/los/mikel/bin /usr/local/bin /usr/ucb /bin /usr/bin .)
prompt  los%
shell   /bin/csh
status  0
term    sun
user    mikel
```

If you want to print the value of an individual variable, give the command:

% echo "$*variable-name*"

(While the example above gives a C shell prompt, this command works in all UNIX shells.)

Whenever you need the value of a shell variable—not just with *echo (9.04)*—you need to put a dollar sign ($) in front of the name. You don't need the dollar sign when you're assigning a new value to a shell variable. You can also stick curly braces ({ }) around the name, if you want (e.g., ${*name*}); when you're writing shell programs, this can often make your code much clearer. Curly braces are mostly used when you need to separate the variable name from what comes after it.

But that's getting us out of the range of interactive variable use and into shell programming *(46.01)*.

—*ML*

7.09 *Special C Shell Variables*

The C shell recognizes and uses environment variables, but it also uses a great many simple shell variables *(7.08)* to control its own operation. These variables don't need to be put into the environment so they can be passed to subshells *(40.04)*, because every instance of the C shell always reads the *.cshrc* file *(2.02)*. Simple shell variables set there are thus propagated to every C shell.

Many of the special C shell variables are simply used as flags; that is, they need not be set to any particular value. The shell simply tests whether they exist or not. They are set simply by saying:

```
set variable
```

rather than:

```
set variable=value
```

Here are some of the special variable names used by the C shell:

- The *cdpath (15.05)* variable stores a list of directories. You can *cd* to subdirectories of these by typing just the subdirectory name.

- If the *echo* (9.13) variable is set, the shell will show the command line, after all variable and history (12.07) substitutions, before executing it. (This is very handy for debugging scripts such as *.cshrc.*)

  If the *verbose* (9.13) variable is set, the shell will show the command line after history substitution but before any other substitutions.

  The Bourne shell *−v* and *−x* options (48.01) work like the *verbose* and *echo* variables.

- If the *filec* or *complete* variable is set, the shell performs filename completion (10.06). The *fignore* (10.07) variable makes filename completion skip filenames that end with certain characters like *.o.*

- The *cwd* (15.14) variable shows the full pathname of the current directory. The *cd*, *pushd*, and *popd* commands set it.

- The *hardpaths* (15.14) variable fixes errors in the *cwd* variable that occur when you *cd* through symbolic links.

- Use the *histchars* (12.17) variable to set different history characters than exclamation point (!) and caret (^).

- The *history* (12.01) variable stores the number of shell command lines to save. The *savehist* (12.12) variable stores the number of lines of shell history to be saved when you log out. This amount of history is saved in a file called *.history* in your home directory, and the lines are restored the next time you log in.

- If you set *ignoreeof* (3.05), the shell won't respond to the end-of-file character (CTRL-d) and will require you to type `logout` or `exit` (40.04) to log out. This can save you from ending the shell accidentally (or logging out).

- The shell can tell you about new electronic mail (1.33) or changes in other files with the *mail* (22.08) variable.

- Stop the > redirection character from overwriting files with *noclobber* (14.06).

- The *noglob* (16.04) variable stops wildcard expansion (16.01).

- Set *nonomatch* when you want the C shell to treat nonmatching wildcards like the Bourne shell does (16.05).

- The *notify* (13.06) variable asks the shell to tell you right away if a background job finishes or is stopped.

- The list of directories that the shell searches for commands is stored in *path* (7.05).

- Your login name from the *USER* or *LOGNAME* (7.03) environment variable is also stored in the C shell variable named *user.*

- The shell's command-line prompt is set by the *prompt* (8.02) variable. (The *PS1* (7.03) environment variable is the Bourne shell equivalent. You can set the Bourne shell's secondary prompt (10.11), too, in *PS2.*)

- The exit status *(46.07)* of the last command is stored in the *csh* variable named *status* and the *sh* *?* (question mark) variable.

- If a job takes more CPU seconds than the number set in the *time (41.03)* variable, the *csh* will print a line of statistics about the job.

—*JP, TOR*

7.10 *Running a Command with a Temporarily Different Environment*

Quite a few UNIX commands set themselves up by reading the environment. For example, the *vi* editor reads startup commands from the *EXINIT* environment variable. Sometimes, you'll want to override the setting of an environment variable for just one command. There's an easier way than setting the variable to a different value and changing it back after you run the command:

- In the Bourne shell, type:

      $ **VARNAME=value command args**

- In the C shell on UNIX systems that have the *env* command, type:

      % **env VARNAME=value command args**

- Or, in any C shell, use a subshell *(14.07)* like this:

      % **(setenv VARNAME value; command args)**

For example, if your *EXINIT* variable has:

    set wrapscan showmatch number

and you want to add `nowrapscan` to the end of it just this once, you could type (to the Bourne shell):

$ 7.01 $ **EXINIT="$EXINIT nowrapscan" vi afile**

After that *vi* command ran, *EXINIT* wouldn't contain `nowrapscan`.

For a great example of this technique, see article 7.07.

—*JP*

8

Setting Your Shell Prompt

8.01 Why Change Your Prompt?

A percent sign (%) is the default C shell prompt on many systems. Not too useful, is it? All that prompt tells you is that you're logged in.

If you're good at remembering your current directory name, the computer you're logged in to, your current login name, and more—and, if you never leave your terminal for long—maybe that prompt is enough. But I forget that kind of stuff. I log in quite a few places and I get interrupted a lot. Without more information in my prompt, I'd always be trying to figure out where I am—typing pwd or who am I.

I've changed my prompt to give me the information I need. My prompt can't do everything I want (at least, not on the C shell), but it makes life a lot easier.

Besides, playing around with your prompt can be *fun*. It's one of the most popular UNIX games, especially for newcomers.

This chapter should get you started. The first few articles cover basics. The rest of the articles show some different prompts and how to make them. Play around. See what works best for you.

—JP

8.02 Basics of Setting the Prompt

The prompt displayed by your shell is contained in a shell variable *(7.08)* called *prompt* in the C shell and *PS1* in the Bourne and Korn shells. As such, it can be set like any other shell variable.

So, for example, if I wanted to change my C shell prompt to include my login name, I might put the following command into my *.cshrc* file:

```
set prompt="tim % "
```

(It's helpful to leave the % at the end so that it remains obvious that this is a C shell. The space after the % makes the command you type stand out from the rest of the prompt.)

Or if I wanted to put in the name of the system I was currently logged in on, I might say:

`...` *10.14*
hostname *52.06*

```
set prompt="`hostname` % "
```

If I wanted to include the history number for each command *(12.01)*, I'd say:

```
set prompt="\! % "
```

Or if I wanted all three things:

```
set prompt="tim@`hostname` \!% "
```

This will give me a prompt like this:

```
tim@isla 43%
```

—TOR

8.03 C Shell Prompt Causes Problems in vi, rsh, etc.

[Stray prompts can cause trouble for many commands that start a non-interactive shell. This problem may have been fixed in your C shell. The point Chris makes about speeding up your .cshrc still applies, though.—JP]

If you *set prompt* in your *.cshrc* file without carefully checking first whether or not *prompt* was already set *(2.09)*, many versions of the C shell will cheerfully print prompts into the pipe *vi* uses to expand glob characters [filename wildcards (*, ?, [ ]) *(1.16)* and the tilde (~) *(15.12)* —JP]. When you type :r abc*, *vi* opens a pipe to the C shell and writes the command echo abc* down the pipe, then reads the response. If the response contains spaces or newlines, *vi* gets confused. If you set your prompt to (n) in your *.cshrc* [i.e., if you show the history number in parentheses as the prompt—TOR], *vi* tends to get:

```
(1) abc.file (2)
```

back from the C shell, instead of just abc.file.

The solution is to kludge your *.cshrc (2.09)* like this:

if *49.03*
$?prompt *49.04*

```
if ($?prompt) then
        # things to do for an interactive shell, like:
        set prompt='(\!) '
endif
```

This works because a noninteractive shell has no initial prompt, while an interactive shell has it set to % .

If you have a large *.cshrc*, this can speed things up quite a bit when programs run other programs with csh -c '*command*', if you put all of it inside that test.

—*CT* in *net.unix-wizards* on Usenet, *22 April 1984*

8.04 *Faster Prompt Setting with Built-in Commands*

To set your prompt, you execute a command (on most shells, the command sets a shell variable). Before setting the prompt, you may run other commands to get information for it: the current directory name, for example. A shell can run two kinds of commands: built-in and external *(1.10)*. Built-in commands usually run faster than external commands. On a slow computer, the difference may be important—waiting a few seconds for your prompt to reset can get irritating. Creative use of your shell's built-in commands might pay off there. Let's look at two examples.

1. *pwd* is an external command that searches the filesystem *(15.04)* to find your current directory name. (*pwd* is built into some shells, but that version doesn't search the filesystem.) However, some shells can give you the current directory name from a variable, usually $cwd or $PWD. On slow computers, the first prompt-setting command below would take more time:

`..` *10.14*

```
set prompt="`pwd`% "
set prompt="${cwd}% "
```

There's a tradeoff here, though—the shell built-in may not *(15.14)* give the right answer.

2. If you're putting your current directory in your prompt, you may only want the tail of the pathname (the name past the last slash). How can you edit a pathname? Most people think of *basename (47.18)* or *sed (35.24)*. Using the current directory from $cwd, they might type:

```
set prompt="`basename $cwd`% "
```

The faster way is with the C shell's built-in "tail" operator, :t :

{} *7.08*

```
set prompt="${cwd:t}% "
```

If your current directory is */usr/users/hanna/projects*, either of those prompts would look like this (with a space after the percent sign):

```
projects%
```

The C shell has several of these built-in string operators *(12.08)* like :t; the Korn Shell has more-powerful string operators.

So, if your prompt takes too long to set, look for built-ins that can save time. As another example, article 8.11 shows how to use *dirs* in a shell prompt.

—JP

8.05 Multi-line Shell Prompts

Lots of people like lots of information in their prompts: hostname, directory name, history number, maybe username. Lots of people spend lots of time trying to make their prompts short enough to fit across the screen and still leave room for typing a command longer than *ls*:

```
<elaineq@applefarm> [/usr/elaineq/projects/april/week4] 23 % ls
```

Even with fairly short prompts, if you look back at a screen after running a few commands, telling the data from the prompts can be a little tough (real terminals don't show user input in boldface, so I won't do it here either):

```
<elaineq@applefarm> [~] 56% cd beta
<elaineq@applefarm> [~/beta] 57% which prog
/usr/tst/applefarm/bin/beta/prog
<elaineq@applefarm> [~/beta] 58% prog
61,102 units inventoried; 3142 to do
<elaineq@applefarm> [~/beta] 59%
```

csh_init

One nice answer is to make a prompt that has more than one line. Here's part of a *.cshrc* file that sets a three-line prompt: one blank line, one line with the hostname and current directory, and a third with the history number and a percent sign:

hostname *52.06*

[..] *7.08*

```
set hostname=`hostname`
alias setprompt 'set prompt="\\
${hostname}:${cwd}\\
\! % "'
alias cd 'chdir \!* && setprompt'
setprompt               # to set the initial prompt
```

The prompts look like this:

```
applefarm:/usr/elaineq/projects/april/week4
23 % prog | tee /dev/tty | mail -s "prog results" bigboss@corpoffice
61,102 units inventoried; 3142 to do

applefarm:/usr/elaineq/projects/april/week4
24 % cd ~/beta

applefarm:/usr/elaineq/beta
25 % prog | mail joanne
```

The blank lines separate each command—though you may want to save space by omitting them. For example, Mike Sierra (here at O'Reilly & Associates) uses a row of asterisks:

```
***** 23 *** <mike@mymac> *** /home/mike/calendar *****
% cd September
***** 24 *** <mike@mymac> *** /home/mike/calendar/September *****
%
```

The nicest part, I think, is that you get a lot of information but have the whole screen width for typing.

Of course, you can put different information in the prompt than I've shown here. The important idea is: if you want more information and need room to type, try a multi-line prompt.

—JP

8.06 Session Information in Your Terminal's Status Line

Some people don't like to put the current directory, hostname, etc. into their prompts because it makes the screen look cluttered to them. Here's another idea. If your terminal or window system has a status line or title bar, you might be able to put the information there. That's nice because you'll be able to see the information while you run programs. The bad side is that the information can get out-of-date if you use a command that takes you to another host or directory without updating the status line.

When you *cd*, an alias uses the *echo* command to write special escape sequences *(6.08)* (terminal commands) to the terminal or window.

Here's a *cd* alias and other commands for your *.cshrc* file. If I were logged in to *sunburn.beach.com* in the directory */home/jerry*, this alias would put:

```
sunburn:/home/jerry
```

in the status area. Of course, you can change the format of the status line. Change the command string below, `${host:h}:${cwd}`, to do what you need.

echo...033 *47.34*

csh_init

&& *46.09*

```
set e="`echo -n x | tr x \\033`"        # Make an ESCape character
set host=`hostname`
# Puts $host and $cwd in VT102 status line. Escape sequences are:
# ${e}7 = save cursor position, ${e}[25;1f = go to start of status
# line (line 25), ${e}[0K = erase line, ${e}8 = restore cursor
alias cd 'chdir \!* && \\
    echo -n "${e}7${e}[25;1f${e}[0K    ${host:h}:${cwd}${e}8"'
```

If you always use a VT102-type terminal (and many people do), that alias will work fine. If you use a different terminal, read its manual or its *termcap/terminfo* entry *(43.11)* and find the escape sequences that work for it.

People who use more than one type of terminal, that aren't all VT102-compatible, can add a *case (46.05)* or *switch (49.06)* to test the terminal type and use a *cd* alias written for that terminal. (The alias can also put the status information in the shell prompt on terminals that don't have a status line.) But you might have some trouble: if the alias is defined in your .cshrc file but your terminal type is set in your .login file, the terminal type may not be set until after the alias has been read. There are workarounds (2.07).

The status line can also get out of sync with reality if you use remote logins (1.12), subshells (40.04), and other things. These might put a new prompt in the status line but not reset the original prompt when it should be reset. The easiest workaround for this is by using the command below to change directory to the current directory (.) and reset the status line:

```
% cd .
```

—JP

8.07 A "Menu Prompt" for Naive Users

Some people don't want to be faced with a UNIX % or $ shell prompt. If you usually run only a few particular UNIX commands, you can put those command names in the shell prompt. Here's a simple one-line Bourne shell prompt for a .profile:

```
PS1='Type "rn", "mailx", "wp", or "logout": '
```

Next, a multi-line prompt (8.05) for the C shell .cshrc file:

($?prompt) **2.09**

(8.03)

```
if ($?prompt) then
set prompt='\\
Type "rn" to read the news,\\
type "mailx" to read and send mail,\\
type "wp" for word processing, or\\
type "logout" to log out.\\
YES, MASTER? '
endif
```

You get the idea.

—JP

8.08 Highlighting in Shell Prompts

If your prompt has some information that you want to stand out—or if you want your whole prompt to stand out from the rest of the text on the screen—you might be able to make it in enhanced characters. If your terminal has special escape sequences (6.08) for enhancing the characters (and most do), you can use them to make part or all of your prompt stand out.

csh_init

Let's say that you want to make sure people notice that they're logged in as root (the superuser) by making part of the root prompt flash. Here are lines for the root .cshrc:

```
# Put ESCape character in $e.  Use to start blinking mode (${e}[5m}
# and go back to normal mode (${e}[0m) on VT100-series terminals:
```

echo...033 *47.34*
hostname *52.06*

```
set e="`echo x | /bin/tr x \\033`"
set prompt="${e}[5mroot${e}[0m@`hostname`# "
```

That prompt might look like this, with the word `root` flashing:

```
root@sys.ora.com#
```

Because the same escape sequences won't work on all terminals, it's probably a good idea to add an *if* test *(49.03)* that only sets the prompt if the terminal type *$TERM* is in the Digital Equipment Corporation VT100 series (or one that emulates it). Table 8-1 shows a few escape sequences for VT100 and compatible terminals. The ESC in each sequence stands for an ESCape character.

Table 8-1. VT100 Escape Sequences for Highlighting

Sequence	What it Does
ESC[1m	Bold, intensify foreground
ESC[4m	Underscore
ESC[5m	Blink
ESC[7m	Reverse video
ESC[0m	All attributes off

Of course, you can use different escape sequences if your terminal needs them. Better, read your terminal's *terminfo* or *termcap* database with a program like *tput* or *tcap (43.10)* to get the correct escape sequences for your terminal. Store the escape sequences in shell variables *(7.08)*.

—JP

8.09 *Show Subshell Level with $cshlevel*

If you're like me, when you start a shell escape *(31.26)* or any subshell *(40.04)*, you can forget that you aren't in your login shell. Your shell history *(12.01)* might get confused, shell variables *(7.08)* may not be set, and other problems may come up. Here's a trick for the C shell that sets a shell variable named *cshlevel*. In your top-level shell, the value of $cshlevel is 0 (zero). In the first subshell, it's 1; in a sub-subshell, it's 2; and so on. You can put $cshlevel in your prompt *(8.01)* (but only during subshells, if you'd like—as a reminder that you aren't in your top-level shell). Test $cshlevel in aliases *(11.02)*, or your *.cshrc*, too. Note that this works only on *csh* (and *ksh*, if you set its *ENV (7.03)* environment variable) because those shells have startup files that are read when any shell starts. The *tcsh (1.08)* has a built-in *shlvl* variable you can use instead of *cshlevel*.

Put these lines in your *.cshrc* file:

```
# STUFF FOR TOP-LEVEL LOGINS AND rsh'S...
if (! $?CSHLEVEL) then
    # THIS PART DONE ON BOTH INTERACTIVE AND NON-INTERACTIVE SHELLS.

    # SHOWS THAT THIS IS TOP-LEVEL SHELL (INCREMENTED TO 0 BELOW).
    setenv CSHLEVEL -1
```

$?prompt *2.09*

```
      ...
      if ($?prompt) then
            # THIS PART DONE ONLY ON INTERACTIVE SHELLS:
            ...
            set prompt=...
      endif
endif


# SET SHELL LEVEL (DEPTH OF NESTED SHELLS).
set cshlevel = $CSHLEVEL
@ cshlevel++
setenv CSHLEVEL $cshlevel
```

@...++ *49.04*

Does your account run a windowing system that's started from your *.login* file? If it does, lines in *.login* like the ones below will reset *CSHLEVEL* so that the shell in the window will start at a *CSHLEVEL* of zero (and act like a top-level shell):

```
# IF ON WORKSTATION CONSOLE, RUN OPEN WINDOWS RIGHT AWAY:
if ("`/bin/tty`" == /dev/console) then
      setenv CSHLEVEL -1
      openwin                  # START WINDOW SYSTEM
endif
```

Now, for example, you can set your prompt to mike% in top-level shells, (1) mike% in a first-level subshell, (2) mike% in a second-level subshell, etc. Here's some sample prompt-setting code for your *.cshrc*:

```
# IF THIS IS A SUB-SHELL, PUT SHELL LEVEL IN PROMPT:
if ($cshlevel == 0) then
      set prompt="${USER}% "
else
      set prompt="($cshlevel) ${USER}% "
endif
```

Getting this to work right in every situation (*rsh* (1.33), *su* (23.23), shell escapes (31.26)—both interactive and noninteractive, subshells, window systems, *at* jobs (42.03), and so on) can be a challenge (2.07)^! It takes a little planning. Sit down and think about:

* All the ways you start subshells.

* Which subshells are interactive and which aren't.

* Whether they'll get *CSHLEVEL* passed from their parent process (if you aren't sure, test that with an *env* or *printenv* command (7.01)).

Then plan which kind of shell needs which *CSHLEVEL* settings. If it gets too complicated, make it work in most cases! If you use many subshells, this trick is too handy to ignore.

—JP

8.10 Shell Prompt for Terminals with Local Editing

Some terminals I've used (like old Hewlett-Packard and Tektronix terminals) had local editing. You could move your cursor up the screen to a previous command line, maybe make some edits to it, then press a SEND LINE key to resend that line to the host. This didn't have anything to do with sophisticated command-line editing *(12.14)* like some UNIX shells have now. Maybe your terminal can do that, too.

The problem was that unless I erased the shell prompt (%) on my screen, it would be sent back to the shell and give the error "%: Command not found." So I set my shell prompt to this:

```
set prompt='    '
```

That's right: four spaces. Most UNIX commands start their output at column 1, so my command lines were easy to find because they were indented. And the shell didn't care if I sent four spaces before the command line. So everything was fine until I got my new terminal without a SEND LINE key . . .

—JP

8.11 dirs in Your Prompt: Better than $cwd

The C shell gives the absolute pathname of your current directory in $cwd *(15.14)*. Many people use that in their prompts. If you use the *pushd* and *popd* *(15.06)* commands, you may not always remember exactly what's in your directory stack (I don't, at least). Also, do you want to shorten your home directory pathname to just a tilde (~) so it takes less room in the prompt? Here's how: run the *dirs* command and use its output in your prompt. A simple alias for *cd* users looks like this:

```
alias cd 'chdir \!* && set prompt="`dirs`% "'
```

and the prompts look like:

```
/work/project % cd
~ % cd bin
~/bin %
```

Here's what to put in *.cshrc* to make a multi-line prompt *(8.05)* that shows the directory stack:

hostname *52.06*

expr *47.28*

csh_init

```
# PUT hostname.domain.name IN $hostname AND hostname IN $HOST:
set hostname=`hostname`
setenv HOST `expr $hostname : '\([^.]*\).*'`
alias setprompt 'set prompt="\\
${USER}@${HOST} `dirs` \\
\! % "'
alias cd   'chdir \!* && setprompt'
alias pushd 'pushd \!* && setprompt'
alias popd 'popd \!* && setprompt'
setprompt                    # SET THE INITIAL PROMPT
```

That makes a blank line before each prompt; if you don't want that, join the first and second lines of the *setprompt* alias. Let's push a couple of directories and watch the prompt:

```
jerry@ora ~
1 % pushd /work/src/perl
/work/src/perl ~

jerry@ora /work/src/perl ~
2 % cd ../cnews

jerry@ora /work/src/cnews ~
3 % pushd ~/bin
~/bin /work/src/cnews ~

jerry@ora ~/bin /work/src/cnews ~
4 %
```

(15.14)

Of course, the prompt looks a little redundant there because each *pushd* command also shows the *dirs* output. A few commands later, though, having your directory stack in the prompt will be handy. If your directory stack has a lot of entries, the first line of the prompt can get wider than the screen. In that case, store the *dirs* output in a shell array *(49.05)* and edit it with a command like *sed* or with the built-in *csh* string editing *(12.08)*. For example, to show just the tail of each path in the *dirs* output, use the alias below; the C shell operator `:gt` globally edits all words, to the tail of each pathname:

csh_init

```
alias setprompt 'set dirs=(`dirs`); set prompt="\\
${USER}@${HOST} $dirs:gt\\
\! % "'
```

Watch the prompt. If you forget what the names in the prompt mean, just type `dirs`:

```
jerry@ora bin cnews jerry
5 % pushd ~/tmp/test
~/tmp/test ~/bin /work/src/cnews ~
...
jerry@ora test bin cnews jerry
12 % dirs
~/tmp/test ~/bin /work/src/cnews ~
```

—*JP*

8.12 Date and Time in Your Bourne Shell Prompt

For interactive use, the C shell beats the old Bourne shell most places. Here's one place the Bourne shell wins.*

The Bourne shell's *trap (46.12)* will run one or more commands when the shell gets a signal *(40.08)*. This trick takes over signal 5, which usually isn't used. When the shell gets signal 5, a *trap* runs a command to get the date and time, then

---

*Newer shells like *tcsh* and *ksh (1.08)* do even better. This trick is good for more than putting the date and time in your prompt: you can use the output of *any* UNIX command in your prompt.

resets the prompt. A background *(1.27)* job springs this trap once a minute. So, every minute, after you type any command, your prompt will change.

If your system's *date* command doesn't understand date formats (like +%a), get one that does—like the version on the Power Tools disk *(53.10)*. Put these lines in your *.profile* file (or just type them in at a Bourne shell prompt):

sh_prompt

```
# Put date and time in prompt; update every 60 seconds:
trap 'PS1=`date "+%a %D %H:%M%n"`\
$\ ' 5
while :
do
    sleep 60
    kill -5 $$
done &
promptpid=$!
```

Now, every minute after you type a command, your prompt will change:

```
Mon 02/17/92 08:59
$ cc bigprog.c
undefined symbol                first referenced in file
xputc                                   bigprog.o
ld fatal: Symbol referencing errors.
Mon 02/17/92 08:59
$ ls
bigprog.c
bigprog.o
Mon 02/17/92 09:00
$
```

The prompt format is up to you. This example makes a two-line prompt *(8.05)*, with backslashes (\) to protect the newline and space from the *trap*; a single-line prompt might be easier to design. The manual page for *date* lists what you can put in the prompt.

This setup starts a *while* loop *(46.10)* in the background. The *promptpid* variable holds the process ID number *(40.03)* of the background shell. Before you log out, you should *kill (40.10)* the loop. You can type the command:

```
kill $promptpid
```

at a prompt or put it in a file that's executed when you log out *(3.02)*.

—JP

## Part Two

Let the Computer Do the Dirty Work

Letting the computer do the dirty work—that's what this entire book is about. However, the next six chapters cover some of the most important ways to do that. The UNIX shells provide many ways to help you avoid typing the same thing over and over again, or typing something long when you could be typing something short, or ...

What is it they say? "Time spent sailing is not subtracted from your life." I don't know about that, but I do know that time spent learning the intricacies of the shell is seldom wasted.

—*TOR*

9

How the Shell Interprets
What You Type

9.01 What the Shell Does

As we've said, the shell is just another program. It's responsible for interpreting the commands you type; there are three or four commonly used shells, and several other variants *(1.08)* kicking around.

Interpreting your commands might seem simple enough, but a lot of things happen between the time you press RETURN and the time the computer actually does what you want. The process of interpretation is very complex: the shell has to break the command into words, expand aliases *(11.02)*, history operators *(12.01)*, and shell and environment variables *(7.08, 7.01)*. It also sets up standard input and output streams *(14.01)* and performs a lot of other tasks. Indeed, if a command looks right but doesn't work right, the cause is probably either:

- File permissions are set incorrectly.

- You don't understand how the shell is processing your command line.

I'd say that file permission problems are more common, but it's a close call. File permission problems are usually easy to understand, once you know what to look for, but the rules by which a shell interprets your command line are another thing altogether. Lest I scare you, we'll try to go slow with this material. Although it's difficult, understanding how the shell parses your commands is important to becoming a power user.

In this chapter, we'll look at how a UNIX shell interprets commands. The standard shells (the C shell, Bourne shell, and Korn shell) have similar interpretation rules. The C shell can be tricky at times, mostly because its behavior isn't as well defined as the others. However, there's nothing "magical" about these rules. Tomorrow morning, you may grab some new shell from the net *(55.01)*, and find out that it has a new and different way of interpreting commands. For better or worse, that's what UNIX is all about.

As part of this discussion, we'll cover quoting, which is the mechanism by which you can turn off the special meanings that the shell assigns to some characters. Quoting is an integral part of command-line processing; it allows you to control what the shell will do to your commands.

—ML

9.02 *Command Evaluation and Accidentally Overwriting Files*

Before getting into the details of command interpretation, I thought I'd give a very simple example of why it's important. Here's an error that occurs all the time. Let's say you have two files, called *file1* and *file2*. You want to create a new version of *file1* that has *file2* added to the end of it. That's what *cat* is all about, so you give the command:

```
% cat file1 file2 > file1                    ...wrong
```

This looks like it should work. If you've ever tried it, you know it doesn't; it erases *file1*, and then dumps *file2* into it. Why? The shell (not *cat*) handles standard input and output.

- As the shell is processing the command, it sees that you're redirecting standard output into *file1*, so it opens the file for writing, destroying the data that's already in it.

- Later, after it's finished interpreting the command line, the shell executes *cat*, passing *file1* and *file2* as arguments. But *file1* is already empty.

- *cat* reads *file1* (which is empty) and writes it on standard output (which goes into *file1*).

- *cat* reads *file2* (which also goes into *file1*). At this point, *cat* is finished, so it exits.

file1 and *file2* are identical, which isn't what you wanted. But it's what you got.

Some versions of *cat* give you a warning message in this situation (`cat: input file1 is output`). This might lead you to believe that somehow *cat* was smart and managed to protect you. Sadly, that's not true. By the time *cat* figures out that an input file and an output file are the same, it's too late: *file1* is already gone. This bit of *cat*ty cleverness does have a function, though: it prevents commands like:

```
% cat file1 file2 >> file2
```

from creating infinitely long files.

—ML

9.03 Command-line Evaluation

With all the different substitution mechanisms available in the C shell, it's important to know which take precedence. Here's the order in which the C shell interprets the command line:

1. History substitution

2. Splitting words (including special characters)

3. Updating the history list

4. Interpreting single quotes (') and double quotes (")

5. Alias substitution

6. Redirection of input and output (e.g., >, <, and |)

7. Variable substitution

8. Command substitution

9. Filename expansion

(The Bourne shell is essentially the same, except that it doesn't perform history substitution or alias substitution.)

History substitutions are always done first. That's why quotes won't protect a ! from the shell; the shell sees the exclamation point and substitutes a command from the history before it's even thought about the quotation marks. To prevent history substitution, you need to use a backslash *(9.11)*.

Let's work through a simple command line that uses several of these features. Nothing in this command line will be difficult, but it will give you a feeling for what we mean by saying that "the shell performs variable substitution after alias substitution." Here's the command line:

```
% ls -l    $HOME/* |    grep "Mar   7"
```

And here's what happens:

1. There are no history operators, so history substitution *(12.02)* doesn't happen. (The Bourne shell wouldn't perform this step.)

2. The command line is split into separate "words." The words are `ls`, `-l`, `$HOME/*`, `|`, `grep`, and `"Mar   7"`. The shell ignores the number of spaces between different words in a command line. Any space creates a new word. The shell doesn't do anything special with options (like `-l`). Options are passed to the command being run, just like any other word;* the command

---

*The convention of starting options with a dash (–) is just that: a convention. Although option handling is being standardized *(46.17)*, each command can interpret its options any way it wants to.

decides how to interpret them. Also, note that quotes *(9.10)* prevent the shell from splitting `"Mar   7"` into two words or eating the two spaces*—even though quote interpretation comes later. At this point, the command line looks like this:

```
ls -l $HOME/* | grep "Mar   7"
```

3. The shell sticks the command line onto the history list. The Bourne shell wouldn't perform this step, either.

4. The shell recognizes the double quotes around `"Mar   7"` and notes that wildcard expansion (yet to come) shouldn't take place inside the quotes.

5. The shell checks whether or not `ls` or `grep` are aliases *(11.02)*. They could be, but we're assuming they aren't.

6. The shell notices the `|`, and does whatever's required *(14.01)* to set up a pipeline.

7. The shell notices the environment variable *(7.01)* `$HOME`, and replaces this variable with its value (`/home/mikel`). At this point, the command line looks like:

```
ls -l /home/mikel/* | grep "Mar   7"
```

8. The shell looks for backquotes *(10.14)*, executes any command inside the backquotes, and inserts its output on the command line. In this case, there's nothing to do. (If there are wildcards or variables inside the backquotes, they aren't interpreted before the shell runs the command inside the backquotes.)

9. The shell looks for wildcards *(1.16)*. In this case, it sees the `*` and expands the filename accordingly, leaving something like this:

```
ls -l /home/mikel/ax ... /home/mikel/zip | grep "Mar   7"
```

10. The shell executes the *ls* command, executes the *grep* command, with the aforementioned pipe sending the *ls* output into *grep*'s input.

One character you'll see often on command lines is ; (semicolon). It's used as a command separator: type one complete command line—then, instead of pressing RETURN, type a semicolon and another complete command line. Chaining commands with semicolons is especially useful in subshells *(14.07)*, aliases, and lists *(14.08)*—this book has lots of examples—in articles 42.02 and 11.02, for instance. There's more about command-line interpretation in the articles on wildcards inside aliases *(9.07)*, *eval* *(9.08)*, conditional execution *(46.09)*, and many others.

—DG, ML

---

*In an *ls –l* listing, dates less than 10 have two spaces before them (they're printed in a field 2 characters wide).

9.04 Output Command-line Arguments with echo

The *echo* command writes its command-line arguments and a newline to the standard output. Shell scripts use *echo* for sending text to the terminal, down a pipe, and into a file. You can use *echo* on the command line to show the value of a variable *(7.01, 7.08)*, to see how filename wildcards will expand without doing anything else to those files, or to check quoting *(48.02)*:

```
% echo "USER is $USER."
USER is jerry.
% echo "All 'a' files are:      " a*
All 'a' files are:      abacus apple axes
```

Portability

The C shell and most other newer shells have a version of *echo* that's built in *(1.10)* so it's faster.

The original *echo* had just one option: *−n*, which tells *echo* not to print a newline after the message. Shell scripts use *−n* to send a question to a user and leave the cursor at the end of the message:

```
echo -n "Enter your name: "
```

(The space at the end makes the prompt look better. The quotes make the shell pass that space on to *echo*.)

Newer versions of *echo* check their arguments for a backslash (\). This marks the start of an *escape sequence*, a character that the backslash and the next letter stand for. For example, when these newer *echo*s see \n, they print a newline character:

```
$ echo "1.\n2.\n3."
1.
2.
3.
$
```

In this version of *echo*, a \c at the end of the last argument suppreses the newline—like the *−n* option does in the other *echo*:

```
echo "Enter your name: \c"
```

Your online *echo* manual page should tell you which version you have and list any escape sequences.

The problem with this newer *echo* is that it's tough to *echo* an arbitrary string that might have a backslash in it. Chris Torek has a workaround: use a here-document *(9.14)* and *cat (26.02)* instead of *echo*. For example:

```
cat << END
The answer is: $variable-whose-value-might-contain-backslashes
END
```

Another utility called *printf* works like the *printf(3)* routine in the C language; it handles escape sequences and more. If we had *printf* and the old *echo*, life would be easier. Article 48.10 shows a way to make *echo* portable.

The C shell *echo* works differently than other versions. For example, to make an empty line with the standard *echo*, don't give any arguments. (This is usually done for readability—to put blank lines between other output.) Standard *echo* will just print a newline:

```
$ echo

$
```

Without arguments, the C shell *echo* doesn't print the newline. To get a newline, you have to give an empty argument:

```
% echo ""

%
```

To use the standard *echo* from the C shell, type */bin/echo* instead.

Making Error Messages

echo writes to standard output. Error messages in shell scripts should be written to the standard error so that redirection *(14.01)* of standard output doesn't accidentally capture the message. The Bourne shell `1>&2` operator *(47.21)* will move *echo*'s output to standard error:

```
echo "progname: choke wheeze complain" 1>&2
```

The C shell can't do that—which is another reason not to write shell scripts with *csh (49.02)*.

—JP

9.05 Setting Your Search Path

Your search path *(7.04, 7.05)* controls what directories—and in what order—the shell searches for external *(1.10)* commands. You can set a search path that takes effect every time you log in by editing your shell setup file *(2.02)*. You might also want to change the path temporarily.

Setting Path in Shell Setup Files

To change the "default" search path used every time you log in, edit the `PATH= . . .` line in your *.profile* file or the `set path=( . . . )` line in your *.cshrc* or *.login* file.

Add the absolute pathname *(15.02)* of the directory to the path. You have a choice:

- You can put the directory at the end of your path. (I think that's the best idea unless you know exactly what you're doing.) Then, commands in the directories you add will be used only if they have unique names that aren't found anywhere else in the path. You can check that with a command like *which (52.07)*.

- If you put the pathname close to the start of the path, before standard system directories *(15.08)* like */bin*, then commands in the directory you add will be used instead of system commands with the same name. That lets you replace commands that don't work the way you want with your own version. For instance, if you had the *cal* script that marks today's date *(50.08)* in your *bin (5.02)*, it would be used instead of the system *cal (50.07)*.

If you set your path this way, you should be especially careful not to accidentally give some random program the same name as a system command—article 46.20 explains how to check for that.

Installing your own version of standard system commands (like *ls* or *rm*) at the front of your path has a serious consequence. Many system programs and shell scripts will call a program like *ls* and expect it to work just like the default system version of that program. If you install a version at the front of your search path that behaves differently, that can cause serious problems for an unsuspecting program.

For example, you might install a version of *rm* that writes messages to standard output like "Do you want to remove this file?" and reads your answer from standard input. The standard system *rm* command won't prompt if its standard input isn't a terminal. If your custom *rm* doesn't work the same way as the system *rm*, other programs that call *rm* can mysteriously lock up while they wait (forever) for your private *rm* to get an answer to its prompt.

If you want to replace a system command, it's better to give your version a different name.

When you log in, as your shell starts, before your setup files are read, your system probably has already set a default search path for you. Your system administrator can change that path. If your system has a default path, you should think about using it as part of your path—ask your administrator. To do that, include the variable $PATH or $path as you set your path. For example, to add your *bin* directory at the end of the system path, use one of the following lines:*

```
set path=($path ~/bin)                 C shell
PATH=$PATH:$HOME/bin                    Bourne shell
```

---

*There's a small problem with this if you set your path in your *.cshrc* or *ksh* *ENV* file. Each time you start a subshell *(40.04)*, your *bin* directory will be added to the path again. That won't cause any errors but it will make the path longer than it needs to be. If you want to work around this, use an environment variable like *ENV_SET (2.07)* as a flag—and set the path only if *ENV_SET* isn't set.

For the Bourne and Korn shells, load the updated *PATH* by typing the command:

```
$ . .profile
```

For the C shell, type one of these commands, depending on which file you changed:

```
% source .cshrc
% source .login
```

Changing Path on the Command Line

As you work, you might need to add a directory to your path temporarily. For example, when I develop new versions of existing programs, I put them in a separate directory named something like *alpha–test*. I don't usually want to run the alpha-test commands---but when I do, I add the *alpha–test* directory to the front of my path temporarily. (It's handy to set the new path in a subshell *(40.04)* so it won't change the path in my other shell.) Use the same path setting command you'd use in a shell setup file:

```
% set path=(~/xxx/alpha-test $path)     C shell
$ PATH=$HOME/xxx/alpha-test:$PATH        Bourne shell
$ export PATH
```

Article 9.06 shows another way to change your path: command-by-command instead of directory-by-directory.

—*JP* from the Nutshell Handbook *MH & xmh: E-Mail for Users & Programmers*

9.06   *A Directory for Commands You Shouldn't Run*

How can you keep yourself from running *some* of the commands in a directory in your search path *(7.04, 7.05)*? For example, I use several different computers. I read and store my electronic mail *(1.33)* on just one computer—on that host, I want to use all the e-mail commands. On the other computers, I want to be able to use mail-sending commands—but I don't want the mail-reading commands to work on my account there.

You might work on a project with shared filesystems where some commands will only work on certain computers. How can you stop the commands from being run accidentally on computers where they shouldn't be? There's a beginner on the system who shouldn't be running dangerous commands. How can you stop him from using just those commands?

You could make aliases *(11.02)* for those commands that just *echo* a message to the terminal. But having tens or hundreds of aliases like that can be a real headache.

Here's how I solved my problem. On all of my computers, the commands for the e-mail system I use (called MH) are stored in the directory */usr/local/mh*. I make a directory named *no_run.hostname* that has short shell scripts. The scripts have the same names as the the commands in */usr/local/mh* that I *don't* want to run. On the computers where I don't want to run those commands, I put the *no_run.hostname* directory before the */usr/local/mh* directory in my path:

switch *49.06*

```
switch (`hostname`)
case cruncher:
        set path=( ... ~/no_run.cruncher /usr/local/mh ... )
        ...
```

(A per-host setup file *(2.13)* can help, too.) When I try to use a command that I shouldn't, the shell will find the shell script in the *no_run* directory before the real command in the *mh* directory. The shell script rings the bell, prints a message with its own name and the name of the computer to use, then quits:

```
% inc
```
beep... You can't run inc here. Use sunspot.

To save disk space, the shell scripts in the *no_run* directory are all hard links *(19.04)* to each other:

```
% ls -li no_run.cruncher
    ...
270156 -rwxr-xr-x 31 jerry       82 Jun 12 09:10 inc
270156 -rwxr-xr-x 31 jerry       82 Jun 12 09:10 mark
270156 -rwxr-xr-x 31 jerry       82 Jun 12 09:10 msgchk
        ...a total of 31 links...
```

no_run

The script uses the command basename $0 *(47.18)* to include its (current) command name with the warning message:

! *46.07*

```
#! /bin/sh
echo "\007You can't run `basename $0` here.  Use sunspot." 1>&2
exit 1
```

The \007 rings the bell on my version of *echo*; your version might need a \a or a real CTRL-g character *(47.34)* instead.

—*JP*

9.07 *Wildcards Inside of Aliases*

Here's another example in which command-line parsing is important. Consider this alias for counting the number of words in all files:

wc *30.06*

```
% alias words "wc -w *"
```

Right away, we can see one effect of command-line parsing. The shell sees the quotation marks, and knows not to expand wildcards inside the quotation marks. Therefore, words is aliased to wc -w *; the * isn't evaluated when you create the alias. (If wildcards were processed before quotes, this won't work.)

Now, think about what happens when you execute the alias. You type:

```
% words
```

The shell starts working through its steps *(9.03)*, and eventually performs alias substitution. When this happens, it converts your command into:

```
wc -w *
```

Now, watch carefully. The shell continues working through the process of interpretation (redirection, variable substitution, command substitution), and eventually gets to filename expansion. At this point, the shell sees the * on the command line, expands it, and substitutes the files in the current directory. Seems simple enough. But think: you didn't type this *; the shell put it there when it expanded the wildcard. What would have happened if the shell expanded wildcards before substituting aliases? The * would never have been expanded; by the time the shell put it on the command line, the wildcard expansion stage would be over, and you'd just count the words in a file named * (which probably doesn't exist).

To me, the amazing thing is that all this works—and works well! The workings of the command line are intricate and complex, but the shell almost always does what you want—and without a lot of thought.

—ML

9.08 eval: When You Need Another Chance

If you read the previous article *(9.07)*, you saw that, most of the time, the shell evaluates the command line "in the right order." But what about when it doesn't? Here's a situation that the shell can't handle. It's admittedly contrived, but not too different from what you might find in a shell program *(1.05)*:

```
% set b=\$a
% set a=foo
% echo $b
$a
```

When we use the variable $b, we'd like to get the variable $a, read it, and use its value. But that doesn't happen. Variable substitution happens once, and it isn't recursive. The value of $b is $a, and that's it. You don't go any further.

But there's a loophole. The *eval* command says, in essence, "Give me another chance. Re-evaluate this line and execute it." Here's what happens if we stick *eval* before the *echo*:

```
% eval echo $b
foo
```

The shell converts $b into $a; then *eval* runs through the command-line evaluation process again, converting echo $a into echo foo—which is what we wanted in the first place!

Here's a more realistic example; you see code like this fairly often in Bourne shell scripts:

```
    ...
    command='grep $grepopts $searchstring $file'
    for opt
```

```
    do
        case "$opt" in
            file) output=' > $ofile' ;;
            read) output=' | more'   ;;
            sort) postproc=' | sort $sortopts';;
        esac
    done
    ...
    eval $command $postproc $output
```

Do you see what's happening? We're constructing a command that will look something like:

```
grep $grepopts $searchstring $file | sort $sortopts > $ofile
```

But the entire command is "hidden" in shell variables, including the I/O redirectors and various options. If the *eval* isn't there, this command will blow up in all sorts of bizarre ways. You'll see messages like | not found, because variable expansion occurs after output redirection. The "nested" variables (like $ofile, which is used inside of $output) won't be expanded either, so you'll also see $ofile not found. Putting an *eval* in front of the command forces the shell to process the line again, guaranteeing that the variables will be expanded properly and that I/O redirection will take place.

eval is incredibly useful if you have shell variables that include other shell variables, shell variables that include aliases, shell variables that include I/O redirectors, or all sorts of perversities. It's commonly used within shell scripts to "evaluate" commands that are built during execution. There are more examples of *eval* in articles 6.04, 11.07, 11.11, 47.17, 47.33, 48.03, and others.

—*ML*

9.09 Is It "2>&1 > file" or "> file 2>&1"? Why?

One of the common questions about the Bourne and Korn shells is why only the second command will redirect both *stdout* and *stderr*(14.01)to a file:

```
$ cat food 2>&1 >file
cat: can't open food
$ cat food >file 2>&1
```

Although lots of *sh* manual pages don't mention this, the shell reads arguments from left to right.

1. On the first command line, the shell sees 2>&1 first. That means "make the standard error (file descriptor 2) go to the same place as the standard output (fd1) is going." There's no effect because both fd2 and fd1 are already going to the terminal. Then >file redirects fd1 (*stdout*) to file. But fd2 (*stderr*) is still going to the terminal.

2. On the second command line, the shell sees >file first and redirects *stdout* to file. Next 2>&1 sends fd2 (*stderr*) to the same place fd1 is going—that's to the file. And that's what you want.

Article 47.21 has much more about the *m>&n* operator.

—JP

9.10 Bourne Shell Quoting

I can't understand why some people see Bourne shell quoting as a scary, mysterious set of many rules. Bourne shell quoting is simple. (C shell quoting is slightly more complicated. See article 9.11.)

The overall idea is: *quoting turns off (disables) the special meaning of characters*. There are three quoting characters: a single quote (`'`), a double quote (`"`), and a backslash (`\`). Note that a backquote (`` ` ``) is *not* a quoting character—it does command substitution *(10.14)*.

Special Characters

Below are the characters that are special to the Bourne shell. You've probably already used some of them. Quoting these characters turns off their special meaning. (Yes, the last three characters are quote marks. You can quote quote marks; more on that later.)

```
# & * ? [ ] ( ) = | ^ ; < > ` $ " ' \
```

Space, tab, and newline also have special meaning: as argument separators. A slash (`/`) has special meaning to UNIX itself, but not the shell—so quoting doesn't change the meaning of slashes.

How Quoting Works

Table 9-1 summarizes the rules; you might want to look back at it while you read the examples.

Table 9-1. Bourne Shell Quoting Characters

Quoting Character	Explanation
`'xxx'`	Disable all special characters in *xxx*.
`"xxx"`	Disable all special characters in *xxx* except $, `` ` `` and \.
`\x`	Disable special meaning of character *x*. At end of line, a \ removes the newline character (continues line).

To understand which characters will be quoted, imagine this: the Bourne shell reads what you type at a prompt, or the lines in a shell script, character by character from first to last. (It's actually more complicated than that, but not for the purposes of quoting.)

When the shell reads one of the three quoting characters, it:

- Strips away that quoting character.

- Turns off (disables) special meaning of some or all other character(s) until the end of the quoted section, by the rules in Table 9-1.

You also need to know how many characters will be quoted. The next few sections have examples to demonstrate those rules. Try typing the examples at a Bourne shell prompt, if you'd like. (Don't use C shell; it's different *(9.11)*.) If you need to start a Bourne-type shell, type *sh*; use CTRL-d when you're done.

- A **backslash** (\) turns off special meaning (if any) of the next character. For example, * is a literal asterisk, not a filename wildcard. So, the first *expr (47.28)* command gets the three arguments 79 * 45 and multiplies those two numbers:

```
$ expr 79 \* 45
3555
$ expr 79 * 45
expr: syntax error
```

In the second example, without the backslash, the shell expanded * into a list of filenames—which confused *expr*. (If you want to see what I mean, repeat those two examples using *echo (9.04)* instead of *expr*.)

- A **single quote** (') turns off special meaning of all characters until the next single quote is found. So, in the command line below, the words between the two single quotes are quoted. The quotes themselves are removed by the shell. Although this mess is probably not what you want, it's a good demonstration of what quoting does:

```
$ echo Hey!      What's next?  Mike's #1 friend has $$.
Hey! Whats next?  Mikes
```

Let's take a close look at what happened. Spaces outside the quotes are treated as argument separators; the shell ignores the multiple spaces. As article 9.04 explains, *echo* prints a single space between each argument it gets. Spaces inside the quotes are passed on to *echo* literally. The question mark (?) is quoted; it's given to *echo* as is, not used as a wildcard.

So, *echo* printed its first argument Hey! and a single space. The second argument to *echo* is Whats next? Mikes; it's all a single argument because the single quotes surrounded the spaces (notice that *echo* prints the two spaces after the question mark: ?   ). The next argument, #1, starts with a hash mark, which is a comment character *(46.02)*. That means the shell will ignore the rest of the string; it isn't passed to *echo*.

- **Double quotes** (") work almost like single quotes. The difference is that double quoting allows the characters $ (dollar sign), ` (backquote), and \ (backslash) to keep their special meanings. That lets you do variable substitution *(7.08, 7.01)* and command substitution *(10.14)* inside double quotes—and also to stop that substitution where you need to.

For now, let's repeat the example above. This time, put double quotes around the single quotes (actually, around the whole string):

```
$ echo "Hey!       What's next?  Mike's #1 friend has $$."
Hey!       What's next?  Mike's #1 friend has 18437.
```

The opening double quote isn't matched until the end of the string. So, all the spaces between the double quotes lose their special meaning—and the shell passes the whole string to *echo* as one argument. The single quotes also lose their special meaning—because double quotes turn off the special meaning of single quotes! So, the single quotes aren't stripped off as they were in the previous example; *echo* prints them.

What else lost its special meaning? The hash mark (#) did; notice that the rest of the string was passed to *echo* this time—because it wasn't "commented out." But the dollar sign ($) didn't lose its meaning; the $$ was expanded into the shell's process ID number *(40.03)* (in this shell, 18437).

In the previous example, what would happen if you put the $ inside the single quotes? (Single quotes turn off the meaning of $, remember.) Would the shell still expand $$ to its value? Yes, it would: the single quotes have lost their special meaning, so they don't affect any characters between themselves:

```
$ echo "What's next?  How many $$ did Mike's friend bring?"
What's next?  How many 18437 did Mike's friend bring?
```

How can you make both the $$ and the single quotes print literally? The easiest way is with a backslash, which still works inside double quotes:

```
$ echo "What's next?  How many \$\$ did Mike's friend bring?"
What's next?  How many $$ did Mike's friend bring?
```

Here's another way to solve the problem. A careful look at this will show a lot about shell quoting:

```
$ echo "What's next?  How many "'$$'" did Mike's friend bring?"
What's next?  How many $$ did Mike's friend bring?
```

To read that example, remember that a double quote quotes characters until the next double quote is found. The same is true for single quotes. So, the string `What's next?  How many ` (including the space at the end) is inside a pair of double quotes. The $$ is inside a pair of single quotes. The rest of the line is inside another pair of double quotes. Both of the double-quoted strings contain a single quote; the double quotes turn off its special meaning and the single quote is printed literally.

Single Quotes Inside Single Quotes?

You can't put single quotes inside single quotes. A single quote turns off *all* special meaning until the next single quote. Use double quotes and backslashes.

Multi-line Quoting

Once you type a single quote or double quote, everything is quoted. The quoting can stretch across many lines. (The C shell doesn't work this way.)

For example, in the short script shown in Figure 9-1, you might think that the $1 is inside quotes... but it isn't.

```
awk '
/foo/ { print '$1' }
'
```

Figure 9-1. Matching Quotes

Actually, everything *but* $1 is in quotes. The grey shaded area shows the quoted parts. So $1 is expanded by the Bourne shell, and not by *awk*.

Here's another example. Let's store a shell variable *(7.08)* with a multi-line message, the kind that might be used in a shell program. A shell variable must be stored as a single argument; any argument separators (spaces, etc.) must be quoted. Inside double quotes, $ and ` are interpreted (*before* the variable is stored, by the way). The opening double quote isn't closed by the end of the first line; the Bourne shell prints secondary prompts *(10.11)* (>) until all quotes are closed:

```
$ greeting="Hi, $USER.
> The date and time now
> are:    `date`."
$ echo "$greeting"
Hi, jerry.
The date and time now
are:    Tue Sep  1 13:48:12 EDT 1992.
$ echo $greeting
Hi, jerry. The date and time now are: Tue Sep 1 13:48:12 EDT 1992.
$
```

The first *echo* command line uses double quotes. So, the shell variable is expanded, but the shell doesn't use the spaces and newlines in the variable as argument separators. (Look at the extra spaces after the word are:.) The second *echo* doesn't use double quotes. The spaces and newlines are treated as argument separators; the shell passes 14 arguments to *echo*, which prints them with single spaces between.

A backslash has a quirk you should know about. If you use it outside quotes, at the end of a line (just before the newline), the newline will be *deleted*. Inside single quotes, though, a backslash at the end of a line is copied as is. Here are examples. I've numbered the prompts (1$, 2$, and so on):

```
1$ echo "a long long long long long long
> line or two"
a long long long long long long
line or two
2$ echo a long long long long long long\
> line
a long long long long long longline
3$ echo a long long long long long long \
> line
a long long long long long long line
4$ echo "a long long long long long long\
> line"
a long long long long long longline
5$ echo 'a long long long long long long\
> line'
a long long long long long long\
line
```

You've seen an example like **example 1** before. The newline is in quotes, so it isn't an argument separator; *echo* prints it with the rest of the (single two-line) argument. In **example 2**, the backslash before the newline tells the shell to delete the newline; the words `long` and `line` are passed to *echo* as one argument. **Example 3** is usually what you want when you're typing long lists of command-line arguments: Type a space (an argument separator) before the backslash and newline. In **example 4**, the backslash inside the double quotes is ignored (compare to example 1). Inside single quotes, as in **example 5**, the backslash has no special meaning; it's passed on to *echo*.

—JP

9.11 Differences Between Bourne and C Shell Quoting

This article explains quoting in the C shell by comparing it to Bourne shell quoting. If you haven't read article 9.10 about Bourne shell quoting, please do.

As in the Bourne shell, the overall idea of C shell quoting is: *quoting turns off (disables) the special meaning of characters.* There are three quoting characters: a single quote (`'`), a double quote (`"`), and a backslash (`\`).

Special Characters

The C shell has several more special characters than the Bourne shell:

```
! { } ~
```

How Quoting Works

Table 9-2 summarizes the rules; you might want to look back at it while you read the examples.

Table 9-2. C Shell Quoting Characters

Quoting Character	Explanation
'xxx'	Disable all special characters in *xxx* except !.
"xxx"	Disable all special characters in *xxx* except $, `, and !.
x	Disable special meaning of character *x*. At end of line, a \ treats the newline character like a space (continues line).

The major differences between C and Bourne shell quoting are:

- The exclamation point (!) character can only be quoted with a backslash. That's true inside and outside single or double quotes. So, you can use history substitution *(12.07)* inside quotes. For example:

  ```
  % grep intelligent engineering file*.txt
  grep: engineering: No such file or directory
  % grep '!:1-2' !:3
  grep 'intelligent engineering' file*.txt
  ...
  ```

- In the Bourne shell, inside double quotes, a backslash (\) stops variable and command substitution (it turns off the special meaning of $ and `).

  In the C shell, you can't disable the special meaning of $ or ` inside double quotes. You'll need a mixture of single and double quotes. For example, searching for the string *use the '–c' switch* takes some work:

  ```
  % fgrep "use the \`-c' switch" *.txt
  Unmatched `.
  % fgrep 'use the \`-c\' switch' *.txt
  Unmatched '.
  % fgrep "use the "'`-c'"' switch" *.txt
  hints.txt:Be sure to use the `-c' switch.
  ```

- In the Bourne shell, single and double quotes include newline characters. Once you open a single or double quote, you can type multiple lines before the closing quote.

  In the C shell, if the quotes on a command line don't match, the shell will print an error. To quote more than one line, type a backslash at the end of each line. Inside single or double quotes, the backslash-newline becomes a newline. Unquoted, backslash-newline is an argument separator:

```
% echo "one\
two" three\
four
one
two three four
```

—JP

9.12   Quoting Handles Special Characters in Filenames

If you want to work with files that have spaces or special characters in the filenames, you may have to use quotes. For instance, if you wanted to create a file that has a space in the name, you could use the following:

```
% cp /dev/null 'a file with spaces in the name'
```

Normally, the shell uses spaces to determine the end of each argument. Quoting *(9.10, 9.11)* changes that—for example, the above example only has two arguments. You can also use a backslash (\) before a special character. The example below will rename a file with a space in the name, changing the space to an underscore (_):

```
% mv a\ file a_file
```

Using the same techniques, you can deal with any character in a filename:

```
% mv '$a' a
```

At worst, a space in a filename makes the filename difficult to use as an argument. Other characters are dangerous to use in a filename. In particular, using ? and * in a filename is playing with fire. If you want to delete the file *a?*, you may end up deleting more than the single file.

—BB

9.13   *verbose and echo Variables Show Quoting*

The C shell has two variables *(7.09)* that, when set, will help you follow the convoluted trail of variable and meta-character expansion. This will echo every command line before shell variables have been evaluated:

set 7.08

```
% set verbose
```

This command will display each line after the variables and meta-characters have been substituted:

```
% set echo
```

If you wish to turn the variables off, use *unset (7.08)* instead of *set*.

The Bourne shell syntax is different. To turn on the verbose flag, use:

```
$ set -v
```

The command `set -x` turns on the echo flag. You can also type them together: `set -xv`.

If your version of UNIX understands *(46.04)* scripts that start with `#!`, here's a convenient way to turn these variables on from the first line of a script:

```
#!/bin/sh -xv
```

It is not necessary to modify the program. You can enable variable tracing in Bourne shell scripts by typing the shell name and options on the command line:

```
$ sh -v script
$ sh -x script
```

Not all Bourne shells let you turn these variables off. If yours does, you can do it by using a plus sign instead of a minus sign:

```
set +xv
```

—*BB*

9.14 *Here Documents*

So far, we've talked about three different kinds of quoting: backslashes (\), single quotes ('), and double quotes ("). The shells support yet one more kind of quoting, called *here documents*. A here document is useful when you need to read something from standard input, but you don't want to create a file to provide that input; you want to put that input right into your shell script (or type it directly on the command line). To do so, use the `<<` operator, followed by a special word:

```
sort >file <<EndOfSort
zygote
abacus
EndOfSort
```

This is very useful because variables *(7.08, 7.01)* are evaluated during this operation. Here is a way to transfer a file using anonymous *ftp (1.33)* from a shell script:

ftpfile

```
#!/bin/sh
# Usage:
#      ftpfile machine file
# set -x
SOURCE=$1
FILE=$2
BFILE=`basename $FILE`
ftp -n $SOURCE <<EndFTP
ascii
user anonymous $USER@`hostname`
get $FILE /tmp/$BFILE
EndFTP
```

As you can see, variables and command substitutions *(10.14)* are done. If you want the quoted text to be left alone, put a backslash in front of the name of the word:

```
cat >file <<\FunkyStriNG
```

Notice the funky string. This is done because it is very unlikely that I will want to put that particular combination of characters in any file. You should be warned that the C shell expects the matching word (at the end of the list) to be escaped the same way, i.e., \FunkyStriNG, while the Bourne shell does not. See article 47.26.

When to Quote?

As you can see, this quoting business can cause a lot of confusion. At this point, you should know how to get the shell to recognize the exact string you want. When we cover regular expressions *(27.04)*, you will be able to follow the quotes without losing your mind.

—BB

9.15 "Special" Characters and Operators

Before you learn about regular expressions *(27.01)*, you should understand how quoting *(9.10)* works in UNIX.

Regular expressions use meta-characters. The shells also have meta-characters. Meta-characters are simply characters that have a special meaning. The problem occurs when you want to use a regular expression in a shell script. Will the shell do something special with the character? Or will it be passed unchanged to the program? The $ character is a good example. It could be the beginning of a variable name, or it could be part of a regular expression *(27.02)*. If you need a regular expression, you must know if any of the characters of the expression are meta-characters, and must know the right way to quote that character, so that it is passed to the program without being modified by the shell.

Table 9-3 is a table of special characters and operators in the C shell (*csh*), Bourne shell (*sh*), and Korn shell (*ksh*). The chart also includes several combinations of characters just to be complete. There is a lot of detail here.

Table 9-3. List of Special Characters and Their Meanings

Character	Where	Meaning	Article
RETURN	*csh, sh, ksh*	Execute command.	43.02
space	*csh, sh, ksh*	Argument separator.	9.03
TAB	*csh, sh, ksh*	Argument separator.	9.03
#	*csh, sh, ksh,* shell scripts	Start a comment.	46.02
`	*csh, sh, ksh*	Command substitution (backquotes).	10.14
"	*sh, ksh*	Weak quotes.	9.10
"	*csh*	Weak quotes.	9.11, 9.10
'	*sh, ksh*	Strong quotes.	9.10
'	*csh*	Strong quotes.	9.11, 9.10

Table 9-3. List of Special Characters and Their Meanings (continued)

Character	Where	Meaning	Article
\	*sh, ksh*	Single-character quote.	9.10
\	*csh*	Single-character quote.	9.11, 9.10
$var	*csh, sh, ksh*	Variable.	7.01, 7.08
${var}	*csh, sh, ksh*	Same as $var.	7.08
${var-default}	*sh, ksh*	If *var* not set, use *default*.	47.12
${var=default}	*sh, ksh*	If *var* not set, set it to *default* and use that value.	47.12
${var+instead}	*sh, ksh*	If *var* set, use *instead*. Otherwise, null string.	47.12
${var?message}	*sh, ksh*	If *var* not set, print *message* (else default). If *var* set, use its value.	47.12
${var#pat}	*ksh*	Value of *var* with smallest *pat* deleted from start.	
${var##pat}	*ksh*	Value of *var* with largest *pat* deleted from start.	
${var%pat}	*ksh*	Value of *var* with smallest *pat* deleted from end.	
${var%%pat}	*ksh*	Value of *var* with largest *pat* deleted from end.	
|	*csh, sh, ksh*	Pipe standard output.	1.04, 14.01
|&	*csh*	Pipe standard output and standard error.	14.05
^	*sh*	Pipe character (obsolete).	
^	*csh*	Edit previous command line.	12.05
&	*csh, sh, ksh*	Run program in background.	1.27, 1.28
?	*csh, sh, ksh*	Match one character.	1.16, 16.02
*	*csh, sh, ksh*	Match zero or more characters.	1.16, 16.02
;	*csh, sh, ksh*	Command separator.	9.03
;;	*sh, ksh*	End of *case* statement.	46.05
~	*csh, ksh*	Home directory.	15.12
~user	*csh, ksh*	Home directory of *user*.	15.12
!	*csh*	Command history.	12.02
-	Programs	Start of optional argument.	9.03
$#	*csh, sh, ksh*	Number of arguments to script.	46.14
"$@"	*sh, ksh*	Original arguments to script.	46.14
$*	*csh, sh, ksh*	Arguments to script.	46.14
$-	*sh, ksh*	Flags passed to shell.	2.11
$?	*sh, ksh*	Status of previous command.	46.07
$$	*csh, sh, ksh*	Process identification number.	9.10
$!	*sh, ksh*	Process identification number of last background job.	8.12
$<	*csh*	Read input from terminal.	10.09
cmd1 && cmd2	*csh, sh, ksh*	Execute *cmd2* if *cmd1* succeeds.	46.09
cmd1 || cmd2	*csh, sh, ksh*	Execute *cmd2* if *cmd1* fails.	46.09

Table 9-3. List of Special Characters and Their Meanings (continued)

Character	Where	Meaning	Article
$(..$)	*ksh*	Command substitution.	
((..))	*ksh*	Arithmetic evaluation.	
. *file*	*sh, ksh*	Execute commands from *file* in this shell.	46.22
:	*sh, ksh*	Evaluate arguments, return true.	47.09
:	*sh, ksh*	Separate values in paths.	7.04, 15.05, 22.08
:	*csh*	Variable modifier.	12.08
[ ]	*csh, sh, ksh*	Match range of characters.	1.16, 16.02
[ ]	*sh, ksh*	Test.	46.19
%*job*	*csh*	Identify job number.	13.01
(*cmd; cmd*)	*csh, sh, ksh*	Run *cmd; cmd* in a subshell.	14.07
{ }	*csh*	In-line expansions.	10.05
{*cmd; cmd;* }	*sh, ksh*	Like (*cmd; cmd*) without a subshell.	14.08
>*file*	*csh, sh, ksh*	Redirect standard output.	14.01
>>*file*	*csh, sh, ksh*	Append standard output.	14.01
<*file*	*csh, sh, ksh*	Redirect standard input.	14.01
<<*word*	*csh, sh, ksh*	Read until *word*, do command and variable substitution.	9.14, 10.12
<<*word*	*csh, sh, ksh*	Read until *word*, no substitution.	9.14
<<-*word*	*sh, ksh*	Read until *word*, ignoring tabs.	9.14
>>! *file*	*csh*	Append to *file*, even if *noclobber* set and *file* doesn't exist.	14.06
>! *file*	*csh*	Output to *file*, even if *noclobber* set and *file* exists.	14.06
>& *file*	*csh*	Redirect standard output and standard error to *file*.	14.05
m> *file*	*sh, ksh*	Redirect output file descriptor *m* to *file*.	47.21
m>> *file*	*sh, ksh*	Append output file descriptor *m* to *file*.	
<*m file*	*sh, ksh*	Redirect input file descriptor *m* from *file*.	
<&*m*	*sh, ksh*	Take standard input from file descriptor *m*.	
<&-	*sh, ksh*	Close standard input.	47.10
>&*m*	*sh, ksh*	Use file descriptor *m* as standard output.	47.21
>&-	*sh, ksh*	Close standard output.	47.21

9.16

Table 9-3. List of Special Characters and Their Meanings (continued)

Character	Where	Meaning	Article
$(..$)	*ksh*	Command substitution.	
m<&*n*	*sh, ksh*	Connect input file descriptor *n* to file descriptor *m*.	47.21
m<&-	*sh, ksh*	Close file descriptor *m*.	47.21
n>&*m*	*sh, ksh*	Connect output file descriptor *n* to file descriptor *m*.	47.21
m>&-	*sh, ksh*	Close file descriptor *m*.	47.21

—BB, JP

9.16 How Many Backslashes?

The problem with backslashes is that many different programs use them as quoting characters. As a result, it's difficult to figure out how many backslashes you need in any situation.

Here's an example, taken from System V Release 4. (Notice that I'm using the standard System V version of *echo* from */bin/echo*. SVR4 has four versions of *echo*!)

```
% /bin/echo hi \\ there
hi \ there
% /bin/echo hi \\\\ there
hi \ there
% /bin/echo hi \\\\\\\\ there
hi \\ there
```

In the first case, the shell converts \\ to \ (as it is supposed to). The *echo* command then echoes the string. (I've heard claims that, on some systems, this command wouldn't print any backslashes, but I wasn't able to reconstruct that situation.)

In the second case, the shell converts each pair of backslashes into a backslash, and runs the command echo hi \\ there. But this is System V, and System V's *echo* interprets backslashes *(9.04)* as special characters. So when *echo* sees the remaining two backslashes, it converts them into a single backslash. So you only see a single backslash, even though you typed four. On BSD systems, *echo* doesn't do this; you'd see two backslashes. For that matter, if you're using SVR4's C shell, with its built-in *echo* command, you'll see the BSD behavior. You'll also see the BSD behavior if you're using SVR4's */usr/ucb/echo*.

The terminal driver *(44.01)* is also capable of "eating" backslashes if they appear before special characters. If a backslash precedes the "erase" character (normally CTRL-h) or the "kill" character (normally CTRL-u), the terminal driver will pass the control character to the shell, rather than interpreting it as an editing character. In the process, it "eats" the backslash. So if you type:

```
% echo \ CTRL-u
```

The shell receives the line echo CTRL-u. See the *termio* manual page for more information; there are certainly system-dependent variations.

What's the point of this article? Well, backslashes are messy. The shell, the terminal driver, *echo* (sometimes), and several other utilities use them. If you think very carefully, you can figure out exactly what's consuming them. If you're not of a rigorous frame of mind, you can just add backslashes until you get what you want. (But, obviously, the non-rigorous approach has pitfalls.) I've seen situations in *troff* (45.14) (which is another story altogether) where you need eight backslashes in order to have a single backslash left at the point where you want it!

—ML

10

Saving Time on the Command Line

10.01 What's Special about the UNIX Command Line

One of UNIX's best features is the shell's command line. Why? Every modern operating system has a command line; we don't use card readers with obscure job setup cards any more. What makes UNIX's special?

The UNIX shell command line allows lots of shortcuts. Some of these you'll find in other operating systems; some you won't. In this chapter, we'll introduce a lot of these shortcuts. Among other things, we'll discuss:

- Faster erasing *(10.02)* of mistakes with the line-kill and word-erase characters. (These aren't just a feature of the shell; they work at many places other than a shell prompt.)

- Filename completion *(10.06, 10.07, 10.08)*, which allows you to type the beginning of a filename and let the shell fill in the rest.

- Command substitution *(10.14)*, which lets you use the output from one command as arguments to another. (Note: this is *different* from pipelining *(1.04)*.)

- Type-ahead *(10.17)*, the ability to type your next command (or commands) while the previous command is still running.

- How to handle command lines that become too long *(10.18, 10.19, 10.21)*.

Some fundamental command-line features that we aren't discussing in this chapter, but which are discussed elsewhere, are:

- Job control *(13.01)*, which lets you run several commands at the same time.

- Aliases *(11.02)*, or abbreviations, for commands.

- History substitution *(12.01)*, the ability to "recall" previous commands.

- Quoting *(9.10, 9.11)*, the way you "protect" special characters from the UNIX shell.

- Wildcards *(16.02)*.

You don't need to be a command-line virtuoso to use UNIX effectively. But you'd be surprised at how much you can do with a few tricks. If all you can do at the command line is type ls or start FrameMaker, you're missing out on a lot.

—ML

10.02 Fix a Line Faster with Line-kill and Word-erase

It's amazing how often you'll see even moderately experienced UNIX users holding down the BACKSPACE or DELETE key to delete a partially completed command line that contains an error.

It's usually easier to use the line-kill character—typically CTRL-u or CTRL-x. (The command *stty –a* or *stty everything (43.03)* will tell you which. Article 6.09 shows how to change them.) The line-kill character will work on a command line (at a shell prompt *(8.01)*) and in other places where the terminal is in cooked mode *(43.02)*. Some UNIX programs that don't run in cooked mode, like *vi*, understand the line-kill character, too.

Even better, many systems have a "word-erase" character, usually CTRL-w, which deletes only back to the previous white space. There's no need to delete the entire command line if you want to change only part of it!

—JP, TOR

10.03 Reprinting Your Command Line with CTRL-r

You're logged in from home, running a program, and answering a prompt. As you're almost done, modem noise prints xDxD@! on your screen. Where were you? Or you're typing a long command line and a friend interrupts you with *write (1.33)* to say it's time for lunch. Do you have to press CTRL-u *(10.02)* and start typing over?

If your system understands the *rprnt* character (usually set to CTRL-r), you can ask for the command line to be reprinted as it was. In fact, you can use CTRL-r any time you want to know what the system thinks you've typed on the current line—not just when you're interrupted. But this only works in the normal *cooked (43.02)* input mode; programs like *vi* that do their own input processing may treat CTRL-r differently. Here's an example:

```
% egrep '(10394|29433|49401)' /work/symtower/
```

```
Message from alison@ruby on ttyp2 at 12:02 ...
how about lunch?
EOF
```
CTRL-r
```
egrep '(10394|29433|49401)' /work/symtower/logs/*
```

After the interruption, I just pressed CTRL-r. It reprinted the stuff I'd started typing. I finished typing and pressed RETURN to run it.

If you use a shell like the Korn shell that has interactive command editing, you can probably use it to reprint the command line, too.

—JP

10.04 *Use Wildcards to Create Files?*

The shells' [ ] (square bracket) wildcards will match a range of files. For instance, if you have files named *afile*, *bfile*, *cfile*, and *dfile*, you can print the first three by typing:

```
% lpr [a-c]file
```

Now, let's say that you want to create some more files called *efile*, *ffile*, *gfile*, and *hfile*. What's wrong with typing the command line below? Try it. Instead of *vi*, you can use your favorite editor or the *touch (22.07)* command:

```
% vi [e-h]file              Doesn't make those four files
% ls
afile    bfile    cfile    dfile
```

Stumped? Take a look at article 1.16 about wildcard matching.

The answer: wildcards can't match names that don't exist yet. That's especially true with a command like touch ?file *(22.07)* or touch *file—think how many filenames those wildcards could possibly create!

Article 10.05 explains C shell { } operators that solve this problem.

—JP

10.05 The Useful csh { } Characters

I've been finding more and more uses for C shell's { } pattern-expansion characters. They're similar to *, ?, and [ ] (16.02), but they don't match filenames exactly the way that *, ?, and [ ] do. So you can give them arbitrary things (not just filenames) to expand—that "expand-anything" ability is what makes them so useful. (Other shells can use { }, too; see article 16.03.)

Here are some ways to use them; they should get you thinking . . .

- To fix a typo in a filename (change *fixbold61.c* to *fixbold6.c*):

  ```
  % mv fixbold{61,6}.c
  ```

  An easy way to see what the shell does with { } is by adding *echo* before the *mv*:

  ```
  % echo mv fixbold{61,6}.c
  mv fixbold61.c fixbold6.c
  ```

- To copy *filename* to *filename.bak* in one easy step:

  ```
  % cp filename{,.bak}
  ```

- To print files from other directory(s) without retyping the whole pathname:

  ```
  % lpr /usr3/hannah/training/{ed,vi,mail}/lab.{ms,out}
  ```

  That would give *lpr*(45.02) all of these files:

  ```
  /usr3/hannah/training/ed/lab.ms
  /usr3/hannah/training/ed/lab.out
  /usr3/hannah/training/vi/lab.ms
  /usr3/hannah/training/vi/lab.out
  /usr3/hannah/training/mail/lab.ms
  /usr3/hannah/training/mail/lab.out
  ```

  . . . in one fell swoop!

- To edit ten new files that don't exist yet:

  ```
  % vi /usr/foo/file{a,b,c,d,e,f,g,h,i,j}
  ```

  That would make */usr/foo/filea, /usr/foo/fileb, . . . /usr/foo/filej*. Because the files don't exist before the command starts, the wildcard vi /usr/foo/file[a-j] would *not* work (10.04).

- An easy way to step through three-digit numbers 000, 001, . . . , 009, 010, 011, . . . , 099, 100, 101, . . . 299 is:

  foreach **10.09**

  ```
  foreach n ({0,1,2}{0,1,2,3,4,5,6,7,8,9}{0,1,2,3,4,5,6,7,8,9})
      ...Do whatever with the number $n...
  end
  ```

  Yes, *csh* also has built-in arithmetic, but that @ operator (49.04) can't make numbers with leading zeros. This nice trick shows that the { } operators are good for more than just filenames.

- To create sets of subdirectories:

```
% mkdir man
% mkdir man/{man,cat}{1,2,3,4,5,6,7,8}
% ls -F man
cat1/    cat3/    cat5/    cat7/    man1/    man3/    man5/    man7/
cat2/    cat4/    cat6/    cat8/    man2/    man4/    man6/    man8/
```

- To print ten copies of the file *project_report* (if your *lpr (45.02)* command doesn't have a *–#10* option):

```
% lpr project_repor{t,t,t,t,t,t,t,t,t,t}
```

—*JP*

10.06 *Filename Completion: Faster Filename Typing*

If you hate typing long filenames, you should know about the C shell's "filename completion" feature. If you set the variable *filec (7.09)* [in some C shells, the variable is named *complete* —*JP*], you can type the initial part of a filename, and then press the ESC key. If the shell can figure out the complete filename from the part that you've typed, it will fill in the rest of the name. If not, it will fill in as much of the name as is unambiguous, and then let you type some more. For example:

```
% ls
file1.c    file1.o    file2.c
% cc file2 ESC
% cc file2.c                      Shell fills in the filename automatically
```

Your terminal will beep if more than one file matches the name you've typed. (If all this beeping drives you crazy, you can set the *nobeep* shell variable; that will turn it off.) In this case, only one filename begins with *file2*, so the shell can fill in the entire name.

If you type part of a filename and then type CTRL-d, the shell lists all the files that match whatever you've typed. It then redisplays your command line and lets you continue typing. For example:

```
% cc file CTRL-d
file1.c    file1.o    file2.c
% cc file
```

Three files begin with the letters "file"; the shell lists them. It then redisplays the *cc* command, letting you finish the filename.

Note: Many C shells don't support filename completion; it's available primarily on systems that are based on BSD 4.3 UNIX.

Also, be forewarned that filename completion is a hack and doesn't always work correctly. For example: if you're using SunOS, you can't use filename completion within a "command tool" (SunOS 4.1). Don't try to mix filename completion with wildcards; it won't work. We can't go into detail about these rough edges, but if you're aware that they exist, you won't have trouble.

Article 15.10 shows an interesting shortcut to filename completion: *cd*ing to a directory by typing its "initials."

—ML

10.07 Don't Match Useless Files in Filename Completion

The shell variable *fignore* lets you tell the shell that you aren't interested in some files when using C shell filename completion *(10.06)*. For example, you are more likely to refer to C language source files (whose names end with *.c*) than object files (*.o* files); you often need to edit your source files, while you may never need to look at your object modules. Set *fignore* to the suffixes that you want to ignore. For example, to ignore *.o* files, type:

set *7.08*
( ) *49.05*

```
% set fignore=(.o)
```

Once you've done this, file completion will ignore your *.o* files when you press the ESC key—unless a *.o* file is the only match it can find.

Most likely, there's a whole list of suffixes that you don't care about: *.o* (object modules), *.out* (random executables), *.Z* (compressed files), and so on. Article 1.17 has a list of them. Here's how to set *fignore* to a list of filenames:

```
% set fignore=(.o .out .Z)
```

Spaces are used to separate items in the list; and the whole list must be enclosed within parentheses.

fignore has no effect when you press CTRL-d to get a listing of the files that match. The shell always gives you a complete list of all possible completions.

—ML

10.08 Filename Completion Isn't Always the Answer

There are a number of times when filename completion *(10.06, 12.14)* isn't appropriate. If you like Sun's "command tool" (*cmdtool*), you can't use filename completion (though you can use it within a Sun *shelltool*—which is one good reason for preferring *shelltool*, even though it's not as fancy). You can't use filename completion within an Emacs shell window *(33.02)*. And, of course, there are plenty of UNIX systems for which filename completion just doesn't work, including SVR3 and BSD 4.2.

When you don't use filename completion, the shell waits to read your command line until you press RETURN. With filename completion, your terminal mode *(43.02)* is changed so the shell can interpret every character as you type it. Bugs, line noise on a modem or network, and other problems can get the shell "out of sync" with what's on your screen.

Easy as it is to get addicted to filename completion, there are times when it isn't appropriate:

- If you want to list many files on the command line, it may be easier to use a carefully constructed wildcard *(1.16)* expression.

- As we mentioned earlier, filename completion and wildcards don't mix. If you need to use a wildcard, you can't use filename completion.

- Filename completion is obviously less worthwhile if you have to type most of the filename before you can use it. For example, if you have a lot of files with similar names, filename completion won't help an awful lot. (This may say something about the way you name files—the remedy might be to think up some more distinctive names.)

—*ML*

10.09 *Repeating a Command with a foreach Loop*

When some people need to repeat a command on several files, the first thing they think of is C shell history *(12.05)*:

```
% cat -t -v /usr/fran/report | pg
    ...
% ^fran/report^rob/file3
cat -t -v /usr/rob/file3 | pg
    ...
% ^3^21
cat -t -v /usr/rob/file21 | pg
    ...
%
```

–v 26.07

That kind of thing can be easier with the C shell's *foreach* loop. (In the Bourne and Korn shells, use a *for(10.10)* loop.) You give the loop a list of the words that will change each time the command line is run. In this example, it's a list of filenames. The loop will step through the words, one by one, storing a word into a shell variable *(7.08)*, then running the command(s). The loop goes on until it has read all the words. For example:

```
% foreach file (/usr/fran/report /usr/rob/file3 /usr/rob/file21)
? cat -t -v $file | pg
? end
        ...Shell runs cat –t –v /usr/fran/report | pg...
        ...Shell runs cat –t –v /usr/rob/file3 | pg...
        ...Shell runs cat –t –v /usr/rob/file21 | pg...
%
```

The question marks (?) are secondary prompts *(10.11)*; the C shell will keep printing them until you type the command *end*. Then the loop runs.

The list between the parentheses doesn't have to be filenames. Among other things, you can use wildcards *(1.16)*, backquotes *(10.14)* (command substitution), variables *(7.08, 7.01)* and the C shell's handy curly brace ({ }) operators *(10.05)* For example, you could have typed the above loop this way:

```
% foreach file (/usr/fran/report /usr/rob/file{3,21})
? cat -t -v $file | pg
? end
```

If you want the loop to stop before or after running each command, add the C shell operator $<. It reads keyboard input and waits for a RETURN. In this case, you can probably ignore the input; you'll use $< to make the loop wait. For example, to make the loop above prompt before each command line:

set *7.08*

```
% foreach file (/usr/fran/report /usr/rob/file{3,21})
? echo -n "Press RETURN to see $file--"
? set x="$<"
? cat -t -v $file | pg
? end
Press RETURN to see /usr/fran/report--[RETURN]
      Shell runs cat –t –v /usr/fran/report | pg...
Press RETURN to see /usr/rob/file3--[RETURN]
      Shell runs cat –t –v /usr/rob/file3 | pg...
Press RETURN to see /usr/rob/file21--[RETURN]
      Shell runs cat –t –v /usr/rob/file21 | pg...
```

The loop parameters don't need to be filenames. For instance, you could send a personalized mail *(1.33)* message to five people this way:*

cat – *14.13*

```
% foreach person (John Cathy Agnes Brett Elma)
? echo "Dear $person," | cat - formletter | mail $person
? end
```

The first line of the first letter will be "Dear John,"; the second letter "Dear Cathy,"; and so on.

Want to take this idea farther? It's a part of shell programming *(46.01)* I usually don't recommend *(49.02)* shell programming with the C shell, but this is a handy technique to use interactively.

—JP

---

*If you're sending lots of mail messages with a loop, your system mailer may get overloaded. In that case, it's a good idea to put a command like sleep 5 *(42.02)* on a separate line before the end. That will give the mailer five seconds to send each message.

10.10 The Bourne Shell for Loop

The Bourne shell *for* loop is like the C shell *foreach* loop *(10.09)*; it loops through a list of words, running one or more commands for each word in the list. This saves time when you want to run the same series of commands, separately, on several files.

Let's use the example from the article about *foreach*:

```
$ for file in /usr/fran/report /usr/rob/file2 /usr/rob/file3
> do
> cat -t -v $file | pg
> done
      ...Shell runs cat –t –v /usr/fran/report | pg...
      ...Shell runs cat –t –v /usr/rob/file2 | pg...
      ...Shell runs cat –t –v /usr/rob/file3 | pg...
$
```

The right angle brackets (>) are secondary prompts *(10.11)*; the Bourne shell will keep printing them until you type the command *done*. Then it runs the loop. You don't have to press RETURN after the do; you can type the first command on the same line after it.

In a shell script, the loop body (the lines between do and done) are usually indented for clarity.

The list after the in doesn't have to be filenames. Among other things, you can use backquotes *(10.14)* (command substitution), variables *(7.08, 7.01)*, or wildcards *(16.01)*. For example, you could have typed the above loop this way:

```
$ for file in /usr/fran/report /usr/rob/file[23]
> do cat -t -v $file | pg
> done
```

If you want the loop to stop before or after running each command, add the Bourne shell *read* command *(46.13)*. It reads keyboard input and waits for a RETURN. In this case, you can probably ignore the input; you'll use *read* to make the loop wait. For example, to make the above loop prompt before each command line:

```
$ for file in /usr/fran/report /usr/rob/file[23]
> do
> echo -n "Press RETURN to see $file--"
> read x
> cat -t -v $file | pg
> done
```
Press RETURN to see /usr/fran/report-- RETURN
      Shell runs cat –t –v /usr/fran/report | pg...
Press RETURN to see /usr/rob/file2-- RETURN
      Shell runs cat –t –v /usr/rob/file2 | pg...
Press RETURN to see /usr/rob/file3-- RETURN
      Shell runs cat –t –v /usr/rob/file3 | pg...

Article 46.15 has more information about the *for* loop. Article 47.16 shows how to make a *for* loop read the standard input instead of a list of arguments.

—JP

10.11 Multi-line Commands, Secondary Prompts

Both the Bourne shell and the C shell support multi-line commands. In the Bourne shell, a newline following an open quote (' or ") , a pipe symbol (|), or a backslash (\) will not cause the command to be executed. Instead, you'll get a secondary prompt (from the *PS2* environment variable, set to > by default) and you can continue the command on the next line. For example, to send a quick *write(1.33)* message without making the other user wait for you to type the message:

```
$ echo "We're leaving in 10 minutes. See you downstairs." |
> write joanne
```

In the C shell, you can continue a line by typing a backslash (\) before the newline *(9.11)*. You won't get the secondary prompt.

Obviously, this is a convenience if you're typing a long command line. It is a minor feature and one easily overlooked; however, it makes it much easier to use a program like *sed (35.24)* from the command line. For example, if you know you chronically make the typos "mvoe" (for "move") and "thier" (for "their"), you might be inspired to type the following command:

```
$ sed '
> s/mvoe/move/g
> s/thier/their/g' myfile | nroff -ms | lp
```

nroff *45.14*
lp *45.02*

More importantly, the ability to issue multi-line commands lets you use the shell's programming features interactively from the command line. In both the Bourne and the C shell, multi-line programming constructs automatically generate a secondary prompt (> in the Bourne shell, ? in the C shell) until the construct is completed.

For example, here's a place to use my favorite programming construct for non-programmers, the *for* loop *(10.10)*:

```
$ for x in file1 file2 file3
> do
> sed 's/thier/their/g' $x > ,$x
> mv ,$x $x
> done
$
```

Or in the C shell with *foreach (10.09)*:

```
% foreach x (file1 file2 file3)
? sed 's/thier/their/g' $x > ,$x
? mv ,$x $x
? end
%
```

While a simple command like this could be saved into a shell script *(1.05)*, it is often even easier to use it interactively.

Users of *sed* should of course make sure their script works correctly before overwriting their original file *(35.03)*.

—TOR

10.12 Using Here Documents for Form Letters, etc.

The here document operator << *(9.14)* is used in shell scripts. It tells the shell to take lines from the script as standard input to a command. The example below shows a loop *(47.17)* that prints three nasty form letters with the *lpr (45.02)* command. Each letter has a different person's name and the current date at the top. You can put this loop into a shell script *(46.02)* or just type it in at a Bourne shell prompt *(10.10, 10.11)*:

```
for person in "Mary Smith" "Doug Jones" "Alison Eddy"
do
        lpr << ENDMSG

        `date`

        Dear $person,

        This is your last notice. Buy me pizza tonight or
        else I'll type "rm -r *" when you're not looking.

        This is not a joak.

        Signed,
        The midnight skulker
ENDMSG
done
```

(47.26)

This loop runs three *lpr* commands; each form letter prints on a separate page. The shell reads the standard input until it finds the terminator word, which in this case is ENDMSG. The word (ENDMSG) has to be on a line all by itself, starting in the first column. (Some Bourne shells ignore indentation if you use <<– instead of <<.) The backquotes *(10.14)* run the *date (53.10)* command and output its date; $person is replaced with the person's name set at the top of the loop. The rest of the text is copied as is to the standard input of the *lpr* command.

—JP

10.13 Throwaway Scripts for Complicated Commands

[If your shell has interactive command-line editing, like the Korn shell (12.14) does, the technique here can still be useful. As Mike says, you might want to save the script and use it later. —JP]

Shell scripts are often handy, even if you never intend to write software. One problem that most users face is typing a complicated command correctly. For example, let's say you need to type the following monstrosity:

```
% soelim a.ms b.ms | pic | eqn | tbl | troff -ms -a | more
```

(This isn't unrealistic; I've typed this particular command a few times.) Rather than spend all that time typing, then backspacing to fix some error, then typing some more, then backspacing again, you can create a very simple "throwaway" shell script with your favorite editor:

```
# shell script "foo" for one-time use
soelim a.ms b.ms | pic | eqn | tbl | troff -ms -a -rz1 | more
```

Use your editor to play with the script until the command looks right—any half-competent text editor will be much easier to work with than the "raw" command line. Then execute it like this:

```
% sh foo
```

If you don't think you'll need this command again, you can delete the file—or use a temporary file *(22.03)* in the first place. But before you use *rm*, think: most things that you do once, you'll need to do again. Give it an intelligent name, and save it in your *bin* directory *(5.02)*. You're now a shell programmer.

This is also a great idea for complex sequences of commands.

—ML

10.14 Command Substitution

A pair of backquotes (` `` `) does *command substitution*. This is really useful—it lets you use the standard output from one command as arguments to another command.

Here's an example. Assume you want to edit all files in the current directory that contain the word "error." Type this:

```
$ vi `grep -l error *.c`
3 files to edit
"bar.c" 254 lines, 28338 characters
    ...
$
```

–| 16.08

But why does this work? How did we build the incantation above? First, think about how you'd do this without using any special techniques. You'd use *grep* to find out which commands contain the word "error"; then you'd use *vi* to edit this list:

```
$ grep error *.c
bar.c:   error("input too long");
bar.c:   error("input too long");
baz.c:   error("data formatted incorrectly");
foo.c:   error("can't divide by zero"):
foo.c:   error("insufficient memory"):
$ vi bar.c baz.c foo.c
```

Is there any way to compress these into one command? Yes, by using command substitution. First, we need to modify our *grep* command so that it only produces a list of filenames, rather than filenames and text. That's easy; use *grep −l*:

```
$ grep -l error *.c
bar.c
baz.c
foo.c
```

The −*l* option lists each filename only once, even if many lines in the file match. (This makes me think that *grep −l* was designed with precisely this application in mind.) Now, we want to edit these files; so we put the *grep* command inside backquotes, and use it as the argument to *vi*:

```
$ vi `grep -l error *.c`
3 files to edit
"bar.c" 254 lines, 28338 characters
    ...
$
```

You might be wondering about the difference between the "vertical" output from *grep*, and the "horizontal" way that people usually type arguments on a command line. The shell handles this with no problems. Inside backquotes, both a newline and a space are argument separators.

The list you use with command substitution doesn't have to be filenames. Let's see how to send a mail message *(1.33)* to all the users logged on to the system now. You want a command line like this:

```
% mail joe lisa franka mondo bozo harpo ...
```

Getting there takes a little thinking about what UNIX commands you need to run to get the output you want. (This is real "Power Tools" stuff!) To get a list of those users, you could use *who (53.04)*. The *who* output also lists login time and other information—but you can cut that off with a command like *cut (36.12)*:

```
% who | cut -c1-8
joe
lisa
franka
lisa
joe
mondo
joe
...
```

Some users are logged on more than once. To get a unique list, use *sort* −*u* *(37.06)*. You're done. Just put the name-making command line between backquotes:

```
% mail `who | cut -c1-8 | sort -u`
```

If you aren't sure how this works, replace the command you want to run with *echo* *(9.04)*:

```
% echo `who | cut -c1-8 | sort -u`
bozo franka harpo joe lisa mondo
```

After using UNIX for awhile, you'll find that this is one of its most useful features. You'll find many situations where you use one command to generate a list of words, then put that command in backquotes and use it as an argument to something else. There are some problems *(10.18)* with command substitution but you usually won't run into them.

This book has many, many examples of command substitution. Here are some of them: making unique filenames *(17.17)*, removing some files from a list *(24.20)*, counting words *(30.06)*, getting a list of files *(16.10)*, setting your shell prompt *(8.04, 8.06, 8.11)*, setting variables *(6.04, 47.30)*, making a wildcard *(16.06)*, and running a loop *(42.02)*.

—*JP*

10.15 *Handling Lots of Text with Temporary Files*

Sometimes, you need to execute a command with a long list of files for arguments. Here's an easy way to create that list without having to type each filename yourself—put the list in a temporary file *(22.03)*:

```
% ls > /tmp/mikel
% vi /tmp/mikel
   ...edit out any files you don't want...
```
`\`.. 10.14`
```
% process-the-files `cat /tmp/mikel`
% rm /tmp/mikel
```

I added the *vi* step to remind you that you can edit this list; for example, you may want to delete a few files that you don't want to process.

Possible problems: if the list is long enough, you may end up with a command line that's too long for your shell to process. If this happens, use *xargs* *(10.19)*. If your system doesn't have *xargs*, there are other workarounds *(10.21)* that should solve the problem. Article 10.22 shows another way to use temporary files for commands.

—*ML*

10.16   Backquotes Plus: Automatic Temporary Files with !

Do you find yourself making temporary files, then giving those files to some commands to read? For example, maybe you want to compare two files with *comm (29.11)*—but *comm* needs sorted files, and these files aren't sorted. So you have to type:

```
% sort file1 > /tmp/file1.sort
% sort file2 > /tmp/file2.sort
% comm /tmp/file1.sort /tmp/file2.sort
```

Here's a neater way to do it: a shell script named *!* (an exclamation point)* that runs a command, stores its output in a temporary file, then puts the temporary filename on its standard output. You use it with backquotes *(10.14)* (` `). Here's an example that shows two unsorted files and the result:

```
% cat file1
rcsdiff.log
runsed
runsed.new
echo.where
foo
% cat file2
newprogram
runsed
echo.where
foo
% comm `! sort file1` `! sort file2`
                echo.where
                foo
        newprogram
rcsdiff.log
                runsed
runsed.new
```

(In the first column, *comm* shows lines only in *file1*. The second column shows lines only in *file2*. The third column shows lines that were in both files.)

Why didn't I use the command line below, without the *!* script?

```
% comm `sort file1` `sort file2`
```

That's because the *comm* program (like most UNIX programs) needs filename arguments. Using backquotes by themselves would place the list of names (the sorted contents of the files *file1* and *file2*) on the *comm* command line.

Let's take a closer look at how that works. By using a Bourne shell and setting its −*x* option *(9.13)*, the shell will display the commands it runs with a + before each one:

```
$ set -x
$ comm `! sort file1` `! sort file2`
+ ! sort file1
```

---

*The C shell also uses an exclamation point as its history character *(12.01, 12.17)*, but not if there's a space after the exclamation point. This script doesn't conflict with *csh* history.

```
+ ! sort file2
+ comm /tmp/bang3969 /tmp/bang3971
                   echo.where
                   foo
           newprogram
rcsdiff.log
                   runsed
runsed.new
```

The script made its temporary files *(22.03)* in */tmp*. You should probably remove them. If you're the only one using this script, you might be able to get away with a command like:

```
% rm /tmp/bang[1-9]*
```

If your system has more than one user, it's safer to use *find (18.01)*:

```
% find /tmp -name 'bang*' -user myname -exec rm {} \;
```

If you use this script much, you might make that cleanup command into an alias *(11.02)* or a shell script—or start it in the background *(1.26)* from your *.logout* file *(3.01, 3.02)*.

Here's the *!* script. Of course, you can change the name to something besides *!* if you want.

```
#! /bin/sh

temp=/tmp/bang$$

case $# in
0)   echo "Usage: `basename $0` command [args]" 1>&2
     echo $temp
     exit 1
     ;;
*)   "$@" > $temp
     echo $temp
     ;;
esac
```

"$@" 46.14

—*JP*

10.17 For the Impatient: Type-ahead

The UNIX shells have a feature called *type–ahead* that allows you to continue typing while the computer is thinking about something. This is convenient if you have a sequence of commands that need to run in order, and you don't like waiting for the last command to finish before typing the next one.

Basically, type-ahead just means that the shell lets you keep typing, even when it's apparently "busy" (i.e., even when you don't have a prompt). You can even continue typing while the current command (in the foreground *(1.26)*) is spraying data to the screen—although you may find that confusing. Any further commands you type will be executed as soon as the foreground command finishes.

The easiest way to demonstrate type-ahead is with the *sleep (42.02)* command, which just waits:

```
% sleep 25
lpr article
% %
```

This *sleep* command does nothing for 25 seconds. Therefore, you don't see a prompt after pressing RETURN at the end of the `sleep` command line. However, you can type the next command (*lpr*), which will be executed as soon as the *sleep* is finished. The terminal driver *(44.01)* reads the characters you type, sticks them in a buffer, and hands them to the shell whenever the shell is ready.

What happens if something goes wrong? You can press your interrupt key *(40.09)* (like CTRL-c) at any time to cancel the foreground job. In this case, UNIX will discard the type-ahead, rather than execute it. (The same goes for CTRL-z, or any other signal the foreground job receives from the terminal.*) This is *usually* what you want; that is, if you press CTRL-c to terminate the foreground job, you usually don't want to execute any jobs that you've queued up afterwards. Type-ahead isn't only good for giving additional commands. If your command takes a long time to start, you can type its input while you're waiting. Here's an example that's about as extreme as you're likely to see. It uses *ftp (1.33)*, a program for connecting to a remote host:

```
% ftp
open golgonooza
loukides
ftp> Connected to golgonooza.
220 golgonooza FTP server ready.
Name (golgonooza:mikel):  331 Password required for loukides.
Password:
```

I managed to enter my first *ftp* command and my login name (which I knew *ftp* would ask for) before *ftp* started. You probably can't use type-ahead for your password, though I've seen some odd systems on which this would work. Even if it works on your system, you shouldn't try it; *ftp* hasn't had time to turn keyboard echoing off, so your password will appear on your terminal, where anyone can read it.

Using type-ahead like this takes some guts; you have to know exactly what input your application will want, and when it will want it. But it's also fun in a perverse sense. You will find occasional applications (particularly applications that take over the screen) that don't allow type-ahead. However, there's no way to predict what will and what won't. I've seen some Emacs implementations that would let you start editing the file before the editor "came up" on the screen; I've seen others that wouldn't. [*vi* almost always lets you type commands as it starts. —*JP*]

---

*There are some situations—like executing commands within an Emacs "shell window"—where stopping the foreground command may not flush the type-ahead commands.

I have a really terrible way of using type-ahead—I don't recommend it, but it shows what you can do. Rather than use a news reader *(1.33)*, I often *cd* to a news directory and use *grep (28.01)* to search for interesting articles. While I watch pages of *grep* output scroll by, I start typing a *more (26.03)* command, using the article numbers that I'm interested in. By the time *grep* has worked through the whole newsgroup, I've finished the *more* command, and I'm ready to read the articles that *grep* told me about. (I didn't say this wasn't perverse. And it's easier on terminals that use a slow data rate.)

—*ML*

10.18 Too Many Files for the Command Line

A pair of backquotes (` ` `) *(10.14)* lets you run a command like *find (18.01)* and put its output onto another command's command line. For example:

pr 45.07
lpr 45.02

```
% pr -n `find . -type f -mtime -1 -print` | lpr
```

would give a list of all the files you edited today to *pr* and pipe *pr*'s output to the printer.

One day I was making global substitutions to a lot of files *(35.03, 29.08)* and got the error `Arguments too long` when I tried to print the files I had edited. Turned out that *find* output such a long list of files that it overflowed the command line:

```
% pr -n ./path/file1 ./path/path/file2 ./path/file3 ... | lpr
```

(This can happen for any command inside backquotes, not just *find*.)

I had to split *find*'s standard output into chunks that wouldn't be too long. This was on a UNIX that didn't have the great *xargs (10.19)*, so I decided to use *fmt (31.37)* instead. *fmt* reads its standard input and collects enough text to fill an output line. I used *fmt –1000*, which makes output lines about 1000 characters wide—long enough so I wouldn't need too many *pr* commands, but not too long . . . I started a Bourne shell, which lets you pipe to the input of a loop *(47.23)*. The shell prints secondary prompts *(10.11)* until you finish entering the loop:

```
% sh
$ find . -type f -mtime -1 -print |
> fmt -1000 |
> while read files
> do pr -n $files
> done | lpr
$ exit
%
```

read 46.13
exit 40.04

The shell put each line of filenames from *fmt –1000* into the *files* shell variable, ran *pr* with those filenames, and piped the output of all the *prs* to the standard input of *lpr*. The *lpr* command didn't know that it was being fed by lots of *pr* commands—all it saw was a series of 66-line pages that the *prs* output.

If you have *xargs* on your system, you can do the same thing this way:

```
% find . -type f -mtime -1 -print | xargs pr -n | lpr
```

(10.20)

xargs reads text from its standard input, collects a reasonable amount, then runs the command line pr -n *path/file path/file*.... Then *xargs* reads more text and runs *pr* again, over and over, until it's read all the text. The output of the *xargs* command (which is actually the output of all those *pr*s) is fed to a single *lpr* command.

Parting shot (by ML): there's really no excuse for *xargs* or any of these other tricks; they're just a patch for a design error. UNIX should be able to handle arbitrarily long command lines; maybe in some future version, it will.

—JP

10.19 *Handle Too-long Command Lines with xargs*

xargs is one of those UNIX utilities that seems pretty useless when you first hear about it—but turns into one of the handiest tools you can have.

xargs

If your system doesn't already have *xargs*, be sure to install it from the Power Tools disk.

xargs reads a group of arguments from its standard input, then runs a UNIX command with that group of arguments. It keeps reading arguments and running the command until it runs out of arguments. The shell's backquotes *(10.14)* do the same kind of thing, but they give all the arguments to the command at once. This can give you a Too many arguments *(10.18)* error.

Here are a couple of examples:

- If you want to print most of the files in a large directory, put the output of *ls* into a file. Edit the file to leave just the filenames you want printed. Give the file to *xargs'* standard input:

  ```
  % ls > allfiles.tmp
  % vi allfiles.tmp
  % xargs lpr < allfiles.tmp
  ```

  What did that do? With lines like these in *allfiles.tmp*:

  ```
  % cat allfiles.tmp
  afile
  application
      ...
  yoyotest
  zapme
  ```

  xargs ran one or more *lpr* commands, each with a group of arguments, until it had read every word in the file:

  ```
  lpr afile application ...
      ...
  lpr ... yoyotest zapme
  ```

- The standard output of *xargs* is the standard output of the commands it runs. So, if you'd created *allfiles.tmp* above but you wanted to format the files with *pr(45.07)* first, you could type:

  ```
  % xargs pr < allfiles.tmp | lpr
  ```

  Then *xargs* would run all of these *pr* commands. The shell would pipe their standard outputs* to a single *lpr* command:

  ```
  pr afile application ...
      ...
  pr ... yoyotest zapme
  ```

  In this next example, *find (18.01)* gets a list of all files in the directory tree. Next, we use *xargs* to read those filenames and run *grep −l (16.08)* to find which files contain the word "WARNING". Next, we pipe that to a setup with *pr* and *lpr*, like the one in the previous example:

  ```
  % find . -type f -print | xargs grep -l WARNING | xargs pr | lpr
  ```

  "Huh?" you might say. Just take that step by step. The output of *find* is a list of filenames, like `./afile ./bfile ... ./adir/zfile` and so on. The first *xargs* gives those filenames to one or more *grep −l* commands:

  ```
  grep -l WARNING ./afile ./bfile ...
      ...
  grep -l WARNING ./adir/zfile ...
  ```

  (14.14)

  The standard output of all those *grep*s is a (shortened) list of filenames that match. That's piped to another *xargs*—it runs *pr* commands with the filenames that *grep* found.

  UNIX is weird and wonderful!

- Sometimes you don't want *xargs* to run its command with as many arguments as it can fit on the command line. The −*n* option sets the maximum number of arguments *xargs* will give to each command. Another handy option, −*p*, prompts you before running each command.

  Here's a directory full of files with errors (whose names end with .*bad*) and corrected versions (named .*fixed*). I use *ls* to give the list of files to *xargs*; it reads two filenames at once, then asks whether I want to run *diff −c* to compare those two files. It keeps prompting me and running *diff −c* until it runs out of file pairs:

  ```
  % ls
  chap1.bad
  chap1.fixed
  chap2.bad
  chap2.fixed
      ...
  chap9.bad
  chap9.fixed
  ```

---

*Actually, the shell is piping the standard output of *xargs*. As I said above, *xargs* sends the standard output of commands it runs to its own standard output.

```
% ls | xargs -p -n2 diff -c
diff -c chap1.bad chap1.fixed ?...y
    ...Output of diff command for chap1...
diff -c chap2.bad chap2.fixed ?...n
diff -c chap3.bad chap3.fixed ?...y
    ...Output of diff command for chap3...
    ...
```

As the next article *(10.20)* explains, *xargs* can have trouble if an argument has white space inside a word. Luckily, this doesn't happen much.

—JP

10.20 *xargs: Problems with Spaces and Newlines*

The *xargs (10.19)* command reads its input and splits the arguments at spaces or newlines. It's legal (though pretty unusual) for UNIX filenames to have spaces or newline characters in them. Those filenames can cause *xargs* trouble.

For example, I have a directory full of copies of Usenet *(1.33)* articles. The filenames are the same as the subjects of the articles:

(1.15)

```
% ls
A use for the "yes" command
Beware UNIX Security Holes
Causes of 'test' errors
    ...
```

The problem comes when I run a command like this:

```
% find . -type f -mtime +7 -print | xargs rm
```

If *find* outputs the pathname *./Beware UNIX Security Holes*, the *xargs* command would most likely tell *rm* to remove four filenames: *./Beware, UNIX, Security,* and *Holes.* I'd probably get four error messages from *rm* because no files with those names exist. If they *did* exist, though, they'd be removed when they shouldn't! Newlines in filenames can cause the same problems.

Some versions of *xargs* are better at handling this problem, but almost none can be perfect. Here's a simple test to see how well your system's version works.

Make an empty directory, a filename with spaces, and a filename with a newline. Try to remove the file:

touch *22.07*
\ *9.11*

```
% mkdir temp
% cd temp
% touch 'Just testing'
% touch 'some\
file'
% find . -print | xargs rm
./Just: No such file or directory
testing: No such file or directory
some: No such file or directory
file: No such file or directory
```

That *xargs* broke the filenames at the space and newline. If it hadn't broken the filenames, the files would have been removed.

If your version of *xargs* has options that tell it whether to split arguments at spaces or newlines, that can help some. It still doesn't solve the problem completely. The only complete answer is not to use *xargs* with unknown arguments. But, depending on the command you're running and the problems that these errors could cause, it may be just fine to watch for error messages as you run the command and fix up any problems later, by hand.

—JP

10.21 *Workaround for "Arguments Too Long" Error*

When the shell matches a wildcard *(16.01)* in a big directory or with long path-names *(15.02, 16.07)*, it can sometimes run out of room. You'll get an error like this:

pr *45.07*

```
% pr */* | lpr
Arguments too long.
```

Sometimes you can work around that. The trick is to split the command line into pieces with semicolons *(9.03)*—and use a subshell *(14.07)* to combine the outputs. For example, I rewrote the previous command like this:

```
% (pr [a-f]*/*;pr [g-m]*/*;pr [n-z]*/*) | lpr
```

The first command prints the files in directories whose names start with "a" through "f," and so on.

How did I decide where to split? There's no magic formula. The number of pieces you'll need and the way you divide them will depend on how many directories and files you're trying to match—and your version of UNIX. Do it by experiment. A dummy command like *true* that ignores its arguments is good for this. In the example above, I first tried splitting the arguments in half. Then I split them more. I did the same for other chunks until the shell was happy with all of them:

```
% true [a-m]*/*
Arguments too long.
% true [a-f]*/*
% true [g-z]*/*
Arguments too long.
% true [g-m]*/*
% true [n-z]*/*
```

This trick works fine for commands like *pr* that make regular output which is consistent whether you run separate chunks of files or do all at the same time. Some commands start each listing with a separate heading—for instance, *ls –l* prints total *n* before it lists a directory. That kind of command won't work as neatly with this trick because you'll get several headings mixed in with the output instead of just one. Still, it might be better than nothing!

—JP

10.22 Get File List by Editing Output of ls –l, grep, etc.

It seems like I'm always using *ls*—also, usually, *–l* and maybe other options—to find out which of my files I need to do something to. I also use *grep* or one of the other *greps (28.01)* to search for files that have certain text in them. No matter what command I use, I redirect the output *(14.01)* to a temporary file *(22.02, 22.03),* then edit the file. After the editing, I have a list of filenames that I can use inside backquotes *(10.14)* with some other command—or store in a shell variable *(7.08).*

Here are two examples. These show the *vi* editor, but you can use any other UNIX editor that handles plain text files. Depending on what you need, there are probably UNIX utilities that can help.

What Files Have I Just Edited?

While I was working on this book, my current directory could have around 1000 files. If I wanted to find out which files I'd edited today, I would use *ls –lt* *(17.02)* to get a listing of files with the most recently modified listed first. Edit the file, delete all lines except files I'd edited today, then remove everything from each line except the filename. Finally, use backquotes and *rcp (1.33)* to copy the files to the *ptbackup* directory on the *fserver* computer:

1. Make the file list and start the editor:

   !$ 12.03
   ```
   % ls -lt > /tmp/bk$$
   % vi !$
   vi /tmp/bk28182
   ```

2. Delete all lines except the ones for files from February 29:

   ```
   total 4294                                      << delete
   -rw-r--r--  1 jerry       1529 Feb 29 17:25 a7630
   -rw-r--r--  1 jerry       1864 Feb 29 16:29 a0147
       ...Keep these lines...
   -rw-r--r--  1 jerry       1772 Feb 29 09:01 a1900
   -rw-r--r--  1 jerry       2693 Feb 29 08:51 a0031
   -rw-r--r--  1 jerry        744 Feb 28 23:35 a7600  << delete
   -rw-r--r--  1 jerry       1957 Feb 28 22:18 a5210  << delete
       ...Delete the rest...
   ```

3. In *vi*, use the | (vertical bar) command *(31.34)* to find the column number just before the filenames start. For example, here's where the commands 30|, 39|, and 45| moved the cursor:

   ```
   -rw-r--r--  1 jerry       1529 Feb 29 17:25 a7630
                            30^        39^   45^
   ```

4. So, I want to delete columns 1-45 from every line. The easiest way is a filter-through *(31.22)* with *colrm 1 45 (36.13)* or *cut –c46– (36.12).*

   ```
   :%!cut -c46-
   ```

5. Now the file looks like this—just the filenames:

```
a7630
a0147
  ...
a1900
a0031
```

I can sort it with `:%!sort` if I want to—or do more editing. Then I write the file and quit.

6. Feed the list of filenames to the UNIX command I want to run:

```
% rcp `cat /tmp/bk$$` fserver:ptbackup
```

This works with most any UNIX command—not just *rcp*. For example, if I want to print the files, I can use:

```
% lpr `cat /tmp/bk$$`
```

7. If I'll be doing a lot of work with the filenames, typing the backquotes over and over is a pain. I'll store the filenames in a shell variable *(7.08)*:

   • First, pick a name for the shell variable. I usually choose *temp* because it's not used on my account. You should check the name you choose before you set it by typing `echo "$varname"`; be sure it's empty or useless.

   • Store the filenames from your temporary file:

     ```
     % set temp=(`cat /tmp/bk$$`)
     $ temp="`cat /tmp/bk$$`"
     ```

   • Use the shell variable. For example:

     ```
     % cp $temp backupdir
     % vi $temp
     % ...
     ```

[Sometimes, *find* with operators like *−newer* *(18.08)* is easier—but *find* searches subdirectories too, unless you use *−prune* *(18.24)*. —*JP*] Oh, try to remember to *rm* the temp file when you're done with it.

Search for Text with grep

The *grep −l* option *(16.08)* gives you a list of filenames that match a string—that might be all I need. But sometimes I need to see the lines that *grep* found to decide whether to include that file or not. Here's how:

1. Search the files. Be sure that your *grep*-like command will print the filename before each matching line:

```
% egrep -i "summar(y|ies)" * > /tmp/bk$$
```

2. Edit the temporary file. The lines will look something like this:

```
a0066:Here is a summary of the different components:
a0183:Summary: String functions in awk
a0183:for a summary of all the string functions
```

```
a0184:Let's start wlth a short summary how awk treats command
a1000:Here's a summary of the rules that UNIX uses to interpret paths:
a1000:Here's a summary of the different sorts of wildcards available:
a1680:cumulative summary files and ASCII reports in
a2710:In summary, \fIcomm\fP is similar to \fIdiff\fP:
    ...
```

Leave a line for each file that you want to operate on; delete the rest:

```
a0066:Here is a summary of the different components:
a0183:Summary: String functions in awk
a1000:Here's a summary of the different sorts of wildcards available:
    ...
```

3. Strip off everything after the filenames. Unless any of your filenames have colons (:) in them, you can tell *vi* to strip off the colons and everything after them. That command is:

```
:%s/:.*//
```

If there's a chance that a filename might be repeated (because *grep* matched more than one line), filter the filenames through *sort −u* to get rid of duplicates. In *vi*, type:

```
:%!sort -u
```

Like before, what's left is a list of filenames:

```
a0066
a0183
a1000
  ...
```

You can feed them to whatever command you need to run, as in the previous example.

I hope those two examples give you the idea, which is: learn what UNIX utilities are "out there"—and how to grab and edit their output to do what you want.

—*JP*

10.23 *The C Shell repeat Command*

The C shell has a built-in command that lets you execute a command repeatedly:

```
% repeat n command
```

All you do is specify the number of repetitions, followed by the command you want to re-execute. A trivial example would be:

```
% repeat 4 echo Enter name:
Enter name:
Enter name:
Enter name:
Enter name:
```

Simple, right? Just imagine what Jack Nicholson could have done in the movie *The Shining* if he had traded in his typewriter for a UNIX system:

```
% repeat 500 echo "All work and no play makes Jack a dull boy."
```

Ok, this is fun at first, but you may soon wonder whether this command has any down-to-earth uses. It does, and I'll conclude with some more useful examples:

a. Print three copies of *memo*:

```
% repeat 3 pr memo | lp
```

b. Run *popd* (15.06) four times to clear a directory stack:

```
% repeat 4 popd
```

c. Append 50 boilerplate files to *report*:

```
% repeat 50 cat template >> report
```

Some versions of the C shell *repeat* command have a quoting bug. See the end of article 49.02.

—*DG*

11

Aliases

11.01 Creating Custom Commands

- If you use the C shell or Korn shell, aliases *(11.02, 11.03, 11.04)* are an easy way to shorten a long command line or do a short series of commands.

- The Korn shell and newer Bourne shells have shell functions *(11.10)*. These are a cross between aliases and shell scripts. They're good both for shortening command lines and for running a short or long series of commands.

- You can simulate shell functions *(11.11)* on older Bourne shells. These "fake functions" don't have much more power than aliases—but they're better than nothing!

—*JP*

11.02 Aliases for Common Commands

The C shell and Korn shell have an "alias" facility that lets you define abbreviations for commonly used commands. Aliases can get very complicated, so we'll give just an introduction here. We'll use the *csh* alias syntax here; article 11.04 shows *ksh*.

Simple Aliases

The simplest kind of alias is simply a new name for an old command. For example, you might want to rename the *ls* command as *dir* because you're used to DOS or VMS systems. That's easily done:

```
alias dir ls
```

---

dir is the new name; from now on, typing `dir` as a command is equivalent to typing `ls`. Some other commonly used aliases are:

```
alias la ls -a      # include "hidden" files in listings
alias lf ls -F      # show whether files are directories, etc.
alias lr ls -R      # list recursively--show directory contents
alias ri rm -i      # ask before deleting
alias mi mv -i      # ask before moving over an existing file
```

In a *.cshrc* file, the hash mark (#) means that the rest of the line is a comment. Describing your aliases can help you remember what they're for. That's an especially good idea for complicated aliases you write—like the aliases in the next section.

Using More Complex Aliases

Here are a few aliases that I find useful; you'll have to adapt them to your own circumstances:

```
alias emacs /home/src/emacs/bin/emacs
alias clean "rm *~ .*~ core *.bak"
alias vtext 'setenv EXINIT "source $HOME/.exrc.text" ; vi'
alias vprog 'setenv EXINIT "source $HOME/.exrc.prog" ; vi'
```

Let's look at these aliases more closely. The *emacs* alias isn't anything fancy; it's just a way of remembering a long command name, without having to add another directory to your search path *(9.05)* for a single command. (I find long search paths aesthetically unappealing. They can also slow your system down, although the C shell uses a hash table *(55.01)* to speed up searching. On the other hand, it takes time to read aliases like *emacs* from your *.cshrc* file into the shell. Defining lots of aliases, instead of simply changing your search path, can delay logins and subshells *(40.04)*. If you have a fast computer, it may not matter whether you use lots of aliases or have a long search path.)

The *clean* alias is great; it deletes GNU Emacs backup files and *core (55.01)* files (which I usually don't keep around) and other miscellany. Rather than have some complex "auto-cleaning" system that runs from *cron*, I just occasionally type `clean` in my current directory. Everyone should have an alias like this and doctor it so that it gets rid of as much junk as possible. (A lot of people, though, would tell you not to be so quick to delete your editor's backup files. Use your own judgment.)

The third and fourth aliases are a bit clever, in a primitive sort of way. You type the command `vtext afile`; the shell separates the commands at the semicolon and executes one after the other:

$HOME *15.12*
```
setenv EXINIT "source $HOME/.exrc.text"
vi afile
```

The first command sets the *EXINIT* environment variable *(7.01)*; this makes *vi* read a particular setup file *(5.09)* named *.exrc.text* in the home directory. The second command starts *vi* with whatever arguments you type. You aren't limited to just one filename. You can type whatever arguments you want, including more filenames and *vi* options; they're all tacked on after `vi`. There are more graceful ways to get command-line arguments into aliases *(11.03)* but this does the trick when the arguments go on the end of an alias.

Note that we put this alias in quotes. Why? Because it's a compound command (*setenv*, then *vi*). We want the alias to include both stages of the command. Think about what this means if we don't put quotes around the alias definition when defining the alias:

```
alias vtext setenv EXINIT "source $HOME/.exrc.text" ; vi      Wrong!
```

The shell sees the semicolon *(9.03)*(a command separator) outside of quotes, so it separates the command line into two commands. The first command defines the *vtext* alias to run *setenv*, not *vi*. After the alias is defined, the shell runs the second command: *vi* with no filename. In any case, the results have nothing to do with what you want.

The way we originally defined the *vtext* alias, with quotes around the whole definition, is what we want. The outer quotes tell the shell to put everything into the alias definition. The semicolon in the alias will be interpreted, and separate the two commands, any time you use the alias.

Next, look at the *clean* alias. As with the *vtext* alias, this one needs to be quoted. The reason now is a bit different; the quotes prevent the shell from expanding the * wildcard immediately. That is, if you just typed:

```
% alias clean rm *~
```

the shell would expand the wildcard immediately. So if a file named *foo˜* is in your current directory, the *clean* alias will be `rm foo~`. That (most likely) isn't what you want; a *clean* alias that will only delete one particular file isn't very interesting.

So you need a way to prevent the shell from interpreting the * right now (when you define the alias); you want the shell to interpret * later, when you use the alias. There are plenty of articles in this book about quoting *(9.10, 9.11)* but the simplest way to write an alias that uses wildcards (or other special characters) is to put it inside of quotation marks.

Setting Aliases Automatically, Unsetting Aliases

Any aliases you define can be placed in your *.cshrc* file, so that they'll be available whenever you're using the C shell. (Note: aliases are *not* passed to subprocesses *(2.02)* so putting them in your *.login* file probably isn't wise.)

Some people like to use aliases to redefine UNIX commands. For instance, you could make an alias named *rm* that actually runs *mv*, moving a file to a "trashcan" directory instead of actually removing it.* Redefining commands can be confusing or dangerous *(11.06)* Still, in some cases, aliases that redefine commands can be useful.

---

*Article 24.08 shows the *delete* programs, a better way to do this.

To temporarily use the default *rm* (not your alias named *rm*), type a backslash (\) before the name:

```
% \rm filename
```

To use the default *rm* for the rest of your login session:

```
% unalias rm
```

Unless you remove the definition from *.cshrc*, the alias is restored the next time you log in (or the next time you create any new C shell).

A final piece of trivia: the C shell manual page tells us that aliases can be nested; that is, they can refer to other aliases. Personally, I think this would get too complicated too quickly to be very useful, so I don't do it and can't recommend it. But you can try.

—ML, JP, DG

11.03 Aliases that Use Command-line Arguments

It's convenient for your aliases to use command-line arguments. For example, let's think about an alias named *phone*:

```
alias phone 'cat ~/phonelist | grep -i'
```

For example, after you define that alias, you could type *phone smith*. The shell would find the *phone* alias and execute it with the argument (*smith*) at the end *(11.02)* this way:

```
cat ~/phonelist | grep -i smith
```

Using *cat* and a pipe that way is inefficient *(14.02)*. It might be more sensible to have an alias that worked like this:

```
grep -i name ~/phonelist
```

How do we do this? The C shell's history *(12.07)* facility lets us use the notation ! $ to refer to the last word in the previous command; the notation ! * refers to all the arguments of the previous command. Assuming that we only want to look up aliases one at a time, we can use ! $ and write our alias like this:

```
alias phone grep -i \!$ ~/phonelist
```

When we use the *phone* command, its final argument will be substituted into the alias. That is, when we type phone bill, the shell executes the command grep -i bill ~/phonelist.

In this example, we needed another kind of quoting. We had to put a backslash before the exclamation point to prevent the shell from replacing ! $ with the previous command's last argument. That is, we don't want the shell to expand ! $ when we define the alias—that's nonsense. We want the shell to insert the previous argument when we use the alias (in which case, the previous argument is just the argument for the alias itself—clear?).

But why couldn't we just use single quotes or double quotes *(9.10)*? This isn't the right place for a full explanation, but neither single quotes nor double quotes protect the exclamation point. The backslash does *(9.11)*. If you want to be convinced, experiment with some commands like:

```
% echo '!!'        Print your last command
% echo '\!!'       Print !!
```

The first *echo* command shows that the shell performs history substitution (i.e., replaces ! ! with your previous command) in spite of the single quotes. The second example shows that the backslash can prevent the shell from interpreting ! as a special character.

Let's look at another alias. We want to pipe the output of *ls −l* into *more (26.03)*. In this case, we would want all the arguments from the command line, instead of merely the last argument (or the only argument). Here's the alias:

```
alias lm 'ls -l \!* | more'
```

This time, we needed both kinds of quoting: A backslash prevents the shell from interpreting the exclamation point immediately. Single quotes protect the pipe symbol and the asterisk (*). If you don't protect them both, and only protect the pipe (with a backslash), look what happens:

```
% alias lm ls -1 \!* \| more
alias: No match.
```

Because the backslash temporarily stops the special meaning of the !, the shell next tries to find filenames that match the wildcard *(1.16)* pattern ! *. That fails (except in the unusual case when you have a file in the current directory whose name starts with a *!*).

Note: Here's a good general rule for quoting aliases. Unless you're trying to do something special with an alias and you understand quoting well, put single quotes (') around the whole definition and put a backslash before every exclamation point (\ !).

Finally, if you want to pick one argument from the command line, use \ ! : *n*, where *n* is the number of the argument. Here's one final alias. It uses *cat (26.02)* to add a header file to the file named in the first argument, then write them both into the file named in the second argument:

~ *15.12*
```
alias addhead 'cat ~/txt/header \!:1 > \!:2'
```

This alias has two arguments: the file to which you want to add a header, and the output file. When you type:

```
% addhead foo bar
```

the C shell substitutes the filename foo for \!:1, and the filename bar for \!:2, executing the command:

```
cat ~/txt/header foo > bar
```

—ML, JP

11.04 Korn Shell Aliases

Virtually everything we've said about aliases applies to the Korn shell (*ksh*). The one thing that's different is the syntax of the *alias* command, which is:

```
$ alias name=definition
```

That is, you need an equal sign (no spaces) between the name and the definition. A good guideline is to use single quotes (') around the *definition* unless you're doing something specialized and you understand how quoting *(9.10)* works in aliases.

Also, Korn shell aliasing is "overloaded" with a few other functions—like keeping track of the locations of executables. However, this shouldn't prevent you from defining your own aliases as you need them.

—ML

11.05 Sourceable Scripts

A powerful concept in *csh* is that of aliases. Another great capability is shell scripts. Each has its strengths. An alias is just right for common sequences of commands, calling a command by a different name, and so on. Scripts are great for more flexible processing and batch processing. There are limitations to both, and I will show a way around them.

The limitation to aliases is that you are working pretty much with one command line. Consider this example:

```
alias pp 'set o2=$cwd; popd; set old=$o2; dir_number; record_dir pp; \\
    prompt_set; set cd_attempt=(\!*); if ($#cd_attempt > 0) cd $cd_attempt'
```

Now this works fine for me, and it served me well for a few years and thousands of invocations, but it's at the point where I start thinking that a script is more suited to the job. This brings me to the limitation of scripts . . .

Shell scripts are great for accomplishing some task that might change a file, start a program, etc. They are limited by the fact that any changes they make to shell or environment variables are not visible *(40.03)* to the parent shell that started them. In other words, you can write some really cool script that will change directories for you if you don't touch the keyboard for five seconds, but once the script exits, you are still in the same place you started.

The answer is to combine the best of both worlds. Consider this:

( ) 49.05
```
alias pp 'set cd_attempt=(\!*); source ~/bin/pp_csh'
```

We set up a variable, and source a script. The concept is to put your command-line arguments into a variable, and then *source (46.22)* a script in order to accomplish something. The difference here is that because you are not starting a sub-shell *(40.04)* for the script, it can do everything an alias can and more. This is much like Bourne shell functions *(11.10)*.

Some hints on using this technique:

- **Naming:** I like to name the script that is doing all of the work after the alias, with *_csh* or *.csh* at the end of its name. I put all of the scripts in my ~/bin *(5.02)*. [Instead of names ending in *.csh*, I put mine in a directory named ~/.lib/csh.—JP]

- **Feedback:** You don't want to execute the script directly. You want to source it. Here's a good first line that detects this:

#! 47.05
```
#! /bin/echo sorry,try:source
```

- **Usage statement:** Check the variable that you expect to see from the alias. If it isn't there, you can show a usage statement, and do a *goto* to the end of the script:

$# 49.04
<< 9.14
```
if ($#lg_args == 0) then
    cat << +++
usage: lg [-a] [-p] pattern [command]
    -a  lists all (.dot files)
    -p  pipe resulting list into command
+++
    goto lg_end
endif
    ...
lg_end:
```

- **Alias options:** You aren't limited to what an alias can do, since you are sourcing a script. You gain some flexibility here. Here's one way of handling options:

switch 49.06
[1] 49.05
set 7.08
shift 49.05
```
unset ls_arg
while (! $?ls_arg)
    switch ("$lg_args[1]")
        case "-a":
            set ls_arg="-a"
            shift lg_args
        case "-p":
            set use_pipe
            shift lg_args
        default:
            set ls_arg
            breaksw
    endsw
end
```

Have fun with this! You may find yourself tossing some old aliases and rewriting them as sourceable scripts. They're also easier to maintain.

—DS

11.06 Avoiding Alias Loops

Here's a situation that came up on the net awhile ago. Someone wanted an *exit* *(40.04)* alias that would run a ⁀/.*exit* file *(15.15)* before leaving the shell. The obvious solution is:

```
alias exit "source ~/.exit; exit"
```

This doesn't work; when you use the *exit* alias, the C shell thinks that the alias is trying to execute itself. Recursive aliases aren't allowed, so the C shell prints an error message (`Alias loop`) and gives up.

There are many, many ways to break the loop. Here's the best (in my opinion):

```
alias exit 'source ~/.exit; ""exit'
```

The pair of quotes before the last *exit* prevents the shell from interpreting *exit* as an alias. Consequently, the shell has no trouble finding *exit* among its built-in commands. I like this because it's simple; it doesn't require a second alias or an auxiliary file, it doesn't require sending signals to yourself, and so on. There are many ways to accomplish this task, but this is the neatest.

All right, then, here's something else that won't work. The big trick is figuring out why:

```
alias exit 'source ~/.exit; \exit'
```

What's the difference between preceding *exit* with quotes and quoting the first letter? If any letter of a command is quoted, the shell won't search its built-in commands; it only searches the "external" commands (i.e., executables and shell scripts that are on the search path). *exit* is a built-in *(1.10)*, not an executable command; so when the shell sees \\`exit`, it can't find the command.

So, if you need to use the alias' name within an alias, you can use:

""*name*   where *name* is the name of a built-in command or any "regular" command.

name   where *name* is the name of any "regular" command, but not a built-in command.

Tempting as this all may sound (and I have to admit, if it didn't sound a bit tempting, I wouldn't be writing this article), I can't really recommend the practice of "redefining" commands with aliases. You should leave the original commands as they are. The original author could have avoided all these problems by calling his alias *quit* rather than *exit*.

If you redefine commands with aliases—then use another account where your alias isn't defined (or, if you let someone type a command on your account)—it's easy for things to go wrong. That's especially true for commands that do something permanent—overwriting or removing files, for example.

Let me give one more example to show you what problems you can have. Let's say you've aliased the *exit* command to *source* a *.exit* file before quitting. Fair enough. But now, let's say that you're not in your login shell, that you've *set ignoreeof* *(7.09)*, and that, for no apparent reason, your *.exit* file disappears (maybe it develops a bad block, so the system can't read it; such things happen).

Now you're stuck. If you type exit, the *source* command will fail, and the "real" *exit* command will never be executed. You can't leave the shell. Of course, if you remember what you did, you can always type unalias exit and get the original command back. Or you can type ""exit. But if you've foisted this alias on an beginner, he or she might not know that. All of a sudden, you're stuck in some shell that you apparently can't get out of.

The biggest virtue of UNIX is that it's infinitely extendable. However, you aren't helping if your extensions hide the basic operations that make everything work. So—extend all you want. But when you write your extensions, give them *new names*. End of sermon.

—*ML*

11.07 *How to Put if-then-else in a C Shell Alias*

The C shell's brain damage *(49.02)* keeps you from using an *if (49.03)* with an *else* in an alias. You have to use a sourceable script *(11.05)*. Or that's what I thought until I saw an article by Lloyd Zusman on *comp.unix.questions* in December 1987. He'd saved an earlier posting on that group (but without its author's name) that showed how. The trick: use enough backslashes (\) and the *eval (9.08)* command.

As an example, here's an alias named *C* for compiling *(54.08)* C programs. It needs the *executable* filename (like C prog), not the source filename (like C prog.c). If you type a filename ending in *.c*, it complains and quits. Else, it:

- Renames any old *prog* file to *prog.old*,

- Prints the message *prog* SENT TO cc,

- Compiles *prog.c*,

- And—if there's a *prog* file (if the compile succeeded)—runs *chmod 311 prog* to protect the file from accidental reading with a command like *cat ** or *more **.

Your alias doesn't need to be as complicated. But this one shows some tricks, like putting an *if* inside the *if*, that you might want to use. The expressions like =~ and -e are explained in article 49.04. Watch your quoting—remember that the shell strips off one level of quoting when you set the alias *(11.03)* and another during the first pass of the *eval*. Follow this example and you'll probably be fine:

csh_init

```
# COMPILE AND chmod C PROGRAMS; DON'T USE .c ON END OF FILENAME.
alias C 'eval "if (\!* =~ *.c) then \\
    echo "C quitting: no .c on end of \!* please." \\
else \\
    if (-e \!*) mv \!* \!*.old \\
    echo \!*.c SENT TO cc \\
```

```
      cc -s \!*.c -o \!* \\
      if (-e \!*) chmod 311 \!* \\
endif"'
```

—*JP*

11.08 *Shell Variables as Aliases*

The Bourne shell doesn't have an *alias* command. (The Korn shell does *(11.04)*.) However, if you like the idea of aliases, shell variables *(7.08)* make a good substitute. For example, let's say that you want aliases for common versions of *ls*. Just stick this in your *.profile*:

```
la="ls -a"
lf="ls -F"
lr="ls -R"
export la lf lr
```

Once you've defined these variables, you can use these variables to execute commands: for example, type $la to execute ls -a:

```
$ $la
.emacs      Mail      gnu     rcs
.login      adb       ksh     sendmail
.profile    before    net     tuning
```

I took the liberty of "exporting" *(7.01)* these aliases because shell variables aren't inherited by subshells *(40.04)*, and the *.profile* is only read when you log in. To make sure that you can use these variables whenever you start a new shell, *export* them. (Yes, C shell aliases aren't inherited by subshells; but aliases are usually defined in *.cshrc*, which *is* read by all subshells.)

By the way, this is a very common trick in shell programming; it's very common to see scripts that start like this:

```
# the versions we're going to use
troff=/usr/sqps/bin/sqtroff
tbl=/usr/sqps/bin/sqtbl
eqn=/usr/ucb/eqn
# whatever setup junk we need to do
    ...
# run it
$eqn $file | $tbl | $troff $options > $output
```

In fact, all my scripts start this way. (I've even been known to write ls=/bin/ls!) The "shell variable" definitions are, essentially, aliases. This may look a little awkward, but it's much easier to adapt the scripts when something changes—for example, when you install *groff* and decide to use it instead of *sqtroff*. It's also a great trick for makefiles *(29.12)*.

Now, let's make this a bit more complicated. The mock-alias facility we've defined above helps, but doesn't take us where we want to go. It's fine for a single command with options and arguments. But if you want anything even remotely complicated, like a compound command (a pipe, for example), this won't work. When interpreting the command line, the shell only interprets the *first* word in the variable as a command. (This has to do with the shell's command-line parsing *(9.03)*; it's not a topic we can discuss here.)

You can get out of this bind by using *eval (9.08)*. *eval* interprets its arguments as a UNIX command line and executes that line. For example, let's say we want an alias to look up a phone number in a list:

```
phone="eval cat $HOME/phonelist | grep -i"
```

Now we can give the command:

```
$ $phone dave
Dave Anderson     235-8686
```

Admittedly, there are things you can't do; for example, you can't get at any command-line arguments, as you can with the C shell's *alias* facility. But this is better than nothing.

—ML

11.09 Fix Quoting in csh Aliases with makealias and quote

Getting quoting right in aliases can be a real problem. Dan Bernstein wrote two aliases called *makealias* and *quote* that take care of this for you.

For example, here I use *makealias* to avoid having to quote ! and *:

```
% makealias mycat
cat `ls | sed '1,/!*/d'` | less
CTRL-d
alias mycat 'cat `ls | sed '\''1,/\!*/d'\''` | less'
```

I typed the `makealias mycat` command and the line starting with `cat` and got back an alias definition with all of the quoting done correctly.

The properly quoted alias definition is sent to the standard output. That line is what you would use to define the alias.*

And here are the *quote* and *makealias* aliases themselves:

csh_init

```
alias quote     "/bin/sed -e 's/\\!/\\\\\!/g' \\
    -e 's/'\\''/'\\'\\\\\\'\\''/g' \\
    -e 's/^/'''/' -e 's/"\$"/'''/'"
alias makealias "quote | /bin/sed 's/^/alias \!:1 /' \!:2*"
```

Pretty gross, but they do the job. . . .

—JIK in *comp.unix.questions* on Usenet, *17 February 1991*

---

*[The *mycat* alias runs *cat* on all files with names later in the alphabet than the argument you type. The output of *cat* is piped to the *less (26.04)* pager. For example, let's say your current directory has the files *afile*, *count*, *jim*, and *report*. Typing `mycat count` would display the files *jim* and *report.—JP*]

11.10 Bourne and Korn Shell Functions

The C shell has aliases *(11.02)*. But until System V Release 2, the Bourne Shell had almost *(11.11, 11.08)* no way for users to set up their own built-in commands. Functions are like aliases, but better. For instance, functions can return a status *(46.07)* and have much more reasonable syntax *(11.07)*. To find out all about functions, check a shell programming book. Here are the examples from articles 11.02 and 11.03 changed into Bourne shell aliases:

• The *la* function includes "hidden" files in *ls* listings. The *lf* function labels the names as directories, executable files, and so on:

```
la () { ls -a "$@"; }
lf () { ls -F "$@"; }
```

The spaces and the semicolon (;) are both important!* The "$@" *(46.14)* is replaced by the command-line arguments (other options, or directory and filenames), if you use any:

```
$ la -l somedir                    ...runs ls -a -l somedir
```

• This next simple function, *cur*, gives the name of your current directory and then lists it:

```
cur()
{
      pwd
      ls
}
```

That example shows how to write a function with more than one line. In that style, with the ending curly brace on its own line, you don't need a semicolon after the last command.

—*JP*

11.11 Simulated Bourne Shell Functions and Aliases

If you have a Bourne shell with no functions *(11.10)* or aliases *(11.02)*, you can do a lot of the same things with shell variables and the *eval* *(9.08)* command.

Let's look at an example. First, here's a shell function named *scp* (safe copy). If the destination file exists and isn't empty, the function prints an error message instead of copying:

```
scp()
{
      if test ! -s "$2"
      then cp "$1" "$2"
      else echo "scp: cannot copy $1: $2 exists"
      fi
}
```

test *46.19*

---

* A function is a Bourne shell list construct *(14.08)*.

If you use the same *scp* twice, the first time you'll make *bfile*. The second time you try, you see the error:

```
$ scp afile bfile
   ...
$ scp afile bfile
scp: cannot copy afile: bfile exists
```

Here's the same *scp*—stored in a shell variable instead of a function:

```
scp='
if test ! -s "$2"
then cp "$1" "$2"
else echo "scp: cannot copy $1: $2 exists"
fi
'
```

Because this fake function uses shell parameters, you have to add an extra step: setting the parameters. Simpler functions are easier to use:

set *46.18*

```
$ set afile bfile
$ eval "$scp"
   ...
$ eval "$scp"
scp: cannot copy afile: bfile exists
```

—*JP*

12

The Lessons of History

12.01 The Lessons of History

It has been said that "the only thing we learn from history is that people don't learn from history."

Fortunately, the original maxim that "history repeats itself" is more appropriate to UNIX.

The C and Korn shells both include a powerful history mechanism that lets you easily recall and repeat past commands, potentially editing them before execution. This can be a godsend, especially when typing a long or complex command.

All that is needed to set C shell history in motion is a command like this in your *.cshrc* file:

```
set history=n
```

where *n* is the number of past commands that you want to save. I typically save 100; a maniac like Jerry Peek saves 1000!

The *history* command lists the saved commands, each with an identifying number. [You can show just the last few commands by typing a number, too. For instance, *history 20* shows your last 20 commands. That's why I save my last 1000 commands... who knows what I'll need?—*JP*] (It's also possible to configure the C shell to print the history number of each command as part of your prompt *(8.02)*.)

You can repeat a past command by typing its number preceded by an exclamation point. You can also select only parts of the command to be repeated, and use various editing operators to modify it. Articles 12.07 and 12.08 give a quick tutorial summary of some of the wonderful things you can do. Most of the rest of the chapter gives a miscellany of tips for using and abusing the C shell history mechanism. The Korn shell's command-line editing is covered in article 12.14.

—TOR

12.02 *History in a Nutshell*

The C shell can save copies of the previous command lines you type. Later, you can ask for a copy of some or all of a previous command line. That can save time and retyping.

This feature is called *history substitution,* and it's done when you type a string that starts with an exclamation point (! *command*). You can think of it like variable substitution ($*varname*) *(7.08)* or command substitution (\`*command*\`) *(10.14)*: the shell replaces what you type (like ! $) with something else (in this case, part or all of a previous command line).

Article 12.01 is an introduction to C shell history. These articles show lots of ways to use history substitution:

- We start with favorite uses from several contributors—articles 12.03, 12.04, 12.05, 12.06.

- Article 12.07 starts with a quick introduction, then covers the full range of history substitutions with a series of examples that show the different kinds of things you can do with history.

- Next, in article 12.08, are examples of the C shell's colon (:) operators, like :r. These can edit history substitutions (and shell variables *(7.08)*, too).

- See an easy way to repeat a set of commands in article 12.09.

- Each C shell saves its own history. To pass a shell's history to another shell, see article 12.13.

- You don't have to use an exclamation point (!) for history. Article 12.17 shows how to use some other character.

- The Korn shell does history in a different way. Article 12.14 introduces part of that: *ksh* command-line editing.

- Article 12.15 shows how to simulate Korn shell command-line editing (*vi* mode) in the C shell.

One last note: putting the history number in your prompt *(8.02)* makes it easy to re-use commands that haven't scrolled off your screen.

—JP

12.03 My Favorite is !$

When using the C shell, I use !$ so much that it's almost a single character to
me. It means "take the last thing on the previous command line." Since most
UNIX commands have the filename last, you often need to type filenames only
once, and then you can use !$ in subsequent lines. Here are some examples of
where it comes in handy:

- I get a lot of *tar* archives *(20.05)* that are compressed *(25.06)*. To unpack them, I
  do the following:

```
% uncompress groff.1.05.tar
% tar xvf !$
tar xvf groff.1.05.tar
```

The same trick can be used for uuencoded *shar* files *(20.02)*. It's also good
when you've edited a file with *vi*, and then want to check its spelling:

```
% vi fred.letter.txt
% spell !$
spell fred.letter.txt
```

- You often want to move a file to another directory and then change directory to that directory. The !$ sequence can also be used to refer to a direc-
  tory:

```
% mv grmacs.tar /usr/lib/tmac
% cd !$
cd /usr/lib/tmac
```

—AN

12.04 My Favorite is !:n*

I use !$ *(12.03)* a lot. But my favorite history substitution is !:n* (where n is a
number from 0 to 9). It means "take arguments n through the last argument on
the previous command line." Since I tend to use more than one argument with
UNIX commands, this lets me type the arguments (usually filenames) only once.
For example, to use RCS *(21.14)* and make an edit to article files named *1171*,
6830, and *2340* for this book, I did:

```
% co -l 1171 6830 2340
RCS/1171,v  -->  1171
    ...
RCS/2340,v  -->  2340
revision 1.8 (locked)
done
% vi !:2*
vi 1171 6830 2340
3 files to edit
    ...
% ci -m"Changed TERM xref." !*
ci -m"Changed TERM xref." 1171 6830 2340
    ...
```

In the first command line (co), I typed the filenames as arguments 2, 3, and 4. In the second command line (vi), I used !:2*; that grabbed arguments 2 through the last (in this case, argument 4) from the first command line. The result was a second command line that had those three filenames as its arguments 1, 2, and 3. So, in the third command line (ci), I used !* to pick arguments 1 through the last from the previous (second) command line. (!* is shorthand for !:1*.)

You can also grab arguments from previous command lines. For example, !em:2* grabs the second through last arguments on the previous *emacs* command line (command line starting with "em"). There are lots more of these in article 12.07.

If those look complicated, they won't be for long. Just learn to count to the first argument you want to grab. It took me years to start using these substitutions—but they've saved me so much typing in the last month that I'm sorry I didn't get started earlier!

—*JP*

12.05 *My Favorite is* ^^

Well, maybe it's not my favorite, but it's probably the history substitution I use most often. It's especially handy if you have fumble-fingers on a strange keyboard:

```
% cat myflie
cat: myflie: No such file or directory
% ^li^il
cat myfile
```

Obviously, this doesn't save much typing for a short command, but it can sure be handy with a long one. I also use ^^ with :p *(12.11)* to recall an earlier command so I can change it. For example:

```
% !m:p
more gobbledygook.c
% ^k^k2
more gobbledygook2.c
```

The point is sometimes not to save typing, but to save the effort of remembering. For example, I want to print the file I looked at earlier, but don't remember the exact name . . .

—*TOR*

12.06 Using !$ for Safety with Wildcards

We all know about using *ls* before a wildcarded *rm* to make sure that we're only deleting what we want. But that doesn't really solve the problem: you can type `ls a*` and then mistakenly type `rm s*` with bad consequences—it's just a minor slip of your finger. But what will always work, if you're a *csh* user, is:

```
% ls a*
a1 a2 a3
% rm !$
```

(`ls -d a*` *(17.09)* will make less output if any subdirectory names match the wildcard.)

Using the history mechanism to grab the previous command's arguments is a good way to prevent mistakes.

—ML

12.07 C Shell History Substitutions

[Although most of the examples here use echo *to demonstrate clearly just what is going on, you'll normally use* history *with other UNIX commands.—JP]*

The exclamation point (!) is the C shell's default *(12.17)* history substitution character. This allows you to recall previously entered commands and re-execute them without retyping. The number of commands saved is up to you. To set this number, look in your *.cshrc* file for something like:

```
set history=40
```

This means that the C shell will save the last 40 commands. To list out these 40 commands use:

```
% history
```

You can also list out the commands in reverse:

```
% history -r
```

Or see just the last few commands:

```
% history 10
```

That will give that last ten commands instead of the entire list.

To use the ! in a command line, you have several choices. Some of the following examples are more of a headache than they may be worth. But they are used mostly in aliases to select arguments from the command line. Here they are:

% !!　　　　Repeats last command.

% !:　　　　Repeats last command. This form is used if you want to add a modifier *(12.08)* like:

```
% echo xy
xy
% !:s/xy/yx
echo yx
yx
```

The second ! was left out.

% !so　　　　Repeats last command that starts with so.

% !?fn?　　　Repeats last command that has fn anywhere in it. The string could be found in an argument or in the command name. This is opposed to !fn, in which !fn must be in a command name. (The last ? need not be there. Thus !?fn means the same thing.)

% !34　　　　Executes command number 34. You can find the appropriate history number when you list your history using the *history* command, or by putting the history number in your prompt *(8.02)*.

% !! &　　　Appends an ampersand (&) to the end of the last command, which executes it and places it into the background. You can append anything to the end of a previous command. For example:

```
% cat -v foo
    ...
% !! | more
cat -v foo | more
    ...
```

In this case the shell will repeat the command to be executed and run it, adding the pipe through the *more (26.03)* pager. Another common usage is:

```
% cat -v foo
    ...
% !! > out
cat -v foo > out
```

which returns the command but redirects the output into a file.

% !:0　　　　Selects only the command name; rather than the entire command line.

```
% /usr/bin/grep Ah fn1
    ...
```

```
% !:0 Bh fn2
/usr/bin/grep Bh fn2
```

Note that as an operator *(12.08)* :0 can be appended to these history substitutions as well. For example, !!:0 will give the last command name, and a colon followed by any number will give the corresponding argument. For example:

```
% cat fn fn1 fn2
    ...
% more !:3
more fn2
    ...
```

gives the third argument.

% **!:2-4**   Gives the second through the fourth argument, or any numbers you choose:

```
% echo 1 2 3 4 5
1 2 3 4 5
% echo !:2-4
echo 2 3 4
2 3 4
```

% **!:-3**   Gives zero through the third argument, or any number you wish:

```
% echo 1 2 3 4
1 2 3 4
% echo !:-3
echo echo 1 2 3
echo 1 2 3
```

% **!^**   Gives the first argument of the previous command. This is the same as !:1. Remember that, just as the ^ (caret) is the beginning-of-line anchor in regular expressions *(27.04)*, !^ gives the beginning history argument.

```
% cat fn fn1 fn2
    ...
% more !^
more fn
    ...
```

% **!$**   Gives the last argument of the last command, in the same way that $ (dollar sign) is the end-of-line anchor in regular expressions, !$ gives the ending history argument. Thus:

```
% cat fn
    ...
% more !$
more fn
    ...
```

The new command (more) is given the last argument of the previous command.

% **!***   Is shorthand for the first through the last argument. This is used a lot in aliases:

```
% echo 1 2 3 4 5
1 2 3 4 5
% echo !*
echo 1 2 3 4 5
1 2 3 4 5
```

In an alias:

```
alias vcat 'cat -v \!* | more'
```

which will pipe the output of *cat −v (26.07)* command through *more*. The backslash (\) has to be there to hide the history character, !, until the alias is used—see article 11.03 for more information.

% **!:2***   Gives the second through the last arguments:

```
% echo 1 2 3 4 5
1 2 3 4 5
% echo !:2*
echo 2 3 4 5
2 3 4 5
```

% **!:2−**   Like 2* but the last argument is dropped:

```
% echo 1 2 3 4 5
1 2 3 4 5
% echo !:2-
echo 2 3 4
2 3 4
```

% **!?fn?%**   Gives the first word found that has fn in it:

```
% sort fn1 fn2 fn3
    ...
% echo !?fn?%
echo fn1
fn1
```

That found the fn in fn1. You can get wilder with:

```
% echo 1 2 3 4 5
1 2 3 4 5
% echo !?ec?^
echo 1
1
```

That selected the command that had ec in it, and the caret (^) said to give the first argument of that command. You can also do something like:

```
% echo fn fn1 fn2
fn fn1 fn2
```

```
% echo !?fn1?^ !$
echo fn fn2
fn fn2
```

That cryptic command told the shell to look for a command that had fn1 in it (!?fn1?), and gave the first argument of that command (^). Then it gave the last argument (!$).

% ^xy^yx   Is the shorthand substitution (12.03, 12.06) command. In the case of:

```
% echo xxyyzzxx
xxyyzzxx
% ^xx^ab
echo abyyzzxx
abyyzzxx
```

it replaced the characters xx with ab. This makes editing the previous command much easier.

% !!:s/xx/ab/

This is doing the same thing as the previous example, but it is using the substitute command instead of the ^. This works for any previous command, as in:

```
% more afile bfile
    ...
% echo xy
xy
% !m:s/b/c/
more afile cfile
```

You do not have to use the slashes (/); any character can act as a delimiter.

% !!:s:xy:yx

There we used the colons (:) [good when the word you're trying to edit contains a slash—JP]. If you want to add more to the replacement, use & to "replay it" and then add on whatever you like:

```
% echo xy
xy
% !!:s/xy/&xy
echo xyxy
xyxy
```

The & in the replacement part said to give what the search part found, which was the xy characters.

The search part, or left side, cannot include meta-characters (27.03). You must type the actual string you are looking for.

Also, the example above only replaces the first occurrence of xy. To replace them all, use g:

```
% echo xy xy xy xy
xy xy xy xy
```

```
% !!:s/xy/yx/
echo yx xy xy xy
yx xy xy xy
% !!:gs/xy/yx/
echo yx yx yx yx
yx yx yx yx
```

The *g* command in this case meant do all the xys. And oddly enough, the *g* has to come before the *s* command.

Or you could have done:

```
% echo xy xy xy xy
xy xy xy xy
% !!:s/xy/yx/
echo yx xy xy xy
yx xy xy xy
% !!:g&
echo yx yx yx yx
yx yx yx yx
```

In that case, we told the shell to globally (:g) replace every matched string from the last command with the last substitution (&). Without the *g* command, the shells would have replaced just one more xy with yx.

[A "global" substitution works just once per word:

```
% echo xyzzy
xyzzy
% !!:gs/y/p/
echo xpzzy
xpzzy
```

The substitution above changed only the first y. *—TC*]

—DR

12.08   *C Shell String Editing (Colon) Operators*

When the C shell does history substitutions *(12.07)* and variable substitutions *(7.08)*, it can also edit the substitution. For instance, in the first example below, when !$ contains /a/b/c, adding the "head" operator :h will give just the head of the pathname, /a/b.

For a complete but very terse list of these operators, see the *csh* manual page. We hope the examples below will help you understand these useful operators.

:h   Gives the head of a pathname *(15.02)*, as follows:

```
% echo /a/b/c
/a/b/c
% echo !$:h
echo /a/b
/a/b
```

That took off the filename and left the header. This also could be used with variables *(49.05)* as:

```
% set x=(/a/b/c)
% echo $x
/a/b/c
% echo $x:h
/a/b
```

:r   Returns the root of a filename:

```
% echo xyz.c abc.c
xyz.c abc.c
% echo !$:r
echo abc
abc
```

The :r removed the .c from the last argument, leaving the root name. This could also be used in variable names:

```
% set x=(abc.c)
% echo $x:r
abc
```

:g   For more than one name, you can add the *g* operator to make the operation global. For example:

```
% set x=(a.a b.b c.c)
% echo $x:gr
a b c
```

The :gr operator stripped off all dot (.) suffixes. By the way, this use of *g* does not work with the history commands.

This is the C shell's answer to the *basename(47.18)* command.

:e   Returns the extension (the part of the name after a dot). Using variables:

```
% set x=(abc.c)
% echo $x:e
c
```

No luck using that within history, either.

:t   Gives the tail of a pathname—the actual filename without the path:

```
% echo /a/b/c
/a/b/c
% echo !$:t
c
```

With variables:

```
% set x=(/a/b/c)
% echo $x:t
c
```

And with multiple pathnames, you can do it globally with:

```
% set x=(/a/b/c /d/e/f /g/h/i)
% echo $x:gt
c f i
```

While the corresponding heads would be:

```
% set x=(/a/b/c /d/e/f /g/h/i)
% echo $x:gh
/a/b /d/e /g/h
```

:p   Prints the command, but does not execute it:

```
% echo *
fn1 fn2 fn3
% !:p
echo fn1 fn2 fn3
```

The command is printed, but it is not executed *(12.11)*.

:q   Prevents further filename expansion, or prints the command as is:

```
% echo *
fn1 fn2 fn3
% !:q
echo *
*
```

The first command echoed the files in the directory, and when the :q was applied, it echoed only the special character.

:x   Like :q, but it breaks the line up in words. That is, when using :q, it is all one word, while :x will break it up into multiple words. [:q and :x are more often used with C shell arrays *(49.05)*. —*JP*]

—*DR*

12.09   *Repeating a Cycle of Commands*

The C shell !! history substitution gives a copy of the previous command. Most people use it to re-execute the previous command line. Sometimes I want to repeat a cycle of two commands, one after the other. To do that, I just type !-2 (second-previous command) over and over:

```
% vi plot
    ...
% vtroff -w plot
    ...
% !-2
vi plot
    ...
% !-2
vtroff -w plot
    ...
```

You can cycle through three commands with !-3, four commands with !-4, and so on. The best part is that if you can count, you never have to remember what to do next. :-)

—JP

12.10 Running a Series of Commands on a File

[There are times when history is not the best way to repeat commands. Here, Jerry gives an example where a few well-chosen aliases can make a sequence of commands, all run on the same file, even easier to execute.— TOR]

While I was writing the articles for this book, I needed to look through a set of files, one by one, and run certain commands on some of those files. I couldn't know which files would need which commands, or in what order. So I typed a few temporary aliases on the command line. Most of these run RCS *(21.14)* commands, but they could run any UNIX command (compilers, debuggers, printers, and so on):

```
% alias h 'set f="\!*";co -p "$f" | grep NOTE'
% alias o 'co -l "$f"'
% alias v 'vi "$f"'
% alias i 'ci -m"Fixed title." "$f"'
```

The *h* alias stores the filename in a shell variable *(7.08)*. Then it runs a command on that file. What's nice is that, after I use *h* once, I don't need to type the filename again. Other aliases get the filename from $f:

```
% h ch01_summary
% o
RCS/ch01_summary,v  -->  ch01_summary
revision 1.3 (locked)
done
% v
"ch01_summary" 23 lines, 1243 characters
    ...
```

Typing a new *h* command stores a new filename.

If you always want to do the same commands on a file, you can store all the commands in one alias:

```
% alias d 'set f="\!*"; co -l "$f" && vi "$f" && ci "$f"'
% d ch01_summary
```

The && (two ampersands) *(46.09)* means that the following command won't run unless the previous command returns a zero ("success") status. If you don't want that, use ; (semicolon) *(9.03)* instead of &&.

—JP

12.11 Check Your History First with :p

Here's how to be more sure of your history before you use it. First, some review of C shell history substitutions:

- !/ and !fra are replaced with the most recent command lines that started with / and fra, respectively.

- !?afile? is replaced with the most recent command line that contained afile anywhere on the line.

But if your memory is like mine (not very good), you might not be sure that !?afile? will bring back the command you want. You can test it by adding :p to the end. The shell will print the substitution but won't execute the command line. If you like what you got, type !! to execute it. For example:

```
% !?afile?:p
lp afile bfile cfile
% !!
lp afile bfile cfile
request id is 676
```

At the first prompt, the :p meant the command line was just printed. At the second prompt, I didn't use :p and the *lp* command was executed. The :p works with all history operators, not just with !? . . . ?.

—JP

12.12 Picking Up Where You Left Off

If you want your command history to be remembered even when you log out, set the *savehist* variable *(7.09)* to the number of lines of history you want saved.

When you log out, the specified number of lines from the history list will be saved in a file called *.history* in your home directory.

Sounds easy, and in the old days, it was. On modern windowing systems, this isn't as trivial as it sounds. On an old-style terminal, people usually started only one main shell, so they could set *savehist* in their *.login* file and have it apply to their login shell.

However, under window systems like X or networked filesystems that share your home directory between several hosts, you have multiple top-level shells. If you set *savehist* in each of them (e.g., by setting it in your *.cshrc*), they will all try to write *.history* at once, leading to trouble. And even if that weren't true, you'd get the history from every window or host, which might not be what you want.

Of course, you could set *savehist* manually in a single window when you thought you might be doing work you might want to pick up later. But there is another way: use the command *history −h* (which prints the history list without leading numbers, so it can be read back in later) and redirect the output to a file. Then use *source −h* to read it back into your history list when you log in.

Do you want to automate this? First, you'll need to choose a system of filenames, like ˜/.*history.window* or ˜/.*history.hostname*, to match each file to its window or host. If each of your C shells is a login shell* *(2.08)*, you can run *history −h* from your *.logout* file and *source −h* from your *.login* file. For non-login shells, automation is tougher—try this:

- Set the *ignoreeof* variable *(3.05)* to force you to leave the shell with an *exit* *(40.04)* command.

- Set an alias for *exit (11.06)* that runs *history −h* before exiting.

- Run *source −h* from your *.cshrc* file. Use a `$?prompt` test *(2.09)* to be sure this only runs in interactive shells.

If you choose to run *history −h* and *source −h* by hand occasionally, they will allow you the kind of control you need to write a script *(12.13)* that saves and restores only what you want.

—*TOR, JP*

12.13 Pass History to Another C Shell

The C shell automatically saves a history of the commands you type. You can add your own commands to that history list without retyping them. Why would you do that?

- You might have a set of commands that you want to be able to recall and reuse every time you log in. This can be more convenient than aliases because you don't have to think of names for the aliases. It's handier than a shell script if you need to do a series of commands but they aren't always in the same order.

- You might have several shells running (say, in several windows) and want to pass the history from one shell to another shell *(12.12)*.

Here's an example. Use the *history −h* command to save the history from a shell to a file. (Here, I'll add the number 20 to get just the most recent 20 commands, but you don't have to do that.) Edit the file to take out commands you don't want:

```
foo% mailx -s "Status report" bigboss
     ...
foo% history -h 20 > history.std
foo% vi history.std
     ...Clean up history...
```

---

*In the X Window System *(1.31)*, set the *xterm +ut* option (with a +, not a −) to force a login shell.

Read that file into another shell's history list with *source -h*:

```
bar% source -h history.std
bar% !ma
mailx -s "Status report" bigboss
```

—*JP*

12.14 Korn Shell Command-line Editing

If you make a typing mistake in your shell command line and press RETURN, it's gone. After you get the pesky error message, you'll have to type the whole thing in again—unless you happen to be using the C shell *and* happen to remember its Byzantine "history" commands *(12.02)*. If you use the Korn shell, you may know that it gives you a *vi*-like editing capability; if you've actually tried this, you probably agree that *vi* makes a lousy command-line editor. [I don't agree. :-) —*JP*]

However, fewer people know that the Korn shell has another editing mode, one that emulates the Emacs *(33.01)* editor. Although the Korn shell manual page used to describe emacs mode, for some reason it doesn't anymore (as of the version dated 11/16/88d, at least). The emacs mode editing commands act like a natural extension to traditional, simple shell editing commands (like Delete or Backspace for character erase), so even if you aren't familiar with the *emacs* editor, you should find emacs mode useful. To use emacs mode, put this line in your *.profile*:

```
set -o emacs
```

We'll cover only the most useful emacs mode commands here. For a more complete description, see the Nutshell Handbook *Learning the Korn Shell*, by Bill Rosenblatt.

Emacs mode figures out what your character-erase key *(6.09)* is and lets you use it in the same way. In addition, it gives you the basic commands for editing a line listed in Table 12-1.

Table 12-1. Korn Shell Emacs Mode Line Editing Commands

Command	Function
CTRL-b	Move backward one character (without deleting).
CTRL-f	Move forward one character.
CTRL-d	Delete one character forward.
CTRL-z	Move to beginning of line.
CTRL-e	Move to end of line.
CTRL-k	Delete ("kill") forward to end of line.
CTRL-w	Delete ("wipe") backward to beginning of line.
CTRL-y	Retrieve ("yank") last deleted item.
CTRL-c	Delete entire line.

In addition, emacs mode maintains a history file that enables you to recall previous commands. The commands in Table 12-2 are the most important of those that let you navigate the history file:

Table 12-2. Korn Shell Emacs Mode History Commands

Command	Function
CTRL-p	Go to previous command.
CTRL-n	Go to next command.
CTRL-r *string*	Search backward for command containing *string*.

The first of these is the most useful by far—it's the "I made a mistake, so I'll go back and fix it" key. The search capability lets you bring back specific commands you may have typed awhile ago without having to go through the history file line by line with CTRL-p. Just enter CTRL-r followed by a search string and RETURN, and the Korn shell will bring back the *most recent* command that contains the search string (or beep at you if it finds no match). Assuming it is the command you want, you would then press RETURN again to run the command. If you begin your search string with a caret (^), it will only match commands that begin with the search string; this will be familiar behavior to users of such UNIX tools as *grep, sed,* and *awk*.

Another extremely useful feature of emacs mode is the *filename completion* facility, which should be familiar to C shell experts as well as Emacs users (see article 10.06). Emacs mode supports two completion commands, the most useful of which is ESC ESC (the Escape key pressed twice). If you type in a word and press ESC ESC, the shell will search for a filename that begins with what you typed and try to finish it. If there is only one filename that begins with your word, the shell will complete the name. If there is more than one, it will only complete out as far as it can without having to make a choice.

For example, if your directory contained the file *program.c* and you typed `pro` followed by ESC ESC, the shell would automatically complete the filename and leave you an extra space. But if your directory also contained the file *program.o*, the shell would only complete out to `program.` and let you complete the filename yourself.

—*BR*

12.15 Editing Previous C Shell Command Lines

C shell history *(12.02)* isn't always easy to use. It's not interactive—that is, it's not easy to see the command you're about to execute until you run it. But there are some ways to make history manipulation a little easier.

One approach is to define some aliases to help you edit and re-execute a previous command line using the *ex* editor and its open mode *(31.36)*. These aliases were suggested by Dave Patterson. In 1987 on Usenet, he wrote: The following are the set of aliases I use for command-line editing in *csh*: *he* stands for "edit history number"—for example, he !121 will edit the 121st history command. [You can use the command name, too—as in he !grep, which will edit the previous *grep* command.—*JP*] *he* may also be used to edit an arbitrary string which then gets *sourced (46.22)*. *le* stands for "edit last command." *redo* will allow you to re-edit the last command you edited.

Here is an example. To start, I type a long *cp* command, press RETURN, then decide to copy another file from the same directory:

Keystrokes   **Result**

```
% cp /usr/foo/somedir/bar /tmp
% le
```
```
              "/home/jerry/.cmd" 1 line, 29 characters
              cp /usr/foo/somedir/bar /tmp
```
Start *ex* editor in its open mode on last command line.

```
2T/
```
```
              cp /usr/foo/somedir/bar /tmp
```
Move cursor back to the filename I want to change. (2T/ means "move back to the character just after the second-previous slash.")

```
cwblat ESC
```
```
              cp /usr/foo/somedir/blat /tmp
```
Change the word *bar* to *blat*.

```
ZZ
```
```
              "/home/jerry/.cmd" 1 line, 30 characters
```
Save the file with the ZZ command (:x or other commands would work, too). Execute the edited *cp* command line.

Here are the aliases:

csh_init

```
alias he 'echo \!*:q > ~/.cmd; ex - +open ~/.cmd; source ~/.cmd'
alias le 'echo \!-1:q > ~/.cmd; ex - +open ~/.cmd; source ~/.cmd'
alias redo 'ex - +open ~/.cmd; source ~/.cmd'
```

The thing I like about these aliases is that you can edit the command without clearing the screen. Often, all the editing takes place on one line at the bottom of the screen (or wherever the shell prompt is).

***

Note: Those aliases may have some problems on your system:

- The aliases use the command *ex* – to make the *ex* editor quieter. On some systems, that dash option changes the way that *ex* handles your terminal; the terminal can lock up or lines of text can march across the screen instead of starting at the left-hand side. If that happens to you, change the `ex` – to plain `ex`.

- The screen may clear when *ex* starts. An easy way to fix this is to temporarily use a terminal type *(6.11)* like *dumb* that doesn't have a screen-clear capability. Change the `ex` - `+open ~/.cmd` to (`setenv TERM dumb; ex` - `+open ~/.cmd`) instead.

- Some versions of *ex* don't understand the + command. The `ex +open` won't work. If that happens, use `ex` -`c open` instead.

***

[Another approach to this problem is to use *ksh* or *tcsh* *(1.08)* (a public-domain variation on *csh*), both of which have interactive history editing built-in. Still another approach is provided by the *redo* and *mced* commands *(12.16)*, which use a full-screen editor to edit any command from your saved history list.—*LM*]

—*JP, DP*

12.16 *More Ways to Do Interactive History Editing*

tcsh (1.08) is a version of *csh* that provides history editing (among other things). If you don't want to switch to *tcsh*, you can simulate history editing using either *redo* or *mced.*

redo is a C shell script that is run by being sourced into the current shell using an alias. The original version was posted to Usenet in the 1980s, author unknown. The version shown here was reposted in 1987 by Dave Patterson. The alias puts you in an *ex* editing buffer, a comfortable environment for *vi* users. You can browse through the previous 22 commands and press RETURN when you want to execute the current line. Before executing, you can edit the commands as you would in *vi.* You can even search for strings using /; just remember to press ESC instead of RETURN after the search string.

To use *redo*, first install it read-only with *no* execute permission *(23.02)*, and then create an alias with the script's absolute pathname *(15.02)* to execute it.

```
alias r source ~/.lib/redo
```

When you run the alias, it reads a set of commands from the sourceable script file *(11.05)*.

redo

Here's the *redo* script:

```
history -h 22 >! /tmp/redo.$$

# Put CR in $c[1] and ESC in $c[2]:
set c=(`echo "m e" | tr me '\015\033'`)
# Make CR map to :wq! and start ex quietly at 2nd to last line in open mode.
(setenv EXINIT "map $c[1] :.wq\!$c[2]|map! $c[1] ${c[2]}:.wq\!$c[2]";\
     ex '+$-1 open' /tmp/redo.$$)
tail -1 /tmp/redo.$$ >! /tmp/cmd.$$

# Insert into history without executing.
source -h /tmp/cmd.$$

# Clear out temporaries.
/bin/rm -f /tmp/{cmd,redo}.$$
unset c

# If thing chosen to redo is the redo alias itself then DON'T redo it.
if (!-2:0 != !!:0) !!
```

Type r to invoke the alias. Then use cursor motion keys (jk) to get to the line you want to edit. Edit the line (remember that you're in the open mode *(31.36)* of *ex*). When you're done, press RETURN. (Don't type ZZ or q.)

mced

redo effectively simulates using the *vi* editor on your C shell history. The other alternative, *mced*, provides support for both *vi* and *emacs* users.

Like *redo*, *mced* requires an alias to use it. This alias is lengthy, but just put it in your *.cshrc* and you'll only have to type it once:

csh_init

```
alias = "history -h 50 >\! /tmp/eh$$;mced \!*; source -h /tmp/ec$$;
     source /tmp/ec$$;/bin/rm /tmp/ec$$"
```

(Type all of that alias on a single line—or get it from the Power Tools disk. We've broken it onto two lines for printing.)

Then when you want to edit your command history, type the = command:

```
% =
```

mced takes over your screen and your last command appears with the %McEd% prompt:

```
%McEd% more README
```

You can use either *vi* or *emacs* commands to go up to another command and edit it. (*mced* will read the *EDITOR (7.03)* environment variable to decide which editor to use.) Then you can execute the edited command by pressing RETURN.

—*LM*

12.17 Changing C Shell History Characters with histchars

The existence of special characters (particularly !) can be a pain; you may often need to type commands that have exclamation points in them, and occasionally need commands with carets (^). These get the C shell confused unless you "quote" them properly. If you use these special characters often, you can choose different ones by setting the *histchars* variable. *histchars* is a two-character string; the first character replaces the exclamation point (the "history" character), and the second character replaces the caret (the "modification" character *(12.05)*). For example:

```
% set histchars='@#'
% ls file*
file1    file2    file3
% @@                              Repeat previous command (was !!)
ls file*
file1    file2    file3
% #file#data                      Edit previous command (was ^file^data^)
ls data*
data4    data5
```

An obvious point: you can set *histchars* to any characters you like, but it's a good idea to choose characters that you aren't likely to use often on command lines. Two good choices might be # (hash mark)* and , (comma).

—ML

12.18 Instead of Changing History Characters

If you need to use ! (or your current history character) for a command (most often, a *uucp* or *mail (1.33)* command), you can type a backslash (\) before each history character. You can also drop into the Bourne shell quickly. Either of these are probably easier than changing *histchars*. For example:

```
% mail ora\!ishtar\!sally < file1        Quote the !s
% sh                                      Start the Bourne shell
$ mail ora!ishtar!sally < file1           ! not special here
$ exit                                    Quit the Bourne shell
%                                         And back to the C shell
```

The Bourne shell doesn't have any kind of history substitution, so ! doesn't mean anything special; it's just a regular character.

By the way, if you have a window system, you can probably copy and paste the command line instead of using shell history.

—ML

---

*In the C shell, # is a comment character *(46.02)* only in non-interactive shells. Using it as a history character doesn't conflict because history isn't enabled in non-interactive shells.

13

Job Control

13.01 Job Control: Work Faster; Stop Runaway Jobs

Multi-tasking, letting you run more than one program at a time, is one of the great things about UNIX. Before job control, though, you had to decide ahead of time whether you wanted to run a job in the foreground (on your screen) or in the background (where you couldn't touch the program except to terminate it before it finished).

The C shell—and other shells since it, including some new Bourne shells—have job control built into them. You can start and stop jobs, pop them in and out of the background, and more. Windowing systems, which let you have multiple terminal windows active on the screen at the same time, make this less essential. Still, there are some important areas where you'll get more productivity out of job control than from simply opening another window. This article is an introduction to job control—there's more to learn.

Job control takes more than a shell to work right: the UNIX kernel has to support it. Berkeley UNIX since BSD 4.0 has had job control, so most Berkeley-type UNIXes will have it, too. Most versions of UNIX System V before Release 4 did not have job control. If your UNIX doesn't support job control, you can still put a job in the background—see the last paragraph in this article.

Foreground and Background

UNIX distinguishes between foreground and background programs. This feature allows you to run several programs simultaneously from your terminal. When a program is running in the foreground, anything you type at the keyboard is sent to the program's standard input unless you have redirected it. As a result, you can't do anything else until the program finishes. When you run a program in the background, it is disconnected from the keyboard. Anything you type reaches the UNIX shell and is interpreted as a command. Therefore, you can run many programs simultaneously in the background. You can only run one program at a time in the foreground.

To run a program in the background, type an ampersand (&) at the end of the command line. For example:

```
% f77 program.F &
[1] 9145
%
```

This runs a FORTRAN compilation in the background, letting you continue other work while the compilation proceeds. The shell responds by printing a job number in brackets ([ ]), followed by the process identification (PID) number *(40.03)* for the command. It then prompts you for a new command. Entering the command *jobs* produces a short report describing all the programs you are executing in the background. For example:

```
% f77 program.F &
[1] 9145
% jobs
[1]      + Running        f77 program.F
%
```

To bring a program from the background into the foreground, use the foreground command, *fg*. If you have more than one background job, follow *fg* with a job identifier—a percent sign (%) followed by the job number:

```
% jobs
[1]      - Running        f77 program.F
[2]      + Stopped        vi sinus.F
% fg %1
```

The plus sign (+) in the report from *jobs* indicates which job will return to the foreground by default *(13.03)*.

To suspend a job running in the foreground, press CTRL-z. This stops the program but does *not* terminate it. [You can use this to stop most frozen or runaway programs until you figure out what to do next. Also, CTRL-z can stop programs that interrupt characters *(6.09)* like CTRL-c can't. —*JP*]

Entering the background command, *bg*, lets a stopped program continue execution in the background. The foreground command, *fg*, restores this program to execution in the foreground. For example:

```
% f77 -o program program.F
CTRL-z
Stopped
% bg
[1]      + Running        f77 -o program program.F
%
```

There is no prompt after the *f77* command because the compiler is running in the foreground. After you press CTRL-z, the shell prints the word "Stopped" to indicate that it has stopped execution. At this point, you can enter any command; the *bg* command lets the job continue executing in the background. This feature is useful if you forget to type an & at the end of the command line or if you decide to do something else while the job is running.

To terminate a background job, you can use the command's job number rather than its PID number, as follows:

    % kill %1

Remember to include the % before the job number! If you omit it, UNIX interprets the job number as a process number. This will probably be the process number of some operating system function. UNIX will not let you make such a mistake unless you are superuser *(1.24)*. If you are superuser, the command is fatal. You may be superuser from time to time and therefore should not develop sloppy habits.

In the next few seconds, press RETURN a few times. You should see the message:

    [1] Terminated   f77 -o program program.F

If you don't see that, use the *jobs* command to check whether the job is still running. If it's still running, use the *−9* option as a last resort:

    % kill -9 %1
    [1] Killed   f77 -o program program.F

The *−9* option doesn't give the process a chance to clean up its temporary files and exit gracefully, so don't use it unless you need to.

A program running in the background cannot read input from a terminal. If a background job needs terminal input, it will stop; the *jobs* command will print the message `Stopped (tty input)`. Before the program can continue, you must bring it into the foreground with the *fg* command and type the required input. You can save yourself this trouble by redirecting the program's input so that it reads all its data from a file. You may also want to redirect standard output and standard error. If you don't, any output the program produces will appear on your terminal (unless you've used *stty tostop (13.07)*). Since you will probably be using other commands, having miscellaneous data and other messages flying across your terminal may be confusing.

On systems and shells without job control features, an & will start a command in the background. It is impossible to move a job from the foreground to the background or vice versa. The *ps (40.05)* command is the only tool available for determining what background jobs you have running.

—*ML* from the Nutshell Handbook *UNIX for FORTRAN Programmers*

13.02 Other Ways to Refer to Jobs

If you have several jobs in the background, you can refer to them by job number, as listed by the *jobs (13.01)* command. For example:

```
% jobs
[1]  + Stopped              vi TODO
[2]  - Running              nroff -ms ch01
% kill %2
% fg %1
```

You don't need to look up the job number to select a job, though. Instead, you can specify a job by name. Simply specify the command name instead of the job number after the percent sign. For example, the commands above could have been issued as:

```
% kill %nroff
% fg %vi
```

If you use %?, you can specify any unique part of the job's command line. What the manual fails to point out is that if you do this, you may need to quote *(9.10)* the question mark, since it's also a shell wildcard. If you don't, you may get the message No match. You could type one of the following commands:

```
% kill %?ch01              No quoting (normal)
% kill %\?ch01             Quoted (in some cases)
```

to kill the *nroff* job shown in the example above.

There are a couple of other shortcuts as well. A job number by itself is the same as the *fg* command followed by that job number. Why type:

```
% fg %3
```

when:

```
% %3
```

will do?

You can put a stopped job into the background in a similar way. For example:

```
% %2 &
```

will put job number 2 into the background.

Of course, it's also true that typing fg or bg without a job number can save you time if there is only one job, or if you want to refer to the current job.

The only problem is that the current job isn't always what you expect *(13.03)*.

—TOR

13.03 The "Current Job" isn't Always What You Expect

% is the "current" stopped or background job, but *not* always the *last* one. If you've stopped any jobs, the current job is the most-recently stopped job. Otherwise, it's the most recent background job. For example, try stopping your editor (like *vi*), then putting another job in the background:

```
% vi afile
CTRL-z
Stopped
% sleep 1000 &
[2] 12345
% fg
```

and notice that the fg brings your editor to the foreground.

—JP

13.04 Job Control and autowrite: Real Time Savers!

I see too many people using a series of commands like the ones below. Programmers do this when they write and compile programs. Writers use this when they're making a draft file and running it through the formatter. They're probably wasting a lot of time and effort:

```
% vi somefile
        ...Edit somefile, then quit vi...
% someprog somefile
        ...Process somefile...
% vi somefile
        ...Edit somefile again...
% someprog somefile
        ...Process somefile again...
```

Each time they restart *vi*, they have to reset options and move the cursor to the place they were working before. After they restart, *vi* has forgotten the previous search (the *n* command), the previous action (the **.** command), the previous regular expression, the named and numbered buffers...

If your system has job control *(13.08)*, that'll solve all these problems.* Instead of quitting *vi*, get into command mode and write your buffer with the :w command. Stop the editor with the CTRL-z command. Then, process the file. When you're ready to do more editing, bring your *vi* job back into the foreground with *fg*. The editor will be just where it was.

Even better, you can set *vi*'s option called *autowrite*. If you've made any changes to the buffer before you press CTRL-z, *vi* will automatically write the buffer. You won't need to remember to type :w before you stop the editor. You can set *autowrite* at a colon (:) prompt, but I set it in my *.exrc* file *(5.09)* instead.

---

*If it doesn't, you can still use a shell escape *(31.26)*.

[You don't absolutely have to write your file before suspending *vi*. It's a good piece of advice, but not required by the job control mechanism. Typing CTRL-z will suspend the editor whether you've written out your files or not.— *TOR*]

—JP

13.05 System Overloaded? Try Stopping some Jobs

If your computer is barely crawling, you can *kill (40.10)* some processes . . . but you'll have to start them again later. On a Berkeley system, you can *renice (41.11)* the processes . . . but you won't be able to raise the priority again later, after the system speeds up, unless you're the superuser *(1.24)*.

If you don't need your results right away (and you won't get them, anyway, if the system is crawling!), try stopping *(13.08)* some jobs. The best candidates are "CPU-eaters" like formatters *(45.13)*, compilers *(54.08)*, and any job that runs up a lot of time quickly in the *ps (40.05)* or *time (41.02)* reports. Start them again, later, and the jobs will take up where they left off.

—JP

13.06 Notification when Jobs Change State

Normally, the shell tells you about changes to your background jobs whenever it prints its prompt. That is, when you do something that makes the shell give you a prompt, you'll get a message like:

```
[1]  + Stopped (tty input)    rm -r
%
```

This message tells you that the *rm -r* command, which you're running in the background, needs input; it has probably asked you whether or not to delete a read-only file, or something similar.

This default behavior is usually what you want. By waiting until it prints a prompt, the shell minimizes "damage" to your screen. If you want to be notified immediately when a job changes state, you should set the shell variable *notify*:

```
% set notify
```

The drawback, of course, is that you may be analyzing a screenful of output that you've laboriously constructed, only to have that screen "destroyed" by a lot of messages from the shell. Therefore, most users prefer to leave *notify* off (unset). To stop all background output, use *stty tostop (13.07)*.

—ML

13.07 Stop Background Output with stty tostop

If you put a job in the background *(1.26)* and don't redirect *(14.01)* its output, text that the job writes to its standard output and standard error will come to your screen. Those messages can mess up the screen while you're using another program. You could lose the (maybe important) messages, too—they might scroll off your screen and be lost, or your foreground program may clear the screen and erase them.

Most BSD UNIX systems, and a lot of newer UNIXes with job control, have the command *stty tostop*. Type that command at a prompt, or put it in your *.login* or *.profile* file *(2.01)*.* After that, your shell's background jobs that try to write to your terminal will be stopped. When you want to see the background job's output, bring it into the foreground (with *fg*).

How will you know that the background job has been stopped? The shell will print a message like this just before it prints a prompt:

```
[1] + Stopped (tty output)     somejob
%
```

The shell can also interrupt your foreground job with that message as soon as the background job is stopped. To make it do that, set the *notify (13.06)* shell variable.

You can turn off this feature and let background jobs write to your terminal any time with the command:

```
% stty -tostop
```

Article 43.02 has more about *stty*.

—*JP*

13.08 Job Control in a Nutshell

Unless otherwise noted, these commands apply only to the C shell and the Korn shell:

- *command* & *(1.26, 13.01)*: Run *command* in the background. You can continue to execute jobs in the foreground. All shells.

- CTRL-c *(40.09)*: Kill the current foreground job by sending the *INTR* signal *(40.08)*. All shells.

- CTRL-z *(13.01, 13.04)*: Suspend the current foreground job by sending the *TSTP* signal *(40.08)*.

- bg %*num (13.01)*: Let a stopped job (by job number *num*) continue in the background.

*This command sets the UNIX terminal device driver *(44.01)* for all processes started on it. You don't need to set this for subshells *(2.02)*.

- `fg %num` *(13.01)*: Put a background job or a stopped job (by job number *num*) into the foreground.

- `kill %num` *(13.01)*: Kill an arbitrary background job (by job number *num*).

- `kill pid` *(40.10)*: Kill an arbitrary job (by process ID number *num*). All shells.

- `jobs` *(13.01)*: List background and stopped jobs and their job numbers.

- `set notify` *(13.06)*: Immediate job-state change notices.

- `stty tostop` *(13.07)*: Automatically stop background processes if they try writing to the screen.

—*ML*

13.09 *Running Multiple Shell Sessions with screen*

screen

An interesting alternative to job control *(13.01)* is the *screen* program, which lets you run several shell sessions from the same terminal, switching between them at will.

For example, often when I'm logged in I want to reply to a mail message *(1.33)* but I need to test something first. Currently, I have to get out of *mail* to do it, or start a shell escape *(31.26)* within *mail*. But using the *screen* program, I could just switch back and forth between shells. I could run *mail* in one shell, test things in another, edit a file in a third, etc. — up to 10 shells in all.

Once you start up *screen*, a full screen disclaimer appears (which can be disabled by configuring *$HOME/.screenrc*). After pressing SPACE or RETURN, you'll be placed in an initial shell with your usual system prompt. This shell is screen number 0.

Screen 0:

```
lmui@ruby 26%
```

I can use this shell to read my mail.

Screen 0:

```
lmui@ruby 26% mail
Mail version SMI 4.0 Wed Oct 23 10:38:28 PDT 1991  Type ? for help.
"/usr/spool/mail/lmui": 42 messages 6 new
    ...
  N 38 kramer   Wed Oct 28 10:31   20/654   Posting on comp.unix.que
```

```
N 39 tim      Wed Oct 28 10:46    39/1485   Re: awf
N 40 tim      Wed Oct 28 10:47    26/832    Re: announcement of vol8
&
```

Now, suppose I read a mail message asking my opinion about a news posting. Rather than get out of mail to read news before I respond, I can just start a new shell using CTRL-a CTRL-c and start up a news reader there. This new window is screen number 1.

Screen 1:

```
lmui@ruby 26% rn comp.unix.questions
Unread news in comp.unix.questions                        333 articles

******** 333 unread articles in comp.unix.questions--read now? [ynq]
```

Once I read the article in question, I switch back to the previous shell using CTRL-a CTRL-a and start to respond to the mail message:

Screen 0:

```
>  38 kramer    Wed Oct 28 10:31    20/654    Posting on comp.unix.que
N  39 tim       Wed Oct 28 10:46    39/1485   Re: awf
N  40 tim       Wed Oct 28 10:47    26/832    Re: announcement of vol8
& r
To: kramer@ora.com
Subject: Re: Posting on comp.unix.questions

He's right that you can use -i for interactive prompting, but
I don't think -f disables interactive mode.
```

Now, suppose I want to check my facts before I continue writing the message. Rather than quit my message or start a subshell, I can just start up yet another shell window by pressing CTRL-a CTRL-c again. Then I can run the commands I want to test. Once I have my information, I can go back to the previous shell using CTRL-a CTRL-a again, or using CTRL-a 0 to explicitly call up screen number 0.

One of the really neat things about *screen* is that it even lets you "detach" a screen, so that you can log out, then go home and pick up where you left off, using a different terminal *(3.07)*.

—*LM*

14

Redirecting Input and Output

14.01 Using Standard Input and Output

There is absolutely no difference between reading data from a file and reading data from a terminal.* Likewise, if a program's output consists entirely of alphanumeric characters and punctuation, there is no difference between writing to a file, writing to a terminal, and writing to the input of another program (as in a pipe).

The *standard I/O* facility provides some simple defaults for managing Input/Output. There are three default I/O streams: standard input, standard output, and standard error. By convention, standard output (abbreviated *stdout*) consists of all "normal" output from your program, while standard error (*stderr*) consists of error messages. It is often a convenience to be able to handle error messages and standard output separately. If you don't do anything special, programs will read standard input from your keyboard, and they will send standard output and standard error to your terminal's display.

Standard input (*stdin*) normally comes from your keyboard. Many programs ignore *stdin*; you name files directly on their command line—for instance, the command *cat file1 file2* never reads its standard input; it reads the files directly. But, without filenames on the command line, UNIX commands that need input will usually read *stdin*. Standard input normally comes from your keyboard, but the shell can redirect *stdin* from a file. This is handy for UNIX commands that can't open files directly—for instance, *mail (1.33)*. To mail a file to *joan*, use *< filename*—to tell the shell to attach the file, instead of your keyboard, to *mail*'s standard input:

```
% mail joan < myfile
```

The real virtue of standard I/O is that it allows you to *redirect* input or output away from your terminal to a file. As we said, UNIX is file-based *(1.29)*. Because

---

*If a program's input consists entirely of alphanumeric characters and punctuation (i.e., ASCII data or international (non-English) characters).

terminals and other I/O devices are treated as files, a program doesn't care or even know if it is sending its output to a terminal or to a file. For example, if you want to run the command *cat file1 file2*, but you want to place the output in *file3* rather than sending it to your terminal, give the command:

```
% cat file1 file2 > file3
```

This is called *redirecting* standard output to *file3*. If you give this command and look at *file3* afterward, you will find the contents of *file1*, followed by *file2*—exactly what you would have seen on your screen if you omitted the `> file3` modifier.

One of the best-known forms of redirection in UNIX is the *pipe*. The shell's vertical bar (|) operator makes a pipe. For example, to send both *file1* and *file2* together in a mail message for *joan*, type:

```
% cat file1 file2 | mail joan
```

The pipe says "connect the standard output of the process at the left (`cat`) to the standard input of the process at the right (`mail`)."

Article 47.20 has diagrams and more information about standard I/O and redirection. Table 14-1 shows the most common ways of redirecting standard I/O, for both the C shell and the Bourne shell.

Table 14-1. Common Standard I/O Redirections

Function	csh	sh, ksh
Send *stdout* to *file*	prog > file	prog > file
Send *stderr* to *file*		prog 2> file
Send *stdout* and *stderr* to *file*	prog >& file	prog > file 2>&1
Take *stdin* from *file*	prog < file	prog < file
Send *stdout* to end of *file*	prog >> file	prog >> file
Send *stderr* to end of *file*		prog 2>> file
Send *stdout* and *stderr* to end of *file*	prog >>& file	prog >> file 2>&1
Read *stdin* from keyboard until *c* (see article 9.14)	prog <<c	prog <<c
Pipe *stdout* to *prog2*	prog | prog2	prog | prog2
Pipe *stdout* and *stderr* to *prog2*	prog |& prog2	prog 2>&1 | prog2

Be aware that:

- While standard I/O is a basic feature of UNIX, the syntax used to redirect standard I/O depends on the shell you are using. Bourne shell syntax and C shell syntax differ, particularly when you get into the less commonly used features. The Korn shell is the same as the Bourne shell, but with a few twists of its own.

- You can redirect standard input and standard output in the same command line. For example, to read from the file *input* and write to the file *output*, give the command:

```
% prog < input > output
```

The Bourne shell will let you go further and write *stderr* to a third file:

```
% prog < input > output 2> errors
```

- The C shell doesn't give you an easy way to redirect standard output without redirecting standard error. A simple trick will help you do this. To put standard output and standard error in different files, give a command like:

```
% ( prog > output ) >& errors
```

We'll discuss commands like this in articles 14.03 and 14.05.

- Many implementations of both shells don't care what order the redirections appear in, or even where they appear on the command line. For example, SunOS lets you type `< input > output prog`. However, clarity is always a virtue that computer users have never appreciated enough. It will be easiest to understand what you are doing if you type the command name first—then redirect standard input, followed by standard output, followed by standard error.

There are some more complex forms of standard I/O redirection, particularly for the Bourne shell *(47.21, 47.22, 47.23)*.

Of course, programs aren't restricted to standard I/O. They can open other files, define their own special-purpose pipes, and write directly to the terminal. But standard I/O is the glue that allows you to make big programs out of smaller ones, and is therefore a crucial part of the operating system. Most UNIX utilities read their data from standard input and write their output to standard output, allowing you to combine them easily. A program that creates its own special-purpose pipe may be very useful, but it cannot be used in combination with standard utilities.

—ML, JP

14.02 *One Argument with a cat Isn't Enough*

What's wrong with this command line?

```
% cat filename | tr -d '\015' > newfile
```

As Tom Christiansen wrote in a Usenet article:

> A wise man once said: if you find yourself calling *cat* with just one argument, then you're probably doing something you shouldn't.

That command line only uses *cat* to feed the file to the standard input of *tr*. It's a lot more efficient to have the shell do the redirection for you with its < character *(14.01)*:

```
% tr -d '\015' < filename > newfile
```

—JP, TC

14.03 Send (only) Standard Error Down a Pipe

A vertical bar character (|) on a command line pipes the standard output of a process to another process. How can you pipe the standard error, not the standard output? You might want to put a long-running *cruncher* command in the background, save the output to a file, and mail yourself a copy of the errors. In the C shell, run the command in a subshell *(14.07)*. The standard output of the command is redirected inside the subshell. All that's left outside the subshell is the standard error; the | & operator *(14.05)* redirects it (along with the empty standard output) to the *mail (1.33)* program:

```
% (cruncher > outputfile) |& mail yourname &
[1] 12345
```

Of course, you don't need to put that job in the background *(1.26)*. If you want the standard output to go to your terminal instead of a text file, use */dev/tty (47.20)* as the `outputfile`.

The Bourne shell gives you a lot more flexibility and lets you do just what you need. The disadvantage is the more complicated syntax. Here's how to run your *cruncher* program, route the *stderr* through a pipe to the *mail* program, and leave *stderr* going to your screen:

```
$ (cruncher 3>&1 1>&2 2>&3) | mail yourname &
12345
```

To redirect *stdout* to an output file and send *stderr* down a pipe, try this:

```
$ (cruncher 3>&1 >outputfile 2>&3) | mail yourname &
12345
```

—JP

14.04 Problems Piping to a Pager

If your window onto UNIX (terminal, X window, communications program, whatever) doesn't have a way to show you the previous screenful, using a pager program like *more (26.03)*, *pg*, or *less (26.04)* can be mighty handy. But piping to a pager doesn't always work the way you want it to.

Here's a *grep* command line that searches several files. What's wrong with it?

```
% grep "^set" */.cshrc | more
```

That wasn't a fair question because you can't tell what's wrong. The problem (it turns out) is that the files named *barney/.cshrc*, *edie/.cshrc*, and *gail/.cshrc* are read-protected *(23.02)*. But, as the first part of Figure 14-1 shows, the error messages scroll off your screen and the pager doesn't stop them.

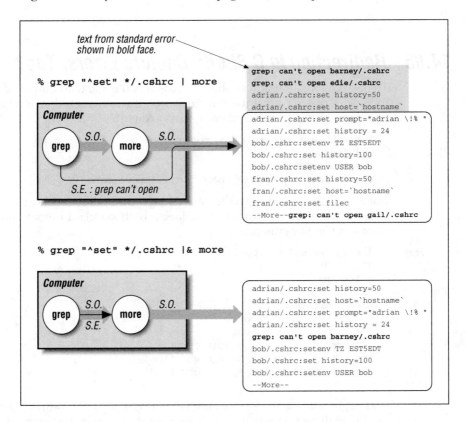

Figure 14-1. *Standard Error Bypassing Pipe, Going Through Pipe*

Unless your display is reallllly sloooowww, the error messages are lost and you never know they were there. Or the errors are jumbled up with the "good" *grep* output. That's because you've told the shell to send only the standard output of *grep* to the pager program. And *grep* writes its errors to the standard error *(47.20)*! But both *stdout* and *stderr* go to the screen at once. The errors on *stderr* scroll away with the output from the pager. The pager can't count the lines of errors so it outputs a complete screenful of *stdout* (the "good stuff"). If *grep*'s standard output (from the files it could read) is at least a screenful, as it is here, there are too many lines to fit on the screen—and some lines will scroll off.

The better way to do this is to combine *grep*'s *stdout* and *stderr* and give them both to the pager. These command lines (in *csh* and *sh*) both do that:

```
% grep "^set" */.cshrc |& more
$ grep "^set" */.cshrc 2>&1 | more
```

The second part of Figure 14-1 shows how this works. Any time I pipe a command's output to a pager, I usually combine the *stdout* and *stderr* this way.

—*JP*

14.05 *Redirection in C Shell: Capture Errors, Too?*

The > (right angle bracket) operator redirects the standard output of a process to a file. It doesn't affect the standard error. If you're logged in and can see any messages written to standard error, that's okay:

```
% nroff -ms report.ms > report.out &
[1] 10316
     ...Later...
nroff: can't open file /hoem/jerry/report.data
```

But if you log out and leave the job running, you'll never see those errors unless you use the *csh* operator >&. It redirects both standard output and standard error to a file. For example:

make *29.12*
```
% make >& make.output &
[1] 10329
% logout
      ...Later...
% cat make.output
         cc -O -c random.c
         cc -O -c output.c
"output.c", line 46: syntax error
"output.c", line 50: time_e undefined
"output.c", line 50: syntax error
     ...
```

You might also use the >& operator while you're logged in—and watch the output file with *tail* −*f (26.17)*. If you don't want the errors mixed with other output, you can split them to two files; see article 14.01.

The C shell also has a pipe operator, | &, that redirects both standard output and standard error. It's great for running a job in the background, or on another computer, and mailing *(1.33)* any output to me:

```
% make |& mailx -s "'make bigprog' output" jerry@ora.com &
[1] 29182 29183
```

If I'd used plain | instead of | &, any text on the standard error wouldn't go into the mail message.

—*JP*

14.06 Safe I/O Redirection with csh noclobber Variable

Have you ever destroyed a file accidentally? The *noclobber* shell variable can help you avoid these mistakes. It prevents you from destroying a file when you are redirecting standard output *(14.01)*.

Consider the following situation:

```
% anycommand > outputfile
```

The command above destroys the old *outputfile* and creates a new one. If you have misspelled the name of your output file, or if you have forgotten that the file already exists and contains important data, or (most common) if you really meant to type >> instead of > (i.e., if you really meant to append to the end of *outputfile*, rather than start a new one), tough luck; your old data is gone.

Setting the variable *noclobber* prevents this problem. If *noclobber* exists, the C shell will not allow I/O redirection to destroy an existing file, unless you explicitly tell it to by adding an exclamation point (!) after the redirect symbol. Here's an example:

```
% ls
filea fileb
% anyprogram > fileb
fileb: File exists.
% anyprogram >! fileb
%
```

[Be sure to put space after the !. If you don't, the shell thinks you're making a history reference and it (usually) prints an error like `fileb: Event not found.` —JP]

Note: In some C shells, *noclobber* will prevent you from redirecting standard output to */dev/null(14.14)* or to a terminal unless you add the !.

The *noclobber* variable has one other feature that's worth noting. Normally, the C shell lets you append to a file that doesn't exist. If *noclobber* is set, it won't; you can only append to files that already exist unless you use an exclamation point:

```
% ls
filea fileb
% anyprogram >> filec
filec: No such file or directory
% anyprogram >>! filec
%
```

Remember that *noclobber* is a shell variable, not an environment variable. Therefore, any new shells you create won't inherit it *(7.08)*. If you want to enable *noclobber* for every shell you create, add the line `set noclobber` to the *.cshrc* file *(2.02)* in your home directory.

—ML

14.07 The ( ) Subshell Operators

A useful shell trick is to use parentheses, ( ), to group commands.

Combining Several Commands

The output of the entire group can be passed together into a single pipeline. For example:

echo *9.04*

```
$ (cat file1; echo .bp; cat file2) | nroff
```

This will interpose the *nroff (45.14)* .bp (break page) request between two files to be formatted.*

Parentheses are also very useful in the Bourne shell if you want to put an entire sequence of commands separated by semicolons into the background. In the C shell, the command line below will go immediately into the background.

& 1.26

```
% nroff -ms file1; nroff -ms file2 &
```

But in the Bourne shell, the background request (&) will only apply to the second command, forcing you to wait for completion of the first job before you get back the system prompt. To get right back to work, you can type:

```
$ (nroff -ms file1; nroff -ms file2) &
```

Temporary Change of Directory and Environment

The parentheses start a subshell *(40.04)*. Commands that run between the parentheses won't affect the parent shell's environment. For instance, to run a command in another directory without changing your active shell's current directory *(40.03)*:

```
% pwd
/home/trent
% (cd /somewhere/else; nroff -ms file1 > file.out) &
[1] 22670
% pwd
/home/trent
```

The file *file.out* will be created in the */somewhere/else* directory.

—*TOR*

---

*If you're using only *cat* and a single *echo*, you can use this command instead:

```
$ echo .bp | cat file1 - file2 | nroff
```

The *cat* – option *(14.13)* tells *cat* to read its standard input (in this case, from the pipe and the *echo*) at that point. *nroff* gets exactly the same input.

14.08   Using {list} to Group Bourne Shell Commands

A lot of people know that you can group the output of a series of commands by using a subshell *(14.07)*. That is, instead of this:

```
$ date > log
$ who >> log
$ ls >> log
```

they start a subshell with parentheses:

> *10.11*

```
$ (date
> who
> ls) > log
```

and only redirect once to *log*. But a subshell takes an extra process and takes time to start on a busy system. If all you need to do is redirect output (or input) of a set of commands, use the Bourne shell's list operators { } (curly braces):

```
$ { date
> who
> ls
> } > log
```

Notice the spaces and the extra RETURN at the end. Each command in a list has to be separated from others. You can also write:

```
$ { date; who; ls; } > log
```

Notice the semicolon after the last command.

Two other differences between the subshell (parentheses) and list (curly braces) operators are:

- A *cd* command in the subshell doesn't change the parent shell's current directory; it does in a list.

- A variable set in a subshell isn't passed to the parent shell; from a list, the variable is passed out.

Note: Jonathan I. Kamens points out that some Bourne shells may run a list in a subshell anyway, especially if there's a pipe involved. If your Bourne shell works like the example below, it's using a subshell, too:

```
$ { echo frep; foo=bar; } | cat
frep
$ echo $foo

$ { echo frep; foo=bar; }
frep
$ echo $foo
bar
```

–JP

14.09 Send Output Two or More Places with tee

If you're running a program and you want to send its output to a file—but you want to see the output on your screen, too, so you can stop the program if something goes wrong—you can use *tee*. The *tee* program reads its standard input and writes it to one or more files.

Note: A pipe may *buffer* the output of a program, collecting it in chunks and spitting it out every so often. If the program's output comes slowly and feeds *tee* through a pipe, there might be long delays before you see any output. In that case, it's better to use > to redirect output to a file, put the program into the background, and watch the output with *tail –f (26.17)*. Or use a program like *script (53.05)*.

Use *tee* for saving results in the middle of a long pipeline of commands. That's especially good for debugging. For example, you could type:

```
% prog | tee prog.out | sed -f sedscr | tee sed.out | ...
```

to save the output of *prog* in the file *prog.out* and also pipe it to the *sed* command, save *sed*'s output in *sed.out* and also pipe it . . .

If you want to add to a file that already exists, use the *–a* option:

```
... tee -a filename ...
```

—*JP*

14.10 How to tee Several Commands into One File

The *tee (14.09)* command writes its standard input to a file and writes the same text to its standard output. You might want to collect several commands' output and *tee* them all to the same file, one after another. The obvious way to do that is with the *–a* option:

```
$ some-command | tee teefile
$ another-command | tee -a teefile
$ a-third-command | tee -a teefile
```

A more efficient way is:

```
$ (some-command
> another-command
> a-third-command) | tee teefile
```

> 10.11

The subshell operators *(14.07)* collect the standard output of the three commands. The output all goes to one *tee* command. The effect is the same—but with two less pipes, two fewer *tee*s (and one more subshell).

Unfortunately, the C shell doesn't make this quite as easy. If you can type all the commands on one line, you can do it this way (the same thing works in the Bourne shell):

```
% (command1; command2; command3) | tee teefile
```

Otherwise, use a semicolon and backslash (; \) at the end of each line:

```
% (some-command ;\
another-command ;\
a-third-command) | tee teefile
```

—*JP*

14.11 tpipe—Redirecting stdout to More than One Place

tpipe

What if you want to use the output of a program twice, and you don't want to deal with an intermediary file? Try the *tpipe* program.

tpipe is similar to *tee (14.09)*, but instead of putting a copy of standard input in a file, it passes the input to a new pipe. You could simulate *tpipe* by using *tee* and running the commands on the *tee* file, but there are instances when you don't want to clutter up your disk with files.

For example, suppose I have some large, compressed PostScript files. I want to print the files, but I also want to know how many pages they are. I know that the number of pages appears on a line following %%Pages: at the end of the file. Using *zcat (25.06)* to uncompress the file to standard output, I can type the following commands into a *for* loop *(10.10)* (or put them into a shell script). This loop sends each file to the printer and uses *sed* to capture the correct line:

```
for f
do
        zcat $f | lpr
        zcat $f | sed -n "s/^%%Pages: \([0-9][0-9]*\)/$f:    \1 pages/p"
done
```

But this ends up running *zcat* twice, which takes some time. I can *uncompress* the file first, but frankly I'm not sure I have the disk space for that.

Using *tpipe*, I can do it in one line, without wasting processes and without eating disk space:

```
for f
do
    zcat $f | tpipe lpr | sed -n "s/^%%Pages: \([0-9][0-9]*\)/$f: \1 pages/p"
done
```

From running this script, as each file is sent to the printer I receive the following messages on my screen:

```
ch01.ps.Z: 44 pages
ch02.ps.Z: 51 pages
ch03.ps.Z: 23 pages
    ...
```

If you don't have *tpipe*, you can also simulate it using *awk (38.01)*:

```
zcat $f | awk "{ print | \"lpr\" ; print }" | \
   sed -n "s/^%%Pages: \([0-9][0-9]*\)/$f:   \1 pages/p"
```

This is much slower and only works on text files, but it does the job.

—LM

14.12 *Writing to Multiple Terminals for Demonstrations*

To show what one person is typing, and let people watch at other terminals:

1. The person doing the demonstration starts an interactive shell with a command like:

```
% csh -i |& tee /tmp/log
$ csh -i 2>&1 | tee /tmp/log
```

Use *exit* to leave the shell. To start a Bourne shell, type *sh* instead of *csh*.

2. Everyone who wants to watch types:

tail –f *26.17*

```
% tail -f /tmp/log
```

and uses CTRL-c to kill *tail –f* when they're done.

There are a couple of gotchas:

- The person who's doing the demonstration won't be able to use full-screen programs like *vi* that expect their outputs to go to a terminal (instead of a pipe).

- Commands may echo onto the screen but not into the log file. If that happens, type `csh -iv` to start the demonstrator's C shell or `sh -iv` for a Bourne shell.

—JP

14.13 *The "Filename" –*

If you put filenames on the command line, a typical UNIX command will read those files. With no filenames, the command will read its standard input. How can you make the command read both files and standard input? Newer UNIX systems have a special file *(1.29)* named something like */dev/stdin*. Some older UNIX commands, like *cat (26.02)* and *diff (29.01)*, will accept a "filename" of – (dash). There's not actually a file named –; it's just a shorthand for "read standard input."

Note: This syntax might change in the future.

For instance, here's how to compare two files on different computers. The rsh snooze cat bin/aprog command sends a copy of the file *bin/aprog* from the remote host *snooze* down the pipe here on the local computer. *diff* compares the local file *aprog.new* to the standard input from the pipe:

rsh 1.33
```
% rsh snooze cat bin/aprog | diff - aprog.new
```

For more examples, see articles 10.09 and 14.07.

—*JP*

14.14 What Can You Do with an Empty File?

It isn't a file, actually, though you can use it like one. */dev/null* is a UNIX device.* It's not a physical device. */dev/null* is a special device that "eats" any text written to it and returns "end-of-file" (a file of length 0) when you read from it. So what the heck can you use it for??

* Empty another file. Just copy */dev/null* "on top of" the other file *(25.01)*.

* Make another program "quiet" by redirecting its output there. For instance, if you're putting a program into the background and you don't want it to bother you, type:

  ```
  % progname > /dev/null &
  ```

  That redirects *(14.01)* standard output but leaves standard error hooked to your terminal, in case there is an error.

* Answer a program that asks a lot of questions *(24.04)*—you know you'll just press RETURN at each prompt. In a lot of cases, you can redirect the program's standard input from */dev/null*:

  ```
  % progname < /dev/null
  Want the default setup? If yes, press RETURN:
  Enter filename or press RETURN for default:
      ...
  ```

  You should test that with each program, though, before you assume this trick will work. (If it doesn't work, try *yes (24.04)*.)

* Where a program needs an extra filename but you don't want it to read or write an actual file. For instance, the *grep (28.01)* programs won't give the name of the file where they find a match unless there are at least two filenames on the command line. When you use a wildcard in a directory where maybe only one file will match, use */dev/null* to be sure that *grep* will always see more than one *(18.21)*:

  ```
  % grep "whatever" * /dev/null
  ```

  You're guaranteed that *grep* won't match its regular expression in */dev/null*.
  :-)

---

*Well, okay. It's a *device file*.

- Article 25.02 shows even more uses for /dev/null.

Another interesting device (mostly for programmers) is /dev/zero. When you read it, you'll get ASCII zeros (NUL characters) *(53.03)* forever. There are no newlines either. For both of those reasons, many UNIX commands have trouble reading it. If you want to play, the command below will give you a start (and *head (26.21)* will give you a stop!)*:

fold *45.08*
od *26.07*

```
% fold -20 /dev/zero | od -c | head
```

—*JP*

14.15 What to do with a Full Bit Bucket :-)

[The techniques in this article should be performed carefully, and only by a fully qualified and inexperienced system administrator. —JP]

Q: Our Sun SPARCstation 1+ 4.1 OW2 started running very slowly. When I logged out, I got the message "/dev/null full: empty bit bucket."

A: The problem is that *null* is full. Your void space is no longer void; it's full up.

The top ways to empty an overflowing bit bucket:

✓ Open the computer. Look for the bit bucket, find the *red* stopper at the bottom of it and open it over a *large* wastebasket.

✓ Take the ethernet terminator off. Type the command:

```
% cat /dev/null > le0
```

This spits the bits into the ether.

✓ When you write to /dev/null, the 0's (zeros) don't take up any space, but the 1's (ones) do. Try writing a file full of 0's to /dev/null. Use binary 0, *not* ASCII 0; ASCII 0 will start overfilling the partition.

✓ This is a common problem *only* if you use the computer. If you stop using it, it won't have many problems at all. Kick the other users off, too.

✓ Run lots of C programs. They have null-terminated strings that will use up the extra bits in /dev/null.

✓ Consider upgrading to a byte bucket or even a word bucket.

✓ Bring the computer to Mr. Goodwrench. He will drain the bit bucket, change the oil, and add windshield fluid, all in 29 minutes or less. Now that's a deal.

—*XX (We wish we knew who wrote this!)*

---

*On some UNIX versions, the *head* program may not terminate after it's printed the first ten lines. In that case, use sed 10q instead of head.

14.16 Store and Show Errors with logerrs

This simple script by Maarten Litmaath runs a command, logs any error messages to a file and also sends them to standard error. Because the standard error usually goes to your screen, this lets you see the errors and log them in a file, too.

The script's first argument is the log filename. Then type the command and any other arguments for it. Here's an example of running *cat foo bar* and logging errors to a file named *errors*. The *foo* file exists; the *bar* file doesn't:

```
$ cat foo
hello world
$ logerrs errors cat foo bar
hello world
bar: No such file or directory
$ cat errors
bar: No such file or directory
```

Now for the script:

logerrs

```
#!/bin/sh
# @(#)log 1.0 89/06/10 Maarten Litmaath
#
###    logerrs - save error messages in a logfile, duplicate on stderr
###    Usage: logerrs error-logfile command

case $# in
[012])
        echo "Usage: `basename $0` <error logfile> <command>" >&2
        exit 1
        ;;
esac

ERRLOG="$1"
shift

exec 3>&1
"$@" 2>&1 >&3 | tee -a "$ERRLOG" >&2
```

—*MAL, JP*

## Part Three

Working with the Filesystem

What's a filesystem anyway? A set of data structures that tell the system how the physical data storage on the disk is organized into files? The organizing principles that make it possible to store data in a predictable way, so it can be retrieved easily not just by one person but by many? A fruitless battle against entropy, as the established hierarchy gets overgrown, overthrown, and fragmented?

The next eight chapters deal with this enormous subject, so central to the art of working with UNIX:

- How to get around the filesystem.

- How to use wildcards effectively to point to more than one file.

- How to find the files you've stored in the filesystem—using *ls* in all its forms.

- How to use *find*, the "power saw" of file search operations.

- How to link, rename, and copy files effectively.

- How to create archives for storing and moving many files.

- How and why to make backups—not just a job for the system administrator.

- All the miscellaneous hints we couldn't fit into the other chapters.

—TOR

15

Moving Around in a Hurry

15.01 Getting Around the Filesystem

How quickly can you move around the UNIX filesystem? Can you locate any file or directory on your filesystem with both its absolute and relative pathnames? How can symbolic links help you and hurt you?

A lot of UNIX users don't realize how much they'll be helped by completely understanding a few filesystem basics. Here are some of the most important concepts and tricks to know:

- Using relative and absolute pathnames: article 15.02.

- What good is a current directory? article 15.03.

- Saving time and typing when you change directories with *cdpath*: article 15.05.

- Directory stacks keep a list of directories you're using and let you get to them quickly: articles 15.06, 15.07.

- Important directories on the UNIX filesystem: article 15.08.

- Quick *cd* aliases: article 15.09.

- Using variables and a tilde (~) to help you find directories and files: articles 15.11, 15.12.

- A *mark* alias to mark directory for *cd*'ing back: article 15.13.

- Problems when *cd*'ing through symbolic links: article 15.14.

- Automatic setup for entering and exiting a directory: article 15.15.

—*JP*

15.02 Using Relative and Absolute Pathnames

Everything in the UNIX filesystem—files, directories, devices, named pipes, and so on—has two pathnames: absolute and relative. If you know how to find those names, you'll know the best way to locate the file (or whatever) and use it. Even though pathnames are amazingly simple, they're one of the biggest problems beginners have. Studying this article carefully can save you a lot of time and frustration.

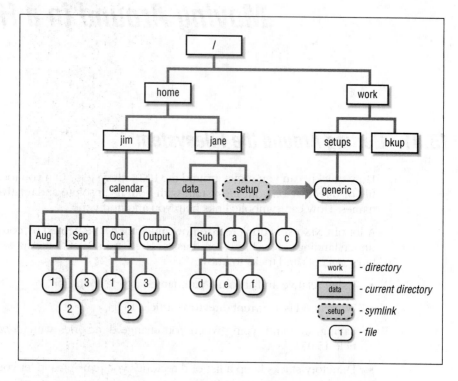

Figure 15-1. A UNIX Filesystem Tree

Table 15-1 describes the two kinds of pathnames.

Table 15-1. Absolute and Relative Pathnames

Absolute Pathnames	Relative Pathnames
Start at the root directory.	Start at your current directory (1.21).
Always start with a slash (/).	Never start with a slash.
The absolute pathname to some object (file, etc.) is always the same.	The relative pathname to an object depends on your current directory.

To make an absolute pathname:

- Start at the root directory (/) and work down.

- Put a slash (/) after every directory name—though if the path ends at a directory, the slash after the last name is optional.

For example, to get a listing of the directory highlighted in Figure 15-2, no matter what your current directory is, you'd use an absolute pathname like this:

```
% ls /home/jane/data
Sub    a    b    c
```

To make a relative pathname:

- Start at your current directory.

- As you move down the tree, away from root, add subdirectory names.

- As you move up the tree toward root, add . . (two dots) for each directory.

- Put a slash (/) after every directory name—though if the path is to a directory, the slash after the last name is optional.

For example, if your current directory is the one shown in Figure 15-1, to get a listing of the *Sub* subdirectory, use a relative pathname:

```
% ls Sub
d    e    f
```

Without changing your current directory, you can use a relative pathname to read the file *d* in the *Sub* subdirectory:

```
% cat Sub/d
```

To change the current directory to Jim's home directory, you could use a relative pathname to it:

```
% cd ../../jim
```

Using the absolute pathname, */home/jim*, might be easier there.

The symbolic link *(19.04)* adds a twist to pathnames. What two absolute pathnames would read the file that the symlink points to? The answer: */home/jane/.setup* or */work/setups/generic*. (The second pathname points directly to the file, so it's a little more efficient.) If your current directory was the one shown in Figure 15-2, what would be the easiest way to read that file with the *more (26.03)* pager? It's probably through the symlink:

```
% more ../.setup
```

Remember, when you need to use something in the filesystem, you don't always need to use *cd* first. Think about using a relative or absolute pathname with the command; that'll almost always work. If you get an error message, check your pathname carefully; that's almost always the problem. If it's hard to visualize the filesystem, a program that makes a diagram of the directory tree *(17.20, 17.21)* can help.

—JP

15.03 What Good is a Current Directory?

People who think the *cd* command is all they need to know about current directories should read this article! Understanding how UNIX uses the current directory can save you work.

Each UNIX process has its own current directory. For instance, your shell has a current directory. So do *vi*, *ls*, *sed*, and every other UNIX process. When your shell starts a process running, that child process starts with the same current directory as its parent. So how does *ls* know which directory to list? It uses the current directory it inherited from its parent process, the shell:

```
% ls
       ...Listing of ls's current directory appears
       that's the same current directory as the shell...
```

Each process can change its current directory and that won't change the current directory of other processes that are already running. So:

- Your shell script (which runs in a separate process) can *cd* to another directory without affecting the shell that started it (the script doesn't need to *cd* back before it exits).

- If you have more than one window or login session to the same computer, they probably run separate processes. So, they have independent current directories.

- When you use a subshell *(14.07, 40.04)* or a shell escape, you can *cd* anywhere you want. After you exit that shell, the parent shell's current directory won't have changed.

  For example, if you want to run a command in another directory without *cd*ing there first (and having to *cd* back), do it in a subshell:

```
% pwd
/foo/bar
% (cd baz; somecommand > somefile)
% pwd
/foo/bar
```

When you really get down to it, what good is a current directory? Here it is: relative pathnames start at the current directory. Having a current directory means you can refer to a file by its relative pathname, like *afile*. Without a current directory and relative pathnames, you'd always have to use absolute pathnames *(15.02)* like */usr/joe/projects/alpha/afile*.

—JP

15.04 How Does UNIX Find Your Current Directory?

A command like *pwd* inherits the current directory of the process that started it (usually, a shell). It could be started from anywhere. How does *pwd* find out where it is in the filesystem? See Figure 15-2 for a picture of the current directory */usr/joe* and its parent directories.

The current directory doesn't contain its own name, so that doesn't help *pwd*. But it has an entry named . (dot), which gives the i-number of the directory (19.02).

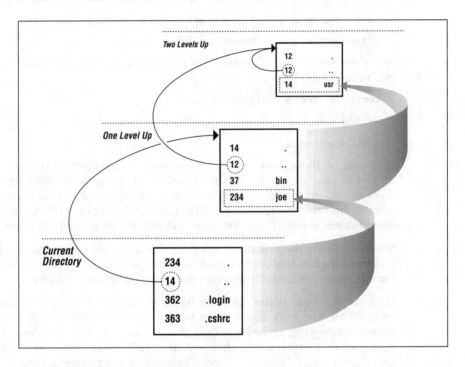

Figure 15-2. Finding the Current Directory Name

The current directory has i-number 234. Next, *pwd* asks UNIX to open the parent directory file, the directory one level up, through the relative pathname (..). It's looking for the name that goes with i-number 234. Aha; the current directory is named *joe*. So the end of the pathname must be *joe*.

Next step. *pwd* looks at the . entry in the directory one level up to get its i-number: 14. Like always, the name of the one-level up directory is in its parent (.., i-number 12). To get its name, *pwd* opens the directory two levels up and looks for i-number 14: *usr*. Now *pwd* has the pathname *usr/joe*.

Same steps: look in the parent, i-number 12. What's its name? Hmmm. The i-number of its parent, 12, is the same as its own—and there's only one directory on the filesystem like this: the root directory. So, *pwd* adds a slash to the start of the pathname and it's done: */usr/joe*.

That's really missing one or two parts: Filesystems can be mounted on other filesystems, or can be mounted across the network from other hosts. So, at each step, *pwd* also needs to check the device that the current directory is mounted on. If you're curious, see the *stat*(2) manual page or check a UNIX internals book.

—JP

15.05 *Saving Time when You Change Directories: cdpath*

Some people make a shell alias *(11.02)* for directories they *cd* to often:

```
alias pwrtools 'cd /books/troff/pwrtools'
```

Other people set shell variables *(7.08)* to hold the pathnames of directories they don't want to retype:

```
pwrtools=/books/troff/pwrtools
```

Later they type:

```
$ cd $pwrtools
```

But both of those tricks make you remember directory abbreviations—and make you put new aliases or shell variables in *.cshrc* or *.profile* each time you want to add or change one. There's an easier way: the C shell's *cdpath* shell variable and the Bourne shell's *CDPATH* variable (*CDPATH* doesn't work in some Bourne shells). I'll use the term "cdpath" to talk about both shells.

When you type the command cd *foo*, the shell first tries to go to the exact pathname *foo*. If that doesn't work, and if *foo* is a relative pathname, the shell tries the same command from every directory listed in the *cdpath*.

Let's say that your home directory is */home/lisa* and your current directory is somewhere else. Let's also say that your *cdpath* has the directories */home/lisa*, */home/lisa/projects*, and */books/troff*. If your cd *foo* command doesn't work in your current directory, then your shell will try, in this order, cd /home/lisa/*foo*, cd /home/lisa/projects/*foo*, and cd /books/troff/*foo*. If the C shell finds one, it shows the pathname:

```
% cd foo
/home/lisa/foo
%
```

Some Bourne shells don't show the directory name. All shells print an error, though, if they can't find any *foo* directory.

So, set your *cdpath* to a list of the parent directories that contain directories you might want to *cd* to. *Don't list the exact directories—list the parent directories (1.21).* This list goes in your *.cshrc* or *.profile* file. For example, *lisa*'s *.cshrc* could have:

~ 15.12
```
set cdpath=(~ ~/projects /books/troff)
```

A Bourne shell user would have this in *.profile*:

```
CDPATH=$HOME:$HOME/projects:/books/troff
export CDPATH
```

(If your system doesn't define $HOME, try $LOGDIR.)

—JP

15.06 *The C Shell's pushd and popd Commands*

How often do you need to move to some other directory temporarily, look at some file, and then move back to the directory where you started? If you're like most users, you do this all the time. The C shell's *pushd* and *popd* commands make this a lot easier. By themselves, they're one great reason for using the C shell.

These commands implement a "directory stack." The classical analogy for a stack is one of those spring-loaded plate stackers in a school cafeteria. The last plate put ("pushed") onto the stack is the first plate taken ("popped") from the stack. It's just the same with directories: each time you use *pushd*, the shell adds your directory to the stack and moves you to the new directory. When you use *popd*, the shell takes the top directory off of the stack, and moves you to the directory underneath.

You may as well learn about *pushd* the way I did: by watching. Let's say that I'm in the directory `˜/power`, working on this book. I want to change to my *Mail* directory briefly, to look at some old correspondence. Here's how:*

```
los% pushd ~/Mail        --current directory becomes ˜/Mail
~/Mail ~/power
```

pushd prints the entire stack, giving me some confirmation about where I am, and where I can get. When I'm done reading the old mail, I want to move back:

```
los% popd                --current directory becomes ˜/power
~/power
```

We're back where we started; the *Mail* directory is no longer on the stack.

What if you want to move back and forth repeatedly? *pushd*, with no arguments, just switches the two top directories on the stack. Like this:

```
los% pwd                 --current directory is ˜/power
/home/los/mikel/power
los% pushd ~/Mail        --current directory becomes ˜/Mail
~/Mail ~/power
los% pushd               --current directory becomes ˜/power
~/power ~/Mail
los% pushd               --current directory becomes ˜/Mail
~/Mail ~/power
```

And so on.

---

*If you've set a cdpath *(15.05)* you can use those short directory names with *pushd*.

If you like, you can let your directory stack get really long. In this case, two special commands are useful. popd +*n* deletes the *n* entry in the stack. Entries are counted "down" from the top, starting with zero; that is, your current directory is 0. So popd +0 and popd are the same. If *n* is greater than 0, your current directory does not change. This may seem surprising, but it isn't; after all, you haven't changed the top of the stack.

The command pushd +*n* "rotates" the stack, so that the *n*th directory moves to the top, becoming the current directory. Note that this is a "rotation": the whole stack moves. I don't find the +*n* commands too useful, but you should know about them.

The *dirs* command prints the directory stack. It's a good way to find out where you are. Some people like to put the *dirs* command in their prompt *(8.11)*, but I personally find incredibly long prompts more annoying than helpful.

The one drawback to *pushd* and *popd* is that you can easily build up a gigantic directory stack full of useless directories. I suppose this doesn't really hurt anything, but it's needless clutter. The only way to clear the stack is to *popd* repeatedly. More to the point, the directories you're most likely to *want* are at the top of the stack. There's no really convenient way to save them. I mean, with 7 directories in the stack, you could conceivably do something like:

```
% pushd +5 ; popd ; popd
```

to get rid of the bottom two elements. The *pushd* moves the bottom two elements of a 7-directory stack to the top. A bit inconvenient. [Clearing the whole stack is a good use for the C shell *repeat (10.23)* command. For example, if the stack has 7 directories, type:

```
% repeat 6 popd
```

That's an easy way to start over when the stack gets too messy. —*JP*]

Note: The Korn shell has some similar (but not quite as general) features. It keeps track of your previous working directory, and then defines the special command cd – as "change to the previous working directory."

—*ML*

15.07 *Nice Aliases for pushd*

The *pushd* command *(15.06)* is nice for jumping around the filesystem. But some of the commands you might type a lot, like *pushd +4*, are sort of a pain to type. I saw these aliases *(11.02)* in Daniel Gilly's setup file. They looked so handy that I decided to steal them for this book:

```
alias pd pushd
alias pd2 'pushd +2'
alias pd3 'pushd +3'
alias pd4 'pushd +4'
```

So, for example, to swap the fourth directory on the stack, just type pd4.

—*JP*

15.08 The UNIX Filesystem Layout

Here is a brief tour of the UNIX filesystem. We will begin with the root directory and its most important subdirectories.

The basic layout of traditional UNIX filesystems is illustrated in Figure 15-3, which shows an idealized BSD directory structure.

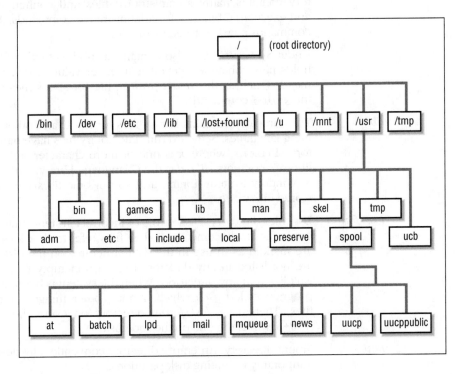

Figure 15-3. BSD Directory Structure

The layouts under UNIX System V Release 3.2, XENIX, and AIX are quite similar. We will point out differences as we proceed.

/   The root directory. This is the base of the filesystem's tree structure; all other files and directories, regardless of their physical disk locations, are logically contained within the root directory.

/bin   Command binaries directory. This directory includes executable public programs that are part of the UNIX operating system and its utilities. Other directories which hold UNIX commands are */usr/bin* and (in many UNIX versions) */usr/ucb*.

/dev	Device directory, containing special files for ttys *(3.08)*, ptys *(43.08)*, tape drives, and so on. The /dev directory is divided into sub-directories in some System V Release 3 implementations and in standard System V Release 4. Each subdirectory holds special files of a given type and is named for the type of devices it contains: *dsk* and *rdsk* for disks accessed in block and raw mode, *mt* and *rmt* for tape drives, *term* for terminals, *pts* and *ptc* for pseudo-terminals (the latter three under System V Release 4 only), and so on.
/etc	System configuration files and executables directory. This directory contains many administrative files and configuration files, and executable binaries for administrative commands. Additional commands may be stored in /usr/etc.

Under System V, /etc also contains a subdirectory *default* which holds files containing default parameter values for various commands (such as the /etc/default/su file for status messages from the *su (23.23)* command). |
/lib	This directory contains library files for the C and other programming languages. Standard run-time library files have names of the form libx.a, where *x* is one or more characters related to the library's contents: *libc.a* is the C language library, *libX11.a* is the X Window System library, and so on. ome library files are also stored in /usr/lib.
/lost+found	Lost files directory. Disk errors or incorrect system shutdown may cause files to become "lost": lost files refer to disk locations that are marked as in use in the data structures on the disk, but that are not listed in any directory (e.g., a nonempty inode *(1.22)* that isn't listed in any directory). When the system is booting, it runs a program called *fsck* which, among other things, "finds" these files. There is a *lost+found* directory on every disk partition; /lost+found is the one on the root disk.
/mnt	Mount directory. An empty directory conventionally designed for temporarily mounting disk partitions.
/u	This directory is a conventional location for users' home directories. For example, user *chavez'* home directory would often be /u/chavez. The name is completely arbitrary, however, and is often changed by the local site. Another common name for this directory is /home, which is the name defined under System V Release 4. On older systems, user home directories were placed under /usr.
/usr	This directory contains subdirectories for spooling, mail, locally generated programs, executables for user commands, and other parts of the UNIX system. The subdirectories of /usr are discussed in more detail in the next section.

/tmp   Temporary directory, available to all users as a scratch directory
                  (22.02, 22.03).

The /usr Directory

The directory */usr* contains a number of important subdirectories:

/usr/adm   Administrative directory (home directory of the special *adm*
                  user). This directory contains the UNIX accounting files and vari-
                  ous system logging files.

/usr/bin   Command binary files and shell scripts directory. This directory
                  contains public executable programs that are part of the UNIX sys-
                  tem, similar to */bin*. On many systems, executables for layered
                  products are also sometimes stored in */usr/bin* (or subdirectories
                  under it).

/usr/etc   On most systems, a few additional administrative commands are
                  stored here. Under SunOS, the administrative commands usually
                  found in */etc* are stored here.

/usr/games   This directory contains the standard UNIX games collection. Some
                  sites choose to remove this directory.

/usr/include   Include files directory. This directory contains C language header
                  files that define the C programmer's interface to standard system
                  features and program libraries. For example, this directory con-
                  tains the file *stdio.h*, which defines the user's interface to the C
                  standard I/O library. The directory */usr/include/sys* contains
                  operating system *include* files.

/usr/lib   Library directory, for public library files. Among other things, this
                  directory contains the standard C libraries for mathematics and
                  I/O. This directory may also contain certain configuration files for
                  UNIX services such as mail. Finally, subdirectories of */usr/lib* con-
                  tain command and configuration files for various standard UNIX
                  facilities like *uucp* and *lex* and optional software products.

/usr/local   Local files directory. By convention, the directory */usr/local/bin* is
                  reserved for any public executable programs developed on your
                  system.

/usr/man   Manual pages directory. This directory contains the online ver-
                  sion of the UNIX reference manuals. It is divided into subdirec-
                  tories for each section of the manual. Under BSD and some Sys-
                  tem V implementations, */usr/man* contains several man*n* sub-
                  directories holding the raw source for the manual pages in that
                  section and cat*n* subdirectories storing the processed versions.
                  The latter can be cleared to save space *(24.18)*; they will be filled
                  only as manual pages are actually accessed. If present, the file
                  /usr/man/whatis contains a database used by the *whatis (52.04)* and
                  apropos (52.02) (*man −k*) commands. The significance of the sec-
                  tions is described in the table in article 52.01.

An older organizational scheme is used by many System V systems. It adds another layer of structure to the BSD plan. The directories */usr/man* and */usr/catman* both have several subdirectories of the form x_man, where x is a code letter indicating the directory's contents: a for administrative, p for programming, u for user commands (other codes are present on some systems). Under each of these directories there are several subdirectories named mann or catn, holding the actual manual pages.

/usr/spool   Spooling directory. This directory contains subdirectories for UNIX subsystems that provide different kinds of spooling services. Some of the tools using */usr/spool* are *uucp (1.33)*, the print spooling system (45.02), and the *cron (42.12)* facility.

/usr/ucb   A directory that contains standard UNIX commands originally developed at the University of California, Berkeley. This directory sometimes includes subdirectories for separate file types (*bin* for binaries, *lib* for libraries, and so on).

/usr/5bin   Under SunOS, executables for System V-compatibility commands are stored here.

/usr/lpp   Under AIX 3.1, "licensed program products" (optional products) are stored in subdirectories of */usr/lpp*. Another important subdirectory is */usr/lpp/bos* (for *b*ase *o*perating *s*ystem), which holds information about the current operating system release.

System V.4 Filesystem Organization

System V Release 4 reorganizes the UNIX directory structure in several ways. Besides adding new subdirectories to */dev* for terminal devices (discussed previously), the following major changes occur:

- Executable files are moved out of */etc* into a new directory named */sbin* or to */usr/sbin* (which was formerly named */usr/etc*). However, many systems set up links to the old locations, so the commands may seem to be in both places.

- Virtually all system configuration files are placed in */etc*. Some new subdirectories are created there to organize files by facility.

- Certain types of static data files (such as the online manual pages, font directories, the files for *spell*, and the like) are stored in subdirectories under */usr/share*. The name "share" reflects the idea that such files could be shared among a group of networked systems, eliminating the need for separate copies on every system.

- A new top-level directory, */var*, holds the volatile spooling directories formerly placed under */usr/spool*. If *var* is placed on a separate disk partition (or even a separate disk) from the root disk partition, then the latter can remain relatively static after initial system setup. This is an important step toward full support for read-only system disks. SunOS also uses a */var* directory.

- The contents of */bin* and */lib* are moved to */usr/bin* and */usr/lib*, respectively.

The basic layout of the System V Release 4 filesystem is illustrated in Figure 15-4.

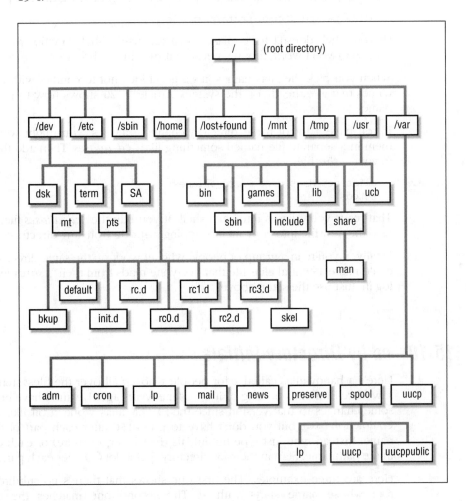

Figure 15-4. Typical System V Release 4 Directory Structure

—*AF* from the Nutshell Handbook *Essential System Administration*

15.09 Quick cd's with Aliases

If you do a lot of work in some particular directories, it can be handy to make aliases *(11.02)* that take you to each directory quickly. For example, this C shell alias lets you type `pwr` to change to the */books/troff/pwrtools* directory:

```
alias pwr cd /books/troff/pwrtools
```

(If your shell doesn't have aliases, you can use a shell function *(11.10)*. A shell script *(1.05)* won't work, though, because it runs in a subshell *(40.04)*.)

When you pick the alias names, it's a good idea not to conflict with command names that are already on the system. Article 46.20 shows how to pick a new name.

If you have a lot of these directory-changing aliases, you might want to put them in a separate file named something like *.cd_aliases*. Then add these lines to your *.cshrc* file:

source *46.22*
~ *15.12*

```
alias setcds source ~/.cd_aliases
setcds
```

That reads your aliases into each shell. If you edit the *.cd_aliases* file, you can read the new file into your shell by typing `setcds` from any directory.

Finally, if you're in a group of people who all work on the same directories, you could make a central alias file that everyone reads from their *.cshrc* files as they log in. Just use the setup above.

—JP

15.10 cd by Directory Initials

Here's a handy alias called *c* for people who *cd* all over the filesystem. (I first saw Marc Brumlik's posting of it on Usenet years ago. He and I have both made some changes to that version since then.) This alias works a bit like filename completion *(10.06)*, but you don't have to press ESC after each part of the pathname. Instead, you just type the initials (first letter, or more) of each directory in the pathname. Start at the root directory. Put a dot (`.`) after each part.

Here are three examples. The first one shows that there's no subdirectory of root whose name starts with *q*. The second one matches the directory */usr/include/hsfs* and *cd*s there:

```
% c q.
No match.
% c u.i.h.
/usr/include/hsfs/
```

In the next example, trying to change to */usr/include/pascal*, the abbreviations aren't unique the first time. The alias shows me all the matches; the second time, I add another letter ("a") to make the name unique:

```
% c u.i.p.
/usr/include/pascal/ /usr/include/pixrect/ /usr/include/protocols/
```

```
cd: Too many arguments.
% c u.i.pa.
/usr/include/pascal/
```

Do you have an alias for your *cd* command? If you do, your alias may not work with the C shell *if* (49.03) used in this *c* alias. Although the *csh* manual page admits it won't work, I'd call that another C shell bug (49.02). So, here are two versions—the first for people who don't use an alias for *cd*, the second for people with *cd* aliases:

csh_init

```
# THIS VERSION PRINTS No match IF NO MATCH, BUT cd ALIAS WON'T WORK...
alias c 'set d=`echo \!^* | sed "s/\([^.]*\)\./\/\1*/g"`/; echo $d; \\
        if ("$d" == "") echo No match.; if ("$d" != "") cd $d'
# THIS VERSION WORKS WITH cd ALIAS, BUT DOUBLE cd AT THE END IS A KLUDGE:
alias c 'set d=`echo \!^* | sed "s/\([^.]*\)\./\/\1*/g"`/; echo $d; \\
        if ("$d" == "") echo No match.; if ("$d" != "") chdir $d; cd .'
```

The second version uses the C shell's *chdir* command to change directory, then runs your *cd* alias to "change to the current directory (.)." It's ugly, but it works. The other ugly thing in these *c* aliases is the two similar *if* tests; I used them because it's tough (but not impossible) to use an *else* inside an alias (11.07).

One way to get around these problems is a sourceable script (11.05).

If you do that, you also might add a test that makes the periods in the initials optional. If you don't use periods (so you can say c uih instead of c u.i.h. as in the example above), the script would run the command:

```
set d=`echo \!^* | sed "s/./\/&*/g"`/
```

Marc and I are leaving that as "an exercise for the reader." :-)

—*JP*

15.11 *Variables Help You Find Directories and Files*

A UNIX system can have hundreds or thousands of directories—and a lot more files. Even if you remember all the pathnames, typing them over and over can be a pain.

Your account probably already has some helpful shell and environment variables (7.08, 7.01) set up. You can add more from the command line or from your shell setup files (2.02) (like *.cshrc* or *.profile*). To see what environment variables are set, use the *env* (System V) or *printenv* (Berkeley) command. The command *set* should show shell variables (some of these might be repeated in the environment). Here's part of what happens on my account:

```
% env
HOME=/home/jerry
MH=/work/jerry_mail/.mh_profile
PATH=/home/jerry/.bin:/home/jerry/.bin/show:/work/bin:...
RNINIT=/home/jerry/.rnswitches
PAGER=/usr/local/bin/less
% set
active  /usr/lib/news/active
cwd     /home/jerry/pwrtools
```

```
mail    (60 /usr/mail/jerry)
maillog /usr/spool/smail/log/logfile
```

UNIX programs use a lot of those environment variables. For instance, my e-mail system finds its setup file from *MH*. But I can use environment variables for other things, too. For instance, when I want to edit my e-mail setup file, I can type `vi $MH` from any directory. The shell expands `$MH` to */work/jerry_mail/.mh_profile* and starts the editor. Check your environment and see what you've got; the names usually explain the variables pretty well.

The shell uses shell variables like `$mail`. I can check incoming messages with the command `tail $mail[2]` *(26.15, 49.05)* (the [2] tells the C shell to pick the second word from the list in `$mail`).

I've set other shell variables for myself. When I send some mail messages, I want to watch the system mail log to see the message being delivered. I just type:

–f 26.17
```
% tail -f $maillog
   ...
09/08/91 17:13:27: [m0kJN4x-0000AKC] new msg: from jerry@ora.com
09/08/91 17:13:28: [m0kJN4x-0000AKC] <jim> ... delivered
09/08/91 17:13:42: [m0kJN4x-0000AKC] <allan@comex.com> ... delivered
```

Are there files or directories that you refer to a lot—ones that aren't right for the *cdpath* *(15.05)* or a shell alias? Pick a likely shell variable name and add the variable to your *.cshrc* or *.profile*. You can store more than one pathname in the same variable—either by separating them with spaces or by using wildcards:

```
# C shell variables:
set worklog=~/todays_worklog              Single file, defined when set
set projfiles=(/work/beta/data_3.9*)      Many files, defined when set
set currdata='/work/beta/data_5*'         Many files, defined when used
# Bourne shell variables:
worklog=$HOME/todays_worklog              Single file, defined when set
```
echo 9.04
```
projfiles="`echo /work/beta/data_3.9_*`"  Many files, defined when set
currdata='/work/beta/data_5*'             Many files, defined when used
```

Then:

- You could type `vi + $worklog` any time you want to add a note to the end of the file *todays_worklog* in your home directory. (The + tells *vi* to start at the end of the file.)

- The shell expands the asterisk (*) when it sets the *projfiles* variable and stores a list of the files *as they were when the variable was set*. (If the list of files changes, it'll be reset when you start your next shell.) You could print all those files any time you wanted to by typing a command like `lpr $projfiles`. The C shell also lets you pick individual files *(49.05)* from the list—for instance, `lpr $projfiles[9]` would print the ninth file from the list.

- When the *currdata* variable is set, the single quotes (' ') around it prevent expansion *(9.10)* of the wildcard (*). Instead, the pathname */work/beta/data_5* is expanded when you use the variable—like pg $currdata—to show you the files as they are at the time you use the variable.

You can also use variables to store the paths to directories. Use *cd*, *ls*, or any other command with the variables.

—JP

15.12 Finding (Anyone's) Home Directory, Quickly

The C shell and Korn shell have a shortcut for the pathname to your home directory: a tilde (~), often called "twiddle" by UNIX-heads. You can use ~ in a pathname to the home directory from wherever you are. For example, from any directory, you can list your home directory or edit your *.cshrc* file in it by typing:

```
% ls ~
    ...
% vi ~/.cshrc
```

Bourne shell users—try the $HOME or $LOGDIR variables instead.

You could change your current directory to your home directory by typing cd ~ or cd $HOME although all shells have a shorter shortcut: typing plain cd with no argument also takes you home.

The C and Korn shells also have an abbreviation for other users' home directories: a tilde with the username on the end. For example, the home directory for *mandi*, which might really be */usr3/users/mfg/mandi*, could be abbreviated ~*mandi*. On your account, if Mandi told you to copy the file named *menu.c* from her *src* directory, you could type:

```
% cp ~mandi/src/menu.c .
```

Don't confuse this with filenames like *report~*. Some programs, like the GNU Emacs *(33.04)* editor, create temporary filenames that end with a ~ (tilde).

The Bourne shell doesn't have anything like ~*mandi*. A couple of workarounds:

- If your system has symbolic links *(19.04)*, your system administrator can make a directory with a short name like */u*. In it, put symbolic links to each user's home directory. Then Bourne shell users and shell programmers could type /u/mandi to refer to Mandi's home directory.

- Here's a trick that's probably too ugly to type a lot—but it's useful in Bourne shell scripts, where you don't want to "hardcode" users' home directory pathnames. This command calls the C shell to put *mandi*'s home directory pathname into *$dir*:

```
username=mandi
dir=`csh -fc "echo ~$username"`
```

The tilde is a good thing to use in your *.cshrc* and *ENV* files *(2.02)*, too.

—JP

15.13 Marking Your Place with a C Shell Variable

The following alias will store the current directory name in a variable:

```
alias mark 'set \!:1=$cwd'
```

so as to use a feature of the C shell:

```
% mark here
    ...
% cd here
```

One need not even type $*here*. If a directory does not exist, *csh* tries searching its *cdpath* (15.05), then tries evaluating the name as a variable (7.08, 7.09).

(I generally use *pushd* and *popd* (15.06) to store directory names; *mark* is more useful with commands that need to look in two different paths, and there $*here* is necessary anyway. Ah well.)

[The MH mail system has a command named *mark*. If you use MH, you might rename the alias *keep*, *save*, or something else. —*JP*]

—*CT* in *comp.unix.wizards* on Usenet, *14 February 1987*

15.14 Which Directory am I in, Really?

The C shell, and some other shells too, keep their own idea of what your current directory is. The *csh* will give you the current directory's full pathname in $cwd. But sometimes it can give you the wrong pathname.

Why? Because the *cwd* variable was added before many versions of UNIX had symlinks (19.04) (symbolic links). As article 19.07 explains, symlinks can point to directories any place else on the filesystem or even (for some UNIXes) directories on another computer. Poor *cwd* couldn't cope: it assumed that the current directory was the name of the symlink itself (instead of the directory that the link points to). That led to problems like the one below: *cd*ing to a "directory" named *wpa* that's actually a symlink to */work/pwrtools/articles*. The value of $cwd, shown in the prompt, is wrong. The */bin/pwd* command shows the real current directory (15.04) (you should type all of /bin/pwd because some shells and users have plain pwd aliased to do echo $cwd):

```
/home/jerry% pwd
/home/jerry% ls -l wpa
lrwxrwxrwx  1 jerry  23 Sep 8 13:55 wpa -> /work/pwrtools/articles
/home/jerry% cd wpa
/home/jerry/wpa% /bin/pwd
/work/pwrtools/articles
/home/jerry/wpa%
```

By now, a lot of C shells have a variable named *hardpaths*. If you set it (usually in your *.cshrc* file), the shell won't be fooled by symlinks. Watch:

```
/home/jerry/wpa% cd
/home/jerry% set hardpaths
```

```
/home/jerry% cd wpa
/work/pwrtools/articles%
```

Setting the *hardpaths* variable makes the shell do extra work, so don't bother with it unless you use $cwd.

The *dirs (15.06)* command has the same problem as the *cwd* variable does. Setting *hardpaths* helps there, too.

If your system has symlinks but your shell doesn't recognize a variable like *hardpaths*, here are workarounds for your *.cshrc* file:

csh_init

```
alias setprompt 'set prompt="${cwd}% "'
alias cd       'chdir \!* && set cwd=`/bin/pwd` && setprompt'
alias pushd    'pushd \!* && cd .'
alias popd     'popd \!* && cd .'
```

When you *cd*, that alias resets the *cwd* variable to the output of */bin/pwd*, then resets the prompt to the new *cwd*. Using *pushd* or *popd (15.06)* runs the *cd* alias, too—this changes to the current directory (.), which fixes *cwd* (as well as the *dirs* command) and resets the prompt.

Whew. Are symlinks worth the work? (I think they are.)

—*JP*

15.15 *Automatic Setup when You Enter/Exit a Directory*

If you work in a lot of different directories, here's a way to make the shell do automatic setup when you enter a directory or cleanup as you leave:

csh_init

```
alias cd 'if (-o .exit) source .exit; chdir \!*; if (-o .enter) source .enter'
```

Then create *.enter* and/or *.exit* files in the directories where you want a custom setup. When you *cd* to a new directory, an *.exit* file is *sourced (46.22)* into your current shell before you leave the old directory. As you enter the new directory, an *.enter* file will be read if it exists. If you use *pushd* and *popd (15.06)*, you might want to make the same kind of aliases for them.

The alias tests to be sure you own the files—this helps to stop other users from leaving surprises for you! But if lots of users will be sharing the directory, they may all want to share the same files—in that case, replace the *-o* tests with *-r* (true if the file is readable). Article 49.04 describes tests like *-o*.

Here's a sample *.enter* file:

umask *23.04*

.enter

```
# Save previous umask; reset in .exit:
set prevumask=`umask`
# Let everyone in the group edit my files here:
umask 002
echo ".enter: setting umask to 002"
# Prompt (with blank line before) to keep me awake:
set prompt="\
$cwd - PROJECT DEVELOPMENT DIRECTORY.  EDIT CAREFULLY...\
% "
```

and the .*exit* to go with it:

if **49.03**
$? **49.04**

.exit

```
# .enter file may put old umask in shell variable:
if ($?prevumask) then
    umask $prevumask
    echo ".exit: setting umask to $prevumask"
    unset prevumask
endif
# Reminder to come back here if need to:
echo "If you didn't check in the RCS files, type 'cd $cwd'."
# Set generic prompt (setprompt alias comes from .cshrc file):
setprompt
```

setprompt **8.05**

Note: The *umask* set in the .*enter* file for some directory will also set the permissions for files you create in other directories with commands that use pathnames—like vi /*somedir*/*somefile*.

Can more than one of your directories use the same .*enter* or .*exit* file? If they can, you'll save disk space and redundant editing by making hard links *(19.04)* between the files. If the directories are on different filesystems, you'll have to use a symbolic link *(19.04)*—though that probably won't save disk space. If you link the files, you should probably add a comment that reminds you of the links when you make your next edit. When your .*enter* files get really long, you might be able to put a command like this in them:

source **46.22**

```
source ~/.global_enter
```

where the .*global_enter* file in your home directory has a procedure that you want to run from a lot of your .*enter* files. (Same goes for .*exit*, of course.)

One last idea: if a lot of users share the same directory, they can make files with names like .*enter.joanne*, .*exit.allan*, and so on. Your aliases can test for a file named .enter.$user *(7.09)* (if your UNIX has a 14-character filename limit, you'll need a shorter name).

—*JP*

16

Wildcards

16.01 File Naming Wildcards

Wildcards *(1.16)* are the shell's way of abbreviating filenames. Just as in poker, where a wildcard is a special card that can match any card in the deck, filename wildcards are capable of matching letters, or groups of letters, in the alphabet. Rather than typing a long filename, or a long chain of filenames, a wildcard lets you provide parts of names, and then use some "wildcard characters" for the rest. For example, if you want to delete all files whose names end in *.o*, you can give the command:

```
% rm *.o
```

You don't have to list every filename.

I'm sure you already know that wildcards are useful in many situations. If not, they are summarized in article 16.02. Here are a few of my favorite wildcard applications:

- If you remember part of a filename, but not the whole name, you can use wildcards to help you find it. If I have a file on genetics saved in a directory with several hundred other files, a command like:

  ```
  % ls *gene*
  ```

  will often find what I want. It's quicker and easier than *find (18.01)*.

- Wildcards are a natural when you want to work with groups of files. If I have a general purpose directory that's full of filenames ending in *.c* and *.h*, I can make new subdirectories and use wildcards to move the files easily:

  ```
  % mkdir c h
  % mv *.c c
  % mv *.h h
  ```

- Wildcards often help you to work with files with inconvenient characters in their names. Let's say you have a file named abc*x*e, where *x* is some unknown control character. You can delete or rename that file by using the wildcarded name abc?e. (When you do this, be careful that your wildcard doesn't match more than you intend.)

- Wildcards can appear in any component of a pathname. This can often be used to your advantage. For example, let's say that you have a directory named */work*, split into subdirectories for a dozen different projects. For each project, you have a schedule, in a file called (obviously enough) *schedule.txt*. You can print all the schedules with the command:

```
% lpr /work/*/schedule.txt        BSD UNIX
% lp  /work/*/schedule.txt        System V UNIX
```

(However, you can occasionally run into problems *(16.07)*.)

It's a common misconception, particularly among new users, that application programs and utilities have something to do with wildcards. Given a command like grep ident *.c, many users think that *grep* handles the * and looks to see which files have names that end in *.c*. If you're at all familiar with UNIX's workings, you'll realize that this is the wrong picture. The shell interprets wildcards. That is, the shell figures out which files have names ending in *.c*, puts them in a list, puts that list on the command line, and then hands that command line to *grep*. As it processes the command line, the shell turns grep ident *.c into grep ident file1.c file2.c ....

Since there are several shells, one might think (or fear!) that there should be several different sets of wildcards. Fortunately, there aren't. The C shell has made one significant extension (the curly brace operators *(10.05)*), and the Korn shell has made a few more, but the basic wildcards work the same for all shells.

—*ML*

16.02 Filename Wildcards in a Nutshell

This section summarizes the wildcards that are used for filename expansion. For the most part, the three shells use the same basic wildcards, though the Korn shell and C shell have added some extensions. Unless otherwise noted, assume that wildcards are valid for all shells.

*	Match zero or more characters. For example, a* matches the files *a*, *ab*, *abc*, *abc.d*, and so on.
?	Match exactly one character. For example, a? matches *aa*, *ab*, *ac*, etc.
[12..a..z]	Match any character listed in the brackets. For example, a[ab] matches *aa* or *ab*.
[a-z]	Match all characters between a and z. For example, a[0-9] matches *a0*, *a1*, and so on, up to *a9*.
[!ab..z]	Match any character that does *not* appear within the brackets. For example, a[!0-9] doesn't match *a0*, but does match *aa*. Korn and newer Bourne shells only.

{word1,word2 . . . }

Match *word1*, *word2*, etc. E.g., a_{dog,cat,horse} matches the filenames *a_dog*, *a_cat*, and *a_horse*. C shell only.

These *(10.05)* actually aren't filename-matching wildcards. They expand *any* string, including filenames that don't exist yet, e-mail addresses, and more.

?(abc)

Match zero or one instance of *abc*. For example, x?(abc)x matches *xx* or *xabcx*. Korn shell only.

*(abc)

Match zero or more instances of *abc*. For example, x*(abc)x matches *xx*, *xabcx*, *xabcabcx*, etc. Korn shell only.

+(abc)

Match one or more instances of *abc*. For example, x+(abc)x matches *xabcx*, *xabcabcx*, etc. Korn shell only.

!(abc)

Match anything that doesn't contain *abc*. For example, x!(abc)x doesn't match *xabcx* or *xabcabcx*, but does match practically anything else that begins or ends with *x*. Korn shell only.

Note: wildcards *do not* match files whose names begin with a dot (.), like *.cshrc*. This prevents you from deleting (or otherwise mucking around with) these files by accident. To match those files, type the dot literally. For example, .[a-z]* matches anything whose name starts with a dot and a lowercase letter. Watch out for plain .*, though; it matches the directory entries . and ..—article 16.06 has suggestions for solving that problem.

And a final note: many operating systems (VAX/VMS and DOS included) consider a file's *name* and *extension* to be different entities; therefore, you can't use a single wildcard to match both. What do I mean? Consider the file *abc.def*. Under DOS or VMS, to match this filename you'd need the wildcard expression *.*. The first * matches the name (the part before the period), and the second matches the extension (the part after the period). Although UNIX uses extensions, they aren't considered a separate part of the filename, so a single * will match the entire name.

—ML

16.03 *Adding { } Operators to Korn (and Bourne) Shells*

The C shell's curly brace operators *(10.05)* are handy for working with strings. Some versions of the Korn shell can be configured to make these work.* If your

---

*If your system has Korn shell sources, your system administrator can edit the file *OPTIONS* and set BRACEPAT=1, then recompile.

Korn shell can't do that, or if you use the Bourne shell, you can use the shell function *(11.10)* I wrote called *qcsh*. It writes the command line you type into a temporary file, then gives the file to the C shell.* Type *qcsh*, a space, and the command line you want to run. Here are two examples from article 10.05: to fix a typo in a filename (change *fixbold61.c* to *fixbold6.c*):

```
$ qcsh mv fixbold{61,6}.c
```

To edit ten new files that don't exist yet:

```
$ qcsh vi /usr/foo/file{a,b,c,d,e,f,g,h,i,j}
```

Here's the function:

qcsh

–f *24.09*

```
qcsh()
{
    echo "$@" > /tmp/q$$
    csh -f /tmp/q$$
    rm -f /tmp/q$$
}
```

—*JP*

16.04 Glob

For some arcane reason, using shell wildcards is called "globbing." This gives you a hint about what the C shell *noglob* variable does: it stops interpretation of shell wildcards. For example:

```
% lpr *
    ...All files in directory are printed...
% set noglob
% lpr *
lpr: *: No such file or directory
```

The first *lpr* command printed all the files in the current directory, as we'd expect: the shell expands * to all filenames in the current directory. The second *lpr* command didn't find anything. We had set *noglob*, so wildcard expansion was disabled; and there is no file named * in the directory.

You almost never need to use *noglob*. If you need to use an asterisk as part of a command, it's almost always easier to quote it or put it within a quoted string, as in the following commands:

```
% grep A\*B myfile
% grep "A*B" myfile
```

The backslash and the quotation marks prevent the shell from expanding the asterisk; instead, it gets passed to *grep*, which is what you want.

---

*In some versions of UNIX, passing the command line to the C shell with csh –fc "$@" wouldn't expand the braces. That's why I used a temporary file.

There's only one good reason to turn off wildcard expansion: when there isn't any other workaround. There's only one situation in which this is commonly used. Many *.login* scripts use the command *set noglob; eval `tset –s ...`* to set the terminal type correctly. *tset(6.03)* can output terminal-setup characters like * and [ ] that should not be treated as wildcards. The *set noglob* at the beginning means that the shell won't try to expand those characters into filenames. *tset* outputs the command *unset noglob* (to restore wildcards) when it's done.

Why, then, worry about *noglob* at all? You may log in to a system one day and find that wildcards don't work. This has happened to me. For some reason that was never explained adequately, the *eval `tset –s ...`* command was bombing rather than setting my terminal properly. Therefore, it never had a chance to turn globbing back on. If you're in this situation, just type `unset noglob`, and wildcards should work normally again.

—ML

16.05 *What if a Wildcard Doesn't Match?*

I ran into a strange situation the other day. I was compiling a program that was core dumping *(55.01)*. At some point, I decided to delete the object files and the *core* file, and start over, so I gave the command:

```
% rm *.o core
```

It works as expected most of the time, *except when* no object files exist. (I don't remember why I did this, but it was probably by using ! ! *(12.07)* when I knew there weren't any *.o*'s around.) In this case, you get No match, and the *core* file is *not* deleted.

It turns out, for C shell users, that if none of the wildcards can be expanded, you get a No match error. It doesn't matter that there's a perfectly good match for other name(s). That's because, when *csh* can't match a wildcard, it aborts and prints an error—it won't run the command. If you create one *.o* file or remove the *.o* from the command line, *core* will disappear happily.

On the other hand, if the Bourne shell can't match a wildcard, it just passes the unmatched wildcard and other filenames:

```
*.o core
```

to the command (in this case, to *rm*) and lets the command decide what to do with it. So, with Bourne shell, what happens will depend on what your command does when it sees the literal characters *.o.

You can make *csh* act a lot like *sh* by using:

```
set nonomatch
```

—ML, JP

16.06 Matching All "Dot Files" with Wildcards

If you want to match all files in a directory whose names do not start with a dot (.), it's easy: just use an asterisk (*). But what about files that *do* start with a dot? That's harder because dot-asterisk (.*) matches the directory links named . and .. that are in every directory; you usually won't want to match those.

Here's how:

    .??* .[^A--/-^?]

That first expression matches all filenames that start with a dot and have at least two more characters. The second one matches all two-character filenames in the ASCII chart *(53.03)* except .. (if you have "international" non-ASCII characters in your filenames, you'll need to extend this). The range starts with CTRL-a (^A is an actual CTRL-a character, *not* the two characters ^ and A) and runs through a dash (-). Then it covers the range from slash (/) through DEL or CTRL-? (make by pressing your DELETE or RUBOUT key; you may have to type CTRL-v or a backslash (\) first).

Yuck—that's sort of complicated. To make it easy, I set that sequence in a shell variable named *dots* from my *.cshrc* file:

csh_init

```
# variable with wildcards to match all names starting with "."
set dots=".??* .[`echo Y--/-Z | tr YZ \\001\\177`]"
```

(The *tr* command in backquotes *(10.14)* turns the expression Y--/-Z into the range with CTRL-a and DEL that we want. That keeps ugly, unprintable characters out of the *.cshrc* file. See article 47.34.) So, for example, I could move all files out of the current directory to another directory by typing:

```
% mv * $dots /somedir
```

Note: Newer Bourne shells let you use the sequence .??* .[!.] to match all dot files, where [!.] means "anything but a dot." Other shells, including *tcsh (1.08)*, will allow .??* .[^.] instead.

—*JP*

16.07 Maybe You Shouldn't Use Wildcards in Pathnames

Suppose you're giving a command like the one below (not necessarily *rm*—this applies to any UNIX command):

```
% rm /somedir/otherdir/*
```

Let's say that matches 100 files. The *rm* command gets 100 complete pathnames from the shell: */somedir/otherdir/afile, /somedir/otherdir/bfile,* and so on. For each of these files, the UNIX kernel has to start at the root directory, then search the *somedir* and *otherdir* directories before it finds the file to remove.

That can make a significant difference, especially if your disk is already busy. It's better to *cd* to the directory first and run the *rm* from there. You can do it in a subshell (with parentheses) *(14.07)* if you want to, so you won't have to *cd* back to where you started:

```
% (cd /somedir/otherdir; rm *)
```

There's one more benefit to this second way: you're not as likely to get the error `Arguments too long`. (Another way to handle long command lines is with the *xargs (10.19)* command.)

—JP

16.08 Getting a List of Matching Files with grep –l

Normally when you run *grep (28.01)* on a group of files, the output lists the filename along with the line containing the search pattern. Sometimes you want to know only the names of the files, and you don't care to know the line (or lines) that match. In this case, use the *–l* (lowercase letter "l") option to list only filenames where matches occur. For example, the command:

```
% grep -l "R5" file1 file2 ... > r5.filelist
```

searches the files for a line containing the string R5, produces a list of those filenames, and stores the list in *r5.filelist*. (This list might represent the files containing Release 5 documentation of a particular product.) Because these Release 5 files can now be referenced by one list, you can treat them as a single entity and run various commands on them all at once:

```
% print `cat r5.filelist`          Print only the Release 5 files
% grep UNIX `cat r5.filelist`      Search limited to the Release 5 files
```

You don't have to create a file list, though. You can insert the output of a *grep* directly into a command line with command substitution *(10.14)*. For example, to edit only the subset of files containing R5, you would type:

```
% vi `grep -l R5 files`
```

—DG

16.09 Getting a List of Non-matching Files with grep –c

You can use the *grep (28.02)* option *–c* to tell you how many occurrences of a pattern appear in a given file, so you can also use it to find files that *don't* contain a pattern (i.e., zero occurrences of the pattern). Let's say you're indexing a *troff (45.14)* document and you want to make a list of files that don't yet contain indexing macros. What you need to find are files with zero occurrences of the string .XX. The command:

```
% grep -c "\.XX" chapter*
```

might produce the following output:

```
chapter1:10
chapter2:27
chapter3:19
chapter4:0
chapter5:39
   ...
```

This is all well and good, but suppose you need to check index entries in hundreds of reference pages? Well, just filter *grep*'s output by piping it through another *grep*. The above command can be modified as follows:

```
% grep -c "\.XX" chapter* | grep :0
```

This results in the following output:

```
chapter4:0
```

Using *sed* *(35.24)* to truncate the :0, you can save the output as a list of files. For example, here's a trick for creating a list of files that *don't* contain index macros:

```
% grep -c "\.XX" * | sed -n s/:0//p > ../not_indexed.list
```

The *sed −n* command prints only the lines that contain :0; it also strips the :0 from the output so that *../not_indexed.list* contains a list of files, one per line. The .. pathname *(1.21)* puts the *not_indexed.list* file into the parent directory—this is one easy way to keep *grep* from searching that file, but may not be worth the bother.

[To edit all files that need index macros added, you could type:

```
% vi `grep -c "\.XX" * | sed -n s/:0//p`
```

which is more obvious once you start using backquotes a lot. You can put this into a little script named *vgrep* with a couple of safety features added:

vgrep

`$@` *46.14*

```
#!/bin/sh
case $# in
0|1) echo "Usage: `basename $0` pattern file [files...]" 1>&2 ;;
*)   pat="$1"; shift
     grep -c "$pat" "$@" | sed -n 's/:0$//p'
     ;;
esac
```

Then you can type, for example, vi `vgrep "\.XX" *`.—*JP*]

—*DG*

16.10 nom: List Files that Don't Match a Wildcard

The *nom* (no match) script takes filenames (usually, expanded by the shell) from its command line. It outputs all filenames in the current directory that *don't* match. Some newer shells have an ! (exclamation point) operator that works like *nom*, but a lot don't. Here are some examples:

- To get the names of all files that *don't* end with .ms:

      % nom *.ms

- To edit all files whose names don't have any lowercase letters:

      % vi `nom *[a-z]*`

- To copy all files to a directory named *Backup* (except *Backup* itself):

      % cp `nom Backup` Backup

Note that *nom* doesn't know about files whose names begin with a dot (.). Here's the script:

nom

trap *46.12*

case *46.06*
$ * *46.14*

comm *29.11*
— *14.13*

```
#! /bin/sh
temp=/tmp/NOM$$
stat=1   # ERROR EXIT STATUS (SET TO 0 BEFORE NORMAL EXIT)
trap 'rm -f $temp; exit $stat' 0 1 2 15

# MUST HAVE AT LEAST ONE ARGUMENT.  ALL MUST BE IN CURRENT DIRECTORY:
case "$*" in
"") echo Usage: `basename $0` pattern 1>&2; exit ;;
*/*) echo "`basename $0` quitting: I can't handle '/'s." 1>&2; exit ;;
esac

# GET NAMES WE DON'T WANT TO MATCH; REPLACE BLANKS WITH NEWLINES:
echo "$*" | tr ' ' '\012' | sort > $temp
# COMPARE TO CURRENT DIRECTORY (-1 = ONE NAME PER LINE); OUTPUT NAMES WE WANT:
ls -1 | comm -23 - $temp
stat=0
```

You can remove the -1 option on the script's ls command line if your version of *ls* lists one filename per line by default. The script line with *tr (36.09)* will split filenames containing space characters. You can replace that line with the following three lines; they run more slowly on some shells but will fix this (unlikely) problem:

for *46.15*

done | *47.23*

```
for file
do echo "$file"
done | sort > $temp
```

—*JP*

16.11 Wildcards that Match Only Directories

It's not news that the shell turns `.*` (dot asterisk) into every name in the current directory that starts with a dot: *.login*, *.profile*, *.bin* (I name my directory that way), and so on—including `.` and `..` too.

Also, many people know that the shell turns `*/.*` into a list of the dot files in subdirectories: *foo/.exrc, foo/.hidden, bar/.xxx*—as well as *foo/., foo/.., bar/.*, and *bar/..*, too. (If that surprises you, look at the wildcard pattern closely—or try it on your account with the *echo* command: `echo */.*`.)

What if you're trying to match just the subdirectory names, but not the files in them? The most direct way is: `*/.`—that matches *foo/., bar/.*, and so on. The dot (`.`) entry in each directory is a link to the directory itself *(19.02, 15.04)*, so you can use it wherever you use the directory name. For example, to get a list of the names of your subdirectories, type:

```
$ ls -d */.
bar/.        foo/.
```

(The *–d* option *(17.09)* tells *ls* to list the names of directories, not their contents.) With some C shells (but not all), you don't need the trailing dot (`.`):

```
% ls -d */
bar/        foo/
```

(The shell passes the slashes (`/`) to *ls*. So, if you use the *ls –F* option *(17.13)* to put a slash after directory names, the listing will show *two* slashes after each directory name.)

When matching directory names that start with a dot, the shells expand the `.*/` or `.*/.` and pass the result to *ls*—so you really don't need the *ls –a* option *(17.12)*. The *–a* is useful only when you ask *ls* (not the shell) to read a directory and list the entries in it. You don't have to use *ls*, of course. The *echo (9.04)* command will show the same list more simply.

Here's another example: a Bourne shell loop that runs a command in each subdirectory of your home directory:

```
for dir in $HOME/*/.
do
    cd $dir
    ...Do something...
done
```

That doesn't take care of subdirectories whose names begin with a dot, like my *.bin*—but article 16.06 shows a way to do that too.

Article 22.12 shows a related trick that doesn't involve the shell or wildcards: making a pathname that will only match a directory.

—*JP*

17

Where Did I Put That?

17.01 Everything But the find Command

A computer isn't that much different from a house or an office; unless you're incredibly orderly, you spend a lot of time looking for things that you've misplaced. Even if you are incredibly orderly, you still spend some time looking for things you need—you just have a better idea of where to find them. After all, librarians don't memorize the location of every book in the stacks, but they do know how to find any book, quickly and efficiently, using whatever tools are available. A key to becoming a proficient user of any system, then, is knowing how to find things.

This chapter is about how to find things. We're excluding the *find (18.01)* utility itself because it's complicated and deserves a chapter of its own. We'll concentrate on simpler ways to find files, beginning with some different ways to use *ls*.

—*ML*

17.02 Finding Oldest or Newest Files with ls –t and ls –u

Your directory might have 50, 100, or more files. Which files haven't been used for a while? You might be able to save space by removing them. You read or edited a file yesterday but you can't remember its name? These commands will help you find it.

In this example, I'll show you my *bin (5.02)* directory full of shell scripts and other programs—I want to see which programs I don't use very often. You can use the same technique for directories with text or other files.

The *ls* command has options to change the way it orders files. By default, *ls* lists files alphabetically—that probably won't help you find old files, but it's a good place to start this explanation. For finding old files, use the –*t* option. This sorts files by their *modification time*, or the last time the file was changed. The newest files are listed first. Here's what happens:

```
jerry@ora ~/.bin
60 % ls -t
weather      unshar       scandrafts   rn2mh        recomp
crontab      zloop        tofrom       rmmer        mhprofile
rhyes        showpr       incc         mhadd        append
rhno         rfl          drmm         fixsubj      README
pickthis     maillog      reheader     distprompter rtfm
cgrep        c-w          zrefile      xmhprint     saveart
dirtop       cw           zscan        replf        echoerr
which        cx           zfolders     fols
tcx          showmult     alifile      incs
```

I just added a shell script named *weather* yesterday; you can see it as the first file in the first column. I also made a change to my script named *crontab* last week; it's shown next. The oldest program in here is *echoerr*; it's listed last.*

[Personally, I find *ls –t* most useful when I've forgotten whether or not I've edited a file recently. If I've changed a file, it will be at, or near, the top of the *ls –t* listing. For example, I might ask, "Have I made the changes to that letter I was going to send?" If I haven't made the changes (but only think I have), my letter will most likely appear somewhere in the middle of the listing. —*ML*]

The *–u* option shows the files' last-access time instead of the last-modification time. The *–u* option doesn't do anything with plain *ls*—you have to use it with another option like *–t* or *–l*. The next listing shows that I've recently used the *rtfm* and *rmmer* files. I haven't read *README* in a long time, though—oops:

```
jerry@ora ~/.bin
62 % ls -tu
rtfm         cx           drmm         saveart      fixsubj
rmmer        c-w          zscan        scandrafts   echoerr
rfl          cw           zrefile      rhno         dirtop
mhprofile    distprompter xmhprint     rhyes        cgrep
showmult     recomp       zloop        replf        append
tcx          crontab      zfolders     reheader     alifile
tofrom       mhadd        which        incs         README
rn2mh        pickthis     unshar       maillog
weather      incc         showpr       fols
```

(Some UNIXes don't update the last-access time of executable files *(22.05)* when you run them. Shell scripts are always read, so their last-access times will always be updated.)

The *–c* option shows when the file's inode information *(1.22, 22.06)* was last changed. The inode time tells when the file was created, when you used *chmod* to change the permissions, and so on. That doesn't help you find "stale" files:

---

*If you're a System V user, *ls –t* will probably list the files in one column, with the newest file first. Although that's usually a pain, I actually find that more convenient when I'm interested in the most recent files. If you're a System V user and don't like this single-column display, you can use *ls –Ct*. If you're a BSD user and think that a single column display might be handy, use *ls –1t*. Throughout this article, we'll assume you're using a multi-column display.

```
jerry@ora ~/.bin
64 % ls -tc
weather      maillog     reheader     recomp        incs
crontab      tcx         rn2mh        fols          cx
cgrep        zscan       tofrom       rmmer         cw
zloop        zrefile     mhadd        fixsubj       c-w
dirtop       rfl         drmm         mhprofile     echoerr
pickthis     showmult    alifile      append        which
rhno         rtfm        showpr       saveart       README
unshar       incc        scandrafts   distprompter
rhyes        zfolders    xmhprint     replf
```

If you're wondering just how long ago a file was modified (or accessed), add the *−l* option for a long listing. As before, adding *−u* shows the last-access time; *−c* shows inode change time. If I look at the access times of a few specific files, I find that I haven't read *README* since 1989 . . .

```
jerry@ora ~/.bin
65 % ls -ltu README alifile maillog
-rwxr-xr-x  1 jerry    ora          59 Feb  2  1991 maillog
-rwxrwxr-x  1 jerry    ora         213 Nov 29  1989 alifile
-rw-r--r--  1 jerry    ora        3654 Nov 27  1989 README
```

—JP

17.03 *Reordering ls Listings*

In the previous tutorial *(17.02)*, I introduced you to several different ways of sorting *ls*' output, based on file time. There was one constant: *ls* listings were always from first (most recent) to last, moving (first) down each column and then across the page.

That's often not the most convenient way to look at the world. For example, if you're going to look at a directory with many, many files, it might be easier to list the files *across* the screen first, and then down. This would be particularly nice if you're using a pager (like *pg* or *more (26.03)*) to read the listing. Then the first screenful will show the files at the top of the list. Here's an example:

```
jerry@ora ~/.bin
59 % ls -x | pg
README       alifile     append       c-w           cgrep
crontab      cw          cx           dirtop        distprompter
drmm         echoerr     fixsubj      fols          incc
incs         maillog     mhadd        mhprofile     pickthis
recomp       reheader    replf        rfl           rhno
rhyes        rmmer       rn2mh        rtfm          saveart
scandrafts   showmult    showpr       tcx           tofrom
unshar       weather     which        xmhprint      zfolders
zloop        zrefile     zscan
```

This listing is "alphabetic"—not sorted by time. So *README* is first in the list (uppercase comes below lowercase), and *alifile* is next to it. The *−x* flag makes the output multi-column. BSD doesn't have *−x*. To get the same sorting order under BSD, pipe *ls* output through the *cols (36.14)* script.

Both BSD and System V have the −C option; it sorts filenames down columns instead of across. In fact, −C is the default on BSD when you *aren't* redirecting the output of *ls*. If BSD *ls* detects that it's writing anywhere other than a terminal, it defaults to single-column output, rather than multi-column. Under BSD, you'll need to use −C (or another technique like the *cols* script or *pr −number* (36.15)) to get output in columns when you pipe *ls* output.

The −r option lists the files in reverse order. I find this particularly useful when I'm looking at modification times. Because −t shows files by modification time, newest first—using −tr shows files by modification time, oldest first:

```
jerry@ora ~/.bin
61 % ls -tr
echoerr       replf          zscan        c-w        dirtop
saveart       xmhprint       zrefile      cx         cgrep
rtfm          distprompter   reheader     maillog    pickthis
README        fixsubj        drmm         rfl        rhyes
append        mhadd          incc         showpr     rhno
fols          rmmer          tofrom       zloop      crontab
mhprofile     rn2mh          scandrafts   unshar     weather
recomp        alifile        showmult     tcx
incs          zfolders       cw           which
```

Adding the −u option shows the least recently accessed files first:

```
jerry@ora ~/.bin
63 % ls -tur
README        maillog        which        mhadd          tofrom
alifile       replf          zfolders     crontab        tcx
append        reheader       zloop        recomp         showmult
cgrep         rhyes          xmhprint     distprompter   mhprofile
dirtop        rhno           zscan        cw             rmmer
fixsubj       showpr         zrefile      cx             rfl
echoerr       scandrafts     drmm         c-w            rtfm
fols          saveart        incc         weather
incs          unshar         pickthis     rn2mh
```

—*JP, ML*

17.04 List All Subdirectories with ls −R

By default, *ls* lists just one directory. If you name one or more directories on the command line, *ls* will list each one. The −R (uppercase R) option lists all subdirectories, recursively. That shows you the whole directory tree starting at the current directory (or the directories you name on the command line).

This list can get pretty long; you might want to pipe the output to a pager program like *more* (26.03). The *ls* −C option is a good idea, too, to list the output in columns. (When the *ls* output goes to a pipe, BSD versions of *ls* won't make output in columns automatically.)

—*JP*

17.05 The Three UNIX File Times

When you're talking to experienced UNIX users, you often hear the terms "change time" and "modification time" thrown around cavalierly. [We've done that ourselves; take a look at article 17.02. —*ML*] To most people (and most dictionaries), a change and a modification are the same thing. What's the difference here?

The difference between a change and a modification is the difference between altering the label on a package and altering its contents. If someone says *chmod a–w myfile*, that is a change; if someone says *echo foo >> myfile*, that is a modification. A change modifies the file's inode; a modification modifies the contents of the file itself.

As long as we're talking about change times and modification times, we might as well mention "access times," too. The access time is the last time the file was read or written. So reading a file updates its access time, but not its change time (information about the file wasn't changed) or its modification time (the file itself wasn't changed).

Incidentally, the change time or "ctime" is incorrectly documented as the "creation time" in many places, including some UNIX manuals. Do not believe them.

—*CT*

17.06 Using ls –t to Compare Two File Dates

[BSD and some other UNIXes have .hushlogin files that this article uses as an example. The file-comparison technique will work on all UNIXes and it's useful any time you need to compare two files.—JP]

The *ls* option *–t (17.02)* sorts a list of files with the most recently modified file first. You can test *ls –t* output to find which of two files was modified first. The following lines use a *csh* array *(49.05)* to store the output of *ls –t* comparing two files' modification times. If the */etc/motd* file is newer than the `~/.hushlogin` file, two commands are run. I use these lines in my *.login* file *(2.02)*, though they'll work anywhere in the C shell:

csh_init

```
set files=(`ls -t /etc/motd ~/.hushlogin`)
if ( $files[1] == /etc/motd ) then
    cat /etc/motd
    touch ~/.hushlogin
endif
unset files
```

Note: If you have *ls* aliased *(11.02)* to output anything but filenames (for instance, to print the sizes of files with *–s*) you'll need to use the system version with `/bin/ls` instead of just `ls`.

Let's look at what the example does. The *.hushlogin* file in my home directory keeps *login* from showing the system message file, */etc/motd*, every time I log in. *ls −t* compares the dates on the two files and outputs the newer filename first; it's stored in the first array member, `$files[1]`.

Next, the *if (49.03)* checks to see if the first file is */etc/motd*. If it is, the *motd* has been modified since my *.hushlogin* was. I display the new *motd*. Then I *touch (22.07)* the *.hushlogin* file to update its modification time and flag that I just saw the *motd*.

You can use the same technique to mark the time that something has happened to any file—or to compare any two files or directories. (Use the *ls −d* option *(17.09)* for directories.) Articles 2.16 and 17.28 show other ways to compare file dates.

—JP

17.07 clf, cls: "Compressed" ls Listings

Most newer UNIX systems let you make filenames that are hundreds of characters long. The bad thing about that is that when *ls* lists the filenames in columns, it can't fit many columns across the screen. If your directory has a lot of files, the listing can scroll off the screen.

I wrote a script that lists a directory in five columns. If a filename doesn't fit, the script truncates the name and prints a right angle bracket (>) at the end of the name. Here's a demo. It starts with the standard *ls* and its *−F* option *(17.13)* to mark directories with a trailing / and executable files with a *. Next, *clf* gives the same listing, compressed. Third, *cls* gives a listing without the / and *:

```
% ls -F
HOMEDIR_backup/                         more*
adir/                                   projects.1990/
afile                                   projects.1991/
cfile                                   updatedb.client
dfile                                   zfile
file_with_a_very_long_name_what_a_mess* zoo.tar.Z
jerryp_MH.tar.Z
% clf
HOMEDIR_back>/ cfile          jerryp_MH.tar> projects.1991/ zoo.tar.Z
adir/          dfile          more*          updatedb.clie>
afile          file_with_a_>* projects.1990/ zfile
% cls
HOMEDIR_backup cfile          jerryp_MH.tar> projects.1991  zoo.tar.Z
adir           dfile          more           updatedb.clie>
afile          file_with_a_v> projects.1990  zfile
```

cls

The script has a total of four names (links). *cls* lists in columns that are sorted top to bottom. *clf* is like *cls*, but marks directories and executable files. *cls2* and *clf2* are like *cls* and *clf*, but they sort filenames side to side instead; this is faster but maybe not as easy to read. The script tests its name and does the right commands in a *case* structure *(46.06)* that starts like this:

```
case "$0" in
*clf2)  $ls -F ${1+"$@"} | sed -e "$sed" | $pr -l1; exit ;;
    ...
```

The `${1+"$@"}` passes in quoted filenames from the command line without breaking them into pieces at the spaces. This is a workaround for differences in the way some old Bourne shells handle an empty `"$@"` parameter *(48.07)*.

The "guts" of the shell script is the two-line *sed* *(35.24)* command below (the single quotes around the expression pass both lines into the shell variable at once):

```
sed='/[/@*=]$/s/^\(.............\)...*\([/@*=][/@*=]*\)$/\1>\2/
s/^\(.............\)...*/\1>/'
```

The *ls* output is piped to *sed*'s standard input:

- The first *sed* script line matches lines that are more than 14 characters long and end with one of the symbols `*`, `/`, `@`, or `=`. The "escaped parenthesis" operators `\( . . . \)` *(35.10)* grab the first 12 characters into `\1` and the symbol into `\2`—then print them both together with a > between.

- The second *sed* line matches other filenames over 14 characters that don't end with a symbol. (It won't match filenames that the first line matched because the first line shortened them.) The second line grabs the first 13 characters, prints them with a > on the end.

If you figured that out yourself, tell your manager that I think you deserve a promotion :-).

The other tricky part is this line:

```
$pr -l`expr \( \`wc -l < $temp\` / 5 \) + 1` $temp
```

It's used when you call the script *clf* or *cls* and the filenames need to be printed down columns instead of across. The same kind of line is used in article 36.14—it's explained there. The time that line takes to run is why *clf* and *cls* are a little slower than *clf2* and *cls2*.

You can install this script from the Power Tools disk or from the online archive *(54.07)*. If you get it from the archive, ask tar to install *cls* and its three other links:

```
% tar xvf archive.tar cls clf cls2 clf2
x cls, 1282 bytes, 3 tape blocks
clf linked to cols
cls2 linked to cols
clf2 linked to cols
```

—*JP*

17.08 ls Shortcuts: ll, lf, lg, etc.

The old 4.1BSD UNIX system I worked on in the early 1980s had commands named *ll*, for *ls –l*; *lf*, for *ls –F*; and *lm*, for the (defunct, on BSD at least . . . RIP) *ls –m* command. [For those of us who don't remember it, *ls –m* listed files separated by commas, rather than spaces.—*ML*] When they left my system, I made my own shell script to do the same things. If your system doesn't have these, you can install the script from the Power Tools disk.

This is the single script file for all the commands:

lf

H *35.13*

```
#! /bin/sh
case $0 in
*lf)    exec ls -F "$@";;
*lg)    exec ls -lg "$@";;
*ll)    exec ls -l "$@";;
*lm)    # THIS IS A HACK!   IF THE DIRECTORY IS TOO BIG, IT OVERFLOWS.
        ls -1 "$@" |
        sed -n -e 's/$/,/' -e H -e '$g' -e 's/\n//g' -e '$s/,$//p'
        ;;
*lr)    exec ls -lR "$@";;
*)      echo "$0: Help!  Shouldn't get here!" 1>&2; exit 1;;
esac
```

System V still has the *–m* option, so you won't need the dirty hack there that I used to make comma-separated output. (That command is the BSD *ls –1*, with a digit 1, by the way.) The *exec (47.07)* commands saves a process—this was important on my overloaded VAX 11/750, and doesn't hurt on faster systems.

You can install this script from the Power Tools disk or you can just type it in. If you type it in, don't forget to make the four other links *(19.05)*. Put it in a file named *lf*. Then type:

```
% chmod 755 lf
% ln lf lg
% ln lf ll
% ln lf lm
% ln lf lr
```

The script tests the name it was called with, in $0, to decide which *ls* command to run. This trick saves disk space. You can add other commands, too, by adding a line to the *case* and another link. (For more on shell programming, start with article 46.01.)

—*JP*

17.09 The ls −d Option

If you give *ls* the pathname of a directory, *ls* lists the entries in the directory:

```
% ls -l /home/joanne
total 554
-rw-r--r--  1 joanne       15329 Oct  5 14:33 catalog
-rw-------  1 joanne       58381 Oct 10 09:08 mail
    ...
```

With the −d option, *ls* lists the directory itself:

```
% ls -ld /home/joanne
drwxr-x--x  7 joanne        4608 Oct 10 10:13 /home/joanne
```

The −d option is especially handy when you're trying to list the names of some directories that match a wildcard. Compare the listing with and without the −d option:

```
% ls -Fd [a-c]*
arc/                    bm/                     ctrl/
atcat.c                 cdecl/
atl.c.Z                 cleanscript.c
% ls -F [a-c]*
atcat.c                 atl.c.Z                 cleanscript.c

arc:
BugsEtc.Z     arcadd.c        arcext.c.Z      arcmisc.c.Z
    ...
bm:
Execute.c.Z   MakeDesc.c.Z    MkDescVec.c.Z   Search.c.Z
    ...
```

To list only the directory names, see the tip in article 16.11.

—JP

17.10 An Alias to List Recently Changed Files

Looking for a recently changed file? Not sure of the name? Trying to do this in a directory with lots of files? Try the *lr* alias:

```
alias lr "ls -lagFqt \!* | head"
```

The alias takes advantage of the −*t* option *(17.02)* to *ls*, so that recent files can float to the top of the listing. *head (26.21)* shows just the first ten lines.

A simple *lr* in my home directory gives me:

```
bermuda:home/dansmith :-) lr
total 1616
-rw-------  1 dansmith staff  445092 Oct  7 20:11 .mush256
-rw-r--r--  1 dansmith staff    1762 Oct  7 20:11 .history
drwxr-xr-x 30 dansmith staff    1024 Oct  7 12:59 text/
-rw-------  1 dansmith staff  201389 Oct  7 12:42 .record
drwxr-xr-x 31 dansmith staff    1024 Oct  4 09:41 src/
-rw-r--r--  1 dansmith staff    4284 Oct  4 09:02 .mushrc
    ...
```

You can also give a wildcarded pattern, in order to narrow the search. For example, here's the command to show me the dot files that have changed lately:

.??* 16.06

```
bermuda:home/dansmith :-) lr .??*
-rw-------  1 dansmith staff    445092 Oct  7 20:11 .mush256
-rw-r--r--  1 dansmith staff      1762 Oct  7 20:11 .history
-rw-------  1 dansmith staff    201389 Oct  7 12:42 .record
-rw-r--r--  1 dansmith staff      4284 Oct  4 09:02 .mushrc
   ...
```

—DS

17.11 findcmd: Find a Command in Your Search Path

UNIX has utilities like *whereis* (52.05) and *which* (52.07) to look for a command on the system. But *whereis* doesn't look in your shell's search path, so it may not find shell scripts in local system directories or your *bin* directory (5.02). And to use *which*, you have to know the exact name of the command, because *which* only shows the first command with that name in your path.

If you're like me, you can't always remember the name of the command you're looking for. "Wasn't it called *reference* or *refer* or something like that?" The *findcmd* script saves me a lot of guessing. It shows all command names, in all directories in my search path, that contain some string. So, I'll look for command names that have "ref" in them:

```
% findcmd ref
/home/jerry/.bin/zrefile
/usr/bin/X11/xrefresh
/usr/local/bin/grefer
/bin/cxref
/bin/refer
/usr/bin/cxref
/usr/bin/refer
./preferences
```

findcmd

After a couple of tries, I usually find the command I want. The *findcmd* script is on the Power Tools disk.

First the script edits a copy of your *PATH* (7.04) to change any current directory entry to a dot (:.:). Next, a colon in the *IFS* (36.19) variable lets the shell split the *PATH* at the colons; a *for* loop (46.15) steps through each directory in the *PATH* and runs *ls −l* to find matching files. Finally, a *sed* (35.24) script reads through the output of all the *ls* commands in the loop, editing and printing matching lines (executable files with the program name we want).

—JP

17.12 Showing Hidden Files with ls –A and –a

The *ls* command normally ignores any files whose names begin with a dot (.). This is often very convenient: UNIX has lots of small configuration files, scratch files, etc. that you really don't care about and don't want to be bothered about most of the time. However, there are some times when you care very much about these files. If you want to see "hidden" files, use the command *ls –a*. For example:

```
% cd
% ls            Don't show hidden files
Mail      mail.txt      performance    powertools
% ls -a         This time, show me EVERYTHING
.          .emacs       Mail           powertools
..         .login       mail.txt
.cshrc     .mailrc      performance
```

With the *–a* option, we see four additional files: the C shell initialization file, the login initialization file, the customization files for the GNU Emacs editor, and mail. We also see two "special" entries, . and .., which represent the current directory and the parent of the current directory. All UNIX directories contain these two entries *(19.02)*.

If you don't want to be bothered with . and .., Berkeley UNIX systems also have a *–A* option:

```
% ls -A         Show me everything but . and ..
.cshrc     .login       Mail           performance
.emacs     .mailrc      mail.txt       powertools
```

—ML

17.13 Useful ls Aliases

Because *ls* is one of the most commonly used UNIX commands and provides numerous options, it's a good idea to create aliases for the display formats that best suit your needs. For example, many users *always* want to know about their "hidden" files. That's reasonable—they're just as important as any other files you have. In some cases, they can grow to take up lots of room (for example, some editors hide backup files), so it's worth being aware of them.

Rather than typing `ls -a` every time, you can create a convenient alias that supplies the *–a* or *–A* option *(17.12)* automatically:

```
alias la "ls -aF"
```

or:

```
alias la "ls -AF"
```

Two things to note here. First, I recommend using *la* as the name of the alias, rather than just renaming *ls*. I personally think it's dangerous to hide the pure, unadulterated command underneath an alias; it's better to pick a new name, and get used to using that name. If you ever need the original *ls* for some reason, you'll be able to get at it without problems.

Second, what's with the *−F* option? I just threw it in to see if you were paying attention. It's actually quite useful; many users add it to their *ls* aliases. The *−F* option shows you the *type* of file in each directory by printing an extra character after each filename. Table 17-1 lists what the extra character can be.

Table 17-1. Filename Types Listed by ls −F

Character	Definition
(nothing)	The file is a regular file.
*	The file is an executable.
/	The file is a directory.
@	The file is a symbolic link (19.04) (BSD and SVR4 only).
=	The file is a "socket" (don't worry about this).

For example:

```
% la              Alias includes −F functionality
.cshrc    .login       Mail/        performance/
.emacs    .mailrc      mail.txt     powertools@
```

This says that *Mail* and *performance* are directories. *powertools* is a symbolic link (*ls −l* will show you what it's linked to). There are no executables or "sockets" in this directory.

You may want this version instead:

```
alias la ls -aFC
```

The *−C* option lists the files in multiple columns. This option isn't needed on systems where multi-column output is the normal behavior (for example, in SVR4). Note, however, that when piped to another command, *ls* output is single-column unless *−C* is used. For example, use `ls -C | more` to preserve multiple columns.

Finally, if you often need the full listing, use the alias:

```
alias ll ls -l
```

This alias may not seem like much of a shortcut until after you've typed it a dozen times. In addition, it's easy to remember as "long listing." Some UNIX systems even include *ll* as a regular command.

—*DG, ML*

17.14 Can't Access a File? Look for Spaces in the Name

What's wrong here?

```
% ls
afile    exefiles   j        toobig
% lpr afile
lpr: afile: No such file or directory
```

Huh?? *ls* shows that the file is there, doesn't it? Try using:

–v 26.07
–t –e 26.06

```
% ls -l | cat -v -t -e
total 89$
-rw-rw-rw-  1 jerry           28 Mar  7 19:46 afile $
-rw-r--r--  1 root         25179 Mar  4 20:34 exefiles$
-rw-rw-rw-  1 jerry          794 Mar  7 14:23 j$
-rw-r--r--  1 root           100 Mar  5 18:24 toobig$
```

The *cat –e* option marks the ends of lines with a $. Notice that `afile` has a $ out past the start of the column. Aha . . . the filename ends with a space. White-space characters like TABs have the same problem, though the default *ls –q* (17.15) option (on many UNIX versions) shows them as ? if you're using a terminal.

To rename *afile*, giving it a name without the space, type:

```
% mv "afile " afile
```

The quotes (9.10) tell the shell to include the space as part of the first argument it passes to *mv*. The same quoting works for other UNIX commands like *rm*, too.

—JP

17.15 Showing Non-printable Characters in Filenames

From time to time, you may get files with non-printing characters, spaces, and other garbage in them. This usually is the result of some mistake—but it's a pain nevertheless.

If you're using BSD UNIX, the *ls* command gives you some help; it will convert all non-printing characters to a question mark (?), giving you some idea that something funny is there.* For example:

```
% ls
ab??cd
```

This shows that there are two non-printing characters between `ab` and `cd`. To delete (or rename) this file, you can use a wildcard pattern like *ab??cd*.

---

*The *–q* option is the default only when *ls*'s standard output is a terminal. If you pipe the output or redirect it to a file, remember to add *–q*.

BE CAREFUL. When I was new to UNIX, I once accidentally generated a lot of weird filenames. *ls* told me that they all began with *????*, so I naively typed rm ????*. That's when my troubles began. See article 24.02 for the rest of the gruesome story. (I spent the next day and night trying to undo the damage.) THE MORAL IS: It's always a good idea to use *echo* to test filenames with wildcards in them.

If you're using System V UNIX, you have a different set of problems. System V's *ls* doesn't convert the non-printing characters to question marks. In fact, it doesn't do anything at all—it just spits these weird characters at your terminal, which can respond in any number of strange and hostile ways. Most of the non-printing characters have special meanings—ranging from "don't take any more input" to "clear the screen."

To prevent this, use the *−b* option.* This tells *ls* to print the octal value of any non-printing characters, preceded by a backslash. For example, on System V:

```
% ls -b
ab\013\014cd
```

This shows that the non-printing characters have octal values 13 and 14, respectively. If you look up these values in an ASCII table *(53.03)*, you'll see that they correspond to CTRL-k and CTRL-l. And—if you think about what's happening—you'll realize that CTRL-l is a formfeed character, which tells many terminals to clear the screen. That's why the regular *ls* command behaved so strangely.

Once you know what you're dealing with, you can use a wildcard pattern to delete or rename the file.

—ML

17.16 Alias with a :-) for UNIX Converts: dir

I've switched back and forth between UNIX, VMS, MS/DOS, and other OSes. Others use *DIR* to do what *ls* does on UNIX. This alias and ones like it save me retyping a command and give me a grin, too:

```
% dir
Hey! This is UNIX! Well, okay... but just this once...
total 265
-rw-rw-r--  1 ellie      47279 Dec 16 13:22 2edit.2
-rw-r--r--  1 jerry      21802 Nov 12 18:24 7911.ps
drwxrwsr-x  2 jerry      14848 Dec 24 07:17 RCS
-r-xr-xr-x  1 ruth         649 Oct 25 13:11 artnums
-rw-rw-r--  1 len        86345 Oct 30 12:19 bmb.bug
-r--r--r--  1 ellie      19900 Dec 23 13:22 ellie.disk
    ...
```

---

*On BSD, pipe the *ls −q* output through *cat −v* or *od −c (26.07)* to see what the non-printing characters are.

The alias is below. I've broken the alias onto two lines for printing; you can type it all on one line if you'd like.

csh_init

```
alias dir 'echo Hey! This is UNIX! \\
           Well, okay... but just this once...; ls -l'
```

—JP

17.17 Picking a Unique Filename Automatically

Shell scripts, aliases, and other programs can need temporary files to hold data used later. If the program will be run more than once, or if the temp file needs to stay around after the program is done, you need some way to make a unique filename.

One way is with the shell's process ID number *(40.03)*, available in the *$$* parameter and often used in the */tmp* directory *(22.03)*. You might name a file */tmp/MYPROG$$*; the shell will turn that into something like */tmp/MYPROG1234* or */tmp/MYPROG28471*. If your program needs more than one temporary file, add an extra unique character to the names:

```
errs=/tmp/MYPROGe$$
output=/tmp/MYPROGo$$
```

Remember the 14-character filename limit on some older UNIXes. *$$* usually makes two to five characters.

If your UNIX doesn't have a *date* command that takes a + parameter to change its output format, you should get one *(53.10)*. For example, to output the *month*, *day*, *Hour*, *Minute*, and *Second*:

```
% date
Thu May 30 07:21:13 EDT 1991
% date +'%m%d%H%M%S'
0530072124
```

Use a + parameter and backquotes (` `` `) *(10.14)* to get a temp file named for the current date and/or time. For instance, on May 31 the command below would store *foo.0531* in the Bourne shell variable *temp*. On December 7, it would store *foo.1207*:

```
temp=foo.`date +'%m%d'`
```

Article 22.03 shows another system for temporary files.

—JP

17.18 Getting Directory Name From a File's Pathname

When you write shell scripts or functions, sometimes you have a file's absolute pathname but need the parent directory's name. (You might need the parent's name to see if you have write permission in the directory—say, to remove or rename the file.)

If the pathname is stored in a *csh* shell (not environment) variable, use the modifier : h *(12.08)*. In the Bourne shell, see if your system has the *dirname (47.18)* command. If it doesn't, use *expr (47.28)* with a regular expression *(27.04)* that gives you everything up to (but not including) the last slash. For example, if the pathname */home/mktg/fred/afile* is stored in the shell variable *file*, these *csh* and *sh* commands would store */home/mktg/fred* into the variable *dir*:

```
% set dir=$file:h
$ dir=`dirname "$file"`
$ dir=`expr "$file" : '\(.*\)/[^/][^/]*$'`
```

To handle multiple pathnames, give this regular expression to *sed (35.24)*:

@ 35.07

```
% ... sed 's@/[^/][^/]*$@@' ...
```

—JP

17.19 Listing Files You've Created/Edited Today

If your directory is full of files and you're trying to find out which files you've made changes to (and created) today, here's how.* Make a shell script that stores today's date in the shell's command-line parameters. Pipe the output of *ls −l* to an *awk* script. In the *awk* script, put the month (which was the second word in the *date* output) into the *awk* string variable *m*. Put the date into the *awk* integer variable *d*—use an integer variable so *date* outputs like Jun 04 will match *ls* outputs like Jun   4. Print any line where the two dates match.

ls_today

```
#!/bin/sh
set `date`
ls -l | awk "BEGIN { m = \"$2\"; d = $3 } \$5 == m && \$6 == d  {print}"
```

If your version of *ls −l* gives both the file's owner and group, change $5 to $6 and $6 to $7. You can make your life simpler by getting *sls (17.30)*—it lets you set the output format (including the date format) exactly.

—JP

---

*Using *find* with *−mtime −1 (18.07)* will list files modified within the last 24 hours. That's not quite the same thing.

17.20 stree: Simple Directory Tree

Here's a simple script that prints a directory tree. It works on any terminal, can be printed or sent in a mail message, and so on. If you don't give *stree* a directory name, it starts at the current directory. If you give it a *–a* (all) option, the *stree* script lists all files, directories, symbolic links, etc. Otherwise, it just lists directories. For example:

```
% stree lib
Tree for directory lib:

lib
    "        at_cron
    "        "        RCS
    "        "        test
    "        csh
    "        ksh
    "        RCS.Z
    "        tmac
    "        "        mm
    "        "        "        RCS
    "        "        ms
    "        "        "        RCS
```

The top-level directory is listed along the left-hand edge. The first level of sub-directories is indented by one tabstop. A ditto mark (") below a name means "same parent directory as above." So, for example, the last directory in that listing is *lib/tmac/ms/RCS.*

Here's the script:

stree

${1-.} *47.12*

```
#! /bin/sh

case "$1" in
-a) shift
    dir=${1-.}   # DEFAULT TO CURRENT DIRECTORY
    echo Tree for directory $dir and its files:
    ;;
*)  findtype="-type d"   # IF NO -a FLAG, MAKE find USE "-type d"
    dir=${1-.}
    echo Tree for directory $dir:
    ;;
esac
```

"newline *9.10*

@ *35.07*

```
echo "
$dir"
find $dir $findtype -print |
tr / \\001 | sort -f | tr \\001 / |
sed -e s@\^$dir@@ -e /\^$/d -e 's@[^/]*@ TAB @g'
```

The script uses *tr (36.09)* to change slash (/) characters into CTRL-a (octal 001 *(53.03)*) during the sort. That makes the slashes sort before letters and other characters so the directory names will always come out before their contents.

—*JP*

17.21 The vtree Visual Directory Tree Programs

vtree

The *vtree* program is similar to *stree* (17.20), but it has a few extra features that might make it worth your while. You can use *vtree* to get information not only about the directories, but about how much disk space they use:

```
% vtree /usr
/usr : 0
    lost+found : 0
    local : 13880
        lost+found : 0
        bin : 23673
            RCS : 41
        lib : 6421
            news : 28896
                bin : 2
            newsbin : 269
                batch : 97
                expire : 138
                input : 91
```

vtree also has options to show how many inodes *(1.22)* are in each directory and to control how many levels down to display. The *-v* option tells *vtree* to give a "visual" display, showing the directory structure:

```
% vtree -v /usr
/usr ------+-> lost+found
           +-> local -----+-> lost+found
           |              +-> bin -------+-> RCS
           |              +-> lib -------+-> news ------+-> bin
           |              |              +-> newsbin ---+-> batch
           |              |              |              +-> expire
           |              |              |              +-> input
           ...
```

—LM

17.22 Finding All Directories with the Same Name

Time for a confession. I collect a lot of software. I have one disk filled with public-domain software. Some directories are "collections" like the Sun User Group tapes. It is likely that I might have the same program in two different directories. To prevent this waste of space, I create an index of directories and the path needed to reach them. If I have two directories with the same name, I would like to know about it. I might be able to delete one of the directories. A simple way to search for redundant directories is with the following command:

```
find . -type d -print | \
awk -F/ '{printf("%s\t%s\n",$NF,$0);}' | \
sort
```

[You might want to make this into an alias or function *(11.01)*. *—JP*] The *find* *(18.01)* command prints out all directories. The *awk* *(38.18)* command uses the slash (/) as the field separator. NF is the number of fields, and $NF the last field. $0 is the *awk* variable for the entire line. The output would tell you where all of the directories named *misc* are located:

```
misc    ./X11/lib/X11/fonts/misc
misc    ./misc
misc    ./src/XView2/contrib/examples/misc
misc    ./src/XView2/fonts/bdf/misc
misc    ./src/XView2/lib/libxvin/misc
misc    ./src/XView2/lib/libxvol/misc
misc    ./src/XView2/misc
```

This could be converted into a shell script that takes arguments. If no arguments are specified, I want it to default to the argument **.** (dot):

dir_path
${*-.} *47.12*

```
#!/bin/sh
# usage: dir_path [directory ...]
# list directory and path to directory
find ${*-.} -type d -print | awk -F/ '
{
    printf ("%s\t%s\n",$NF,$0);
}' | sort
```

[You could also use this great idea for finding duplicate files. Change the -type d to -type f. If you (or all the users on your system) want to use this a lot, run *dir_path* nightly with *cron (42.12)* or *at (42.03)*. Save the output to a "database" file. Use the speedy *look* command *(28.18)* to search the database file. Article 18.19 shows another *find* database. —*JIK, JP*]

—*BB*

17.23 *Comparing Two Directory Trees with dircmp*

You have an original directory. You copy the files in it to another directory, edit some of them, and add a few others. Later, you want to know the differences between the two directories. If your system's *diff (29.01)* has a –*r* (recursive) option, you can use that. System V has *dircmp*. The output of *dircmp* is formatted with *pr(45.07)*; you get 66-line-long pages with headings:

```
% dircmp a b

Sep 16 09:26 1991   a only and b only Page 1

./foo.tmp                              ./defs.h
        ...

Sep 16 09:26 1991   Comparison of a b Page 1

directory   .
same        ./Makefile
directory   ./data
same        ./data/test1
same        ./data/test2
        ...
```

```
different    ./pqp.help
same         ./pqs.help
             ...
```

In the a only and b only listing, files only in the first directory are in the first column and files only in the second directory are in the second column. The Comparison of a b listing compares files that are in both directories. The comparison is recursive—if there are any subdirectories, *dircmp* checks those, too.

The *dircmp* *−s* option stops the "identical file" messages. Use *−d* to run *diff* on files that are different; *dircmp* prints a new page for each *diff* it runs:

```
% dircmp -d -s a b
Sep 16 09:35 1991  a only and b only Page 1
   ...
Sep 16 09:35 1991  Comparison of a b Page 1
   ...
Sep 16 09:35 1991  diff of ./pqp.help in a and b Page 1

3c3,4
< -#     "Only this printer"... 'pqp -3' would print on #3.
---
> -#     "Only this printer"... 'pqp -3' would print only on #3;
>        other printer queues will be held.
   ...
```

The designers assumed you'd want to send the output to a printer. I usually read it on my screen with the *less (26.04)* pager and its *−s* option, which squeezes out the multiple blank lines. If you don't have *less* or *more −s*, try piping the output through *cat −s (26.10)* or a *sed* filter *(35.18)*.

—JP

17.24 *Comparing Filenames in Two Directory Trees*

Do you have two directory trees full of subdirectories and files? Would you like to compare the filenames to see if there are some files only in one tree or the other? If you don't have *dircmp (17.23)*, look at the quick-and-dirty substitute in the example below. The numbered prompts *(8.02)* like 3% are just for reference:

```
1% cd directory1
2% find . -type f -print | sort >/tmp/dir1
3% cd directory2
4% find . -type f -print | sort >/tmp/dir2
5% comm -3 /tmp/dir[12]
6% rm /tmp/dir[12]
```

[..] *16.02*

The *comm (29.11)* command will give you two columns: files in the left-hand column are only in *directory1*. Files in the right-hand column are only in *directory2*. You can get other information, too, like a list of files that are in both trees.

This works nicely for directory trees on other computers, too. Run one find | sort on the remote system. Transfer that file to the computer with the other directory tree and run *comm* there. Or do the *diff* across the network by replacing commands 3-5 above with:

rsh *1.33*

```
% rsh host \
    'cd directory2; find . -type f -print | sort' | \
    comm -e /tmp/dir1 -
```

The - argument tells *comm* to read its standard input (from the remote *find* command). Article 14.13 shows a similar trick for a filesystem across a network. Articles 17.20 and 17.21 are about programs that help you see a directory tree.

—*JP*

17.25 *Counting Files by Types*

I use *awk (38.18)* a lot. One of my favorite features of *awk* is its associative arrays. This means *awk* can use anything as an index into an array. In the next example, I use the output of the *file (26.08)* command as the index into an array to count how many files there are of each type:

count_types

${*-.} *47.12*
xargs *10.19*

```
#!/bin/sh
# usage: count_types [directory ...]
# Counts how many files there are of each type
# Original by Bruce Barnett
# Updated version by yu@math.duke.edu (Yunliang Yu)
find ${*-.} -type f -print | xargs file |
awk '{
        $1=NULL;
        t[$0]++;
}
END {
        for (i in t) printf("%d\t%s\n", t[i], i);
}' | sort -nr    # Sort the result numerically, in reverse
```

The output of this might look like:

```
38   ascii text
32   English text
20   c program text
17   sparc executable not stripped
12   compressed data block compressed 16 bits
8    executable shell script
1    sparc demand paged dynamically linked executable
1    executable /bin/make script
```

—*BB*

17.26 Listing Files by Age and Size

If you find a large directory, and most of the files are new, that directory may not be suitable for removal, as it is still being used. Here is a script that lists a summary of file sizes, broken down into the time of last modification. You may remember that *ls* −*l* will list the month, day, hour, and minute if the file is less than six months old, and show the month, day, and year if the file is more than six months old. Using this, the script creates a summary for each of the last six months, and each year for files older than that:

age_files

```
#!/bin/sh
# usage: age_files [directory ...]
# lists size of files by age
#
# pick which version of ls you use
#    System V
#LS="ls -ls"
#    Berkeley
LS="ls -lsg"
#
find ${*:-.} -type f -print | xargs $LS | awk '
# argument 7 is the month; argument 9 is either hh:mm or yyyy
# test if argument is hh:mm or yyyy format
{ if (split($9,junk,":") == 1) {
      sz[$9]+=$1;
      } else {
      sz[$7]+=$1;
      }
}
END {
      for (i in sz) printf("%d\t%s\n", sz[i], i);
}' | sort -nr
```

${*:-.} *47.12*
xargs *10.19*

The program might generate results like this:

```
5715   1991
3434   1992
2929   1989
1738   Dec
1495   1990
1227   Jan
1119   Nov
953    Oct
61     Aug
40     Sep
```

—BB

17.27 Finding Text Files with findtext

Some of my directories—my *bin (5.02)*, for instance—have some text files (like shell scripts and documentation) as well as non-text files (executable binary files, compressed files, archives, etc.). If I'm trying to find a certain file—with *grep (28.01)* or a pager *(26.03, 26.04)*—the non-text files can print garbage on my screen. I want some way to say "only look at the files that have text in them."

The *findtext* shell script does that. It runs *file (26.08)* to guess what's in each file. It only prints filenames of text files.

So, for example, instead of typing:

```
% egrep something *
```

I type:

10.14

```
% egrep something `findtext *`
```

Here's the script, then some explanation of how to set it up on your system:

findtext

```
#!/bin/sh

# PIPE OUTPUT OF file THROUGH sed TO PRINT FILENAMES FROM LINES
# WE LIKE.  NOTE: DIFFERENT VERSIONS OF file RETURN DIFFERENT
# MESSAGES.  CHECK YOUR SYSTEM WITH strings /usr/bin/file OR
# cat /etc/magic AND ADAPT THIS.
/usr/bin/file "$@" |
sed -n '
/MMDF mailbox/b print
/Interleaf ASCII document/b print
/PostScript document/b print
/Frame Maker MIF file/b print
/c program text/b print
/fortran program text/b print
/assembler program text/b print
/shell script/b print
/c-shell script/b print
/shell commands/b print
/c-shell commands/b print
/English text/b print
/ascii text/b print
/\[nt\]roff, tbl, or eqn input text/b print
/executable .* script/b print
b
:print
s/:TAB.*//p'
```

The script is simple: It runs *file* on the command-line arguments. The output of *file* looks like this:

```
COPY2PC:          directory
Ex24348:          empty
FROM_consult.tar.Z:        compressed data block compressed 16 bits
```

```
GET_THIS:       ascii text
hmo:            English text
msg:            English text
1991.ok:        [nt]roff, tbl, or eqn input text
```

The output is piped to a *sed (35.24)* script which selects the lines that seem to be from text files—after the print label, the script strips off everything after the filename (starting at the colon) and prints the filename.

Different versions of *file* produce different output. Some versions also read an */etc/magic* file. To find the kinds of names your *file* calls text files, use commands like:

```
% strings /usr/bin/file > possible
% cat /etc/magic >> possible
% vi possible
```

The *possible* file will have a list of descriptions that *strings* found in the *file* binary; some of them are for text files. If your system has an */etc/magic* file, it will have lines like these:

```
0    long      0x1010101      MMDF mailbox
0    string    <!OPS          Interleaf ASCII document
0    string    %!             PostScript document
0    string    <MIFFile       Frame Maker MIF file
```

Save the descriptions of text-type files from the right-hand column.

Then, turn each line of your edited *possible* file into a *sed* command:

b print *35.19*   **/description/b print**

Watch for special characters in the *file* descriptions. I had to handle two special cases in the last two lines of the script above:

- I had to change the string executable %s script from our *file* command to /executable .* script/b print in the *sed* script. That's because our *file* command replaces %s with a name like /bin/ksh.

- Characters that *sed* will treat as a regular expression, such as the brackets in [nt]roff, need to be escaped with backslashes. I used \[nt\]troff in the script.

If you have *perl (39.01)*, you can do all this much more simply, since *perl* has a built-in test for whether or not a file is a text file. (Of course, you have to agree with *perl*'s choice of what a "text file" is.) The *perl* command looks like this:

```
% perl -le '-T && print while $_ = shift' *
```

csh_init

If you want to put that into an alias *(11.02)*, the C shell's quoting problems *(49.02, 9.11)* make it tough to do. Thanks to *makealias (11.09)*, though, here's an alias that does the job:

```
alias findtext 'perl -le '\''-T && print while $_ = shift'\'' *'
```

—*JP*

17.28 newer: Print the Name of the Newest File

Here's a quick alias that figures out which file in a group is the newest:

-d *17.09*

```
alias newer "ls -dt \!* | head -1"
```

If your system doesn't have a *head (26.21)* command, use *sed 1q* instead.

For example, let's say that you have two files named *plan.v1* and and *plan.v2*. If you're like me, you (often) edit the wrong version by mistake—and then, a few hours later, can't remember what you did. You can use this alias to figure out which file you changed most recently:

* *16.02*

```
% newer plan.v*
plan.v1
```

Oops. I edited the wrong version by mistake. I could also have used backquotes *(10.14)* to handle this in one step:

```
% emacs `newer plan.*`
```

—*ML*

17.29 oldlinks: Find Unconnected Symbolic Links

One problem with symbolic links is that they're relatively "fragile" *(19.06)*. The link and the file itself are different kinds of entities; the link only stores the name of the "real" file. Therefore, if you delete or rename the real file, you can be left with a "dead" or "old" link: a link that points to a file that doesn't exist.

This causes no end of confusion, particularly for new users. For example, you'll see things like this:

```
% ls nolink
nolink
% cat nolink
cat: nolink: No such file or directory
```

The file's obviously there, but *cat* tells you that it doesn't exist.

There's no real solution to this problem, except to be careful. One way to be careful is to write a script that checks links to see whether or not they exist. Here's one such script; it uses *find* to track down all links, and then uses *sed* to write a short C shell script that tests the links and lists any that aren't properly "resolved."

```
#! /bin/csh -f
# csh script to find and print outdated symbolic links, searching
# (recursively) downwards into the specified directories.
#     By Mike Schwartz, 11-20-85.
#     University of Washington Computer Science Department

set temp=/tmp/TSTLINKS$$
```

oldlinks

```
if $#argv == 0 then
    /bin/sh -c "echo 'Usage: oldlinks <directory> [<directory>, ...]' 1>&2"
    exit 1
endif

onintr cleanup
find $* -type l -print | sed 's/.*/if !(-e &) echo &/' > $temp
source $temp

cleanup:
rm -f $temp
```

The script only lists "dead" links; it doesn't try to delete them or do anything drastic. If you want to take some other action (like deleting these links automatically), you can use the output of the script in backquotes. For example:

```
% rm `oldlinks`
```

[The strange-looking *sh* and *echo* line line that makes the script's error message works around a *csh* programming nightmare *(49.02)*: the C shell can only write error messages to standard output. If you'd run the script from inside backquotes without this Bourne shell trick, and the script printed an error message, the backquotes would make *rm* try to remove files named *Usage:*, *oldlinks*, *<directory>*, and so on. —JP]

Tom Christiansen offers the following alternative, using *perl (39.01)*:

```
% find . -type l -print | perl -nle '-e || print'
```

—ML

17.30 sls: Super ls with Format You Can Choose

The *ls* −*l* command, and related commands like *stat (22.13)*, give lots of information about a file (more exactly, about a file's inode *(1.22)*). The information is printed in a way that's (sort of) nice to look at. But the format might not be exactly what you want. That format can be tough for shell programmers to use: parsing the output with *sed*, *awk*, and others is tricky and a pain (articles 38.10 and 17.26 have examples). Finally, the *ls* −*l* output is different on BSD and System V systems.

sls

The *sls* command solves those problems and more. It lets you:

- Make your own output format: pick the information you want to see and the order it's shown.

- Sort the output on one or more fields.

- Make a consistent date format: numeric or in words, include the seconds if you want to, and more. Best of all, the date format won't change for files more than six months old (unless you use the −*u* option).

- There's much more.

The manual page on the disk explains *sls* formatting in detail. Here are a few examples. Let's start with the normal Berkeley *ls* −*l* output. (The default *sls* −*l* gives a standard date without the six-month format switch or another shell programmer's headache, the *total* line.)

```
% ls -l
total 3
-rw-r-----   1 jerry          1641 Feb 29  1992 afile
lrwxrwxrwx   1 jerry             8 Nov 18 00:38 bfile -> ../bfile
```

Here's a more user-friendly format for people who aren't UNIX hackers (it might be best to put this into an alias or shell function *(11.01)*). The date and time are shown, followed by the owner's name, the size in kbytes, and the filename without the symbolic link information like -> ../bfile:

```
% sls -p '%m"%F %d, 19%y  %r"  %u %4skK %n'
February 29, 1992  03:43:00 PM   jerry   2K afile
November 18, 1992  00:38:22 AM   jerry   1K bfile
```

How about a simple *ls* output that shows all three file dates *(17.05)*: modification, access, and inode change? We'll use *echo(9.04)* to print a title first:

```
% echo 'modify   access   inode'; \
sls -p '%m"%D" %a"%D" %c"%D" %n'
modify   access   inode
02/29/92 09/17/92 11/18/92 afile
11/18/92 11/18/92 11/18/92 bfile
```

Finally, let's ask *sls* to make a set of UNIX commands that could be used at the end of a shell archive *(20.02)* file. These commands would recreate the modes, date and owner (with a numeric UID) as the files are extracted from the archive:

touch 22.07
```
% sls -p 'chmod %P %n; chown %U %n; touch %m"%m%d%H%M%y" %n'
chmod 640 afile; chown  225 afile; touch 0229154392 afile
chmod 777 bfile; chown  225 bfile; touch 1118003892 bfile
```

I didn't show the sorting options or many of the other output format characters. But I hope I've given you an idea (or ten).

—JP

18

Finding Files with find

18.01 *The find Command is Great;*
The Problem is Finding How to Use It

find is one of UNIX's most useful and important utilities. It finds files that match a given set of parameters, ranging from the file's name to its modification date. In this chapter, we'll be looking at many of the things it can do. As an introduction, here's a quick summary of its features and operators:

```
% find path operators
```

where *path* is the directory in which *find* will begin to search and *operators* (or, in more customary jargon, *options*) tell *find* which files you're interested in. The *operators* are:

-name *filename*
: Find files with the given *filename*. This is the most commonly used operator. *filename* may include wildcards *(16.02)*, but if it does, it must be quoted to prevent the shell from interpreting the wildcards. See article 18.04.

-perm *mode*
: Find files with the given access *mode (23.02)*. You must give the access mode in octal *(1.23)*. See articles 18.10 and 18.15.

-type *c*
: The files of the given type, specified by *c*. *c* is a one-digit code; for example, f for a plain file, b for a block special file, l for a symbolic link, etc. See article 18.13.

-user *name*
: Find files belonging to user *name*. *name* may also be a user ID number *(40.03)*. See article 18.16.

-group *name*
: Find files belonging to group *name*. *name* may also be a group ID number *(40.03)*. See article 18.16.

-size *n*
: Find files that are *n* blocks long. A block equals 512 bytes. The notation +*n* says "find files that are over

n blocks long." The notation *nc* says "find files that are *n* characters long." Can you guess what +*nc* means? See article 18.14.

-inum *n*   Find files with the inode number *(1.22)* *n*. See article 18.10.

-atime *n*   Find files that were accessed *n* days ago. +*n* means "find files that were accessed over *n* days ago" (i.e., not accessed in the last *n* days). -*n* means "find files that were accessed less than *n* days ago" (i.e., accessed in the last *n* days). See articles 18.05 and 18.07.

-mtime *n*   Similar to *atime*, except that it checks the time the file's contents were modified. See articles 18.05 and 18.07.

-ctime *n*   Similar to *atime*, except that it checks the time the inode *(1.22)* was last changed. "Changed" means that the file was modified or that one of its attributes (for example, its owner) was changed. See articles 18.05 and 18.07.

-newer *file*   Find files that have been modified more recently than the given *file*. See articles 18.08 and 18.09.

Of course, you often want to take some action on files that match several criteria. So we need some way to combine several operators:

operator1 -a *operator2*
                    Find files that match both *operator1* and *operator2*. The -a isn't necessary; when two search parameters are juxtaposed, *find* assumes you want files that match both of them. See article 18.12.

operator1 -o *operator2*
                    Find files that match either *operator1* or *operator2*. See article 18.06.

! *operator*   Find all files that do *not* match the given *operator*. The ! performs a logical NOT operation. See article 18.06.

\(*expression* \)
                    Logical precedence; in a complex expression, evaluate this part of the *expression* before the rest. See article 18.06.

Another group of operators tells *find* what action to take when it locates a file:

-print   Print the file's name on standard output. See articles 18.02 and 18.03.

| -exec *command* | Execute *command*. To include the pathname of the file that's just been found in *command*, use the special symbol { }. *command* must end with a backslash followed by a semicolon (\ ;). For example: |

```
% find -name "*.o" -exec rm -f {} \;
```

tells *find* to delete any files whose names end in *.o*. See article 18.10.

| -ok *command* | Same as *–exec*, except that *find* prompts you for permission before executing *command*. This is a useful way to test *find* commands. See article 18.10. |

A last word: *find* is one of the tools that vendors frequently fiddle with, adding (or deleting) a few operators that they like (or dislike). The operators listed above should be valid on virtually any system. If you check your system's manual page, you may find a few others.

—ML

18.02 *Delving Through a Deep Directory Tree*

The first, and most obvious, use is *find*'s ability to locate old, big, or unused files whose locations you've forgotten. However, what may be *find*'s most fundamentally important characteristic is its ability to travel down subdirectories.

Normally the shell provides the argument list to a command. That is, UNIX programs are frequently given filenames and not directory names. Only a few programs can be given a directory name and march down the directory searching for subdirectories. The programs *find, tar, du,* and *diff* do this. Some versions of *chmod, chgrp, ls, rm,* and *cp* will, but only if a *–r* or *–R* option is specified.

In general, most commands do not understand directory structures, and rely on the shell to expand wildcards *(16.02)* to directory names. That is, to delete all files whose names end with a *.o* in a group of directories, you could type:

```
% rm *.o */*.o */*/*.o
```

Not only is this tedious to type, it may not find all of the files you are searching for. The shell has certain blind spots. It will not match files in directories whose names start with a dot. And, if any files match */*/*/*.o, they would not be deleted.

Another problem is typing the above and getting the error Arguments too long. This means the shell would expand too many arguments from the wildcards you typed.

find is the answer to these problems.

A simple example of *find* is using it to print the names of all the files in the directory and all subdirectories. This is done with the simple command:

```
% find . -print
```

The first argument to *find* is a directory or filename—in that example, a dot (.) is one name for the current directory *(1.21)*. The arguments after the pathnames always start with a minus sign (–) and tell *find* what to do once it finds a file. These are the search operators. In this case, the filename is printed. Any number of directories can be specified. You can use the tilde (~) *(15.12)* supported by the C shell, as well as particular paths. For example:

```
% find ~ ~barnett /usr/local -print
```

And if you have a very slow day, you can type:

```
% find / -print
```

which will list every file on the system. [This command is okay on single-user workstations with their own disks. It can tie up disks on multi-user systems enough to make users think of gruesome crimes! If you really need that list and your system has fast *find (18.18)*, try the command find '/*' instead.—*JP*]

find sends its output to standard output, so once you've "found" a list of filenames, you can pass them to other commands. One way to use this is with command substitution *(10.14)*:

–d *17.09*
```
% ls -ld `find . -print`
```

The *find* command is executed, and its output replaces the backquoted string. *ls* sees the output of *find*, and doesn't even know *find* was used.

(10.20)
An alternate method uses the *xargs (10.19)* command. *xargs* and *find* work together beautifully. *xargs* executes its arguments as commands and reads standard input to specify arguments to that command. *xargs* knows the maximum number or arguments each command line can handle and does not exceed that limit. While the command:

```
% ls -ld `find / -print`
```

might generate an error when the command line is too large, the equivalent command using *xargs* will never generate that error:

```
% find / -print | xargs ls -ld
```

—*BB*

18.03 Don't Forget –print

"Why didn't *find* find my file?" I wondered sometimes. "I know it's there!"

More often than not, I'd forgotten to use *–print*. Without *–print* (or *–ls*, on versions of *find* that have it), *find* doesn't print any pathnames. [This is probably the feature that confuses and "turns off" more beginning *find* users than any other.— *TOR*]

—*JP*

18.04 Looking for Files with Particular Names

You can look for particular files by using a regular expression with meta-characters (shell wildcards, not *grep*-like expressions *(27.02)*) as an argument to the *–name* operator. Because the shell also understands these meta-characters, it is necessary to quote *(9.10)* them so they are passed to *find* unchanged. Any kind of quoting can be used:

```
% find . -name \*.o -print
% find . -name '*.o' -print
% find . -name "[a-zA-Z]*.o" -print
```

Any directory along the path to the file is not matched with the *–name* operator, merely the name at the end of the path. For example, the commands above would not match the pathname *./subdir.o/afile*—but they would match *./subdir.o* and *./src/subdir/prog.o*. Article 18.25 shows a way to match directories in the middle of a path.

—BB

18.05 Searching for Old Files

If you want to find a file that is seven days old, use the *–mtime* operator:

```
% find . -mtime 7 -print
```

An alternate way is to specify a range of times:

```
% find . -mtime +6 -mtime -8 -print
```

mtime is the last modified time of a file. If you want to look for files that have not been used, check the access time with the *–atime* argument. A command to list all files that have not been read in 30 days or more is:

```
% find . -type f -atime +30 -print
```

It is difficult to find directories that have not been accessed because the *find* command modifies the directory's access time.

There is another time associated with each file, called the *ctime*, the inode *(1.22)* change time. Access it with the *–ctime* operator. The *ctime* will have a more recent value if the owner, group, permission, or number of links has changed, while the file itself does not. If you want to search for files with a specific number of links, use the *–links* operator.

Article 17.05 has more information about these three times. Article 18.07 explains how *find* checks them.

—BB

18.06 Be an Expert on find Search Operators

find is admittedly tricky. Once you get a handle on its abilities, you'll learn to appreciate its trickiness. But before thinking about anything remotely tricky, let's look at a simple *find* command:

```
% find . -name "*.c" -print
```

The `.` tells *find* to start its search in the current directory (`.`) *(1.21)*, and to search all subdirectories of the current directory. The `-name "*.c"` *(18.04)* tells *find* to find files whose names end in *.c*. The *–print* operator tells *find* how to handle what it finds: print the names on standard output.

All *find* commands, no matter how complicated, are really just variations on the one above. You can specify many different names, look for old files, and so on; no matter how complex, you're really only specifying a starting point, some search parameters, and what to do with the files (or directories or links or . . .) you find.

The key to using *find* in a more sophisticated way is realizing that search parameters are really "logical expressions" that *find* evaluates. That is, *find* works by:

- Looking at every file, one at a time.

- Using the information in the file's inode *(1.22)* to evaluate an expression given by the command-line operators.

- Taking the specified action (e.g., printing the file's name) if the expression's value is "true."

So, something like `-name "*.c"` is really a logical expression that evaluates to true if the file's name ends in *.c*.

Once you've gotten used to thinking this way, it's easy to use the AND, OR, NOT, and grouping operators. So let's think about a more complicated *find* command. Let's look for files that end in *.o* or *.tmp* AND that are more than five days old, AND print them. We want an expression that evaluates true for files whose names match either **.o* OR **.tmp*:

```
-name "*.o" -o -name "*.tmp"
```

If either condition is true, we want to check the access time. So we put the expression above within parentheses (quoted *(9.10)* with backslashes so the shell doesn't treat the parentheses as subshell operators *(14.07)*). We also add a *–atime* operator *(18.05)*:

```
-atime +5 \( -name "*.o" -o -name "*.tmp" \)
```

The parentheses force *find* to evaluate what's inside as a unit. The expression is true if "the access time is more than 5 days ago and \(either the name ends with *.o* or the name ends with *.tmp* \)." If you didn't use parentheses, the expression would mean something different:

```
-atime +5 -name "*.o" -o -name "*.tmp"          Wrong!
```

When *find* sees two operators next to each other with no *−o* between, that means AND. So the "wrong" expression is true if "either \(the access time is more than 5 days ago and the name ends with *.o* \) or the name ends with *.tmp*." This incorrect expression would be true for any name ending with *.tmp*, no matter how recently the file was accessed—the -atime doesn't apply. (There's nothing really "wrong" or illegal in this second expression—except that it's not what we want. *find* will accept the expression and do what we asked—it just won't do what we want.)

The following command, which is what we want, lists files in the current directory and subdirectories that match our criteria:

```
% find . -atime +5 \( -name "*.o" -o -name "*.tmp" \) -print
```

What if we wanted to list all files that do *not* match these criteria? All we want is the logical inverse of this expression. The NOT operator is ! (exclamation point). The ! operator applies to the expression on its right. Since we want it to apply to the entire expression, and not just the *−atime* operator, we'll have to group everything from -atime to "*.tmp" within another set of parentheses.

```
% find . ! \( -atime +5 \( -name "*.o" -o -name "*.tmp" \) \) -print
```

For that matter, even *−print* is an expression; it always evaluates to true. So are *−exec* and *−ok* *(18.10)*, they evaluate to true when the command they execute returns a zero status. (There are a few situations in which this can be used to good effect; see article 18.11 for some of those.) Article 18.12 has more about *find* expressions.

But before you try anything too complicated, you need to realize one thing. *find* isn't as sophisticated as you might like it to be. You can't squeeze all the spaces out of expressions, as if it were a real programming language. You need spaces before and after operators like !, \ (, \ ), and { }, in addition to spaces before and after every other operator. Therefore, a command line like the following won't work:

```
% find . !\(-atime +5 \(-name "*.o" -o -name "*.tmp"\)\) -print
```

A true power user will realize that *find* is relying on the shell to separate the command line into meaningful chunks *(9.03)*, or *tokens*. And the shell, in turn, is assuming that tokens are separated by spaces. When the shell gives *find* a chunk of characters like *.tmp)) (without the double quotes or backslashes—the shell took them away), *find* gets confused; it thinks you're talking about a weird filename that includes an asterisk and a couple of parentheses.

Once you start thinking about expressions, *find*'s syntax ceases to be obscure—in some ways, it's even elegant. It certainly allows you to say what you need to say with reasonable efficiency.

—ML, JP

18.07 The Times that find Finds

The times that go with the *find* operators *−mtime*, *−atime*, and *−ctime* (18.04) aren't documented very well. The times are in days:

- A number with no sign, for example, 3 (as in *−mtime 3* or *−atime 3*), means the 24-hour period that *ended* exactly three days ago (in other words, between 96 and 72 hours ago).

- A number with a minus sign (−) refers to the period *since* that time. For example, −3 (as in *−mtime −3*) is any time between now and three days ago (in other words, between 0 and 72 hours ago).

- Naturally, a number with a plus sign (+) refers to the 24-hour period *before* that time. For example, +3 (as in *−mtime +3*) is any time more than three days ago (in other words, more than 72 hours ago).

Got that? Then you should see that *−atime −2* and *−atime 1* are both true on files that have been accessed between 48 and 24 hours ago. (*−atime −2* is also true on files accessed 24 hours or less ago.)

For more exact comparisons, use *find −newer* with *touch* (18.08).

—*JP*

18.08 Exact File Time Comparisons

One problem with *find*'s time operators (18.05, 18.07) (*−atime* and its brethren) is that they don't allow very exact comparisons. They only allow you to specify time to within a day. Sometimes that's just not good enough. You think that your system was corrupted at roughly 4 p.m. yesterday (March 20); you want to find any files that were modified after that point, so you can inspect them. Obviously, you'd like something more precise than "give me all the files that were modified in the last 24 hours."

Some versions of *touch* (22.07), and other freely available commands like it, can create a file with an arbitrary timestamp. That is, you can use *touch* to make a file that's backdated to any point in the past (or, for that matter, postdated to some point in the future). This feature, combined with *find*'s *−newer* operator, lets you make comparisons accurate to one minute or less.

For example, to create a file dated 4 p.m., March 20, give the command:

```
% touch 03201600 4PMyesterday
```

Then to find the files created after this, give the command:

```
% find . -newer 4PMyesterday -print
```

What about "older" files? Older files are "not newer" files, and *find* has a convenient NOT operator (!) for just this purpose. So let's say that you want to find files that were created between 10:46 a.m. on July 3, 1982, and 9:37 p.m. on August 4, 1985. You could use the following commands:

```
% touch 0703104682 file1
% touch 0804213785 file2
% find . -newer file1 ! -newer file2 -print
```

(18.09)

—*ML*

18.09 Problems with –newer

You may run into problems with the –*newer* *(18.08)* operator if you try to use it twice in the same command. Let's say that you want to find all files that are newer than *filea* but older than *fileb*. The obvious way to do this would be with the command:

```
% find . -newer filea ! -newer fileb -print
```

However, most versions of *find* can only work with one date at a time. When *find* reads the date of *fileb*, it discards the date of *filea*, and uses *fileb*'s date in both places. So it's really trying to find files that are newer than *fileb* but older than *fileb*, and will (obviously) find nothing at all.

You can work around this by figuring out the number of days since *filea* and *fileb* were modified, and rewriting the command using two –*mtime* operators. –*mtime* isn't afflicted by the same bug.

As with all bugs (or "features"), some vendors may have fixed it. So your system may not be afflicted with the problem. A *find* expression with two –*newer* operators apparently works under SunOS 4.1, but not under previous SunOS releases. It also seems to work under SVR4.

—*ML*

18.10 Running Commands on What You Find

[Often, when you find a file, you don't just want to see its name; you want to do something, like grep *for a text string. To do this, use the* –exec *operator. This allows you to specify a command that is executed upon each file that is found.—* TOR *]*

The syntax is peculiar and in many cases, it is simpler just to pipe the output of *find* to *xargs* *(18.02)*. However, there are cases where –*exec* is just the thing, so let's plunge in and explain its peculiarities.

The –*exec* operator allows you to execute any command, including another *find* command. If you consider that for a moment, you realize that *find* needs some way to distinguish the command it's executing from its own arguments. The obvious choice is to use the same end-of-command character as the shell (i.e., the semicolon). Since the shell uses the semicolon *(9.03)* itself, it is necessary to escape the character with a backslash or quotes.

Therefore, every *–exec* operator ends with the characters \ ; . There is one more special argument that *find* treats differently: { }. These two characters are used as the variable whose name is the file *find* found. Don't bother rereading that last line. An example will clarify the usage. The following is a trivial case, and uses the *–exec* operator with *echo(9.04)* to mimic the *–print* operator:

```
% find . -exec echo {} \;
```

The C shell uses the characters { and } *(10.05)* but doesn't change { } together, which is why it is not necessary to quote these characters. The semicolon must be quoted, however. Quotes can be used instead of a backslash:

```
% find . -exec echo {} ';'
```

as both will sneak the semicolon past the shell and get it to the *find* command. As I said before, *find* can even call *find*. If you wanted to list every symbolic link in every directory owned by a group *staff*, you could execute:

`` ..` 10.14``
```
% find `pwd` -type d -group staff -exec find {} -type l -print \;
```

To search for all files with group-write permission and remove the permission, you can use:

–perm *18.15*
```
% find . -perm -20 -exec chmod g-w {} \;
```

or:

```
% find . -perm -20 -print | xargs chmod g-w
```

The difference between *–exec* and *xargs* is subtle. The first one will execute the program once per file, while *xargs* can handle several files with each process. However, *xargs* may have problems *(10.20)* with filenames that contain embedded spaces.

Occasionally people create a strange file that they can't delete. This could be caused by accidentally creating a file with a space or some control character in the name. *find* and *–exec* can delete this file, while *xargs* could not. In this case, use *ls –il* to list the files and i-numbers *(1.22)*, and use the *–inum* operator with *–exec* to delete the file:

```
% find . -inum 31246 -exec rm {} ';'
```

If you wish, you can use *–ok* which does the same as *–exec*, except the program asks you first to confirm the action before executing the command. It is a good idea to be cautious when using *find*, because the program can make a mistake into a disaster. When in doubt, use *echo* as the command. Or send the output to a file and examine the file before using the file as input to *xargs*. This is how I discovered that *find* can only use one { } in the arguments to *–exec*. I wanted to rename some files using `-exec mv {} {}.orig` but I learned that I have to write a shell script *(18.11)* that I tell *find* to execute.

Articles 18.12 and 18.25 have more examples of *–exec*.

—*BB*

18.11 Using –exec to Create Custom Tests

Here's something that will really make your head spin. Remember that –*exec* doesn't necessarily evaluate to "true"; it only evaluates to true if the command it executes returns a zero exit status *(46.07)*. You can use this to construct custom *find* tests.

Assume that you want to list files that are "beautiful." You have written a program called *beauty* that returns zero if a file is beautiful, and non-zero otherwise. (This program can be a shell script *(46.11)*, a *perl (39.01)* script, an executable from a C program, anything you like.) Here's an example:

```
% find . -exec beauty {} \; -print
```

In this command, –*exec* is just another *find* operator. The only difference is that we care about its value; we're not assuming that it will always be "true." *find* executes the *beauty* command for every file. Then –*exec* evaluates to true when *find* is looking at a "beautiful" program, causing *find* to print the filename. (Excuse me, causing *find* to evaluate the –*print*. :-))

Of course, this ability is capable of infinite variation. If you're interested in finding beautiful C code, you could use the command:

```
% find . -name "*.[ch]" -exec beauty {} \; -print
```

And so on. For performance reasons, it's a good idea to put the –*exec* operator as close to the end as possible. This avoids starting processes unnecessarily; the –*exec* command will only execute when the previous operators evaluate to true.

—*JP, ML*

18.12 Finding Many Things with One Command

Running *find* is fairly time-consuming, and for good reason: it has to read every inode *(1.22)* in the directory tree that it's searching. Therefore, it's a good idea to combine as many things as you can into a single *find* command. If you're going to walk the entire tree, you may as well accomplish as much as possible in the process.

Let's work from an example. Assume that you want to write a command (eventually for inclusion in a shell script) that sets file access modes *(23.02)* correctly. You want to change all directories to 771 access, 600 access for all backup files (**.BAK*), 755 access for all shell scripts (**.sh*), and 644 access for all text files (**.txt*). You can do all this with one command:

```
$ find . \( -type d     -a -exec chmod 771 {} \; \) -o \
         \( -name "*.BAK" -a -exec chmod 600 {} \; \) -o \
         \( -name "*.sh"  -a -exec chmod 755 {} \; \) -o \
         \( -name "*.txt" -a -exec chmod 644 {} \; \)
```

Why does this work? Remember that –*exec* is really just another part of the expression; it evaluates to true when the following command is successful. It isn't an independent action that somehow applies to the whole *find* operation.

Therefore, *exec* can be mixed freely with *–type*, *–name*, and so on. (Also, see article 18.11.)

However, there's another important trick here. Look at the first chunk of the command. It says: "If this file is a directory and the *chmod* command executes successfully . . . " Wait. Why doesn't the *–exec* execute a *chmod* on every file in the directory, trying to see whether or not it's successful?

Logical expressions are evaluated from left to right; and, in any chunk of the expression, evaluation stops once it's clear what the outcome is. Consider the logical expression "'A AND B' is true." If A is false, you know that the result of "'A AND B' is true" will also be false—so there's no need to look at B.

So in the multi-layered expression above, when *find* is looking at a file, it checks whether or not the file is a directory. If it is, -type d is true, and *find* evaluates the *–exec* (changing the file's mode). If the file is not a directory, *find* knows that the result of the entire statement will be false, so it doesn't bother wasting time with the *–exec*. *find* goes on to the next chunk.

And, of course, there's no need for the *–exec*s to run the same kind of command. Some could delete files, some could change modes, some could move them to another directory, and so on.

One final point. Although understanding our multi-layered *find* expression was difficult, it really was no different than a "garden variety" command. Think about what the following command means:

```
% find . -name "*.c" -print
```

There are two operators: *–name* (which evaluates to true if the file's name ends in *.c*) and *–print* (which is always true). The two operators are ANDed together; we could stick a *–a* between the two without changing the result at all. If *–name* evaluates to false (i.e., if the file's name doesn't end in *.c*), *find* knows that the entire expression will be false. So it doesn't bother with *–print*. But if *–name* evaluates to true, *find* evaluates *–print*—which, as a side effect, prints the name.

As we said in article 18.06, *find*'s business is evaluating expressions—not locating files. Yes, *find* certainly locates files; but that's really just a side effect. For me, understanding this point was the conceptual breakthrough that made *find* much more useful.

—ML

18.13 Searching for Files by Type

If you are only interested in files of a certain type, use the *–type* argument, followed by one of the characters in Table 18-1 [some versions of *find* don't have all of these —*JP*].

Table 18-1. find –type Characters

Character	Meaning
b	Block special file ("device file")
c	Character special file ("device file")
d	Directory
f	Plain file
l	Symbolic link
p	Named pipe file
s	Socket

Unless you are a system administrator, the important types are directories, plain files, or symbolic links (i.e., types d, f, or l).

Using the *–type* operator, another way to list files recursively is:

xargs *10.19*

```
% find . -type f -print | xargs ls -l
```

It can be difficult to keep track of all the symbolic links in a directory. The next command will find all the symbolic links in your home directory and print the files that your symbolic links point to. If your *find* doesn't have a *–ls* operator, pipe to *xargs* as above and have *awk* print $10 (the tenth field).

```
% find $HOME -type l -ls | awk '{print $13}'
```

—BB

18.14 Searching for Files by Size

find has several operators that take a decimal integer. One such argument is *–size*. The number after this argument is the size of the files in disk blocks. Unfortunately, this is a vague number. Earlier versions of UNIX used disk blocks of 512 bytes. Newer versions allow larger block sizes, so a "block" of 512 bytes is misleading.

This confusion is aggravated when the command *ls –s* is used. The *–s* option supposedly lists the size of the file in blocks. But if your system has a different block size than *ls –s* has been programmed to assume, it can give a misleading answer. You can put a c after the number, and specify the size in bytes. To find a file with exactly 1234 bytes (as in an *ls –l* listing), type:

```
% find . -size 1234c -print
```

To search for files using a range of file sizes, a minus or plus sign can be specified before the number. The minus sign (–) means less than, and the plus sign

(+) means greater than. This next example lists all files that are greater than 10,000 bytes, but less than 32,000 bytes:

```
% find . -size +10000c -size -32000c -print
```

When more than one qualifier is given, both must be true *(18.06)*.

—BB

18.15 Searching for Files by Permission

find can look for files with a specific permission. It uses an octal number for these permissions. The string rw-rw-r-- indicates that you and members of your group have read and write permission, while the world has read-only privilege. The same permissions, when expressed as an octal number *(1.23)*, is 664. To find all *.o* files with the above permission, use:

```
% find . -name \*.o -perm 664 -print
```

To see if you have any directories with write permission for everyone, use:

```
% find . -type d -perm 777 -print
```

The examples above only match an exact combination of permissions. If you wanted to find all directories with group write permission, you want to match the pattern ----w----. There are several combinations that can match. You could list each combination, but *find* allows you to specify a pattern that can be bit-wise ANDed with the permissions of the file. Simply put a minus sign before the octal value. The group write permission bit is octal 20, so the following negative value:

```
% find . -perm -20 -print
```

will match the following common permissions:

Permission	Octal Value
rwxrwxrwx	777
rwxrwxr-x	775
rw-rw-rw-	666
rw-rw-r-	664
rw-rw----	660

If you wanted to look for files that you can execute (i.e., shell scripts or programs), you want to match the pattern --x------ by typing:

```
% find . -perm -100 -print
```

When the *–perm* argument has a minus sign, all of the permission bits are examined, including the set user ID bits *(1.23)*.

—BB

18.16 Searching by Owner and Group

Often you need to look for a file belonging to a certain user or group. This is done with the *–user* and *–group* search operators. You often need to combine this with a search for particular permissions. To find all files that are set user ID *(1.23)* to root, use:

```
% find . -user root -perm -4000 -print
```

To find all files that are set group ID *(1.23)* to *staff*, use:

```
% find . -group staff -perm -2000 -print
```

Instead of using a name or group from */etc/passwd (37.03)* or */etc/group (23.14)*, you can use the UID or GID number *(40.03)*:

```
% find . -user 0 -perm -4000 -print
% find . -group 10 -perm -2000 -print
```

Often, when a user leaves a site, his account is deleted, but his files are still on the computer. Some versions of *find* have *–nouser* or *–nogroup* operators to find files with an unknown user or group ID.

—BB

18.17 Duplicating a Directory Tree (No Pathnames with find {} Operator)

The *find* operator { }, used with the *–exec (18.10)* operator, only works when it's separated from other arguments by white space. So, for example, the following command will *not* do what you thought it would:

```
% find . -type d -exec mkdir /usr/project/{} \;
```

You might have thought this command would make a duplicate set of (empty) directories, from the current directory and down, starting at the directory */usr/project*. For instance, when the *find* command finds the directory *./adir*, you would have it execute mkdir /usr/project/./adir (ignore the dot; the result is */usr/project/adir*) *(1.21)*.

That doesn't work because *find* doesn't recognize the { } in the pathname. The trick is to pass the directory names to *sed (35.24)*, which substitutes in the leading pathname:

```
% find . -type d -print | sed 's@^@/usr/project/@' | xargs mkdir
% find . -type d -print | sed 's@^@mkdir @' | (cd /usr/project; sh)
```

The first example above uses *xargs (10.19)*. If you don't have *xargs*, try the second example. It uses *sed* to insert the *mkdir* command, then changes to the target directory in a subshell *(14.07)* where the *mkdir* commands will actually be executed. (Given a list of directory names, *sed* substitutes the desired path to that directory at the beginning of the line before passing the completed filenames to *xargs* and *mkdir*. An @ is used as a *sed* delimiter because slashes are needed in the actual text of the substitution. See article 35.07.)

—JP

18.18 Using "Fast find"

Berkeley added a handy feature to its *find* command—if you give it a single argument, it will search a database for file or directory names that match. For example, if you know there's a file named *MH.eps* somewhere on the computer but you don't know where, type:

```
% find MH.eps
/nutshell/graphics/cover/MH.eps
```

The database is usually rebuilt every night. So, it's not completely up-to-date, but it's usually close enough. If your system administrator has set this up, the database usually lists all files on the filesystem—although it may not list files in directories that don't have world-access permission. If the database isn't set up at all, you'll get an error like `/usr/lib/find/find.codes: No such file or directory`. (If that's the case, you can set up a "fast *find*" database yourself. Article 18.19 explains how to create the database, and also how to create an alias equivalent for fast *find*. Another relative of fast *find* is called *finder* *(18.20)*.)

Unless you use wildcards, fast *find* does a simple string search, like *fgrep (28.06)*, through a list of absolute pathnames *(15.02)*. Here's an extreme example:

```
% find bin
/bin
/bin/ar
     ...
/home/robin
/home/robin/afile
/home/sally/bin
     ...
```

You can cut down this output by piping it through *grep (28.01)*, *sed (35.24)*, and so on. All the fast *find* commands I've used have an undocumented feature, though: they can match shell wildcards (*, ?, [ ]) *(16.02)*. If you use a wildcard on one end of the pattern, the search pattern is automatically "anchored" to the opposite end of the string (the end where the wildcard isn't). The shell matches filenames in the same way.

The difference between the shell's wildcard matching and fast *find*'s matching is that the shell treats slashes (/) specially: you have to type them as part of the expression. In fast *find*, a wildcard matches slashes and any other character. When you use a wildcard, be sure to put quotes around the pattern so the shell won't touch it.

Here are some examples:

- To find any pathname that ends with *bin*:

  ```
  % find '*bin'
  /bin
  /home/robin
  /home/robin/bin
  ...
  ```

- To find any pathname that ends with */bin* (a good way to find a file or directory named exactly *bin*):

  ```
  % find '*/bin'
  /bin
  /home/robin/bin
  /usr/bin
  ...
  ```

- Typing find '*bin*' is the same as typing find bin.

- To match the files in a directory named *bin*, but not the directory itself, try something like:

  ```
  % find '*/bin/*'
  /bin/ar
  /bin/cat
  ...
  /home/robin/bin/prog
  ```

- To find the files in */home* whose names end with a tilde (~) (these are probably backup files from the Emacs editor):

  ```
  % find '/home/*~'
  /home/testfile~
  /home/allan/.cshrc~
  /home/allan/.login~
  /home/dave/.profile~
  ...
  ```

  Notice that the fast *find* asterisk matches "dot files," too.

- The ? (question mark) and [] (square brackets) operators work, too. They're not quite as useful as they are in the shell because they match the slashes (/) in the pathnames. A couple of quick examples:

  ```
  % find '????'
  /bin
  /etc
  /lib
  /src
  /sys
  /usr
  % find '/[bel]??'
  /bin
  /etc
  /lib
  ```

Because fast *find* is so fast, it's worth trying to use whenever you can. Pipe its output to *xargs* *(10.19)* and any other UNIX command, run a shell or *awk* script to test its output—almost anything will be faster than running a standard *find*. For example, if you want a long listing of the files, use one of these commands:

−d *17.09*
`..` *10.14*

```
% ls -ld `find whatever`
% find whatever | xargs ls -ld
```

There's one problem with that trick. The fast *find* list may be built by *root*, which can see all the files on the filesystem; your *ls −l* command may not be able to access all files in the list.

—JP

18.19 Finding Files (much) Faster with a find Database

If you use *find* *(18.02)* to search for files, you know that it can take a long time to work, especially when there are lots of directories to search. Here are some ideas for speeding up your *find*s.

Note: By design, setups like these that build a file database won't have absolutely up-to-date information about all your files.

If your system has the BSD-type "fast *find*" *(18.18)* command, that's probably all you need. It lets you search a list of all pathnames on the system.

Even if you have the fast *find* command, it still might not do what you need. For example, fast *find* only searches for pathnames. To find files by the owner's name, the number of links, the size, and so on, you have to use "slow" *find*. In that case—or, when you don't have fast *find* at all—you may want to set up your own version.

The basic fast *find* has two parts. One part is a command, a shell script named */usr/lib/find/updatedb*, that builds a database of the files on your system—if your system has it, take a look to see a fancy way to build the database. The other part is the *find* command itself—it searches the database for pathnames that match the name (regular expression) you type.

To make your own fast *find*:

1. Pick a filename for the database. We'll use *$HOME/.fastfind* (some systems use $LOGDIR instead of $HOME).

2. Design the *find* command you want to use. The command to build a database of all the files in your home directory might look like this:

    ```
    cd
    find . -print | sed "s@^./@@" > $HOME/.fastfind
    ```

If you're short on disk space, use this instead:

compress *25.06*

```
cd
find . -print | sed "s@^./@@" | compress > $HOME/.fastfind.Z
```

To save disk space, the script starts from your home directory, then uses *sed* *(35.24)* to strip the start of the pathname (like *. /*) from every entry. (If you're building a database of the whole filesystem, don't do that!)

3. Set up *cron (42.12)* or *at (42.03)* to run that *find* as often as you want—usually once early every morning is fine.

4. Finally, make a shell script *(1.05)* (I call mine *ffind*) to search the database. It's usually fastest to use *egrep (28.05)*—and that lets you search with flexible regular expressions *(27.04)*, too:

```
egrep "$1" $HOME/.fastfind | sed "s@^@$HOME/@"
```

or, for a compressed database:

zcat *25.06*

```
zcat $HOME/.fastfind.Z | egrep "$1" | sed "s@^@$HOME/@"
```

The *sed* expressions add your home directory's pathname (like */usr/freddie*) to each line.

To search the database, type:

```
% ffind somefile
/usr/freddie/lib/somefile
% ffind '/(sep|oct)[^/]*$'
/usr/freddie/misc/project/september
/usr/freddie/misc/project/october
```

You can do much more. I'll get you started. If you have room to store more information than just pathnames, you can feed your *find* output to a command like *ls −l* or *sls (17.30)*. For example, if you do a lot of work with links *(19.03)*, you might want to keep the files' i-numbers *(1.22)* as well as their names. You'd build your database with a command like the one below. Use *xargs (10.19)* or something like it *(10.18)*:

```
cd
find . -print | xargs ls -id > $HOME/.fastfind
```

Or, if your version of *find* has the handy *−ls* operator, use the next script. Watch out for really large i-numbers; they might shift the columns and make *cut* *(36.12)* give wrong output.

```
cd
find . -ls | cut -c1-7,67- > $HOME/.fastfind
```

The exact column numbers will depend on your system. Then, your *ffind* script could search for files by i-number. For instance, if you had a file with i-number 1234 and you wanted to find all its links:

```
% ffind "^1234 "
```

(The space at the end prevents matches with i-numbers like 12345.) You could also search by pathname.

The *finder* (18.20) program has a database like this one. Article 17.22 shows another *find* database setup, a list of directories or files with the same names.

With some information about UNIX shell programming and utilities like *awk* (38.18), the techniques in this article should let you build and search a sophisticated file database—and get information much faster than with plain old *find*.

—JP

18.20 Finding Directories

A relative of the fast *find* (18.18) utility is the *finder* program, which only reports directory names. This comes in handy in lots of situations, since there are plenty of times when you're only interested in directory names.

finder

```
% finder ddx /work/source
/work/source/X11R5/mit/server/ddx
/work/source/X11R4/R4src/src/mit/server/ddx
```

Like "fast *find*," *finder* depends on a listing having been set up, in this case using the *mkfindex* script which comes with *finder*. *mkfindex* creates a file called *.findex* in the uppermost directory it is called on, listing each of its sub-directories. The *finder* script simply searches for the given string the *.findex* file. Naturally, the results are only as up-to-date as the last time *mkfindex* was called, but you can set up *mkfindex* to run on multiple directories overnight using *cron* (42.12), as you would for updating the "fast *find*" database using */usr/lib/find/updatedb* (18.19).

There are a couple of advantages to *finder* that can make it much faster than either standard *find* or "fast *find*." One advantage is that you can restrict yourself to only directory names, greatly reducing the number of names that have to be searched through. Another advantage is that you restrict yourself to a given directory tree—which you can do with regular *find*, but not with "fast *find*," since it uses a system-wide database. *finder* is functionally equivalent to *find . –type d –print*, but it is much, much faster.

—LM

18.21 grepping a Directory Tree (and a Gotcha)

Want to search every file, in some directory and all its subdirectories, to find the file that has a particular word or string in it? That's a job for *find* and one of the *grep* (28.01) commands.

For example, to search all the files for lines starting with a number and containing the words "SALE PRICE," you could use:

```
% egrep '^[0-9].*SALE PRICE' `find . -type f -print`
./archive/ad.1290: 1.99 a special SALE PRICE
./archive/ad.0191: 2.49 a special SALE PRICE
```

Using the backquotes *(10.14)* (` `) might not work. If *find* finds too many files, *egrep*'s command-line arguments can get too long *(10.18)*. Using *xargs (10.19)* can solve that; it splits long sets of arguments into smaller chunks. There's a problem with that: if the last "chunk" has just one filename and the *grep* command finds a match there, *grep* won't print the filename:

fgrep *28.06*

```
% find . -type f -print | xargs fgrep '$12.99'
./old_sales/ad.0489: Get it for only $12.99!
./old_sales/ad.0589: Last chance at $12.99, this month!
Get it for only $12.99 today.
```

The answer is to add the UNIX "empty file," */dev/null (14.14)*. It's a filename that's guaranteed never to match but always to leave *grep* with at least two filenames:

```
% find . -type f -print | xargs fgrep '$12.99' /dev/null
```

Then *xargs* will run commands like:

```
fgrep '$12.99' /dev/null ./afile ./bfile ...
fgrep '$12.99' /dev/null ./archives/ad.0190 ./archives/ad.0290 ...
fgrep '$12.99' /dev/null ./old_sales/ad.1289
```

That trick is also good when you use a wildcard and only one file might match it. *grep* won't always print the file's name unless you add */dev/null*:

```
% grep "whatever" /dev/null /x/y/z/a*
```

—*JP*

18.22 lookfor: Which File has that Word?

The following simple shell script, *lookfor*, uses *find (18.01)* to look for all files in the specified directory hierarchy modified within a certain time, and it passes the resulting names to *grep (28.02)* to scan for a particular pattern. For example, the command:

```
% lookfor /work -7 tamale enchildada
```

would search through the entire */work* filesystem and print the names of all files modified within the past week that contain the words "tamale" or "enchilada". (So, for example: if this article is stored on */work*, *lookfor* should find it.)

The arguments to the script are the pathname of a directory hierarchy to search in ($1), a time ($2), and one or more text patterns (the other arguments). This simple but slow version will search for an (almost) unlimited number of words:

lookfor

```
#!/bin/sh
temp=/tmp/lookfor$$
trap 'rm -f $temp; exit' 0 1 2 15
find $1 -mtime $2 -print > $temp
shift; shift
for word
do grep -i "$word" `cat $temp` /dev/null
done
```

That version runs *grep* once to search for each word. The *–i* option makes the search find either uppercase or lowercase letters. Using */dev/null* makes sure that *grep* will print the filename *(14.14)*. Watch out: the list of filenames may get too long *(10.18)*.

The next version is more limited but faster. It builds a regular expression for *egrep (28.05)* that finds all the words in one pass through the files. If you use too many words, *egrep* will say Regular expression too long. Your *egrep* may not have a *—i* option; you can just omit it. This version also uses *xargs* *(10.19)*, though *xargs* has its problems *(10.20)*.

elookfor

```
#!/bin/sh
where="$1"
when="$2"
shift; shift
# Build egrep expression like (word1|word2|...) in $expr
for word
do
    case "$expr" in
    "") expr="($word" ;;
    *) expr="$expr|$word" ;;
    esac
done
expr="$expr)"

find $where -mtime $when -print | xargs egrep -i "$expr" /dev/null
```

—JP, TOR

18.23 Finding the Links to a File

Here is how to find links—and a brief look at the UNIX filesystem from the user's viewpoint. Suppose you are given the following:

```
% ls -li /usr/foo
2076 -rw-r--r--  3 chris        326 Sep 16 03:23 /usr/foo
```

In other words, there are three links, and */usr/foo* is one of three names for inode *(1.22)* 2076. You can find the full names of the other two links by using */etc/ncheck* and/or *find*. However, just knowing the inode number does not tell you everything.

The whole truth is that there is another number hiding away in there. This is the *device number*, and it tells which *filesystem* holds the file. There can be any number of inode 2076s, as long as each one is on a different filesystem. (More recent UNIX systems use a *filesystem ID number* in place of a device number, so that they can represent filesystems on other machines. They may also use a *vnode number* rather than an inode number. The effect is the same, although you often cannot run */etc/ncheck* on anything but a local disk.)

You can find out which filesystem */usr/foo* is in by running *df (25.08)* or *mount*. Suppose it is on */dev/sd0g*. If */dev/sd0g* shows up as:

```
% df
Filesystem     kbytes     used   avail capacity  Mounted on
/dev/sd0g      179423   152202    9278    94%    /usr
```

```
% ls -l /dev/sd0g
brw------- 1 root      2,   6 Dec 27 07:17 /dev/sd0g
```

then it is "major device 2, minor device 6." These numbers are smashed together with the *makedev* macro in one of the kernel source files. Typically this is just *major**256 + *minor*; here we have 2*256+6, or 518. Another way to find this same number is to use the *stat*(2) system call on the original file */usr/foo*; the device number appears in the st_dev field. [The *stat (22.13)* program does this for you.—*JP*]

So if you do a find / -inum 2076 -print to find every file with inode number 2076, you may find more than three files. Only three of them will be on *sd0g*, though.

—*CT* in *net.unix* on Usenet, *15 January 1985*

18.24 *Finding Files with −prune*

find has lots of operators for finding some particular kinds of files. But *find* won't stop at your current directory—if there are subdirectories, it looks there, too. How can you tell it "only the current directory"? Use *−prune*.

find

Note: If your version of *find* doesn't have *−prune*, this won't work. Try GNU *find* on the Power Tools disk.

−prune prunes *find*'s search tree at the current pathname. So, if the current pathname is a directory, *find* won't descend into that directory for any further searches. The command line looks kind of hairy. Here's one to find all files from the current directory modified in the last 24 hours:

```
% find . \( -type d ! -name . -prune \) -o \( -mtime -1 -print \)
./afile
./cfile
```

I'll put that into an alias in a minute. First let's try to understand it—once you see the pattern, you'll understand some important things *(9.03, 18.12)* about *find* that many people don't. Let's follow *find* as it looks at a few pathnames.

find looks at each entry, one by one, in the current directory (.). For each entry, *find* tries to match the expression from left to right. As soon as some part matches, it quits and ignores the rest (if any) of the expression.

1. When *find* is looking at the file named *./afile*: The first part of the expression, \(-type d ! -name . -prune \), doesn't match (*./afile* isn't a directory). So *find* tries the other part, after the -o (or).

   Has *./afile* been modified in the last day? In this case, it has—so the -print (which is always true) prints the pathname.

2. Next, *./bfile*: Like the previous step, the first part of the expression won't match. In the second part, \(-mtime -1 -print \), the file's modification time is more than one day ago. So this part of the expression is false; *find* stops and doesn't bother with the -print operator.

3. Finally, let's look at *./adir*, a directory: The first part of the expression, \(-type d ! -name . -prune \), matches. That's because *./adir* is a directory (-type d), its name is not . (! -name .)—and so -prune, which is always true, makes this part of the expression true. *find* skips *./adir*.

Whew! Let's put that into a couple of aliases. The first one, named *find.* (with a dot on the end of its name), just prints names with *–print*. The second alias gives a listing like *ls –gilds*. They work like this:

```
% find. -mtime -1
./afile
./cfile
% find.ls -mtime -1
43073   0 -r--------  1 jerry    ora          0 Mar 27 18:16 ./afile
43139   2 -r--r--r--  1 jerry    ora       1025 Mar 24 02:33 ./cfile
```

The *find.* alias is handy inside backquotes *(10.14)*, feeding a pipe, and other places you need a list of filenames. Here are the aliases. The second one, *find.ls*, uses *–ls* instead of *–print*:

csh_init

```
alias find. 'find . \( -type d ! -name . -prune \) -o \( \!* -print \)'
alias find.ls 'find . \( -type d ! -name . -prune \) -o \( \!* -ls \)'
```

If you don't want the ./ at the start of each name, add a pipe through colrm 1 2 *(36.13)* or cut -c3- *(36.12)* to the end of the alias definition.

—*JP*

18.25 Skipping Some Parts of a Tree in find (a More Selective –prune)

Q: I want to run *find* across a directory tree, skipping standard directories like */usr/spool* and */usr/local/bin*. A -name *dirname* -prune clause won't do it because *–name* doesn't match the whole pathname—just each part of it, such as *spool* or *local*. How can I make *find* match the whole pathname, like */usr/local/bin/*, instead of *all* directories named *bin*?

A: It cannot be done directly. You *can* do this:

test 46.19

```
find /path -exec test {} = /foo/bar -o {} = /foo/baz \; -prune -o pred
```

This will not perform *pred* on /foo/bar and /foo/baz; if you want them done, but not any files within them, try:

```
find path \( -exec test test-exprs \; ! -prune \) -o pred
```

The second version is worth close study, keeping the manual for *find* at hand for reference. It shows a great deal about how *find* works.

The *–prune* operator simply says "do not search the current path any deeper," and then succeeds a la *–print*.

Q: I only want a list of pathnames; the *pred* I use in your answer above will be just *–print*. I think I could solve my particular problem by piping the *find* output through a *sed* or *egrep –v* filter that deletes the pathnames I don't want to see.

A: That would probably be fastest. Using *test* runs the *test* program for each file name, which is quite slow. [There's more about complex *find* expressions in other articles, especially 18.06 and 18.12. —*JP*]

—*CT, JP*

18.26 Keeping find from Searching Networked Filesystems

The most painful aspect of a large NFS *(1.33)* environment is avoiding the access of files on NFS servers that are down. *find* is particularly sensitive to this, because it is very easy to access dozens of machines with a single command. If *find* tries to explore a file server that happens to be down, it will time out. It is important to understand how to prevent *find* from going too far.

To do this, use *–prune* with *–fstype* or *–xdev*. [Unfortunately, not all *find*s have all of these.—*JP*] *fstype* tests for filesystem types, and expects an argument like *nfs* or *4.2*. The latter refers to the "fast filesystem" introduced in the 4.2 release of the Berkeley Software Distribution. To limit *find* to files only on a local disk or disks, use the clause *–fstype 4.2 –prune* or *–o –fstype nfs –prune*.

To limit the search to one particular disk partition, use *–xdev*. For example, if you need to clear out a congested disk partition, you could look for all files greater than 40 blocks on the current disk partition with this command:

```
% find . -size +40 -xdev -print
```

—*BB*

19

Linking, Renaming, and Copying Files

19.01 What's so Complicated about Copying Files?

It hardly seems that there should be enough material to fill an entire chapter with information about renaming, moving, and copying files. There are several things that make the topic more complex (and more interesting) than you might expect:

- In addition to moving and copying files, UNIX systems also allow you to link them—to have two filenames, perhaps in different directories or even on different filesystems, that point to the same file. We talk about why you'd want to do that (article 19.03), the difference between "hard" and "soft" links (article 19.04), how to create links (article 19.05), and various issues that can come up when using links (articles 19.06, 19.07, and 19.08).

- It is non-trivial to rename a group of files all at once, but as usual, UNIX provides many ways to circumvent the tedium of renaming files one by one. We show you many different ways to do this, exploring the variety in the UNIX toolbox along the way.

- In a hierarchical filesystem, you're sometimes faced with the problem of moving not only files but entire directory hierarchies from one place to another. Articles 19.16 and 19.17 show you two ways to do that. Of course, this discussion starts to get into the territory covered by the next two chapters. Chapter 20 covers "archives"—large files that include many other files and directories, with instructions for recreating copies of the original files and directories. Chapter 21 covers backups—which are typically archive files copied to tape.

—TOR

19.02 What's Really in a Directory

Before you can understand moving and copying files, you need to know a bit more about how files are represented in directories. What does it mean to say that a file is really "in" a directory? It's easy to imagine that files are actually inside of something (some special chunk of the disk that's called a directory). But that's precisely wrong, and it's one place where the filing cabinet model *(1.19)* of a filesystem doesn't apply.

A directory really is just another file, and really isn't different from any other data file. If you want to prove this, type the command cat -v ., which dumps the current directory to the screen in raw form. It will certainly look ugly (it's not a text file—it has lots of binary characters). But the *cat -v (26.07)* will probably let you see the names of the files that are in the current directory.

So a directory is really just a list of files. It contains filenames and inode numbers *(1.22)*. That is, we can visualize a directory like this:

```
The file named     .            is inode 34346
The file named     ..           is inode 987
The file named     mr.ed        is inode 10674
The file named     joe.txt      is inode 8767
The file named     grok         is inode 67871
The file named     otherdir     is inode 2345
```

So when you give a filename like *grok*, the kernel looks up *grok* in the current directory and finds out that this file has inode 67871; it looks up this inode to find out who owns the file, where the data blocks are, and so on.

What's more, some of these "files" may be directories in their own right. In particular, that's true of the first two entries: . and . . These entries are in *every* directory. Single . just refers to the current directory, while double . . refers to the "parent" of the current directory (i.e., the directory that "contains" the current directory). The file *otherdir* is yet another directory that happens to be "within" the current directory. But there's no way you can tell that from its directory entry—UNIX doesn't know it's different until it looks up its inode.

Now that you know what a directory is, let's think about some basic operations. What does it mean to move, or rename, a file? If the file is staying in the same directory, the *mv* command just changes the file's name in the directory; it doesn't touch the data at all.

Moving a file into another directory takes a little more work, but not much. A command like *mv dir1/foo dir2/foo* means "delete *foo*'s entry in *dir1*, and create a new entry for *foo* in *dir2*." Again, UNIX doesn't have to touch the data blocks or the inode at all.

The only time you actually need to copy data is if you're moving a file into another filesystem. In that case, you have to copy the file to the new filesystem; delete its old directory entry; return the file's data blocks to the "free list," which means that they can be re-used; and so on. It's a fairly complicated operation, but (still) relatively rare. (On some old versions of UNIX, *mv* won't let you move files between filesystems.)

Now let's see if you've understood. How does UNIX find out the name of the current directory? In our "current directory," there's an entry for ., which tells us that the current directory has inode 34346. Is the directory's name part of the inode? Sorry—it isn't. The directory's name is included in the parent directory. The parent directory is .., which is inode 987. So UNIX looks up inode 987, finds out where the data is, and starts reading every entry in the parent directory. Sooner or later, it will find one that corresponds to inode 34346. When it does that, it knows that it has found the directory entry for the current directory, and can read its name. Article 15.04 has a diagram and more explanation.

Complicated? Yes, but if you understand this, you have a pretty good idea of how UNIX directories work.

—ML

19.03 Files with Two or More Names

We talk about hard links and symbolic links in a number of places (19.04, 19.05, 25.04). However, we've never really said *why* you'd want a file with several names. When I was learning UNIX, this was a big stumbling block. It was easy to understand what a link would *do*, but why would you want one?

With time, I acquired wisdom. There are many situations that links (and only links) are able to handle. Once you've seen a few of the problems that a link can solve, you'll start seeing even more situations in which they are appropriate.

Consider a company phone list on a system that is shared by several users. Every user might want a copy of the phone list in his or her home directory. However, you wouldn't want to give each user a different phone list. In addition to wasting disk space, it would be a pain to modify all of the individual lists whenever you made a change. Giving each user a "link" to a master phone list is one way to solve the problem.

Similarly, assume that you use several different systems that share files via NFS (1.33). Eventually, you get tired of editing five or six different *.login* and *.cshrc* (2.02) files whenever you decide to add a new alias or change some element in your startup file; you'd like to have the exact same file appear in each of your home directories. You might also want to give several systems access to the same master database files.

How about this: you have a program or script that performs several related functions. Why not perform them all with the same executable? All the script or program needs to do is check the name it's called by, and act accordingly. Article 47.13 explains how this works; articles 23.10 and 26.05 show scripts that test their name.

Yet another example. Assume that you have two versions of a file: a current version, which changes from time to time, and one or more older versions. One good convention would be to name the files data.*date*, where *date* shows when the file was created. For example, you might have the files *data.jul1*, *data.jul2*, *data.jul5*, and so on. However, when you access these files, you don't necessarily want to figure out the date—not unless you have a better chronological sense than I do. To make it easier on yourself, create a link (either symbolic or hard) named *data.cur* that always refers to your most recent file. The following script runs the program *output*, puts the data into a dated file, and resets *data.cur*:

```
#!/bin/sh
curfile=data.`date +%h%d`
linkname=data.cur
output > $curfile
rm -f $linkname
ln -s $curfile $linkname
```

Here's an analogous problem. When writing technical manuals at one company, I had two classes of readers: some insisted on referring to the manuals by name, and the others by (believe it or not) part number. Rather than looking up part numbers all the time, I created a set of links so that I could look up a manual online either via its name or via its part number. For example, if the manual was named "Programming" and had the part number 046-56-3343, I would create the file */manuals/byname/programming*. I would then create the link */manuals/bynumber/046-56-3343*:

```
% cd /manuals/bynumber
% ln -s ../byname/programming 046-56-3343
```

Sometimes you simply want to collect an assortment of files in one directory. These files may really belong in other places, but you want to collect them for some temporary purpose: for example, to make a tape. For example, let's say that you want to make a tape that includes manual pages from */development/doc/man/man1*, a manual from */development/doc/product*, source files from */src/ccode*, and a set of executables from */release/68000/execs*. The shell script below creates links for all of these directories within the */tmp/tape* directory, and then creates a *tar (21.01)* tape that can be sent to a customer or friend. Note that the *tar h* option tells *tar* to follow symbolic links and archive whatever is at the end of the link; otherwise, *tar* makes a copy of just the symbolic link:

/tmp 22.02

```
#!/bin/sh
mkdir /tmp/tape
cd /tmp/tape
rm -rf ./man1 ./product ./ccode ./execs
ln -s /development/doc/man/man1 ./man1
ln -s /development/doc/product ./product
ln -s /src/ccode ./ccode
ln -s /release/68000/execs ./execs
tar ch ./man1 ./product ./ccode ./execs
```

This really only scrapes the surface. Links provide neat solutions to many problems, including source control, filesystem layout, etc.

—*ML*

19.04 Hard vs. Soft Links

UNIX provides two different kinds of links:

1. **Hard links:** With a hard link, two filenames (i.e., two directory entries *(19.02)*) point to the same inode and the same set of data blocks. All UNIX versions support hard links. They have two important limitations: a hard link can't cross a filesystem (i.e., both filenames must be in the same filesystem), and you can't create a hard link to a directory (i.e., a directory can only have one name). They have two important advantages: the link and the original file are absolutely and always identical, and the extra link takes no disk space (except an occasional extra disk block in the directory file).

2. **Symbolic links** (also called **soft links** or **symlinks**): With a symbolic link, there really are two different files. One file contains the actual data; the other file just contains the name of the first file and serves as a "pointer." We call the pointer the *link.* The system knows that whenever it opens a link, it should read the contents of the link, and then access the file that really holds the data you want. All Berkeley UNIX systems and System V.4 support symbolic links. Symbolic links are infinitely more flexible than hard links. They can cross filesystems, or even computer systems (if you are using NFS or RFS). You can make a symbolic link to a directory. A symbolic link has its own inode and takes a small amount of disk space to store.

You obviously can't do without copies of files: copies are important whenever users need their own "private version" of some master file. But it is also important to know about links. With links, there's only one set of data and many different names that can access it. Article 19.05 shows how to make links.

There are some important differences between hard and symbolic links. With a hard link, the two filenames are identical in every way. You can delete one without harming the other. The system deletes the directory entry for one filename, leaves the data blocks (which are shared) untouched. The only thing *rm* does to the inode is decrement its "link count" which (as the name implies) counts the number of hard links to the file. The data blocks are only deleted when the link count goes to zero—meaning that there are no more directory entries that point to this inode. Article 18.23 shows how to find the hard links to a file.

With a symbolic link, the two filenames are really not the same. Deleting the link with *rm* leaves the original file untouched, which is what you'd expect. But deleting or renaming the original file removes both the filename and the data. You are left with a link that doesn't point anywhere. (Article 17.29 has a script that finds unconnected symlinks.) Remember that the link itself doesn't have any data associated with it. Despite this disadvantage, you rarely see hard links on UNIX versions that support symbolic links. Symbolic links are so much more versatile that they have become omnipresent.

—ML

19.05 Creating and Removing Links

The *ln* command creates both hard and soft (symbolic) links *(19.04)*. You use it as follows:

```
% ln filename linkname        To create a hard link
% ln -s filename linkname      To create a symbolic link
```

The *–s* option is only valid for Berkeley UNIX and System V.4.

In either case, `filename` must already exist. Otherwise you will get an error message. If you are using Berkeley UNIX, `linkname` must not exist—if it does, you will get an error. Under System V, `linkname` may already exist; if you are allowed to write the file, *ln* destroys its old contents and creates your link. If you don't have write access for `linkname`, *ln* asks whether or not it is OK to override the file's protection. For example:

```
% ln foo bar
ln: override protection 444 for bar? y
```

Typing y gives *ln* permission to destroy the file *bar* and create the link. Note that this will still fail if you don't have write access to the directory.

You are allowed to omit the `linkname` argument from the *ln* command. In this case, *ln* takes the last component of `filename` (i.e., everything after the last slash) and uses it for `linkname`. Of course, this assumes that `filename` doesn't refer to the current directory. If it does, the command will fail: the link will already exist. For example, the commands below are the same:

```
% ln -s ../archive/file.c
% ln -s ../archive/file.c file.c
```

Both create a link from *file.c* in the current directory to *../archive/file.c*.

ln also lets you create a group of links with one command, provided that all of the links are in the same directory. Here's how:

```
% ln file1 file2 file3 ... filen directory
```

This command strips the last component (everything after the last slash) from each filename and uses it as the name for the link. It then creates all the links within the given `directory`. For example, the first command below is equivalent to the next two:

```
% ln ../s/f1 ../s/f2 current
% ln ../s/f1 current/f1
% ln ../s/f2 current/f2
```

You can replace this list of files with a wildcard expression *(16.02)*, as in:

```
% ln -s ../newversion/*.[ch] .
```

One word of caution about symbolic links: it's possible for them to get out-of-date *(19.06)*.

—*ML*

19.06 *Stale Symbolic Links*

Symbolic links have one problem. Like good bread, they become "stale" fairly easily. What does that mean?

Consider the following commands:

```
% ln -s foo bar
% rm foo
```

What happens when you do this? Remember that the link *bar* is a pointer: it doesn't have any real data of its own. Its data is the name of the file *foo*. After deleting *foo*, the link *bar* still exists, but it points to a nonexistent file. Commands that refer to *bar* will get a confusing error message:

```
% cat bar
cat: bar: No such file or directory
```

This will drive you crazy if you're not careful. An *ls* will show you that *bar* still exists. You won't understand what's going on until you realize that *bar* is only a pointer to a file that no longer exists. [The command *ls −Ll* or *ls −LF* will show an unconnected symbolic link. The −*L* option means "list the file that this link points to instead of the link itself." If the link points nowhere, *ls −L* will still list the link. —*JP*]

There are many innocuous ways of creating invalid symbolic links. For example, you could simply *mv* the data file *foo*. Or you could move *foo, bar,* or both to some other part of the filesystem where the pointer wouldn't be valid anymore.

One way to avoid problems with invalid links is to use relative pathnames (1.21) when it is appropriate. For example, using relative pathnames will let you move entire directory trees around without invalidating links (providing that both the file and the link are in the same tree). Here's an example. Assume that you have the file */home/mars/john/project/datastash/input123.txt*. Assume that you want to link this file to */home/mars/john/test/input.txt*. You create a link by giving the command:

```
% cd /home/mars/john/test
% ln -s ../project/datastash/input123.txt input.txt
```

At some later date, you hand the project over to *mary*, who copies (19.17) the entire *project* and *test* data trees into her home directory. The link between *input.txt* and the real file, *input123.txt*, will still be valid. Although both file's names have changed, the relationship between the two (i.e., the relative path from one directory to the other) is still the same. Alternatively, assume that you are assigned to a different computer named *jupiter* and that you copy your entire home directory when you move. Again, the link remains valid: the relative path from your *test* directory to your *datastash* directory hasn't changed, even though the absolute paths of both directories are different.

On the other hand, there is certainly room for absolute pathnames (15.02). They're useful if you're more likely to move the link than the original file. Assume that you are creating a link from your working directory to a file in a master directory (let's say */corp/masterdata/input345.txt*). It is much more likely that you will rearrange your working directory than that someone will move the master set of files. In this case, you would link as follows:

```
% ln -s /corp/masterdata/input345.txt input.txt
```

Now you can move the link *input.txt* anywhere in the filesystem: it will still be valid, provided that *input345.txt* never moves.

In article 17.29, we give a script for detecting stale symbolic links.

Note that hard links *(19.04)* never have this problem. With a hard link, there is no difference at all between the link and the original—in fact, it's unfair to call one file the link and the other the original.

—ML

19.07 *Linking Directories*

One feature of symbolic links *(19.04)* (a.k.a. *symlinks*) is that unlike hard links, you can use symbolic links to link directories as well as files. Since symbolic links can span between filesystems, this can become enormously useful.

For example, sometimes administrators want to install a package in a directory tree that's different from where users and other programs expect it to be. On our site, we like to keep */usr/bin* pure—that is, we like to be sure that all the programs in */usr/bin* came with the operating system. That way, when we install a new OS, we know for sure that we can overwrite the entirety of */usr/bin* and not lose any "local" programs. We install all local programs in */usr/local.*

The X11 *(1.31)* package poses a problem, though. X11 programs are expected to be installed in */usr/bin/X11*. But X isn't distributed as part of our OS, so we'd prefer not to put it there. Instead, we install X programs in */usr/local/X11/bin*, and create a symbolic link named */usr/bin/X11*. We do the same for */usr/include/X11* and */usr/lib/X11*:

```
# ln -s /usr/local/X11/bin /usr/bin/X11
# ln -s /usr/local/X11/lib /usr/lib/X11
# ln -s /usr/local/X11/include /usr/include/X11
```

By using symlinks, we can have it both ways: we installed the package where we wanted to, but kept it invisible to any users or programs that expected the X programs, libraries, or include files to be in the standard directories.

Directory links can result in some unexpected behavior, however. For example, let's suppose I want to look at files in */usr/bin/X11*. I can just *cd* to */usr/bin/X11* even though the files are really in */usr/local/X11/bin*:

```
% cd /usr/bin/X11
% ls -F
X@        mkfontdir*      xcalc*        xinit*        xset*
    ...
```

−F *17.13*

But when I do a *pwd*, I see that I'm really in */usr/local/X11/bin*. If I didn't know about the symlink, this might be confusing for me:

```
% pwd
/usr/local/X11/bin
```

Now suppose I want to look at files in */usr/bin*. Since I did a *cd* to */usr/bin/X11*, I might think I can just go up a level. But that doesn't work:

```
% cd ..
% ls -F
bin/        include/        lib/
% pwd
/usr/local/X11
```

What happened? Remember that a symbolic link is just a *pointer* to another file or directory. So when I went to the */usr/bin/X11* directory, my current working directory became the directory */usr/bin/X11* points to, */usr/local/X11/bin*. The C shell's *hardpaths* variable (15.14) works around this problem.

lndir

As a solution to this problem and others, the X distribution provides a program called *lndir*. *lndir* is also provided on our Power Tools disk. *lndir* makes symlinks between directories by creating links for each individual file. It's cheesy, but it works. We can use *lndir* instead of *ln −s*:

```
# lndir /usr/local/X11/bin /usr/bin/X11
# ls -F /usr/bin/X11
X@          mkfontdir@      xcalc@          xinit@          xset@
...
```

—*LM*

19.08 *Showing the Actual Filenames for Symbolic Links*

sl

The *sl* program is a *perl* (39.01) script that traverses the pathnames supplied on the command line, and for each one, tells you if it had to follow any symbolic links to find the actual filename. Symbolic links to absolute pathnames start over at the left margin. Symbolic links to relative pathnames are aligned vertically with the path element they replace. For example:

```
$ sl /usr/lib/libXw.a

/usr/lib/libXw.a:
/usr/lib/libXw.a -> /usr/lib/X11/libXw.a
/usr/lib/X11 -> /X11/lib
/X11 -> /usr/local/X11R4
/usr/local/X11R4/lib/libXw.a

$ sl /bin/rnews
```

```
/bin -> /usr/bin
/usr/bin/rnews -> /usr/lib/news/rnews
/usr/lib/news -> ../local/lib/news
     local/lib/news/rnews -> inews
                  inews
```

—*LW, RS* from the Nutshell Handbook *Programming Perl*

19.09 *Renaming Multiple Files*

One frustrating deficiency of UNIX is that it won't let you rename a group of files at one time. Let's say that a novice programmer has written a bunch of files called *grp.c*, *chk.c*, *boric.c*, and so on. When you review them, you realize that they're really C header files and should have names ending in *.h*. To fix this, you'd really like to give a command like *mv *.c *.h*. But if you've used UNIX for more than a week, you probably realize that this won't work. (You've probably tried it already!) And if you're used to an operating system like VAX/VMS, which does allow this kind of multi-file rename, you can become fairly frustrated, indeed.

rename.sh

The Power Tools disk has a shell script to do the job. You can name it anything you want (*fred*?), but I call it *rename*. The comments within the script pretty much say it all; read them carefully, particularly the gotchas. Here's an example. This takes all files whose names end in the extension *.txt*, and changes the *.txt* to *.ms*:

```
% rename '\.txt$' .ms *.txt
```

The first argument should usually be in single quotes (9.10) so the shell won't try to expand it. The first argument is a regular expression for *sed*—not a shell wildcard expression (27.02). The $ says "the *.txt* must occur at the end of the filename"; the \ says "don't treat this period as a special character." Two backslashes are needed; the shell strips away the first one, and the second one does the work (inside the *sed* (35.24) command). If this is confusing, read up on regular expressions (27.01) before trying anything too complicated.

The second argument is just a replacement string. There's nothing particularly mysterious here.

The third argument (and, optionally, others) is a list of files to work on. It's just there for a few special cases, and can usually be omitted, in which case *rename* searches through all the files in the directory. The script will ignore any files that *don't* match the first argument (the string you want to change). The third argument lets you handle situations like this: you have a bunch of *.txt* files. You want to change some of them, but not all of them. List the files you want or use a shell wildcard (16.02) expression.

The part of the script that handles the filenames is below:

```
# If no filenames on command line, use all files.
# The set x and shift stop errors if first filename starts with a "-"
case "$#" in
```

```
x 36.19    0)       set x *; shift ;;
           esac
           # rename files, one at a time
           for file
           do
                   # generate the new filename with sed
                   newname=`echo $file | sed -e "s/$regexp/$replace/"`
                   ...
```

If you don't give the script any filenames to rename, the *set (46.18)* command puts a list of all files in the directory (expanded from the `*`) into the command-line arguments. The *for* loop *(46.15)* steps through the filenames one by one. A *sed (35.24)* command does the substitution you specified in the first two command-line arguments (which have been stored into shell variables). Backquotes *(10.14)* grab *sed*'s output for the *newname* shell variable.

—ML, JP

19.10 *Renaming, Copying, or Comparing a Set of Files*

If you have a group of files whose names end with *.new* and you want to rename them to end with *.old*, this won't work:

```
% mv *.new *.old
```

because the shell can't match `*.old` *(1.18)*, and because the *mv* command just doesn't work that way. Here's how to do it:

–d *17.09*
\(..\)..\1 *35.10*

```
% ls -d *.new | sed 's/\(.*\)\.new$/mv & \1.old/' | sh
```

That outputs a series of *mv* commands, one per file, and pipes them to a shell:

```
mv afile.new afile.old
mv bfile.new bfile.old
       ...
```

(To see the commands that will be generated rather than executing them, leave off the `| sh` or use `sh -v` *(9.13)*.) To copy, change `mv` to `cp`. For safety, use `mv -i` or `cp -i` if your versions have the `-i` options *(22.11)*.

This method works for any UNIX command that takes a pair of filenames. For instance, to compare a set of files in the current directory with the original files in the */usr/local/src* directory, use *diff (29.01)*:

```
% ls -d *.c *.h | sed 's@.*@diff -c & /usr/local/src/&@' | sh
```

—JP

19.11 There's More than One Way to Do It

[In article 19.09, Mike Loukides showed a shell script that lets you change one set of filenames to another according to some regular pattern. In article 19.10, Jerry Peek showed how if you really understand the shell and utilities like sed, you can easily construct custom commands to do the same thing. Here, Larry Wall and Randal Schwartz present a Perl (39.01) script that gives you even more power and flexibility. By the way, that's the Perl slogan: "There's more than one way to do it."—TOR]

rename

There are many ways of renaming multiple files under UNIX. Most of these ways are kludges. They force you to use ad hoc shell variable modifiers or multiple processes. With the *rename* Perl script, you can rename files according to the rule specified as the first argument. The argument is simply a Perl expression that is expected to modify the $_ string in Perl [the current input line— *TOR*] for at least some of the filenames specified. Thus you can rename files using the very same s/// notation you're already familiar with (35.24). If a given filename is not modified by the expression, it will not be renamed. If no filenames are given on the command line, filenames will be read via standard input.

For example, to rename all files matching *.bak to strip the extension, you might say:

```
% rename 's/\.bak$//' *.bak
```

But you're not limited to simple substitutions—you have at your disposal the full expressive power of Perl. To add those extensions back on, for instance, say this:

```
% rename '$_ .= ".bak"' *
```

or even:

```
% rename 's/$/.bak/' *
```

To translate uppercase names to lowercase, you'd use:

```
% rename 'tr/A-Z/a-z/' *
```

And how about these?

```
% rename 's/foo/bar/; $_ = $was if -e' *foo*

% find . -print | rename 's/readme/README/i'

% find . -print | rename 's/$/.old/ if -M $_ > 0.5'

% find . -name '*,v' -print | \
    rename 's#(.*)/#$1/RCS/#, $x{$1}++ || mkdir("$1/RCS", 0777)'
```

[Of course, to even understand some of these more complex incantations, you have to learn more about Perl, which is just the point... It's worth taking the time to learn.— TOR]

—*LW, RS* from the Nutshell Handbook *Programming Perl*

19.12 *Renaming Files with ren*

The Power Tools disk contains a command called *ren* that you can use to rename multiple files. The advantage of *ren* is that it can be used to rename files in a flexible fashion. For example, I have a set of PostScript files that are named *ps.ch01, ps.ch02,* and so on. I need these files to follow the usual convention of having the *ps* extension as a suffix, not a prefix—i.e. *ch01.ps, ch02.ps, ch03.ps,* etc. I could do this with a simple shell script, but it's much easier to just use *ren*.

ren

ren recognizes the metacharacters * and ?, and uses each instance of their use in replacement patterns. The first string in the filename that matches a wildcard is taken as argument 1, or #1. The second is taken as #2, and so on. The best way to explain this is to simply show how *ren* can be used.

```
% ls
ps.ch01 ps.ch02 ps.ch03 ps.ch04 ps.ch05 ps.ch06 ps.ch07
```

Use the * wildcard in the search string, and then use #1 where you want that string included the replacement string. Because * is also a shell wildcard that should be interpreted by *ren* and not the shell, you need to protect it within quotes *(9.10)*. In the Bourne shell, # is also a comment character and needs to be quoted; an interactive C shell doesn't treat # as a comment but, to be consistent, we show it quoted:

```
% ren "ps.*" "#1.ps"
```

If *ren* completes execution silently, everything worked just fine and the files were renamed. Check by listing the directory again:

```
% ls
ch01.ps ch02.ps ch03.ps ch04.ps ch05.ps ch06.ps ch07.ps
```

ren doesn't let you overwrite existing files without warning. Suppose we had another file in the same directory called *ch07.ps*:

```
% ls
ch07.ps ps.ch01 ps.ch02 ps.ch03 ps.ch04 ps.ch05 ps.ch06 ps.ch07
```

Now when we try renaming the files, *ren* warns you about overwriting the *ch07.ps* file:

```
% ren "ps.*" #1.ps
ps.ch07 -> ch07.ps ; remove old ch07.ps?
```

This feature can be suppressed with the *−d* option, which says to overwrite files without prompting. Related options are *−k*, which says *not* to overwrite any files, also without prompting; and *−a*, which says to abort the entire procedure if any files will be overwritten. Using *−a, ren* aborts before any files are renamed, so you can start all over again.

ren is also smart enough to detect internal naming conflicts before it actually renames any files. For example, suppose we had both files with both *ps.* and

---

eps. prefixes that we wanted renamed with *.ps* suffixes. If there were any conflicts, *ren* would tell us right away, and none of the files would be renamed:

```
% ls
README          ps.ch01     ps.ch03     ps.ch05     ps.ch07
eps.ch07        ps.ch02     ps.ch04     ps.ch06
% ren "*ps.*" "#2.ps"
Two or more files would have to be renamed to 'ch07.ps'.
Aborting, no renames done.
```

ren has the restriction that it can only be used to move files within a single directory. Although this makes it inconvenient for some applications, it also makes it more secure.

To show *ren* in a more complicated situation, let's take another example. Every week I write a report and then store it in a directory under the name *month.day.year*. After a while, I realized that because of the default sorting used by *ls*, the files weren't being listed in chronological order.

```
% ls
1.13.92         1.27.92         12.23.91        2.3.92
1.20.92         1.6.92          12.30.91
```

What I needed to do was to rename them *year.month.day*, and use leading 0s for the first nine months. This can be quickly done with two *ren* commands:

```
% ren "?.*.*" "#3.0#1.#2"
% ren "1?.*.9?" "9#3.1#1.#2"
% ls
91.12.23        92.01.13        92.01.27        92.02.3
91.12.30        92.01.20        92.01.6
```

The first command renames any reports for single-digit months (0-9). In the second command, I'm careful not to match any of the names of files I've already moved.

—LM

19.13 *Renaming a List of Files Interactively*

Article 19.10 shows how to rename a set of files, like changing `*.new` to `*.old`. Here's a different way, done from inside *vi*. This gives you a chance to review and edit the commands before you run them. Here are the steps:

```
% vi                    Start vi without a filename
:r !ls *.new            Read in the list of files, one filename per line
:%s/.*/mv & &/          Make mv command lines
:%s/new$/old/           Change second filenames; ready to review
:w !sh                  Run commands by writing them to a shell
:q!                     Quit vi without saving
```

If you've made an alias *(11.02)* for *ls* that changes its output format, that can cause trouble here. If your alias gives more than a plain list of filenames in a column, use !/bin/ls instead of just !ls.

—JP

19.14 *One More Way to Do It*

I couldn't resist throwing my hat into this ring. I can imagine an unsophisticated user who might not trust himself to replace one pattern with another, but doesn't want to repeat a long list of *mv* commands. Here's a simple script *(1.05)* that takes a list of filenames (perhaps provided by wildcards) as input, and prompts the user for a new name for each file:

```
#!/bin/sh
# Usage:  newname files
for x
do
    echo -n "old name is $x, new name is: "
    read newname
    mv "$x" "$newname"
done
```

-n *9.04*

For example:

touch *22.07*

```
% touch junk1 junk2 junk3
% newname junk*
old name is junk1, new name is: test1
old name is junk2, new name is: test2
old name is junk3, new name is: test3
```

This script is so simple, it's not included on the disk. I just thought I'd throw it in to demonstrate that there's more than one way to do it, even if you aren't using Perl *(19.11)*.

—TOR

19.15 *Relinking Multiple Symbolic Links*

relink

Like the *rename* program in article 19.11, the *relink* program (a Perl script) relinks the symbolic links given according to the rule specified as the first argument. The argument is a Perl expression that is expected to modify the $_ string in Perl for at least some of the names specified. For each symbolic link named on the command line, the Perl expression will be executed on the contents of the symbolic link with that name. If a given symbolic link's contents is not modified by the expression, it will not be changed. If a name given on the command line is not a symbolic link, it will be ignored. If no names are given on the command line, names will be read via standard input.

For example, to relink all symbolic links in the current directory pointing to somewhere in *X11R3* so that they point to *X11R4*, you might say:

```
$ relink 's/X11R3/X11R4/' *
```

To change all occurrences of links in the system from */usr/spool* to */var/spool*, you'd say:

–type l *18.13*

```
$ find / -type l -print | relink 's#^/usr/spool#/var/spool#'
```

—*LW, RS* from the Nutshell Handbook *Programming Perl*

19.16 *Copying Directory Trees with cp −r*

Some versions of *cp* have a *−r* (recursive) flag. It copies all the files in a directory tree—that is, all the files in a directory and its subdirectories.

Note: One of our UNIX systems has a *cp* without a *−r* option. But it also has an *rcp (1.33)* command that *does* have *−r*. *rcp* can copy to any machine, not just remote machines. When I need *cp −r* on that host, I use *rcp −r*.

The first argument(s) to *cp −r* can be directory(s)—or, if you name any file(s), they'll be copied just the way they would without the *−r*. The last argument should be a directory. So, you can use *cp −r* in two ways:

1. Give *cp −r* directory(s) to copy. They'll be created as subdirectories of the directory named at the end.

2. Give *cp −r* file(s) to copy. They'll be copied to the directory named at the end.

Those two methods are really doing the same thing. They're both copying the tail of the first pathname(s) to the end of the last pathname.

*   Here's how to do the copy shown in Figure 19-1. This copies the directory */home/jane*, with all its files and subdirectories, and creates a subdirectory named *jane* in the current directory:

    ```
    % cd /work/bkup
    % cp -r /home/jane .
    ```

*   How can you copy the contents of the subdirectory called *data* and all its files (but not the subdirectory itself) into a duplicate directory named *data.bak*? First create the destination directory. That's because the last argument to *cp −r* must be a directory that already exists:

    ```
    % cd /home/jane
    % mkdir data.bak
    % cp -r data/* data.bak
    ```

    That doesn't copy any files in *data* whose names start with a dot (.). There's a way *(16.06)* to do that though.

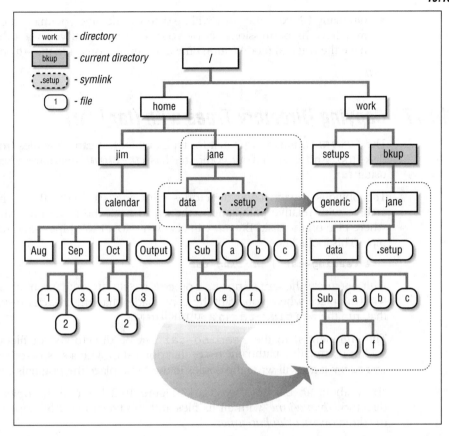

Figure 19-1. Copying /home/jane to Current Directory (/work/bkup) with cp

- To copy the subdirectories *Sep* and *Oct* and their files, as well as the file *Output*, from the directory */home/jim/calendar* into the current directory (.):

[..]* *16.02*

```
% cp -r /home/jim/calendar/[SO]* .
```

If you use the C shell, you can copy just the directories by using the handy *csh* curly brace operators *(10.05)*:

```
% cp -r /home/jim/calendar/{Sep,Oct} .
```

Some gotchas:

- Symbolic and hard links *(19.04)* are copied as files. That can be good because, at the destination, a symbolic link might point to the wrong place. It can be bad if the link pointed to a really big file; the copy can take a lot of disk space. (In Figure 19-1 notice that the symbolic link in *jane's* home directory was converted to a file named *.setup* with a copy of the contents of *generic*.)

- On many UNIXes, the copy will be dated at the time you made the copy and may have its permissions set by your *umask (23.04)*. If you want the copy to have the original modification time and permissions, add the –*p* option.

—*JP*

19.17 Copying Directory Trees with (tar | tar)

The *tar (20.05)* command isn't just for tape archives. It can copy files from disk to disk, too. And even if your computer has *cp* –*r (19.16)*, there are advantages to using *tar*.

The obvious way to copy directories with *tar* is to write them onto a tape archive with relative pathnames—then read back the tape and write it somewhere else on the disk. But *tar* can also write to a UNIX pipe—and read from a pipe. This looks like:

```
% reading-tar | writing-tar
```

with one trick: the `writing-tar` process has a different current directory *(40.03, 40.04)* (the place where you want the copy made) than the `reading-tar`. To do that, run the `writing-tar` in a subshell *(14.07)*.

The argument(s) to the `reading-tar` can be directory(s) or file(s). Just be sure to use relative pathnames *(15.02)* that don't start with a slash—otherwise, the `writing-tar` will write the copies in the same place the originals came from!

"How about an example," you ask? Figure 19-2 has one. It copies from the directory */home/jane*, with all its files and subdirectories. The copy is made in the directory */work/bkup/jane*:

```
% mkdir /work/bkup/jane
% cd /home/jane
% tar cf - . | (cd /work/bkup/jane; tar xBf -)
```

If your *tar* has a *B* (reblocking) option, use it to help be sure that the copy is made correctly. If your *tar* doesn't have a reblocking option, you can use this trick suggested by Chris Torek:

```
% tar cf - . | cat | (cd /work/backup/jane; tar xbf 1 -)
```

 At least one *tar* version has a *v* (verbose) option that writes the verbose text to standard output instead of standard error *(20.08)*! If your *tar* does that, don't use *v* on the `reading-tar` (the *tar* that feeds the pipe)—use *v* on the `writing-tar`.

You can use other options that your *tar* might have—like excluding files or directories *(21.08)*—on the `reading-tar`, too.

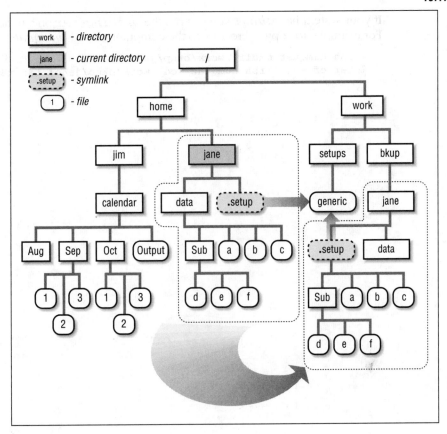

Figure 19-2. Copying /home/jane to /work/bkup with tar

Some gotchas:

- Symbolic links *(19.04)* will be copied exactly. If they point to relative path-names, the copied links might point to locations that don't exist. You can search for these symbolic links with *find —type l(18.13)* or *oldlinks(17.29)*.

- A hard link *(19.04)* will be copied as a file. If there are more hard links to that file in the files you're copying, they will be linked to the copy of the first link. That can be good because the destination might be on a different filesystem (a hard link can't work then). It can be bad if the link pointed to a really big file; the copy can take a lot of disk space. You can search for these hard links by:

  - Searching the directory you're copying from with *find —links +1 —type f (18.05)* to find all files that have more than one link, and

  - Running the *reading-tar* with its *l* (lowercase letter L) option to complain if it didn't copy all links to a file.

If your system has *rsh* (1.33), you can run the *writing-tar* on a remote system. For example, to copy a directory to the computer named *kumquat*:

```
% rsh kumquat mkdir /work/bkup/jane
% tar cf - . | rsh kumquat 'cd /work/bkup/jane; tar xBf -'
```

—JP

20

Creating and Reading Archives

20.01 Packing Up and Moving

The worst part of living in a nice big house is the headache of moving. The more stuff you've got room for, the more trouble it is to pack it up and take it with you.

The UNIX operating system is a little bit like that. One of its real advantages is a filesystem that lets you organize your personal files into a hierarchical directory tree just like the much bigger tree that encompasses the entire filesystem. You can squirrel away all kinds of useful information into neat pigeonholes.

While your personal directory hierarchy is usually only two or three levels deep, for all practical purposes it can have as many levels as you like. And, as is true of any powerful and flexible tool, problems lie in wait for the sorcerer's apprentice. Directories and files grow increasingly complex the longer you use the system, with more forgotten files and more detailed organization.

This chapter will tackle the problems that can arise when you want to move a block of files (in one or many directories) from one place to another.

Maybe you're writing the files to a tape for safety *(21.02)*. In many cases though, this is a "backup and restore" problem. For example, if you were moving your account to another system, you might just ask the system administrator (if there is one) to archive your files to tape or floppy and restore them in the new location. Many new users are less aware that you can use the backup programs *tar (21.01)* and *cpio (20.09)* (as well as some common archive programs like *shar (20.02)*) to create online archives that you can move from one place to another.

This situation is most likely to arise in a networked environment. You might be packaging files to ship as a package to another user. The files might be going to an archive site on the Internet or Usenet, for distribution to many users. Even though we've made a conscious decision *(1.32)* to omit networking information from this book these programs are so useful even on a single system (let alone one without the artificial boundaries we've put on this book) that we decided we ought to keep at least this chapter in the book.

—TOR

20.02 *Introduction to Shell Archives*

A shell archive or *shar* file is a single file that contains one or more other files. Files are extracted from the archive with the standard UNIX Bourne shell *(46.03)*. A shell archive usually doesn't let you save and restore complete directory hierarchies like *cpio (20.09)* and *tar (20.05)* do, but it is completely portable and, as a result, is used extensively on Usenet, an international network with many UNIX systems.

In the Bourne shell, the operator << *(9.14)* means to take the following lines, up to a specified string, as input to a command. (This is often called a *here document*.) Using this syntax and the *cat (26.02)* and *echo (9.04)* commands, you can write a simple shell archiver (*shar*) like the one below. Incidentally, many systems already have *shar* programs in place; there are several freely-available versions, including the one on the Power Tools disk. Just about any of them are likely to be more sophisticated than the version shown here—but this version shows the essence of how they work:

shar

for *46.15*

<< *9.14*

```
#!/bin/sh
for file
do
        echo "echo restoring $file"
        echo "cat > $file << 'XxXxXxXxXx-EOF-XxXxXxXxXx'"
        cat $file
        echo "XxXxXxXxXx-EOF-XxXxXxXxXx"
done
```

The string XxXxXxXxXx-EOF-XxXxXxXxXx is entirely arbitrary—it just needs to be a string that won't otherwise appear in the input and can be used by the shell to recognize when the here document is finished.

When you give *shar* a list of filenames, it will string those files together on standard output, separating them with that arbitrary string and the commands to split them up again. Simply redirect this output stream to a file to create the archive. For example, the command:

```
$ shar file1 file2 > archive.shar
```

will produce a file called *archive.shar* that contains the following data:

'...' *47.26*

```
echo restoring file1
cat > file1 << 'XxXxXxXxXx-EOF-XxXxXxXxXx'
    . . .
```
Text of file1 will be stored here
```
    . . .
XxXxXxXxXx-EOF-XxXxXxXxXx
echo restoring file2
cat > file2 << 'XxXxXxXxXx-EOF-XxXxXxXxXx'
```

```
. . .
```
Text of file2 will be stored here
```
. . .
XxXxXxXxXx-EOF-XxXxXxXxXx
```

When this archive is run through *sh*, the commands it contains will be executed. Each here document (the lines from each `cat` up to the next `XxXxXxXxXx-EOF-XxXxXxXxXx`) will be output to a file:

```
$ sh archive.shar
restoring file1
restoring file2
$ ls
archive.shar
file1
file2
```

The *unshar* (20.03) program does essentially the same thing.

You should never blindly run a shell archive supplied by someone you don't know personally. An unscrupulous prankster could easily include a "Trojan horse" command (like `rm *`) in the middle of a seemingly innocuous archive, and cause you a lot of trouble. An easy way to do this is by browsing through the archive with the search command in a program like *more* (26.03). Use the search command (in *more*, the command is `/`) to find each end-of-file string (like `XxXxXxXxXx`); look carefully at the commands between it and the `cat` that starts the next file.

Of course, if the files in the shell archive are programs themselves, you should also check them before they're executed.

—TOR

20.03 unshar: Unarchive a Shell Archive

Article 20.02 explained how to extract files from a shell archive by executing it as a shell script with *sh*. There are a few drawbacks to this. One of them is that *shar* files are often sent through e-mail, and have an e-mail header ahead of shell commands. One can strip out the header manually after saving the file—but why bother?

shar

The *unshar* program, which is distributed with *shar* on the Power Tools disk, is more intelligent about ignoring leading garbage and checking out the *shar* file for problems.

—TOR

20.04 A Simple Version of unshar

This little script is a great example of how something simple in UNIX can do a lot. It skips past the mail header and comments that come before some shell archives *(20.02)*, then feeds the archive to a shell. You can use it while you're reading a message with most UNIX mail programs *(1.33)*:

```
& save | unshar
```

or give it the name of an archive file on its command line:

```
% unshar somefile.shar
```

and so on. Here's a version of the script:

```
#! /bin/sh
# IGNORE LINES BEFORE FIRST "#" COMMENT STARTING IN FIRST COLUMN:
sed -n '/^#/,$p' $1 | sh
```

The script reads from its standard input or a single file. It skips all lines until the comment (#) that starts most shell archives; the rest of the lines are piped to the shell. It doesn't read from multiple files; that would add another couple of lines for a loop—and make the script too long! :-) In the last few years, much fancier *unshar* programs *(20.03)* have come out. They protect against "Trojan horses" buried in *shar* files and let systems without a Bourne shell (like DOS) unpack shell archives. This basic script still does a fine job though. [It also gives one more demonstration of why at least basic knowledge of *sed* *(35.24)* is so important to would-be power users. It's an incredibly handy utility.— *TOR*]

—*JP*

20.05 Using tar to Create Archives

Many UNIX users think of *tar* *(21.01)* as a utility for creating tapes. Like most UNIX utilities though, that's only the beginning. For example, you can use *tar* for copying directory trees *(19.17)*.

One common use for *tar* is creating archive files that can be shipped to other systems. We've already seen a utility for creating shell archives *(20.02)*, but there are a lot of things that a shell archive can't do. *tar* is very useful when you're sending binary data; I've seen some *shar* utilities that can handle binary data, but they're rare, and I don't particularly like the way they do it. If you use *tar*, you can package several directories into an archive, you can send directories that include links, you can preserve file ownership and access permissions, etc.

To create a *tar* archive, use the *c* (create) and *f* (filename) options to save *tar*'s output in a file:

```
% cd /home/src/fsf
% tar cf gnuemacs.tar gnuemacs/*
```

This command puts everything in the *gnuemacs* directory into a file (called a *tar file*) named *gnuemacs.tar*. You can then give this file to other users, via FTP, UUCP *(1.33)*, or any other means.

Archives (no matter how you make them) are usually rather large, so it's common to *compress (25.06)* them, with a command like:

```
% compress gnuemacs.tar
```

This creates the file *gnuemacs.tar.Z*, which should be significantly smaller than the original *tar* archive.

If you're going to use UUCP or FTP to transfer the file, this is good enough; both UUCP and FTP know how to handle binary data. Often though, you'd like to send the archive via electronic mail *(1.33)*, and mail only knows how to handle ASCII *(53.03)* data. So you need to create an ASCII version. To do this, use the *uuencode (55.01)* command. To read the file directly, repeat its name twice:

```
% uuencode gnuemacs.tar.Z gnuemacs.tar.Z > gnuemacs.tar.Z.uu
```

You can then insert *gnuemacs.tar.Z.uu* into a mail message and send it to someone. Of course, the ASCII-only encoding won't be as efficient as the original binary file. It's about 33 percent larger.*

What happens when you receive a uuencoded, compressed *tar* file? The same thing, in reverse. You'll get a mail message that (after the various header lines) looks something like this:

```
begin 644 gnuemacs.tar.Z
M+DDQ0"D
M+DDQ0"D="D
M-DDK
M
M
```

So you save the message in a file, complete with headers. Let's say you call this file *mailstuff.* How do you get the original files back? Use the following sequence of commands:

```
% uudecode mailstuff
% uncompress gnuemacs.tar.Z
% tar xf gnuemacs.tar
```

The *uudecode* command creates the file *gnuemacs.tar.Z.* Then *uncompress* recreates your original *tar* file, and *tar xf* extracts the individual files from the archive. Article 20.07 shows a more efficient method.

By the way, *tar* is so flexible precisely because of UNIX's file-oriented design: everything, even a tape drive, "looks like" a file. So *tar* creates a certain kind of file and sends it out into the world; it usually lands on a tape, but you can put it somewhere else if you want. With most operating systems, a tape utility would know how to talk to a tape drive, and that's all.

—*ML*

---

*If so, why bother compressing? Why not forget about both *compress* and *uuencode*? Well, you can't. Remember that *tar* files are binary files to start with—even if every file in the archive is an ASCII text file. You'd need to *uuencode* a file before mailing it, anyway—so you'd still pay the 33-percent size penalty that *uuencode* incurs. Using *compress* minimizes the damage.

20.06 GNU tar Can Compress an Archive

tar

Article 20.05 describes how to compress an archive file you've created. If you're using GNU *tar*, this is even easier, since *tar* itself can do the compression. Simply use the *z* option when writing or reading archives. For example:

```
% tar cvzf /dev/rst0
```

will create a compressed tar archive on the tape attached to */dev/rst0*. Try this when you need to fit more data on the tape than the manufacturer intended.

—*TOR*

20.07 Extracting Files from a Compressed Archive

In article 20.05, we discussed how to create and unpack compressed *tar* archives: run *uncompress (25.06)*, and then use *tar*. You can combine these into one step by using *zcat*, and then piping the output into *tar*:

```
% zcat archive.tar.Z | tar xf - pathnames
```

The *zcat* command uncompresses a file, sending the result to standard output. With the *f* option, and – listed as a filename, *tar* reads from standard input. You don't need to create the larger, uncompressed file; you can store the archive permanently in its compressed form. To extract only some of the files in the archive, give the *pathnames* on the command line *exactly* as they're stored in the archive. Otherwise, *tar* will extract all the files. (For a list of the exact pathnames, use tar tf -.)

If you need to do this often, you could create an alias easily enough:

```
alias ztar "zcat \!^ | tar xf -"
```

You can use this same technique to create a compressed archive:

```
% tar cf - list-of-files | compress > archive.tar.Z
```

(20.08)

Instead of cf, you can use cvf so *tar* will list each file as it's processed.

If you have an archive compressed with the older *pack* utility, try this:

```
% pcat archive.tar.z | tar xf -
```

Note: If you extract files from an archive that you didn't create, the files you extract may not belong to you. Here's why. On many non-BSD systems, when *tar* extracts a file, the file will be owned by the same UID *(40.03)* that owned the file when the archive was created. If that UID isn't yours, *tar* may extract directories you can't modify and files you can't edit.

On systems with that problem, you can add the *o* option (for example, tar xof) to be sure that files extracted will belong to you.

—*ML, JIK, JP*

20.08   Problems with Verbose tar

I've heard of one *tar* version with a *v* (verbose) option that writes the verbose information to its standard output, rather than standard error. If your *tar* does that, be sure not to use *v* when you're using *tar* to write to a pipeline. For example, the command below would be a disaster if your version of *tar* has this bug:

```
% tar cvf - *.txt | compress > archive.tar.Z
```

The filenames would appear in standard output, along with the *tar* file itself. The result would be a compressed archive that couldn't be extracted. (You would probably get a "checksum error" from *tar*, or something similar, if you tried.)

You can test for this problem by typing:

```
% tar cvf - somefile > /dev/null              tar without v bug
a somefile 23 blocks, 44567 characters
```

That redirects standard output to */dev/null (14.14)*. If you don't see any verbose output, your *tar* has the bug.

—JP

20.09   A System V Tape Archiver: cpio

There was a time when people used to debate whether the BSD *tar (21.01, 20.05)* (tape archiver) or the System V *cpio* (copy in/out) was the better file archive and backup program. At this point, there's no question. No one ships out *cpio* archives over the net *(1.33)*. *tar* is widespread, and because there are free versions available, including GNU *tar (20.06)*, there's no reason why you should have to read a *cpio* archive from someone else.

Still, if you're on an older System V machine, you might use *cpio*. Though we don't give it much air time in this book, here are a few basics:

- To write out an archive, use the *−o* option, and redirect output either to a tape device or to an archive file. The list of files to be archived is often specified with *find (18.01)*, but can be generated in other ways—*cpio* expects a list of filenames on its standard input. For example:

```
% find . -name "*.old" -print | cpio -ocBv > /dev/rst8
```

or:

```
% find . -print | cpio -ocBv > mydir.cpio
```

- To read an archive in, use the *−i* option, and redirect input from the file or tape drive containing the archive. The *−d* option is often important; it tells *cpio* to create directories as needed when copying files in. You can restore all files from the archive or specify a filename pattern (with wildcards quoted to protect them from the shell) to select only some of the files. For example, the following command will restore from a tape drive all C source files:

```
% cpio -icdv "*.c" < /dev/rst8
```

Subdirectories are created if needed (*−d*), and *cpio* will be verbose (*−v*), announcing the name of each file that it successfully reads in.

- To copy an archive to another directory, use the *−o* option, followed by the name of the destination directory. (This is one of the nicer features of *cpio*.) For example, you could use the following command to copy the contents of the current directory (including all subdirectories) to another directory:

```
% find . -depth -print | cpio -pd newdir
```

- There are lots of other options, for things like resetting file access times or ownership, or changing the blocking factor on the tape. See your friendly neighborhood manual page for details. Notice that options are typically "squashed together" into an option string rather than written out as separate options.

—*TOR*

21

Backing Up Files

21.01 tar in a Nutshell

When many UNIX users think of file archives, on tape or in an archive file, they think of the *tar* utility. There are other ways to make archives and handle tapes—including *cpio (20.09)*, *shar (20.02)*, and *dd (21.06)*. This article summarizes articles about *tar*—in this chapter and others.

- Although *tar* is a *tape ar*chiver, one of its common uses is making an archive file on disk *(20.05)*. Because *tar* "pads" its archives with NUL characters *(53.03)*, on-disk *tar* archive files can be much bigger than the size of the individual files put together. The file can be compressed—so you may need to uncompress an archive *(20.07)*. The GNU *tar (20.06)* can compress files while storing them. If you make on-disk archives, be careful with *tar*'s *v* (verbose) flag or you could end up with a corrupted archive that holds more than your files *(20.08)*.

  With compression, a *tar* archive can take less disk space *(25.07)* than compressing individual small files.

  Because *tar* keeps most of a file's inode *(1.22)* information, it can make a more complete copy *(19.17)* of a file or directory tree than utilities like *cp*.

- Yes, we do have articles about archives on tape. Bruce Barnett's article 21.02 has enough information to make your own archive . . . although you might need the details from article 21.03, too. After you've made an archive, you'll probably want to restore it—at least as a test to be sure your archive is okay. Article 21.04 explains how.

  If there isn't a tape drive on your computer, read article 21.05 about using a drive on another computer. If that isn't enough information, read the gory details from another of our long-time UNIX and tape experts, Chris Torek, in article 21.06.

> • *tar* copies a directory tree, recursively, from top to bottom. What if you don't want to archive everything? You can back up just some files by combining *ls –lt* and *find (21.07)*. Some versions of *tar* have options for including or excluding certain files and directories *(21.08)*.
>
> —JP

21.02 Make Your Own Backups

As someone who has been an end user and a system administrator, I strongly believe that every user should understand the importance of backups.

If you have data that is important to you, you should have a known backup.

Accidents and oversights happen. Tapes can be damaged, lost, or mislabeled. Assume that your system administrator is top-notch. The best administrator can recover your lost data 99 percent of the time. There is still a small chance that the files you need might not be recovered. Can you afford to duplicate months of effort 1 percent of the time? No.

An experienced user learns to be pessimistic. Typically, this important fact is learned the hard way. Perhaps a few hours are lost. Perhaps days. Sometimes months are lost.

Here are some common situations:

• A user works on a file all day. At the end of the day, the file is deleted by accident. The system manager cannot recover the file. A day's work has been lost.

• A programmer tries to clean up a project directory. Instead of typing `rm *.o` the programmer types `rm * .o` and the entire directory is lost.

• A user deletes a file by accident. After a few days, the user asks the system administrator to recover the file. The incremental backup system has re-used the only tape the missing file was on.

• A large project is archived on a magnetic tape and deleted from the disk. A year later, some of the information is needed. The tape has a bad block at the beginning. The system manager must learn how to recover data from a bad tape. The attempt is often unsuccessful. The information is lost forever, and must be re-created, at the cost of months of effort.

• Someone breaks into a computer and accesses confidential information.

• A fire breaks out in the computer room. The disks and *all* of the backup tapes are lost.

Gulp! I scared myself. Excuse me for a few minutes while I load a tape....

Ah! I feel better now. As I was saying, being pessimistic has its advantages.

Making a backup is easy. Get a blank tape and put a label on it. Learn how to load it onto the tape drive. Then do the following:

```
% cd
% tar c .
```

Take the tape off. Write-protect the tape (slide the tab, turn the knob, or put in the ring). That's all.

[Not quite! Bruce also points out that you can get even more protection by using a version control system like SCCS *(21.12)* or RCS *(21.14)* to save every version of a file you are updating frequently.— *TOR*]

—BB

21.03 *How to Make Backups with a Local Tape Drive*

As we said in article 21.02, making a backup is easy:

```
% cd
% tar c .
```

The *cd* command moves you to your home directory. You could back up any directory the same way.

The *tar (21.01)* command, which is an abbreviation of *tape archive*, copies the current directory (specified by the .) to the default tape drive. The c argument specifies the *create* mode of *tar.*

You might get an error. Something about device *rmt8* off line. Don't worry. I exaggerated slightly when I said *tar* was easy to use. The tape device that Sun *tar* uses by default is */dev/rmt8* (yours may be different). There are several types of tape units, and not all can be referred to using that name. Some system administrators will link that name to the actual device, which makes *tar* easier to use. But if that doesn't work, you need to specify additional arguments to *tar.*

Syntax of the tar Command

Most UNIX commands follow a certain style when arguments are specified. *tar* does not follow this convention, so you must be careful to use *tar* properly. If the standard was followed, then the following might be an example of dumping the current directory to the 1/2-inch tape cartridge, verbose mode, block size of 20:

```
% tapedump -c -v -b 20 -f /dev/rmt8 .          Wrong!
```

Instead, all the flags are in the first argument, and the parameters to those flags follow the first argument, in order of the flags specified:

```
% tar cvbf 20 /dev/rmt8 .
```

The same command can be specified in a different way by changing the order of the letters in the first argument:

```
% tar cvfb /dev/rmt8 20 .
```

(Article 21.11 has diagrams and more information about the order of arguments.) The only key letter that has a fixed location is the first one, which must specify if you are reading or writing an archive. The most common key letters, and the functions they perform are listed in Table 21-1.

Table 21-1. Common tar Key Letters

Key Letter	Function
c	Create an archive.
x	Extract files from an archive.
t	Table of contents.
v	Give verbose information.

Some versions of *tar* require a hyphen before the letter. It is optional on SunOS.

What is the Name of the Tape Drive?

Part of the difficulty in using *tar* is figuring out which filename to use for which device. The best way to find out is by asking your system administrator. If you can't, here are some ideas for Sun computers. If you have a 1/2-inch tape drive, try:

```
% tar cf /dev/rmt8 .
```

If you have a 1/4-inch tape cartridge [or any drive connected by SCSI—*JP*], try:

```
% tar cf /dev/rst8 .
```

If this doesn't work, then try changing the 8 to a 0. You can also list the devices in the */dev* directory and look for one that has the most recent usage:

[ ] *16.02*
```
% ls -lut /dev/r[ms]t*
```

Some UNIX systems use different standards for naming magnetic tapes. There might be an *h* at the end of a name for *high density*. When in doubt, examine the major and minor numbers (using the *ls −l* command) and read the appropriate manual page, which can be found by searching through the possible entries using *man −k* or *apropos* (52.02):

```
% man -k mt
% man -k tape
```

More on Tape Names

The names of tape devices always start with an *r* by convention, which suggests this is a *raw* device that does not support a filesystem. If the first two letters are *nr*, then this suggests a *no-rewind* operation. Normally the tape is automatically rewound when you are done. If you repeat the *tar* command, it will overwrite the first dump.* As this can waste large amounts of tape if the dumps are small, use the *nr* name of the tape to put several dumps on one tape. As an example, if you wanted to dump three separate directories to a 1/4-inch tape cartridge, you can type:

```
% cd dir1
% tar cf /dev/nrst8 .
% cd dir2
% tar cf /dev/nrst8 .
% cd dir3
% tar cf /dev/rst8 .
```

Note that the third dump does not use the no-rewind name of the device, so that it will rewind when done.

To examine a tape without extracting any files, get a table of contents and use the key letter t or tv instead of the c . Adding the v flag gives a more verbose listing.

If you want to examine the third dump file, you can either use *tar* twice with the no-rewind names or skip forward one or more dump files by using the *mt* (magnetic tape) command to skip forward two. Be sure to use the no-rewind name:

```
% mt -f /dev/nrst8 fsf 2
```

SunOS 4.1 has added a new convenience to the *tar* command. If you defined an environment variable *TAPE*:

```
setenv TAPE /dev/rst8
```

then you don't have to specify it for the *mt* or *tar* commands.

[Some versions of *tar*, like the one from GNU *(55.01)* on the Power Tools disk, handle remote drives automatically.—*JIK*]

—*BB*

---

*This is probably not what you want. You could use a new tape for each dump.

21.04 Restoring Files from Tape with tar

When you create an archive, there are several ways to specify the directory. If the directory is under the current directory, you could type:

```
% tar c project
```

A similar way to specify the same directory is:

```
% tar c ./project
```

If you are currently in the directory you want archived, you can type:

```
% tar c .
```

Another way to archive the current directory is to type:

```
% tar c *
```

Here, the shell expands the * (asterisk) to the files in the current directory. However, it does not match files starting with a . (dot), which is why the previous technique is preferred.

This causes a problem when restoring a directory from a *tar* archive. You may not know if an archive was created using . or the directory name.

I always check the names of the files before restoring an archive:

```
% tar t
```

If the archive loads the files into the current directory, I create a new directory, change to it, and extract the files.

If the archive restores the directory by name, then I restore the files into the current directory.

Restoring a Few Files

If you want to restore a single file, get the pathname of the file as *tar* knows it, using the *t* flag. You must specify the exact filename, because `filename` and `./filename` are not the same. You can combine these two steps into one command by using [this may run very slowly—*JP*]:

```
% tar xvf /dev/rst0 `tar tf /dev/rst0 | grep filename`
```

Whenever you use *tar* to restore a directory, you must always specify *some* filename. If none is specified, no files are restored.

There is still the problem of restoring a directory whose pathname starts with /(slash). Because *tar* restores a file to the pathname specified in the archive, you cannot change *where* the file will be restored. The danger is that either you may overwrite some existing files or you will not be able to restore the files because you don't have permission.

You can ask the system administrator to rename a directory and temporarily create a symbolic link pointing to a directory where you can restore the files. Other solutions exist, including editing the *tar* archive and creating a new directory structure with a C program executing the *chroot*(2) system call.

Another solution is to use the version from the Free Software Foundation (55.01) that allows you to remap pathnames starting with /(slash). It also allows you to create archives that are too large for a single tape, incremental archives, and a dozen other advantages. This freely-available version of *tar* is also called GNU *tar* (20.06). (It's on the disk.)

But the best solution is to never create an archive of a directory that starts with /(slash) *or* ~(tilde).

Remote Restoring

To restore a directory from a remote host, use the following command:

rsh 1.33

```
% rsh -n host dd if=/dev/rst0 bs=20b | tar xvBfb - 20 files
```

Because of its nature, it is difficult to read fixed-size blocks over a network. This is why *tar* uses the *B* flag to force it to read from the pipe until a block is completely filled.

—BB

21.05 *Using tar to a Remote Tape Drive*

If your computer doesn't have a tape drive connected, creating *tar* (21.01) backup files is slightly more complicated. If you have an account on a machine with a tape drive, and the directory is mounted via NFS (1.33), you can just *rlogin* (1.33) to the other machine and use *tar* to back up your directory.

If the directory is not NFS mounted, or it is mounted but you have permission problems accessing your own files, you can use *tar*, *rsh* (1.33), and *dd* (36.04) to solve this dilemma. The syntax is confusing, but if you forget, you can use *man tar* (52.01) to refresh your memory. The command to dump the current directory to a tape in a remote machine called *zephyrus* is:

```
% tar cvfb - 20 . | rsh zephyrus dd of=/dev/rmt0 obs=20b
```

Here, the output file of *tar* is – (14.13), which *tar* interprets as standard input if *tar* is reading an archive or standard output if *tar* is creating an archive.

The *dd* command copies data from standard input to the device */dev/rmt0*. Article 21.06 explains more about how this works.

This example assumes you can use *rsh* without requiring a password. You can add your current machine's name to the remote *.rhosts* file (1.33) if you get a Password: prompt when you use *rlogin* to access this machine.

—BB

21.06 Writing a Tape Drive on a Remote Machine

[Bruce Barnett introduces this topic in article 21.05. —JP]

In news posting *<5932@tahoe.unr.edu> malc@equinox.unr.edu* (Malcolm Car-lock) asked how to make *tar* write a remote tape drive via *rsh* (1.33) and *dd* (36.04). Here's the answer:

```
% tar cf - . | rsh foo dd of=/dev/device obs=20b
```

Be forewarned that most incarnations of *dd* are extremely slow at handling this.

What is going on? This answer requires some background:

- Tapes have "block sizes." Not all tapes, mind you—most SCSI tapes have a fixed block size that can, for the most part, be ignored. Nine-track tapes, however, typically record data in "records" separated by "gaps," and only whole records can be reread later.

- In order to accommodate this, UNIX tape drivers generally translate each *read( )* or *write( )* system call into a single record transfer. The size of a written record is the number of bytes passed to *write( )*. (There may be some additional constraints, such as "the size must be even" or "the size must be no more than 32768 bytes." Note that phase-encoded (1600-bpi) blocks should be no longer than 10240 bytes, and GCR (6250-bpi) blocks should be no longer than 32768 bytes, to reduce the chance of an unrecoverable error.) Each *read( )* call must ask for at least one whole record (many drivers get this wrong and silently drop trailing portions of a record that was longer than the byte count given to *read( )*); each *read( )* returns the actual number of bytes in the record.

- Network connections are generally "byte streams": the two host "peers" (above, the machine running *tar*, and the machine with the tape drive) will exchange data but will drop any "record boundary" notion at the protocol-interface level. If record boundaries are to be preserved, this must be done in a layer above the network protocol itself. (Not all network protocols are stream-oriented, not even flow-controlled, error-recovering protocols. Internet RDP and XNS SPP are two examples of reliable record-oriented protocols. Many of these, however, impose fairly small record sizes.)

- *rsh* simply opens a stream protocol, and does no work to preserve "packet boundaries."

- *dd* works in mysterious ways:

  ```
  dd if=x of=y
  ```

  is the same as:

  ```
  dd if=x of=y ibs=512 obs=512
  ```

  which means: open files *x* and *y*, then loop doing *read(fd_x)* with a byte count of 512, take whatever you got, copy it into an output buffer for file *y*, and each time that buffer reaches 512 bytes, do a single *write(fd_y)* with 512 bytes.

On the other hand:

```
dd if=x of=y bs=512
```

means something completely different: open files x and y, then loop doing *read(fd_x)* with a byte count of 512, take whatever you got, and do a single *write(fd_y)* with that count. All of this means that:

```
% tar cf - . | rsh otherhost dd of=/dev/device
```

will write 512-byte blocks (not what you wanted), while:

```
% tar cf - . | rsh otherhost dd of=/dev/device bs=20b
```

will be even worse: it will take whatever it gets from *stdin*—which, being a TCP connection, will be arbitrarily lumpy depending on the underlying network parameters and the particular TCP implementation—and write essentially random-sized records. On purely "local" (Ethernet) connections, with typical implementations, you will wind up with 1024-byte blocks (a *tar* "block factor" of 2).

If a blocking factor of 2 is acceptable, and if *cat* forces 1024-byte blocks (both true in some cases), you can use:

```
% tar cf - . | rsh otherhost "cat >/dev/device"
```

but this depends on undocumented features in *cat*. In any case, on nine-track tapes, since each gap occupies approximately 0.7 inches of otherwise useful tape space, a block size of 1024 has ten times as many gaps as a block size of 10240, wasting 9x1600x0.7 = 10 kbytes of tape at 1600 bpi, or 32 times as many as a size of 32768, wasting 31x6250x0.7 = 136 kbytes of tape at 6250 bpi.

I say "approximately" because actual gap sizes vary. In particular, certain "streaming" drives (all too often called streaming because they do not—in some cases the controller is too "smart" to be able to keep up with the required data rate, even when fed back-to-back DMA requests) have been known to stretch the gaps to 0.9 inches.

In general, because of tape gaps, you should use the largest record size that permits error recovery. Note, however, that some olid* hardware (such as that found on certain AT&T 3B systems) puts a ridiculous upper limit (5K) on tape blocks.

—*CT* in *comp.unix.questions* on Usenet, *3 April 1991*

---

*Go ahead, look it up ... it is a perfectly good crossword puzzle word. :-)

21.07 Creating a Timestamp File for Selective Backups

Whenever I upgraded to a new version of UNIX, one common problem was making sure I maintained all of the changes made to the standard release of UNIX. Previously, I did an *ls* −*lt (17.02)* in each directory, and then I examined the modification date. The files that were changed have an obviously newer date than the original programs. Even so, finding every change was tedious, as there were dozens of directories to be searched.

A better solution is to create a file as the first step in upgrading. I usually call this *FirstFile*. *find* has a −*newer* option *(18.08)* that tests each file and compares the modification date to the newer file. If you then wanted to list all files in */usr* that need to be saved when the operating system is upgraded, use:

```
% find /usr -newer /usr/FirstFile -print
```

This could then be used to create a *tar (20.05)* or *cpio (20.09)* file that would be restored after the upgrade.

—BB

21.08 Telling tar which Files to Exclude or Include

[This article was written for SunOS. Many versions of tar don't have some or all of these features. Some do it in a different way. Check your tar manual page, or use the GNU tar (20.06) that we provide on the disk.—JP]

On some systems, *make (29.12)* creates files starting with a comma (,) to keep track of dependencies. Various editors create backup files ending with a percent sign (%) or a tilde (~). I often keep the original copy of a program with the *.orig* extension and old versions with a *.old* extension.

I often don't want to save these files on my backups. There may be some binary files that I don't want to archive, but don't want to delete either.

A solution is to use the *X* flag to *tar (21.01)*. [Check your *tar* manual page for the *F* and *FF* options, too. —*JIK*] This flag specifies that the matching argument to *tar* is a filename that lists files to exclude from the archive. Here is an example:

```
% find project ! -type d -print | \
egrep '/,|%$|~$|\.old$|SCCS|/core$|\.o$|\.orig$' > Exclude
% tar cvfX project.tar Exclude project
```

In this example, *find (18.01)* lists all files in the directories, but does not print the directory names explicitly. If you have a directory name in an excluded list, it will also exclude all the files inside the directory. *egrep (28.05)* is then used as a filter to exclude certain files from the archive. Here, *egrep* is given several regular expressions to match certain files. This expression seems complex but is simple once you understand a few special characters:

/   The slash is not a special character. However, since no filename can contain a slash, it matches the beginning of a filename, as output by the *find* command.

| The vertical bar separates each regular expression.

$ The dollar sign is one of the two regular expression "anchors" and specifies the end of the line, or filename in this case. The other anchor, which specifies the beginning of the line, is ^ (caret). But because we are matching filenames output by *find*, the only filenames that can match ^ are those in the top directory.

\. Normally the dot matches any character in a regular expression. Here, we want to match the actual character . (dot), which is why the backslash is used to quote or escape the normal meaning.

A breakdown of the patterns and examples of the files that match these patterns is given below:

Pattern	Matches Files	Used by
/,	starting with ,	*make* dependency files
%$	ending with %	*textedit* backup files
~$	ending with ~	*emacs* backup files
\.old$	ending with *.old*	old copies
SCCS	in *SCCS* directory	Source Code Control System
/core$	with name of *core*	core dump *(55.01)*
\.o$	ending with *.o*	object files
\.orig$	ending with *.orig*	original version

Instead of specifying which files are to be excluded, you can specify which files to archive using the *−I* option. As with the exclude flag, specifying a directory tells *tar* to include (or exclude) the entire directory. You should also note that the syntax of the *−I* option is different than the typical *tar* flag. This example archives all C files and makefiles:

```
% find project -type f -print | \
egrep '\.c|\.h|[Mm]akefile$' > Include
% tar cvf project.tar -I Include
```

I suggest using *find* to create the include or exclude file. You can edit it afterward, if you wish. One caution: extra spaces at the end of any line will cause that file to be ignored.

One way to debug the output of the *find* command is to use */dev/null* *(14.14)* as the output file:

```
% tar cvfX /dev/null Exclude project
```

Including Other Directories

There are times when you want to make an archive of several directories. You may want to archive a source directory and another directory like */usr/local*. The natural, but wrong way to do this is to use the command:

```
% tar cvf /dev/rmt8 project /usr/local
```

When using tar, you must never specify a directory name starting with a slash (/). This will cause problems when you restore a directory, as you will see later.

The proper way to handle the incorrect example above is to use the *–C* flag:

```
% tar cvf /dev/rmt8 project -C /usr local
```

This will archive */usr/local/* . . . as *local/* . . . . Article 21.10 has more information.

Type Pathnames Exactly

For the above options to work when you extract files from an archive, the pathname given in the include or exclude file must exactly match the pathname on the tape.

Here's a sample run. I'm extracting from a file named *appe.tar.* Of course, this example applies to tapes, too:

```
% tar tf appe.tar
appe
code/appendix/font_styles.c
code/appendix/xmemo.c
code/appendix/xshowbitmap.c
code/appendix/zcard.c
code/appendix/zcard.icon
```

Next, I create an exclude file, named *exclude,* that contains the lines:

```
code/appendix/zcard.c
code/appendix/zcard.icon
```

Now, I run the following *tar* command:

```
% tar xvfX appe.tar exclude
x appe, 6421 bytes, 13 tape blocks
x code/appendix/font_styles.c, 3457 bytes, 7 tape blocks
x code/appendix/xmemo.c, 10920 bytes, 22 tape blocks
x code/appendix/xshowbitmap.c, 20906 bytes, 41 tape blocks
code/appendix/zcard.c excluded
code/appendix/zcard.icon excluded
```

Exclude the Archive File!

If you're archiving the current directory (.) instead of starting at a subdirectory, remember to start with two pathnames in the *Exclude* file: the archive that *tar* creates and the *Exclude* file itself. That keeps *tar* from trying to archive its own output!

```
% cat > Exclude
./somedir.tar
./Exclude
CTRL-d
```

```
% find . -type f -print | \
egrep '/,|%$|~$|\.old$|SCCS|/core$|\.o$|\.orig$' >>Exclude
% tar cvfX somedir.tar Exclude .
```

In that example, we used `cat >` *(26.02)* to create the file quickly; you could use a text editor instead. Notice that the pathnames in the *Exclude* file start with `./`; that's what the *tar* command expects when you tell it to archive the current directory (`.`). The long *find/egrep* command line uses the `>>` operator *(14.01)* to add other pathnames to the end of the *Exclude* file.

Or, instead of adding the archive and exclude file's pathnames to the exclude file, you can move those two files somewhere out of the directory tree that *tar* will read.

—BB, TOR

21.09 *When a Program Doesn't Understand Wildcards*

When extracting files from a *tar* archive, it's handy to be able to use wildcards. You have to protect them *(9.10)* from the shell, so that they are passed directly to *tar.*

However, some versions of *tar* don't understand wildcards. There's a terribly ugly hack that you can use to select the files you want anyway. Try a command like this:

`10.14`
```
% tar xvf /dev/rst0 `tar tf /dev/rst0 | grep 'pattern'`
```

What you're doing here is using *tar* twice. *tar t* will print the names of all the files on the tape. The pattern supplied to *grep* selects the file(s) you want, and the resulting filenames are passed to the first *tar* command, which actually extracts the files from the archive.

—TOR

21.10 *Avoid Absolute Paths with tar*

One problem with *tar*: it can't change a file's pathname when restoring. Let's say that you put your home directory in an archive (tape or otherwise) with a command like this:

```
% tar c /home/mike
```

What will these files be named when you restore them, either on your own system or on some other system? They will have *exactly* the same pathnames that they had originally. So if */home/mike* already exists, it will be destroyed. There's no way to tell *tar* that it should be careful about overwriting files; there's no way to tell *tar* to put the files in some other directory when it takes them off the tape, etc. If you use absolute pathnames *(15.02)* when you create a tape, you're stuck. If you use relative paths *(15.02)* (for example, `tar c ./*`), you can restore the files in any directory you want.

This means that you should:

- Avoid using absolute paths when you create an archive. (See below.)

- Use *tar t* to see what files are on the tape before restoring the archive.

- Use GNU *tar* (on the Power Tools disk). It can ignore the leading / as it extracts files.

Rather than giving a command like **tar c /home/mike**, do something like:

```
% cd /home/mike
% tar c ./*
```

Or, even more elegant, use *–C* on the *tar* command line:

```
% tar c -C /home/mike .
```

This command tells *tar* to *cd* to the directory */home/mike* before creating the archive. If you want to archive several directories, you can use several *–C* options:

```
% tar c -C /home/mike ./docs  -C /home/susan ./test
```

This command archives *mike*'s *docs* directory and *susan*'s *test* directory.

—ML

21.11 *Getting tar's Arguments in the Right Order*

tar's command line is one of UNIX's little mysteries. It's difficult to associate arguments with options. Let's say you want to specify the block size (*b*), the output file (*f*), and an "exclude" file (*X*). Where do you put all this information? It's easy enough to glob the option letters into a lump and put them into a command (**tar cXbf**). But where do you put the block size, the name of the exclude file, and so on?

List any arguments that you need *after* the block of key letters. You must place the arguments in the *same order* as the key letters, as shown in Figure 21-1.

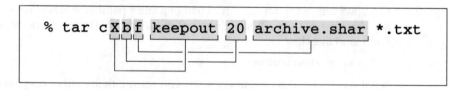

Figure 21-1. *tar Options and Arguments*

In this command, *keepout* goes with the *X* option, *20* goes with the *b* option, and *archive.shar* goes with the *f* option. If we put the options in a different order, we also have to put the arguments in a different order (see Figure 21-2).

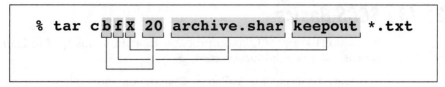

Figure 21-2. The Same Command, Rearranged

Note that the files you want to put on the tape (or the files you want to extract from the tape) always go at the *end* of the command. These are not arguments to *c* or *X*; they are part of the command itself.

The *dump* command and a few others work the same way.

—*ML*

21.12 Protecting Files with SCCS or RCS

You don't need to ask the system manager to restore files. When you do need a file, you can get it right away, without waiting. What's more, you can recover any version you want, with one command, and get the file back immediately.

Sounds great, doesn't it?

All you need to do is use either SCCS (Source Code Control System) or RCS (Revision Control System). SCCS comes standard on most System V UNIXes; RCS is available on many BSD-based systems, and is also available on the Power Tools disk.

Of course, SCCS and RCS won't protect you from a disk crash, but they can protect you from many cases of accidental file deletion or corruption. These tools were developed to manage multi-person development projects, ensuring that only one person has write access to a file at one time, and making it possible to go back to any previous version of a file. But as it turns out, they are handy for any user who has important files that change frequently.

Article 21.13 tells how to use SCCS to protect your files. Article 21.14 does the same for RCS. Article 21.15 gives a fuller introduction to RCS.

—*BB, TOR*

21.13 SCCS Basics

If you don't know SCCS, you probably thought it was hard to learn. Not true. Here is a simple introduction to SCCS.

1. Create a subdirectory called *SCCS* in the directory where you keep the code or other text files you want to protect.

2. Add the characters %W%   %G% somewhere in the file you want to place under SCCS. Put this in a comment field. That is, use /* %W%   %G% */ in a C program and # %W%   %G% in a shell script.

3. Place the file under source code control. This is done by typing:

```
% sccs create filename
```

That's it. You're done. There are three more commands you need to know:

```
% sccs get filename
% sccs edit filename
% sccs delta filename
```

You may also want to add the following to your list of C shell aliases *(11.02)*:

```
alias Create 'sccs create'
alias Get 'sccs get'
alias Edit 'sccs edit'
alias Delta 'sccs delta'
```

The *get* command will get a copy of the file from the Source Code Control System. The file will be marked read-only *(23.02)*. If you want to edit the file, use the *edit* command. Once you are done, return the file to the *SCCS* directory with the command *delta*. Each time you store the file, you'll get a new version number, or "delta."

There are only two more commands that you will need to know. If you checked out a file for editing, and later on decided you didn't want to edit, use:

```
% sccs unedit filename
```

and if you want a list of all files currently checked out, use:

```
% sccs check
```

That's all there is to it! If you are not using SCCS, you should. It is the best way to protect yourself. It does not require dozens of tapes.

It is much easier to just type:

```
% sccs get -r1.12 filename
```

One command, and version 1.12 is restored. If it's not the right one, restore the version before or after the one you just grabbed. If you are worried that you are keeping 12 versions of the file on the disk, and that this will use up a lot of disk space, don't. SCCS stores the differences in a clever manner that allows it to recover any version of the file in a single pass through the file.

Suppose you delete a file by accident? Well, if the file is just checked out with a *get*, it will be retrieved and marked read-only, so deleting the file will cause *rm* to ask you for confirmation. If you do delete it, you can recover it with another *get* command. Suppose you check out a file with *edit*, because you planned to change it. Well, if this file gets deleted accidentally, you would lose the most recent changes. This is why you should check your files back into SCCS frequently—several times a day, if you wish. Do it whenever you make significant changes to the file, and it would be difficult to remember all of the changes. Making hundreds of changes to a file without checking it back into the system is just begging for trouble.

Good luck, and may you never delete another important file by accident. [There are several other revision control systems—including RCS *(21.15)*, which is widely used and available on the Power Tools disk. You can probably get the most help on whatever revision control system your colleagues or classmates use.—*JP*]

—*BB*

21.14 *RCS Basics*

[I've patterned this article after the article on SCCS (21.13) by Bruce Barnett. This one shows how to do the same things with the Revision Control System, RCS, in case that's what you have on your system. —JP]

You don't need to ask the system manager to restore files. You can recover any version you want with one command. Here is a simple introduction to RCS.

1. Create a subdirectory called *RCS* in the directory where you keep the code or other text files you want to protect.

2. It's a good idea (but not required) to add the characters Id somewhere in the file you want to place under RCS. Put this in a comment field. That is, use /* Id */ in a C program and # Id in a shell script.

3. Place the file under Revision Control. This is done by typing:

```
% ci filename
```

The *ci* (checkin) program will prompt you for a short description of the file. (You can read the description later, if you want to, with the *rlog* command.) That's it. You're done. There is another command and an option you need to know:

```
% co filename
% co -l filename
```

The *co* (checkout) command will get a copy of the file from RCS. The file will be marked read-only. If you want to edit the file, use the *co –l* command (the option is a lowercase L)—then, when you're done, return the file to the *RCS* directory with the command *ci*.

There are only two more commands that you will need to know. If you checked out a file for editing, and later on decided you didn't want to change it, use:

```
% rcs -u filename
% rm filename
```

and if you want a list of all files currently checked out, use:

```
% rlog -L -R RCS/*
```

(If you don't use RCS often, you may want to store those command lines in aliases or shell functions *(11.01)* with names like *Checkout, Checkedout,* and so on.) That's all there is to it! If you are not using RCS or SCCS, you should. They are the best way to protect yourself and do not require dozens of tapes.

It is much easier to just type:

```
% co -r1.12 filename
```

One command, and version 1.12 is restored. If it's not the right one, restore the version before or after the one you just grabbed. If you are worried that you are keeping 12 versions of the file on the disk, and that this will use up a lot of disk space, don't. RCS stores the differences between versions, not 12 separate copies of the file. It can recover any version of the file.

Suppose you delete a file by accident? Well, if the file is just checked out with a *co*, it will be retrieved and marked read-only, so deleting the file will cause *rm* to ask you for confirmation. If you do delete it, you can recover it with another *co* command. Suppose you check out a file with *co −l*, because you planned to change it. Well, if this file gets deleted accidentally, you would lose the most recent changes. This is why you should check your files back into RCS frequently—several times a day, if you wish. Do it whenever you make significant changes to the file, and it would be difficult to remember all of the changes. Making hundreds of changes to a file without checking it back into the system is just begging for trouble.

For more information, see the tutorial on RCS *(21.15)*.

—*BB, JP*

21.15 *File Management with RCS*

[Both RCS and SCCS are good for one-person file protection and backup. This article goes into more detail about RCS (including how a group of people might use it) than the SCCS article (21.13) does.—JP]

rcs

RCS (Revision Control System) is a file management tool designed to aid development of text files (programs, documents, almost any printable file) under UNIX. It is not a standard part of UNIX per se but is distributed with the rest of the system as part of the user-contributed software (along with the manual entries for the *UNIX Programmer's Reference Manual*). More recently, the Free Software Foundation has published a version of RCS (it's on the Power Tools disk). Many UNIX versions provide a collection of tools called SCCS. SCCS is functionally identical to RCS but has a completely different user interface. If your site uses SCCS, this article will still be a useful conceptual introduction; however, you will need to learn a different set of commands.

RCS meets an important need in managing large projects. It allows you to automate many of the tasks involved in coordinating a team of people who are editing and using files. These tasks include maintaining all versions of a file in a recoverable form, preventing several people from modifying the same code simultaneously, helping people to merge two different development tracks into a single version, ensuring that a single program is not undergoing multiple simultaneous versions, and maintaining logs for versions and other changes.

Revision Numbers

The first version of a file under RCS control is given number 1.1. Succeeding versions that descend linearly from this file are numbered 1.2, 1.3, etc.

A new development branch can begin at any point on this tree. [You don't need to make new branches for basic RCS use.—*JP*] RCS gives the first "branch" beginning at version 1.3 the number 1.3.1. It numbers the second branch beginning at this point 1.3.2, etc. The first version along the first branch is 1.3.1.1, the second is 1.3.1.2, etc.

The tool *rcsmerge* exists to help you merge versions from different branches of development. This tool can be very useful if two developers have been working in different directions on the same program. One programmer might be fixing bugs in an old release, and another might be adding some new features. *rcsmerge* helps you to integrate both of their changes painlessly, so that you can produce a new version containing both the bug fixes and the new features. It will not be described further here.

Basic Operations

The two fundamental commands for using RCS are *ci* and *co*. These commands "check in" and "check out" software that RCS is maintaining. When you check a file in, RCS deletes your source file and creates or modifies a file called *source*,v where *source* is the name of the original and ,v is an extension that indicates an RCS file. By deleting *source*, RCS prevents you from doing any further editing without using *co* again. When you check out a file, RCS extracts a version of the file—usually the most recent version—from the corresponding RCS file. To do a simple checkin, use the following command:

```
% ci filename
```

This creates a new RCS version of your file. If the file is not currently managed by RCS, this command places the file under RCS management, gives it the version number 1.1, and prompts for a description of the file. If the file is already being managed by RCS, this command will assign the next higher version number in the sequence (1.2 follows 1.1) and will prompt you for a description of the changes you have made since the last checkin. The following example shows what happens when you check in version 1.4 of a file called *mytest*:

```
% ci mytest
mytest,v  <--  mytest
new revision: 1.4; previous revision: 1.3
enter log message:
(terminate with ^D or single '.')
>> fixed a trivial error on the last line
>> .
done
%
```

The prompt >> indicates that RCS is waiting for a line of text. Typing a . (dot) or pressing CTRL-d on an unused line terminates the log message. At this point, RCS enters the message in its file and prints the word done. RCS will warn you if you check in a file that has not been modified since it was last checked out. You can force it to check the file in anyway by typing y in response to its warning message:

```
% ci mytest
mytest,v  <--  mytest
new revision: 1.8; previous revision: 1.7
File mytest is unchanged with respect to revision 1.7
check in anyway? [ny](n): y
    ...
```

Used by itself, the command *ci* deletes your working version of the file. If you want to retain a read-only version of the file, enter the command:

```
% ci -u filename
```

In this case, you retain a copy of *filename* for reference. You cannot modify the file, however; see below.

In order to use a file that has been placed under the control of RCS, use the checkout command, *co*, as follows:

```
% co filename
```

where *filename* is the name of the file you want to work on. This retrieves the latest version of your file from the RCS file in which it has been stored.

By itself, *co* is sufficient if you only want to read, compile, or otherwise use the file without changing it. However, *co* restores your source file with read-only access: you cannot edit it or make changes. If you want to modify the file, use the command:

```
% co -l filename
```

This not only creates a file that you can modify but also installs a lock. This means that no one else can modify the file until you return it to RCS with *ci*. Other people can still use *co*, getting a read-only version of the file. Conversely, if someone else has already locked the file, *co* −*l* will not let you check it out. If you try to check out a file that someone else has already locked, *co* will reply:

```
% co -l lockedfile
co error: revision n already locked by someone-else
```

where *someone-else* is the username of whoever locked the file. If you see this message, negotiate with the lock's owner to find out when he or she will be finished. [You can also use the *rcs -u* command to take away the lock. I do *not* recommend that until you know exactly what you're doing!—*JP*]

Note: It is possible to circumvent this protection by using the UNIX commands for changing file access modes, etc. Please don't. If you do not want the protection that RCS gives, don't use RCS in the first place. One person who refuses to play by the rules can quickly confuse a large development effort.

RCS Directories and Files

Before checking a file in or out, RCS always looks for a subdirectory named *RCS* within the current directory. If this directory exists, RCS will keep all the files it creates within that directory, keeping your working directories free from extra clutter.

RCS creates a separate RCS file for every file under its management. This file stores a description of the file you are managing, the entire change log, the current version of the file, a list of users who are allowed to access the file, the file's date and time, and a list of changes that lets RCS reproduce any obsolete version of the file at will. Despite the information they maintain, RCS files are not substantially larger than the source files they manage. However, they do grow with time. If you need to reduce your disk requirements, you can use the *rcs -o* command to eliminate old versions of the file that are no longer needed.

The Revision Log

Whenever you check in a file, RCS prompts you for a log message describing the changes you have made since the last version. This log exists so that you can easily find out who changed the program, when, and why.

The command *rlog* displays the entire log for a file. For example:

```
% rlog mytest
rcs file:        mytest,v;  Working file:    mytest
head:            1.2
locks:
access list:
symbolic names:
comment leader:  "# "
total revisions: 2;    selected revisions: 2
description:
this is a simple test of rcs
to play with it
----------------------------
revision 1.2
date: 86/06/26 10:00:15; author: mike; state: Exp; lines added/del: 2/0
another version to demonstrate the features of a log.
----------------------------
revision 1.1
date: 86/06/26 08:24:14;  author: mike;  state: Exp;
```

```
This is the initial version of the program.
=======================================================
%
```

In addition to the version number and the log of comments, this display shows the date and time at which each version was checked in, the author of the modifications, the total number of lines added and deleted in this modification, and the file's current state. Note that RCS considers a modification to a line to be deleting the old line and adding the new line. The `state:` field shows the file's status at each version. By default, the `state:` field will always be `Exp`, which stands for experimental. By using the command:

```
% rcs -sstate:revnum filename
```

you can give any version (*revnum*) any state (*state*) you wish. This is described in the section "Other Features" later in this article.

Identification Strings

If you wish, RCS can put identification strings into your source code and object files. These strings contain information about the current version number, the author, and the time the file was last checked in. Here is a typical identification string:

```
$Header: /u/mike/C/RCS/lin.F,v 1.1 86/06/27 11:28:37 mike Exp $
```

It shows the pathname, the version number, the modification date and time, the person who checked in this version, and the state.

To include an identification string in a file, insert the marker:

```
$Header$
```

If the file is a program, the marker should be within a comment statement to let the program compile correctly. RCS will replace this marker with the identification string whenever you check out the file. RCS will replace the marker `$Log$` with the accumulated version log messages. In programs, this marker should be contained within a comment. For example:

```
/*
 * $Log$
 */
```

Other markers with similar functions are `$Author$`, `$Date$`, `$Locker$`, `$Revision$`, `$Source$`, and `$State$`. RCS replaces `$Source$` with the complete pathname of the RCS file storing this version. The meanings of the other markers should be self-evident.

Strict Access

On many systems, by default,* RCS is in the strict-access mode. This mode has two important features:

1. No one is allowed to check in a file without locking it first.

2. No one can modify a file unless that person checked it out locked.

To take a particular RCS file out of the strict-access mode, use the command:

```
% rcs -U filename
```

where *filename* is the name of a particular file under RCS management. This places RCS in the open-access mode for this file. In this mode, the owner of *filename* can modify the file without locking it first. All other users must still lock a file before modifying it. Only use RCS in the open-access mode if you are the only person modifying this file. Otherwise, you risk multiple simultaneous modifications by different people and thus defeat one of RCS' primary aims.

Return that RCS file to strict access with the command:

```
% rcs -L filename
```

More About Checking In

The *ci* command may refuse to let you check in a file, printing the message:

```
ci error: no lock set by your-name
```

This can only occur under two circumstances:

1. If you did not lock the file upon checkout in the strict-access mode.

2. If someone locked the file after you checked it out in open-access mode.

ci will not tell you who locked the file. As far as it is concerned, you are the one who is at fault for not locking a file you intended to modify and replace. If this situation occurs, lock the file by using the following command:

```
% rcs -l filename
```

At this point, two things can happen. In the first situation, where no one else locked the file, RCS retroactively locks the file so that you can check in your file normally with the *ci* command. In the second situation, RCS will print the warning:

```
rcs error: revision n already locked by someone-else
```

where *someone-else* is the username of whoever has locked your file. You need to negotiate with him or her to reach a solution. [As a last resort, you can also use the *rcs −u* command to take away the lock. This will send a mail message (1.33) to *someone-else*. As before, I do *not* recommend *rcs −u* unless you can't find the lock owner and have to edit the file.—*JP*] Tools like *rcsdiff* and *rcsmerge* will help you find out the differences between the two files and create

---

*The default is set when the RCS commands are installed on your system.

a new version that incorporates the modifications to both files. Neither of these situations should occur unless you or your colleagues are playing "fast and loose" with file access. RCS does not eliminate the need for discipline and coordination. It only makes discipline and coordination easier to live with.

At times, you may want to do a checkin, followed immediately by a checkout. You may want to install a version reflecting the current state of your program (possibly as a backup), then continue editing immediately. Rather than using two operations, RCS lets you perform both with the command:

```
% ci -l filename
```

This updates the RCS file and gives you a lock with a fresh copy of your working file, allowing you to continue editing immediately.

New and Old Generations

At points in the development cycle, you will decide that your program has reached a decisively different stage. You may want your version numbering to reflect this new state: for example, by changing from version 1.x to version 2.1. To do this, use the *–r* option when you check in the program, as shown in the following example:

```
% ci -rn filename
```

This assigns the version number *n* to the most recent version of *filename*. For example, the command:

```
% ci -r2.3 makefile
```

checks in *makefile* with version number 2.3.

If you want to check out an old version of this file, use the *–r* option with *co*. For example:

```
% co -r1.4 makefile
```

retrieves version 1.4 of *makefile*. There are several reasons for retrieving an old version: nostalgia and recovering from disastrous modifications are only two of the more likely ones.

Other Features

RCS has quite a few other features. Look at your RCS manual pages or the full version of this article, Chapter 7 in the Nutshell Handbook, *UNIX for FORTRAN Programmers*, by Mike Loukides. Here is a brief summary:

States   You can assign a *state* to any version of a file. A state can be any string of characters that has some meaning for you. For example, you can assign the state Exp for experimental software, Stab for stable software, Rel for released software, and so on.

Names   You can assign a *symbolic name* to any version. This name can be used in place of a version number in all commands within the RCS system. For instance, if you give version 2.4 the symbolic name *betatest*, you can check in version 2.4 with the command:

```
% co -rbetatest filename
```

The -r means "version number."

Access Lists

An *access list* is a list of users who are allowed to use RCS to manipulate a file. In most cases, RCS will refuse to allow anyone not on the access list to lock or otherwise modify a file. There are only three exceptions to this rule:

1. The owner of a file can lock it (and check it in after getting the lock).

2. A superuser can always lock any file and check it in.

3. If the access list is empty, anyone can lock the file.

Any user can check out a read-only version of the file, whether or not they are on the access list.

—*ML* from the Nutshell Handbook *UNIX for FORTRAN Programmers*

22

More about Managing Files

22.01 A Grab-bag

Let's face it, even in a book as loosely structured as this one, there are things that don't quite fit. This chapter gave us a place to say a few things about files that we just didn't manage to cover anywhere else.

The chapter is short, and it's late, so I'm not even going to bother with the summary I might otherwise attempt in a situation like this. Just dive in.

—*TOR*

22.02 A Better Place for Temporary Files: /tmp

How many times have you made a little test file for something:

```
% grep foo bar > baz
```

then forgotten to remove *baz*—and found it, weeks later, cluttering up your directory and wasting disk space? Yeah, me too. So I decided to make my temporary files in the system temporary-file directory, */tmp*.

Everyone on the system has permission to write files there. Because there are lots of temporary files, it's good to use a name that won't conflict with other people's files *(22.03)*.

If your file doesn't have world permission *(23.04, 23.02)*, other people on the system won't be able to read or write it. But they may be able to rename or remove it *(24.09)* unless the */tmp* directory's sticky bit *(23.06)* is set. That usually isn't a problem, but you should know that it can happen.

Most systems delete leftover files in */tmp* every day or so, when the filesystem fills up, or at least when the system is rebooted. So, don't use */tmp* for a file that you want to keep for a while. Your system may have other directories for temporary files, like */usr/tmp (22.04)*, that aren't erased as often.

—*JP*

22.03 *Unique Names for Temporary Files*

All users share */tmp (22.02)*, so you should make unique filenames there. The best way to do this is by putting $$ in the filename. For example:

```
% vi /tmp/jerry.$$
"/tmp/jerry.12345" [New file]
% lpr /tmp/jerry.$$
% rm /tmp/jerry.$$
```

The shell replaces $$ with the shell's PID number *(40.03)* (in this case, `12345`).

If you use a subshell *(40.04)*, or have more than one login session or window, and want to share the same temp file, $$ won't work for you. In that case, just pick a unique name. You could use today's date instead.

To give myself both options with a minimum of work, I set this line in my *.cshrc* file *(2.02)*:

```
set tf=/tmp/jp$$
```

and this in my *.login*:

```
set date = (`date`)
setenv TF /tmp/jp$date[4]
```

(Those lines use C shell arrays *(49.05)* and command substitution *(10.14)* to grab the fourth word—the current time—from the output of the *date (53.10)* command.) When I want a temporary file in my current shell, I type:

```
% grep foo bar > $tf-1
% grep wheeze bar > $tf-2
% more $tf-*
```

* *16.02*

The shell expands the shell variable *(7.08)* `$tf-1` into a filename like `/tmp/jp2345-1`, and `$tf-*` expands into all my temporary files in this shell. Usually, that's great. But if I go to a subshell, do a shell escape, and so on, the temporary files I make with `$tf` won't be the same as the ones I make in my login shell because the PIDs are different. If I need them to be the same, I use `$TF`, the environment variable *(7.01)*. It's set to the time I logged in. And because environment variables are passed to child shells, the name (like */tmp/jp09:34:56*) will be the same in subshells:

```
% someprog > $TF-1
    ...
% otherprog > $TF-6
% sh
$ head $TF-[16]
```

[..] *16.02*

csh_logout
nonomatch **16.05**
-d **17.09**
|& **14.05**

$< **10.09**
=~ **49.04**

To clean up when I log out, I added these lines to my .logout file:

```
# CLEAN FILES (IF ANY) OUT OF /tmp:
set nonomatch
set tmpf="`ls -d $tf-* $TF-* |& grep -v ' not found'`"
if ( "$tmpf" =~ ?* ) then
        echo; echo "Your files in /tmp:"
        ls -d $tmpf
        echo -n "'rm -rf' them? [ny] (n) "
        if ( "$<" =~ y* ) rm -rf $tmpf
endif
```

If I made any temporary files from my login shell or any subshells, I get this message when I log out:

```
% logout

Your files in /tmp:
/tmp/jp2345-1   /tmp/jp2345-2   /tmp/jp2748-1   /tmp/09:23:45-1
'rm -rf' them? y
```

Another way to do this is with a script like *del* (24.05).

—JP

22.04 *Why Both /tmp and /usr/tmp?*

[UNIX traditionally has two places to put temporary files: /tmp and /usr/tmp. This article explains how that started.—JP]

As I understand it, the reason for the */tmp–/usr/tmp* split is identical to the reason for the */bin–/usr/bin* and */lib–/usr/lib* splits and is a historical accident of hardware configuration at the Research system.

At one time (circa the time of the original UNIX paper in CACM), the Research machine was a PDP 11/45 with a fixed-head disk, some RK05s, and an RP03. The root went on the fixed-head disk, since the absence of seek times made it fast. But fixed-head disks (anybody remember them?) were *tiny*. Two megabytes [sic] was a big fixed-head disk. So you had to be fairly careful to avoid overflowing the root filesystem (which included */tmp*—it wasn't a separate filesystem). */usr*, on the other hand, was the main filesystem on the 40-MB RP03.

So you had a very sharp split of hardware: things directly under /, like */tmp*, */bin*, and */lib*, were fast but had to be small; things under */usr* could be big but accesses to them were slower. So you put the heavily used commands in */bin*, the heavily used libraries in */lib*, and [flourish of trumpets] the small temporary files in */tmp*. All the other slush went under */usr*, including a */usr/tmp* directory for big temporaries. This is why a few programs like *sort* (37.01) put their temporaries in */usr/tmp*: they expect them to be big. [Though most */usr* filesystems are fast these days, a lot of systems still have much more room on */usr/tmp* than */tmp*.—JP]

In practice, fixed-head disks are historical relics now, and much of the justification for the various /x–/usr/x splits has disappeared. There is one reason why you might retain a /tmp–/usr/tmp split, however. If your /tmp filesystem is kept in "RAM disk" or something similar for speed, you might want to keep your editor temp files somewhere else if your editor has crash recovery *(31.24)*. Crash recovery definitely works better when the files it is looking for are kept in nonvolatile memory!

—HS in *net.unix* on Usenet, *19 March 1984*

22.05 *What Good is a File's Last Access Time?*

UNIX keeps three times for each file: last modification, last inode change, and last access. Here are some things you can do with the last-access time:

- Find files that have been forgotten. This information comes from commands like *ls –lu (17.02)* and *find –atime +180 (18.05)*. (If you use the MH e-mail system, you can find mail messages that haven't been read or scanned in a long time.) You can save disk space by cleaning up unused files; see article 24.18.

- Automatically compress *(25.06)* files to save disk space. Some users run a shell script named *compresser* which looks for nonexecutable files (except files and directories in a personal "skip" list) that haven't been accessed in 90 days. The program runs *compress* on these files:

xargs *10.19*
```
find $HOME -type f ! -name '*.[zZ]' -atime +90 -print | xargs compress -v
```

A system like this could automatically archive files to tape and delete them. It could also create a shell script that the user can run, later, to say "yes" or "no" about compressing each file. And so on . . .

- Check a directory to see which files are being read by programs, compilers, etc. This "sanity check" can help you debug programs by confirming which files are being accessed.

Note: Some UNIX systems, including versions of BSD and SunOS, do not update the access time of executable files (programs) when they're executed. To test yours, use *ls –lu* on a pure-executable file (not a shell script) before and after you run it.

—JP

22.06 A File's Inode Change (not "Creation"!) Time

An old *ls* manual page I have says that the *ls −c* option lists the "time of file creation." Boo, hiss! That's an old UNIX myth. UNIX keeps three times for each file: last modification (*mtime*), last access (*atime*) *(22.05)*, and *last inode (1.22)* modification (*ctime*). A file's *ctime* is changed when the file is modified or when something kept in the inode (number of hard links, owner, group, etc.) has been changed. If you need to find out when that time was changed, use *ls −lcr* or *find −ctime (18.05, 18.07)*.

Many computer sites check the *ctime* to decide which files to back up.

—JP

22.07 Setting File Modification Time with touch

How can you make a file quickly (often for some kind of test)? In the Bourne shell, use the command below. Because this command uses a built-in *(1.10)* operator, it's fast and efficient. This creates a new file or empties an existing file:

```
$ > filename
```

The C shell doesn't allow that. From the C shell, you can empty a file by copying */dev/null* onto it *(25.01)*. The easiest way to create an empty file is with the *touch* command. *touch* is also useful from any shell to change an existing file's modification time to "now"—without changing the file's contents (usually for an automatic file time comparison *(18.08, 29.12, 22.09)*). You can touch more than one file at a time. Just type:

```
% touch filename1 filename2 ...
```

Some versions of *touch* (and other freely available commands like it) can create a file with an arbitrary timestamp. That is, you can use *touch* to make a file that's backdated to any point in the past (or, for that matter, postdated to some point in the future). If your version can do that, the syntax is probably like:

```
% touch date filename1 filename2 ...
```

where *date* has the form:

```
modyhrmiyy
```

and:

mo is two digits, representing the month.

dy is two digits, representing the day of the month.

hr is two digits, representing the hour (on a 24-hour clock).

mi is two digits, representing the minute within the hour.

    yy   is two digits, representing the year (within the twentieth century). These two digits are optional; if you omit them, *date* assumes the current year.

For example, to create a file dated 4 p.m., March 20, give the command:

```
% touch 03201600 foo
```

(Under SunOS 4.1, if */usr/5bin* is after */bin* or */usr/bin* in your search path *(7.04)*, you'll need to use the command */usr/5bin/touch.*) Article 23.17 explains *cpmod*, a program on the Power Tools disk for copying dates and permissions from file to file.

—ML, JP

22.08 The MAILCHECK and mail Variables Check more than Mail

Depending on how your system is set up, you may notice that it periodically says something like You have new mail. When you run your mail program *(1.33)*, the mail will be waiting for you in your mailbox. You can also use this feature to check for changes in several mailboxes, as well as changes in files and directories that don't hold mail—more about that in a minute.

For C Shell Users

If you use the C shell, this feature is controlled by the *mail* shell variable (usually set in your *.cshrc* file *(2.03)*).

The shell normally checks your mailbox every five minutes. However, you can set a different interval at the start of the list. For example, the command below tells the shell to check my mailbox every 60 seconds:

```
% set mail=(60 /usr/spool/mail/mikel)
```

Note that the exact filename depends upon how your mail system is set up. For example, many systems use */usr/mail* instead of */usr/spool/mail*. Checking for mail takes time and can delay your prompt on busy systems. Don't set a short interval unless you need to.

Multiple Mailboxes

Many users need to watch more than one mailbox. For example, I need to watch */usr/spool/mail/mikel*; but if I'm responsible for product support, and my company maintains a special mail ID for support questions, I might also want to watch */usr/spool/mail/prodsupport*. To do this, we set the *mail* variable so that it's a list of important files and directories:

```
% set mail=(/usr/spool/mail/mikel /usr/spool/mail/prodsupport)
```

When the list has more than one file, the shell will tell you which file has changed with a message like `new mail in /usr/spool/mail/prodsupport`.

Watching Other Files

All *mail* is doing is looking to see whether or not the file has changed; it doesn't know that it's looking at a "mail" file. Therefore, you can use it to watch anything you want; your list can even include directories. Let's say that you're running a program that periodically writes to the file */home/los/mikel/radio/log.out.* Then you can set *mail* as follows:

```
% set mail=(/home/los/mikel/radio/log.out other-files)
```

Watching Directories

Watching a directory is the same as watching a file; you'll be notified whenever the directory changes (whenever a file is added or deleted in the directory). So let's modify our previous example slightly; let's say that your reports are named */home/los/mikel/radio/log/date*, where the *date* indicates when the report was created. Every report thus generates a new file. In this case, you'd want to watch the log directory for the creation of new files.

```
% set mail=(/home/los/mikel/radio/log other-files)
```

Here's another example. Let's say that you suspect someone is using UUCP *(1.33)* to send company secrets to a system named *somewhere.* You want to watch this systems's UUCP traffic very carefully. To do so, you can tell the shell to inform you whenever the logfile changes:

```
% set mail=(5 /usr/spool/uucp/.Log/uucico/somewhere)
```

We've told the shell to check the log every five seconds because, given that we suspect security problems, we want to get our reports immediately.

If the directory you're watching is actually a symbolic link *(19.04)* to another directory, be sure to check the actual directory and not the link. The *sl (19.08)* script is handy for this—or you can use *ls −ld (17.09)*:

```
% ls -ld /usr/local/logs
lrwxrwxrwx  1 root     15 Jul 10  1990 /usr/local/logs -> /foo/bar/logs
% ls -ld /foo/bar/logs
drwxrwxr-x  2 root   512 Aug 10 12:20 /foo/bar/logs
% set mail=(/foo/bar/logs)
```

For Bourne Shell Users

Now, let's assume that you're a Bourne shell user, and go through everything once more. The Bourne shell uses three variables to control mail notification. (These are usually set in users' *.profile (2.02)* files. To make them work in sub-shells *(40.04)*, *export (7.01)* the variables.) We'll assume that you read the C shell description above, and move a bit faster.

First, if you want to check only one file or directory, set the variable *MAIL* accordingly.

```
$ MAIL=/usr/spool/mail/mikel
$ export MAIL
```

Note: The next three features don't work on some Bourne shells. They do work on the Korn Shell.

By default, the Bourne shell checks every ten minutes. To check at some other interval, set the variable *MAILCHECK* to your new interval, in seconds: for example, the command below tells the shell to check every 55 seconds:

```
$ MAILCHECK=55
```

One useful trick: if you set *MAILCHECK* to 0, the shell will check whenever it prints the "primary" prompt (by default, $). In other words, it will check after each command. This may be slow on busy systems.

If you want to watch several files, use the *MAILPATH* variable. Its value must be a list of file or directory names, separated by colons. For example:

```
$ MAILPATH=/usr/spool/mail/mikel:/usr/spool/mail/prodsupport
```

If *MAILPATH* is set, the shell will ignore the *MAIL* variable. You can't use both.

Normally, the Bourne shell prints you have mail whenever any file that it's watching changes. However, if you follow a filename in *MAILPATH* with a percent sign (%) and a message, the shell will print the message whenever the file changes. For example, let's have the shell print you have mail when mail comes in and New log! when a log file changes:

```
$ MAILPATH=/usr/spool/mail/mikel:/home/mikel/Z/log%"New log!"
```

You can create a different message for every file that you care about.

—*ML*

22.09 Keep File Printouts Up-to-Date Automatically with make

A lot of people think that the *make (29.12)* utility is just for programmers. But it's also good for people who need to do something when files have been modified.

Here's a *makefile* that lets you be sure you have printouts of the latest versions of certain files in a directory. Any time you think files have been modified, just type:

```
% make print
pr chap1 chap5 | lpr -Pxyz
touch print
```

make saw that the files *chap1* and *chap5* had been modified since the last print job. So it used *pr* and *lpr* to print the files. Then it ran *touch* (22.07) to create or update the empty file named *print*; the "timestamp" (modification time) of this empty file keeps a record of when these other files were printed. Or, the command *make printall* will print all files any time without updating the *print* timestamp file.

Here's the *makefile*. Change the names and the print commands to do what you want. Remember that each command line (here, the lines starting with pr and touch) *must* start with a TAB character:

make_print

```
LPR = lpr -Pxyz
FILES = preface chap1 chap2 chap3 chap4 chap5 appendix

print: $(FILES)
        pr $? | $(LPR)
        touch print

printall:
        pr $(FILES) | $(LPR)
```

Article 2.16 shows another use of *make*: displaying a changed file.

—JP

22.10 *Keep a Directory Listing at Top of the Screen: dirtop*

When I'm cleaning out a directory, I'm always using *ls* to see what files are there. When I have a terminal with windows, I can keep an *ls* listing in one window and do cleanup in another. In a terminal without windows, I use this script named *dirtop*. It clears the screen, puts an *ls* listing at the top of the screen, and sends an escape sequence to the terminal that makes the screen top nonscrolling. So, as I type my commands, they scroll "underneath" the *ls* listing at the top without disturbing it. If I use a command like *vi* that resets the screen, I just use *dirtop* again when the command is done. When I'm done, the command *dirtop −c* clears the screen and makes the whole screen scrollable again.

This script works only on VT100-type terminals and compatibles because the escape sequences are hardcoded into it. It should probably be rewritten to use *termcap* or *terminfo* information so it'd work on more terminals. Luckily, there are lots of VT100-compatible terminals and communications programs.

dirtop

echo...33' **47.34**

```
#! /bin/sh

ls="/bin/ls -CF"                # ls command to use
maxlines=10      # if more lines in listing than this, quit
# UNCOMMENT THE LINE FOR YOUR SYSTEM:
cmd=echo     c='\c'   e='\033'   n=                        # SysV
#cmd=/usr/5bin/echo   c='\c'   e='\033'   n=               # SunOS
#cmd=/bin/echo   c=   e="`echo e | tr e '\033'`"   n=-n # BSD

case "$1" in
```

```
-c) $cmd $n "${e}[r${e}[2J${c}"; exit 0;; # just reset screen
"") ;;
*) echo "Usage: `basename $0` [-c]" 1>&2; exit 1 ;;
esac

temp=/tmp/DIRTOP$$
trap 'rm -f $temp; exit' 0 1 2 15

$ls > $temp
# set number of lines to clear: one more than length of ls listing:
lines=`expr 1 + \`wc -l < $temp\``
if [ $lines -gt $maxlines ]
then
    echo "`basename $0`: Directory listing > $maxlines lines" 1>&2
    exit 1
else
    # CLEAR SCREEN.   SET NO-SCROLL AREA:
    $cmd $n "${e}[2J${c}"
    $cmd $n "${e}[${lines};24r${c}"
    # MOVE CURSOR TO TOP-LEFT CORNER, THEN PRINT LISTING:
    $cmd $n "${e}[0;0f${c}"
    cat $temp
    exit
fi
```

—JP

22.11 Safer Removing, Moving, and Copying with –i

Some people add the following aliases *(11.02)* to their *.cshrc* files *(2.02)*:

```
alias rm rm -i
alias cp cp -i
alias mv mv -i
```

The *–i* argument to the *cp* and *mv* commands will warn you if the action will overwrite any existing file. Aliasing the *rm* command will also change the behavior so that it always asks you to confirm every deletion. If you want to override this action, you can defeat the alias *(11.06)* by typing:

```
% \rm *.o
```

This is a very convenient way to protect yourself from accidental deletions. There is a danger with these aliases. You become used to the actions, and if aliases are not in place, you can delete files before you realize the alias wasn't in place. I recommend that you always look at the command line containing a *rm* command very carefully before you press the RETURN key.

[*mv* and *cp* on the Sun systems Bruce is writing about have a *–i* option, but not all UNIXes do. As Bruce says, it might be safer to get in the habit of checking what you type before you press RETURN.—*JP*]

—BB

22.12 Copying Files to a Directory

Several commands like *cp* and *mv* will let you copy a file to a directory. That is, given the command:

```
% cp file1 somewhere
```

if *somewhere* is a directory, *cp* copies *file1* into the directory, leaving its name unchanged. You get a new file whose relative pathname *(1.21)* is *somewhere/file1*. A few commands, for example, *mv* and *ln*, have the same behavior.

Of course, this version of the command looks the same as a "regular" *cp* command. This leads to a common frustration: what if the directory *somewhere* doesn't exist? Maybe you forgot to create it; maybe you misspelled the name. *cp* doesn't know that you really meant a directory, so it just copies *file1* into a new file, *somewhere*, in the current directory. There are plenty of situations in which this can be plenty confusing, and even (if you're unlucky) lead to errors.

There's an easy safeguard, though. If you're copying files into a directory, add a slash and dot (/ .) after the directory's pathname:

```
% cp file1 path-to-directory/.
```

This makes a pathname to the special entry named . (dot) *(1.21, 19.02)* in the directory *somewhere*—which is a link to the directory itself. If the directory named *somewhere* doesn't exist, you'll get an error message:

```
% cp file1 somewhere/.
cp: somewhere/.: No such file or directory
```

—*ML*

22.13 Read an Inode with stat

The *stat* program reads an inode *(1.22)*. *stat* shows you the information that the *stat*(2) system call gives about a file (or directory or socket or . . .). The *atime* *(22.05)*, *mtime* *(17.02)*, and *ctime* *(22.06)* are shown, along with the elapsed time since. For example:

stat

```
% ls -l ptco
-r-xr-xr-x  2 jerry        3203 Mar 24 05:33 ptco
% stat ptco
  File: "ptco"
  Size: 3203     Allocated Blocks: 8     Filetype: Regular File
  Mode: (0555/-r-xr-xr-x)   Uid: (115/jerry)  Gid: (100/staff)
Device:  7,18  Inode: 172255    Links: 2
Access: Fri May  8 01:00:30 1992(00000.05:48:13)
Modify: Tue Mar 24 05:33:43 1992(00045.00:15:01)
Change: Fri May  8 06:48:42 1992(00000.00:00:02)
```

—*JP*

22.14 *Automatically Appending the Date to a Filename*

I suppose this falls into the category of "stupid tricks" but I still find it useful sometimes. I created a simple alias called *vid*, which I use to create and edit a file with a date as part of the filename.

I find it handy for repetitive reports and memos.

The alias looks like this:

csh_init

```
alias vid "vi \!:1.`date +%m.%d`"
```

and given an argument like *memo* or *status*, appends the date as an extension. Using wildcards, I can then list all my memos of a particular date or a particular subject:

```
% ls status*
status.02.18
status.03.10
% ls *3.10
budget.03.10
status.03.10
```

If I wanted to add the year, I'd put a dot or other separator, followed by %y in the specification to the *date* command.

If you understand backquote interpolation *(10.14)* and the formats for the *date* *(53.10)* command, you can easily develop variations of this alias that work with other commands besides *vi*.

—*TOR*

23

File Security, Ownership, and Sharing

23.01 Introduction to File Ownership and Security

Because UNIX is a multi-user system, you need some way of protecting users from each other: you don't want other users to look at the wrong files and find out compromising information about you or raising their salaries or doing something equivalently antisocial. Even if you're on a single-user system, file ownership still has value: it can often protect you from making mistakes, like deleting important executables.

In this chapter, we'll describe how file ownership works: who owns files, how to change ownership, how to specify which kinds of file access are allowed, and so on. We'll also discuss some other ways to prevent people from "prying," like encryption and clearing your screen. In my opinion, most security breaches arise from mistakes that could easily have been avoided: someone discovers that *anyone* can read the boss's e-mail, including the messages to his bookie. Once you've read this chapter, you'll understand how to avoid the common mistakes and protect yourself from most intruders.

—ML

23.02 *Tutorial on File and Directory Permissions*

[Think you know all about permissions? Even if you do, skim through this article. Bruce has some good tips.—JP]

There are three basic attributes for plain file permissions: read, write, and execute. Read and write permission obviously let you read the data from a file or write new data to the file. When you have execute permission, you can use the file as a program or shell script. The characters used to describe these permissions are r, w, and x, for e*x*ecute.

Directories use these same permissions, but they have a different meaning. If a directory has read permission, you can see what files are in the directory. Write permission means you can add, remove, or rename files in the directory. Execute allows you to use the directory name when accessing files inside that directory. (Article 19.02 has more information about what's in a directory.) Let's examine this more closely.

Suppose you have execute access to a directory, but you do not have read access to the files in the directory. You can still read the directory, or *inode* (1.22) information for that file, as returned by the *stat*(2) system call. That is, you can see the file's name, permissions, size, access times, owner and group, and number of links. You cannot read the contents of the file.

Write permission in a directory allows you to change the contents of a directory. Because the name of the file is stored in the directory, and not the file, *write permission in a directory allows creation, renaming, or deletion of files.* To be specific, if someone has write permission to your home directory, they can rename or delete your *.login* file and put a new file in its place. The permissions of your *.login* file do not matter. Someone can rename a file even if they can't read the contents of a file. (See article 23.11.)

Execute permission on a directory is sometimes called search permission. If you found a directory that gave you execute permission, but not read permission, you could use any file in that directory. However, you *must* know the name. You cannot look inside the directory to find out the names of the files. Think of this type of directory as a black box. You can throw filenames at this directory, and sometimes you find a file, sometimes you don't. (See article 23.13.)

User, Group, and World

All files have an owner and group associated with them. There are three sets of read/write/execute permissions: one set for the user or owner of the file, one set for the group of the file, and one set for everyone else. These permissions are determined by nine bits in the inode information, and are represented by the characters rwxrwxrwx in an *ls* −*l* listing:*

---

*Note that on a Berkeley UNIX system, *ls* −*l* produces an eight-column listing without the group name (here, books). Use *ls* −*lg* to get the listing format shown here.

```
% ls -l
drwxr-xr-x  3 jerry    books       512 Feb 14 11:31 manpages
-rw-r--r--  1 jerry    books     17233 Dec 10  1990 misc.Z
-rwxr-xr-x  1 tim      books       195 Mar 29 18:55 myhead
```

The first character in the *ls −l* listing specifies the type of file *(18.13)*. The first three of the nine permissions characters that follow specify the user, the middle three the group, and the last three the world. If the permission is not true, a dash is used to indicate lack of privilege. If you wanted to have a data file that you could read or write, but don't want anyone else to access, the permissions would be rw-------.

An easier way to specify these nine bits is with three octal digits instead of nine characters. (Article 1.23 has diagrams of permission bits and explains how to write permissions as an octal number.) The order is the same, so the above permissions can be described by the octal number 600. The first number specifies the owner's permission. The second number specifies the group *(23.14)* permission. The last number specifies permission to everyone who is not the owner or not in the group of the file [although permissions don't apply to the superuser *(1.24)*, who can do anything to any file or directory—*JP*].

This last point is subtle. When testing for permissions, the system looks at the groups in order. If you are denied permission, UNIX does not examine the next group. Consider the case of a file that is owned by user *jo*, is in the group *guests*, and has the permissions -----xrwx, or 017 in octal. This has the result that user *jo* cannot use the file, anyone in group *guests* can execute the program, and everyone else besides *jo* and *guests* can read, write, and execute the program. This is not a very common set of permissions. But some people use a similar mechanism *(23.15)* to deny one group of users from accessing or using a file. In the above case, *jo* cannot read or write the file she owns. She could use the *chmod* *(23.07)* command to grant herself permission to read the file. However, if the file was in a directory owned by someone else, and the directory did not give *jo* read or search permission, she would not be able to find the file to change its permission.

The above example is an extreme case. Most of the time permissions fall into four cases:

1. The information is personal. Many people have a directory or two in which they store information they do not wish to be public. Mail should probably be confidential, and all of your mailbox files should be in a directory with permissions of 700, denying everyone but yourself and the superuser read access to your letters. (See article 5.05.)

2. The information is not personal, yet no one should be able to modify the information. Most of my directories are set up this way, with the permissions of 755.

3. The files are managed by a team of people. This means group-write permission, or directories with the mode 775.

4. In the previous case, for confidential projects, you may want to deny access to people outside the group. In this case, make directories with mode 770.

You could just create a directory with the proper permissions, and put the files inside the directory, hoping the permissions of the directory will "protect" the files in the directory. This is not adequate. Suppose you had a directory with permissions 755 and a file with permissions 666 inside the directory. Anyone could change the contents of this file because the world has search access on the directory and write access to the file.

What is needed is a mechanism to prevent any new file from having world-write access. This mechanism exists with the *umask* command *(23.04)*. If you consider that a new directory would get permissions of 777, and new files get permissions of 666, the *umask* command specifies permissions to "take away" from all new files. To "subtract" world-write permission from a file, 666 must have 002 "subtracted" from the default value to get 664. To subtract group and world write, 666 must have 022 removed to leave 644 as the permissions of the file. These two values of *umask* are so common that it is useful to have some aliases *(11.02)* defined:

csh_init

```
alias open umask 002
alias shut umask 022
```

With these two values of *umask*, new directories will have permissions of 775 or 755. Most people have a *umask* value of one of these two values.

In a friendly work group, people tend to use the *umask* of 002, which allows others in your group to make changes to your files. Someone who uses the mask of 022 will cause grief to others working on a project. Trying to compile a program is frustrating when someone else owns files that you must delete but can't. You can rename files if this is the case or ask the system administrator for help.

Members of a team who normally use a default umask of 022 should find a means to change the mask value when working on the project. (Or else risk flames from your fellow workers!) Besides the *open* alias above, some people have an alias that changes directories and sets the mask to group-write permission:

```
alias proj "cd /usr/projects/proj;umask 002"
```

This isn't perfect, because people forget to use aliases. You could have a special *cd* alias and a private shell file in each project directory that sets the *umask* when you *cd* there. Other people could have similar files in the project directory with different names. Article 15.15 shows how.

Still another method is to run *find (18.01)* three times a day and search for files owned by you in the project directory that have the wrong permission:

$USER *7.03*
xargs *10.19*
chmod *23.07*

```
% find /usr/projects -user $USER ! -perm -020 -print | \
xargs chmod g+w
```

You can use the command *crontab* −e *(42.16, 42.12)* to define when to run this command. [If your system doesn't have personal *crontabs*, use a self-restarting *at* job *(42.08)*. —JP]

Which Group is Which?

Since group-write permission is so important in a team project, you might be wondering how the group of a new file is determined? The answer depends on several factors. Before I cover these, you should note that Berkeley and AT&T-based systems would use different mechanisms to determine the default group.

Originally UNIX required you to specify a new group with the *newgrp* command. If there was a password for this group in the */etc/group* file, and you were not listed as one of the members of the group, you had to type the password to change your group.

Berkeley-based versions of UNIX would use the current directory to determine the group of the new file. That is, if the current directory has *cad* as the group of the directory, any file created in that directory would be in the same group. To change the default group, just change to a different directory.

Both mechanisms had their good points and bad points. The Berkeley-based mechanism made it convenient to change groups automatically. However, there is a fixed limit of groups one could belong to. SunOS 4 has a limit of 16 groups. Earlier versions had a limit of eight groups.

SunOS and System V Release 4 support both mechanisms. The entire disk can be mounted with either the AT&T or the Berkeley mechanism. If it is necessary to control this on a directory-by-directory basis, a special bit *(23.05)* in the file permissions is used. If a disk partition is mounted without the Berkeley group mechanism, then a directory with this special bit will make new files have the same group as the directory. Without the special bit, the group of all new files depends on the current group of the user.

—BB

23.03 Who'll Own a New File?

If you share files with other users, it's good to be able to tell who will own each file. On BSD-based systems, this is even more important because only the superuser can change file ownership *(23.21, 23.22)*.

1. When you create a new file, it belongs to you.

2. When you append to a file with *>>file*, the owner doesn't change because UNIX doesn't have to create a new file.

3. When you rename a file with *mv*, the ownership doesn't change.

   Exception: if you use *mv* to move a file to another filesystem *(1.22)*, the moved file will belong to you—because, to move across filesystems, *mv* actually has to copy the file and delete the original.

4. When you copy a file, the copy belongs to you because you created it *(23.11)*.

5. When you edit a file:

- With an editor like *vi (31.02)*, the file keeps its original owner because a new file is never created.

- An editor like Emacs *(33.01)*, which makes a backup copy, can be different. The backup copy could belong to you or to the original owner. If you replace the edited file with its backup, the file's ownership might have changed:

```
% emacs filea
...Edit a lot, then decide you don't want your changes...
% mv filea~ filea
```

If you aren't sure, use *ls* *−l (23.02)*.

—JP

23.04 *Setting an Exact umask*

You can use the *umask* command to set the default mode for newly created files. Its argument is a three-digit numeric mode that represents the access to be *inhibited*—masked out—when a file is created. Thus, the value it wants is the octal complement of the numeric file mode you want. To determine this, you simply figure out the numeric equivalent *(1.23)* for the file mode you want and then subtract it from 777. For example, to get the mode 751 by default, compute 777–751 = 026; this is the value you give to *umask*:

```
% umask 026
```

Once this command is executed, all future files created will be given this protection automatically. System administrators can put a *umask* command in the system initialization file to set a default for all users. You can set your own *umask* in your shell setup files *(2.01)*.

—AF from the Nutshell Handbook Essential System Administration

23.05 *Group Permissions in a Directory with the setgid Bit*

If you work on a UNIX system with lots of users, you may be taking advantage of UNIX group permissions *(23.02)* to let users in one group write to files in a directory—but not let people in other groups write there.

How does UNIX determine what group should own the files you create? There are three ways:

1. On most System V-based systems, your *primary group membership (23.14)* determines the ownership of the files you create.

2. On most BSD UNIXes, files are owned by *the group that owns the directory in which you create the file.*

3. The rules under SunOS 4.*x* and System V Release 4 are more complicated. The system administrator decides which of the two above methods a

filesystem will use for group ownership. There are other wrinkles, too. It's probably easiest to create an empty new file *(22.07)* then check the group ownership with *ls −l* or *−lg (23.02)*.

You may be able to use the directory's *set group ID* (setgid) bit to control group ownership. In those cases, if the bit is set, the BSD rules apply. if the bit is not set, the System V rules apply. To set and remove the setgid bit, use the commands *chmod g+s (23.07)* and *chmod g−s*, respectively.

You can use the *chgrp (1.23)* command to change a file's group. However, you must own the file. And you must also be a member of the file's new group.

—JP, ML

23.06 *Protecting Files with the Sticky Bit*

UNIX directory access permissions say that if a user has write permission on a directory, she can rename or remove files there—even files that don't belong to her (see article 23.11). Many newer versions of UNIX have a way to stop that. The owner of a directory can set its *sticky bit* (mode *(1.23)* 1000). The only people who can rename or remove any file in that directory are the file's owner, the directory's owner, and the superuser.

Here's an example: the user *jerry* makes a world-writable directory and sets the sticky bit (shown as t here):

```
jerry% mkdir share
jerry% chmod 1777 share
jerry% ls -ld share
drwxrwxrwt   2 jerry    ora          32 Nov 19 10:31 share
```

Other people create files in it. When *jennifer* tries to remove a file that belongs to *ellie*, she can't:

```
jennifer% ls -l
total 2
-rw-r--r--   1 ellie    ora         120 Nov 19 11:32 data.ellie
-rw-r--r--   1 jennifer ora        3421 Nov 19 15:34 data.jennifer
-rw-r--r--   1 peter    ora         728 Nov 20 12:29 data.peter
jennifer% rm data.ellie
data.ellie: 644 mode ? y
rm: data.ellie not removed.
Permission denied
```

—JP

777
744
―――
033

23.07 Using chmod to Change File Permission

To change a file's permissions, you need to use the *chmod* command and you must be the file's owner or root. The command's syntax is pretty simple:

```
% chmod new-mode file(s)
```

The `new-mode` describes the access permissions you want *after* the change. There are two ways to specify the mode: you can use either a *numeric mode* or some symbols that describe the changes. I generally prefer the numeric mode (because I'm strange, I suppose). Anyway, to use a numeric mode, decide what permissions you want to have, express them as an octal number *(1.23, 23.02)*, and give a command like:

```
% chmod 644 report.txt
```

This gives read and write access to the owner of *report.txt* and read-only access to everyone else.

Most users prefer to use the *symbolic mode* to specify permissions. A symbolic *chmod* command looks like this:

```
% chmod g-w report.txt
```

This means "take away write access for group members." The symbols used in mode specifications are shown in Table 23-1.

Table 23-1. chmod Symbolic Modes

Category	Mode	Description
Who:	u	User (owner) of the file.
	g	Group members.
	o	Others.
	a	All (i.e., user, group, and others).
What to do:	–	Take away this permission.
	+	Add the indicated permission.
	=	Set exactly this permission *(23.08)*.
Permissions:	r	Read access.
	w	Write access.
	x	Execute access.
	X	Give (or deny) execute permission to directories, or to files that have another "execute" bit set.
	s	Set user or group ID (only valid with + or –).
	t	Set the "sticky bit" *(23.06, 1.23)*.

(Article 23.02 explains the "Who" and "Permissions" categories.) Here are a few example symbolic modes:

o=r   Set others access to read-only, regardless of what other bits are set.
o+r   Add read access for others.
go-w   Take away write access for group members and others.

> a=rw   Give everyone (user, group, and others) read-write (but not exe-
> cute) access.

Remember that + and − add or delete certain permissions, but leave the others untouched. The commands below show how permissions are added and subtracted:

```
% ls -l foo
-rwx-----x  1 mikel           0 Mar 30 11:02 foo
% chmod a+x foo
% ls -l foo
-rwx--x--x  1 mikel           0 Mar 30 11:02 foo
% chmod o-x,g+r foo
% ls -l foo
-rwxr-x---  1 mikel           0 Mar 30 11:02 foo
%
```

Note the last *chmod* command. It shows something we haven't mentioned before. With symbolic mode, you're allowed to combine two (or more) specifications, separated by commas. This command says "take away execute permission for others, and add read access for group members."

On occasion, I've wanted to change the permissions of a whole directory tree: all the files in a directory and all of its subdirectories. In this case, you want to use *chmod −R* (the R stands for recursive) or *find −exec* (18.10). You won't need this often, but when you do, it's a real lifesaver.

—*ML*

23.08 *The Handy chmod = Operator*

Let's say you have a set of files. Some are writable by you, others are read-only. You want to give people in your group the same permissions you have—that is, they can write writable files but can only read the read-only files. It's easy with an underdocumented feature of *chmod*:

```
% chmod g=u *
```

That means "for all files (*), set the group permissions (g) to be the same as the owner permissions (u)." You can also use the letter o for others, which is everyone who's not the owner or in the owner's group. Article 23.02 explains these categories.

If your *chmod* has a −R (recursive) option, you can make the same change to all files and directories in your current directory and beneath. If you don't have *chmod −R*, use this *find* (18.10):

```
% find . -exec chmod g=u {} \;
```

The *cpmod* (23.17) program on the Power Tools disk can copy all file permissions.

—*JP*

23.09 Protect Important Files: Make Them Unwritable

A good way to prevent yourself from making mistakes is to make certain files read-only. If you try to delete a read-only file, you will get a warning. You will also get a warning if you try to move a file onto another file that is write-protected. If you know you want to remove or move a file, even though the file is read-only, you can use the *−f* option with *rm* or *mv* to *force* the change without warnings.

Manually changing the permissions of files all the time is counterproductive. You could create two aliases to make it easier to type:

csh_init

```
# change mode to read only
alias -w chmod -w
# change mode to add write permission
alias +w chmod u+w
```

[These are really handy! I use a script named *c−w* and *cw*, respectively, instead. For shell programming, I also added *cx* that does *chmod +x*. Article 23.10 explains the script.—*JP*] It is a good idea to remove write permission from some files. Occasionally some files contain information difficult to replace. These files might be included with other, easily replaceable files. Or you might want to protect some files that rarely change. Combined with directory permissions, and the current value of *umask (23.04)*, you can find some file that might be protected in this manner. You can always create a script that adds write permission, edits the file, and removes write permission:

chmod_edit

```
#!/bin/sh
# add write permission to the files
chmod u+w "$@"
# edit the files; use vi if VISUAL not defined
${VISUAL=vi} "$@"
# remove write permission
chmod -w "$@"
```

"$@" 46.14

${..=..} 47.12

—*BB*

23.10 cx, cw, c−w: Quick File Permission Changes

Here's a short script that I use a lot. To make a new shell script executable, for example, I type:

```
% cx scriptfile
```

Using *cw* adds write permission; *c−w* takes it away. This is the single script file for all three commands:

```
#! /bin/sh
case "$0" in
*cx)   chmod +x "$@" ;;
*cw)   chmod +w "$@" ;;
*c-w)  chmod -w "$@" ;;
*)     echo "$0: Help!  Shouldn't get here!" 1>&2; exit 1 ;;
esac
```

The script has three links. Put it in a file named *cx*. Then type:

```
% chmod +x cx
% ln cx cw
% ln cx c-w
```

The script tests the name it was called with, in $0, to decide which *chmod* command to run. This trick saves disk space. You can add other commands, too, by adding a line to the *case* and another link. Or you can use aliases *(23.09)*.

—*JP*

23.11 A Loophole: Modifying Files without Write Access

No one said that UNIX is perfect *(1.34)*, and one of its nagging problems has always been security. Here's one glitch that you should be aware of. If you don't have write access to a file, you can't modify it. However, if you have write access to the directory, you can get around this as follows:

```
% ls -l unwritable
-r--r--r--  1 john            334 Mar 30 14:57 unwritable
% cat > unwritable
unwritable: permission denied
% cat unwritable > temp
% vi temp
    ...
% mv temp unwritable
override protection 444 for unwritable? y
% cat unwritable
John wrote this originally, and made the file read-only.
But then Mike came along and wrote:
I should not have been able to do this!!!
```

I couldn't write the file *unwritable* directly. But I was able to copy it, and then use *vi* to make whatever changes I wanted. After all, I had read access, and to copy a file, you only need to be able to read it. When I had my own copy, I could (of course) edit it to my heart's content. When I was done, I was able to *mv* the new file on top of *unwritable*. Why? Renaming a file only requires that you be able to write the file's directory. You don't need to be able to write the file itself. (Note that a *cp* wouldn't work—copying requires *unwritable* to be writable, if it already exists.) This is one reason to watch directory access fairly closely.

As you can see, allowing directory-write access to others can be dangerous. If this is a problem for you, solve it by setting your *umask* *(23.04)* correctly and using *chmod* *(23.07)* to fix permissions of existing directories. Or, you may be able to leave the directory writable and set the directory's sticky bit *(23.06)*.

—*ML*

23.12 Directory Read and Execute Permissions

This book says that, in general, directories need both read and execute permission *(23.02)*. What happens if you take away one or the other? Let's experiment.

Note: You need the default *ls* for this experiment. If your *ls* has been aliased or changed to use some of its options, stop that temporarily. Or, to be sure, type */bin/ls* instead of just *ls*.

Make a directory, a subdirectory, and a file, like this:

```
% mkdir junk
% cd junk
% mkdir sub
% echo this is a file > sub/afile
% ls -lR
total 1
drwxr-xr-x   2 jerry         512 Apr 18 14:46 sub

sub:
total 1
-rw-r--r--   1 jerry          15 Apr 18 14:46 afile
% ls sub
afile
% cat sub/afile
this is a file
```

echo *9.04*
–R *17.04*

(The directory's exact permissions don't matter in this experiment, as long as you have read and execute permission to start.) Next, take away execute permission from the subdirectory. List the subdirectory with plain *ls* and also with *–l*. Try to read the file:

```
% chmod a-x sub
% ls sub
afile
% cat sub/afile
cat: sub/afile: Permission denied
% ls -lR
total 1
drw-r--r--   2 jerry         512 Apr 18 14:46 sub

ls: sub/afile: Permission denied
sub:
total 0
```

You can see that *afile* is in the subdirectory, but you can't "get to it." What happened? (Usually, I'd tell you. But this is an experiment!) Now, let's turn things around: give the directory execute permission but no read permission:

```
% chmod a=x sub
% ls sub
ls: sub unreadable
% cat sub/afile
this is a file
% ls -lR
```

```
total 1
d--x--x--x  2 jerry         512 Apr 18 14:46 sub
```

```
ls: sub unreadable
```

You can read *afile*, but you can't list its directory. Hmmmmmmm... One more experiment: change into the *sub* directory and try this again:

```
% cd sub
% ls
ls: . unreadable
% cat afile
this is a file
% ls -l
ls: . unreadable
% ls -l afile
-rw-r--r--  1 jerry         15 Apr 18 14:46 afile
```

Okay, Sherlock. Solve this mystery and you'll win the "filesystem wizard" cap. (Article 23.02 might help... or it might not!)

1. When a directory is readable, the *ls* command can read what's in the directory file (the filenames). But, without execute permission, the contents of the directory are not accessible.

   If plain *ls* can show you *afile*, why can't *ls –l* show it? Because plain *ls* only has to read the directory file *(19.02)*. If you add *–l* (or *–F* or *–s* or almost any option that gives more information about a file), then *ls* has to open the file's inode *(1.22)* to get the information. Without execute permission, *ls* can't access the inode.

2. When a directory is executable, its contents are accessible. So, if you know the name of an entry in the directory, you can access it. But, without read permission, commands can't read the directory file to find the names of things in it.

   This trick is good for hiding things in a directory *(23.13)*.

—*JP*

23.13 A Directory that People Can Access but Can't List

Do you need to let someone use a file of yours, but you don't want everyone on the system to be able to snoop around in the directory? You can give execute permission, but not read permission, to a directory. Then, if a file in the directory is accessible, a person can use the file by typing the exact filename. *ls* will say the directory is "unreadable." Wildcards won't work.

Here's an example. Let's say that your home directory has `rwxr-xr-x` permissions (everyone can access and list files in it). Your username is *hanna*. You have a subdirectory named *project*; you set its permissions so that everyone else on the system has execute-only permission:

```
hanna% pwd
/home/hanna
hanna% chmod 711 project
hanna% ls -ld project project/plan711
drwx--x--x  2    hanna    512  Jul 26 12:14 project
-rw-r--r--  1    hanna   9284  Jul 27 17:34 project/plan711
```

—d 17.09 appears in the left margin.

Now you tell the other user, *toria*, the exact name of your file, *plan711*. Like everyone else on the system, she can access your *project* directory. She can't list it because she doesn't have read permission. Because she knows the exact filename, she can read the file because the file is readable (anyone else could read the file, too, if they knew its exact name):

```
toria% cd /home/hanna/project
toria% pwd
pwd: can't read .
toria% ls
ls: . unreadable
toria% more plan711
    ...File appears...
toria% ln plan711 /home/toria/project.hanna/plan
```

toria made a hard link *(19.05)* to the *plan711* file, with a different name, in her own *project.hanna* directory. (She could have copied, printed, or used any other command that reads the file.) Now, if you (*hanna*) want to, you can deny everyone's permission to your *project* directory. *toria* still has her link to the file, though. She can read it any time she wants to, follow the changes you make to it, and so on:

```
toria% cd
toria% ls -ld project.hanna project.hanna/plan
drwx------  2    toria    512  Jul 27 16:43 project.hanna
-rw-r--r--  2    hanna   9284  Jul 27 17:34 project.hanna/plan
toria% more project.hanna/plan
    ...File appears...
```

toria has protected her *project.hanna* directory so that other users can't find her link to *hanna*'s file.

Note: If *hanna* denies permission to her directory, *toria* can still read the file through her hard link. If *toria* had made a symbolic link, though, she wouldn't be able to access the file any more. That's because a hard link keeps the file's i-number *(1.22, 19.02)* but a symbolic link doesn't.

You might also want to give other users permission to list and access the files in a directory, but not make the directory open to all users. One way to do this is to put a fully accessible directory with an unusual name inside an unreadable directory. Users who know the exact name of the fully accessible directory can *cd* to it; other users can't find it without its name:

```
hanna% chmod 711 project
hanna% chmod 777 project/pLaN
```

```
hanna% ls -ld project project/pLaN
drwx--x--x  3    hanna     512  Jul 27 17:36 project
drwxrwxrwx  2    hanna     512  Jul 27 17:37 project/pLaN
```

Users who type cd /home/hanna/project/pLaN can list the directory's contents with *ls*. With the permissions you've set, other users can also create, delete, and rename files inside the *pLaN* directory—though you could have used more restrictive permissions like drwxr-xr-x instead.

This setup can still be a little confusing. For instance, as article 15.04 explains, the *pwd* command won't work for users in the *pLaN* directory because *pwd* can't read the *project* directory. Variables like $cwd *(15.14)* and $PWD *(7.03)* will probably have the full pathname. If another user gets lost in a restricted directory like this, the best thing to do is *cd* to the home directory and start again.

—*JP*

23.14 *Groups and Group Ownership*

Group membership is an important part of UNIX security. All users are members of one or more groups, as determined by your entry in */etc/passwd (37.03)* and the */etc/group* file.

To find out what groups you belong to, "*grep (28.01)* for" your entry in */etc/passwd*:

```
% grep mikel /etc/passwd
mikel:sflghjraloweor:50:100:Mike Loukides:/home/mikel:/bin/csh
```

The fourth field (the second number) is your *primary group ID*. Look up this number in the */etc/group* file:

```
% grep 100 /etc/group
staff:*:100:root
```

My primary group is *staff*. Therefore, when I log in, my group ID is set to 100. To see what other groups you belong to, use the *groups* command if your UNIX version has it. Otherwise, look for your name in */etc/group*:

```
% grep mikel /etc/group
power:*:55:mikel,jerry,tim
weakness:*:60:mikel,harry,susan
```

I'm also a member of the groups *power* and *weakness*, with group IDs 55 and 60.

With BSD UNIX, you're always a member of all your groups. This means that I can access files that are owned by the *staff, power,* and *weakness* groups, without doing anything in particular. Under System V UNIX, you can only be "in" one group at a time, even though you can be a member of several. (I suppose this is like social clubs; you can belong to the Elks and the Odd Fellows, but you can only wear one silly hat at a time.) If you need to access files that are owned by another group, use the *newgrp* command:

```
% newgrp groupname
```

(System V even lets you change to groups that you don't belong to. In this case, you have to give a *group password*. Group passwords are rarely used—usually, the password field is filled with a `*`, which effectively says that there are no valid passwords for this group.)

On most systems, there are groups for major projects or departments, groups for system administration, and maybe one or two groups for visitors. Some BSD-based systems have a *wheel* group; to become root *(1.24)*, you must belong to *wheel*. Many systems make terminals writable only by the owner and a special group named *tty*; this prevents other users from sending characters to your terminal without using an approved *setgid (1.23)* program like *write (1.33)*.

—ML

23.15 Add Users to a Group to Deny Permission

Usually, UNIX group access *(23.14)* allows a group of users to access a directory or file that they couldn't otherwise access. You can turn this around though, with groups that *deny* permission.

Note: This trick works only on UNIX systems, like BSD, that let a user belong to more than one group at the same time.

For example, you might work on a computer that has some proprietary files and software that three "guest" accounts shouldn't be able to use. Everyone else on the computer should have access. To do this, put the software in a directory owned by a group named something like *deny*. Then use *chmod* to deny permission to that group:

```
# chmod 705 /usr/local/somedir
# ls -lgd /usr/local/somedir
drwx---r-x 2    root    deny         512  Mar 26 12:14 /usr/local/somedir
```

Finally, add the guest accounts to the *deny* group (in the */etc/group* file).

UNIX checks permissions in the order *user-group-other*. The first applicable permission is the one used, even if it denies permission rather than grant it. In this case, none of the guest accounts are *root* (we hope! `:-)`). They're members of the group called *deny*, however—so that permission (`---`) is checked and the group members are shut out. Other users who aren't members of *deny* are checked for "other" access (`r-x`); they can get into the directory.

The same setup works for individual files (like programs). Just be careful about changing system programs that are SUID or SGID *(1.23)*.

—JP, JIK

23.16 Juggling Permissions

Like any security feature, UNIX permissions occasionally get in your way. When you want to let people use your apartment, you have to make sure you can get them a key; and when you want to let someone into your files, you have to make sure they have read and write access.

In the ideal world, each file would have a list of users who can access it, and the file's owner could just add or delete users from that list at will. Some secure versions of UNIX are configured this way, but standard UNIX systems don't provide that degree of control. Instead, we have to know how to juggle UNIX file permissions to achieve our ends.

For example, suppose I have a file called *ch01* which I want edited by another user, *val*. I tell her that the file is */books/ptools/ch01*, but she reports to me that she can't access it:

```
val % cd /books/ptools
val % more ch01
ch01: Permission denied
```

The reason *val* can't read the file is that it is set to be readable only by me. *val* can check the permissions on the file using the *–l* option to the *ls* command:

```
val % ls -l ch01
-rw-------  1 lmui        13727 Sep 21 07:43 ch01
```

val asks me (*lmui*) to give her read and write permission on the file. Only the file owner and *root* can change permission for a file.

Now, what's the best way to give *val* access to *ch01*?

The fastest and most sure-fire way to give another user permission is to extend read and write permission to everyone:

```
lmui % chmod 666 ch01
lmui % ls -l ch01
-rw-rw-rw-  1 lmui        13727 Sep 21 07:43 ch01
```

But this is sort of like leaving your front door wide open so your cat can get in and out. It's far better to extend read and write access to a common group instead of to the entire world. I try to give *val* access to the file by giving group read and write access:

```
lmui % chmod 660 ch01
lmui % ls -l ch01
-rw-rw----  1 lmui        13727 Sep 21 07:43 ch01
```

But *val* reports that it still doesn't work:

```
val % more ch01
ch01: Permission denied
```

What happened? Well, I gave read and write permission to the file's group, but *val* doesn't belong to that group. You can find out the group a file belongs to using the *–lg* option to *ls* (this is the default on System V when you type `ls –l`):

```
val % ls -lg ch01
-rw-rw----  1 lmui     power          13727 Sep 21 07:43 ch01
```

You can use the *groups* command to find out what groups a user belongs to:

```
% groups val
val : authors ora
% groups lmui
lmui : authors power wheel ora
```

The *ch01* file belongs to group *power*. *val* isn't a member of this group, but both *lmui* and *val* are in the *authors* group.

To give *val* access to the file *ch01*, therefore, I need to put the file in group *authors*. To do that, I use the *chgrp(1.23)* command:

```
lmui % chgrp authors ch01
lmui % ls -lg ch01
-rw-rw----  1 lmui     authors        13727 Sep 21 07:43 ch01
```

Now *val* can read and write the file. (On System V systems, she may need to run *newgrp(23.14)* first.)

—*LM*

23.17 *Copying Permissions with cpmod*

A utility to help facilitate permission juggling is *cpmod*. This program lets you copy the group ownership and permission modes of one file to another.

For example, suppose you just juggled permissions *(23.16)* using *chmod* and *chgrp* to give another user access to a file called *ch01*, and now she wants permission for three more files in the same directory. You could repeat the process, or you could just use *cpmod* to copy the permissions from the first file:

cpmod

[..] *16.02*

```
% ls -lg ch01
-rw-rw----  1 lmui     authors        13727 Sep 21 07:43 ch01
% ls -lg ch0[234]
-rw-------  1 lmui     book           34020 Oct 15 11:13 ch02
-rw-r-----  1 lmui     acct           11207 Oct 13 09:49 ch03
-rw-r--r--  1 lmui     book           29239 Oct 07 18:12 ch03
% cpmod ch01 ch0[234]
% ls -lg ch0?
-rw-rw----  1 lmui     authors        13727 Sep 21 07:43 ch01
-rw-rw----  1 lmui     authors        34020 Sep 21 07:43 ch02
-rw-rw----  1 lmui     authors        11207 Sep 21 07:43 ch03
-rw-rw----  1 lmui     authors        29239 Sep 21 07:43 ch04
```

Use *cpmod* to say, "Make these files just like this other one."

In this example, we used it to quickly give write permission to several files at once. But notice that the new files also inherit the same modification times. This is another feature of *cpmod*, which comes in useful for programmers and other users of *make (29.12)*. The *make* program uses modification dates on files to determine whether it should recompile source code. *cpmod* provides a way to manipulate the modification dates when you need to. Article 22.07 explains the version of the *touch* command that can set a file to have any modification date.

—*LM*

23.18 *Ways of Improving the Security of crypt*

Files encrypted with *crypt* are exceedingly easy for a cryptographer to break. For several years, it has been possible for noncryptographers to break messages encrypted with *crypt* as well, thanks to a program developed in 1986 by Robert Baldwin at the MIT Laboratory for Computer Science. Baldwin's program, Crypt Breaker's Workbench (*cbw*), automatically decrypts text files encrypted with *crypt* within a matter of minutes.

cbw has been widely distributed; as a result, files encrypted with *crypt* should not be considered secure. (They weren't secure before *cbw* was distributed; it was simply that fewer people had the technical skill necessary to break them.)

Although we recommend that you do not use *crypt* to encrypt files, you may have no other encryption system readily available to you. If this is the case, there are a few simple precautions that you can take to decrease the chances that your encrypted files will be decrypted:

- Encrypt the file multiple times, using different keys at each stage. This essentially changes the transformation.

- Compress *(25.06)* your files before encrypting them. Compressing a file alters the information—the plain ASCII *(53.03)* text—that programs like *cbw* use to know when they have correctly guessed part of the encryption key. If your message does not decrypt into plain text, *cbw* will not know when it has correctly decrypted your message. However, if your attackers know you have done this, they can modify their version of *cbw* accordingly.

- If you use *compress* or *pack* to compress your file, remove the three-byte header. Files compressed with *compress* contain a three-byte signature, or header, consisting of the hexadecimal values 1f, 9d, and 90 (in that order). If your attacker believes that your file was compressed before it was encrypted, knowing how the first three bytes decrypt can help him to decrypt the rest of the file. You can strip these three bytes with the *dd (36.04)* command:*

```
% compress -c <plaintext | dd bs=3 skip=1 | crypt >encrypted
```

---

*Using *dd* this way is very slow and inefficient. If you are going to be encrypting a lot of compressed files, you may wish to write a small program to remove the header more efficiently.

Of course, you must remember to put the three-byte header back on before you attempt to uncompress the file with *zcat.* You can get a header by compressing */dev/null (14.14)*:

() *14.07*

```
% (compress -cf /dev/null; crypt <encrypted) | zcat >plaintext
```

- If you do not have *compress,* use *tar (20.05)* to bundle your file to be encrypted with other files containing random data; then encrypt the *tar* file. The presence of random data will make it more difficult for decryption programs such as *cbw* to isolate your plain text.

—*SG, GS* from the Nutshell Handbook *Practical UNIX Security*

23.19 *Clear Your Terminal for Security, to Stop Burn-in*

The *clear* command reads your *termcap* or *terminfo (6.02)* entry to find out how to erase your screen, then it sends that command. If you're typing something confidential that other people shouldn't read, just type `clear` at a shell prompt when you can. Many UNIX programs let you do a shell escape *(31.26)* to run a single UNIX command—you can clear your screen that way, by typing something like `!clear` from inside the program.

Note: Some terminals and window systems have memories—scrolling buffers that save previous screens or the current one. The *clear* command probably won't clear those. Check your manual to find out how—or, if you're desperate, log off UNIX, then turn off your screen's power for a minute.

If you leave your desk for a long meeting or for the day, then remember that you didn't erase your screen, you can probably clear your screen from another user's terminal. (If your system has the tty-group-write protection *(23.14)*, then you'll have to log in or *su (23.23)* to your account from the other terminal first.) If the other terminal has the same terminal type, use the command:

who *53.04*

```
% who | grep yourname
yourname    ttyp3    Jun 24 10:44
% clear > /dev/ttyp3
```

If you're on a different type of terminal, you'll need to set the *TERM* environment variable temporarily *(7.10)* before you use that command.

—*JP*

23.20 Shell Scripts Must be Readable and (usually) Executable

Almost everyone knows that you need to make a program file executable—otherwise, UNIX won't execute it. Well, that's true for directly executable binary files like C and Pascal programs, but it's not quite true for interpreted programs like shell scripts.

The UNIX kernel can read an executable binary directly—if there's execute permission, the kernel is happy; it doesn't need read permission. But a shell script has to be read by a user's UNIX program (a shell). To read a file, any UNIX program has to have read permission. So, shell scripts must be readable.

Shell scripts don't need execute permission if you start the shell and give it the script file to read:

```
% sh scriptfile
% sh < scriptfile
```

(47.24) The execute permission is a signal to the kernel that it can try to execute the file when you type only the filename:

```
% scriptfile
```

So shell scripts don't need to be executable—it's just handy.

—JP

23.21 Why Can't You Change File Ownership under BSD UNIX?

[Chris is explaining why Berkeley UNIX systems allow only root (1.24) to change a file's ownership. If you need to change ownership, there is a workaround (23.22). —JP]

This restriction is not bogus, because the system supports disk quotas (25.17). If you could give away your own files, you could:

```
mkdir .hide; chmod 700 .hide
cd .hide
create_huge_file >foo
chown prof1 foo
create_huge_file >bar
chown prof2 bar
create_huge_file >baz
chown prof3 baz
```

All you would need do is find someone with a high quota or no quota (such as a professor) who does not often check his own usage (such as a professor) and probably does not care that the disk is 99 percent full (such as a, er, well, never mind), and then give away files as necessary to keep under your own quota.

You could regain ownership of the file by copying it to another disk partition, removing the original, and copying it back.

—*CT in comp.unix.questions on Usenet, 6 July 1989*

23.22 How to Change File Ownership without chown

UNIX systems with disk quotas *(25.17)* won't let you change the owner *(23.21)* of a file; only the superuser can use *chown.* Here's a workaround for those systems.

1. The file's current owner should make sure that the new owner has write permission on the directory where the file is and read permission on the file itself:

```
jerry% ls -ld . afile
drwxr-xr-x   2 jerry    512  Aug 10 12:20 .
-rw-r--r--   1 jerry   1934  Aug 10 09:34 afile
jerry% chmod go+w .
```

2. The new owner (logged in as herself) should rename the file, make a copy, and delete the original file. If the new owner is there at the same time, *su (23.23)* is probably the fastest way to change accounts:

```
jerry% su laura
Password:
laura% mv afile afile.tmp
laura% cp -p afile.tmp afile
laura% ls -l afile
-rw-r--r--   1 laura   1934  Aug 10 09:34 afile
laura% rm -f afile.tmp
laura% exit
jerry% chmod go-w .
```

–f 24.09

The *cp –p (19.16)* command preserves the file's original permissions and last modification time. After the new owner (*laura*) is done copying, the old owner (*jerry*) takes away the directory's write permission again.

—*JP*

23.23 The su Command Isn't Just for the Superuser

System administrators use the *su* command to become the superuser *(1.24)*. But you can use it for lots more:

- Become another user temporarily, without logging off your account.

- Become another user without tying up another terminal port.

- Switch between multiple users any time (on systems with job control).

- Do a "quick login" to another user's account, especially when the system is busy.

When you type:

```
youraccount% su whoever
Password:
whoever%
```

UNIX starts a subshell *(40.04)* that runs as the user *whoever*. After you use the *cd* command to go to the user's home directory, you can run commands as if you'd logged into that account (more or less . . . see below).

Ending or Suspending

End the subshell and go back to the account where you typed su with the *exit (40.04)* command or a CTRL-d.

Or, on systems with job control *(13.08)*, you can stop the subshell temporarily and go back to the account where you started the *su*. To do that, type suspend if *whoever*'s shell has job control (most C shells do); otherwise, enter CTRL-z at the shell prompt.

Note: If the *su* subshell doesn't have job control but your starting shell does, entering CTRL-z to *any* command you run from the subshell will stop the command *and the subshell.*

You can use *suspend* to start multiple *su* sessions from the same shell. You can go back to your original login, from any of those sessions, without losing your shell history, current directory, etc. Because these shells run on the same tty *(3.08)* as your login shell, *su* doesn't tie up other tty/pty ports like multiple logins or multiple windows can. This is helpful on busy machines with lots of users.

On any UNIX system, you can type exit (or use CTRL-d) to go back to the original login. But on systems with job control, you can *su* to several other users and jump back to your original login at any time. Job control lets you suspend the other *su*'s and go back to the place you left off without typing another *su* (and password). The C shell has a *suspend* command that lets you do that. On other shells, you may be able to enter CTRL-z (your job suspend character) or make a command alias *(11.04)* to stop the current shell:

kill *40.10*
$$ *9.15*

```
alias stop='kill -STOP $$'
```

Here's a demo. I'm logged in to the account *jerry* on the computer *wheeze.* I've *su*ed to the superuser, *sarah*, and *manuals* accounts, too. I'm using job control to switch users:

```
jerry@wheeze% jobs
[1]    Stopped      su
[2] -  Stopped      su sarah
[3] +  Stopped      su manuals
jerry@wheeze% fg
su manuals
      ...Do stuff as manuals...
manuals@wheeze% suspend
Stopped
jerry@wheeze% fg %1
```

```
su
wheeze#
        ...Do stuff as root...
wheeze# suspend
Stopped
jerry@wheeze%
```

I use that so much that I've made a single-letter alias *(11.02)* named *z* that does a *suspend*.

Who are You Now?

It's easier to jump between accounts if the shells' prompts *(8.01)* have the username in them, as shown above. If not, use the command *whoami* or *id* to see which user you are. Also, to see your original login name (the account where you started the *su*), try who am i (with spaces).

Problems You Might Have

Some System V versions don't change the environment variable *HOME* (*LOGDIR*) *(15.12)* to the right value for the account you *su* to. That means a *cd* command will take you to the home directory of your original login, not the home directory of your *sued* account. Also, a C shell you start on the other account won't read your *.cshrc* file. The best fix for that is a shell script named *su* that sets the variable for you. It's written in the C shell because *csh* has the ~ (tilde) operator *(15.12)* for finding the account's home directory. Add this script to a directory before */bin* in your path *(9.05)* or make an alias or shell function that runs the script instead of the standard *su*.

```
#!/bin/csh -f
# su - fix incorrect $HOME with system 'su' command
foreach arg ($argv)
        # find first non-option argument
        if ("x$arg" !~ x-*) then
                setenv HOME ~$arg
                exec /bin/su $argv:q
        endif
end
echo "$0 ERROR: can't find username."
exit 1
```

Another workaround for that is an alias with the name of the account I'm *suing* to:

```
alias randi '(setenv HOME ~randi; su randi)'
```

There's another problem that can happen on any version of UNIX: the account you *su* to doesn't have permission *(23.02)* to access the current directory where you ran the *su* command. Then, you may get an error like getwd: can't stat . from the C shell on the account you *su* to. Or you may get no error but the *su* will fail. The fix for both problems is to *cd* to a world-access directory like / or */tmp* before you run *su*. An alias can make that easy:

\su *11.06*

```
alias su '(cd /; \su \!*)'
```

You can also add the cd / command to the shell script above if you want.

If the account you *su* to runs the C shell (and you don't use the –*f* option—see below), it will read the *.cshrc* file. If that *.cshrc* has hardcoded pathnames or commands that only the other account can run, the commands might fail. That can cause a variety of "fun" problems. Try replacing hardcoded pathnames like /home/*oldacct*/bin with paths that use account-specific variables like $home/bin, ~/bin, and so on.

Plain su *whoever* doesn't read a C shell user's *.login* file or a Bourne shell user's *.profile*. Using su – *whoever* (see the section "Other su Features" below) solves that, but you can't suspend an *su* – shell (at least not on my systems).

Finally, because the *su* command runs in a subshell *(40.04)*, environment variables *(7.01)* set in the account you *su* from will be passed into the subshell. That can be good or bad. For instance, your favorite EDITOR *(7.03)* (*vi*, Emacs, or whatever) can be passed to the account you *su* to. But that account might also set a variable that you want to use. If you're wondering what's set after you *su*, type set for a list of shell variables and either env (System V) or printenv (BSD) to see environment variables.

Quick Changes to Other Accounts

If your system is busy, it can take time to run through all the commands in the other user's *.cshrc* file. The *su* command can pass arguments to the subshell it starts, though. If the other account uses C shell, the –*f* option tells it not to read the *.cshrc* file (for example, su -f *whoever*). You won't get that account's *.cshrc* setup, but you will start to work on it sooner.

If logging in on your system takes a long time and you want to switch to another account permanently, you can *exec (47.07)* the *su* command:

```
% exec su whoever
```

That makes a weird situation where the *who (53.04)* command will show you logged on as your original account, but you'll be running as *whoever* (the *whoami* or *id* command will tell you that). Also, because the *su* shell isn't a login shell *(2.08)*, the *logout* command won't work; you'll need to type exit instead. So, *exec su* is a little tricky—but it's fast.

Other su Features

The command *su* *−e* switches to the other user's account but keeps the environment you have now. That's handy when you're having trouble with the other user's environment or want to keep your own.

The command *su* *−* simulates a full login to the other account. If the other account runs the Bourne shell, the *.profile* will be read. For the C shell, both *.cshrc* and *.login* will be read. You can't *suspend* a *su* *−* subshell. When you log out though, you'll be back in your original account's shell.

—JP

24

Removing Files

24.01 *The Cycle of Creation and Destruction*

As a computer user, you spend lots of time creating files. Just as the necessary counterpart of life is death, the other side of file creation is deletion. If you never delete any files, you soon have a computer's equivalent of a population explosion: your disks get full, and you have to either spend money (buy and install more disk drives) or figure out which files you don't really need.

In this chapter, we'll talk about ways to get rid of files: how to do it safely, how to get rid of files that don't want to die, and how to find "stale" files, or unused files that have been around for a long time. "Safe" deletion is a particularly interesting topic, because UNIX's *rm* command is extreme: once you delete a file, it's gone permanently. There are several solutions for working around this problem, letting you (possibly) reclaim files from the dead.

—*ML*

24.02 *rm and its Dangers*

Under UNIX, you use the *rm* command to delete files. The command itself is simple enough; you just type rm followed by a list of files. If anything, *rm* is too simple. It's easy to delete more than you want, and once something is gone, it's permanently gone. There are a few hacks that make *rm* somewhat safer, and we'll get to those momentarily. But first, a lecture on some of the dangers.

To understand why it's impossible to reclaim deleted files, you need to know a bit about how the UNIX filesystem works. The system contains a "free list," which is a list of disk blocks that aren't used. When you delete a file, its directory entry (which gives it its name) is removed. If there are no more links to the file (i.e., if the file only has one name), its inode *(1.22)* is added to the list of free inodes, and its datablocks are added to the free list.

Well, why can't you get the file back from the free list? After all, there are DOS utilities that can reclaim deleted files by doing something similar. Remember, though, UNIX is a multi-tasking operating system. Even if you think your system is a single-user system, there are a lot of things going on "behind your back": daemons are writing to log files, handling network connections, processing electronic mail, and so on. You could theoretically reclaim a file if you could "freeze" the filesystem the instant your file was deleted—but that's not possible. With UNIX, everything is always active. By the time you realize you made a mistake, your file's data blocks may well have been re-used for something else.

When you're deleting files, it's particularly important to use wildcards carefully. Simple typing errors can have disastrous consequences. Let's say you want to delete all your object (.o) files. But because of a nervous twitch, you add an extra space and type:

```
% rm * .o
```

It looks right, and you might not even notice the error. But before you know it, all the files in the current directory will be gone. Irretrievably.

If you don't think this can happen to you, here's something that actually did happen to me. At one point, when I was a relatively new UNIX user, I was working on my company's business plan. The executives thought that, to be "secure," they'd set business plan's permissions so you had to be root (1.24) to modify it. (A mistake in its own right, but that's another story.) I was using a terminal I wasn't familiar with, and accidentally managed to create a bunch of files with four control characters at the beginning of their name. To get rid of these, I typed (as *root*):

```
# rm ????*
```

This command took a *long* time to execute. When about two-thirds of the directory was gone, I realized (with horror) what was happening: I was deleting all files with four or more characters in the filename.

The story got worse. They hadn't made a backup in about five months. (By the way, this article should give you plenty of reasons for making regular backups *(21.02)*) By the time I had restored the files I had deleted (a several-hour process in itself; this was on an ancient version of UNIX with a horrible *backup* utility) and checked (by hand) all the files against our printed copy of the business plan, I had resolved to be *very careful* with my *rm* commands.

—*ML*

24.03 Tricks for Making rm Safer

Here's a summary of ways to protect yourself from accidentally deleting files:

- Use *rm −i*, possibly as an alias (articles 22.11 and 24.06).

- Make *rm −i* less painful (article 24.05).

- Write a "delete" script that moves "deleted" files to a temporary directory (article 24.07).

- The *tcsh (1.08)* shell has an *rmstar* variable that makes the shell ask for confirmation when you type something like rm *.

- Use a more comprehensive "safe delete" program, like the one described in article 24.08.

- Use revision control (article 21.12).

- Make your own backups, as explained in article 21.02.

If you want to delete with wild abandon, use *rm −f* (article 24.09).

—*ML*

24.04 Answer "Yes" or "No" Forever with yes

Some commands—like *rm −i*, *find −ok*, and so on—ask users to answer a "do it or not?" question from the keyboard. For example, you might use a file-deleting program named *del* that asks before deleting each file:

```
% del *
Remove file1? y
Remove file2? y
    ...
```

If you answer y, then the file will be deleted.

What if you want to run a command that's going to ask you 200 questions and you want to answer y to all of them, but you don't want to type all those y's in from the keyboard? Pipe the output of yes to the command; it will answer y for you:

```
% yes | del *
Remove file1?
Remove file2?
    ...
```

If you want to answer n to all the questions, you can do:

```
% yes n | del *
```

> **Note:** Not all UNIX commands read their standard input for answers to prompts. If a command opens your terminal (*/dev/tty* (47.20)) directly to read your answer, **yes** won't work.

yes knows how to say more than just *y* or *n*. Article 44.07 shows how to test a terminal with *yes*.

—JP

24.05 A Faster Way to Remove Files Interactively

[The rm –i *command asks you about each file, separately. The method in this article can give you the safety without the hassle of typing* y *as much.—JP]*

Another approach, which I recommend, is that you create a new script or alias, and use that alias whenever you delete files. Call the alias *del* or *Rm*, for instance. This way, if you ever execute your special delete command when it doesn't exist, no harm is done—you just get an error. If you get into this habit, you can start making your delete script smarter. Here is one that asks you about each file if there are three or less files specified. For more than three files, it displays them all and asks you once if you wish to delete them all:

del

```
#!/bin/sh
case $# in
0)      echo "`basename $0`: you didn't say which file(s) to delete"; exit 1;;
[123]) /bin/rm -i "$@" ;;
*)      echo "$*"
        echo do you want to delete these files\?
        read a
        case "$a" in
        [yY]*) /bin/rm "$@" ;;
        esac
        ;;
esac
```

—BB

24.06 Safer File Deletion in some Directories

Using *noclobber* (14.06) and read-only files only protects you from a few occasional mistakes. A potentially catastrophic error is typing:

```
% rm * .o
```

instead of:

```
% rm *.o
```

In the blink of an eye, all of your files would be gone. A simple, yet effective, preventive measure is to create a file called *−i* in the particular directory in which you want extra protection:

touch *22.07*
./- *24.13*

```
% touch ./-i
```

In the above case, the * is expanded to match all of the filenames in the directory. Because the file *−i* is alphabetically listed *(53.03)* before any file except those that start with one of these characters: !#$%&`()*+,, the *rm* command sees the *−i* file as a command-line argument. When *rm* is executed with its *−i* option *(22.11)*, files will not be deleted unless you verify the action. This still isn't perfect. If you have a file that starts with a comma (,) in the directory, it will come before the file starting with a dash, and *rm* will not get the *−i* argument first.

The *−i* file also won't save you from errors like:

```
% rm [a-z]* .o
```

[Two comments about Bruce's classic and handy tip: first, if lots of users each make a *−i* file in each of their zillions of subdirectories, that could waste a lot of disk inodes *(1.22)*. It might be better to make one *−i* file in your home directory and hard link *(25.04)* the rest to it, like:

~ *15.12*

```
% cd
% touch ./-i
% cd somedir
% ln ~/-i .
    ...
```

Second, to save disk blocks, make sure the *−i* file is zero-length—use the *touch* command, not *vi* or some other command that puts characters in the file.—*JP*]

—*BB*

24.07 *Safe Delete: Pros and Cons*

To protect themselves from accidentally deleting files, some users create a "trash" directory somewhere, and then write a "safe delete" program that, instead of *rm*ing a file, moves it into the *trash* directory. The implementation can be quite complex, but a simple alias will do most of what you want:

```
alias del "mv \!* ~/trash"
```

Of course, now your deleted files collect in your *trash* directory, so you have to clean that out from time to time. You can do this either by hand or automatically, via a *cron (42.12)* entry like:

&& *46.09*
−r *24.16*

```
23 2 * * * cd $HOME/trash && rm -rf *
```

This deletes everything in the trash directory at midnight daily. To restore a file that you deleted, you have to look through your trash directory by hand and put the file back in the right place. That may not be much more pleasant than poking through your garbage to find the tax return you threw out by mistake, but (hopefully) you don't make lots of mistakes.

There are plenty of problems with this approach. Obviously, if you delete two files with the same name in the same day, you're going to lose one of them. A shell script could (presumably) handle this problem, though you'd have to generate a new name for the deleted file. There are also lots of nasty side effects and "gotchas," particularly if you want an *rm −r* equivalent, if you want this approach to work on a network of workstations, or if you use it to delete files that are shared by a team of users.

Unfortunately, this is precisely the problem. A "safe delete" that isn't really safe may not be worth the effort. A safety net with holes in it is only good if you can guarantee in advance that you won't land in one of the holes. You can patch some of the holes by replacing this simple alias with a shell script. But you can't fix all of them. For a real solution, see Jonathan Kamens' article on *delete (24.08)*.

—ML

24.08 delete: Protecting Files from Accidental Deletion

The problem of protecting users from accidental file deletion is one that many people have encountered, and therefore there are many solutions of different types already implemented and available. Which solution you choose depends on the features you want it to have and on how you want it to do its job. Many people do not use the shell-script solutions described above *(24.07)*, because they are too slow or too unreliable or because they don't allow deleted files to be recovered for long enough.

For example, Purdue University runs a large network of many different machines that utilize some local file space and some NFS *(1.33)* file space. Their file recovery system, *entomb*, replaces certain system calls (for example, *open*(2), *unlink*(2)) with *entomb* functions which check to see if a file would be destroyed by the requested system call; if so, the file is backed up (by asking a local or remote *entomb* daemon to do so) before the actual system call is performed.

The advantages of this system are that you don't have to create any new applications to do safe file removal—the standard *rm* program will automatically do the right thing, as will *mv* and any other programs that have the potential of erasing files. Even *cat a b > a* is recoverable.

A disadvantage of this system is that you have to have the source code for your UNIX system and be able to recompile its utilities, in order to link them against the *entomb* libraries. Furthermore, if you wish to install this system on your machines, you have to be able to install it on *all* of them. If someone learns *entomb* on a machine you manage and then wants to use it on a workstation in a private lab for which you do not have source code, it can't be done. Also, there is a danger of people getting used to *entomb* being there to save them if they make mistakes, and then losing a file when they use *rm* or *mv* on a system that doesn't have *entomb*.

If you don't have strict control over all the machines on which you want to have file-deletion protection, or if you don't have source code and therefore can't use something like *entomb*, there are several other options available. One of them is the *delete* package, written at MIT.

delete overcomes several of the disadvantages of *entomb*. It is very simple, compiles on virtually any machine, and doesn't require any sort of superuser access to install. This means that if you learn to use *delete* on one system and then move somewhere else, you can take it with you by getting the source code and simply recompiling it on the new system. Furthermore, *delete* intentionally isn't named *rm*, so that people who use it know they are using it and therefore don't end up believing that files removed with *rm* can be recovered. However, this means that users have to be educated to use *delete* instead of *rm* when removing files.

delete works by renaming files with a prefix that marks them as deleted. For example, *delete foo* would simply rename the file *foo* to *.#foo*. Here's an example of the *delete*, *undelete*, *lsdel*, and *expunge* commands in action:

The directory starts with three files:
```
% ls
a        b        c
```

One of the files is deleted:
```
% delete a
```

*The deleted file doesn't show up with normal ls because the name
now starts with a dot (.). However, it shows up when files starting with .
are listed or when the lsdel command is used:*
```
% ls
b        c
```
−A 17.12
```
% ls -A
.#a      b        c
% lsdel
a
```

Bringing the file back with undelete leaves us back where we started:
```
% undelete a
% ls
a        b        c
```

We can delete everything:
```
% delete *
% lsdel
a  b  c
```

We can expunge individual files or the current working directory:
```
% expunge a
% lsdel
b  c
% expunge
```

After the last expunge, there are no files left at all:
```
% lsdel
% ls -A
%
```

The technique used by *delete* has some advantages and some disadvantages.

The advantages include:

- It works on any filesystem type—local, NFS, AFS, RFS, whatever. You don't have to have special daemons running on your file servers in order for it to work, and there are no daemons to go down and prevent deleted file archiving from taking place.

- It maintains the directory locations in which deleted files are stored so that they can be undeleted in the same locations.

- It maintains file permissions and ownership so that undeleted files can be restored with them. Furthermore, deleted files can be undeleted by anyone who had permission to delete them in the first place, not just by the one individual who deleted them.

Disadvantages include:

- Deleted files are counted against a user's disk quota *(25.17)* until they are actually permanently removed (either by the system, a few days after they are deleted, or by the user with the *expunge* command that is part of the *delete* package). Some people would actually call this an advantage, because it prevents people from using deleted file space to store large files (something which is possible with *entomb*).

- Deleted files show up when a user does *ls −a*. This is considered a relatively minor disadvantage by most people, especially since files starting with a dot (.) are supposed to be hidden *(17.12)* most of the time.

- Deleted files have to be searched for in filesystem trees in order to expunge them, rather than all residing in one location as they do with *entomb*. This, too, is usually considered a minor disadvantage, since most systems already search the entire filesystem *(24.21)* each night automatically in order to delete certain temporary files.

- Only the *entomb* program protects files. A user can still blow away a file with *mv, cat a b > a*, etc. If your main concern is eliminating accidental file deletions with *rm*, this isn't much of a problem; furthermore, it is not clear that the extra overhead required to run something like *entomb* is worth the advantage gained (even if it is possible to do what *entomb* needs at your site).

entomb and *delete* represent the two main approaches to the problem of protection from accidental file erasure. Other packages of this sort choose one or the other of these basic techniques in order to accomplish their purposes.

delete

[Because we assume that you don't have access to source for the entire UNIX operating system, we provide only *delete* (and its associated programs, *lsdel*, *undelete*, and *expunge*), on the Power Tools disk.— *TOR*]

—JIK

24.09 Deletion with Prejudice: rm –f

The –f option to rm is the extreme opposite of –i (22.11). It says "just delete the file; don't ask me any questions." The "f" stands (allegedly) for "force," but this isn't quite right. rm –f won't force the deletion of something that you aren't allowed to delete. (To understand what you're allowed to delete, you need to understand file access permissions (23.02).)

What, then, does rm –f do, and why would you want to use it?

- Normally, rm asks you for confirmation if you tell it to delete files to which you don't have write access—you'll get a message like Override protection 444 for foo? (The UNIX filesystem allows you to delete read-only files, provided you own the file and provided you have write access to the directory.) With –f, these files will be deleted silently.

- Normally, rm's exit status (46.07) is 0 if it succeeded and 1 if it failed to delete the file. With –f, rm's return status is always 0.

I find that I rarely use rm –f on the UNIX command line, but I almost always use it within shell scripts. In a shell script, you (probably) don't want to be interrupted by lots of prompts should rm find a bunch of read-only files.

—ML

24.10 Deleting Files with Odd Names

A perennial problem is deleting files that have strange characters (or other oddities) in their names. The next few articles contain some hints for:

- Deleting files with random control characters in their names (article 24.11).

- Deleting files with a "null" name (article 24.12).

- Deleting files whose names that start with a dash (article 24.13).

- Deleting files with "unprintable" filenames (article 24.14).

- Deleting files by using the inode number (article 24.15).

- Deleting directories, and problems that can arise (article 24.16).

We'll also give hints for:

- Deleting unused (or rarely used) files (articles 24.18 and 24.19).

- Deleting all the files in a directory, except for one or two (article 24.20).

—ML

24.11 Using Wildcards to Delete Files with Strange Names

Filenames can be hard to handle if their names include control characters or characters that are special to the shell. Here's a directory with three oddball filenames:

```
% ls
What now
a$file
prog|.c
program.c
```

When you type those filenames on the command line, the shell interprets the special characters (space, dollar sign, and vertical bar) instead of including them as part of the filename. There are several ways *(24.10)* to handle this problem. One is with wildcards *(16.02)*. Type a part of the filename without the weird characters and use a wildcard to match the rest. As article 9.03 explains, the shell doesn't scan the filenames for other special characters after it interprets the wildcards, so you're (usually) safe if you can get a wildcard to match. For example, here's how to rename *What now* to *Whatnow*, remove *a$file*, and rename *prog|.c* to *prog.c*:

```
% mv What* Whatnow
% rm -i a*
rm: remove a$file? y
% mv prog?.c prog.c
```

Filenames with control characters are just another version of the same problem. Use a wildcard to match the part of the file that's troubling you. The real problem with control characters with filenames is that some control characters do weird things to your screen. Once I accidentally got a file with a CTRL-L in its name. Whenever I ran *ls*, it erased the screen before I could see what the filename was! Article 17.15 explains that on a BSD-based UNIX system, you can use *ls –q* instead of a plain *ls*; on System V, use *ls –b*. It should be easy to spot the offensive file and construct a wildcard expression to rename or delete it. (*ls –q* is the default on many modern BSD UNIX implementations. So if you're a BSD user, you may never see this problem.)

—*JP*

24.12 Deleting Files with the Null Name

I write this article with fear and trepidation; I've never done this, and *clri* is strong medicine. However, it's something that needs to be said.

I've seen several reports about files with null names—they evidently arise through some bad interaction between PCs running NFS *(1.33)* and UNIX systems. For lots of reasons, it's virtually impossible to delete a null-named file. The following technique has been recommended:

- Use *ls –ailF* to find out the inode number *(1.22)* of the directory with the null filename.

- Become superuser and dismount the filesystem that contains the directory with the null filename.

- Use the command `clri filesystem inode` to "clear" the *directory's* inode, where *inode* is the inode number of the directory that contains the null filename and *filesystem* is the name of the filesystem that contains this directory.

- Run *fsck*, and let it repair the damage.

—ML

24.13 *Handling a Filename Starting with a Dash (–)*

Sometimes you can slip and create a file whose name starts with a dash (–), like *–output* or *–f*. That's a perfectly legal filename. The problem is that UNIX command options usually start with a dash (–). If you try to type that filename on a command line, the command might think you're trying to type a command option.

In almost every case, all you need to do is "hide" the dash from the command. Start the filename with . / (dot slash). This doesn't change anything as far as the command is concerned; . / just means "look in the current directory" *(1.21)*. So here's how to remove the file *–f*:

```
% rm ./-f
```

(Most *rm* commands have a special option for dealing with filenames that start with a dash, but this trick should work on *all* UNIX commands.)

—JP

24.14 *Using unlink to Remove a File with a Strange Name*

Some versions of UNIX have a lot of trouble with eight-bit filenames—that is, filenames that contain non-ASCII *(53.03)* characters. The *ls –q (17.15)* command shows the non-ASCII characters as question marks (?), but usual tricks like *rm –i * (24.11)* skip right over the file. You can at least see exactly what the filename is by using *od –c (26.07)* to dump the current directory, using its relative pathname . (dot) *(1.21)*, character by character. (Note: some versions of UNIX have an *ls –b (17.15)* option that will do the same thing as *od –c*, but a lot more easily.)

```
% ls -q
   ????
afile
bfile
% rm -i *
afile: ? n
bfile: ? n
% od -c .
   ...
00.....   \t 360 207 005 254   \0  \0  \0  \0  ...
```

If you can find the filename in the *od* listing of the directory (it will probably end with a series of NUL characters, like \0 \0 \0 . . .), you might be able to remove it directly by using the system call *unlink*(2) in a little C program *(54.08)* Put a backslash (\) before each of the octal bytes shown in the *od* output:

```
% vi unlink.c
    ...
% cat unlink.c
main()
{
    unlink("\t\360\207\005\254");
}
% cc unlink.c
% a.out
```

Another *ls* will tell you whether your program worked (there probably won't be any error messages if it doesn't work).

—*JP*

24.15 *Removing a Strange File by its I-number*

If wildcards don't work *(24.11)* to remove a file with a strange name, try getting the file's i-number *(1.22)*. Then use *find*'s *—inum* operator *(18.10)* to remove the file.

Here's a directory with a weird filename. *ls* (with its default *—q* option *(17.15)* on BSD UNIX) shows that it has three unusual characters in it. Running *ls —i* shows each file's i-number. The strange file has i-number 6239. Give the i-number to *find* and the file is gone:

```
% ls
adir        afile       b???file  bfile     cfile     dfile
% ls -i
   6253 adir          6239 b???file    6249 cfile
   9291 afile         6248 bfile       9245 dfile
% find . -inum 6239 -exec rm {} \;
% ls
adir    afile  bfile  cfile  dfile
```

Instead of deleting the file, I could also have renamed it to *newname* with the command:

```
% find . -inum 6239 -exec mv {} newname \;
```

If the current directory has large subdirectories, you'll probably want to add the *find* *—prune* operator *(18.24)* for speed.

—*JP*

24.16 Problems Deleting Directories

What if you want to get rid of a directory? The standard way, and the safest way, to do this is to use *rmdir* (remove directory):

```
% rmdir files
```

The *rmdir* command often confuses new users. It will *only* remove a directory if it is completely empty; otherwise, you'll get an error message:

```
% rmdir files
rmdir: files: Directory not empty
% ls files
%
```

As in the example, *ls* will often show that the directory is empty. What's going on?

It's common for editors and other programs to create "invisible" files (files with names beginning with a dot). The *ls* command normally doesn't list them; if you want to see them, you have to use *ls* −a (17.12):

```
% rmdir files
rmdir: files: Directory not empty
% ls -a files
.    ..    .BAK.textfile2
```

Here, we see that the directory wasn't empty after all: there's a backup file that was left behind by some editor. You may have used `rm` * to clean the directory out, but that won't work: *rm* also ignores files beginning with dots, unless you explicitly tell it to delete them. We really need a wildcard pattern like .??* (or more) (16.06):

```
% rmdir files
rmdir: files: Directory not empty
% ls -a files
.    ..    .BAK.textfile2
% rm files/.??*
% rmdir files
%
```

Other pitfalls might be files whose names consist of "non-printing" characters or blank spaces—sometimes these get created by accident or by malice (yes, some people think this is funny). Such files will usually give you "suspicious" *ls* output (17.14) (like a blank line).

If you don't want to worry about all these special cases, just use *rm* −*r*:

```
% rm -r files
```

This command removes the directory and everything that's in it, including other directories. A lot of people warn you about it; it's dangerous because it's easy to delete more than you realize. Personally, I use it all the time, and I've never made a mistake. I *never* bother with *rmdir*.

—*ML*

24.17 How Making and Deleting Directories Works

Every file in the UNIX filesystem—and a directory is just a file, albeit a rather special one—is represented by one *inode (1.22)* and one or more names (directory entries *(19.02)*). In a sense the inode *is* the file; each name is a *link (19.04)* to this inode. An ordinary file may have anywhere from one to several thousand links (the exact limit is system dependent), but a directory never has any fewer than two. Every directory has at least two names.

Suppose you start in */usr/tmp* and do a *mkdir x*. What are the two links to *x*? They are */usr/tmp/x* and */usr/tmp/x/.*, directory entries in */usr/tmp* and */usr/tmp/x*, respectively. This might seem rather odd at first: how can a directory name itself? It's not hard: first you create */usr/tmp/x*, a completely empty directory, then link */usr/tmp/x* to */usr/tmp/x/.*. All *link* does is take its first name and turn it into an inode—the file itself—then make a new entry for the second name, pointing to that inode. You must also link */usr/tmp* to */usr/tmp/x/..* to make a properly formed directory. The *mkdir* program and system call both do all this properly; and there is no other way for anyone except the superuser *(1.24)* to create a directory.

Here is where the trouble creeps in. All *unlink*(2) does is take the name it is given, convert it to an inode, and remove the name. If the name was the last link to that inode, the file itself is destroyed as well; if not, it is left intact and may still be accessed by its other name(s). So what happens if you unlink a directory? Well, if it is completely empty, it goes away and everything is fine. However, if it still has . and .. in it—and it almost certainly will—things are not so good. The . link to the directory itself still exists, so the file that is the directory is not deleted. The name */usr/tmp/x is* deleted, and that leaves us with a pretty problem: how can we get rid of that last . and ..?

The answer is that we cannot. That directory will stick around forever. Worse, it has in it another name for, or link to, */usr/tmp*, which means that that, too, cannot be deleted. Of course, *fsck* (which does not use the regular filesystem mechanisms) can clean this up, but this usually requires a system shutdown. [*fsck* is a filesystem-checking program that the system administrator runs.—*JP*] For this reason, again, only the superuser may unlink a directory. Ordinary processes must use use the *rmdir* program or system call.

Incidentally, the *mkdir*(2) and *rmdir*(2) system calls do not exist on older UNIX systems. On these systems, you must use careful *fork–exec (40.02)* sequences to run the *mkdir* and *rmdir* programs.

—CT in *net.unix* on Usenet, *25 July 1986*

24.18 Deleting (BSD) Manual Pages that Aren't Read

The BSD *man (52.01)* command comes with unformatted manual pages in directories named */usr/man/man* ... or */usr/share/man* .... It also has empty directories for formatted manual pages named */usr/man/cat* ... or */usr/share/cat* ....
As people use *man* to read different pages, the *man* command puts each formatted manual page in these *cat* directories so they don't have to be formatted the next time they're read.*

The formatted manual pages can take a lot of disk space, though. You can keep preformatted copies of "high-demand" manual entries by removing those that prove not to be in high demand:

–atime *22.05*

```
find /usr/man/cat? -atime +5 -exec rm -f {} \;
```

—*CT* in *comp.unix.questions* on Usenet, *19 April 1987*

24.19 Deleting Stale Files

Sooner or later, a lot of junk collects in your directories: files that you don't really care about and never use. It's possible to write *find (18.01)* commands that will automatically clean these up. If you want to clean up regularly, you can add some *find* commands to your *crontab* file *(42.12)*.

Basically, all you need to do is write a *find* command that locates files based on their last access time (*–atime (18.05)*), and use *–ok* or *–exec (18.10)* to delete them. Such a command might look like this:

```
% find . -atime +60 -ok rm -f {} \;
```

This locates files that haven't been accessed in the last 60 days, asks if you want to delete the file, and then deletes the file. (If you run it from *cron*, make sure you use *–exec* instead of *–ok*; and make *absolutely sure* that the *find* won't delete files that you think are important.)

Of course, you can modify this *find* command to exclude (or select) files with particular names; for example, the command below deletes old core dumps and GNU Emacs backup files (whose names end in ~), but leaves all others alone:

```
% find . \( -name core -o -name "*~" \) -atime +60 -ok rm -f {} \;
```

If you take an automated approach to deleting stale files, here are some things to watch out for:

- There are plenty of files (for example, UNIX utilities and log files) that should *never* be removed. Never run any "automatic deletion" script on */usr* or / or any other "system" directory.

---

*Newer BSD releases, Net.2 and 4.4BSD, use a new manual page scheme. Only the preformatted "*cat*" files are used. (The unformatted versions are kept with the source, so that they will be updated to match any changes in the source ... or at least, to encourage this.)

- On some systems, executing a binary executable doesn't update the last access time. Since there's no reason to read these files, you can expect them to get pretty stale, even if they're used often. You don't want to delete them. If you cook up a complicated enough *find* command, you should be able to handle this automatically. Something like this should (at least partially) do the trick:

! *18.06*
–perm *18.15*

```
% find . -atime +30 ! -perm -111 ... -exec rm {} \;
```

- Along the same lines, you'd probably never want to delete C source code, so you might modify your *find* command to look like this:

```
% find . -atime +30 ! -perm -111 ! -name "*.c" ... -exec rm {} \;
```

- I personally find that automatically deleting files is an extreme and bizarre solution. I can't imagine deleting files without knowing exactly what I've deleted or without (somehow) saving the "trash" somewhere just in case I accidentally removed something important. You can use the *find –cpio* operator (if your system has it) to archive *(20.09)* the deleted files on tape.

OK, I've said that I don't really think that automated deletion scripts are a good idea. What's my solution, then?

I don't have a good comprehensive solution. I spend a reasonable amount of time (maybe an hour a month) going through directories and deleting stale files by hand. I also have a *clean* alias that I type whenever I think about it. It looks like this:

```
alias clean "rm *~ junk *.BAK core #*"
```

That is, this alias deletes all of my Emacs *(33.01)* backup files, Emacs autosave files (I admit, that's risky), files named *junk*, some other backup files, and core dumps *(55.01)*. I'll admit that since I *never* want to save these files, I could probably live with something like:

```
% find ~ \( -name "*~" -o -name core \) -atime +1 -exec rm {} \;
```

But still: automated deletion commands make me really nervous, and I'd prefer to live without them.

—ML

24.20 Removing Every File but One

One problem with UNIX: it's not terribly good at "excluding" things. There's no option to *rm* that says "do what you will with everything else, but please don't delete these files." You can sometimes create a complex wildcard expression *(1.16)* that does what you want—but sometimes that's a lot of work, or maybe even impossible.

Here's one place where UNIX's command substitution *(10.14)* operators (backquotes) come to the rescue. You can use use *ls* to list all the files, pipe the output into a *grep −v* or *egrep −v (28.03)* command, and then use backquotes to give the resulting list to *rm*. Here's what this command would look like:

```
% rm -i `ls -d *.txt | grep -v '^john\.txt$'`
```

[Actually, when you're matching just one filename, *fgrep −v −x (28.06)* might be better.—*JP*] This command deletes all files whose names end in *.txt*, except for *john.txt*. I've probably been more careful than you need to be about making sure there aren't any extraneous matches; in most cases, *grep −v john* would probably suffice. Using *ls −d (17.09)* makes sure that *ls* doesn't look into any sub-directories and give you those filenames. The *rm −i (22.11)* asks you before removing each file; if you're sure of yourself, omit the *−i*.

Of course, if you want to exclude two files, you can do that with *egrep*:

```
% rm `ls -d *.txt | egrep -v 'john|mary'`
```

(Not all *egrep* implementations support the *−v* option. Don't forget to quote the vertical bar (|), to prevent the shell from piping *egrep*'s output to *mary*.)

Another solution is the *nom (16.10)* script.

—ML

24.21 *Using find to Clear Out Unneeded Files*

Do you run *find* on your machine every night? Do you know what it has to go through just to find out if a file is three days old and smaller than 10 blocks or owned by "fred" or setuid root? This is why I tried to combine all the things we need done for removal of files into one big *find* script:

cleanup

```
#! /bin/sh
#
# cleanup - find files that should be removed and clean them
# out of the file system.

find / \(      \( -name '#*'                -atime +1 \)  \
         -o   \( -name ',*'                -atime +1 \)  \
         -o   \( -name rogue.sav           -atime +7 \)  \
         -o   \(       \( -name '*.bak'                   \
                    -o -name '*.dvi'                   \
                    -o -name '*.CKP'                   \
                    -o -name '.*.bak'                  \
                    -o -name '.*.CKP' \)  -atime +3 \)  \
         -o   \( -name '.emacs_[0-9]*'     -atime +7 \)  \
         -o   \( -name core                          \)  \
         -o   \( -user guest              -atime +9 \)  \
   \) -print -exec rm -f {} \; > /tmp/.cleanup 2>&1
```

2>&1 47.21

[This is an example of using a single *find* command to search for files with different names and last-access times (see article 18.05). As Chris points out, doing it all with one *find* is much faster, and less work for the disk, than running a lot of separate *find*s. The parentheses group each part of the expression. The neat indentation makes this big thing easier to read. The −print −exec at the end removes each file and also writes the filenames to standard output, where they're collected into a file named */tmp/.cleanup*—people can read it to see what files were removed. You should probably be aware that printing the names to */tmp/.cleanup* lets everyone see pathnames, like */home/joe/personal/resume.bak*, that some people might consider sensitive. Another thing to be aware of is that this *find* command starts at the root directory; you can do the same thing for your own directories.—*JP*]

—*CT* in *net.unix-wizards* on Usenet, *9 June 1985*

25

Other Ways to Get Disk Space

25.01 Instead of Removing a File, Empty it

Sometimes you don't want to remove a file completely—you just want to empty it:

- When you remove a file and create a new one with the same name, the new file will have your default permissions *(23.04)* and ownership *(23.03)*. It's better to empty the file now, then add new text later; this won't change the permissions and ownership.

- Completely empty files (ones that *ls* −*l* says have zero characters) don't take any disk space to store. (Except the few bytes that the directory entry *(19.02)* uses.)

- You can use the empty files as "place markers," to remind you that something was there or belongs there. Some UNIX logging programs won't write errors to their log files unless the log files already exist. Empty files work fine for that.

- Empty files hold a "timestamp" (just like files with text do) that shows when the file was last modified. I use empty files in some directories to remind me when I've last done something (backups, printouts *(22.09)*, etc.). The *find* −*newer (18.08, 18.09)* command can compare other files to a timestamp file.

Well, you get the idea by now.

How can you empty a file? Watch out: when some editors like *vi* say that a file has "no lines," *vi* may still append a newline character when it writes the file. Just one character still takes a block of disk space to store. Better:

- In the Bourne shell, the most efficient way is to redirect the output of a null command:

```
$ > afile
```

If the file already exists, that command will truncate the file without needing a subprocess.

- In the C shell copy the UNIX empty file, */dev/null (14.14)*, on top of the file:

```
% cp /dev/null afile
```

You can also "almost" empty the file, leaving just a few lines, this way:

tail 26.15
```
% tail afile > tmpfile
% cat tmpfile > afile
% rm tmpfile
```

That's especially good for log files that you never want to delete completely. Use *cat* and *rm*, not *mv*—*mv* will break the link to the original file (`afile`) and replace it with the temporary file.

—*JP*

25.02 Save Space with "Bit Bucket" Log Files and Mailboxes

Some UNIX programs—usually background or daemon programs—insist on writing a log file. You might not want the log file itself as much as you want the disk space that the log file takes. Here are a few tips:

- Some daemons will write to a log file only if the log file exists. If the daemon isn't running, try removing the log file.

- If you remove a log file and the daemon recreates it, look for command-line options or a configuration file setup that tells the daemon not to make the log file.

- If your system has symbolic links *(19.04)*, try replacing the log file with a symbolic link to */dev/null (14.14)*:

```
# rm logfile
# ln -s /dev/null logfile
```

If you're lucky, the daemon won't complain and will throw all its messages in the bit bucket. Watch out for programs that run at reboot or from the system *crontab (42.12)* to truncate and replace the log file. These programs might replace the symbolic link with a small regular file that will start growing again.

- Does a system mailbox for a user like *uucp* keep getting mail *(1.33)* that you want to throw away? You may be able to add a *.forward* file to the account's home directory with this single line:

```
/dev/null
```

Or add an alias in the system mail alias file that does the same thing:

```
uucp: /dev/null
```

If your system has a command like *newaliases* to rebuild the alias database, don't forget to use it after you make the change.

—JP

25.03   Unlinking Open Files isn't a Good Idea

[Some programmers write programs that make temporary files, open them, then unlink (remove) each file before they're done reading it (47.10). This keeps other people from deleting, reading, or overwriting a file. Because the file is opened by a process, UNIX removes the file's directory entry (its link*) but doesn't actually free the disk space until the process is done with the file.*

Here's why you shouldn't do that. (By the way, the point Chris makes about system administrators cleaning up full filesystems by emptying open files is a good one.) —JP]

To give people another reason not to unlink open files (besides that it does, er, "interesting" things under NFS *(1.33)*), consider the following:

```
multi 1000 </usr/dict/words >/tmp/file1
```

(*multi* is a program that makes *n* copies of its input; here *n* is 1000.) Now suppose */tmp (22.02)* runs out of space. You can:

```
rm /tmp/file1        # oops, file didn't actually go away
ps ax                # find the "multi" process
kill pid             # get rid of it
```

or you can:

/dev/null **14.14**
```
cp /dev/null /tmp/file1 # now have some time to fix things up
```

Bending the example a bit, suppose that */tmp* runs out of file space and there are a bunch of unlinked but open *(47.20)* files. To get rid of the space these occupy, you must kill the processes holding them open. However, if they are ordinary files, you can just trim them down to zero bytes.

There is one good reason to unlink open temporary files: if anything goes wrong, the temporary files will vanish. There is no other way to guarantee this absolutely. You must balance this advantage against the disadvantages.

—CT in net.unix-wizards *on Usenet, 9 September 1985*

25.04 Save Space with a Link

You might have copies of the same file in several directories because:

- Several different users need to read it (a data file, a program setup file, a telephone list, etc.).

- It's a program that more than one person wants to use. For some reason, you don't want to keep one central copy and put its directory in your search path *(9.05)*.

- The file has a strange name or it's in a directory you don't usually use. You want a name that's easier to type, but you can't use *mv*.

Instead of running *cp*, think about *ln*. There are lots of advantages to links *(19.03)*. One big advantage of hard links is that they don't use any disk space.* The bigger the file, the more space you save with a link. A symbolic link always takes some disk space, so a hard link might be better (unless you have to link across filesystems).

Some people don't use links because they think all links to a file need to have the same name. That's not true. A link can be named *myfile* in one directory and *file.allan* in another directory—UNIX keeps it all straight.

—JP

25.05 Limiting File Sizes

Here is a technique to keep you from creating large files (which can happen by accident, such as runaway programs). To set a maximum file size, use the C shell command (usually in your *.cshrc* file):

```
limit filesize max-size
```

In the Korn shell, use `ulimit -f` *max-size*. You can change the limit from the command line, too. For example, the *csh* and *ksh* commands below keep you from creating any files larger than 2 megabytes:

```
% limit filesize 2m
$ ulimit -f 2000
```

With this command, UNIX will refuse to allocate more disk space to any file that grows larger than 2 MB.

Similarly, on Berkeley systems, you can use *limit* and *ulimit* to restrict the size of core dump files *(55.01)*. Core dumps are generally large files and are often gen-

---

* The link entry takes a few characters in the directory where you make the link. Unless this makes the directory occupy another disk block, the space available on the disk doesn't change.

erated for innocuous reasons, such as invoking commands incorrectly. To set a maximum size for core dumps, execute one of these commands:

```
% limit coredumpsize max-size
$ ulimit -c max-size
```

To eliminate core dumps entirely, use 0 (zero) for *max-size*. Because core dumps are essential for effective debugging, any users who are actively debugging programs should know the command *unlimit coredumpsize*, which removes this restriction.

—*ML from the Nutshell Handbook System Performance Tuning*

25.06 *Compressing Files to Save Space*

Most files can be "squeezed" to take up less space. Let's say you have a text file. Each letter occupies a byte, but almost all of the characters in the file are alphanumeric or punctuation, and there are only about 70 such characters. Furthermore, most of the characters are (usually) lowercase; furthermore, the letter "e" turns up more often than "z," the letter "e" often shows up in pairs, and so on. All in all, you don't really need a full eight-bit byte per character. If you're clever, you can reduce the amount of space a file occupies by 50 percent or more.

compress

Compression algorithms are a complex topic that we can't discuss here. Fortunately, you don't need to know anything about them. Many UNIX systems have a good compression utility built in. It's called *compress*. Those of you who don't have it can find it on the Power Tools disk.

To compress a file, just give the command:

```
% compress filename
```

The file's name is changed to *filename*.Z. Some versions of *compress* tell you how much space you saved. In other cases, the *–v* option should force *compress* to tell you how much space you saved. The savings are usually between 30 and 70 percent.

If the file *shouldn't* be compressed—that is, if compressing the file wouldn't result in a savings—*compress* prints a message and leaves the file alone. You can use the *–f* option to "force" *compress* to compress such a file. This might be better if you're using *compress* within a shell script and don't want to worry about files that might *not* be compressed.

Compressed files are always binary files; even if they started out as text files, you can't read them. To get back the original file, use the *uncompress* utility:

```
% uncompress filename
```

You can omit the .Z at the end of the filename. If you just want to read the file but don't want to restore the original version, use the command *zcat*; this just decodes the file and dumps it to standard output. It's particularly convenient to pipe *zcat* into *more (26.03)* or *grep (28.01)*. The Power Tools disk has several scripts that work on compressed files, uncompressing and recompressing them automatically: editing with *zvi*, *zex*, and *zed* (25.10); viewing with *zview* (25.11) or *zmore*, *zless*, and *zpg* (26.05); or running almost any command that can read from a pipe with *zloop* (25.09).

There are a number of other compression utilities floating around the UNIX world. Of those that are commonly available, *compress* is the best. Unfortunately, it's the subject of a patent suit, so its future is in question; if the bad guys win, *compress* may become prohibitively expensive—in which case, UNIX vendors would probably stop shipping it, or make it an added-cost option. A poor second is a utility called *pack*. It works the same way (except that it uses a lowercase *.z* to indicate a compressed file). It just isn't as good at squeezing the last bit of space out of a file.

—*ML*

25.07 Save Space: tar and compress a Directory Tree

In the UNIX filesystem, files are stored in blocks (55.01). Each nonempty file, no matter how small, takes at least one block.* A directory tree full of little files can fill up a lot of partly empty blocks. A big file is more efficient because it fills all (except possibly the last) of its blocks completely.

The *tar* (20.05) command can read lots of little files and put them into one big file. Later, when you need one of the little files, you can extract it from the *tar* archive. Seems like a good space-saving idea, doesn't it? But *tar*, which was really designed for magnetic *tape archives*, adds "garbage" characters at the end of each file to make it an even size. So, a big *tar* archive uses about as many blocks as the separate little files do.

Okay, then why am I writing this article? Because the *compress* (25.06) utility can solve the problems. It squeezes files down—especially, compressing a file gets rid of repeated characters. Compressing a *tar* archive saves about 50 percent.

Making a compressed archive of a directory and all of its subdirectories is easy: *tar* copies the whole tree when you give it the top directory name. Just be sure to save the archive in some directory that won't be copied—so *tar* won't try to archive its own archive! I usually put the archive in the parent directory. For example, to archive my directory named *project*, I'd use the commands below. If you work on a system that has 14-character filename length limits, be sure that the archive filename (here, `project.tar.Z`) won't be too long. The *.tar.Z* extension isn't required, just a convention. Watch carefully for errors:

```
                 % cd project
    .. 1.21      % tar clf - . | compress > ../project.tar.Z
                 % cd ..
    −r 24.16     % rm -r project
```

The *tar l* (lowercase letter L) option will print messages if any of the files you're archiving have other hard links (19.04). If a lot of your files have other links,

---

*Completely empty files (zero characters) don't take a block.

archiving the directory may not save much disk space—the other links will keep the file on the disk, even after your *rm −r* command.

Any time you want a list of the files in the archive, use *tar t* or *tar tv*:

more 26.03

```
% zcat project.tar.Z | tar tvf - | more
rw-r--r--239/100      485 Oct  5 19:03 1991 ./Imakefile
rw-rw-r--239/100     4703 Oct  5 21:17 1991 ./scalefonts.c
rw-rw-r--239/100     3358 Oct  5 21:55 1991 ./xcms.c
rw-rw-r--239/100    12385 Oct  5 22:07 1991 ./io/input.c
rw-rw-r--239/100     7048 Oct  5 21:59 1991 ./io/output.c
    ...
```

To extract all the files from the archive, type:

```
% mkdir project
% cd project
% zcat ../project.tar.Z | tar xf -
```

Of course, you don't have to extract the files into a directory named *project*. You can read the archive file from other directories, move it to other computers, and so on.

You can also extract just a few files and/or directories from the archive. Be sure to use exactly the name shown by the *tar tv* command above. For instance, to restore the old subdirectory named *project/io* (and everything that was in it), you'd type:

```
% mkdir project
% cd project
% zcat ../project.tar.Z | tar xf - ./io
```

—JP

25.08 *How Much Disk Space?*

Two tools, *df* and *du*, report how much disk space is free and how much is used by any given directory. For each filesystem, *df* tells you the capacity, how much space is in use, and how much is free. By default, it lists both local and remote (i.e., NFS *(1.33)*) filesystems. Under BSD UNIX, the output from *df* looks like this:

```
% df
Filesystem    kbytes    used    avail  capacity  Mounted on
/dev/disk0a   889924  724308   76620    90%      /
/dev/disk3d   505463  376854   78062    83%      /benchmarks
/dev/disk5e   635287  553121   18637    97%      /field
/dev/disk2d   505463  444714   10202    98%      /research
/dev/disk1e   956094  623534  236950    72%      /homes
toy:/usr      498295  341419  107046    76%      /usr
toy:/           7495    5883     862    87%      /root
    ...
```

This report shows information about five local filesystems and two remote filesystems (from the system *toy*). The */research* and */field* filesystems are close to capacity (98 and 97 percent, respectively), while the other filesystems still have a lot of room left. You might want to take some action to free up some storage on these two filesystems. Note that a BSD filesystem that is 100 percent full really has 10 percent free space—but only the superuser *(1.24)* can use this last 10 percent, and that usually isn't a good idea.

df can be invoked in several other ways:

- If you already know that you're interested in a particular filesystem, you can use a command such as *df /homes* or *df . (.* means "the current directory" *(1.21))*.

- If your system uses NFS and you are interested only in local filesystems, use the command *df –t 4.2.* You should always use this command if remote file servers are down. If you have mounted remote disks that are unavailable, *df* will be extremely slow.

- If you are interested in inode *(1.22)* usage rather than filesystem data capacity, use the command *df –i.* This produces a similar report showing inode statistics.

If you are using the older System V filesystem, the report from *df* will look different. The information it presents, however, is substantially the same. Here is a typical report, taken from a XENIX system:

```
% df
/        (/dev/root ):      1758 blocks     3165 i-nodes
/u       (/dev/u    ):       108 blocks    13475 i-nodes
/us      (/dev/us   ):     15694 blocks     8810 i-nodes
```

There are 1758 physical blocks (always measured as 512-byte blocks, regardless of the filesystem's logical block size) and 3165 inodes available on the root filesystem. To find out the filesystem's total capacity, use *df –t.* The command *df –l* only reports on your system's local filesystems, omitting filesystems mounted by NFS or RFS. The *dfspace* command (available on Systems V.3 and V.4) produces a significantly nicer report that's similar to the BSD-style *df.* For each filesystem, *dfspace* shows the amount of free storage both in kilobytes and as a percentage of the filesystem's size.

It is often useful to know how much storage a specific directory requires. This can help you to determine if any users are occupying more than their share of storage. The *du* utility provides such a report. Here's a simple report from *du*:

```
% du
107     ./reports
888     ./stuff
32      ./howard/private
33      ./howard/work
868     ./howard
258     ./project/code
769     ./project
2634    .
```

This command shows that the current directory and all of its subdirectories occupy about 2.5 MB (2634 KB). The biggest directories in this group are *stuff* and *howard*, which have a total of 888 KB and 868 KB, respectively. The report also shows storage occupied by sub-subdirectories (*/howard/work*, etc.). *du* does not show individual files as separate items, unless you invoke it with the *−a* option. Note that System V reports disk usage in 512-byte blocks, not KB.

The *−s* option tells *du* to report the total amount of storage occupied by a directory; it suppresses individual reports for all subdirectories. For example:

```
% du -s
2634   .
```

This is essentially the last line of the previous report.

—*ML* from the Nutshell Handbook *System Performance Tuning*

25.09 *zloop: Run a Command on Compressed Files*

The good thing about compressing files *(25.06)* is that it saves disk space. The bad thing is that if there are lots of compressed files you want to access separately, typing all those *zcat* commands can get tedious and waste time.

I wrote a script named *zloop* that takes a command you want to run and a list of compressed files. It runs *zcat* on each file, separately, and pipes each *zcat* output to the command you gave. It shows the command line it ran and the output (if any) of the command. If the command returned nonzero status *(46.07)*, *zloop* prints a warning.

```
% ls
185.Z   187.Z   189.Z   191.Z   193.Z   195.Z   197.Z
186.Z   188.Z   190.Z   192.Z   194.Z   196.Z   198.Z
% zloop 'egrep "^Subject:.*group"' *.Z

==== zloop: zcat 185.Z | egrep "^Subject:.*group" ====
Subject: List of Active Newsgroups

==== zloop: zcat 186.Z | egrep "^Subject:.*group" ====
Subject: Alternative Newsgroup Hierarchies

==== zloop: zcat 187.Z | egrep "^Subject:.*group" ====
zloop: note: that command returned 1 (non-zero) status:
       'zcat 187.Z | egrep "^Subject:.*group"'

==== zloop: zcat 188.Z | egrep "^Subject:.*group" ====
Subject: Checkgroups message (with INET groups)
Subject: Checkgroups message (without INET groups)
Subject: Monthly checkgroups posting
    ...
```

zloop is sort of verbose for a UNIX command—but you can make the script quieter if you want to. The status messages are sent to standard error. So, if you want to send *zloop* output through a pager like *more*, tell the shell to merge standard output and standard error:

|& *14.05*
```
% zloop 'egrep "^Subject:.*group"' *.Z |& more
```

With a plain pipe (|), the status messages and command output can be jumbled *(14.04)*.

In case it isn't clear: when you redirect the output of *zloop*, you're redirecting the output of all the commands that *zloop* runs. For instance, typing this command:

tr 36.09
-2 36.15

```
% zloop 'tr "[A-Z]" "[a-z]" | pr -2' *.Z > toprint
```

is like typing these commands by hand:

(14.07

```
( zcat file1.Z | tr "[A-Z]" "[a-z]" | pr -2
  zcat file2.Z | tr "[A-Z]" "[a-z]" | pr -2
  zcat file3.Z | tr "[A-Z]" "[a-z]" | pr -2
) > toprint
```

zloop

and feeding the standard output of that subshell *(14.07)*, and all of the commands, to the *toprint* file. You may never do anything that fancy with *zloop*. The script is on the Power Tools disk.

—JP

25.10 *Edit Compressed Files with zvi, zex, and zed*

Compressed files *(25.06)* save disk space. But compressed files aren't as convenient to work with: you have to uncompress them before you can read or edit them. This script makes editing easier. It uncompresses the files and starts a text editor: *vi*, *ex*, or *ed*. (It's easy to modify this to use other editors.) The *vi* and *ex* editors can edit several files *(31.04)*; this script handles that. After you edit all the files, the script recompresses them in the background so that you don't have to wait. There's one more bit of trickery here: instead of uncompressing all files you specify before it starts the editor, the script uncompresses just the first file—it does the rest in the background while you're editing the first file. (It figures out what all the uncompressed files will be named. By the time the editor gets to them, they should have been uncompressed.)

This makes it easy to save a lot of disk space by keeping your files compressed most of the time. The response is almost as fast as editing an uncompressed file, especially if the first file on the command line is a small one. Here's an example. I'll edit the files *qlog.Z* and */usr/central/data.Z* with *vi*. Next, I'll run *zed* on *bigfile.Z*:

```
% zvi qlog.Z /usr/central/data        The .Z isn't required
```

   ...Edit the two files like a normal vi multiple-file session...

```
zvi: recompressing qlog /usr/central/data in the background...
% zed bigfile < edscr
173571                                  ed's file size counts
183079
zed: recompressing bigfile in the background...
```

If there are any errors, the program prompts you when it can—otherwise you'll get e-mail *(1.33)* with a copy of the error messages. Please test this script carefully

zvi

on your system before you use it. All this trickery could need a little tweaking to work right.

Most of the script is pretty straightforward. Here's one trick it uses to help performance: if you give more than one filename on the command line, it uncompresses the first file, starts the editor with a list of all the filenames—then uncompresses the rest of the files in the background. This means the script won't work with editors like *Emacs (33.01)* that open all the files right away.

This section is interesting. It's the part that uncompresses background files. If there's an error in the background, how can the script catch it?

```
test -n "$bgfiles" && $uncompress $bgfiles >$t 2>&1 &

$prog $files
if [ -s $t ]
then
    echo "$myname: 'uncompress $bgfiles' bombed:" 1>&2
    cat $t 1>&2
    $echo "Should I try to compress all files [ny](n)? $nnl"
    read ans
```

The standard output and standard error of the background job goes to a temporary file, `$t`. The editor (`$prog`) runs. After you quit the editor, the *test* ([ ]) *(46.19)* −*s* option checks the temporary file. If the file isn't empty, the script shows you the errors and asks you whether the files should be recompressed.

The script is written to have two other links *(19.03)*. You may want to make more or fewer links though, depending on the editors your system has. If you install the script from the Power Tools disk, the links will be made for you. If you type in the script, put it in an executable file named *zvi*. Then make the links:

```
% chmod 755 zvi
% ln zvi zex
% ln zvi zed
```

The script tests the name it was called with, from `$0`, to decide which editor to use. This trick saves disk space. You can change the editors it uses by modifying the script and adding or removing links.

The absolute pathnames at the start of the script may need to be changed for your system.

—*JP*

25.11 Read-only Editing of Compressed Files with zview

The *zvi* *(25.10)* script edits compressed files *(25.06)*. If you use the read-only version of *vi* called *view*, you really don't need to use *zvi*. The script *zview* doesn't need the tricks that *zvi* uses because read-only files don't need to be recompressed. This script puts a temporary copy of each file in the */tmp* *(22.02)* directory and gives all those filenames to *view*. Instead of uncompressing all files you specify before it starts the editor, the script uncompresses just the first file—it does the rest in the background while you're editing the first file. Use the *vi* commands for editing multiple files *(31.04)*. When you finish *zview*, it deletes the temporary uncompressed copies.

The */tmp* filesystem is shared by everyone, so filenames there need to be unique *(22.03)*. *zview* translates the filenames you give it into names that should be unique but still easy for you to recognize. For example, this command line:

```
% zview afile bin/aprog
```

would edit files named something like */tmp/ZV99990_afile* and */tmp/ZV99991_bin_aprog*. (The first 14 characters will be unique, and *view* will display the whole filename. There shouldn't be problems on filesystems with 14-character filename length limits.)

zview

Like the *compress* utilities, *zview* doesn't make you type the *.Z* filename extension—though you can if you want to. That lets the script work with wildcards *(16.02)*. The first part of the script fragment below does that. Handling filename extensions is one of the things *expr*(47.28) is good at. The script also uses *expr* for arithmetic—to make a series of temporary filenames, as explained above. The second chunk of code below also uses a *case* to match *(46.06)* a slash (/) in the pathname; if there is one, the script uses *echo* and *tr (36.09)* to turn slashes into underscores (_).

```
case "$arg" in
*.Z) file="`/bin/expr $arg : '\(.*\).Z'`" ;;  # $arg WITHOUT THE .Z
*) file="$arg" ;;  # ASSUME FILE HAS A .Z ON END
esac

# GET TEMPORARY FILENAME (NO SLASHES EXCEPT IN $t PART).
n="`/bin/expr $n + 1`"
# USE case TO SEE IF WE NEED tr (SAVES TIME; case IS BUILT IN):
case "$file" in
*/*) tfile=${t}${n}_"`echo $file | tr / _`" ;;
*) tfile=${t}${n}_"$file" ;;
esac
```

You should check the portable *echo*(48.10) and the *zcat=* pathname at the start of the script; they may need to be changed for your system.

—*JP*

25.12 Compressing a Directory Tree: Fine-tuning

Here's a quick little command that will compress *(25.06)* files in the current directory and below. It uses *find (18.02)* to find the files, recursively, and pick the files it should compress:

−size *18.14*
xargs *10.19*

```
% find . ! -perm -0100 -size +1 -type f -print | xargs compress -v
```

This command finds all files that:

- Are not executable (! -perm -0100), so we don't compress shell scripts and other program files.

- Are bigger than one block, since it won't save any disk space to compress a file that takes one disk block or less. But, depending on your filesystem, the -size +1 may not really match files that are one block long. You may need to use -size +2, -size +1024c, or something else.

- Are regular files (-type f) and not directories, named pipes, etc.

The *−v* switch to *compress* tells you the names of the files and how much they're being compressed. If your system doesn't have *xargs*, use:

```
% find . ! -perm -0100 -size +1 -type f -exec compress -v {} \;
```

Tune the *find* expressions to do what you want. Here are some ideas—for more, read your system's *find* manual page:

! -name *.Z	Skip any file that's already compressed (filename ends with *.Z*).
-links 1	Only compress files that have no other (hard) links.
-user *yourname*	Only compress files that belong to you.
-atime +60	Only compress files that haven't been accessed (read, edited, etc.) for more than 60 days.

You might want to put this in a job that's run every month or so by *at (42.03)* or *cron (42.12)*.

—*JP*

25.13 Save Space in Executable Files with strip

(25.14)

After you compile *(54.08)* and debug a program, there's a part of the executable binary that you can delete to save disk space. The *strip* command does the job. Note that once you strip a file, you can't use a symbolic debugger like *dbx* on it!

Here's an example. I'll compile a C program and list it. Then I'll strip it and list it again. How much space you save depends on several factors, but you'll almost always save something.

−s 18.14

```
% cc -o echoerr echoerr.c
% ls -ls echoerr
  52 -rwxr-xr-x   1 jerry      24706 Nov 18 15:49 echoerr
% strip echoerr
% ls -ls echoerr
  36 -rwxr-xr-x   1 jerry      16656 Nov 18 15:49 echoerr
```

If you know that you want a file stripped when you compile it, use *cc* with its −s option. If you use *ld*—say, in a *makefile (29.12)*—use the −s option there.

Here's a shell script named *stripper* that finds all the unstripped executable files in your *bin* directory *(5.02)* and strips them. It's a quick way to save space on your account. (The same script, searching the whole filesystem, will save even more space for system administrators—but watch out for unusual filenames *(10.20)*):

stripper

xargs *10.19*

```
#! /bin/sh
skipug="! -perm -4000 ! -perm -2000"  # SKIP SETUID, SETGID FILES
find $HOME/bin -type f \( -perm -0100 $skipug \) -print |
xargs file |
sed -n '/executable .*not stripped/s/:TAB.*//p' |
xargs -t strip
```

The *find (18.02)* finds all executable files that aren't setuid or setgid *(25.14)* and runs *file (26.08)* to get a description of each. The *sed* command skips shell scripts and other files that can't be stripped. *sed* searches for lines from *file* like:

```
/usr/local/bin/xemacs:TABxxx... executable xxx... not stripped
```

with the word "executable" followed by "not stripped"—*sed* removes the colon, tab, and description, then passes the filename to *strip*.

—*JP*

25.14 Don't Strip Carelessly

One nice way to save space in your filesystem is by running *strip (25.13)* on directly-executable (binary) files. You'll probably think of running it recursively with *find (18.02)*. Be careful. On some operating systems, using *strip* on a setuid file *(1.23)* will strip the setuid bit; the program won't be setuid anymore. It's best to tell *find* to skip setuid and setgid files. For instance, the command below finds all world-executable files *(18.15)* that are not setuid or setgid *(18.16)*:

```
% find . -type f -perm -0001 ! -perm -4000 ! -perm -2000 ...
```

Other files that shouldn't be stripped include the UNIX kernel (like */vmunix*) and files that programmers need to debug.

—*JP*

25.15 Trimming a Directory

In article 5.07, we mentioned that it's good to keep directories relatively small. Large directories can make your system seem slower because it takes more time to look up files. How small is "small"? Under 60 files is great.

However, there's a problem: the size of a directory can *only* increase. That is, creating new files can make a directory bigger; deleting new files doesn't, in itself, make the directory any smaller. I'm not saying that a directory grows every time you create a new file. That's not true; if you've deleted a file, the directory will have an empty entry in it, and UNIX can re-use the empty entry. But the fact remains: a directory can only get bigger; it can never get smaller, unless you delete it. [Some BSD systems will "squeeze" directories smaller. —*JP*]

So let's say you've been sloppy and have a few directories around with hundreds of files, a lot of which is junk you don't need (I've been there). You could just delete the junk, which would make your disk happier, but you haven't reduced the directory's size. What do you do? Here's a trick:

1. Rename the old directory:

   % **mv project project.toobig**

2. Create a new directory with the old directory's name:

   % **mkdir project**

3. Move *only* the files you want from the old directory into the new directory:

   % **mv project.toobig/*.txt project**

4. Now the old directory contains only junk. Delete the old obese directory and everything in it:

   % **rm -r project.toobig**

—*ML*

25.16 Trimming a Huge Directory

Some implementations of the BSD fast filesystem never truncate directories. That is, when you delete a file, the filesystem marks its directory entry as "invalid," but doesn't actually delete the entry. The old entry can be re-used when someone creates a new file, but will never go away. Therefore, the directories themselves can only get larger with time. Directories usually don't occupy a huge amount of space, but searching through a large directory is noticeably slow. So you should avoid letting directories get too large.

On many UNIX systems, the only way to "shrink a directory" is to move all of its files somewhere else and then remove it; for example:

```
ls -lgd old                                Get old owner, group, and mode
mkdir new; chown user new; chgrp group new; chmod mode new
```

.[^A--/-^?] *16.06*

```
mv old/.??* old/.[^A--/-^?] old/* new     ^A and ^? are CTRL-a and DEL
rmdir old
mv new old
```

This method also works on V7-ish filesystems. It cannot be applied to the root of a filesystem.

Other implementations of the BSD fast filesystem do truncate directories. They do this after a complete scan of the directory has shown that some number of trailing fragments are empty. Complete scans are forced for any operation that places a new name into the directory—such as *creat*(2) or *link*(2). In addition, new names are always placed in the earliest possible free slot. Hence, on these systems there is another way to shrink a directory. [How do you know if your BSD filesystem truncates directories? Try the pseudo-code below (but use actual commands), and see if it has an effect.—*ML*]

```
while (the directory can be shrunk) {
    mv (file in last slot) (some short name)
    mv (the short name) (original name)
}
```

This works on the root of a filesystem as well as subdirectories.

Neither method should be used if some external agent (for example, a daemon) is busy looking at the directory. The first method will also fail if the external agent is quiet but will resume *and* hold the existing directory open (for example, a daemon program, like *sendmail*, that rescans the directory, but which is currently stopped or idle). The second method requires knowing a "safe" short name—i.e., a name that doesn't duplicate any other name in the directory.

I have found the second method useful enough to write a shell script to do the job. I call the script *squoze*:

squoze

IFS *36.19*

: *47.09*

-r *26.16*

-i *22.11*
&& *46.09*

```
#! /bin/sh
#
# squoze
last=
ls -ldg
IFS='
'
while :
do
    set `ls -f | tail -10r`
    for i do
        case "$i" in "$last"|.|..) break 2;; esac
        # _ (underscore) is the "safe, short" filename
        /bin/mv -i "$i" _ && /bin/mv _ "$i"
    done
    last="$i"
done
ls -ldg
```

[The *ls* −*f* option lists entries in the order they appear in the directory; it doesn't sort. —*JP*] This script does not handle filenames with embedded newlines. It is, however, safe to apply to a *sendmail* queue while *sendmail* is stopped.

—*CT* in *comp.unix.admin* on Usenet, *22 August 1991*

25.17 Disk Quotas

No matter how much disk space you have, you will eventually run out. One way the system administrator can force users to clean up is to impose quotas on disk usage. BSD UNIX supports a disk quota system which will enforce the quotas the system administrator sets up. Prior to V.4, System V had no quota system at all. In Release V.4, System V supports quotas for BSD-style (UFS) filesystems.

If you're a user, how do quotas affect you? Sooner or later, you may find that you're over your quota. Quotas are maintained on a per-filesystem basis. They may be placed on disk storage (the number of blocks) and on inodes (the number of files). The quota system maintains the concept of *hard* and *soft* limits. When you exceed a soft limit, you'll get a warning (WARNING: disk quota exceeded), but you can continue to accumulate more storage. The warning will be repeated whenever you log in. At some point (i.e., after some number of sessions in which the storage stays above the soft limit), the system loses patience and refuses to allocate any more storage. You'll get a message like OVER DISK QUOTA: NO MORE DISK SPACE. At this point, you must delete files until you're again within the soft limit. Users are never allowed to exceed their hard limit. This design allows you to have large temporary files without penalty, provided that they do not occupy too much disk space long-term.

There may also be a quota on the number of files (i.e., inodes *(1.22)*) you can own per filesystem. It works exactly the same way; you'll get a warning when you exceed the soft limit; if you don't delete some files, the system will eventually refuse to create new files.

—*ML*

25.18 Huge Files Might Not Take a Lot of Disk Space

If you're doing filesystem cleanup, you use *ls* −*l*, and see a file with ten million bytes... "Yipes!" you say, "That must be eating a lot of disk space!" But if you remove the file, *df* *(25.08)* shows almost no difference in disk space. Why?

It could be a *sparse file*, a file with a lot more NUL characters in it than anything else (that's a general definition, but it's basically correct). The command *ls* −*ls* *(18.14)* will show you sparse files; the disk usage in the first column will be relatively much smaller than the character count:

```
% ls -ls
total 128
   64 -rw-r--r--  1 jerry     8413616 Nov  9 16:49 core
   64 -rw-r--r--  1 jerry       64251 Nov  7 18:22 dns.tar
```

Programs that use *dbm* (*data base management* subroutines) often create sparse files because *dbm* uses file location as part of its hashing and tries to spread out entries in the database file so there is lots of blank space between them.

Many UNIX filesystems (although not all—the Andrew File System, for example does not) support the ability to greatly reduce the amount of space taken up by a file that is mostly NULs by not really storing the file blocks that are filled with NULs. Instead, the OS keeps track of how many blocks of NULs there are between each block that has something other than NULs in it, and feeds NULs to anybody who tries to read the file, even though they're not really being read off a disk.

You can create a sparse file in C by using *fopen*(3) to open a file and *fseek*(3) to move the file pointer far past the end of the file without writing anything. The file up to where you *fseek* will contain NULs, and the kernel (probably) won't save all of those NULs to disk.

By the way, sparse files can be a problem to copy. The kernel isn't smart enough to figure out you're feeding it a sparse file if you actually feed it the NULs. Therefore, standard file copying programs like *cp* that just read the file in and write it out in a different location lose, because they end up creating a file that really does take up as much as space physically as there are NULs in the abstract file object. Then your disk space might really be in trouble. [Some operating systems have a *cp* −*z* option to solve this problem.— *TC*]

—*JIK, JP*

Part Four

Looking Inside Files

It's amazing how much there is to know about files without ever opening them. But all the cataloging and organizing and finding of files is simply a prelude to using them—and that usually means dealing with what's inside.

Chapter 26 talks about various ways to dump the entire contents of a file to your screen—all at once, or in manageable pieces.

Chapter 27 describes the essential prelude to any more precise look at just parts of a file—the regular expressions that allow you to match textual patterns rather than fixed words or phrases.

Chapter 28 describes the *grep* family of programs, which use regular expressions to find and print individual matching lines from a file or files. *grep* is the program that people ignorant of UNIX like to pick on for its seemingly obscure name, yet it is one of the handiest tools UNIX provides.

Chapter 29 tells how to compare two files that might have a great deal in common, how to isolate the differences, and how to put Humpty back together again when versions have become skewed with multiple incompatible edits.

Chapter 30 describes some specialized ways to look at files—spell checking, word counting, and various kinds of simple proofreading.

—TOR

26

Showing What's in a File

26.01 Cracking the Nut

This chapter talks about the many ways of dumping a file to the screen. Most users know the brute force approach provided by *cat (26.02)*, but there's more to it than that:

- Pagers like *more (26.03)* and *less (26.04)* that give you more control when looking through long files.

- Looking at files that are compressed or otherwise unviewable (article 26.05).

- Finding out what type of data a file contains before opening it (article 26.08).

- Adding and deleting blank lines or other white space before displaying a file (articles 26.09 through 26.14).

- Looking at just the beginning or just the end of a file (articles 26.15 through 26.21).

- Numbering lines (article 26.22).

—*TOR*

26.02 Four Ways to Skin a cat

The *cat* command may well be the first command new users hear about, if only because of its odd name. *cat* stands for con*cat*enate or, as some would say, catenate. Both words mean the same thing: to connect in a series. The *cat* command takes its filename arguments, and strings their contents together. Essentially, *cat* takes its input and spits it out again.

cat has many uses, but the four most basic applications are described below. In many ways, they don't illustrate *cat* so much as they illustrate the shell's output redirection *(14.01)* mechanism.

1. First form:

   ```
   % cat file
   % cat file1 file2 file...
   ```

   Use this form to display one or more files on the screen. The output doesn't pause when the screen is full. As a result, if your files are more than one screenful long, the output will whiz by without giving you a chance to read it.* To read output by screenfuls, use the *more (26.03)* command or some other pager, like *less (26.04)*.

2. Second form:

   ```
   % cat files > new_file
   ```

   Use this form when you want to combine several smaller files into one large file. Be sure the destination file does not already exist; otherwise, it will be replaced by the new contents (effectively destroying the original). For example, the command:

   ```
   % cat chap1 chap2 chap3 > book
   ```

   creates a new file, *book*, composed of three files, one after the other. The three component files still exist as *chap1*, *chap2*, and *chap3*.

3. Third form:

   ```
   % cat file >> existing_file
   % cat files >> existing_file
   ```

   Use this form to add one or more files to the end of an existing file. For example:

   ```
   % cat note1 note2 > note_list
   % cat note3 >> note_list
   ```

4. Fourth form:

   ```
   % cat > newfile
   ```

---

*You may think this command form is pointless. The truth is, this form is rarely used in such a basic way. More often, you'll use this form along with some of *cat*'s display options or connect this command to other UNIX commands via a pipe *(1.03)*.

Use this form as a quick-and-dirty way to create a new file. This is useful when you aren't yet familiar with any of the standard text editors. With this command, everything you type at the keyboard goes into the new file. (You won't be able to back up to a previous line.) To finish your input, enter CTRL-d on a line by itself.

Well, that was just in case there are some beginners on board. Articles 14.13, 26.07, 26.10, and 26.22 give some more useful tips about *cat* options.

—DG

26.03 *Using more to Page through Files*

The *more* utility is light-years ahead of *cat (26.02)*. It lets you read files one page at a time. If you had only *cat* and wanted to read long files, you'd have to read very fast or have a quick trigger finger (on CTRL-s *(43.02)*) to stop the text—or get used to reading the last few lines of a file, and no more. In fact, even the most backward versions of *more* are infinitely preferable to *cat* for reading a file—so much so that I don't understand why anyone uses *cat* for this purpose. [I *cat* tiny files because I have *more* and *less (26.04)* set up to clear my screen (with the −c option) before displaying a file.— *TC*]

When you start *more*, it displays the first screen of the file. To move to the next page, press the space bar. You can continue to move forward through the file by pressing the space bar or by pressing RETURN (which moves you forward one line). More recent versions of *more* allow you to "back up" to previous pages in the file by typing b.

Some other features:

- If you list several files on the command line, you can type :n to move to the next file and :p to move to the previous one.

- You can get a "help" screen at any time by typing h.

- You can jump from *more* into the *vi* editor by typing v.

- You can search for a string by typing /, followed by the string you want. The search string can be a full regular expression *(27.01)*. You can find the next occurrence of a string by typing n.

If you invoke *more* with two or more files, it will display a short header at the beginning of each file. This little nicety is strangely useful. Let's say you want to print all of your .h files with a single command, and you'd like some kind of label before each file. You can use *more* to create the labels *(45.11)* for you:

pr *45.07*
lpr *45.02*

```
% more *.h | pr | lpr
```

(When *more* isn't writing to a terminal, it doesn't expect you to type spaces; it dumps the whole file to standard output.)

more has a few defects:

- Even the best versions can't back up while reading a pipe. So if you pipe the output from some command into *more*, b won't work.

- When you get to the end of the last file, *more* quits. I guess there's nothing wrong with this behavior, but I don't like it; I'd rather have the chance to back up or move to an earlier file.

- Some implementations of *more* (System V) terminate if you search for a string that it can't find.

A program called *less* *(26.04)* solves all of these problems.

[Some versions of System V support a somewhat equivalent program called *pg* instead of *more*. And some people like to look at files with a read-only version of *vi* called *view*. I prefer *more* or *less*. :-) — *TOR*]

—*ML*

26.04 The "less" Pager: More than "more"

less

less is one of those classic file-listing programs, like *list* on MS-DOS, that does so much you never realized you needed to do. It does so much more than *more* *(26.03)*, and does it so much better, that it's one of the first programs I port to a new computer. If I tried to cover all the features, this article would be ten pages long. Luckily, *less* comes with online help (type h) and a comprehensive manual page, which is stored with the software on the disk.

Some of the features and advantages:

- No relearning: *less* does the right thing when you use *more*, *vi* *(31.02)*, or *emacs* *(33.01)* file-browsing commands.

- While reading from pipes *(1.03)*, *less* can redraw the screen and read previous pages.

- Lots of ways to move to certain parts of the file: by line number, percentage, screen, with a search. Can mark and return to lines.

- For programmers: handles nonstandard tabstops *(43.04)*. Finds matching braces and parentheses.

- An incredible number of screen-control settings and options to make the screen look like you want it, including position after searches. Customizable prompt to give you the information you want.

The *lesskey* program (which is included with the *less* distribution on the disk) lets you make custom key definitions. You can store your favorite setup options in the *LESS* environment variable *(7.01)*.

—*JP, TOR*

26.05 Page through Compressed and Unprintable Files

zmore

Compressed *(25.06)* files save disk space. But compressed files aren't as convenient to work with: you have to uncompress them before you can read or edit them. The *zmore* script (also named *zpg* and *zless*) makes the job easier. It uncompresses one or more files and feeds them to a pager: *more (26.03)*, *pg*, or *less (26.04)*.

Note: The *compress* utility on the Power Tools disk comes with a different program that is also named *zmore*. If you install both, you'll want to rename one.

The script can also page through files that have been made printable by *cat −v −t −e (26.07, 26.06)*. This is a safe way to page through files that might have unprintable characters that could mess up your terminal if they weren't filtered.

Here's an example. Let's page through the compressed files *data.Z* and *../summary.Z*. Then we'll read the suspiciously-named file *Ex034912* to see what's in it:

```
% zmore data ../summary       You don't need to type the .Z

      ...First screen of data.Z, uncompressed...

--More--

      ...The rest of data.Z, uncompressed...

zmore: Press RETURN to see next file, '../summary':

      ...First screen of ../summary.Z, uncompressed...

% vmore Ex034912

      ...First screen of Ex034912, filtered with cat −t −v −e...
```

The same script file does all those things. It's written to have five other links *(19.03)*. You may want to make more or fewer links though, depending on the pagers your system has. To set up the script as shown here, just install it from the Power Tools disk. Or, if you type in the script, put it in a file named *zmore* and use a *foreach (10.09)* or *for (10.10)* loop to make the links:

```
% foreach n (zpg zless vmore vpg vless)
? ln zmore $n
? end
```

The script tests the name it was called with, from $0, to decide whether to use *zcat* or *cat −t −v −e* and which pager to run. This trick saves disk space. You can change the pagers used by modifying the script and adding or removing links to it. The absolute pathnames at the start of the script may need to be changed for your system.

Most pager programs can't back up or move around as easily when they're reading from a pipe. You can use a temporary file instead. That's not as efficient as using a pipe, but it's good to be able to do. To do that, add the following two lines after the second *case* structure:

/tmp..$$ *22.03*
trap *46.12*

```
temp=/tmp/$myname$$
trap 'rm -f $temp; exit' 0 1 2 15
```

And change this line inside the *while* loop, around line 38:

```
*) $cat "$1" | $prog $opts ;;
```

to these three lines:

```
*) $cat "$1" > $temp
   $prog $opts $temp
   ;;
```

—*JP*

26.06   What's in that White Space?

The *cat −v* option *(26.07)* shows non-printable characters in a printable way. *cat* has two options for displaying white space in a line. If you use the *−t* option with *−v*, TAB characters are shown as ^I. The *−e* option combined with *−v* marks the end of each line with a $ character. Some versions of *cat* don't require the *−v* with those options. Let's compare a one-line file without and with the *−t −e* (which have to be typed separately, by the way; *−te* won't work):

```
% cat afile
This is a one-line file -- boring, eh?
% cat -v -t -e afile
ThiS^Hs is^Ia one-line file^I-- boring, eh?        $
```

Although you can't tell it from plain *cat*, there's a Backspace (CTRL-h) before the first s, two TABs that take up only one column of white space each, and seven spaces at the end of the line. Knowing this can help you debug problems in printing and displaying files. It's also a help for shell programmers who need to parse or sort the output of other programs.

—*JP*

26.07   Show Non-printing Characters with cat −v or od −c

Especially if you use an ASCII-based terminal, files can have characters that your terminal can't display. Some characters will lock up your communications software or hardware, make your screen look strange, or cause other weird problems. So if you'd like to look at a file and you aren't sure what's in there, it's not a good idea to just *cat* the file!

Instead, try *cat −v*. It turns non-printable characters into a printable form. In fact, although most manual pages don't explain how, you can read the output and see what's in the file. Another utility for displaying non-printable files is *od*. I usually use its *−c* option when I need to look at a file character by character.

Let's look at a file that's almost guaranteed to be unprintable: a directory file. This example is on a standard V7 (UNIX Version 7) filesystem. A directory usually has some long lines, so it's a good idea to pipe *cat*'s output through *fold* *(45.08)*:

–f 25.16

```
% ls -fa
.
..
comp
% cat -v . | fold -62
M-^?^N.^@^@^@^@^@^@^@^@^@^@^@^@^@>^G..^@^@^@^@^@^@^@^@^@^@^@^@
M-a
comp^@^@^@^@^@^@^@^@^@^@^@@MassAveFood^@^@^@^@^@hist^@^@^
@^@^@^@^@^@^@^@
% od -c .
0000000 377 016   .  \0  \0  \0  \0  \0  \0  \0  \0  \0  \0  \0  \0  \0
0000020   > 007   .   .  \0  \0  \0  \0  \0  \0  \0  \0  \0  \0  \0  \0
0000040 341  \n   c   o   m   p  \0  \0  \0  \0  \0  \0  \0  \0  \0  \0
0000060  \0  \0   M   a   s   s   A   v   e   F   o   o   d  \0  \0  \0
0000100  \0  \0   h   i   s   t  \0  \0  \0  \0  \0  \0  \0  \0  \0  \0
0000120
```

Each entry in a V7-type directory is 16 bytes long (that's also 16 characters, in the ASCII *(53.03)* system). The *od –c* command starts each line with the number of bytes, in octal, shown since the start of the file. The first line starts at byte 0. The second line starts at byte 20 (that's the sixteenth in decimal, the way most of us count). And so on. Enough about *od* for now, though. We'll come back in a minute. Time to dissect the *cat –v* output:

- You've probably seen sequences like ^N and ^G. Those are control characters. (Find them in the *cat –v* output, please.)

  Another character like this is ^@, the character NUL (ASCII 0). There are a lot of NULs in the directory; more about that below. A DEL character (ASCII 177 octal) is shown as ^?. Check an ASCII chart.

- *cat –v* has its own symbol for characters outside the ASCII range with their high bits set, also called meta-characters. *cat –v* prints those as M- followed by another character. There are two of them in the *cat –v* output: M-^? and M-a.

  To get a meta-character, you add 200 octal. "Say what?" Let's look at M-a first. The octal value of the letter a is 141. When *cat –v* prints M-a, it means the character you get by adding 141+200, or 341 octal.

  You can decode the character *cat* prints as M-^? in the same way. The ^? stands for the DEL character, which is octal 177. Add 200+177 to get 377 octal.

- If a character isn't M-*something* or ^*something*, it's a regular printable character. The entries in the directory (., .., comp, MassAveFood, and hist) are all made of regular ASCII characters.

  If you're wondering where the entries MassAveFood and hist are in the *ls* listing, the answer is: they aren't. Those entries have been deleted from the directory. UNIX puts two NUL (ASCII 0, or ^@) bytes in front of the name when a file has been deleted.

cat has two options, *–t* and *–e*, for displaying white space in a line. The *–v* option doesn't convert TAB and trailing space characters to a visible form without those options. See article 26.06.

Next, time for *od –c*; it's easier to explain than *cat –v*:

- *od –c* shows some characters starting with a backslash (\). It uses the standard UNIX and C abbreviations for control characters *(55.01)* where it can. For instance, \n stands for a newline character, \t for a tab, etc. There's a newline at the start of the comp entry—see it in the *od –c* output? That explains why the *cat –v* output was broken onto a new line at that place: *cat –v* doesn't translate newlines when it finds them.

  The \0 is a NUL character (ASCII 0). It's used to pad the ends of entries in V7 directories when a name isn't the full 14 characters long.

- *od –c* shows the octal value of other characters as three digits. For instance, the 007 means "the character 7 octal." *cat –v* shows this as ^G (CTRL-g).

  Meta-characters, the ones with octal values 200 and above, are shown as M-*something* by *cat –v*. In *od –c*, you'll see their octal values—like 341.

  Each directory entry on a UNIX Version 7 filesystem starts with a two-byte "pointer" to its location in the disk's inode table. When you type a filename, UNIX uses this pointer to find the actual file information on the disk. The entry for this directory (named .) is 377 016. Its parent (named ..) is at > 007. And *comp*'s entry is 341 \n. Find those in the *cat –v* output, if you want—and compare the two outputs.

- Like *cat –v*, regular printable characters are shown as is by *od –c*.

The *strings (28.19)* program finds printable strings of characters (such as filenames) inside mostly-non-printable files (like executable binaries).

—JP

26.08 Finding File Types

Many different kinds of files live on the typical UNIX system: database files, executable files, regular text files, files for fancy editors like Interleaf, *tar* files, mail messages, directories, font files, and so on.

You often want to check to make sure you have the right "kind" of file before doing something. For example, you'd like to read the file *tar*. But before typing more tar, you'd like to know whether this file is your set of notes on carbon-based sludge, or the *tar* executable. If you're wrong, the consequences might be unpleasant. Sending the *tar* executable to your screen might screw up your terminal settings *(44.04)*, log you off, or do any number of hostile things.

The *file* utility tells you what sort of file something is.* It's fairly self-explanatory:

```
% file /bin/sh
/bin/sh:        sparc demand paged executable
% file 2650
2650:           [nt]roff, tbl, or eqn input text
% file 0001,v
0001,v:         ascii text
% file foo.sh
foo.sh:         shell commands
```

file is actually quite clever [though it isn't always correct—some versions are better than others—*JP*]. It doesn't just tell you if something's binary or text; it looks at the beginning of the file and tries to figure out what it's doing. So, for example, you see that file *2650* is an *nroff* (45.14) file and *foo.sh* is a shell script. It isn't quite clever enough to figure out that *0001,v* is an RCS (21.14) archive, but it does know that it's a plain ASCII (53.03) text file.

System V and SunOS let you customize the *file* command so that it will recognize additional file types. The file */etc/magic* tells *file* how to recognize different kinds of files. It's capable of a lot (and should be capable of even more), but we'll satisfy ourselves with an introductory explanation. Our goal will be to teach *file* to recognize RCS archives.

/etc/magic has four fields:

> *offset   data-type   value   file-type*

These are:

offset   The offset into the file at which *magic* will try to find something. If you're looking for something right at the beginning of the file, the offset should be 0. (This is usually what you want.)

data-type   The type of test to make. Use `string` for text comparisons, `byte` for byte comparisons, `short` for two-byte comparisons, and `long` for four-byte comparisons.

value   The value you want to find. For string comparisons, any text string will do; you can use the standard UNIX escape sequences (like `\n` for newline). For numeric comparisons (byte, short, long), this field should be a number, expressed as a C constant (e.g., `0x77` for the hexadecimal byte 77).

file-type   The string that *file* will print if this test succeeds.

So, we know that RCS archives begin with the word `head`. This word is right at the beginning of the file (offset 0). And we obviously want a string comparison. So we make the the following addition to */etc/magic*:

```
0     string     head     RCS archive
```

---

*Another solution to this problem is *findtext* (17.27).

This says, "The file is an RCS archive if you find the string head at an offset of 0 bytes from the beginning of the file." Does it work?

```
% file RCS/0002,v
RCS/0002,v:        RCS archive
```

As I said, the tests can be much more complicated, particularly if you're working with binary files. To recognize simple text files, this is all you need to know.

—ML

26.09 Adding and Deleting White Space

There are a lot of ways to change the amount of white space (space and tab characters) in a line:

- Berkeley systems have *cat −s (26.10)* to replace sets of two or more blank lines with single blank lines. If you don't have *cat −s* or need something different, look at article 35.18.

- The *crush (26.11)* script removes all blank lines.

- Use *doublespace (26.12)* to double space text and *triplespace (26.13)* to triple space text.

- The *pushin (26.14)* script replaces multiple white space characters with a single space. This can shorten long lines.

- You can use *sed* to indent lines of text before printing *(45.10)*. The *offset (36.05)* shell script does that more easily.

- For other jobs, utilities like *awk (38.18)* and *sed (35.24)* will probably do what you want. You have to understand how to program them before you use them.

—JP

26.10 Squash Extra Blank Lines with cat −s

Reading output with lots of empty lines can be a waste of screen space. For instance, some System V versions of *man (52.01)* show all the blank lines between manual pages. To stop that, read your file or pipe it through *cat −s*. (Many versions of *more (26.03)* have a similar −s option.) The −s option replaces multiple blank lines with a single blank line.

This might not always seem to work. The problem is usually that the "empty" lines have SPACE, TAB, or CTRL-m characters on them. The fix is to let *sed* "erase" lines with those invisible characters on them:

```
% sed 's/^[ SPACE  TAB  CTRL-v  CTRL-m ]*$//' somefile | cat -s
```

In *vi (32.05)* and many terminal drivers *(44.01)*, the CTRL-v character quotes the CTRL-m (RETURN) so that character doesn't end the current line.

—JP

26.11 crush: A cat that Skips all Blank Lines

Sometimes I have a series of files, or just one file, with lots of blank lines. Some systems have a *–s* option to cat that causes it to compress adjacent blank lines into one. If that option isn't available, you can use *crush*. The *crush* script skips all lines that are empty or have only blanks and/or TABs. Here it is:

crush

```
#!/bin/sed -f
/^[    ]*$/d
```

The brackets, [   ], have a TAB and a space in them. That file doesn't even use a shell, so it's efficient; the kernel starts *sed* directly *(47.03)* and gives it the script itself as the input file expected with the *–f* option. If your UNIX can't execute files directly with #!, type in this version instead:

```
:
exec sed '/^[    ]*$/d' ${1+"$@"}
```

It starts a shell, then *exec* replaces the shell with *sed (47.07)*. The ${1+"$@"} works around a problem with argument handling *(48.07)* in some Bourne shells.

—*JP*

26.12 doublespace: Double Space Text

Here's a script that's handy for printing drafts of files. It double spaces file(s) or standard input. For example:

```
% doublespace afile | lp
% prog | doublespace | lp
```

Here it is:

doublespace

```
#!/bin/sed -f
G
```

No, that isn't a typo: *doublespace* just uses the *sed* command *G*. The *G* command appends a newline and the contents of *sed*'s hold space, which will be empty in this script. The effect is to add a newline after every newline.

That file doesn't even use a shell, so it's efficient; the kernel starts *sed* directly *(47.03)* and gives it the script itself as the input file expected with the *–f* option. If your UNIX can't execute files directly with #!, type in this version instead:

```
:
exec /bin/sed G ${1+"$@"}
```

It starts a shell, then *exec* replaces the shell with *sed (47.07)*. The ${1+"$@"} works around a problem with argument handling *(48.07)* in some Bourne shells.

—*JP*

26.13 triplespace: Triple Space Text

To print or view a file and add two empty lines after every line of text, use the *triplespace* script. It reads from file(s) or standard input and writes to standard output. In the example below, the line numbers to the left of each line (like *2>*) are not part of the file; they are for reference only.

triplespace

```
1>  #!/bin/sed -f
2>  a\
3>  \
4>
```

That *sed a* command adds two newlines to the end of each line of text. That file doesn't use a shell; the kernel starts *sed* directly *(47.03)* and gives it the script itself as the input file expected with the *-f* option. Note that the line 4 of the file is empty. If your UNIX can't execute files directly with #!, type in this version instead:

```
1>  :
2>  exec sed 'a\
3>  \
4>  ' ${1+"$@"}
```

It starts a shell, then *exec* replaces the shell with *sed (47.07)*. The ${1+"$@"} works around a problem with argument handling *(48.07)* in some Bourne shells.

And now you know how to make *quadruplespace, quintuplespace,* ... :-).

—*JP*

26.14 pushin: Squeeze Out Extra White Space

If you're viewing or printing a file with lines that are too long to read, you can use a program like *fold (45.08)* to fold the lines. Or, if there's lots of white space in each line—multiple spaces and/or TABs next to each other—you can use the script at the end of this article. The *pushin* script replaces series of spaces and/or TABs with a single space, "pushing in" each line as much as it can. It reads from files or standard input and writes to standard output.

Here's an example of lines in a file that aren't too long (we can't print long lines in this book, anyway) but that do have a lot of white space. Imagine how *pushin* would help with longer lines:

```
% cat data
resistor          349-4991-02               23
capacitor         385-2981-49               16
diode             405-3951-58                8
% pushin data
resistor 349-4991-02 23
capacitor 385-2981-49 16
diode 405-3951-58 8
```

Here's the script:

pushin

```
#!/bin/sed -f
s/[ ][    ]*/ /g
```

Inside each pair of brackets, [   ], the *sed* substitute command has a space and a TAB. The replacement string is a single space.

That file doesn't use a shell; the kernel starts *sed* directly *(47.03)* and gives it the script itself as the input file expected with the −*f* option. If your UNIX can't execute files directly with # !, type in this version instead:

```
:
exec sed 's/[    ][    ]*/ /g' ${1+"$@"}
```

It starts a shell, then *exec* replaces the shell with *sed* *(47.07)*. The ${1+"$@"} works around a problem with argument handling *(48.07)* in some Bourne shells.

—*JP*

26.15 How to Look at the End of a File: tail

Let's say that you want to look at the end of some large file. For example, you've just sent some mail via UUCP *(1.33)* and want to find out whether it was handled correctly. But when you give the *uulog* command, you find out that the UUCP log file is 30 or 40 KB long, and you don't care about the whole thing—you certainly don't want to page through it until you get to the end. How do you handle this?

The *tail* command is just what you need in this situation. *tail* reads its input and discards everything except for the last ten lines (by default). Therefore, if you're pretty sure that the information you want is at the end of the file, you can use *tail* to get rid of the junk that you don't want. To use the *uulog* example:

```
% uulog | tail
```

This will give you the last ten lines of the UUCP log. If you need more or less than ten lines, look at article 26.16.

You can give *tail* one (and *only* one!) filename:

```
% tail somefile
```

There are many other situations in which *tail* is useful: I've used it to make sure that a job that produces a big output file has finished correctly, to remind me what the last piece of mail in my mailbox was about, and so on. You'll find *tail* important whenever you're interested only in the end of something.

—*ML*

26.16 Finer Control on tail

What if you need to look at the last 11 lines of the file? The command `tail -n` shows the final *n* lines. The command `tail +n` discards the first *n*–1 lines, giving you line *n* and everything that follows it.

You can also tell *tail* to count the number of characters or the number of 512-byte blocks. To do so, use the *–c* option (count characters) or the *–b* option (count blocks). If you want to state explicitly that you're interested in lines, give the *–l* option.

Note: *tail* is one of the UNIX programs that likes its arguments to be smashed together. In other words, if you want to look at the last three blocks of a file, give the command *tail –3b*. If you give the command *tail –3 –b*, *tail* will happily assume that you want to look at the file *–b*. This also applies to the *–f* option, which we'll discuss a bit in article 26.17.

For example, the command *tail –4b mail.txt* dumps the last 2048 bytes (four blocks, each 512 bytes) of my *mail.txt* file to the screen.

Many versions of *tail* also have a *–r* option that shows the file in reverse order, starting from the last line. (Also see article 26.20.)

Some versions of UNIX may limit the maximum number of lines that *tail*, especially *tail –r*, can display.

—ML

26.17 How to Look at a File as it Grows

One of the best things that you can do with *tail* is look at a file as it is growing. For example, I once was debugging a program named *totroff* that converted a manual from a plain text format to *troff*. It was rather slow, so that you didn't want to wait until the program finished running before looking at the output. But you didn't want to be typing more *(26.03)* every 20 seconds either, to find out whether or not the part of the file that you were debugging had made it through yet. (*more* quits when you "run out" of file, so it can't really help you look for a part of a file that hasn't been written yet.) The *tail –f* command solves this problem. For example:

```
% totroff < file.txt > file.ms &
[1] 12345
% tail -f file.ms
.LP
Tail produces output as
the file grows.
    . . .
CTRL-c
```

Other applications for *tail –f*: lets you watch any system log file (*/usr/adm/messages*, *sendmail* log file, news log, etc.) as it grows.

What's actually happening here?

When you invoke *tail –f*, *tail* behaves just like it normally does: it reads the file and dumps the last ten (or whatever) lines to the screen. But, unlike most applications, *tail* doesn't quit at this point. Instead, *tail* goes into an infinite loop. It sleeps for a second, then wakes up and looks to see if the file is any longer, then sleeps again, and so on. Because this is an infinite loop, you have to enter CTRL-c (or whatever your interrupt key *(40.09)* is) when you've seen the data you're interested in, or when the file you're watching has been completed. *tail* has no way of knowing when the file has stopped growing.

tail ignores the *–f* option when it is reading from a pipe. For example, *totroff < file.txt | tail –f* wouldn't work.

—ML

26.18 An Alias in Case You Don't Have tail

Some System V UNIX versions don't support the *tail* command *(26.15)*. Here's an alias *(11.02)* that gives you (sort of) an equivalent:

wc *30.06*

```
alias ptail 'set end=(`wc -l \!^`); set start; @ start = $end[1] - 9; \\
sed -n $start,\$p \!^ ; unset start end'
```

csh_init

This prints the last ten lines of a file. It's probably more interesting as an example of an alias than as a real replacement for *tail*, but does about 80 percent of what you want. It will break if the file has less than ten lines.

—JP

26.19 Watching Several Files Grow

Now here's a useful tool: suppose you want to monitor several files at once. Administrators, for example, might want to keep track of several log files, such as */usr/adm/messages*, */usr/adm/lpd-errs*, UUCP error files, etc.

xtail

The *xtail* program comes in useful for keeping an eye on several administrative log files at once. But it also comes in useful for non-administrators. It's sort of a *tail –f* for several files as once.

For example, suppose you want to perform several *grep*s through many files, saving the output in different files. You can then monitor the files using *xtail*. For example:

```
% grep Berkeley ch?? > Berkeley.grep &
% grep BSD ch?? > BSD.grep &
% grep "System V" ch?? > SystemV.grep &
% grep SysV ch?? > SysV.grep &
% xtail Berkeley.grep BSD.grep SystemV.grep SysV.grep
```

When new text appears in the files called with *xtail*, it also appears on the screen:

```
*** SysV.grep ***
ch01:using a SysV-based UNIX system, you must

*** Berkeley.grep ***
ch01:at the University of California at Berkeley, where

*** BSD.grep ***
ch03:prefer BSD UNIX systems because they are less likely to
ch04:who use a BSD-based UNIX systems must run the

*** SysV.grep ***
ch04:is a SysV derivative sold by Acme Products Inc.
```

(When text is written to a new file, the filename is printed surrounded by ***.)

If you press your interrupt key *(6.09)* (usually CTRL-c or DEL), *xtail* will tell you which files have been modified most recently:

```
CTRL-c
*** recently changed files ***
   1   4-Nov-92 18:21:12   BSD.grep
   2   4-Nov-92 18:19:52   Berkeley.grep
   3   4-Nov-92 17:42:45   SysV.grep
```

To exit *xtail*, you must send the *QUIT* signal (usually CTRL-\, control-backslash).

If an argument given to *xtail* is a directory name and not a filename, then *xtail* monitors all files in that directory. For administrators, this comes in very useful for monitoring the UUCP *(1.33)* log files in all the subdirectories of */usr/spool/uucp/.Log*:

```
% xtail /usr/spool/uucp/.Log/*
```

—LM

26.20 Reverse Lines in Long Files with flip

If you're looking at a long log file and you want to see the most recent lines first, you might use the *tail −r (26.16)* command. It shows the lines of a file in reverse order, last line first. It will give up if your file is too big, though. How big "too big" is depends on your version of *tail*. To find out, try a very big text file and see how far *tail −r* goes:

```
% tail -r /usr/dict/words > /tmp/words.tailr
% ls -l /tmp/words.tailr /usr/dict/words
-rw-r--r--  1 jerry      32768 Dec  5 09:49 /tmp/words.tailr
-rw-r--r--  1 root      206672 Feb  8  1990 /usr/dict/words
```

flip

tail −r quit after 32768 characters on our system. The *flip* program has a much bigger limit; it uses the *ed* editor to reverse all the lines in the file with this command:

```
g/^/m0
```

The command means "globally move this line to the top of the file." It starts at the first line of the file and keeps flipping lines onto the top. There's still a length limit, but it's usually much bigger than the limit in *tail −r*. If you need an even bigger limit, make the script use *ex (31.02)* instead of *ed*.

[The one-line *perl (39.01)* script below has no limits, though it will take a lot of memory on a big file:

```
perl -e 'print reverse <>'
```

It's yet another one-line *perl* script that replaces a big *sh/sed/awk* script. —*TC*]
[*perl* isn't always better than *sh, sed, awk*, and so on. Sometimes, it's worse; the trick is to know when *perl* is best. Tom is right in this case! The *perl* script is also much faster than *flip*. —*JP*]

The *flip* script's *−f* option flips a file in place—reads it and writes it back. Use *flip −f* carefully with large files—over the file size limit, it might corrupt the file if your *ed* doesn't handle big files well. If *ed* doesn't like something, it prints a cryptic error, just a question mark (?) or worse—and it may write the error to standard output instead of standard error.

```
% flip -f somefile
```

With no *−f* and one file argument, *flip* reads the file and writes to standard output. With no arguments, it reads standard input and writes standard output—so you can pipe to *flip*.

Flipping a big file can take a while. You might run *flip* in the background and save its output to another file.

—JP

26.21 *Using sed to Print the Top of a File*

Many versions of BSD UNIX include a nice program called *head* that prints the top *n* (default: 10) lines of a file. System V or other users without *head* can emulate its behavior with *sed*.

The easiest way is simply to use *sed*'s *q* command *(35.21)*:

```
% sed 10q file
```

head

If you want to get fancy, you can use a shell script to emulate all of the behavior of the BSD *head* command, including taking an option for the number of lines to be printed, and printing a separator line if multiple filenames are specified on the same command line.

Showing What's in a File

The Power Tools disk has that script. Most of it is straightforward. One interesting part is below. It's the *sed* command that prints the separator when more than one file is shown:

```
sed "
1i\\
==> $1 <==
${show}q" $1
```

The *sed* command *1i* inserts the separator before line 1. The *sed* command *q* quits after the number of lines (by default, 10) in the $show shell variable *(7.08)*. The shell substitutes $1 with the filename being read. The double quotes (") around the *sed* commands let the shell build the commands on-the-fly before starting *sed*.

—JP, TOR

26.22 Numbering Lines with cat −n and pr −n

There are times when you want to print out a file with the lines numbered—perhaps because you are showing a script or program in documentation and want to refer to individual lines in the course of your discussion.

This is one of the handy things *cat* can do for you, with the *−n* option.

cat −n precedes each line with some leading spaces, the line number, and a TAB. How many leading spaces? It depends on how high the line numbers go. The line numbers are right justified at column 6, which means that a six-digit number will go all the way back to the margin. I only belabor this point in case you're tempted to trim the leading spaces with something like *cut(36.12)*.

If you have a version of *cat* that doesn't support *−n*, you may be able to achieve a similar effect with *pr −t −n*. (This only works on System V versions of *pr*.) If it works, it's even better than *cat −n*, since you don't have to number every line.

For example:

```
% pr -t -n5 somefile > numbered_file
```

will number only every fifth line.

(The *−t* keeps *pr* from inserting the header and footer *(45.07)* it normally uses to break its output into pages.)

—TOR

27

Regular Expressions (Pattern Matching)

27.01 *That's an Expression*

When my young daughter is struggling to understand the meaning of an idiomatic expression, such as, "Someone let the cat out of the bag," before I tell her what it means, I have to tell her that it's an *expression*, that she's not to interpret it literally. (As a consequence, she also uses "That's just an expression" to qualify her own remarks, especially when she is unsure about what she has just said.)

An expression, even in computer terminology, is not something to be interpreted literally. It is something that needs to be evaluated.

Many UNIX programs use a special "regular expression syntax" for specifying what you could think of as "wildcard searches" through files. Regular expressions describe patterns, or sequences of characters, without necessarily specifying the characters literally. You'll also hear this referred to as "pattern matching."

In this chapter, we depart a bit from the usual "tips and tricks" style of the book to provide an extended tutorial about regular expressions in article 27.04. We did this because regular expressions are so important to many of the tips and tricks elsewhere in the book, and we wanted to make sure that they are covered thoroughly.

This tutorial article is accompanied by a few snippets of advice (articles 27.05 and 27.07), and a few tools that help you see what your expressions are matching (article 27.06). There's also a quick reference (article 27.10) for those of you who just need a refresher.

For tips, tricks and tools that rely on an understanding of regular expression syntax, you have only to look at:

- Chapter 28, *Searching Through Files*
- Chapter 31, *vi Tips and Tricks*
- Chapter 34, *Batch Editing*
- Chapter 35, *The sed Stream Editor*
- Chapter 38, *The awk Programming Language*
- Chapter 39, *Perl, A Pathologically Eclectic Rubbish Lister*

—DD, TOR (Dale wrote the good part, in the Nutshell Handbook *sed & awk)*

27.02 *Don't Confuse Regular Expressions with Wildcards*

Before we even start talking about regular expressions, a word of caution for beginners: regular expressions can be confusing because they look a lot like the file matching patterns the shell uses. Both the shell and programs that use regular expressions have special meanings for the asterisk (*), question mark (?), parentheses (( )), square brackets ([ ]), and vertical bar (|, the "pipe").

Some of these characters even act the same way—almost.

Just remember, the Bourne shell, C shell, *find*, and *cpio* use filename matching patterns and not regular expressions.

You also have to remember that shell meta-characters are expanded before the shell passes the arguments to the program. To prevent this expansion, the special characters in a regular expression must be quoted *(9.10)* when passed as an argument from the shell.

The command:

```
$ grep [A-Z]*.c chap[12]
```

could, for example, be interpreted by the shell as:

```
grep Array.c Bug.c Comp.c chap1 chap2
```

and so *grep* would then try to find the pattern "Array.c" in files *Bug.c, Comp.c, chap1,* and *chap2.*

The simplest solution in most cases is to surround the regular expression with single quotes (').

—BB, DG, TOR

27.03 Understanding Expressions

You are probably familiar with the kinds of expressions that a calculator interprets. Look at the following arithmetic expression:

    2 + 4

"Two plus four" consists of several constants or literal values and an operator. A calculator program must recognize, for instance, that 2 is a numeric constant and that the plus sign represents an operator, not to be interpreted as the + character.

An expression tells the computer how to produce a result. Although it is the result of "two plus four" that we really want, we don't simply tell the computer to return a six. We instruct the computer to evaluate the expression and return a value.

An expression can be more complicated than 2+4; in fact, it might consist of multiple simple expressions, such as the following:

    2 + 3 * 4

A calculator normally evaluates an expression from left to right. However, certain operators have precedence over others: that is, they will be performed first. Thus, the above expression will evaluate to 14 and not 20 because multiplication takes precedence over addition. Precedence can be overridden by placing the simple expression in parentheses. Thus, (2+3)*4 or "the sum of two plus three times four" will evaluate to 20. The parentheses are symbols that instruct the calculator to change the order in which the expression is evaluated.

A regular expression, by contrast, is descriptive of a pattern or sequence of characters. Concatenation is the basic operation implied in every regular expression. That is, a pattern matches adjacent characters. Look at the following example of a regular expression:

    ABE

Each literal character is a regular expression that matches only that single character. This expression describes an "A followed by a B then followed by an E" or simply the string ABE. The term "string" means each character concatenated to the one preceding it. That a regular expression describes a *sequence* of characters can't be emphasized enough. (Novice users are inclined to think in higher-level units such as words, and not individual characters.) Regular expressions are case-sensitive; A does not match a.

Programs such as *grep (28.02)* that accept regular expressions must first evaluate the syntax of the regular expression to produce a pattern. They then read the input line by line trying to match the pattern. An input line is a string, and to see if a string matches the pattern, a program compares the first character in the string to the first character of the pattern. If there is a match, it compares the second character in the string to the second character of the pattern. Whenever it fails to make a match, it compares the next character in the string to the first character of the pattern. Figure 27-1 illustrates this process, trying to match the pattern abe on an input line.

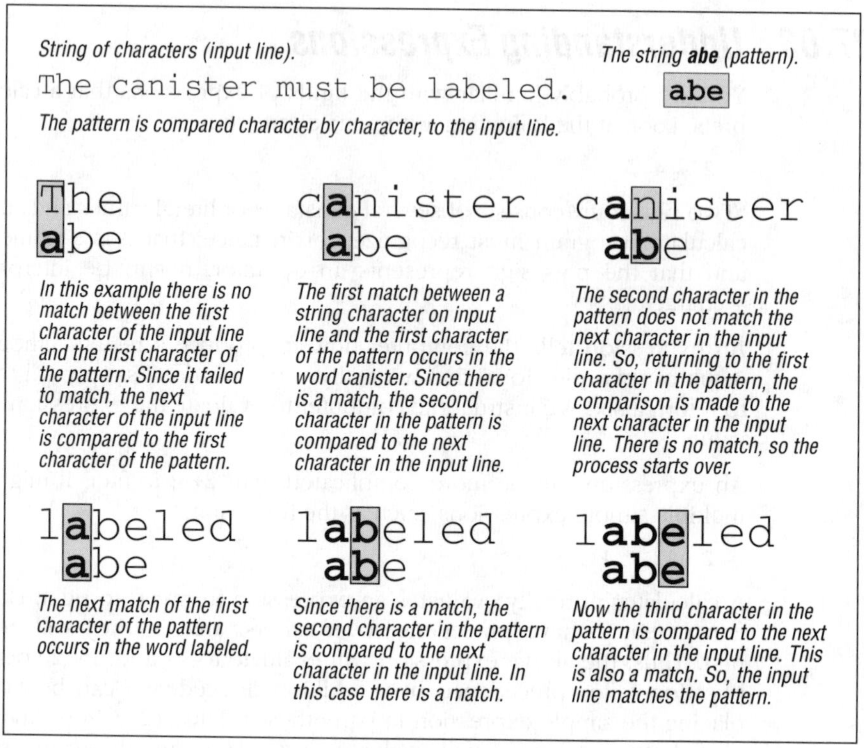

String of characters (input line).   The string **abe** (pattern).

`The canister must be labeled.`   `abe`

The pattern is compared character by character, to the input line.

`The`
`abe`

In this example there is no match between the first character of the input line and the first character of the pattern. Since it failed to match, the next character of the input line is compared to the first character of the pattern.

`canister`
`abe`

The first match between a string character on input line and the first character of the pattern occurs in the word canister. Since there is a match, the second character in the pattern is compared to the next character in the input line.

`canister`
`abe`

The second character in the pattern does not match the next character in the input line. So, returning to the first character in the pattern, the comparison is made to the next character in the input line. There is no match, so the process starts over.

`labeled`
`abe`

The next match of the first character of the pattern occurs in the word labeled.

`labeled`
`abe`

Since there is a match, the second character in the pattern is compared to the next character in the input line. In this case there is a match.

`labeled`
`abe`

Now the third character in the pattern is compared to the next character in the input line. This is also a match. So, the input line matches the pattern.

Figure 27-1. Interpreting a regular expression

A regular expression is not limited to literal characters. There is, for instance, a meta-character—the dot (`.`)—that can be used as a "wildcard" to match any single character. You can think of this wildcard as analogous to a blank tile in Scrabble™ where it means any letter. Thus, we can specify the regular expression `A.E` and it will match `ACE`, `ABE`, and `ALE`. It will match any character in the position following `A`.

The meta-character `*` (the asterisk) is used to match zero or more occurrences of the *preceding* regular expression, which typically is a single character. You may be familiar with `*` as a *shell* meta-character, where it also means "zero or more characters." But that meaning is very different from `*` in a regular expression. By itself, the meta-character `*` does not match anything in a regular expression; it modifies what goes before it. The regular expression `.*` matches any number of characters. The regular expression `A.*E` matches any string that matches `A.E` but it will also match any number of characters between A and E: `AIRPLANE`, `A FINE`, `AFFABLE`, or `A LONG WAY HOME`, for example.

If you understand the difference between `.` and `*` in regular expressions, you already know about the two basic types of meta-characters: those that can be evaluated to a single character, and those that modify how characters that precede it are evaluated.

It should also be apparent that by use of meta-characters you can expand or limit the possible matches. You have more control over what is matched and what is not. In article 27.04, Bruce Barnett explains in detail how to use regular expression meta-characters.

—DD from the Nutshell Handbook sed & awk

27.04 *Using Meta-characters in Regular Expressions*

There are three important parts to a regular expression:

1. *Anchors* are used to specify the position of the pattern in relation to a line of text.

2. *Character sets* match one or more characters in a single position.

3. *Modifiers* specify how many times the previous character set is repeated.

A simple example that demonstrates all three parts is the regular expression:

```
^#*
```

The caret (^) is an anchor that indicates the beginning of the line. The hash mark is a simple character set that matches the single character #. The asterisk (*) is a modifier. In a regular expression it specifies that the previous character set can appear any number of times, including zero. As you will see shortly, this is a useless regular expression (except for demonstrating the syntax!).

There are two main types of regular expressions: *simple* regular expressions and *extended* regular expressions. (As we'll see later in the article, the boundaries between the two types have become blurred as regular expressions have evolved.) A few utilities like *awk* and *egrep* use the extended regular expression. Most use the simple regular expression. From now on, if I talk about a "regular expression" (without specifying simple or extended), I am describing a feature common to both types.

The commands that understand just simple regular expressions are: *vi, sed, grep, csplit, dbx, more, ed, expr, lex, pg, nl*, and *rdist*. The utilities *awk, nawk,* and *egrep* understand extended regular expressions.

[The situation is complicated by the fact that simple regular expressions have evolved over time, and so there are versions of "simple regular expressions" that support extensions missing from extended regular expressions! Bruce explains the incompatibility at the end of his article. — *TOR*]

The Anchor Characters: ^ and $

Most UNIX text facilities are line-oriented. Searching for patterns that span several lines is not easy to do. You see, the end-of-line character is not included in the block of text that is searched. It is a separator. Regular expressions examine the text between the separators. If you want to search for a pattern that is at one end or the other, you use *anchors*. The caret (^) is the starting anchor, and the dollar sign ($) is the end anchor. The regular expression ^A will match all lines that start with an uppercase A. The expression A$ will match all lines that end with uppercase A. If the anchor characters are not used at the proper end of the pattern, then they no longer act as anchors. That is, the ^ is only an anchor if it is the first character in a regular expression. The $ is only an anchor if it is the last character. The expression $1 does not have an anchor. Neither does 1^. If you need to match a ^ at the beginning of the line or a $ at the end of a line, you must *escape* the special character by typing a backslash (\) before it. Table 27-1 has a summary.

Table 27-1. *Regular Expression Anchor Character Examples*

Pattern	Matches
^A	An A at the beginning of a line.
A$	An A at the end of a line.
A^	An A^ anywhere on a line.
$A	A $A anywhere on a line.
^\^	A ^ at the beginning of a line.
^^	Same as ^\^.
\$$	A $ at the end of a line.
$$	Same as \$$.

The use of ^ and $ as indicators of the beginning or end of a line is a convention other utilities use. The *vi* editor uses these two characters as commands to go to the beginning or end of a line. The C shell uses !^ to specify the first argument of the previous line, and !$ is the last argument on the previous line (article 12.07 explains).

It is one of those choices that other utilities go along with to maintain consistency. For instance, $ can refer to the last line of a file when using *ed* and *sed*. *cat −v −e (26.06, 26.07)* marks ends of lines with a $. You might see it in other programs as well.

Matching a Character with a Character Set

The simplest character set is a character. The regular expression the contains three character sets: t, h, and e. It will match any line that contains the string the, including the word other. To prevent this, put spaces (□) before and after the pattern: □the□. You can combine the string with an anchor. The pattern ^From:□ will match the lines of a mail message *(1.33)* that identify the sender. Use this pattern with *grep* to print every address in your incoming mailbox:

```
% grep '^From: ' /usr/spool/mail/$USER
```

Some characters have a special meaning in regular expressions. If you want to search for such a character as itself, escape it with a backslash (\).

Match any Character with . (Dot)

The dot (.) is one of those special meta-characters. By itself it will match any character, except the end-of-line character. The pattern that will match a line with any single character is: ^.$.

Specifying a Range of Characters with [. . .]

If you want to match specific characters, you can use square brackets, [], to identify the exact characters you are searching for. The pattern that will match any line of text that contains exactly one digit is: ^[0123456789]$. This is longer than it has to be. You can use the hyphen between two characters to specify a range: ^[0-9]$. You can intermix explicit characters with character ranges. This pattern will match a single character that is a letter, digit, or underscore: [A-Za-z0-9_]. Character sets can be combined by placing them next to each other. If you wanted to search for a word that:

- started with an uppercase T,

- was the first word on a line,

- the second letter was a lowercase letter,

- was three letters long (followed by a space character(□)), and

- the third letter was a lowercase vowel,

the regular expression would be: ^T[a-z][aeiou]□.

Exceptions in a Character Set

You can easily search for all characters except those in square brackets by putting a caret (^) as the first character after the left square bracket ([). To match all characters except lowercase vowels use: [^aeiou].

Like the anchors in places that can't be considered an anchor, the right square bracket (]) and dash (-) do not have a special meaning if they directly follow a [. Table 27-2 has some examples.

Table 27-2. Regular Expression Character Set Examples

Regular Expression	Matches
[0-9]	Any digit.
[^0-9]	Any character other than a digit.
[-0-9]	Any digit or a -.
[0-9-]	Any digit or a -.
[^-0-9]	Any character except a digit or a -.
[]0-9]	Any digit or a].
[0-9]]	Any digit followed by a].

Table 27-2. Regular Expression Character Set Examples (continued)

Regular Expression	Matches
[0-99-z]	Any digit or any character between 9 and z *(53.03)*.
[]0-9-]	Any digit, a -, or a].

Repeating Character Sets with *

The third part of a regular expression is the modifier. It is used to specify how many times you expect to see the previous character set. The special character * (asterisk) matches *zero or more* copies. That is, the regular expression 0* matches zero or more zeros, while the expression [0-9]* matches zero or more digits.

This explains why the pattern ^#* is useless, as it matches any number of #'s at the beginning of the line, including *zero*. Therefore, this will match every line, because every line starts with zero or more #'s.

At first glance, it might seem that starting the count at zero is stupid. Not so. Looking for an unknown number of characters is very important. Suppose you wanted to look for a digit at the beginning of a line, and there may or may not be spaces before the digit. Just use ^□* to match zero or more spaces at the beginning of the line. If you need to match one or more, just repeat the character set. That is, [0-9]* matches zero or more digits and [0-9][0-9]* matches one or more digits.

Matching a Specific Number of Sets with \{ and \}

You cannot specify a maximum number of sets with the * modifier. However, some programs *(27.09)* recognize a special pattern you can use to specify the minimum and maximum number of repeats. This is done by putting those two numbers between \{ and \}.

The backslashes deserve a special discussion. Normally a backslash *turns off* the special meaning for a character. For example, a literal period is matched by \. and a literal asterisk is matched by *.

However, if a backslash is placed before a <, >, {, }, (, or) or before a digit, the backslash *turns on* a special meaning. This was done because these special functions were added late in the life of regular expressions. Changing the meaning of {, }, (,), <, and > would have broken old expressions. (This is a horrible crime punishable by a year of hard labor writing COBOL programs.) Instead, adding a backslash added functionality without breaking old programs. Rather than complain about the change, view it as evolution.

Having convinced you that \{ isn't a plot to confuse you, an example is in order. The regular expression to match four, five, six, seven, or eight lowercase letters is: [a-z]\{4,8\}. Any numbers between 0 and 255 can be used. The second number may be omitted, which removes the upper limit. If the comma and the second number are omitted, the pattern must be duplicated the exact number of times specified by the first number.

You must remember that modifiers like * and \{1,5\} only act as modifiers if they follow a character set. If they were at the beginning of a pattern, they would not be modifiers. Table 27-3 is a list of examples, and the exceptions.

Table 27-3. Regular Expression Pattern Repetition Examples

Regular Expression	Matches
*	Any line with a *.
*	Any line with a *.
\\	Any line with a \.
^*	Any line starting with a *.
^A*	Any line.
^A*	Any line starting with an A*.
^AA*	Any line starting with one A.
^AA*B	Any line starting with one or more A's followed by a B.
^A\{4,8\}B	Any line starting with four, five, six, seven, or eight A's followed by a B.
^A\{4,\}B	Any line starting with four or more A's followed by a B.
^A\{4\}B	Any line starting with an AAAAB.
\{4,8\}	Any line with a {4,8}.
A{4,8}	Any line with an A{4,8}.

Matching Words with \< and \>

Searching for a word isn't quite as simple as it at first appears. The string the will match the word other. You can put spaces before and after the letters and use this regular expression: □the□. However, this does not match words at the beginning or the end of the line. And it does not match the case where there is a punctuation mark after the word.

There is an easy solution—at least in many versions of *ed, ex,* and *vi.* The characters \< and \> are similar to the ^ and $ anchors, as they don't occupy a position of a character. They do *anchor* the expression between to match only if it is on a word boundary. The pattern to search for the words the and The would be: \<[tT]he\>.

Let's define a "word boundary." The character before the t or T must be either a newline character or anything except a letter, digit, or underscore (_). The character after the e must also be a character other than a digit, letter, or underscore, or it could be the end-of-line character.

Remembering Patterns with \(, \), and \1

Another pattern that requires a special mechanism is searching for repeated words. The expression [a-z][a-z] will match any two lowercase letters. If you wanted to search for lines that had two adjoining identical letters, the above pattern wouldn't help. You need a way to remember what you found and see if the same pattern occurs again. In some programs, you can mark part of a pattern using \(and \). You can recall the remembered pattern with \ followed by a single digit. Therefore, to search for two identical letters, use: \([a-z]\)\1. You can have nine different remembered patterns. Each occurrence of \(starts a new pattern. The regular expression to match a five-letter palindrome (e.g., "radar") is: \([a-z]\)\([a-z]\)[a-z]\2\1. [Some versions of some programs can't handle \(\) in the same regular expression as \n. In all versions of *sed*, you're safe if you use \(\) on the pattern side of an s command and \n on the replacement side *(35.10)*. —*JP*]

Potential Problems

That completes a discussion of simple regular expressions. Before I discuss the extensions that extended expressions offer, I want to mention two potential problem areas.

The \< and \> characters were introduced in the *vi* editor. The other programs didn't have this ability at that time. Also, the \{*min,max*\}´modifier is new, and earlier utilities didn't have this ability. This makes it difficult for the novice user of regular expressions, because it seems as if each utility has a different convention. Sun has retrofitted the newest regular expression library to all of their programs, so they all have the same ability. If you try to use these newer features on other vendors' machines, you might find they don't work the same way.

The other potential point of confusion is the extent of the pattern matches *(27.06)*. Regular expressions match the longest possible pattern. That is, the regular expression A.*B matches AAB as well as AAAABBBBABCCCCBBBAAAB. This doesn't cause many problems using *grep*, because an oversight in a regular expression will just match more lines than desired. If you use *sed*, and your patterns get carried away, you may end up deleting or changing more than you want to.

Extended Regular Expressions

Two programs use extended regular expressions: *egrep* and *awk*. With these extensions, those special characters preceded by a backslash no longer have special meaning: \{, \}, \<, \>, \(, \), as well as *digit*. There is a very good reason for this, which I will delay explaining to build up suspense.

The question mark (?) matches zero or one instances of the character set before it, and the plus sign (+) matches one or more copies of the character set. You can't use \{ and \} in extended regular expressions, but if you could, you might consider ? to be the same as \{0,1\} and + to be the same as \{1,\}.

By now, you are wondering why the extended regular expressions are even worth using. Except for two abbreviations, there seem to be no advantages and a lot of disadvantages. Therefore, examples would be useful.

The three important characters in the expanded regular expressions are (, |, and). Parentheses are used to group expressions; the vertical bar acts an an OR operator. Together, they let you match a *choice* of patterns. As an example, you can use *egrep* to print all From: and Subject: lines from your incoming mail:

```
% egrep '^(From|Subject): ' /usr/spool/mail/$USER
```

All lines starting with From: or Subject: will be printed. There is no easy way to do this with simple regular expressions. You could try something like ^[FS][ru][ob][mj]e*c*t*: and hope you don't have any lines that start with Sromeet:. Extended expressions don't have the \< and \> characters. You can compensate by using the alternation mechanism. Matching the word "the" in the beginning, middle, or end of a sentence or at the end of a line can be done with the extended regular expression: (^|)the([^a-z]|$). There are two choices before the word: a space or the beginining of a line. After the word, there must be something besides a lowercase letter or else the end of the line. One extra bonus with extended regular expressions is the ability to use the *, +, and ? modifiers after a (. . .) grouping. The following will match "a simple problem", "an easy problem", as well as "a problem":

```
% egrep "a[n]? (simple|easy)? ?problem" data
```

I promised to explain why the backslash characters don't work in extended regular expressions. Well, perhaps the \{ . . . \} and \< . . . \> could be added to the extended expressions, but it might confuse people if those characters are added and the \(. . . \) are not. And there is no way to add that functionality to the extended expressions without changing the current usage. Do you see why? It's quite simple. If (has a special meaning, then \(must be the ordinary character. This is the opposite of the simple regular expressions, where (is ordinary and \(is special. The usage of the parentheses is incompatible, and any change could break old programs.

If the extended expression used (. . .|. . .) as regular characters, and \(. . .\|. . .\) for specifying alternate patterns, then it is possible to have one set of regular expressions that has full functionality. This is exactly what GNU Emacs *(33.01)* does, by the way—it combines all of the features of regular and extended expressions with one syntax.

—*BB*

27.05 Getting Regular Expressions Right

Writing regular expressions involves more than learning the mechanics. You not only have to learn how to describe patterns, you also have to recognize the context in which they appear. You have to be able to think through the level of detail that is necessary in a regular expression, based on the context in which the pattern will be applied.

The same thing that makes writing regular expressions difficult is what makes writing them interesting: the variety of occurrences or contexts in which a pattern appears. This complexity is inherent in language itself, just as you can't always understand an expression *(27.01)* by looking up each word in the dictionary.

The process of writing a regular expression involves three steps:

1. Knowing what it is you want to match and how it might appear in the text.

2. Writing a pattern to describe what you want to match.

3. Testing the pattern to see what it matches.

This process is virtually the same kind of process that a programmer follows to develop a program. Step 1 might be considered the specification, which should reflect an understanding of the problem to be solved as well as how to solve it. Step 2 is analogous to the actual coding of the program, and step 3 involves running the program and testing it against the specification. Steps 2 and 3 form a loop that is repeated until the program works satisfactorily.

Testing your description of what you want to match ensures that the description works as expected. It usually uncovers a few surprises. Carefully examining the results of a test, comparing the output against the input, will greatly improve your understanding of regular expressions. You might consider evaluating the results of a pattern-matching operation as follows:

Hits	*The lines that I wanted to match.*
Misses	*The lines that I didn't want to match.*
Misses that should be hits	*The lines that I didn't match but wanted to match.*
Hits that should be misses	*The lines that I matched but didn't want to match.*

Trying to perfect your description of a pattern is something that you work at from opposite ends: you try to eliminate the "hits that should be misses" by limiting the possible matches and you try to capture the "misses that should be hits" by expanding the possible matches.

The difficulty is especially apparent when you must describe patterns using fixed strings. Each character you remove from the fixed-string pattern increases the number of possible matches. For instance, while searching for the string what, you determine that you'd like to match What as well. The only fixed-string pattern that will match What and what is hat, the longest string common to both. It is obvious, though, that searching for hat will produce unwanted matches. Each character you add to a fixed-string pattern decreases the number of possible matches. The string them is going to produce fewer matches than the string the.

Using meta-characters in patterns provides greater flexibility in extending or narrowing the range of matches. Meta-characters, used in combination with literals or other meta-characters, can be used to expand the range of matches while still eliminating the matches that you do not want.

—*DD* from the Nutshell Handbook *sed & awk*

27.06 *Just What Does a Regular Expression Match?*

One of the toughest things to learn about regular expressions is just what they do match. The problem is that a regular expression tends to find the longest possible match—which can be more than you want.

showmatch

Here's a simple script called *showmatch* that is useful for testing regular expressions, when writing *sed* scripts, etc. Given a regular expression and a filename, it finds lines in the file matching that expression, just like *grep*, but it uses a row of carets (^^^^) to highlight the portion of the line that was actually matched.

```
#! /bin/sh

pattern="$1"; shift
```

gawk 38.05

```
gawk '# showmatch -- mark string that matches pattern
{# find starting position and length of matching string in input
# print the line where the match was found
#
    if (match($0, pattern)) {
        print
        # create a string of ^ the length of the match.
        patmatch = ""
        for (k = 1; k <= RLENGTH; k++)
            patmatch = patmatch "^"
        # print a blank column followed by string of ^
        printf("%"RSTART-1"s" "%-s\n","", patmatch)
    }
}' pattern="$pattern" $*
```

For example:

```
% showmatch CD-... mbox
and CD-ROM publishing. We have recognized
   ^^^^^^
that documentation will be shipped on CD-ROM; however,
                                       ^^^^^^
```

This is a quick-and-dirty script with a few problems. First, it highlights only the first instance of the pattern on a line; second, if the portion of the line before the pattern contains a TAB, the carets won't line up properly. There's a work-around: first expand the TABs to spaces with *expand (43.04)*. We didn't put this into the script though, because then you'll have a problem if the pattern you're matching contains a TAB.

If you're confident that the pattern doesn't contain a TAB, but the early part of the line might, just do this:

```
% expand files | showmatch pattern
```

getmatch

getmatch is a related script that simply retrieves only the matched text. It was our first cut at this problem; the only drawback is that you see only the matched pattern, and not the rest of the line. This can actually be handy—it allows you to extract patterned data from a file. For example, you could extract only the numbers from a table containing both text and numbers:

```
#! /bin/sh

pattern="$1"; shift

gawk '# getmatch -- print string that matches line
{        # extract string matching pattern using
         # starting position and length of string in $0
         if match($0, pattern)
                 print substr($0, RSTART, RLENGTH)
}' pattern="$pattern" $*
```

Like *showmatch*, this script extracts only the first instance of the pattern on the line.

—DD, TOR, JP

27.07 Limiting the Extent of a Match

A regular expression tries to match the longest string possible; that can cause unexpected problems. For instance, look at the following regular expression, which matches any number of characters inside of quotation marks:

```
".*"
```

Let's look at a *troff* macro that has two quoted arguments, as shown below:

```
.Se "Appendix" "Full Program Listings"
```

To match the first argument, a novice might describe the pattern with the following regular expression:

```
\.Se ".*"
```

However, the pattern ends up matching the whole line because the second quotation mark in the pattern matches the last quotation mark on the line. If you know how many arguments there are, you can specify each of them:

```
\.Se ".*" ".*"
```

Although this works as you'd expect, each line might not have the same number of arguments, causing misses that should be hits—you simply want the first argument. Here's a different regular expression that matches the shortest possible extent between two quotation marks:

```
"[^"]*"
```

It matches "a quote, followed by any number of characters that do not match a quote, followed by a quote." The use of what we might call "negated character classes" like this is one of the things that distinguishes the journeyman regular expression user from the novice.

—DD from the Nutshell Handbook *sed & awk*

27.08 *I Never Meta Character I Didn't Like*

Once you know regular expression syntax, you can match almost anything. But sometimes, it's a pain to think through how to get what you want. Here are some useful regular expressions that match various kinds of data you might have to deal with in the UNIX environment. Some of these examples work in any program that uses regular expressions; others only work with a specific program such as *egrep*. (Article 27.09 lists the metacharacters that each program accepts.) The □ means to use a space as part of the regular expression.

US Postal Abbreviation for State (NM)	`□[A-Z][A-Z]□`
US City, State (Portland, OR)	`^.*,□[A-Z][A-Z]`
Month Day, Year (JAN 05, 1993) (January 5, 1993)	`[A-Z][A-Za-z]\{2,8\}□[0-9]\{1,2\},□[0-9]\{4\}`
US Social Security Number (123-45-6789)	`[0-9]\{3\}-[0-9]\{2\}-[0-9]\{4\}`
US Telephone Number (547-5800)	`[0-9]\{3\}-[0-9]\{4\}`
Formatted Dollar Amounts ($1) ($ 1000000.00)	`\$□*[0-9]+(\.[0-9][0-9])?`
troff In-line Font Requests (\f(CB)	`\\f[(BIRP]C*[BW]*`
troff Requests (.bp)	`^\.[a-z][a-z]□`
troff Macros (.B1)	`^\.[A-Z12].□`

---

troff Macro with Arguments (.Ah "Tips for" "ex & vi")	`^\.[A-Z12].□".*"`
Blank Lines	`^$`
Entire Line	`^.*$`
One or More Spaces	`□□*`

—*DD* from the Nutshell Handbook *sed & awk*

27.09 Valid Meta-characters for Different UNIX Programs

Some regular expression meta-characters are valid for one program but not for another. Those that are available to a particular UNIX program are marked by a bullet (•) in Table 27-4 below. Quick reference descriptions of each of the characters can be found in article 27.10.

[Unfortunately, even this table doesn't give the whole story. For example, in recent releases, Sun has taken some of the extensions originally developed for *ed*, *ex*, and *vi* (such as the \< \> and \{*min,max*\} modifiers) and added them to other programs that use regular expressions. So don't be bashful—try things out, but just don't be surprised if every possible regular expression feature isn't supported by every program. In addition, there are many programs that recognize regular expressions, such as *csplit, more, dbx, expr, lex, pg,* and *less,* that aren't covered in Daniel's table.—*TOR*]

Table 27-4. Valid Meta-characters for Different Programs

Symbol	ed	ex	vi	sed	awk	grep	egrep	Action
.	•	•	•	•	•	•	•	Match any character.
*	•	•	•	•	•	•	•	Match zero or more preceding.
^	•	•	•	•	•	•	•	Match beginning of line.
$	•	•	•	•	•	•	•	Match end of line.
\	•	•	•	•	•	•	•	Escape character following.
[ ]	•	•	•	•	•	•	•	Match one from a set.
\(\)	•	•	•					Store pattern for later replay.
\{ \}	•			•		•		Match a range of instances.
\< \>	•	•	•					Match word's beginning or end.
+					•		•	Match one or more preceding.
?					•		•	Match zero or one preceding.

Table 27-4. Valid Meta-characters for Different Programs (continued)

Symbol	ed	ex	vi	sed	awk	grep	egrep	Action
|					•		•	Separate choices to match.
( )					•		•	Group expressions to match.

In *ed*, *ex*, and *sed*, note that you specify both a search pattern (on the left) and a replacement pattern (on the right). The meta-characters in Table 27-4 above are meaningful only in a search pattern. *ed*, *ex*, and *sed* support the additional meta-characters in Table 27-5 that are valid only in a replacement pattern.

Table 27-5. Valid Meta-characters for Replacement Patterns

Symbol	ex	sed	ed	Action
\	•	•	•	Escape character following.
\n	•	•	•	Reuse pattern stored in \ (\ ) .
&	•	•		Reuse previous search pattern.
~	•			Reuse previous replacement pattern.
\u \U	•			Change character(s) to uppercase.
\l \L	•			Change character(s) to lowercase.
\E	•			Turn off previous \U or \L.
\e	•			Turn off previous \u or \l.

—DG

27.10 *Pattern Matching Quick Reference with Examples*

Article 27.04 gives a tutorial introduction to regular expressions. This article is intended for those of you who just need a quick listing of regular expression syntax as a refresher from time to time. It also includes some simple examples.

The characters in Table 27-6 have special meaning only in search patterns.

Table 27-6. Special Characters in Search Patterns

.	Match any *single* character except newline.
*	Match any number (or none) of the single characters that immediately precede it. The preceding character can also be a regular expression. For example, since . (dot) means any character, .* means "match any number of any character."
^	Match the following regular expression at the beginning of the line.

Table 27-6. Special Characters in Search Patterns (continued)

$	Match the preceding regular expression at the end of the line.
[ ]	Match any *one* of the enclosed characters.
	A hyphen (–) indicates a range of consecutive characters. A caret (^) as the first character in the brackets reverses the sense: it matches any one character *not* in the list. A hyphen or a right square bracket (]) as the first character is treated as a member of the list. All other meta-characters are treated as members of the list.
\{*n*,*m*\}	Match a range of occurrences of the single character that immediately precedes it. The preceding character can also be a regular expression. \{*n*\} will match exactly *n* occurrences; \{*n*,\} will match at least *n* occurrences; and \{*n*,*m*\} will match any number of occurrences between *n* and *m*.
\	Turn off the special meaning of the character that follows.
\(\)	Save the pattern enclosed between \(and \) into a special holding space. Up to nine patterns can be saved on a single line. They can be "replayed" in substitutions by the escape sequences \1 to \9.
\< \>	Match characters at beginning (\<) or end (\>) of a word.
+	Match one or more instances of preceding regular expression.
?	Match zero or one instances of preceding regular expression.
|	Match the regular expression specified before or after.
( )	Apply a match to the enclosed group of regular expressions.

The characters in Table 27-7 have special meaning only in replacement patterns.

Table 27-7. Special Characters in Replacement Patterns

\	Turn off the special meaning of the character that follows.
n	Restore the *n*th pattern previously saved by \(and \). *n* is a number from 1 to 9, with 1 starting on the left.
&	Re-use the search pattern as part of the replacement pattern.
~	Re-use the previous replacement pattern in the current replacement pattern.
\u	Convert first character of replacement pattern to uppercase.
\U	Convert replacement pattern to uppercase.
\l	Convert first character of replacement pattern to lowercase.
\L	Convert replacement pattern to lowercase.

Examples of Searching

When used with *grep* or *egrep*, regular expressions are surrounded by quotes. (If the pattern contains a $, you must use single quotes; e.g., `'pattern'`.) When used with *ed*, *ex*, *sed*, and *awk*, regular expressions are usually surrounded by / (although any delimiter works). Table 27-8 has some example patterns.

Table 27-8. Search Pattern Examples

Pattern	What Does it Match?
bag	The string bag.
^bag	bag at beginning of line.
bag$	bag at end of line.
^bag$	bag as the only word on line.
[Bb]ag	Bag or bag.
b[aeiou]g	Second letter is a vowel.
b[^aeiou]g	Second letter is a consonant (or uppercase or symbol).
b.g	Second letter is any character.
^...$	Any line containing exactly three characters.
^\.	Any line that begins with a . (dot).
^\.[a-z][a-z]	Same, followed by two lowercase letters (e.g., *troff* requests).
^\.[a-z]\{2\}	Same as previous, *grep* or *sed* only.
^[^.]	Any line that doesn't begin with a . (dot).
bugs*	bug, bugs, bugss, etc.
"word"	A word in quotes.
"*word"*	A word, with or without quotes.
[A-Z][A-Z]*	One or more uppercase letters.
[A-Z]+	Same, *egrep* or *awk* only.
[A-Z].*	An uppercase letter, followed by zero or more characters.
[A-Z]*	Zero or more uppercase letters.
[a-zA-Z]	Any letter.
[^0-9A-Za-z]	Any symbol (not a letter or a number).
[567]	One of the numbers 5, 6, or 7.

egrep or awk pattern:

five|six|seven	One of the words five, six, or seven.
80[23]?86	One of the numbers 8086, 80286, or 80386.
compan(y|ies)	One of the words company or companies.

ex or vi pattern:

\<the	Words like theater or the.
the\>	Words like breathe or the.
\<the\>	The word the.

Table 27-8. Search Pattern Examples (continued)

sed or grep pattern:

```
0\{5,\}                    Five or more zeros in a row.
[0-9]\{3\}-[0-9]\{2\}-[0-9]\{4\}
                           US social security number (nnn-nn-nnnn).
```

Examples of Searching and Replacing

The following examples show the meta-characters available to *sed* or *ex*. (*ex* commands begin with a colon.) A space is marked by □; a TAB is marked by *tab*.

Command	Result
`s/.*/( & )/`	Redo the entire line, but add parentheses.
`s/.*/mv & &.old/`	Change a wordlist into *mv* commands.
`/^$/d`	Delete blank lines.
`:g/^$/d`	*ex* version of previous.
`/^[□tab]*$/d`	Delete blank lines, plus lines containing spaces or TABs.
`:g/^[□tab]*$/d`	*ex* version of previous.
`s/□□*/□/g`	Turn one or more spaces into one space.
`:%s/□□*/□/g`	*ex* version of previous.
`:s/[0-9]/Item &:/`	Turn a number into an item label (on the current line).
`:s`	Repeat the substitution on the first occurrence.
`:&`	Same.
`:sg`	Same, but for all occurrences on the line.
`:&g`	Same.
`:%&g`	Repeat the substitution globally.
`:.,$s/Fortran/\U&/g`	Change word to uppercase, on current line to last line.
`:%s/.*/\L&/`	Lowercase entire file.
`:s/\<./\u&/g`	Uppercase first letter of each word on current line (useful for titles).
`:%s/yes/No/g`	Globally change a word to No.
`:%s/Yes/~/g`	Globally change a different word to No (previous replacement).
`s/die or do/do or die/`	Transpose words.
`s/\([Dd]ie\) or \([Dd]o\)/\2 or \1/`	Transpose, using hold buffers to preserve case.

—*DG* from the Nutshell Handbook *UNIX in a Nutshell (SVR4/Solaris)*

28

Searching Through Files

28.01 Different Versions of grep

grep is one of UNIX's most useful tools. As a result, everyone seems to want their own, slightly different version that solves a different piece of the problem. (Maybe this is a problem in itself; there really should be only one *grep*, as the manual page says.) Three versions of *grep* come with every UNIX system; in addition, there are six or seven freely-available versions that we'll mention here, and probably dozens of others that you can find kicking around the net.

Here are the different versions of *grep* and what they offer. We'll start with the standard versions:

- Plain old *grep*: great for searching with regular expressions (article 28.02).

- Extended *grep* (or *egrep*): handles extended regular expressions. It is also, arguably, the fastest of the standard *grep*s (article 28.05).

- So-called "fast *grep*," or *fgrep*. Actually, this is the slowest of them all. Useful to search for patterns with literal backslashes, asterisks, and so on that you'd otherwise have to escape somehow. Has the interesting ability to search for multiple strings (articles 28.06, 28.07).

Now for the public domain versions:

- *agrep*, or "approximate *grep*"; a tool that finds lines that "more or less" match your search string. A very interesting and useful tool (article 28.08).

- Very fast versions of *grep*, such as the Free Software Foundation's *egrep* (article 28.09).

- *rcsgrep*, which searches through RCS files *(21.15)* (article 28.10).

In addition, you can simulate the action of *grep* with *sed*, *awk*, and *perl*. These utilities allow you to write such variations as a *grep* that searches for a phrase that might be split across two lines *(28.11)*, or context *grep* programs *(28.12, 28.13)*, which show you a few lines before and after the text you find. (Normal *greps* just show the lines that match.)

—*ML*

28.02 *Searching for Text with grep*

There are many well-known benefits provided by *grep* to the user who doesn't remember what his or her files contain. Even users of non-UNIX systems who make fun of its obscure name wish they had a utility with its power to search through a set of files for an arbitrary text pattern, known as a regular expression *(27.04)*.

The main function of *grep* is to look for strings matching a regular expression and print only the lines found. Use *grep* when you want to look at how a particular word is used in one or more files. For example, here's how to list the lines in the file *ch04* that contain either *run-time* or *run time*:

".." 9.10

```
$ grep "run[- ]time" ch04
This procedure avoids run-time errors for not-assigned
and a run-time error message is produced.
run-time error message is produced.
program aborts and a run-time error message is produced.
DIMENSION statement in BASIC is executable at run time.
This means that arrays can be redimensioned at run time.
accessible or not open, the program aborts and a run-time
```

Another use might be to look for a specific *nroff/troff* macro *(45.15)* in a file. In a file coded with mm macros, the following command will list top-level (.H1) and second-level (.H2) headings:

[..] 16.02

```
$ grep "^\.H[12]" ch0[12]
ch01:.H1 "Introduction"
ch01:.H1 "Windows, Screens, and Images"
ch01:.H2 "The Standard Screen-stdscr"
ch01:.H2 "Adding Characters"
ch02:.H1 "Introduction"
ch02:.H1 "What Is Terminal Independence?"
ch02:.H2 "Termcap"
ch02:.H2 "Terminfo"
```

In effect, it produces a quick outline of the contents of these files.

grep is also often used as a filter *(1.03)*, to select from the output of some other program. For example, not all versions of *ps (40.05)* allow you to print out the processes belonging to another user, but it's easy to simulate this behavior by listing all processes and piping the output to *grep*:

```
% ps -aux | grep jerry
```

There are several options commonly used with *grep*. The *–i* option specifies that the search ignore the distinction between uppercase and lowercase. The *–c* option tells *grep* to return only a count of the number of lines matched. The *–w* option searches for the pattern "as a word." For example, `grep if` would match words like *cliff* or *knife*, but `grep -w if` wouldn't. The *–l* option *(16.08)* returns only the name of the file when *grep* finds a match. This can be used to prepare a list of files for another command. The *–v* option *(28.03)* reverses the normal action, and only prints out lines that don't match the search pattern.

—*DD* from *UNIX Text Processing*, Hayden Books, 1987

28.03 Finding Text that Doesn't Match

The *grep* programs have one very handy feature: they can select lines that don't match a pattern just as they can select the lines that do. Simply use the *–v* option.

I used this most recently when working on this book. We have thousands of separate files under RCS *(21.15)* and I sometimes forget which ones I've got checked out. Since there's a lot of clutter in the directory, and several people working there, a simple *ls* won't do. So I use a *find* alias to list only the files belonging to me. (It's a version of the *find* alias described in article 18.24, with *–user tim* added to select only my own files.)

Believe it or not, even that isn't specific enough. There are a variety of temporary files created by some of our printing scripts that I don't want to see. All of these files have names beginning with a comma, so when I want to see which files I might have forgotten to check back in to RCS, I type:

```
% find. | grep -v ,
```

Obviously, that's about as specific, non-reproducible an example as you're likely to find anywhere! But it's precisely these kind of special cases that call for a rich vocabulary of tips and tricks. You'll never have to use *grep –v* for this particular purpose, but you'll find a use for it someday.

—*TOR*

28.04 Finding a Pattern Only When It's a Word

One very useful *grep* option is *–w*, which tells it to report a line containing the pattern only when the pattern appears as a separate word. This is just like the \< and \> *(27.04)* pattern-matching characters, but a lot easier to type.

—*TOR*

28.05 Extended Searching for Text with egrep

The *egrep* command is yet another version of *grep (28.02)*, one that extends the syntax of regular expressions *(27.04)*. A plus sign (+) following a regular expression matches one or more occurrences of the regular expression; a question mark (?) matches zero or one occurrences. In addition, regular expressions can be nested within parentheses:

```
% egrep "Lab(oratorie)?s" name.list
AT&T Bell Laboratories
AT&T Bell Labs
Symtel Labs of Chicago
```

Parentheses surround a second regular expression and ? modifies this expression. The nesting helps to eliminate unwanted matches; for instance, the word *Labors* or *oratories* would not be matched.

Another special feature of *egrep* is the vertical bar (|), which serves as an *or* operator between two expressions. Lines matching either expression are printed, as in the next example:

```
% egrep "stdscr|curscr" ch03
into the stdscr, a character array.
When stdscr is refreshed, the
stdscr is refreshed.
curscr.
initscr() creates two windows: stdscr
and curscr.
```

Remember to put the expression inside quotation marks to protect the vertical bar from being interpreted by the shell as a pipe symbol. Look at the next example:

```
% egrep "Alcuin (User|Programmer)('s)? Guide" docguide
Alcuin Progammer's Guide is a thorough
refer to the Alcuin User Guide
Alcuin User's Guide introduces new users to
```

You can see the flexibility that *egrep*'s syntax can give you, matching either User or Programmer and matching them whether or not they had an 's. Article 21.08 has another example and explanation of *egrep*.

Both *egrep* and *fgrep (28.06)* can read search patterns from a file using the *-f* option *(28.07)*. The *calendar (50.05)* utility makes a file full of complicated expressions for matching dates.

—*DD* from *UNIX Text Processing*, Hayden Books, 1987

28.06 Fast grep Isn't

Have you heard this old saw:

> UNIX beginners use *grep* because it's all they know about.

> Intermediate users use *fgrep* because the manual says it's faster.

> Advanced users use *egrep* because they've tried it.

Yes, despite what the manual page says (or rather, used to say, because nowadays, many *grep* manual pages have been rewritten to acknowledge the fact), *fgrep* is usually the slowest of the three standard *grep*s.

If you want to prove this to yourself, try using the *runtime* program (shown in article 41.04) to give you the average execution time of a search. Here's the result of my search for the string *Waldo* in a large directory crowded with saved mail files.

```
% runtime -10 grep Waldo  *
  ...
AVERAGES:
 4.13u  0.83s 0:04 0+203k 21+0io 19pf+0w
% runtime -10 fgrep Waldo *
  ...
AVERAGES:
 5.19u  0.80s 0:05 0+195k 4+0io 2pf+0w
% runtime -10 egrep Waldo
  ...
AVERAGES:
 2.61u  0.76s 0:02 0+244k 0+0io 0pf+0w
```

On my Sparcstation IPC, *grep* managed the search in four seconds, *fgrep* in five, and *egrep* in only two. *egrep* also used the least CPU time.

Just for the heck of it, let's see how some other search programs stack up. *sed*, *awk*, and *perl* can also emulate the action of *grep*:

```
% runtime -10 sed -n '/Waldo/p' *
  ...
AVERAGES:
 3.64u  1.20s 0:04 0+227k 2+0io 1pf+0w
% runtime -10 awk '/Waldo/' *
  ...
AVERAGES:
 4.86u  0.76s 0:05 0+279k 1+0io 0pf+0w
% runtime -10 perl -ne \'print if \(/Waldo/\) \; \' *
  ...
AVERAGES:
 2.94u  0.69s 0:03 0+498k 28+4io 27pf+0w
```

(Note that we have to escape any characters that the shell might interpret in the *perl* command line.)

perl is faster than all but *egrep*, but even *sed* edges your basic *grep* by a hair. And *fgrep* is by far the slowest—it even lost to *awk*!

---

fgrep

This doesn't mean that *fgrep* is useless, though. It has a couple of handy options: *–x* requires a line to be exactly the same as the search pattern; *–f (28.07)* takes one or many search patterns from a file. You can sometimes exploit the fact that *fgrep* doesn't understand regular expressions, and so using it to search for literal asterisks or other regular expression meta-characters can save you a bit of quoting. The time saved on the command line can be worth the slower execution speed.

—TOR

28.07 grepping for a List of Patterns

egrep (28.05) lets you look for multiple patterns using its grouping and alternation operators (big words for parentheses and a vertical bar). But sometimes, even that isn't enough.

Both *egrep* and *fgrep (28.06)* support a *–f* option, which allows you to save a list of patterns (fixed strings in the case of *fgrep*) in a file, and search for all the items in the list with a single invocation of the program. For example, in writing this book, we've used this feature to check for consistent usage for a list of terms across all articles:

```
% egrep -f terms *
```

(To be more accurate, we used rcsegrep *(28.10)*, since the articles are all kept under RCS *(21.15)*, but you get the idea.)

—TOR

28.08 agrep: Searching for Approximate Matches (and More)

agrep

[Sun Wu and Udi Manber of the University of Arizona have made one of the nicer additions to the grep *family.* agrep *is not only one of the faster greps around, it has the unique feature that it will look for approximate matches. It's also record-oriented rather than line-oriented.... But why don't I let the authors tell the story.— TOR]*

The three most significant features of *agrep* that are not supported by the *grep* family are:

1. The ability to search for approximate patterns, with a user-definable level of accuracy. For example,

```
% agrep -2 homogenos foo
```

will find "homogeneous" as well as any other word that can be obtained from "homogenos" with at most 2 substitutions, insertions, or deletions.

```
% agrep -B homogenos foo
```

will generate a message of the form:

```
best match has 2 errors, there are 5 matches, output them? (y/n)
```

2. *agrep* is record-oriented rather than just line oriented; a record is by default a line, but it can be user-defined with the *−d* option specifying a pattern that will be used as a record delimiter. For example,

```
% agrep -d '^From ' 'pizza' mbox
```

outputs all mail messages *(1.33)* (delimited by a line beginning with *From* and a space) in the file *mbox* that contain the keyword *pizza*. Another example:

```
% agrep -d '$$' pattern foo
```

will output all paragraphs (separated by an empty line) that contain *pattern*.

3. *agrep* allows multiple patterns with AND (or OR) logic queries. For example,

```
% agrep -d '^From ' 'burger,pizza' mbox
```

outputs all mail messages containing at least one of the two keywords (, stands for OR).

```
% agrep -d '^From ' 'good;pizza' mbox
```

outputs all mail messages containing both keywords.

Putting these options together one can write queries like:

```
% agrep -d '$$' -2 '<CACM>;TheAuthor;Curriculum;<198[5-9]>' bib
```

which outputs all paragraphs referencing articles in CACM between 1985 and 1989 by *TheAuthor* dealing with Curriculum. Two errors are allowed, but they cannot be in either CACM or the year. (The <> brackets forbid errors in the pattern between them.)

Other features include searching for regular expressions (with or without errors), unlimited wildcards, limiting the errors to only insertions or only substitutions or any combination, allowing each deletion, for example, to be counted as, say, 2 substitutions or 3 insertions, restricting parts of the query to be exact and parts to be approximate, and many more.

Please mail bug reports (or any other comments) to *sw@cs.arizona.edu* or *udi@cs.arizona.edu*. We would appreciate if users notify us (at the address above) of any extensions, improvements, or interesting uses of this software.

—SW, UM

28.09 New greps are much Faster

grep

Many of the newer, public domain greps such as *agrep* *(28.08)* and GNU *egrep*, use the much faster Boyer-Moore search algorithm. Both *agrep* and GNU *egrep* are on the Power Tools disk.*

In article 28.06, we used the *time* program to compare the execution times of *fgrep*, *egrep*, and *grep*. This time we'll use the *runtime* program (shown in article 41.04) to show the average time needed to search for the string *Waldo* in a large directory of files. First, let's show the results using *agrep*:

```
% runtime -10 agrep Waldo *
    ...
AVERAGES:
 0.48u  0.73s 0:01 0+261k 0+0io 0pf+0w
```

Here's the same output for GNU *egrep*:

```
% runtime -10 egrep Waldo *
    ...
AVERAGES:
 0.62u  0.62s 0:01 0+242k 0+0io 0pf+0w
```

Now compare these numbers against those in article 28.06. For example, here's what we get from the much-maligned everyday *grep*:

```
% runtime -10 grep Waldo *
    ...
AVERAGES:
 4.13u  0.83s 0:04 0+203k 21+0io 19pf+0w
```

grep took four clock seconds to search all the files, while both *agrep* and GNU *egrep* breezed by in one. So are you a believer yet?

—TOR, LM

28.10 Search RCS files with rcsgrep

rcsgrep

Storing multiple versions of a file in RCS *(21.14)* saves space. How can you search a lot of those files at once? You could check out all the files, then run *grep*—but you'll have to remove the files after you're done searching. Or, you could search the RCS files themselves with a command like `grep foo RCS/*,v`—but that can show you garbage lines from previous revisions, log messages, and other text that isn't in the latest revision of your file.

The *rcsgrep* script—and two links to it named *rcsegrep* and *rcsfgrep*—run *grep*, *egrep* *(28.05)*, and *fgrep* *(28.06)* on all files in the RCS directory. (You can also choose the files to search.) The script checks out each file, pipes it to the version of grep you chose, then uses *sed* to add the matching filename. The output looks just like *grep*'s—although, by default, you'll also see the messages from the *co* command (the *–s* option silences those messages).

---

*The GNU *egrep* executable is also installed under the name *grep*—so don't get confused!

Some *grep* options need special handling to work right in the script: *−e*, *−f*, and *−l*. (For instance, *−e* and *−f* have an argument after them. The script has to pass both the option and its argument.) The script passes any other options you type to the grep command. Your grep versions may have some other options that need special handling, too. Just edit the script to handle them.

You can install this script from the Power Tools disk or from the online archive *(54.07)*. If you get it from the archive, ask tar to install *rcsgrep* and its two other links:

```
% tar xvf archive.tar rcsgrep rcsegrep rcsfgrep
x rcsgrep, 2587 bytes, 6 tape blocks
rcsegrep linked to rcsgrep
rcsfgrep linked to rcsgrep
```

The script tests its name to decide whether to act like *grep*, *egrep*, or *fgrep*.

—JP

28.11 Searching for a Pattern Across Two Lines

One weakness of the *grep* family of programs is that they are line-oriented. They only read one line at a time, and so they can't find patterns (such as phrases) that are split across two lines.

phrase

This is a job for *sed (35.24)*, *awk (38.18)*, or *perl (39.01)*. The disk includes a *sed* version of a program we call *phrase*. (Article 35.17 explains how *phrase* works.)

Here's the result when the program is run on a sample file:

```
$ phrase "the procedure is followed" sect3
If a pattern is followed by a \f(CW!\fP, then the procedure
is followed for all lines that do \fInot\fP match the pattern.
so that the procedure is followed only if there is no match.
```

[*agrep (28.08)* can also do multi-line searches. One advantage of the *phrase* script is that it shows how to handle multiple-line patterns in *sed*—and can be adapted for work other than searches.—*JP*]

—TOR

28.12 Make Custom grep Commands (etc.) with perl

All of the various *grep*-like utilities perform pretty much the same function, with minor differences—they search for a specified pattern in some or all of a file, and then display that pattern with varying amounts of surrounding context.

As you use UNIX more and more, you will find yourself wanting to do an increasing number of *grep*-like tasks, but no particular UNIX utility will quite suit them all (hence the need for the various *grep* utilities discussed earlier in this section). You'll start accumulating C programs, *awk* scripts, and shell scripts to do these different tasks, and you'll be craving one utility that can easily encompass them all so you don't have to waste the disk space for all of those binaries. That utility is Perl *(39.01)*, the "Practical Extraction and Report Language" developed by Larry Wall. According to the documentation accompanying Perl, it is "an interpreted language optimized for scanning arbitrary text files, extracting information from those text files, and printing reports based on that information." If you don't already have *perl* installed on your system, you can get it from the Power Tools disk.

perl

For example, to search for a pattern in the header of a Usenet message:

```
perl -ne 'exit if (/^$/); print if (/pattern/);' filename
```

[This works because mail and Usenet *(1.33)* messages always use a blank line—indicated by ^$ in regular expression syntax—to separate the header from the body of the message.—*TOR*]

To do a search for a pattern and print the paragraphs in which it appears:

```
perl -ne '$/ = "\n\n"; print if (/pattern/);' filename
```

[This assumes that paragraphs are delimited by a double linefeed—that is, a blank line. You'd have to adjust this script for a *troff* or TeX document where paragraphs are separated by special codes.—*TOR*]

To do a simple context *grep* that prints the line before, including, and after a pattern:

#! *47.03*

```
#!/usr/bin/perl

$before = "";
$including = "";
$print = 0;
$pattern = shift || die "$0: No pattern specified.\n";

while (<>) {
    if ($print) {
        print "$before$including$_";
        $print = 0;
    }
    $before = $including;
    $including = $_;
    $print = 1 if (/$pattern/o);
}
```

Note that special Perl operators like the <> operator used above make file I/O and other common operations very easy.

Searching through files is one of Perl's strengths, but certainly not its only strength. Perl encompasses all of the functionality of *sed, awk, grep, find,* and other UNIX utilities. Furthermore, a Perl program to do something originally done with one or more of these utilities is usually faster and easier to read than the non-Perl solution.

—*JIK*

28.13 More grep-like Programs Written in Perl

[Article 28.12 gave a sense of how easy it might be to write custom search programs in Perl . . . but until you learn the language, you can't rip these off whenever you find yourself in need. This article describes a few more custom greps written in Perl. It doesn't show the scripts themselves, just how to use them. If you like them, they are on the disk.— TOR]

tgrep

The *tgrep* program *greps* only those files containing textual data. It's useful in a directory that has mixed binary and textual files, when the filenames aren't a sufficient clue to the nature of the file. *tgrep* has one option, –*l*, which causes it to list the files containing the pattern rather than listing the lines containing the pattern.

pipegrep

The *pipegrep* program *greps* the output of a series of commands. The difficulty with doing this using the normal *grep* program is that you lose track of which file was being processed. This program prints out the command it was executing at the time, including the filename. The command, which is a single argument, will be executed once for each file in the list. If you give the string { } anywhere in the command, the filename will be substituted at that point. Otherwise the filename will be added onto the end of the command. This program has one option, –*l*, which causes it to list the files containing the pattern. For example [*nm* is a programmers' utility that prints symbol name lists—*JP*]:

```
$ cd /usr/lib
$ pipegrep 'sys_nerr' nm lib*.a
nm /usr/lib/libX11.a |:        U _sys_nerr
nm /usr/lib/libXaw.a |:        U _sys_nerr
nm /usr/lib/libXaw.a |:        U _sys_nerr
nm /usr/lib/libc.a |:          U _sys_nerr
                    .
                    .
                    .
```

cgrep

The *cgrep* program *greps* for a pattern in the specified files, and prints out that line with several lines of surrounding context. If invoked on itself with this command:

```
$ cgrep eval cgrep
```

cgrep will print out two sets of lines, with the line containing "eval" in the middle of each set of lines, like this:

```
$pat =~ s#/#\\/#g;

# First line of input will be middle of array.
# In the eval below, it will be $ary[$context].

$_ = <>;
push(@ary,$_);


------


# Now use @ary as a silo, shifting and pushing.
```

```
eval <<LOOP_END;
    while (\$ary[$context]) {
        if (\$ary[$context] =~ /$pat/) {
            print "------\n" if \$seq++;
```

This context grep script is more powerful than the one shown in article 28.12 because it lets you specify how many lines of context you want if you want more or less than the default. For example:

```
$ cgrep -3 pattern files
```

would give you three lines of context above and below the matching line. Each occurrence is separated from the next by a short horizontal line (--------).

—*LW, RS* from the Nutshell Handbook *Programming Perl*

28.14 Compound Searches

The *grep* commands can match a pattern on a single line. None (except *agrep* match files that contain two patterns on different lines. Sometimes I need that.

Here's an example. I wanted to search all my Korn shell script files (which start with the line #! /bin/ksh) for lines that started with the word *if*. I didn't want to see lines with *if* in other files. The answer: have one *grep* –*l (16.08)* find the files with #! /bin/ksh—and output those filenames. Use backquotes to pass those filenames to another *grep*; it searches for the lines with *if*:

```
$ grep -w "if" `grep -l "^#! /bin/ksh" *`
bar:if [ -w "$file" ]
bkedit:    if cp "$1" "$1.bak"
    ...
```

It might be more efficient to do that with a program like *awk* that can open and search each file just once. This method is probably easier to do quickly.

—*JP*

28.15 Narrowing a Search Quickly

If you're searching a long file to find a particular word or name, or you're running a program like *ls* –*l* and you want to filter some lines, here's a quick way to narrow down the search. As an example, say your phone file has 20,000 lines like these:

```
Smith, Nancy:MFG:50 Park Place:Huntsville:(205)234-5678
```

and you want to find someone named Nancy. When you see more information, you know you can find which of the Nancys she is:

```
% grep Nancy phones
```

Use the C shell's history mechanism *(12.02)* and *sed (35.24)* to cut out lines you don't want. For example, about a third of the Nancys are in Huntsville, and you know she doesn't work there:

```
% !! | sed -e /Huntsville/d
grep Nancy phones | sed -e /Huntsville/d
```

The shell shows the command it's executing: the previous command (!!) piped to *sed*, which deletes lines in the *grep* output that have the word *Huntsville*.

Okay. You know Nancy doesn't work in the MFG or SLS groups, so delete those lines, too:

```
% !! -e /MFG/d -e /SLS/d
grep Nancy phones | sed -e /Huntsville/d -e /MFG/d -e /SLS/d
```

Keep using !! to repeat the previous command line, and adding more *sed* expressions, until the list gets short enough. The same thing works for other commands—when you're hunting for errors in *uulog (1.33)* output, for example, and you want to skip lines with SUCCEEDED and OK:

```
% uulog | sed -e /SUCCEEDED/d -e /OK/d
...
```

If the matching pattern has anything but letters and numbers in it, you'll have to understand shell quoting *(9.10)* and *sed* regular expressions *(27.04)*. Most times, though, this quick-and-dirty way works just fine.

—*JP*

28.16 *Faking Case-insensitive Searches*

This may be the simplest tip in the book, but it's something that doesn't occur to lots of users.

On most UNIX implementations, the *egrep* command doesn't support the $-i$ option, which requests case-insensitive searches. I find that case-insensitive searches are absolutely essential, particularly to writers. You never know whether or not any particular word will be capitalized.

To fake a case-insensitive search with *egrep*, just eliminate any letters that might be uppercase. Instead of searching for *Example*, just search for *xample*. If the letter that might be capitalized occurs in the middle of a phrase, you can replace the missing letter with a "dot" (single character) wildcard, rather than omitting it.

Sure, you could do this the "right way" with a command like:

```
% egrep '[eE]xample' *
```

But our shortcut is easier.

This tip obviously isn't limited to *egrep*; it applies to any utility that only implements case-sensitive searches, like *more*.

—*ML*

28.17 Finding a Character in a Column

Here's an idea for finding lines that have a given character in a column. Use the following simple *awk (38.18)* command:

```
% awk 'substr($0,n,1) == "c"' filename
```

where *c* is the character you're searching for, and *n* is the column you care about.

Where would you do this? If you're processing a file with very strict formatting, this might be useful; for example, you might have a telephone list with a # in column 2 for "audio" telephone numbers, $ for dial-up modems, and % for fax machines. A script for looking up phone numbers might use an *awk* command like this to prevent you from mistakenly talking to a FAX machine.

If your data has any TAB characters, the columns might not be where you expect. In that case, use *expand (43.04)* on the file, then pipe it to *awk*.

—*JP, ML*

28.18 Fast Searches and Spelling Checks with "look"

Every so often, someone has designed a new, faster *grep*-type program. Public domain software archives have more than a few of them. One of the fastest search programs has been around for years: *look*. It uses a binary search method that's very fast. But *look* won't solve all your problems: it works only on files that have been sorted *(37.01)*. If you have a big file or database that can be sorted, searching it with *look* will save a lot of time. For example, to search for all lines that start with *Alpha*:

```
% look Alpha filename
Alpha particle
Alphanumeric
```

look

The *look* program can also be used to check the spelling of a word or find a related word; see article 30.03. If you don't have *look* installed on your system, you can get it from the Power Tools disk.

—*JP*

28.19 Finding Words Inside Binaries and Other Non-printable Files: strings

If you try to read binaries *(55.01)* on your screen with, say, *cat −v (26.07)*, you'll see a lot of non-printable characters. Buried in there somewhere though are words and strings of characters that might make some sense. For example, if the code is copyrighted, you can usually find that information in the binary. The pathnames of special files that the program reads will probably show up. If you're trying to figure out which program printed an error message, use *strings* on the binaries and look for the error. Some versions of *strings* do a better job of getting just the useful information; others may write a lot of junk, too. But what the heck—pipe the output to a pager *(26.03, 26.04)* or *grep (28.02)*, redirect it to a file—ignore the stuff you don't want.

Here's a (shortened) example on SunOS:

```
% strings /bin/write
@(#)write.c 1.10 88/05/10 SMI
Usage: write user [ttyname]
/etc/utmp
write: Can't open /etc/utmp
write: Can't find your tty
        ...
Message from %s@%s on %s at %d:%02d ...
Write failed (%s logged out?)
/bin/sh
        (((((
DDDDDDDDDD
AAAAAA
BBBBBB
```

The first line comes from SCCS *(21.12)*—you can see the version number, the date the code was last modified or released, and so on. The `%s`, `%d`, and `%02d` are special places that the *printf*(3) function will replace with values like the username, hostname, hour, and minute.

—JP

28.20 A Highlighting grep

Does it happen to you that you *grep* for a word, lines scroll down your screen, and it's hard to find the word on each line? For example, suppose I'm looking for any mail messages I've saved that say anything about the *perl* programming language. But when I *grep* the file, most of it seems useless:

```
% grep perl ~/Mail/save
> and some of it wouldn't compile properly.  I wonder if
Subject: install script, for perl scripts
perl itself is installed?
> run but dies with a read error because it isn't properly
> if I can get it installed properly on another machine I
> run but dies with a read error because it isn't properly
> if I can get it installed properly on another machine I
```

hgrep

Well, as described on its own manual page, here's a program that's "trivial, but cute." *hgrep* runs a *grep* and highlights the string being searched for, to make it easier for us to find what we're looking for.

```
% hgrep perl ~/Mail/save
> and some of it wouldn't compile properly.  I wonder if
Subject: install script, for perl scripts
perl itself is installed?
> run but dies with a read error because it isn't properly
> if I can get it installed properly on another machine I
> run but dies with a read error because it isn't properly
> if I can get it installed properly on another machine I
```

And now we know why the output looked useless: because most of it is! Luckily, *hgrep* is just a front-end; it simply passes all its arguments to *grep*. So *hgrep* necessarily accepts all of *grep*'s options, and I can just use the −*w* option *(28.04)* to weed the output down to what I want:

```
% hgrep -w perl ~/Mail/save
Subject: install script, for perl scripts
perl itself is installed?
```

—LM

29

Comparing Files

29.01 Checking Differences with diff

The *diff* command displays different versions of lines that are found when comparing two files. It prints a message that uses *ed*-like notation (*a* for append, *c* for change, and *d* for delete) to describe how a set of lines has changed. This is followed by the lines themselves. The < character precedes lines from the first file and > precedes lines from the second file.

Let's create an example to explain the output produced by *diff*. Look at the contents of three sample files:

test1	*test2*	*test3*
apples	apples	oranges
oranges	oranges	walnuts
walnuts	grapes	chestnuts

When you run *diff* on *test1* and *test2*, the following output is produced:

```
$ diff test1 test2
3c3
< walnuts
---
> grapes
```

The *diff* command displays the only line that differs between the two files. To understand the report, remember that *diff* is prescriptive, describing what changes need to be made to the first file to make it the same as the second file. This report specifies that only the third line is affected, exchanging walnuts for grapes. This is more apparent if you use the −*e* option, which produces an editing script that can be submitted to *ed*, the UNIX line editor. (You must redirect standard output *(14.01)* to capture this script in a file.)

```
$ diff -e test1 test2
3c
grapes
.
```

This script, if run on *test1*, will bring *test1* into agreement with *test2*. (Article 29.08 describes how to get *ed* to execute this script.)

If you compare the first and third files, you find more differences:

```
$ diff test1 test3
1d0
< apples
3a3
> chestnuts
```

To make *test1* the same as *test3*, you'd have to delete the first line (apples) and append the third line from *test3* after the third line in *test1*. Again, this can be seen more clearly in the editing script produced by the *–e* option. Notice that the script specifies editing lines in reverse order; otherwise, changing the first line would alter all succeeding line numbers.

```
$ diff -e test1 test3
3a
chestnuts
.
1d
```

So what's this good for? Here's one example.

When working on a document, it is not an uncommon practice to make a copy of a file and edit the copy rather than the original. This might be done, for example, if someone other than the writer is inputing edits from a written copy. The *diff* command can be used to compare the two versions of a document. A writer could use it to proof an edited copy against the original.

```
$ diff brochure brochure.edits
49c43,44
< environment for program development and communications,
---
> environment for multiprocessing, program development
> and communications, programmers
56c51
< offering even more power and productivity for commericial
---
> offering even more power and productivity for commercial
76c69
< Languages such as FORTRAN, COBOL, Pascal, and C can be
---
> Additional languages such as FORTRAN, COBOL, Pascal, and
```

Using *diff* in this manner is a simple way for a writer to examine changes without reading the entire document. By redirecting *diff* output to a file, you can keep a record of changes made to any document. In fact, just that technique is used by SCCS and RCS *(21.12)* to manage multiple revisions of source code and documents.

—DD from *UNIX Text Processing*, Hayden Books, 1987

29.02 Comparing Three Different Versions with diff3

You can use the *diff3* command to look at differences between three files. Here are three sample files, repeated from article 29.01:

test1	test2	test3
apples	apples	oranges
oranges	oranges	walnuts
walnuts	grapes	chestnuts

For each set of differences, *diff3* displays a row of equal signs (====) followed by 1, 2, or 3, indicating which file is different; if no number is specified, then all three files differ. Then, using *ed*-like notation *(29.01)*, the differences are described for each file.

```
$ diff3 test1 test2 test3
====3
1:1c
2:1c
  apples
3:0a
====
1:3c
  walnuts
2:3c
  grapes
3:2,3c
  walnuts
  chestnuts
```

With the output of *diff3*, it is easy to keep track of which file is which; however, the prescription given is a little harder to decipher. To bring these files into agreement, the first range of text (after ====3) shows that you would have to add apples at the beginning of the third file (3:0a). The second range tells you to change line 3 of the second file to line 3 of the first file; and change lines 2 and 3 of the third file, effectively dropping the last line.

The *diff3* command also has a *−e* option for creating an editing script for *ed*. It doesn't work quite the way you might think. Basically, it creates a script for building the first file from the second and third files.

```
$ diff3 -e test1 test2 test3
3c
walnuts
chestnuts
.
1d
w
q
```

If you reverse the second and third files, a different script is produced:

```
$ diff3 -e test1 test3 test2
3c
grapes
```

w

q

As you might guess, this is basically the same output as doing a *diff* on the first and third files. (The only difference in the output is the result of a rather errant inconsistency between *diff* and *diff3*. The System V version of *diff3* produces an *ed* script that ends with the commands that save the edited version of the file. The Berkeley *diff3*, and both versions of *diff*, require that you supply the w and q. We show the System V version of *diff3* here.)

—DD from *UNIX Text Processing*, Hayden Books, 1987

29.03 *Side-by-Side diffs: sdiff*

After you've used *diff* for a while, the output is easy to read. Sometimes, though, it's just easier to see two files side-by-side. The *sdiff* command does that. Between the files, it prints < to point to lines that are only in the first file, > for lines only in the second file, and | for lines that are in both, but different. By default, *sdiff* shows all the lines in both files. Here's a fairly bogus example that compares two files that contain the output of *who (53.04)* at different times:

```
$ sdiff -w75 who1 who2
jake     vt01      Sep 10 10:37       jake     vt01      Sep 10 10:37
uunmv    ttyi1i    Sep 16 11:43    <
jerry    ttyi1j    Sep 15 22:38       jerry    ttyi1j    Sep 15 22:38
jake     ttyp1     Sep  9 14:55       jake     ttyp1     Sep  9 14:55
jake     ttyp2     Sep  9 15:19    |  ellen    ttyp2     Sep 16 12:07
                                   >  carolo   ttyp5     Sep 16 13:03
alison   ttyp8     Sep  9 12:49       alison   ttyp8     Sep  9 12:49
```

To see only lines that are different, use −*s* (silent):

```
$ sdiff -s -w75 who1 who2
2d1
uunmv    ttyi1i    Sep 16 11:43    <
5c4,5
jake     ttyp2     Sep  9 15:19    |  ellen    ttyp2     Sep 16 12:07
                                   >  carolo   ttyp5     Sep 16 13:03
```

The output lines are usually 130 characters long. That's too long for 80-column-wide screens; if you can put your terminal in 132-column mode or stretch your window, fine. If you can't, use the −*w* option to set a narrower width, like −*w80* for 80-column lines; *sdiff* will show the first 37 characters from each line (it doesn't write quite all 80 columns). If you can set your printer to compressed type or have a very wide window, use an option like −*w170* to get all of each line.

Article 29.05 explains a very useful feature of *sdiff*: building one file interactively from two files you compare.

—JP

29.04 Comparing Files Alongside One Another

twin

sdiff (29.03) can be used to show *diff*ed files side-by-side, so that you can compare them in context. The *twin* program on the Power Tools disk is similar to *sdiff*, but it allows you to scroll through files alongside each other. *twin* is also a nicer about wrapping lines to make the files easier to read.

The *twin* program displays the two files in a split screen, with line numbers in the left margin:

```
1                                      |
2 You can use the bc program to        |You can also use bc to
3 convert from decimal to hex.         |convert from decimal to hex.
4 To do so, use obase to               |To do so, use obase to
5 set the base for output:             |set the base for output:
6                                      |
7  obase=16                            | obase=16
        . . .
```

The highlighted line might be underlined on your terminal. This line is the one that *twin* notices is different between the files.

twin uses a limited number of commands to move around in the files, which are shown when you first start up the program. You can use the u command to move both files up, and the v command to move both files down. There are also commands for moving only one side of the screen—for example, j to move the right-side text down.

—LM

29.05 Choosing Sides with sdiff

One problem you might be tempted to tackle with *diff3 (29.02)* is sorting out the mess that can happen if two people make copies of the same file, and then make changes to their copies. You often find that one version has some things right and another version has other things right. What if you wanted to compile a single version of this document that reflects the changes made to each copy? You want to select which version is correct for each set of differences. An effective way to do this would be to use *sdiff (29.03)*. (Of course, the best thing to do is to prevent the problem in the first place, by using SCCS or RCS (21.12).)

One of the most powerful uses of *sdiff* is to build an output file by interactively choosing between different versions of two files. To do this, you have to specify the *–o* option and the name of an output file to be created. The *sdiff* command then displays a % prompt after each set of differences.

You can compare the different versions and select the one that will be sent to the output file. Some of the possible responses are l to choose the left column, r to choose the right column, and q to exit the program.

—TOR, JP

29.06 diff for Very Long Files: bdiff

The *diff* command has trouble comparing very long files. Its *−h* option does a half-hearted and fast job, but it can miss changes in some cases. System V users have an alternative: *bdiff*. It ignores lines common to the beginning of both files, splits the remainder of each file into chunks, and runs *diff* on corresponding segments. (BSD users can probably make a shell script that does this, more or less. I haven't tried, though.) *bdiff* also adjusts the line numbers for each chunk to make it look like one *diff* did the whole job.

The good part of this is that *bdiff* will find all the differences. The bad part is that it might find "differences" that really aren't differences at all. This extra output is usually caused by uneven-length files. Here's an example of two files that aren't quite too long for the regular *diff*—it finds the single difference correctly. But *bdiff* finds another "difference" that isn't really a difference:

```
% diff log1 log2
11580a11581
> 15:25:42: ERROR: printer offline
% bdiff log1 log2
11580a11581
> 15:25:42: ERROR: printer offline
15080d15080
< 17:22:59: WARNING: queue too long; waiting
15080a15081
> 17:22:59: WARNING: queue too long; waiting
```

Even with that wart, sometimes you can't get along without *bdiff*.

—JP

29.07 More Friendly diff Output

ediff

If you find the output of the *diff*(29.01) program to be hard to follow, try using the *ediff* program to filter *diff* output into something more readable. For example, the *diff* program might produce the following output:

```
% diff chapter2 chapter2.new
i22,26d21
< Use the bc program to convert from decimal to hexadecimal.
< To do so, use the obase command to set the base for output:
<
<        obase=16
<
<
39c34,35
< See Section 5.6 for more examples of using bc.
---
> See Section 5.6 for information on how to use the bc command to
> convert decimal to hexadecimal.
```

This is a little hard to follow until you get used to the format. Now try filtering the output through *ediff*:

```
% diff chapter2 chapter2.new | ediff
```

```
-------- 5 lines deleted at 22:
Use the bc program to convert decimal to hexadecimal.
To do so, use the obase command to set the base for output:

        obase=16


-------- 1 line changed to 2 lines at 39 from:
See Section 5.6 for more examples of using bc.
-------- to:
See Section 5.6 for information on how to use the bc command to
convert decimal to hexadecimal.
```

Now you see why *ediff* describes itself as a "*diff* to English translator."

—LM

29.08 *ex Scripts Built by diff*

The *−e* option of *diff* produces an editing script usable with either *ex (34.04)* or *ed*, instead of the usual output. This script consists of a sequence of a (add), c (change), and d (delete) commands necessary to re-create *file1* from *file2* (the first and second files specified on the *diff* command line).

Obviously there is no need to completely re-create the first file from the second, because you could do that easily with *cp*. However, by editing the script produced by *diff*, you can come up with some desired combination of the two versions.

It might take you a moment to think of a case in which you might have use for this feature. Consider this one: two people have unknowingly made edits to different copies of a file, and you need the two versions merged. (This can happen especially easily in a networked environment, in which people copy files between machines. Poor coordination can easily result in this kind of problem.)

To make this situation concrete, let's take a look at two versions of the same paragraph, that we want to combine:

Version 1:
```
The Book of Kells, now one of the treasures of the Trinity
College Library in Dublin, was found in the ancient
monastery at Ceannanus Mor, now called Kells. It is a
beautifully illustrated manuscript of the Latin Gospels,
and also contains notes on local history. It was written in the eighth century.
The manuscript is generally regarded as the finest example
of Celtic illumination.
```

Version 2:
```
The Book of Kells was found in the ancient
monastery at Ceannanus Mor, now called Kells. It is a
beautifully illustrated manuscript of the Latin Gospels,
and also contains notes on local history.
It is believed to have been written in the eighth century.
The manuscript is generally regarded as the finest example
of Celtic illumination.
```

As you can see, there is one additional phrase in each of the two files. We can merge them into one file that incorporates both edits. Typing:

```
$ diff -e version1 version2 > exscript
```

will yield the following output in the file *exscript*:

```
6c
It is believed to have been written in the eighth century.
.
1,2c
The Book of Kells was found in the ancient
.
```

You'll notice that the script appears in reverse order, with the changes later in the file appearing first. This is essential whenever you're making changes based on line numbers; otherwise, changes made earlier in the file may change the numbering, rendering the later parts of the script ineffective. You'll also notice that, as mentioned, this script will simply recreate *version1*, which is not what we want. We want the change to line 5, but not the change to lines 1 and 2. We want to edit the script so that it looks like this:

```
6c
It is believed to have been written in the eighth century.
.
w
```

(Notice that we had to add the w command to write the results of the edit back into the file.) Now we can type:

```
$ ex - version1 < exscript
```

to get the resulting merged file:

```
The Book of Kells, now one of the treasures of the Trinity
College Library in Dublin, was found in the ancient
monastery at Ceannanus Mor, now called Kells. It is a
beautifully illustrated manuscript of the Latin Gospels,
and also contains notes on local history.
It is believed to have been written in the eighth century.
The manuscript is generally regarded as the finest example
of Celtic illumination.
```

Using *diff* like this can get confusing, especially when there are many changes. It is easy to get the direction of changes confused or to make the wrong edits. Just remember to do the following:

- Specify the file that is closest in content to your eventual target as the first file on the *diff* command line. This will minimize the size of the editing script that is produced.

- After you have corrected the editing script so that it makes only the changes that you want, apply it to that same file (the first file).

Nonetheless, because there is so much room for error, it is better not to have your script write the changes back directly into one of your source files. Instead of adding a w command at the end of the script, add the command %p (or 1,$p) to write the results to standard output *(14.01)*. This is almost always preferable when you are using a complex editing script.

If we use this command in the editing script, the command line to actually make the edits would look like this:

```
$ ex - version1 < exscript > version3
```

Writers often find themselves making extensive changes and then wishing they could go back and recover some part of an earlier version. Obviously, frequent backups will help. However, if backup storage space is at a premium, it is possible to save only some older version of a file and then keep incremental *diff –e* scripts to mark the differences between each successive version. (As it turns out, this is what version control systems like SCCS and RCS *(21.12)* do.)

To apply multiple scripts to a single file, you can simply pipe them to *ex* rather than redirecting input:

cat *26.02*
```
$ cat script1 script2 script3 | ex - oldfile
```

But wait! How do you get your w (or %p) command into the pipeline? You could edit the last script to include one of these commands. But there's another trick that we ought to look at because it illustrates another useful feature of the shell that many people are unaware of. If you enclose a semicolon-separated list of commands in parentheses *(14.07)*, the standard output of all of the commands are combined, and can be redirected together. The immediate application is that, if you type:

echo *9.04*
```
$ cat script1 script2 script3; echo '%p' | ex - oldfile
```

the results of the *cat* command will be sent, as usual, to standard output, and only the results of *echo* will be piped to *ex*. But if you type:

```
$ (cat script1 script2 script3; echo '%p') | ex - oldfile
```

the output of the entire sequence will make it into the pipeline, which is what we want.

—*TOR* from *UNIX Text Processing*, Hayden Books, 1987

29.09 Problems with diff and Tabstops

The *diff* *(29.01)* utility adds extra characters (>, <, +, and so on) to the beginning of lines. That can cause you real grief with tabstops because the extra characters *diff* adds can shift lines enough to make the indentation look wrong. The *diff* *−t* option expands TABs to 8-character tabstops and solves the problem.

If you use non-standard tabstops, though, piping *diff*'s output through *expand* or *pr* *−e* (see article 43.04):

```
% diff afile bfile | expand -4
```

doesn't help because *diff* has already added the extra characters.

The best answer I've seen is the *!* (exclamation point) script *(10.16)*. It can expand TABs before *diff* sees them. For example, to show the differences between two files with 4-column tabstops:

```
% diff `! expand -4 afile` `! expand -4 bfile`
    ...
```

—*JP*

29.10 cmp and diff

cmp is another program for comparing files. It's a lot simpler than *diff* *(29.01)*; it tells you whether the files are equivalent, and the byte offset at which the first difference occurs. You don't get a detailed analysis of where the two files differ. For this reason, *cmp* is often faster, particularly when you're comparing ASCII *(53.03)* files: it doesn't have to generate a long report summarizing the differences. If all you want to know is whether two files are different, it's the right tool for the job.

It's worth noting, though, that *cmp* isn't *always* faster. Some versions of *diff* make some simple checks first, like comparing file length. If two binary files have different lengths, they are obviously different; some *diff* implementations will tell you so without doing any further processing.

Both *diff* and *cmp* return an exit status *(46.07)* that shows what they found:

Exit Status	Meaning
0	The files were the same.
1	The files differed.
2	An error occurred.

Within a shell script, the exit status from *diff* and *cmp* is often more important than their actual output.

—*ML*

29.11 Comparing Two Files with comm

The *comm* command can tell you what information is common to two lists, and what information appears uniquely in one list or the other. For example, let's say you're compiling information on the favorite movies of critics Siskel and Ebert. The movies are listed in separate files (and must be sorted *(37.01)*—if they aren't sorted, the *!* script *(10.16)* will help). For the sake of illustration, assume each list is short:

```
% cat siskel
Citizen Kane
Halloween VI
Ninja III
Rambo II
Star Trek V
Zelig
% cat ebert
Cat People
Citizen Kane
My Life as a Dog
Q
Z
Zelig
```

To compare the favorite movies of your favorite critics, type:

```
% comm siskel ebert
                Cat People
                                        Citizen Kane
Halloween VI
                My Life as a Dog
Ninja III
                Q
Rambo II
Star Trek V
                Z
                                        Zelig
```

Column 1 shows the movies that only Siskel likes; Column 2 shows those that only Ebert likes; and Column 3 shows the movies that they both like. You can suppress one or more columns of output by specifying that column as a command-line option. For example, to suppress Columns 1 and 2 (displaying only the movies *both* critics like), you would type:

```
% comm -12 siskel ebert
Citizen Kane
Zelig
```

As another example, say you've just received a new software release (Release 4), and it's your job to figure out which library functions have been added so that they can be documented along with the old ones. Let's assume you already have a list of the Release 3 functions (*r3_list*) and a list of the Release 4 functions (*r4_list*). (If you didn't, you could create them by changing to the directory that has the function manual pages, listing the files with *ls*, and saving each list to a file.) In the lists below, we've used letters of the alphabet to represent the functions:

```
% cat r3_list
b
c
d
f
g
h

% cat r4_list
a
b
c
d
e
f
```

You can now use the *comm* command to answer several questions you might have:

- Which functions are new to Release 4? Answer:

  ```
  % comm -13 r3_list r4_list      show 2nd column, which is "Release 4 only"
  a
  e
  ```

- Which Release 3 functions have been dropped in Release 4? Answer:

  ```
  % comm -23 r3_list r4_list      show 1st column, which is "Release 3 only"
  g
  h
  ```

- Which Release 3 functions have been retained in Release 4? Answer:

  ```
  % comm -12 r3_list r4_list      show 3rd column, which is "common functions"
  b
  c
  d
  f
  ```

You can create partial lists by saving the above output to three separate files.

comm can only compare sorted files. If you can't sort the files, look at the trick in article 2.15: using *diff* and *grep*.

—DG

29.12 make Isn't Just for Programmers!

The *make* program is a UNIX facility for describing dependencies among a group of related files, usually ones that are part of the same project. This facility has enjoyed widespread use in software development projects. Programmers use *make* to describe how to "make" a program—what source files need to be compiled, what libraries must be included, and which object files need to be linked. By keeping track of these relationships in a single place, individual members of a software development team can make changes to a single module, run *make*, and be assured that the program reflects the latest changes made by others on the team.

We group *make* with the other commands for keeping track of differences between files only by a leap of the imagination. However, although it does not compare two versions of the same source file, it can be used to compare versions such as a source file and the formatted output.

Part of what makes UNIX a productive environment for text processing is discovering other uses for standard programs. The *make* utility has many possible applications for a documentation project. One such use is to maintain up-to-date copies of formatted files that make up a single manual and provide users with a way of obtaining a printed copy of the entire manual without having to know which preprocessors or *nroff/troff* (45.14) options need to be invoked.

The basic operation that *make* performs is to compare two sets of files, for example, formatted and unformatted files, and determine if any members of one set, the unformatted files, are more recent than their counterpart in the other set, the formatted files. This is accomplished by simply comparing the last-modification date ("timestamp") of pairs of files. If the unformatted source file has been modified since the formatted file was made, *make* executes the specified command to "remake" the formatted file.

To use *make*, you have to write a description file, usually named *makefile* (or *Makefile*), that resides in the working directory for the project. The *makefile* specifies a hierarchy of dependencies among individual files, called components. At the top of this hierarchy is a target. For our purposes, you can think of the target as a printed copy of a book; the components are formatted files generated by processing an unformatted file with *nroff*.

Here's the *makefile* that reflects these dependencies:

```
manual: ch01.fmt ch02.fmt ch03.fmt
        lp ch0[1-3].fmt
ch01.fmt: ch01
        nroff -mm ch01 > ch01.fmt
ch02.fmt: ch02
        tbl ch02 | nroff -mm > ch01.fmt
ch03.fmt: ch03a ch03b ch03c
        nroff -mm ch03? > ch03.fmt
```

lp *45.02*

tbl *45.17*

This hierarchy is represented in Figure 29-1.

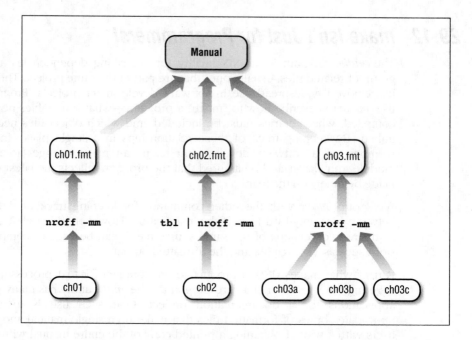

Figure 29-1. What makefile Describes: Files and Commands to Make Manual

The target is *manual*, which is made up of three formatted files whose names appear after the colon. Each of these components has its own dependency line. For instance, *ch01.fmt* is dependent upon a coded file named *ch01*. Underneath the dependency line is the command that generates *ch01.fmt*. Each command line must begin with a TAB.

When you enter the command make, the end result is that the three formatted files are spooled to the printer. However, a sequence of operations is performed before this final action. The dependency line for each component is evaluated, determining if the coded file has been modified since the last time the formatted file was made. The formatting command will be executed only if the coded file is more recent. After all the components are made, the *lp (45.02)* command is executed.

As an example of this process, we'll assume that all the formatted files are up-to-date. Then by editing the source file *ch03a*, we change the modification time. When you execute the *make* command, any output files dependent on *ch03a* are reformatted:

```
$ make
nroff -mm ch03? > ch03.fmt
lp ch0[1-3].fmt
```

Only *ch03.fmt* needs to be remade. As soon as that formatting command finishes, the command underneath the target *manual* is executed, spooling the files to the printer.

Although this example has actually made only limited use of *make*'s facilities, we hope it suggests more ways to use *make* in a documention project. You can keep your *makefiles* just this simple, or you can go on to learn additional notation, such as internal macros and suffixes, in an effort to generalize the description file for increased usefulness.

—*TOR* from *UNIX Text Processing*, Hayden Books, 1987

29.13 *Even more Uses for make*

Thinking about *make* will pay off in many ways. One way to get ideas about how to use it is to look at other *makefiles*.

One of my favorites is the *makefile* for NIS *(1.33)* (formerly called yp, or "Yellow Pages"). I like this *makefile* because it does something that you'd never think of doing, even though it suits *make* perfectly: updating a distributed database.

The *makefile* is fairly complicated, so I don't want to get into a line-by-line explication of the *makefile*; but I will give you a sketch of how it works. Here's the problem. A system administrator updates one or more files (we'll say the *passwd* file), and wants to get his changes into the *yp* database. So you need to check whether or not the new password file is more recent than the database. Unfortunately, the database isn't represented by a single file, so there's nothing to "check" against. The NIS *makefile* handles this situation by creating empty files that serve as timestamps. There's a separate *.time* file for every database that NIS serves. When you type *make*, *make* checks every master file against the corresponding timestamp. If a master file is newer than the timestamp, *make* knows that it has to rebuild part of the database. After rebuilding the database, the *makefile* "touches" the timestamp, so that it reflects the time at which the database was built.

The *makefile* looks something like this:

```
passwd: passwd.time
passwd.time:   /etc/master/passwd
               @ lots of commands that rebuild the database
               @ touch passwd.time
               @ more commands to distribute the new database


hosts: hosts.time
hosts.time:   similar stuff
```

touch *22.07*

You may never need to write a *makefile* this complicated; but you should look for situations in which you can use *make* profitably. It isn't just for programming.

—*ML*

29.14 Show Changes in a troff File with diffmk

Whenever you produce multiple drafts of a document for review, "change marks" in the newer draft are useful for showing where additions and deletions have occurred. The *troff (45.14)* request .mc (margin character) can be used to print change marks in the margin of any document that is formatted through *troff*, and the UNIX command *diffmk* uses .mc requests to produce marked drafts. *diffmk* has the following syntax:

```
% diffmk version.1 version.2 marked_file
```

The above command line compares an old version of a file (*version.1*) to a new version (*version.2*) and creates a third file, *marked_file. marked_file* consists of the contents of *version.2* plus .mc requests that show where that file differs from *version.1*. When *marked_file* is formatted, additions and changes will be indicated by vertical bars (|) in the margin, while deleted text will be indicated by an asterisk (*) in the margin.

There are times when you'll want the *diffmk* command to run on many files at once. For example, suppose you have a project directory containing eight chapter files from a first draft:

```
% ls project
chapters.old/          stuff
% ls project/chapters.old
ch01     ch03     ch05     ch07
ch02     ch04     ch06     ch08
```

Before making second-draft revisions, you copy the chapter files into a directory named *chapters.new*:

```
% ls project
chapters.new/          chapters.old/          stuff
% cd project/chapters.new
% ls
ch01     ch03     ch05     ch07
ch02     ch04     ch06     ch08
```

Copying the files allows you to edit new versions while preserving the original files in the old directory. After you've edited the files in the new directory, you want to run *diffmk* on all of them. In the new directory, you would want to type:

```
% diffmk   ../chapters.old/ch01   ch01   ch01.diffmk
% diffmk   ../chapters.old/ch02   ch02   ch02.diffmk
% diffmk   ../chapters.old/ch03   ch03   ch03.diffmk
   ...
```

A shell loop *(10.09, 10.10)* would simplify the amount of typing you need to do. You can save disk space by using a version control utility such as SCCS or RCS *(21.12)*.

—*DG*

30

Spell Checking, Word Counting, and Textual Analysis

30.01 The UNIX spell Command

The *spell* command reads one or more files and prints a list of words that may be misspelled. You can redirect the output to a file, use *grep(28.01)* to locate each of the words, and then use *vi* or *ex* to make the edits. It's also possible to hack up a shell and *sed* script that interactively displays the misspellings and fixes them on command, but realistically, this is too tedious for most users. (The *ispell(30.02)* program solves many—though not all—of these problems.)

When you run *spell* on a file, the list of words it produces usually includes a number of legitimate words or terms that the program does not recognize. *spell* is case sensitive; it's happy with *Aaron* but complains about *aaron*. You must cull out the proper nouns and other words *spell* doesn't know about to arrive at a list of true misspellings. For instance, look at the results on this sample sentence:

```
Alcuin uses TranScript to convert ditroff into
PostScript output for the LaserWriter printerr.
$ spell sample
Alcuin
ditroff
printerr
LaserWriter
PostScript
TranScript
```

Only one word in this list is actually misspelled.

On many UNIX systems, you can supply a local dictionary file so that *spell* recognizes special words and terms specific to your site or application. After you have run *spell* and looked through the word list, you can create a file containing the words that were not actual misspellings. The *spell* command will check this list after it has gone through its own dictionary.

If you added the special terms in a file named *dict*, you could specify that file on the command line using the + option:

```
$ spell +dict sample
printerr
```

The output is reduced to the single misspelling.

The *spell* command will also miss words specified as arguments to *nroff* or *troff* macros *(45.14)*, and like any spelling checker, will make some errors based on incorrect derivation of spellings from the root words contained in its dictionary. If you understand how *spell* works *(30.04)*, you may be less surprised by some of these errors.

—DD from *UNIX Text Processing*, Hayden Books, 1987

30.02 Check Spelling Interactively with ispell

The original UNIX spell checking program, *spell (30.01)*, is fine for quick checks of spelling in a short document, but it makes you cry out for a real spelling checker, which not only shows you the misspelled words in context, but offers to change them for you.

ispell

ispell, a very useful program that's been ported to UNIX and enhanced over the years, does all this and more. Here's the basic usage.

Just as with *spell*, you spell check a document by giving *ispell* a filename. But there the similarities cease. *ispell* takes over your screen or window, printing two lines of context at the bottom of the screen. If your terminal can do reverse video, the offending word is highlighted. Several alternate possibilities are presented in the upper-left corner of the screen—any word in *ispell*'s dictionary that differs by only one letter, has a missing or extra letter, or transposed letters.

Faced with a highlighted word, you have eight choices:

SPACE   Press the spacebar to accept the current spelling.

A   Type A to accept the current spelling, now and for the rest of this input file.

I   Type I to accept the current spelling now and for the rest of this input file, and also instruct *ispell* to add the word to your private dictionary. By default, the private dictionary is the file *.ispell_words* in your home directory, but can be changed with the –p option or by setting the environment variable *(7.01)* WORDLIST to the name of some other file. If you work with computers, this option will come in handy, since we use so much jargon in this business! It makes a lot more sense to "teach" all those words to *ispell* than to keep being offered them for possible correction. (One gotcha: when specifying an alternate file, you must use an absolute pathname *(1.19)* or *ispell* will look for the file in your home directory.)

0-9   Type the digit corresponding to one of *ispell*'s alternate suggestions to use that spelling instead. For example, if you've typed "hnadle," as I did when writing this article, *ispell* will offer 0: handle in the upper-left corner of your screen. Typing 0 makes the change and moves on to the next misspelling, if any.

R   Type R if none of *ispell*'s offerings do the trick, and you want to be prompted for a replacement. Type in the new word, and the replacement is made.

L   Type L if *ispell* didn't make any helpful suggestions, and you're at a loss how to spell the word correctly. *ispell* will prompt you for a lookup string. You can use * as a wildcard character (it appears to substitute for zero or one characters); *ispell* will print a list of matching words from its dictionary.

Q   Type Q to quit, writing any changes made so far, but ignoring any mispellings later in the input file.

X   Type X to quit without writing any changes.

But that's not all! *ispell* also saves a copy of your original file with a *.bak* extension, just in case you regret any of your changes. (This is starting to sound like a Ginsu knife commercial!) If you don't want it making *.bak* files, invoke it with the *−x* option.

How about this: *ispell* knows about capitalization. It already knows about proper names and a lot of common acronyms—it can even handle words like "TeX" that have oddball capitalization. Speaking of TeX *(45.17)*, it even has a special mode in which it recognizes TeX constructions. (Too bad it doesn't know about *troff (45.14)*.)

For even more features, see the manual pages stored with the program on the disk.

—TOR

30.03   *How Do I Spell that Word?*

If you aren't sure which of two possible spellings is right, you can use *spell* command with no arguments to find out. Type the name of the command, followed by a RETURN, then type the alternative spellings you are considering. Press CTRL-d (on a line by itself) to end the list. The *spell* command will echo back the word(s) in the list that it considers to be in error:

```
$ spell
misspelling
mispelling
CTRL-d
mispelling
```

You can invoke *spell* in this way from within *vi*, by typing:

:! *31.26*

```
:!spell
misspelling
mispelling
```

```
CTRL-d
mispelling
[Hit return to continue]
```

If you're using *ispell (30.02)*, you need to add the *–l* option, since *ispell* doesn't read from standard input by default. (Even *–l* doesn't let *ispell* read from a pipe. The purpose of this option is to let you type in a list of words, just as shown above for *spell*; when you end the list, *ispell* will echo back the misspelled word, just like *spell*. There's no additional functionality there, except that *ispell* will use its local dictionaries and improved spelling rules.)

An even better way to do the same thing may be with *look (28.18)*. With just one argument, *look* searches the system word file, */usr/dict/words*, for words starting with the characters in that one argument. That's a good way to check spelling or find a related word:

```
% look help
help
helpful
helpmate
```

look uses its *–df* options automatically when it searches the word list. *–d* ignores any character that isn't a letter, number, space or tab; *–f* treats uppercase and lowercase letters the same.

—DD, JP

30.04 *Inside spell*

[If you have ispell (30.02), there's not a whole lot of reason for using spell *any more. Not only is it more powerful, it's a heck of a lot easier to update its spelling dictionaries. Nonetheless, we decided to keep this article, because it makes clear the kinds of rules that spelling checkers go through to expand on the words in their dictionaries. — TOR]*

On many UNIX systems, the directory */usr/lib/spell* contains the main program invoked by the *spell* command along with auxiliary programs and data files.

```
$ ls -l /usr/lib/spell
total 888
-rwxr-xr-x   1 bin        545 Dec  9  1988 compress
-rwxr-xr-x   1 bin      16324 Dec  9  1988 hashcheck
-rwxr-xr-x   1 bin      14828 Dec  9  1988 hashmake
-rw-r--r--   1 bin      53872 Dec  9  1988 hlista
-rw-r--r--   1 bin      53840 Dec  9  1988 hlistb
-rw-r--r--   1 bin       6336 Dec  9  1988 hstop
-rw-rw-rw-   1 root    252312 Nov 27 16:24 spellhist
-rwxr-xr-x   1 bin      21634 Dec  9  1988 spellin
-rwxr-xr-x   1 bin      23428 Dec  9  1988 spellprog
```

On some systems, the *spell* command is a shell script that pipes its input through *deroff –w (30.11)* and *sort –u (37.06)* to remove formatting codes and prepare a sorted word list, one word per line. On other systems, it is a standalone program that does these steps internally. Two separate spelling lists are maintained, one for American usage and one for British usage (invoked with the *−b* option to *spell*). These lists, *blista* and *blistb*, cannot be read or updated directly. They are compressed files, compiled from a list of words represented as nine-digit hash codes. (Hash coding is a special technique used to quick search for information.)

The main program invoked by *spell* is *spellprog*. It loads the list of hash codes from either *blista* or *blistb* into a table, and looks for the hash code corresponding to each word on the sorted word list. This eliminates all words (or hash codes) actually found in the spelling list. For the remaining words, *spellprog* tries to see if it can derive a recognizable word by performing various operations on the word stem, based on suffix and prefix rules. A few of these manipulations follow:

```
−y+iness
+ness
−y+i+less
+less
−y+ies
−t+ce
−t+cy
```

The new words created as a result of these manipulations will be checked once more against the spell table. However, before the stem-derivative rules are applied, the remaining words are checked against a table of hash codes built from the file *hstop*. The stop list contains typical misspellings that stem-derivative operations might allow to pass. For instance, the misspelled word *thier* would be converted into *thy* using the suffix rule −y+ier. The *hstop* file accounts for as many cases of this type of error as possible.

The final output consists of words not found in the spell list, even after the program tried to search for their stems, and words that were found in the stop list.

You can get a better sense of these rules in action by using the *−v* or *−x* option. The *−v* option eliminates the last lookup in the table, and produces a list of words that are not actually in the spelling list along with possible derivatives. It allows you to see which words were found as a result of stem-derivative operations, and prints the rule used.

```
% spell -v sample
Alcuin
ditroff
LaserWriter
PostScript
printerr
TranScript
+out    output
+s      uses
```

The *−x* option makes *spell* begin at the stem-derivative stage, and prints the various attempts it makes to find the word stem of each word.

```
% spell -x sample
...
```

```
=into
=LaserWriter
=LaserWrite
=LaserWrit
=laserWriter
=laserWrite
=laserWrit
=output
=put
...
LaserWriter
...
```

The stem is preceded by an equal sign (=). At the end of the output are the words whose stem does not appear in the spell list.

One other file you should know about is *spellhist*. On some systems, each time you run *spell*, the output is appended through *tee (14.09)* into *spellhist*, in effect creating a list of all the misspelled or unrecognized words for your site. The *spellhist* file is something of a "garbage" file that keeps on growing. You will want to reduce it or remove it periodically. To extract useful information from this *spellhist*, you might use the *sort* and *uniq −c (36.18)* commands to compile a list of misspelled words or special terms that occur most frequently (see article 30.08 for a similar example). It is possible to add these words back into the basic spelling dictionary, but this is too complex a process to describe here. It's probably easier just to use a local spelling dictionary *(30.01)*. Even better, use *ispell*; not only is it a more powerful spelling program, it is much easier to update the word lists it uses *(30.05)*.

—*DD* from *UNIX Text Processing*, Hayden Books, 1987

30.05 *Adding Words to ispell's Dictionary*

ispell (30.02) uses two lists for spelling verification: a master wordlist and a supplemental personal wordlist.

The master wordlist for *ispell* is normally the file */usr/local/lib/ispell/ispell.hash*. This is a "hashed" dictionary file. That is, it has been converted to a condensed, program-readable form using the *buildhash* program (which comes with *ispell*), to speed the spell-checking process.

The personal wordlist is normally a file called *.ispell_words* in your home directory. (You can override this default with either the *−p* command-line option or the *WORDLIST* environment variable *(7.01)*.) This file is simply a list of words, one per line, so you can readily edit it to add, alter, or remove entries. The personal wordlist is normally used in addition to the master wordlist, so if a word usage is permitted by either list it is not flagged by *ispell*.

Custom personal wordlists are particularly useful for checking documents that use jargon, or special technical words that are not in the master wordlist, and for personal needs such as holding the names of your correspondents. You may choose to keep more than one custom wordlist, to meet various special requirements.

You can add to your personal wordlist any time you use *ispell*: simply use the I command to tell *ispell* that the word it offered as a misspelling is actually correct, and should be added to the dictionary. You can also add a list of words from a file using the *ispell −a* option. The words must be one to a line, but need not be sorted. Each word to be added must be preceded with an asterisk. (Why? Because *ispell −a* has other functions as well.) So, for example, we could have added a list of UNIX utility names to our personal dictionaries all at once, rather than one by one as they were encountered during spell-checking.

Obviously, though, in an environment where many people are working with the same set of technical terms, it doesn't make sense for each individual to add the same word list to his or her own private *.ispell_words* file. It would make far more sense for a group to agree on a common dictionary for specialized terms and always to set *WORDLIST* to point to that common dictionary.

If the private wordlist gets too long, you can create a "munched" wordlist. The *munchlist* script that comes with *ispell* reduces the names in a wordlist to a set of word roots and permitted suffixes according to rules described in the *ispell*(4) reference page that will be installed with *ispell* from the Power Tools disk. This creates a more compact but still editable wordlist.

Another option is to provide an alternate master spelling list using the *−d* option. This has two problems, though:

1. The master spelling list should include spellings that are always valid, regardless of context. You do not want to overload your master wordlist with terms that might be misspellings in a different context. For example, *perl* is a powerful programming language, but in other contexts, *perl* might be a misspelling of *pearl*. You may want to place *perl* in a supplemental wordlist when documenting UNIX utilities, but probably wouldn't want it in the master wordlist unless you are documenting UNIX utilities most of the time that you use *ispell*.

2. The *−d* option must point to a hashed dictionary file. This is a large file and time-consuming to build. What's more, you cannot edit a hashed dictionary; you will have to edit a master word list and use (or have the system administrator use) *buildhash* to hash the new dictionary to optimize spelling checker performance.

To build a new hashed wordlist, provide *buildhash* with a complete list of the words you want included, one per line. (The *buildhash* utility can only process a raw wordlist, not a munched wordlist.) The standard system wordlist, */usr/dict/words* on many systems, can provide a good starting point. This file is writeable only by the system administrator, and probably shouldn't be changed in any case. So make a copy of this file, and edit or add to the copy. After processing the file with *buildhash*, you can either replace the default *ispell.hash* file, or point to your new hashed file with the *−d* option.

—*TOR, LK*

30.06 Counting Lines, Words, and Characters: wc

The *wc* (word count) command counts the number of lines, words, and characters in the files you specify. (Like most UNIX utilities *(1.30)*, *wc* reads from its standard input if you don't specify a filename.) For example, the file *letter* has 120 lines, 734 words, and 4297 characters:

```
% wc letter
      120     734    4297 letter
```

You can restrict what is counted by specifying the options *−l* (count lines only), *−w* (count words only), and *−c* (count characters only). For example, you can count the number of words in a file:

```
% wc -w letter
      734 letter
```

or you can count the number of files in a directory:

```
% cd man_pages
% ls | wc -l
      233
```

The first example uses a file as input; the second example pipes the output of an *ls* command to the input of *wc*. (Be aware that the *−a* option to *ls* causes *ls* to list dot files. If your *ls* command is aliased *(11.02)* to include *−a (17.12)* or other options that add lines to the normal output (such as *−s*), then you may not get the results you want.)

The fact that you can pipe the output of a command through *wc* lets you use *wc* to perform addition and subtraction. For example, I once wrote a shell script that involved, among other things, splitting files into several pieces, and I needed the script to keep track of how many files were created. (The script ran *csplit (36.08)* on each file, producing an arbitrary number of new files named *file.00, file.01, file.02*, etc.) Here's the code I used to solve this problem:

```
beforesplit="`ls $file* | wc -l`"          # count the file
    split the file by running it through csplit
aftersplit="`ls $file* | wc -l`"           # count file plus new splits
num_files="`expr $aftersplit - $beforesplit`"  # evaluate the difference
```

As another trick, the following command will tell you how many more words are in *new.file* than in *old.file*:

expr 51.07

```
% expr `wc -w < new.file`    -    `wc -w < old.file`
```

[The C and Korn shells have built-in arithmetic commands and don't really need *expr*—but *expr* works in all shells.—*JP*] Notice that you should have *wc* read the input files by using a < character. If instead you say:

```
% expr `wc -w new.file` - `wc -w old.file`
```

the filenames will show up in the expressions and produce a syntax error.*

---

*You could also type cat new.file | wc -w, but this involves two commands, so it's less efficient *(14.02)*.

Taking this concept further, here's a simple shell script to calculate the differences in word length between two files:

count.it

```
count_1=`wc -w < $1`                    # number of words in file 1
count_2=`wc -w < $2`                    # number of words in file 2

diff_12=`expr $count_1 - $count_2`      # difference in word count

# if $diff_12 is negative, reverse order and don't show the minus sign:
case "$diff_12" in
-*) echo "$2 has `expr $diff_12 : '-\(.*\)'` more words than $1" ;;
*)  echo "$1 has $diff_12 more words than $2" ;;
esac
```

echo **9.04**
... **10.14**

If this script were called *count.it*, then you could invoke it like this:

```
% count.it draft.2 draft.1
draft.1 has 23 more words than draft.2
```

You could modify this script to count lines or characters.

Note: Unless the counts are very large, the output of *wc* will have leading spaces. This can cause trouble in scripts if you aren't careful. For instance, in the script above, the command:

```
echo "$1 has $count_1 words"
```

might print:

```
draft.2 has        79 words
```

See the extra spaces? Understanding how the shell handles quoting *(9.10)* will help here. If you can, let the shell read the *wc* output and remove extra spaces. For example, without quotes, the shell passes four separate words to *echo*—and *echo* adds a single space between each word:

```
echo $1 has $count_1 words
```

that might print:

```
draft.2 has 79 words
```

That's especially important to understand when you use *wc* with commands like *test* or *expr* which don't expect spaces in their arguments. If you can't use the shell to strip out the spaces, delete them by piping the *wc* output through `tr -d ' '` *(36.09)*.

—*DG, JP*

30.07 Count How many Times each Word is Used

The *wordfreq* script counts the number of occurrences of each word in its input. If you give it files, it reads from them; otherwise it reads standard input. The *−i* option folds uppercase into lowercase (uppercase letters will count the same as lowercase).

The script is simple. The *sed (35.24)* code to strip off extra punctuation around words does a pretty good job—you can adapt it if you want to. The script uses *awk (38.18)* associative arrays to store the word counts, then prints them out in what seems like random order. Its output could be sorted by word or count—though you can do that yourself, on the command line. Here's the first part of this article run through *wordfreq* and sorted by count:

```
% wordfreq article | sort +1nr
the 7
of 5
it 3
word 3
The 2
awk 2
case 2
in 2
input 2
more 2
output 2
    ...
```

wordfreq

Next, the shell script. It stores *awk* and *sed* routines in shell variables *(7.08)* because those routines are used in more than one place; the shell expands the variables before starting *awk* and *sed*.

```
#! /bin/sh

awkscr='{
    for (i = 1; i <= NF; i++)
        num[$i]++
}
END {
    for (word in num)
        print word, num[word]
}'

strippunc='s/[,.-?!)"]* / /g
s/[,.-?!)"]*$//g
s/ ["(]/ /g
s/^["(]//g'

case "$1" in
-i) shift
    sed "
    y/ABCDEFGHIJKLMNOPQRSTUVWXYZ/abcdefghijklmnopqrstuvwxyz/
    $strippunc
    " ${1+"$@"} |
    awk -e "$awkscr"
```

```
    ;;
*)  sed "$strippunc" ${1+"$@"} | awk -e "$awkscr" ;;
esac
```

The `${1+"$@"}` works around a quoting problem *(48.07)* on some Bourne shells.

—JP

30.08 Another Word Counter

concordance

Here's another version of *wordfreq (30.07)*, using completely different tools (and included for that very reason—to show that there are many ways to do the same thing). This version was taken from a long-ago Usenet *(1.33)* posting by Carl Brandauer. We call it *concordance*, after the apt and suggestive title Carl prints at the top of the report.

According to the dictionary, a concordance is an alphabetical listing of the principal words in a book. For example, they have concordances to the Bible, in which every word used is listed—with an index to exactly where it is used. This tool just counts them, doesn't index them. Nonetheless, the title is suggestive. For those of us who write books, a tool like this could be a wonderful way to check for the consistency of special terminology.

Here's the script:

```
                cat $* |                     # tr reads the standard input
  tr 36.09      tr "[A-Z]" "[a-z]" |          # Convert all uppercase to lowercase
                tr -cs "[a-z']" "\012" |      # replace all characters not a-z or '
                                              # with a new line. i.e. one word per line
 sort 37.01     sort |                        # uniq expects sorted input
 uniq 36.18     uniq -c |                      # Count number of times each word appears
                sort +0nr +1d |               # Sort first from most to least frequent,
                                              # then alphabetically
  -4 36.15      pr -w80 -4 -h "Concordance for $*"      # Print in four columns
```

Carl notes that the precise syntax of *tr* varies among versions, so some diddling may be needed on the *tr* command that puts each word on its own line. (See article 36.09.) You could use *deroff (30.11)* instead.

—TOR

30.09 Find a a Doubled Word

One type of error that's hard to catch when proofreading is a doubled word. It's hard to miss the double "a" in the title of this article, but you might find yourself from time to time with a "the" on the end of one line and the beginning of another.

csh_init

uniq 36.18

We've seen *awk* scripts to catch this, but nothing so simple as this alias that Brian Fitzgerald posted to the newsgroup *comp.unix.questions* last year:

```
alias ww 'deroff -w \!* | uniq -d'
```

Oddly enough, my choice of a demonstration in the title of this article turned up a weakness of this script: *deroff(30.11)* doesn't consider a single character to be a word, and so it doesn't catch that error.

—TOR

30.10 Looking for Closure

A common problem in text processing is making sure that items that need to occur in pairs actually do so.

Most UNIX text editors include support for making sure that elements of C syntax such as parentheses and braces are closed properly. There's much less support for making sure that textual documents, such as *troff(45.14)* source files, have the proper structure.

For example, tables must start with a .TS macro, and end with .TE.

UNIX provides a number of tools that might help you to tackle this problem. Here's a shell script written by Dale Dougherty that uses *awk* to make sure that .TS and .TE macros come in pairs:

gawk 38.05

paircheck

```
gawk '
BEGIN    {
     TSlineno = 0
     TElineno = 0
     prevFile=""
}
# check for
FILENAME != prevFile {
     if (inTable)
        printf ("found .TS at File %s: %d without .TE before end of file\n",
                 prevFile, TSlineno)
        inTable = 0
        prevFile = FILENAME
}
# match TS and see if we are in table
/^\.TS/ {
     if (inTable){
        printf("%s: nested starts, File %s: line %d and %d\n",
                $0, FILENAME, TSlineno,FNR)
        }
        inTable=1
        TSlineno=FNR
}
/^\.TE/ {
     if (! inTable)
        printf("%s: too many ends, File %s: line %d and %d\n",
                 $0, FILENAME, TElineno,FNR)
        else
             inTable=0
        TElineno = FNR
}
# this catches end of input, not end of file.
END  {
```

```
        if (inTable)
            printf ("found .TS at File %s: %d without .TE before end of file\n",
                FILENAME, TSlineno)
    }
    ' $*
```

You can adapt this type of script for any place you need to check for something that has a start and finish.

A more complete syntax checking program could be written with the help of a lexical analyzer like *lex*. *lex* is normally used by experienced C programmers, but it can be used profitably by someone who has mastered *awk* and is just beginning with C, since it combines an *awk*-like pattern-matching process using regular expression syntax, with actions written in the more powerful and flexible C language.

And of course, this kind of problem could be very easily tackled in *perl (39.01)*.

—TOR

30.11 *Just the Words, Please*

In various kinds of textual analysis scripts, you sometimes need just the words *(30.09)*.

There are two ways I know how to do this. The *deroff* command was designed to strip out *troff (45.17)* constructs and punctuation from files. The command *deroff —w* will give you a list of just the words in a document; pipe to *uniq (37.06)* if you want only one of each.

deroff has one major failing, though. It only considers a word to be a string of characters beginning with a letter of the alphabet. A single character won't do, which leaves out one-letter words like the indefinite article "A."

A substitute is *tr (36.09)*, which can perform various kinds of character-by-character conversions.

To produce a list of all the individual words in a file, type:

< 14.01   `% tr -cs A-Za-z '\012' < file`

The *—c* option "complements" the first string passed to *tr*; *—s* squeezes out repeated characters. This has the effect of saying: "Take any non-alphabetic characters you find (one or more) and convert them to newlines (\012)."

(Wouldn't it be nice if *tr* just recognized standard UNIX regular expression syntax *(27.04)*? Then, instead of `-c A-Za-z`, you'd say `'[^A-Za-z]'`. It's not any less obscure, but at least it's used by other programs, so there's one less thing to learn.)

The System V version of *tr* has slightly different syntax. You'd get the same effect with:

```
% tr -cs '[A-Z][a-z]' '[\012*]' < file
```

—TOR

Part Five

Text Editing

On many systems, when you talk about editing, you're talking about word processing, more or less. And while modern word processing programs have many nifty features and can be very easy to learn and use, it can be quite striking just how much they lack.

When you talk about text editing under UNIX, you are talking about some real power tools—"word processors" that let you write what amount to "editing programs" that automate repetitive editing and give you enormous power to make global changes to many files at once.

If you're coming to UNIX from a system with a friendly modern word processor, you're likely to be appalled at your first encounter with *vi* or Emacs—but if you stick with it, and go on from there to programs like *sed* and *awk*, you'll look back on your former smugness with chagrin. Yes, there are many features you'll miss when using these relics of an earlier age. And yes, "There were giants on the earth in those days."

For all their features, modern text processing programs still have a lot of catching up to do.

—*TOR*

31

vi Tips and Tricks

31.01 The vi and ex Editors: Why so much Material?

We're giving a lot of pages to the *vi* editor. People who use another editor, like Emacs, might wonder why. Here's why.

I've watched people (including myself) learn and use *vi* for ten years. It's the standard editor that comes with almost every UNIX system these days, but most people have no idea that *vi* can do so much. People are surprised, over and over, when I show them features that their editor has. Even with its warts, *vi* is a Power Tool. If you work with files, you probably use it constantly. Knowing how to use it well will save you lots of time and work.

But why not give the same coverage to another editor that lots of people use: GNU Emacs *(33.01)?* That's because GNU Emacs comes with source code. Its commands have descriptive names that you can understand by reading through a list. *vi*'s commands are usually no more than a few characters long; many of the option names are short and not too descriptive either. Lots of UNIX systems don't even have *vi* source code these days.

I hope that you *vi* users will learn a lot in this section, and that people who don't use *vi* will at least browse through to see some of *vi*'s less obvious features.

—JP

31.02 What We Cover

The articles in this chapter show you how to get the most for your money from *vi* and *ex*. If you've been using *vi* for a while, you may already know a lot of these things—but take a quick look at this list of topics to see if there's anything new to you:

- Travel between files, save text into buffers, and move it around without leaving *vi*: articles 31.04, 31.05, and 31.07.

- Recover deletions from up to nine numbered buffers: article 31.08.

- Do global search and replacement with pattern matching: articles 31.09, 31.14, 31.17, 31.15, and 31.27.

- Save a lot of typing with word abbreviations: articles 31.31, 31.32, and 31.33.

- "Prettify" lines of text that don't fit on the screen the way you want them to: article 31.37.

- Run other UNIX commands without leaving *vi* (called a filter-through): articles 31.22, 31.26, and 31.23.

- Keep track of functions and included files with *ctags* and *tags*: articles 31.28 and 31.29.

- Change your *vi* and *ex* options in your *.exrc* file for all files or just for files in a local directory: articles 31.06 and 31.18.

—*EK*

31.03 Mice vs. vi

[This article is taken from a posting on Usenet (1.33). Those of you who aren't familiar with Usenet might not know that people who post replies to articles by others often include sections of the previous postings to which they are replying. These included sections are "quoted" by preceding them with >. Sometimes, as in this article, you'll see a quote within a quote, indicated by >>.

Here, the original posting was from John Bruner (>>). Pierce Wetter (>) replied to John. Chris Torek then replied to Pierce, including some of John's original posting.

Chris later called this article "largely religious flamage"—an argument based largely on opinion rather than fact, with no real resolution possible. But I think it has some important points to make about editors like vi: an editor that requires a mouse is not always fastest or best for the job. Besides, flames are fun to read. :-) —JP]

From: Chris Torek <chris%umcp-cs.uucp@BRL.ARPA>
Subject: Re: Porting UNIX Applications to the Mac
Date: 16 Sep 86 09:02:17 GMT
To: info-unix@brl-sem.arpa

>In article <15372@mordor.ARPA> jdb@mordor.UUCP (John Bruner) writes:
>>I am far more productive with "vi" on UNIX than with any of
>>the mouse-based editors I've run across on the Mac.

In article <981@cit-vax.Caltech.Edu> wetter@tybalt.caltech.edu.UUCP
(Pierce T. Wetter) responds:
[much laughter]
>Considering my experiences ... this is the most hilarious thing I've
>ever heard. When I'm programming the thing I do most often is move
>around in the file. You can't tell me that pointing and clicking
>with the mouse isn't faster then banging away on random cursor keys.

Yes I can, and yes it is—for me. If it is not for you, fine. (To expound a bit, I do
not "bang away on random cursor keys." If I want to get three lines down from
the middle of the screen, to the end of the seventh word, I might type Mjjj7E. I
can type that sequence in about a half-second. When I use a Sun, it typically
takes me about four seconds to find the mouse, point, click, and find the keyboard again.)

>It's true that you can go directly to a specific line number but
>you can't easily go up five lines and over twenty characters.

5k20l took about a second. The real problem with this is converting a visual
representation to a number of characters. It is an acquired skill, as is using a
mouse.

>a mouse based editor is much easier to cut & paste in (which
>if you looked at code I've written you'll know why I like this—
>"Who needs a for next loop I'll just paste it in five times")

That depends on a number of things. I do indeed use the Sun mouse for this at
times, whenever I think it will be faster or easier.

>, you need to move your hands away from the "home row" whenever you
>hit the escape key or any other "control key."

I do not. I *do* need to move my hands significantly to use the mouse.

>The mouse isn't any worse (unless you have an infinite typing speed).

>However, there is one small thing I should mention, I'm using a trackball
>instead of a mouse ...

Actually, I would like to have a keyboard, a mouse, a trackball, a light pen, a
bitpad, a touch screen, an eye tracker, and voice input, and be able to choose
among these as I wish. Indeed, I think the only reasonable approach is to program for a virtual input device, and allow the connection of just about anything.

>Nuff Said

Indeed.

—*CT* in *net.unix* on Usenet, *16 September 1986*

31.04 *Editing Multiple Files with vi*

ex commands enable you to switch between multiple files. The advantage is speed. When you are sharing the system with other users, it takes time to exit and re-enter *vi* for each file you want to edit. Staying in the same editing session and traveling between files is not only faster for access, but you also save abbreviations and command sequences that you have defined, and you keep yank buffers *(31.05)* so that you can copy text from one file to another.

When you first invoke *vi*, you can name more than one file to edit, and then use *ex* commands to travel between the files:

    % vi file1 file2

This edits *file1* first. After you have finished editing the first file, the *ex* command :w writes (saves) *file1* and :n calls in the next file (*file2*). You can even say vi * to edit all the files in a directory. If you don't modify a file, just use :n to go on to the next file.

You can also switch at any time to another file that you didn't specify on the command line with the *ex* command :e. If you want to edit another file within *vi*, you first need to save your current file (:w), then give the command:

    :e filename

vi "remembers" two filenames at a time as the current and alternate filenames. These can be referred to by the symbols % (current filename) and # (alternate filename). # is particularly useful with :e, since it allows you to switch easily back and forth between two files. The command :e# is always "switch to the other one." (On some systems, the *vi* command CTRL-^ (control-caret) is a synonym for :e#.)

If you have not first saved the current file, *vi* will not allow you to switch files with :e or :n unless you tell it imperatively to do so by adding an exclamation point after the command.

The command:

    :e!

is also useful. It discards your edits and returns to the last saved version of the current file.

In contrast to the # symbol, % is useful mainly when writing out the contents of the current buffer to a new file. For example, you could save a second version of the file *letter* with the command:

    :w %.new

instead of:

`:w letter.new`

when you switch to another file.

—*LL* from the Nutshell Handbook *Learning the vi Editor*

31.05 *Edits Between Files*

When you give a yank buffer a one-letter name, you have a convenient way to move text from one file to another. Named buffers are not cleared when a new file is loaded into the *vi* buffer with the `:e` command *(31.04)*. Thus, by yanking (copying) or deleting text from one file (into multiple named buffers if necessary), calling in a new file with `:e`, and putting the named buffer into the new file, you can transfer material between files.

The following example illustrates how to transfer text from one file to another.

Keystrokes	Result

`"f4yy`

```
With a screen editor you can scroll
the page, move the cursor, delete lines,
insert characters, and more, while seeing
the results of the edits as you make them
```

Yank four lines into buffer f.

`:w`

```
"practice" 6 lines 238 characters
```

Save the file.

`:e letter`

```
Dear Mr.
Henshaw:
I thought that you would
be interested to know that:
Yours truly,
```

Enter the file *letter* with `:e`. Move cursor to where the copied text will be placed.

`"fp`

```
Dear Mr.
Henshaw:
I thought that you would
be interested to know that:
With a screen editor you can scroll
the page, move the cursor, delete lines,
insert characters, and more, while seeing
the results of the edits as you make them
Yours truly,
```

Place yanked text from named buffer f below the cursor.

If you yank into a buffer and type the buffer name as an uppercase letter, your new text will be added to the text already in the buffer. For example, you might use `"f4yy` to yank four lines into the buffer named *f*. If you then move somewhere else and type `"F6yy`, with an uppercase *F*, that will add six more lines to the same *f* buffer—for a total of ten lines. You can yank into the uppercase buffer name over and over. To output all of the yanked text, use the lowercase letter—like `"fp`. To clear the buffer and start over, use its lowercase name (`"fy . . .`) again.

—*LL, JP* from the Nutshell Handbook *Learning the vi Editor*

31.06 *Local Settings for vi and ex*

In addition to reading the *.exrc* file in your home directory *(5.09)*, *vi* will read a file called *.exrc* in the current directory. This allows you to set options that are appropriate to a particular project.

For example, you might want to have one set of options in a directory mainly used for programming:

```
set number lisp autoindent sw=4 terse
set tags=/usr/lib/tags
```

and another set of options in a directory used for text editing:

```
set wrapmargin=15 ignorecase
```

Note that you can set certain options in the *.exrc* file in your home directory and unset them (for example, set `wrapmargin=0 noignorecase`) in a local directory.

Note: In System V, Release 3.2 and later, *vi* doesn't read *.exrc* files in the current directory unless you first set the `exrc` option in your home directory's *.exrc* file:

```
set exrc
```

This mechanism prevents other people from placing, in your working directory, an *.exrc* file whose commands might jeopardize the security of your system.

You can also define alternate *vi* environments by saving option settings in a file other than *.exrc* and reading in that file with the `:so` command. For example:

```
:so .progoptions
```

Local *.exrc* files are also useful for defining abbreviations *(31.31)* and key mappings *(32.02)*. When we write a book or manual, we save all abbreviations to be used in that book in an *.exrc* file in the directory in which the book is being created.

You can also store settings and startup commands for *vi* and *ex* in an environment variable *(7.01)* called *EXINIT (7.03)*. If there is a conflict between settings in *EXINIT* and an *.exrc* file, *EXINIT* settings take precedence.

—*TOR* from the Nutshell Handbook *Learning the vi Editor*

31.07 Using Buffers to Move or Copy Text

In a *vi* editing session, your last deletion (d or x) or yank (y) is saved in a buffer. You can access the contents of that buffer and put the saved text back in your file with the put command (p or P). A frequent sequence of commands is:

5dd	*delete 5 lines*
	move somewhere else
p	*put the 5 deleted lines back in a new*
	location, below the current line

What fewer new users are aware of is that *vi* stores the last nine *(31.08)* deletions in numbered buffers. You can access any of these numbered buffers to restore any (or all) of the last nine deletions. (Small deletions, of only parts of lines, are not saved in numbered buffers, however.) Small deletions can be recovered only by using the p or P command immediately after you've made the deletion.

vi also allows you to yank (copy) text to "named" buffers identified by letters. You can fill up to 26 (a-z) buffers with yanked text and restore that text with a put command at any time in your editing session. This is especially important if you want to transfer data between two files, because all buffers except named buffers are lost when you change files. See article 31.05.

—*TOR* from the Nutshell Handbook *Learning the vi Editor*

31.08 Get Back what You Deleted with Numbered Buffers

Being able to delete large blocks of text at a single bound is all very well and good, but what if you mistakenly delete 53 lines that you need? There's a way to recover any of your past *nine* deletions, because they're saved in numbered buffers. The last delete is saved in buffer 1, the second-to-last in buffer 2, and so on.

To recover a deletion, type " (double quote), identify the buffered text by number, then give the put command. To recover your second-to-last deletion from buffer 2, type:

"2p

The deletion in buffer 2 is placed on the line below the cursor.

If you're not sure which buffer contains the deletion you want to restore, you don't have to keep typing " *n*p over and over again. If you use the repeat command (.) with p after u, it automatically increments the buffer number. As a result, you can search through the numbered buffers as follows:

"1pu.u.u *etc.*

to put the contents of each succeeding buffer in the file one after the other. Each time you type u, the restored text is removed; when you type a dot (.), the contents of the *next* buffer is restored to your file. Keep typing u and . until you've recovered the text you're looking for.

—*TOR* from the Nutshell Handbook *Learning the vi Editor*

31.09 *Using Search Patterns and Global Commands*

Besides using line numbers and address symbols (., $, %), *ex* (including the *ex* mode of *vi*, of course) can address lines by using search patterns *(27.01)*. For example:

`:/pattern/d`	Deletes the next line containing *pattern*.
`:/pattern/+d`	Deletes the line *below* the next line containing *pattern*. (You could also use +1 instead of + alone.)
`:/pattern1/,/pattern2/d`	Deletes from the next line (after the current line) that contains *pattern1* through the next following line that contains *pattern2*.
`:.,/pattern/m23`	Takes text from current line (.) through the next line containing *pattern* and puts it after line 23.

Note that patterns are marked by a slash both *before* and *after*.

Deletion-by-pattern works differently in *vi* and *ex*. Suppose you have a file containing the lines:

```
With a screen editor you can scroll the
page, move the cursor, delete lines, insert
characters and more, while seeing results
of your edits as you make them.
```

Keystrokes	*Result*
| d/while | ```
With a screen editor you can scroll the
page, move the cursor, while seeing results
of your edits as you make them.
``` |

In *vi*, the delete-to-*pattern* command deletes from the cursor up to the word *while* but leaves the remainder of both lines.

`:.,/while/d`

```
With a screen editor you can scroll the
of your edits as you make them.
```

The *ex* command deletes the entire range of addressed lines; in this case both the current line and the line containing the pattern. All lines are deleted in their entirety.
```

Global Searches

In *vi* you use a / (slash) to search for patterns of characters in your files. By contrast, *ex* has a global command, g, that lets you search for a pattern and display all lines containing the pattern when it finds them. The command :g! does the opposite of :g. Use :g! (or its synonym :v) to search for all lines that do *not* contain *pattern*.

You can use the global command on all lines in the file, or you can use line addresses to limit a global search to specified lines or to a range of lines.

:g/*pattern*/	Finds (moves to) the last occurrence of *pattern* in the file.
:g/*pattern*/p	Finds and displays all lines in the file containing *pattern*.
:g!/*pattern*/nu	Finds and displays all lines in the file that don't contain *pattern*; also displays line number for each line found.

:60,124g/*pattern*/p

Finds and displays any lines between lines 60 and 124 containing *pattern*.

g can also be used for global replacements. For example, to search for all lines that begin with WARNING: and change the first word not on those lines to NOT:

\<..\> *27.04*   :g/^WARNING:/s/\<not\>/NOT/

—*LL* from the Nutshell Handbook *Learning the vi Editor*

31.10 *Confirming Substitutions in ex and vi*

It makes sense to be overly careful when using a search and replace command. It sometimes happens that what you get is not what you expect. You can undo any search and replacement command by entering u, provided that the command was intended for the most recent edit you made. But you don't always catch undesired changes until it is too late to undo them. Another way to protect your edited file is to save the file with :w before performing a global replacement. Then at least you can quit the file without saving your edits and go back to where you were before the change was made. You can also read the previous version of the buffer back in with :e! *(31.04)*.

It's wise to be cautious and know exactly what is going to be changed in your file. If you'd like to see what the search turns up and confirm each replacement before it is made, add the c option (for confirm) at the end of the substitute command:

:1,30s/his/the/gc

This command will display the entire line where the string has been located, and the string will be marked by a series of carets (^^^^).

```
copyists at his school
          ^^^ -
```

If you want to make the replacement, you must enter y (for yes) and press RETURN. If you don't want to make a change, simply press RETURN.

```
this can be used for invitations, signs, and menus.
     ^^^
```

The combination of the *vi* commands, n (repeat last search) and dot (.) (repeat last command), is also an extraordinarily useful and quick way to page through a file and make repetitive changes that you may not want to make globally. So, for example, if your editor has told you that you're using *which* when you should be using *that*, you can spot-check every occurrence of *which*, changing only those that are incorrect:

```
/which          Search for which.
cwthat ESC      Change to that.
n               Repeat search.
.               Repeat change (if appropriate).

                .

                .

                .
```

This often turns out to be faster than using a global substitution with confirmation. [It also lets you see other lines near the text you're checking.—*JP*]

—*DD, TOR* from the Nutshell Handbook *Learning the vi Editor*

31.11 *Keep Your Original File, Write to a New File*

You can use :w to save an entire buffer (the copy of the file you are editing) under a new filename.

Suppose you have a file *practice*, containing 600 lines. You open the file and make extensive edits. You want to quit but save *both* the old version of *practice* and your new edits for comparison. To save the edited buffer in a file called *check_me*, give the command:

```
:w check_me
```

Your old version, in the file *practice*, remains unchanged (provided that you didn't previously use :w). You can now quit the old version by typing :q.

—*LL* from the Nutshell Handbook *Learning the vi Editor*

31.12 Saving Part of a File

While editing, you will sometimes want to save just part of your file as a separate, new file. For example, you might have entered formatting codes and text that you want to use as a header for several files.

You can combine *ex* line addressing with the write command, w, to save part of a file. For example, if you are in the file *practice* and want to save part of practice as the file *newfile*, you could enter:

`:230,$w newfile`   Saves from line 230 to end-of-file in *newfile*.

`:.,600w newfile`   Saves from the current line to line 600 in *newfile*.

[To write *newfile* again, you'll need w! instead of w. —*JP*]

—*LL* from the Nutshell Handbook *Learning the vi Editor*

31.13 Appending to an Existing File

You can use the UNIX redirect and append operator (>>) with w to append all or part of the contents of the buffer to an existing file. For example, if you entered:

`:1,10w newfile`

and then:

`:340,$w >>newfile`

newfile would contain lines 1-10 and line 340 to the end of the buffer.

—*TOR* from the Nutshell Handbook *Learning the vi Editor*

31.14 Moving Blocks of Text by Patterns

You can move blocks of text delimited by patterns *(31.09)*. For example, assume you have a 150-page reference manual. All references pages are organized into three paragraphs with the same three headings: SYNTAX, DESCRIPTION, and PARAMETERS. A sample of one reference page follows:

```
.Rh 0 "Get status of named file" "STAT"
.Rh "SYNTAX"
.nf
integer*4 stat, retval
integer*4 status(11)
character*123 filename
...
retval = stat (filename, status)
.fi
.Rh "DESCRIPTION"
Writes the fields of a system data structure into the
status array.
These fields contain (among other
things) information about the file's location, access
```

```
privileges, owner, and time of last modification.
.Rh "PARAMETERS"
.IP "\fBfilename\fR" 15n
A character string variable or constant containing
the UNIX pathname for the file whose status you want
to retrieve.
You can give the ...
```

Suppose that it is decided to move the SYNTAX paragraph below the DESCRIP-
TION paragraph. Using pattern matching, you can move blocks of text on all 150
pages with one command!

```
:g/SYNTAX/,/DESCRIPTION/-1 mo /PARAMETERS/-1
```

This command operates on the block of text between the line containing the
word *SYNTAX* and the line just before the word *DESCRIPTION* (/DESCRIP-
TION/-1). The block is moved (using mo) to the line just before *PARAMETERS*
(/PARAMETERS/-1). Note that *ex* can place text only below the line specified.
To tell *ex* to place text above a line, you first have to move up a line with -1,
and then place your text below. In a case like this, one command saves literally
hours of work. (This is a real-life example—we once used a pattern match like
this to rearrange a reference manual containing hundreds of pages.)

Block definition by patterns can be used equally well with other *ex* commands.
For example, if you wanted to delete all DESCRIPTION paragraphs in the reference chapter, you could enter:

```
:g/DESCRIPTION/,/PARAMETERS/-1d
```

This very powerful kind of change is implicit in *ex*'s line addressing syntax, but
it is not readily apparent even to experienced users. For this reason, whenever
you are faced with a complex, repetitive editing task, take the time to analyze
the problem and find out if you can apply pattern-matching tools to get the job
done.

—*TOR* from the Nutshell Handbook *Learning the vi Editor*

31.15 Useful Global Commands (with Pattern Matches)

The best way to learn pattern matching is by example, so here's a short list of
pattern-matching examples, with explanations. (Article 27.10 has a list of these
patterns.) Study the syntax carefully so you understand the principles at work.
You should then be able to adapt these examples to your own situation.

1. Change all occurrences of the word *help* (or *Help*) to *HELP*:

    ```
    :%s/[Hh]elp/HELP/g
    ```

    or:

    ```
    :%s/[Hh]elp/\U&/g
    ```

    The \U changes the pattern that follows to all uppercase. The pattern that
    follows is the repeated search pattern, which is either *help* or *Help*.

---

2. Replace one or more spaces following a period or a colon with two spaces (here a space is marked by a □):

   `:%s/\([:.]\)□□*/\1□□/g`

   Either of the two characters within brackets can be matched. This character is saved into a hold buffer, using `\(` and `\)`, and restored on the right-hand side by the `\1`. Note that within brackets a special character such as a dot does not need to be escaped with a backslash (`\`).

3. Delete all blank lines:

   `:g/^$/d`

   What you are actually matching here is the beginning of the line (`^`) followed by the end of the line (`$`), with nothing in between.

4. Delete all blank lines, plus any lines that contain only white space:

   `:g/^[□tab]*$/d`

   (In the line above, a tab is shown as *tab*.) A line may appear to be blank but may in fact contain spaces or tabs. The previous example will not delete such a line. This example, like the one above it, searches for the beginning and end of the line. But instead of having nothing in between, the pattern tries to find any number of spaces or tabs. If no spaces or tabs are matched, the line is blank. To delete lines that contain white space but that *aren't* blank, you would have to match lines with *at least* one space or tab:

   `:g/^[□tab][□tab]*$/d`

5. Match the first quoted argument of all section header (`.Ah`) macros *(45.14)*, and replace each line with this argument:

   `:%s/^\.Ah "\([^"]*\)" .*/\1/`

   The substitution assumes that the `.Ah` macro can have more than one argument surrounded by quotes. You want to match everything between quotes, but only up to the *first* closing quote. Using `".*"` would be wrong because it would match all arguments on the line. What you do is to match a series of characters that *aren't* quotes, `[^"]*`. The pattern `"[^"]*"` matches a quote, followed by any number of non-quote characters, followed by a quote. Enclose the first argument in `\(` and `\)` so it can be replayed using `\1`.

6. Same as previous, except preserve the original lines by copying them.

   `:g/^\.Ah/t$ | s/\.Ah "\([^"]*\)" .*/\1/`

   In *ex*, the vertical bar (`|`) is a command separator that works like a semicolon (`;`) *(9.03)* on a UNIX command line. The first part, `:g/^\.Ah/t$`, matches all lines that begin with a `.Ah` macro, uses the `t` command to copy these lines, and places them after the last line (`$`) of the file. The second part is the same as in the previous example, except that the substitutions are performed on copies at the end of the file. The original lines are unchanged.

   —*TOR, DG from the Nutshell Handbook Learning the vi Editor*

31.16 Counting Occurrences; Stopping Search Wraps

Want to see how many times you used the word *very* in a file? There are a couple of easy ways.

First, tell *vi* to stop searching when you get to the end of the file. Type the command `:set nowrapscan` or put it in your *.exrc* file *(5.09)*.

1. Move to the top of the file with the 1G command. Search for the first *very* with the command `/very` (HINT: using the word-limiting regular expression `/\<very\>` *(27.04)* instead will keep you from matching words like *every*). To find the next *very*, type the n (next) command.

   When *vi* says `Address search hit BOTTOM without matching pattern`, you've found all of the words.

2. Use the command:

   `:g/very/p`

   The matching lines will scroll down your screen.

To find the line numbers, too, type `:set number` before your searches.

—*JP*

31.17 Capitalizing Every Word on a Line

Are you typing the title of an article or something else that needs an uppercase letter at the start of every word? Do you need to capitalize some text that isn't? It can be tedious to press the SHIFT key as you enter the text, or to use ~ (tilde) and w commands to change the text. The command below capitalizes the first character of every word that starts with a lowercase English letter:

`\< 27.04`   `:s/\<[a-z]/\u&/g`

That does only the current line. You can add a range of lines after the colon. For example, to edit all lines in the file:

`:%s/\<[a-z]/\u&/g`

To do the current line and the next five, use:

`:.,+5s/\<[a-z]/\u&/g`

To make the first character of each word uppercase and the rest lowercase, try:

`\u..\l.. 27.10`   `:s/\<\([A-Za-z]\)\([A-Za-z]*\)\>/\u\1\l\2/g`

Those commands can be a pain to type. If you use one of them a lot, try putting it in a keymap *(32.02)*.

—*JP*

31.18 Setting vi Options Automatically for Individual Files

The *.exrc file (5.09)* can set *vi* options for all files—or for files in a certain directory *(31.06)*. The articles listed below show other ways to set your *vi* setup.

- A controversial feature because of security problems, *modelines (31.19)* are still handy if you use them carefully. They let you store setup commands for each file, in the file itself.

- Instead of modelines, you can make separate setup files for each file you want to edit. These don't have the security problems of modelines because you can make the setup files read-only. See article 31.21.

- Article 31.20 lets you choose any one of a number of setups by typing a setup-choosing command from the shell prompt. All *vi* commands you start afterwards will use that setup. You can start a new setup any time.

—JP

31.19 Modelines: Bug or Feature?

Some versions of *vi* and *ex* have a *modeline* or *modelines* option. When that option is set in your *.exrc* file *(5.09)*, you can store setup commands at the top or bottom of any file you edit. When you start the editor, it will read the setup commands and run them. This is a lot like having a separate *.exrc* for each file you edit.

Modelines can be a security problem. If any troublemakers should edit your files and change your modelines, think about the difficulties they can cause you.

Most newer versions of *vi* disable modelines by default.

Here's a sample file—a shell script *(46.01)* with a modeline on the second line:

```
#! /bin/sh
# vi:set number wrapmargin=0 autoindent showmatch:

while read line
do
    ...
```

The mode line has #, the shell's comment character, at the start of it—so, the shell will ignore the line but *vi* will still read it. This is only necessary in a shell script, but it demonstrates that the modeline need not start in column 1. The modeline itself consists of a space or tab, the string *vi:* or *ex:*, the commands to be executed, and a closing colon. The space or tab before the modeline and the closing colon are both important—they tell the editor where the modeline begins and ends. You can put modelines on the first five or last five lines of a file (or both).

When you start *vi* on the file shown in the example above, it sets the options *number, wrapmargin=0, autoindent*, and *showmatch*.

Note: Any time you open a file with a modeline, *vi* changes the file status to "modified"—even if you haven't actually made any changes. To leave the file without writing it, you have to use the :q! command. This is a hassle when you use UNIX tools that depend on a file's modification time, like *make (29.12)*, especially if you also have the *autowrite* option set.

To find out whether your version of *vi* supports modelines—and whether the option is called *modeline* or *modelines*—get a list of all options with the command :set all. If the option is available, but not set, you'll see *nomodeline* (or *nomodelines*) as one of the options. Put the command

```
set modeline(s)
```

in your *.exrc* file to enable the option. Unfortunately, some versions list the option but don't support it!

—JP

31.20 *Multiple Editor Setup Files; Starting with a Search*

[This article shows vi, *but the same thing will work for other editors that read a setup file when they start up.—JP]*

Like many people, I want different *vi* options set for writing a program than for working on a text file. Here's how I do it.

Instead of putting mode lines *(31.19)* within each file, or writing extensions to the filenames *(31.21)*, I've got several different *.exrc (5.09)* startup files . . . one for each *vi* mode I'd like to use. I have aliases *(11.02)* that let me select the *.exrc* file I want. And, I have *vi* aliased so that, when I start it up, it tells me which *.exrc* file is in use. Here are the lines (with comments) from my *.cshrc (2.01)* file:

csh_init

~ 15.12
setenv *7.01*

```
setenv EXSTAT text          # INITIALIZATION FOR 'vi' ALIAS

        # --- THESE ALIASES RESET THE .exrc FILE --- #
# SET 'vi' FOR 4-CHARACTER TABS/SHIFTS:
alias 4vi 'cp ~/lib/vi/exrc4 ~/.exrc; setenv EXSTAT programming'
# SET 'vi' FOR 8-CHARACTER TABS/SHIFTS:
alias 8vi 'cp ~/lib/vi/exrc8 ~/.exrc; setenv EXSTAT text'
# SET 'vi' FOR QUICK WORK WHEN SYSTEM IS SLOW (NO .exrc FILE):
alias qvi 'rm ~/.exrc; setenv EXSTAT quick'

        # --- THESE ARE THE vi ALIASES. ONE SETS THE vi MODE FIRST --- #
alias vi 'echo "MODE: $EXSTAT"; /usr/ucb/vi \!*'
# CALL vi WITH A SEARCH:
alias vs '8vi; vi +/\!*'
```

The *EXSTAT* variable remembers which setup file has been stored in the *.exrc* file. Also, because you can't start *vi* with a search (`vi +/PATTERN`) unless the *wrapscan* option has been set ... so, I start the *vs* alias with an 8vi because my *exrc8* file sets *wrapscan*. Here's an example. I'll edit the file *report* and search for a line that has the word *misteak*:

```
% vs misteak report
MODE: text
"report" 45 lines, 2734 characters
```

—JP

31.21 Per File Setups in Separate Files

Do you need to set certain editor options for certain files—but *not* use the same setup for every file you edit? Make a special setup file with the same name and an underscore (_) at the end. For instance, a file named *report* could have a corresponding setup file named *report_*. (You don't have to use an underscore at the end of the filename. It's convenient though, because it's not a shell special character *(9.15)*.)

The setup file has the same format as a *.exrc* file *(5.09)*. To make the editor read it, map *(32.02)* a function key like F1 (or any other key sequence):

^[*32.05*   map #1 :source %_^[

When you start *vi*, tap that key to read the setup file. (The percent sign stands for the current filename *(31.04)*.)

If you want to use the same setup file for several files in a directory, you might want to make hard links *(19.03)* between them. That will save disk space. It also means that if you decide to change a setup option, you can edit one of the links to the setup file and the others will have the same change.

—JP

31.22 Filtering Text through a UNIX Command

(31.23)

When you're editing in *vi*, you can send a block of text as standard input to a UNIX command. The output from this command replaces the block of text in the buffer. You can filter text through a command from either *ex* or *vi*. The main difference between the two methods is that you indicate the block of text with line addresses in *ex* and with text objects (movement commands) in *vi*.

Filtering Text with ex

The first example demonstrates how to filter text with *ex*. Assume that the list of names in the preceding example, instead of being contained in a separate file called *phone*, is already contained in the current file on lines 96 through 99. You simply type the addresses of the lines you want to filter, followed by an exclamation mark and the UNIX command to be executed. For example, the command:

```
:96,99!sort
```

will pass lines 96 through 99 through the *sort (37.01)* filter and replace those lines with the output of *sort*.

The *ex %* operator is the easiest way to filter all the lines in your buffer. If you're editing a C program, for instance, you could feed it all through the formatting program named *indent* by typing:

```
:%!indent
```

Filtering Text with vi

In *vi*, text is filtered through a UNIX command by typing an exclamation mark (!) followed by any of *vi*'s movement keystrokes that indicate a block of text, and then by the UNIX command line to be executed. For example:

```
!)command
```

will pass the next sentence through *command*.

There are a couple of unusual features about how *vi* acts when you use this structure.

- First, the exclamation mark doesn't appear on your screen right away. When you type the keystroke(s) for the text object you want to filter, the exclamation mark appears at the bottom of the screen, *but the character you type to reference the object does not.*

- Second, text blocks must be more than one line, so you can use only the keystrokes that would move more than one line (G, { }, ( ), [[ ]], +, -). To repeat the effect, a number may precede either the exclamation mark or the text object. (For example, both !10+ and 10!+ would indicate the next ten lines.) Objects such as w do not work unless enough of them are specified so as to exceed a single line. You can also use a slash (/) followed by a *pattern* and a carriage return to specify the object. This takes the text up to the pattern as input to the command.

- Third, there is a special text object that can be used only with this command syntax; you can specify the current line by entering a second exclamation mark:

```
!!command
```

Remember that either the entire sequence or the text object can be preceded by a number to repeat the effect. For instance, to change lines 96 through 99 as in the above example, you could position the cursor on line 96 and enter either:

```
4!!sort
```

or:

```
!4!sort
```

As another example, assume you have a portion of text in a message that you're going to send to the Usenet *(1.33)* "net news." On Usenet, text that might be offensive or would give away the answer to a question is "rotated." The letter *a* is changed to *n*, *b* is changed to *o*, and so on. There are programs for rotating text, but it's also easy to rotate text with the *tr (36.09)* command. In this example, the second sentence is the block of text that will be filtered to the command.

```
One sentence before.
With a screen editor you can scroll the page
move the cursor, delete lines, insert characters,
and more, while seeing the results of your edits
as you make them.
One sentence after.
```

Keystrokes	***Result***
| `!)` | ```
One sentence after.
~
~
~
!_
``` |

An exclamation mark appears on the last line to prompt you for the UNIX command.

```
tr '[a-m][n-z][A-M][N-Z]' '[n-z][a-m][N-Z][A-M]'
```

```
One sentence before.
Jvgu n fperra rqvgbe lbh pna fpebyy gur cntr
zbir gur phefbe, qryrgr yvarf, vafreg punenpgref,
naq zber, juvyr frrvat gur erfhygf bs lbhe rqvgf
nf lbh znxr gurz.
One sentence after.
```

Enter the UNIX command and press RETURN. The input is replaced by the output.

To repeat the previous command, the syntax is:

```
! object !
```

It is sometimes useful to send sections of a coded document to *nroff (45.14)* to be replaced by formatted output. Remember that the "original" input is replaced by the output. Fortunately, if there is a mistake, such as an error message being sent instead of the expected output, you can undo the command and restore the lines.

—TOR from the Nutshell Handbook Learning the vi Editor
```

31.23 Safer vi Filter-throughs

Sometimes when I do a filter-through—especially on some buggy, old versions of *vi*—it completely scrambles and trashes my text. Things can be so bad that the *u* (undo) command won't work. Unless I've been careful to write my buffer before the filter-through, I can lose the whole file! I've seen the same problem on several versions of *vi* and read articles on Usenet from people who've been bitten by it.

If you've been burned, too, you might want to use the keymaps *(32.02)* below. Map one of your keys—a numbered function key like F4, if you can—to do filter-throughs of your whole file. To start a filter-through, press the F4 key—this invokes the first map below. Next, type the UNIX command you want to run. To run the filter-through, press F4 again.

The maps are shown below. Enter the control characters ^M ^V, and ^ [by typing CTRL-v first *(32.05)*.

exrc

```
map #4 :se noaw^M:w^M:%d^M:r !
map! #4 ^V '%'^M:1d^[:se aw^[
```

The first one (`map #4`) maps the F4 key during command mode to set the *noautowrite* option (`:se noaw`), write the buffer to your file (`:w`), delete all lines in the buffer (`:%d`), and start a shell command line (`:r !`). After pressing F4 from command mode, your cursor should be on the bottom line, ready for you to type the filter-through:

```
:r !
```

Type the UNIX command (like `expand`, `fmt -75`, and so on). Then press F4 again. Because you're in text-input mode, the second map above (`map! #4`) will be used this time.

The map starts with CTRL-v and a space; this trick puts a space between the command line you type and the filename. Next, the current filename (`%`)—in single quotes, to protect special characters from the shell—is output, followed by a RETURN to execute the command. Reading a UNIX command with `:r !` leaves a blank line above; the `:1d` deletes that line (it'll be the line 1 in the buffer). Finally, the `:se aw` command turns on the *autowrite* option again.

If you never set the *autowrite* option, you can leave out the `:se noaw^M` and `:se aw^M`. But be sure—if autowrite is set when you use this map, all lines in your file will be deleted! (The empty buffer will be auto-written when the shell command runs.)

I guess it figures :-(—this tricky set of keymaps doesn't work perfectly on every version of *vi*. On my SunOS 4.1 version of *vi*, for instance, it leaves me in text-input mode; I have to hit ESC after pressing F4 the second time.

Still, this is a lot more reliable than the normal way to do filter-throughs. It's been especially nice because I've always been able to undo the filter-through with the *u* (undo) or :e! commands (so far, at least . . .).

—JP

31.24 vi/ex File Recovery vs. Networked Filesystems

Have you ever used the *vi −r* command to recover a file? It lets you get back a file you were editing when the system crashed or something else killed your editor before you could save. The system will send you a mail message *(1.33)* something like this:

```
Date: Tue, 19 Nov 91 09:59:00 EST
To: jerry

A copy of an editor buffer of your file "afile"
was saved when the system went down.
This buffer can be retrieved using the "recover" command of the editor.
An easy way to do this is to give the command "vi -r afile".
This works for "edit" and "ex" also.
```

(31.25)

Your files are saved under a directory named something like */usr/preserve*. Follow the instructions and you'll get back your file, more or less the way it was when you lost it.

If your computers have networked filesystems, such as NFS, there's a wrinkle in the way that *vi −r* works. It may only work right on the specific computer where you were editing a file. For example, if you're editing the file *foo* on the host named *artemis* and it crashes . . . you may not be able to log onto another host and do *vi −r foo* to recover that file. That's because, on many hosts, temporary files (like editor buffers) are stored on a local filesystem instead of on the networked (shared) filesystems. On this kind of system, you may need to log onto *artemis* to recover your lost editor buffer.

If you don't remember what files are saved on a machine, you can usually get a list of your saved files by typing *vi −r* without a filename:

```
% vi -r
/var/preserve/jerry:
On Wed Jul 17 at 08:02 saved 15 lines of file "/u/jerry/Mail/drafts/1"
On Sun Aug 25 at 18:42 saved 157 lines of file "doit"
/tmp:
No files saved.
```

/tmp *22.02*

Don't wait too long. Most UNIX systems remove these saved editor buffers every month, week, or even more often.

—JP

31.25 vi –r May not Write Recovered Buffer when You Exit

Usually, when you're editing a file with *vi*, if you type the command *ZZ*, it saves your file. But, on some versions of *vi*, if you recover a file with *vi –r*(31.24), typing *ZZ* may not save your edits!

That might be a good thing. When you recover a buffer, you need to decide whether the recovered buffer is really what you want. Maybe you've made other changes to the file since then. Maybe something went wrong as the buffer was being saved (say, the system crashed). You shouldn't just save without checking first.

You can use the `:w!` command to write the recovered version after you're sure that you want it. Use the `:q!` command if you don't want the recovered version.

—JP

31.26 Shell Escapes: Running One UNIX Command while Using Another

Some UNIX commands, usually interactive commands like *vi*, let you run another UNIX command temporarily. To do that, you type a special command character—usually an exclamation point (`!`)—then type the UNIX command line you want to run. In this article, I'll show examples for the *vi* editor. To see if this works on another utility, check its documentation or just try typing `!`*UNIXcommand* when the utility is waiting for you to type a command.

You can run any UNIX command without quitting *vi*. That's handy, for example, if you want to read your mail or look at some other file . . . then go back to the file you were editing without losing your place. It's called a "shell escape." (By the way, there's a another way to do this, called job control (13.01), that works on many UNIX systems with the C and Korn shells. I think that job control is a lot more convenient and flexible than shell escapes.)

Let's say you're editing the file named *foo* and you need to run *grep* to get someone's phone number from your phone file. The steps are:

1. Be sure you're in command mode (press the ESC key if you aren't sure).

2. If you want to run a command that needs the file you're editing, remember to write out your *vi* buffer with the `:w` command. (So, you probably wouldn't need to write before the *grep* command below.) Type `:!` followed by the UNIX command, then press RETURN. For example:

~ 15.12

```
:!grep tim ~/phone
```

3. The *grep* program will run. When it finishes, *vi* will say:

```
[Hit return to continue]
```

After you press RETURN, you'll be right back where you were.

Other examples:

`:!pg somefile`	Page through *somefile* on your screen.
`:!ptroff %`	Run this file through the *ptroff* formatter program. *vi* replaces `%` with the name of the file you're editing now.
`:!mail`	Read your mail. Be careful about this if you were already running the *mail* program, and you used the command ˜v to edit a message with *vi* from inside the *mail* program. This shell escape starts a subshell *(40.04)*; it will *not* take you back to the same *mail* session before you started editing!
`:!sh`	Start a completely new shell. (If you are using the C shell or Korn shell instead of the Bourne shell, you'd almost always want to use job control to temporarily suspend *vi* instead *(13.04)*!)

Basically: anything you can do at a shell prompt, you can do with a shell escape. You'll be in a subshell though, not your original login shell. So, commands like *cd* won't affect the program where you started the subshell or any other shell. On the bright side, changing directories or resetting anything in your environment won't affect *vi* or the shell where you started *vi*. Terminating the program you're running in the subshell will bring you right back where you were.

—*JP*

31.27 *vi Compound Searches*

You probably know that you can search for a word or phrase with the *vi* command / (slash):

/treasure

If you have a file that uses the same word over and over again, you might want to find one particular place that the word is used. You can repeat the search with the *n* command until you find the place you want. That can take time and work, though.

For example, supose you want to find the word "treasure" in the sentence that has words something like "Los Alamos residents . . . treasure," but you can't remember exactly how the sentence is written. You could use wildcards in your regular expression *(27.04)*:

/Los Alamos.*treasure

but then the phrases "Los Alamos" and "treasure" have to be on the same line of the file you're searching—and they won't always be. Also, you want your cursor on the word *treasure*, but that search would put the cursor on *Los* instead.

"Hmmm," you say, "How about two separate searches, like this?"

```
/Los Alamos
/treasure
```

The problem there is: the file might have the phrase "Los Alamos" all through it; you might have to type *n* over and over until you get to the sentence with *treasure*.

Here's the easy way: a compound search. Say your cursor is on line 1 of the following file:

```
Before the second World War, there was a treasured boys school in
what was to become the city of Los Alamos, New Mexico. The school at
Los Alamos changed the lives and made a lifelong impression on most boys
who attended. One of the boys who attended the Los Alamos school went on
to propose that remote set of mesas as a site for the U.S. Government's
     ...
Since the war ended, most of the boys school ranch buildings have been torn
down or replaced. But there's one building that Los Alamos residents still
use and treasure. It's The Lodge, a log building on the edge of what's now
     ...
```

Type the command:

`/Los Alamos/;/treasure/`

That means "find the first occurrence of *treasure* just after *Los Alamos*." Starting at the top of the example above, that search will skip past all the *treasure* and *Los Alamos* words until it finds the word *treasure* on the last line shown. (It's probably smarter to type just `/Alamos/;/treasure/` in case the *Los Alamos* is split across two lines of the file.)

Another example: a C programmer who wants to find the *printf* function call just after the line where *i* is incremented by two (`i += 2`). She could type:

`/i += 2/;/printf/`

Note: You can't repeat a compound search by typing n. The easiest way is to define the search as a key map *(32.02)*:

_{`M 32.05`}

        `:map g /Los Alamos/;/treasure/^M`

and use (in this case) g to repeat the search.

—JP

31.28 Keep Track of Functions and Included Files with ctags and tags

The source code for a large C program will usually be spread over several files. Sometimes, it is difficult to keep track of which file contains which function definitions. To simplify matters, a UNIX command called *ctags* can be used together with the `:tag` command of *vi*.

ctags creates an information file (a database) that *vi* uses later to determine which files define which functions. By default, this database file is called *tags*. This file contains lines of the form:

```
tag_ID     file     context
```

where `tag_ID` is the name of the C function or macro, `file` is the source file in which `tag_ID` is defined, and `context` is a search pattern that shows the line of code containing `tag_ID`.

From within *vi*, a command such as:

:! 31.26

```
:!ctags file.c
```

creates a file named *tags* under your current directory. *tags* is a database containing information on the functions defined in *file.c*. A command like:

```
:!ctags *.c
```

creates a *tags* file describing all the C source files under the directory. [If you'll be using the tags file while you're in some other directory, be sure to use a full pathname, like this:

10.14

```
:!ctags `pwd`/*.c
```

That will store full pathnames in the *tags* file.—*JP*]

Now suppose your *tags* file contains information on all the source files that make up a C program. Also suppose that you want to look at or edit a function in the program but do not know where the function is. From within *vi*, the command:

```
:tag name
```

will look at the *tags* file to find out which file contains the definition of the function *name*. It will then read in the file and position the cursor on the line where the name is defined. In this way, you don't have to know which file you have to edit; you only have to decide which function you want to edit. [My favorite *tags* shortcut is to put the cursor on the first letter of a function name in your buffer. Then press CTRL-] (Control-right square bracket). *vi* will read the *tags* file and open to the function name that was under your cursor. At least, my version of *vi* will do that!—*JP*]

Note: If *tags* isn't working, that may be because you have the *vi* option *nowrapscan* set. That's a problem on many versions of *vi*. If typing the following command fixes *tags* for you:

```
:set wrapscan
```

---

then add that command to your *.exrc* file *(5.09)* or *EXINIT* variable *(7.03)*. (Thanks to Chris Torek for this tip.)

—*JS from the Nutshell Handbook* Learning the vi Editor

31.29 Setting Multiple tags Files

You might have a *tags* file in your current directory. You might also have another system-wide or group-wide *tags* file. How can you make *vi* search both of them?

In your *.exrc* file *(5.09)* or at the colon (:) prompt, type a backslash (\) between the *tag* filenames:*

```
set tags=tags\ /usr/local/lib/tags
```

—*JP*

31.30 vi Outsmarts Dual-function Function Keys

[This tip is about a Digital Equipment VT220 terminal, specifically—but you can probably use the same idea on other terminals.—JP]

I worked at a university with labs full of VT220 terminals. VT220s can be set to act as either VT220s or VT100s. The top row on the keyboard has a key marked ESC, for "escape." Unfortunately, the key sends a real ESC character only when the terminal is in its VT100 mode. As a VT220, that function key sends ESC followed by the four characters " [23~"—these make *vi* beep and change character case.

You can solve that problem by putting this command in your *.exrc* *(5.09)* file:

```
map [23~ mm
```

Then, whenever you press that key in the VT220 mode, the ESC character will do what ESC should and the [23~ will execute the *vi* command *mm*. That command marks *(31.39)* the current cursor position as "m"—nothing useful, but it keeps *vi* quiet.

—*JP*

---

*Thanks to Eli Taub, on the Usenet *comp.editors* newsgroup in 1990, for this tip. He says it worked under AIX then; it works for me under SunOS, too. I haven't seen it in any *ex/vi* documentation, though I've heard since that it's common knowledge.

31.31 vi Word Abbreviation

You can define abbreviations that *vi* will automatically expand into the full text whenever you type the abbreviation in insert mode. To define an abbreviation, use the *ex* command:

```
:ab abbr phrase
```

abbr is an abbreviation for the specified *phrase*. The sequence of characters that make up the abbreviation will be expanded in insert mode only if you type it as a full word; *abbr* will not be expanded within a word. [I abbreviate *Covnex* to *Convex*, my company's name, because I have dyslexic fingers. —*TC*]

Suppose in the file *practice* you want to enter text that contains a frequently recurring phrase such as a difficult product or company name. The command:

```
:ab ns the Nutshell Handbook
```

abbreviates *the Nutshell Handbook* to the initials *ns*. Now whenever you type *ns* as a separate word in insert mode, *ns* expands to the full text.

Abbreviations expand as soon as you press a non-alphanumeric character* (e.g., punctuation), a carriage return, or ESC (returning to command mode). When you are choosing abbreviations, choose combinations of characters that don't ordinarily occur while you are typing text. If you create an abbreviation that ends up expanding in places where you don't want it to, you can disable the abbreviation by typing:

```
:unab abbr
```

To list your currently defined abbreviations, type:

```
:ab
```

The characters that compose your abbreviation cannot also appear at the end of your phrase. For example, if you issue the command:

```
:ab PG This movie is rated PG
```

you'll get the message No tail recursion, and the abbreviation won't be set. The message means that you have tried to define something that will expand itself repeatedly, creating an infinite loop. If you issue the command:

```
:ab PG the PG rating system
```

you may or may not produce an infinite loop, but in either case you won't get a warning message. For example, when the above command was tested on a System V version of UNIX, the expansion worked. On a Berkeley version though, the abbreviation expanded repeatedly, like this:

```
the the the the the ...
```

---

*An abbreviation won't expand when you type an underscore (_); it's treated as part of the abbreviation.

until a memory error occurred and *vi* quit. We recommend that you avoid repeating your abbreviation as part of the defined phrase.

—DD, DG from the Nutshell Handbook *Learning the vi Editor*

31.32 Using vi Abbreviations as Commands (Cut and Paste Between vi's)

The *vi* command ab *(31.31)* is for abbreviating words. But it's also good for abbreviating *ex*-mode commands that you type over and over. In fact, for *ex*-mode commands (commands that start with a colon (:)), abbreviations can be better than keymaps *(32.02)*. That's because you can choose almost any command name; you don't have to worry about conflicts with existing *vi* commands.

Here's an example. If you have a windowing terminal or have more than one terminal, you might have *vi* sessions running in more than one place. Your system might have a way to transfer text between windows, but it can be easier to use files in */tmp (22.02)*—especially for handling lots of text. Here are some abbreviations from my *.exrc (5.09)* file:

exrc

```
ab aW w! /tmp/jerry.temp.a
ab aR r /tmp/jerry.temp.a
ab bW w! /tmp/jerry.temp.b
ab bR r /tmp/jerry.temp.b
...
```

I use those abbreviations this way. To write the current and next 45 lines to temporary file *a*, I type this command in one *vi* session:

```
:.,+45 aW
```

To read those saved lines into another *vi* session, I use:

```
:aR
```

You can do the same thing in a single *vi* session by using named buffers *(31.04)*, but temporary files are the only method that works between two separate *vi* sessions.

—JP

31.33 Fixing Typos with vi Abbreviations

Abbreviations are a handy way to fix common typos. Try a few abbreviations like this:

```
ab teh the
ab taht that
```

in your *.exrc (5.09)* file.

Any time you find yourself transposing letters or saying, "Darn, I always misspell that word," add an abbreviation to *.exrc*. (Of course, you do have to worry about performance if the file gets too big.)

You can do the same thing to enforce conventions. For example, we type command names in italics, so creating a list of abbreviations like:

```
ab vi \fIvi\fP
```

saves us from having to type lots of *troff (45.14)* codes.

(This abbreviation is not recursive *(31.31)* because the vi is sandwiched between other alphanumeric characters, not standing alone as a word.)

—*TOR*

31.34 *vi Line Commands vs. Character Commands*

[Quite a few vi *users understand how to build* vi *commands with the* (number*)*(command*)*(text object*) model. But not too many people understand the difference between line commands and character commands. This article explains that and gives some examples.—JP]*

The _ (underscore) command is very similar to the ^ (caret) command in that it moves to the first non-blank character of the current line. The key difference is that _ is a *line* command while ^ is a *character* command. This is important for all functions that read an "address," for example, d, y, and c.

In fact, delete, yank, and so on all call a common internal routine in *vi* to get an "address." If the address is of a particular character, *vi* does a character-mode delete or yank or whatever. If it is a line address, *vi* does a line-mode operation. The "address" command may be any of the regular positioning commands (e.g., W, b, $, or /pattern/) or the original character repeated (as in dd or yy).

Some examples are in Table 31-1.

Table 31-1. Examples of vi Character and Line Commands

Keystrokes	Results
dd	Deletes the current line.
d'a	Deletes all lines between the current line and the line containing mark a, inclusive.
d`a	Deletes all characters between the current character and the character at mark a. This works much like an Emacs ^W in that the two endpoints are considered to be between two characters. Note that a character-oriented delete may delete newlines.
c/accord/	Changes all characters (*not* lines!) between the current character up to but not including the a in accord. (However, see the Note below.)
c?accord?	Changes all characters between the current character and the accord, including the word accord.
yj	Yanks two lines, the current line and the one below.

yH	Yanks all the lines from the top of the screen to the current line, inclusive.
<G	Unindents or "dedents" the lines between the current line and the last line, inclusive. (The variable shiftwidth determines the amount of dedenting.) Note that this command turns character addresses into line addresses (so does >).
!}fmt	Runs the lines between the current line and the end of the paragraph through the program *fmt (31.37)*.

Note: If you have wrapscan set, a search like c?accord? may wrap from the beginning of the file to the end. This can cause unexpected results, and is one reason why I have set nows in my .exrc. Unfortunately, turning off wrapscan breaks *tags (31.28)* in many versions of *vi*.

---

vi combines the repeat count, if any, on the command character with the repeat count on the motion command, so that 2y2j yanks five lines. Interestingly, 2y2_ yanks 4 lines (so does 2y2y) since the _ command moves down (repeat count minus 1) lines. Beware, however, of using repeat counts on all of the motion commands; they're not all implemented in the same way. 4$ moves to the end of the third line below the current; 4^ merely moves to the first non-blank character of the current line. | (vertical bar) is a synonym for 0 (zero); given a repeat count it goes that many characters to the right of the beginning of the line (as if you had typed | (*rept-1*) l). (Exercise for the reader: why can't you give a repeat count to 0?)

Uppercase letters do different things depending on the command. The exact actions may not always seem sensible, but typically they affect the "current line": D acts like d$; C acts like c$; Y acts like yy. The list must merely be memorized, or you can use a good *vi* reference guide.

—*CT* in *net.unix* on Usenet, *19 March 1984*

31.35 *Out of Temporary Space? Use Another Directory*

vi keeps its temporary copy of the file you're editing in a temporary-file directory *(22.02)*—usually */tmp*, */usr/tmp*, or */var/tmp*. If you're editing a big file or if the temporary filesystem runs out of space, *vi* may not be able to make your temporary file. When that happens, you can use *vi*'s set directory command to set the pathname of a different temporary directory. (If this happens a lot though, you should talk to the system administrator and see if the standard area can be cleaned up or made bigger.)

First, you'll need the absolute pathname *(15.02)* of a directory on a filesystem with enough room *(25.08)*. Use an existing directory or make a new one.

The *vi* command is `set` directory—for example,

```
set directory=/usr1/jim/vitemp
```

You have to type that command before giving *vi* a filename to edit—after that, *vi* has made the temporary file and you'll be too late. But if you type that command while using *vi* and then use the `: e` command *(31.04)*, all files from then on will use the new temporary directory.

To set the directory temporarily, it's probably easiest to add that command to the *EXINIT* environment variable:

```
setenv EXINIT 'set directory=/usr1/jim/vitemp'
```

There are other ways to change *EXINIT*, too—see article 7.10.

If you already have a *.exrc* file *(5.09)*, setting *EXINIT* will make *vi* ignore your *.exrc* file. To make the temporary `set directory` work, too, use a command with a vertical bar (|) like this:

```
setenv EXINIT 'source /usr1/jim/.exrc|set directory=/usr1/jim/vitemp'
```

—JP

31.36 *The ex Open Mode Can be Handy*

Most *vi* users hate it when they start the editor and get a message like one of these:

```
Visual needs addressable cursor or upline capability
[Using open mode]
```

Those folks usually say (or think) something choice like "how the #&@! do I get to fullscreen mode?" If you're one of those people, wait. You might get to *like* the *ex* open mode!

Before I show you an example of open mode, I'll mention another place where it's nice: on slow dialup lines or sluggish network connections, where your screen fills slowly and you're always waiting for it to redraw. It's also very useful if you're using a window system and *vi* doesn't seem to understand how many lines are in your window—for quick editing, it can be easier to switch to open mode for a minute than to try to fix the window.

The open mode is something like *vi* on a one-line screen. It's different than other UNIX line-mode editors like *ed* or the standard colon-prompt mode of *ex*, though. In open mode, you use the normal fullscreen *vi* commands—one line at a time. For example, to exit, type ZZ just like you do in fullscreen mode.

If you've got a fair amount of experience with *vi*, the easiest way to learn about open mode is to jump in and try it—after a little explanation, that is. There are three ways to get into open mode:

- If you're thrown into *ex* mode and given a colon (:) prompt, type this command and press RETURN:

    ```
    :open
    ```

- If you have a choice—on a slow network connection, for example—start open mode from the command line. Depending on your version of *vi*, use one of the following commands:

```
% ex +open filename
% ex -c open filename
```

- If you're already in *vi*'s fullscreen mode, switch to open mode by typing Q to get an *ex* colon (:) prompt. Then type the command open and press RETURN.

When you start open mode, the editor will display the current line and put your cursor at the start of it.

Keystrokes	*Result*

ex +open afile

```
[Using open mode]
"afile" 47 lines, 1943 characters
In the beginning, there was a cursor.
```

Open the file *afile* in open mode. Notice that the prompt line, which shows the filename and size at the bottom of the screen in *vi*, is printed first during open mode. That's because open mode always prints line by line. Next, the first line of the file is displayed. Your cursor is at the start of the line.

2w

```
[Using open mode]
"afile" 47 lines, 1943 characters
In the beginning, there was a cursor.
```

The *vi* command 2w moves the cursor forward two words.

j

```
[Using open mode]
"afile" 47 lines, 1943 characters
In the beginning, there was a cursor.
The screen was blank and without characters.
```

The *vi* command j moves the cursor down one line. NOTE: On some versions, this command will print only the first few characters of the new line—up to the place where the cursor sits. So, instead of j, I usually use the RETURN command to paint a whole line and move the cursor to the front of it.

k

```
[Using open mode]
"afile" 47 lines, 1943 characters
In the beginning, there was a cursor.
The screen was blank and without characters.
In the beginning, there was a cursor.
```

The *vi* command k moves the cursor up one line—to the previous line. This is open mode, so the previous lines scroll away. To keep from getting confused, remember: the line with the cursor is the one you're editing now. NOTE: As in the previous step, the k command may not print all of the line. In that case, the minus (–) command is better.

cwend

```
[Using open mode]
"afile" 47 lines, 1943 characters
In the beginning, there was a cursor.
The screen was blank and without characters.
In the end, there was a cursor.
```

Typing cw puts you into *vi*'s text-input mode to change the word *beginning* to *end*.
Press ESC to go back to command mode.

This might take some getting used to. But once you learn the idea behind open
mode, it can be handy to know.

—JP

31.37 *Neatening Lines*

Many versions of UNIX have a handy program named *fmt*. It reformats lines of
text to fit on the screen. You can use *fmt* for things like neatening lines of a
mail message or a file that you're editing with *vi*. (Emacs has its own built-in
line-neatener.) It's also great for shell programming and almost any place you
have lines that are too long or too short for your screen.

 On at least one version of UNIX, *fmt* is a disk initializer (disk formatter) command. Don't run *that* command accidentally! Check
your on-line manual page and see the *fmt* equivalents below.

Here's an example. Let's say you're editing a file (e-mail message, whatever) in
vi and the lines aren't even. They look like this:

```
This file is a mess
with some short lines
and some lines that are too long -- like this one, which goes on and on for qu
```

```
Let's see what 'fmt' does with it.
```

You put your cursor on the first line and type (in command mode):

5!!fmt

which means "feed 5 lines to *fmt*." Then the lines will look like this:

```
This file is a mess with some short lines and some lines that are too
long -- like this one, which goes on and on for quite a while and etc.
```

```
Let's see what 'fmt' does with it.
```

This is handiest for formatting paragraphs. Put your cursor on the first line of
the paragraph and type (in command mode):

!} *31.22*   **!}fmt**

If you don't have any text in your file that needs to be kept as is, you can neaten the whole file at once by typing:

```
:% ! fmt
```

There are a few different versions of *fmt*, some fancier than others. In general, the program assumes that:

- Paragraphs have blank lines between them.

- If a line is indented, keep the indentation.

- The output lines should be about 70 characters wide. Some have a command line option to let you set this. For example, fmt -132 (or, on some versions, fmt -l 132) would reformat your file to have lines with no more than 132 characters on each.

- Lines should be written to its standard output.

If you don't have *fmt*, there are a couple of freely-available versions. Alternatively, you can make your own simple (and a little slower) version with *sed* and *nroff*—see article 31.38. The *recomment (36.02)* script uses *fmt* with *sed* to do a different kind of reformatting: program comment blocks.

—*JP, TOR*

31.38 *Faking fmt with nroff in System V*

fmt (31.37) is hard to do without once you've learned about it. Unfortunately, it's not available in many versions of System V. However, it's relatively easy to emulate with *sed (35.24)* and *nroff (45.14)*.

Here's the script:

fmt.sh

```
#!/bin/sh
sed '1i\
.ll 72\
.na\
.hy 0\
.pl 1' $* | nroff
```

The reason this is so complicated is that by default, *nroff* makes some assumptions you need to change. For example, it assumes an 11-inch page (66 lines), and will add blank lines to a short file (or the end of a long file). The quick-and-dirty workaround to this is to manually put the *nroff* request *.pl 1* (page length 1 line) at the top of the text you want to reformat. *nroff* also tends to justify lines; you want to turn this off with the .na request. You also want to turn off hyphenation (.hy 0), and you may want to set the line length to 72 instead of *nroff*'s default 65, if only for consistency with the real *fmt* program. All these *nroff* requests get inserted before the first line of input by the *sed* 1i command.

A fancier script would take a –*nn* line-length option and turn it into a *.ll* request for *nroff*, etc.

—*TOR*

31.39 *Finding Your Place with Undo*

Often, you're editing one part of a file, and need to go to another point to look at something. How do you get back?

You can mark your place with the m command. In command mode, type m followed by any letter. (We'll use **x** in the example.) Then to return to your place, type:

m**x**	Marks current position with *x* (*x* can be any letter).
'x	Moves cursor to first character of line marked by *x*.
`x	Moves cursor to character marked by *x*.
``	Returns to exact position of previous mark or context after a move.
''	Returns to the beginning of the line of the previous mark or context.

But I often find it just as easy to simply type u to undo my last edit. That pops me right back to the place where I was editing. Then I type u again to restore the edit. (I still use m if I want to mark more than one place.)

—TOR

32

Creating Custom Commands in vi

32.01 Why Type More Than You Have To?

Keymapping—storing complex command sequences so that they can be executed with a single keystroke—is one of my favorite timesavers. There's nothing like typing one key and watching a whole string of work take place. For repetitive edits (e.g., font changes) it's a real wrist-saver, too. In this chapter we show you how to:

- Save time by mapping keys: articles 32.02, 32.06, and 32.07.

- Know when to map a key and when not to: article 32.03.

- Map keys like ESC and RETURN: article 32.05.

- Move around the file without leaving insert mode: articles 32.11 and 32.12.

- Protect the text you're pasting in from another window: article 32.04.

- Put custom commands in your *.exrc* file: articles 32.08, 32.09, and 32.13.

- Wrap long lines of text: article 32.15.

—EK

32.02 Save Time and Typing with the vi map Command

While you're editing, you may find that you are using a command sequence frequently, or you may occasionally use a very complex command sequence. To save yourself keystrokes, or the time that it takes to remember the sequence, you can assign the sequence to an unused key by using the map command.

The map command acts a lot like ab *(31.31)* except that you define a macro for command mode instead of insert mode.

map *x sequence*	Define *x* as a *sequence* of editing commands.
unmap *x*	Disable the *x* definition.
map	List the characters that are currently mapped.

As with other *ex*-mode commands, these map commands can be saved in your *.exrc* file *(5.09)*—or typed in after a colon (:).

Before you can start creating your own maps, you need to know the keys not used in command mode that are available for user-defined commands:

Letters:	g K q V v
Control keys:	^A ^K ^O ^T ^W ^X
Symbols:	_ * \ =

(Note: the = is used by *vi* if Lisp mode is set.)

With maps you can create simple or complex command sequences. As a simple example, you could define a command to reverse the order of words. In *vi*, with the cursor as shown:

    you can t̲he scroll page

the sequence to put *the* after *scroll* would be dwwP: delete word, dw; move to the next word, w; put the deleted word before that word, P. (You can also use W instead of w.) Saving this sequence:

    map v dwwP

enables you to reverse the order of two words at any time in the editing session with the single keystroke v.

You can also map certain multiple-character sequences. Start the map with one of the symbols in the list above. For example, to map the keystrokes *s to put single quotes around a word (*'word'*), and *d to use double quotes (*"word"*):

^[32.05

    map *s Ea'^[Bi'^[
    map *d Ea"^[Bi"^[

Now you'll be able to make hundreds of key maps (though your version of *vi* probably has a limit). Article 32.08 has lots of examples.

You may also be able to associate map sequences with your terminal's function keys if your *termcap* or *terminfo* entry *(6.02)* defines those keys. For example, to make function key F1 transpose words:

```
map #1 dwelp
```

A final note: map assignments are not really limited to unused keys. You can map keys that are defined as other *vi* commands, but then the key's original meaning in inaccessible. But this is probably okay if the key is tied to a command that you rarely use. There's more information in article 32.13 about the *noremap* option.

—DG, JP, LL

32.03 What You Lose when You Use map!

Back in the old days (when bread cost five cents and my grandfather was just a boy...) a terminal's arrow keys didn't work during *vi* text-input mode. To move around in the file, you pressed ESC and used command-mode commands like *5k* and *4w*. Since then, lots of vendors and users have modified *vi* so that you can use arrow keys during text-input mode. In fact, we've shown you how to do it yourself in articles 32.11 and 32.12. These days, lots of folks think the newfangled way that *vi* works is the right way. Here are some reasons to do it the old way instead:

- In most cases, the u (undo) command will be useless after text-input mode because the arrow keymap does several hidden commands. The only "undo" command that will do much good is U—it undoes all changes on the current line, and it doesn't work if you've moved off the line since you made the change you want to undo.

- Beginners can get confused by this. They need to learn that *vi* is a moded editor, that you enter text in text-input mode and make changes in command mode. Movement through the file is with commands.

  When people start using *vi* and they find that some motion commands (the cursor keys) work in text-input mode, *vi* seems inconsistent.

- If your map! runs commands that start with an ESC (and it almost always will), your ESC key may work more slowly. That's because every time you press the ESC key, *vi* will wait one second (or so) to be sure that the ESC is just an ESC alone and not the beginning of a map!ped sequence. Some vendors have changed this, though.

  The fast alternative is to press ESC twice. That rings the terminal bell, though.

—JP

32.04 Keymaps for Pasting into a Window Running vi

I usually run *vi* inside windows on a system like X, Sunview, or the Macintosh. The window systems can copy and paste text between windows. Pasting into a *vi* window may be tricky if you use *vi* options like *wrapmargin* or *autoindent*—the text you paste can be rearranged or indented in weird ways.

I've fixed that with the keymaps below. If I'm pasting in text that should be copied exactly with no changes, I go into text-input mode and type CTRL-x. That shuts off autoindent (noai) and the wrapmargin (wm=0). When I'm done pasting, I type CTRL-n while I'm still in text-input mode.

A different kind of "pasted" input is with CTRL-r. It starts the *fmt (31.37)* utility to reformat and clean up lines while I'm pasting them. To use it, go to text-input mode and type CTRL-r. Then paste the text—*fmt* will read it but not display it. Press RETURN, then CTRL-d to end the standard input to *fmt*. The reformatted text will be read into your *vi* buffer.

^[*32.05*

exrc

```
" Set 'exact' input mode for pasting exactly what is entered:
map! ^X ^[:se noai wm=0^[a
" Set 'normal' input mode with usual autoindent and wrapmargin:
map! ^N ^[:se ai wm=8^[a
" Read pasted text, clean up lines with fmt. Type CTRL-d when done:
map! ^R ^[:r!fmt^M
```

—*JP*

32.05 Protecting Keys from Interpretation by ex

Note that when defining a map, you cannot simply type certain keys, such as RETURN, ESC, BACKSPACE, and DELETE as part of the command to be mapped, because these keys already have meaning within *ex*. If you want to include one of these keys as part of the command sequence, you must escape the normal meaning by preceding the key with ^V (CTRL-v). The keystroke ^V appears in the map as the ^ character. Characters following the ^V also do not appear as you expect. For example, a carriage return appears as ^M, escape as ^[, backspace as ^H, and so on.

On the other hand, if you want to use a control character as the character to be mapped, in most cases all you have to do is hold down the CTRL key and press the letter key at the same time. So, for example, all you need to do in order to map ^A is to type:

:map CTRL-a *sequence*

There are, however, a few other control characters that must be escaped with a ^V. One is ^T. The others are:

- The characters that your account uses for erasing parts of the input you type at a command line, ^W for erasing words and ^U for erasing lines (see article 10.02).

- The characters for interrupting jobs *(40.09)* and stopping jobs *(13.08)*.

So, for example, if you want to map ^T, you must type:

```
:map CTRL-v CTRL-t sequence
```

The use of CTRL-v applies to any *ex* command, not just a map command. This means that you can type a carriage return in an abbreviation or a substitution command. For example, the abbreviation:

```
:ab 123 one^Mtwo^Mthree
```

expands to this:

```
one
two
three
```

(Here we show the sequence CTRL-v RETURN as ^M, the way it would appear on your screen.)

You can also add lines globally at certain locations. The command:

```
:g/^Section/s//As you recall, in^M&/
```

inserts a phrase on a separate line before any line beginning with the word *Section*. The & restores the search pattern.

Unfortunately, one character always has special meaning in *ex* commands, even if you try to quote it with CTRL-v. Recall that the vertical bar (|) has special meaning as a separator of multiple *ex* commands. You cannot use a vertical bar in insert mode maps.

Now that you've seen how to use CTRL-v to protect certain keys inside *ex* commands, you're ready to define some powerful map sequences.

—*LL, DG* from the Nutshell Handbook *Learning the vi Editor*

32.06 *Maps for Repeated Edits*

Not every keymap is something you want to save in your *.exrc* file. Some maps are handy just because you have to do a repetitive series of edits. Developing a complex map to repeat your edits can save more time than it takes. For example, assume that you have a glossary with entries like this:

```
map - an ex command which allows you to associate
a complex command sequence with a single key.
```

You would like to convert this glossary list to *nroff*(45.14) format, so that it looks like this:

```
.IP "map" 10n
An ex command which allows you to associate
a complex command sequence with a single key.
```

The best way to define a complex map is to do the edit once manually, writing down each keystroke that you must type. Then re-create these keystrokes as a map. You want to:

1. Insert the *ms* macro for an indented paragraph (.IP) at the beginning of the line. Insert the first quotation mark as well (I.IP ").

2. Press ESC to terminate insert mode.

3. Move to the end of the first word (e) and add a second quotation mark, followed by a space and the size of the indent (a" 10n).

4. Press RETURN to insert a new line.

5. Press ESC to terminate insert mode.

6. Remove the hyphen and two surrounding spaces (3x) and capitalize the next word (~).

That's quite an editing chore if you have to repeat it more than a few times. With map you can save the entire sequence so that it can be re-executed with a single keystroke:

```
map g I.IP "^[ea" 10n^M^[3x~
```

(To set that option during a *vi* session, type a colon (:) first.) Note that you have to "quote" both the ESC and RETURN characters with CTRL-v *(32.05)*. ^[is the sequence that appears when you type CTRL-v followed by ESC . ^M is the sequence shown when you type CTRL-v RETURN .

Now, simply typing g will perform the entire series of edits. At a slow data rate you can actually see the edits happening individually. At a fast data rate it will seem to happen by magic.

Don't be discouraged if your first attempt at keymapping fails. A small error in defining the map can give very different results from the ones you expect. Type u to undo the edit, and try again.

—*TOR* from the Nutshell Handbook *Learning the vi Editor*

32.07 *More Examples of Mapping Keys in vi*

The examples below will give you an idea of the clever shortcuts possible when defining keyboard maps.

1. Add text whenever you move to the end of a word:

```
map e ea
```

Most of the time, the only reason you want to move to the end of a word is to add text. This map sequence puts you in insert mode automatically. Note that the mapped key, e, has meaning in *vi*. You're allowed to map a key that is already used by *vi*, but the key's normal function will be unavailable as long as the map is in effect. This isn't so bad in this case, since the E command is often identical to e.

In the remaining examples, we assume that e has been mapped to ea.

2. Save a file and edit the next one in a series *(31.04)*:

```
map q :w^M:n^M
```

Notice that you can map keys to *ex* commands, but be sure to finish each *ex* command with a RETURN. This sequence makes it easy to move from one file to the next and is useful when you've opened many short files with one *vi* command. Mapping the letter q helps you remember that the sequence is similar to a "quit."

3. Put *troff* emboldening codes (\fB and \fP) around a word:

```
map v i\fB^[e\fP^[
```

This sequence assumes that the cursor is at the beginning of the word. First, you enter insert mode, then you type the code for bold font. (In *map* commands, you don't need to type two backslashes to produce one backslash.) Next, you return to command mode by typing a "quoted" *(32.05)* ESC. Finally, you append the closing *troff* code at the end of the word, and you return to command mode. Of course, the map is not limited to *troff* font codes. You can use it to enclose a word in parentheses or C comment characters, to name just a few applications.

This example shows you that map sequences are allowed to contain other map commands (the e is already mapped to ea). The ability to use nested map sequences is controlled by *vi*'s remap option *(32.13)*, which is normally enabled.

4. Put *troff* emboldening codes around a word, even when the cursor is not at the beginning of the word:

```
map V lbi\fB^[e\fP^[
```

This sequence is the same as the previous one, except that it uses lb to handle the additional task of positioning the cursor at the beginning of the word. The cursor might be in the middle of the word, so you want to move to the beginning with the b command.

But if the cursor were already at the beginning of the word, the b command would move the cursor to the previous word instead. To guard against that case, type an l before moving back with b, so that the cursor never starts on the first letter of the word. You can define variations of this sequence by replacing the b with B and the e with Ea. In all cases though, the l command prevents this sequence from working if the cursor is at the end of a line. (To get around this, you could add a space to the end of the word before typing the keymap.)

—*DG* from the Nutshell Handbook *Learning the vi Editor*

32.08 Good Stuff for Your .exrc File

[You probably won't want all of these keymaps and abbreviations. I always hate to re-map keys unless I really have to—I'd rather remember the real command instead of my special map that works only from my account. But not everyone agrees with me. And I've gotta admit that Tom has some pretty useful-looking customizations in this file.

Wherever you see ^V in this printout, that means that you type CTRL-v to protect the next key from interpretation by ex (32.05). In that case, the ^V is not stored in the macro. If you see two of them (^V^V) that sequence will store an actual CTRL-v in the macro. The file on the Power Tools disk is ready to use: it has the real control characters stored in it.

One more note: if your fancy hacks to the .exrc file don't seem to be working, watch carefully for error messages just as vi starts, before it clears your screen. If you can't read them quickly enough, try the tricks in article 44.08. —JP]

exrc

```
"       INPUT MACROS that i always want active
"
map! ^Z ^[:stop^M
"       so i can stop in input mode.  note that autowrite is set, so
map! ^A ^[:stop!^M
"       will stop me without writing.
"
map! ^K ^V^[O
"       lets me do kindof a negative carriage return in input mode.
map! ^V^[^B ^[bi
"       non-destructive ^W
map! ^V^[^F ^[Ea
"       and its inverse
"
"       EMACS Style ARROW MACROS
"
map! ^B ^V^[i
map! ^F ^V^[lli
map! ^A ^V^[I
map! ^E ^V^[A
"
"
"       EXCHANGE MACROS -- for exchanging things
"
map v xp
"       exchange current char with next one in edit mode
map V :m+1^M
"       exchange current line with next one in edit mode
map! ^P ^V^[hxpa
"       exchange last typed char with penultimate one in insert mode
map = ^^
"       edit previously editted file
"
"       OTHER MACROS
"
map ^W :w^M
"       write out the file
"
```

```
map * i^M^[
"     split line
"
map ^A :stop!^M
"     unconditional stop
map Y y$
"     so Y is analagous to C and D
map ^R ddu
"     single-line redraw
map ^N :n +/^M
"     go to next file in arg list, same position
"     useful for "vi +/string file1 file2 file3"
"
"
"     META MACROS, all begin with meta-key '\' ; more later in file
"
map ^V^I \
"     so can use both ^I and \ for meta-key
"
map \/ dePo/\<^V^[pA\>^V^["wdd@w
"     find current word, uses w buffer
"
map \C o^V^[k:co.^V^M:s/./ /g^V^Mo^V^[80a ^V^[:-1s;^;:s/;^V^M:s;$;
//;^V^M"mdd@m:s/\(.\)./\1/g^V^M:s;^;:-1s/^/;^V^M"mdd@mjdd
"     [NOTE: We split the macro above onto two lines for printing.
"     Type it on one line in your .exrc file. —JP ]
"     center text.  there's a better way, but i lost the short version.
"
"     INVERT WORD CASE -- V is like W, v is like w.  3V is ok, only to EOL.
"     uses both register n and mark n.
map \v ywmno^[P:s/./\~/g^M0"nDdd`n@n
"     abc -> ABC     ABC->abc
map \V yWmno^[P:s/./\~/g^M0"nDdd`n@n
"     abc.xyz -> ABC.XYZ    ABC.XYZ->abc.xyz
"
"
"     EXECUTION MACROS --these two are for executing existing lines.
"
map \@ ^V^["mdd@m
"     xqt line as a straight vi command (buffer m, use @@ to repeat)
map \! 0i:r!^V^["ndd@n
"     xqt line as :r! command (buffer n, use @@ to repeat)
"
```

cat **26.02**
/dev/tty **47.20**

```
map \t :r!cat /dev/tty^M
"     read in stuff from X put buffer [in X window system —JP ]
"
"
"     BLOCK MACROS -- these help when dealing with C blocks
"
map! ^O ^V^V^V{^M^V^V^V} ^V^[O^T
"     this will begin a block, leaving in insert mode
map! ^] ^V^[/^V^V^V}^V^Ma
"     and this will take you past its end, leaving in insert mode
"
"
"     LINT MACRO.  deletes all text from "lint output:" and below, (if any)
"     replacing it with lint output in pretty block comment form.  could
"     do sed work myself, but this is faster.
```

```
"        the map! is for subsequent map, not by people,
"        though /^Lo would make sense.
"        this is one of those famous time/space tradeoffs
"
map! ^Lo lint output
"
"        and now for the real work
map \l Go^M/* ^Lo^M^[/^Lo^MdG:w^Mo/*** ^Lo^[<<
:r!lint -u -lc %^V|sed 's/^/ *   /'^MGo***/^[N
"        [NOTE: We split the macro above onto two lines for printing.
"        Type it on one line in your .exrc file. —JP ]
"
"        indent this for me
"
map \i :%!indent -i4^M
"
"        COMMENTING MACROS -- these are actually pretty amazing
"
"        from edit mode, this comments a line
map ^X ^i/* ^[A */^[^
"
"        and this undoes it
map ^Y :s/\/\* \([^*]*\) \*\//\1^[
"
"        this next one defeats vi's tail-recursion defeatism
"        called by 2 maps following this one
map! ^N ^V^[:unmap! ^V^V^M^[
"
"        while in insert mode, this will put you "inside" a comment
map! ^X ^V^[:map! ^V^V^M ^V^V^[a^V^V^V^No^[a /*   */^[hhi
"
"        while in edit mode, this begins a block comment -- ^N to escape
map \cO/*^M *  ^M*/^[k:map! ^V^V^M ^V^V^M*  ^MA
"
"        and this is for adding more lines to a block comment -- ^N to escape
map \o:map! ^V^V^M ^V^V^M*  ^MA
"
"
map _ i_^V^V^V^H^V^[ll
"        this character will now be underlined when less'd, rn'd, etc.
"
"        SPELL MACROS
"
map \s :w^Mgo^V^[:$r!spell %^M
"        spell the file, placing errors at bottom, use \w to find
map \n Gdd\/
"        for find next spelling error
"
"
"        FORMATING MACROS
"
map \P :.,$!fmt -75^M
"        format thru end of document
map \p !}fmt -75^M
"        format paragraph
map \f 1G/---^Mj:.,$!fmt -75^M
"        format message (assumes MH Mail "comp" format)
```

less *26.04*

spell *30.01*

fmt *31.37*

expand 43.04
```
map \e :%!expand -4^M
"      expand tabs to 4 stops
```

sed 35.24
```
map \r 1G/^-/^[:r!sed -e '1,/^$/d' -e 's/^./> &/' @ ^[/^-/^[j
"      read in @, quoted (for MH replies, who link @ to current file)
map \d :s/$/ $/^M$r 74^V|? ^V^Ms^M^[$xx0
"      split line, like !!fmt but cheaper
"
"
ab Jan January
ab jan january
ab Feb February
ab feb february
ab Sep September
ab sep september
ab Oct October
ab oct october
ab Nov November
ab nov november
ab Dec December
ab dec december
ab Xmas Christmas
ab xmas christmas
ab Mon Monday
ab mon monday
ab Tue Tuesday
ab tue tuesday
ab Wed Wednesday
ab wed wednesday
ab Thu Thursday
ab thu thursday
ab Fri Friday
ab fri friday
ab Sat Saturday
ab Sun Sunday
ab Int International
ab info information
```

—TC

32.09 *Repeating a vi Keymap*

The *vi* (actually, *ex*) command map *(32.02)* lets you build custom *vi* commands.
For example, this map redefines the – key to run the *vi* commands *o* (open a
new line below), *ESCAPE*, *75a-* (add 75 dashes), and *ESCAPE* again:

```
:map - o^[75a-^[
```

So typing – draws a row of dashes below the current line. The problem is that
on many versions of *vi*, you can't add a repetition number—that is, you can't
type the command 10- to add 10 dashed lines.

The workaround is to define another macro that calls the first macro ten times.
For example, to make the v key draw ten rows of dashes:

```
:map v - - - - - - - - - -
```

(Ugly, eh? But it works.) You might want to put the – map in your *.exrc* file and define "multi-maps" like *v* while you're running *vi*.

—JP

32.10   *Typing in Uppercase without CAPS LOCK*

[You may want to input text in all uppercase letters—maybe for a FORTRAN program. Using CAPS LOCK in vi *can be a pain because you have to release CAPS LOCK almost every time you want to type a* vi *command. Here's a nice way to type lowercase letters during input and* ex *modes; they'll be mapped to uppercase automatically.—JP]*

Try putting this in your *.exrc (5.09)* file:

```
map! a A
map! b B
map! c C
   ...
map! z Z
```

Anytime you type (in insert mode) an a, the editor will map it into A. What's that you say? You don't want this all the time? Just put it in a file called *.f* (for FORTRAN), and type:

```
:source .f
```

when you want FORTRAN mode. Of course, you can define a function key *(32.02)* to `:source` this.

[After that, the only way to write your file and quit is with the *vi* command ZZ. If you try typing a command like `:q`, it'll be mapped to uppercase letters and you'll get the error `Q: Not an editor command.`

To quit without writing, go into the *ex* command mode by typing the *vi* command Q. That takes you to the *ex* colon (`:`) prompt—where the *map!* macros won't affect what you type. Enter q! and press RETURN.—*JP*]

—BB in *net.unix* on Usenet, *9 October 1986*

32.11   *Insert Mode Cursor Motion with no Arrow Keys*

Some people don't like to press ESC first to move the cursor while they're using *vi*. These keymaps change CTRL-h, CTRL-j, CTRL-k, and CTRL-l to do the same things during input mode as the commands h, j, k, and l do in command mode.

Note: Is your erase character set to CTRL-h *(6.09)* outside *vi*? If it is, mapping CTRL-h (usually labelled BACKSPACE on your keyboard) will change the way CTRL-h works during text-input mode: Instead of erasing the characters you've typed since you entered text-input mode, now CTRL-h will move backwards over what you type without erasing it.

One workaround is to change your UNIX erase character to the DELETE or RUBOUT key by typing the command `stty erase '^?'` before you start *vi*. Then your DELETE key will erase what you type and the BACK-SPACE key will jump back over it without deleting.

exrc

The lines for your *.exrc* file *(5.09)* are below:

```
map! ^H ^[i
map! ^K ^[ka
map! ^L ^[la
map! ^V
 ^[ja
" Note: the two lines above map ^J (LINEFEED)
```

That last map takes two lines; it's tricky and may not work right on all versions of *vi*. No, it isn't a map for CTRL-v, though that's what it looks like. It maps `^J`, the LINEFEED key. The `^V` comes at the very end of its line. When you're entering that keymap, type CTRL-v and then press LINEFEED or CTRL-j. The cursor will move to the start of the next line; type a SPACE and the rest of the macro. It's a good idea to add the reminder comment (starting with the comment character, a double quote (`"`)), on the line below the map.

Note: This map for CTRL-j is pretty obviously something that the *vi* designers didn't plan for. For example, look at the mess it makes when I ask for a list of my text-input keymaps:

```
:map!
^H      ^H      ^[i
^K      ^K      ^[ka
^L      ^L      ^[la

        ^[ja
```

Before you use this map on important files, you should probably test it carefully.

—JP

32.12 *Making Cursor Keys Work in vi Text-input Mode*

Here is my *.exrc* file, which I customized for a VT100 terminal. It is set up for C and *nroff* *–me* macros. [Strings like `^[OD` are set by the cursor keys *(43.12)* on VT100-type terminals. Make the `^[` by typing CTRL-v ESC . Many *vi* versions make this easier; they understand `map #1` to mean "map function key F1."—*JP*]

exrc

```
set ai redraw sm wm=1
set tabstop=4
set shiftwidth=4
map! {} {^M}^[O^V        great for auto indenting { } pairs
map! ^[OD ^[ha           cursor down while inserting
```

map!	^[OA ^[ka	*vt100 up arrow while inserting*
map!	^[OB ^[ja	*cursor left while inserting*
map!	^[OC ^[la	*cursor right*
map	^[OP A	*mapped pf1 to append to end of line*
map!	^[OP ^[A	*insert mode of the above*
map	^[OQ 0i	*mapped pf2 to insert before line*
map!	^[OQ ^[0i	*insert mode of the above*
map!	`` *(lq	*troff left quote*
map!	'' *(rq	*troff right quote*

troff **45.14**

I can use the cursor keys while inserting. This is handy because I can back up and insert without pressing ESC. [Though you may not be able to *(32.03)* undo your previous change with the *u* command. —*JP*]

Also, I have defined PF1 to append at the end of the line. This is useful because it doesn't matter what mode you are in, it always puts you in insert mode.

At one time, I mapped the entire numeric keypad to emulate the EDT editor.

—*BB* in *net.unix* on Usenet, *9 October 1986*

32.13 Don't Lose Important Functions with vi Maps: Use noremap

For years, I assumed that I could map *(32.02)* only a few keys in *vi*—the characters like *v* and *^A* that aren't used. For instance, if I mapped *^F* to do something else, I thought I'd lose that handy "forward one screen" command. You think the same thing? Then we're both wrong!

Just use the *noremap* option. Here's a simple example. You can make *^F* the "show file information" (normally *^G*) command. Then, make *^A* take over the "forward (ahead) one screen" function. Put these lines in your *.exrc* file *(5.09)*:

```
set noremap
map ^F ^G
map ^A ^F
```

—*JP*

32.14 Fooling vi into Allowing Complex Macros

vi wants undo to work for macros. Unfortunately, *vi*'s undo is very simple. Rather than allow complex macros to break undo, *vi* disallows complex macros. I believe this is a *big* mistake. I'd much rather give up undo than powerful macros.

Fortunately (for those who want real macros), the code that figures out whether a macro will break undo is "very" broken.

For instance, throwing in an `mx` (mark location **x**) at the front of the rhs ["right-hand side"—*JP*] of a macro often calms *vi* down. For some reason, this sends *vi* through an alternate path on which the macro checking is not as strict.

Likewise, breaking a single macro into multiple macros that call each other can also fool *vi*. For example, to do one complex macro, I define:

```
map X "bY
```

and then use:

```
1GkwEX@b
```

instead of:

```
1GkwE"bY@b
```

Using `"bY` directly doesn't work, but (on most systems anyway) using the macro X does.

So what does it mean that you get the message `can't put inside a glo-bal/macro`? Probably it means that your UNIX vendor "fixed" *vi* to recognize that a yank can break undo, even if it's in a called macro.

So rise up. Tell your UNIX vendor that you're tired of being coddled like an MS-DOS user! If you intended to undo that macro, you wouldn't have executed it in the first place. Don't let meddling johnny-come-lately UNIX vendors destroy the venerable screw-the-user tradition that has made UNIX great. Make them put it back the way it was.

—*DH*

32.15 *vi Macro for Splitting Long Lines*

When you add text to the start of a line and make the line longer than your screen's width, *vi* won't break ("wrap") the line unless your cursor crosses the *wrapmargin* point near the right-hand edge of the screen. You can get lines that are too long.

exrc

Here are two macros that cut (Kut) the current line:

```
map K 78^V|1Bhr^M
map K 0781F r^M
```

The first macro doesn't seem to work on some versions of *vi*. It's the better one though, because it uses the | (vertical bar) command to move to column 78, even if there are TABs in the line. Then it moves one more character to the right (if it can), moves back to the start of the word, moves back one more character onto the blank or tab before the word, and replaces that character with a RETURN.

The second macro counts TABs as single characters, but it works on every version of *vi* I've tried. It moves to the left edge, then to the 79th character, then back to the previous space. Finally, it replaces that space with a carriage return.

You might try adding a J to the start of either macro. That'll join the next line to the current one before cutting; it might make a nicer "wrap." Another way to do this is with a filter-through *(31.22)* and the *fmt (31.37)* command:

```
!!fmt
```

That will break the current line at the 72nd column or before, though it also might change the spacing after periods or replace leading TABs with spaces.

—*JP*

33

GNU Emacs

33.01 Emacs: the Other Editor

The "other" interactive editor that's commonly used is Emacs. Emacs actually refers to a family of editors; versions of Emacs run under almost any operating system available. However, the most important (and most commonly used) version of Emacs is "GNU Emacs," developed by the Free Software Foundation.

emacs

GNU Emacs is popular because it's the most powerful editor in the Emacs family; it is also available for free, under the terms of the FSF's General Public License. (You can also get it from the Power Tools disk.) Although there are certainly religious differences between Emacs users and *vi* users, most people agree that Emacs provides a much more powerful and richer working environment.

What's so good about Emacs, aside from the fact that it's free? There are any number of individual features that I could mention. (I'll give a list of favorite features in article 33.02.) In a word, though, the best feature of Emacs is the extent to which it interacts with other UNIX features. For example, it has a built-in e-mail *(1.33)* system so you can send and receive mail without leaving the editor. It has tools for "editing" (deleting, copying, renaming) files, for running a UNIX shell within Emacs, and so on. The C shell has a rather awkward command history mechanism; the Korn shell has something more elaborate. But imagine being able to recall and edit your commands as easily as you edit a letter! That's far beyond the abilities of any shell, but it's simple when you run a shell inside your editor.

In this book, we can't give anywhere near as much attention to Emacs as we can to *vi (31.02)*, but we will point out some of its best features and a few tricks that will help you get the most out of it.

—*ML, BR, DC* from the Nutshell Handbook *Learning GNU Emacs*

33.02 Emacs Features: a Laundry List

Here's the list we promised—my personal list of favorite features:

Windows Emacs is a "windowed editor." Before anyone heard of the X Window System or the Macintosh, Emacs had the ability to divide a terminal's screen into several "windows," allowing you to do different things in each window. You can edit a different file in each window or read mail in one window, answer mail in another, issue shell commands in a third, and so on.

Now that we all have nice workstations with mice and other crawly things for navigating around a bitmapped screen, why do you care? First, you may not have a bitmapped screen, and even if you have one in the office, you probably don't at home. Second, I still find Emacs preferable to most "modern" window systems because I don't have to use a mouse. If I want to create another window, I just type CTRL-x 2 (which splits the current window, whatever it is, into two); if I want to work in another window, I just type CTRL-x o; if I want to delete a window, I type CTRL-x 0. Is this faster than reaching for my mouse and moving it around? You bet. Particularly since my mouse is hidden under a pile of paper. (Of course, it's hidden because I hardly ever need it.) Once you've created a window, it's equivalently easy to start editing a new file, initiate a shell session, and so on.

Shells You can start an interactive shell within any Emacs window; just type ESC x shell, and you'll see your familiar shell prompt. It's easy to see why this is so useful. It's trivial to return to earlier comands, copy them, and edit them. Even more important, you can easily take the output of a command and copy it into a text file that you're editing—obviously an extremely useful feature when you're writing a book like this. Emacs also lets you issue commands that operate on the contents of a window or a selected region within a window.

Keyboard Macros
Emacs lets you define "keyboard macros," sequences of commands that can be executed automatically. This is similar to *vi*'s *map* facility, with one extra twist: Emacs actually executes the commands while you're defining the macro, while *vi* expects you to figure out what you need to do, type it in without any feedback, and hope that the macro doesn't do anything hostile when you edit it. With Emacs, it's much easier to get the macro right. You can see what it's going to do as you're defining it, and if you make a mistake, you can correct it immediately.

Editing Modes
Emacs has a large number of special editing "modes" that provide "context sensitive" help while you're writing. For example, if you're writing a C program, the C mode will help you to observe

conventions for indentation and commenting. It automatically lines up braces for you, and tells you when parentheses are unbalanced. There are special modes for virtually every programming language I've ever heard of. There are also special modes for *troff*, TeX, outlines, stick figures, etc.

Mail   Although I often use Emacs' mail facility as an example, I'm not personally fond of it. However, if you really like working within the Emacs environment, you should try it.

Customization

Emacs is the most customizable tool I've ever seen. Customization is based on the LISP programming language, so you need to learn some LISP before you can work with it much. However, once you know LISP, you can do virtually anything. For example, I have no doubt that you could write a complete spreadsheet program within Emacs—which means that you could use your normal Emacs commands to edit the spreadsheet and incorporate it (in whole or in part) into your documents. (An Emacs-based spreadsheet may already exist, though I'm not aware of it.) And, because of the FSF's *(55.01)* General Public License, virtually all special-purpose packages are available for free.

—ML

33.03 *Customizations and How to Avoid Them*

Emacs customizations are usually stored in a file called *.emacs*, in your home directory. In article 33.08, we've given a few customizations that I personally find convenient; if you're like most people, you'll add customizations over time. You'll end up doing this even if you're not a LISP programmer; if you know any other Emacs users, you'll soon be borrowing their shortcuts. The best way to customize Emacs to your taste is to find out what works for others, and then steal it. For that matter, many—if not most—of the customizations in my file were stolen from other users over the years. I hope I've gotten this process off to a good start.

However, you should also be aware of the "dark side" of customization. What happens if you sit down at someone else's terminal, start Emacs, and find out that he's customized it so extensively that it's unrecognizable? Or that a "helpful" administrator has installed some system-wide hacks that are getting in your way? Here's what will help. First, start *emacs* with the option *–q*; that tells Emacs not to load any *.emacs* initialization file. (If you want to load your initialization file, instead of someone else's, try the option *–u yourname*).

That still doesn't solve the problem of system-wide customizations. To keep those from getting in the way, put the following line at the beginning of your *.emacs* file:

```
(inhibit-default-init t)
```

This turns off all "global" initializations. (If you're sharing someone else's terminal, you may still need the *–u* option to force Emacs to read your initialization file.)

—*ML, DC, BR*

33.04 *Backup and Auto-save Files*

If you're like most people, you often spend a few hours editing a file, only to decide that you liked your original version better. Or you press some strange sequence of keys that makes Emacs do something extremely weird and that you can't "undo." Emacs provides several ways to get out of these tight spots.

First, try the command ESC x revert-buffer. Emacs will ask one of two questions: either "Buffer has been auto-saved recently. Revert from auto-save file? (y or n)" or "Revert buffer from file *your-filename*? (yes or no)".

Before deciding what to do, it's important to understand the difference between these two questions. Emacs creates an auto-save* file every 300 keystrokes you type. So, if you're reverting to the auto-save file, you'll at most lose your last 300 keystrokes. Maybe this is what you want—but maybe you made the mistake a long time ago. In that case, you don't want to use the auto-save file; type n, and you'll see the second question, asking if you want to revert to the last copy of the file that you saved. Type yes to go back to your most recent saved version.

It's possible that you'll only see the second question ("Revert buffer from file ..."). This means that you have saved the file sometime within the last 300 keystrokes. As soon as you save a file, Emacs deletes the auto-save file. It will create a new one every 300 keystrokes.

It's worth noting that Emacs is *very* picky about what you type. If it asks for a y or an n, you've got to type y or n. If it asks for yes or no, you've got to type yes or no. In situations like this, where the two styles are mixed up, you've got to get it right.

If you're in real trouble, and you want to go back to your *original file*—the way it was when you started editing—you need to recover Emacs' *backup file*. If you're editing a file that already exists, Emacs will create a backup file as soon as it starts. If you're editing a new file, Emacs will create a backup the *second* time you save the file. Once it's created, the backup file is never touched; it stays there until the next time you start Emacs, at which point you'll get a new backup, reflecting the file's contents at the start of your editing session.

---

*For reference, the name of the auto-save file is #*your-filename*#; that is, it sticks a hash mark (#) before and after the file's "regular" name.

Now that we're over the preliminaries, how do you recover the backup file? Emacs doesn't have any special command for doing this; you have to do it by hand. The backup file's name is the same as your original filename, with a tilde (~) added to it. So quit Emacs (or start a shell), and type:

```
% mv your-filename~ your-filename
```

Note that Emacs has the ability to save "numbered" backup files, like the VAX/VMS operating system. We've never played with this feature and don't particularly think it's a good idea. But it's there if you want it.

—ML, DC

33.05 *Putting Emacs in Overwrite Mode*

Many users are used to editors that are normally in *overwrite mode*: when you backspace and start typing, you "type over" the character that is underneath the cursor.* By default, Emacs works in *insertion mode*, where new characters are inserted just before the cursor's position.

If you prefer overwrite mode, just give the command ESC x overwrite-mode. You can use command abbreviation *(33.06)* to shorten this to ESC x ov. If you get tired of overwrite mode, use the same command to turn it off.

If you *always* want to use overwrite mode, create a file named *.emacs* in your home directory, and put the following line in it:

```
(setq-default overwrite-mode t)
```

This is a simple Emacs customization; for a lot more about customization, see the Nutshell Handbook *Learning GNU Emacs*, by Debra Cameron and Bill Rosenblatt.

—ML, DC

33.06 *Command Completion*

Emacs has a great feature called *command completion*. Basically, command completion means that Emacs will let you type the absolute minimum and it will fill in the rest. You can use Emacs whenever you're typing a filename, a buffer name, a command name, or a variable name. Simply type enough of the name to be "unique" (usually the first few letters), followed by a TAB. Emacs will fill in the rest of the name for you. If the name isn't unique—that is, if there are other filenames that start with the same letters—Emacs will show you the alternatives. Type a few more letters to select the file you want, then press TAB again.

---

*This includes some mainframe editors, like XEDIT, and (in my memory) a lot of older tools for word processing and general editing.

For example, if I'm trying to load the file *outline.txt*, I can simply give the command CTRL-x CTRL-f out TAB. Providing that there are no other filenames beginning with the letters *out*, Emacs will fill in the rest of the filename. When I see that it's correct, I press RETURN, and I'm done.

When you use command completion, always make sure that Emacs has successfully found the file you want. If you don't, the results may be strange: you may end up with a partial filename or with the wrong file.

—ML, BR

33.07 Disabling Harmful Commands

One common and annoying mistake is pressing ESC twice instead of once. On many terminals, the ESC key will even repeat if you hold it too long—so you can press it twice (or a dozen times) accidentally. When this happens, you get dumped into the *eval-expression* command, which is useful only to LISP programmers. By default, this command is disabled, though, which is even worse: Emacs shows you a window asking if you want to try the command, you get this long dialog, and so on. It's really a drag.

There's an easy way to fix this; just tell Emacs that ESC ESC means nothing to you. This is called "unbinding" the key sequence. Add this line to your *.emacs* file:

```
(global-unset-key "\e\e")
```

Exit Emacs and start over. When you do, you'll find that ESC ESC no longer has any special meaning.

By the way, when you need the *eval-expression* command, you can still use it; just type ESC x eval-expression.

—ML, DC, BR

33.08 Mike's Favorite Time Savers

I'm a very fast typist—which means that I hate using special function keys, arrow keys, and especially mice. I deeply resent anything that moves me away from the basic alphanumeric keyboard. Even Backspace and Delete are obnoxious, since they force me to shift my hand position.

With this in mind, I've customized Emacs so that I can do virtually anything with the basic alphabetic keys, plus the CONTROL key. Here are some extracts from my *.emacs* file:

.emacs_ml

```
;; Make CTRL-h delete the previous character. Normally, this gets
;; you into the "help" system.
  (define-key global-map "\C-h" 'backward-delete-char)
;; make sure CTRL-h works in searches, too
  (setq search-delete-char (string-to-char "\C-h"))
;; bind the "help" facility somewhere else (CTRL-underscore).
;; NOTE:  CTRL-underscore is not defined on some terminals.
```

```
(define-key global-map "\C-_" 'help-command) ;; replacement
(setq help-char (string-to-char "\C-_"))
;; Make ESC-h delete the previous word.
(define-key global-map "\M-h" 'backward-kill-word)
;; Make CTRL-x CTRL-u the "undo" command; this is better than "CTRL-x u"
;; because you don't have to release the CTRL key.
(define-key global-map "\C-x\C-u" 'undo)
;; scroll the screen "up" or "down" one line with CTRL-z and ESC z
(defun scroll-up-one () "Scroll up 1 line." (interactive)
  (scroll-up (prefix-numeric-value current-prefix-arg)))
(defun scroll-down-one () "Scroll down 1 line." (interactive)
  (scroll-down (prefix-numeric-value current-prefix-arg)))
(define-key global-map "\C-z" 'scroll-up-one)
(define-key global-map "\M-z" 'scroll-down-one)
;; Use CTRL-x CTRL-v to "visit" a new file, keeping the current file
;; on the screen
(define-key global-map "\C-x\C-v" 'find-file-other-window)
```

The comments (lines beginning with two semicolons) should adequately explain what these commands do. Figure out which you need, and add them to your *.emacs* file. The most important commands are at the *top* of the file.

—ML

33.09 *Rational Searches*

Emacs has, oh, a hundred or so different search commands. (Well, really, the number's probably more like 32, but who's counting?) There are searches of absolutely every flavor you could ever imagine: incremental searches, word searches,* regular expression searches, and so on.

However, when it comes to your plain, old garden-variety search, Emacs is strangely deficient. There is a simple search that just looks for some arbitrary sequence of characters; but it's rather well hidden. And it lacks one very important feature: you can't search for the same string repeatedly. That is, you can't say "OK, you found the right sequence of letters; give me the next occurrence"; you have to retype your search string every time.

search.el

I thought this was an incredible pain until a friend of mine wrote a special search command. It's in the file *search.el.* Just stick this into your directory for Emacs hacks *(5.04)*, and add something like the following to your *.emacs* file:

```
;; real searches, courtesy of Chris Genly
;; substitute your own Emacs hack directory for /home/los/mikel/emacs
(load-file "/home/los/mikel/emacs/search.el")
```

Now you can type CTRL-s to search forward and CTRL-r to search back. Emacs will prompt you for a search string and start searching when you press RETURN. Typing another CTRL-s or CTRL-r repeats your previous search. When you try

---

*These are especially nice because they can search for phrases that cross linebreaks; most searches assume that all the text you want will all be on the same line. However, you can only search for whole words, and if you use *troff* or TeX *(45.17)*, Emacs may be confused by your "markup."

this, you'll see one other useful feature: unlike the other Emacs searches, this kind of search displays the "default" (i.e., most recent) search string in the mini-buffer. It's exactly the kind of search I want.

It's conceivable that you'll occasionally want incremental searches. You'll have to "rebind" them in order to use them conveniently. Here are the key bindings that I use:

```
;; rebind incremental search as ESC-s and ESC-r
(define-key global-map "M-s" 'isearch-forward)
(define-key global-map "M-r" 'isearch-backward)
;; have to rebind ESC s separately for text-mode. It's normally
;; bound to 'center-line'.
(define-key text-mode-map "M-s" 'isearch-forward)
```

That is: ESC s and ESC r now give you forward and reverse incremental searches. And once you've started an incremental search, CTRL-s and CTRL-r still repeat the previous incremental search, just like they're supposed to.

Of course, now you'll have to rebind the "center-line" command if you're fond of it. In my opinion, it's not worth the trouble. The game of "musical key-bindings" stops here.

—*ML*

33.10 *Unset PWD Before Using Emacs*

I've seen a number of strange situations in which Emacs can't find files unless you type a complete ("absolute") pathname *(1.21)*, starting from the root (/). When you try to "visit" a file, you'll get the message `File not found` and `directory doesn't exist`.

In my experience, this usually means that the C shell's *PWD* environment variable has gotten set incorrectly. There are a few (relatively pathological) ways of tricking the C shell into making a mistake. More commonly though, I've seen a few systems on which the C shell sticks an extra slash into *PWD*: that is, its value will be something like */home/mike//Mail* rather than */home/mike/Mail*. UNIX doesn't care; it lets you stack up extra slashes without trouble. But Emacs interprets // as the root directory—that is, it discards everything to the left of the double slash. So if you're trying to edit the file */home/mike//Mail/output.txt*, Emacs will look for */Mail/output.txt*. Even if this file exists, it's not what you want. [This also happens when Emacs is called from a (Bourne) shell script that has changed its current directory.—*JP*]

This problem is particularly annoying because the shell will automatically reset *PWD* every time you change directories—so the obvious solution, sticking `unsetenv PWD` in your *.cshrc* file, doesn't do any good.

What will work is defining an alias *(11.01)*:

(..) *14.07*

```
alias gmacs "(unsetenv PWD; emacs \!*)"
```

A better solution might be to switch to another shell that doesn't have this problem. The Bourne shell (*sh*) obviously doesn't, since it doesn't keep track of your current directory.

—ML

33.11 *Inserting Binary Characters into Files*

I remember being driven absolutely crazy by a guy (who hopefully won't read this) who called me every other week and asked me how to stick a page break into some text file he was writing. He was only printing on a garden-variety daisy wheel printer, for which inserting a page break is a simple matter: just add a formfeed character, CTRL-l. But CTRL-l already means something to Emacs ("redraw the screen"). How do you get the character into your file, without Emacs thinking that you're typing a command?

Simple. Precede CTRL-l with the "quoting" command, CTRL-q. CTRL-q tells Emacs that the next character you type is text, not a part of some command. So the sequence CTRL-q CTRL-l inserts the character CTRL-l into your file; you'll see ^L on your screen. (Note that this represents a single character, instead of two characters.) In turn, when you print the file on a daisy wheel printer, the CTRL-l will cause a page eject at the appropriate point.

You can use this technique to get any "control character" into an Emacs file. In fact, under pressure I've done some pretty bizarre binary editing—not a task I'd recommend, but certainly one that's possible.

—ML

33.12 *Using Word Abbreviation Mode*

Like *vi*, Emacs provides an "abbreviation" facility. Its traditional usage lets you define abbreviations for long words or phrases so you don't have to type them in their entirety. For example, let's say you are writing a contract which repeatedly references the National Institute of Standards and Technology. Rather than typing the full name, you can define the abbreviation `nist`. Emacs inserts the full name whenever you type `nist`, followed by a space or punctuation mark. Emacs watches for you to type an abbreviation, then expands it automatically as soon as you press the space bar or type a punctuation mark (such as . , ! ? ; :).

One use for word abbreviation mode is to correct misspellings as you type. Almost everyone has a dozen or so words that they habitually type incorrectly, due to some worn neural pathways. You can simply tell Emacs that these misspellings are "abbreviations" for the correct versions, and Emacs fixes the misspellings every time you type them. If you take time to define your common typos as abbreviations, you'll never have to be bothered with teh, adn, and recieve when you run the spellchecker. Emacs sweeps up behind your typos and corrects them. For example, let's say that you define `teh` as an abbreviation for `the`. When you press the space bar after you type `teh`, Emacs fixes it immediately while you continue happily typing. You may not even notice that you typed the word wrong before Emacs fixes it.

Trying Word Abbreviations for One Session

Usually, if you go to the trouble of defining a word abbreviation, you will use it in more than one Emacs session. But if you'd like to try out abbreviation mode to see if you want to make it part of your startup, you can use the following procedure.

To define word abbreviations for this session:

1. Enter word abbreviation mode by typing ESC x abbrev-mode. abbrev appears on the mode line.

2. Type the abbreviation you want to use and press C-x -. Emacs then asks you for the expansion.

3. Type the definition for the abbreviation and press RETURN. Emacs then expands the abbreviation and will do so each time you type it followed by a space or punctuation mark. The abbreviations you've defined will work only during this Emacs session.

If you find that you like using word abbreviation mode, you may want to make it part of your startup, as described in the following section.

Making Word Abbreviations Part of Your Startup

Once you become hooked on abbreviation mode, make it part of your *.emacs* file so that you enter abbreviation mode and load the file of your word abbreviations and their definitions automatically.

To define word abbreviations and make them part of your startup:

1. Add these lines to your *.emacs* file:

```
(setq-default abbrev-mode t)
(read-abbrev-file "~/.abbrev_defs")
(setq save-abbrevs 't)
```

2. Save the *.emacs* file and reenter Emacs. abbrev appears on the mode line.

3. Type an abbreviation you want to use and then type C-x - following the abbreviation. Emacs asks you for the expansion.

4. Type the definition for the abbreviation and press RETURN. Emacs expands the abbreviation and will do so each time you type it followed by a space or punctuation mark. You can define as many abbreviations as you want to by repeating steps 3 and 4.

5. Type ESC x write-abbrev-file to save your abbreviations file. Emacs asks for the filename.

6. Type /~.abbrev_defs. Emacs then writes the file. You need only take this step the first time you define abbreviations using this procedure. After

this file exists, the lines in your *.emacs* file load the abbreviations file automatically.

After you've followed this procedure the first time, you only need to use steps 3 and 4 to define more abbreviations. When you add word abbreviations in subsequent sessions, Emacs asks whether you want to save the abbreviations file. Respond with a y to save the new abbreviations you've defined and have them take effect automatically.

If you define an abbreviation and later regret it, use *edit–word–abbrevs* to delete it.

—DC

33.13 *Getting Around Emacs Flow Control Problems*

A common annoyance among Emacs users is the *flow control(43.02)* problem that occurs in some situations involving terminals (as opposed to PCs or workstations). Some operating systems and data communications devices (terminals, modems, networks, etc.) use the characters CTRL-s and CTRL-q to act as "stop" and "go" signs for terminal input and output, to prevent buffer overflow.

Many more modern systems use other means of flow control, such as extra hardware, but others still use the CTRL-s/CTRL-q convention. This is especially likely in situations where there are multiple data communications devices between you and the actual computer (for example, a terminal talking to a modem, talking to another modem, talking to a terminal server, talking to a local area network, talking to a computer, remotely logged in to another computer . . .).

In general, the more pieces of hardware between you and the computer, the more likely that CTRL-s and CTRL-q are used as flow control characters; this means that those two characters are not accessible to Emacs. Unfortunately, Emacs is not set up to get around this problem easily.

To find out whether the problem affects you, simply invoke Emacs and type CTRL-s. If you see the `Isearch:` prompt in the minibuffer, all is probably well. Otherwise, nothing will happen and your terminal will appear to hang—any other keys you type will have no effect. Actually, you will have told some piece of hardware not to accept any more input. To get out of this, just type CTRL-q. Any keys you press in between will then take effect.

An easy way to get around this problem is to set up your Emacs so that different keystroke sequences are bound to the commands normally bound to CTRL-s and CTRL-q, i.e., *isearch–forward* and *quoted–insert*, respectively. It will also be necessary to reset the "forward search repeat" character to something other than CTRL-s. For example, you could use ESCAPE S for *isearch–forward*,

ESCAPE Q for *quoted–insert,* and CTRL-f as the "forward search repeat" character. To do this, put the following in your *.emacs* file:

```
(define-key esc-map "s" 'isearch-forward)
(define-key esc-map "q" 'quoted-insert)
(setq search-repeat-char ?\C-f)
```

Remember that you should exit and restart Emacs to make changes to your *.emacs* file take effect.

There are certain pathological cases in which flow control problems can be even worse. If Emacs has to do lots of continuous terminal output (e.g., if you are scrolling through a file with lots of long lines of text), the operating system or some piece of data communications hardware might start sending CTRL-s/CTRL-q pairs to the computer to stem the flood of data. When this happens, Emacs will usually try to interpret the flow control characters as an incremental search command (since CTRL-s is bound to *isearch–forward*).

You can prevent Emacs from interpreting CTRL-s/CTRL-q as any commands by removing the two keys' bindings with the *global–unset–key* function, and by overriding the option in which any control character can be used to exit incremental search. Just put the following lines in your *.emacs* file:

```
(global-unset-key "\C-s")
(global-unset-key "\C-q")
(setq search-exit-option nil)
```

The last of these lines makes ESC the only character you can use to end an incremental search.

This code will solve most but not all of your problems. For example, you may be in the middle of an "interactive" command that does lots of I/O (such as *query–replace* or incremental search), and a stray CTRL-s/CTRL-q might have annoying effects. For example, if you are in the middle of an incremental search, you might hear a beep and see ^S^Q (for CTRL-s CTRL-q) appended to your search string in the minibuffer. You can counteract this by doing the following: press any key (since CTRL-q is the "quote" character in incremental search), and that key will appear in place of the ^Q. Then press DELETE twice to delete the key you pressed and the preceding ^S from your search string. Once you have done this, you can resume your search.

—BR

33.14 An Absurd Amusement

If you have time to waste (and I mean "really waste"), Emacs has things to keep you occupied. There are lots of interesting special effects, like "disassociated text." My favorite is a command called "psychoanalyze-pinhead." It's based on "doctor," which is a variation classic artificial intelligence demonstration called "Eliza": the computer plays psychotherapist, asks you questions, you reply, and your answers are the basis for new questions. Nothing new, really; I remember it from my high-school days, in the early 70's. If you think you might be in need of a psychotherapist, save your money and try ESC x doctor RETURN.

If you want to see something really interesting, try ESC x psychoanalyze-pinhead. This takes the built-in "doctor" program and feeds it with quotations from the cult comic strip *Zippy the Pinhead*. The result is indeed bizarre. Here's some typical output:

```
I am the psychotherapist.  Please, describe your problems.  Each time
you are finished talking, type RET twice.

YOU PICKED KARL MALDEN'S NOSE!!

Why do you say I picked karl malden's nose?

Am I SHOPLIFTING?

Is it because of your plans that you say are you shoplifting?

Are you selling NYLON OIL WELLS??  If so, we can use TWO DOZEN!!
```

—ML

34

Batch Editing

34.01 *Why Line Editors Aren't Dinosaurs*

In the "old days," when programmers worked on printing terminals, editing was done one line at a time. Editors that let you move a cursor around the screen to select text to edit weren't invented, because there weren't any screens to look at text on!

In these days of even more advanced WYSIWYG (What You See Is What You Get) word processors and editing programs, it's easy for novices to think of line editors as a bizarre relic. Perhaps they are—but if so, they are a relic of extraordinary power.

You see, line editors lend themselves to *scripting*—the ability to write what in effect are editing programs that can be applied over and over to different files.

When we talk about "batch editing" or scripts, here are some of the programs you might use:

- *ed* is the original UNIX line editor.

- *ex* supports a superset of *ed* commands; it is widely used from within *vi*, which is the *ex* "visual" or "screen" mode.

- *sed* is an editor that can *only* be run with scripts; while it has many similar commands, it has some important differences *(35.01)* from *ed* and *ex*.

- *patch (34.09)* is a specialized editor designed to apply editing scripts created with *diff (29.01)*. You can do this with *ed* or *ex* as well, but *patch* is especially clever at it.

Of course, editing is a continuum, and beyond *sed*, you can think of *awk (38.01)* and *perl (39.01)* as even more powerful editing programs.

—*TOR*

34.02 Writing Editing Scripts

When you write a script that contains a series of editing actions and then run the script on an input file, you take what would be a *hands-on* procedure in an editor such as *vi* and transform it into a *look-no-hands* procedure.

When performing edits manually, you get to trust the cause-and-effect relationship of entering an editing command and seeing the immediate result. There is usually an "undo" command that allows you to reverse the effect of a command and return the text file to its previous state. Once you learn an interactive text editor, you have the feeling of making changes in a safe and controlled manner, one step at a time.

Most people new to "power editing" will feel there is greater risk in writing a script to perform a series of edits than in making those changes manually. The fear is that by automating the task, something will happen that cannot be reversed. The object of learning scripting with *ex* or *sed* is to understand the commands well enough to see that your results are predictable. In other words, you come to understand the cause-and-effect relationship between your editing script and the output that you get.

This requires using the editor in a controlled, methodical way. Gradually, you will develop methods for creating and testing editing scripts. You will come to rely upon these methods and gain confidence that you know what your script is doing and why.

Here are a few tips:

1. Carefully examine your input file, using *grep*, before designing your script.

2. Start with a small sample of occurrences in a test file. Run your script on the sample and make sure the script is working. Remember, it's just as important to make sure the script *doesn't* work where you *don't* want it to. Then increase the size of the sample. Try to increase the complexity of the input.

3. Work carefully, testing each command that you add to a script. Compare the output against the input file to see what has changed. Prove to yourself that your script is complete. Your script may work perfectly, based on your assumptions of what is in the input file, but your assumptions may be wrong.

4. *Be pragmatic!* Try to accomplish what you can with your script but understand that it doesn't have to do 100 percent of the job. If you encounter difficult situations, check and see how frequently they occur. Sometimes it's better to do a few remaining edits manually.

If you can add to these tips with your experience, tack them on.

[Okay, I will: use a revision control system *(21.12)* to keep previous versions. That makes it easy to undo your edits. —*JP*]

—*DD* from the Nutshell Handbook *sed & awk*

34.03 Line Addressing

The key to making line editors work for you is understanding how to select (or "address") the lines that will be affected by the commands in your script.

In most line editors, a command affects only the "current" line—the first line of the file to begin with, and later the site of the last edit or movement command—unless you precede the command with an address to indicate some other line or lines.

Most line editors address lines in three ways:

- with line numbers
- with regular expression patterns
- with special symbols

It's possible to address single lines or a range of lines.

Table 34-1 describes the addresses you can use with *ex*.

Table 34-1. Line Addressing in the ex Editor

1,$	All lines in the file.
%	All lines; same as 1,$.
x,y	Lines *x* through *y*.
x;y	Lines *x* through *y*, with current line reset to *x*.
1	Top of file.
0	"Before the top" of file. Used to add text above top line: 0r, *x*m0, etc.
.	Current line.
n	Absolute line number *n*.
$	Last line.
x-n	*n* lines before *x*.
x+n	*n* lines after *x*.
-*n*	*n* lines previous.
-	Previous line.
+*n*	*n* lines ahead.
+	Next line.
'*x*	Line marked with *x*.
' '	Previous mark.
/pattern/	Next line matching *pattern*.
?pattern?	Previous line matching *pattern*.

If the address specifies a range of lines, the format is:

x,y

where *x* and *y* are the first and last addressed lines. *x* must precede *y* in the file.

—*TOR, DG, JP*

34.04 Useful ex Commands

Many line editor commands are not particularly useful in scripts. The two commands that you will use far and away the most often are **s** (substitute), to replace one pattern with another, and **d** (delete) to delete one or more lines. On occasion, though, you'll want to insert text from a script. (Editing scripts built by *diff(29.08)* make heavy use of insert, append, delete, and change commands.) And of course, you need commands to write and quit the editor.

Here's the syntax of most of the commands you may encounter in editing scripts. Elements in [brackets] are optional; don't type the [or]. (The leading colon is the *ex* command character used to issue an *ex* command from *vi*; in a script, the colon would be omitted.)

append   [address] a[!]
             text

             .

             Append *text* at specified *address*, or at present address if none is specified. Add a ! to switch the **autoindent** setting that will be used during input. For example, if **autoindent** was enabled, ! disables it.

change   [address] c[!]
             text

             .

             Replace the specified lines with *text*. Add a ! to switch the **autoindent** setting during input of *text*.

copy   [address] co destination

             Copy the lines included in *address* to the specified *destination* address.

                 :1,10 co 50

delete   [address] d [buffer]

             Delete the lines included in *address*. If *buffer* is specified, save or append the text to the named buffer.

                 :/Part I/,/Part II/-1d   *Delete to line above "Part II"*
                 :/main/+d   *Delete line below "main"*
                 :.,$/d   *Delete from this line to last line*

global	[address] g[!]/*pattern*/[*commands*]

Execute *commands* on all lines that contain *pattern* or, if *address* is specified, on all lines within that range. If *commands* are not specified, print all such lines. If ! is used, execute *commands* on all lines that *don't* contain *pattern*.

```
:g/Unix/p
:g/Name:/s/tom/Tom/
```

insert	[address] i[!]
	text
	.

Insert *text* at line before the specified address, or at present address if none is specified. Add a ! to switch the **autoindent** setting during input of *text*.

move	[address] **m** destination

Move the lines specified by *address* to the *destination* address.

```
:.,/Note/m /END/                Move block after line containing "END"
```

print	[address] **p** [count]

Print the lines specified by *address. count* specifies the number of lines to print, starting with *address.*

```
:100;+5p                        Show line 100 and the next five lines
```

quit	q[!]

Terminate current editing session. Use ! to discard changes made since the last save. If the editing session includes additional files in the argument list that were never accessed, quit by typing **q!** or by typing **q** twice.

read	[address] **r** *file*

Copy in the text from *file* on the line below the specified *address.* If *file* is not specified, the current filename is used.

```
:0r $HOME/data                  Read file in at top of current file
```

read	[address] **r** !*command*

Read the output of UNIX *command* into the text after the line specified by *address.*

```
:$r !cal                        Place a calendar at end of file
```

source	so file

Read and execute *ex* commands from *file.*

```
:so $HOME/.exrc
```

substitute   [address] s [/*pattern*/*replacement*/] [*options*] [*count*]

Replace each instance of *pattern* on the specified lines with *replacement*. If *pattern* and *replacement* are omitted, repeat last substitution. *count* specifies the number of lines on which to substitute, starting with *address*.

Options

c   Prompt for confirmation before each change.

g   Substitute all instances of *pattern* on each line.

p   Print the last line on which a substitution was made.

```
:1,10s/yes/no/g       Substitute on first 10 lines
:%s/[Hh]ello/Hi/gc    Confirm global substitutions
:s/Fortran/\U&/ 3     Uppercase "Fortran" on next 3 lines
```

write   [address] w[!] [[>>] *file*]

Write lines specified by *address* to *file*, or write full contents of buffer if *address* is not specified. If *file* is also omitted, save the contents of the buffer to the current filename. If >> *file* is used, write contents to the end of an existing *file*. The ! flag forces the editor to write over any current contents of *file*.

write   [address] w !*command*

Write lines specified by *address* to *command*.

```
:1,10w name_list      Copy first 10 lines to name_list
:50w >> name_list     Now append line 50
```

—*TOR, DG*

34.05   *Running Editing Scripts Within vi*

Because *vi* is built on top of the *ex* line editor, you get all the power of a line editor as well. Any experienced *vi* user issues *ex* commands all the time—but usually one by one, at the colon prompt.

The one exception is the *.exrc* file *(31.06)*, which is, at bottom, a list of commands for *ex* to run on startup—in short, an editor script.

What many beginners don't know is that you can save a sequence of *ex* commands in any file, and execute it with the :so command. For example, Bruce Barnett uses this trick to set himself up specially for editing FORTRAN programs *(32.10)*.

In general, *sed (35.24)* is better for general-purpose batch editing—such as making a set of global substitutions over and over again on multiple files—therefore, :so is most often used for reading in setup commands. Keep in mind though; any time you find yourself issuing the same commands over and over again, *think script!*

—*TOR*

34.06 *Change Many Files by Editing Just One*

(34.08)

The *diff* command can make an editing script *(29.08)* that you give to the *ex* or *ed* editors or the *patch (34.09)* program. They'll apply your same edits to other copies of the same file. This is handy if you have a lot of copies of a big file, spread around a network or on a lot of disks, and you want to make the same small change to all the files. Instead of sending new copies of the whole file, just have *diff* make a script—and use that little script to update all the big files.

Here's a demo. I'm going to modify a program called *pqs.c*. Then I'll use *diff* and *ed* to apply the same changes to a copy of the file named *remote-pqs.c* (which might be at a remote computer):

(29.06)

```
1% cp pqs.c remote-pqs.c
2% cp pqs.c pqs.c.new
3% vi pqs.c.new
4% diff pqs.c pqs.c.new
106,107c106
<         fprintf(stderr,
<             "%s: quitting: notable to %s your .pq_profile file.\n",
---
>         fprintf(stderr, "%s: quitting: can't %s your .pq_profile file.\n",
390a390
>                 "WARNING:",
5% diff -e pqs.c pqs.c.new > edscr
6% cat edscr
390a
                "WARNING:",
.
106,107c
        fprintf(stderr, "%s: quitting: can't %s your .pq_profile file.\n",
.
7% echo w >> edscr
8% ed remote-pqs.c < edscr
19176
19184
9% diff pqs.c.new remote-pqs.c
10%
```

At prompt 1%, I make the simulated "remote" copy of the *pqs.c* file. At prompt 2%, I make another copy of it; at prompt 3%, I edit the copy. Prompt 4% has a *diff* that shows the changes I made. Then, at prompt 5%, I run diff -e *(29.01)*; I save the result in *edscr*, which I show at prompt 6.

Prompt 7% is important because *diff -e* doesn't add a w command to the script file. That tells *ed* to write its changes to the file. I use echo w *(9.04)* to add the command.

In prompt 8%, I give *ed* the name of the "remote" file to edit as a command-line argument and give it the script file on its standard input. At prompt 9%, I do a *diff* that shows the changes have been made and the two versions are the same.

—JP

34.07 ed/ex Batch Edits: Avoid Errors when No Match

Q: My Bourne shell script calls *ed* to edit a set of files:

= 7.08

for 10.10

<< 9.14
\ 9.10

```
site=something
cmty=somethingelse
for i in file1 file2 file3
do
    ed $i << end
    1,\$s/pat1/$site/g
    1,\$s/pat2/$cmty/g
    w
    q
end
done
```

It works fine except when one of the files does not contain *pat1*. *ed* doesn't update that file, even though it could have matched *pat2*. The other files are edited as they should be.

A: On an error—including "no matches"—*ed* attempts to discard any unread commands. If you are running *ed* "by hand" this has no effect, but if its input is from a file, this makes EOF (end-of-file) the next thing it sees. You could remove the q command and you would see the same behavior, as *ed* automatically quits at end-of-file.

There is a simple workaround. Unlike the s command, the *global* command g does not report an error if no lines match. Thus:

```
ed - $i << end
g/pat1/s//$site/g
g/pat2/s//$cmty/g
w
end
```

The – (dash) flag suppresses the two numbers that *ed* normally prints when reading and writing files. These are the number of characters in the file, and are usually irrelevant. [As Chris explained, the q in the original script isn't needed. *—JP*]

—CT in comp.unix.questions on Usenet, 16 May 1989

34.08 Batch Editing Gotcha: Editors Bomb on Big Files

People use the *ed* editor with script files to make global edits. But many versions of *ed* can't handle large files. The *ex* editor is usually better, but it has limits, too. How large is "large"? That depends on your version. Most *ed*s I've seen can't handle more than about 100,000 characters.

There are no limits on *sed (35.24)*, although you'll need to save its output somehow *(35.03)*, and your editing script may have to be changed to work with *sed*.* Here's what you'll see when *ed* bombs:

```
% cat edscr
s/Unix/UNIX/g
w
% ed - words < edscr
?
%
```

The ? is *ed*'s verbose way of telling you that something's wrong. This obscure message is especially bad if you write a shell script that edits multiple files in a loop; you may not notice the error or be able to tell which file had the problem. Be sure your script checks for errors!

Unfortunately for programmers, *ed* may not return an error status that you can test. There are workarounds *(34.08, 48.09)*, though. When the `ed` - command succeeds, it doesn't display anything. The simplest way to find errors is to check for any output on *stdout* or *stderr*. This chunk of a Bourne shell script shows how (your filename is in the shell variable `$filename` *(7.08)*):

2>&1 *47.21*
[] *46.19*
$? *46.07*
```
edout="`ed - $filename < edscr 2>&1`"
if [ -n "$edout" -o $? -ne 0 ]
then
        echo "QUITTING: 'ed - $filename < edscr' bombed?!?" 1>&2
        exit 1
fi
```

—*JP*

34.09 patch: Generalized Updating of Files that Differ

patch

Like all of Larry Wall's widely-used programs (including *perl (39.01)*, a software configuration script called *Configure*, and the *rn* news reader), *patch* betrays a whimsical intelligence of its own. Feed it any kind of *diff* listing *(29.01)* (not just an editing script produced with the *−e* option *(29.08)*). *patch* figures out what it needs to do to apply the diff, and updates the file, supplying all the while a breezy commentary on what it's doing:

```
% patch < testfile.diff
Hmm... Looks like a normal diff to me...
File to patch: testfile
```

---

*By default, *ed* commands apply to the current line. *sed* commands are global. Also, line addresses like −5 don't work in *sed*.

```
Patching file testfile using Plan A...
Hunk #1 succeeded at 2.
done
```

As Larry once noted, *patch* has done an awful lot to "change the culture of computing." Almost all free software is now updated by means of patches rather than complete new releases. *patch* is smart enough to discard any leading or trailing garbage (such as mail headers or signatures) so that a program source file can be updated by piping a mail message containing a diff listing between old and new versions directly to *patch*.

Here are a few of the other things *patch* is smart enough to do:

- Figure out the name of the file to be updated and do it without asking (usually only if the diff file is a "context diff" produced with the −*c* option).

- Look for a suitable SCCS or RCS *(21.12)* file and check it out, if the filename itself can't be found.

- Handle diff listings that don't quite match. This makes it possible for *patch* to update a file that the recipient has already changed from the one that the diff was based on.

- Save any pieces of the diff file that don't end up being used, in a file named by adding the suffix *.rej* (reject) to the name of the file being patched.

- Back up the file that is being patched, appending the suffix *.orig* to the name of the file being patched.

- Recognize that its input may actually apply to several files, and patch each of them separately. So, for example, a whole directory might be updated by a "patch" file that contained diff listings for each of the files in the directory. (By the way, the −*d* option to *patch* tells it to *cd* to a specified directory before starting work.)

- Recognize (or at least speculate) that a patch might have been created incorrectly, with the old and new files swapped. Larry says: "Yes, I'm afraid that does happen occasionally, human nature being what it is." *patch*'s −*R* option will force *patch* to reverse the sense of the patch; what's really amusing is to see *patch* suggest that this might be the thing to do, when things seem out of sync.

If you are a programmer, *patch* is worth studying just to see how much a program can do to anticipate errors, deal with fuzzy input, and in general "make the computer do the dirty work." But if you're a programmer, you doubtless already know about *patch* . . . .

One last note: *patch* is so useful that it's been added to many UNIX systems. Check to see if your system has it before installing it from the Power Tools disk.

—*TOR*

34.10 Quick Globals from the Command Line with qsubst

Users at our office frequently have to make global changes across multiple files. For that purpose we encourage them to use *sed* *(35.24)*, but *sed* syntax is tricky for new users (or even some experienced users!).

qsubst

As an alternative, try the *qsubst* program, available on our Power Tools disk. *qsubst* is a simple query-replace program that anyone can use. For example, to change the string "Unix" into "UNIX" in the files *ch01* and *ch02*, you can do:

```
% qsubst Unix UNIX ch01 ch02
```

You'll be prompted with each line to be changed, in context. That is, the line containing the string will be surrounded by both the previous and the next lines in the file. The string to be changed is underlined:

```
Unlike emacs, vi is available on
every Unix system.
So you can
think of vi as the
```

To approve the change, press the space bar. You'll then be prompted with the next occurrence in the file. To refuse the change, press n to go on to the next occurrence of the string. You can also use the exclamation point (!) to approve this change and all future changes in this file, and CTRL-g to reject this change and all future changes.

You can also have *qsubst* replace all occurrences without prompting, using the *–noask* command-line option:

```
% qsubst Unix UNIX -noask ch01 ch02
(file: ch01)
(file: ch02)
```

Both files are edited without prompting.

qsubst is clearly not as powerful as *sed*. It doesn't understand regular expressions: you can only use *qsubst* to replace simple strings. But *qsubst* is clearly a useful tool for users who just want to make a simple global change without learning *sed*.

One word of warning about *qsubst*: if you interrupt *qsubst* midstream (e.g., using CTRL-c), your *stty* settings are likely to be garbled. If this happens, try the tips in article 44.04 to get your *stty* settings correct again.

—LM

35

The sed Stream Editor

35.01 Two Things You Must Know about sed

If you are already familiar with global edits in other editors like *vi* or *ex*, you know most of what you need to know to begin to use *sed*. There are two things, though, that make it very different:

1. It doesn't change the file it edits. It is just what its name says: a "*stream editor*"—designed to take a stream of data from standard input or a file, transform it, and pass it to standard output. If you want to edit a file, you have to write a shell wrapper *(35.03)* to capture standard output and write it back into your original file.

2. *sed* commands are implicitly global. In an editor like *ex*, the command:

   ```
   s/old/new/
   ```

   will change "old" to "new" only on the current line unless you use the global command or various addressing symbols to apply it to additional lines. In *sed*, exactly the opposite is true. A command like the one above will be applied to all lines in a file. Addressing symbols are used to *limit* the extent of the match. (However, like *ex*, only the first occurrence of a pattern on a given line will be changed unless the *g* flag is added to the end of the substitution command.)

If all you want to do is make simple substitutions, you're ready to go. If you want to do more than that, *sed* has some unique and powerful commands.

This chapter makes no attempt to cover everything there is to know about *sed*. Article 35.24 contains a complete quick reference to *sed* commands, with many examples, because we use so many *sed* scripts elsewhere in this book, and we need a "dictionary" so beginners can interpret them. But for the most part, this chapter contains advice on working with *sed* and extended explanations of how to use some of its more difficult commands.

—*TOR*

35.02 Invoking sed

If you were using *sed* on the fly, as a stream editor *(35.01)*, you might execute it as simply as this:

```
% somecommand | sed 's/old/new/' | othercommand
```

Given a filename, *sed* will read that instead of standard input:

```
% sed 's/old/new/' myfile
```

A simple script can go right on the command line. If you want to execute more than one editing command, you can use the *–e* option:

```
% sed -e 's/old/new/' -e '/bad/d' myfile
```

or (especially useful in shell scripts *(1.05)*) you can use the Bourne shell's ability to understand multi-line commands:

```
sed '
s/old/new/
/bad/d' myfile
```

or you can put your commands into a file, and tell *sed* to read that file with the *–f* option:

```
% sed -f scriptfile myfile
```

There's only one other command line option: *–n*. *sed* normally prints every line of its input (except those that have been deleted by the editing script). But there are times when you only want lines that your script has affected, or that you explicitly ask for with the *p* command. In these cases, use *–n* to suppress the normal output.

—TOR

35.03 Testing and Using a sed Script: testsed, runsed

All but the simplest *sed* scripts are usually invoked from a "shell wrapper," a shell script *(46.01)* that invokes *sed* and also contains the editing commands that *sed* executes. A shell wrapper is an easy way to turn what could be a complex command line into a single-word command. The fact that *sed* is being used might be transparent to users of the command.

Two shell scripts that you should immediately arm yourself with are described here. Both use a shell *for* loop *(46.15)* to apply the same edits to any number of files. But the first just creates temporary files, so you can make sure that your edits were made correctly. The second writes the edits back into the original file, making them permanent.

testsed

testsed

The shell script *testsed* automates the process of saving the output of *sed* in a temporary file. It expects to find the script file, *sedscr*, in the current directory and applies these instructions to the input file named on the command line. The output is placed in a temporary file.

```
for x
do
    sed -f sedscr $x > tmp.$x
done
```

The name of a file must be specified on the command line. As a result, this shell script saves the output in a temporary file with the prefix *tmp.*. You can examine the temporary file to determine if your edits were made correctly. If you approve of the results, you could then use *mv* to overwrite the original file with the temporary.

You might also incorporate the *diff* command into the shell script. (Add the line `diff $x tmp.$x` after the `sed` command line.)

If you find that your script did not produce the results you expected, remember that the easiest "fix" is usually to perfect the editing script and run it again on the original input file. Don't write a new script to "undo" or improve upon changes made in the temporary file.

runsed

runsed

The shell script *runsed* was developed to make changes to an input file permanently. In other words, it is used in cases when you would want the input file and the output file to be the same. Like *testsed*, it creates a temporary file, but then it takes the next step: copying the file over the original.

```
temp=/tmp/runsed$$
for x
do
    echo "editing $x: \c"
    if test "$x" = sedscr; then
        echo "not editing sedscript!"
    elif test -s $x; then
        sed -f sedscr $x > $temp
        if test -s $temp; then
            if cmp -s $x $temp; then
                echo "file not changed: \c"
            else
                cp $temp $x
            fi
            echo "done"
        else
            echo "sed produced an empty file - check your sedscript."
        fi
    else
        echo "original file is empty."
    fi
done
```

\c 9.04
if 46.08
test 46.19

cmp 29.10

```
        echo "all done"
-f 24.09    rm -f $temp
```

To use *runsed*, create a *sed* script named *sedscr* in the directory where you want to make the edits. Supply the name or names of the files to edit on the command line. Shell meta-characters *(16.02)* can be used to specify a set of files:

$ runsed ch0?

runsed simply invokes *sed –f sedscr* on the named files, one at a time, and redirects the output to a temporary file. *runsed* then tests this temporary file to make sure that output was produced before copying it over the original.

The muscle of this shell script is essentially the same as *testsed*. The additional lines are intended to test for unsuccessful runs, for instance, when no output is produced. It compares the two files to see if changes were actually made or to see if an empty output file was produced before overwriting the original.

However, *runsed* does not protect you from imperfect editing scripts. You should use *testsed* first to verify your changes before actually making them permanent with *runsed*.

—*DD, TOR* from the Nutshell Handbook *sed & awk*

35.04 *sed Addressing Basics*

A *sed* command can specify zero, one, or two addresses. An address can be a regular expression *(27.04)* that describes a pattern, a line number, or a line addressing symbol.

- If no address is specified, then the command is applied to each line.

- If there is only one address, the command is applied to any line matching the address.

- If two comma-separated addresses are specified, the command is performed on the first matching line and all succeeding lines up to and including a line matching the second address.

- If an address is followed by an exclamation mark (!), the command is applied to all lines that do *not* match the address.

To illustrate how addressing works, let's look at examples using the delete command, *d*. A script consisting of simply the *d* command and no address:

```
d
```

produces no output since it deletes *all* lines.

When a line number is supplied as an address, the command affects only that line. For instance, the following example deletes only the first line:

```
1d
```

The line number refers to an internal line count maintained by *sed*. This counter is not reset for multiple input files. Thus, no matter how many files were specified as input, there is only one line 1 in the input stream.

Similarly, the input stream has only one last line. It can be specified using the addressing symbol, $. The following example deletes the last line of input:

```
$d
```

The $ symbol should not be confused with the $ used in regular expressions, where it means the end of the line.

When a regular expression is supplied as an address, the command affects only the lines matching that pattern. The regular expression must be enclosed by slashes (/). The following delete command:

```
/^$/d
```

deletes only blank lines. All other lines are passed through untouched.

If you supply two addresses, then you specify a range of lines over which the command is executed. The following example shows how to delete all lines blocked by a pair of macros, in this case, .TS and .TE, that mark *tbl (45.17)* input:

```
/\.TS/,/\.TE/d
```

It deletes all lines beginning with the line matched by the first pattern up to and including the line matched by the second pattern. Lines outside this range are not affected. The following command deletes from line 50 to the last line in the file:

```
50,$d
```

You can mix a line address and a pattern address:

```
1,/^$/d
```

This example deletes from the first line up to the first blank line, which, for instance, will delete a mail header from a mail message *(1.33)* that you have saved in a file.

You can think of the first address as enabling the action and the second address as disabling it. *sed* has no way of looking ahead to determine if the second match will be made. The action will be applied to lines once the first match is made. The command will be applied to *all* subsequent lines until the second match is made. In the previous example, if the file did not contain a blank line, then all lines would be deleted.

An exclamation mark following an address reverses the sense of the match. For instance, the following script deletes all lines *except* those inside *tbl* input:

```
/\.TS/,/\.TE/!d
```

This script, in effect, extracts *tbl* input from a source file. (This can be handy for testing the format of tables.)

Curly braces ({ }) let you give more than one command with an address. For example, to search every line of a table, capitalize the word Caution on any of those lines, and delete any line with .sp 2p:

```
/\.TS/,/\.TE/{
    s/Caution/CAUTION/g
    /^\.sp 2p/d
}
```

—*DD* from the Nutshell Handbook *sed & awk*

35.05 *Order of Commands in a Script*

Combining a series of edits in a script can have unexpected results. You might not think of the consequences one edit can have on another. New users typically think that *sed* applies an individual editing command to all lines of input before applying the next editing command. But the opposite is true. *sed* applies every editing command to the first input line before reading the second input line and applying the editing script to it. Because *sed* is always working with the latest version of the original line, any edit that is made changes the line for subsequent commands. *sed* doesn't retain the original. This means that a pattern that might have matched the original input line may no longer match the line after an edit has been made.

Let's look at an example that uses the substitute command. Suppose someone quickly wrote the following script to change pig to cow and cow to horse:

```
s/pig/cow/
s/cow/horse/
```

The first command would change pig to cow as expected. However, when the second command changed cow to horse on the same line, it also changed the cow that had been a pig. So, where the input file contained pigs and cows, the output file has only horses!

This mistake is simply a problem of the order of the commands in the script. Reversing the order of the commands—changing cow into horse before changing pig into cow—does the trick.

Some *sed* commands change the flow through the script. For example, the *N* command reads another line into the pattern space without removing the current line, so you can test for patterns across multiple lines. Other commands tell *sed* to exit before reaching the bottom of the script or to go to a labeled command. *sed* also maintains a second temporary buffer called the *hold space*. You can copy the contents of the pattern space to the hold space and retrieve it later. The commands that make use of the hold space are discussed in article 35.13 and other articles after it.

—*DD* from the Nutshell Handbook *sed & awk*

35.06 One Thing at a Time

I find that when I begin to tackle a problem using *sed*, I do best if I make a mental list of all the things I want to do. When I begin coding, I write a script containing a single command that does one thing. I test that it works, then I add another command, repeating this cycle until I've done all that's obvious to do. I say what's obvious because my list is not always complete, and the cycle of implement-and-test often adds other items to the list.

It may seem to be a rather tedious process to work this way, and indeed there are a number of scripts where it's fine to take a crack at writing the whole script in one pass and then begin testing it. However, the one-step-at-a-time is highly recommended for beginners because you isolate each command and get to easily see what is working and what is not. When you try to do several commands at once, you might find that when problems arise you end up recreating the recommended process in reverse; that is, removing commands one by one until you locate the problem.

—*DD* from the Nutshell Handbook *sed & awk*

35.07 Delimiting a Regular Expression

Whether in *sed* or *vi*, when using the substitution command, a delimiter is required to separate the search pattern from the replacement string. The usual practice is to use the slash (/) as a delimiter (for example, s/*search*/*replacement*/). However, the delimiter can be any character except blank or a newline. (*vi* seems to be more restrictive than *sed*.)

When either the search pattern or the replacement string contains a slash, it is easier to change the delimiter character rather than escape the slash. Thus, if the pattern was attempting to match UNIX pathnames, which contain slashes, you could choose another character, such as a colon, as the delimiter:

```
s:/usr/mail:/usr2/mail:
```

Note that the delimiter appears three times and is required after the *replacement*. Regardless of which delimiter you use, if it does appear in the regular expression, use a backslash (\) to escape it.

If you don't know what characters the search pattern might have (in a shell program that handles any kind of input, for instance), the safest choice for the delimiter can be a control character. Article 47.34 shows how to make and use a control character as the delimiter in a shell script—without having to store the control character in the file.

Pattern addresses in *sed* require a slash as a delimiter.

—*DD* from the Nutshell Handbook *sed & awk*

35.08 Newlines in a sed Replacement

The backslash (\) in the replacement string of the *sed* substitution command is generally used to escape other meta-characters, but it is also used to include a newline in a replacement string.

Given the following input line where each item is separated by a tab:

```
Column1    Column2    Column3    Column4
```

we can replace the second tab character on each line with a newline character:

2 35.11

```
s/TAB/\
/2
```

Note that no spaces are permitted after the backslash. This script produces the following result:

```
Column1    Column2
Column3    Column4
```

Another example comes from the conversion of a file for *troff* to an ASCII input format for Ventura Publisher™. It converts the following line for *troff*:

```
.Ah "Major Heading"
```

to a similar line for Ventura:

```
@A HEAD = Major Heading
```

The twist in this problem is that the line needs to be preceded and followed by a blank line. It is an example of writing a multi-line replacement string:

```
/^\.Ah/{
s/\.Ah */\
\
@A HEAD = /
s/"//g
s/$/\
/
}
```

The first substitute command replaces `.Ah` with two newlines and `@A HEAD = `. Each backslash at the end of the line is necessary to escape the newline. The second substitution removes the quotation marks. The last command matches the end of line in the pattern space (not the embedded newlines) and adds a newline after it.

—*DD* from the Nutshell Handbook *sed & awk*

35.09 Referencing the Search String in a Replacement

As a meta-character, the ampersand (&) represents the extent of the pattern match, not the line that was matched. For instance, you might use it to match a word and surround it with *troff* requests. The following example surrounds a word with point-size requests:

```
s/UNIX/\\s-2&\\s0/g
```

Because backslashes are also replacement meta-characters, two backslashes are necessary to output a single backslash. The & in the replacement string refers to UNIX. If the input line is:

```
on the UNIX Operating System.
```

then the substitute command produces:

```
on the \s-2UNIX\s0 Operating System.
```

The ampersand is particularly useful when the regular expression matches variations of a word. It allows you to specify a variable replacement string that corresponds to what was actually matched. For instance, let's say that you wanted to surround with parentheses any cross-reference to a numbered section in a document. In other words, any reference such as See Section 1.4 or See Section 12.9 should appear in parentheses, as (See Section 12.9). A regular expression can match the different combination of numbers, so we use & in the replacement string and surround whatever was matched:

```
s/See Section [1-9][1-9]*\.[1-9][1-9]*/(&)/
```

The ampersand makes it possible to reference the entire match in the replacement string.

In the next example, the backslash is used to escape the ampersand, which appears literally in the replacement section:

```
s/ORA/O'Reilly \& Associates, Inc./g
```

It's easy to forget about the ampersand appearing literally in the replacement string. If we had not escaped it in this example, the output would have been O'Reilly ORA Associates, Inc.

—*DD* from the Nutshell Handbook *sed & awk*

35.10 Referencing Portions of a Search String

In *sed*, the substitution command provides meta-characters to select any individual portion of a string that is matched and recall it in the replacement string. A pair of escaped parentheses are used in *sed* to enclose any part of a regular expression and save it for recall. Up to nine "saves" are permitted for a single line. \n is used to recall the portion of the match that was saved, where *n* is a number from 1 to 9 referencing a particular "saved" string in order of use. (The section of article 27.04 called "Remembering Patterns with \ (, \ ), and \1" has more information.)

For example, to embolden the section numbers when they appeared as a cross-reference, we could write the following substitution:

```
s/\(See Section \)\([1-9][1-9]*\.[1-9][1-9]*\)/\1\\fB\2\\fP/
```

Two pairs of escaped parentheses are specified. The first captures "See Section" (because this is a fixed string, it could have been simply retyped in the replacement string). The second captures the section number. The replacement string recalls the first saved substring as \1 and the second as \2, which is surrounded by bold-font requests—for example, `See Section \fB12.9\fP`.

We can use a similar technique to match parts of a line and swap them. For instance, let's say there are two parts of a line separated by a colon. We can match each part, putting them within escaped parentheses and swapping them in the replacement:

```
% cat test1
first:second
one:two
% sed 's/\(.*\):\(.*\)/\2:\1/' test1
second:first
two:one
```

The larger point is that you can recall a saved substring in any order, and multiple times.

Articles 14.11, 15.10, 17.07, 19.10, 47.30, and 53.03 have examples.

—*DD* from the Nutshell Handbook *sed & awk*

35.11 *Search & Replacement: One Match among Many*

One of the more unusual options of *sed*'s substitution command is the numeric flag that allows you to point to one particular match when there are many possible matches on a particular line. It is used where a pattern repeats itself on a line and the replacement must be made for only one of those occurrences by position. For instance, a line, perhaps containing *tbl* input, might contain multiple tabs. Let's say that there are three tabs per line, and you'd like to replace the second tab with >. The following substitute command would do it:

```
s/TAB/>/2
```

TAB represents an actual tab character, which is otherwise invisible on the screen. If the input is a one-line file such as the following:

```
Column1 TAB Column2 TAB Column3 TAB Column4
```

the output produced by running the script on this file will be:

```
Column1 TAB Column2>Column3 TAB Column4
```

Note that without the numeric flag, the substitute command would replace only the first tab. (Therefore, 1 can be considered the default numeric flag.) The range of the numeric value is from 1 to 512.

—*DD* from the Nutshell Handbook *sed & awk*

35.12 Transformations on Text

The transform command (*y*) is useful for exchanging lowercase letters for uppercase letters on a line. Effectively, it performs a similar function to *tr (36.09)*. It replaces any character found in the first string with the equivalent character in the second string. The command:

```
y/abcdefghijklmnopqrstuvwxyz/ABCDEFGHIJKLMNOPQRSTUVWXYZ/
```

will convert any lowercase letter into the corresponding uppercase letter. The following:

```
y/abcdefghijklmnopqrstuvwxyz/nopqrstuvwxyzabcdefghijklm/
```

would perform a *rot13* transformation—a simple form of encryption in which each alphabetic character is replaced by the character halfway through the alphabet. (*rot13* encryption is sometimes used to keep offensive news postings *(1.33)* from being read except by someone who really means to. Encryption and decryption are automatically supported by most news readers, but it's fun to see how simple the encryption is. By the way, the command above handles only lower case letters; if we'd shown upper case as well, the command would have run past the margins!)

—TOR

35.13 Hold Space: the Set-aside Buffer

The *pattern space* is a buffer *(55.01)* that contains the current input line. There is also a set-aside buffer called the *hold space*. The contents of the pattern space can be copied to the hold space, and the contents of the hold space can be copied to the pattern space. A group of commands allows you to move data between the hold space and the pattern space. The hold space is used for temporary storage, and that's it. Individual commands can't address the hold space or alter its contents.

The most frequent use of the hold space is to have it retain a duplicate of the current input line while you change the original in the pattern space. The commands that affect the pattern space are:

Hold	*h* or *H*	Copy or append contents of pattern space to hold space.
Get	*g* or *G*	Copy or append contents of hold space to pattern space.
Exchange	*x*	Swap contents of hold space and pattern space.

Each of these commands can take an address that specifies a single line or a range of lines. The hold commands (*h,H*) move data into the hold space and the get commands (*g,G*) move data from the hold space back into the pattern space. The difference between the lowercase and uppercase versions of the same command is that the lowercase command overwrites the contents of the target buffer, while the uppercase command appends to the existing contents.

The hold command replaces the contents of the hold space with the contents of the pattern space. The get command replaces the contents of the pattern space with the contents of the hold space.

The Hold command puts a newline followed by the contents of the pattern space after the contents of the hold space. (The newline is appended to the hold space even if the hold space is empty.) The Get command puts a newline followed by the contents of the hold space after the contents of the pattern space.

The exchange command (*x*) swaps the contents of the two buffers. It has no side effects on either buffer.

Let's use a trivial example to illustrate putting lines into the hold space and retrieving them later. We are going to write a script that reverses pairs of lines. For a sample file, we'll use a list of numbers:

```
1
2
11
22
111
222
```

The object is to reverse the order of the lines beginning with 1 and the lines beginning with 2. Here's how we use the hold space: we copy the first line to the hold space—and hold onto it—while we clear the pattern space. Then we get the second line and append the line in the hold space to it. Look at the script:

```
#Reverse flip
/1/{
h
d
}
/2/{
G
}
```

Any line matching a 1 is copied to the hold space and deleted from the pattern space. Control passes to the top of the script and the line is not printed. When the next line is read, it matches the pattern 2 and the line which had been copied to the hold space is now appended to the pattern space. Then both lines are printed [because, by default, *sed* prints the pattern space after it has finished all commands in the script—*JP*]. In other words, we save the first line of the pair and don't output it until we match the second line. Here's the result of running the script on the sample file:

```
% sed -f sed.flip test.flip
2
1
22
11
222
111
```

The hold command followed by the delete command is a fairly common pairing. Without the delete command, control would reach the bottom of the script and the contents of the pattern space would be output. If the script used the next command (n), instead of the delete command (d), the contents of the pattern space would also be output. You can experiment with this script by removing the delete command altogether or by putting a next command in its place. You could also see what happens if you use g instead of G.

Note that the logic of this script is poor, though the script is useful for demonstration purposes. If a line matches the first instruction and the next line fails to match the second instruction, the first line will not be output. This is a hole down which lines disappear.

For scripts that make practical use of the hold space, see articles 35.17 and 26.12. For a fanciful analogy that makes clear how it works, see article 35.16.

—*DD* from the Nutshell Handbook *sed & awk*

35.14 *Transforming Part of a Line*

The transform command, *y (35.12)*, acts on the entire contents of the pattern space. It is something of a chore to do a letter-by-letter transformation of a portion of the line, but it is possible (though convoluted) as the following example will demonstrate. [The real importance of this example is probably not the use of the *y* command, but the use of the hold space to isolate and preserve part of the line.— *TOR*]

While working on a programming guide, we found that the names of statements were entered inconsistently. They needed to be uppercase, but some were lowercase while others had an initial capital letter. While the task was simple—to capitalize the name of the statement—there were nearly a hundred statements and it seemed a tedious project to write that many explicit substitutions of the form:

```
s/find the Match statement/find the MATCH statement/g
```

The transform command could do the lowercase-to-uppercase conversion but it applies the conversion to the entire line. The hold space makes this task possible because we use it to store a copy of the input line while we isolate and convert the statement name in the pattern space. Look at the script first:

```
# capitalize statement names
/the .* statement/{
h
s/.*the \(.*\) statement.*/\1/
y/abcdefghijklmnopqrstuvwxyz/ABCDEFGHIJKLMNOPQRSTUVWXYZ/
G
s/\(.*\)\n\(.*the \).*\( statement.*\)/\2\1\3/
}
```

The address limits the procedure to lines that match the `.*` statement. Let's look at what each command does:

h The hold command copies the current input line into the hold space. Using the sample line `find the Match statement`, we'll show what the contents of the pattern space and hold space contain. After the *h* command, both the pattern space and the hold space are identical.

> *Pattern space*: `find the Match statement`
> *Hold space*: `find the Match statement`

`s/.*the \(.*\) statement.*/\1/`
The substitute command extracts the name of the statement from the line and replaces the entire line with it.

> *Pattern space*: `Match`
> *Hold space*: `find the Match statement`

`y/abcdefghijklmnopqrstuvwxyz/ABCDEFGHIJKLMNOPQRSTUVWXYZ/`
The transform command changes each lowercase letter to an uppercase letter.

> *Pattern space*: `MATCH`
> *Hold space*: `find the Match statement`

G The Get command appends the line saved in the hold space to the pattern space. The embedded newline from the Get command is shown as \n.

> *Pattern space*: `MATCH\nfind the Match statement`
> *Hold space*: `find the Match statement`

`s/\(.*\)\n\(.*the \).*\( statement.*\)/\2\1\3/`
The substitute command matches three different parts of the pattern space: 1) all characters up to the embedded newline, 2) all characters following the embedded newline and up to and including the followed by a space, and 3) all characters beginning with a space and followed by `statement` up to the end of the pattern space. The name of the statement as it appeared in the original line is matched but not saved. The replacement section of this command recalls the saved portions and reassembles them in a different order, putting the capitalized name of the command in between the and `statement`.

> *Pattern space*: `find the MATCH statement`
> *Hold space*: `find the Match statement`

Let's look at a test run. Here's our sample file:

```
find the Match statement
Consult the Get statement.
using the Read statement to retrieve data
```

Running the script on the sample file produces:

```
find the MATCH statement
Consult the GET statement.
using the READ statement to retrieve data
```

As you can see from this script, the hold space can be skillfully used to isolate and manipulate portions of the input line.

—*DD* from the Nutshell Handbook *sed & awk*

35.15 *Making Edits across Line Boundaries*

Most programs that use regular expressions are able to match a pattern only on a single line of input. This makes it difficult to find or change a phrase, for instance, because it can start near the end of one line and finish near the beginning of the next line. Other patterns might be significant only when repeated on multiple lines.

sed has the ability to load more than one line into the pattern space. This allows you to match (and change) patterns that extend over multiple lines. In this article, we show how to create a multi-line pattern space and manipulate its contents.

The multi-line Next command, *N*, creates a multi-line pattern space by reading a new line of input and appending it to the contents of the pattern space. The original contents of pattern space and the new input line are separated by a newline. The embedded newline character can be matched in patterns by the escape sequence \n. In a multi-line pattern space, only the meta-character ^ matches the newline at the beginning of the pattern space and $ matches the newline at the end. After the Next command is executed, control is then passed to subsequent commands in the script.

The Next command differs from the next command, *n*, which outputs the contents of the pattern space and then reads a new line of input. The next command does not create a multi-line pattern space.

For our first example, let's suppose that we wanted to change "Owner and Operator Guide" to "Installation Guide" but we found that it appears in the file on two lines, splitting between `Operator` and `Guide`. For instance, here are a few lines of sample text:

```
Consult Section 3.1 in the Owner and Operator
Guide for a description of the tape drives
available on your system.
```

The following script looks for `Operator` at the end of a line, reads the next line of input, and then makes the replacement:

```
/Operator$/{
N
s/Owner and Operator\nGuide/Installation Guide/
}
```

In this example, we know where the two lines split and where to specify the embedded newline. When the script is run on the sample file, it produces the two lines of output, one of which combines the first and second lines and is too long to show here. This happens because the substitute command matches the embedded newline but does not replace it. Unfortunately, you cannot use \n to insert a newline in the replacement string. You must use the backslash to escape the newline, as follows:

```
s/Owner and Operator\nGuide /Installation Guide\
/
```

This command restores the newline after Installation Guide. It is also necessary to match a blank space following Guide so the new line won't begin with a space. Now we can show the output:

```
Consult Section 3.1 in the Installation Guide
for a description of the tape drives
available on your system.
```

Remember, you don't have to replace the newline, but if you don't, it can make for some long lines.

What if there are other occurrences of "Owner and Operator Guide" that break over multiple lines in different places? You could change the address to match Owner, the first word in the pattern instead of the last, and then modify the regular expression to look for a space or a newline between words, as shown below:

```
/Owner/{
N
s/Owner *\n*and *\n*Operator *\n*Guide/Installation Guide/
}
```

The asterisk (*) indicates that the space or newline is optional. This seems like hard work though, and indeed there is a more general way. We can read the newline into the pattern space and then use a substitute command to remove the embedded newline, wherever it is:

```
s/Owner and Operator Guide/Installation Guide/
/Owner/{
N
s/ *\n/ /
s/Owner and Operator Guide */Installation Guide\
/
}
```

The first line of the script matches Owner and Operator Guide when it appears on a line by itself. (See the discussion at the end of the article about why this is necessary.) If we match the string Owner, we read the next line into the pattern space and replace the embedded newline with a space. Then we attempt to match the whole pattern and make the replacement followed by a newline. This script will match `Owner and Operator Guide` regardless of how it is broken across two lines. Here's our expanded test file:

```
Consult Section 3.1 in the Owner and Operator
Guide for a description of the tape drives
available on your system.

Look in the Owner and Operator Guide shipped with your system.

Two manuals are provided, including the Owner and
Operator Guide and the User Guide.

The Owner and Operator Guide is shipped with your system.
```

Running the above script on the sample file produces the following result:

```
% sed -f sedscr sample
Consult Section 3.1 in the Installation Guide
for a description of the tape drives
available on your system.

Look in the Installation Guide shipped with your system.

Two manuals are provided, including the Installation Guide
and the User Guide.

The Installation Guide is shipped with your system.
```

In this sample script, it might seem redundant to have two substitute commands that match the pattern. The first command matches it when the pattern is found already on one line, and the second matches the pattern after two lines have been read into the pattern space. Why the first command is necessary is perhaps best demonstrated by removing that command from the script and running it on the sample file:

```
% sed -f sedscr2 sample
Consult Section 3.1 in the Installation Guide
for a description of the tape drives
available on your system.

Look in the Installation Guide
shipped with your system.
Two manuals are provided, including the Installation Guide
and the User Guide.
```

Do you see the two problems? The most obvious problem is that the last line did not print. The last line matches `Owner` and when *N* is executed, there is not another input line to read, so *sed* quits. It does not even output the line. If this is the normal behavior, the Next command should be used as follows to be safe:

```
$!N
```

It excludes the last line (`$`) from the Next command. As it is in our script, by matching `Owner and Operator Guide` on the last line, we avoid matching `Owner` and applying the *N* command. However, if the word `Owner` appeared on the last line we'd have the same problem unless we implement the `$!N` syntax.

The second problem is a little less conspicuous. It has to do with the occurrence of Owner and Operator Guide in the second paragraph. In the input file, it is found on a line by itself:

    Look in the Owner and Operator Guide shipped with your system.

In the output shown above, the blank line following shipped with your system is missing. The reason for this is that this line matches Owner and the next line, a blank line, is appended to the pattern space. The substitute command removes the embedded newline, and the blank line has in effect vanished. (If the line were not blank, the newline would still be removed but the text would appear on the same line with shipped with your system.) The best solution seems to be to avoid reading the next line when the pattern can be matched on one line. So, that is why the first instruction attempts to match the case where the string appears all on one line.

—*DD* from the Nutshell Handbook *sed & awk*

35.16 *The Deliberate Scrivener*

The operations of *sed*'s most difficult commands—hold (*h* or *H*), get (*g* or *G*), and exchange (*x*)—can be explained, somewhat fancifully, in terms of an extremely deliberate medieval scrivener or amanuensis toiling to make a copy of a manuscript. His work is bound by several spatial restrictions: the original manuscript is displayed in one room; the set of instructions for copying the manuscript are stored in a middle room; and the quill, ink, and folio are set up in yet another room. The original manuscript as well as the set of instructions are written in stone and cannot be moved about. The dutiful scrivener, being sounder of body than mind, is able to make a copy by going from room to room, working on only one line at a time. Entering the room where the original manuscript is, he removes from his robes a scrap of paper to take down the first line of the manuscript. Then he moves to the room containing the list of editing instructions. He reads each instruction to see if it applies to the single line he has scribbled down.

Each instruction, written in special notation, consists of two parts: a *pattern* and a *procedure*. The scrivener reads the first instruction and checks the pattern against his line. If there is no match, he doesn't have to worry about the procedure, so he goes to the next instruction. If he finds a match, then the scrivener follows the action or actions specified in the procedure.

He makes the edit on his piece of paper before trying to match the pattern in the next instruction. Remember, the scrivener has to read through a series of instructions, and he reads all of them, not just the first instruction that matches the pattern. Because he makes his edits as he goes, he is always trying to match the latest version against the next pattern; he doesn't remember the original line.

When he gets to the bottom of the list of instructions, and has made any edits that were necessary on his piece of paper, he goes into the next room to copy out the line. (He doesn't need to be told to print out the line.) After that is done, he returns to the first room and takes down the next line on a new scrap of paper. When he goes to the second room, once again he reads every instruction from first to last before leaving.

This is what he normally does, that is, unless he is told otherwise. For instance, before he starts, he can be told *not* to write out every line (the −*n* option). In this case, he must wait for an instruction that tells him to print (*p*). If he does not get that instruction, he throws away his piece of paper and starts over. By the way, regardless of whether or not he is told to write out the line, he always gets to the last instruction on the list.

Let's look at other kinds of instructions the scrivener has to interpret. First of all, an instruction can have zero, one, or two patterns specified: if no pattern is specified, then the same procedure is followed for each line. If there is only one pattern, he will follow the procedure for any line matching the pattern. If a pattern is followed by a !, then the procedure is followed for all lines that do *not* match the pattern. If two patterns are specified, the actions described in the procedure are performed on the first matching line and all succeeding lines until a line matches the second pattern. The scrivener can work on only one line at a time, so you might wonder how he handles a range of lines. Each time he goes through the instructions, he tries to match only the first of two patterns. Now, after he has found a line that matches the first pattern, each time through with a new line he tries to match the second pattern. He interprets the second pattern as *pattern!*, so that the procedure is followed only if there is no match. When the second pattern is matched, he starts looking again for the first pattern.

Each procedure contains one or more commands or *actions*. Remember, if a pattern is specified with a procedure, the pattern must be matched before the procedure is executed. We have already shown many of the usual commands that are similar to other editing commands. However, there are several highly unusual commands.

For instance, the *N* command tells the scrivener to go, right now, and get another line, adding it to the same piece of paper. The scrivener can be instructed to "hold" onto a single piece of scrap paper. The *h* command tells him to make a copy of the line on another piece of paper and put it in his pocket. The *x* command tells him to exchange the extra piece of paper in his pocket with the one in his hand. The *g* command tells him to throw out the paper in his hand and replace it with the one in his pocket. The *G* command tells him to append the line he is holding to the paper in front of him. If he encounters a *d* command, he throws out the scrap of paper and begins again at the top of the list of instructions. A *D* command has effect when he has been instructed to append two lines on his piece of paper. The *D* command tells him to delete the first of those lines.

If you want the analogy converted back to computers, the first and last rooms in this medieval manor are standard input and standard output. Thus, the original file is never changed. The line on the scrivener's piece of scrap paper is in the *pattern space*; the line on the piece of paper that he holds in his pocket is in the *hold space*. The hold space allows you to retain a duplicate of a line while you change the original in the pattern space.

Article 35.17 shows a practical application of the scrivener's work, a *sed* program that searches for a particular phrase that might be split across two lines.

—*DD*

35.17 *Searching for Patterns Split Across Lines*

Article 28.11 showed a script called *phrase*. It is a general-purpose, *grep*-like program built with *sed* that allows you to look for a series of multiple words that might appear across two lines. This article explains the *sed* tricks that are necessary to do this kind of thing. It gets into territory that is essential for any advanced applications of this obscure yet wonderful editor. (Articles 35.13 through 35.16 have background information.)

An essential element of the *phrase* program is that, like *grep*, it only prints out the lines that match the pattern. You might think we'd use *sed*'s *−n* option to suppress the default output of lines. However, what is unusual about this *sed* script is that it creates an input/output loop, controlling whether a line is output or not.

The logic of this script is to look first for the pattern on one line and print the line if it matches. If no match is found, we read another line into the pattern space (as in previous multi-line scripts). Then we copy the two-line pattern space to the hold space for safekeeping. Now the new line that was read into the pattern space previously could match the search pattern on its own, so the next match we attempt is on the second line only. Once we've determined that the pattern is not found on either the first or the second lines, we remove the newline between the two lines and look for the pattern spanning those lines.

The script is designed to accept arguments from the command line. The first argument is the search pattern. All other command-line arguments will be interpreted as filenames. Let's look at the entire script before analyzing it:

phrase

shift *46.16*

for *46.15*

```
#!/bin/sh
# phrase -- search for words across lines
#         $1 = search string; remaining args = filenames
search="$1"
shift
for file
do
sed '
/'"$search"'/b
N
h
s/.*\n//
/'"$search"'/b
g
s/ *\n/ /
/'"$search"'/{
g
b
}
g
```

```
D' $file
done
```

A shell variable named *search* is assigned the first argument on the command line, which should be the search pattern. This script shows another method of passing a shell variable into a script. Here we surround the variable reference with a pair of double quotes. Other parts of the script are enclosed in pairs of single quotes, which protect characters that are normally special to the shell from being interpreted. Each double-quote pair makes sure the enclosed argument is evaluated first by the shell before the *sed* script is evaluated by *sed*.* Article 9.10 explains multi-line shell quoting.

The *sed* script tries to match the search string at three different points, each marked by the address that looks for the search pattern. The first line of the script looks for the search pattern on a line by itself:

```
/'"$search"'/b
```

If the search pattern matches the line, the branch command transfers control to the bottom of the script where the line is printed. This makes use of *sed*'s normal control-flow so that the next input line is read into the pattern space and control then returns to the top of the script. The branch command is used in the same way each time we try to match the pattern.

If a single input line does not match the pattern, we begin our next procedure to create a multi-line pattern space. It is possible that the new line, by itself, will match the search string. It may not be apparent why this step is necessary—why not just look immediately for the pattern anywhere across two lines? The reason is that if the pattern is actually matched on the second line, we'd still output the pair of lines. In other words, the user would see the line preceding the matched line and might be confused by it. This way we output the second line by itself if that is what matches the pattern:

```
N
h
s/.*\n//
/'"$search"'/b
```

The Next command, *N*, appends the next input line to the pattern space. The hold command, *h*, places a copy of the two-line pattern space into the hold space. The next action will change the pattern space, and we want to preserve the original intact. Before looking for the pattern, we use the substitute command to remove the previous line, up to and including the embedded newline. There are several reasons for doing it this way and not another way, so let's consider some of the alternatives. You could write a pattern that matches the search pattern only if it occurs after the embedded newline:

```
/\n.*'"$search"'/b
```

---

*You can also use shell variables to pass a series of commands into a *sed* script. This somewhat simulates a procedure call but it makes the script more difficult to read.

However, if a match is found, we don't want to print the entire pattern space, just the second portion of it. Using the above construct would print both lines when only the second line matches.

You might want to use the Delete command, *D*, to remove the first line in the pattern space before trying to match the pattern. A side effect of the Delete command is a change in flow-control that would resume execution at the top of the script. (The Delete command could conceivably be used, but not without changing the logic of this script.)

So, we try to match the pattern on the second line, and if that is unsuccessful, then we try to match it across two lines:

```
g
s/ *\n/ /
/'"$search"'/{
g
b
}
```

The get command, *g*, retrieves a copy of the original line from the hold space, overwriting the line we had worked with in the pattern space. The substitute command replaces the embedded newline and any spaces preceding it with a single space. Then we attempt to match the pattern. If the match is made, we don't want to print the contents of the pattern space, but rather get the duplicate from the hold space (which preserves the newline) and print it. Thus, before branching to the end of the script, the get command, *g*, retrieves the copy from the hold space.

The last part of the script is executed only if the pattern has not been matched:

```
g
D
```

The get command retrieves the duplicate, that preserves the newline, from the hold space. The Delete command removes the first line in the pattern space and passes control back to the top of the script. We delete only the first part of the pattern space, instead of clearing it, because after reading another input line, it is possible to match the pattern spanning across both lines.

—*DD* from the Nutshell Handbook *sed & awk*

35.18 *Multi-line Delete*

The *sed* delete command, *d*, deletes the contents of the pattern space *(35.13)* and causes a new line of input to be read, with editing resuming at the top of the script. The Delete command, *D*, works slightly differently: it deletes a portion of the pattern space, up to the first embedded newline. It does not cause a new line of input to be read; instead, it returns to the top of the script, applying these instructions to what remains in the pattern space. We can see the difference by writing a script that looks for a series of blank lines and outputs a single blank line. The version below uses the delete command:

```
# reduce multiple blank lines to one; version using d command
/^$/{
     N
     /^\n$/d
}
```

When a blank line is encountered, the next line is appended to the pattern space. Then we try to match the embedded newline. Note that the positional meta-characters, ^ and $, match the beginning and the end of the pattern space, respectively. Here's a test file:

```
This line is followed by 1 blank line.

This line is followed by 2 blank lines.


This line is followed by 3 blank lines.



This line is followed by 4 blank lines.



This is the end.
```

Running the script on the test file produces the following result:

```
% sed -f sed.blank test.blank
This line is followed by 1 blank line.

This line is followed by 2 blank lines.
This line is followed by 3 blank lines.

This line is followed by 4 blank lines.
This is the end.
```

Where there was an even number of blank lines, all the blank lines were removed. Only when there was an odd number was a single blank line preserved. That is because the delete command clears the entire pattern space. Once the first blank line is encountered, the next line is read in, and both are deleted. If a third blank line is encountered, and the next line is not blank, the delete command is not applied, and thus a blank line is output.

If we use the multi-line Delete command, we get a different result, and the one that we wanted:

```
/^\n$/D
```

The reason the multi-line Delete command gets the job done is that when we encounter two blank lines, the Delete command removes only the first of the two. The next time through the script, the blank line will cause another line to be read into the pattern space. If that line is not blank, then both lines are output, thus ensuring that a single blank line will be output. In other words, when there are two blank lines in the pattern space, only the first one is deleted. When there is a blank line followed by text, the pattern space is output normally.

—*DD* from the Nutshell Handbook *sed & awk*

35.19 *Making Edits Everywhere Except . . .*

There are two ways in *sed* to avoid specified portions of a document while making the edits everywhere else. You can use the *!* command to specify that the edit applies only to lines that *do not* match the pattern. Another approach is to use the *b* (branch) command to skip over portions of the editing script. Let's look at an example.

As described in article 45.23, we use *sed* to preprocess the input to *troff* so that double dashes (– –) are converted automatically to em-dashes (—) and straight quotes (" ") are converted to curly quotes (" "). However, program examples in technical books are usually shown in a constant-width font that clearly shows each character as it appears on the computer screen. When typesetting a document, we don't want *sed* to apply the same editing rules within these examples as it does to the rest of the document. For instance, straight quotes should not be replaced by curly quotes.

Because program examples are set off by a pair of macros (something like .ES and .EE, for "Example Start" and "Example End"), we can use those as the basis for exclusion.

So you can say:

```
/^\.ES/,/^\.EE/!{
s/^"/``/
    . . .
s/\\(em"/\\(em``/g
}
```

All of the commands enclosed in braces ({ }) will be subject to the initial pattern address.

There is another way to accomplish the same thing. The *b* command allows you to transfer control to another line in the script that is marked with an optional label. Using this feature, you could write the above script like this:

```
/^\.ES/,/^\.EE/bend
s/^"/``/
    . . .
s/\\(em"/\\(em``/g
:end
```

A label consists of a colon (:), followed by up to eight characters. If the label is missing, the *b* command branches to the end of the script. (In the example above, the label end was included just to show how to use one, but a label is not really necessary here.)

The *b* command is designed for flow control within the script. It allows you to create subscripts that will only be applied to lines matching certain patterns and will not be applied elsewhere. However, as in this case, it also provides a powerful way to exempt part of the text from the action of a single-level script.

The advantage of *b* over *!* for this application is that you can more easily specify multiple conditions to avoid. The *!* command can be applied to a single line or to the set of commands, enclosed in brackets, that immediately follows. On the other hand, *b* gives you almost unlimited control over movement around the script.

—TOR

35.20 *The sed Test Command*

The test command, *t*, branches to a label (or the end of the script) if a successful substitution has been made on the currently addressed line. It implies a conditional branch. Its syntax is as follows:

[*address*]t[*label*]

If no *label* is supplied, control falls through to the end of the script. If *label* is supplied, then execution resumes at the line following the label.

Let's look at an example suggested by Tim O'Reilly. He needed to generate automatic index entries based on evaluating the arguments in a macro *(45.15)* that produced the top of a command manual page for a BASIC manual. If there were three quoted arguments, he wanted to do something different than if there were two or only one. (One reference page might list one language statement; another might list two, or three. He wanted to index each of the statements, regardless of how many there were.) The task was to try to match each of these cases in succession (3,2,1), and when a successful substitution was made, to avoid making any further matches.

Here's Tim's script. It uses \ (\ ) to select each of the arguments to the .Rh macro, so that they can be replayed in the .XX macro, but it uses & to replay the original line as well. Note how a substitution command can span several lines:

```
/^\.Rh/{
s/"\(.*\)" "\(.*\)" "\(.*\)"/&\
.XX "\1"\
.XX "\2"\
.XX "\3"/
t
s/"\(.*\)" "\(.*\)"/&\
.XX "\1"\
.XX "\2"/
t
s/"\(.*\)"/&\
.XX "\1"/
}
```

If there are three arguments on the .Rh line, the test command after the first substitute command will be true, control will branch to the end of the script, and *sed* will go on to the next input line. If there are fewer than three arguments, no substitution will be made, the test command will be evaluated false, and the next substitute command will be tried. This will be repeated until all the possibilities are used up.

Without the test command, subsequent substitutions would also match. Because regular expressions always select the longest match, a line with three arguments would also be selected by the subsitute command designed for the line with two or one.

—*DD, TOR* from the Nutshell Handbook *sed & awk*

35.21   *Uses of the sed Quit Command*

The quit command, *q*, causes *sed* to stop reading new input lines (and stop sending them to the output). Its syntax is:

> [*line-address*]q

It can take only a single-line address. Once the line matching address (*line-address*) is reached, the script will be terminated.

For instance, the following one-liner uses the quit command to print the first ten lines from a file:

```
% sed '10q' myfile
    ...
```

sed prints each line until it gets to line 10 and quits.

This is much more efficient than the functionally equivalent:

```
% sed -n '1,10p' myfile
```

(especially if *myfile* is a long file) because *sed* doesn't need to keep reading its input once the patterns in the script are satisfied.

One possible use of *q* is to quit a script after you've extracted what you want from a file. For instance, in a script like *getmac (45.22)*, there is some inefficiency in continuing to scan through a large file after *sed* has found what it is looking for.

So, for example, you could revise the *sed* script in the *getmac* shell script as follows:

```
sed -n "
/^\.de *$1/,/^\.\./{
p
/^\.\./q
}" $file
done
```

The grouping of commands keeps the line:

```
/^\.\./q
```

from being executed until *sed* reaches the end of the macro we're looking for, at a line starting with two dots (..). (This line by itself would terminate the script at the conclusion of the first macro definition.) The *sed* program quits on the spot, and doesn't continue through the rest of the file looking for other possible matches.

Because the macro definition files are not that long, and the script itself not that complex, the actual time saved from this version of the script is negligible. However, with a very large file, or a complex, multi-line script that needs to be applied to only a small part of the file, this script could be a significant timesaver.

—TOR

35.22 Dangers of the sed Quit Command

The *sed* quit command, *q (35.21)*, is very useful for getting *sed* to stop processing any more input once you've done what you want.

However, you need to be very careful not to use *q* in any *sed* script that writes its edits back to the original file. After *q* is executed, no further output is produced. It should not be used in any case where you want to edit the front of the file and pass the remainder through unchanged. Using *q* in this case is a dangerous beginner's mistake.

—TOR

35.23 sed Newlines, Quoting, and Backslashes in a Shell Script

Feeding *sed (35.24)* newlines is easy; the real trick is getting them past the C shell.

The *sed* documentation says that in order to insert newlines in substitute commands, you should quote them with backslashes:

```
sed -e 's/foo/b\
a\
r/'
```

Indeed, this works quite well in the Bourne shell, which does what I consider the proper thing *(9.10)* with this input. The C shell, however, thinks it is smarter than you are, and *removes* the trailing backslashes *(9.11)*, and instead you must type:

```
sed -e 's/foo/b\\
a\\
r/'
```

Probably the best solution is to place your *sed* commands in a separate file, to keep the shell's sticky fingers off them.

—CT in *net.unix* on Usenet, *20 November 1985*

35.24 Quick Reference: sed

How sed operates:

- Each line of input is copied into a pattern space.

- All editing commands in a *sed* script are applied in order to each line of input.

- Editing commands are applied to all lines (globally) unless line addressing restricts the lines affected.

- If a command changes the input, subsequent command-addresses will be applied to the current line in the pattern space, not the original input line.

- The original input file is unchanged because the editing commands modify a copy of the original input line. The copy is sent to standard output (but can be redirected to a file).

Syntax of sed Commands

sed commands have the general form:

[*address*][, *address*][!]*command* [*arguments*]

sed commands consist of *addresses* and editing *commands*. *commands* consist of a single letter or symbol; they are described later, alphabetically and by group. *arguments* include the label supplied to *b* or *t*, the filename supplied to *r* or *w*, and the substitution flags for *s*. *addresses* are described below. Elements in [brackets] are optional; don't type the brackets.

Pattern Addressing

A *sed* command can specify zero, one, or two addresses. An address can be a line number, the symbol $ (for last line), or a regular expression enclosed in slashes (/*pattern*/). Regular expressions are described in Chapter 27. Additionally, \n can be used to match any newline in the pattern space (resulting from the *N* command), but not the newline at the end of the pattern space. See article 35.04.

If the command specifies:	Then it is applied to:
No address	Each input line.
One address	Any line matching the address. Some commands accept only one address: *a*, *i*, *r*, *q*, and =.
Two comma-separated addresses	First matching line and all succeeding lines up to and including a line matching the second address.
An address followed by !	All lines that do *not* match the address.

Examples

Substitute on all lines (all occurrences):

    s/xx/yy/g

Delete lines containing BSD:

    /BSD/d

Print between BEGIN and END, inclusive:

    /^BEGIN/,/^END/p@

Delete any line that doesn't contain SAVE:

    /SAVE/!d

Substitute on all lines, except between BEGIN and END:

    /BEGIN/,/END/!s/xx/yy/g

Braces ({}) are used in *sed* to nest one address inside another or to apply multiple commands at the same address:

    [/pattern/][,/pattern/]{
    command1
    command2
    }

The left curly brace ({) must end a line, and the right curly brace (}) must be on a line by itself. Be sure there are no blank spaces after the braces.

Alphabetical Summary of sed Commands

Begin a comment in a *sed* script. Valid only as the first character of the first line.

:   *:label*
       Label a line in the script for the transfer of control by *b* or *t*. *label* may contain up to seven characters.

=   *[/pattern/]=*
       Write to standard output the line number of each line addressed by *pattern*.

a   *[address]a*
       text

       Append *text* following each line matched by *address*. If *text* goes over more than one line, newlines must be "hidden" by preceding them with a backslash. *text* will be terminated by the first newline that is not hidden in this way. *text* is not available in the pattern space, and subsequent commands cannot be applied to it. The results of this command are sent to standard output when the list of editing commands is finished, regardless of what happens to the current line in the pattern space.

Example

```
$a\
This goes after the last line in the file\
(marked by $). This text is escaped at the\
end of each line, except for the last one.
```

b   [*address1*][, *address2*]b[*label*]

Transfer control unconditionally to :*label* elsewhere in script. That is, the command following the *label* is the next command applied to the current line. If no *label* is specified, control falls through to the end of the script, so no more commands are applied to the current line. See articles 35.19 and 35.17.

Example

```
# Ignore tbl tables; resume script after TE:
/^\.TS/,/^\.TE/b
```

c   [*address1*][, *address2*]c\
    text

Replace the lines selected by the address with *text*. When a range of lines is specified, all lines as a group are replaced by a single copy of *text*. The newline following each line of *text* must be escaped by a backslash, except the last line. The contents of the pattern space are, in effect, deleted and no subsequent editing commands can be applied to it (or *text*).

Example

```
# Replace first 100 lines in a file:
1,100c\
\
<First 100 names to be supplied>
```

d   [*address1*][, *address2*]d

Delete the addressed line (or lines) from the pattern space. Thus, the line is not passed to standard output. A new line of input is read, and editing resumes with the first command in the script. See articles 35.04 and 35.18.

Example

```
# delete all blank lines:
/^$/d
```

D   [*address1*][, *address2*]D

Delete first part (up to embedded newline) of multi-line pattern space created by *N* command and resume editing with first command in script. If this command empties the pattern space, then a new line of input is read, as if *d* had been executed. See article 35.18.

Example

```
# Strip multiple blank lines, leaving only one:
/^$/{
N
```

```
/^\n$/D
}
```

g   [*address1*][,*address2*]g
Paste the contents of the hold space (see *h* or *H*) back into the pattern space, wiping out the previous contents of the pattern space. See articles 35.13 and 35.16. The example shows a simple way to copy lines.

Example

This script collects all lines containing the word Item: and copies them to a place marker later in the file. The place marker is overwritten.

```
/Item:/H
/<Replace this line with the item list>/g
```

G   [*address1*][,*address2*]G
Same as *g*, except that the hold space is pasted below the address instead of overwriting it. The example shows a simple way to "cut and paste" lines. See articles 35.13 and 35.16.

Example

This script collects all lines containing the word Item: and moves them after a place marker later in the file. The original Item: lines are deleted.

```
/Item:/{
H
d
}
/Summary of items:/G
```

h   [*address1*][,*address2*]h
Copy the pattern space into the hold space, a special temporary buffer. The previous contents of the hold space are obliterated. You can use *h* to save a line before editing it. See articles 35.13 and 35.16.

Example

```
# Edit a line; print the change; replay the original
/UNIX/{
h
s/.* UNIX \(.*\) .*/\1:/
p
x
}
```

Sample input:

```
This describes the UNIX ls command.
This describes the UNIX cp command.
```

Sample output:

```
ls:
This describes the UNIX ls command.
```

```
cp:
This describes the UNIX cp command.
```

H   [*address1*][, *address2*]H
Append the contents of the pattern space (preceded by a newline) to the contents of the hold space. Even if the hold space is empty, *H* still appends a newline. *H* is like an incremental copy. See examples under *g* and *G*, also articles 35.13 and 35.16.

i   [*address*]i\
     text

Insert *text* before each line matched by *address*. (See *a* for details on *text*.)

Example

```
/Item 1/i\
The five items are listed below:
```

l   [*address1*][, *address2*]l
List the contents of the pattern space, showing non-printing characters as ASCII codes *(53.03, 26.07)*. Long lines are wrapped.

n   [*address1*][, *address2*]n
Read next line of input into pattern space. The current line is sent to standard output, and the next line becomes the current line. Control passes to the command following *n* instead of resuming at the top of the script.

Example

In the *ms* macros *(45.15)*, a section header occurs on the line below an .NH macro. To print all lines of header text, invoke this script with *sed −n*:

```
/^\.NH/{
n
p
}
```

N   [*address1*][, *address2*]N
Append next input line to contents of pattern space; the two lines are separated by an embedded newline. (This command is designed to allow pattern matches across two lines.) Using \n to match the embedded newline, you can match patterns across multiple lines. See example under *D*, also article 35.15.

Examples

Like previous example, but print .NH line as well as header title:

```
/^\.NH/{
N
p
}
```

Join two lines (replace newline with space):

```
/^\.NH/{
N
s/\n/ /
p
}
```

p   [*address1*][, *address2*]p
Print the addressed line(s). Unless the −*n* command-line option is used, this command will cause duplicate lines to be output. Also, it is typically used before commands that change flow control (*d*, *N*, *b*) and that might prevent the current line from being output. See examples under *b*, *n*, and *N*.

P   [*address1*][, *address2*]P
Print first part (up to embedded newline) of multi-line pattern created by *N* command. Same as *p* if *N* has not been applied to a line.

Example

Suppose you have function references in two formats:

```
function(a,b,c)
function(a,
        b,
        c)
```

The following script changes argument c, regardless of whether it appears on the same line as the function name:

```
s/function(a,b,c)/function(a,b,XX)/
/function(/{
N
s/c/XX/
P
D
}
```

q   [*address*]q
Quit when *address* is encountered. The addressed line is first written to output (if default output is not suppressed), along with any text appended to it by previous *a* or *r* commands. See articles 35.21 and 35.22.

Example

Delete everything after the addressed line:

```
/Garbled text follows:/q
```

Print only the first 50 lines of a file:

```
50q
```

r   [*address*]r *file*
Read contents of *file* and append after the contents of the pattern space. Exactly one space must be put between the r and *file*.

Example

> /The list of items follow:/r item_file

s   [*address1*][, *address2*]s/*pattern*/*replacement*/[*flags*]
Substitute *replacement* for *pattern* on each addressed line. If pattern addresses are used, the pattern // represents the last pattern address specified. The following flags can be specified:

   n   Replace *n*th instance of /*pattern*/ on each addressed line. *n* is any number in the range 1 to 512 (default is 1). See article 35.11.

   g   Replace all instances of /*pattern*/ on each addressed line, not just the first instance.

   p   Print the line if a successful substitution is done. If several successful substitutions are done, multiple copies of the line will be printed. Often used in scripts with the −*n* command-line option *(35.02)*.

   w *file* Write the line to a *file* if a replacement was done. A maximum of ten different files can be opened.

See articles 35.07 through 35.10.

Examples

Here are some short, commented scripts:

```
# Change third and fourth quote to ( and ):
/function/{
s/"/(/3
s/"/)/4
}

# Remove all quotes on a given line:
/Title/s/"//g

# Remove first colon or all quotes; print resulting lines:
s/://p
s/"//gp

# Change first "if" but leave "ifdef" alone:
/ifdef/!s/if/    if/
```

t   [*address1*][, *address2*]t [*label*]
Test if any substitutions have been made on addressed lines, and if so, branch to line marked by :*label*. (See *b* and :.) If *label* is not specified, control falls through to bottom of script. The *t* command is like a *case* statement in the C programming language or the shell programming languages. You test each case: when it's true, you exit the construct. See article 35.20.

Example

Suppose you want to fill empty fields of a database. You have this:

```
ID: 1    Name: greg    Rate: 45
ID: 2    Name: dale
ID: 3
```

You want this:

```
ID: 1    Name: greg    Rate: 45    Phone: ??
ID: 2    Name: dale    Rate: ??    Phone: ??
ID: 3    Name: ????    Rate: ??    Phone: ??
```

You need to test the number of fields already there. Here's the script (fields are tab-separated):

```
/ID/{
s/ID: .* Name: .* Rate: .*/&    Phone: ??/p
t
s/ID: .* Name: .*/&    Rate: ??    Phone: ??/p
t
s/ID: .*/&    Name: ??    Rate: ??    Phone: ??/p
}
```

w   *[address1][,address2]*w *file*

Append contents of pattern space to *file*. This action occurs when the command is encountered rather than when the pattern space is output. Exactly one space must separate the w and *file*. A maximum of ten different files can be opened in a script. This command will create the file if it does not exist; if the file exists, its contents will be overwritten each time the script is executed. Multiple write commands that direct output to the same file append to the end of the file.

Example

```
# Store tbl and eqn blocks in a file:
/^\.TS/,/^\.TE/w troff_stuff
/^\.EQ/,/^\.EN/w troff_stuff
```

x   *[address1][,address2]*x

Exchange contents of the pattern space with the contents of the hold space. For examples, see *h* and articles 35.13 and 35.16.

y   *[address1][,address2]*y*/abc/xyz/*

Translate characters. Change every instance of *a* to *x*, *b* to *y*, *c* to *z*, etc. See article 35.12.

Example

```
# Change item 1, 2, 3 to Item A, B, C ...
/^item [1-9]/y/i123456789/IABCDEFGHI/
```

—*DG* from the Nutshell Handbook *UNIX in a Nutshell (SVR4/Solaris)*

36

You Can't Quite Call this Editing

36.01 And Why Not?

There are many specialized forms of editing that happen frequently enough that they sometimes want to be saved into a script. Examples of this kind of thing include:

- *recomment (36.02)*, a script for reformatting comment blocks within programs and scripts.

- *behead (36.03)*, a script for removing the headers from mail and news messages.

- *center (36.06)*, a script for centering lines of text in a file.

In addition, there are a number of programs that provide some useful ways of modifying files but that you don't normally think of as editors:

- *split (36.07)* and *csplit (36.08)* let you split a big file into smaller pieces.

- *tr (36.09)* lets you substitute one character for another—including non-printing characters that you specify by their octal values.

- *dd (36.04, 36.10, 36.11)* lets you perform various data conversions on a file.

- *cut (36.12)* and *colrm (36.13)* let you cut columns or fields out of a file, and *paste (36.16)* lets you put them back, perhaps in a different order.

This chapter covers all that and more.

—TOR

36.02 recomment: Clean up Program Comment Blocks

Lines in a program's comment block usually start with one or more special characters, like:

```
# line 1 of the comment
# line 2 of the comment
# line 3 of the comment
    ...
```

It can be a hassle to add more text to one of the comment lines in a block because the line can get too long, which requires you to fold that line onto the next line, which means you have to work around the leading comment character(s).

The *fmt (31.37)* program neatens lines of a text file. It doesn't help programmers who want to "neaten" blocks of comments though, because *fmt* mixes the comment characters from the starts of lines with the words. The *recomment* script is *fmt* for comment blocks. It's for people who write shell, *awk*, C, or almost any other kind of program with comment blocks several lines long.

recomment reads the lines that you feed its standard input. It looks at the first line and figures out what characters you're using to comment the line (see the $cchars variable for a list—typically SPACEs, TABs, #, or *). Then, *recomment* strips those comment characters off each line, feeds the remaining block of text to the *fmt* utility, and uses *sed (35.24)* to add the comment characters again.

I usually use *recomment* from inside *vi*, with filter-through *(31.22)* commands like:

```
!}recomment        reformat to the next blank line
5!!recomment       reformat this line and the next 4
```

Normally, *recomment* lets *fmt* choose the width of the comment block (72 characters, typically). To get another width, you can either:

- Give the width on the command line, like:

    ```
    recomment -50
    ```

- Set an environment variable named *CBLKWID*. Give the maximum width, in characters, for the comment text. For example, in the C shell, use:

    ```
    % setenv CBLKWID 50
    ```

recomment isn't perfect, but it's usually much better than nothing!

recomment

```
#! /bin/sh
umask 077    # MAKE $temp PRIVATE
temp=/tmp/RECOMMENT$$
trap 'rm -f $temp; exit' 0 1 2 15

cchars='    #*'    # LEADING CHARACTERS TO PRESERVE (INCL. SPACE, TAB)

case "$1" in
-[0-9]|-[0-9][0-9]|-[0-9][0-9][0-9]) widopt="$1" ;;
"") # CHECK ENVARIABLE (SILENTLY IGNORE ERRORS SO DON'T SCREW UP TEXT):
    case "$CBLKWID" in
    [0-9]|[0-9][0-9]|[0-9][0-9][0-9]) widopt="-$CBLKWID" ;;
```

```
          esac
          ;;
    *)    # PRINT ERROR, THEN GIVE THEM TEXT BACK (SO vi WON'T DELETE LINES):
          echo "Usage: `basename $0` [-widthnum].
              (Text output with no reformatting.)" 1>&2
          cat
          exit
          ;;
    esac

    cat > $temp

    # GET COMMENT CHARACTERS USED ON FIRST LINE; STORE IN $comment:
    comment="`sed -n \"1s/^\([$cchars]*\).*/\1/p\" $temp`"
    # GET NUMBER OF CHARACTERS IN COMMENT CHARACTER STRING:
    cwidth=`expr "$comment" : '.*'`
```

expr 47.29

```
    # RE-FORMAT THE COMMENT BLOCK.  IF $widopt SET, USE IT:
    colrm 1 $cwidth < $temp |       # STRIP OFF COMMENT LEADER FROM LINES
    fmt $widopt |                   # RE-FORMAT THE TEXT, AND
    sed "s/^/$comment/"            # PUT THE COMMENT CHARACTERS BACK
```

If your system doesn't have the *colrm (36.13)* utility, change the third-to-last line to use *cut (36.12)* instead:

```
    cut -c`expr $cwidth + 1`- < $temp |  # STRIP OFF COMMENT LEADER
```

That makes a command like cut -c4- instead of colrm 1 3.

—JP

36.03 *Remove Mail/News Headers with behead*

When you're saving or re-sending a news article or mail message, you might want to the remove header lines (*Subject:*, *Received:*, and so on). This little script will handle standard input, one or many files. It writes to standard output. Here are a few examples:

- With saved messages, at a shell prompt:

      % **behead** *msg** **| mail -s "Did you see these?" fredf**

- To save an article, from a pipe, without a header, from a program (here, the old *readnews*) that can't cut off headers itself:

      What now? [ynq] **s-** **| behead > *filename***

Here's the script, adapted a little from the original by Arthur David Olson:

behead

```
#! /bin/sh
case $# in
0)  exec sed '1,/^$/d' ;;
*)  for i
    do sed '1,/^$/d' "$i"
    done
    ;;
esac
```

The script relies on the fact that mail messages use a blank line to separate the header from the body of the message. As a result, the script simply deletes the text from the beginning up to the first blank line.

—JP

36.04 Low-level File Butchery with dd

Want to strip off some arbitrary number of characters from the front of a file?

dd provides an unexpectedly easy answer. Let's say you wanted to delete the first 100 characters in a file. Here's the command that will do the trick (assuming of course that you give *dd* a filename with the *if=* option or data from a pipe):

```
% dd bs=100 skip=1
```

Or you could try:

```
% dd bs=1 skip=100
```

dd normally reads and writes data in 512-byte blocks; the input block size can be changed with the *ibs=* option, and the output block size with *obs=*. Use *bs=* to set both. *skip=* sets the number of blocks to skip at the start of the file.

Why would you want to do this? Article 23.18 gives an interesting example when encrypting files. Article 21.06 explains using *dd* over a network with a tape drive. To convert files between ASCII and EBCDIC, see article 36.10. Article 36.11 shows even more uses for *dd*.

—TOR

36.05 offset: Indent Text

Do you have a printer that starts each line too close to the left margin? You might want to indent text to make it look better on the screen or a printed page. Here's a shell script that does that. It reads from files or standard input and writes to standard output. The default indentation is 5 spaces. For example, to send a copy of a file named *graph* to the *lp* printer, indented 12 spaces:

```
% offset -12 graph | lp
```

There are easier ways to do this (with *awk (38.18)*, for instance). This script uses the Bourne shell *case* structure in an interesting way though, and that might give you ideas for other work.

offset

```
#! /bin/sh

# GET INDENTATION (IF ANY) AND CHECK FOR BOGUS NUMBERS:
case "$1" in
-[0-9]|-[0-9][0-9]) indent="$1"; shift ;;
-*) echo "`basename $0`: '$1' isn't -number or is > 99." 1>&2; exit 1 ;;
esac
```

```
# SET DEFAULT:
case "$indent" in
"") indent=-5 ;;
esac

# BUILD THE SPACES FOR sed.
# FIRST case DOES MULTIPLES OF 10; SECOND case DOES SINGLE SPACES:
s="          "  # TEN SPACES
case "$indent" in
-?) ;;  # LESS THAN 10; SKIP IT
-1?) pad="$s" ;;
-2?) pad="$s$s" ;;
-3?) pad="$s$s$s" ;;
-4?) pad="$s$s$s$s" ;;
-5?) pad="$s$s$s$s$s" ;;
-6?) pad="$s$s$s$s$s$s" ;;
-7?) pad="$s$s$s$s$s$s$s" ;;
-8?) pad="$s$s$s$s$s$s$s$s" ;;
-9?) pad="$s$s$s$s$s$s$s$s$s" ;;
*)  echo "`basename $0`: Help! \$indent is '$indent'!?!" 1>&2; exit 1 ;;
esac

case "$indent" in
-0|-?0) ;;  # SKIP IT; IT'S A MULTIPLE OF 10
-1|-?1) pad="$pad " ;;
-2|-?2) pad="$pad  " ;;
-3|-?3) pad="$pad   " ;;
-4|-?4) pad="$pad    " ;;
-5|-?5) pad="$pad     " ;;
-6|-?6) pad="$pad      " ;;
-7|-?7) pad="$pad       " ;;
-8|-?8) pad="$pad        " ;;
-9|-?9) pad="$pad         " ;;
*)  echo "`basename $0`: Help! \$indent is '$indent'!?!" 1>&2; exit 1 ;;
esac

# MIGHT ADD expand FIRST TO TAKE CARE OF TABS:
sed "s/^/$pad/" $*
```

First, the script sets the indentation amount, like −12 or −5, in the *indent* variable. Next, it builds a shell variable, *pad*, with just enough spaces to indent the text. One *case* checks the first digit of $indent to find out how many tenspace chunks of spaces to put in *pad*. The next *case* finishes the job with a few more spaces. A *sed (35.24)* command adds the spaces to the start of each line. If your lines have TABs in them, change the last line to use *expand* or *pr −e −t (43.04)* and pipe the result to *sed*:

```
expand $* | sed "s/^/$pad"
```

—*JP*

36.06 Centering Lines in a File

Here's an *awk* script that centers lines across an 80-character line. It builds a variable full of spaces, enough to center the line. Then it prints the spaces and the line.

In *vi*, you can use a filter-through *(31.22)* command to center lines while you're editing. Or just use *center* from the command line. For example:

```
% center afile > afile.centered
% sort party_list | center | lp
```

Here it is. If your system understands #! *(46.04, 47.03)*, this script will be passed directly to *awk* without a shell. Otherwise, put this into a Bourne shell script *(38.15)*.

center

```
#! /bin/awk -f
# center - center lines in file(s) or standard input
# Usage: center [filenames]
{
    spaces = ""
    for (i = 1; i < (80 - length($0)) / 2; i++)
        spaces = spaces " "
    print spaces $0
}
```

—JP

36.07 Splitting Files at Fixed Points: split

Most versions of UNIX come with a program called *split* whose purpose is to split large files into smaller files for tasks such as editing them in an editor that cannot handle large files, or mailing them if they are so big that some mailers will refuse to deal with them. For example, let's say you have a really big text file that you want to mail to someone:

```
% ls -l bigfile
-r--r--r--  1 jik        139070 Oct 15 21:02 bigfile
```

Running *split* on that file will (by default, with most versions of *split*) break it up into pieces that are each no more than 1000 lines long:

```
% ls -l
total 283
-r--r--r--  1 jik        139070 Oct 15 21:02 bigfile
-rw-rw-r--  1 jik         46444 Oct 15 21:04 xaa
-rw-rw-r--  1 jik         51619 Oct 15 21:04 xab
-rw-rw-r--  1 jik         41007 Oct 15 21:04 xac
```
wc *30.06*
```
% wc -l x*
    1000 xaa
    1000 xab
     932 xac
    2932 total
```

Note the default naming scheme, which is to append "aa," "ab," "ac," etc. to the letter "x" for each subsequent filename. It is possible to modify the default behavior. For example, you can make it create files that are 1500 lines long instead of 1000:

```
% rm x??
% split -1500 bigfile
% ls -l
total 288
-r--r--r--  1 jik          139070 Oct 15 21:02 bigfile
-rw-rw-r--  1 jik           74016 Oct 15 21:06 xaa
-rw-rw-r--  1 jik           65054 Oct 15 21:06 xab
```

You can also get it to use a name prefix other than "x":

```
% rm x??
% split -1500 bigfile bigfile.split.
% ls -l
total 288
-r--r--r--  1 jik          139070 Oct 15 21:02 bigfile
-rw-rw-r--  1 jik           74016 Oct 15 21:07 bigfile.split.aa
-rw-rw-r--  1 jik           65054 Oct 15 21:07 bigfile.split.ab
```

Although the simple behavior described above tends to be relatively universal, there are differences in the functionality of *split* on different UNIX systems. There are four basic variants of *split* as shipped with various implementations of UNIX:

1. A *split* that understands only how to deal with splitting text files into chunks of *n* lines or less each.

bsplit

2. A *split*, usually called *bsplit*, that understands only how to deal with splitting non-text files into *n*-character chunks. A public domain version of *bsplit* is available on the Power Tools disk.

3. A *split* that will split text files into *n*-line chunks, or non-text files into *n*-character chunks, and tries to figure out automatically whether it's working on a text file or a non-text file.

4. A *split* that will do either text files or non-text files, but needs to be told explicitly when it is working on a non-text file.

The only way to tell which version you've got is to read the manual page for it on your system, which will also tell you the exact syntax for using it.

The problem with the third variant is that although it tries to be smart and automatically do the right thing with both text and non-text files, it sometimes guesses wrong and splits a text file as a non-text file or vice versa, with completely unsatisfactory results. Therefore, if the variant on your system is (3), you probably want to get your hands on one of the many *split* clones out there that is closer to one of the other variants (see below).

Variants (1) and (2) listed above are OK as far as they go, but they aren't adequate if your environment provides only one of them rather than both. If you find yourself needing to split a non-text file when you have only a text *split*, or needing to split a text file when you have only *bsplit*, you need to get one of the clones that will perform the function you need.

Variant (4) is the most reliable and versatile of the four listed, and is therefore what you should go with if you find it necessary to get a clone and install it on your system. There are several such clones in the various source archives, including the freely-available BSD UNIX version. Alternatively, if you have installed *perl (39.01)*, it is quite easy to write a simple *split* clone in *perl*, and you don't have to worry about compiling a C program to do it; this is an especially significant advantage if you need to run your *split* on multiple architectures that would need separate binaries.

If you need to split a non-text file and don't feel like going to all of the trouble of finding a *split* clone that handles them, one standard UNIX tool you can use to do the splitting is *dd (36.04)*. For example, if *bigfile* above were a non-text file and you wanted to split it into 20000-byte pieces, you could do something like this:

```
$ ls -l bigfile
-r--r--r--  1 jik        139070 Oct 23 08:58 bigfile
$ for i in 1 2 3 4 5 6 7                          # *
> do
>         dd of=x$i bs=20000 count=1 2>/dev/null  # †
> done < bigfile
$ ls -l
total 279
-r--r--r--  1 jik        139070 Oct 23 08:58 bigfile
-rw-rw-r--  1 jik         20000 Oct 23 09:00 x1
-rw-rw-r--  1 jik         20000 Oct 23 09:00 x2
-rw-rw-r--  1 jik         20000 Oct 23 09:00 x3
-rw-rw-r--  1 jik         20000 Oct 23 09:00 x4
-rw-rw-r--  1 jik         20000 Oct 23 09:00 x5
-rw-rw-r--  1 jik         20000 Oct 23 09:00 x6
-rw-rw-r--  1 jik         19070 Oct 23 09:00 x7
```

for *46.15*

> *10.11*

done < *47.23*

—*JIK*

36.08 *Splitting Files by Context: csplit*

csplit

Like *split (36.07)*, *csplit* lets you break a file into smaller pieces, but *csplit* (context split) also allows the file to be broken into different-sized pieces, according to context. With *csplit*, you give the locations (line numbers or search patterns) at which to break each section. *csplit* comes with System V, but there are also freely-available versions.

Let's look at search patterns first. Suppose you have an outline consisting of three main sections. You could create a separate file for each section by typing:

```
% csplit outline /I./ /II./ /III./
28     number of characters in each file
```

---

*To figure out how many numbers to count up to, divide the total size of the file by the block size you want and add one if there's a remainder. The *jot* program *(47.11)* can help here.

†The output file size I want is denoted by the *bs* or "block size" parameter to *dd*. The 2>/dev/null *(47.21, 14.14)* gets rid of *dd*'s diagnostic output, which isn't useful here and takes up space.

```
415            .
372            .
554            .
% ls
outline
xx00    outline title, etc.
xx01    Section I
xx02    Section II
xx03    Section III
```

This command creates four new files (*outline* remains intact). *csplit* displays the character counts for each file. Note that the first file (*xx00*) contains any text up to *but not including* the first pattern, and that *xx01* contains the first section, as you'd expect. This is why the naming scheme begins with *00*. (Even if *outline* had begun immediately with a I., *xx01* would still contain Section I, but *xx00* would be empty in this case.)

If you don't want to save the text that occurs before a specified pattern, use a percent sign as the pattern delimiter:

```
% csplit outline %I.% /II./ /III./
415
372
554
% ls
outline
xx00    Section I
xx01    Section II
xx02    Section III
```

The preliminary text file has been suppressed, and the created files now begin where the actual outline starts (the file numbering is off, however).

Let's make some further refinements. We'll use the *−s* option to suppress the display of the character counts, and we'll use the *−f* option to specify a file prefix other than the conventional *xx*:

```
% csplit -s -f part. outline /I./ /II./ /III./
% ls
outline
part.00
part.01
part.02
part.03
```

There's still a slight problem though. In search patterns, a period is a meta-character *(27.10)* that matches any single character, so the pattern /I./ may inadvertently match words like *Introduction*. We need to escape the period with a backslash; however, the backslash has meaning both to the pattern and to the shell, so in fact, we need either to use a double backslash or to surround the pattern in quotes *(9.10)*. A subtlety, yes, but one that can drive you crazy if you don't remember it. Our command line becomes:

```
% csplit -s -f part. outline "/I\./" /II./ /III./
```

You can also break a file at repeated occurrences of the same pattern. Let's say you have a file that describes 50 ways to cook a chicken, and you want each method stored in a separate file. Each section begins with headings *WAY #1*, *WAY #2*, and so on. To divide the file, use *csplit*'s repeat argument:

```
% csplit -s -f dump. fifty_ways /^WAY/ "{49}"
```

This command splits the file at the first occurrence of *WAY*, and the number in braces tells *csplit* to repeat the split 49 more times. Note that a caret is used to match the beginning of the line and that the C shell requires quotes around the braces *(10.05)*. The command has created 50 files:

```
% ls cook.*
cook.00
cook.01
    ...
cook.48
cook.49
```

Quite often, when you want to split a file repeatedly, you don't know or don't care how many files will be created; you just want to make sure that the necessary number of splits takes place. In this case, it makes sense to specify a repeat count that is slightly higher than what you need (maximum is 99). Unfortunately, if you tell *csplit* to create more files than it's able to, this produces an "out of range" error. Furthermore, when *csplit* encounters an error, it exits by removing any files it created along the way. (A bug, if you ask me.) This is where the *−k* option comes in. Specify *−k* to *k*eep the files around, even when the "out of range" message occurs.

csplit allows you to break a file at some number of lines above or below a given search pattern. For example, to break a file at the line that is five lines below the one containing *Sincerely,* you could type:

```
% csplit -s -f letter. all_letters /Sincerely/+5
```

This situation might arise if you have a series of business letters strung together in one file. Each letter begins differently, but each one begins five lines after the previous letter's *Sincerely* line. Here's another example, adapted from AT&T's UNIX *User's Reference Manual*:

```
% csplit -s -k -f routine. prog.c '%main(%' '/^}/+1' '{99}'
```

The idea is that the file *prog.c* contains a group of C routines, and we want to place each one in a separate file (*routine.00, routine.01*, etc.). The first pattern uses % because we want to discard anything before *main*. The next argument says, "Look for a closing brace at the beginning of a line (the conventional end of a routine) and split on the following line (the assumed beginning of the next routine)." Repeat this split up to 99 times,* using *−k* to preserve the created files.

The *csplit* command takes line-number arguments in addition to patterns. You can say:

```
% csplit stuff 50 373 955
```

---

*In this case, the repeat can actually occur only 98 times, since we've already specified two arguments and the maximum number is 100.

to create files split at some arbitrary line numbers. In that example, the new file *xx00* will have lines 1–49 (49 lines total), *xx01* will have lines 50–372 (323 lines total), *xx02* will have lines 373–954 (582 lines total), and *xx03* will hold the rest of *stuff*.

csplit works like *split* if you repeat the argument. The command:

```
% csplit top_ten_list 10 "{18}"
```

breaks the list into 19 segments of 10 lines each.*

—DG

36.09 *Hacking on Characters with tr*

The *tr* command is a character translation filter, reading standard input and either deleting specific characters or substituting one character for another.

The most common use of *tr* is to change each character in one string to the corresponding character in a second string. (A string of consecutive ASCII *(53.03)* characters can be represented as a hyphen-separated range.)

For example, the command:

```
$ tr "A-Z" "a-z" < file
```
                                              BSD version

will convert all uppercase characters in *file* to the equivalent lowercase characters. The result is printed on standard output.

In the System V version of *tr*, square brackets must surround any range of characters. That is, you have to say: [a-z] instead of simply a-z. And of course, because square brackets are meaningful to the shell, you must protect them from interpretation by putting the string in quotes.

The System V version also has one other nice feature: the syntax [a*n], where *n* is some digit, means that the string should consist of *n* repetitions of character "a." If *n* isn't specified, or is 0, it is taken to be some indefinitely large number. This is useful if you don't know how many characters might be included in the first string.

As described in article 31.22, this translation (and the reverse) can be useful from within *vi* for translating a string. You can also delete specific characters. The −*d* option deletes from the input each occurrence of one or more characters specified in a string (special characters should be placed within quotation marks to protect them from the shell). For instance, the following command passes to standard output the contents of *file* with all punctuation deleted [and is a great exercise in shell quoting *(9.10)*—*JP*]:

```
$ tr -d ",.!?;:'"'"'`' < file
```

---

*Not really. The first file contains only nine lines (1-9); the rest contain 10. In this case, you're better off saying split -10 top_ten_list.

The –s (*squeeze*) option of *tr* removes multiple consecutive occurrences of the same character. For example, the command:

```
$ tr -s " " < file
```

will print on standard output a copy of *file* in which multiple spaces in sequence have been replaced with a single space.

We've also found *tr* useful when converting documents created on other systems for use under UNIX. For example, as described in article 1.05, *tr* can be used to change the carriage returns at the end of each line in a Macintosh text file into the newline UNIX expects. *tr* allows you to specify characters as octal values by preceding the value with a backslash, so the command:

```
$ tr '\015' '\012' < file.mac > file.unix
```

does the trick.

The command:

```
$  tr -d '\015' < pc.file
```

will remove the carriage return from the carriage return/newline pair that a PC file uses as a line terminator. (This command is also handy for removing the excess carriage returns from a file created with *script (53.05)*.)

Article 30.11 uses *tr* to split sentences into words.

—*TOR* from *UNIX Text Processing*, Hayden Books, 1987

36.10 *Converting Between ASCII and EBCDIC*

The first time I was handed an EBCDIC tape, I discovered the wonders of *dd*. It is great for reading tapes generated on non-UNIX systems.

You do need to understand a bit about the blocking factors on the foreign tape *(21.06)*, but once you've got that down, you can handle just about anything.

For example, to read an EBCDIC tape on tape device */dev/rmt0* and convert it to ASCII, putting the output in file *was_ibm*:

```
% dd if=/dev/rmt0 of=was_ibm ibs=800 cbs=80 conv=ascii
```

dd reads standard input and writes to standard output, but if you want to specify file or device names, you can use the fairly non-standard *if=* and *of=* options to specify the input file and output file, respectively.

If you wanted to convert the other way, you could use this command:

```
% dd if=was_unix of=/dev/rmt0 obs=800 cbs=80 conv=ebcdic
```

There's also a *conv=ibm* option, which uses a different ASCII to EBCDIC conversion table. According to the *dd* manual page, "The ASCII/EBCDIC conversion tables are taken from the 256 character standard in the CACM Nov, 1968. The ibm conversion, while less blessed as a standard, corresponds better to certain IBM print train conventions. There is no universal solution."

Some gotchas:

- You need to be able to read the raw device *(21.03)* to do the conversion, since the tape probably doesn't use standard UNIX tape block sizes.

- You need to know the blocking factor of the foreign tape, so you can tell *dd* about it.

- If the foreign tape has multiple files on it, you'll have to use the tape device name that allows "no rewind on close" *(21.03)* to read past the first file.

One last thing to mention about *dd*: all options that refer to sizes expect counts in bytes, unless otherwise mentioned. However, you can use keyletters to indicate various types of multiplication: *k* means to multiply by 1024; *b* to multiply by 512 (a block); and *w* to multiply by 4 (word). You can also show an arbitrary multiplication by separating two numbers with an *x*.

—TOR

36.11 Other Conversions with dd

Besides converting between ASCII and EBCDIC *(36.10)*, you can use *dd* to convert:

- fixed length to variable-length records (*conv=unblock*), and the reverse (*conv=block*)

- uppercase to lowercase (*conv=lcase*), and the reverse (*conv=ucase*)

- the byte order of every pair of bytes (*conv=swab*)

The `cbs=` option must be used to specify a conversion buffer size when using *block* and *unblock*. (This is also true when using conversions between ASCII and EBCDIC.) The specified number of characters are put into the conversion buffer. For *ascii* and *unblock* conversion, trailing blanks are trimmed and a newline is added to each buffer before it is output. For *ebcdic*, *ibm*, and *block*, the input is padded with blanks up to the specified conversion buffer size.

—TOR

36.12 Cutting Columns or Fields with cut

cut+paste

System V includes a nifty command called *cut* that lets you select a list of columns or fields from one or more files. We've also included a public-domain version on the disk, for those of you whose systems do without.

You must specify either the *−c* option to cut by column or *−f* to cut by fields. (Fields are separated by tabs unless you specify a different field separator with *−d*. Use quotes *(9.10)* if you want a space or other special character as the delimiter.)

The column(s) or field(s) to cut must follow the option immediately, without any space. Use a comma between separate values and a hyphen to specify a range (e.g., 1–10, 15, 20, or 50–).

cut is incredibly handy. Here are a couple of examples:

- Find out who is logged in, but list only login names:

who *53.04*

```
% who | cut -d" " -f1
```

- Extract usernames and real names from */etc/passwd (37.03):*

```
% cut -d: -f1,5 /etc/passwd
```

- Cut characters in the fourth column of *file*, and paste them back as the first column in the same file:

paste *36.16*

```
% cut -c4 file | paste - file
```

—TOR, DG

36.13 *Cutting Columns with colrm*

BSD's (somewhat limited) alternative to *cut (36.12)* is *colrm*.

It can cut only by column position, not by field. All you have to give it is a starting column position and an optional ending position. The text is read from standard input. (*colrm* can't read files directly; redirect input with < or | *(14.01)*.)

If you give just one column number, all columns from that position to the end of the line are removed. With two column number arguments, all columns between the starting column position and the ending position, inclusive, are removed.

The following command will print just the permissions (columns 1 to 10) and filenames (columns 45 to the end of the line, including the space before names) from BSD *ls –l* output *(23.02)*:

```
% ls -l | colrm 11 44
drwxr-xr-x manpages
-rw-r--r-- misc.Z
-rwxr-xr-x myhead
```

The following command will remove the remote hostname, if any, that starts at column 33 of *who (53.04)* output:

```
% who | colrm 33
```

—JP, TOR

36.14 Make Columns Automatically with cols

cols

If the output from some program runs down the left-hand side of your screen and takes more than one screen to display, you can pipe the program output to a pager *(26.03, 26.04)*. If the lines of text are short, you can see more of that text on the screen at once by reformatting the text into columns. The *pr* command can make columns *(36.15)*. But it's not easy to use if you want the input text to be ordered down a column instead of across columns. And it's tough to use if you want as many columns as will fit across your screen—you have to find the widest piece of data before you can figure each column's width.

Some UNIX systems have a program specifically for making data into columns—but many don't. The *cols* script takes care of that. It reads your text, finds the widest piece, and chooses *pr* options to make as many columns as will fit on the screen. *cols* also has seven other names—links *(19.03)* named *c2, c3, c4, c5, c6, c7,* and *c8*—that make output in 2, 3, 4, 5, 6, 7, or 8 columns. If you call the script with one of those names, it will fill the screen with that number of columns.

For example, to list misspelled words in columns:

```
% spell somefile | cols
word1    word2    word3    word4    word5    word6    word7    word8
word9    word10   word11   word12   word13   word14   word15   word16
```

Without the *−d* option, like the example above, *cols* and the others order the input words across the screen; that's the fastest way. If you need output going down each column, use the *−d* option. Then the scripts will calculate column length and order items down the screen:

```
% spell somefile | cols -d
word1    word3    word5    word7    word9    word11   word13   word15
word2    word4    word6    word8    word10   word12   word14   word16
```

The script will read from files you name; otherwise it reads standard input. It figures your screen width from the *COLUMNS* environment variable if it's set; otherwise, it calls *tcap (43.10)* to read your *termcap*. (On *terminfo* systems, use *tput (43.10)* instead of *tcap*.) If you use a windowing system with adjustable-width windows, the script could be hacked to check the output of *stty size*.

A few programming details: the number of columns, *nc*, is taken from the script name (*c2*, etc.)—or, if you call *cols*, the script uses *awk (38.01)* to find the longest input line and calculate the number of columns. (A *case* structure *(46.05)* tests $0 *(46.21)* to decide.) *expr (47.28)* does other calculations. Without the *−d* flag, the *pr* command line for making the columns is simple:

```
pr -$nc -t -w$width -l1 $temp
```

The $temp file holds the input text. With *−d*, the command line is more complicated. It uses *wc −l (30.06)* to count the number of input lines, then *expr* to divide by the number of columns and add 1:

```
pr -$nc -t -w$width -l`expr \( \`wc -l < $temp\` / $nc \) + 1` $temp
```

The escaped backquotes (\\`) mean that wc -l < $temp will run first. The line count from *wc* will be substituted onto the *expr* command line. The result from *expr* will be glued after the -1 to complete the *pr* page length option. If you don't like condensing the command line that much, you can move the *wc* and *expr* commands to other lines and pass the values with shell variables.

You can install this script from the Power Tools disk or from the online archive (54.07). If you get it from the archive, ask tar to install *cols* and its seven other links:

```
% tar xvf archive.tar cols c2 c3 c4 c5 c6 c7 c8
x cols, 2160 bytes, 5 tape blocks
c2 linked to cols
c3 linked to cols
   ...
```

—*JP*

36.15 Making Text in Columns with pr

The *pr* command is famous for printing a file neatly on a page—with margins at top and bottom, filename, date, and page numbers. It can also print text in columns: one file per column or many columns for each file.

The –*t* option takes away the heading and margins at the top and bottom of each page. That's useful when you want data "pasted" into columns with no interruptions.

One File per Column: –m

The –*m* option reads all files on the command line simultaneously and prints each in its own column, like this:

```
% pr -m file1 file2 file3

Nov  1 19:40 1992    Page 1

The lines           The lines           The lines
of file1            of file2            of file3
are here            are here            are here
   ...                 ...                 ...
```

One File, Several Columns: –number

An option that's a number will print a file in that number of columns. For instance, the –*3* option prints a file in three columns. The file is read, line by line, until the first column is full (by default, that takes 56 lines). Next, the second column is filled. Then, the third column is filled. If there's more of the file, the first column of page 2 is filled—and the cycle repeats:

```
% pr -3 file1

Nov  1 19:44 1992   file1   Page 1
```

```
Line 1 here          Line 57 here          Line 115 here
Line 2 here          Line 58 here          Line 116 here
Line 3 here          Line 59 here          Line 117 here
   ...                   ...                   ...
```

The columns aren't balanced—if the file will fit into one column, the other columns aren't used. You can change that by adjusting *–l*, the page length option; see the section below.

Order Lines Across Columns with –l

Do you want to arrange your data across the columns, so that the first three lines print across the top of each column, the next three lines are the second in each column, and so on, like this?

```
% pr -l1 -t -3 file1
Line 1 here          Line 2 here          Line 3 here
Line 4 here          Line 5 here          Line 6 here
Line 7 here          Line 8 here          Line 9 here
   ...                   ...                   ...
```

Use the *–l1* (page length 1 line) and *–t* (no title) options. Each "page" will be filled by three lines (or however many columns you set). You have to use *–t*; otherwise, *pr* will silently ignore any page lengths that don't leave room for the header and footer. That's just what you want if you want data in columns with no headings.

If you want headings too, pipe the output of *pr* through another *pr*:

```
% pr -l1 -t -3 file1 | pr -h file1

Nov  1 19:48 1992  file1  Page 1

Line 1 here          Line 2 here          Line 3 here
Line 4 here          Line 5 here          Line 6 here
Line 7 here          Line 8 here          Line 9 here
   ...                   ...                   ...
```

The `-h file1` puts the filename into the heading.

Also see *paste (36.16)* and *cols (36.14)*. Of course, programming languages like *awk (38.18)* and *perl (39.01)* can also make text into columns.

—JP

36.16 Pasting Things in Columns

cut+paste

Do you ever wish you could paste two (or even three) files side by side? You can, if you have the System V *paste* program (or the public-domain implementation on the disk).

For example, to create a three-column *file* from files *x*, *y*, and *z*:

```
$ paste x y z > file
```

To make *paste* read standard input, use the – option, and repeat – for every column you want. For example, to make an old broken System V *ls* (which lists files in a single column) list files in four columns:

```
$ ls | paste - - - -
```

The "standard input" option is also handy when used with *cut (36.12)*. You can cut data from one position on a line and paste it back on another.

The separate data streams being merged are separated by default with a tab, but you can change this with the *–d* option. Unlike the *–d* option to *cut*, you need not specify a single character; instead, you can specify a list of characters, which will be used in a circular fashion. (I haven't figured a use for this—maybe you can.)

The characters in the list can be any regular character or the following escape sequences:

```
\n    newline
\t    tab
\\    backslash
\0    empty string
```

Use quoting, if necessary, to protect characters from the shell.

There's also a *–s* option that lets you merge subsequent lines from one file. For example, to merge each pair of lines onto a single line:

```
$ paste -s -d"\t\n" list
```

—*TOR, DG*

36.17 Joining Lines with join

If you've worked with databases, you'll probably know what to do with the UNIX *join* command; see your online manual page. If you don't have a database (as far as you know!), you'll still probably have a use for *join*: combining or "joining" two column-format files. *join* searches certain columns in the files; when it finds columns that match each other, it "glues the lines together" at that column. This is easiest to show with an example.

I needed to summarize the information in thousands of e-mail messages under the MH mail system. MH made that easy: it has one command (*scan*) that gave me almost all the information I wanted about each message in the format I wanted. But I also had to use *wc –l (30.06)* to count the number of lines in each message. I ended up with two files, one with *scan* output and the other with *wc* output. One field in both lines was the message number; I used *sort (37.01)* to sort the files on that field. I used `awk '{print $1 "," $2}'` to massage *wc* output into comma-separated fields. Then I used *join* to "glue" the two lines together on the message-number field. (Next I fed the file to a PC running *dBASE*, but that's another story.)

Here's the file that I told *scan* to output. The columns (message number, e-mail address, comment, name, and date sent) are separated with commas (,):

```
0001,andrewe@isc.uci.edu,,Andy Ernbaum,19901219
0002,bc3170x@cornell.bitnet,,Zoe Doan,19910104
0003,zcode!postman@uunet.uu.net,,Head Honcho,19910105
   ...
```

Here's the file from *wc* and *awk* with the message number and number of lines:

```
0001,11
0002,5
0003,187
   ...
```

Then, this *join* command joined the two files at their first columns (-t, tells *join* that the fields are comma-separated):

```
% join -t, scanfile wcfile
```

The output file looked like:

```
0001,andrewe@isc.uci.edu,,Andy Ernbaum,19901219,11
0002,bc3170x@cornell.bitnet,,Zoe Doan,19910104,5
0003,zcode!postman@uunet.uu.net,,Head Honcho,19910105,187
   ...
```

Of course, *join* can do a lot more than this simple example shows. See your online manual page.

—*JP*

36.18 *Quick Reference: uniq*

uniq is used to remove duplicate adjacent lines from a sorted file, sending one copy of each line to standard output or to a second file, if one is specified on the command line. Be warned:

```
% uniq file1 file2
```

will not print the unique lines from both *file1* and *file2* to standard output! It will replace the contents of *file2* with the unique lines from *file1*. *uniq* is often used as a filter *(1.30)*. See also *comm (29.11)* and *sort (37.01)*.

options

    -c   Print each line once, counting instances of each.

-d	Print duplicate lines once, but no unique lines.
-u	Print only unique lines (no copy of duplicate entries is kept).
-n	Ignore first *n* fields of a line. Fields are separated by spaces or by tabs.
+n	Ignore first *n* characters of a field.

You can specify only one of the options **-c**, **-d**, or **-u**.

Examples

To send only one copy of each line from **list** to output file **list.new**:

```
uniq list list.new
```

To show which names appear more than once:

```
sort names | uniq -d
```

To show which lines appear exactly three times:

grep 28.01

```
sort names | uniq -c | grep " 3 "
```

—*DG* from the Nutshell Handbook *UNIX in a Nutshell (SVR4/Solaris)*

36.19 *Using IFS to Split Strings*

It might not be obvious why the Bourne shell has an *IFS* (internal field separator) shell variable. By default, it holds three characters: SPACE, TAB, and NEWLINE. These are the places that the shell parses command lines. So what?

If you have a line of text—say, from a database—and you want to split it into fields, the *IFS* variable can help. Put the field separator into *IFS* temporarily, use the shell's *set* (46.18) command to store the fields in command-line parameters; then restore the old *IFS*.

For example, the chunk of a shell script below gets the UID number for the user *nathan*. In the next-to-last line, *grep* grabs *nathan's* entry from */etc/passwd*, which looks like this:

```
nathan::128:100:Nathan Hale:/home/nathan:/bin/csh
```

The shell parses the line returned from *grep* by the backquotes (10.14). It stores *x* in $1. This trick stops errors if *grep* fails for some reason—without the *x*, if *grep* made no standard output, the shell's *set* command would print a list of all shell variables. Then *nathan* goes into $2, an empty field* into $3, and so on:

```
who=nathan
oldifs="$IFS"
# Change IFS to a colon:
IFS=:
# Put x in $1, username in $2, password in $3, UID in $4, etc.:
set x `grep "^${who}:" /etc/passwd`
IFS="$oldifs"
```

---

*Nathan has a password; it's in the system's "shadow password" file.

Because you don't need a subprocess to parse the output of *grep*, this can be faster than using an external command like *cut (36.12)* or *awk (38.18)*. (Of course, using *sed*'s escaped parentheses *(35.10)* to do the searching and the parsing may be faster and easier.)

—JP

36.20 *Straightening Jagged Columns*

As we were writing this book, I decided to make a list of all the articles, the numbers of lines and characters in each—then combine that with the description, a status code, and the article's title. After a few minutes with *wc –l –c* *(30.06)*, *cut (36.12)*, *sort (37.01)*, and *join (36.17)*, I had a file that looked like this:

```
% cat messfile
2850 2095 51441 ~BB A sed tutorial
3120 868 21259 +BB mail - lots of basics
6480 732 31034 + How to find sources - JIK's periodic posting
    ...900 lines...
5630 14 453 +JP Running Commands on Directory Stacks
1600 12 420 !JP With find, Don't Forget -print
0495 9 399 + Make 'xargs -i' use more than one filename
```

Yuck. It was tough to read. The columns needed to be straightened. A little *awk* *(38.18)* script turned the mess into this:

```
% cat cleanfile
2850 2095   51441 ~BB  A sed tutorial
3120  868   21259 +BB  mail - lots of basics
6480  732   31034 +     How to find sources - JIK's periodic posting
     ...900 lines...
5630   14     453 +JP  Running Commands on Directory Stacks
1600   12     420 !JP  With find, Don't Forget -print
0495    9     399 +     Make 'xargs -i' use more than one filename
```

Here's the simple script I used and the command I typed to run it:

```
% cat neatcols
{
printf "%4s %4s %6s %-4s %s\n", \
    $1, $2, $3, $4, substr($0, index($0,$5))
}
% awk -f neatcols messfile > cleanfile
```

You can adapt that script for whatever kinds of columns you need to clean up. In case you don't know *awk*, here's a quick summary:

- The first line of the *printf*, between double quotes (`"`), tells the field widths and alignments. For example, the first column should be right-aligned in 4 characters (`%4s`). The fourth column should be 4 characters wide left-adjusted (`%-4s`). The fifth column is big enough to just fit (`%s`). I used string (`%s`) instead of decimal (`%d`) so *awk* wouldn't strip off the leading zeros in the columns.

- The second line arranges the input data fields onto the output line. Here, input and output are in the same order, but I could have reordered them. The first four columns get the first four fields ($1, $2, $3, $4,).

The fifth column is a catch-all; it gets everything else. substr($0, index($0,$5)) means "find the fifth input column; print it and everything after it." That trick works only if you're sure that the first word in the fifth column could never be repeated in one of the columns before it.

—*JP*

36.21 *Rotating Text*

Every now and then you come across something and say, "Gee, that might come in handy someday, but I have no idea for what." This might happen to you when you're browsing at a flea market or garage sale; or if you're like us, it might happen when you're browsing through public domain software.

Which brings us to the *rot* program. *rot* basically just rotates text columns and rows. For example, if you have the following input file:

rot

```
abcde
1
2
3
4
5
```

rot will rotate the text 90 degrees, to produce:

```
54321
       a
       b
       c
       d
       e
```

What is this useful for? Well, *rot* can be used to apply programs like *sed (35.24)* or *grep (28.01)* on columns instead of rows. After scratching my head for awhile, I came up with an example—a contrived one, alas, but it may suggest a real application to some inspired or desperate reader. Suppose you have a series of files containing lists like the following:

```
a  is for Apples
b  is for Balloons
c  is for Cats
d  is for Donkeys
e  is for Egrep
     ...
```

and you decide that you'd rather use uppercase letters at the beginning of lines instead of lowercase letters. One possibility is to just manually edit each file. In *vi*, this is a fairly straightforward global substitution:

```
:%s/^[a-z]/\U&/
```

But for the sake of argument, let's say that there are too many files to make using *vi* practical. You could use an *ex (31.02)* script, but you're stubborn and want to use *sed* (so you have an excuse for trying *rot!*). *sed* doesn't support those handy \U and \L escape sequences for changing the case in a substitute command. And since you need to make sure the letter is substituted only as the first character on each line, you can't use a global transform (*y*) *(35.12)* command. Instead, you have to write a separate *sed* command for each letter:

```
s/^a/A/
s/^b/B/
    ...
```

This may not be a giant investment in time, but there's got to be a better way. As you might guess, you can solve this problem using *rot*. Since you know that all the characters you want to change are in the first column, you can write a shell script like this:

```
for file
do
    rot $file |
    sed '1 y/abcdefghijklmnopqrstuvwxyz/ABCDEFGHIJKLMNOPQRSTUVWXYZ/' |
    rot -r > $file.done
done
```

Here we use *rot* to rotate the columns into rows, and then we call *sed* on the first line, which is actually the first column. We use the *sed* y command to translate all the lowercase letters into their uppercase equivalents. After *sed* is completed, we use *rot* again with the *-r* option to reverse the direction of the rotation and revert the file to its original orientation. The resulting file reads:

```
A  is for Apples
B  is for Balloons
C  is for Cats
D  is for Donkeys
E  is for Egrep
    ...
```

—LM

37

Sorting

37.01 *Putting Things in Order*

Sorting a file under UNIX is easy, right? Of course it is, if all you want to do is sort a list of single words, or sort lines starting with the first character in the line. But if you want to do more than that, there's a lot more to the *sort* command than typing:

> `% sort filename`

- Article 37.02 describes how to select individual fields from a line for *sort* to operate on.

- Article 37.03 describes how to change the field delimiter from "white space" to some other character.

- Article 37.04 describes the kinds of problems that you can encounter if fields *are* delimited by white space.

- Article 37.05 clarifies the distinctions between alphabetic and numeric sorting.

- Article 37.06 gives miscellaneous hints about useful *sort* options.

But learning the mechanics of *sort* isn't the end of the story. Like most of the other things you'll find in the UNIX toolbox, *sort* is even more powerful when it's used with other programs. For example, you can:

- Sort paragraphs, or other multi-line entries (article 37.07).

- Sort lines by how long they are (article 37.08).

- Sort a list of names by last name, whether or not there's a middle name as well (article 37.09).

—TOR

37.02 Sort Fields: How sort Sorts

Unless you tell it otherwise, *sort* divides each line into fields at white space (blanks or tabs), and sorts the lines, by field, from left to right.

That is, it sorts on the basis of field 0 (leftmost); but when the leftmost fields are the same, it sorts on the basis of field 1; and so on. This is hard to put into words, but it's really just common sense. Suppose your office inventory manager created a file like this:

```
supplies    pencils   148
furniture   chairs    40
kitchen     knives    22
kitchen     forks     20
supplies    pens      236
furniture   couches   10
furniture   tables    7
supplies    paper     29
```

You'd want all the supplies sorted into categories and within each category, you'd want them sorted alphabetically:

```
% sort supplies
furniture   chairs    40
furniture   couches   10
furniture   tables    7
kitchen     forks     20
kitchen     knives    22
supplies    paper     29
supplies    pencils   148
supplies    pens      236
```

Of course, you don't always want to sort from left to right. The command line option +*n* tells *sort* to start sorting on field *n*; −*n* tells *sort* to stop sorting on field *n*. Remember (again) that *sort* counts fields from left to right, starting with 0.* Here's an example. We want to sort a list of telephone numbers of authors, presidents, and blues singers:

```
Robert M Johnson     344-0909
Lyndon B Johnson     933-1423
Samuel H Johnson     754-2542
Michael K Loukides   112-2535
Jerry O Peek         267-2345
Timothy F O'Reilly   443-2434
```

According to standard "telephone book rules," we want these names sorted by last name, first name, and middle initial. We don't want the phone number to play a part in the sorting. So we want to start sorting on field 2, stop sorting on field 3, continue sorting on field 0, sort on field 1, and (just to make sure) stop sorting on field 2 (the last name). We can code this as follows:

```
% sort +2 -3 +0 -2 phonelist
Lyndon B Johnson     933-1423
```

---

*I harp on this because I always get confused and have to look it up in the manual page.

```
Robert M Johnson      344-0909
Samuel H Johnson      754-2542
Michael K Loukides    112-2535
Timothy F O'Reilly    443-2434
Jerry O Peek          267-2345
```

A few notes:

- We need the −3 option to prevent *sort* from sorting on the telephone number after sorting on the last name. Without −3, the "Robert Johnson" entry would appear before "Lyndon Johnson" because it has a lower phone number.

- We don't need to state +1 explicitly. Unless you give an explicit "stop" field, +1 is implied after +0.

- If two names are completely identical, we probably don't care what happens next. However, just to be sure that something unexpected doesn't take place, we end the option list with −2, which says, "After sorting on the middle initial, don't do any further sorting."

There are a couple of variations that are worth mentioning. You may never need them unless you're really serious about sorting data files, but it's good to keep them in the back of your mind. First, you can add any "collation" operations (discard blanks, numeric sort, etc.) to the end of a field specifier to describe how you want that field sorted. Using our previous example, let's say that if two names *are* identical, you want them sorted in numeric phone number order. The following command does the trick:

```
% sort +2 -3 +0 -2 +3n phonelist
```

The +3n option says "do a numeric sort on the fourth field." If you're worried about initial blanks (perhaps some of the phone numbers have area codes), use +3nb.

Second, you can specify individual columns within any field for sorting, using the notation +n.c, where n is a field number, and c is a character position within the field. Likewise, the notation −n.c says "stop sorting at the character before character c." If you're counting characters, be sure to use the −b (ignore white space) option—otherwise, it will be very difficult to figure out what character you're counting.

—*ML*

37.03 *Changing the Field Delimiter*

Article 37.02 explained how *sort* separates a line of input into two or more fields using "white space" (spaces or tabs) as field delimiters. The *–t* option lets you change the field delimiter to some other character.

For example, if you wanted to sort the login names on your system by the login shell they use, you could issue a command like this:

/etc..wd *37.03*

```
% sort -t: +6 /etc/passwd
root:SndEKOs9H7YLm:0:1:Operator:/:/bin/csh
sys:*:2:2::/:/bin/csh
jim:LjKwcUt816kZK:2391:1004:Jim O'Callahan:/u/jim:/bin/csh
    ...
bart:2DPD8rCOKBbUu:2665:1004:Bart Buus:/u/bart:/bin/tcsh
tap:xY7oeuJ8WxyGO:2943:1004:Tap Bronman:/u/tap:/bin/tcsh
```

The option *–t:* tells *sort* to use a colon as a field separator—so, in this example, field 0 is the login name, field 1 is the encoded password, field 2 is the user ID number, field 3 is the group ID number, and so on. By this numbering, the login shell is in the sixth field.

Remember that *sort* numbers fields starting with zero—this will save you lots of grief. Two consecutive colons indicate a "null" field that still must be counted.

—ML, TOR

37.04 *Confusion with White Space Field Delimiters*

One would hope that a simple task like sorting would be relatively unambiguous. Unfortunately, it isn't. The behavior of. *sort* can be very puzzling. I'll try to straighten out some of the confusion—at the same time, I'll be leaving myself open to abuse by the real *sort* experts. I hope you appreciate this! Seriously, though: if we find any new wrinkles to the story, we'll add them in the next edition.

The trouble with *sort* is figuring out where one field ends and another begins. It's simplest if you can specify an explicit field delimiter *(37.03)*. This makes it easy to tell where fields end and begin. But by default, *sort* uses white space characters (tabs and spaces) to separate fields, and the rules for interpreting white space field delimiters are unfortunately complicated. As I see them, here they are:

* The first white space character you encounter is a "field delimiter"; it marks the end of the old field and the beginning of the next field.

* Any white space character following a field delimiter is *part of* the new field. That is—if you have two or more white space characters in a row, the first one is used as a field delimiter, and isn't sorted. The remainder *are* sorted, as part of the next field.

- Every field has at least one non-whitespace character, unless you're at the end of the line. (That is: null fields only occur when you've reached the end of a line.)

- All white space is not equal. Sorting is done according to the ASCII *(53.03)* collating sequence. Therefore, TABs are sorted before spaces.

Here is a silly but instructive example that demonstrates most of the hard cases. We'll sort the file *sortme*, which is:

```
        apple   Fruit shipment
20      beta    beta test sites
 5              Something or other
```

All is not as it seems— *cat −t −v (26.06, 26.07)* shows that the file really looks like this:

```
^Iapple^IFruit shipment
20^Ibeta^Ibeta test sites
 5^I^ISomething or other
```

^I indicates a tab character. Before showing you what *sort* does with this file, let's break it into fields, being very careful to apply the rules above. In the table, we use quotes to show exactly where each field begins and ends:

Field	0	1	2	3
Line				
1	"^Iapple"	"Fruit"	"shipment"	null (no more data)
2	"20"	"beta"	"beta"	"test"
3	" 5"	"^Isomething"	"or"	"other"

OK, now let's try some *sort* commands; I've added annotations on the right, showing what character the "sort" was based on. First, we'll sort on field zero—that is, the first field in each line:

```
% sort sortme               sort on field zero
        apple   Fruit shipments       field 0, first character: TAB
 5              Something or other     field 0, first character: SPACE
20      beta    beta test sites        field 0, first character: 2
```

As I noted earlier, a TAB precedes a space in the collating sequence. Everything is as expected. Now let's try another, this time sorting on field 1 (the second field):

```
% sort +1 sortme            sort on field 1
 5              Something or other     field 1, first character: TAB
        apple   Fruit shipments       field 1, first character: F
20      beta    beta test sites        field 1, first character: b
```

Again, the initial TAB causes "something or other" to appear first. "Fruit shipments" preceded "beta" because in the ASCII table, uppercase letters precede lowercase letters. Now, let's sort on the next field:

```
% sort +2 sortme          sort on field 2
20    beta    beta test sites      field 2, first character: b
 5            Something or other    field 2, first character: o
      apple   Fruit shipments       field 2, first character: s
```

No surprises here. And finally, sort on field 3 (the "fourth" field):

```
% sort +3 sortme          sort on field 3
      apple   Fruit shipments       field 3:  NULL
 5            Something or other     field 3, first character: o
20    beta    beta test sites       field 3, first character: t
```

The only surprise here is that the NULL field gets sorted first. That's really no surprise, though: NULL has the ASCII value zero, so we should expect it to come first.

OK, this was a silly example. But it was a difficult one; a casual understanding of what sort "ought to do" won't explain any of these cases. Which leads to another point. If someone tells you to sort some terrible mess of a data file, you could be heading for a nightmare. But often, you're not just sorting; you're also *designing* the data file you want to sort. If you get to design the format for the input data, a little bit of care will save you lots of headaches. If you have a choice, *never* allow tabs in the file. And be careful of leading spaces; a word with an extra space before it will be sorted *before* other words. Therefore, use an explicit delimiter between fields (like a colon), or use the −b option (and an explicit sort field), which tells *sort* to ignore initial white space.

—ML

37.05 Alphabetic and Numeric Sorting

sort performs two fundamentally different kinds of sorting operations: alphabetic sorts and numeric sorts. An alphabetic sort is performed according to the traditional "dictionary order," using the ASCII *(53.03)* collating sequence. Uppercase letters come before lowercase letters (unless you specify the −f option, which "folds" uppercase and lowercase together), with numerals and punctuation interspersed.

This is all fairly trivial and common-sense. However, it's worth belaboring the difference, because it's a frequent source of bugs in shell scripts. Say you sort the numbers 1 through 12. A numeric sort gives you these numbers "in order," just like you'd expect. An alphabetic sort gives you:

```
1
11
12
2
...
```

Of course, this is how you'd sort the numbers if you applied dictionary rules to the list. Numeric sorts can handle decimal numbers (for example, numbers like 123.44565778); they can't handle floating-point numbers (for example, 1.2344565778E+02).

What happens if you include alphabetic characters in a numeric sort? Although the results are predictable, I would prefer to say that they're "undefined." Including alphabetic characters in a numeric sort is a mistake, and there's no guarantee that different versions of *sort* will handle them the same way. As far as I know, there is no provision for sorting hexadecimal numbers.

One final note: Under System V, the numeric sort treats initial blanks as significant—so numbers with additional spaces before them will be sorted ahead of numbers without the additional spaces. This is an incredibly stupid misfeature. There is a workaround; use the *−b* (ignore leading blanks) and always specify a sort field.* That is: `sort -nb +0` will do what you expect; `sort -n` won't.

—ML

37.06 Miscellaneous sort Hints

Here is a grab-bag of useful, if not exactly interesting, *sort* features. The utility will actually do quite a bit, if you let it.

Dealing with Repeated Lines

sort −u sorts the file and eliminates duplicate lines. It's more powerful than *uniq (36.18)* because:

- It sorts the file for you; *uniq* assumes that the file is already sorted, and won't do you any good if it isn't.

- It is much more flexible. *sort −u* considers lines "unique" if the sort fields *(37.02)* you've selected match. So the lines don't even have to be (strictly speaking) unique; differences outside of the sort fields are ignored.

In return, there are a few things that *uniq* does that *sort* won't do—like print only those lines that aren't repeated, or count the number of times each line is repeated. But on the whole, I find *sort −u* more useful.

Here's one idea for using *sort −u*. When I was writing a manual, I often needed to make tables of error messages. The easiest way to do this was to *grep* the source code for *printf* statements; write some Emacs *(33.01)* macros to eliminate junk that I didn't care about; use *sort −u* to put the messages in order and get rid of duplicates; and write some more Emacs macros to format the error messages into a table. All I had to do was write the descriptions.

---

*Stupid misfeature number 2: *−b* doesn't work unless you specify a sort field explicitly, with a *+n* option.

Ignoring Blanks

One important option (that I've mentioned a number of times) is *−b*; this tells *sort* to ignore extra white space at the beginning of each field. This is absolutely essential; otherwise, your sorts will have rather strange results. In my opinion, *−b* should be the default. But they didn't ask me.

Another thing to remember about *−b*: It only works if you explicitly specify which fields you want to sort. By itself, *sort −b* is the same as *sort*: white space characters are counted. I call this a bug, don't you?

Case-insensitive Sorts

If you don't care about the difference between uppercase and lowercase letters, invoke *sort* with the *−f* (case-fold) option. This treats uppercase and lowercase letters identically.

A quick inspection of *sort*'s output shows that *sort −f* treats all letters as if they were lowercase; that is, numbers come before letters in the collating sequence.

Dictionary Order

The *−d* option tells *sort* to ignore all characters except for letters, digits, and white space. In particular, *sort −d* ignores punctuation.

Month Order

The *−M* option tells *sort* to treat the first three non-blank characters of a field as a three-letter month abbreviation, and to sort accordingly. That is, JAN comes before FEB, which comes before MAR. This option isn't available on all versions of UNIX.

Reverse Sort

The *−r* option tells *sort* to "reverse" the order of the sort; i.e., Z comes before A, 9 comes before 1, and so on. You'll find that this option is really useful. For example, imagine you have a program running in the background that records the number of free blocks in the filesystem at midnight each night. Your log file might look like this:

```
Jan 1 1992:  108 free blocks
Jan 2 1992:  308 free blocks
Jan 3 1992: 1232 free blocks
Jan 4 1992:   76 free blocks
...
```

The script below finds the smallest and largest number of free blocks in your log file:

```
#!/bin/sh
echo "Minimum free blocks"
sort -t: +1nb  logfile | head -1
```

head *26.21*

```
echo "Maximum free blocks"
sort -t: +1nbr logfile | head -1
```

It's not profound, but it's an example of what you can do.

—ML

37.07 *Sorting Multi-line Entries*

There's one limitation to *sort*. It works a line at a time. If you want to sort a file with multi-line entries, you're in tough shape. For example, let's say you have a list of addresses:

```
Doe, John and Jane
30 Anywhere St
Anytown, New York
10023


Buck, Jane and John
40 Anywhere St
Nowheresville, Alaska
90023
```

chunksort

How would you sort these? Certainly not with *sort*—whatever you do, you'll end up with a mish-mash of unmatched addresses, names, and zip codes. Here's a tool, called *chunksort*, that will do the trick:

echo..1' 47.34

```
#! /bin/sh
###     chunksort - sort multi-line records (separated by single blank lines)
###     Usage: chunksort [-a] [sort options] [files]
ctrla=`echo a | tr a '\001'`
files=""
sortopts=""

# parse command line:
while :
do
        case "$1" in
        "")    # out of arguments (we hope...)
               break  ;;
        -a)    # use ctrl-a as sort field separator (so can pick which line of
               # the record to sort on -- for example, +1 to sort on line 2):
               sortopts="$sortopts -t$ctrla" ;;
        -o)    # we can't pass -o to sort because user would get wrong output:
               echo "`basename $0` quitting: I don't have a -o option." 1>&2
               exit 1 ;;
        -[Tyz]) # these options to 'sort' have an argument after them.
               sortopts="$sortopts $1 $2"
               shift  ;; # get rid of one (we'll do other below)
        [-+]*)  # some other option or sort field:
               sortopts="$sortopts $1";;
        *)      # IT'S A FILENAME (WE HOPE...)
               files="$files $1" ;;
        esac
        shift
done
```

```
# completely empty lines separate records.
# the $ctrla is not quoted, so shell substitutes it:
sed -n '
/^$/ {
        x
        s/'$ctrla'$//
        p
        b
}
H
g
s/\n//
s/$/'$ctrla'/
h' $files |
sort $sortopts |
sed "
s/$ctrla/\\
/g
G"
```

The script starts with a lot of option processing—it's incredibly thorough, and allows you to use any *sort* options, except *−o*. [Jerry wrote this script; my own version isn't anywhere near as complete.*—ML*] It also adds a new *−a* option, which allows you to sort based on different lines of a multi-line entry. Say you're sorting an address file, and the street address is on the second line of each entry. The command `chunksort −a +3` would sort the file based on the zip codes. I'm not sure if this is really useful (you can't, for example, sort on the third field of the second line), but it's a nice bit of additional functionality.

The body of the script (after the option processing) is conceptually simple. It uses *sed* (35.24) to collapse each multi-line record into a single line, with the CTRL-a character to mark where the line breaks were. After this processing, a few addresses from a typical address list might look like this:

```
Doe, John and Jane^A30 Anywhere St^AAnytown, New York^A10023
Buck, Jane and John^A40 Anywhere St^ANowheresville, Alaska^A90023
```

Now that we've converted the original file into a list of one-line entries, we have something that *sort* can handle. So we just use *sort*, with whatever options were supplied on the command line. After sorting, another *sed* script "unpacks" this single-line representation, restoring the file to its original form.

There are lots of interesting variations on this script. You can substitute *grep* for the *sort* command, allowing you to search for multi-line entries—for example, to look up addresses in an address file. This would require slightly different option processing, but the script would be essentially the same.

Finally, it's worth pointing out some shell tricks that should be in your toolchest. First, note the use of *echo* and *tr* to shove CTRL-a into a shell variable. This is a good, portable way to use control characters within shell scripts without sticking non-printable characters into the file. Second, note the careful use of single and double quotes within the *sed* scripts. These allow the shell to expand the variable $crtla properly, without interfering with *sed*—which also wants to use $ as a special character. And finally—note Jerry's careful command-line processing. Yes, it's a pain to be so careful. But, in the long run, it gives you a much more useful script.

—JP, ML

37.08 lensort: Sort Lines by Length

A nice little script to sort lines from shortest to longest can be handy when you're writing and want to find your big words:

deroff 30.11
uniq 36.18

```
% deroff -w report | uniq -d | lensort
a
an
  ...
deoxyribonucleic
```

Once I used it to sort a list of pathnames:

find 18.01

```
% find adir -type f -print | lensort
adir/.x
adir/.temp
  ...
adir/subdir/part1/somefile
adir/subdir/part1/a_test_case
```

The script uses *awk* *(38.18)* to print each line's length and a TAB before the line. Next, *sort* sorts the lengths numerically *(37.05)*. Then *sed* *(35.24)* strips off the lengths and the TABs—and prints the lines:

lensort

```
#! /bin/sh
awk '{ printf "%d\t%s\n", length($0), $0 }' |
sort +0n -1 |
sed 's/^[0-9][0-9]*TAB//'
```

—JP

37.09 Sorting a List of People by Last Name

It's hard to sort any old list of peoples' names because some people have one-word first and last names like Joe Smith, but other people have multi-part names like Mary Jo Appleton. This program handles all sorts of names; it sorts on the last word in each name. That won't take care of the way that names are used everywhere in the world, but it might give you some ideas . . .

The script reads from a file or its standard input; it writes to standard output.

namesort

```
#! /bin/sh
# awk script that reverses fields:
awkscr='BEGIN {
    IFS = " "
}
{
    for (n = NF; n > 1; n--)
        printf "%s ", $n
    print $1
```

```
}'
# reverse fields, then sort, then reverse fields again:
awk "
$awkscr
" $1 |
sort |
awk "
$awkscr
"
```

—*JP*

37.10 *Handling Sequentially Numbered Files*

I have a problem. You might call it VMS-envy. I like to save old, sequentially numbered copies of my files. For example, given *ch01.txt*, I might want to call the next version *ch01.2.txt*, the third version *ch01.3.txt*, and so on. I could explain at some length why, for my particular application, RCS and SCCS *(21.12)* are less than ideal—but I'll spare you that insanity. Instead, I'll show you a script that's incredibly useful when you have a directory littered with files of this type. It's also a good example of some simple uses for *sort*.

Here's a listing of a slightly worse-than-average directory:

```
% ls *.txt
appb.txt       ch02.txt       ch04.txt       ch07.txt
bibliog.txt    ch03.2.txt     ch05.2.txt     ch08.2.txt
ch01.2.txt     ch03.3.txt     ch05.3.txt     gloss.txt
ch01.3.txt     ch03.4.txt     ch05.4.txt     optimized.2.txt
ch01.txt       ch03.txt       ch05.txt       optimized.3.txt
ch02.2.txt     ch04.2.txt     ch06.2.txt     optimized.txt
ch02.4.txt     ch04.3.txt     ch06.txt
ch02.5.txt     ch04.4.txt     ch07.3.txt
```

There are a lot of things you might want to do with these files, like:

- Print the current version of each file.

- Make a *tar* archive of the current version of each file.

- Move the current (i.e., highest numbered) version of each of them into a directory.

And so on. For any of these tasks, no matter how simple or how complicated, you need a list of the "current version" files. Here's a relatively simple script called *curver* that plods through a directory like this and writes a list of current files on standard output:

```
#!/bin/sh
# Given files  named name.txt through name.n.txt (n integer), print
# the filename with highest "n," or name.txt if no "n" versions exist.
#
# Get a list of relevant filename "bases," with all suffixes trimmed
basenames=`ls *.txt | sed -e 's/.[0-9]*//g; s/xt//g' | uniq`
# For each basename, use sort to find the one with highest "n"
```

for *46.15*

tail *26.16*

```
# echo $basenames   #testing only
for name in $basenames
do
        ls $name.*txt | sort -n -t. +1 -2 | tail -1
done
```

First, we find out what files we're actually dealing with: we strip all the suffixes, leaving a list like "ch01 ch01 ch01 ch02 ch02 ch03 ... " Then we use *uniq*(36.18) to squeeze out the duplicates, leaving us with the "bases" of the files we care about (ch01 ch02 ch03 ...).

Once we have a list of filename bases, we start another loop. For each base, we use *ls* to list all the files starting with that base. Then we use *sort* again. This time, we use a dot as the field delimiter, and do a numeric sort on the second field (+1 -2; remember that *sort* numbers fields beginning with zero). We then use *tail* to grab the last name in the list, which is the file with the highest sequence number.

So, running this script in the directory above produces the following:

```
% curver
ch01.3.txt
ch02.5.txt
ch03.4.txt
...
```

And, once you have this, it's easy to use *curver* within other commands. A few examples:

`..` *10.14*

```
% lpr `curver`
% tar c `curver`
% mkdir current; mv `curver` current
```

There are some obvious improvements to make: as presented, this script is hard-wired to look for *.txt* files, but that's certainly not necessary. A simple rewrite would allow you to supply the suffix as a command-line argument. An even better improvement might be to let you provide any command (on the command line) that produces a list of filenames. But these are "exercises left to the reader." As written, the script meets my needs.

By the way—99% of the time, RCS and SCCS are ideal for storing successive versions of text files. Take a good look at these utilities before coming up with a harebrained naming scheme like mine.

—*ML*

38

The awk Programming Language

38.01 A Pattern-matching Programming Language

awk, named after its developers, Aho, Weinberger, and Kernighan, is a programming language that permits easy manipulation of structured data and the generation of formatted reports.

Identifying *awk* as a programming language scares some people away from it. If you are one of these people, consider *awk* a different approach to problem solving, one in which you have a lot more control over what you want the computer to do.

sed is easily seen as the flip side of interactive editing. A *sed* procedure corresponds closely enough to how you would apply the editing commands manually. *sed* limits you to the methods you use in a text editor. *awk* offers a more general model for processing a file.

A typical example of an *awk* program is one that transforms data into a formatted report. The data might be a log file generated by a UNIX program such as *uucp (1.33)*, and the report might summarize the data in a format useful to a system administrator. Another example is a data processing application consisting of separate data entry and data retrieval programs. Data entry is the process of recording data in a structured way. Data retrieval is the process of extracting data from a file and generating a report.

The key to all of these operations is that the data has some kind of structure. Let me illustrate this by making the analogy to a bureau. A bureau consists of multiple drawers, and each drawer has a certain set of contents: socks in one drawer, underwear in another, and sweaters in a third drawer. Sometimes drawers have compartments allowing different kinds of things to be stored together. These are all structures that determine where things go—when you are sorting the laundry—and where things can be found—when you are getting dressed. *awk* allows you to use the structure of a text file in writing the procedures for putting things in and taking things out.

Thus, the benefits of *awk* are best realized when the data has some kind of structure. A text file can be loosely or tightly structured. A chapter containing major and minor sections has some structure. We'll look at a script that extracts the section headings, and numbers them to produce an outline. A table consisting of tab-separated items in columns might be considered very structured. You could use an *awk* script to re-order columns of data, or even change columns into rows and rows into columns.

Like *sed* scripts, *awk* scripts are typically invoked by means of a shell wrapper. This is a shell script that usually contains the command line that invokes *awk* as well as the script that *awk* interprets. Of course, simple one-line *awk* scripts can be entered from the command line.

Some of the features of *awk* are:

- Ability to view a text file as made up of records and fields in a textual database.

- Use of variables to manipulate the database.

- Use of arithmetic and string operators.

- Use of common programming constructs such as loops and conditionals.

- Ability to generate formatted reports.

With *nawk* and *gawk (38.05)*, additional features make it easier to write larger scripts. Using *nawk* and *gawk*, you can:

- Define functions.

- Execute UNIX commands from a script.

- Process the result of UNIX commands.

- Process command-line arguments more gracefully.

- Work more easily with multiple input streams.

Because of these new features, *awk* now has the power and range that users might rely upon to do the kinds of tasks performed by shell scripts. [Of course, there are many people who say that *awk* has now been completely obsoleted by *perl (39.01)*, which is even more powerful.— *TOR*]

The capabilities of *awk* extend the idea of text editing into computation, making it possible to perform a variety of data processing tasks, including analysis, extraction, and reporting of data. These are, indeed, the most common uses of *awk* but there are also many unusual applications: one person told me he had written a LISP interpreter in *awk* and another had written a compiler!

—*DD* from the Nutshell Handbook *sed & awk*

38.02 awk in a Nutshell

awk was developed as a programmable editor that, like *sed*, is stream-oriented and interprets a script of editing commands. Where *awk* departs from *sed* is in discarding the line-editor command set. It offers in its place a programming language modeled on the C language. The *print* statement replaces the "p" command, for example. The concept of addressing is carried over, such that:

```
/regular/ { print }
```

prints those lines matching `regular`. The braces ({}) surround a series of one or more statements that are applied to the same address.

The advantage of using a programming language in scripts is that it offers a lot more ways to control what the programmable editor can do. *awk* offers conditional statements, loops, and other programming constructs.

One of the distinctive features of *awk* that makes it useful for many tasks that *sed* can't touch is that it *parses*, or breaks up, each input line and makes individual words available for processing with a script. Thus, *awk* parses the input file into records and fields so you can refer to, and manipulate, these structures. (An editor such as *vi* also recognizes words, allowing you to move word by word, or make a word the object of an action, but these features can only be used interactively.)

—*DD* from the Nutshell Handbook *sed & awk*

38.03 The Rules of the Game

To write an *awk* script, you must become familiar with the rules of the game. The rules can be stated plainly and you will find them described in article 38.04. The goal of this chapter is not to describe the rules but to show you how to play the game. We don't cover every feature of *awk*, but sample those that might be most appealing to the non-programmer or that show off a few practical applications.

In this way, you will become acquainted with many of the features of the language and see examples that illustrate how scripts actually work. Some people prefer to begin by reading the rules, which is roughly equivalent to learning to use a program from its manual page or learning to speak a language by scanning its rules of grammar—not an easy task. Having a good grasp of the rules, however, is essential once you begin to use *awk* regularly. But that is to say that the more you use *awk*, the faster the rules of the game become second nature. You learn them through trial and error—spending a long time trying to fix a silly syntax error such as a missing space or brace has a magical effect upon long-term memory. Thus, the best way to learn to write scripts is to begin writing them.

—*DD* from the Nutshell Handbook *sed & awk*

38.04 awk's Programming Model

It's important to understand the basic model that *awk* offers the programmer. Part of the reason why *awk* is easier to learn than many programming languages is that it offers such a well-defined and useful model to the programmer.

An *awk* program consists of what we will call a *main input loop*. A *loop* is a routine that is executed over and over again until some condition exists that terminates it. You don't write this loop; it is given—it exists as the framework within which the code that you do write will be executed. The main input loop in *awk* is a routine that reads one line of input from a file and makes it available for processing. The actions you write to do the processing assume that there is a line of input available. In another programming language, you would have to create the main input loop as part of your program. It would have to open the input file and read one line at a time. This is not necessarily a lot of work but it illustrates that *awk* is "setting you up," making it easier for you to write your program.

The main input loop is executed as many times as there are lines of input. This loop does not execute until there is a line of input. It terminates when there is no more input to be read.

awk allows you to write two special routines that can be executed *before* any input is read and *after* all input is read. These are the procedures associated with the *BEGIN* and *END* rules, respectively. In other words, you can do some preprocessing before the main input loop is ever executed and you can do some postprocessing after the main input loop has been terminated. The *BEGIN* and *END* procedures are optional and they do not need to be defined.

You can think of an *awk* script as potentially having three major parts: what happens before, what happens during, and what happens after processing the input. Figure 38-1 shows the relationship of these parts in the flow of control of an *awk* script.

Of these three parts, the main input loop or "what happens during processing" is where most of the work gets done. Inside the main input loop, your instructions are written as a series of pattern/action procedures. A pattern is a rule for testing the input line to determine whether the action should be applied to it. The actions, as we shall see, can be quite complex, consisting of statements, functions, and expressions.

The main thing to remember is that each pattern/action procedure sits in the main input loop, which takes care of reading the input line. The procedures that you write will be applied to each input line, one line at a time.

Pattern Matching

In this section, we look at a number of small, even trivial examples that demonstrate the power of pattern-matching rules.

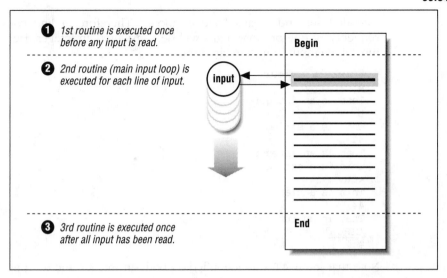

Figure 38-1. Flow of Control in awk Scripts

When *awk* reads an input line, it attempts to match each pattern-matching rule in a script. Only the lines matching the particular pattern are the object of an action. If no action is specified, the line that matches the pattern is printed (executing the *print* statement is the default action). Consider the following script:

```
/^$/ { print "This is a blank line." }
```

This script reads: *if the input line is blank, then print "This is a blank line."* The pattern is written as a regular expression *(27.01)* that identifies a blank line. The action, like most of those we've seen so far, contains a single *print* statement.

If we place this script in a file named *awkscr* and use an input file named *test* that contains three blank lines, then the following command executes the script:

```
$ awk -f awkscr test
This is a blank line
This is a blank line
This is a blank line
```

(From this point on, we'll assume that our scripts are placed in a separate file and invoked using the *–f* command-line option.) The result tells us that there are three blank lines in *test*. This script ignores lines that are not blank.

Let's add several new rules to the script. This script is now going to analyze the input and classify it as an integer, a string, or a blank line.

```
# test for integer, string or empty line.
/[0-9]+$/ { print "That is an integer" }
/[A-z]+/ { print "This is a string" }
/^$/     { print "This is a blank." }
```

The general idea is that if a line of input matches any of these patterns, the associated *print* statement will be executed. The + meta-character is part of the extended set and means "one or more." Therefore, a line consisting of a sequence of one or more digits will be considered an integer. Here's a sample run, taking input from standard input:

```
% awk -f awkscr
4
That is an integer
t
This is a string
4T
That is an integer
This is a string
<CR>
This is a blank.
44
That is an integer
CTRL-d
%
```

Note that input **4T** was identified as both an integer and a string. A line can match more than one rule. You can write a stricter rule set to prevent a line from matching more than one rule. You can also write actions that are designed to skip other parts of the script.

Describing Your Script

Adding comments as you write the script is a good practice. A comment begins with the # character and ends at a newline. Unlike *sed*, *awk* allows comments anywhere in the script.

Note: If you surround your *awk* script with single quotes (') and store it in a shell script, do not use a single quote in a comment. The shell interprets it and causes the program to stop. See article 38.16.

As we begin writing scripts, we'll use comments to describe the action:

```
# blank.awk -- Print message for each blank line.
/^$/ { print "This is a blank line" }
```

This comment offers the name of the script *blank.awk* and briefly describes what the script does. A particularly useful comment for longer scripts is one that identifies the expected structure of the input file. For instance, in the next section, we are going to look at writing a script that reads a file containing names and phone numbers. The introductory comments for this program should be:

```
# blocklist.awk -- print name and address in block form.
# fields: name, company, street, city, state and zip, phone
```

It is useful to embed this information in the script because the script won't work unless the structure of the input file corresponds to that expected by the person who wrote the script.

As *awk* interprets a script at runtime, there is undoubtedly some small penalty incurred by placing comments in scripts. However, in most cases, that should not have significant impact on *awk* applications.* One approach to take in those circumstances is to document the program in another file.

Records and Fields

awk makes the assumption that its input is structured and not just an endless string of characters. In the simplest case, it takes each input line as a record and each word, delimited by blank spaces or tabs, as a field.

You can change the field separator with the *–F* option on the command line. It is followed immediately by the delimiter character. In the following example, the field separator is changed to a tab:

```
% awk -F"\t" '{ print $2 }' names
666-111-5555
```

\t is a valid escape sequence that indicates a tab. You can also enter a tab by pressing the TAB key. In any case, you must surround the tab by single or double quotes.

Commas delimit fields in the following two address records:

```
John Robinson,Koren Inc.,978 4th Ave.,Boston,MA 01760,696-0987
Phyllis Chapman,GVE Corp.,34 Sea Drive,Amesbury,MA 01881,879-0900
```

—*DD* from the Nutshell Handbook *sed & awk*

38.05 Versions of awk

awk was introduced as part of UNIX's seventh edition and has been part of the standard distribution ever since.

In 1985, the authors of *awk* extended the language, adding many useful features. Unfortunately, this new version remained inside AT&T for several years. It became a regular part of AT&T's System V as of Release 3.1. It can be found under the name of *nawk* (for new *awk*); the older version still exists under its original name.

gawk

Unfortunately, *nawk* is not available on all systems. The good news is that the Free Software Foundation *(55.01)* GNU project's version of *awk*, called *gawk*, implements all the features of the new *awk*.

In this book, we show both *nawk* and *gawk* scripts. In general, you can assume that what is true for *nawk* is true for *gawk*, unless *gawk* is explicitly called out. Scripts written for *nawk* are 100 percent compatible with *gawk*. If you want to

---

*I have found a couple of circumstances where larger scripts failed, reporting syntax errors that I could not track down. Removing all the comments made the program run fine. I conclude from this that the size of the program was the problem, which seemed to be a machine-specific limitation of *awk*. The program, comments included, ran fine on two other systems.

use one of the *nawk* scripts, and don't have *nawk* on your system, simply change the script to invoke *gawk* instead.

There are a few areas where *gawk* has introduced *gawk*-specific features; however, recent versions of *nawk* support many of these features, suggesting that the remaining differences are really very minor. This shouldn't matter in any case, since we do supply *gawk* on the disk.

—DD, TOR

38.06 *Expressions*

The use of expressions in which you can store, manipulate, and retrieve data is quite different from anything you can do in *sed*, yet it is a common feature of most programming languages, including *awk*.

The use of expressions makes *awk* able to handle many types of tasks that would be unthinkable in *sed*. Look at the following example which counts each blank line in a file:

```
# Count blank lines.
/^$/ {
        print x += 1
      }
```

Although we didn't initialize the value of *x*, we can safely assume that its value is 0 up until the first blank line is encountered. The expression `x += 1` is evaluated each time a blank line is matched and the value of *x* is incremented by 1. The *print* statement prints the value returned by the expression.

There are different ways to write expressions, some more terse than others. The expression `x += 1` is more concise than the following equivalent expression:

```
x = x + 1
```

But both of these expressions are not as terse as the following expression:

```
++x
```

`++` is the increment operator. (`--` is the decrement operator.) Each time the expression is evaluated the value of the variable is incremented by one. The increment and decrement operators can appear on either side of the operand, as *prefix* or *postfix* operators. The position has a different effect.

```
++x     increment x before returning value (prefix)
x++     increment x after returning value (postfix)
```

For instance, suppose our example was written:

```
/^$/ {
        print x++
      }
```

When the first blank line is matched, the expression returns the value 0; the second blank line returns 1, and so on. If we put the increment operator before *x*, then the first time the expression is evaluated, it will return 1.

Let's implement that expression in our example. In addition, instead of printing a count each time a blank line is matched, we'll accumulate the value of *x* and print only the total number of blank lines. The *END* pattern is the place to put the *print* that displays the value of *x* after the last input line is read.

```
# Count blank lines.
/^$/ {
        ++x
}
END {
        print x
}
```

—*DD* from the Nutshell Handbook *sed & awk*

38.07 *System Variables*

awk has two types of built-in system variables. The first type defines values whose default can be changed, such as the default field and record separators. The second type defines values that can be used in reports or processing, such as the number of fields found in the current record, the count of the current record, and others.

There are a set of default values that affect the recognition of records and fields on input and their display on output. The system variable *FS* defines the field separator. By default, it is a space or a tab. You might change the field separator to a comma in order to read a list of names and addresses, or to a colon to read the UNIX passwd *(1.09)* file.

The output equivalent of *FS* is *OFS*, which is a space by default. We'll see an example of redefining *OFS* shortly. *awk* defines its variable *NF* to be the number of fields for the current input record. This value can't be changed but it is useful to access in order to determine how many fields there are.

awk also defines *RS*, the record separator, as a newline. Its output equivalent is *ORS*, which is also a newline by default. In the section "Working with Multi-line Records," we'll show how to change the default record separator. *awk* sets the variable *NR* to the number of the current input record. It can be used to number records in a list. The variable *FILENAME* contains the name of the current input file. *nawk (38.05)* also defines the variable *FNR*. It is useful when multiple files are open as it provides the number of the current record relative to the current input file.

Typically, the field and record separators are defined in the *BEGIN* procedure because you want these values redefined before the first input line is read. However, you can redefine these values anywhere in the script, but you should test whether it affects the current input line. (With *nawk*, setting the field separator causes the current input line to be re-evaluated using the new value. With *gawk (38.05)* and *awk*, this has no effect on the current input line; rather it affects the next input line.)

—*DD* from the Nutshell Handbook *sed & awk*

38.08 Working with Multi-line Records

All of our examples have used input files whose records consisted of a single line. How do you read a record where each *field* consists of a single line?

Let's suppose that a file of names and addresses is stored in block format. Instead of having all the information on one line, the person's name is on one line, followed by the company's name on the next line and so on. Here's a sample record:

```
John Robinson
Koren Inc.
978 Commonwealth Ave.
Boston
MA 01760
696-0987
```

This record has six fields. After each record, a blank line is output.

To process this data, we can specify a multi-line record by defining the field separator to be a newline, represented as \n; and set the record separator to null, which stands for a blank line.

```
BEGIN { FS = "\n"; RS = "" }
```

We can print the first and last fields using the following script:

```
# block.awk - print first and last fields
# $1 = name; $NF = phone number

BEGIN { FS = "\n"; RS = "" }

{ print $1, $NF }
```

Here's a sample run:

```
% awk -f block.awk phones.block
John Robinson 696-0987
Phyllis Chapman 879-0900
Jeffrey Willis 914-636-0000
Alice Gold (707) 724-0000
Bill Gold 1-707-724-0000
```

The two fields are printed on the same line because the default output separator (*OFS*) remains a single space. If you want the fields to be output on separate lines, change *OFS* to a newline. If you want to preserve the blank space between records, you must specify the output record separator *ORS* to be two newlines:

```
OFS = "\n"; ORS = "\n\n"
```

Article 50.11 shows another way to handle multi-line records: the *getline* function.

—*DD* from the Nutshell Handbook *sed & awk*

38.09 Substitution Functions

It was a real weakness in the original *awk* that it didn't offer a simple regular expression-based substitution capability, similar to the *s* command in *sed*.

nawk and *gawk* (38.05) provide two substitution functions: *sub( )* and *gsub( )*. The difference between them is that *gsub( )* performs its substitution globally on the input string whereas *sub( )* makes only the first substitution possible. This makes *gsub( )* equivalent to the *sed* substitution command with the *g* (global) flag.

Both functions take at least two arguments. The first is a regular expression (surrounded by slashes) that matches a pattern and the second argument is a string that replaces what the pattern matches. The regular expression can be supplied by a variable in which case the slashes are omitted. An optional third argument specifies the string which is the target of the substitution. If there is no third argument, the substitution is made for the current input record ($0).

The substitution functions change the specified string directly. (You might expect, given the way functions work, that the function returns the new string created when the substitution is made.) The substitution functions actually return the *number* of substitutions made. *sub( )* will always return 1 if successful; both return 0 if unsuccessful. Thus, you can test the result to see if a substitution was made.

For example, the following example uses *gsub( )* to replace all occurrences of "UNIX" with "POSIX."

```
if (gsub(/UNIX/,"POSIX"))
        print
```

The conditional statement tests the return value of *gsub( )* such that the current input line is printed only if a change is made.

—*DD* from the Nutshell Handbook *sed & awk*

38.10 Getting Information about Files

[The filesum *program developed in this article demonstrates many of the basic constructs used in* awk. *What's more, it gives you a pretty good idea of the process of developing a program (although syntax errors produced by typos and hasty thinking have been gracefully omitted). If you wish to tinker with this program, you might add a counter for directories, or a rule that handles symbolic links* (27.01)—DD].

The following is a sample of the long listing produced by the command *ls −l:**

```
% ls -l
-rw-rw-rw-   1 dale     project   6041 Jan  1 12:31 com.tmp
```

---

* Note that on a Berkeley UNIX system, *ls −l* produces an eight-column report; use *ls −lg* to get the same report format shown here.

```
-rwxrwxrwx   1 dale      project    1778 Jan  1 11:55 combine.idx*
-rw-rw-rw-   1 dale      project    1446 Feb 15 22:32 dang
-rwxrwxrwx   1 dale      project    1202 Jan  2 23:06 format.idx*
```

This listing is a report in which data is presented in rows and columns. Each file is presented across a single row. The file listing consists of nine columns. The file's permissions appear in the first column, the size of the file in bytes in the fifth column, and the filename is found in the last column. Because one or more spaces separate the data in columns, we can treat each column as a field.

In our first example, we're going to pipe the output of this command to an *awk* script that prints selected fields from the file listing. To do this, we'll create a shell script so that we can make the pipe transparent to the user. Thus, the structure of the shell script is:

```
ls -l $* | awk 'script' -
```

The $* parameter *(46.14)* is used by the shell and expands to all arguments passed from the command line. (We could use $1 here, which would pass the first argument, but passing *all* the arguments provides greater flexibility.) These arguments can be the names of files or directories or additional options to the *ls* command. If no arguments are specified, the $* will be ignored and the current directory will be listed. Thus, the output of that command will be directed to *awk*, and we've specified – in place of a filename *(14.13)* to indicate standard input.

We'd like our *awk* script to print the size and name of the file. That is, print field 5 ($5) and field 9 ($9):

```
ls -l $* | awk '{
       print $5,"\t", $9 }
}' -
```

If we put the above lines in a file named *fls* and make that file executable, we can enter *fls* as a command:

```
% fls
6041       com.tmp
1778       combine.idx
1446       dang
1202       format.idx
% fls com*
6041       com.tmp
1778       combine.idx
```

So what our program does is take the long listing and reduce it to two fields. Now, let's add new functionality to our report by producing some information that the *ls* –*l* listing does not provide. We can store the size of each file and accumulate it to produce the total number of bytes used by all files in the listing: we can also keep track of the number of files and produce that total. There are two parts to adding this functionality. The first is to accumulate the totals for each input line. We create the variable *sum* to accumulate the size of files and the variable *filenum* to accumulate the number of files in the listing.

```
{
       sum += $5
```

```
        ++filenum
        print $5,"\t", $9
}
```

The first expression uses the assignment operator +=. It adds the value of field 5 to the present value of the variable *sum*. The second expression increments the present value of the variable *filenum*. This variable is used as a *counter*, and each time the expression is evaluated, 1 is added to the count.

The action we've written will be applied to all input lines. The totals that are accumulated in this action must be printed after *awk* has read all the input lines. Therefore, we write an action that is controlled by the END rule:

```
END { print "Total: ", sum, "bytes (" filenum " files)"
}
```

We can also use the BEGIN rule to add column headings to the report:

```
BEGIN { print "BYTES" "\t" "FILE"
}
```

Now we can put this script in an executable file *(1.05)* named *filesum* and execute it as a single-word command:

```
% filesum c*
BYTES    FILE
882      ch01
1771     ch03
1987     ch04
6041     com.tmp
1778     combine.idx
Total:   12459 bytes (5 files)
```

What's nice about this command is that it allows you to determine the size of all files in a directory or any group of files.

While the basic mechanism works, there are a few problems to be taken care of. The first problem occurs when you list the entire directory using the *ls* –*l* command. The listing contains a line that specifies the total number of blocks in the directory. The partial listing (all files beginning with "c") in the previous example does not have this line. But the following line would be included in the output if the full directory was listed:

```
total 555
```

The block total does not interest us because the program displays the total file size in bytes. Currently, *filesum* does not print this line; however, it does read this line and cause the *filenum* counter to be incremented.

There is also a problem with this script in how it handles subdirectories. Look at the following line from an *ls* –*l*:

```
drwxrwxrwx   3 dale     project        960 Feb  1 15:47 sed
```

"d" as the first character in column 1 (file permissions) indicates that the file is a subdirectory. The size of this file (960 bytes) does not indicate the size of files in that subdirectory and therefore, it is slightly misleading to add it to the file size totals. Also, it might be helpful to indicate that it is a directory.

If you want to list the files in subdirectories, supply the *–R* option on the command line. It will be passed to the *ls* command. However, the listing is slightly different as it identifies each directory. For instance, to identify the subdirectory *old*, the *ls –l –R* listing produces a blank line followed by:

```
./old:
```

filesum

Our script ignores that line and a blank line preceding it but nonetheless they increment the file counter. Fortunately, we can devise rules to handle these cases. Let's look at the revised, commented script:

```
ls -l $* | awk '
# filesum: list files and total size in bytes
# input: long listing produced by System V "ls -l"

#1 output column headers
BEGIN { print "BYTES" "\t" "FILE"
}
#2 test for 9 fields; files begin with -
NF == 9 && /^-/ {
        sum += $5        # accumulate size of file
        ++filenum        # count number of files
        print $5,"\t", $9        # print size and filename
}

#3 test for 9 fields; directory begins with "d"
NF == 9 && /^d/ {
        print "<dir>", "\t", $9   #print <dir> and name
}

#4 test for ls -1R line ./dir:
$1 ~ /^\..*:$/ {
        print "\t" $0 # print that line preceded by tab
}

#5 once all is done,
END {
        #print total file size and number of files
        print "Total: ", sum, "bytes (" filenum " files)"
}' -
```

The rules and their associated actions have been numbered to make it easier to discuss them. The listing produced by *ls –l* contains nine fields for a file. *awk* supplies the number of fields for a record in the system variable *NF*. Therefore, rules 2 and 3 test that *NF* is equal to 9. This helps us avoid matching odd blank lines or the line stating the block total. Because we want to handle directories and files differently, we use another pattern to match the first character of the line. In rule 2 we test for – in the first position on the line, which indicates a file. The associated action increments the file counter and adds the file size to the previous total. In rule 3, we test for a directory, indicated by d as the first character. The associated action prints <dir> in place of the file size. Rules 2 and 3 are *compound* expressions, specifying two patterns that are combined using the && operator. Both patterns must be matched for the expression to be true.

Rule 4 tests for the special case produced by the *ls −lR* listing (`./old:`). There are a number of patterns that we can write to match that line, using regular expressions or relational expressions:

`NF == 1`	*If the number of fields equals 1 ...*
`/^\..*:$/`	*If the line begins with a period*
	followed by any number of characters and
	ends in a colon...
`$1 ~ /^\..*:$/`	*If field 1 matches the regular expression...*

We used the latter expression because it seems to be the most specific. It employs the match operator (~) to test the first field against a regular expression. The associated action consists of only a *print* statement.

Rule 5 is the END pattern and its action is only executed once, printing the sum of file sizes as well as the number of files.

The *sls (17.30)* command on the Power Tools disk can set almost any output format. Using it instead of *ls −l −R* would avoid most of the special-case testing in *filesum*.

—DD from the Nutshell Handbook sed & awk

38.11 *Date Conversion: mm-dd-yy or mm/dd/yy to Month Day, Year*

Here's a script that converts dates in the form "mm-dd-yy" or "mm/dd/yy" to "month day, year." Here's a sample run:

```
% echo 5/11/55 | date-month
May 11, 1955
```

[If this simple script doesn't do exactly what you want, change it! You could add a test that tries to find reversed dates like *dd/mm/yy* or *yy/mm/dd*. Of course, you can also change the script to use a different default date order. *—JP*]

date-month

```
awk '# date-month -- convert mm/dd/yy to month day, year

# build list of months and put in array.
BEGIN {
    # the 2-step assignment is done for printing in book
    listmonths="January,February,March,April,May,June,July,August,"
    listmonths=listmonths "September,October,November,December"
    split( listmonths,month,"," )
}

# check that there is input
$1 != "" {
# split on "/" the first input field into elements of array
    sizeOfArray = split($1,date,"/")
# check that only one field is returned
    if (sizeOfArray == 1)
        # try to split on "-"
        sizeOfArray = split($1,date,"-")
```

```
# must be invalid
    if (sizeOfArray == 1)
        exit
# add 0 to number of month to coerce numeric type
    date[1] += 0
# print month day, year
    print month[date[1]], date[2]", 19" date[3]
}' -
```

This script reads from standard input. The BEGIN action creates an array named *month* whose elements are the names of the months of the year. The second rule verifies that we have a non-empty input line. The first statement in the associated action splits the first field of input looking for / (a slash) as the delimiter. *sizeOfArray* contains the number of elements in the array. If *awk* is unable to parse the string, it creates the array with only one element. Thus, we can test the value of *sizeOfArray* to determine if we have several elements. If we do not, we assume that perhaps – (dash) was used as the delimiter. If that fails to produce an array with multiple elements, we assume the input is invalid, and exit. If we have successfully parsed the input, date[1] contains the number of the month. This value can be used as the index to the array *month*, nesting one array inside another. However, before using date[1], we coerce the type of date[1] by adding 0 to it. [*awk* has both numeric and string variables. The trick of adding zero to a variable makes sure *awk* will treat the variable as numeric. Appending an empty string to a variable, like *varname* "", forces a string variable.—*JP*] While *awk* will correctly interpret "11" as a number, leading zeros may cause a number to be treated as a string. Thus, "06" might not be recognized properly without type coercion. The element referenced by date[1] is used as the subscript for *month*.

—*DD* from the Nutshell Handbook *sed & awk*

38.12 *Writing Your Own Functions*

With the addition of user-defined functions, *nawk* and *gawk* allow the *awk* programmer to take another step towards C programming by writing programs that make use of self-contained functions. When you write a function properly, you have defined a program component that can be re-used in other programs. The real benefit of modularity becomes apparent as programs grow in size or in age, and as the number of programs you write increases significantly.

A function definition can be placed anywhere in a script that a pattern-action rule appears. Typically, we put the function definitions at the top of the script before the pattern-action rules. A function is defined using the following syntax:

```
function name(parameter-list) {
        statements
}
```

The newlines after the left brace and before the right brace are optional.

The *parameter-list* is a comma-separated list of variables that are passed as arguments into the function when it is called. The body of the function consists of one or more statements. The function typically contains a *return* statement that returns control to that point in the script where the function was called; it often has an expression that returns a value as well.

```
return expression
```

Writing a Sort Function

For example, here's a *sort* function that sorts the elements of an array.

We define a function that takes two arguments, the name of the array and the number of elements in the array. This function can be called as such:

```
sort(pick,NUM)
```

The function definition lists the two arguments and three local variables used in the function.

```
# sort numbers in ascending order
function sort(ARRAY,ELEMENTS,    temp,i,j) {
     for ( i = 2; i <= ELEMENTS; ++i )
          for ( j = i; ARRAY[j-1] > ARRAY[j]; --j ) {
               temp = ARRAY[j]
               ARRAY[j] = ARRAY[j-1]
               ARRAY[j-1] = temp
     }
return
}
```

The body of the function implements an insertion sort. This sorting algorithm is very simple. We loop through each element of the array and compare it to the value preceding it. If the first element is greater than the second, the first and second elements are swapped. To actually swap the values, we use a temporary variable to hold a copy of the value while we overwrite the original. The loop continues swapping adjacent elements until all are in order. At the end of the function, we use the *return* to simply return control. It does not need to pass the array back to the main routine because the array itself is changed and it can be accessed directly.

—DD from the Nutshell Handbook *sed & awk*

38.13 Maintaining a Function Library

You might want to put a useful function in its own file and store it in a central directory. *nawk (38.05)* permits multiple uses of the *–f* option to specify more than one program file. For instance, we could have written the previous example such that the sort function was placed in a separate file from the main program *grade.awk*. The following command specifies both program files:

```
% awk -f grade.awk -f /usr/local/lib/awk/sort.awk grades.test
```

This command assumes that *grade.awk* is in the working directory and that the sort function is defined in *sort.awk* in the directory */usr/local/lib/awk*.

gawk allows you to specify an environment variable named *AWKPATH* that defines a search path for *awk* program files. By default, it is defined to be `.:/usr/lib/awk:/usr/local/lib/awk`. Thus, when a filename is specified with the *–f* option, the three default directories will be searched, beginning with the current directory. Note that if the filename contains a /, then no search is performed. Use of *AWKPATH* would permit us to omit the absolute pathname of *sort.awk* in the previous example.

Remember to document functions clearly so that you will understand how they work when you want to re-use them.

—*DD* from the Nutshell Handbook *sed & awk*

38.14 Passing Parameters into a Script

One of the more confusing subtleties of programming in *awk* is passing parameters into a script. A parameter assigns a value to a variable that can be accessed within the *awk* script. The variable can be set on the command line, after the script and before the filename.

```
awk 'script' var=value inputfile
```

Each parameter must be interpreted as a single argument. Therefore, spaces are not permitted on either side of the equal sign. Multiple parameters can be passed this way. For instance, if you wanted to define the variables *high* and *low* from the command line, you could invoke *awk* as follows:

```
% awk -f scriptfile high=100 low=60 datafile
```

Inside the script, these two variables are available and can be accessed as any *awk* variable. If you were to put this script in a shell script wrapper, then you could pass the shell's command-line arguments as values. (The shell makes available command-line arguments in the positional variables—$1 for the first parameter, 2 for the second, and so on.) For instance, look at the shell script version of the previous command:

```
awk -f scriptfile high=$1 low=$2 datafile
```

If this shell script were named "awket," it could be invoked as:

```
% awket 100 60
```

100 would be $1 and passed as the value assigned to the variable *high*.

In addition, environment variables or the output of a command can be passed as the value of a variable. Here are two examples:

```
directory=$cwd
directory=`pwd`
```

$cwd returns the value of the variable *cwd* which is the current working directory. The second example uses backquotes to execute the *pwd* command and assign its result to the variable *directory*.

You can also use command-line parameters to define system variables, as in the following example:

```
% awk '{print NR, $0 }' OFS='. ' names
1. Tom 656-5789
2. Dale 653-2133
3. Mary 543-1122
4. Joe 543-2211
```

The output field separator is redefined to be a period followed by a space.

An important restriction on command-line parameters is that they are not available in the BEGIN procedure. That is, they are not available until *after* the first line of input is read.

One consequence of the way parameters are evaluated is that you cannot use the BEGIN procedure to test or verify parameters that are supplied on the command line. You can get around this limitation by composing the rule NR == 1 and using its procedure to verify the assignment. Another way is to test the command-line parameters in the shell script before invoking *awk*.

nawk (38.05) provides a solution to the problem of defining parameters before any input is read. The *−v* option* specifies command-line arguments that you want available in the BEGIN procedure (i.e., before the first line of input is read). The *−v* option must be specified before the script or the *−f progfile* arguments. For instance, the following command uses the *−v* option to set the record separator for multi-line records:

```
% nawk -F"\n" -v RS="\n\n" '{print}' phones.block
```

A separate *−v* option is required for each argument passed to the program.

—DD from the Nutshell Handbook *sed & awk*

---

*Judging from release notes distributed with the version of *nawk* by the UNIX Toolchest, the *−v* option was added in the summer of 1989. It was not supported on a version of *nawk* running under System V Release 3 (Interactive Systems V/386) that I tested. However, it does appear in the System V Release 4 documentation for *nawk*.

38.15 Putting awk, sed, etc. inside Shell Scripts

In *SunExpert* magazine, in his article on *awk* (January, 1991), Peter Collinson suggests a stylization similar to this for *awk* programs in shell scripts *(46.01)*:

```
#!/bin/sh
awkprog='
/foo/{print $3}
/bar/{print $4}'

awk "$awkprog" $*
```

He argues that this is more intelligible in long pipelines because it separates the program from the command. For example:

```
grep foo $input | sed .... | awk "$awkprog" - | ...
```

Not everyone is thrilled by the "advantages" of writing *awk* this way, but it's true that there are disadvantages to writing *awk* in the standard way.

Here's an even more complex variation:

```
#!/bin/sh
temp=/tmp/awk.prog.$$
cat > $temp <<\END
/foo/{print $3}
/bar/{print $4}
END
awk -f $temp $1
rm -f $temp
```

<<\ *9.14*

This version makes it a bit easier to create complex programs dynamically. The final *awk* command becomes the equivalent of a shell *eval (9.08)*; it executes something that has been built up at runtime. The first strategy (program in shell variable) could also be massaged to work this way.

As another example a program that I used once was really just one long pipeline, about 200 lines long. Huge *awk* scripts and *sed* scripts intervened in the middle. As a result, it was almost completely unintelligible. But if you start each program with a comment block and end it with a pipe, the result can be fairly easy to read. It's more direct than using big shell variables or temporary files, especially if there are several scripts.

```
#
# READ THE FILE AND DO XXX WITH awk:
#
awk '
       ...the indented awk program...
       ...
       ...
' |
#
# SORT BY THE FIRST FIELD, THEN BY XXX:
#
sort +0n -1 +3r |
#
# MASSAGE THE LINES WITH sed AND XXX:
```

```
#
sed '
    ...
```

Multi-line pipes like that one are uglier in the C shell because each line has to end with a backslash (\).

—*ML, JP*

38.16 *Printing a Single Quote from awk in a Shell Script*

The usual way to run an *awk* script from inside a Bourne shell script *(38.15)* is by putting single quotes (') around the whole *awk* script:

```
#!/bin/sh
    ...
awk '
{
    ...
} '
    ...
```

But it's tough to use a single quote inside the *awk* script itself. The Bourne shell won't let you unless you do some fancy work with double quote (") characters—and a simple backslash first (\ ') doesn't help.

The best trick is to print a single quote by using its ASCII value *(53.03)* and the *printf* function:

```
awk '
{ printf "Here is a single quote: %c\n", 39 }
'
```

or, if you need lots of quotes, you can store a single quote in a string variable:

```
awk '
BEGIN { S = sprintf("%c",39) }
{ print "That" S "s all, folks." }
'
```

The command prints: That's all, folks..

—*JP*

38.17 *Debugging*

No aspect of programming is more frustrating or more essential than debugging. In this article, we'll look at ways to debug *awk* scripts and offer advice on how to correct an *awk* program that fails to do what it is supposed to do.

nawk is a significant improvement on *awk* in reporting syntax errors in a way that helps you locate the problem. As mentioned earlier, *awk*'s standard error message ("bailing out") is hardly any help. But even with improved error detection, it is often difficult to isolate the problem. The techniques for discovering the source of the problem are a modest few and are fairly obvious.

There are two classes of problems with a program. The first is really a bug in the program's logic. The program runs—that is, it finishes without reporting any error messages, but it does not produce the result you wanted. For instance, perhaps it does not create any output. This bug could be caused by failing to use a *print* statement to output the result of a calculation. Program errors are mental errors, if you will.

The second class of errors is one in which the program fails to execute or complete execution. This could result from a syntax error and cause *awk* to spit code at you that it is unable to interpret. Many syntax errors are the result of a typo or a missing brace ({ }) or parenthesis (( )). Syntax errors usually generate error messages that help direct you to the problem. Sometimes, however, a program may fail (or core dump *(55.01)*) without producing any reasonable error message. This may also be caused by a syntax error, but there could be problems specific to the machine. I have had a few larger scripts that dumped core on one machine while they ran without a problem on another. You could, for instance, be running up against limitations set for *awk* for that particular implementation.

You should be clear in your mind which type of program bug you are trying to find: an error in the script's logic or an error in its syntax.

Make a Copy

Before you begin debugging a program, make a copy of it. This is extremely important. To debug an *awk* script, you have to change it. These modifications may point you to the error but many changes will have no effect or may introduce new problems. It's good to be able to restore changes that you make. However, it is bothersome to restore each change that you make, so I like to continue making changes until I have found the problem. When I know what it is, I go back to the original and make the change. In effect, that restores all the other inconsequential changes that were made in the copy.

It is also helpful to view the process of creating a program as a series of stages. Look at a core set of features as a single stage. Once you have implemented these features and tested them, make a copy of the program before going to the next stage to develop new features. That way, you can always return to the previous stage if you have problems with the new code that you added.

Before and After Photos

What is difficult in debugging *awk* is that you don't always know what is happening during the course of the program. You can inspect the input and the output, but there is no way to stop the program in mid-course and examine its state. Thus, it is difficult to know which part of the program is causing a problem.

A common problem is determining when or where in the program the assignment of a variable takes place. The first method of attack is to use the *print* statement to print the value of the variable at various points in the program. For instance, it is common to use a variable as a flag to determine that a certain condition has occurred. At the beginning of the program, the flag might be set to 0. At one or more points in the program, the value of this flag might be set to 1. The problem is to find where the change actually occurs. If you want to check the flag at a particular part of the program, use *print* statements before and after the assignment. For instance:

```
print flag, "before"
if (something) {
        .
        .
        .
        flag = 1
}
print flag, "after"
```

If you are unsure about the result of a substitution command or any function, print the string before and after the function is called:

```
print $2
sub(/ *\(/,"(", $2)
print $2
```

The value of printing the value before the substitution command is to make sure that the command sees the value that you think should be there. A previous command might have changed that variable. The problem may turn out to be that the format of the input record is not as you thought. Checking the input carefully is a very important step in debugging. In particular, use *print* statements to verify that the sequence of fields is as you expect. When you find that input is causing the problem, you can either fix the input or write new code to accommodate it.

Find Out Where the Problem Is

The more modular a script is—that is, the more it can be broken down into separate parts, the easier it is to test and debug the program. One of the advantages of writing functions is that you can isolate what is going on inside the function and test it without affecting other parts of the program. You can omit an entire action and see what happens.

If a program has a number of branching constructs, you might find that an input line falls through one of the branches. Test that the input reaches part of a program. For instance, when debugging a program called *masterindex* in my Nutshell Handbook *sed & awk*, I wanted to know if an entry containing the word "retrieving" was being handled in a particular part of the program where I thought it should be encountered:

/dev/tty *47.20*
```
if ($0 ~ /retrieving/) print ">> retrieving" > "/dev/tty"
```

When the program runs, if it encounters the string "retrieving," it will print the message. I like to use some pair of characters that will instantly call my attention to the output. Here I use >> but ! ! is also a good one.

Sometimes you might not be sure which of several *print* statements are causing a problem. Insert identifiers into the *print* statement that will alert you to the *print* statement being executed. In the following example, we simply use the variable name to identify what is printed with a label:

```
if (PRIMARY)
        print (">>PRIMARY:%s", PRIMARY)
else
        if (SECONDARY)
                print (">>TERTIARY:%s", TERTIARY)
```

This technique is also useful for investigating whether parts of the program are executed at all. Some programs get to be like remodeled homes: a room is added here, a wall is taken down there. Trying to understand the basic structure can be difficult. You might wonder if each of the parts is truly needed or indeed if it is ever executed at all.

If an *awk* program is part of a pipeline of several programs, even other *awk* programs, you can use the *tee (14.09)* command to redirect output to a file, while also piping the output to the next command. For instance, look at the shell script for running a *masterindex* program:

sort **37.01**
uniq **36.18**

```
$INDEXDIR/input.idx $FILES |
sort -bdf -t:  +0 -1 +1 -2 +3 -4 +2n -3n | uniq |
$INDEXDIR/pagenums.idx | tee page.tmp |
$INDEXDIR/combine.idx |
$INDEXDIR/format.idx
```

By adding | `tee page.tmp`, we are able to capture the output of the *page-nums.idx* program in a file named *page.tmp*. The same output is also piped to *combine.idx*.

Comment Out Loud

Another technique is simply commenting out a series of lines that may be causing problems. This is useful in determining which lines are really causing the problem.

I recommend developing a consistent two-character symbol such as `#%` to comment out lines temporarily. Then you will notice them on subsequent editing and remember to deal with them. It also becomes easier to remove the symbols and restore the lines with a single editing command that does not affect permanent program comments:

```
#% if ( thisFails )
        print "I give up"
```

Using the comment here eliminates the conditional, so the `print` statement is executed unconditionally.

Slash and Burn

When all else fails, arm yourself with your editor's delete command and begin deleting portions of the program until the error disappears. Of course, make a copy of the program and delete lines from the temporary copy. This is a very crude technique, but an effective one to use before giving up altogether or starting over from scratch. It is sometimes the only way to discover what is wrong when the only result you get is that the program dumps core. The idea is the same as above, to isolate the problem code. Remove a function, for instance, or a *for* loop to see if it is the cause of the problem. Be sure to cut out complete units: for instance, all the statements within braces and the matching braces. If the problem persists—the program continues to break—then cut out another large section of the program. Sooner or later, you will find the line that is causing the problem.

You can use "slash and burn" to learn how a program works. First, run the original program on sample input, saving the output. Begin by removing a part of the program that you don't understand. Then run the modified program on sample input and compare the output to the original. Look to see what changed.

Get Defensive about Your Script

There are all types of input errors and inconsistencies that will turn up bugs in your script. You probably didn't consider that *user* errors will be pointed to as problems with *your* program. Therefore, it is a good idea to surround your core program with "defensive" procedures designed to trap inconsistent input records and prevent the program from failing unexpectedly. For instance, you might want to verify each input record before processing it, making sure that the proper number of fields exist or that the kind of data that you expect is found in a particular field.

Another aspect of incorporating defensive techniques is error handling. In others words, what do you want to have happen once the program detects an error? While in some cases you can have the program continue, in other cases it may be preferable that the program print an error message and/or halt if such an error is encountered.

It is also appropriate to recognize that *awk* scripts are typically confined to the realm of quick fixes, programs that solve a particular problem rather than solving a class of problems encountered by many different users. Because of the nature of these programs, it is not really necessary that they be professional quality. Thus, it is not necessary to write 100% user-proof programs. For one thing, defensive programming is quite time-consuming and frequently tedious. Secondly, as amateurs, we are at liberty to write programs that perform the way we expect them to; a professsional has to write for an audience and must account for their expectations. In brief, if you are writing the script for others to use, consider the possible uses and possible problems encountered by users before considering the program complete. If you are not writing for other users, maybe the fact that the script works—even for a very narrow set of circumstances—is good enough and all there is time for.

—*DD* from the Nutshell Handbook *sed & awk*

38.18 Quick Reference: awk

This article also covers *nawk* and *gawk(38.05)*. Values in [brackets] are optional; don't type the [or].

Command-line Syntax

awk can be invoked in two ways:

```
awk [options] 'script' var=value file(s)
awk [options] -f scriptfile var=value file(s)
```

You can specify a *script* directly on the command line, or you can store a script in a *scriptfile* and specify it with *–f*. The variable *var* can be assigned a value on the command line. The value can be a literal, a shell variable (*$name*), or a command substitution (`` `cmd` ``), but the value is available only after a line of input is read (i.e., after the BEGIN statement). *awk* operates on one or more *file(s)*. If none are specified (or if – is specified), *awk* reads from the standard input.

The recognized *options* are:

-F*c* Set the field separator to character *c*. This is the same as setting the system variable *FS. nawk* allows *c* to be a regular expression. Each input line, or record, is divided into fields by white space (blanks or tabs) or by some other user-definable record separator. Fields are referred to by the variables $1, $2,...$*n*. $0 refers to the entire record.

For example, to print the first three (colon-separated) fields on a separate line:

```
% awk -F: '{print $1; print $2; print $3}' /etc/passwd
```

-v *var=value*
Assign a *value* to variable *var*. This allows assignment before the script begins execution. (Available in *nawk* only.)

Patterns and Procedures

awk scripts consist of patterns and procedures:

```
pattern {procedure}
```

Both are optional. If *pattern* is missing, {*procedure*} is applied to all lines. If {*procedure*} is missing, the matched line is printed.

Patterns

pattern can be any of the following:

```
/regular expression/
relational expression
pattern-matching expression
BEGIN
END
```

- Expressions can be composed of quoted strings, numbers, operators, functions, defined variables, or any of the predefined variables described later under the section "awk System Variables."

- Regular expressions use the extended set of meta-characters as described in article 27.04.

- In addition, ^ and $ can be used to refer to the beginning and end of a field, respectively, rather than the beginning and end of a line.

- Relational expressions use the relational operators listed under the section "Operators" later in this article. Comparisons can be either string or numeric. For example, $2 > $1 selects lines for which the second field is greater than the first.

- Pattern-matching expressions use the operators ~ (match) and !~ (don't match). See the section "Operators" later in this article.

- The BEGIN pattern lets you specify procedures that will take place *before* the first input line is processed. (Generally, you set global variables here.)

- The END pattern lets you specify procedures that will take place *after* the last input record is read.

Except for BEGIN and END, patterns can be combined with the Boolean operators || (OR), && (AND), and ! (NOT). A range of lines can also be specified using comma-separated patterns:

```
pattern,pattern
```

Procedures

procedure can consist of one or more commands, functions, or variable assignments, separated by newlines or semicolons, and contained within curly braces. Commands fall into four groups:

- Variable or array assignments

- Printing commands

- Built-in functions
- Control-flow commands

Simple Pattern-Procedure Examples

1. Print first field of each line:

   ```
   { print $1 }
   ```

2. Print all lines that contain `pattern`:

   ```
   /pattern/
   ```

3. Print first field of lines that contain `pattern`:

   ```
   /pattern/{ print $1 }
   ```

4. Select records containing more than two fields:

   ```
   NF > 2
   ```

5. Interpret input records as a group of lines up to a blank line:

   ```
   BEGIN { FS = "\n"; RS = "" }
   ```

6. Print fields 2 and 3 in switched order, but only on lines whose first field matches the string URGENT:

   ```
   $1 ~ /URGENT/ { print $3, $2 }
   ```

7. Count and print the number of `pattern` found:

   ```
   /pattern/ { ++x }
   END { print x }
   ```

8. Add numbers in second column and print total:

   ```
   {total += $2 };
   END { print "column total is", total}
   ```

9. Print lines that contain less than 20 characters:

   ```
   length < 20
   ```

10. Print each line that begins with `Name:` and that contains exactly seven fields:

    ```
    NF == 7 && /^Name:/
    ```

11. Reverse the order of fields:

    ```
    { for (i = NF; i >= 1; i--) print $i }
    ```

awk System Variables

Version	Variable	Description
awk	FILENAME	Current filename.
	FS	Field separator (default is a blank).
	NF	Number of fields in current record.
	NR	Number of the current record.
	OFS	Output field separator (default is a blank).

Version	Variable	Description
	ORS	Output record separator (default is a newline).
	RS	Record separator (default is a newline).
	$0	Entire input record.
	$n	*n*th field in current record; fields are separated by *FS*.
nawk	ARGC	Number of arguments on command line.
	ARGV	An array containing the command-line arguments.
	FNR	Like *NR*, but relative to the current file.
	OFMT	Output format for numbers (default is %.6g).
	RSTART	First position in the string matched by *match* function.
	RLENGTH	Length of the string matched by *match* function.
	SUBSEP	Separator character for array subscripts (default is \034).
gawk	ENVIRON	An associative array of environment variables.
	IGNORECASE	If non-zero, pattern matches are case-independent.

Operators

The table below lists the operators, in order of increasing precedence, that are available in *awk*:

Symbol	Meaning
= =+ -= *= /= %= ^=	Assignment.
? :	C conditional expression (*nawk* and *gawk*).
||	Logical OR.
&&	Logical AND.
~ !~	Match regular expression and negation.
< <= > >= != ==	Relational operators.
(blank)	Concatenation.
+ -	Addition, subtraction.
* / %	Multiplication, division, and modulus.
+ - !	Unary plus and minus, and logical negation.
^	Exponentiation.
++ --	Increment and decrement, either prefix or postfix.
$	Field reference.

Variables and Array Assignments

Variables can be assigned a value with an equal sign (=). For example:

```
FS = ","
```

Expressions using the operators +, -, /, and % (modulo) can be assigned to variables.

Arrays can be created with the *split* function (see below), or they can simply be named in an assignment statement. ++, +=, and -= are used to increment or decrement an array, as in the C language. Array elements can be subscripted with numbers (`array[1],...array[n]`) or with names. For example, to count the number of occurrences of a pattern, you could use the following script:

```
/pattern/ { array["/pattern/"]++ }
END { print array["/pattern/"] }
```

Group Listing of awk Commands

awk commands may be classified as follows:

Arithmetic Functions	String Functions	Control Flow Statements	Input/Output Processing
atan2*	gsub*	break	close*
cos	index	continue	delete*
exp	length	do/while*	getline*
int	match*	exit	next
log	split	for	print
rand*	sub*	if	printf
sin	substr	return*	sprintf
sqrt	tolower†	while	system*
srand*	toupper†		

*Not in original *awk*
†*gawk* only

Alphabetical Summary of Commands

The following alphabetical list of statements and functions includes all that are available in *awk*, *nawk*, or *gawk*. Unless otherwise mentioned, the statement or function is found in all versions. New statements and functions introduced with *nawk* are also found in *gawk*.

atan2 atan2(*y*, *x*)
    Returns the arctangent of *y*/*x* in radians. (*nawk*)

break Exit from a *while* or *for* loop.

close close(*filename-expr*)
    close(*command-expr*)

    In most implementations of *awk*, you can have only ten files open simultaneously and one pipe. Therefore, *nawk* provides a *close* statement that allows you to close a file or a pipe. *close* takes as an argument the same expression that opened the pipe or file. (*nawk*)

continue Begin next iteration of *while* or *for* loop without reaching the bottom.

cos   cos(*x*)
Return cosine of **x**.

delete   delete(*array*[element])

Delete element of array. (*nawk*)

do

do
   body
while (*expr*)

Looping statement. Execute statements in *body*, then evaluate *expr*. If *expr* is true, execute *body* again. (*nawk*)

exit   Do not execute remaining instruction and do not read new input. END procedures will be executed.

exp   exp(*arg*)
Return exponent of *arg*.

for   for (*i=lower* ; *i<=upper* ; *i++*)
   command

While the value of variable *i* is in the range between *lower* and *upper*, do *command*. A series of commands must be put within braces ({ }). <= or any relational operator can be used; ++ or – – can be used to increment or decrement the variable.

for   for (*item* in *array*)
   command

For each *item* in an associative *array*, do *command*. More than one *command* must be put inside braces ({ }). Refer to each element of the array as *array*[*item*].

getline   [*var*][<*file*]
     or
command | getline [*var*]

Read next line of input. Original *awk* does not support the syntax to open multiple input streams. The first form reads input from *file*, and the second form reads the output of *command*. Both forms read one line at a time, and each time the statement is executed it gets the next line of input. The line of input is assigned to $0, and it is parsed into fields, setting *NF*, *NR*, and *FNR*. If *var* is specified, the result is assigned to *var* and the $0 is not changed. Thus, if the result is assigned to a variable, the current line does not change. It is actually a function and it returns 1 if it reads a record successfully, 0 if end-of-line is encountered, and –1 if for some reason it is otherwise unsuccessful. (*nawk*)

gsub   gsub(*r*, *s*, *t*)
Globally substitute *s* for each match of the regular expression *r* in the string *t*. Return the number of substitutions. If *t* is not supplied, defaults to $0. (*nawk*)

if   (*condition*)
     command
[else]
     [*command*]

If *condition* is true, do *command(s)*, otherwise do *command* in *else* clause. Condition can be an expression using any of the relational operators <, <=, ==, !=, >=, or >, as well as the pattern-matching operator ~ (e.g., if $1 ~ /[Aa].*/). A series of commands must be put within braces ({}).

index   index(*substr*, *str*)
Return position of substring *substr* in string *str*.

int   int(*arg*)
Return integer value of *arg*.

length   length(*arg*)
Return the length of *arg*. If *arg* is not supplied, $0 is assumed. Therefore, *length* can be used as a predefined variable that contains the length of the current record.

log   log(*arg*)
Return logarithm of.*arg*.

match   match(*s*, *r*)
Function that matches the pattern, specified by the regular expression *r*, in the string *s* and returns either the position in *s* where the match begins or 0 if no occurrences are found. Sets the value of *RSTART* and *RLENGTH*. (*nawk*)

next   Read next input line and start new cycle through pattern/procedures statements.

print   print [*args*][*destination*]
Print *args* on output. *args* is usually one or more fields, but may also be one or more of the predefined variables. Literal strings must be quoted. Fields are printed in the order they are listed. If separated by commas in the argument list, they are separated in the output by the character specified by *OFS*. If separated by spaces, they are concatenated in the output. *destination* is a UNIX redirection or pipe expression (e.g., > *file*) that redirects the default output.

printf   *[format [, expression(s)]*

Formatted print statement. Fields or variables can be formatted according to instructions in the *format* argument. The number of arguments must correspond to the number specified in the format sections.

format follows the conventions of the C-language *printf* statement. Here are a few of the most common formats:

%s	A string.
%d	A decimal number.
%*n.mf*	A floating-point number, where *n* is the total number of digits and *m* is the number of digits after the decimal point.
%[-]*nc*	*n* specifies minimum field length for format type *c*, while – justifies value in field; otherwise value is right justified.

format can also contain embedded escape sequences: \n (newline) or \t (tab) being the most common.

Spaces and literal text can be placed in the *format* argument by quoting the entire argument. If there are multiple expressions to be printed, there should be multiple formats specified.

Example

Using the script:

```
{printf ("The sum on line %s is %d \n", NR, $1+$2)}
```

The following input line:

```
5   5
```

produces this output, followed by a newline:

```
The sum on line 1 is 10.
```

rand   rand()

Generate a random number between 0 and 1. This function returns the same number each time the script is executed, unless the random number generator is seeded using the *srand( )* function. (*nawk*)

return   return [*expr*]

Used at end of user-defined functions to exit function, returning value of expression *expr*. (*nawk*)

sin   sin(*x*)

Return sine of *x*.

split	split(*string*, *array*[, *sep*]) Split *string* into elements of *array* array[1], . . . array[n]. *string* is split at each occurrence of separator *sep*. If *sep* is not specified, *FS* is used. The number of array elements created is returned.
sprintf	[*format*[, *expression(s)*]] Return the value of *expression(s)*, using the specified *format* (see *printf*). Data is formatted but not printed.
sqrt	sqrt(*arg*) Return square root of *arg*.
srand	srand(*expr*) Use *expr* to set a new seed for random number generator. Default is time of day. (*nawk*)
sub	sub(*r*, *s*, *t*) Substitute *s* for first match of the regular expression *r* in the string *t*. Return 1 if successful; 0 otherwise. If *t* is not supplied, defaults to $0. (*nawk*)
substr	substr(*string*, *m*, [*n*]) Return substring of *string* beginning at character position *m* and consisting of the next *n* characters. If *n* is omitted, include all char- acters to the end of string.
system	system(*command*) Function that executes the specified *command* and returns its status. The status of the command that is executed typically indicates its success (1), completion (0), or unexpected error (–1). The output of the command is not available for processing within the *awk* script. Use *command* | getline to read the output of the command into the script. (*nawk*)
tolower	tolower(*str*) Translate all uppercase characters in *str* to lowercase and return the new string. (*gawk*)
toupper	toupper(*str*) Translate all lowercase characters in *str* to uppercase and return the new string. (*gawk*)

```
while     (condition)
          command
```

Do *command* while *condition* is true (see if for a description of allowable conditions). A series of commands must be put within braces ({ }).

—*DG* from the Nutshell Handbook *UNIX in a Nutshell (SVR4/Solaris)*

39

Perl, a Pathologically Eclectic Rubbish Lister

39.01 What We Do and Don't Tell You about Perl

Unlike most of the chapters in this book, this one really doesn't say very much about what Perl does or how to use it. *perl* (the program) is quite easy to use; Perl (the language, for which *perl* is an interpreter) is also easy to learn, especially if you know some of the other tools that it is designed to replace. However, it is also quite large and complex—sufficiently so that even the quick reference treatment we gave to *sed* *(35.24)* and *awk* *(38.18)* would be difficult to fit in here.

Instead, we've contented ourselves with two "arguments" for using Perl, both of which will give you a sense of what the language contains and why its users are so passionate about it.

Throughout the book, you'll also find sprinkled a few Perl scripts—though unfortunately, not as many as we'd like. (Maybe more in the next edition.)

perl

If you are interested in learning more about Perl, try the Nutshell Handbook, *Programming Perl*...or just start in, using the extensive manual page stored with *perl* itself on the Power Tools disk.

—*TOR*

39.02 Why Learn Perl

Perl is a language for easily manipulating text, files, and processes. Perl provides a more concise and readable way to do many jobs that were formerly accomplished (with difficulty) by programming in the C language or one of the shells. While this book is primarily intended for users of the UNIX operating system, Perl runs on several other operating systems, and provides a portable model of computing across diverse architectures.

In the beginning, Perl was intended to be a data reduction language: a language for navigating among various files in an arbitrary fashion, scanning large amounts of text efficiently, invoking commands to obtain dynamic data, and printing easily-formatted reports based on the information gleaned. And it does these things quite well—the pattern matching and textual manipulation capabilities of Perl often outperform dedicated C programs. But as Perl developed, it also became a convenient file manipulation language—that is, a language in which you can deal with the files themselves apart from their contents, moving them, renaming them, changing their permissions, and so on. And it also became a convenient process manipulation language, allowing you to create and destroy processes, to control the flow of data between them, to preprocess their input and postprocess their output, and to clean up after them when they blow up. And it became a networking language, with the ability to communicate to other processes on other machines via sockets.

These things can be done in other languages, such as C or one of the shells. But the solutions are difficult and ugly, because C can't easily do many of the things that a shell can do, and a shell can't do many of the things that C lets you do. Perl fills a rather large niche between them—providing you with those things that are easy to do in both languages (all in one convenient place), thus bridging the gap between shell programming and C programming.

On the other hand, knowledge of Perl can actually help you in learning the C language, if that is your goal. And if you already know C, then learning Perl will be easy, since the languages are structured quite similarly. Perl also shares features with many of the UNIX utilities that a shell would invoke, and this can ease your learning of both Perl and UNIX.

It has been stated that a language is not worth knowing unless it teaches you to think differently. Perl is the exception to that rule (for those who know UNIX), because much of Perl is derived in spirit from other portions of UNIX. To those who merely like Perl, it is the Practical Extraction and Report Language. To those who love it, it's the Pathologically Eclectic Rubbish Lister. And to the minimalists in the crowd who think there should only be one way to do something, Perl looks hopelessly redundant and derivative. But somehow, by a grave violation of the minimalistic UNIX toolbox philosophy, Perl has become the UNIX tool of choice for many tasks of small-to-medium complexity, and ends up fitting quite happily back into the toolbox. Perl can be said to be the toolsmith's workbench from which new tools are derived.

Perl is in many ways a simple language. The types and structures used by Perl are easy to use and understand, and you can often tell what a well-written piece of Perl code is doing just by glancing at it. You don't have to know any special incantations to compile a Perl program—you can just execute it like a shell script *(47.03)*. You don't have to know everything there is to know about Perl before you can write useful programs.

Though simple in many ways, Perl is also a rich language, and there is much to be learned about it. Although it will take some time for you to absorb all that Perl can do, you will be glad that you have access to the extensive capabilities of Perl when the time comes that you need them. We noted above that Perl borrows many capabilities from the shells and C, but Perl also possesses a strict superset of *sed* and *awk* capabilities. There are, in fact, translators supplied with Perl to turn your old *sed* and *awk* (and *nawk*, and *gawk*) scripts into Perl scripts, so you can see how the features you may already be familiar with correspond to those of Perl.

There are other more mundane reasons why people like Perl. Many UNIX utilities have undocumented limitations: they don't like lines longer than n, where n is some mysterious power of two, or they blow up if you feed them binary data. These limitations are to some extent encouraged by the C language in which they are written. Perl, however, does not have these limitations. Your lines (and arrays) may grow as long as you like. Your subroutine recursion may go as deep as you like. Variable names can be as long as you like. Binary data will not cause problems. The hashed tables used by associative arrays expand as necessary to avoid degradation of performance. And if you don't know what associative arrays are, that's okay; we'll explain them. You can emulate all kinds of fancy data structures with them. And you can keep them in database files called DBM files.

You might also like to learn Perl because it will allow you to write programs more securely. Through a dataflow tracing mechanism, Perl can determine which data is derived from insecure sources, and prevent dangerous operations before they happen. System administrators will particularly love this feature.

You might like Perl because it lets you develop programs quickly. As an interpreted script language, you get instant feedback when something isn't right. And there's a built-in symbolic debugger that understands any Perl expression because it's written in Perl (and because a running Perl script is itself good at executing random bits of Perl code).

People have been calling Perl a "system administration language" primarily because system administrators have been talking about it, but we think it has a much broader appeal.

[Perl is too complex (or should we say "complete") a language to describe in this chapter. There is an extensive manual page on the disk along with the software, but if what we've said here intrigues you, you should probably get Larry and Randal's book *Programming Perl*. As they say in the preface of the book (from which this article was taken): "Whether you are learning Perl because you are curious, or because your boss told you to, this handbook will lead you through both the basics and the intricacies. And although we don't intend to teach you how to program, the perceptive reader will be able to absorb some of the art, and a little of the science, of programming. You will also learn much about UNIX, and how to balance the benefits of the integrated-tool approach with the benefits of the toolbox approach. We will encourage you to develop the three great virtues of a programmer: laziness, impatience, and hubris. Along the way, we hope you find the book mildly amusing in some spots (and wildly amusing in others). And while we're at it, we firmly believe that learning Perl will increase the value of your resume."—*TOR*]

—*LW, RS* from the Nutshell Handbook *Programming Perl*

39.03 *Three Great Virtues of a Programmer*

Laziness
> The quality that makes you go to great effort to reduce overall energy expenditure. It makes you write labor-saving programs that other people will find useful, and document what you wrote so you don't have to answer so many questions about it. Hence, the first great virtue of a programmer. Also hence, this book.

Impatience
> The anger you feel when the computer is being lazy. This makes you write programs that don't just react to your needs, but actually anticipate them. Or at least that pretend to. Hence, the second great virtue of a programmer.

Hubris Excessive pride, the sort of thing Zeus zaps you for. Also the quality that makes you write (and maintain) programs that other people won't want to say bad things about. Hence, the third great virtue of a programmer.

—*LW, RS* from the Nutshell Handbook *Programming Perl*

39.04 *Why Learn Perl #2*

Donning my vestments as devil's advocate, let me start by saying that just because you learn something new, you shouldn't entirely forget the old. UNIX is a pluralistic environment in which many paths can lead to the solution, some more circuitously than others. Different problems can call for different solutions. If you force yourself to program in nothing but Perl, you may be short-changing yourself and taking the more tortuous route for some problems.

Now, that being said, I shall now reveal my true colors as Perl disciple and perhaps not infrequent evangelist. Perl is without question the greatest single program to appear in the UNIX community (although it runs elsewhere, too) in the last ten years. It makes programming fun again. It's simple enough to get a quick start on, but rich enough for some very complex tasks. I frequently learn new things about it despite having used it nearly daily since Larry Wall first released it to the general public about six years ago. Heck, sometimes even Larry learns something new about Perl! The Artist is not always aware of the breadth and depth of his own work.

It is indeed the case that Perl is a strict superset of *sed* and *awk*, so much so that *s2p* and *a2p* translators exist for these utilities. You can do anything in Perl that you can do in the shell, although Perl is strictly speaking not a command interpreter. It's more of a programming language.

Most of us have written, or at least seen, shell scripts from hell. While often touted as one of UNIX's strengths because they're conglomerations of small, single-purpose tools, these shell scripts quickly grow so complex that they're cumbersome and hard to understand, modify, and maintain. After a certain point of complexity, the strength of the UNIX philosophy of having many programs that each does one thing well becomes its weakness.

The big problem with piping tools together is that there is only one pipe. This means that several different data streams have to get multiplexed into a single data stream, then demuxed on the other end of the pipe. This wastes processor time as well as human brain power.

For example, you might be shuffling a list of filenames through a pipe, but you also want to indicate that certain files have a particular attribute, and others don't. (For example, certain files are more than ten days old.) Typically, this information is encoded in the data stream by appending or prepending some special marker string to the filename. This means that both the pipe feeder and the pipe reader need to know about it. Not a pretty sight.

Because *perl* is one program rather than a dozen others (*sh, awk, sed, tr, wc, sort, grep*, and so on), it is usually clearer to express yourself in *perl* than in *sh* and allies, and often more efficient as well. You don't need as many pipes, temporary files, or separate processes to do the job. You don't need to go shoving your data stream out to *tr* and back, and to *sed* and back, and to *awk* and back, and to *sort* and back, and then back to *sed*, and back again. Doing so can often be slow, awkward, and/or confusing.

Anyone who's ever tried to pass command-line arguments into a *sed* script of moderate complexity or above can attest to the fact that getting the quoting right is not a pleasant task. In fact, quoting in general in the shell is just not a pleasant thing to code or to read.

In a heterogeneous computing environment, the available versions of many tools vary too much from one system to the next to be utterly reliable. Does your *sh* understand functions on all your machines? What about your *awk*? What about local variables? It is very difficult to do complex programming without being able to break a problem up into subproblems of lesser complexity. You're forced to resort to using the shell to call other shell scripts and allow UNIX's power of spawning processes *(40.02)* to serve as your subroutine mechanism, which is inefficient at best. That means your script will require several separate scripts to run, and getting all these installed, working, and maintained on all the different machines in your local configuration is painful. With *perl*, all you need to do is get it installed on the system—which is really pretty easy thanks to Larry's *Configure* program—and after that you're home free.

Perl is even beginning to be included by some software and hardware vendors' standard software distributions. I predict we'll see a lot more of this in the next couple of years.

Besides being faster, *perl* is a more powerful tool than *sh*, *sed*, or *awk*. I realize these are fighting words in some camps, but so be it. There exists a substantial niche between shell programming and C programming that *perl* conveniently fills. Tasks of this nature seem to arise with extreme frequency in the realm of system administration. Since system administrators almost invariably have far too much to do to devote a week to coding up every task before them in C, *perl* is especially useful for them. Larry Wall, Perl's author, has been known to call it "a shell for C programmers." I like to think of it as a "BASIC for UNIX." I realize that this carries both good and bad connotations.

In what ways is *perl* more powerful than the individual tools? This list is pretty long, so what follows is not necessarily an exhaustive list. To begin with, you don't have to worry about arbitrary and annoying restrictions on string length, input line length, or number of elements in an array. These are all virtually unlimited; i.e., limited to your system's address space and virtual memory size.

Perl's regular expression *(27.04)* handling is far and above the best I've ever seen. For one thing, you don't have to remember which tool wants which particular flavor of regular expressions, or lament the fact that one tool doesn't allow (..|..) constructs or +'s \b's or whatever. With Perl, it's all the same—and, as far as I can tell, a proper superset of all the others.

Perl has a fully functional symbolic debugger (written, of course, in Perl) that is an indispensable aid in debugging complex programs. Neither the shell nor *sed/awk/sort/tr/* ... have such a thing.

Perl has a loop control mechanism that's more powerful even than C's. You can do the equivalent of a *break* or *continue* (*last* and *next* in Perl) of any arbitrary loop, not merely the nearest enclosing one. You can even do a kind of *continue* that doesn't trigger the re-initialization part of a loop, something you may, from time to time, want to do.

Perl's data types and operators are richer than the shells' or *awk*'s, because you have scalars, numerically-indexed arrays (lists), and string-indexed (hashed) arrays. Each of these holds arbitrary data values, including floating-point numbers, for which mathematic built-in subroutines and power operators are available. It can handle binary data of arbitrary size.

Speaking of LISP, you can generate strings, perhaps with *sprintf( )*, and then *eval* them. That way you can generate code on the fly. You can even do lambda-type functions that return newly-created functions that you can call later. The scoping of variables is dynamic; fully recursive subroutines are supported; and you can pass or return any type of data into or out of your subroutines.

You have a built-in automatic formatter for generating pretty-printed forms with automatic pagination and headers and center-justified and text-filled fields like %(|fmt)s, if you can imagine what that would actually be were it legal.

There's a mechanism for writing SUID *(1.23)* programs that can be made more secure than even C programs thanks to an elaborate data-tracing mechanism that understands the "taintedness" of data derived from external sources. It won't let you do anything really stupid that you might not have thought of.

You have access to just about any system-related function or system call, like *ioctls, fcntl, select, pipe* and *fork, getc, socket* and *bind,* and *connect* and *attach,* and indirect *syscall* invocation, as well as things like *getpwuid, gethost-byname,* etc. You can read in binary data laid out by a C program or system call using structure-conversion templates.

At the same time you can get at the high-level shell-type operations like the *−r* or *−w* tests *(46.19)* on files or \`backquote\` *(10.14)* command interpolation. You can do file-globbing with the `<*.[ch]>` *(16.01)* notation or do low-level *readdir*s as suits your fancy.

DBM files can be accessed using simple array notation. This is really nice for dealing with system databases (aliases, news, . . .), efficient access mechanisms over large data sets, and for keeping persistent data.

Don't be dismayed by the apparent complexity of what I've just discussed. Perl is actually very easy to learn because so much of it derives from existing tools. It's like interpreter C with *sh, sed, awk,* and a lot more built into it. And, finally, there's a lot of code out there already written in Perl, including libraries to handle things you don't feel like re-implementing.

—TC

## Part Six

Managing Processes

In one of his more famous lines, poet William Butler Yeats asked, "How can you tell the dancer from the dance?"

If it didn't sound so pretentious, you might get away with asking the same question about programs and processes. A process is the image of a program as it executes rather than lies there on the disk, a process *in potentia*.

Really, this whole book is about processes; we're not talking about program design but about using the darn things.

Perhaps we're splitting hairs to break off this section. The chapters it contains could have fit in elsewhere. In the end, though, it seemed right to honor the somewhat tenuous link between the topics of managing processes (Chapter 40), program and system performance (Chapter 41), and offline execution (Chapter 42).

—TOR

40

Starting, Stopping, and Killing Processes

40.01 What's in this Chapter

We've already talked about so many of the topics in this chapter, here or there, that it may seem like a real hodgepodge. It's a grab-bag of important things to know about processes—which you can think of as programs that are actually running, rather than sitting on the disk somewhere.

The chapter starts out with a couple of conceptual articles. They define some important terms that you're likely to encounter in this chapter.

Then we talk about the *ps* command, which tells you what processes you have running and just what they are up to (articles 40.05, 40.06, 40.07).

The next few articles cover signals, which are how processes communicate with each other. We cover topics like:

- What are signals (articles 40.08, 40.09)?

- How to send signals from the keyboard (article 40.10; also see article 6.09).

- How shell programs can "handle" signals (article 40.11; also see article 46.12).

We go from there to a more general discussion of ways to kill processes:

- How to kill all your processes (article 40.12).

- How to kill processes by name rather than by process id (article 40.13).

- How to stop runaway jobs (article 40.14).

- Why some processes don't seem to go away when you kill them (articles 40.15, 40.16).

40.02 fork and exec

We've already discussed *fork* and *exec* way back in article 1.11, but the concept comes up so often in this chapter that we thought we ought to have a closer cross-reference.

Put simply, *fork* and *exec* are the UNIX system calls (requests for operating system services) that UNIX programs use to create new processes. When you start up a UNIX system, it starts with only one process, a program called *init*.

How does *init* magically turn into the hundreds or perhaps even thousands of processes that make up a working UNIX system? That's where *fork* and *exec* come in.

One process spawns another ("spawn" is another term you should get used to seeing) either by replacing itself when it's done—an *exec*—or if it needs to stay around, by making a copy of itself—a *fork*. In the latter case, the forked copy commits polite suicide by *exec*ing the desired second program.

A good example of this whole sequence can be seen in the way a UNIX system's login procedure for terminals (non-network *(1.33)* logins) works. The *init* process spawns a series of *getty* processes, each of which monitors a serial port (a *tty*) looking for activity. It's the *getty* program that actually puts up the first `login:` prompt.

Once someone actually types a login name, *getty*'s job is done; it *exec*s the *login* command. *login* prompts for a password (if the account has one) and, if the password is okay, *exec*s the login shell. Whenever you start another program, the shell *fork*s itself, and the copy *exec*s whatever program you asked to run.

That's why some commands are built-in to the shell *(1.10)*. There's overhead involved in starting a new process. What's more, because a child process can't affect its parent's environment *(40.03)*, some commands don't make sense as separate processes. For example, *cd* must be built in, or it couldn't change the working directory for the current shell.

There's an *exec* command that you can type at a shell prompt; see article 47.07. Watch out, though, it will replace your shell with whatever command you *exec*, with no going back. This is useful only if you want to replace your shell with some other interactive command interpreter with similar powers (as in article 23.23), or if you'll be ready to log out when the command you *exec* finishes.

—*TOR*

40.03 Managing Processes: Overall Concepts

As you know, when you log into your UNIX account and start typing, you're talking to the shell *(9.01)*. The shell you use may be a variant of the Bourne shell (such as a standard *sh*, or *ksh* or the GNU shell *bash*), or perhaps it is a variant of the C shell, *csh* (such as, perhaps, the *tcsh* shell that includes line- and history-editing features). Alternatively, you may be using a somewhat less common shell such as *rc*.

Your shell is a **process**, one of many individual programs running at the same time on the machine. Every process has certain pieces of information associated with it, including:

- The **process ID** (PID) is a number assigned to the process when it is started up. Process IDs are unique (that is, they cycle and are eventually re-used, but no two processes have the same process ID at the same time).

- The **user ID** (UID) tells who the process belongs to. This determines what files and directories the process is allowed to read to or write from *(23.01)*, as well as who is allowed to *kill* the process *(40.10)* (tell it to stop running).

- The **group ID** (GID) is similar to the user ID, but tells which group the process belongs to. On some systems, this controls the group assigned to files created by the process. See articles 23.05, 23.14, and 23.02.

- The **environment** contains a list of variables and associated values. For example, when you type echo $HOME at the shell and it prints out the name of your home directory *(1.20)*, it has told you the contents of the environment variable *(7.01)* called *HOME*.

- The **current working directory** *(15.03)* is the directory that is currently the default. When you specify a filename to a program but do not say explicitly where to look for it [with a pathname *(15.02)* —*JP*], the program will look in the current working directory.

- **File descriptors** are a record of which files a process has opened for reading or writing, as well as the current position in each file. Articles 47.20 through 47.23 explain file descriptor use in the Bourne shell.

- Versions of UNIX with job control *(13.08)* have **process groups**. A process group is used for distribution of signals *(40.09, 40.12, 40.14)*. It's also used to control which process can read from a terminal. A process that has the same process group as the terminal is "in the foreground" and can read from the terminal. Other processes are stopped when they try to read from the terminal.

When you're typing commands at the shell, it is the **controlling process** of your terminal, meaning that it (the shell) is the process that gets the input you type. See article 40.06.

Normally, when you type a command at the shell prompt, that command runs and is allowed by the shell to take over the terminal for its lifetime. For example, if you type `more .login` to view your *.login* file, the shell starts up the *more (26.03)* program and then sits around waiting for it to finish; while *more* is running, you can type commands to page through the file and *more* will see them instead of the shell. The command you run is called a **child** or **subprocess** of the shell process, which is its **parent**. All process information (user ID, group ID, etc.) is inherited by the child from its parent, except for the process ID, since the child is assigned a new one. [Built-in shell commands *(1.10)* like *cd* don't start a child process. —*JP*]

Although the normal behavior is for the shell to wait until any command you run has finished before it becomes active again, there are some situations in which you don't want this to occur. For example, if you're using a window system such as X *(1.31)* and want to start up a new *xterm* window from your shell, you don't want to type just `xterm`, because then your original shell will wait until the *xterm* finishes before allowing you to type any more commands. This would mean that you still have only one shell to work in, thus defeating the purpose of starting the new *xterm*.

When you don't want a process to finish before getting back to the shell, you can run it in the background *(1.26)*. You do this by putting an ampersand (&) character at the end of the command, for example, `xterm &`. The shell will start the child process and then immediately prompt you for another command. Note that in this situation, the shell retains control of the terminal and the newly created background process cannot read input. Some shells have additional job control *(13.08)* features (processes that are running in the background are often described as **background jobs** or just jobs) that enable you to do things such as kill jobs or bring a job from the background into the **foreground** so that it becomes the controlling process of the terminal and you can type input at it.

An important thing to remember is that although process information is inherited by children *when they are started*, it is impossible for the parent to affect its child's process information (or vice versa) after that point. For example, if you start up the editor *vi*, suspend it *(13.04)*, and then use the *cd* command in the shell to change directories, *vi* will still have the old working directory when you bring it back into the foreground. Similarly, if you write a shell script that changes some environment variables, those variables will contain their old values in the shell when the shell script exits. This is sometimes confusing to MS-DOS users, since information such as the current directory is stored in a global area which is referenced by all programs. If it is necessary to communicate information from a child back to a parent shell, other methods are needed *(9.08, 46.22)*.

Just as there are ways to modify the environment and the current working directory of the shell, there are also useful ways to manipulate file descriptors *(47.20, 47.21, 47.22)*.

—JIK

40.04 Subshells

In UNIX, when a program starts another program (more exactly, when a process starts another process), the new process runs as a subprocess *(40.03)* or child process.* When a shell starts another shell, the new shell is called a *subshell.*†

So what? There are some important things to know *(7.02)* about it: the child process gets a copy of its parent's environment. Any changes in the environment of the child process aren't passed to its parent. "Still," I hear you say, "so what??"

- Shell scripts are run in a subshell (unless you use the *source* or . commands *(46.22)* to start the script). If the script makes changes to the environment of its (sub)shell, the parent shell won't see those changes. If the script uses *cd*, it doesn't change the current directory in the parent shell. If the script changes the value of the *TZ* (or any) environment variable *(7.07)*, that won't change *TZ* in the parent shell. The script can set a different *umask (23.04)* than the parent shell—no problem.

- There are times you might want to start a subshell from your current shell. Maybe you're working on a special project where you want to work in a different current directory, set new values of environment variables, set a new home directory, reset some aliases, use a different *PATH (7.04)*, whatever. When you end the subshell, the parent shell's environment will be the way it was.

  If your parent shell has job control *(13.01)*, you can stop the subshell and pop back to your parent shell without losing the changes in the subshell. If the child shell has job control, too, the *suspend (23.23)* command will stop it. Otherwise, just type CTRL-z at the subshell's prompt. For example:

prompt 8.02

```
myprompt% csh
myprompt% set prompt="project% "
project% cd project-directory
project% setenv PRINTER plotter
project% set path=($path some-new-directories)
project% setenv EXINIT "se ts=4 sw=4 aw wm=0"
    ...do some work...
project% suspend

Stopped
myprompt%
    ...back to parent shell...
```

---

*This isn't true when the subprocess is *exec*d from the parent process without a *fork* first. Article 40.02 explains.

†When you use the shell's *exec (47.07)* command, it does not start a subprocess.

```
myprompt% fg %csh
    ...back to subshell...
%
```

I use *suspend* so much that I've made a CTRL-z-like alias named *z*.

- A shell escape *(31.26)* starts a subshell. Do whatever you want to the subshell's environment. When you end the shell escape, the changes go away.

- The *su (23.23)* command starts a subshell. *cd* anywhere, change environment variables, and so on . . .

If you use the *exit* command, a subshell (or any shell) will terminate. In a script, when the shell reads the end of file, that does an implicit *exit*. On the command line, an end-of-input character (usually CTRL-d) will do the same thing. Article 46.11 explains how *exit* sets a shell's exit status.

—JP

40.05 *The ps Command*

The *ps* command produces a report summarizing execution statistics for current processes. The bare *ps* command lists the process ID, the terminal the command was started from, how much CPU time it has used, and the command itself. The output looks something like this (it differs from system to system):

```
PID TT STAT   TIME COMMAND
1803 p5 IW    0:00 -csh (csh)
1883 p5 IW    0:04 vi outline
1811 p6 IW    0:01 -csh (csh)
5353 p6 TW    0:01 vi 4890
```

By default, *ps* lists only your own processes. There are many times, though, when it's desirable to have a more complete listing, with a lot of data about all of the processes currently running on the system. The options required to do this differ between BSD UNIX and System V. Under BSD UNIX, the command is *ps –aux*, which produces a table of all processes, arranged in order of decreasing CPU usage at the moment when the *ps* command was executed. [The *–a* option gives processes belonging to all users, *–u* gives a more detailed listing, and *–x* lists processes that no longer have a controlling terminal *(40.06)*. *— TOR*] It is often useful to pipe this output to *head (26.21)*, which will display the most active processes:

```
% ps -aux | head -5
USER       PID %CPU %MEM   SZ  RSS TTY STAT   TIME COMMAND
martin   12923 74.2 22.5  223  376 p5  R      2:12 f77 -o foo foo.F
chavez   16725 10.9 50.8 1146 1826 p6  R N   56:04 g94 HgO.dat
ng       17026  3.5  1.2  354  240 co  I      0:19 vi benzene.txt
gull      7997  0.2  0.3  142   46 p3  S      0:04 csh
```

The meanings of the fields in this output (as well as others displayed by the *–l* option to *ps*) are given in Table 40-1.

The first line of Table 40-1 shows that user *martin* is running a FORTRAN compilation (f77). This process has PID *(40.03)* 12923 and is currently running or runable. User *chavez'* process (PID 16725), executing the program *g94*, is also running or runable, though at a lowered priority. From this display, it's obvious who is using most system resources at this instant: *martin* and *chavez* have about 85% of the CPU and 73% of the memory between them. However, although it does display total CPU time, *ps* does not average the %CPU or %MEM values over time in any way.

Table 40-1. ps Command Output Fields

Column*	Contents
USER (BSD)	Username of process owner.
UID (System V)	Username of process owner.
PID	Process ID.
%CPU	Estimated fraction of CPU consumed (BSD).
%MEM	Estimated fraction of system memory consumed (BSD).
SZ	Virtual memory used in K (BSD) or pages (System V).
RSS	Real memory used (in same units as SZ).
TT, TTY	Terminal port associated with process.
STAT (BSD), S (System V)	Current process state; one (or more under BSD) of:
	R: Running or runnable.
	S: Sleeping.
	I: Idle (BSD). Intermediate state (System V).
	T: Stopped *(13.08)*.
	Z: Zombie process *(40.16)*.
	D (BSD): Disk wait.
	P (BSD): Page wait.
	X (System V): Growing: waiting for memory.
	K (AIX): Available kernel process.
	W (BSD): Swapped out.
	N (BSD): Niced *(41.09, 41.11)*: execution priority lowered.
	> (BSD): Execution priority artificially raised *(41.11)*.
TIME	Total CPU time used.
COMMAND	Command line being executed (truncated).
STIME (System V)	Time or date process started.
C (System V), CP (BSD)	Short term CPU-use factor; used by scheduler for computing execution priority (PRI below).
F	Flags associated with process (see *ps* manual page).
PPID	Parent's PID.

Table 40-1. ps Command Output Fields (continued)

Column*	Contents
PRI	Actual execution priority (recomputed dynamically).
NI	Process nice number.
WCHAN	Event process is waiting for.

*Some vendors add other fields, such as the processor number for multiprocessors and additional or different process states (as in the AIX K field). These codes may differ from vendor to vendor: for example, the 0 code under Stardent UNIX means a process that is actually running (and R means runable) while 0 under AIX means a nonexistent process.

A vaguely similar listing is produced by the System V *ps -ef* command:

```
$ ps -ef
    UID   PID  PPID   C    STIME    TTY  TIME CMD
   root     0     0   0 09:36:35      ?  0:00 sched
   root     1     0   0 09:36:35      ?  0:02 /etc/init
  . . .
   gull  7997     1  10 09:49:32  ttyp3  0:04 csh
 martin 12923 11324   9 10:19:49  ttyp5 56:12 f77 -o foo foo.F
 chavez 16725 16652  15 17:02:43  ttyp6 10:04 g94 <HgO.dat >HgO.log
     ng 17026 17012  14 17:23:12 console 0:19 vi benzene.txt
```

The columns hold the username, process ID, parent's PID (the PID of the process that created it), the current scheduler value, the time the process started, its associated terminal, its accumulated CPU time, and the command it is running. Note that the ordering is by PID, not resource usage.

AIX's version of the *ps* command supports both BSD and System V options. The BSD options are not preceded by a hyphen (which is a legal syntax variation), and the System V options are. Thus, under AIX, `ps -au` is not the same as `ps au`. The command is the System V version, however, even if its output is displayed with the BSD column headings. Thus, *ps aux* output is displayed in PID rather than %CPU order.

ps is also useful in pipes; a common use is:

```
% ps -aux | grep chavez
```

to see what user *chavez* has currently running.

—AF from the Nutshell Handbook *Essential System Administration*

40.06 The Controlling Terminal

In article 40.05, we pointed out that the *ps* command needs special options (*–x* for BSD and *–e* for System V) to list processes without a controlling terminal.

But just what is a controlling terminal? Just what it sounds like: the terminal from which the process was started. In the *ps* listing, this is usually given as a *tty*, or terminal id. That *ps* entry usually corresponds to a serial port, or a *pty* *(43.08)*. A *pty* or "pseudo-terminal" is a construct that makes a window or network login *(1.33)* look to the operating system just like a terminal.

In the *ps* listing, a tty might appear as t1 for */dev/tty1*, p3 for */dev/ttyp3*, or as some other designation, such as co for */dev/console*, the full screen display of a workstation before any window system is started. Processes without a controlling terminal show a question mark (?).

How does a process "lose" its controlling terminal? Easy. Some processes, such as system "daemons" *(1.14)* never had one—they were started by system scripts that weren't started from any terminal, or they disconnected themselves from their controlling terminals. But it's also possible that you started a process running in the background, logged out, and logged back later or on another terminal to find it still running without a controlling terminal.

The *tty* command can be used to report which "terminal" you're currently connected to. For example:

```
% tty
/dev/ttyp2
```

Running *tty* without a controlling terminal gives the message not a tty.

—TOR

40.07 Why ps Prints Some Commands in Parentheses

The reason that some versions of *ps*, and thus derivatives such as *w*, sometimes print commands in parentheses [one of our UNIX systems uses square brackets—*JP*]:

```
% ps -f -u jerry
    UID   PID  PPID  C    STIME TTY     TIME COMMAND
  jerry 29240 29235  0 07:56:19 ttyp1   0:01 sh find_mh_dupes
  jerry 29259 29240 23 07:57:52 ttyp1   0:07 (egrep)
```

is that whoever wrote *ps* liked it that way. The parentheses indicate that the command overwrote its name, or that *ps* could not find the name, and that *ps* is printing instead the "accounting name." (The accounting name is the last component of the name given to the *exec (40.02)* system call, and is the name used in the system resource usage accounting file.) Basically, *ps* does this [in the C language—*JP*]:

```
if (proc->argv == NULL || strcmp(proc->acct_name, proc->argv[0]) != 0)
    printf("(%s)", proc->acct_name);
```

In the case of a large environment, *ps* is unable to find the argument vector. This is because it reads only the last few stack pages of each process.

Other versions of *ps* use completely different mechanisms for locating the command arguments and may never print parentheses.

—*CT* in *net.unix-wizards* on Usenet, *13 November 1983*

40.08 *What are Signals?*

Signals are a simple, but important means of interprocess communication. Interprocess communication sounds fancy, but it's really a simple concept: it's the means by which one program sends a message to another program. It's common to think of signals as special messages sent by the UNIX kernel *(1.14)* but, in fact, any program can signal any other program.

What kinds of messages can you send with a signal? Relatively few, in reality. Signals aren't "arbitrary" messages, like letters; they are a small group of predefined messages, each with its own special meaning. System V UNIX supports 16 signals, each of which is assigned a number; BSD-derived UNIX implementations and SVR4 have 32 signals. Table 40-2 lists some of the more commonly used signals. It also lists keyboard characters that send common signals on BSD systems (these can be changed; see article 6.09).

Table 40-2. Common Signals

Signal Name	Number	Meaning and Typical Use
HUP	1	Hangup—stop running. Sent when you log out or disconnect a modem.
INT	2	Interrupt—stop running. Sent when you type CTRL-c.
QUIT	3	Quit—stop running (and dump core *(55.01)*). Sent when you type CTRL-\ .
KILL	9	Kill—stop unconditionally and immediately; a good "emergency kill."
SEGV	11	Segmentation violation—You have tried to access illegal memory.
TERM	15	Terminate—terminate nicely, if possible.
STOP	17	Stop unconditionally and immediately; continue with CONT.
TSTP	18	Stop—Stop executing, ready to continue (in either background or foreground). Sent when you type CTRL-z. *stty (6.09)* calls this *susp*.
CONT	19	Continue—Continue executing after STOP or TSTP.
CHLD	20	Child—a child process's status has changed.
USR1	30	User-defined signal.

While this list isn't definitive, it shows you the types of things signals can do. Many signals, like *SIGSEGV*, are warning or error messages. You've probably seen the frustrating "segmentation violation" message. That message came when the kernel detected something wrong and sent your program a *SIGSEGV* signal; in response, your program quit. Others signals, like *SIGTSTP*, are generated in response to special characters on the keyboard. And a lot of signals just say, "Your time is up, goodbye!"

When a process receives a signal, it can take a number of actions; for example:

- It can take whatever default action is specified for the signal. By default, some signals kill the process that receives them. For some signals, the default action is to stop running and dump core. (*SIGQUIT* is an example of this.) Other signals have no effect by default.

- It can trap *(46.12)* the signal and run a special "signal handling" function—in which case, it can do whatever it wants. A signal handler often does whatever's necessary to shut the program down nicely: make sure that files are closed and left in a consistent state, and so on.

- It can ignore the signal, in which case nothing happens.

You've probably read that the command *kill –9* is guaranteed to kill a process. Why? Two special signals in Table 40-2 can't be caught or ignored: the *KILL* and *STOP* signals.

The *kill (40.10)* command doesn't kill—it really does nothing more than send signals. As you now know, signals often bring death and destruction—but there's no necessary reason for them to do so.

—ML

40.09 Killing Foreground Jobs

You probably know that typing CTRL-c *(40.08)* will terminate your foreground job. But what actually happens when you type CTRL-c?

When you type CTRL-c, you're sending the INT (interrupt) signal *(40.08)* to the foreground process. Most well-designed programs "catch" the interrupt signal—which means that the program installs some special function (a "signal handler") that is called whenever a signal arrives. The signal handler normally closes all open files, resets your terminal properly (if needed), and does anything else necessary so that the program can depart from this world at peace. Then the program terminates. The QUIT signal, sent by CTRL-\, works similarly but also makes a *core* file *(55.01)* for debugging.

Of course, it's possible for the signal handler to do something else entirely: it's possible for the program to decide not to quit, or to implement some truly bizarre feature. In fact, editors like *vi* or Emacs almost always ignore most signals. The *trap (46.12)* command handles signals in the Bourne shell.

Whenever you send a signal from the keyboard, it's sent to all processes in the same process group *(40.03)*. This may include the program's child processes, but may not. And, of course, child processes can choose to ignore signals on their own. But more often than not, killing the parent process kills its children.

Article 6.09 explains how to set the key that sends these and other signals. The *kill (40.10)* command also sends signals.

—*ML, JP*

40.10 *Destroying Processes with kill*

Sometimes it's necessary to eliminate a process entirely or to signal a process *(40.11)*; this is the purpose of the *kill* command. You can use the *kill* command with or without a signal id:

```
% kill pid
% kill -signal pid
```

where *pid* is the process' identification number, and *signal* (which is optional) is the signal to send to the process. The default signal is number 15, the *TERM* signal, which tells the process to terminate. Under System V, the signal must be specified numerically; under BSD, either the signal number or its symbolic name may be used. [Use *kill –l* for a list of signal names; unfortunately, the listing doesn't shown the correspondence of names and numbers. However, they are in order, so if you can count, you can figure it out.— *TOR*]

Sometimes, a process may still exist after a *kill* command. If this happens, execute the *kill* command with the *–9* option, which sends the process signal 9, appropriately named *KILL*. This almost always guarantees that the process will be destroyed. However, it does not allow the dying process to clean up, and therefore may leave the process' files in an inconsistent state.

Occasionally, processes will not die even after being sent the *KILL* signal. The vast majority of such processes fall into one of three categories:

- Zombies. A process in the zombie state *(40.16)* is displayed as *Z* status in BSD *ps* displays and as *<defunct>* under System V *(40.05)*. When a process is exiting, it informs its parent of its imminent death; when it receives an acknowledgment, its PID is removed from the process table. A zombie process is one whose total resources have been freed, but the parent process' acknowledgment has not occurred. Usually, *init* will step in when the parent is gone, but very occasionally this fails to happen. Zombies are always cleared the next time the system is booted and do not adversely affect system performance.

- Processes waiting for unavailable NFS *(1.33)* resources (for example, trying to write to a remote file on a system that has crashed) will not die if sent a *KILL* signal. Use the *QUIT* signal(3) or the *INT* (interrupt) signal(2) to kill such processes.

- Processes waiting for a device to complete an operation before exiting. Often this means waiting for a tape to finish rewinding.

Killing a process may also kill all of its children. Child processes may not die if they're blocking or "catching" the signal you use—although, as explained above, the *KILL* signal will usually terminate those processes. Killing a shell can therefore kill all the foreground and stopped background processes initiated from that shell (including other shells). Killing a user's login shell is equivalent to logging the user out. This is a useful (if somewhat painful) way to recover from certain kinds of problems. For example, if a user manages to confuse his editor by mistyping control keys and escape sequences, or enters an infinite loop that he can't terminate by normal means, killing his shell will let him regain control of the situation, possibly at the cost of some work. Use the *ps* command to determine which process is the offending user's shell. Remember that you must be superuser *(1.24)* in order to kill someone else's process.

—*AF* from the Nutshell Handbook *Essential System Administration*

40.11 *Printer Queue Watcher: a Restartable Daemon Shell Script*

[This article may not appear to have a lot to do with the subject of this chapter, but it illustrates the other side of signal handling—what a program or shell script can do when it receives a signal. Jerry's script uses the trap (46.12) command to catch several different signals, and act differently depending on whether the signal is a "hangup" (HUP, or signal 1) or a TERM (signal 15).—TOR]

UNIX systems run "daemon" programs like *cron*(8) and *syslogd*(8) that wait in the background, looking for work to do. Many daemons read configuration files when they start up. System administrators sometimes change the configuration files and want the daemon to re-read the file. One way to do that is by terminating and restarting the program—but that's ugly and also means the daemon won't be running for a few seconds until it's restarted. So, many daemons are designed to re-read their configuration files and/or restart themselves when they get a signal (usually, the HUP signal, signal 1). System administrators do this by getting the daemon's process ID number and sending the signal with the *kill* command. Because the daemon "catches" the signal, the daemon isn't actually killed.

You can run a shell script as a daemon by putting it in the background.* Here's a simple example, a shell script named *watchq*. It reads a file full of printer queue names and stores it in a shell variable. Every 30 seconds, it runs *lpq* *(45.02)* on all printer queues listed. If any queues have an error, the script echoes a message and the output of *lpq* to a particular user with the *write* *(1.33)* command.

---

*It's usually also a good idea to be sure that the input and outputs are redirected *(14.01, 47.21)* away from the terminal, maybe to the system console instead. On systems and shells that kill background jobs when you log out, use *nohup* *(40.18).*

After the script has run for a while, the printer named *office* goes down. I edit the *watchqs* file and remove that printer so the poor user *lisa* won't keep getting complaints about it. Then I send a signal to have the file re-read:

watchq

```
% cat watchq
#! /bin/sh
# watchq - "daemon" script that watches printer queue(s) for errors
temp=/tmp/WATCHQ$$                # Holds output of lpq
watch=/usr/local/lib/watchqs     # Queue names to watch
writeto=lisa                     # User who gets notices about printer
queues="`cat $watch`"            # Put list of queue names in $queues
trap 'queues="`cat $watch`"' 1   # Reset $queues if we get a SIGHUP
trap 'rm -f $temp; exit' 0 15    # Clean up temp file when killed

# Loop forever (until someone kills script):
while :
do
     for queue in $queues
     do
          lpq -P$queue >$temp
          if egrep '(out of paper|error|warning)' $temp >/dev/null
          then echo "PRINTER QUEUE $queue:" | cat - $temp | write $writeto
          fi
     done
     sleep 30
done
% echo office main lobby > /usr/local/lib/watchqs
% watchq &
[1] 4363
    ...
% echo main lobby > /usr/local/lib/watchqs
% kill -1 4363
    ...
% kill 4363
[1]    Exit -48            watchq
```

/dev/null 14.14
− 14.13

kill 40.10

In real life, the *watchq* script might be started from a system file like */etc/rc.local* when the system reboots. Lisa would probably edit the *watchqs* file herself. The username that's notified by *write* might also be resettable with a *kill −1*.

This isn't foolproof and you can run into subtle problems. For instance, the *write* command may not work on some UNIXes if it's running from a daemon without a controlling tty *(40.06)*. Also, the error messages that *egrep (28.05)* searches for may not catch all problems and are system-dependent. But this script is just a demonstration—to show a great way to write a quick-and-dirty daemon.

—JP

40.12 Killing All Your Processes

On many UNIX systems, *kill (40.10)* interprets the special "process ID" −1 as a command to signal all your processes (all processes with your user ID), *except* for the process sending the signal. So, for example, the command:

```
% kill -TERM -1
```

will terminate all your processes.* To see if your system supports this feature, type man 2 kill to read the *kill*(2) manual page.

You can use this to prevent background jobs from continuing after you logout; just stick kill -TERM -1 into your *.logout* file. There are some good reasons *not* to do this though: if you use several terminals, this will kill *all* your processes when you log out from *any* terminal.

This command is also useful in desperate situations. If processes are spawning out of control, or if your terminal is locked, you can log in from another terminal and kill everything, without having to dig through *ps (40.05)* to find the right process. [The *zap (40.13)* script searches process lists and kills processes automatically.—JP]

The special −1 process ID is defined differently for the superuser; if you're root, it means "all processes *except* system processes."

If you can't use the −1 process ID, and you use the Bourne shell or another shell without job control, you can use a 0 (zero) process ID. That sends the signal to all members of the process group (that is, processes resulting from the current login). A 0 doesn't work on shells, like the C shell, that have job control *(13.01)*.

—ML, JP, JIK

40.13 Interactively Kill Processes Matching a Pattern

When you want to kill processes, it's a pain in the neck to run *ps (40.05)*, figure out the process ID, and then kill the process. This article explains two versions of *zap*. The Perl version is fast and fancy. The shell version is slower—but it's a great example of elegant Bourne shell programming.

Perl zap

zap

zap is a *perl (39.01)* script that runs *ps* for you and selects those processes that match the regular expression pattern you supply. (The pattern can match anything on the line that *ps* prints out, not just the command name.)

zap then asks you whether you want to kill each of the selected processes. Type y or Y to kill the process, anything else to leave it alone. Type q or Q to quit. The terminal is put into "single character" mode, so you don't have to type a RETURN.

---

*Signal 15 is *SIGTERM*, which is the signal *kill* sends by default. In this command, you need to specify it explicitly, for obvious syntactic reasons.

zap normally sends a *TERM* signal *(40.08)* (number 15), which gives processes time to exit gracefully, but you can specify another signal by name or number. For example:

```
% zap -9 roff
sqtroff? y
```

Bourne Shell zap

The Perl *zap* emulates a shell script of the same name presented by Brian Kernighan and Rob Pike in their classic book *The UNIX Programming Environment*. The original shell version uses *egrep (28.05)* to pick the processes to kill; you can type extended expressions that match more than one process, such as:

```
% zap 'troff|fmat'
   PID TTY TIME CMD
 22117  01 0:02 fmat somefile? n
 22126  01 0:15 sqtroff -ms somefile? y
```

We've reprinted the script by permission of the authors:

```
#! /bin/sh
zap pattern:  kill all processes matching pattern

PATH=/bin:/usr/bin
IFS='
'                       # just a newline
case $1 in
"")    echo 'Usage: zap [-2] pattern' 1>&2; exit 1 ;;
-*)    SIG=$1; shift
esac

echo '   PID TTY TIME CMD'
kill $SIG `pick \`ps -ag | egrep "$*"\` | awk '{print $1}'`
```

The `ps -ag` command displays all processes on the system. Leave off the `a` to get just your processes. Your version of *ps* may need different options *(40.05)*.

This shell version of *zap* calls another script, *pick,** shown below. *pick* shows each line of its standard input and waits for you to type *y*, *q*, or anything else. Answering *y* writes the line to standard output, answering *q* aborts *pick* without showing more lines, and any other answer shows the next input line without printing the current one. *zap* uses *awk (38.18)* to print the first argument (the process ID number) from any *ps* line you've selected with *pick*. The inner set of nested backquotes *(10.14)* in *zap* pass *pick* the output of *ps*, filtered through *egrep*. Because the *zap* script has set the *IFS* variable *(36.19)* to just a newline, *pick* gets and displays each line of *ps* output as a single argument. The outer set of backquotes pass *kill (40.10)* the output of *pick*, filtered through *awk*.

If you're interested in shell programming and that explanation wasn't detailed enough, take a careful look at the scripts—they're really worth studying. (This

---

*The MH mail system also has a command named *pick*. If you use MH, you could rename this script to something like *choose*.

book's shell programming chapters, 46 through 48, may help, too.) Here's the
pick script:

```
#!/bin/sh
# pick:  select arguments

PATH=/bin:/usr/bin

for i
do
        echo -n "$i? " >/dev/tty
        read response
        case $response in
        y*)     echo $i ;;
        q*)     break
        esac
done </dev/tty
```

—LW, RS, JP

−n *48.10*
/dev/tty *47.20*

done < *47.22*

40.14 *Processes Out of Control? Just STOP Them*

Especially if you're a programmer, you can run into a situation where you have
processes forking *(40.02)* out of control—more and more of them. By the time you
kill one, fifty more fork.

- On systems with job control, there's a good answer: use the *STOP* signal to
  stop the processes:

  ```
  % kill -STOP ...
  ```

  Stop any process you can. Then it won't be able to fork more processes.
  Stop them all. *Then* start cleaning up with *kill –9.*

- If your system manager has set a per-user process limit on your computer,
  the good news is that your processes won't eventually crash the system. But
  the bad news is, when you try to run any command that isn't built into the
  shell:

  ```
  % ps
  No more processes.
  ```

  you can't because you're already at your limit.

  If that happens, log onto another account or ask someone to run a command
  that will give a list of your processes. Depending on your system, the command is probably like one of these two:

  ```
  % ps -u yourname               System V
  % ps aux | grep yourname       BSD
  ```

  Then go back to your terminal and start stopping :-). If you get the No
  more processes error, your shell must not have a built-in *kill* command.
  The C shell does. *Carefully* type the next command to replace your shell

with a C shell. Don't make a mistake (if you do, you may not be able to log in again):

exec *47.07*

```
$ exec /bin/csh
% kill ...
```

—*JP*

40.15 Cleaning Up an Unkillable Process

You or another user might have a process that (according to *ps (40.05)*) has been sleeping for several days, waiting for input. If you can't kill *(40.10)* the process, even with *kill* –9, there may be a bug or some other problem.

✓ These processes can be unkillable because they've made a request for a hardware device or network resource. UNIX has put them to sleep at a very high priority and the event that they are waiting on hasn't happened (because of a network problem, for example). This causes *all* other signals to be held until the hardware event occurs. The signal sent by *kill* doesn't do any good.

✓ If the problem is with a terminal and you can get to the back of the terminal or the back of the computer, try unplugging the line from the port. Also, try typing CTRL-q on the keyboard—if the user typed CTRL-s while getting a lot of output, this may free the process.

✓ Ask your vendor if there's a special command to reset the device driver *(44.01)*. If there isn't, you may have to reboot the computer.

—*JP*

40.16 Why You Can't Kill a Zombie

[Processes in your ps *output that are in the <exiting> status are called zombies.—JP]*

You cannot kill zombies; they are already dead.

"What is a zombie?" I hear you ask. "Why should a dead process stay around?"

Dead processes stick around for two principal reasons. The lesser of these is that they provide a sort of "context" for closing open file descriptors *(40.03)*, and shutting down other resources (memory, swap space, and so forth). This generally happens immediately, and the process remains only for its major purpose: to hold onto its name and exit status *(46.07)*.

A process is named by its *process ID* or PID. Each process also has associated with it a *Parent Process ID*. The parent PID is the PID of the process that created it via *fork (40.02)*, or, if that particular process has since vanished, 1 (the PID of *init (40.02)*). While the original parent is around, it can remember the PIDs of its children. These PIDs cannot be re-used until the parent knows the children are done. The parent can also get a single byte of status *(46.07)* from each child. The *wait* system call looks for a zombie child, then "collects" it, making its PID available and returning that status. The *init*(8) program is always waiting, so that once a parent exits, *init* will collect all its children as they exit, and promptly ignore each status.

So, to get rid of a zombie, you must wait for it. If you have already done so or if the process' PPID is 1, the process is almost certainly stuck in a device driver *(44.01)* close routine, and if it remains that way forever, the driver has a bug.

—*CT in comp.unix.questions* on Usenet, *16 January 1989*

40.17 *Automatically Kill Background Processes on Logout in csh*

In many versions of the Bourne shell, background processes *(1.26)* are automatically killed with a HANGUP signal (signal 1) on logout. But the C shell makes background processes immune to signals and a HANGUP signal at logout doesn't affect the processes; they keep running.

If you want the C shell to work like the Bourne shell, put lines like these in your *.logout* file *(3.01)*:

```
/tmp 22.02    set tf=/tmp/k$$
              jobs >$tf
! -z 49.04    if (! -z $tf) then       # there are jobs
                  jobs >$tf.1          # rerun it to dump `Done' jobs
                                       # skip Stopped jobs (killed by default)
-v 28.03          grep -v Stopped <$tf.1 >$tf; rm $tf.1
                                       # cannot use a pipe here
                  if (! -z $tf) then   # there are running jobs
eval 9.08             eval `echo kill -1; sed 's/.\([0-9]*\).*/%\1/' <$tf`
                  endif
              endif
              rm $tf
```

Warning: this may run afoul of various *csh* quirks *(49.02)*. [To watch this work, put `set verbose echo` *(9.13)* at the top of your *.logout* file. If the logout process clears your screen or closes the window, you can give yourself *n* seconds to read the debugging output by adding `sleep n` *(42.02)* to the end of your *.logout* file.—*JP*] The important trick is to run `jobs >file`, not `jobs | command`, as the latter runs *jobs* in a subshell *(40.04)* and thus produces no output, although `jobs | any-csh-builtin` is good for a laugh :-) .

—*CT in comp.unix.questions* on Usenet, *5 August 1989*

40.18 nohup

When UNIX first started, even local terminals often communicated with the system via short-haul modems. (After all, UNIX was invented by the phone company.) When someone logged out, the modem hung up the phone—and conversely, if the modem hung up, a "hangup" signal was sent to the login shell, whereupon it terminated, bringing down all its child processes *(40.03)* with it.

In the C shell, processes that you run in the background are immune to hangups, but in the Bourne shell, a process that you started in the background might be abruptly terminated.

The *nohup* command (*"no hangup"*) allows you to circumvent this. Simply type:

```
$ nohup command &
```

Any output from *command* that would normally go to the terminal (i.e., has not been redirected) goes to a file named *nohup.out* in the current directory.

Of course, if you want to run jobs at off hours, you might do even better using *at, cron,* or *batch (42.01).*

nohup is sometimes handy in shell scripts to make them ignore the HUP and TERM signals *(40.08)*, though *trap (46.12)* is more versatile. (In System V, *nohup* causes a command to ignore HUP and QUIT, but not TERM.)

—*TOR*

41

Time and Performance

41.01 Which Time is it?

When we talk about "time" on UNIX systems, we could be talking about two things:

1. What time it is, as shown by the *date(53.10)* command, and recorded in countless ways—as file creation and modification times, as the time of last login, and so on.

2. How long things take.

This chapter is concerned with the latter. It talks about how long programs take to run, what makes them faster or slower, and what you can (or more often can't) do about it.

—TOR

41.02 Timing Programs

Two commands, *time* and */bin/time*, provide simple timings. Their information is highly accurate, because no profiling overhead distorts the program's performance. Neither program provides any analysis on the routine or trace level. They report the total execution time, some other global statistics, and nothing more. You can use them on any program.

time and */bin/time* differ primarily in that *time* is built into the C shell. Therefore, it cannot be used in Bourne shell scripts or in makefiles. It also cannot be used if you prefer the Bourne shell (*sh*). */bin/time* is an independent executable file and therefore can be used in any situation. To get a simple program timing, enter either *time* or */bin/time*, followed by the command you would normally use to execute the program. For example, to time a program named *analyze*, enter the following command:

```
% time analyze inputdata outputfile
9.0u 6.7s 0:30 18% 23+24k 285+148io 625pf+0w
```

This indicates that the program spent 9.0 seconds on behalf of the user (user time), 6.7 seconds on behalf of the system (system time, or time spent executing UNIX kernel routines on the user's behalf), and a total of 30 seconds elapsed time. Elapsed time is the wall clock time from the moment you enter the command until it terminates, including time spent waiting for other users, I/O time, etc. By definition, the elapsed time is greater than your total CPU time and can even be several times larger. You can set programs to be timed automatically (without typing *time* first) or change the output format by setting the *csh time* variable *(41.03)*.

The example above shows the CPU time as a percentage of the elapsed time (18 percent). The remaining data report virtual memory management and I/O statistics. The meaning varies, depending on your shell; check your online *csh* manual page or article 41.03. In this example, under SunOS 4.1.1, the other fields show the amount of shared memory used, the amount of nonshared memory used (k), the number of block input and output operations (io), and the number of page faults plus the number of swaps (pf and w). The memory management figures are unreliable in many implementations, so take them with a grain of salt.

/bin/time reports only the real time (elapsed time), user time, and system time. For example:

```
% /bin/time analyze inputdata outputfile
      60.8 real        11.4 user        4.6 sys
```

[If you use the Bourne shell, you can just type time.—*JP*] This reports that the program ran for 60.8 seconds before terminating, using 11.4 seconds of user time and 4.6 seconds of system time, for a total of 16 seconds of CPU time.

Article 41.05 has more about the terms used in this article.

—*ML* from the Nutshell Handbook *UNIX for FORTRAN Programmers*

41.03 *The csh time variable*

The C shell's variable named *time* controls the built-in *csh time* command *(41.02)*. It lets you run *time* by default on commands that take more than a certain number of CPU seconds, and it lets you control the format of *time*'s output.

We'll start with the simple stuff. On virtually any UNIX system, you can use the *time* shell variable *(7.08)* to run *time* automatically when commands take more than a set amount of CPU time. Decide what your threshhold is (i.e., the point at which you want *time* to run automatically), in CPU seconds. Then set the *time* shell variable to this number. For example, if you want to run *time* automatically on programs that require more than 10 CPU seconds, give the command:

```
% set time=10
% ls
file1.ms    file2.ms    file3.ms
% nroff -ms *.ms | lpr
4.3u 9.8s 0:23 60% 0+200k 106+103io 143pf+0w
```

nroff 45.14

The *ls* command didn't generate a *time* report because it ran in well under 10 seconds. The *nroff* command took about 14.1 CPU seconds, so it did generate a report.

Why would you want to do this? It lets you monitor the performance of long jobs automatically without being bothered by statistics for the small jobs.

On many C shells, you can also use the *time* variable to customize the timing report. Sometimes this is useful; the standard report gives you a lot of information, but it's pretty ugly. For some reason, this feature often goes undocumented.

To customize a timing report, give a command like this:

```
% set time=(threshold "format-string")
```

Note that you have to give a threshold, whether you want one or not. If you don't want execution times reported automatically, set *threshold* to some large number.

The format string can be any combination of text and tags. Each tag causes *time* to insert particular statistics. The valid tags seem to vary some from system-to-system (and are undocumented some places, so you may not be able to tell). We've used two sources: a version for 4.1BSD written by Mark Wittenberg and one supplied with SunOS 4.1.2. Where the two are different, Mark's is labeled **A>** and Sun's is **B>**.

%D   **A>** Average kilobytes of resident data+stack pages.
     B> The average amount of memory required by the program's data segment, in kilobytes. This excludes any "shared data." Shared memory is a relatively new feature, so most programs probably don't use it.

%E   The elapsed time required to execute the program. This is the amount of time you'd measure if you sat with a stopwatch and waited for the program to finish; it's often called "wall clock" time.

%F   The number of page faults; i.e., the number of times UNIX had to bring a page of virtual memory in from disk. A large number of page faults may mean that your program is taking an unnecessarily long time to run, and you can fix the problem by buying more memory.

%I   The number of block input operations. This is the number of times the program needed to read data from disk.

%K   **A>** Average kilobytes of resident text+data+stack pages.
     B> The average amount of memory required by the program's stack segment, in kilobytes.

%M The maximum amount of real memory (physical memory) used by the program during execution, in kilobytes. (On 17 October 1986, Daniel V. Klein reported on Usenet *net.unix* that the amount %M gives is really just *half* the maximum. The number does seem to be smaller than %K sometimes, so Daniel is probably right. Don't you love undocumented features?)

%O The number of block output operations.

%P The program's total CPU time, as a percentage of elapsed time. If you're the only user on the system and the program does little I/O, this should be close to 100%. It will decrease as the program's I/O requirements and the system's overall load increase.

%S CPU system time; the number of seconds the CPU spent in the "system" state on behalf of your program—i.e., how much time the system spent executing system calls on behalf of your program.

%U CPU user time; the number of seconds the CPU spent in the "user" state on behalf of your program—i.e., how much time the system spent executing your program itself.

%W The number of "swaps"; the number of times the system needed to move your whole program to disk in order to free memory. If this is non-zero, your system needs more memory.

%X **A>** Average kilobytes of resident text pages.
B> The average amount of shared memory that your program required, in kilobytes.

For example, let's say that we want time statistics for programs that require more than 10 seconds of CPU time, and that we want to report the system time, the user time, and the elapsed time. Despite the huge number of statistics you can get, these are all that you really care about, unless you're a performance expert. To do so, we'll set the *time* variable like this (you can also set it in your *.cshrc* file *(2.02)*):

```
% set time=(10 "System time: %S  User time: %U  Elapsed time: %E")
% nroff -man * > /dev/null
System time: 0.3  User time: 41.2  Elapsed time: 0:43
```

This report is much clearer than the mess you get by default. It shows clearly that the *nroff* command required 0.3 seconds of system-state CPU time, 41.2 seconds of user-state CPU time, and a total elapsed time of 43 seconds.

Note: I have seen a note somewhere saying that many of *time*'s more obscure statistics weren't reported correctly. By "obscure statistics," I mean page faults, average amount of unshared stack space, and the like. You can trust the user and system CPU time, the elapsed time, and other basic statistics, but if you really care about the fancy statistics, beware. I seriously doubt that any vendor has fixed these problems.

—*ML, JP*

41.04 Average Command Runtimes with runtime

runtime

The *time* command *(41.02)* will time a single run of a command—but the results can vary from run to run. The *runtime* script runs a command the number of times you specify, then averages the results. For example:

```
% runtime -5 getdata 0.5 outfile
        ...wait a while...
runtime summary -- 5 runs of
    % getdata 0.5 outfile
(working directory = /users/jerry/.src/getdata)

First run started at: Thu Mar 19 09:33:58 EST 1992
Last run finished at: Thu Mar 19 09:36:41 EST 1992
------------------------------------------------

RUN #      ***INDIVIDUAL RESULTS***
    1    1.0u 7.4s 1:06 12% 0+108k 0+0io 0pf+0w
    2    0.2u 0.8s 0:05 16% 0+128k 0+0io 0pf+0w
    3    0.2u 1.3s 0:11 13% 0+116k 0+0io 0pf+0w
    4    0.4u 2.7s 0:25 12% 0+108k 0+0io 0pf+0w
    5    0.9u 5.9s 0:53 12% 0+108k 0+0io 0pf+0w

AVERAGES:
  0.54u  3.62s 0:32 0+113k 0+0io 0pf+0w
```

It's good for testing different versions of a program to find the fastest (or slowest!). If you're writing a program that will run a lot, shaving 10% or 20% off its time can be worth the work.

Note that the command you run can't have any redirection in it; that's because *runtime* does some redirection of its own. You can redirect the output of runtime into a log file though, and run the whole mess in the background. For example:

```
% runtime -5 getdata 0.5 outfile > runtime.out &
[1] 12233
```

The summary will go to the *runtime.out* file.

—JP

41.05 Why is the System so Slow?

To a user, performance means: "How much time does it take to run my job?" For a system manager, this question is much too simple: a user's job may take a long time to execute because it is badly written or because it doesn't really use the computer appropriately. Furthermore, a system manager must optimize performance for all system users—which is much more complicated than optimizing performance for a single user. Here are some of the things that affect performance.

Time and Performance

The UNIX utility */bin/time* reports the amount of time required to execute a program, breaking down the total time into several important components. For example, consider the report below:

```
% /bin/time application
    4.8 real        0.5 user        0.7 sys
```

This report shows that the program ran in roughly 4.8 seconds. This is the *elapsed* or *wallclock* time: it is the actual time that the program runs as it would be measured by a user sitting at the terminal with a stopwatch. The amount of time that the system spent working on your program is much smaller. It spent 0.5 seconds of *user time*, which is time spent executing code in the user state, and about 0.7 seconds of *system time*, which is time spent in the system state (i.e., time spent executing UNIX system code) on behalf of the user. The total amount of CPU time (actual execution time on the main processor) was only 1.2 seconds, or only one-quarter of the elapsed time.*

Where did the rest of the time go? Some time was spent performing I/O (text input/output) operations, which */bin/time* doesn't report. Handling I/O requires some computation, which is attributed to system time. But time that is spent by disk drives, network interfaces, terminal controllers, or other hardware isn't accounted for; most of the time was spent running jobs on behalf of other users. This entails its own performance overhead (context-switch time, swapping time, etc.).

Many different components contribute to a program's total running time. When you understand the role these components play, you will understand the problem. Here is a summary of the different components:

- **User-state CPU time.** The actual amount of time the CPU spends running your program in the user state. It includes time spent executing library functions but excludes time spent executing system calls (i.e., time spent in the UNIX kernel on behalf of the process). Programmers can control user-state time by knowing which library routines are efficient and which aren't, and they should know how to run profilers on the program to find out where it's spending its time.

- **System-state CPU time.** The amount of time the CPU spends in the system state (i.e., the amount of time spent executing kernel code) on behalf of the program. This includes time spent executing system calls and performing administrative functions on the program's behalf. The distinction between time spent in simple library routines and time spent in system services is important and often confused. A call to *strcpy*, which copies a character string, executes entirely in the user state because it doesn't require any special handling by the kernel. Calls to *printf*, *fork*, and many other routines are much more complex. These functions do require services from the UNIX kernel so they spend part of their time, if not most of it, in the system state. All I/O routines require the kernel's services.

---

*Note that BSD and System V versions of */bin/time* have different output formats but provide the same information. */bin/time* also differs from the C shell's *time* command **(41.03)**, which provides a more elaborate report.

System-state CPU time is partially under the programmer's control. Although programmers cannot change the amount of time it takes to service any system call, they can rewrite the program to issue system calls more efficiently (for example, to make I/O transfers in larger blocks).

- **I/O time**. The amount of time the I/O subsystem spends servicing the I/O requests that the job issues. Under UNIX, I/O time is difficult to measure; however, there are some tools for determining whether the I/O system is overloaded and some configuration considerations that can help alleviate load problems.

- **Network time**. The amount of time that the I/O subsystem spends servicing network requests that the job issues. This is really a subcategory of I/O time and depends critically on configuration and usage issues.

- **Time spent running other programs**. As system load increases, the CPU spends less time working on any given job, thus increasing the elapsed time required to run the job. This is an annoyance, but barring some problem with I/O or virtual memory performance, there is little you can do about it.

- **Virtual memory performance**. This is by far the most complex aspect of system performance. Ideally, all active jobs would remain in the system's physical memory at all times. But when physical memory is fully occupied, the operating system starts moving parts of jobs to disk, thus freeing memory for the job it wants to run. This takes time. It also takes time when these disk-bound jobs need to run again and therefore need to be moved back into memory. When running jobs with extremely large memory requirements, system performance can degrade significantly.

If you spend most of your time running standard utilities and commercial applications, you can't do much about user-state or system-state time. To make a significant dent in these, you have to rewrite the program. But you can do a lot to improve your memory and I/O performance, and you can do a lot to run your big applications more efficiently.

Keyboard response is an extremely important issue to users, although it really doesn't contribute to a program's execution time. If there is a noticeable gap between the time when a user types a character and the time when the system echoes that character, the user will think performance is bad, regardless of how much time it takes to run a job. In order to prevent terminal buffers from overflowing and losing characters, most UNIX systems give terminal drivers *(44.01)* very high priority. As a side effect, the high priority of terminals means that keyboard response should be bad only under exceptionally high loads. If you are accessing a remote system across a network, however, network delays can cause poor keyboard response. Network performance is an extremely complex issue.

—*ML* from the Nutshell Handbook *System Performance Tuning*

41.06 *lastcomm:* What Commands are Running and How Long do They Take?

When you're debugging a problem with a program, trying to figure out why your CPU usage bill is so high, or curious what commands someone (including yourself) is running, the *lastcomm* command on Berkeley-like UNIXes can help (if your computer has its process accounting system running, that is). Here's an example that lists the user *lesleys*:

```
% date
Wed Sep  4 16:38:13 EDT 1991
% lastcomm lesleys
emacs             lesleys  ttyp1       1.41 secs Wed Sep  4 16:28
cat             X lesleys  ttyp1       0.06 secs Wed Sep  4 16:37
stty              lesleys  ttypa       0.02 secs Wed Sep  4 16:36
tset              lesleys  ttypa       0.12 secs Wed Sep  4 16:36
sed               lesleys  ttypa       0.02 secs Wed Sep  4 16:36
hostname          lesleys  ttypa       0.00 secs Wed Sep  4 16:36
quota             lesleys  ttypa       0.16 secs Wed Sep  4 16:35
    ...
```

The processes are listed in the order completed, most-recent first. The `emacs` process on the tty `ttyp1` *(3.08)* started ten minutes ago and took 1.41 seconds of CPU time. Sometime while *emacs* was on ttyp1, *lesleys* ran *cat* and killed it (the X shows that). Because *emacs* ran on the same terminal as *cat* but finished later, Lesley might have stopped *emacs* (with CTRL-z) *(13.01)* to run *cat*. The processes on `ttypa` are the ones run from her *.cshrc* and *.login* files (though you can't tell that from *lastcomm*). You don't see the login shell for `ttypa` (*csh*) here because it hasn't terminated yet; it'll be listed after Lesley logs out of ttypa.

lastcomm can do more. See its manual page.

Here's a hint: on a busy system with lots of users and commands being logged, *lastcomm* is pretty slow. If you pipe the output or redirect it into a file, like this:

```
% lastcomm lesleys > lesley.cmds &
% cat lesley.cmds
    ...nothing...
```

tee 14.09

```
% lastcomm lesleys | tee lesley.cmds
    ...nothing...
```

then the *lastcomm* output may be written to the file or pipe in big chunks instead of line-by-line. That can make it look as if nothing's happening. To grab the output into a file, if you can tie up a terminal while *lastcomm* runs, first start *script (53.05)* and then run *lastcomm*:

```
% script lesley.cmds
Script started, file is lesley.cmds
% lastcomm lesleys
emacs             lesleys  ttyp1       1.41 secs Wed Sep  4 16:28
cat             X lesleys  ttyp1       0.06 secs Wed Sep  4 16:37
    ...
```

```
% exit
Script done, file is lesley.cmds
%
```

—JP

41.07 Checking System Load: uptime

The BSD command *uptime*, also available under System V Release 4, AIX, and some System V Release 3 implementations, will give you a rough estimate of the system load:

```
% uptime
3:24pm up 2 days, 2:41, 16 users, load average: 1.90, 1.43, 1.33
```

uptime reports the current time, the amount of time the system has been up, and three load average figures. The load average is a rough measure of CPU use. These three figures report the average number of processes active during the last minute, the last five minutes, and the last 15 minutes. High load averages usually mean that the system is being used heavily and the response time is correspondingly slow. Note that the system's load average does not take into account the priorities and *niceness (41.09)* of the processes that are running.

What's high? As usual, that depends on your system. Ideally, you'd like a load average under, say, 3, but that's not always possible given what some systems are required to do. Higher load averages are usually more tolerable on machines with more than one processor. Ultimately, "high" means high enough so that you don't need *uptime* to tell you that the system is overloaded—you can tell from its response time.

Furthermore, different systems will behave differently under the same load average. For example, on some workstations, running a single CPU-bound background job at the same time as the X Window System *(1.31)* will bring response to a crawl even though the load average remains quite "low." In the end, load averages are significant only when they differ from whatever is "normal" on your system.

—AF from the Nutshell Handbook *Essential System Administration*

41.08 A Big Environment Can Slow You Down

Part of starting a new child process (starting a program, for instance) is making a copy of the environment from the parent process. Some computers, especially busy ones, aren't very fast at making new processes. (In the early 1980s, I worked on a VAX 11/750 running 4.1 BSD; the load average got above 40. Sometimes, after a command finished, it could take 10 or 20 seconds just to get the next shell prompt. Sheesh!)

Filling up your environment with lots of variables (the *csh* command *setenv* or the *sh* command *export*) can be handy. But it can slow you down—especially in shell scripts that run loops, starting lots of subprocesses.

I did a test on our 386-based computer running Interactive UNIX System V/386 Release 3.2 late one night when I was the only user logged on. First, I cleaned out my environment to around 300 characters. Then I did:

env *7.01*
wc *30.06*

time *41.03*
repeat *10.23*

```
% env | wc -c
     335
% set time
% repeat 50 /bin/true
0.0u 0.1s 0:00 15%
0.1u 0.1s 0:00 18%
0.0u 0.2s 0:00 20%
   . . .
```

That started the short */bin/true* shell script 50 times. I added up the system times (from the second column) and got 6.9 CPU seconds. Then I used a C shell *while* loop to quickly add a bunch of huge environment variables named *FOO1*, *FOO2*, and so on, like this:

set *7.08*

@ *49.04*

```
% set n = 0
% while ($n < 30)
? @ n++
? setenv FOO$n xxxxxxxxxxxxxxxxxxxxxxxxxxxxxxxxxxxxxxxxxxxxxxxxxxx...
? end
   . . .
% env | wc -c
    4934
```

and ran `repeat 50 /bin/true` again. With a 5000-character environment, it took 8.9 system CPU seconds—that's about 30% longer.

A thorough test? Nope. But if you have a big environment on a slow computer, you might run a test like this to see whether cleaning it out—replacing environment variables with shell variables, for instance—can make your subprocesses start faster.

Article 40.07 explains the problem a big environment can cause for *ps.* Article 2.09 shows how to start C shells more quickly.

—JP

41.09 Know When to Be "nice" to Other Users . . . and When Not to

The *nice* command modifies the scheduling priority of time-sharing processes (for BSD and pre-V.4 releases of System V, all processes). If you're not familiar with UNIX, you will find its definition of priority confusing—it's the opposite of what you would expect. A process with a high *nice* number runs at low priority, getting relatively little of the processor's attention; similarly, jobs with a low *nice* number run at high priority. This is why the *nice* number is usually called *niceness*: a job with a lot of niceness is very kind to the other users of your system (i.e., it runs at low priority), while a job with little niceness will hog the CPU. The term "niceness" is awkward, like the priority system itself. Unfortunately, it's the only term that is both accurate (*nice* numbers are used to compute priorities but are not the priorities themselves) and avoids horrible circumlocutions ("increasing the priority means lowering the priority . . . ").

Many supposedly experienced users claim that *nice* has virtually no effect. Don't listen to them. As a general rule, reducing the priority of an I/O-bound job (a job that's waiting for I/O a lot of the time) won't change things very much. The system rewards jobs that spend most of their time waiting for I/O by increasing their priority. But reducing the priority of a CPU-bound process can have a significant effect. Compilations, batch typesetting programs (*troff*, TeX, etc.), applications that do a lot of math, and similar programs are good candidates for *nice*. On a moderately loaded system, I have found that *nice* typically makes a CPU-intensive job roughly 30 percent slower and consequently frees that much time for higher priority jobs. You can often significantly improve keyboard response by running CPU-intensive jobs at low priority.

Note that System V Release 4 has a much more complex priority system, including real-time priorities. Priorities are managed with the *priocntl* command. The older *nice* command is available for compatibility. Other UNIX implementations (including HP and Concurrent) support real-time scheduling. These implementations have their own tools for managing the scheduler.

The *nice* command sets a job's niceness, which is used to compute its priority. It may be one of the most non-uniform commands in the universe. There are four versions, each slightly different from the others. BSD UNIX has one *nice* that is built into the C shell, and another standalone version can be used by other shells. System V also has one *nice* that is built into the C shell and a separate standalone version.

Under BSD UNIX, you must also know about the *renice*(8) command *(41.11)*; this lets you change the niceness of a job after it is running. Under System V, you can't modify a job's niceness once it has started, so there is no equivalent.

Note: Think carefully before you *nice* an interactive job like a text editor. See article 41.10.

We'll tackle the different variations of *nice* in order.

BSD C Shell nice

Under BSD UNIX, *nice* numbers run from −20 to 20. The −20 designation corresponds to the highest priority; 20 corresponds to the lowest. By default, UNIX assigns the *nice* number 0 to user-executed jobs. The lowest *nice* numbers (−20 to −17) are unofficially reserved for system processes. Assigning a user's job to these *nice* numbers can cause problems. Users can always request a higher *nice* number (i.e., a lower priority) for their jobs. Only the superuser *(1.24)* can raise a job's priority.

To submit a job at a lower niceness, precede it with the modifier *nice*. For example, the command:

```
% nice awk -f proc.awk datafile > awk.out
```

runs an *awk* command at low priority. By default, *csh* version of *nice* will submit this job with a *nice* level of 4. To submit a job with an arbitrary *nice* number, use *nice* one of these ways:

```
% nice +n command
% nice -n command
```

where *n* is an integer between 0 and 20. The +*n* designation requests a positive *nice* number (low priority); −*n* request a negative *nice* number. Only a superuser may request a negative *nice* number.

BSD Standalone nice

The standalone version of *nice* differs from C shell *nice* in that it is a separate program, not a command built in to the C shell. You can therefore use the standalone version in any situation: within makefiles *(29.12)*, when you are running the Bourne shell, etc. The principles are the same. *nice* numbers run from −20 to 20, with the default being zero. Only the syntax has been changed to confuse you. For the standalone version, −*n* requests a positive *nice* number (lower priority) and −−*n* requests a negative *nice* number (higher priority—superuser only). Consider these commands:

```
$ nice -6 awk -f proc.awk datafile > awk.out
# nice --6 awk -f proc.awk datafile > awk.out
```

The first command runs *awk* with a high *nice* number (i.e., 6). The second command, which can be issued only by a superuser, runs *awk* with a low *nice* number (i.e., −6).

System V C Shell nice

System V takes a slightly different view of *nice* numbers. *nice* levels run from 0 to 39; the default is 20. The numbers are different but their meanings are the same: 39 corresponds to the lowest possible priority, and 0 is the highest. A few System V implementations support real-time submission via *nice*. Jobs submitted by root with extremely low *nice* numbers (−20 or below) allegedly get all of the CPU's time. Systems on which this works properly are very rare and usually advertise support for real-time processing. In any case, running jobs this way will destroy multi-user performance. This feature is completely different from real-time priorities in System V Release 4.

With these exceptions, the C shell version of *nice* is the same as its BSD cousin. To submit a job at a low priority, use the command:

```
% nice command
```

This increases the command's niceness by the default amount (4, the same as BSD UNIX); *command* will run at *nice* level 24. To run a job at an arbitrary priority, use one of the following commands:

```
% nice +n command
% nice -n command
```

where *n* is an integer between 0 and 19. The +*n* entry requests a higher *nice* level (a decreased priority), while −*n* requests a lower *nice* level (a higher priority). Again, this is similar to BSD UNIX, with one important difference: *n* is now relative to the default *nice* level. That is, the command:

```
% nice +6 awk -f proc.awk datafile > awk.out
```

runs *awk* at *nice* level 26.

System V Standalone nice

Once again, the standalone version of *nice* is useful if you are writing makefiles or shell scripts or if you use the Bourne shell as your interactive shell. It is similar to the C shell version, with these differences:

- With no arguments, standalone *nice* increases the *nice* number by 10 instead of by 4; this is a significantly greater reduction in the program's priority.

- With the argument *−n, nice* increases the *nice* number by *n* (reducing priority).

- With the argument *− −n, nice* decreases the *nice* number by *n* (increasing priority; superuser only).

Consider these commands:

```
$ nice -6 awk -f proc.awk datafile > awk.out
# nice --6 awk -f proc.awk datafile > awk.out
```

The first command runs *awk* at a higher *nice* level (i.e., 26, which corresponds to a lower priority). The second command, which can be given only by the superuser, runs *awk* at a lower *nice* level (i.e., 14).

—ML from the Nutshell Handbook System Performance Tuning

41.10 A nice Gotcha

It's NOT a good idea to *nice* a foreground job. If the system gets busy, your terminal could "freeze" waiting to get enough CPU time do do something. You may not even be able to kill a nice'd job on a very busy system because the CPU may never give the process enough CPU time to recognize the signal waiting for it! And, of course, don't *nice* an interactive program like a text editor unless you like to wait . . . :-)

—JP

41.11 Changing a Job's Priority under BSD UNIX

Once a job is running, you can use the *renice*(8) command to change the job's priority:

```
% /etc/renice priority -p pid
% /etc/renice priority -g pgrp
% /etc/renice priority -u uname
```

where *priority* is the new *nice* level *(41.09)* for the job. It must be a signed integer between –20 and 20. *pid* is the ID number *(40.03)* (as shown by *ps (40.05)*) of the process you want to change. *pgrp* is the number of a process group *(40.03)*, as shown by *ps –l*; this version of the command modifies the priority of all commands in a process group. *uname* may be a user's name, as shown in */etc/passwd*; this form of the command modifies the priority of all jobs submitted by the user. Again, only the superuser can lower the *nice* number (raise a process' priority). Users can only raise the *nice* number (lower the priority) and can modify the priorities of only the jobs they started.

BSD UNIX systems automatically *nice* jobs after they have accumulated a certain amount of CPU time. This implicitly gives priority to jobs that don't run for a long time, sacrificing users who run long jobs in favor of users who run many short commands. The autonice time varies from system to system, but is usually 10 minutes.

—ML

41.12 What Makes Your Computer Slow? How do You Fix it?

Article 41.05 discussed the various components that make up a user's perception of system performance. There is another equally important approach to this issue: the computer's view of performance. All system performance issues are basically resource contention issues. In any computer system, there are three fundamental resources: the CPU, memory, and the I/O subsystem (e.g., disks and networks). From this standpoint, performance tuning means ensuring that every user gets a fair share of available resources.

Each resource has its own particular set of problems. Resource problems are complicated because all resources interact with each other. Your best approach is to consider carefully what each system resource does: CPU, I/O, and memory. To get you started, here's a quick summary of each system resource and the problems it can have.

The CPU

On any time-sharing system, even single-user time-sharing systems (such as UNIX on a personal computer), many programs want to use the CPU at the same time. Under most circumstances the UNIX kernel is able to allocate the CPU fairly; however, each process (or program) requires a certain number of CPU cycles to execute and there are only so many cycles in a day. At some point the CPU just can't get all the work done.

There are a few ways to measure CPU contention. The simplest is the UNIX load average, reported by the BSD *uptime* (41.07) command. Under System V, *sar −q* provides the same sort of information. The load average tries to measure the number of active processes at any time (a *process* is a single stream of instructions). As a measure of CPU utilization, the load average is simplistic, poorly defined, but far from useless.

Before you blame the CPU for your performance problems, think a bit about what we *don't* mean by CPU contention. We don't mean that the system is short of memory or that it can't do I/O fast enough. Either of these situations can make your system appear very slow. But the CPU may be spending most of its time idle; therefore, you can't just look at the load average and decide that you need a faster processor. Your programs won't run a bit faster. Before you understand your system, you also need to find out what your memory and I/O subsystems are doing. Users often point their fingers at the CPU, but I would be willing to bet that in most situations memory and I/O are equally (if not more) to blame.

Given that you are short of CPU cycles, you have three basic alternatives:

- You can get users to run jobs at night or at other low-usage times (ensuring the computer is doing useful work 24 hours a day) with *batch* or *at* (42.01).

- You can prevent your system from doing unnecessary work.

- You can get users to run their big jobs at lower priority (41.09).

If none of these options is viable, you may need to upgrade your system.

The Memory Subsystem

Memory contention arises when the memory requirements of the active processes exceed the physical memory available on the system; at this point, the system is out of memory. To handle this lack of memory without crashing the system or killing processes, the system starts *paging*: moving portions of active processes to disk in order to reclaim physical memory. At this point, performance decreases dramatically. Paging is distinguished from *swapping*, which means moving entire processes to disk and reclaiming their space. Paging and swapping indicate that the system can't provide enough memory for the processes that are currently running, although under some circumstances swapping can be a part of normal housekeeping. Under BSD UNIX, tools such as *vmstat* and *pstat* show whether the system is paging; *ps* can report the memory requirements of each process. The System V utility *sar* provides information about virtualiy all aspects of memory performance.

To prevent paging, you must either make more memory available or decrease the extent to which jobs compete. To do this, you can tune system parameters, which is beyond the scope of this book (see the Nutshell Handbook *System Performance Tuning* by Mike Loukides for help). You can also terminate *(40.10)* the jobs with the largest memory requirements. If your system has a lot of memory, the kernel's memory requirements will be relatively small; the typical antagonists are very large application programs.

The I/O Subsystem

The I/O subsystem is a common source of resource contention problems. A finite amount of I/O bandwidth must be shared by all the programs (including the UNIX kernel) that currently run. The system's I/O buses can transfer only so many megabytes per second; individual devices are even more limited. Each kind of device has its own peculiarities and, therefore, its own problems. Unfortunately, UNIX has poor tools for analyzing the I/O subsystem. Under BSD UNIX, *iostat* can give you information about the transfer rates for each disk drive; *ps* and *vmstat* can give some information about how many processes are blocked waiting for I/O; and *netstat* and *nfsstat* report various network statistics. Under System V, *sar* can provide voluminous information about I/O efficiency, and *sadp* (V.4) can give detailed information about disk access patterns. However, there is no standard tool to measure the I/O subsystem's response to a heavy load.

The disk and network subsystems are particularly important to overall performance. Disk bandwidth issues have two general forms: maximizing per-process transfer rates and maximizing aggregate transfer rates. The per-process transfer rate is the rate at which a single program can read or write data. The aggregate transfer rate is the maximum total bandwidth that the system can provide to all programs that run.

Network I/O problems have two basic forms: a network can be overloaded or a network can lose data integrity. When a network is overloaded, the amount of data that needs to be transferred across the network is greater than the network's capacity; therefore, the actual transfer rate for any task is relatively slow. Network load problems can usually be solved by changing the network's configuration. Integrity problems occur when the network is faulty and intermittently transfers data incorrectly. In order to deliver correct data to the applications using the network, the network protocols may have to transmit each block of data many times. Consequently, programs using the network will run very slowly. The only way to solve a data integrity problem is to isolate the faulty part of the network and replace it.

User Communities

So far we have discussed the different factors that contribute to overall system performance. But we have ignored one of the most important factors: the users who submit the jobs.

In talking about the relationship between users and performance, it is easy to start seeing users as problems: the creatures who keep your system from running the way it ought to. Nothing is further from the truth. Computers are tools: they exist to help users do their work and not vice versa.

Limitations on memory requirements, file size, job priorities, etc., are effective only when everyone cooperates. Likewise, you can't force people to submit their jobs to a batch queue *(42.06)*. Most people will cooperate when they understand a problem and what they can do to solve it. Most people will resist a solution that is imposed from above, that they don't understand, or that seems to get in the way of their work.

The nature of your system's users has a big effect on your system's performance. We can divide users into several classes:

- Users who run a large number of relatively small jobs: for example, users who spend most of their time editing or running UNIX utilities.

- Users who run a small number of relatively large jobs: for example, users who run large simulation programs with huge data files.

- Users who run a small number of CPU-intensive jobs that don't require a lot of I/O but do require a lot of memory and CPU time. Program developers fall into this category. Compilers tend to be large programs that build large data structures and can be a source of memory contention problems.

All three groups can cause problems. Several dozen users running *grep* and accessing remote filesystems can be as bad for overall performance as a few users accessing gigabyte files. However, the types of problems these groups cause are not the same. For example, setting up a "striped filesystem" will help disk performance for large, I/O-bound jobs but won't help (and may hurt) users who run many small jobs. Setting up batch queues will help reduce contention among large jobs, which can often be run overnight, but it won't help the system if its problems arise from users typing at their text editors and reading their mail.

Modern systems with network facilities *(1.33)* complicate the picture even more. In addition to knowing what kinds of work users do, you also need to know what kind of equipment they use: a standard terminal over an RS-232 line, an X terminal over Ethernet, or a diskless workstation? The X Window System requires a lot of memory and puts a heavy load on the network. Likewise, diskless workstations place a load on the network. Similarly, do users access local files or remote files via NFS or RFS?

—*ML* from the Nutshell Handbook *System Performance Tuning*

42

Delayed Execution

42.01 Off-peak Job Submission

Now that time sharing and interactive programming have become universal, many UNIX users have forgotten one of the best ways to get the most out of the system: running jobs at nights or on the weekend. Most people tend to work from 9 to 5, which is roughly one-third of the day. (Though many programmers do keep later hours!) If you can make use of the other hours (night and weekends), you can almost quadruple your system's throughput. Running jobs at night is less fun than running them interactively, but it is a lot less expensive than three new machines. If you can use off-peak hours, you will get a lot more work from your hardware.

There are a few mechanisms to take advantage of off-peak hours:

- The *at* command *(42.03)* lets you submit jobs for execution at an arbitrary later date; it is standard on almost all UNIX systems.

- The *batch* command *(42.06)*, which is available in System V.4 and SunOS 4.1, provides a simple (and simplistic) batch queueing system. Some more fully featured batch systems are available for other UNIX systems.

- Although it serves an entirely different purpose, you should also be aware of the *crontab (42.12)* facility, which provides a way to schedule jobs for periodic execution on a regular basis.

- Finally, don't forget *sleep (42.02)*, which can be helpful if you want to delay or space out execution just a little bit.

—ML

42.02 Waiting a Little While: sleep

The *sleep* command waits. That's all it does. So, what good is it?

- A quick-and-dirty reminder service when you don't have *leave (50.06)*. This will print the message Time to go now.... in 10 minutes (600 seconds):

( ) & *14.07*

```
% (sleep 600; echo Time to go now....) &
```

- You can't use *at (42.03)* and you have to run a job later (say, three hours):

```
% (sleep 10800; someprog) &
```

- To watch a program (usually a shell script) that's running in the background and see what processes it runs:

```
% prog &
[1] 12345
% sleep 5;ps
  PID TT STAT   TIME COMMAND
18305 p4 S      0:01 -csh (csh)
18435 p4 S      0:00 /bin/sh prog
18437 p4 D      0:00 /bin/sort -r temp
18438 p4 R      0:00 ps
```

!! *12.07*

```
% !!;!!;!!;!!;!!
sleep 5; ps; sleep 5; ps; sleep 5; ps; sleep 5; ps; sleep 5; ps
  PID TT STAT   TIME COMMAND
    ...
    ...5 seconds pass...
  PID TT STAT   TIME COMMAND
    ...
```

- When you're running a series of commands that could swamp the computer, give it time to catch up. For instance, the *mail (1.33)* program starts background processes to deliver the mail. If you're sending a bunch of form letters, sleep five or ten seconds after each one:

foreach *10.09*

```
% foreach name (`cat people`)
? formltrprog $name | mail $name
? sleep 10
? end
```

Or, to send print jobs while you're at lunch—but give other people a chance to print between yours:

```
% lp bigfile1;sleep 600;lp bigfile2;sleep 600;lp bigfile3
```

—*JP*

42.03 The at Command

The *at* facility submits a command line (or a script) for execution at an arbitrary later time. It has the form:

```
% at options time < scriptfile
```

This submits the *scriptfile* for execution at a later *time*. The redirection (<) isn't required on BSD and some other UNIX systems. If you don't want to write a script, you can omit it and type your commands on the terminal, terminated by CTRL-d:

```
% at options time
Command 1
Command 2
...
CTRL-d
```

The *time* is most commonly a four-digit number representing a time on a 24-hour clock. For example, `0130` represents 1:30 a.m. and `1400` represents 2 p.m. You can also use abbreviations such as `1am`, `130pm`, and so on.

—*ML* from the Nutshell Handbook *System Performance Tuning*

42.04 Choosing Which Shell at Should Run

If you are using BSD UNIX, the −c option tells *at (42.03)* to execute your script via the C shell; the −s option tells *at* to use the Bourne shell. *at* defaults to the shell you log in with.

> *at* jobs are run by a system program in an environment that's much different than your normal login sessions. Be careful about using command aliases, shell functions and variables, and other things that may not be set for you by the system.

The easiest way to find out what's happening is by having your job write its environment into some temporary files, then read them in the morning:

```
% at 0234
set > $HOME/at.set
printenv > $HOME/at.env
CTRL-d
```
set 7.08
printenv 7.01

On some systems you'll need `$LOGDIR` instead of `$HOME` and *env* instead of *printenv*.

If you use the C shell, the shell will read your *.cshrc* file *(2.02)* when the job starts running. This is good news and bad news. The good news is that you can set shell parameters to be used by your *at* job. If you have interactive commands in your *.cshrc*, though, your *at* job might ignore them or might hang forever, waiting for an answer. For instance, the *tty (3.08)* command will print the error `not a tty`; if you try to use *tty* to set a shell variable, it can cause *unset variable* errors, which can abort your *.cshrc* file . . . and so on. That's the bad news.

You can use a *set prompt* test *(2.09)* in your *.cshrc* file to make sure that there are no interactive commands run by *at*, but unless I need *csh* features, I usually just use *at −s* to run the job under the Bourne shell.

—*ML* from the Nutshell Handbook *System Performance Tuning*

42.05 *Avoiding Other at and cron Jobs*

atq and *at −l (42.09)* are more important than they seem. They give you a way to decide when to run your jobs. I suggest that you check *atq* before picking a time to run your job. If you don't, the system may have a dozen huge jobs starting at midnight or 1 a.m. They will bring the system to its knees when there's no one around to help out. Here's an example of what can happen, using the BSD-style *at* commands:

```
% atq
Rank       Execution Date     Owner   Job#   Queue   Job Name
1st    Sep 21, 1990 01:00     mikel   4529     a      trashsys.sh
2nd    Sep 21, 1990 01:00     johnt   4531     a      flame.sh
3rd    Sep 21, 1990 01:00     davek   4532     a      stdin
4th    Sep 21, 1990 01:00     joek    4533     a      troffit
5th    Sep 21, 1990 02:00     bobr    4534     a      stdin
```

Four of the five users happened to pick 1 a.m. as their submission time. Therefore, four big jobs will start in the middle of the night. Will your system survive? Will any of these be done in the morning? These are good questions. Instead of submitting your jobs to run at 1 a.m., at midnight, or at some other integral number, start them at different times, and make them times like 3:48 a.m. If your system administrator notices lots of jobs running at the same times on your system, she might delete some of them and ask you to reschedule.

If your system has personal *crontab* files *(42.12)*, you won't be able to see other users' *cron* jobs. The best way to cut system load is to pick strange times like 4:37 a.m. for your *cron* jobs.

—*ML* from the Nutshell Handbook *System Performance Tuning*

42.06 *System V.4 Batch Queues*

At many UNIX sites, batch submission systems are considered a thing of the past. This is unfortunate. Batch execution is an effective way to get a lot of work done, particularly in a production-oriented environment. A batch queue is one of the best ways to ensure that a computer remains active during off hours. The *at* command leads to "bursty" execution: you will see a lot of activity at midnight, 1 a.m., 2 a.m., and other popular submission times, trailing off as the jobs complete. A batch queue will keep the system running on an even keel as long as there is work left to do.

System V.4 and SunOS have added a very simple batch queue facility. This facility is really just a variation of the *at* command, except that you can't specify when you want to run the job. The system has a single batch queue that executes jobs in the order in which they are entered into the queue. Submit a job to the queue with the command:

```
% batch
Command 1
Command 2
CTRL-d
```

If you have written your job as a shell script, you can submit it as:

```
% batch script-name
```

But check your online *batch* manual page to be sure that your system will run it with the right shell. To delete jobs from the queue, use *atq* and *atrm* (SunOS) or *at −l* and *at −r* (V.4).

The queue facility is so simple that it's pathetic: it doesn't support multiple queues, queue priorities, and other features that you really need if you want batch submission. But it will do one important thing. If users use batch queues for their big jobs, they will guarantee that, at most, one large program (whether it is the compiler, an engineering application, or whatever) is running at a time. That may be all you need to restore order to a troubled system.

—*ML* from the Nutshell Handbook *System Performance Tuning*

42.07 *Making Your at Jobs Quiet*

Most modern versions of *at* will mail *(1.33)* you any output that your commands make. Some people try the command line below to throw that output into the UNIX trash can, */dev/null (14.14)*:

>& *14.05*

```
% at sometime... >& /dev/null
```

But that won't work because it throws away the output of the *at* command itself. *at* just saves your job in a file to be run later by a system program. The commands you want quiet are the commands stored in that file. One way to keep *at* quiet, if you use the C shell, is:

```
% at sometime...
at> some command >& /dev/null
at> another command >& /dev/null
at> ...etc... >& /dev/null
at> CTRL-d
```

The Bourne shell makes it easier:

exec > *47.07*

```
$ at sometime...
at> exec > /dev/null 2>&1
at> some command
at> another command
at> ...etc...
at> CTRL-d
```

Two notes:

- Some versions of *at* have a *−s* option that runs your job with the Bourne shell.

- Not all versions of *at* prompt you with at> as I showed above.

—JP

42.08 Automatically Restarting at Jobs

In some situations, it's convenient to create jobs that do their work, finish, and automatically reschedule themselves at some time in the future. Here's how to do this:

```
#!/bin/sh
myself=/home/mikel/bin/restarter
# Add any commands you want to do real work here
...
sleep 60
at -s 1 AM tomorrow $myself
```

Once you've started this script, it will run every day at 1 a.m. The *sleep (42.02)* makes sure that the following *at* command is executed after 1 a.m.; this guarantees that the next job will run at 1 a.m. tomorrow instead of 1 a.m. today. This trick isn't needed on most versions of *at*, but it isn't a bad idea.

Note that self-restarting jobs really are an artifact of an earlier era, when mortal users were supposed to stay away from the *cron (42.12)* facility. Now that users can have personal *crontab* files, the need for self-restarting jobs should diminish.

If you find that you do need to create scripts that reschedule themselves, please make sure to clean up after yourself! When your program is no longer needed, remember to delete it with *atq* and *atrm (42.09)*.

—ML

42.09 Checking and Removing Jobs

From time to time, you'll submit an *at* job and realize that there's something wrong with it. How do you get it out of the queue? Two tools help you do this: *atq*, which reports the jobs that are in the queue, and *atrm*, which deletes jobs that are already in the queue.

atq is pretty simple; by default, it reports on all jobs that have been queued. Optionally, you can give it a user name as an argument; in this case it reports all the jobs queued by the given user. The report looks like this:

```
los% atq
 Rank     Execution Date      Owner    Job #   Queue   Job Name
 1st    Oct  9, 1992 22:00    mikel     4637      a     stdin
 2nd    Oct 10, 1992 01:00    mikel     4641      a     stdin
 3rd    Oct 10, 1992 02:00    judy      4663      a     stdin
```

Note that *atq* has no objection to telling you about other users' jobs. Although this might seem like a security hole, it's actually useful—see article 42.05. The jobs are ordered according to their execution date. With the *–c* option, *atq* orders jobs according to when they were queued—conceivably a useful feature. (*atq −n* just prints the number of jobs that are queued; I'm not sure when this would be useful.)

Once you've found out the job number, you can delete it with the command *atrm*. You can only delete your own jobs, not someone else's:

```
% atrm 4637
4637: removed
% atrm 4663
4663: permission denied
```

The command *atrm −* removes all the jobs you submitted; it's good for cleaning out your queue completely.

Note: On System V prior to SVR4, use *at −l* to list your jobs (instead of *atq*), and *at −r* to delete your jobs (instead of *atrm*). SunOS and SVR4 support both versions.

Some older BSD-based implementations may not support any of these options. Once you submit a job, you can delete it by finding its filename in the */usr/spool/at* directory and emptying the file *(25.01)*. Or the superuser *(1.24)* can go to the spool directory and delete the file by hand.

—ML

42.10 *nextday, nextweekday: Tomorrow or Next Weekday*

nextday

Before my UNIX systems had personal crontabs *(42.12)*, I wanted a way to make an *at* job *(42.03)* repeat itself the next weekday (skipping Saturday and Sunday) or, sometimes, every day. Our *at* was simple-minded and didn't understand dates like *now + 1 day*. This script with two names, *nextday* and *nextweekday*, did the job. I called it from inside my *at* job, like this:

```
% cat atjob
somecommand
sleep 60
at 2325 `nextweekday` < atjob
```

`... ` 10.14

On Thursday, the result will be a command like at 2325 Friday atjob. On Friday, the command will be at 2325 Monday atjob; using *nextday* instead, the result would be at 2325 Saturday atjob.

The *−n* option returns a numeric weekday.

Note: This script only works with some versions of *date*. If your version doesn't understand format strings like +%*format*, install the *date (53.10)* from the Power Tools disk.

You can install this script from the Power Tools disk or from the online archive *(54.07)*. If you get it from the archive, ask *tar* to install *nextday* and its other link:

```
% tar xvf archive.tar nextday nextweekday
x nextday, 1564 bytes, 4 tape blocks
nextweekday linked to nextday
```

The script tests the name it was called with, in $0, to decide which command to run.

—JP

42.11 *Send Yourself Reminder Mail*

I use the *at* command *(42.07)* to send myself reminders. The *at* job runs a mail program *(1.33)* and feeds the body of the message to the mailer's standard input. Examples:

1. To send a one-line reminder, I use a one-line command like this:

    ```
    % at 0427 tuesday
    at> echo "send summary to Tim today" | mail jerry
    at> CTRL-d
    %
    ```

    It sends mail at (in this case) 4:27 a.m. on the next Tuesday. The mail says: "send summary to Tim today."

2. To send more than one line, you can use a temporary file:

    ```
    % vi msgfile
         ...put message body in msgfile...
    % at 0808 feb 28
    at> mail jerry < msgfile
    at> rm msgfile
    at> CTRL-d
    %
    ```

3. Combine the output of UNIX commands and text with backquotes *(10.14)* and a here document *(9.14)*:

    ```
    % at 0115
    at> Mail -s "Hard-working People" jerry << END
    at> These employees are working late. Give them a raise:
    at> `w`
    at> END
    at> CTRL-d
    %
    ```

    That sends me a message at 1:15 a.m. tonight. (My mailer lets me add a subject on the command line with its *–s* option. The output of the *w* command gives detailed information about logged-in users; not all systems have it.) Unless you understand how to quote here-document text *(47.26)*, the message shouldn't have anything but letters, numbers, commas, and periods.

If your system administrator has set up the *calendar* *(50.05)* program, it's good for easy one-line reminders on particular days. If your UNIX has personal crontabs *(42.12)* that can send periodic reminders every Tuesday, every hour, or whatever: use the commands in items 1 or 2 above.

—*JP*

42.12 *Periodic Program Execution: the cron Facility*

cron allows you to schedule programs for periodic execution. For example, you can use *cron* to call a particular UUCP *(1.33)* site every hour, to clean up editor backup files every night, or to perform any number of other tasks. However, *cron* is not a general facility for scheduling program execution off-hours; use the *at* command *(42.03)*.

With redirection *(14.01)*, *cron* can send program output to a log file or to any user-name via the mail system *(1.33)*.

Execution Scheduling

The *cron* system is serviced by the *cron* daemon. What to run and when to run it are specified to *cron* by *crontab* entries, which are stored in the system's *cron* schedule. Under BSD, this consists of the files */usr/lib/crontab* and */usr/lib/crontab.local*; either file may be used to store *crontab* entries. Both are ASCII files and may be modified with any text editor. Since usually only *root* has access to these files, all *cron* scheduling must go through the system administrator. This can be either an advantage or a disadvantage, depending on the needs and personality of your site.

Under System V (and AIX, XENIX, and SunOS), any user may add entries to the *cron* schedule. *crontab* entries are stored in separate files for each user. The *crontab* files are not edited directly by ordinary users, but are placed there with the *crontab* command (described later in this section). [In my experience, the *cron* jobs are run from your home directory. If you read a file or redirect output to a file with a relative pathname *(15.02)*, that'll probably be in your home directory. Check your system to be sure.—*JP*]

crontab entries direct *cron* to run commands at regular intervals. Each one-line entry in the *crontab* file has the following format:

> *mins hrs day-of-month month weekday username cmd*   (BSD)
> *mins hrs day-of-month month weekday cmd*   (System V)

Spaces separate the fields. However, the final field, *cmd*, can contain spaces within it (i.e., the *cmd* field consists of everything after the space following *weekday*); the other fields must not contain spaces. The *username* field is used in the BSD version only and specifies the username under which to run the command. Under System V, commands are run by the user who owns the *crontab* in which they appear (and for whom it is named).

The first five fields specify the times at which *cron* should execute *cmd*. Their meanings are described in Table 42-1.

Table 42-1. *crontab Entry Time Fields*

Field	Meaning	Range
mins	The minutes after the hour.	0-59
hrs	The hours of the day.	0-23 (0 = midnight)
day-of-month	The day within a month.	1-31
month	The month of the year.	1-12
weekday	The day of the week.	1-7 (1 = Monday) *BSD*
		0-6 (0=Sunday) *System V*

An entry in any of these fields can be a single number, a pair of numbers separated by a dash (indicating a range of numbers), a comma-separated list of numbers and ranges, or an asterisk (a wildcard that represents all valid values for that field).

If the first character in an entry is a number sign (#), *cron* will treat the entry as a comment and ignore it. This is an easy way to temporarily disable an entry without permanently deleting it.

Here are some example *crontab* entries (shown in System V format):

```
0,15,30,45 * * * *  (echo -n '   '; date; echo "") >/dev/console
0,10,20,30,40,50 7-18 * * * /usr/lib/atrun
7 0 * * *  find / -name "*.bak" -type f -atime +7 -exec rm {} \;
12 4 * * *  /bin/sh /usr/adm/ckdsk 2>&1 >/usr/adm/disk.log
22 2 * * *  /bin/sh /usr/adm/ckpwd 2>&1 | mail root
30 3 * * 1 /bin/csh -f /usr/lib/uucp/uu.weekly 2>&1 >/dev/null
#30 2 * * 0,6  /usr/lib/newsbin/news.weekend
```

The first entry displays the date on the console terminal every fifteen minutes (on the quarter hour); notice that multiple commands are enclosed in parentheses in order to redirect their output as a group. (Technically, this says to run the commands together in a subshell *(14.07).*) The second entry runs */usr/lib/atrun* every ten minutes from 7:00 a.m. to 6:00 p.m. daily. The third entry runs a *find* command at seven minutes after midnight to remove all *.bak* files not accessed in seven days. [To cut wear and tear and load on your disk, try to combine *find* jobs *(24.21).* Also, as article 42.05 explains, try not to schedule your jobs at often-chosen times like 1:00 a.m., 2:00 a.m., and so on; pick oddball times like 4:12 a.m.—*JP*]

The fourth and fifth lines run a shell script every day, at 4:12 a.m. and 2:22 a.m., respectively. The shell to execute the script is specified explicitly on the command line in both cases; the system default shell, usually the Bourne shell, is used if none is explicitly specified. Both lines' entries redirect standard output and standard error, sending it to a file in one case and mailing it to *root* in the other.

The sixth entry executes a C shell script named *uu.weekly*, stored in */usr/lib/uucp*, at 3:30 a.m. on Monday mornings. Notice that the command format—specifically the output redirection—is for the Bourne shell even though the script itself will be run under the C shell. The final entry would run the command */usr/lib/newsbin/news.weekend* at 2:30 a.m. on Saturday and Sunday mornings if it were not disabled.

The final three active entries illustrate three output-handling alternatives: redirecting it to a file, piping it through mail, and discarding it to */dev/null (14.14)*. If no output redirection is performed, the output is sent via mail to the user who ran the command.

The *cmd* field can be any UNIX command or group of commands (properly separated with semicolons). The entire *crontab* entry can be arbitrarily long, but it must be a single physical line in the file.

The *cron* command starts the *cron* program. It has no options. Once started, *cron* never terminates. It is normally started automatically by one of the system initialization scripts. *cron* reads the *crontab* file(s) every minute to see whether there have been changes. Therefore, any change to its schedule will take effect within one minute.

—*AF* from the Nutshell Handbook *Essential System Administration*

42.13 *Adding crontab Entries*

Most recent versions of UNIX—System V, AIX, SunOS, and XENIX—have a special command for maintaining the *crontab* file. To create a new *crontab* file, create a file containing the desired *crontab* entries. Then run the *crontab* command to install the file in the *cron* spool area. For example, if user *chavez* executes the command below, the file *mycron* will be installed as */usr/spool/cron/crontabs/chavez*:

```
$ crontab mycron
```

If *chavez* had previously installed *crontab* entries, they will be *replaced* by those in *mycron*; thus, any current entries that *chavez* wishes to keep must also be present in *mycron*.

The *–l* option to *crontab* lists the current *crontab* entries, and redirecting its output to a file will allow them to be captured and edited:

```
$ crontab -l >mycron
$ vi mycron
$ crontab mycron
```

The *–r* option will remove all current *crontab* entries. Under SunOS, *crontab* has an additional *–e* option which lets you directly edit your current *crontab* entries in a single step (see article 42.16 for a script like that).

On BSD-based UNIX implementations, there is no separate *crontab* command, nor does each user get a personal *crontab* file. BSD does distinguish between "global" *crontab* entries (in */usr/lib/crontab*) and "local" entries (in

/usr/lib/crontab.local)—however, you have to edit these files directly, which will probably require you to become superuser. It's a good idea to collect personal and site-specific *crontab* entries in the *crontab.local* file.

—*AF* from the Nutshell Handbook *Essential System Administration*

42.14 Including Standard Input within a cron Entry

Since *crontab* entries must be a single line long, it's hard to include any standard input with them. Sure, you can use commands like:

```
0 22 * * * echo "It's 10PM; do you know where your children are?" | wall
```

but you can't use "here documents" and other methods of generating multi-line input; they intrinsically take several lines.

To solve this problem, *cron* allows you to include standard input directly on the command line. If the command contains a percent sign (%), *cron* uses any text following the sign as standard input for *cmd*. Additional percent signs can be used to subdivide this text into lines. For example, the following *crontab* entry:

```
30 11 31 12 * /etc/wall%Happy New Year!%Let's make next year great!
```

runs the *wall* command at 11:30 a.m. on December 31st, using the text:

```
Happy New Year!
Let's make next year great!
```

as standard input.

—*AF* from the Nutshell Handbook *Essential System Administration*

42.15 Getting the "Third Monday" into a crontab

One problem with the *crontab* syntax is that it lets you specify any day of the month, and any day of the week; but it doesn't let you construct cases like "the third Monday of every month." You might think that the *crontab* entry:

```
0 0 15-21 * 1 your-command
```

would do the trick, but it won't; this *crontab* entry runs your command on every Monday, plus the 15th through the 21st of each month.*

To solve this problem, let's write a short script that accepts two arguments: the number of some week in the month, and an arbitrarily long command. (To be accurate, the command is really many arguments—but we'll play fast and loose

---

*Some historical research leads me to believe that this strange behavior is a System V peculiarity that somehow infected the rest of the world. "True" BSD systems behave the way you'd expect them to. However, SunOS 4.X systems have incorporated System V's behavior; and, with the advent of Solaris, there are relatively few true commercial BSD systems left in the world.

with our terminology.) The script figures out if the current date falls into the correct week; if so, it executes the command:

whichweek

+%d *53.10*

```
#!/bin/sh
# whichweek.sh:  runs a command only in a given week of the month.
#      $1 is the week number
#      $2 ... $n are a command
week=$1
shift
command=$*
# get today's date (day in month) into a variable
today=`date +%d`
# figure out when the week begins and ends
startdate=`expr \( $week - 1 \) \* 7 + 1`
enddate=`expr $week \* 7`
if [ $today -lt $startdate -o $today -gt $enddate ]; then exit 0; fi
$command
```

With this script, your *crontab* entry would look like this:

```
# Run on the third Monday of every month
0 0 * * 1 whichweek.sh 3 your-command
```

That is, you rely on *cron* to select every Monday; and you use *whichweek* to select the particular Monday that you want.

—*ML*

42.16 *crontab Script Makes crontab Editing Easier/Safer*

I've made mistakes with the *crontab* command, accidentally deleting my *crontab* file and not being able to get it back. I like the SunOS *crontab –e* command for interactive editing. So, I made a shell script that does it. To help keep me from using the system version, I store this script in a directory near the start of my PATH *(9.05)*; if I really need the system version, I type its absolute pathname.

crontab

umask *23.04*

trap *46.12*

```
#! /bin/sh
cmd=/usr/bin/crontab     # THE SYSTEM VERSION

# MAKE SURE EVERYONE KNOWS WHAT THEY'RE RUNNING:
echo "Running Jerry's crontab command..." 1>&2

case $# in
1)  ;; # OK
*)  echo "Usage: `/bin/basename $0` -e | -l | -d"; exit 1 ;;
esac

case "$1" in
-[ld]) $cmd $1 ;;    # EXIT WITH STATUS OF REAL COMMAND
-e) # EDIT IT:
    umask 077
    stat=1 # DEFAULT EXIT STATUS; RESET TO 0 FOR NORMAL EXIT
    start=/tmp/CRONTAB$$s    end=/tmp/CRONTAB$$e
    trap 'rm -f $start $end; exit $stat' 0 1 2 15
```

```
$cmd -l > $start || exit      # GET COPY OF CRONTAB
/bin/cp $start $end
${VISUAL-${EDITOR-vi}} $end
if cmp -s $start $end
then echo "The crontab file was not changed." 1>&2; exit
else
    $cmd $end
    stat=$? # EXIT WITH STATUS FROM REAL crontab COMMAND
    exit
fi
;;
*)  echo "Usage: `/bin/basename $0` -e | -l | -d"; exit 1;;
esac
```

|| *46.09*

${..-..} *47.12*

cmp *29.10*

—*JP*

Part Seven

Terminals and Printers

We don't spend a whole lot of time on UNIX hardware in this book, but we can't avoid spending some on terminals and printers. Without these input/output devices, everything else becomes rather irrelevant.

We talked a bit about terminal setup back in Chapter 6. Chapters 43 and 44 pick up the thread. Chapter 43 describes some of the underpinnings of the UNIX terminal interface—the way things work. Chapter 44 focuses on problems that might occur and how to solve them.

Chapter 45 talks about how printing works under UNIX, including not only the basics of the print spooler but also ways to get formatted output. Among other things, it includes some nifty PostScript and image conversion utilities.

—*TOR*

43

Terminal and Serial Line Settings

43.01 *Delving a Little Deeper*

Article 6.02 and others introduce parts of UNIX terminal handling. This chapter contains several articles that show a little more about how UNIX handles terminals and other serial devices. Beginners don't always realize that there are several overlapping mechanisms at work. Programs like *tset* and *tput*, and the *termcap* and *terminfo* databases they depend on, actually configure the terminal or window (or tell other programs about their characteristics), while *stty* affects the operation of the UNIX device drivers that handle the serial line. From a user's point of view, the distinction isn't always clear, especially since *tset* does some of its work on both levels.

Perhaps we're continuing the confusion by putting information about both of these topics into the same chapters. Oh well. What we have here are a miscellany of topics that delve a little deeper than we've gone before into how terminals work under UNIX.

- Article 43.02 explains why *stty* is as complex as it is. Article 43.03 shows how to check *stty*'s settings.

- Article 43.04 explains some of the mysteries of terminal tab handling.

- Article 43.05 lists differences in the way that System V and BSD UNIX handle what you type on the command line.

- Articles 43.06 and 43.07 give two practical uses of *stty*.

- Article 43.08 explains how software designed for terminals still runs under window systems, using "pseudo-terminals" or *ptys*.

- Articles 43.09 and 43.10 describe how to issue escape sequences to change the behavior of your terminal.

- Article 43.11 describes how to read a *termcap* or *terminfo* entry.

- Article 43.12 describes how to avoid reading *termcap* and *terminfo* entries.

- Article 44.01 introduces more low-level concepts.

—*TOR*

43.02 stty and All that Stuff

[. . . all that useful *stuff! This article has a lot of good background for under-standing how communications works between the UNIX host and your terminal or window. Chris has been in the business since way back; there's lots of interesting history in here, too.*

You might want a copy of your system's stty *manual page close by while you read this article.—JP]*

Q: What is *stty* all about? Why does it have so many options?

A: Serial ports—indeed, computer communications in general—are a tangled and complicated area. The demands made for serial port communication, and hence the support for it in UNIX systems, began simply, but then grew in raging, uncontrolled bursts.

How we Made it this Far (Back?)

Originally, UNIX ran on a small machine that talked only to *teletypes*, or *ttys* for short. The UNIX kernel had to collect up input lines, allowing minor corrections—erasing the previous character and killing (erasing wholly) the input line—and translating a few "special" characters for controlling programs. Teletypes were printers, incapable of erasing, so the erase and kill characters were just ordinary printing characters, namely # and @. The original special characters were CTRL-d (for end-of-file), DEL (to interrupt), and CTRL-\ (to quit). The kernel also mapped input RETURN codes to the newline character, so that users could push the big RETURN key, on teletypes that had those.

These teletypes had some peculiarities. In particular, they used a moving print head (or *carriage*), and this print head took a noticeable amount of time to return from the right margin to the left. If sent continuous printing text, a teletype could smear characters all over the paper during a carriage return.* The UNIX kernel therefore had to allow for a delay after a carriage return. At the same time, the kernel did "output processing" by changing newlines to the teletype's carriage return and linefeed codes, if necessary.† A few teletypes allowed only uppercase characters, and UNIX grew support for these as well. UNIX did

---

*This is an exaggeration. Printing during a carriage return was occasionally used as a diagnostic for checking the motor speed. The character printed during the return was supposed to appear exactly halfway along the line.

†Some teletypes really processed a newline as a "new line," i.e., a carriage return and linefeed, but most left this up to the host computer.

get away without something common to other operating systems, however: UNIX systems assumed that all teletypes were "full duplex" and used "remote echo." This meant, in essence, that both the teletype and the UNIX system could send to each other at the same time; and the teletype would not print what you typed until told to do so by the UNIX host.*

UNIX also had to provide a way for special applications, such as UUCP *(1.33)*, to get input characters without any processing. This was the so-called "raw" mode. The kernel service was all-or-nothing: in raw mode, every input and output character was left alone, and passed directly—and immediately—to the application. In "cooked" mode, the kernel did input and output translations and delays.

Along with the ability to set raw or cooked mode, the kernel allowed changing each of the special characters *(6.09)* and allowed control of some of the simpler aspects of the serial port interface, such as parity† and baud rate. The baud rate, perhaps better called the bit rate, of the original teletype was 110 bits per second (bps), or 11 characters per second. (The machines really did print exactly 11 times each second, with one possibility being quietly to print nothing.) Early computer modems ran at 110 and 300 baud, and there were a standard set of serial port speeds: 50, 75, 110, 134.5, 150, 200, 300, 600, 1200, 1800, 2400, 4800, and even 9600 bps, which was considered terribly fast. UNIX systems used serial cards with two additional "external control" rates labelled A and B; these became *exta* and *extb*. Some UNIX systems still support exactly (and only) these rates, and tie *exta* to 19200 bps and *extb* to 38400 bps.

Eventually, teletype printers began to be displaced. First there came so-called "glass ttys"—CRT displays that tried to act just like a teletype—and then smarter terminals, ones that could (gasp) move a cursor around the screen, and edit the display in place. These used special control and escape codes to do the editing. They also provided the opportunity to write full-screen editors. UNIX had to evolve to adapt to these new constraints. Unfortunately, by this time there were two main branches of UNIX. One would eventually become 4BSD, or Berkeley UNIX; the other was to become System V.

The goals for both systems were similar, and thus both wound up with comparable approaches. Berkeley UNIX, however, attempted both to retain backwards compatibility and to provide a nice user interface, while the original System V system discarded compatibility in favor of efficiency and a "complete" interface—one that allowed doing everything a serial port could do.

---

*Full duplex/remote echo and half duplex/local echo tended to go together. In particular, a half duplex system—which was not the same as a simplex system—had to have local echo to avoid being annoying to use. Fortunately, this is irrelevant today. The concept of "duplex" has fallen by the wayside, and everything is full duplex, or at least simulates it internally.

†Parity is used for error checking. Parity is simply the number of "1" bits. If you have the value 1001001, and even parity, the parity bit should be 1, because 1001001 has three 1 bits—an odd number—and adding another 1 makes this even. If the parity bit fails to match, at least one bit is wrong. It could, of course, be the parity bit itself. Moreover, with a *tty* port, there may not be anything you can do to fix the error—most UNIX kernels just drop the bad input character—but the check is available.

Berkeley UNIX thus acquired *three* terminal modes. It retained the original *raw* and *cooked* modes, and added a new one called *cbreak*.* In cbreak mode, some input processing was done, but most characters were sent on to the application as they arrived. Since the kernel was not collecting lines, the erase and line-kill characters were unneeded; these were sent on unchanged. Most of the process control characters—interrupt, quit, and a new *stop* or *suspend* code—were still interpreted. To allow users to type these codes, a new "literal next" or "quote" character was introduced. Berkeley UNIX also added more output processing, including a special translation option for certain Hazeltine Corporation displays and features such as proper tab handling, output flush, and word erase.

The System V base, on the other hand, dropped the idea of raw mode entirely. Instead, this system provided an individual control for each option. The *icanon* option, for instance, controlled whether input lines were to be collected or "canonicalized." The *isig* option controlled signals: when off, the *interrupt* (DEL, or in modern systems, CTRL-c) and *quit* characters were just ordinary characters. The *inpchk* option controlled input parity checking, and so forth. Similarly, output processing had individual flags: *ocrnl* for carriage return-newline control, *opost* for output processing in general. By turning everything off individually, an application could get the same effect as the old system's raw mode. The kernel also allowed control over the number of data bits in each serial frame,† the number of stop bits, and so forth. Thus, while Berkeley UNIX had nice line editing, it was incapable of attaching to five-bit Baudot systems. System V lacked the user interface features, but could talk to almost anything.

Since then, the world has become simpler in one way—those old printing teletypes are gone nearly everywhere, for instance—but more complicated in another. These days, many computers use bitmapped displays rather than individual remote terminals. UNIX systems now support networking, and use windowing systems such as MIT's X Window System *(1.31)*. These in turn bring a myriad of options, window managers, look-and-feel, and so on. But they all have one thing in common: To run old applications, each window or network login must provide a *virtual terminal* interface. UNIX systems generally do this with *pseudo teletypes* or *ptys (43.08)*. Each pty exists to emulate a display terminal, which in turn is mainly pretending to be a teletype printer. (Sometimes one has to wonder where the progress lies.)

Recently, a POSIX standardization committee has settled on a standard interface, both at the UNIX kernel level and for the *stty* command. Most UNIX systems, including Berkeley UNIX, have moved to embrace this standard. While it leaves a few loose ends—mainly for reasons involving backwards compatibility for System V—it allows systems both the flexibility of the System V interface and the features of the Berkeley approach. This means that, while windows and

---

*This *cbreak* mode has sometimes been referred to as "half-baked."

†Different systems use anything from five to nine bits in a serial-port "byte." Most people, however, do not need to care about all this. Most systems just use eight bits, either as seven data bits and a parity check, or as eight data bits without parity. Thus, most people can ignore these options, and stick with either "seven bits, even parity" or "eight bits, no parity."

networks may be emulating ancient teletypes, at least they are all doing it the same way.

Handling Most Characters

With all that as background, let's take a look at what happens to an input character, from the time you type it until an application can react. The details may vary—often wildly—depending on your system and whether you are using a window, a terminal, a network, or some combination of all three, but the overall idea is the same. For simplicity, we will assume you have an ordinary terminal. We will call this "the terminal" and the kernel's idea of it "the tty."

Suppose you type the letter x. The terminal sends the ASCII code *(53.03)* for a lowercase X (120) to the UNIX kernel's tty. The kernel then looks at the *tty* state. Assume for the sake of discussion that the tty is in cooked or icanon mode, and that none of the special characters has been set to x. Then the letter x is placed in an input buffer and echoed back to the terminal, causing an x to be displayed on your screen. But if you really wanted to type a c, you would now type your erase character *(6.09)* (usually CTRL-h, BACKSPACE, or DELETE, which may or may not all be the same or all different, depending on your particular terminal or keyboard). The code for this character will also be sent to the tty; this time it will match your erase character. The kernel will then remove the last character from the input buffer. Since this—a lowercase X—is an ordinary printing character, the kernel will send a single backspace, or the sequence "backspace space backspace," to the terminal. This will generally back the cursor up over the character and then erase it from the screen. (On a POSIX system, you get the latter by setting *echoe* mode.) Finally, when you type RETURN or ENTER, your terminal sends an ASCII code 13. Since *icrnl* is set, the kernel changes this to 10 (newline), which it then echoes to the terminal. Since *onlcr* is set, this sends both a code 13 (carriage return) and a 10 (linefeed) to the terminal. The kernel sees that 10 is a newline, wraps up the collected buffer, and passes it on to whatever application is currently reading from the tty.

If you turn off *icanon* (or turn on *cbreak*), the kernel takes any partially collected buffer and passes those characters to the application, then passes on each ordinary input character as it comes in. The kernel still echoes input back to the terminal. If you turn off the *echo* flag in the tty, the kernel will stop doing echoing. This is how a full-screen editor like *vi* works: it turns off *icanon*, turns off *echo*, and turns off some, but not all, of the special characters. The *vi* program can then do its own echoing, so that when you type i to go into insert mode, no i appears on your terminal.

One of several difficult areas involves turning *icanon* back on. In particular, there may be some characters you typed at the terminal while *icanon* was off. These reached the tty, which packaged them up and sent them off to an application. The application may not have read them yet, but as far as the *tty* is concerned, they are gone. Thus, you may not be able to recover them for your current input line. Older Berkeley UNIX systems are able to handle this case, but System V systems that use the STREAMS interface are not. As long as your system is fast enough, though, you will never notice, because applications will always turn *icanon* on before you can type anything at the terminal.

What about TABs?

Tabs are another difficult issue. The history here predates computing; typewriter tabs are sometimes used as the "right" model. Nonetheless, different terminals behave differently, and different people make different assumptions about how tabs should work. The ASCII code for TAB, code 9, is intended to move the cursor right to the next tabstop. But where *is* that? Moreover, once the cursor has gone there, how does the kernel move it back if you decided to erase the tab?

Many UNIX kernels can be told to expand tabs. When they do this, they set the tabstops at every eight characters. This is where they think tabstops belong. That is, if you print a newline, two ordinary letters, and a tab, the tab will turn into six spaces. If a *tty* is in icanon/cooked mode, and is expanding tabs, it can "unexpand" them to backspace over the tab. Berkeley kernels will do this, and it works fairly well. They can get it wrong, however, under certain conditions. For instance, if you set the *tty* to pass tabs unmodified, and if the terminal itself puts tabstops at every ten characters—this would be the proper setting for dealing with a DEC-10, for instance—the kernel *tty* code will put out fewer backspaces than needed.

Even if the terminal sets its tabstops at eight, the kernel's *tty* code and the terminal can get different ideas of the current cursor column. Most Berkeley kernels count control codes as "ordinary" output characters, for instance, even though those characters are likely to have no effect on the cursor, or might even move it to an arbitrary position. To help prevent *input* control characters from goofing up backspacing, Berkeley kernels can echo them as two-character sequences. For instance, CTRL-g will normally echo as ^G. Erasing such a control character works properly: the *tty* code puts out *two* backspaces, *two* spaces, and two more backspaces. Erasing more characters, possibly including a TAB, then still works. This "control echo" can be switched on and off individually as well.

In addition to carriage return delays, which exist to allow time for the teletype's print carriage to move left, some UNIX systems also support tab delays, for more or less the same reason. Like return-delays, these are pretty much outmoded and useless. The POSIX standard leaves room for both kinds of delay, but does not mandate either one. You may see them in *stty* output, as *cr2*, *cr3*, *tab1*, and the like, but your system's default is probably "no delay," and few people are likely to change this deliberately.

Article 43.04 has some higher-level information about TABs.

Flow Control (We Hope)

Finally, flow control—avoiding lost input and output characters—is perhaps the dirtiest swamp of all. Most of the terminals built in the 1980s support, and at higher speeds require, something called *XON/XOFF* flow control. Here, when the terminal falls behind in printing characters, it shouts "stop!" by sending an XOFF character—ASCII code 19, or CTRL-s—to the UNIX system. If the UNIX machine does not stop soon enough, some text will be lost. When the terminal is ready for more, it sends a "go" character—an XON, ASCII code 17, or CTRL-q. These were never intended as a general flow control mechanism—on some of the original teletypes, they turned the paper tape punch off and on—but they have that meaning now. Unfortunately, most terminals also allow users to type CTRL-s and CTRL-q, but they provide no way to distinguish between the terminal yelling "stop" and the user pushing CTRL-s. The result is a constant battle between people who want to use CTRL-s and computer systems that want to take it for themselves.

Other systems, notably HP-based systems, use something called *ENQ/ACK* flow control. Here the terminal and the host system must agree up-front on a minimum buffer size. Then either system is allowed to send that many characters to the other, after which it must stop and wait for a "go-ahead" signal. Each system requests such a signal by sending an "enquire": ASCII code 5, or CTRL-e. When the listening system encounters the ENQ, and is ready for more, it sends an acknowledgement: ASCII code 6, or CTRL-f. This system is superior to the XON/XOFF system in one way, as it never has problems with a busy system failing to stop immediately on command, but it still does not prevent users from typing CTRL-e and CTRL-f. Moreover, it is not implemented on most UNIX systems.

A third method of flow control, and the most reliable where it is available, is the so-called *out of band* approach. "Out of band" simply means that users cannot accidentally simulate it by typing control characters. Out of band control can be done in software, using something similar to HP's ENQ/ACK and some encoding tricks, but in practice, most UNIX machines that support any kind of out of band flow control use something called either "hardware flow control" or "*RTS/CTS* flow control." (This can be implemented with no special hardware at all on many systems, so the latter name is better.)

With RTS/CTS flow control, two existing serial-cable wires, RTS and CTS, are "taken over." (RTS and CTS—which stand for Request to Send and Clear to Send respectively—were originally intended for use with half duplex modems. Since half duplex modems are today merely museum pieces, this is a sensible approach, but it does violate the RS232 standard.) RTS at the terminal is cross-connected to CTS at the host computer, and vice versa. The terminal and the computer both assert RTS whenever they are ready to receive data, and wait for CTS before sending. Unfortunately, not enough systems implement this, and of those that do, many get it wrong.* Thus, while RTS/CTS flow control offers the possibility of working perfectly, you cannot count on it. Still, it is worth looking for an *rts/cts* option in your UNIX's *stty*.

---

*For instance, on Sun workstations, RTS/CTS is supported in hardware, but the particular Zilog chip that does this also uses the DCD (Data Carrier Detect) line to control the receiver. Thus, if you set *stty crtscts*, you cannot tell a modem to dial out, because DCD is off. It is possible to work around this, but only with control over both the hardware and the UNIX kernel.

Then what?

If you think this is complicated, just hope you never have to deal with synchronous transmission, RS422, DIN connectors, lightning strike protection, and many of the other hardware and electrical aspects that surround computer communications. Getting two arbitrary computers to talk to each other can be excessively difficult. Here again, standards come to the rescue. If everything you have is proper RS232—modulo *(55.01)*, perhaps, RTS/CTS flow control—and POSIX, things should usually go smoothly.

—CT

43.03 Find Out Terminal Settings with stty

It may hardly seem appropriate to follow Chris Torek's learned article about how *stty* works *(43.02)* with some basics, but this book is designed for beginners as well as those who already know everything. :-) *(53.12)* So:

To find out what settings your terminal line currently has, type:

```
% stty
```

For a more complete listing, type:

```
% stty -a
```

on System V-ish systems, and:

```
% stty -everything
```

on BSD systems.

As Jerry Peek said in an editorial aside to Chris's article, be sure to have your *stty* manual page handy!

—TOR

43.04 How UNIX Handles TAB Characters

TAB characters are used in a lot of places: tables, indented paragraphs, source code for programs, the output of many programs, and so on. UNIX handles TABs in a flexible way that's different than some other computer systems.

Most UNIX programs, printers, and terminals are set up to assume tabstops every 8 columns. That is, if the terminal or printer gets a TAB character on its input, it moves to the next tabstop position: column 9, 17, 25, etc. The UNIX system (kernel, device driver *(44.01)*) usually doesn't interpret TAB characters or set tabstops; it treats the TABs like any other character, passing them on to utilities or hardware like terminals.

You might want to use tabstop intervals other than 8. When I write programs, for example, an 8-character indent wastes space, so I use a 4-character indent. If you want to use different tabstops, too, you need to understand how TABs are handled.

TAB is Just Another Character to UNIX

Typing TAB sends a single TAB character to the UNIX system. If you're editing a file, the editor probably puts that single TAB character into the file. Later, when you use *cat (26.02)*, *pr (45.07)*, *lp (45.02)*, and so on, they read each TAB and send out that single character to your terminal, printer, or whatever. The TAB is usually interpreted by the hardware device itself. Before that, it's a single character like any other. (But see the *stty –tabs* command below.)

If your terminal has a setup mode, enter setup mode and look at the tabstop settings. They're probably set at columns 9, 17, 25, and so on. When your terminal receives a TAB from the UNIX system, the terminal moves the cursor to the terminal's next tabstop.

For example, your terminal might have different tabstops—maybe 11, 21, 31, and so on. Let's say that you're *cat*ting a file. The programmer who made the file had her terminal tabstops set at the default 8-column intervals. When she typed it, she used TABs (shown as ▶ in this example) to indent the lines. Her terminal showed the file this way:

```
% cat prog
while read line; do
▶        set $line
▶        for word in line; do
▶        ▶        case "$1" in
 . . .
```

If your terminal has tabstops set at 12 characters, the same file would look like this:

```
% cat prog
while read line; do
▶            set $line
▶            for word in line; do
▶            ▶            case "$1" in
 . . .
```

Neither the UNIX kernel nor the *cat* program did anything different to the *prog* file. The terminal interprets the TABs.

If you want to display or edit a file that has different tabstops than your terminal, what can you do?

- Use a UNIX utility that "expands" (converts) TABs into spaces. On BSD systems, *expand* does the job. The terminal never sees the TABs in this case, so its tabstop settings are never used:

```
% expand prog
while read line; do
        set $line
        for word in line; do
                case "$1" in
 . . .
```

On System V, use *pr* with its *–t –e* options:

```
% pr -t -e prog
while read line; do
        set $line
        for word in line; do
                case "$1" in
  ...
```

So, no matter what your terminal tabstops are, the file will look normal.

If you want to use other tabstops, use an option. For instance, get 4-character tabstops with *expand –4* or *pr –e4*.

- Tell your text editor to use different tabstops. The editor will probably "expand" the TABs into spaces before it sends them to your terminal. For instance, in *vi*, type:

```
:set tabstop=4
```

to edit programs with 4-character tabstops. The *prog* file from above would look like:

```
% vi prog
while read line; do
►       set $line
►       for word in line; do
►    ►      case "$1" in
  ...
```

although it has TAB characters in exactly the same places. If you have a text editor handy, try changing its tabstops while you display a file.

If you make a file with non-standard tabstops, it's a good idea to put a comment in the file so people will know. Or, before you save the file for the last time, expand the TABs into spaces. With *vi* on a system that has *expand*, for example, this command would convert TABs to spaces at 4-column tabstops:

:%! *31.22*   `:%!expand -4`

Telling UNIX to Expand TABs

I said above that the UNIX kernel and device drivers don't usually expand TABs into spaces. Sometimes, if you're having a lot of trouble with funny-looking tabstop settings, you might ask the device driver to expand the TABs into spaces. The command is:

```
% stty -tabs
```

Now in most cases, UNIX will not send TABs to your terminal. It's better to fix your terminal's tabstops, if you can.

—JP

43.05 *Why some Systems Backspace over Prompts*

[One curiosity that some people notice is that on BSD systems, you can't back-space over shell prompts, but on System V, you can go right back to the edge of your screen or window, erasing the prompt. Brandon Allberry explains that here.—TOR]

You can make the BSD system behave like the System V one with *stty old*. But I don't think that's what you want . . . .

The System V terminal driver *(44.01)* makes no assumptions about the sanity or configuration of the terminal, and therefore doesn't try to get fancy with echo-ing. It can be annoying at times to see the system acting so stupidly, but it won't suddenly act up on you.

The BSD tty driver makes the assumption that the terminal is behaving sanely, and that nothing is playing games with escape sequences, etc., so it can get away with assuming how to stop at the prompt. To this end, it echoes control characters in "uparrow format" [like ^A for CTRL-a—*JP*] and assumes you have the *stty tabs* setting correct for the terminal (`stty tabs` only if the terminal has 8-character hardware tabs set, otherwise `stty -tabs`). But it also requires various other trickery (such as `stty tilde` to compensate for old Hazeltine terminals that use ~ instead of the ASCII ESC character) to stay in sync with strange terminals.

The BSD method mostly works, but has some drawbacks: for example, on a DEC-compatible terminal I sometimes have to echo a control character *(43.09)* to get the terminal to display ASCII instead of graphics characters. Under System V, this is convenient: it can be done by typing the control character at the shell command line, then backspace, then RETURN to redisplay the prompt as some-thing other than Greek. Under BSD I have to resort to *cat (26.02)*. Also, while BSD will echo "typed" control characters in uparrow format, it won't help you if a backgrounded program splatters control characters at the terminal. (Well, you can *stty tostop(13.07)*, but sometimes you "want" that behavior from some particu-lar backgrounded program: a status message, for example.)

Programs like *ksh* and *tcsh* also do "smart" echoing. They have the same prob-lems, plus an additional one: the BSD tty driver can tell when another program scribbles on the terminal while doing a line-buffered read and automatically redisplays the input line after the next keystroke. A user program has no way to find out about such scribbling, however, so you can get into a decidedly non-WYSIWYG situation despite every attempt by the program to make things look right. At least System V is honest in not promising anything.

Such are the problems with non-regulated access by a multi-tasking system to a non-multiplexed device like a terminal, and such are the possible solutions. You choose the one that works best in your particular situation.

—BA in comp.unix.misc on Usenet, 12 October 1991

43.06 Using sleep to Keep Port Settings

It's sometimes desirable to use *stty (43.03)* to set values for a serial port other than the one your tty may be on (for example, a printer or modem port). But without a program "hanging onto" a port, the settings are pretty much useless in many UNIXes. A tty that is not attached to a process typically gets reset to some default whenever you open it. The only way to set it some way and make it stay that way is to open it and hold onto it, then set the modes.

The standard trick is to use:

```
% sleep 1000000 > /dev/ttyXX &
```

before setting things up. You can kill *(40.10)* the *sleep (42.02)* later, when you are done.

—CT in *net.unix* on Usenet, *30 January 1984*

43.07 Reading Verrrry Long Lines from the Terminal

Sometimes you can have a very long line of input that you want to write to a file. It might come from your personal computer, a device hooked to your terminal, or just an especially long set of characters that you have to type on the keyboard. Normally the UNIX terminal driver *(44.01)* holds all characters you type until it sees a line terminator or interrupt character. Most buffers have room for 256 characters.

To make UNIX pass each character it reads without buffering, use *stty (43.03)* to set your terminal to *cbreak* (or *non-canonical*) input mode. For example:

```
% stty cbreak
% cat > file
enter the very long line.........
CTRL-c
% stty -cbreak
```

On System V, start with `stty -icanon` and end with `stty icanon`.

While you're in *cbreak* mode, special keys like BACKSPACE or DELETE won't be processed; they'll be stored in the file. Typing CTRL-d will not make *cat* quit. To quit, kill *cat* by pressing your normal interrupt key—say, CTRL-c.

(If you accidentally type a backspace or press RETURN when you didn't want to, you can see those characters in the file with the octal dump command, *od (26.07)*, and its −c option. Filter them out with *tr −d (36.09)* or a text editor (the GNU Emacs *(33.01)* editor can handle very long lines).

One more problem: if you use a shell with built-in command line editing *(12.14)* and/or filename completion *(10.06)*, they might cause you trouble because they use *stty*-like commands to let you edit. In that case, start a plain Bourne shell (type *sh* or */bin/sh*) before you give the *stty* command.

—JP

43.08 ptys and Window Systems

When window systems came along, UNIX needed a workaround, so that all the software that was written for ASCII terminals could continue to run in windows.

From the window system side, what it took was a terminal emulator—a program that makes a window act like a terminal. Most emulators imitate a DEC VT100 or VT102 terminal; they respond to its escape sequences, and in general masquerade pretty well.

But there's another side to the equation. The system needs to know what "terminal" a program is running on, so it can read input and send output to the right place. There's normally an association between a *tty* file and a physical device attached to a serial line. But what's the association for an abstraction on a workstation screen, on a device that's nothing like a serial line?

The answer was to come up with a "terminal-like" construct on the system side. It's called a *pty*, for pseudo-terminal, instead of a *tty*.

—TOR

43.09 Aliases to Adjust Your Terminal

Most terminals and window systems read every character that the host computer sends to them. They're watching for an *escape sequence*, a series of characters that give commands to the terminal or window. (From now on, I'll just say "terminal." But this article applies to windows, too.) When the terminal sees an escape sequence, it performs the command instead of showing you the characters.

You can send these escape sequences yourself, from your UNIX account. For instance, maybe some program has accidentally left your terminal set to reverse video. If you're using an ANSI terminal (like a VT100) you could type an *echo* command to send the sequence ^[[0m (where ^[is an ESCape character) to turn off reverse video. However, it's usually easier to make aliases or a shell script that does the same thing.

These escape sequences should be documented in your terminal's manual. In this article, I'll use sequences for a VT102 or compatible terminal. If you're trying to make your setup more general so that it works on lots of terminals, you should use a command like *tput* or *tcap(43.10)* that reads your terminal's *terminfo* or *termcap* information.

For example, you might decide that it's easier to read a complicated display when it's in reverse video. To put it in reverse video and go back to normal video later:

```
% Revvid
%      ...type commands; all text shows in reverse video...
% Normal
%      ...now everything is in normal video...
```

Most full-screen programs (*vi*, etc.) re-initialize your terminal. That can undo some of what these aliases do.

C Shell Aliases

The first line stores an ESC character in a shell variable named *e*. It's used in all the other aliases as `${e}`:

csh_init

```
# VT102 AND COMPATIBLE TERMINAL CONTROL ESCAPE SEQUENCES

set e = "`echo X | tr X '\033'`"          # ESCape character

alias Clear 'echo -n "${e}[;H${e}[2J"'    # move to top left, clear screen

# ALTERNATE CHARACTER SETS.  YOU USUALLY WANT "NOG" TO CLEAR THESE
# WHEN YOUR TERMINAL GETS IN THIS MODE ACCIDENTALLY:
#

alias NOG 'echo -n "${e}(B"'        # cancel graphics
alias Graphics 'echo -n "${e}(0"'   # lowercase letters become graphics

# NOTE: THESE WON'T WORK FOR FULL-SCREEN APPLICATIONS LIKE vi.
# BETTER TO RESET YOUR TERMINAL PARAMETERS (tset, stty):
alias C132 'echo -n "${e}[?3;h"'    # 132-column mode
alias C80 'echo -n "${e}[?3;1"'     # 80-column mode

alias Revvid 'echo -n "${e}[?5;h"' # Reverse video
alias Normal 'echo -n "${e}[?5;1"' # Normal video

# WRITE MESSAGE TO TERMINAL STATUS LINE (NICE FOR REMINDERS) --
#       EXAMPLE:  ToStatus Clean out your files\!
# CLEAR IT.
alias ToStatus 'echo -n "${e}7${e}[25;1f${e}[0K\!*${e}8"'
alias ClrStatus 'echo -n "${e}7${e}[25;1f${e}[0K${e}8"'
```

Be careful to type those exactly if you don't get them off the disk. The *Graphics* alias uses the digit 0, not the letter O. The *Normal, ToStatus,* and *ClrStatus* aliases use the digit 1 (one), not the letter l (L).

Shell Script

If you need to use a shell script instead of aliases, here's how. One advantage of a shell script is that other users can put the directory it's in—like your *bin*—in their search paths. Then they can use the same scripts. Or, your system administrator can install the script in a system directory for everyone to use. In that case, though, the script should probably test the *TERM (6.11)* environment variable and print an error if the escape sequences in the script aren't right for the current terminal type. A shell script can also be called from other shell scripts—to, say, put a message into the status line and erase it later.

To write the script, make a file named for one of the aliases, like *Clear*:

Clear

```
#! /bin/sh
# SENDS VT102 AND COMPATIBLE TERMINAL CONTROL ESCAPE SEQUENCES

e="`echo e | tr e '\033'`"  # Make an ESCape character portably
```

```
case "$0" in
*Clear) seq="${e}[;H${e}[2J"  ;;# move to top left, clear screen

# ALTERNATE CHARACTER SETS.  YOU USUALLY WANT "NOG" TO CLEAR THESE
# WHEN YOUR TERMINAL GETS IN THIS MODE ACCIDENTALLY:

*NOG) seq="${e}(B" ;;        # cancel graphics and European
*Graphics) seq="${e}(0" ;;   # lower-case letters become graphics
*Eur) seq="${e}(1" ;;        # lower-case letters become European

# NOTE: THESE WON'T WORK FOR FULL-SCREEN APPLICATIONS LIKE vi.
# BETTER TO RESET YOUR TERMINAL PARAMETERS (tset, stty):

*C132) seq="${e}[?3;h" ;;    # 132-column mode
*C80) seq="${e}[?3;l" ;;     # 80-column mode

*Revvid) seq="${e}[?5;h" ;; # Reverse video
*Normal) seq="${e}[?5;l" ;; # Normal video

# WRITE MESSAGE TO TERMINAL STATUS LINE (NICE FOR REMINDERS)
#        EXAMPLE:  ToStatus Clean out your files\!
# CLEAR IT.

*ToStatus) seq="${e}7${e}[25;1f${e}[0K$*${e}8" ;;
*ClrStatus) seq="${e}7${e}[25;1f${e}[0K${e}8" ;;
*) echo "$0: HELP -- can't run myself." 1>&2; exit 1;;
esac

# SEND $seq TO TERMINAL WITHOUT INTERPRETATION BY SYSTEM V echo:
cat << END_OF_seq
$seq
END_OF_seq
exit 0
```

You can install this script from the Power Tools disk or you can just type it in. If you type it in, first put it in a file named *Clear* and make the script file executable with *chmod +x (46.02)*. The script has several links *(19.05)*. They're easiest to make with a *foreach* loop *(10.09)*:

```
% foreach link (NOG Graphics C132 C80 Revvid Normal ToStatus ClrStatus)
? ln Clear $link
? end
%
```

The script tests the name it was called with *(46.21)*, in $0, to decide which string to output (the asterisk (*) matches any pathname before the command name). This trick saves disk space. You can add other commands, too, by adding a line to the case and another link.

—JP based on a suggestion and aliases by Bruce Barnett

43.10 Using terminfo Capabilities in Shell Programs

The weakness of the technique described in article 43.09 is that it requires you to hardcode the escape sequences for a particular terminal. If you use more than one kind of terminal, you have to create separate aliases for each one. That's exactly the kind of problem that the *termcap* and *terminfo* databases were designed to solve.

tcap

For each terminal in the database, there is a list of terminal capabilities *(43.11)*. The *tput* program (standard on any system with *terminfo*) lets you print out the value of any individual capability. The *tcap* program does the same for systems using *termcap*. (*tcap* was originally named *tc*. We renamed it to avoid conflicts with *tc*, the *ditroff* interpreter program for Tektronix 4015 terminals.) This makes it possible to use terminal capabilities such as those for standout mode in shell programs.

For example, a prompt issued by a shell program could be highlighted by the following code using *tput*:

```
# Store the terminfo capability to start standout mode into
# the variable HIGHLIGHT; this might be bold, or inverse video
HIGHLIGHT=`tput smso`
# Store the terminfo capability to end standout mode into
# the variable NORMAL
NORMAL=`tput rmso`
# Echo a highlighted prompt
echo "${HIGHLIGHT}Press Return to accept value: ${NORMAL}\c"
```

Capabilities that accept arguments (such as cursor movement sequences) will interpolate values that follow the capability name on the command line. For example, to issue the cursor motion sequence to move to the upper-left corner of the screen (row 0, column 0), you could type:

```
$ tput cup 0 0
```

Another case where *tput* comes in useful is when command sequences accidentally get sent to the screen, leaving output garbled or in a distracting highlight mode. It sometimes happens that a user reads a non-ASCII file, or reads a mail message with a control character accidentally imbedded, and ends up with gibberish. This is often because the sequence for entering an alternate character set has been sent to the terminal, and the screen is no longer readable to the human eye. The user can return to the normal character set two ways: by rebooting the terminal, or by entering *tput init (6.13)* on the command line. Using *tput*, obviously, is much more efficient.

—*JS, TOR* from the Nutshell Handbook *termcap & terminfo*

43.11 How termcap and terminfo Describe Terminals

The *termcap* and *terminfo* databases *(6.02)* describe the capabilities of terminals using a rather obscure and compact language. At this point, the ASCII terminal market has slowed down and standardized, so it is not as essential as it used to be to write new terminal entries. However, there are still times when it's useful to know how to read an entry. For example, you may want to use particular capabilities in a shell program *(43.10)* or in a function key map *(43.12)*.

We won't give you a detailed list of all of the possible capabilities—that you can get from the *termcap* or *terminfo* manual page on your system. However, we do want to give you an introduction to the language of *termcap* and *terminfo*.

Here's a simplified entry for the Wyse Technology Wyse-50 terminal. The capabilities described here are only a subset sufficient to introduce the basic syntax of the language:

```
# incomplete termcap entry for the Wyse WY-50
n9|wy50|WY50| Wyse Technology WY-50:\
    :bs:am:co#80:li#24:\
    :up=^K:cl=^Z:ho=^^:nd=^L:cm=\E=%+ %+ :
```

And here is the corresponding *terminfo* source file:

```
# incomplete terminfo entry for Wyse WY-50
wy50|WY50|Wyse Technology WY-50,
    am, cols#80, lines#24, cuu1=^K, clear=^Z,
    home=^^, cuf1=^L, cup=\E=%p1%'\s'%+%c%p2%'\s'%+%c,
```

The backslash (\) character is used to suppress the newline in *termcap*. *termcap* entries must be defined on a single logical line, with colons (:) separating each field. *terminfo* does not require the entry to be on a single line, so backslashes are not necessary. In *terminfo*, commas are used as the field separator.

The language certainly is not verbose! However, if we work through it methodically, it might begin to make sense.

There are three types of lines in a *termcap* or *terminfo* file: comment lines, lines that list alias names for the terminal, and lines that specify terminal capabilities.

- *Comment lines:*
  The first line in both the *termcap* and *terminfo* entries shown above is a comment line.

  ```
  # incomplete termcap entry for the Wyse WY-50
  # incomplete terminfo entry for the Wyse WY-50
  ```

All comment lines begin with a hash mark (#). Embedded comments are not allowed: a line is either a comment or part of an entry. In *termcap* and *terminfo*, the convention is that comments precede the terminal they describe.

- *Name lines:*

  The second line is a list of alias names for the terminal, separated by the vertical bar character.

  ```
  n9|wy50|WY50| Wyse Technology WY-50:\          ...termcap
  ```

  ```
  wy50|WY50|Wyse Technology WY-50,               ...terminfo
  ```

  Multiple aliases are provided as a convenience to the user. The environment variable TERM *(6.11)* can be set to any one of the aliases. By convention, the last alias is the full name of the terminal.

  The alias list is the first field of the terminal description, with a colon (*termcap*) or comma (*terminfo*) marking the end of the alias list and the start of the capabilities list. You could begin listing the capabilities immediately after this field, but it makes reading much easier if all the aliases are on one line and the capabilities start on the next.

  When a *terminfo* source file is compiled with *tic*, the compiled data is placed in a file corresponding to the first alias (in this case, */usr/lib/terminfo/w/wy50*), and a link is created for all other aliases but the last. In this example, TERM could be set to either *wy50* or *WY50* to access the compiled terminal description.

- *Capability lines:*

  The remaining lines are the list of the actual terminal capabilities. These lines are indented (using a tab or blank spaces) to distinguish them from the line of terminal aliases. Note that the indentation of continued capability lines is not just cosmetic but is a required part of the syntax.

  In *termcap*, capabilities are identified by a two-character name; in *terminfo*, the capability names may have anywhere between two and five characters. The capability name is the first thing in each capability field and describes a feature of the terminal.

There are three types of capability:

- **Boolean capabilities** consist of a capability name with no arguments. For example, *am* (both *termcap* and *terminfo*) specifies that the terminal performs automatic right margins, wrapping the cursor to the start of the next line when the cursor reaches the last position on the current line. If *am* is not specified, programs will assume that your terminal does not have this feature.

  am is an example of a boolean feature which is advantageous, but booleans are also used to specify negative features of your terminal—for example, if your terminal does not perform newlines in the expected way, you might have what is called the "newline glitch," and the entry may need to specify *xn* (*termcap*) or ***xenl*** (*terminfo*) to tell programs to adjust for the terminal's peculiarity.

- **Numeric capabilities** consist of a capability name, a sharp sign, and a number. For example, co#80 (*termcap*) and cols#80 (*terminfo*) says that the terminal has 80 columns. All numeric values are non-negative.

- **String capabilities** tell how to issue a command to the terminal. The format of a string capability is the capability name, followed by an equal sign, followed by the command sequence. For example, up=^K (*termcap*) or cuu1=^K (*terminfo*) specifies that the sequence CTRL-k will move the cursor up one line.

Now the Wyse-50 example should make more sense. First *termcap*:

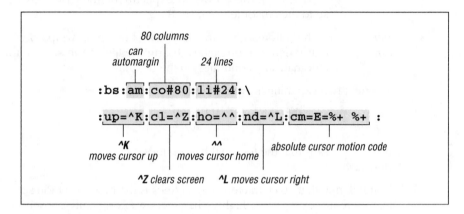

Figure 43-1. A Simplified termcap Entry

Now *terminfo*:

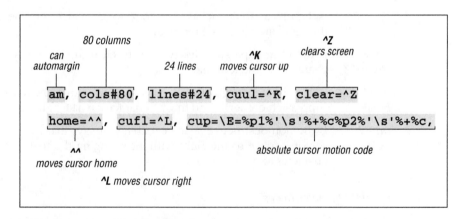

Figure 43-2. A Simplified terminfo Entry

The examples demonstrate all three kinds of capabilities: boolean, numeric, and string.

The first two capabilities in the *termcap* entry, and the first capability in the *terminfo* entry, are boolean.

bs   is the *termcap* backspace capability, which means that the terminal will backspace when sent the CTRL-h (^H) character. There is no *terminfo* capability directly equivalent to *bs*, so it is considered obsolete by *terminfo* and by BSD 4.3 *termcap*. In place of the *bs* capability, *terminfo* would explicitly define CTRL-h as the string to send the cursor left (*cul1=^H*).

am   is the automargin capability, also known as wraparound. It means
am   that when a line reaches the right edge of the screen, the terminal automatically continues on the next line.

The next two capabilities are numeric.

co#80   says that the terminal has 80 columns.
cols#80

li#24   says that the terminal has 24 lines.
lines#24

You will find that 80 characters and 24 lines is the most common screen size but that there are exceptions. Eighty characters was originally chosen because it is the width of a punch card, and 24 lines was chosen to take advantage of cheap television screen technology.

The remainder of the fields in the Wyse-50 entry contain string capabilities. The first four of these are fairly simple:

up=^K   is the up capability; it says that to move the cursor up one line, send
cuu1=^K   the ^K character to the terminal.

cl=^Z   is the clear capability; it says that to clear the screen, send the ^Z
clear=^Z   character to the terminal.

*ho=^^*   is the home capability; it says that to move the cursor Home
*home=^^*   (upper-left corner), send the ^^ character (CTRL-^) to the terminal.

nd=^L   is the non-destructive space capability; it says that to move the cur-
cuf1=^L   sor one space to the right without changing the text, send the ^L character to the terminal.

Special Character Codes

No doubt the symbols ^K, ^Z, ^^, and ^L shown above are familiar to you. A caret (^) followed by a letter is a convention for representing an unprintable control character generated by holding down the CONTROL (CTRL) key on the keyboard while typing another. Note that control characters are entered into a terminal description as two characters by typing the caret character (^) followed by a letter, rather than by inserting the actual control character.

Both *termcap* and *terminfo* use other codes to write other unprintable characters, as well as characters that have special meaning in *termcap* or *terminfo* syntax. The other codes, most of which should be familiar to C programmers, are listed in Table 43-1 below.

Table 43-1. Termcap and Terminfo Special Character Codes

Code	Description	Comment
\E	escape	*termcap and terminfo*
\e	escape	*terminfo only*
^*x*	control-*x*	*where **x** is any letter*
\n	newline	
\r	return	
\t	tab	
\b	backspace	
\f	formfeed	
\s	space	*terminfo only*
\l	linefeed	*terminfo only*
xxx	octal value of **xxx**	*must be three characters*
\041	exclamation point !	*C shell history uses* !
\072	the character :	*termcap uses ordinary : as separator*
\200	null	*\000 for null does not work*
\0	null	*terminfo only*
\^	caret	*terminfo only*
\\	backslash	*terminfo only*
\,	comma	*terminfo only*
\:	colon	*terminfo only*

Encoding Arguments

The last capability in the Wyse-50 example is the most complicated. *cm=* (*termcap*) and *cup=* (*terminfo*) specify the cursor motion capability, which describes how to move the cursor directly to a specific location. Since the desired location is specified by the program at run time, the capability must provide some mechanism for encoding arguments. The program uses this description to figure out what string it needs to send to move the cursor to the desired location.

Because we aren't telling you how to write *termcap* or *terminfo* entries, but just to read them, all you need to know is that the percent sign (%) is used for encoding, and when it appears in a terminal entry, the capability is using run time parameters.

If you need to write an entry, see the Nutshell Handbook *termcap and terminfo*.

—*JS, TOR* from the Nutshell Handbook *termcap and terminfo*

43.12 Finding Out what Characters your Terminal's Special Keys Send

Sometimes, when writing *vi* keymaps *(32.02, 32.12)*, you need to find out what characters are generated by labeled keys like arrows, HOME, and Function Keys.

If you have a terminal manual handy, the information should be listed somewhere in there. If not, you can read the *termcap* or *terminfo* entry *(43.11)*. Unfortunately, not every entry is complete—a terminal may have capabilities that aren't described in its entry. In any event, if you don't know the syntax well, finding the right information can be difficult.

However, there are several online techniques for finding out what character is sent by a special key. Each has drawbacks, but between them, you can almost always find out what character a key generates.

- Enter insert mode in *vi* and use the ^V control sequence to quote each special key. That is, type CTRL-v followed by the key whose identity you are trying to discover. A printable representation of the key should appear on the screen.

  This will not work if the key generates a sequence containing more than one non-printing character, since ^V will only quote the first one. It also will not work for keys that generate a newline (such as the down-arrow key on the Wyse-50 keyboard)—but in such a case, the action of the key should be obvious.

- At the command line, print:

  ```
  % stty -echo; cat -v; stty echo
  ```

  and then type the special keys, each followed by a carriage return. *cat −v* *(26.07)* will echo the translated version on the screen. When you are finished, type CTRL-d.

- Simply type the special key at the shell prompt. As long as the key does not have meaning to the shell (for example, ^C or ^D), the command generated by the key will be executed on the terminal. Depending on the version of UNIX you use, a printable equivalent to the command generated by the key you pressed may also be printed as the command is executed. (Keep in mind that with full-duplex communications, characters are not sent from your keyboard directly to your terminal but are sent to the system and echoed back to the terminal.)

On some systems, the control character is recognized on input and is echoed in two separate ways: as a printable representation of the control character (e.g., ^Z—literally, caret-Z) and as the actual control character. Other systems echo only the actual control character, which means that you see the effect but not the character that caused it.

In either case, the shell will give an error message containing the character(s) typed as soon as you press RETURN. The message should read something like this:

```
^[[U : Command not found.
```

If, on the other hand, the key generates a sequence that is meaningful to the device, some standard function, such as interrupt, end-of-file, or suspend, will be executed. You can find out what command invokes each of these functions using *stty* *(43.03)*.

—*JS, TOR* from the Nutshell Handbook *termcap & terminfo*

44

Problems with Terminals

44.01 *Making Sense out of the Terminal Mess*

When you're sitting in front of a terminal, it's sometimes hard to realize that you're face to face with about twenty years of accumulated history, with hack piled upon hack to deal with evolutions in hardware.

When you type at a terminal, you are really dealing with four things:

1. The shell, utility, or application that interprets and responds to what you type.

2. The UNIX kernel, or more specifically, the serial line driver, which may perform some low-level conversions on what you type before it's even passed to the program you think you're talking to.

3. The terminal, which has behavior of its own—and may locally interpret or respond to some of what you type instead of, or as well as, passing it through to the system.

4. The communication link between the terminal and the system.

Some of the confusion about UNIX terminal handling comes from the fact that there are mechanisms for dealing with each of these layers. Let's take the list in the reverse order this time:

*   Most ASCII terminals, or *ttys*, are connected to the system by a *serial line*—a set of up to 24 wires defined by the RS-232 standard. A remote terminal may be connected to a modem by a serial line; if this is the case, the computer too must be connected to a modem, and the two modems talk to each other over the telephone. Some serial line configuration happens at the hardware level. For example, not every cable includes every wire called for in the RS-232 standard, and both the terminal and the system or modem have to agree to such things as which one will talk over which wire. (Actually, both computer systems and terminals are quite stubborn about this; they have fixed ideas about which wire to talk on, and which to listen on,

and if both want to use the same one, it's up to the system administrator to trick them by crossing the wires.)

There's more to the communications link than just the wires, though. For example, both the terminal and the system or modem have to be configured to agree on such things as how many data bits make up a character (a byte is made up of eight bits, but ASCII characters only require seven), whether or not to use parity (a simple form of error checking), how to "frame" each character with "start" and "stop" bits, and how fast to communicate (the baud rate).

All of these things are usually configured in advance—if they weren't, the system and terminal couldn't talk to each other. However, the *stty* command *(43.02, 43.03)* does let you change these parameters on the fly (at least on the system side—your terminal may have a setup key and a built-in setup menu). You'd better know what you're doing, though, or you may render your terminal and computer unable to communicate.

- At least when UNIX started out, there were no standards for how terminals worked. A screen size of 24 lines and 80 columns became a (fairly) common denominator, but the special keys on terminal keyboards generate different characters, and each terminal might respond to different escape sequences *(6.08)* for moving the cursor around the screen, highlighting text in inverse video, underlining, and so on. The *termcap* and *terminfo* databases *(6.02)* were developed to make sense out of this babel. Once a terminal's characteristics are described in the database, a screen-oriented program like *vi* can look up the information it needs to clear the screen, move around, and so on. Programs like *tset (6.12)* and *tput (6.13, 43.10)* were created to read the terminal database and use the information it contains to issue commands (in the form of escape sequences) to the terminal. If you always use the same kind of terminal, you can configure your terminal by issuing the escape sequences directly *(43.09)*. You don't need to look them up in the terminal database. (That's only important if you want a program or script to work with a variety of terminals.)

- The serial line driver does various things to the characters it gets from the terminal. For example, in normal use, it changes the carriage return (ASCII character \015) generated by the RETURN key on your keyboard into a linefeed (ASCII character \012). Chris Torek talks about some of these conversions in article 43.02. For the most part, unless you are a programmer or a system administrator, you don't need to know a whole lot about all of the possibilities—but you do need to know that they are configurable, and that *stty (43.03)* is the program that reports (and changes *(6.09)*) the settings.

Not all of the terminal driver settings are obscure. Some of them you use every day, and must be sure to set in your *.login* or *.profile* file *(2.03)*. For example, how does the system know that you want to use CTRL-c to interrupt a program or CTRL-s to stop output, or CTRL-z to suspend execution? This happens at a level below even the shell—the shell never even sees these characters, because they are interpreted and acted on by the serial line driver. However, there are times when they *aren't* interpreted. Have you ever typed CTRL-z when you're in *vi*'s insert mode? Instead of *vi* being suspended, the character is input. That's because *vi* needs to reset the serial driver to a different mode *(43.02)* so that it has control over which characters are echoed and which are interpreted as commands.

All of this is by way of saying that there's an awful lot of complexity under the skin.

• And, of course, as we've talked about at length in the discussion of wildcards and quoting *(9.10)*, the shell may intercept and act on various characters before passing them on to another program.

The point of this long excursion is to suggest that when you are trying to figure out problems with terminals, you owe it to yourself to know about all the levels where the problems can occur. (For example, article 9.16 is about backslash handling.)

Are the terminal and computer system properly configured? Has the cable come loose? Is the terminal type set correctly so that programs know how to make that particular terminal do their bidding? Has an interrupted program sent out unfinished commands that left the terminal in an inconsistent or unusual state? Is it really a terminal problem, or is it just that things aren't working quite the way you expect?

—TOR

44.02 *Fixing a Hung Terminal or Job*

Here are a lot of techniques for unlocking a locked-up terminal or window session.

Output Stopped?

If your terminal has a HOLD SCREEN or SCROLL LOCK button, did you accidentally press it? Try pressing it and see if things start working. If pressing the button once doesn't fix the problem, you should probably press it once more to undo the screen hold. Otherwise, you may lock up your session worse than it was before!

Another way to stop output is by pressing CTRL-s. The way to restart stopped output is with CTRL-q—try pressing that now. (Unlike a SCROLL LOCK button, though, if CTRL-q doesn't help, you don't need to undo it.)

Job Stopped?

If you have a shell prompt *(8.01)* instead of being in the program you thought you were running—and if your UNIX has job control—you may have stopped a job. Try the *jobs* command; if the job is stopped, restart it *(13.08)*.

Program Waiting for Input?

The program may be waiting for you to answer a question or type text to its standard input.

> If the program you were running does something that's hard to undo—like removing files—*don't* try this step unless you've thought about it carefully.

If your system has job control, you can find out by putting the job in the background with CTRL-z and *bg*. If the job was waiting for input, you'll see the message:

```
[1]  + Stopped (tty input)  grep pat
```

You can bring the job back into the foreground and answer its question, if you know what that question is. Otherwise, now that the job is stopped, you can kill it. See the directions below.

On systems without job control, you may be able to satisfy the program by pressing RETURN or some other key that the program is expecting, like *y* or *n*. You could also try pressing CTRL-d or whatever your "end of input" character is set to. That might log you out, though, unless you've set the *ignoreeof* variable *(3.05)*.

Stalled Data Connection?

If your terminal is hooked to a computer, modem, or network, be sure that the wires haven't come loose.

If you're using a modem and the modem has function lights, try pressing keys and see if the SD or Send Data light flashes. If it does, your terminal is sending data to the host computer. If the RD or Receive Data light flashes, the computer is sending data to your terminal—if you don't see anything, there might be something wrong on your terminal.

If you're connected with *rlogin* or *telnet* *(1.33)*, the network to the remote computer might be down or be really slow. Try opening another connection to the same remote host—if you get a response like `Connection timed out`, you have two choices:

1. Wait for your original connection to unfreeze. The connection may come back and let you keep working where you left off. Or the connection may end when *rlogin* or *telnet* notices the network problem.

2. Quit the session and try later.

Aborting Programs

To abort a program, most users press CTRL-c. Your account may be set up to use a different interrupt character, like DELETE or RUBOUT. If these don't work, try CTRL-\ (CTRL-backslash). Under most circumstances, this will force the program to terminate. Otherwise, do the following:

1. Log in at another terminal or window.

2. Enter the command ps -x. On System V, use ps -u *yourname*, where *yourname* is your UNIX username. This displays a list of the programs you are running, something like this:

    ```
    % ps -x
    PID     TTY     STAT    TIME    COMMAND
    163     i26     I       0:41    -csh (csh)
    8532    i26     TW      2:17    vi ts.ms
    22202   i26     S       12:50   vi UNIXintro.ms
    8963    pb      R       0:00    ps -x
    24077   pb      S       0:05    -bin/csh (csh)
    %
    ```

3. Search through this list to find the command that has backfired. Note the process identification (PID) number for this command.

4. Enter the command kill *PID(40.10)*, where *PID* is the identification number from the previous step. If that doesn't work, try kill -1 *PID* to send a HUP signal. You may need *kill –9*, but try the other *kills* first.

5. If the UNIX shell prompt (like % or $) has appeared at your original terminal, things are probably back to normal. You may still have to take the terminal out of a strange mode *(44.04)*though.

    If the shell prompt hasn't come back, find the shell associated with your terminal (identified by a tty number) and *kill* it. The command name for the C shell is *csh*. For the Bourne shell, it is *sh*. In most cases, this will destroy any other commands running from your terminal. Be sure to *kill* the shell on your own terminal, not the terminal you borrowed to enter these commands. The tty you borrowed is the one running *ps*; look at the example above and check the TTY column. In this case, the borrowed terminal is TTYpb.

    Check *ps* to ensure that your shell has died. If it is still there, take more drastic action with the command kill -9 *PID*.

6. Run *ps –x* again to be sure that all processes on the other tty have died. (In some cases, processes will remain.) If there are still processes on the other tty, kill them.

7. At this point, you should be able to log in again from your own terminal.

The *ps (40.05)* command, which lists all the programs you are running, also gives you useful information about the status of each program and the amount of CPU time it has consumed. Note that *ps* lists all the programs you are running, including programs you may not know about (e.g., programs that other programs execute automatically).

—JP, ML from the Nutshell Handbook UNIX for FORTRAN Programmers

44.03 Why Changing TERM Sometimes Doesn't Work

The use of *tset* to set the TERMCAP environment variable *(6.04)* can cause problems for new users who do not understand it completely. For example, as long as the TERMCAP variable is not set, programs look by default in */etc/termcap*. However, once the TERMCAP variable contains the actual *termcap* entry, changing the value of TERM will no longer have any effect on a program like *vi*.

If you set the value of TERM correctly but *vi* or other programs that depend on TERM still do not seem to work, check to make sure that TERMCAP is not set to the actual *termcap* entry. You can clear this condition with the command:

```
% unsetenv TERMCAP
```

or:

```
$ TERMCAP=
```

or:

```
$ unset TERMCAP          (newer Bourne shells)
```

—TOR

44.04 Checklist for Resetting a Messed Up Terminal

Gremlins (like line noise on a modem, a bug in a program, a really long line of output, non-printable characters in a file you *cat* to your screen, etc.) can sneak into your system somewhere and mess up your terminal screen or window. The screen could have a bunch of flashing junk, the character set could turn into hieroglyphics, words could start coming out underlined or in inverse video, the line could lock up . . . well, there are lots of possibilities.

Here's a rough list of things to try. This might be worth reading through right now. Some things in here need to be ready *before* your terminal locks up.

✓ If you can get to a shell prompt (% or $), the first command you should try is probably:

clear *23.19* | `% clear`   *systems with termcap*
tput *43.10* | `% tput clear`   *systems with terminfo*

That will try to erase the screen and may also cancel other problems like inverse video.

✓ If running *clear* doesn't clear up your screen completely and your terminal has a setup menu, look for a "clear screen" function and try it. (If you don't know how your terminal's setup mode works, find the manual or find an expert. Write down the steps and keep them close to your terminal.)

✓ If you have a shell prompt and you're on a system using *terminfo*, try these commands. Don't use *tput init* unless *tput reset* doesn't fix things:

```
% tput reset
% tput init
```

If you're using a *termcap* system, there's no command quite like those two. You can simulate them by making an alias *(11.02)* that runs the *tset (6.04)* command from your login setup files. (Why not do it now, for the next time you get into this mess?) Here's a simple alias:

```
alias newterm 'set noglob; eval `tset -srQ \!*`; unset noglob'
```

The *tset* command usually sends resetting or initialization commands to your terminal.

✓ If every character you type shows up on a different line, characters don't appear as you type them, a RETURN does nothing or prints a ^M on your screen, the backspace, interrupt, and kill keys don't work, or lines

```
jump down
        the screen
                like this
```

you've probably got trouble with the settings of your port (UNIX terminal device). One of the following commands can make your terminal usable. It might not be set up the way you're used to, but at least you'll be able to log out and log in again:

```
% reset
% CTRL-j reset CTRL-j
% stty sane
% CTRL-j stty sane CTRL-j
```

(If your terminal has a LINEFEED key, you can use it instead of CTRL-j.)

If the system says that those commands don't exist or are an "unknown mode," you should make yourself an alias *(11.02)*, shell function *(11.10)*, or shell script *(46.02)* that executes an *stty* command similar to the one below. The exact parameters you use will depend on your normal UNIX setup:

```
stty echo -nl -cbreak
```

Call it something like *sane*. You may need to execute it by typing LINEFEED or CTRL-j before and after.

If that doesn't work perfectly, here's what to do. The next time you log in and your screen works just right, typing *stty everything* or *stty –g* (see below) should help you decide exactly what parameters to use in your *sane* command.

✓ If the system seems to treat every character you type as a separate command (and you may not be able to see the characters you type):

```
% reset
r: Command not found.
: No previous regular expression
: No current filename
```

```
: No lines in the bufferq
%
```

(It actually doesn't look quite like that, but the first **e** started the editor named *e*. The **s**, **e**, and **t** are all read as commands by *e*. You have to quit *e* by typing its q command. Sheesh!)

You should make a shell function or alias—or, put a symbolic link *(19.04)* or shell script in your *bin* directory *(5.02)*—that lets you run the command from the previous step (*reset, stty sane*, etc.) by typing a single character. I picked] (right square bracket) as the name of mine. To make mine, I made a symlink in my *bin*:

```
% ln -s /usr/ucb/reset ]
```

(Your system's *reset* command may have a different pathname.) Now, to fix a goofed-up terminal, I just type a] at a shell prompt (it may need a LINEFEED or CTRL-j before and after).

✓ Best of all, if your system has the command *stty –g*, you can use it to save your favorite terminal settings in a file. Then, when your terminal is goofed up, read those settings in again from the file. Here's how. First, when your terminal is working just the way you want it, type:

```
% stty -g >$HOME/.stty
```

Then make your alias, shell script, or shell function named *sane,]*, etc. (as explained above) that runs the command:

```
% stty `cat $HOME/.stty`
```

This should restore your terminal the way it was when you first ran the *stty –g* command.

If your system doesn't have *stty –g*, you can fake it. Run the command *stty everything* and look at the settings:

```
% stty everything
speed 38400 baud, 0 rows, 0 columns
parenb -parodd cs7 -cstopb -hupcl cread -clocal -crtscts
-ignbrk brkint ignpar -parmrk -inpck istrip -inlcr -igncr icrnl -iuclc
ixon -ixany -ixoff imaxbel
isig iexten icanon -xcase echo echoe echok -echonl -noflsh -tostop
echoctl -echoprt echoke
opost -olcuc onlcr -ocrnl -onocr -onlret -ofill -ofdel -tabs
erase  kill   werase rprnt  flush  lnext  susp   intr   quit   stop    eof
^?     ^U     ^W     ^R     ^O     ^V     ^Z/^Y  ^C     ^\     ^S/^Q   ^D
```

Then check your *stty* manual page and read about those settings (some of them, like the parity settings, might not be appropriate for all your login sessions). Put the settings in your *sane* or *]* command:

```
stty icanon echo erase '^?' kill '^u' ...
```

Note that if you use several different terminals, each may have different settings. Make yourself several *sane* commands; you might select one automatically as you log in *(2.12)*.

If worse comes to worst, try the steps from article 44.02. Find another place to log in to your account. Run *ps* to find your processes on the hung-up terminal or window and kill them. Then turn off the terminal or close the window and log in again. (If you didn't have a way to kill the processes before you logged in again, be sure to kill your old processes right away after you log in.)

—JP

44.05 Checklist: Screen Size Messed Up?

The termcap and terminfo *(6.02)* systems used to be the only place where the size of your terminal screen (number of lines and characters) was set. These days, screen-oriented commands like *vi* and *more* on most UNIXes need to work with window systems. Users can shrink or stretch their windows without changing the *termcap* or *terminfo* definition. Depending on the command and version of UNIX you're using, you can run into window-size problems even if you aren't using a window system.

Window systems don't cause all the problems though. "Classic" problems, such as files with lines that are longer than the terminal is wide, were around before UNIX did windows.

Here's a checklist of things to try. Once you figure out what's wrong and how to fix it on your terminal and version of UNIX, you'll probably be able to fix problems with other programs you run.

✓ Displaying or editing a file with lines longer than the screen is wide can cause strange problems if everything isn't set up right. There are two places that may try to split a line into pieces when it thinks that the line is too long. The problem, of course, is when these don't work together or one of them has a wrong idea about the line length:

- Your terminal or window may be set to autowrap lines that would cross the right edge: The line is broken and the rest is shown beginning at the left margin on the next line below.

- If you use a screen-oriented program like *vi* or *more*, they may wrap long lines. The *termcap* and *terminfo* definitions tell screen-oriented programs whether to wrap lines. (For more information, see the Nutshell Handbook *termcap & terminfo*.)

To find out what your terminal is doing, display a file with long lines like *longlines (44.06)*. The *cat (26.02)* and *head (26.21)* programs don't use *termcap* or *terminfo*—they spit the file directly to your screen. So, for example, a single 200-character line from *longlines* should be shown as three lines on an 80-column screen. You shouldn't lose any of the characters at either side. Two lines would look like this:

```
% head -2 longlines
1   4567890123456789012345678901234567890123456789012345678901234567890
1234567890123456789012345678901234567890123456789012345678901234567890
1234567890123456789012345678901234567890
2   4567890123456789012345678901234567890123456789012345678901234567890
```

```
12345678901234567890123456789012345678901234567890123456789012345678901234567890
12345678901234567890123456789012345678901234567890
```

If you see only two "chopped" lines, your terminal isn't wrapping lines. You may want to go into its setup mode and enable line-wrapping. If you do though, be sure that your termcap/terminfo definition lists the terminal as autowrapping.

If your terminal autowraps but the *termcap/terminfo* definition doesn't say that, screen-oriented applications may try to wrap lines for you. Exactly what happens depends on the application you're using and your terminal. One common problem is that the screen may look double-spaced—each part of a single long line that's "wrapped" has a blank line after it. For instance, the *longlines* file might look like this:

```
1   45678901234567890123456789012345678901234567890123456789012345678901234567890

12345678901234567890123456789012345678901234567890123456789012345678901234567890

12345678901234567890123456789012345678901234567890
    ...
```

In that case, both the terminal and the application are probably trying to wrap the lines for you. Usually, then, the application won't know exactly how many lines your terminal is displaying and will send twice as many lines as your screen can show.

What a mess! Try to use another value of the *TERM (6.11)* environment variable that defines your terminal as autowrapping. These can have names that end with *am* or *aw*, like *vt100aw*. (For more information, see article 43.11 or the Nutshell Handbook *termcap & terminfo*.)

✓ Your screen can be mixed up when a full-screen application—a pager like *pg*, for example—is displaying the standard output of some program. The program writes some messages to its standard error. These extra lines aren't counted by the application, but they show on your screen.

If the application has a redraw screen command like CTRL-l you may be able to get a fresh copy of the lines from standard output. Or, you can pipe both stdout and stderr to the pager *(14.04)*.

✓ Some applications let you set their screen size in a configuration file or environment variable. For example, Berkeley *mail* (*mailx (1.33)* on System V) has a *screen* variable that might be set in its *.mailrc* file or in a system file like */usr/lib/Mail.rc*. The *vi* editor has a *window* variable that might be set in your *.exrc (5.09)* file.

Unless you set those variables correctly for all the terminals you use, you'll usually be better off to let the application set its own window size.

✓ Your version of UNIX may keep the screen size as part of the device settings. To find out, type the command:

```
% stty size
24 80
```

The command shows that UNIX thinks your screen has 24 lines and 80 columns. Or, the screen size may be stored in environment variables called *COLUMNS* and *LINES*:

env *7.01*
egrep *28.05*

```
% env | egrep '(COLUMNS|LINES)='
COLUMNS=80
LINES=24
```

If the current settings don't match your screen size *(44.06)* you can change the screen size settings. See the suggestions below.

✓ If UNIX doesn't know your screen size and your system has the *stty size* command, you can use *stty* to change the settings. For example, if your window has 43 rows and 80 columns, type:

```
% stty rows 43 columns 80
```

If applications are using the *COLUMNS* and *LINES* environment variables, just reset them *(7.01)*.

Note: Any jobs that are stopped or in the background when you change the screen size may not work anymore because they'll still have the old window size. If that's a problem, quit and restart the applications or send them a *SIGWINCH* signal (below).

✓ If you're running *xterm* in the X Window System *(1.31)*, use *resize*. It asks your *xterm* to report (silently) on how big the window is now, then it resets the *stty* parameters or environment variables, depending on which your system needs. When it sets environment variables, *resize* needs to give commands to the shell. In the C shell, type:

eval *9.08*

```
% set noglob; eval `resize`
```

(You don't need to use `unset noglob` *(16.04)* because *resize* outputs that command.) In the Bourne shell,

```
$ eval `resize`
```

Both of these are easier to use if you define an alias *(11.02)* or a shell function *(11.10)* named something like *rs*:

```
alias rs 'set noglob; eval `resize`'
rs()
{
    eval `/usr/bin/X11/resize`
}
```

✓ In UNIXes that store the window size as part of the device settings (not in environment variables), here's another thing you can do. First, use *stty* to set the right sizes (see above). Then send a *SIGWINCH* (window changed) signal to the shell and/or job that has a wrong idea of the window size:

```
% kill -WINCH $$        ...send signal to the shell
% kill -WINCH %1        ...send signal to job 1
```

✓ In some window systems, you can make your window a little taller or shorter. That will reset things.

✓ You're using the *telnet (1.33)* command to log into a remote machine. You didn't have trouble with the window size on your local machine—what's wrong?

Not all versions of *telnet* pass your correct window size to the remote host. If both the local and remote machines support *rlogin (1.33)*, use it instead. Otherwise, use one of the tips above to set the window size on the remote system.

—*JP*

44.06 Screen Size Testing Files

How many lines and columns are there on your screen or window? The answer can be important to some programs *(44.05)*. I've got a directory named *testing_files* with a few files I've developed to test and set screen sizes.

Single Line Screen Width: 80cols

80cols

The *80cols* file has a line of 80 numbers. I use it to see if the window has exactly 80 columns, as in Figure 44-1.

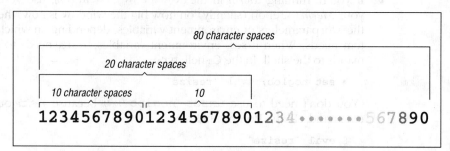

Figure 44-1. The 80cols File

The pattern repeats every ten characters, making it easy to count how many columns the window has.

Some UNIX programs are set for 80-column screens—even if you can make wider windows, you may not want to. If you want other widths, you can make *cols* files for them, too.

Screen Width and Height: screensize

screensize

The *screensize* file has 69 lines of numbers, starting at 69 and ending at 1. Type cat screensize. As shown in Figure 44-2, when the file has all been displayed, count the number of lines filled on the screen.

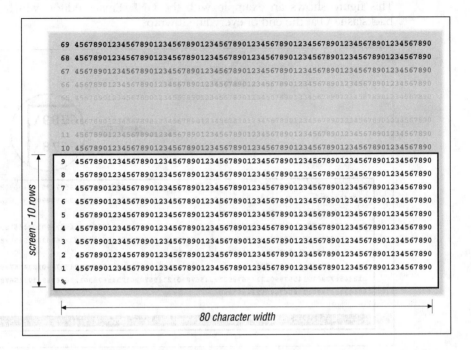

Figure 44-2. Checking Window Height and Width with screensize

In Figure 44-2 the top number is 9. So, the window has 10 lines (counting the prompt on the last line).

The *screensize* file is also handy with a full-screen application like *more (26.03)* to see if the right number of lines and columns are displayed. When *more* shows the first screenful, the line labeled 69 should be at the top of the screen (the command line might be displayed above it). The last line should have the prompt, like --More--. When you ask for the next screenful, you should see the next consecutive line at the top of the screen, maybe with a line or two from the previous screen.

The same thing should work with editors like *vi*.

Set Width, Test Line Wrapping: longlines

longlines

The file *longlines* in Figure 44-3 is like *screensize,* but the 200-character lines in it are too long for most screens. You can use it for two things: to adjust windows to a particular size and to see if long-line wrapping is working right *(44.05).* This figure shows an example with the GNU Emacs editor, which shows a backslash (\) at the end of every line it wraps.

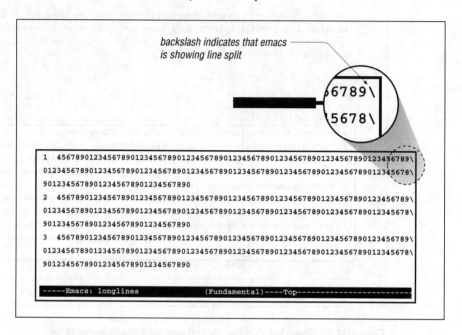

Figure 44-3. Using longlines File with the Emacs Editor

On an 80-column screen, if line wrapping is working right, each line of *longlines* should take exactly two and one-half lines to display. (If you're using Emacs, remember that because it adds a backslash at the line break, the third part of each line will have two more characters.) As Figure 44-3 shows, there shouldn't be any missing numbers or blank lines.

If you're using a windowing system like X *(1.31),* look for a resize or window info function. For example, in the X Window System, the *twm* window manager will show a small box with the window dimensions as you hold down the mouse button to resize a window. You don't have to resize the window; just look at the size-box. The X command *xwininfo* gives lots of information—including the window size in pixels.

—JP

44.07 termtest: Send Repeated Characters to Terminal

This script uses the *yes (24.04)* command to send 79-character lines of columns to the terminal over and over, as fast as possible. It's been useful for me when I'm looking for dropped characters, dialup noise, and other problems on a terminal or connection. The −*b* (blanks) option sends a screen full of space characters with an asterisk (*) in column 77—watching this column is an easy way to look for added or dropped characters without distractions. Use your interrupt key *(6.09)* (like CTRL-c) to kill the script when you're done.

termtest

The two *yes* command lines below have been broken into two pieces for printing. You should enter them all on one line.

exec 47.07

```
#! /bin/sh
# USE yes PROGRAM TO PRINT CHARACTER STRINGS FOREVER:
case "$1" in
"") exec yes '()*+,-./ 01234567 89:;<=>? @ABCDEFG
HIJKLMNO PQRSTUVW XYZ[]^_ `abcdefg hijklmn' ;;
-b) exec yes '
                                    *' ;;
*)  echo "Usage: `basename $0` [-b]" 1>&2; exit 1;;
esac
```

—*JP*

44.08 Errors Erased Too Soon? Try These Workarounds

I just made a change to my *.exrc* file *(5.09)*. Then I started *vi* and noticed a message in reverse video before the screen cleared and my file was displayed. It was probably an error message. But *vi*, like some other programs, will show errors and then clear (erase) the screen before you can see them. Great design, eh?

Here are some workarounds I've found in ten years of error-hunting:

✓ When my terminal used to run at a slow data rate (1200 baud or less), I could usually read an error message before the screen cleared. In these days of 9600 bps and above, you can still fake that. Log out. Then set your terminal or communications package to a slow data rate and log in again. Now look fast.

✓ Way back, when ttys were real teletypes *(43.02)*, finding errors was easy: there was no screen to clear; the error was right there on the paper.

So, if your terminal has a printer, turn it on. (On DOS, try doing CTRL + PrtSC .) Re-run your program and read the error on the paper.

✓ If your window or communications program has a "capture to file" function, turn it on. Make the error happen. Turn off the capture function (important!). Then read the file—you'll probably need to use a program like *cat −v* *(26.07)* or *vmore (26.05)* to keep the screen-clearing characters stored in the file from erasing your screen as you read the file!

✓ If you don't have a screen-capture function, but you do have the *script (53.05)* program, use it with the technique in the step above.

✓ If your window has a scroll bar or a "page up" command, try it. Some screen-clear commands won't clear the scrolling memory.

✓ Restart the program and get to the point just before the error will happen. Try to hit CTRL-s or HOLD SCREEN between the time the error is output and the screen clears. That can be tough to do over a network or on a high-speed connection, though, because of the delay between the time you press the key and the time when all the output finally stops coming.

✓ Temporarily switch *(7.10)* to a *termcap/terminfo* definition that doesn't have a clear-screen capability. Two good settings for TERM are *dumb* and *unknown*.

✓ That previous trick will leave your program almost useless, if it runs at all. If you do a lot of troubleshooting of full-screen programs like *vi* (or writing startup files such as *.exrc*), it's worth your time to find a *termcap* or *terminfo* definition that has all the capabilities of the usual definition—except that it won't clear the screen.* If you don't know how, read the Nutshell Handbook *termcap & terminfo*—or lure a UNIX guru from down the hall somewhere.†

—*JP*

---

*You'll probably want to check the termcap capabilities *cl=*, *is=*, *if=*, *rs=*, *rf=*, *r2=*, and maybe *ti=*. Or, for *terminfo*, look at *clear=*, *iprog=*, *is2=*, *if=*, *rs2=*, *rf=*, and maybe *smcup=*.

†Hint: all computer gurus like pizza.

45

Printing

45.01 *Introduction to Printing*

This chapter discusses printing, which is a surprisingly complicated subject. To understand why printing is so complicated, though, let's think a little bit about what you might want to print.

First, in the "olden days" we had line printers and their relatives: daisy wheel printers, dot matrix printers, and other pieces of equipment that generated typewriter-like output. Printing a simple text file was easy: you didn't need any special processing, you only needed some software to shove the file into the printer. If you wanted, you might add a banner page and do a little simple formatting, but that was really pretty trivial.

The one area of complexity in the printing system was the "spooling system," which had to do several things in addition to force-feeding the printer. Most printers were (and still are) shared devices. This means that many people can send jobs to the printer at the same time. There may also be several printers on which your file gets printed; you may care which one is used, you may not. The spooling system needs to manage all this: receiving data from users, figuring out whether or not an appropriate printer is in use, and sending the file to the printer (if it's free) or storing the file somewhere (if the printer isn't free).

Historical note: why is this called the "spooling system"? My understanding (I'm not that old) is that in the "really olden days" when computers had tubes that glowed in the dark, the "spooler" just took everything that was sent its way and stuck it on a spool of magnetic tape. (Maybe even paper tape.) There was no printer at all. When the tape got full, the operator would go over to a different machine, mount the tape, and print everything on the tape, from start to finish. Several hours later, your "output" would magically appear in a wooden box with your name on it.

The first few articles in this chapter, 45.02, 45.03, 45.04, and 45.05, discuss the basic UNIX spooling system, and how to work with it as a user. (We don't discuss the administrative aspects of spooling; that's a much more complicated topic, and not really appropriate for this book.) Article 45.06 shows one way to print to a terminal with its own printer.

The next few articles talk about how to format articles for printing—not the kind of fancy formatting people think of nowadays, but simpler things like pagination, margins, and so on, for text files that are to be sent to the line printer. Articles 45.07 through 45.12 describe this kind of simple formatting.

Historical note number two: why is the print spooler called *lp* or *lpr*? Because it typically spooled text to a line printer, a fast printer that used a wide head to print an entire line at a time. These printers are still common in data processing applications, and they can really fly!

In the mid-70s, lots of UNIX people got excited about typesetting. Some typesetters were available that could be connected to computers, most notably the C/A/T phototypesetter. Programs like *troff* and TeX were developed to format texts for phototypesetters: letting computer people think that, because they could produce fancy output, they actually had some sense of design. Most of them didn't; if you go back to the early days of typesetting, or even of laser printers, you probably remember lots of incredibly ugly documents masquerading as "good designs." (Gothic fonts on a dot matrix printer? Get real.) But that's another story. Tools like *troff*, *nroff* (a *troff* equivalent that produces output for a standard terminal), and TeX are still with us, and still very valuable. They're discussed in articles 45.13 through 45.23.

Laser printers became commonplace in the mid-80s, allowing common people to do high-quality printing: almost as good (but not quite) as true typesetting. With laser printers came a widely used standard language, called PostScript, to drive the printer. Tools like *troff* and TeX now generated PostScript output files, which could be printed on any printer that understood the PostScript language. This was a big advantage: if you bought a new printer, you didn't have to change your software; you could ship a PostScript file cross-country and be reasonably sure the recipient could print it correctly.* However, another problem appeared. PostScript is a complicated language; things that were easy with a simple text file were now rather difficult. You can't just type up a letter and send it to your daisy wheel printer; you need to convert it into PostScript. It used to be easy to print "just a few pages" from the middle of a file, *grep* through a file to find something interesting, or to look at the file on your screen and read it. Not any more. We've ended this chapter with a few utilities for working with PostScript files. Unfortunately, not enough; I played with lots of them, and while there were some winners, there were many more losers: programs that worked sometimes but not most of the time. The winners are discussed in articles 45.24, 45.25, and 45.26. One particular loser is discussed in article 45.27, which is really a desperate plea for a tool that would reliably convert PostScript back into a plain ASCII text: a tool I'd very much like to have.

---

*Documents were reasonably "portable" back in the line-printer era. Portability disappeared in the early days of computer typesetting, and only reappeared when PostScript became the dominant page description language.

Finally, article 45.28 is about the *pbm* package. It's a useful tool for people who deal with graphics files. *pbm* converts between different graphics formats.

—*ML*

45.02 *Introduction to Printing on UNIX*

Personal computers often have dedicated printers. A dedicated printer is connected to your machine and only you can use it. You can send it only one print job at a time and have to wait until the printing finishes before you can go back to work.

UNIX uses a print spooler to allow many users to share a single printer. A user can make a printing request at any time, even if the printer is currently busy. Requests are queued and processed in order as the printer becomes available.

UNIX permits multiple printers to be connected to the same system. If there is more than one printer, one printer is set up as the default printer and print jobs are automatically sent there.

System V Printing Commands

In System V, the *lp* command is used to queue a print job. (Berkeley systems' printer commands are explained below.) When you use *lp*, it spools the file for printing and returns the request id of your print job. The request id can later be used to cancel the print job, if you decide to do so.

```
$ lp notes
request-id is lp-2354 (1 file)
```

The *lpstat* command can be used to check on the status of your print jobs. The *lpstat* command will tell whether your job is in the queue.

```
$ lpstat
lp-2354          14519 fred      on lp
```

The message on lp indicates that the job is currently printing. If your job does not appear at all on the listing, it means your job has finished printing. If the job is listed, but the on lp message does not appear, then the job is still in the queue. You can see the status of all jobs in the queue with the *–u* option. You can cancel a job with the *cancel* command.

```
$ lpstat -u
lp-2354          14519 fred      on lp
lp-2355          21321 alice
lp-2356           9065 john
$ cancel lp-2356
lp-2356: cancelled
```

The *lpstat* command can be used to determine what printers are connected to your system and their names. If there is more than one printer, you can then use

---

the −*d* option with *lp* to specify a printer destination other than the default. For instance, if a laser printer is configured as *laserp*, then you can enter:

```
$ lp -dlaserp myfile
```

Berkeley Printing Commands

BSD UNIX uses the *lpr* command to queue a print job. When you use *lpr*, it spools the file for printing.

```
$ lpr notes
```

Unlike System V *lp*, the *lpr* command doesn't print a request id. If you need to kill the job, use *lpq* first. The *lpq* command tells you the status of your print jobs.

```
$ lpq
lp is ready and printing
Rank    Owner     Job  Files              Total Size
active  fred      876  notes              7122 bytes
1st     alice     877  standard input     28372 bytes
2nd     john      878  afile bfile ...    985733 bytes
```

The word `active` in the Rank column shows the job that's currently printing. If your job does not appear at all on the listing, it means your job has finished printing. If a job is not *active*, it's still in the queue.

You can remove a job with the *lprm* command. (First, run *lpq* to get the job number.)

```
$ lprm 877
dfA877host dequeued
cfA877host dequeued
```

The command *lpc status (45.03)* can be used to determine which printers are connected to your system and their names. If there is more than one printer, you can then use the −*P* option with *lpr* to specify a printer destination other than the default. For instance, if a laser printer is configured as *laserp*, then you can enter:

```
$ lpr -Plaserp myfile
```

The −*P* option also works with *lpq* and *lprm*. If you'll be using a certain printer often, put its name in the *PRINTER* environment variable *(45.04)*.

—*DD, TOR, JP* from the Nutshell Handbook *DOS Meets UNIX*

45.03 Printer Control with lpc

The Berkeley *lpc*(8) command is mostly for the superuser. Everyone can use a few of its commands; this article covers those.

You probably don't have the */etc* or */usr/etc* directory in your search path *(9.05)*, so you'll need to start *lpc* with its absolute pathname. You can type *lpc* commands at the `lpc>` prompt—then, when you're done, type *exit* (or CTRL-d).

lpc controls only printers on your local host. *lpc* won't control printers connected to other hosts, though you can check the queue of jobs (if any) waiting on your local computer for the remote printer.

```
% /etc/lpc
lpc> help status
status            show status of daemon and queue
lpc> ...
lpc> exit
%
```

Or you can type a single *lpc* command from the shell prompt:

```
% /etc/lpc status imagen
imagen:
        queuing is enabled
        printing is enabled
        no entries
        no daemon present
%
```

The printer daemon *(1.14)* watches the queue for jobs that people submit with *lpr* *(45.02)*. If queueing is disabled (usually by the system administrator), *lpr* won't accept new jobs.

The commands anyone can use are:

restart [*printer*]

> This tries to start a new printer daemon. Do this if something makes the daemon die while there are still jobs in the queue (*lpq* or *lpc status* will tell you this). It's worth trying when the system administrator is gone and the printer doesn't seem to be working.
>
> The printer name can be *all* to restart all printers. The printer name doesn't need an extra *P*. For example, to specify the *foobar* printer to *lpr*, you'd type *lpr -Pfoobar*. With *lpc*, use a command like *restart foobar*.

status [*printer*]

> Shows the status of daemons and queues on the local computer (see example above). The printer name can be *all* to show all printers.

help [*command*]

> By default, gives a list of *lpc* commands, including ones for the superuser only. Give it a command name and it explains that command.

exit   Quits from *lpc.*

—JP

45.04 *Using Different Printers*

By default, commands that send a file to a printer assume that the printer is named *lp*—which probably stands for "line printer" (though it could stand for "laser printer"). If you're using a single-user workstation, and have a printer connected directly to your workstation, you can name your printer *lp* and forget about it.

However, in most environments, there are more options available: e.g., there are several printers in different parts of the building that you can choose from. Often, only one printer will be able to print your documents: you may need to send your print jobs to a PostScript printer, not the line printer that the accounting department uses for billing.

There are two ways to choose a printer:

- Printing commands that originated with BSD UNIX accept the option -P*printer*. This includes *lpr (45.02)*, various scripts to format typeset documents, etc. For example, lpr -Pps file.ps sends the file *file.ps* to the printer named *ps*. (By the way, *ps* is probably the second most common printer name, after *lp*.)

- Commands that originate with BSD UNIX recognize the *PRINTER* environment variable *(7.01)*; if *PRINTER* is defined, the command will read its value and choose a printer accordingly. So the command:

  ```
  % setenv PRINTER ps                    --or
  $ PRINTER=ps ; export PRINTER
  ```

  ensures that the BSD print commands will send your documents to the printer named *ps*.

- Commands that originate with System V UNIX (such as *lp*) use the *−d* option to select a printer. So lp -d pr file.ps sends *file.ps* to the printer named *lp*; it's equivalent to the previous *lpr* example.

- Commands that originate with System V UNIX look for an environment variable named *LPDEST*, rather than *PRINTER*. So:

  ```
  % setenv LPDEST ps                     --or
  $ LPDEST=ps ; export LPDEST
  ```

  ensures that the System V print commands will send your documents to the printer named *ps*.

Note that System V Release 4 includes both the System V and BSD print commands (*lp* and *lpr*). This can make things confusing, particularly if you're using a script to process *troff* or TeX documents, and that script automatically sends your documents to the printer. Unless you know how the script works, you won't know which variable to set. I'd suggest setting both *PRINTER* and *LPDEST*.

By the way, if you only have one printer, but you've given it some name other than *lp*, the same solution works: just set *PRINTER* or *LPDEST* to the appropriate name.

—ML

45.05 Using Symbolic Links for Spooling

When you print a file, the file is copied to a "spooling directory." This can be a problem if you want to print a very large file: the copy operation might take a long time, or the act of copying might fill the spooling directory's filesystem.

On BSD UNIX systems, the *lpr* command provides a workaround for this problem. The *–s* option makes a symbolic link *(19.04)* to your file from the spooling directory. Here's such a command:

```
% lpr -s directions
```

Rather than copying *directions*, *lpr* creates a symbolic link to *directions*. The symbolic link is much faster, and you're unlikely to get a "filesystem full" error.

Using a symbolic link has one important side effect. Because the file isn't hidden away in a special spooling directory, you can delete or modify it after you give the *lpr* command, and before the printer is finished with it. This can have interesting side effects; be careful not to do it.

Of course, this warning applies only to the file that actually goes to the printer. For example, when you format a *troff (45.14)* file for a PostScript printer, you can continue to modify the *troff* file. If the PostScript file is spooled with *lpr –s*, you'd have to be careful about it. However, this isn't likely to be a problem. Most users use some kind of formatting script to run *troff*, and the formatting script prevents you from seeing, or mucking with, the PostScript file.

—ML

45.06 Printing to a Terminal Printer

Does your terminal have an extra port on the back for plugging in a printer? You might be able to hook up a serial printer to the port. Then you can make a little shell script named something like *myprint* and use it this way:

```
% myprint somefile
% someprogram | myprint
```

The *myprint* shell script can be as simple as this:

```
echo "\033[5i\c"
cat $*
echo "\033[4i\c"
```

or this:

```
escape=`echo -n e | tr e '\033'`
echo -n "$escape[5i"
cat $*
echo -n "$escape[4i"
```

depending on what version of *echo* your UNIX has *(48.10)*. Your terminal may need different escape sequences; these are for a VT100-compatible terminal. (Articles 43.10 and 6.02 can help.) If your printer seems to lose a lot of characters, you may have flow-control problems. Try using a slower data rate to the terminal.

—JP

45.07 Quick-and-Dirty Formatting Before Printing

The line printer spooler *(45.02)* prints what you send it. If you send it a continuous stream of text (and the printer is set up to print text files rather than PostScript), that's just what you'll get: no page breaks, indenting, or other formatting features.

That's where *pr* comes in. It's a simple formatter that breaks its input into "pages" that will fit onto a standard 66-line page. (Well, US standard anyway.) It adds a header that automatically includes the date and time, the file name, and a page number. It also adds a footer that ensures that text doesn't run off the bottom of the page.

This is just what you want if you are sending program source code or other streams of unbroken text to a printer. For that matter, *pr* is often very handy for sending text to your screen. In addition to its default behavior, it has quite a few useful options:

-f
: Separate pages using formfeed character (^L) instead of a series of blank lines.

-h*str*
: Replace default header with string *str*. See article 36.15.

-l*n*
: Set page length to *n* (default is 66).

-m
: Merge files, printing one in each column (can't be used with *−num* and *−a*). Text is chopped to fit. See article 36.15. This is a poor man's *paste (36.16)*.

-s*c*
: Separate columns with *c* (default is a tab).

-t
: Omit the page header and trailing blank lines.

-w*num*
: Set line width for output made into columns to *num* (default is 72).

+*num*   Begin printing at page *num* (default is 1).

-*n*   Produce output having *n* columns (default is 1). See article 36.15.

There are also options that apply only to the System V version:

-**a**   Multi-column format; list items in rows going across.

-**d**   Double-spaced format.

-**e**cn   Set input tabs to every *n*th position (default is 8), and use *c* as field delimiter (default is a tab).

-**F**   Fold input lines (avoids truncation by *−a* or *−m*).

-**i**cn   For output, replace white space with field delimiter *c* (default is a tab) every *n*th position (default is 8).

-**n**cn   Number lines with numbers *n* digits in length (default is 5), followed by field separator *c* (default is a tab). See also *nl*.

-**o**n   Offset each line *n* spaces (default is 0).

-**p**   Pause before each page.

-**r**   Suppress messages for files that can't be found.

Let's put this all together with a couple of examples:

- Print a side-by-side list, omitting heading and extra lines:

```
pr -m -t list.1 list.2 list.3
```

- Alphabetize a list of states; number the lines in five columns. First, with the System V options:

```
sort states_50 | pr -n -5
```

On a BSD system, which doesn't support *−n*, you can use *cat -n (26.22)* to supply the line numbers:

```
sort states_50 | cat -n | pr -5
```

—*TOR, DG from the Nutshell Handbook UNIX in a Nutshell (SVR4/Solaris)*

45.08 *Fixing Margins with pr and fold*

The System V version of *pr (45.07)* has a *−F* option for folding lines that are too wide for the output page: the printer won't truncate them. If you print lots of random data and stuff that may have long lines and your *pr* doesn't have *−F*, try the *fold* command instead.

fold arbitrarily breaks lines that are too long, by default at 80 columns. Use *−width* where *width* is the desired column to fold at for some other breaking point.

I made an alias *(11.02)* called *prF* to do that. It prints a single file and puts the filename in the *pr* heading (usually, if you pipe to *pr*, it won't know the filename). You might want to add | lpr onto the end of this, too:

csh_init

```
alias prF 'fold \!^ | pr -h "\!^"'
```

A good way to see which lines are folded is with line numbering. *pr* versions without *–F* usually don't have *–n* either. You can add it to your alias with *cat –n* *(26.22)*. The lines will be numbered before they're folded:

csh_init

```
alias prnF 'cat -n \!^ | fold | pr -h "\!^"'
```

—JP

45.09 Fold without Cutting Words in Half

One of the problems with *fold (45.08)* is that it breaks text at an arbitrary column position—even if that position happens to be in the middle of a word. It's a pretty primitive utility, designed to keep long lines from printing off the edge of a line printer page, and not much more.

fmt (31.37) can do a better job because it thinks in terms of language constructs like paragraphs. *fmt* wraps lines continuously, rather than just folding the long ones. It assumes that paragraphs end at blank lines. Many versions of *fmt* can also handle program source code or other structured data. Their *–s* option breaks long lines at white space but doesn't join short lines to form longer ones.

By default, *fmt* breaks lines at or before column 72. You can set a different length with the option *–n* or *–l n*. For example, *–40* or *–l 40* will output lines no longer than 40 characters.

—TOR, JP

45.10 Indenting Text for Printing

If you want to print a file that has plain text (not PostScript or some other page description language), you can indent the printout by adding some spaces to the start of each line. Use *sed (35.24)* to add a TAB or two (if your printer can handle TABs)—otherwise, spaces—to the start of each line. Here's a simple command that adds four spaces to the start of each line of the *logdata* file, then prints with *lpr*:

```
% sed 's/^/    /' logdata | lpr
```

You'll run into trouble if the file you're printing has any TABs in it though, because the extra spaces at the start of each line will mess up the tabstops. In that case, expand tabs *(43.04)* first:

```
% expand logdata | sed 's/^/    /' | lpr
```

The *pr (45.07)* command makes a nicely formatted printout. You can indent its output, too:

```
% pr logdata | sed 's/^/    /' | lpr
```

That doesn't always work. If there are TABs in the file, *pr* may not expand them—though some versions of *pr* have a *-e* switch to do that. Also, your indentation will indent the heading on each page—too much indentation can shove the heading off the right-hand side of the paper. Here's a better command to handle those problems. It expands the TABs and indents the body but doesn't indent the heading:

```
% expand logdata | sed 's/^/    /' | pr -h logdata | lpr
```

The *-h* logdata puts the filename at the top of each page (because *pr* can't get the name otherwise). Omit that if you don't want it.

The *offset (36.05)* script lets you set the indentation with a command-line option.

—JP

45.11 Filename Headers above Files without pr

The *pr* command *(45.07)* displays your files with a nice header above them. But it can also add a bunch of blank lines to fill a page and break the file to add more headers in the middle if the file is longer than a page. You might want a string of your files with the filename above each, like this:

```
*** header for file1 ***

file1 contents

*** header for file2 ***

file2 contents
   ...
```

Here are some ways to do that. You'll usually be piping these commands to a printer, redirecting them to a file, and so on:

1. One feature of *head (26.21)* (not always documented) is that when you give multiple filenames, it adds a header above each. To be sure *head* gives you all of your file (not just the head), use a line count bigger than any of your files, like 10,000. The output will be:

```
% head -10000 file*
==> file1 <==
...contents of file1....

==> file2 <==
...contents of file2....


   ...
```

2. When you redirect the output of *more (26.03)* somewhere besides a terminal, it doesn't stop at the end of a screenful. It prints a little header above each file and outputs all the files at once:

```
% more file* > package
% cat package
```

```
::::::::::::::
file1
::::::::::::::
...contents of file1....
::::::::::::::
file2
::::::::::::::
...contents of file2....
...
```

3. Use *wc −l* *(30.06)* to count the number of lines in each file, then set *pr* to print a page just a little longer. I'll show that with a C shell *foreach* loop *(10.09)*, but you could use a Bourne shell *for* loop *(10.10)* instead.

(30.06)

```
% foreach f (file*)
? set length = `wc -l < $f`
? @ length = $length + 11
? pr -1$length $f >> printme
? end
% cat printme

Oct 28 07:28 1992   file1 Page 1

...contents of file1....

Nov  3 09:35 1992   file2 Page 1

...contents of file2....
...
```

Note that some versions of *pr* won't put headers on very short files.

4. Bourne shell *for* loops with redirected output *(47.22)* let you combine a bunch of commands and grab the output of all of them at once. Here's a loop that runs *ls −l* on each file. It uses *cut* *(36.12)* to print just the file's permissions (columns 1-11, including a space), last modification date, and name (columns 42-end). (You could pipe *ls −l* into something like *sed*, instead, to make a fancier heading—and get rid of the *echo* commands, too.) The output is redirected to a file named *printme*; as above, a pipe to your printer program will also work.

```
$ for f in file*
> do
> echo =====================================
> ls -l $f | cut -c1-11,42-
> echo =====================================
> cat $f
> done > printme
$ cat printme
=====================================
-rw-r----- Oct 28 07:28 file1
=====================================
...contents of file1....
=====================================
-r--r--r-- Nov  3 09:35 file2
=====================================
```

...contents of file2....

...

If you use those last two tricks a lot, you might put them into an alias, function, or shell script *(11.01)*.

—JP

45.12 Big Letters: banner

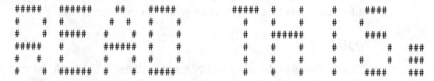

I made that with the System V version of *banner* by typing:

```
banner "read this."
```

Each argument (10 characters or less) is printed to the standard output *(14.01)* in letters like those. I quoted my two words to keep them together. If you type separate arguments, *banner* will print them down the page.

The Berkeley version of *banner* prints big letters, too. But they're much bigger and they're output sideways for a continuous-form printer. These banners are great for parties. The default is 132 characters high, enough for a wide printer or a smaller printer in compressed-type mode. Use the *–w* option to get 80-column width; add a number for a different width, like *–100*, to get 100-character width.

This program is usually in the */usr/games* directory. Although you can type the message on the command line, it's easier to type at the (undocumented) `Message:` prompt because you won't have to quote special characters. For example:

```
% /usr/games/banner -w | lpr -Ptractor
Message: * * Happy Birthday, Alice!! * *
```

If you don't have a continuous-form printer, you can piece together separate pages with a *csh foreach* loop *(10.09)* or an *sh for* loop *(10.10)*, some scissors, and a roll of tape ;-):

'..' 9.11

```
% foreach page (Pay me '$10,' 000)
? /usr/games/banner -w "$page" | lpr -Plaser
? end
```

Remember to quote special characters.

—JP

45.13 Typesetting Overview

In the early '80s, one thing that made UNIX popular was that it came with its own typesetting system. It was the first operating system that could really let users produce high-quality documents using laser printers. Although there are probably more fancy editors available for Macintosh systems, high-quality printing is still a part of the UNIX experience.

In this article, we'll discuss briefly the different typesetters that are available for UNIX. We won't describe any of the systems in detail, but we'll give enough information so that you'll know what options are available.

troff

This is the grand-daddy of UNIX typesetters. It's the oldest program that we'll discuss. It's a batch-oriented, markup-based language. This means that you insert typesetting commands directly into your document. You write documents with a regular text editor, like *vi* or *emacs*, process them with the *troff* command (or, more likely, by invoking some kind of "format" shell script), and see the output on a laser printer. In fact, *troff* files are really more like "programs" than traditional "text files."

troff comes with three preprocessors that handle equations (*eqn*), tables (*tbl*), and simple line drawings (*pic*). The equation and table processors are reasonably good; the drawing program has some interesting features, but really isn't worth the trouble. If you need a lot of illustrations (or high-quality illustrations), use a tool like FrameMaker or Interleaf, or some dedicated illustration program, and insert the results into your *troff* document.

troff is surprisingly flexible, although taking advantage of its flexibility is difficult. For example, this book was written with *troff*; we've added index, cross-reference, and table-of-contents packages. Although it's obsolete, quirky, and difficult, we find that *troff* is still better for large typesetting jobs, particularly books.

At one time, *troff* was supplied with all UNIX systems. That's no longer true; these days, you often have to buy it as an extra-cost product, particularly if you're using System V. Unfortunately, if *troff* comes with your system, it's probably the old and moldy version that was designed to work with a particular obsolete phototypesetter. By hacking it to death, it has been made to work with modern printers of all sorts. But you're better off spending the money and getting *device independent troff*; you'll get much better results

Of course, now that vendors are making money from *troff*, some third party vendors such as SoftQuad and Elan are selling enhanced versions. Given the language's basic warts, this is probably a good thing. The Free Software Foundation also has a version of *troff* called *groff (45.18)*. I haven't used it, but I generally have a high opinion of their software. And you can't beat the price.

TeX

TeX is a typesetting language that was designed in the '70s by Donald Knuth, primarily so he could write his *Art of Computer Programming* books. I am not a fan of TeX, and readers of this section should be forewarned. Really, in my opinion, TeX is not much worse than *troff*. But it's also not much better, despite many claims to the contrary.

TeX is a complete programming language. Like *troff*, you add typesetting commands to your text as you write it, and then process the document with some kind of formatting command. TeX's syntax is much more like a programming language than a "simple markup language." However, if *troff*'s syntax is graceless, TeX's is decidely ugly. If you write a lot of software, you might like it. If you don't write software, you might get used to it with time. I don't find LaTeX (a macro package that makes TeX look like Scribe, which we'll discuss below) to be a significant improvement, though it's admittedly simpler. If you want to write your own macro package, the difference between TeX and *troff* is a toss-up; whichever you choose, the task requires a lot of black magic.

TeX's biggest strength is typesetting equations, for which it really doesn't have an equal. (*troff*'s *eqn* preprocessor will do the job, but isn't anywhere near as flexible.) It doesn't have a drawing processor, though I have seen versions of *troff*'s *pic* preprocessor that work with TeX. However, if you need illustrations, you'll need to develop them with some other tools and insert the results into your TeX document.

I think TeX's biggest drawback is its error messages. *troff* has virtually no error messages. But TeX's error messages are incomprehensible or misleading, and I think that's worse. TeX messages typically complain about something going wrong inside a macro package. So you get an error message about a line of code that you've never seen. Yes, your input *did* cause the error—but, unless you know in detail how TeX works, you may never figure out why. Another drawback: TeX gives you incredible flexibility. Unfortunately, you get altogether too much flexibility, and this gives people who are long on intellect but short on good taste the ability to create horrendously ugly output. There's no need for *anyone* to play with the algorithm for putting spaces between letters or words. In short: it's possible to create beautiful documents with TeX, but it's very easy to create ugly ones.

TeX's biggest advantage is that it's distributed for free by the American Mathematical Society. So if you need a low-cost typesetting solution, it's definitely worth considering. [There are also commercial versions available from Ready-to-Run (for UNIX), ArborText (for both UNIX and DOS), and Blue Sky Research (for the Mac). These may be preferable on the strength of their technical support.—*EK*]

Scribe

A few words on Scribe, only because I really thought it was a good tool. Scribe was another "batch" typesetting system, like TeX and *troff*. However, the authors of Scribe had a great knack for hiding complexity from the mortal user. Someone with no technical training could make good-looking documents very quickly.

Scribe was horribly overpriced, and never (to my knowledge) priced realistically for workstations. (I'm sure I'll hear if this is untrue!) This limited its acceptance in the workstation market.

WYSIWYG Document Processors

In the last decade, we've been bombarded with WYSIWYG documentation tools. WYSIWYG stands for "What You See Is What You Get," and means that your workstation or X terminal *(1.31)* displays a realistic approximation of the printed document on the screen. When you make changes, you get immediate feedback on what happened; you don't have to wait for the document to come out of the printer. Such tools are very good for drawings and illustrations. They aren't quite as good at handling equations, but some of them have special equation processors built-in. The drawback of the WYSIWYG is (of course) that you can't use a WYSIWYG processor effectively on an ASCII terminal.

The leading WYSIWYG processors for UNIX are FrameMaker and Interleaf. In terms of features, they tend to leap-frog each other. In my opinion, a lot of these features (like self-modifying, or "live," documents) exist mostly for marketing value. They're surprisingly weak at handling large (book-length) documents; yes, they can do it, but the battle-scarred batch tools (Scribe, TeX, and *troff*) do as good a job, or better.

Frame and Interleaf are arguably easier to learn than the batch-oriented typesetters. However, it's easy to overstate the advantages of a graphical interface. While they're certainly easier to learn than *troff* or TeX, I'm not sure how either would stack up against a well-designed batch document processor, like Scribe.

WYSIWYG processors are all added-cost products; they can be quite expensive. I'm not aware of any public domain or "free" tools, though such may exist.

—ML

45.14 The Text Formatters nroff, troff, ditroff, . . .

Have you used a WYSIWYG (What You See Is What You Get) word processor like FrameMaker, WordPerfect, Interleaf, and so on? Then you might not have much experience with the original UNIX formatters, *nroff* and *troff*.

Instead of showing a picture of the completed document on your screen as you type, these formatters read a *source file* full of text and special formatting commands. The formatted output goes into a file (text, PostScript, or some other format) or straight to a printer. You create and edit the source file with any text editor (like *vi*). O'Reilly & Associates still uses *troff* to produce many of its books. For example, the start of the source file for this article looks like:

```
.Ah 2520 "The Text Formatters nroff, troff, ditroff, ..."
Have you used a WYSIWYG (What You See Is What You Get) word
processor like FrameMaker, WordPerfect, Interleaf and so on?
Then you might not have much experience with the original UNIX
formatters, \fInroff\fP and \fItroff\fP.
.LP
Instead of showing a picture of the completed document on your
screen as you type, these formatters read a \fIsource file\fP full
...
```

You might wonder, "Why use these dinosaurs?"

- All UNIX systems have them or can get them, so they're portable.

- The source files are usually much smaller than WYSIWYG formatters' files.

- The source files are plain text with no non-printable characters; they're easy to copy from computer to computer.

- The formatting language that's used has a powerful set of features that gives professional typesetters (like O'Reilly & Associates) excellent control over the way the output page looks.

- You can use UNIX utilities—*grep*, *awk*, shell scripts, and many others—to process the text. This adds even more power to the formatting setup. For example, that 2520 following the .Ah in the example above is the filename. Each article in this book has an arbitrary four digit filename; this is mapped into the section number printed in the margin and in all the cross-references throughout the book using a system of scripts I wrote. I also built a crude outline processor so that we could control the organization of the book by changing a single file. All this was possible only because *troff* wasn't forced to work alone—we could apply the full power of the UNIX environment.

Batch formatters like *nroff* and *troff* aren't the answer for all formatting jobs, but they're worth looking into—especially for small or very complex jobs.

—*JP*

45.15 nroff/troff and Macro Packages

nroff and *troff* have a set of built-in commands, but what makes them truly powerful is the ability to define *macros*. Think of macros as batch files or command scripts, written in *nroff* and *troff's* arcane language.

Macros are difficult to write and even harder to debug. Luckily, several *macro packages* are available for everyday use. Macro packages are sets of macros designed to work together. For example, manual pages for UNIX are written with the *man* macro package, which is called on the command line using the *—man* option:

```
% nroff -man cat.1
```

We wrote this book with our own proprietary macro package which is based on *ms*. *ms* was one of the original macro packages written at Bell Labs, but it was dropped by AT&T in System V. It is still available on BSD-based systems, as is another macro package called *me*. The System V replacement for *ms* is called *mm*.

—LM

45.16 Determining the troff Macro Package

Ever *troff* a file with the wrong macro package, or without using *tbl (45.17)?* You quickly regret it: you end up with a printout of gibberish. To avoid that happening again, try out the *dtp* program, which looks at the files and generates the command line needed to format it correctly.

dtp

dtp just scans the source file for *troff* macros in order to decide what macro package *(45.15)* or preprocessors *(45.17)* are needed to format it. For example, if *dtp* comes across a .TP macro, it knows that it is written using the *man* macros. If it comes across a .OF macro, it knows that the file is probably written in *ms*.

dtp also looks for macros used for preprocessors. For example, tables meant to be processed by *tbl* need to be surrounded by .TS and .TE, so when *dtp* sees a .TS it knows that *tbl* is required. Similarly for .PS/.PE for *pic* and .EQ/EN for *eqn*.

dtp does not actually run the commands, it just generates the commands needed. For example, if you call *dtp* on a file that's written using *ms* macros and uses *tbl*, *dtp* will just spit out the command line:

```
% dtp appf
tbl appf | ditroff -ms > dtp.out
```

To actually run the commands, you could use backquotes:

eval *9.08*

```
% eval `dtp appf`
```

Or you can use *dtp* in a shell script.

```
# Format file:
eval `dtp $1`
```

```
# Convert ditroff to postscript and print
devps dtp.out | lpr
```

You can use command-line options to have *dtp* use *pstroff* or *iptroff* instead of *ditroff*. In those instances, the output is not redirected to the *dtp.out* file, since output is sent directly to the printer.

Of course, *dtp* needs to make the assumption that you're using unmodified standard macro sets. If you modify your *troff* macros, or if you use an unsupported version of *troff* or *tbl*, it's likely that *dtp* will need to be customized at the source level before it works right for you.

Also, be aware that *dtp* just looks for the first macro recognized as part of the *ms*, *man*, or *me* macro sets and makes its determination based on that. This method isn't foolproof. For example, I tried *dtp* on a file that was written using *ms*, but *dtp* reported it as being *me*. When I looked at the file, I saw that, before any *ms* macros, were some commented-out lines:

```
.ig ++
This document could use some more work.
.++
```

The .ig ++ line says to ignore everything up to the next .++. I could have used any two-character string, but I chose to use ++. But then *dtp* recognized the .++ code as an *me* macro!

—LM

45.17 *From a Source File to the Printer*

The path from a TeX or *troff* source file to your printer is surprisingly complex. It's often useful to know exactly what is happening. It isn't knowledge that will help you "do anything" (i.e., you won't be able to make fancier documents), but it will come in handy—particularly when something goes wrong.

For TeX and *troff*, the processing is surprisingly similar, as shown in Figure 45-1.

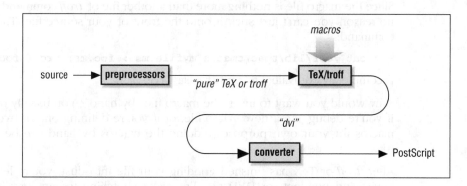

Figure 45-1. Processing Path for TeX or troff Source File

You start with a source file, containing your text and markup. First, it's processed by one or more *preprocessors* to handle figures, tables, and so on. Preprocessors are essential to *troff*; they aren't used that often with TeX, but they do exist. What a preprocessor does is provide a simpler language for formatting complex elements like tables, equations, or figures; the preprocessor interprets this language, and outputs the low-level *troff* requests needed to implement the desired result.

The most commonly used preprocessors are listed in Table 45-1.

Table 45-1. Common troff and TeX Preprocessors

Name	Used with	Function
pic	*troff*	Illustrations
grap	*troff*	Graphs; not frequently used
tbl	*troff*	Tables
eqn	*troff*	Equations
tpic	*TeX*	Illustrations; equivalent to *pic*

After going through the preprocessors, you're left with a "pure" document that consists of basic commands and macros. This is fed into the TeX or *troff* processor, which starts by adding a "macro definition file" to the beginning of your text. The processor then produces a device independent file; this is a generic representation of your document in terms of low-level commands. You can't do much with device-independent output except (possibly) inspect it for bugs.

Before going on, a word about macro files. A macro file is nothing more than a file of *troff* or TeX commands that defines macros, sets up page borders, headers, footers, and so on. Basically, a macro file defines the look of your document, together with any "high-level" (e.g., paragraph or heading) commands that you use. For *troff*, these files are kept in the directory */usr/lib/tmac* and have filenames like *tmac.name*; when you invoke *troff*, you give the option -m*name* to select a macro package.

Since the macro file is nothing more than another file of *troff* commands, there's no reason you can't just stick it onto the front of your source file. That is, the command:

```
% cat /usr/lib/tmac/tmac.s myfile.ms > foo.ms; troff foo.ms
```

is completely equivalent to `troff -ms foo.ms`.

Why would you want to insert the macro file "by hand"? You usually don't; but if you're debugging a new macro file, or if you're defining one or two special macros for your own purposes, adding the macros by hand can be a useful trick.

After *troff* or TeX has finished grinding your file into dust, you're left with a device independent (or DVI) file. I'm really stretching terminology here, but (conceptually) this is the right way to think. The problem is that there are two versions of *troff*: device independent *troff*, or *ditroff*, and "old" *troff*. *ditroff* is the only one that really generates device independent output: i.e., generic output that can easily be translated into a file for any printer. The old *troff* generates output for a C/A/T phototypesetter, an archaic beast that probably exists only in museums. C/A/T output is not device independent by any means: it reflects lots of C/A/T idiosyncracies that are a pain to deal with. However, conceptually, you can think of C/A/T output as device independent output with a botched design; it's certainly independent of any device you're likely to see! :-)

The concept of device independent output really originated with TeX; TeX's DVI files are very well defined and quite elegant. Unfortunately, they're completely different from *ditroff*'s DVI files. And if you're using some "third-party" version of *troff*, like SoftQuad's *sqtroff* or the FSF's *groff*, you probably have yet another kind of device independent output to deal with. Although they sound like they're standardized, device independent formats aren't.

At any rate, once your processor is finished, its device independent output (of whatever type) needs to be converted to commands for your printer. This is done by a postprocessor. The name of the postprocessor depends entirely on what kind of printer you're using, which version of TeX or *troff* you're using, and where you bought your software. One such program is *psroff*, which is part of Adobe's *transcript* package; it converts *ditroff* output to PostScript.

Although this may seem complex, most of this is invisible to you; most often, you'll invoke *troff* through a script that will handle all the postprocessing (and possibly even the preprocessing) for you. However, when you need to debug something that isn't working, there's no substitute for understanding the machinery.

—ML

45.18 groff

troff (45.13) was originally designed for a now-obsolete typesetter. One of the main limitations of this typesetter was that it could only use a total of four fonts on the same page—usually the Roman, **Bold**, and *Italic* versions of the same typeface, plus a special font that included math characters and various other symbols. It doesn't let you do things like you see on these pages, which typically include seven or eight fonts: the four listed above, plus a completely different typeface for the headings, plus a constant width font (with bold and italic variations) for use in showing scripts and examples.

The original *troff* was replaced with a device independent version called *ditroff* (45.17), which addressed these limitations and added a lot of other new features as well. Unfortunately, *ditroff* was unbundled from UNIX and sold as a separate product, so all that many systems offer is the old version.

groff

Fortunately, there is a solution. The Free Software Foundation's *groff* has all of the nice features of *ditroff*. It also includes postprocessors that convert its device independent output *(45.17)* to PostScript.

—*TOR*

45.19 Don't have nroff? Try awf

Some UNIX systems are distributed without *nroff*. Your operating system vendor may sell *nroff* separately as part of a text formatting package that isn't included with the base operating system. Or your operating system vendor may not provide *nroff* at all, meaning that you'd need to buy it from a third-party vendor such as Elan or SoftQuad. For systems without *nroff* installed, manual pages are supplied in a formatted (*cat*) form so that users can still read them without *nroff*.

The problem arises when you want to want to install third-party packages, either commercial or public domain, which don't supply formatted versions of their documentation. You can try to weed through *nroff* source, but you'd be better off if you could get a working version of *nroff*.

awf

The *awf* program is an *awk*-based version of *nroff*. *awf* doesn't provide anywhere near all the functionality of *nroff*, but it does a pretty good simulation, and it's a very clever idea.

awf recognizes both *man* and *ms* macros. To use it, you need to supply the macro package on the command line (as you would for *nroff*):

```
% awf -man cat.1
```

—*LM*

45.20 How nroff Makes Bold and Underline; How to Remove it

The UNIX formatter *nroff* produces output for line printers and CRT displays. To achieve such special effects as emboldening, it outputs the character followed by a backspace and then outputs the same character again. A sample of it viewed with a text editor or *cat −v (26.07)* might look like:

```
N^HN^HN^HNA^HA^HA^HAM^HM^HM^HME^HE^HE^HE
```

which emboldens the word "NAME." There are three overstrikes for each character output. Similarly, underlining is achieved by outputting an underscore, a backspace, and then the character to be underlined. There are many times when it's necessary to strip these special effects; for example, if you want to *grep* through formatted *man pages* (as we do in 52.03). There are a number of ways to get rid of these decorations. The easiest way to do it is to use a utility like *col*, *colcrt*, or *ul*:

- With *col*, use the command:

    ```
    % col -b nroffoutput > strippedoutput
    ```

    The *−b* option tells *col* to strip all backspaces (and the character preceding the backspace) from the file. *col* is available on System V and BSD UNIX.

- With *colcrt*, use a command like:

    ```
    % colcrt - nroffoutput > strippedoutput
    ```

    The − (dash) option (yes, that's an option) says "ignore underlining." If you omit it, *colcrt* tries to save underlining by putting the underscores on a separate line. For example:

    ```
    Refer to Installing System V for information about
    ---------- ------ -
    installing optional software.
    ```

    colcrt is only available under BSD; in any case, *col* is probably preferable.

- *ul* reads your *TERM* environment variable, and tries to translate backspace (underline and overstrike) into something your terminal can understand. It's used like this:

    ```
    % ul nroffoutput
    ```

    The *-t term* option lets you specify a terminal type; it overrides the *TERM* variable. I think that *ul* is probably the least useful of these commands; it tries to be too intelligent, and doesn't always do what you want.

Both *col* and *colcrt* attempt to handle "half linefeeds" (used to print superscripts and subscripts) reasonably. Many printers handle half linefeeds correctly, but most terminals can't deal with them.

Here's one other solution to the problem: a simple *sed* (35.24) script. The virtue of this solution is that you can elaborate on it, adding other features that you'd like, or integrating it into larger *sed* scripts. The following *sed* command removes the sequences for emboldening and underscoring:

```
s/.^H//g
```

It removes any character preceding the backspace along with the backspace itself. In the case of underlining, "." matches the underscore; for emboldening, it matches the overstrike character. Because it is applied repeatedly, multiple occurrences of the overstrike character are removed, leaving a single character for each sequence. Note that ^H is the single character CTRL-h. If you're a *vi* user, enter this character by typing CTRL-v followed by CTRL-h. If you're an *emacs* user, type CTRL-q followed by CTRL-h.

—DD, ML from the Nutshell Handbook *sed & awk*

45.21 Removing Leading Tabs and Other Trivia

In article 45.20 we discussed several techniques for removing overstriking and underlining from *nroff* output. Of course, that's not the only problem you'll face when you're working with *nroff*. Here are some more postprocessing tricks for *nroff* files.

You may also want to remove strange escape sequences that produce formfeeds or various other printer functions. For example, you sometimes see the sequence ^[9 at the top of the formatted manual page. This escape sequence can be removed with the *sed* command:

```
s/^[9//g
```

The ESC character is entered in *vi* by typing CTRL-v *(32.05)* followed by the ESC key. In Emacs, use CTRL-q ESC. The number 9 is literal.

The typical manual page also uses leading spaces to establish the left margin and to indent most of the text. On further inspection, you'll see that leading spaces precede headings (such as "NAME"), but a single tab precedes each line of text. Tabs may also appear unexpectedly in the text. Of course, using tabs wherever possible is a good idea on the whole; on a mechanical printer, and even on modern CRT displays, it's much quicker to print a TAB than to move the cursor over several spaces. However, the tabs can cause trouble if your printer (or terminal) isn't set correctly, or when you're trying to search for something in the text.

To eliminate the left margin and the unwanted tabs, use the following two *sed* commands:

```
s/^[□|-|]*//g
s/|-|/ /g
```

The first command looks for any number of tabs or spaces at the beginning of a line. (A TAB is represented by |—| and a space by □.) The second command looks for a tab and replaces it with a single space.

Now, let's put all these pieces together—including the script to strip underlines and overstrikes (from article 45.20). Here's a script called *sedman* that incorporates all of these tricks.

sedman

```
#!/bin/sed -f
#sedman -- deformat nroff-formatted man page
s/.^H//g
s/^[9//g
s/^[□|-|]*//g
s/|-|/ /g
```

Running this script on a typical manual page produces a file that looks like this:

```
who                                                who



NAME
who - who is on the system?
```

```
SYNOPSIS
who [-a] [-b] [-d] [-H] [-l] [-p] [-q] [-r] [-s] [-t] [-T]
[-u] [file]
who am i

who am I

DESCRIPTION
who can list the user's name, terminal line, login time,
elapsed time since activity occurred on the line, and the
...
```

This doesn't eliminate the unnecessary blank lines *(35.18, 26.11, 26.10)* caused by paging.

—*DD, ML*

45.22 *Displaying a troff Macro Definition*

If you're writing or debugging *troff* macros *(45.14)*, you often need to review the contents of a macro. Rather than searching through the macro definition files with an editor, it is relatively easy to construct a small script that uses *sed (35.24)* and the shell to extract and display a single macro.

The script is easy to construct because the macro definitions have a regular structure that lends itself to easy identification with the regular expressions *(27.04)* used by *sed*. A *troff* macro definition always begins with the string .de, followed by an optional space and the one- or two-letter name of the macro. The definition ends with a line beginning with two dots (. .).

troff macros are defined in a macro package, often a single file that's located in a directory such as */usr/lib/tmac*. The most common macro packages are *mm*, *ms* and *me*—though it is unlikely that a given system will have all three. *mm* is generally found on System V-derived systems, and *ms* and *me* on BSD-derived systems. The *man* macros are found on just about all systems because they are used by the *man* command *(52.01)*.

Here's the *getmac* script:

getmac

```
#!/bin/sh
# Usage: getmac -package macro
case $1 in
  -mm)  file="/usr/lib/macros/mmt";;
  -ms)  file="/usr/lib/tmac/tmac.s";;
  -me)  file="/usr/lib/tmac/tmac.e";;
  -man) file="/usr/lib/tmac/tmac.an";;
esac
echo '.
echo .\
echo '.
sed -n -e "/^.de *$2/,/^..$/p" $file
```

For those unfamiliar with *sed*, here are a few notes on the script:

- *sed* is invoked with the *−n* option to keep it from printing out the entire file.

With this option, *sed* will print only the lines it is explicitly told to print via the print command (p).

- The name of the macro to be extracted is passed into the *sed* script via the shell variable $2 (the second argument). The first argument is the name of the macro package to be searched. For example:

  ```
  % getmac -mm BL
  ```

  would extract the definition of the BL macro from the *mm* macro package.

- The *sed* print command is used to print every line between those two matching pattern addresses: the first matches the start of the macro definition specified on the shell script command line—for example, .deBL—and the second matches its termination, .., on a line by itself. Note that dots appear literally in the two patterns and are escaped using the backslash.

- Some macro packages include a space between .de and the name of the macro, while others do not. Accordingly, following .de, we specify a space followed by an asterisk, which means the space is optional:

  ```
  /^\.de *$2/
  ```

- Double quotes rather than single quotes are used to surround the *sed* script within the shell script because single quotes would not allow interpretation of $2 by the shell. (Article 9.10 explains.)

There's an extension to *getmac* in article 35.21.

—*TOR* from *UNIX Text Processing*, Hayden Books, 1987

45.23 *Preprocessing troff Input with sed*

On a typewriter-like device (including a CRT), an em-dash is typed as a pair of hyphens (--). In typesetting, it is printed as a single, long dash (—). *troff* provides a special character name for the em-dash, but it is inconvenient to type \(em, and the escape sequence is also inappropriate for use with *nroff*.

Similarly, a typesetter provides "curly" quotation marks (" and ") as opposed to a typewriter's straight quotes ("). In standard *troff*, you can substitute two backquote characters (``) for open quote and two frontquote characters ('') for closed quote; these characters would appear as " and ". But it would be much better if we could just continue to type in " and have the computer do the dirty work.

A peculiarity of *troff* is that it generates the space before each word in the font used at the beginning of that word. This means that when we mix a constant-width font such as Courier within text, we get a noticeably large space before each word, which can be distracting for readers—for example:

The following `text` is in `Courier`; note the `spaces`.

The fix for this is to force *troff* to generate the space in the previous font by inserting a no-space character (\&) before each constant-width font change. As you can imagine, this can turn into a large undertaking.

The solution for each of these problems is to preprocess *troff* input with *sed* *(35.24)*. This is an application that shows *sed* in its role as a true stream editor, making edits in a pipeline—edits that are never written back into a file.

We almost never invoke *troff* directly. Instead, we invoke it with a script that strings together a pipeline including the standard preprocessors (when appropriate) as well as doing this special preprocessing with *sed*.

The *sed* commands themselves are fairly simple.

The following command changes two consecutive dashes into an em-dash:

```
s/--/\\(em/g
```

We double the backslashes in the replacement string for \(em, since the backslash has a special meaning to *sed*.

However, there may be cases in which we don't want this substitutiion command to be applied. What if someone is using hyphens to draw a horizontal line? We can refine the script to exclude lines containing three or more consecutive hyphens. To do this, we use the ! address modifier:

```
/---/!s/--/\\(em/g
```

It may take a moment to penetrate this syntax. What's different is that we use a pattern address to restrict the lines that are affected by the substitute command, and we use ! to reverse the sense of the pattern match. It says, simply, "If you find a line containing three consecutive hyphens, don't apply the edit." On all other lines, the substitute command will be applied.

Similarly, to deal with the font change problem, we can use *sed* to search for all strings matching \f(CW, \f(CI, and \f(CB, and insert \& before them. This can be written as follows:

```
s/\\f(C\([WIB]\)/\\\&\\f(C\1/g
```

To deal with the open and closed quote problem, the script needs to be more involved because there are many separate cases that must be accounted for. You need to make *sed* smart enough to change double quotes to open quotes only at the beginning of words and to change them to closed quotes only at the end of words.

Such a script might look like the one below, which obviously could be shortened by judicious application of \([. . .]\) *(35.10)* regular expression syntax, but it is shown in its long form for effect.

```
s/^"/``/
s/"? /''? /g
s/"? /''? /g
s/"?$/''?/g
s/ "/ ``/g
s/" /'' /g
s/ TAB "/ TAB ``/g
s/" TAB /'' TAB /g
s/")/'')/g
s/"]/'']/g
s/("/(``/g
```

```
s/\["/\[``/g
s/";/'';/g
s/":/'':/g
s/,"/,''/g
s/",/'',/g
s/\."/.\\\&''/g
s/"\./''.\\\&/g
s/"\\^\\(em/''\\(em/g
s/\\(em\\^"/\\(em``/g
s/"\\(em/''\\(em/g
s/\\(em"/\\(em``/g
```

cleanup.sed

A more complete "typesetting preprocessor" script written in *sed*, and suitable for integration into a *troff* environment (perhaps with a bit of tweaking), can be found on the disk.

In addition to the changes described above, it tightens up the spacing of ellipses (. . .), and doesn't do anything between certain pairs of *troff* macros **(35.19)**.

—*TOR, LM*

45.24 *Converting Text Files to PostScript*

Printing used to be easy; when all we had were daisy wheel printers and line printers, you could send virtually any text file to a printer without modification. That's no longer possible; fancy "printer languages" like PostScript force you to do a fair amount of processing to get a simple text into some form that the printer can understand.

As always, there are several ways to solve this problem. The first is gross and disgusting, but quite effective. Assume that you have a working version of *troff* with the *–ms* macros. Here's the script:

```
# the name of the script that runs troff for you
roff=lw
# choose your favorite macro package
macros=-ms
sed -e '
1i\
.DS\
.in 0\
.ft CW\
.ps 10\
.vs 12
s/\\/\\e/g
s/^/\\\&/
$a.DE ' | $roff $macros
```

How does it work? It just "wraps" your text with a *troff* incantation that prints the text in a fixed-width font, with no "justification" or "fill." It relies on the *ms* macro package to handle margins, new lines, page numbers, and so on. The *sed* script also massages your file so that it will print anything that *troff* finds confusing—in particular, backslashes and lines beginning with periods or single quotation marks. In fact, it can even print a *troff* macro package; if memory serves me, that's why I originally wrote it.

I like this because it works as well as any other solution I've seen, and better than most; it's extremely simple; and, because it uses UNIX tools to do the work they were designed to do, it's a good demonstration of the UNIX philosophy. It's even elegant in its own bizarre way. And, if you know a little bit (not much) about *troff*, you can customize it for your own situation.

However, there are other solutions. Perhaps the best is to use the *enscript* program, which is part of Adobe's *transcript* package. That's proprietary software, so we can't include it with this book. But at least we can point you in the right direction.

pstext

One option that's "free" is Dan Judd's *pstext* program. Though it's small, it provides a lot of features. It emulates a standard line printer: it interprets form feeds as page breaks, handles backspaces and tabs appropriately, lets you vary the margin, the number of lines per page, and so on. Here's how to use it:

```
% pstext options file1 file2 ... | lpr
```

There are a zillion options, but the most important are:

-l   Print "landscape" (across the page, the long way); by default, printing is "portrait" (down the page).

-ld   Print landscape, "two-up" (two logical pages per physical page)—not too useful, unless your source file has short lines.

-d   Print portrait, "two up."

-s *p*   Use a font of size *p* (in points).

-f *name*
    Use the font with the given *name*.

-n *n*   Print *n* lines per page.

There are a number of other options, but these are the most important. Enjoy!

—*ML*

45.25   psselect: Print Some Pages from a PostScript file

psutils

The *psselect* program allows you to take a PostScript file and select individual pages for printing. It's part of Angus Duggan's *psutils* collection, a group of utilities for working with PostScript files. *psselect* produces a second PostScript file, which you can print using *lpr* or *lp*. It's easy to use; in the simplest form, just type:

```
% psselect -ppage-spec input output
```

where the *page-spec* can be a string of page numbers, or a "range" of page numbers separated by a dash, or even combinations. Pages are counted from 1, which is the first page of the document; *psselect* doesn't try to detect and decode any "page numbers" that may be part of your document. For example, to select pages 1 through 16 of the file *book.ps*, give the command:

```
% psselect -p1-16 book.ps first16.ps
```

Instead of a *–p* option, you can use *–e* to print the even-numbered pages only; or *–o* to print the odd-numbered pages. Add the *–r* option if you want to reverse the order in which pages are printed. On some laser printers (mostly older ones), this is a lot more convenient.

psselect only works on PostScript files that conform to the Adobe Document Structuring Conventions. I won't elaborate on those conventions, but I will say that PostScript files that obey these conventions are the exception, rather than the rule. Unfortunately, the PostScript language is entirely too flexible; it's impossible to write fully general programs for extracting pages (and the like) without processing the entire language.

Fortunately, Angus has written a few scripts that convert PostScript files generated by various word processors into a form that he can deal with. These filters are all written in the *perl* language *(39.01)*; here's a quick summary of what's available:

Name	Function
fixfmps	Fix FrameMaker files
fixwpps	Fix WordPerfect files
fixmacps	Fix Macintosh files
fixpspps	Fix PSPrint files

So to get the odd-numbered pages of a document called *fmdoc.ps*, which was generated with FrameMaker (in my experience, only UNIX versions of FrameMaker), give this command:

```
% fixfmps < fmdoc.ps | psprint -o > oddpages.ps
```

—*ML, AD*

45.26 *Other PostScript Utilities*

psutils

Angus Duggan's *psutils* package contains several interesting tools in addition to psselect *(45.25)*. They're a bit more esoteric, but they can be very useful in some situations: for example, if you're printing a brochure or a bulletin, these tools help to automate the task. I'll only summarize them quickly; you can look at Angus' manual pages for detailed information.

pstops   A general utility for rearranging pages in a PostScript document. You can select individual pages, put several pages on an individual page with different orientations, and so on.

psbook   Rearranges files in a PostScript document into "signatures"; that is, rearranges pages so that folding them "naturally" will result in a book or pamplet.

psnup   Rearranges a PostScript document so that it prints several pages on each sheet of paper, scaling and orienting the pages appropriately for a booklet. Together with *psbook*, *psnup* makes production of a booklet (or even a moderate-sized book) relatively easy.

As with *psbook*, you may need to use a preprocessor to put the PostScript file into an acceptable form. Angus has written filters for PostScript files generated by Frame, WordPerfect, the Macintosh, and PSPrint.

—ML, AD

45.27 *Extracting Text from a PostScript File*

It would be *really nice* to be able to get the text *out* of a PostScript file, wouldn't it? You could *grep* through files and extract interesting data automatically, perhaps even using *sed* or *perl* to do some clever processing on the text. I do this with my *troff* files all the time: write scripts to figure out which order to process them in based on the contents, etc.

Now that I've got you interested, I bet you thought I was going to introduce a PostScript text extractor. Well, sorry. As far as I know, there ain't no such thing. I've seen a number of attempts (you can find them by looking through *alt.sources* and other source code archives on Usenet), but nothing really works correctly. It's easy to write something that works correctly 10% of the time; quite a bit harder to write something that works 50% of the time; and very difficult to write something that works 90% of the time.* While this seems like it ought to be an easy problem, it isn't. I'll spare you the discussion of why.

Well, then, what's the point of this? Simple. I would really like to have a program that extracts the text from a PostScript file. I'm very disappointed that we weren't able to find something acceptable. So—if you've got a solution, and if your program isn't a quick hack that will fall apart on the first (or second) non-trivial test case, send it in. We'll test it, and if it works, you'll be in the next edition.

—ML

---

*It's impossible—or at least extremely difficult—to write something that works 100% of the time. We don't demand perfection, just something that's reasonably reliable.

45.28 The Portable Bitmap Package

There are dozens of formats used for graphics files across the computer industry. There are *tiff* files, *PICT* files, and *gif* files. There are different formats for displaying on different hardware, different formats for printing on different printers, and then there are the internal formats used by graphics programs. This means that importing a graphics file from one platform to another (or from one program to another) can be a large undertaking, requiring a filter written specially to convert from one format to the next.

pbmplus

The *pbmplus* package can be used to convert between a wide variety of graphics formats. The idea behind *pbm* is to use a set of very basic graphics formats that (almost) all formats can be converted into and then converted back from. This is much simpler than having converters to and from each individual format. These formats are known as *pbm*, *pgm*, and *ppm*: the portable bitmap, graymap, and pixmap formats. (A bitmap is a two-dimensional representation of an image; a graymap has additional information encoded that gives grayscale information for each bit; a pixmap encodes color information for each bit.) The name "*pnm*" is a generic name for all three portable interchange formats (with the *n* standing for "a*ny*"), and programs that work with all three are said to be "anymap" programs.

The *pbmplus* package contains well over a hundred conversion programs. There are three basic kind of programs:

- Programs that convert a graphics file to one of the *pnm* formats. For example, if I had a *tiff* file and I wanted to convert it to PostScript, I might start the process by using *tifftopnm*:

```
% tifftopnm Hobbes.tiff > Hobbes.pnm
```

- Programs that convert from one of the *pnm* formats to another format. For example, if I wanted to convert the *Hobbes.pnm* file directly to PostScript, I could use *pnmtops*:

```
% pnmtops Hobbes.pnm > Hobbes.ps
```

- Programs used to manipulate the image in *pnm* format. For example, if I wanted to crop the image, I could use *pnmcut* before I converted the file to PostScript and printed it:

```
% tifftopnm Hobbes.tiff > Hobbes.pnm
% pnmcut 10 10 200 200 Hobbes.pnm > Hobbes.cut
% pnmtops Hobbes.cut > Hobbes.ps
% lpr Hobbes.ps
```

or, on one command line (and without cluttering your disk with intermediary files):

```
% tifftopnm Hobbes.tiff | pnmcut 10 10 200 200 | pnmtops | lpr
```

I frequently like to create X11 bitmaps out of pictures in newspapers or magazines. The way I do this is to first scan the picture in on a Macintosh and save it as *tiff* or *PICT* format. Then I *ftp* the file to our UNIX system and convert it to *pnm* format, and then use *pbmtoxbm* to convert it to X bitmap format. If the picture is too big, I use *pnmscale* on the intermediary *pnm* file. If the picture isn't right-side-up, I can use *pnmrotate* and sometimes *pnmflip* before converting the *pnm* file to X11 bitmap format.

The programs provided with the *pbmplus* package are far too many to discuss in detail, and some of these formats are ones that you've probably never even heard of. But here's a summary of them. Table 45-2 lists the conversion programs. Table 45-3 lists the programs that perform various kinds of editing, enhancement, or transformations on image files.

Table 45-2. Image Format Conversion Programs

Format	To pnm	From pnm
ASCII graphics		*pbmtoascii*
Abekas YUV bytes	*yuvtoppm*	*ppmtoyuv*
Andrew Toolkit raster object	*atktopbm*	*pbmtoatk*
Atari Degas .pi1	*pi1toppm*	*ppmtopi1*
Atari Degas .pi3	*pi3topbm*	*pbmtopi3*
Atari compressed Spectrum file	*spctoppm*	
Atari uncompressed Spectrum file	*sputoppm*	
Bennet Yee "face" file	*ybmtopbm*	*pgmtoybm*
BitGraph graphics		*pbmtobg*
CMU window manager bitmap	*cmuwmtopbm*	*pbmtocmuwm*
DEC sixel format		*ppmtosixel*
Epson printer graphics		*pbmtoepson*
FITS	*fitstopgm*	*pgmtofits*
GEM .img file	*gemtopbm*	*pbmtogem*
GIF	*giftoppm*	*ppmtogif*
Gemini 10X printer graphics		*pbmto10x*
Gould scanner file	*gouldtoppm*	
GraphOn graphics (compressed)		*pbmtogo*
Group 3 fax file	*g3topbm*	*pbmtog3*
HIPS	*hipstopgm*	
HP LaserJet format		*pbmtolj*
HP PaintJet	*pjtoppm*	*ppmtopj*
IFF ILBM	*ilbmtoppm*	*ppmtoilbm*
Img-whatnot	*imgtoppm*	
Lisp Machine bitmap	*lispmtopgm*	*pgmtolispm*
MGR bitmap	*mgrtopbm*	*pbmtomgr*
MacPaint	*macptopbm*	*pbmtomacp*
Macintosh PICT	*picttoppm*	*ppmtopict*
Motif UIL icon file		*ppmtouil*
NCSA ICR format		*ppmtoicr*
PCX	*pcxtoppm*	*ppmtopcx*

Table 45-2. *Image Format Conversion Programs (continued)*

Format	To pnm	From pnm
PostScript "image" data	*psidtopgm*	
PostScript		*pnmtops*
Printronix printer graphics		*pbmtoptx*
Sun icon	*icontopbm*	*pbmtoicon*
Sun rasterfile	*rasttopnm*	*pnmtorast*
TIFF file	*tifftopnm*	*pnmtotiff*
TrueVision Targa file	*tgatoppm*	*ppmtotga*
Unix plot(5) file		*pbmtoplot*
Usenix FaceSaver(tm)	*fstopgm*	*pgmtofs*
X10 bitmap	*xbmtopbm*	*pbmtox10bm*
X10 window dump	*xwdtopnm*	
X11 "puzzle" file		*ppmtopuzz*
X11 bitmap	*xbmtopbm*	*pbmtoxbm*
X11 pixmap	*xpmtoppm*	*ppmtoxpm*
X11 window dump	*xwdtopnm*	*pnmtoxwd*
Xim file	*ximtoppm*	
Zinc bitmap		*pbmtozinc*
doodle brush	*brushtopbm*	
output from the MTV or PRT ray tracers	*mtvtoppm*	
output from the QRT ray tracer	*qrttoppm*	
portable bitmap		*pgmtopbm*
portable graymap		*ppmtopgm*
portable pixmap		*pgmtoppm*
raw RGB bytes	*rawtoppm*	
raw grayscale bytes	*rawtopgm*	
text	*pbmtext*	
three portable graymaps	*rgb3toppm*	*ppmtorgb3*
unknown		*anytopnm*

Table 45-3. Manipulating pnm Files

Program	Purpose
pbmlife	Apply Conway's rules of Life to a portable bitmap.
pbmmake	Create a blank bitmap of a specified size.
pbmmask	Create a mask bitmap from a regular bitmap.
pbmreduce	Read a portable bitmap and reduce it N times.
pbmupc	Create a Universal Product Code bitmap.
pgmbentley	Bentleyize a portable graymap.
pgmedge	Edge-detect a portable graymap.
pgmenhance	Edge-enhance a portable graymap.
pgmhist	Print a histogram of the values in a portable graymap.
pgmnorm	Normalize the contrast in a portable graymap.
pgmoil	Turn a portable graymap into an oil painting.
pgmramp	Generate a grayscale ramp.
pgmtexture	Calculate textural features on a portable graymap.
pnmarith	Perform arithmetic on two portable anymaps.
pnmcat	Concatenate portable anymaps.
pnmconvol	General MxN convolution on a portable anymap.
pnmcrop	Crop a portable anymap.
pnmcut	Cut a rectangle out of a portable anymap.
pnmdepth	Change the maxval in a portable anymap.
pnmenlarge	Read a portable anymap and enlarge it N times.
pnmfile	Describe a portable anymap.
pnmflip	Perform one or more flip operations on a portable anymap.
pnmgamma	Perform gamma correction on a portable anymap.
pnmindex	Build a visual index of a bunch of anymaps.
pnminvert	Invert a portable anymap.
pnmmargin	Add a border to a portable anymap.
pnmnoraw	Force a portable anymap into plain format.
pnmpaste	Paste a rectangle into a portable anymap.
pnmrotate	Rotate a portable anymap by some angle.
pnmscale	Scale a portable anymap.
pnmshear	Shear a portable anymap by some angle.
pnmsmooth	Smooth out an image.
pnmtile	Replicate a portable anymap into a specified size.
ppmdither	Ordered dither for color images.
ppmhist	Print a histogram of a portable pixmap.
ppmmake	Create a pixmap of a specified size and color.
ppmpat	Make a pretty pixmap.

Table 45-3. Manipulating pnm Files (continued)

Program	Purpose
ppmquant	Quantize the colors in a portable pixmap down to a specified number.
ppmquantall	Run *ppmquant* on a bunch of files all at once, so they share a common colormap.
ppmrelief	Run a Laplacian relief filter on a portable pixmap.
sxpm	Show an XPM (X PixMap) file and/or convert XPM2 files to XPM version 3.

bitmaps

The *pbmplus* package is also distributed with a set of public domain bitmaps. We've put these bitmaps on the Power Tools disk as well.

—*LM*

Part Eight

Shell Programming

The shell is the ultimate UNIX power tool.

It is the design of the shell—including basic features like pipes, filters, and redirection, and the idea of an environment where small programs can do big things by working together—that makes all the rest possible.

—TOR

46

Shell Programming
for the Uninitiated

46.01 Everyone Should Learn some Shell Programming

One of the great things about UNIX is that it's made up of individual utilities, "building blocks" like *cat* and *grep*, that you run from a shell prompt. Using pipes, redirection, filters, and so on, you can combine those utilities to do an incredible number of things. Shell programming lets you take the same commands you'd type at a shell prompt—and put them into a file you can run by just typing its name. You can make new programs that combine UNIX programs (and other shell scripts) in your own way to do exactly what you need. If you don't like the way a program works, you can write a shell script to do just what you want.

Because many UNIX users use the shell every day, they don't need to learn a whole new language for programming... just some tips and techniques. In fact, this chapter covers a lot of programming techniques that you'll want to use even when you aren't programming. For example, loops and tests are handy on the command line.

(This series of articles does assume that you've written programs in some language before, or are generally familiar with programming concepts. If you haven't, you should start with a more comprehensive shell programming book like *UNIX Shell Programming* by Kochan and Wood.)

Some of the topics you need to learn about as a beginning shell programmer have already been covered in other chapters. Here are the articles you'll probably want to read—in an order that makes sense if you're looking for something of a tutorial:

- To see how to write a simple shell program, article 46.02.

- For explanation of shells in general, article 46.03.

- To test how your system executes files so you'll know how to write your shell programs, article 46.04.

- To read about environment and shell variables in articles 7.01 and 7.08, respectively.

- The *echo* command is covered by article 9.04.

- Shell quoting is explained in article 9.10.

- Test strings with a *case* structure, article 46.05. Match patterns in a *case* structure, article 46.06.

- Use the output of one command as arguments to another command with command substitution, article 10.14.

- Find out whether a program worked or failed with its exit status, article 46.07.

- Test a program's exit status and do different things if it worked or failed, articles 46.08 and 46.09.

- Loop through a set of commands and use another command to control that loop, article 46.10.

- Set exit status of a shell (shell script), article 46.11.

- Handle interrupts (like CTRL-c) and other signals, article 46.12.

- Read input from the keyboard, article 46.13.

- Handle command line arguments (options, filenames, etc.), article 46.14.

- Step through arguments, or any list of words, with a *for* loop, articles 10.10 and 46.15.

- Handle arguments with the *while* and *shift* commands, article 46.16.

- Handle command-line arguments in a more standard and portable way with *getopt*, article 46.17.

- Set shell options and command-line arguments with the *set* command, article 46.18.

- Test files and strings of characters with the *test* command, article 46.19.

- Pick a name for a new command with no conflict, article 46.20.

- Find the name of a program and use it in the script, article 46.21.

- Use "subprograms" that can change the current environment, article 46.22.

This chapter discusses only Bourne shell programming. In most cases, the C shell isn't great for shell programming *(49.02)*.

A note about command versions: unfortunately, the same commands on different versions of UNIX can have different options. Some Bourne shells are a little different than others. For instance, some *test (46.19)* commands have a –*x* option to test for an executable file; others don't. As article 48.10 explains, some *echo* commands use a –*n* option to mean "no newline at the end of this string"; others have you put \c at the end of the string. And so on. Where there are differences, these articles generally use the commands in Berkeley 4.3 BSD UNIX. If a command doesn't seem to work on your system, check its online manual page or the *sh* manual page.

—JP

46.02 Writing a Simple Shell Program

A shell script need be no more than a complex command line saved in a file. For example, let's assume that you'd like a compact list of all the users who are currently logged in on the system.

A command like this might do the trick:

```
% who | cut -c1-8 | sort -u | pr -l1 -8 -w78 -t
```

A list of logged-in users should come out in columns, looking something like this:

```
abraham   appleton biscuit  charlie  charlott fizzie   howard   howie
hstern    jerry    kosmo    linda    ocshner  peterson root     ross
sutton    yuppie
```

We used four UNIX commands joined with pipes:

1. who gives a list of all users.

2. cut -c1-8 *(36.12)* outputs columns 1-8 of the *who* output—the usernames. If your system doesn't have *cut*, use the command colrm 9 *(36.13)*.

3. The sort -u *(37.06)* puts names in order and takes out names of users who are logged on more than once.

4. The pr -l1 -8 -w78 -t *(36.15)* takes the list of usernames, one per line, and makes it into 8 columns on 78-character-wide lines. (The -l1 is the lowercase letter *L* followed by the digit *1*.)

If you wanted to do this frequently, wouldn't it be better if all you had to do was type something like:

```
% loggedin
```

to get the same result? Here's how:

1. Start your favorite text editor (Emacs, *vi*, whatever) on a new file named *loggedin*.

2. If your system supports the special #! notation *(46.04)*, the first line of the script file should be:

```
#! /bin/sh
```

Otherwise, leave the first line blank. (When the first line of a script is blank, most shells will start a Bourne shell to read it. Articles 47.02 and 47.06 have more information.)

I think that the second line of a shell script should always be a comment to explain what the script does. (Use more than one line, if you want.) A comment starts with a hash mark (#); all characters after it on the line are ignored:

```
# loggedin - list logged-in users, once per user, in 8 columns
```

Put this on the third line, just like you did on the command line:

```
who | cut -c1-8 | sort -u | pr -l1 -8 -w78 -t
```

(As I explained earlier, you might need *colrm* instead of *cut*.)

3. Save the file and leave the editor. You've just written a shell script.

4. Next, you need to make the shell script you just wrote executable. The *chmod (23.07)* (change mode) command is used to change permissions on a file. The plus sign followed by an x (+x) makes the file executable:

```
% chmod +x loggedin
```

5. If your account uses the C shell, you'll need to reset its command search table. To do that, type:

rehash *5.02*

```
% rehash
```

6. Finally, try the script. Just type its name and it should run:

```
% loggedin
```

If that doesn't run, your current directory may not be in your shell's command search path. In that case, try this:

```
% ./loggedin
```

If it still doesn't work, and you started the first line of your script with #!, be sure that the Bourne shell's pathname on that line (like /bin/sh) is correct.

7. If you want to run the script from somewhere other than the current directory, or if you want other programs and scripts you write to be able to use it, you need to put it in a directory that's in your search path *(9.05)*. If you're the only person who plans to use the script, you should put it in your personal *bin* directory *(5.02)*. Otherwise, you might ask your system administrator if there's a systemwide directory for local commands.

—JP

46.03 What's a Shell, Anyway?

A *shell* is a program that interprets your command lines and runs other programs. Another name for the shell is "command interpreter." This article covers the two major UNIX shells, including discussion about how shells run, how they search for programs, and how they read shell script files.

How Shells Run Other Programs

For each command it runs, a shell does a series of steps. First, if the shell is reading commands from a terminal (interactively), it prints a prompt (such as a % or $) and waits for you to type something. Next, the shell reads the command line (like *cat −v afile bfile > cfile*), interprets it *(9.01, 9.03)*, and runs that command line. When the command finishes running (unless the command is in the background *(1.26, 1.27)*), the shell is ready to read another command line.

Interactive Use vs. Shell Scripts

A shell can read command lines from a terminal or it can read them from a file. When you put command lines into a file, that file is called a *shell script* or shell program. The shell handles the shell script just as it handles the commands you type from a terminal (though it doesn't print the % or $ prompts). With this information, you already know how to write simple shell scripts—just put commands in a file and feed them to the shell!

In addition though, there are a number of programming constructs that make it possible to write shell programs that are much more powerful than just a list of commands.

Types of Shells

There are two main kinds of shells in UNIX:

- The *C shell* (*csh*) is especially good for working on a terminal. *csh* will read shell scripts and has some useful features for programmers. Unfortunately, it has some quirks *(49.02)* that can make shell programming tough.

- The *Bourne shell* (*sh*) and shells like it, are probably used more often for shell programming. (Some newer *sh*-like shells, including *ksh* and *bash (1.08)*, combine handy interactive C shell-like features with Bourne shell syntax.)

Shell Search Paths

As article 9.05 explains, if the shell is trying to run a command and the command isn't built-in to the shell itself, it looks in a list of directories called a *search path*. UNIX systems have standard directories with names like */bin* and */usr/bin* that hold standard UNIX programs. Almost everyone's search path has these directories.

If you do much shell programming, you should make a directory on your account for executable files. Most people name theirs *bin* and put it under the home directory. See article 5.02.

Bourne Shell Used Here

Most serious shell programmers write their scripts for the Bourne shell. So do we.

Newer Bourne shells have features—like shell functions *(11.10)*, an *unset* command for shell variables, and others—that the earlier *Version 7* Bourne shell didn't. Most scripts in this book are written to work on all Bourne shells, though—for portability, the scripts don't use these new features.

For the rest of these introductory articles, it may be easier if you have a terminal close by so you can try the examples. If your account uses the Bourne shell or one of its relatives (*ksh*, *bash*, etc.), your prompt probably has a dollar sign ($) in it. If your account isn't running the Bourne shell, start one by typing sh. Your prompt should change to a dollar sign ($). You'll be using the Bourne shell until you type CTRL-d at the start of a line:

```
% sh
$
$ ...Enter commands...
$ CTRL-d
%
```

—*JP* from the Nutshell Handbook *MH & xmh: E-Mail for Users & Programmers*

46.04 Testing How your System Executes Files

Your version of UNIX may understand the #! notation. This is a way to tell UNIX which shell should execute the commands in your file.* If your UNIX doesn't recognize #!, you'll need to be sure that you know how to make it read shell scripts using the Bourne shell—regardless of the shell you use interactively—because most scripts in this book are for the Bourne shell.

To test your system, let's make a two-line file named *testing*.

Note: Do not make programs named *test*. There's an important system command named *test (46.19)*, and your command might be used, accidentally, instead of the system program. Name your test programs *testing*, *atest*, whatever—just not *test*.

Article 46.20 shows how to find a unique filename.

---

1. Make a file named *testing* (use an editor, or just make the file by hand with cat > testing *(26.02)*). Put the following two lines in the file. Be sure to

---

*Actually, you can use #! to specify any interpreter program *(47.03)*, not just a shell.

start on the *first* line of the file, and type this text just as it's shown. Be sure that the hash mark (#) is at the left-hand edge (column 1) of the first line:

```
#! /bin/echo just
export stuff
```

2. Exit the editor and save the file. Make the file executable by typing chmod +x testing *(46.02)*.

Now run the program by typing its name at a shell prompt. There are four kinds of responses:

1. If this happens, then the #! is working. You'll be able to tell your system which shell should run each script:

```
% testing
just testing
%
```

2. If this happens, then your UNIX doesn't understand #!, but it ran your program with the Bourne shell anyhow:

```
% testing
%
```

3. If this happens, then your system ran the program with an older version of the Bourne shell. You should not use comment lines starting with a hash mark (#):

```
% testing
#!: not found
%
```

4. If this happens, then your UNIX doesn't understand #!, and it ran your program with the C shell:

```
% testing
export: Command not found.
%
```

Many UNIX systems, especially newer ones, will answer just testing. That's because, as article 47.05 explains, the UNIX kernel strips off the #! from the start of the line, adds the script file's name to the end of it, and runs it:

```
/bin/echo just testing
```

If your system ran the shell script with the C shell, find a way to make it use the Bourne shell instead. It's best to ask a local expert such as your system administrator.

—*JP* from the Nutshell Handbook *MH & xmh: E-Mail for Users & Programmers*

46.05 Test String Values with Bourne Shell case

Each time you type a command line at a shell prompt, you can see what happens and decide what command to run next. But a shell script needs to make decisions like that itself. A *case* structure helps the script make decisions. A *case* structure compares a string (usually taken from a shell or environment variable *(7.08, 7.01)*) to one or more patterns. The patterns can be simple strings (words, digits, etc.) or they can be *case* wildcard expressions *(46.06)*. When the *case* finds a pattern that matches the string, it executes one or more commands.

Here's an example. It tests your *TERM (6.11)* environment variable. If you're using a vt100 or tk4023 terminal, it runs a command to send some characters to your terminal. If you aren't on either of those, it prints an error and quits:

```
                case "$TERM" in
echo...\027' 47.34   vt100)   echo 'ea[w' | tr 'eaw' '\033\001\027' ;;
                tk4023)  echo "*[p23" ;;
                *)   # Not a VT100 or tk4023.  Print error message:
    1>&2 9.04           echo "progname: quitting: you aren't on a VT100 or tx4023." 1>&2
    exit 40.04          exit
                     ;;
                esac
```

Here are more details about how this works. The structure compares the string between the words `case` and `in` to the strings at the left-hand edge of the lines ending with a `)` (right parenthesis) character. If it matches the first case (in this example, if it's the `vt100`), the command up to the `;;` is executed. The `;;` means "jump to the `esac`" (*esac* is "case" spelled backwards). You can put as many commands as you want before each `;;`, but put each command on a separate line.

If the first pattern doesn't match, the shell tries the next case—here, *tk4023*. As above, a match runs the command and jumps to the *esac*. No match? The next pattern is the wildcard `*`. It matches any answer other than *vt100* or *tk4023* (such as *xterm* or an empty string).

You can use as many patterns as you want to. The first one that matches is used. It's okay if none of them match. The style doesn't matter much. Pick one that's readable and be consistent.

—*JP* from the Nutshell Handbook *MH & xmh: E-Mail for Users & Programmers*

46.06 Pattern Matching in case Structures

A *case* structure *(46.05)* is good at string pattern matching. Its "wildcard" pattern-matching meta-characters work like the filename wildcards in the shell, with a few twists. Here are some examples:

?) Matches a string with exactly one character like a, 3, !, and so on.

?*) Matches a string with one or more characters (a non-empty string).

[yY]|[yY][eE][sS])
  Matches y, Y or yes, YES, YeS, etc. The | means "or."

/*/*[0-9])
  Matches a file pathname, like */xxx/yyy/somedir/file2*, that starts with a slash, contains at least one more slash, and ends with a digit.

'What now?')
  Matches the pattern What now?. The quotes *(9.10)* tell the shell to treat the string literally: not to break it at the space and not to treat the ? as a wildcard.

"$msgs") Matches the contents of the *msgs* variable. The double quotes let the shell substitute the variable's value; the quotes also protect spaces and other special characters from the shell.

—*JP* from the Nutshell Handbook *MH & xmh: E-Mail for Users & Programmers*

46.07 Exit Status of UNIX Processes

When a UNIX process (command) runs, it can return a numeric status value to the process (command) that started it. The status can tell the calling process whether the command succeeded or failed. Many (but not all) UNIX commands return a status of zero if everything was okay or non-zero (1, 2, etc.) if something went wrong. A few commands, like *grep* and *diff*, return a different non-zero status for different kinds of problems; see your online manual pages to find out.

The Bourne shell puts the exit status of the previous command in the question mark (?) variable. You can get its value by preceding it with a dollar sign ($), just like any other shell variable. For example, when *cp* copies a file, it sets the status to 0. If something goes wrong, *cp* sets the status to 1:

```
$ cp afile /tmp
$ echo $?
0
$ cp afiel /tmp
cp: afiel: No such file or directory
$ echo $?
1
```

In the C shell, use the *status* variable instead:

```
% cp afiel /tmp
cp: afiel: No such file or directory
% echo $status
1
```

Of course, you usually don't have to display the exit status in this way, because there are several ways *(46.08, 46.09, 46.19)* to use the exit status of one command as a condition of further execution.

There are a few sticky points. The exit status of pipes *(1.04)* isn't defined everywhere; where it is defined, the definition varies. You can't test the exit status of background jobs in the Bourne shell.

—*JP* from the Nutshell Handbook *MH & xmh: E-Mail for Users & Programmers*

46.08 *Test Exit Status with the "if" Structure*

If you are going to write a shell script of any complexity at all, you need some way to write "conditional expressions." Conditional expressions are nothing more than statements that have a value of "true" or "false": like "Have I gotten dressed today?" or "Is it before 5 p.m.?" or "Does the file *indata* exist?" or "Is the value of $aardvark greater than 60?"

The UNIX shell is a complete programming language. Therefore, it allows you to write "if" statements with conditional expressions—just like C, Basic, Pascal, or any other language. Conditional expressions can also be used in several other situations; but most obviously, they're the basis for any sort of *if* statement. Here's the syntax of an *if* statement for the Bourne shell:

```
if conditional
then
    # do this if conditional returns a zero ("true") status
    one-or-more-commands
else
    # do this if conditional returns non-zero ("false") status
    one-or-more-commands
fi
```

You can omit the *else* and the block of code following it. However, you can't omit the *then* or the *fi*. If you want to omit the *then* (i.e., if you want to do someting special when *condition* is false, but nothing when it is true), write the statement like this:

```
if conditional
then
    :     # do nothing
else
    # do this if conditional returns non-zero ("false") status
    one-or-more-commands
fi
```

Note that this uses a special null command, a colon (:) *(47.09)*. There's another, more useful way of expressing the inverse of a condition (do something if *conditional* is not "true"), the || operator *(46.09)* (two vertical bars).

Don't forget the *fi* terminating the loop. This is a surprisingly common source of bugs. (At least for me.)

Another common debugging problem: the manual pages that discuss this material imply that you can smash the *if*, the *then*, and the *else* onto one line. Well, it's true, but it's not always easy. Do yourself a favor: write your *if* statements *exactly* like the one above. You'll rarely be disappointed, and you may even start writing programs that work correctly the first time.

Here's a real-life example: a shell script named *bkedit* that makes a backup copy of a file before editing it. If *cp* returns a zero status, the script edits the file; otherwise, it prints a message. (The $1 is replaced with the first filename from the command line—see article 46.14.)

```
#! /bin/sh
if cp "$1" "$1.bak"
then
    vi "$1"
else
    echo "bkedit quitting: can't make backup?" 1>&2
fi
```

1>&2 *9.04*

You can try typing in that shell script and running it. Or, just type in the lines (starting with the if) on a terminal running the Bourne shell; use a real filename instead of $1.

The *if* structure is often used with a command named *test* *(46.19)*. The *test* command does a test and returns an exit status of 0 or 1.

—ML, JP

46.09 Testing Your Success

The Bourne and Korn shells let you test for success right on the command line. This gives you a very efficient way to write quick and comprehensible shell scripts.

I'm referring to the || and && operators; in particular, the || operator. *comm1* || *comm2* is typically explained as "execute the command on the right if the command on the left failed." I prefer to explain it as an "either-or" construct: "execute either *comm1* or *comm2*." While this isn't really precise, let's see what it means in context:

```
cat filea fileb > filec || exit
```

This means "either *cat* the files or *exit*." If you can't *cat* the files (if *cat* returns an exit status of 1), you exit *(40.04)*. If you can *cat* the files, you don't exit; you execute the left side *or* the right side.

I'm stretching normal terminology a bit here, but I think it's necessary to clarify the purpose of | |. By the way, we could give the poor user an error message before flaming out:

1>&2 *9.04*

```
cat filea fileb > filec || {
        echo sorry, no dice 1>&2
        exit 1
}
```

Similarly, *comm1* && *comm2* means "execute *comm1* AND *comm2*," or execute *comm2* if *comm1* succeeds. (But if you can't execute the first, don't do any.) This might be helpful if you want to print a temporary file and delete it immediately.

```
lpr file && rm file
```

If *lpr* fails for some reason, you want to leave the file around. Again, I want to stress how to read this: print the file and delete it. (Implicitly: if you don't print it, don't delete it.)

—*ML*

46.10 Loops that Test Exit Status

The Bourne shell has two kinds of loops that run a command and test its exit status. An *until* loop will continue until the command returns a zero status. A *while* loop will continue until the command returns a non-zero status.

Looping until a Command Succeeds

The *until* loop runs a command repeatedly until it succeeds. That is, if the command returns a non-zero status, the shell executes the body of the loop and then runs the loop control command again. The shell keeps running the command until it returns a zero status, as shown in the following example:

```
% cat sysmgr
#! /bin/sh
until who | grep "^barb "
do sleep 60
done
echo The system manager just logged on.
% sysmgr &
[1] 2345
        ...time passes...
barb     ttyp7    Jul 15 09:30
The system manager just logged on.
```

The loop runs *who (53.04)* and pipes that output to *grep (28.01)*, which searches for any line starting with *barb* and a space. (The space makes sure that usernames like *barbara* don't match.) If *grep* returns non-zero* (no lines matched), the shell waits 60 seconds. Then the loop repeats, and the script tries the who | grep command again. It keeps doing this until *grep* returns a zero status—then the loop is broken and control goes past the done line. The *echo* command prints a message and the script quits. (I ran this script in the background *(1.26)* so I could do something else while I waited for Barb.)

[A Bourne shell *until* loop is *not* identical to the *until* construction in most programming languages, because the condition is evaluated at the top of the loop. Virtually all languages with an *until* loop evaluate the condition at the bottom.—*ML*]

Looping until a Command Fails

catsaway

The *while* loop is the opposite of the *until* loop. A *while* loop runs a command and loops until the command fails (returns a non-zero status). The *catsaway* program below uses a *while* loop to watch the *who* output for the system manager to log off. It's the opposite of the *sysmgr* script.

/dev/null *14.14*

```
% cat catsaway
#! /bin/sh
while who | grep "^barb " > /dev/null
do sleep 60
done
echo "The cat's away..."
% catsaway &
[1] 4567
    ...time passes...
The cat's away...
```

—*JP* from the Nutshell Handbook *MH & xmh: E-Mail for Users & Programmers*

46.11 Set Exit Status of a Shell (Script)

Most standard UNIX commands return a status *(46.07)*. Your shell script should, too. This section shows how to set the right exit status for both normal exits and error exits.

To end a shell script and set its exit status, use the *exit* command. Give *exit* the exit status that your script should have. If it has no explicit status, it will exit with the status of the last command run.

---

*The loop is actually testing the exit status of the whole pipeline, a big questionmark that's defined differently in different shells (if it's defined at all). Check your shell's online manual page. If your shell doesn't define the exit status of a pipeline and you're doing something critical, you should probably use a temporary file *(22.03)* and split the pipeline into several commands before the *do* statement *(47.19)*.

Here's an example: a rewrite of the *bkedit* script from article 46.08. If the script can make a backup copy, the editor is run and the script returns the exit status from *vi* (usually 0). If something goes wrong with the copy, the script prints an error and returns an exit status of 1. Here's the script:

bkedit

```
#! /bin/sh
if cp "$1" "$1.bak"
then
    vi "$1"
    exit    # USE STATUS FROM vi
else
    echo "bkedit quitting: can't make backup?"
    exit 1
fi
```

Here's what happens if I run it without a filename:

```
$ bkedit
cp: usage: cp fn1 fn2 or cp fn1 [fn2...] dir
bkedit quitting: can't make backup?
```

And here's what's left in the exit status variable:

```
$ echo $?
1
```

—*JP* from the Nutshell Handbook *MH & xmh: E-Mail for Users & Programmers*

46.12 Trapping Exits Caused by Interrupts

If you're running a shell script and you press your interrupt key *(6.09)* (like CTRL-c), the shell quits right away. That can be a problem if you use temporary files in your script because the sudden exit might leave the temporary files there. The *trap* command lets you tell the shell what to do before it exits. A *trap* can be used for a normal exit, too. See Table 46-1.

Here's a script named *zpg* that uses a temporary file named */tmp/zpg$$* in a system temporary-file directory *(22.03)*. The shell will replace $$ with its process ID number *(40.03)*. Because no other process will have the same ID number, that file should have a unique name. The script uncompresses *(25.06)* the file named on its command line, then starts the *pg* file viewer.* The script uses *trap*s—so it will clean up the temporary files, even if the user presses CTRL-c. The script also sets a default exit status of 1 that's reset to 0 if *pg* quits on its own (without an interrupt).

```
#! /bin/sh
# zpg - UNCOMPRESS FILE, DISPLAY WITH pg
# Usage: zpg file
stat=1  # DEFAULT EXIT STATUS; RESET TO 0 BEFORE NORMAL EXIT
temp=/tmp/zpg$$
trap 'rm -f $temp; exit $stat' 0
trap 'echo "`basename $0`: Ouch! Quitting early." 1>&2' 1 2 15
```
exit 46.11

*The script could run zcat $1 | pg directly, but *pg* can't back up when it's reading from a pipe.

```
case $# in
1) zcat "$1" >$temp
   pg $temp
   stat=0
   ;;
*) echo "Usage: `basename $0` filename" 1>&2 ;;
esac
```

There are two *traps* in the script:

- The first *trap*, ending with the number 0, is executed for all shell exits—normal or interrupted. It runs the command line between the single quotes. In this example, there are two commands separated with a semicolon (;). The first command removes the temporary file (using the –f option *(24.09)*, so *rm* won't give an error message if the file doesn't exist yet). The second command exits with the value stored in the *stat* shell variable. Look ahead at the rest of the script—$stat will always be 1 unless the *pg* command quit on its own, in which case *stat* will be reset to 0. Therefore, this shell script will always return the right exit status—if it's interrupted before it finishes, it'll return 1; otherwise, 0.*

- The second *trap* has the numbers 1 2 15 at the end. These are signal numbers that correspond to different kinds of interrupts. There's a short list in Table 46-1. For a list of all signals, see your online *signal*(3) reference page.

  This trap is done on an abnormal exit (like CTRL-c). It prints a message, but it could run any list of commands.

Table 46-1. Some UNIX Signal Numbers for trap Commands

Signal Number	Signal Name	Explanation
0	Normal exit	*exit* command.
1	SIGHUP	When session disconnected.
2	SIGINT	Interrupt—often CTRL-c.
15	SIGTERM	From *kill* command.

Shell scripts don't always have two *traps*. Look at the *nom (16.10)* script for an example.

Also, notice that the *echo* commands in the script have 1>&2 *(47.21)* at the end. That tells the Bourne shell to put the output of the *echo* command on the standard error instead of the standard output. This is a good idea because it helps to make sure that errors come to your screen instead of being redirected to a file or down a pipe with the other standard output text. (In this particular script,

---

*It's important to use single quotes, rather than double quotes, around the *trap*. That way, the value of $stat won't be interpreted until the trap is actually executed when the script exits.

that doesn't matter much because the script is used interactively. But it's a good habit to get into for all of your scripts.)

—JP from the Nutshell Handbook MH & xmh: E-Mail for Users & Programmers

46.13 *read: Reading from the Keyboard*

The Bourne shell *read* command reads a line of one or more words from the keyboard (or standard input) and stores the words in one or more shell variables. This is usually what you use to read an answer from the keyboard. For example:

```
echo -n "Type the filename: "
read filename
```

- If you give the name of one shell variable, *read* stores everything from the line into that variable:

    ```
    read varname
    ```

- If you name more than one variable, the first word typed goes into the first variable, the second word into the second variable, and so on . . . all leftover words go into the last variable. So, for example, with these commands:

    ```
    echo -n "Enter first and last name: "
    read fn ln
    ```

    If a user types John Smith, the word *John* would be available from $fn and *Smith* would be in $ln. If the user types Jane de Boes, then *Jane* would be in $fn and the two words *de Boes* are in $ln.

The *grabchars* (47.31) program lets you read from the keyboard without needing to press RETURN.

—JP

46.14 *Handling Command-line Arguments in Shell Scripts*

To write flexible shell scripts, you usually want to give them command-line arguments. As you've seen in other articles (46.11, 46.12), $1 holds the first command-line argument. The Bourne shell can give you arguments through the ninth, $9. The Korn Shell and some other newer Bourne-type shells understand ${10} for the tenth argument, and so on. (Article 9.03 has an overview of the shell's command-line handling.)

With the "$@" Parameter

If you've been reading this series (46.01) of articles in order, you saw the *zpg* (46.12) script that accepted just one command-line argument. Wouldn't it be nice to pass *zpg* all the command-line arguments so that it could handle any number of filenames? (Say "yes," please!)

Okay; you talked me into it. If you put `"$@"` in a script, the shell will replace that string with a quoted *(9.10)* set of the script's command-line arguments. Then you can pass as many arguments as you want, including filenames with unusual characters *(24.10)*:

```
% zpg report memo "savearts/What's next?"
```

The third filename is perfectly legal; we see more and more of them on our system—especially filesystems that are networked to computers like the Macintosh, where spaces and other "special" characters in filenames are common. Double-quoting all arguments through the script helps to be sure that the script can handle these unusual (but legal!) filenames.

In this case, we want the arguments to be passed to the *zcat* command. Let's change the *zpg* script to read:

```
zcat "$@" >$temp
```

When the shell runs the script with the arguments shown above, the command line will become:

```
zcat "report" "memo" "savearts/What's next?" >/tmp/zpg12345
```

Note: On some Bourne shells, if there are no command-line arguments, the `"$@"` becomes a single empty argument *(48.07)*, as if you'd typed this:

```
zcat "" >/tmp/zpg12345
```

In this case, the *zcat* command would complain that it can't find a file. (Of course, in this script, the *case* would prevent this problem. But not all scripts test the number of arguments.)

On those shells, you can replace `"$@"` with `${1+"$@"}` *(47.12)*. That means that if `$1` is defined, `"$@"` should be used. A less-good fix is to replace `"$@"` with `$*`. It gives you an unquoted list of command-line arguments; that's usually fine but can cause trouble on filenames with special characters in them.

With a Loop

A *for* loop *(46.15)* can step through all command-line arguments, one by one. You can also use a *while* loop *(46.10)* that tests `$#` (see below) and removes the arguments one by one with the *shift* command *(46.16)*. The *getopt* and *getopts* *(46.17)* commands handle arguments in a more standard way.

Counting Arguments with $#

The `$#` parameter counts the number of command-line arguments. For instance, if there are three arguments, `$#` will contain 3. This is usually used for error-checking (as in the *zpg* script in article 46.12) with *case (46.05)* or *test (46.19)*.

—*JP* from the Nutshell Handbook *MH & xmh: E-Mail for Users & Programmers*

46.15 Handling Command-line Arguments with a for Loop

Sometimes you want a script that will step through the command-line arguments one by one. (The "$@" parameter *(46.14)* gives you all of them at once.) The Bourne shell *for* loop can do this. The *for* loop looks like this:

```
for arg in list
do
    ...handle $arg...
done
```

If you omit the in *list*, the loop steps through the command-line arguments. It puts the first command-line argument in *arg* (or whatever else you choose to call the shell variable *(7.08)*), then executes the commands from do to done. Then it puts the next command-line argument in *arg*, does the loop... and so on... ending the loop after handling all the arguments.

For an example of a *for* loop, let's hack on the *zpg (46.12)* script.

```
#! /bin/sh
# zpg - UNCOMPRESS FILE(S), DISPLAY WITH pg
# Usage: zpg [pg options] file [...files]
stat=1  # DEFAULT EXIT STATUS; RESET TO 0 BEFORE NORMAL EXIT
temp=/tmp/zpg$$
trap 'rm -f $temp; exit $stat' 0
trap 'echo "`basename $0`: Ouch! Quitting early..." 1>&2' 1 2 15

files= switches=
for arg
do
```
case *46.06*
```
    case "$arg" in
    -*) switches="$switches $arg" ;;
    *)  files="$files $arg" ;;
    esac
done

case "$files" in
"") echo "Usage: `basename $0` [pg options] file [files]" 1>&2 ;;
*)  for file in $files
    do zcat "$file" | pg $switches
    done
    stat=0
    ;;
esac
```

We added a *for* loop to get and check each command-line argument. For example, let's say that a user typed:

% zpg -n afile ../bfile

The first pass through the *for* loop, $arg is −n. Because the argument starts with a minus sign (−), the *case* treats it as an option. Now the switches variable is replaced by its previous contents (an empty string), a space, and −n. Control goes to the esac and the loop repeats with the next argument.

The next argument, afile, doesn't look like an option. So now the files variable will contain a space and afile.

The loop starts over once more, with `../bfile` in `$arg`. Again, this looks like a file, so now `$files` has `afile ../bfile`. Because `../bfile` was the last argument, the loop ends; `$switches` has the options and `$files` has all the other arguments.

Next, we added another *for* loop. This one has the word in followed by `$files`, so the loop steps through the contents of `$files`. The loop runs *zcat* on each file, piping it to *pg* with any switches you gave.

Note that `$switches` isn't quoted *(9.10)*. This way, if `$switches` is empty, the shell won't pass an empty argument to *pg*. Also, if `$switches` has more than one switch, the shell will break the switches into separate arguments at the spaces and pass them individually to *pg*.

You can use a *for* loop with any space-separated list of words, not just filenames. You don't have to use a shell variable as the list; you can use command substitution *(10.14)* (backquotes), shell wildcards *(16.02)*, or just "hardcode" the list of words:

```
                for person in Joe Leslie Edie Allan
                do
 – 14.13            echo "Dear $person," | cat - form_letter | lpr
lpr 45.02       done
```

The *getopt* and *getopts* *(46.17)* commands handle command-line arguments in a more standard way than *for* loops.

—JP from the Nutshell Handbook MH & xmh: E-Mail for Users & Programmers

46.16 *Handling Arguments with while and shift*

A *for* loop *(46.15)* is great if you want to handle all of the command-line arguments to a script, one by one. But, as is often the case, some arguments are options that have their own arguments. For example, in the command `grep -f filename`, *filename* is an argument to *–f*; the option and its argument need to be processed together. One good way to handle this is with a combination of *while (46.10)*, *test (46.19)*, *case (46.05)*, and *shift*. Here's the basic construct:

```
                while [ $# -gt 0 ]
                do
                    case "$1" in
                        -a) options="$options $1";;
                            ...
                        -f) options="$options $1"
                            argfile="$2"
                            shift
                            ;;
                         *) files="$files $1";;
                    esac
                    shift
                done
```

The trick is this: *shift* removes an argument from the script's argument list, shifting all the others over by one ($1 disappears, $2 becomes $1, $3 becomes $2 and so on). To handle an option with its own argument, do another *shift*. The *while* loop uses *test (46.19)* to check that $#—the number of arguments—is greater than zero, and keeps going until this is no longer true, which only happens when they have all been used up.

Meanwhile, all the *case* has to do is to test $1 against the desired option strings. In the simple example shown above, we simply assume that anything beginning with a minus sign is an option, which we (presumably) want to pass on to some program that is being invoked by the script. So all we do is build up a shell variable that will eventually contain all of the options. It would be quite possible to do anything else instead, perhaps setting other shell variables or executing commands.

We assume that anything without a minus sign is a file. This last case could be written more robustly with a *test* to be sure the argument is a file. Here's an example of a simple script that uses this construct to pass an option and some files to *pr* and from there to a program that converts text to PostScript and on to the print spooler:

```
while [ $# -ne 0 ]
do
    case $1 in
        +*) pages="$1" ;;
         *) if [ -f "$1" ]; then
                files="$files $1"
            else
                echo "$0: file $1 not found" 1>&2
            fi;;
    esac
    shift
done
pr $pages $files | psprint | lpr
```

This approach is perhaps obsolete if you have *getopts (46.17)*, since *getopts* lets you recognize option strings like -abc as being equivalent to -a -b -c but I still find it handy.

—*TOR*

46.17 *Standard Command-line Parsing*

Most shell scripts need to handle command-line arguments—options, filenames, and so on. Articles 46.14, 46.15, and 46.16 show how to parse command lines with any Bourne shell. Those methods have two problems. You can't combine arguments with a single dash, e.g., -abc instead of -a -b -c. You also can't specify arguments to options without a space in between, e.g., -b*arg* in addition to -b *arg*.*

---

*Although most UNIX commands allow this, it is actually contrary to the Command Syntax Standard Rules in *intro* of the User's Manual. The version of *getopt* on the Power Tools disk supports this syntax. The *getopts* we've seen also support this, but may not in future releases.

Your Bourne shell may have a built-in command named *getopts**. *getopts* lets you deal with multiple complex options without these constraints. To find out whether your shell has *getopts*, see your on-line *sh* or *getopts*(1) manual page.

getopt

If your shell doesn't have *getopts*, you can use the command named *getopt* on the Power Tools disk. *getopts* works differently than *getopt*; we won't cover it here.

getopt takes two or more arguments. The first is a string that can contain letters and colons (:). Each letter names a valid option; if a letter is followed by a colon, the option requires an argument. The second and following arguments are the original command-line options; you'll usually give *"$@"* *(46.14)* to pass all the arguments to *getopt*.

getopt picks each option off the command line, checks to see if the option is valid, and writes the correct option to its standard output. If an option has an argument, *getopt* writes the argument after its option. When *getopt* finds the first non-option argument (the first argument that doesn't start with a - character), it outputs two dashes (--) and the rest of the arguments. If *getopt* finds an invalid option, or an option that should have an argument but doesn't, it prints an error message and returns a non-zero status *(46.07)*.

opttest

Your script can use a loop to parse the *getopt* output. Here's an example script named *opttest* that shows how *getopt* works.

```
#! /bin/sh
set -- `getopt "ab:" "$@"` || {
    echo "Usage: `basename $0` [-a] [-b name] [files]" 1>&2
    exit 1
}
echo "Before loop, command line has: $*"
aflag=0  name=NONE
while :
do
    case "$1" in
    -a) aflag=1 ;;
    -b) shift; name="$1" ;;
    --) break ;;
    esac
    shift
done
shift    # REMOVE THE TRAILING --
echo "aflag=$aflag / name=$name / Files are $*"
```

| | 46.09
| 14.08

The script has two legal options. The *−a* option sets the variable named *aflag* to 1. The *−b* option takes a single argument; the argument is stored in the variable named *name*. Any other arguments are filenames.

---

* *getopts* replaces the old command *getopt*; it is better integrated into the shell's syntax and runs more efficiently. C programmers will recognize *getopts* as very similar to the standard library routine *getopt*(3).

The script starts by running *getopt* inside backquotes *(10.14)*—and using the *set* *(46.18)* command to replace the command-line arguments with the *getopt* output. The first argument to *set*, – – (two dashes), is important: it makes sure that *set* passes the script's options to *getopt* instead of treating them as options to the shell itself. An *echo* command shows the output of *getopt*. Then the loop parses the *getopt* output, setting shell variables as it goes. When the loop finds the – – argument from *getopt*, it quits and leaves the remaining filenames (if any) in the command-line arguments. A second *echo* shows what's in the shell variables and on the command line after the loop. Here are a few examples:

```
% opttest
Before loop, command line has: --
aflag=0 / name=NONE / Files are
% opttest -b file1 -a file2 file3
Before loop, command line has: -b file1 -a -- file2 file3
aflag=1 / name=file1 / Files are file2 file3
% opttest -q -b file1
getopt: illegal option -- q
Usage: opttest [-a] [-b name] [files]
% opttest -bfile1
Before loop, command line has: -b file1 --
aflag=0 / name=file1 / Files are
% opttest -ab
getopt: option requires an argument -- b
Usage: opttest [-a] [-b name] [files]
```

The advantages of *getopt* are that it minimizes extra code necessary to process options and fully supports the standard UNIX option syntax (as specified in *intro* of the User's Manual).

—JP, BR

46.18 *The Bourne Shell set Command*

[Most of this article, except the part about IFS, *also applies to the C shell.—JP]*

The Bourne shell command line can have options like *–e* (exit if any command returns non-zero status). It can also have other arguments; these are passed to shell scripts. You can set new command-line parameters while you're typing interactive commands (at a shell prompt) or in a shell script.

To reset the command-line parameters, just type *set* followed by the new parameters. So, for example, to ask the shell to show expanded versions of command lines after you type them, set the *–v* (verbose) option *(9.13)*:

```
$ set -v
$ mail $group1 < message
mail andy ellen heather steve wilma < message
$ mail $group2 < message
mail lisa@foobar.com randy@xyz.edu yori@mongo.medfly.com < message
$ set +v
```

Typing set +v cancels the *v* option on many Bourne shells.

You can put filenames or any other strings in the command-line parameters interactively or from a shell script. That's handy for storing and parsing the output of a UNIX command with backquotes *(10.14)*. For example, you can get a list of all logged-in users from the parameters $1, $2, and so on. Use *users* if your system has it. Otherwise, use *who (53.04)*—and *cut (36.12)* to strip off everything but the usernames:

```
$ set `users`
$ set `who | cut -c1-8`
$ for u
> do
> ...do something with each user ($u)...
> done
```

for 10.10

You can save the original parameters in another variable and reset them later:

```
oldparms="$*"
set something new
      ...use new settings...
set $oldparms
```

Because the shell parses and scans the new parameters before it stores them, wildcards *(16.02)* and other special characters *(9.15)* will be interpreted—watch your quoting *(9.10)*. You can take advantage of this to parse lines of text into pieces that aren't separated with the usual spaces and TABs—for instance, a line from a database with colon-separated fields—by setting the *IFS (36.19)* variable before the *set* command.

If you want to save any special quoting on the original command line, be careful; the quoting will be lost unless you're clever. For example, if $1 used to be *John Smith*, it'll be split after it's restored: $1 will have *John* and $2 will be *Smith*. A better solution might be to use a subshell *(14.07)* for the part of the script where you need to reset the command-line parameters:

```
# reset command-line parameters during subshell only:
(set some new parameters
      ...do something with new parameters...
)
# original parameters aren't affected from here on...
```

One last note: *set* won't set $0, the name of the script file.

—JP

46.19 test: Testing Files and Strings

UNIX has a command called *test* that does a lot of useful tests. For instance, it can test to see if a file is writable before your script tries to write to it. It can treat the string in a shell variable as a number and do comparisons ("is that number less than 1000?"). You can combine tests, too ("if the file exists *and* it's readable *and* the message number is more than 500 . . ."). For a complete list, read your online *test* manual page.

The *test* command returns a zero status *(46.07)* if the test was true or a non-zero status otherwise. So people usually use *test* with *if, while,* or *until.* Here's a way your program could check to see if the user has a readable file named *.signature* in the home directory:

$HOME *7.03*
```
if test -r $HOME/.signature
then
    ...Do whatever...
else
    echo "Can't read your '.signature'.  Quitting." 1>&2
    exit 1
fi
```

The *test* command also lets you test for something that *isn't* true. Add an exclamation point (!) before the condition you're testing. For example, the following test is true if the *.signature* file is *not* readable:

```
if test ! -r $HOME/.signature
then
    echo "Can't read your '.signature'.  Quitting." 1>&2
    exit 1
fi
```

UNIX also has a version of *test* (a link to the same program, actually) named *[*. Yes, that's a left bracket. You can use it interchangeably with the *test* command with one exception: there has to be a matching right bracket (]) at the end of the test. The second example above could be rewritten this way:

```
if [ ! -r $HOME/.signature ]
then
    echo "Can't read your '.signature'.  Quitting." 1>&2
    exit 1
fi
```

Be sure to leave space between the brackets and other text. There are a couple of other common gotchas caused by empty arguments; articles 48.04 and 48.05 have workarounds.

test can do many kinds of tests. Some versions of *test* have more options than others. Why not take a minute now to look at your system's online *test* manual page?

—*JP* from the Nutshell Handbook *MH & xmh: E-Mail for Users & Programmers*

46.20 Picking a Name for a New Command

When you write a new program or shell script, you'll probably want to be sure that its name doesn't conflict with any other commands on the system. For instance, you might wonder whether there's a command named *tscan*. You can check by typing one of the commands in the following example. If you get output (besides an error) from one of them, there's probably already a command with the same name. (The *whence* command works on the Korn shell; I've shown it with the *ksh* dollar sign ($) prompt.)

```
% man 1 tscan
No manual entry for tscan in section 1.
```

which *52.07*
```
% which tscan
no tscan in . /xxx/ehuser/bin /usr/bin/X11 /usr/local/bin ...
```

whereis *52.05*
```
% whereis tscan
tscan:
```

alias *11.02*
```
% alias tscan
%
```

```
$ whence tscan
```

—*JP* from the Nutshell Handbook *MH & xmh: E-Mail for Users & Programmers*

46.21 Finding Program Name; Multiple Program Names

A UNIX program should use its name as the first word in error messages it prints. That's important when the program is running in the background or as part of a pipeline—you need to know which program has the problem:

```
someprog: quitting: can't read file xxxxxx
```

It's tempting to use just the program name in the *echo* commands:

```
echo "someprog: quitting: can't read file $file" 1>&2
```

but if you ever change the program name, it's easy to forget to fix the messages. A better way is to store the program name in a shell variable at the top of the script file, and then use the variable in all messages:

```
myname=someprog
  ...
echo "$myname: quitting: can't read file $file" 1>&2
```

Even better, use the $0 parameter. The shell automatically puts the script's name there. But $0 can have the full pathname of the script, such as */xxx/yyy/bin/someprog*. The *basename (47.18)* program fixes this: *basename* strips off the head of a pathname—everything but the filename.

For example, if $0 is */u/ehuser/bin/sendit*, then:

```
myname="`basename $0`"
```

would put *sendit* into the *myname* shell variable.

Just as you can make links *(19.03)* to give UNIX files several names, you can use links to give your program several names *(47.13)*. For instance, see the script named *ll, lf, lg* (. . . and so on) in article 17.08. Use $0 to get the current name of the program.

—*JP from the Nutshell Handbook* MH & xmh: E-Mail for Users & Programmers

46.22 *Reading Files with the . and source Commands*

As article 7.02 explains, UNIX programs can *never, ever* modify the environment of their parents. A program can only modify the environment of its children. This is a common mistake that many new UNIX users make: they try to write a program that changes a directory (or does something else involving an environment variable) and try to figure out why it doesn't work. You can't do this. If you write a program that executes the *cd* command, that *cd* will be effective within your program—but when the program finishes, you'll be back in your original (parent) shell.

One workaround is to "source" the program (for *csh*) or run it as a "dot" script (*sh, ksh*): for example,

```
% source change-my-directory
$ . change-my-directory
```

If your shell doesn't have shell functions *(11.10)*, you can simulate them *(11.11)* with the . command. It acts a lot like a subroutine or function in a programming language.

—*ML, JP*

47

Shell Programming
for the Initiated

47.01 Beyond the Basics

This chapter has a bunch of tricks and techniques for programming with the Bourne shell. Some of them are documented but hard to find; others aren't documented at all. Here is a summary of this chapter's articles:

- The first group of articles is about **making a file directly executable with #! on the first line**. On many versions of UNIX (see article 46.04), an executable file can start with a first line like this:

  ```
  #! /path/to/interpreter
  ```

  The kernel will start the program named in that line and give it the file to read. Chris Torek's Usenet classic, article 47.02, explains how #! started. Article 47.03 explains that your "shell scripts" may not need a shell at all. Article 47.04 will give you a few grins as it shows unusual examples of #!—and article 47.05 has experiments to help you understand what #! does. If your UNIX doesn't have #!, the trick in article 47.06 will let you be sure your scripts run with the Bourne shell.

  Scripts using an interpreter that isn't a shell are in articles 26.11, 26.12, 26.13, and 26.14.

- The next five articles are about **processes and commands**. The *exec* command, article 47.07, replaces the shell with another process; it can also be used to change input/output redirection (see below). The *trap* command can control how signals are passed to child processes; see article 47.08. The **:** (colon) operator evaluates its arguments and returns a zero status—article 47.09 explains why you should care. UNIX keeps a file on-disk once it's been opened; as article 47.10 explains, this has its ups and downs. The *jot* command, article 47.11, is useful for all kinds of operations with lists of numbers and characters.

- Next are techniques for handling variables and parameters. Parameter substitution, explained in article 47.12, is a compact way to test, set, and give default values for variables. You can use the $0 parameter and UNIX links to make the same script have multiple names and do multiple things; see article 47.13. Article 47.14 shows the easy way to get the last command-line argument. Article 47.15 has an easy way to remove all the command-line arguments.

- Four articles cover *sh* loops. A *for* loop usually reads a list of single arguments into a single shell variable. Article 47.16 shows how to make the *for* loop read from standard input. Article 47.17 has techniques for making a *for* loop set more than one variable. The *dirname* and *basename* commands can be used split pathnames with a loop; see article 47.18. A *while* loop can have more than one command line at the start; see article 47.19.

- Next is an assortment of articles about input/output. Article 47.20 introduces open files and file descriptors—there's more to know about standard input/output/error than you might have realized! Article 47.21 has a look at file descriptor handling in the Bourne shell, swapping standard output and standard error. The shell can redirect the I/O from all commands in a loop at once; article 47.22 explains one use for this technique and article 47.23 explains good and bad points of doing this.

- The shell can read commands directly from a shell script file. As article 47.24 points out, a shell can also read commands from its standard input, but that can cause some problems. Article 47.25 shows one place scripts from *stdin* are useful: writing a script that creates another script as it goes.

  Next are two articles about miscellaneous I/O. One gotcha with the here-document operator (for redirecting input from a script file) is that the terminators are different in the Bourne and C shells; article 47.26 explains. Article 47.27 shows how to turn off echoing while your script reads a "secret" answer such as a password.

- The last articles in this chapter cover text handling within a script. Three articles—47.28, 47.29, and 47.30—show uses for the versatile *expr* expression-handling command. The *grabchars* program in article 47.31 is similar to *read (46.13)*—but *grabchars* doesn't need a RETURN after the answer; *grabchars* also can prompt and do basic tests on the answer.

  Article 47.32 shows a trick for making one *case* structure *(46.05)* test two things at once. Article 47.33 has a trick for simulating arrays in the Bourne Shell. Finally, article 47.34 uses *echo* and *tr* to get a control character in a script without typing the lateral character into the file.

—*JP*

47.02 The Story of : # #!

Once upon a time, there was the Bourne shell. Since there was only "the" shell, there was no trouble deciding how to run a script: run it with *the* shell. It worked, and everyone was happy.

Along came progress, and wrote another shell. The people thought this was good, for now they could choose their own shell. So some chose the one, and some the other, and they wrote shell scripts and were happy. But one day someone who used the "other" shell ran a script by someone who used the "other other" shell, and alas! it bombed spectacularly. The people wailed and called upon their Guru for help.

"Well," said the Guru, "I see the problem. The one shell and the other are not compatible. We need to make sure that the shells know which other shell to use to run each script. And lo! the one shell has a 'comment' called :, and the other a true comment called #. I hereby decree that henceforth, the one shell will run scripts that start with :, and the other those that start with #." And it was so, and the people were happy.

But progress was not finished. This time he noticed that only shells ran scripts, and thought that if the kernel too could run scripts, that this would be good, and the people would be happy. So he wrote more code, and now the kernel could run scripts, but only if they began with the magic incantation: #!, and told the kernel which shell ran the script. And it was so, and the people were confused.

For the #! looked like a "comment." Though the kernel could see the #! and run a shell, it would not do so unless certain magic bits were set. And if the incantation were mispronounced, that too could stop the kernel, which after all was not omniscient. And so the people wailed, but alas!, the Guru did not respond. And so it was, and still it is today. Anyway, you will get best results from a 4BSD machine by using

    #! /bin/sh

or

    #! /bin/csh

as the first line of your script. #! /bin/csh -f is also helpful on occasion [it's usually faster because *csh* won't read your *.cshrc* file—*JP*].

—*CT*

47.03 Don't Need a Shell for Your Script? Don't Use One

If your UNIX understands *(46.04)* files that start with:

```
#! /interpreter/program
```

You don't have to use those lines to start a shell, such as `#!/bin/sh`. If your script is just starting a program like *awk*, UNIX can start the program directly and save execution time. This is especially useful on small or overloaded computers, or when your script has to be called over and over (such as in a loop).

First, here are two scripts. Both scripts print the second word from each line of text files. One uses a shell; the other runs *awk* directly:

```
% cat with_sh
#!/bin/sh
awk '
{ print $2 }
' $*
% cat no_sh
#!/usr/bin/awk -f
{ print $2 }
% cat afile
one two three four five
```

Let's run both commands and *time (41.02)* them:

```
% time with_sh afile
two
0.1u 0.2s 0:00 26%
% time no_sh afile
two
0.0u 0.1s 0:00 13%
```

One of the things that's really important to understand here is that when the kernel runs the program on the interpreter line, it is given the script as an input file. If the intepreter program understands a file directly, like */bin/sh* does, nothing special needs to be done. But a program like *awk* or *sed* requires the *–f* option if it is to read its script from a file. This leads to the seemingly odd syntax in the example above, with a call to *awk –f* with no following filename. The script itself is the input file!

One implication of this usage is that the interpreter program needs to understand # as a comment, or that first interpreter-selection line itself will be acted upon (and probably rejected by) the interpreter. (Fortunately, the shells and both *sed* and *awk* do recognize this comment character.)

—JP

47.04 Fun with #!

[You might think that the "magic" characters #! *are only for shell scripts. Not true (47.05, 47.03)! Here are some fun examples. Study them and (if your UNIX system understands* #! *) try them; I hope they'll help you see what* #! *really does.—JP]*

Q: Why begin a shell script with #!/bin/sh or #!/bin/csh?

A: Under some systems—principally those with Berkeley influence—this makes the program directly executable. That is, the kernel can start this program, even though it's not machine code; the kernel will invoke the named program after fiddling arguments a bit.

In fact, the script

```
#! /bin/mv
```

will rename itself. Place it in a file called *zap*, and type zap zup, and now you have a shell script called *zup*. Your shell tried to *exec* the program with the argument zup. This succeeded, but actually ran */bin/mv* with the arguments zap zup.

You can make self-removing scripts:

```
#! /bin/rm
```

Or self-printing scripts:

```
#! /bin/awk NR > 1 { print }
text...
```

This last one works because the kernel is willing to do more than insert the filename in the argument list: it will insert one—and only one—optional argument. Normally, this is used for things like the *–f* option to the C shell ("fast", don't read *.cshrcs*), but it works well enough for *awk* too, because blanks no longer matter. Thus, the one argument to *awk* here is NR > 1 { print }.

#! is described, though not completely, in the *execve*(2) manual page. Note that there may be a small limit on the number of characters in the #! line, typically 32. (32 is "magic" because it equals sizeof(struct exec).) Because of that limit, I have to spell that last example differently on a system where *awk* is in */usr/bin*:

```
#! /usr/bin/awk NR>1 { print }
```

Otherwise, the string will be too long.

—CT in net.unix on Usenet, 29 December 1984

47.05 A File that Shows Itself . . . and What #! Does

If your UNIX understands *(46.04)* executable files that start with #!, you can use this nice trick to make executable files that display themselves (or part of themselves). I used this to make a program named *help* on a system that didn't have any online help. A program like *cat (26.02)* isn't what you want because it'll display the #! line as well as the message. Watch what happens:

```
% cat help
#!/bin/cat
For help with UNIX, call the ACS Consulting Hotline at 555-1212.

man command              shows the manual for a command
   . . .
% chmod +x help
% help
#!/bin/cat
For help with UNIX, call the ACS Consulting Hotline at 555-1212.

man command              shows the manual for a command
   . . .
```

The trick is to invoke an interpreter that shows all the lines except the line starting with #!. For example, this file uses *grep (28.02)* and a regular expression *(27.04)* that says "show all lines that don't start with #":

```
% cat help
#!/bin/grep ^[^#]
For help with UNIX, call the ACS Consulting Hotline at 555-1212.

man command              shows the manual for a command
   . . .
% help
For help with UNIX, call the ACS Consulting Hotline at 555-1212.

man command              shows the manual for a command
   . . .
```

For longer files, try using more +2 *(26.03)*; this file will show itself screenful-by-screenful, starting at line 2:

```
% cat help
#!/usr/ucb/more +2
For help with UNIX, call the ACS Consulting Hotline at 555-1212.

man command              shows the manual for a command
   . . .
```

You have to give the full pathname to the interpreter because the kernel doesn't use your search path *(9.05)*. The kernel can pass just one argument to the interpreter. More than one argument probably won't work. In the next example, I try to pass two arguments to *grep*—but the kernel passes the whole string -v ^#

as just one argument. That confuses *grep*, which complains about every character from the space on:

```
% cat help
#!/bin/grep -v ^#
For help with UNIX, call the ACS Consulting Hotline at 555-1212.
```

```
man command                    shows the manual for a command
    . . .
% help
grep: illegal option --
grep: illegal option -- ^
grep: illegal option -- #
Usage: grep -hblcnsvi pattern file . . .
```

(Remember, there's no shell interpreting the arguments here. The kernel does
it.) That's why I wrote the first *help* with the strange-looking
`#!/bin/grep ^[^#]` instead of using the *−v* option: it does the job I need
without trying to pass a second argument.

—JP

47.06 *Making Sure your Script Runs with Bourne Shell, without #!*

Lots of UNIX versions let you start a script file this way:

```
#!/bin/sh
```

That executable file will always be read by a Bourne shell. If some versions of
UNIX you use don't understand #! *(46.04)*, here's how to start your scripts:

```
#!/bin/sh
export PATH || exec /bin/sh $0 $argv:q
```

|| 46.09

If a Bourne shell reads that line (that is, if the `#!/bin/sh` succeeded), the
`export PATH` command will succeed and the rest of the command line will be
skipped. If a C shell reads the line, it will print the error `export: Command
not found`. Then it will run `exec /bin/sh $0 $argv:q`. The *exec (47.07)*
replaces the C shell with a Bourne shell, passes it the name of the script file in
`$0`, and passes a quoted list of the command-line arguments from `$argv:q`
(12.08).

—JP

47.07 The exec Command

The *exec* command will execute a command in place of the current shell; that is, it terminates the current shell and starts a new process *(40.03)* in its place.

Historically, *exec* was often used to execute the last command of a shell script. This would kill the shell slightly earlier; otherwise, the shell would wait until the last command was finished. This practice saved a process and some memory. (Aren't you glad you're using a modern system? This sort of conservation usually isn't necessary any longer unless your system limits the number of processes each user can have.)

exec can be used to replace one shell with another shell:

```
% exec ksh
$
```

without incurring the additional overhead of having an unused shell in the background.

exec also manipulates file descriptors *(47.21, 47.22)* in the Bourne shell. When you use *exec* to manage file descriptors, it does not replace the current process. For example, the following command makes the standard input of all commands come from the file *formfile* instead of the default place (usually, your terminal):

```
exec < formfile
```

—ML, JP

47.08 Handling Signals to Child Processes

The Bourne shell *trap* command *(46.12)* controls what the shell does when it gets an interrupt or signal (from the *kill (40.10)* command, from a keyboard character like CTRL-c, and so on). To run an external command *(1.10)*—like an editor or a simple command such as *sort*—the shell starts a child process *(40.03)* (subprocess). If the program running in the child process wants to handle its own signals, the parent shell should probably pass signals on to the child process. For example, you might be running *vi* as a child process and want to send a CTRL-c to stop *vi* from what it's doing, but not want the CTRL-c to kill the parent shell script.

When the parent process gets a signal, should it die or keep running? Should the child get the signal or not? The Bourne shell gives you a fair amount of flexibility in signal handling. The bad news is that most *sh* manual pages don't say much about this. And no manual page I've seen explains a useful choice: using the : (colon) operator *(47.09)* with *trap*. Table 47-1 shows your choices.

Table 47-1. trap Arguments (for Most Bourne Shells)

Argument	Effect
`" "`	Ignore signal, don't pass signal to child.
`:`	(undocumented) Ignore signal, pass signal to child.
`"command-line"`	Run *command-line* with variable and command substitution done when *trap* set; don't pass signal to child.
`'command-line'`	Run *command-line* with variable and command substitution done when *trap* executed; don't pass signal to child.
`No argument`	Reset signal handling to default (usually, parent terminates). Pass signal to child.

Because so much of this is undocumented, I won't try to give you "the answers" for how it should work with your shell. Instead, here are two shell scripts that let you experiment with your shell's signal handling. One script, named *parent*, starts the second script, *child*. The *child* script sets some traps, then starts *sleep* (42.02) so it'll be there when you send a signal. This lets you use CTRL-c or other interrupts, if *parent* is running in the foreground—or the *kill* command with signal numbers, if you've put *parent* in the background. You can edit the *trap* lines in the two scripts to test the setup you want to use.

Here's an example. I'll start *parent* in the background from the C shell, then send it a signal 1 ("hangup" signal):

```
% parent &
[1] 8669
parent started
child started
% kill -1 %1
child got a signal 1
child exiting
parent still running after child exited
        ...1000 seconds later...
parent exiting
[1]   + Done                        parent
```

%1 *13.01*

Now, the scripts:

```
% cat parent
#! /bin/sh
echo parent started
trap "echo parent exiting; exit" 0
trap : 1                          # pass signal 1 to child but don't die
trap "" 2                         # ignore signal 2, block from child
trap "echo parent got signal 15" 15   # ignore signal 15, send to child
                                  # die on other signals, send to child
child
echo parent still running after child exited
sleep 1000
% cat child
```

```
#! /bin/sh
echo child started
trap 'echo child exiting; exit' 0
trap 'echo child got a signal 1' 1
trap '' 2          # ignore signal 2
trap 'echo child got a signal 3' 3
sleep 1000         # wait a long time for a signal
```

Even with this help, the way that signal handling works might not be too clear. For more about signal handling, see a book that covers UNIX internals on your system.

—JP

47.09 The Under-Appreciated Bourne Shell ":" Operator

Some people think that the Bourne shell's **:** is a comment character. It isn't really. It evaluates its arguments and returns a zero exit status *(46.07)*. Here are a few places to use it:

- Replace the UNIX *true* command to make an endless *while* loop *(46.10)*. This is more efficient because the shell doesn't have to start a new process each time around the loop (as it does when you use `while true`):

      while :
      do
          commands
      done

  (Of course, one of the *commands* will probably be *break*, to end the loop eventually.)

- When you want to use the *else* in an *if (46.08)*, but leave the *then* empty, the **:** makes a nice "do-nothing" place filler:

      if something
      then :
      else
          commands
      fi

- If your Bourne shell doesn't have a true # comment character, you can use **:** to "fake it." It's safest to use quotes so the shell won't try to interpret characters like > or | in your "comment":

      : 'read answer and branch if < 3 or > 6'

- Finally, it's useful with parameter substitution *(47.12)* like ${var?} or ${var=default}. For instance, using this line in your script will print an error and exit if either the *USER* or *HOME* variables aren't set:

      : ${USER?} ${HOME?}

—JP

47.10 Removing a File Once It's Opened—for Security and Easy Cleanup

Once a process has opened a file *(47.20)*, UNIX won't delete the file until the process closes it. (The *rm* command only removes a link to the file from a directory, not the file itself.)

I've heard arguments *(25.03)* about whether removing a file while it's open is a good idea. If you want to run a set of commands from a file, but not let anyone else read the list of commands you're using, you can write a shell script that removes itself before doing anything else. (You should be aware that if you use a filesystem mounted by NFS *(1.33)*, NFS will just rename the "removed" file to a hidden filename *(17.12)* like *.nfsXXXXX.*)

Here's a simple self-removing shell script:

```
% cat doit
rm doit     # by now, shell has opened this file; we can remove it
ls doit
make bigprog
    ...
% sh doit
ls: doit not found
cc    -target sun4 -c  routine.c
    ...
```

Here's a more typical script that opens and removes a file in */tmp (22.03)*

```
% cat delme
#! /bin/sh
temp=/tmp/delme$$                 # file in /tmp (could be anywhere)
echo "This is line1.
This is line2.
This is line3." > $temp           # put three lines in $temp
ls -l $temp; wc $temp            # ls and count lines in the file
```
exec *47.07*
```
exec < $temp                     # take standard input from $temp
read line; echo $line            # read and echo line 1 from $temp
rm $temp; echo rm returned $?    # remove $temp file; show status
ls -l $temp; wc $temp           # the file is gone...?
read line; echo $line            # but file is still open!
read line; echo $line
```
<&– *47.21*
```
exec <&-                         # close standard input (and file)
% delme
-rw-rw-r--  1 jerry    45 Sep 16 12:31 /tmp/delme22743
        3       9      45 /tmp/delme22743
This is line1.
rm returned 0
ls: /tmp/delme22743: No such file or directory
wc: cannot open /tmp/delme22743
This is line2.
This is line3.
```

—*JP*

47.11 The Multi-Purpose jot Command

The *jot* command is an extremely powerful tool for shell programming. People who have used *jot* end up using it all the time, but those who haven't been exposed to it may be perplexed by its function. For that reason, I think the best way to learn *jot* is by example. (If you've been paying attention, then you might notice that I think that example is the best way to learn anything; but for *jot*, it's doubly true!)

jot

In its most basic use, *jot* produces a series of numbers. With only one integer as a command-line argument, it produces the sequential integers from 1 to that number.

```
% jot 4
1
2
3
4
```

Big deal, you might say. Well, it may not be earth-shattering on the surface, but it can make your life much easier if you program in the Bourne shell. Take the instance when you want to increment a number in a loop. The usual way of doing this is:

```
counter=1
while [ $counter -le 10 ]
do
    ...
    counter=`expr $counter + 1`
done
```

This is laborious and quite slow. Because the Bourne shell doesn't have any built-in *(1.10)* number crunching, the only way to increment the counter is to use the *expr* command in each iteration of the loop. But if you have *jot*, the same loop can be written in a simple *for* loop:

```
for counter in `jot 10`
do
    ...
done
```

You can also use *jot* to show any other sequence of numbers. For example, to show the integers between 24 and 28 (inclusive), try:

```
% jot 5 24
24
25
26
27
28
```

The first argument (*5*) is taken to be how many values should be shown. The second number (*24*) is the number to start counting with. This may seem frustrating—why not just let us say "jot 24 28" to specify the beginning and end of the sequence, rather than make us figure out how many numbers will be in the sequence first? Well, the reason is that you might not always want to be counting by whole numbers.

If supplied a third argument, *jot* takes it as the number to end the sequence with. And if you specify either the beginning or end boundary with a decimal point, it will produce fractional numbers in its output:

```
% jot 5 24 28.0
24.0
25.0
26.0
27.0
28.0
% jot 4 24 28.0
24.0
25.3
26.7
28.0
```

You can also use the *–p* option to specify a given precision:

```
% jot -p4 4 24 28
24.0000
25.3333
26.6667
28.0000
```

By default, the values shown are evenly spaced across the interval. You can change this by using a fourth numerical argument, which becomes the size of each step in the iteration. For example:

```
% jot 4 24 28.0 .5
24.0
24.5
25.0
25.5
```

Notice in this example that only the first four iterations are shown, because we asked for only four values in the first argument. This is because any three values determine the fourth automatically, so when the values conflict, *jot* takes the lower value. *jot* stopped after four values regardless of the fact that it would need nine iterations to complete the sequence. However, *jot* will also stop if the sequence is completed *before* the specified number of values are shown.

```
% jot 4 24 28 2
24
26
28
```

To omit any of these values, replace them with a single dash (–). For example, if you know that you just want the digits from 24 to 28, you can omit the field specifying the number of values as long as you tell it to use a step of 1:

```
% jot - 24 28 1
24
25
26
```

27
28

And of course, you can use negative numbers and negative steps:

```
% jot - 1 -3 -2
1
-1
-3
```

If you want the output separated by a string other than a newline, use the −s option. For example, to have the output of the previous command separated by spaces, enter:

```
% jot -s " " - 1 -3 -2
1 -1 -3
```

That's *jot* in its no-frills form, already potentially useful for any writer of shell scripts. However, *jot* does quite a lot more. The −c option can be used to show ASCII (53.03) characters instead of integers. To print out the character for ASCII 65 (decimal), for example, try:

```
% jot -c 1 65
A
```

You can also do the ASCII-to-decimal conversion in reverse, by just specifying a character in place of the lower bound:

```
% jot 1 A
65
```

This can be handy if you want an automatic listing of all 26 letters:

```
% jot -c 26 A
A
B
C
    ...
```

The −r option produces random numbers, which is very useful in shells with no random number generator (such as the Bourne or C shells). To create a 6-digit random number, try:

```
% jot -r 1 100000 999999
523467
```

(Using −r, the fourth numerical argument, if specified, is taken to be a seed for the random number.)

The −b option can be used to repeat a given word, much like the *yes* (24.04) command:

```
% jot -b lunchtime! 3
lunchtime!
lunchtime!
lunchtime!
```

The *jot* manual page suggests a clever way of using this feature: if you want to search for lines in a files that have 40 or more characters, you could do this using regular expressions, but you'd have to count out all those dots.

```
grep "...................................." file
```

Using *jot*, you can pat yourself on the back for being ingenious (or for just reading the manpage!):

```
grep `jot -s "" -b . 40` file
```

But the most powerful feature of *jot* comes with its *−w* option. The *−w* option accepts a word containing format conversion characters as used by the *printf( )* function. (For example, `%d` prints a decimal argument; `%h` prints hexadecimal.) If you aren't familiar with the *printf( )* format conversions, read your *printf*(3) manual page or check any C programming book.

This allows you to combine strings with *jot* output, a useful feature for manipulating temporary files within scripts. For example, suppose you have a shell script that creates multiple temporary files that you want to remove at the end of the script. You might have even created the files using *jot* earlier in the script, as shown previously:

```
for counter in `jot 10 1`
do
        whatever commands > tmp$counter
done
```

Then later on you want to remove the files. You could do another loop, but it's more efficient to just enter:

```
rm `jot -w tmp%d 10 1`
```

The *jot* command expands to the strings *tmp1* through *tmp10*, which are the names of the temporary files created earlier in the script.

—LM

47.12 *Parameter Substitution*

The Bourne shell has a handy set of operators for testing and setting shell variables. They're listed in Table 47-2:

Table 47-2. Bourne Shell Parameter Substitution Operators

Operator	Explanation
`${var-default}`	If *var* not set, use *default* instead.
`${var=default}`	If *var* not set, set it to *default* and use that value.
`${var+instead}`	If *var* is set, use *instead*. Otherwise, use nothing (null string).

Table 47-2. Bourne Shell Parameter Substitution Operators (continued)

Operator	Explanation
${var?message}	If *var* is not set, print *message*, if any—the default message depends on your UNIX version. If *var* is set, use its value.

To see how parameter substitution works, here's another version of the *bkedit* script *(46.08, 46.11)*:

```
#! /bin/sh
if cp "$1" "$1.bak"
then
    ${VISUAL-/usr/ucb/vi} "$1"
    exit   # USE STATUS FROM EDITOR
else
    echo "`basename $0` quitting: can't make backup?"
    exit 1
fi
```

If the *VISUAL* *(7.03)* environment variable is set, its value (like */usr/local/bin/emacs*) is used and the command line becomes /usr/local/bin/emacs "$1". If *VISUAL* isn't set, the command line will default to /usr/ucb/vi "$1".

You can use parameter substitution operators in any command line. You'll see them used with the colon (:) operator *(47.09)*, checking or setting default values.

Most newer versions of the Bourne shell understand a variation of the parameter substitution operators. If you add a colon (:) before the –, =, + or ?, the test will succeed if the variable is set *and the variable's value is not empty*. Let's look at the example below. The first substitution (${nothing=default}) will leave $nothing empty because the variable has been set. The second substitution will set $nothing to *default* because the variable has been set but is empty. The third substitution will leave $something set to *stuff*:

```
nothing=
something=stuff
: ${nothing=default}
: ${nothing:=default}
: ${something:=default}
```

—*JP*

47.13 Save Disk Space and Programming: Multiple Names for a Program

If you're writing:

- several programs that do the same kinds of things,

- programs that use a lot of the same code (as you're writing the second, third, etc. programs, you copy a lot of lines from the first program), or

- a program with several options that make a big change in the way it works,

you might want to write just one program and make links *(19.04, 19.03)*, to it instead. The program can find the name you called it with and, through *case* or *test* commands, work in different ways. For instance, the Berkeley UNIX commands *ex, vi, view, edit*, and others are all links to the same executable file. This takes less disk space and makes maintenance easier. It's usually only sensible when most of the code is the same in each program. If the program is full of name tests and lots of separate code, this technique may be more trouble than it's worth.

Depending on how the script program is called, this name can be a simple relative pathname like `prog` or `./prog`—it can also be a full pathname like `/usr/joe/bin/prog` (article 15.02 explains pathnames). There are a couple of ways to handle this in a shell script. If there's just one main piece of code in the script, as in the *lf* script *(17.08)*, a *case* that tests $0 might be best. The asterisk (`*`) wildcard at the start of each case (see article 46.06) handles the different pathnames that might be used to call the script:

```
case "$0" in
*name1)
    ...do this when called as name1...
    ;;
*name2)
    ...do this when called as name2...
    ;;
    ...
*)  ...print error and exit if $0 doesn't match...
    ;;
esac
```

You might also want to use *basename (47.18)* to strip off any leading pathname and store the cleaned-up $0 in a variable called *myname*. You can test $myname anywhere in the script and also use it for error messages:

```
myname=`basename $0`
    ...
case "$myname" in
    ...
```

```
echo "$myname: aborting; error in xxxxxx" 1>&2
    ...
```

—*JP*

47.14 Finding the Last Command-line Argument

Do you need to pick up the last parameter $1, $2 . . . from the parameter list [the "command line"—*JP*]? It looks like eval \$$# would do it:

```
$ set foo bar baz
$ eval echo \$$#
baz
```

eval *9.08*

except for a small problem with *sh* argument syntax:

```
$ set m n o p q r s t u v w x
$ echo $11
m1
```

$11 means ${1}1, and not ${11}. Trying ${11} directly gives bad sub-stitution.

The only reliable way to get at the last parameter is to use something like

```
for i do last="$i"; done
```

[That *for* loop assigns each parameter to the shell variable named *last*; after the loop ends, $last will have the last parameter. Also, note that you won't need this trick on all *sh*-like shells. The Korn shell understands ${11}.—*JP*]

—*CT* in *comp.unix.questions* on Usenet, *15 January 1990*

47.15 How to Unset all Command-line Parameters

The *shift (46.16)* command "shifts away" one command-line parameter. You can shift three times if there are three command-line parameters; some shells also can take an argument, like *shift 3*, that tells how many times to shift.

The easiest way to unset all command-line parameters is probably to set *(46.18)* a single dummy parameter, then shift it away:

```
set x
shift
```

Setting the single parameter wipes out whatever other parameters were set before.

—*JP*

47.16 Standard Input to a for Loop

An obvious place to use a Bourne shell *for* loop *(46.15)* is to step through a list of arguments—from the command line or a variable. But combine the loop with backquotes *(10.14)* and *cat (26.02)*, and the loop will step through the words on standard input.

Here's an example:

```
for x in `cat`
do
        ...handle $x
done
```

Because this method splits the input into separate words, no matter how many words are on each input line, it can be more convenient than a *while* loop running the *read* command, as in article 10.18. When you use this script interactively though, the loop won't start running until you've typed all of the input; using *while read* will run the loop after each line of input.

—JP

47.17 Making a for Loop with Multiple Variables

The normal Bourne shell *for* loop *(46.15)* lets you take a list of items, store the items one by one in a shell variable, and loop through a set of commands once for each item:

```
for file in prog1 prog2 prog3
do
        ...process $file
done
```

I wanted a *for* loop that stores several different shell variables and makes one pass through the loop for each *set* of variables (instead of one pass for each *item*, as a regular *for* loop does). This loop does the job:

```
for bunch in "ellie file16" "donna file23" "steve file34"
do
        # PUT FIRST WORD (USER) IN $1, SECOND (FILE) IN $2...
        set $bunch
        mail $1 < $2
done
```

set *46.18*

If you have any command-line arguments and still need them, store them in another variable before you do that. Or, you can make the loop this way:

```
for bunch in "u=ellie f=file16 s='your files'" \
    "u=donna f=file23 s='a memo'" "u=steve f=file34 s=report"
do
        # SET $u (USER), $f (FILENAME), $s (SUBJECT):
        eval $bunch
        mail -s "$s" $u < $f
done
```

This script uses the shell's *eval (9.08)* command to re-scan the contents of the *bunch* variable and store it in separate variables. Notice the single quotes like s='your files'; this groups the words for *eval*. The shell removes those single quotes before it stores the value into the *s* variable.

—*JP*

47.18 *Using basename and dirname*

Almost every UNIX command can use relative and absolute pathnames *(15.02)* to find a file or directory. There are times you'll need part of a pathname—the head (everything before the last slash) or the tail (the name after the last slash).

Introduction to basename and dirname

The *basename* command strips any "path" name components from a filename, leaving you with a "pure" filename. For example:

```
% basename /usr/bin/gigiplot
gigiplot
% basename /home/mikel/bin/bvurns.sh
bvurns.sh
```

basename can also strip a suffix from a filename. For example:

```
% basename /home/mikel/bin/bvurns.sh .sh
bvurns
```

The *dirname* command strips the filename itself, giving you the "directory" part of the pathname:

```
% dirname /usr/bin/screenblank
/usr/bin
% dirname local
.
```

If you give *dirname* a "pure" filename (i.e., a filename with no path, as in the second example), it tells you that the directory is . (the current directory).

Note: *dirname* and *basename* have a bug in many System V implementations. They don't recognize the second argument as a filename suffix to strip. Here's a good test:

```
% basename 0.foo .foo
```

If the answer is 0, your *basename* implementation is good. If the answer is 0.foo, the implementation is bad. If *basename* doesn't work, *dirname* won't, either.

Use with Loops

Here's an example of *basename* and *dirname*. There's a directory tree with some very large files—over 100,000 characters. You want to find those files, run *split* *(36.07)* on them, and add *huge.* to the start of the original filename. By default, *split* names the file chunks *xaa*, *xab*, *xac*, and so on; you want to use the original filename and a dot (.) instead of *x*:

```
for path in `find /home/you -type f -size +100000c -print`
do
        cd `dirname $path` || exit
        filename=`basename $path`
        split $filename $filename.
        mv -i $filename huge.$filename
done
```

|| 46.09
exit 46.11

The *find* command will output pathnames like these:

```
/home/you/somefile
/home/you/subdir/anotherfile
```

(The absolute pathnames are important here. The *cd* would fail on the second pass of the loop if you use relative pathnames.) In the loop, the *cd* command uses *dirname* to go to the directory where the file is. The *filename* variable, with the output of *basename*, is used several places—twice on the *split* command line.

If that gives the error `command line too long`, replace the first lines with the two lines below. This makes a redirected-input loop *(47.22)*:

```
find /home/you -type f -size +100000c -print |
while read path
```

—*JP, ML*

47.19 A while Loop with Several Loop Control Commands

Most people think the Bourne shell's *while* loop *(46.10)* looks like this, with a single command controlling the loop:

```
while command
do
        ...whatever
done
```

But *command* can actually be a *list* of commands. The exit status of the last command controls the loop. This is handy for prompting users and reading answers—when the user types an empty answer, the *read* command returns "false" and the loop ends:

```
while echo "Enter command or CTRL-d to quit: \c"
        read command
do
        ...process $command
done
```

Here's a loop that runs *who* and does a quick search on its output. If the *grep* returns non-zero status (because it doesn't find $who in $tempfile), the loop quits—otherwise, the loop does lots of processing:

```
while
    who > $tempfile
    grep "$who" $tempfile >/dev/null
do
    ...process $tempfile...
done
```

—*JP*

47.20 Overview: Open Files and File Descriptors

[This introduction is general and simplified. If you're a technical person who needs a complete and exact description, read a book on UNIX programming like the Nutshell Handbook Using C on the UNIX System.*—JP]*

UNIX shells let you redirect the input and output of programs with operators like > and |. How does that work? How can you use it better? Here's an overview.

When the UNIX kernel starts any process *(40.03)*—for example, *grep*, *ls*, or a shell—it sets up several places for that process to read from and write to. Figure 47-1 shows that.

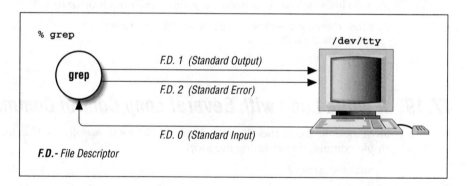

Figure 47-1. *Open Standard I/O Files with no Command-line Redirection*

These places are called *open files*. The kernel gives each file a number called a *file descriptor*. But people usually use names for these places instead of the numbers:

- The *standard input* or *stdin* (File Descriptor (F.D.) number 0) is the place where the process can read text. This might be text from other programs or from your keyboard.

- The *standard output* or *stdout* (F.D. 1) is a place for the process to write its "answers."

- The *standard error* or *stderr* (F.D. 2) is where the process can send error messages.

By default, as Figure 47-1 shows, the file that's opened for *stdin, stdout*, and *stderr* is */dev/tty*—a name for your terminal. This makes life easier for users—and programmers, too. The user doesn't have to tell a program where to read or write because the default is your terminal. A programmer doesn't have to open files to read or write from (in many cases); the programs can just read from *stdin*, write to *stdout*, and send errors to *stderr*.

This gets better. When the shell starts a process (when you type a command at a prompt), you can tell the shell what file to "connect to" any of those file descriptors. For example, Figure 47-2 shows what happens when you run *grep* and make the shell redirect *grep*'s standard output away from the terminal to a file named *grepout*.

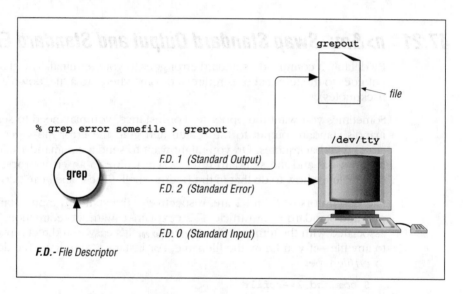

Figure 47-2. Standard Output Redirected to a File

Programs can read and write files besides the ones on *stdin, stdout*, and *stderr*. For instance, in Figure 47-2, *grep* opened the file *somefile* itself—it didn't use any of the standard file descriptors for *somefile*. A UNIX convention is that if you don't name any files on the command line, a program will read from its standard input. Programs that work that way are called *filters (1.30)*.

All shells can do basic redirection with *stdin, stdout*, and *stderr*. But, as you'll see in article 47.21, the Bourne shell also handles file descriptors 3 through 9. That's useful sometimes:

- Maybe you have a few data files that you want to keep reading from or writing to. Instead of giving their names, you can use the file descriptor numbers.

- Once you open a file, the kernel remembers what place in the file you last read from or wrote to. Each time you use that file descriptor number while the file is open, you'll be at the same place in the file. That's especially nice when you want to read from or write to the same file with more than one program. For example, the *line* command on some UNIX systems reads one line from a file—you can call *line* over and over, whenever you want to read the next line from a file. Once the file has been opened, you can remove its link (name) from the directory *(47.10)*; the process can access the file through its descriptor without using the name.

- When UNIX starts a new subprocess *(40.03)*, the open file descriptors are given to that process. A subprocess can read or write from file descriptors opened by its parent process. A redirected-I/O loop, as in articles 47.22 and 47.23, takes advantage of this.

—*JP*

47.21 *n>&m: Swap Standard Output and Standard Error*

By default, a command's standard error goes to your terminal. The standard output goes to the terminal or is redirected somewhere (to a file, down a pipe, into backquotes).

Sometimes you want the opposite. For instance, you may need to send a command's standard output to the screen and grab the error messages (standard error) with backquotes. Or, you might want to send a command's standard output to a file and the standard error down a pipe to an error-processing command. Here's how to do that in the Bourne shell. (The C shell can't do this.)

File descriptors 0, 1, and 2 are, respectively, the standard input, standard output, and standard error (article 47.20 explains). Without redirection, they're all associated with the terminal file */dev/tty (47.20)*. It's easy to redirect any descriptor to any file—if you know the filename. For instance, to redirect file descriptor 2 to *errfile*, type:

```
$ command 2>errfile
```

You know that a pipe and backquotes also redirect the standard output:

```
$ command | ...
$ var=`command`
```

But there's no filename associated with the pipe or backquotes, so you can't use the 2> redirection. You need to rearrange the file descriptors without knowing the file (or whatever) that they're associated with. Here's how.

Let's start slowly: by sending both standard output and standard error to the pipe or backquotes. The Bourne shell operator *n>&m* rearranges the files and file descriptors. It says "make file descriptor *n* point to the same file as file descriptor *m*." Let's use that operator on the previous example. We'll send standard error to the same place standard output is going:

```
$ command 2>&1 | ...
$ var=`command 2>&1`
```

In both those examples, 2>&1 means "send standard error (file descriptor 2) to the same place standard output (file descriptor 1) is going." Simple, eh?

You can use more than one of those *n*>&*m* operators. The shell reads them left-to-right before it executes the command.

"Oh!" you might say, "To swap standard output and standard error—make *stderr* go down a pipe and *stdout* go to the screen—I could do this!"

```
$ command 2>&1 1>&2 | ...        (wrong...)
```

Sorry, Charlie. When the shell sees 2>&1 1>&2, the shell first does 2>&1. You've seen that before—it makes file descriptor 2 (*stderr*) go the same place as file descriptor 1 (*stdout*). Then, the shell does 1>&2. It makes *stdout* (1) go the same place as *stderr* (2)... but *stderr* is already going the same place as *stdout*, down the pipe.

This is one place the other file descriptors, 3 through 9, come in handy. They normally aren't used. You can use one of them as a "holding place," to remember where another file descriptor "pointed." For example, one way to read the operator 3>&2 is "make 3 point the same place as 2." After you use 3>&2 to grab the location of 2, you can make 2 point somewhere else. Then, make 1 point where 2 used to (where 3 points now).

We'll take that step-by-step below. The command line you want is one of these:

```
$ command 3>&2 2>&1 1>&3 | ...
$ var=`command 3>&2 2>&1 1>&3`
```

How does it work? The next four figures break the second command line (with the backquotes) into the same steps the shell follows as it rearranges the file descriptors. You can try these on your terminal, if you'd like. Each figure adds another *n*>&*m* operator and shows the location of each file descriptor after that operator.

The figures use a *grep* command reading two files. *afone* is readable and *grep* finds one matching line in it; the line is written to the standard output. *bfoen* is misspelled and so is not readable; *grep* writes an error message to the standard error. In each figure, you'll see the terminal output (if any) just after the variable-setting command with the backquotes. The text grabbed by the backquotes goes into the shell variable; the *echo* command shows that text.

By Figure 47-6, the redirection is correct. Standard output goes to the screen, and standard error is captured by the backquotes.

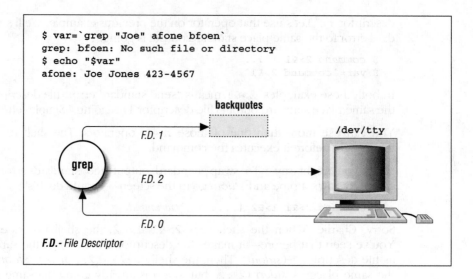

```
$ var=`grep "Joe" afone bfoen`
grep: bfoen: No such file or directory
$ echo "$var"
afone: Joe Jones 423-4567
```

backquotes

/dev/tty

F.D. 1

grep

F.D. 2

F.D. 0

F.D.- *File Descriptor*

Figure 47-3. File Descriptors Before Redirection

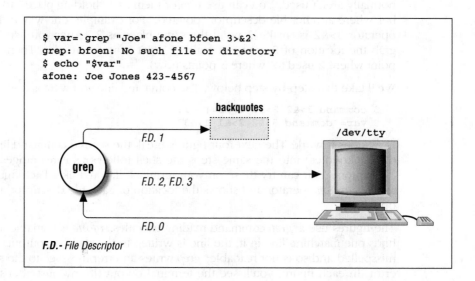

```
$ var=`grep "Joe" afone bfoen 3>&2`
grep: bfoen: No such file or directory
$ echo "$var"
afone: Joe Jones 423-4567
```

backquotes

/dev/tty

F.D. 1

grep

F.D. 2, F.D. 3

F.D. 0

F.D.- *File Descriptor*

Figure 47-4. File Descriptors After 3>&2 Redirection

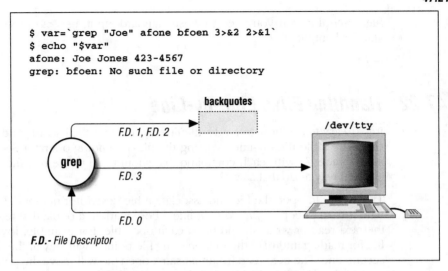

```
$ var=`grep "Joe" afone bfoen 3>&2 2>&1`
$ echo "$var"
afone: Joe Jones 423-4567
grep: bfoen: No such file or directory
```

Figure 47-5. File Descriptors After 3>&2 2>&1 Redirection

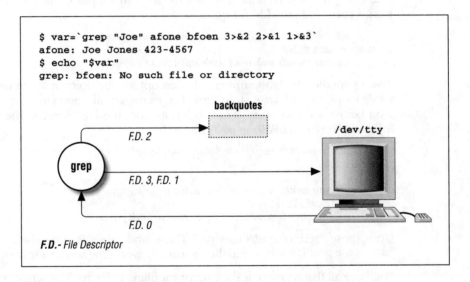

```
$ var=`grep "Joe" afone bfoen 3>&2 2>&1 1>&3`
afone: Joe Jones 423-4567
$ echo "$var"
grep: bfoen: No such file or directory
```

Figure 47-6. File Descriptors After 3>&2 2>&1 1>&3 Redirection

Open files are automatically closed when a process exits. But it's safer to close the files yourself as soon as you're done with them. That way, if you forget and use the same descriptor later for something else (for instance, use F.D. 3 to redirect some other command, or a subprocess uses F.D. 3), you won't run into conflicts. Use *m<&-* to close input file descriptor *m* and *m>&-* to close output file descriptor *m*. If you need to close standard input, use <&–; >&– will close standard output.

—JP

47.22 Handling Files Line-by-Line

It isn't easy to see how to read a file line-by-line in a shell script. And while you can write a file line-by-line by using the file-appending operator >> (two right angle brackets) with each command that should add to the file, there's a more efficient way to do that as well.

The trick is to open the file and associate a file descriptor number (3, 4, ..., 9) with it. UNIX keeps a *file pointer*, like a bookmark in a book, that tells it where the next read or write should be in each open file. For example, if you open a file for reading and read the first line, the file pointer will stay at the start of the second line. The next read from that same open file will move the pointer to the start of the third line. This trick only works with files that stay open; each time you open a file, the file pointer is set to the start of the file.* The Bourne shell *exec* command *(47.07)* can open a file and associate a file descriptor with it. For example, this *exec* command makes the standard input of all following commands come from the file *formfile*:

```
        ...all commands read their stdin from default place
exec < formfile
        ...all commands will read their stdin from formfile
```

There's another way to rearrange file descriptors: by doing it at the last line of *while* loops, *if* and *case* structures. For example, all commands in the *while* loop below will take their standard inputs from the file *formfile*. The standard input outside the *while* loop isn't changed:

```
        ...all commands read their stdin from default place
while ...
do
        ...all commands will read their stdin from formfile
done < formfile
        ...all commands read their stdin from default place
```

I call those "redirected-I/O loops." Those and other Bourne shell structures have some problems *(47.23)*, but they're usually worth the work to solve.

We'll use all that to make a shell script for filling in forms. The script, *formprog*, reads an empty form file like this one, line by line:

```
Name:
Address:
City:
State/Province:
Phone:
FAX:
```

---

*The file-appending operator >> sets the pointer to the end of the file before the first write.

Project: Corporate Decision
Comments:

If a line has just a label, like Name:, the script will prompt you to fill it in. If
you do, the script will add the completed line to an output file; otherwise, no
output line is written. If a form line is already completed, like:

Project: Corporate Decision

the script doesn't prompt you; it just writes the line to the output file:

```
% formprog formfile completed
Name: Jerry Peek
Address: 123 Craigie St.
City: Cambridge
State/Province: MA
Phone: (617)456-7890
FAX:
Project: Corporate Decision
Comments:
% cat completed
Name: Jerry Peek
Address: 123 Craigie St.
City: Cambridge
State/Province: MA
Phone: (617)456-7890
Project: Corporate Decision
```

Here's the *formprog* script. The line numbers are for reference only; don't type
them into the file. There's more explanation after the script:

formprog

(48.10)

```
 1  #! /bin/sh
 2  # formprog - fill in template form from $1, leave completed form in $2
 3  # TABSTOPS ARE SET AT 4 IN THIS SCRIPT
 4
 5  template="$1"   completed="$2"   errors=/tmp/formprog$$
 6  myname=`basename $0`   # BASENAME OF THIS SCRIPT (NO LEADING PATH)
 7  trap 'rm -f $errors; exit' 0 1 2 15
 8
 9  # READ $template LINE-BY-LINE, WRITE COMPLETED LINES TO $completed:
10  exec 4<&0   # SAVE ORIGINAL stdin (USUALLY TTY) AS FD 4
11  while read label line
12  do
13      case "$label" in
14      ?*:) # FIRST WORD ENDS WITH A COLON; LINE IS OKAY
15          case "$line" in
16          ?*) # SHOW LINE ON SCREEN AND PUT INTO completed FILE:
17              echo "$label $line"
18              echo "$label $line" 1>&3
19              ;;
20          *)  # FILL IT IN OURSELVES:
21              echo -n "$label "
22              exec 5<&0   # SAVE template FILE FD; DO NOT CLOSE!
23              exec 0<&4   # RESTORE ORIGINAL stdin TO READ ans
24              read ans
25              exec 0<&5   # RECONNECT template FILE TO stdin
26              case "$ans" in
27              "") ;;      # EMPTY; DO NOTHING
28              *)  echo "$label $ans" 1>&3 ;;
```

```
29              esac
30                ;;
31          esac
32          ;;
33      *)  echo "$myname: bad $1 line:   '$label $line'" 1>&2; break;;
34      esac
35  done <"$template" 2>$errors 3>"$completed"
36
37  if [ -s $errors ]; then
38      /bin/cat $errors 1>&2
39      echo "$myname: should you remove '$completed' file?" 1>&2
40  fi
```

Line 10 uses the 4<&0 operator *(47.21)* to save the location of the original standard input—usually your terminal, but not always*—as file descriptor 4. (We'll need to read that original *stdin* in line 24.)

During **lines 11-35** of the redirected-I/O *while* loop: all commands' standard input comes from the file named in $template, all standard error goes to the $errors file, and anything written to file descriptor 3 is added to the $completed file. UNIX keeps file pointers for all those open files—so each read and write is done just past the end of the previous one.

Here's what happens each time the loop is executed:

1. The *read* command *(46.13)* in **line 11** reads the next line from its standard input—that's the open $template file.

2. The *case (46.05)* in lines 15-31 checks the text from the $template file:

   - If the text has both a label (ending with a colon (:)) and some other text (stored in $line), the complete line is written two places. **Line 17** writes the line to the standard output—which is probably your screen (it's not redirected by the script, anyway). **Line 18** writes the line to file descriptor 3, the open $completed file.

   - If the text has just a label, **line 21** writes the label to standard output (usually your terminal) without a newline. We want to read the answer, at **line 24**, but there's a problem: on some Bourne shells, the *read* command can only read from file descriptor 0 and won't let you use operators like 4<&0 on its command line.

     So, in **line 22**, we save a copy of the open $template file descriptor *and the location of the open file pointer* in file descriptor 5. **Line 23** changes standard input so the *read* in line 24 will read from the right place (usually the terminal). **Line 25** adjusts standard input so the next *read* at the top of the loop (line 11) will come from the $template file.

---

*We can't assume that standard input is coming from a terminal. If we do, it prevents you from running *formprog* this way:

```
% command-generator-program | formprog
% formprog < command-file
```

If line 24 doesn't read an answer, **line 27** does not write a line. Otherwise, **line 28** writes the line to file descriptor 3, the open $completed file.

3. If the template label doesn't end with a colon, **line 33** writes a message to *stderr* (file descriptor 2). These messages, together with messages to *stderr* from any other command in the loop, are redirected into the $errors file. After the loop, if the test *(46.19)* in **line 37** sees any text in the file, the text is displayed in **line 38** and the script prints a warning.

The loop keeps reading and writing line by line until the *read* at the top of the loop reaches the end-of-file of $template.

—*JP* from the Nutshell Handbook *MH & xmh: E-Mail for Users & Programmers*

47.23 *The Ins and Outs of Redirected I/O Loops*

The Bourne shell usually runs a loop with redirected input or output *(47.22)* in a subshell *(40.04)*. For the *formprog* script in article 47.22, this means, among other things, that:

- Any command inside the loop that reads its standard input will read from the pipe or file redirected to the loop's standard input. That's something you have to pay attention to, because the only command that should read from the file is usually the *read* command at the top of the loop. The inputs of other commands inside the loop—like commands that read from the terminal—have to be redirected to read from somewhere other than the loop's standard input.

- In many Bourne shells, if you use the *exit (40.04)* command inside a redirected loop, that will only terminate the subshell that's running the loop; it will *not* terminate the script. It's hard to call this a "feature"; I'd call it a bug. The script in article 47.22 has a workaround for this; see the next paragraph. Later versions of Bourne-like shells have fixed this problem, more or less, but the fix below should work in all Bourne shells.

- If there's any error inside the loop that should terminate the script, an error message is written to file descriptor 2. File descriptor 2 is redirected to an error-holding file at the subshell (loop) output. A *break* command can end the loop right away. After the loop ends, if the error file has anything in it, that means there was an error—if there are more commands to run, the script can terminate before running them.

- You can test the exit status *(46.07)* of the redirected-I/O loop. To end the loop, use a command like exit 0, exit 2, and so on. Just after the done command outside the loop, use case $? *(46.05)* to test the loop's status. For instance, a 0 status might mean the loop worked fine, a 1 could signal one kind of error, a 2 status a different error, and so on.

- If you change the value of any shell or environment variables inside the loop, their values outside the loop (after the *done* command at the end of the loop) will not be changed.

Here's the usual fix for that problem. You use another file descriptor, like file descriptor 6, and write variable-setting commands to it. You redirect that file descriptor to a temporary file. Then, use the shell's dot command (.) (46.22) to read the temporary file into the shell outside the loop. For example, to get the value of a variable named *varname* outside the loop:

```
while whatever
do   ...
      echo "varname='value'" 1>&6
      ...
done 6> var_set_file
. var_set_file
```

—*JP* from the Nutshell Handbook *MH & xmh: E-Mail for Users & Programmers*

47.24 A Shell Can Read a Script from its Standard Input, But . . . 0365 1.21

Q: What is the difference between `sh < file` and `sh file`?

A: The first way keeps the script from reading anything else from its input. Consider the *zip* script:

```
while read word
do   echo $word | sed s/foo/bar/
done
```

If run as `sh zip`, it will read from your terminal, replacing `foo` with `bar`. If run as `sh < zip`, it will exit right away, since after reading the script, there's no input left.

—*CT* in *net.unix* on Usenet, *29 December 1984*

47.25 Shell Scripts On-the-Fly from Standard Input

(47.24)

The shell can read commands from its standard input or from a file. To run a series of commands that can change, you may want to use one program to create the command lines automatically—and pipe that program's output to a shell, which will run those "automatic" commands.

Here's an example.* You want to copy files from a subdirectory and all its subdirectories into a single directory. The filenames in the destination directory can't conflict; no two files can have the same name. An easy way to name the copies is to replace each slash (/) in the file's relative pathname with a minus sign (–).† For instance, the file named *lib/glob/aprog.c* would be copied to a file

---

*This isn't recommended for systems with a 14-character filename limit.

†A replacement like CTRL-a would make filenames that are more unique (but harder to type).

named *lib–glob–aprog.c.* You can use *sed (35.01)* to convert the filenames and output *cp* commands like these:

```
cp from/lib/glob/aprog.c to/lib-glob-aprog.c
cp from/lib/glob/aprog.h to/lib-glob-aprog.h
    ...
```

However, an even better solution can be developed using *nawk (38.05)*. The example below uses *find (18.01)* to make a list of pathnames, one per line, in and below the *copyfrom* directory. Next it runs *nawk* to create the destination file pathnames (like *to*/lib-glob-aprog.c) and write the completed command lines to the standard output. The shell reads the command lines from its standard input, through the pipe.

This example is in a script file because it's a little long to type at a prompt. But you can type commands like these at a prompt, too, if you want to:

```
#! /bin/sh
find copyfrom -type f -print |
nawk '{ out = $0
gsub("/", "-", out)
sub("^copyfrom-", "copyto/", out)
print "cp", $0, out }' |
sh
```

If you change the last line to sh -v, the shell's verbose option *(48.01)* will show each command line before executing it. If the last line has sh -e, the shell will quit immediately after any command returns a non-zero exit status *(46.07)*—that might happen, for instance, if the disk fills up and *cp* can't make the copy.

—JP

47.26 *Quoted hereis Document Terminators: sh vs. csh*

At the times you need to quote your hereis document *(9.14)* terminators there's an annoying problem: *sh* and *csh* demand different conventions. If you are using *sh*, you *must not* quote the terminator. For example,

```
#! /bin/sh
cat << 'eof'
Hi there.
eof
```

If you are using *csh*, however, you *must* quote the terminator. The script:

```
#! /bin/csh
cat << \eof
Hi.  You might expect this to be the only line, but it's not.
eof
'e'of
\eof
```

prints three lines, not one.

—CT in *net.unix-wizards* on Usenet, *20 July 1984*

47.27 Turn off echo for "Secret" Answers

When you type your password, UNIX turns off echoing so what you type won't show on the screen. You can do the same thing in shell scripts with `stty -echo`.

```
#!/bin/sh
    ...
trap 'stty echo; exit' 0 1 2 3 15
# use the right echo for your UNIX:
echo "Enter code name: \c"
#echo -n "Enter code name: "
stty -echo
read ans
stty echo
    ...
```

read *46.13*

The response is stored in $ans. The `trap` *(46.12)* helps to make sure that, if the user presses CTRL-c to abort the script, characters will be echoed again.

—JP

47.28 Quick Reference: expr

expr is a very handy tool in shell programming, since it provides the ability to evaluate a wide range of arithmetic, logical, and relational expressions. It evaluates its arguments as expressions and prints the result. Here's the syntax. The [brackets] mean "optional"; don't type the brackets:

> expr *arg1 operator arg2* [*operator arg3* ...]

Arguments and operators must be separated by spaces. In most cases, an argument is an integer, typed literally or represented by a shell variable. There are three types of operators: arithmetic, relational, and logical.

Exit status *(46.07)* values for *expr* are 0 if the expression evaluates non-zero and non-null, 1 if the expression evaluates to 0 or null, or 2 if the expression is invalid.

Arithmetic operators

Use these to produce mathematical expressions whose results are printed.

+	Add *arg2* to *arg1*.
−	Subtract *arg2* from *arg1*.
*	Multiply the arguments.
/	Divide *arg1* by *arg2*.
%	Take the remainder when *arg1* is divided by *arg2*.

Addition and subtraction are evaluated last, unless they are grouped inside parentheses. The symbols *, (, and) have meaning to the shell, so they must be escaped (preceded by a backslash or enclosed in single quotes).

Relational operators

Use these to compare two arguments. Arguments can also be words, in which case comparisons assume a<z and A<Z. If the comparison statement is true, *expr* writes 1 to standard output; if false, it writes 0. The symbols > and < must be escaped.

=	Are the arguments equal?
!=	Are the arguments different?
>	Is *arg1* greater than *arg2*?
>=	Is *arg1* greater than or equal to *arg2*?
<	Is *arg1* less than *arg2*?
<=	Is *arg1* less than or equal to *arg2*?

Logical operators

Use these to compare two arguments. Depending on the values, the result written to standard output can be *arg1* (or some portion of it), *arg2*, or 0. The symbols | and & must be escaped.

|	Logical OR; if *arg1* has a non-zero (and non-null) value, the output is *arg1*; otherwise, the output is *arg2*.
&	Logical AND; if both *arg1* and *arg2* have a non-zero (and non-null) value, the output is *arg1*; otherwise, the output is 0.
:	Sort of like *grep (28.01)*; *arg2* is a pattern to search for in *arg1*. *arg2* must be a regular expression in this case. If the *arg2* pattern is enclosed in \(\), the output is the portion of *arg1* that matches; otherwise, the output is simply the number of characters that match. A pattern match always applies to the beginning of the argument (the ^ symbol is assumed by default).

Examples

Division happens first; output is 10:

```
% expr 5 + 10 / 2
```

Addition happens first; output is 7 (truncated from 7.5):

```
% expr \( 5 + 10 \) / 2
```

Add 1 to variable *i*; this is how variables are incremented in Bourne shell scripts:

```
i=`expr "$i" + 1`
```

Output 1 (true) if variable *a* is the string "hello":

```
% expr "$a" = hello
```

Output 1 (true) if variable *b* plus 5 equals 10 or more:

```
% expr "$b" + 5 \>= 10
```

In the examples below, variable *p* is the string "version.100". This command returns the number of characters in *p*:

```
% expr "$p" : '.*'            Output is 11
```

Match all characters and print them:

```
% expr "$p" : '\(.*\)'        Output is "version.100"
```

Output the number of lowercase letters matched:

```
% expr "$p" : '[a-z]*'        Output is 7
```

Match a string of lowercase letters:

```
% expr "$p" : '\([a-z]*\)'    Output is "version"
```

Truncate $x if it contains five or more characters; if not, just output $x. (Logical OR uses the second argument when the first one is 0 or null; i.e., when the match fails.)

```
% expr "$x" : '\(.....\)' \| "$x"
```

—*DG from the Nutshell Handbook* UNIX in a Nutshell *(SVR4/Solaris)*

47.29 *Testing Characters in a String with expr*

The *expr (47.28)* command does a lot of different things with expressions. One expression it handles has three arguments: first, a string; second, a colon (:); third, a regular expression *(27.04)*. The string and regular expression usually need quotes.

expr can count the number of characters that match the regular expression. The regular expression is automatically anchored to the start of the string you're matching, as if you'd typed a ^ at the start of it in *grep, sed,* and so on. *expr* is usually run with backquotes *(10.14)* to save its output:

```
$ part="resistor 321-1234-00"  name="Ellen Smith"
    ...
$ expr "$part" : '[a-z ]*[0-9]'    --character position of first number
10
$ len=`expr "$name" : '[a-zA-Z]*'`
$ echo first name has $len characters
first name has 5 characters
```

When a regular expression *(27.04)* matches some character(s), *expr* returns a zero ("true") exit status *(46.07)*. If you want a true/false test like this, throw away the number that *expr* prints and test its exit status:

/dev/null *14.14*
```
$ if expr "$part" : '.*[0-9]' > /dev/null
> then echo \$part has a number in it.
> else echo "it doesn't"
> fi
$part has a number ln it.
```

—*JP*

47.30 Grabbing Parts of a String

How can you parse (split, search) a string of text to find the last word, the second column, and so on? There are a lot of different ways. Pick the one that works best for you—or invent another one! (UNIX has lots of ways to work with strings of text.)

Matching with expr

The *expr* command *(47.28)* can grab part of a string with a regular expression. The example below is from a shell script whose last command-line argument is a filename. The two commands below use *expr* to grab the last argument and all arguments except the last one. The "$*" gives *expr* a list of all command-line arguments in a single word. (Using "$@" *(46.14)* here wouldn't work because it gives individually-quoted arguments. *expr* needs all arguments in one word.)

```
last=`expr "$*" : '.* \(.*\)'`      # LAST ARGUMENT
first=`expr "$*" : '\(.*\) .*`      # ALL BUT LAST ARGUMENT
```

Let's look at the regular expression that gets the last word. The leading part of the expression, .* , matches as many characters as it can, followed by a space. This includes all words up to and including the last space. After that, the end of the expression, \(.*\), matches the last word.

The regular expression that grabs the first words is the same as the previous one—but I've moved the \(\) pair. Now it grabs all words up to but not including the last space. The end of the regular expression, .*, matches the last space and last word—and ignores them.

expr is great when you want to split a string into just two parts. The .* also makes *expr* good for skipping a variable number of words when you don't know how many words a string will have. But *expr* is lousy for getting, say, the fourth word in a string. And it's almost useless for handling more than one line of text at a time.

Using echo with awk, colrm, or cut

awk *(38.02)* can split lines into words. But *awk* has a lot of overhead and can take some time to execute, especially on a busy system. The *cut* *(36.12)* and *colrm* *(36.13)* commands start more quickly than *awk* but they can't do as much.

All of those utilities are designed to handle multiple lines of text, You can tell *awk* to handle a single line with its pattern-matching operators and its *NR* variable. You can also run those utilities with a single line of text, fed to the standard input through a pipe from *echo* *(9.04)*. For example, to get the third field from a colon-separated string:

```
string="this:is:just:a:dummy:string"
field3_awk=`echo "$string" | awk -F: '{print $3}'`
field3_cut=`echo "$string" | cut -d: -f3`
```

Let's combine two *echo* commands. One sends text to *awk*, *cut*, or *colrm* through a pipe; the utility ignores all the text from columns 1-24, then prints columns 25 to the end of the variable *text*. The outer *echo* prints *The answer is* and that answer. Notice that the inner double quotes are escaped with backslashes to keep the Bourne shell from interpreting them before the inner *echo* runs:

```
echo "The answer is `echo \"$text\" | awk '{print substr($0,25)}'`"
echo "The answer is `echo \"$text\" | cut -c25-`"
echo "The answer is `echo \"$text\" | colrm 1 24`"
```

Using set

The Bourne shell *set (46.18)* command can be used to parse a single-line string and store it in the command-line parameters *(46.14)* `"$@"`, `$*`, `$1`, `$2`, and so on. Then you can also loop through the words with a *for* loop *(46.15)* and use everything else the shell has for dealing with command-line parameters. Also, you can set the *IFS* variable *(36.19)* to control how the shell splits the string.

Using sed

The UNIX *sed (35.24)* utility is good at parsing input that you may or may not be able to split into words otherwise, at finding a single line of text in a group and outputting it, and many other things. In this example, I want to get the percentage-used of the filesystem mounted on */home*. That information is buried in the output of the *df (25.08)* command. On my system, *df* output looks like:

```
% df
Filesystem          kbytes    used   avail capacity  Mounted on
    ...
/dev/sd3c           1294854  914230  251139    78%    /work
/dev/sd4c            597759  534123    3861    99%    /home
    ...
```

I want the number *99* from the line ending with */home*. The *sed* address `/ \/home$/` will find that line (including a space before the */home* makes sure the address doesn't match a line ending with */something/home*). The *-n* option keeps *sed* from printing any lines except the line we ask it to print (with its *p* command). I know that the "capacity" is the only word on the line that ends with a percent sign (`%`). A space after the first `.*` makes sure that `.*` doesn't "eat" the first digit of the number that we want to match by `[0-9]`. The *sed* escaped-parenthesis operators *(35.10)* grab that number. Here goes:

```
usage=`df | sed -n '/ \/home$/s/.* \([0-9][0-9]*\)%.*/\1/p'`
```

Combining *sed* with *eval (9.08)* lets you set several shell variables at once from parts of the same line. Here's a command line that sets two shell variables from the *df* output:

```
eval `df |
sed -n '/ \/usr$/s/^[^ ]*  *\([0-9]*\)  * \([0-9]*\).*/kb=\1 u=\2/p'`
```

The left-hand side of that substitution command has a regular expression that uses *sed*'s escaped parenthesis operators. They grab the "kbytes" and "used" columns from the *df* output. The right-hand side outputs the two *df* values with

Bourne shell variable-assignment commands to set the *kb* and *u* variables. After *sed* finishes, the resulting command line looks like this:

```
eval kb=597759 u=534123
```

Now $kb will give you *597759* and $u contains *534123*.

—JP

47.31 A Better read Command: grabchars

grabchars

grabchars gets characters from the user as they are typed in, without having to wait for the RETURN key to be pressed. Among other things, this allows shell scripts to be written with highly interactive menus.

By default, *grabchars* will obtain one character from the standard input, echo that character to the standard output, and return an exit status *(46.07)* of one—meaning one character was read. Options (see the manual page) accept more than one character, accept only certain characters, prompt the user, and more.

Here's an example. With the standard *echo (9.04)* and *read (46.13)* commands, you'd prompt a user this way:

```
echo -n "Answer y or n, then press RETURN: "
read ans
```

With *grabchars*, a prompt can be printed to standard error, the user's answer read as soon as the character is pressed, and backquotes *(10.14)* used to grab the standard output (the user's answer, echoed by *grabchars*):

```
ans=`grabchars -q'Answer y or n: '`
```

By default, the answer that *grabchars* reads and echoes will be "eaten" by the backquotes; the user won't see what she typed. That's nice when the answer needs to be a secret. To show the answer, you have two choices:

- You can use the *−b* option. *grabchars* will echo the answer to both *stdout* (which the backquotes read) and *stderr* (which is usually the terminal).

- You can also use one of my favorite tricks, completing the user's answer before their eyes. For example, if the user types **y**, the script echoes yes. An **n** answer echoes as no. Any other answer (*x*) echoes as: *x*? Please answer y or n. Here's that sample code, including a *while* loop *(46.10)* to repeat until the user types the right answer:

```
          while :
          do
              ans=`grabchars -q'Answer y or n: '`
              case "$ans" in
              y) echo "yes" 1>&2; break ;;
              n) echo "no" 1>&2; break ;;
              *) echo "${ans}?  Please answer y or n." 1>&2 ;;
              esac
          done
```

`: 47.09`

`1>&2 9.04`
`break 47.09`

The option *-cvalid-characters* tells *grabchars* to accept only characters listed in *valid-characters* (this can be a regular expression like [a-z]). If the user types something that isn't listed, *grabchars* will ignore the answer and wait. So, to accept only *y* or *n*:

```
ans=`grabchars -c'yn' -q'Answer y or n: '`
```

There are lots of other options. I'd like to explain two more. (Please look at the manual page for the rest.) You can give *grabchars* a time limit with the *-t* option. If the user doesn't answer by then, *grabchars* can quit—and also give a default answer from the *-d* option. The timeout option lets you write shell scripts where you can offer some assistance if it's obvious that the user might be stuck—or to let a user answer a prompt only if he doesn't want the default. For example:

```
ans=`grabchars -t5 -d'y' -q'To stop, type n within 5 seconds: '`
```

If the user doesn't type anything in 5 seconds, *grabchars* will answer *y* automatically.

—JP, DS

47.32 *Testing Two Strings with One case Structure*

The shell's *case* structure *(46.05)* has some advantages over the *test* command *(46.19)*—for instance, *case* can do pattern matching. But *test* has the *-a* and *-o* "and" and "or" operators; those don't seem easy to do with *case*.

Here's a way to test two things with one *case* structure. It won't solve all your problems. If you think carefully about the possible values the variables you're testing can have, though, this might do the trick. Use a separator (delimiter) character between the two variables.

In the example below, I've picked a slash (/). You could use almost any character that isn't used in *case* pattern matching *(46.06)* and that won't be stored in either $# or $1. The *case* below tests the command-line arguments of a script:

```
case "$#/$1" in
1/-f) redodb=yes ;;
0/) ;;
*)   echo "Usage: $myname [-f]" 1>&2; exit 1 ;;
esac
```

If there's one argument ($# is 1) and the argument ($1) is exactly -f, the first pattern matches, and the *redodb* variable is set. If there's no argument, $# will be 0 and $1 will be empty, so the second pattern matches. Otherwise, something is wrong; the third pattern matches, the script prints an error and exits.

Of course, you can do a lot more this way than just testing command-line arguments.

—JP

47.33 *Arrays in the Bourne Shell*

The C shell *(49.05)*, *awk (38.18)*, the Korn shell, and some other UNIX command interpreters have built-in array support. The standard Bourne shell doesn't, though its command line is a sort-of array that you can store with the *set (46.18)* command—and get stored values through $1, $2, etc.

You can store and use Bourne shell variables—with names like *array1*, *array2*, and so on—to simulate an array with elements 1, 2, and so on. The *eval (9.08)* command does the trick. As an example, if the *n* shell variable stores the array index (1, 2, etc.), you can store an element of the array named *part* this way:

```
eval part$n="value"
```

and use its value this way:

```
eval echo "The part is \$part$n."
```

You need the extra quoting in that last command because *eval* scans the command line twice. The really important part is \$part$n—on the first pass, the shell interprets $n, strips off the backslash, and leaves a line like:

```
echo "The part is $part5."
```

The next pass gives the value of the *part5* variable.

To store a line of text with multiple words into these fake array elements, the *set* command won't work. A *for* loop *(46.15)* usually will. For example, to read a line of text into the *temp* variable and store it in an "array" named *part*:

```
echo "Enter the line: \c"
read temp
n=0
for word in $temp
do
        n=`expr $n + 1`
        eval part$n="$word"
done
```

expr 51.07

The first word from $temp goes into the variable *part1*, the second into *part2*, and so on.

—*JP*

47.34 Using a Control Character in a Script

There are times when you need to use non-printing control characters in a script file. If you type them directly into the file, they can be invisible to printers and on your screen—or, worse, they can cause trouble when you print or display the file.

One time you might need to store control characters in a script is when you're writing *sed* substitution commands; you don't know what delimiters to use because the strings you're substituting could contain almost any text:

```
sed "s/$something/$whoknows/"
```

Because *sed* can use almost any character as the delimiter, you can use a control character like CTRL-a instead of the slash (/). Another time you might also need to use non-printable strings of characters is for controlling a terminal; you won't want to type an Escape character directly into the file.

The answer is to use a command that will create the control characters as the script runs—and store them in shell variables.

With echo

If your version of *echo (9.04, 48.10)* interprets an octal number in a string like \001 as its ASCII value *(53.03)*, the job is easy. An octal-to-ASCII chart shows you that 0001 is CTRL-a. You can store the output of *echo* in a shell variable, and use the variable wherever you need a CTRL-a character:

```
ca=`echo \001`      # control-A character
    ...
sed "s${ca}$something${ca}$whoknows${ca}"
```

With tr and echo

If your *echo* can't make control characters directly, the *tr* utility can do it for you. *tr* understands octal sequences, too. Make your *echo* output characters you don't want, and have *tr* translate them into the control characters you do want. For example, to make the 4-character sequence *ESCape CTRL-a [CTRL-w*, use a command like this:

```
escseq=`echo 'ea[w' | tr 'eaw' '\033\001\027'`
```

tr reads the four characters down the pipe from *echo*; it translates the *e* into ESCape (octal 033), the *a* into CTRL-a (octal 001), and the *w* into CTRL-w (octal 028). The left bracket isn't changed; *tr* prints it as is.

The *script.tidy* script in article 53.06 shows a way to set several control characters in several shell variables with one command—that's efficient because it cuts the number of subprocesses needed. Another way to get control characters is with the handy *jot (47.11)* command on the Power Tools disk.

—*JP*

48

Shell Script Debugging
and Gotchas

48.01 Tips for Debugging Shell Scripts

Depending on the Bourne shell version you have, the error messages it gives can be downright useless. For instance, it can just say End of file unexpected. Here are a few tricks to use to get a little more information about what's going on.

Use −xv

Start your script like this:

```
#! /bin/sh −xv
```

(or, if your UNIX can't handle #!, use the command set −xv *(46.18)*). The −xv shows you what's happening as the shell reads your script. The lines of the script will be shown as the shell reads them. The shell shows each command it executes with a plus sign (+) before the command.

Note that the shell reads an entire loop (*for, while*, etc.) before it executes any commands in the loop.

If you want to run a script with debugging but you don't want to edit the script file, you can also start the shell explicitly from the command line and give the options there:

```
% sh -xv scrfile
```

Debugging output is usually pretty long, more than a screenful. So I pipe it to a pager like *pg*. But the shell sends its debugging output to *stderr*, so I pipe both stdout and stderr *(14.04)*. Using a pager has another advantage: if you want to kill the script before it finishes, just use the pager's "quit" command (like *q*). When the pager quits, UNIX may even kill the shell script (you may see the message Broken pipe *(52.11)*).

Do you want to save the debugging output in a file and see it on your screen, too? Use *tee (14.09)* to snag the *scrfile* stdout and stderr; add *tee* to the pipeline before the pager.

If the script is slow, you can run it in the background. Redirect the shell's output and errors *(14.05, 9.09)* into a temporary file. Use *tail –f (26.17)* to "watch" the log file. If you want to do something else while the script runs, just kill the *tail* command (with CTRL-c or your interrupt key), do something else, then start another *tail –f* when you want to watch again.

Finally, if the script normally writes something to its standard output, you can split the normal and debugging outputs into two files *(14.01)*.

Unmatched Operators

If the shell says `End of file unexpected`, look for a line in your script that has an opening quote but no closing quote. The shell is probably searching for but never finding the matching quote. The same goes for missing parentheses and braces (`{ }`).

Exit Early

If you're getting an `End of file unexpected` error, put these two lines near the top of your script:

```
echo "DEBUG: quitting early..." 1>&2
exit
```

Then run your script. If you don't get the `End of file unexpected` error anymore, you know that the problem is somewhere after the `exit` line. Move those two lines farther down and try again.

Missing or Extra esac, ;;, fi, etc.

A message like `line 23: ;; unexpected` means that you have an unmatched piece of code somewhere before line 23. Look at all nested *if* and *case* constructs and constructs like them to be sure that they end in the right places.

Line Numbers Reset inside Redirected Loops

The shell may give you an error that mentions "line 1" or another line number that seems way too small, when there's no error close to the top of your script. Look at any loops or other structures with redirected inputs or outputs *(47.22)*. Some Bourne shells start a separate shell to run these loops and lose track of the line numbers.

—*JP* from the Nutshell Handbook *MH & xmh: E-Mail for Users & Programmers*

48.02 Quoting Trouble? Think, then Use echo

Q: I can't get the following shell script to work:

```
case $col2 in
"income") awk '{if($2=='$col2') {    /* THIS LINE IS THE PROBLEM */
          /* I CAN'T GET AWK TO RECOGNIZE EITHER '$col2' or '$2' */
              .
              .

          } ' $file1 ;;
```

A: It is clear from this code fragment that *awk* is supposed to compare $2 with
`"income"`. If you think about it (or change awk to echo above), you will see
that you have given the following to *awk*:

```
{if($2==income) { /* THIS LINE IS THE PROBLEM */
```

What does *awk* do with this? It compares $2 with the contents of the variable
income. If *income* has not been set, it compares it with zero or with the null
string. Instead, you want:

```
{ if ($2 == "income") {
```

which you can say with:

```
case $col2 in
income)
        awk '
        {
                if ($2 == "'$col2'") {
                    ... awk code ...
                }
        }' $file1;;
```

Replacing commands with echo in shell scripts is a handy debugging trick.

—*CT* in *net.unix* on Usenet, *1 November 1986*

48.03 Bourne Shell Debugger Shows a Shell Variable

If you have a shell script that sets several variables and you want to show the
value of one of them, you can add a loop that asks you for variable names and
displays their values (47.19):

```
% cat myscript
#!/bin/sh
    ...
while echo "Pick a variable; just RETURN quits: \c"
      read var
do
      case "$var" in
      "") break ;;
      *)  eval echo \$$var ;;
      esac
done
```

The loop prompts `Pick a variable:`, then reads a value; if you type an empty answer, the loop quits. Otherwise, the value of that variable is displayed; the *eval(9.08)* command scans the *echo* command line twice.

This tip isn't just good for debugging. It's good in any shell script where you need to show the value of a variable by typing its name.

—*JP*

48.04 *Stop Syntax Errors in Numeric Tests*

The *test* and *[* (square bracket) commands *(46.19)* can compare two numbers. But it's an error if one of the numbers you test is stored in a shell variable that's empty or doesn't exist. For example, an empty *num* variable here will give you a `Syntax error`:

```
if [ "$num" -gt 0 ]
then ...
```

To stop syntax errors, add a leading zero, like this:

```
if [ "0$num" -gt 0 ]
then ...
```

In that case, if $num is empty, the test will compare 0 to 0. If $num is 1, the test will be true (because 01 is greater than 0)—and so on, just as it should be.

—*JP*

48.05 *Stop Syntax Errors in String Tests*

Using the *test* or *[* (square bracket) command *(46.19)* for a string test can cause errors if the variable starts with a dash (–). For example:

```
if [ "$var" = something ]
then ...
```

If $var starts with -r, the *test* command may think that you want to test for a readable file.

One common fix (that doesn't always work; see below) is to put an extra character at the start of each side of the test. This means the first argument will never start with a dash; it won't look like an option:

```
if [ "X$var" = Xsomething ]
then ...
```

That trick doesn't work if you want the test to fail when the variable is empty or not set. Here's a test that handles empty variables:

```
case "${var+X}" in
X) ...do this if variable is set...
   ;;
```

```
*)   ...do this if variable is not set...
    ;;
esac
```

If `$var` is set (even if it has an empty string), the shell replaces `${var+X}` *(47.12)* with just X and the first part of the *case* succeeds. Otherwise the default case, `*)`, is used.

—JP

48.06 *Watch Out for Bourne Shell –e Bug*

The Bourne shell *–e* option should stop execution when a command returns a non-zero status. Does your *–e* option seem to cause some *if* commands to abort scripts? If so, you have a copy of the Buggy Bourne Shell, as distributed with 4.2BSD, 4.3BSD, and probably several other systems. It can be identified by running:

```
$ set -e
$ if false; then echo yipe; else echo ok; fi
```

and noting that the shell exits instead of printing ok, and by:

```
$ set -e
$ false || echo ok
```

46.09

which also exits and should not, and by:

```
$ set -e
$ while false; do :; done
```

To fix it, first get the source, and then change it in the obvious three places in *xec.c*. You will have to learn Bournegol [the ALGOL-like dialect of C that Steve Bourne used to write the original Bourne shell—*JP*]. Another alternative is to replace */bin/sh* with one of the free *sh* look-alikes *(1.08)*, provided you can find one that is enough alike.

As a workaround, you can `set +e` around all the tests that might fail. Unfortunately, some versions of the Buggy Bourne Shell do not even support `set +e`; here the only workaround is to run a subshell *(40.04)* without the *–e* flag.

—CT in *comp.unix.questions* on Usenet, *20 February 1990*

48.07 *Quoting and Command-line Parameters*

Q: I need to pass a shell script some arguments with multiple words. I thought that putting quotes *(9.10)* around command-line arguments would group them. The shell script seems to ignore the quoting, somehow. Here's a simple example:

```
$ cat script
    ...
for arg in $*
do
```

```
        echo "Argument is $arg"
done
$ script '1 2 3' 4
    ...
Argument is 1
Argument is 2
Argument is 3
Argument is 4
```

A: This is the way $* is defined to work. $* expands to:

```
$1 $2
```

[not "$1" "$2"—*JP*] if there are two arguments. Hence the *for* loop reads:

```
for arg in 1 2 3 4
```

Note that the quotes are gone. What you wanted the shell to see was:

```
for arg in '1 2 3' 4
```

You cannot get that, but you can get something that is Good Enough:

"$@" *46.14*
```
for arg in "$@"
```

In effect, $@ expands to:

```
    $1" "$2
```

Putting " "s around $@, the effect is:

```
for arg in "$1" "$2"
```

Shell quoting is unnecessarily complex. The C shell actually has the right idea (variables can be set to "word lists" *(49.05)*; *argv* is such a list), but its defaults and syntax for suppressing them make for an artless programming language:

```
foreach arg ($argv:q)            # colon q ?!?
```

For the special case of iterating a shell variable over the argument list as it stands at the beginning of the iteration, the Bourne shell provides the construct `for arg do` [i.e., no in *list*—*JP*]:

```
for arg
do echo "Argument is $arg"
done
```

produces:

```
Argument is 1 2 3
Argument is 4
```

"$@" is still needed for passing argument lists to other programs. Unfortunately, since $@ is defined as expanding to:

```
$1" "$2...$n-1" "$n
```

(where n is the number of arguments), when there are no arguments:

```
"$@"
```

expands to:

```
" "
```

and `" "` produces a single argument. [Many UNIX vendors considered this a bug and changed it so that it produces *no* arguments.—*JP*] The best solution for this is to use, for example:

```
% cat bin/okeeffe
#! /bin/sh
exec rsh okeeffe.berkeley.edu -l torek ${1+"$@"}
%
```

The construct `${1+"$@"}` means "expand $1, but if $1 is defined, use `"$@"` instead." [You don't need this on Bourne shells with the "bug fix" I mentioned, but it's a good idea if you want your code to be portable.—*JP*] Hence, if there are no arguments, we get $1 (which is nothing and produces no arguments), otherwise we get `"$@"` (which expands as above). `${var+instead}` is one of several *sh* expansion shortcuts *(47.12)*. Another more generally useful one is `${var-default}`, which expands to $var, but if *var* is not set, to `default` instead. All of these can be found in the manual for *sh*, which is worth reading several times, experimenting as you go.

—*CT* in *comp.unix.questions* on Usenet, *18 March 1988*

48.08 Test Built-in Commands for Failure

Some old-timers in shell programming (myself included) tend to depend on shell "features" that they shouldn't. Here's one bad assumption: the Bourne shell will exit if the *cd* command fails. That wasn't documented (as far as I know), but still people wrote scripts like this:

```
    ...
cd $somedir
rm -rf *
```

The Korn shell didn't have that undocumented behavior. If a *cd* failed, *ksh* would print an error message and keep on reading the script. That caused some infamous problems when Bourne shell users gave their scripts to the Korn shell!

Unless the behavior of a command is documented, don't count on it to keep a disaster from happening. In the script above, for example, the *rm* command removed everything from a directory different than $somedir. One thing that's worth doing: test the exit status of a built-in and quit if it returns non-zero status. For instance, the `||` operator *(46.09)* makes this script abort if the *cd* fails:

```
    ...
cd $somedir || exit
rm -rf *
```

Careful testing of scripts that could do something disastrous—trying to find places where they'll fail—can be worth the time. That's especially true when you run the script on a new system or with another shell: test the built-in commands' exit status after they fail.

—JP

48.09 If Command Doesn't Return a Status, Test the Error Messages

UNIX commands should return a zero exit status *(46.07)* if they succeed or a non-zero status if they fail. Not all commands do. For example, here's a log I found of a test I did back in 1985 to the 4.3BSD version of *touch (22.07)*:

```
$ touch /tmp
touch: /tmp: can only touch regular files
$ echo $?
0
$ touch -f /usr/src/usr.bin/touch.c
touch: /usr/src/usr.bin/touch.c: couldn't chmod: Not owner
$ echo $?
0
$ touch -z
touch: bad option -z
$ echo $?
0
```

Because the status was always zero, as if the command had succeeded, my shell scripts couldn't test the exit status for failure. A workaround* is to make your own shell script version of *touch* (maybe call it *mytouch*)—or to put code like this into a shell script where you need to run *touch*:

```
                       # RUN touch ON THE COMMAND LINE ARGUMENTS (INCLUDING ANY OPTIONS).
                       # MERGE stderr ONTO stdout AND TEST FOR ERROR MESSAGES:
2>&1 47.21             out=`/bin/touch "$@" 2>&1`
                       case "$out" in
                       "")                              exitstat=0;;
                       *bad\ option)                    exitstat=1 ; echo "$out" 1>&2;;
                       *does\ not\ exist)               exitstat=3 ; echo "$out" 1>&2;;
                       *can\ only\ touch\ regular\ files*)  exitstat=4 ; echo "$out" 1>&2;;
                       *couldn\'t\ chmod)               exitstat=5 ; echo "$out" 1>&2;;
                       *couldn\'t\ chmod\ back)         exitstat=6 ; echo "$out" 1>&2;;
                       *cannot\ touch)                  exitstat=7 ; echo "$out" 1>&2;;
                       *)                               exitstat=10; echo "$out" 1>&2;;
                       esac
                       exit $exitstat
```

That code handles many of the error exits; other errors get an exit status of 10. You could simplify the code to return a status of 1 on *any* error. On the other hand, it would be easy to expand that code to cover any possible (or interesting) error output. Article 28.19 shows how to get a list of many of the possible error messages; you can also see the errors by making some typical mistakes like unreadable or unwritable filenames.

---

*Thanks to Richard Doty for this idea and the section of the shell script I've shown here.

That code won't work everywhere. The command you're running might write text to standard output that you don't want mixed together with error messages (on the standard error). Or, worse, some vendors' versions of some commands write errors to the standard output! Still, this technique should give you a good start on working around badly-behaved UNIX commands.

—JP

48.10 A Portable echo Command

One of the frustrating changes to UNIX (for me, at least) is the newer versions of *echo* (9.04) that interpret escape sequences like \c and \007. That feature is actually nice to have—usually, at least. But if the shell script has to work on both Berkeley and System V UNIX, it's a headache to write an *echo* command that prompts a user for an answer—with no newline at the end of the line. With a traditional UNIX *echo* command, you write:

```
echo -n "Answer y for yes or n for no: "
```

but the newer *echo* needs:

```
echo "Answer y for yes or n for no: \c"
```

and giving the wrong command to the wrong *echo* makes messy output.

Since then, I've seen workarounds by Bruce Barnett and Liam R. E. Quin. I've turned them into this version. It sets shell variables that you use this way:

```
$echo "Answer y for yes or n for no: ${nnl}"
```

Can your shell script be set up for a particular UNIX version ahead of time? If it can, write your no-newline *echo* commands like the example above—and put the lines below at the top of your script:

```
# UN-COMMENT THE LINE FOR YOUR SYSTEM:
echo="echo -n"   nnl= ;;                                    # BSD
#echo="echo"      nnl="\c" ;;                               # Sys V
#echo="echo -n"   nnl=      PATH=/usr/bin:$PATH; export PATH # SunOS
```

Lines similar to those let the person who installs the script set the right *echo* version.

But if your script is shared between many UNIX systems (across a networked filesystem) or runs on a system where users can choose BSD or System V features (like SunOS), your script will need to configure *echo* each time it runs. To do that, put the following code at the top of your script:

```
case "`echo 'x\c'`" in
'x\c')  echo="echo -n"   nnl= ;;      # BSD
x)      echo="echo"      nnl="\c" ;;  # Sys V
*)      echo "$0 quitting: Can't set up echo." 1>&2; exit 1 ;;
esac
```

In that code, the shell runs the current *echo* command and tests its output. Newer *echo* commands will interpret the \c and print **x** (with no newline after it; that doesn't matter here). Berkeley *echo* commands will echo the \c literally; this is matched by the first pattern instead.

You can handle other escape sequences and unprintable characters in the same way. For example, to make the code set $esc, a shell variable that makes an ESCape character, you can add lines like one of the two below:

`echo...033` **47.34**

```
esc=`echo -n d | tr "d" "\033"`     # BSD
esc="\033"                          # Sys V
```

—*JP*

49

C Shell Programming ... NOT

49.01 Why Not?

If you've read very much in this book, you'll see that we're very fond of the C shell. History, aliases, and so forth make it far superior to the Bourne shell for interactive use. However, it has some major drawbacks when it comes to shell programming.

Tom Christiansen explains some of the reasons in his famous tract "C Shell Programming Considered Harmful," which we've included as article 49.02. If you find yourself bristling at the tone of this article, remember that it was originally posted to Usenet *(1.33)*. It is an example of that art form known colloquially as a "flame." As flames go, this is actually fairly mild.

We agree with most of Tom's criticisms, and make no attempt to teach C shell programming in this book. We do however include a few quick-reference style articles on constructs that we use in articles about the C shell's setup files *(2.02)*, since they are in effect nothing but C shell programs read when the shell starts up. Specifically, we cover the syntax of *if (49.03)* and *switch (49.06)* statements. We explain how to set and use C shell arrays *(49.05)*—a nice C shell feature that, we admit :-), the Bourne shell is missing. (The *foreach (10.09)* loop, covered in another chapter, could be put in this chapter, too.) C shell expressions *(49.04)* (like $?prompt) can be used in *if, switch,* and *foreach.*

—*TOR, JP*

49.02 C Shell Programming Considered Harmful

Resolved: the *csh* is a tool utterly inadequate for programming, and its use for such purposes should be strictly banned.

I am continually shocked and dismayed to see people write test cases, install scripts, and other random hackery using the *csh*.

The *csh* is seductive because the conditionals are more C-like, so the path of least resistance is chosen and a *csh* script is written. Sadly, this is a lost cause, and the programmer seldom even realizes it, even when he finds that many simple things he wishes to do range from cumbersome to impossible in the *csh*.

What's more, lack of proficiency in the Bourne shell has been known to cause errors in */etc/rc* and *.cronrc* files, which is a problem, because you *must* write these files in that language.

File Descriptors

The most common problem encountered in *csh* programming is that you can't do file-descriptor manipulation. All you are able to do is redirect *stdin*, or *stdout*, or *dup stderr* into *stdout*. Bourne-compatible shells offer you an abundance of more exotic possibilities.

Writing Files

In the Bourne shell, you can open or *dup* random file descriptors. For example,

```
exec 2>errs.out
```

means that from then on, *stderr* goes into the *errs.out* file.

Or what if you just want to throw away *stderr* and leave *stdout* alone? Pretty simple operation, eh?

/dev/null *14.14*

```
cmd 2>/dev/null
```

That works in the Bourne shell. In the C shell, you can only make a pitiful attempt like this:

/dev/tty *47.20*

```
(cmd > /dev/tty) >& /dev/null
```

But who said that *stdout* was my terminal? So it's wrong. This simple operation *cannot be done* in the C shell.

Along these same lines, you can't direct error messages in *csh* scripts on *stderr*, as is considered proper. In the Bourne shell, you might say:

```
echo "$0: cannot find $file" 1>&2
```

but in the C shell, you can't redirect *stdout* onto *stderr* so you end up doing something silly like this:

```
sh -c "echo '${0}: cannot find $file' 1>&2"
```

Reading Files

In the *csh*, all you've got is $<, which reads a line from your *tty*. What if you've redirected *stdin*? Tough noogies, you still get your *tty*, which you really can't redirect. Now, the *read* statement in the Bourne shell allows you to read from *stdin*, which catches redirection. It also means that you can do things like this:

```
exec 3< file1
exec 4< file2
```

Now you can read from file descriptor 3 and get lines from *file1*, or from *file2* through fd 4. In modern, Bourne-like shells, this suffices:

```
read some_var 0<&3
read another_var 0<&4
```

Although in older ones where *read* only goes from 0, you trick it:

```
exec 5<&0  # save old stdin
exec 0<&3; read some_var
exec 0<&4; read another_var
exec 0<&5  # restore it
```

Closing FDs

In the Bourne shell, you can close file descriptors you don't want open, like 2>&-, which isn't the same as redirecting it to */dev/null*.

More Elaborate Combinations

Maybe you want to pipe *stderr* to a command and leave *stdout* alone. Not too hard an idea, right? As I mentioned above, you can't do this in the C shell. In a Bourne shell, you can do things like this:

```
$ exec 3>&1; grep yyy xxx 2>&1 1>&3 3>&- | sed s/file/foobar/ 1>&2 3>&-
grep: xxx: No such foobar or directory
```

Normal output would be unaffected. The fd closes (3>&-) were there in case something really cared about all its FDs. We send *stderr* to *sed*, and then put it back out FD 2.

Consider the pipeline:

```
A | B | C
```

You want to know the status of *C*, well, that's easy: it's in $?, or $status in *csh*. But if you want it from *A*, you're out of luck—if you're in the C shell, that is. In the Bourne shell, you can get it, although doing so is a bit tricky. Here's something I had to do where I ran *dd*'s *stderr* into a *grep* *−v* pipe to get rid of the records in/out noise, but had to return the *dd*'s exit status, not the *grep*'s:

```
device=/dev/rmt8
dd_noise='^[0-9]+ [0-9]+ records (in|out)$'
exec 3>&1
status=`((dd if=$device ibs=64k 2>&1 1>&3 3>&- 4>&-; echo $? >&4) |
    egrep -v "$dd_noise" 1>&2 3>&- 4>&-) 4>&1`
exit $status;
```

Command Orthogonality

Built-ins

The *csh* is a horrid botch with its built-ins. You can't put them together in any reasonable way. Even a simple little thing like this:

```
% time | echo
```

while nonsensical, shouldn't give me this message:

```
Reset tty pgrp from 9341 to 26678
```

Others are more fun:

```
% sleep 1 | while
while: Too few arguments.
[5] 9402
% jobs
[5]      9402 Done                    sleep |
```

Some can even hang your shell. Try typing CTRL-z while you're *source*ing something, or redirecting a *source* command. Just make sure you have another window handy.

Flow Control

You can't mix flow control and commands, like this:

```
who | while read line; do
    echo "gotta $line"
done
```

You can't combine multi-line constructs in a *csh* using semicolons. There's no easy way to do this:

```
alias cmd 'if (foo) then bar; else snark; endif'
```

Stupid Parsing Bugs

Certain reasonable things just don't work, like this:

```
% kill -1 `cat foo`
`cat foo`: Ambiguous.
```

But this is ok:

```
% /bin/kill -1 `cat foo`
```

If you have a stopped job:

```
[2]      Stopped                 rlogin globhost
```

You should be able to kill it with:

```
% kill %?glob
kill: No match
```

but:

```
% fg %?glob
```

works.

White space can matter:

```
if(expr)
```

may fail on some versions of csh, while:

```
if (expr)
```

works!

Signals

In the C shell, all you can do with signals is trap *SIGINT*. In the Bourne shell, you can trap any signal, or the end-of-program exit. For example, to blow away a temporary file on any of a variety of signals:

```
trap 'rm -f /usr/adm/tmp/i$$ ;
      echo "ERROR: abnormal exit";
      exit' 1 2 3 15
trap 'rm tmp.$$' 0    # on program exit
```

Quoting

You can't quote things reasonably in the *csh*:

```
set foo = "Bill asked, \"How's tricks?\""
```

doesn't work. This makes it really hard to construct strings with mixed quotes in them. In the Bourne shell, this works just fine. In fact, so does this:

```
cd /mnt; /usr/ucb/finger -m -s `ls \`u\``
```

Dollar signs ($) cannot be escaped in double quotes in the *csh*. Ugh.

```
set foo = "this is a \$dollar quoted and this is $HOME not quoted"
dollar: Undefined variable.
```

You have to use backslashes (\) for newlines, and it's just darn hard to get them into strings sometimes.

```
% set foo = "this \
and that";
% echo $foo
this  and that
% echo "$foo"
Unmatched ".
```

Say what? You don't have these problems in the Bourne shell, where it's just fine to write things like this:

```
echo  'This is
      some text that contains
      several newlines.'
```

Variable Syntax

There's this big difference between global (environment) and local (shell) variables. In *csh*, you use a totally different syntax to set one from the other.

In Bourne shell, this:

```
VAR=foo cmds args
```

is the same as:

```
(export VAR; VAR=foo; cmd args)
```

or *csh*'s:

```
(setenv VAR; cmd args)
```

You can't use :t, :h, etc. *(12.08)* on environment variables. Watch:

```
% echo Try testing with $SHELL:t
Try testing with /bin/csh:t
```

It's really nice to be able to say ${PAGER-more} or FOO=${BAR:-${BAZ}} *(47.12)* to be able to run the user's *PAGER* if set, and *more* otherwise. You can't do this in the *csh*. It takes more verbiage.

You can't get the process number of the last background command from the C shell, something you might like to do if you're starting up several jobs in the background. In the Bourne shell, the PID of the last command put in the background is available in $!.

The *csh* is also flakey about what it does when it imports an environment variable into a local shell variable, as it does with *HOME, USER, PATH*, and *TERM*. Consider this:

```
% setenv TERM '`/bin/ls -l / > /dev/tty`'
% csh -f
```

And watch the fun!

Expression Evaluation

Consider this statement in the *csh*:

```
if ($?MANPAGER) setenv PAGER $MANPAGER
```

Despite your attempts to set only *PAGER* when you want to, the *csh* aborts:

```
MANPAGER: Undefined variable.
```

That's because it parses the whole line anyway *and evaluates it*! You have to write this:

```
if ($?MANPAGER) then
    setenv PAGER $MANPAGER
endif
```

That's the same problem you have here:

```
% if ($?X && $X == 'foo') echo ok
X: Undefined variable
```

This forces you to write a couple of nested *if* statements. This is highly undesirable because it renders short-circuit Booleans useless in situations like these. If the *csh* were really C-like, you would expect to be able to safely employ this kind of logic. Consider the common C construct:

```
if (p && p->member)
```

Undefined variables are not fatal errors in the Bourne shell, so this issue does not arise there.

While the *csh* does have built-in expression handling, it's not what you might think. In fact, it's space-sensitive. This is an error:

```
@ a = 4/2
```

but this is okay:

```
@ a = 4 / 2
```

Error Handling

Wouldn't it be nice to know you had an error in your script before you ran it? That's what the *−n* flag is for: just check the syntax. This is especially good to make sure seldom taken segments of code are correct. Alas, the *csh* implementation of this doesn't work. Consider this statement:

```
exit (i)
```

Of course, they really meant:

```
exit (1)
```

or just:

```
exit 1
```

Either shell will complain about this. But if you hide this in an *if* clause, like so:

```
#!/bin/csh -fn
if (1) then
    exit (i)
endif
```

the C shell tells you there's nothing wrong with this script. The equivalent construct in the Bourne shell, on the other hand, tells you this:

```
#!/bin/sh -n
if (1) then
    exit (i)
endif

/tmp/x: syntax error at line 3: `(' unexpected
```

Random Bugs

Here's one:

```
!%s%x%s
```

Core dump, or garbage.

If you have an alias with backquotes (` `), and use that in backquotes in another one, you get a core dump.

Try this:

```
% repeat 3 echo "/vmu*"
/vmu*
/vmunix
/vmunix
```

What???

While some vendors have fixed some of the *csh*'s bugs (the *tcsh* *(1.08)* also does much better here), most of its problems can never be solved because they're a result of braindead design decisions. Do yourself a favor, and if you have to write a shell script, do it in the Bourne shell.

—*TC*

49.03 Conditional Statements with if

One piece of *csh* programming that's fairly important in setting up *.login* and *.cshrc* files *(2.02)* is the use of conditionals (*if* statements). This article explains the syntax of *if* statements. Article 49.04 explains the syntax of the expressions you can test with an *if*.

The *if* command is used to begin a conditional statement. The simple format is:

```
if (expr) cmd
```

There are three other possible formats, shown side-by-side:

```
if (expr) then        if (expr) then        if (expr) then
    cmds                  cmds1                 cmds1
endif                 else                  else if (expr) then
                          cmds2                 cmds2
                      endif                 else
                                                cmds3
                                            endif
```

In the simplest form, execute *cmd* if *expr* is true; otherwise do nothing (redirection still occurs; this is a bug). In the other forms, execute one or more commands. If *expr* is true, continue with the commands after then; if *expr* is false, branch to the commands after else (or after the **else if** and continue checking). For example, the following *if* clause will take a default action if no command-line arguments are given:

```
if ($#argv == 0) then
    echo "No filename given. Sending to Report."
    set outfile = Report
else
    set outfile = $argv[1]
endif
```

For more examples, see article 49.04.

—*DG from the Nutshell Handbook* UNIX in a Nutshell (SVR4/Solaris)

49.04 *C Shell Variable Operators and Expressions*

Variables

In the following substitutions, braces ({ }) are optional, except when needed to separate a variable name from following characters that would otherwise be a part of it. The array *argv* (the command-line arguments) is used as an example, but any *csh* array name may be used.

${*var*}	The value of variable *var*.
${*var*[*i*]}	Select word or words in position *i* of *var*. *i* can be a single number, a range *m–n*, a range *–n* (missing *m* implies 1), a range *m–* (missing *n* implies all remaining words), or * (select all words). *i* can also be a variable that expands to one of these values.
${#*var*}	The number of words in *var*.
${#argv}	The number of command-line arguments.
${argv[*n*]}	Individual arguments on command line (positional parameters). *n* is a number (1, 12, etc.).
${*n*}	Same as **${argv[*n*]}**.
${argv[*]}	All arguments on command line.
$*	Same as **$argv[*]**.
${argv[$#argv]}	The last argument.
${?*var*}	Return 1 if *var* is set; 0 if *var* is not set.
! ${?*var*}	Return 0 if *var* is set; 1 if *var* is not set.
$$	Process number of current shell; useful as part of a filename for creating temporary files with unique names.
$<	Read a line from standard input.

Expressions

Expressions are used in C shell *@*, *if,* and *while* statements to perform arithmetic, string comparisons, file testing, etc. *exit* and *set* can also specify expressions. Expressions are formed by combining variables and constants with operators that resemble those in the C programming language. Operator precedence is the same as in C but can be remembered as follows:

1. `*` `/` `%`

2. `+` `-`

Group all other expressions inside ( ). Parentheses are required if the expression contains <, >, &, or | .

Operators

Operators can be one of the following types:

Assignment Operators

=	Assign value.
+= -=	Reassign after addition/subtraction.
*= /= %=	Reassign after multiplication/division/remainder.
&= ^= |=	Reassign after bitwise AND/XOR/OR.
++	Increment
--	Decrement.

Arithmetic Operators

* / %	Multiplication; integer division; modulus (remainder).
+ -	Addition; subtraction.

Bitwise and Logical Operators

~	Binary inversion (one's complement).
!	Logical negation.
<< >>	Bitwise left shift; bitwise right shift.
&	Bitwise AND.
^	Bitwise exclusive OR.
|	Bitwise OR.
&&	Logical AND.
| |	Logical OR.
{ *cmd* }	Return 1 if command *cmd* is successful; 0 otherwise. Note that this is the opposite of *cmd*'s normal return code. The *status* variable may be more practical.

Comparison Operators

== !=	Equality; inequality.
<= >=	Less than or equal to; greater than or equal to.
< >	Less than; greater than.
=~	String on left matches a filename pattern on the right containing *, ?, or [...].
!~	String on left does not match a filename pattern containing *, ?, or [...].

File Inquiry Operators

Command substitution and filename expansion are performed on *file* before the test is performed.

-d *file*	The file is a directory.
-e *file*	The file exists.
-f *file*	The file is a plain file.
-o *file*	The user owns the file.
-r *file*	The user has read permission.
-w *file*	The user has write permission.
-x *file*	The user has execute permission.
-z *file*	The file has zero size.
!	Reverse the sense of any inquiry above.

Examples

The following examples show @ commands and assume *n* = 4:

Expression	Value of $x
@ x = ($n > 10 || $n < 5)	1
@ x = ($n >= 0 && $n < 3)	0
@ x = ($n << 2)	16
@ x = ($n >> 2)	1
@ x = $n % 2	0
@ x = $n % 3	1

The following examples show the first line of *if* or *while* statements:

Expression	Meaning
while ($#argv != 0)	While there are command-line (*argv*) arguments ...
if ($today[1] == Fri)	If the first word is *Fri* ...
if ($file !~ *.[zZ])	If the file doesn't end with *.z* or *.Z* ...
if ($argv[1] =~ chap?)	If the first argument is *chap* followed by a single character ...
if (-f $argv[1])	If the first argument is a plain file ...
if (! -d $tmpdir)	If *tmpdir* is not a directory ...

—*DG* from the Nutshell Handbook *UNIX in a Nutshell (SVR4/Solaris)*

49.05 Using C Shell Arrays

The C shell can treat its shell variables as *word lists*. They're a lot like *arrays* *(55.01)* in other programming languages, so that's what I'll call them. The C shell's *path (7.05)*, *cdpath (15.05)*, and *mail (22.08)* shell variables are arrays, for example. By the way, arrays are great for storing information in your shell setup files *(2.02)*.

To set an array, use parentheses around the value. Put a space between array members. Inside the parentheses, you can use single quotes, backquotes, double quotes, and so on. Here's how to put *fix the report* in the first member of the *job* array and *resign* as the second member:

```
% set job=("Fix the report" resign)
```

A dollar sign ($) before the name of a shell variable gives you its value. That gives all members of an array, too, because the array is stored as a shell variable. To pick out a particular member, put its number in square brackets after the name. For example:

```
% echo $job
Fix the report resign
% echo $job[1]
Fix the report
```

Like the Bourne shell *shift (46.16)* command, the C shell *shift* command shifts the command-line arguments. It also shifts array members. Let's shift the *job* array:

```
% shift job
% echo $job[1]
resign
```

Tom Christiansen told me that putting your directory stack *(15.06)* in an array is really useful. He's right. You might add an alias *(11.02)* for *pushd* and *popd* that stores the *dirs* output into an array named *dirstack*:

csh_init

```
alias pushd 'pushd \!* && set dirstack=(`dirs`)'
alias popd 'popd \!* && set dirstack=(`dirs`)'
```

Then, to look in the third directory in your stack, use a command like `ls $dirstack[3]`. Or, use an array with a *foreach* loop *(10.09)* to step through the members one-by-one. For instance, you might need to find the file *frobozz* that you put in some directory in your stack. Use the *–e* test *(49.04)* to look for a file that exists:

? 10.11
```
% foreach dir ($dirstack)
? if (-e $dir/frobozz) echo "frobozz is in $dir"
? end
frobozz is in /work/vol3/ch02.files/summaries
%
```

—*JP*

49.06 Quick Reference: C Shell switch Structure

The *switch* statement is used to process commands depending on the value of a variable. When you need to handle more than three choices, *switch* is a useful alternative to an *if-then-else* statement.

If the `string` variable matches `pattern1`, the first set of `commands` is executed; if `string` matches `pattern2`, the second set of `commands` is executed; and so on. If no patterns match, execute `commands` under the `default:` case. `string` can be specified using command substitution *(10.14)*, variable substitution *(7.08)*, or filename expansion *(1.16)*. Patterns can be specified using the pattern-matching symbols `*`, `?`, and `[ ]`. `breaksw` is used to exit the `switch` after `commands` are executed. If `breaksw` is omitted (which is rarely done), the `switch` continues to execute another set of `commands` until it reaches a `breaksw` or `endsw`.

Below is the general syntax of *switch*, side by side with an example that processes the first command-line argument.

```
switch (string)                    switch ($argv[1])
    case pattern1:                     case -[nN]:
        commands                           nroff $file | lp
        breaksw                            breaksw
    case pattern2:                     case -[Pp]:
        commands                           pr $file | lp
        breaksw                            breaksw
    case pattern3:                     case -[Mm]:
        commands                           more $file
        breaksw                            breaksw
        .                              case -[Ss]:
        .                                  sort $file
        .                                  breaksw
    default:                           default:
        commands                           echo "Error--no such option"
                                           exit 1
        breaksw                            breaksw
endsw                              endsw
```

—*DG* from the Nutshell Handbook *UNIX in a Nutshell (SVR4/Solaris)*

Part Nine

Miscellaneous

We're getting to the end, so this part of the book has all the things that didn't fit in earlier. That doesn't make it a collection of leftovers, though. In fact, this part of the book has some of the best programs in the whole collection, including a spreadsheet, a business graphics package, and a PostScript calendar-maker you'll wonder how you ever did without.

It's also got information on UNIX's online documentation system and error messages, a miscellanous collection of useful programs and curiosities (now that one is a grab-bag), and a glossary.

It's also got a very important chapter with instructions about how to install the programs from the Power Tools disk!

—TOR

50

Office Automation

50.01 *Well, What Else Could We Call It?*

OK, so maybe the articles in this chapter don't really talk about office automation, but they do talk about things of interest to office workers—things that don't have much to do with computers, but rather with the kinds of things that people wanted the computers for in the first place. Things like:

- Maintaining an online phone and address database *(50.02)*.

- Quick lookup of area codes *(50.03)* or zip codes *(50.04)*.

- Reminding yourself of your appointments with *calendar (50.05)*, or even just when it's time to leave *(50.06)*.

- Printing out calendars for any date (articles 50.07, 50.08, and 50.09) including a super-duper one that includes all your appointments (article 50.10).

- Maintaining simple databases with *awk (50.11)* or *index (50.12, 50.13)*.

If you're looking for office tools, also be sure to check out *sc (51.09)* and *ipl (51.10)* in the next chapter.

—*TOR*

50.02 On-line Phone and Address Lists

Here's a useful little shell script that we've used at O'Reilly & Associates. If you run it as *phone*, it gives you peoples' phone numbers—it searches files named *phone* in your home directory and in a system location. If you run it as *address*, it does the same thing for files named *address*. Lines from the system file are labeled sys>; lines from your personal file are marked pers>. For example:

```
% phone tom
pers>Tom VW's mother, Barbara Van Winkel in Vermont 802-842-1212
pers>Tom Christiansen [5/10/92] 201/555-1212
sys>Flitecom (Dave Stevens, Tom Maddy) (301) 588-1212
```

The script uses *egrep (28.05)* to search the file; the *egrep −i* option means you can type tom and the script will find lines with either *Tom* or *tom* (or *TOM* or . . .). The two names for this script are both links *(19.03)* to the same file. Of course, you can adapt the script for things besides phone numbers and addresses.

phone

```
#!/bin/sh
# LINK BOTH THE phone AND address SCRIPTS TOGETHER; BOTH USE THIS FILE!

myname="`basename $0`"  # NAME OF THIS SCRIPT (USUALLY address OR phone)
case "$myname" in
phone|address)
        sysfile=/work/ora/$myname   # SYSTEM FILE
        persfile=${HOME?}/$myname   # PERSONAL FILE
        ;;
*) echo "$0: HELP!  I don't know how to run myself." 1>&2; exit 1 ;;
esac
```

test *46.19*
touch *22.07*

```
if test ! -f $persfile
then touch $persfile
fi
```

$# *46.14*

```
case $# in
0)   echo "Usage: $myname searchfor [...searchfor]
     (You didn't tell me what you want to search for.)" 1>&2
     exit 1
     ;;
*)   # BUILD egrep EXPRESSION LIKE (arg1|arg2|...) FROM NAME(S) USER TYPES:
     for arg
     do
         case "$expr" in
         "") expr="($arg" ;;
         *) expr="$expr|$arg" ;;
         esac
     done
     expr="$expr)"
esac

# SEARCH WITH egrep, USE sed TO ADD sys> TO START OF FILENAMES FROM
# SYSTEM FILE AND pers> TO START OF FILENAMES FROM HOME LIST:
egrep -i "$expr" $persfile $sysfile |
sed -e "s@^$sysfile:@sys>@" -e "s@^$persfile:@pers>@"
exit
```

The comments in the script explain what each part does. The most interesting part is probably the *for* loop *(46.15)* and *case* structure *(46.05)* that build the *egrep* expression. For instance, if you type the command phone tom mary, the script builds and runs an *egrep* command as if you'd typed this:

```
% egrep -i "(tom|mary)" /u/me/phone /work/ora/phone
/u/me/phone:Tom VW's mother, Barbara Van Winkel in Vermont 802-842-1212
/u/me/phone:Tom Christiansen [5/10/92] 201/555-1212
/work/ora/phone:Flitecom (Dave Stevens, Tom Maddy) (301) 588-1212
   ...
```

The *sed (35.24)* command turns the pathnames from *egrep* into pers> and sys>.

You can install this script from the Power Tools disk or you can just type it in. If you type in the script, put it in an executable file named *phone.* (If all users on your system will share it, your system administrator should put the script in a central directory such as */usr/local/bin.*) Then make a link to it:

```
% chmod 755 phone
% ln phone address
```

—*JP*

50.03 *Where is that Area Code?*

How many times have you gotten a phone message from someone you never heard of, asking you to call a long-distance number and leaving no hint of where you'd actually be calling? Maybe you want to know because you'd like to have an idea what time zone they're in. Maybe you want to know because you don't like the idea of paying for a phone call to Vancouver to talk to a salesperson.

areacode

Now you can use the *areacode* program to quickly find out what area in North America is mapped to what area code. For example, if you get a message to call someone with area code 319:

```
% areacode 319
Area code 319 is Dubuque, Iowa.
```

The area codes are hardcoded into the *areacode* program, so the most recent changes by the phone company may not be known. But it's definitely better than scouring the phone book!

—*LM*

50.04 How About the Same Thing for Zip Codes?

zipcode

areacode (50.03) seemed like a good idea, so we asked Jeff Moskow, who put together the public domain software for the disk, to see if he could find a zip code database out there somewhere and whip up a script that does much the same thing as *areacode*. *zipcode* was his answer. *zipcode* is written in *perl* (39.01), using a listing of zip codes that is available on the Internet.

Like *areacode*, the *zipcode* program takes a five-digit U.S. zip code and returns the region that the zip code corresponds to. For example:

```
% zipcode 10467
Bronx, NY
```

Now, you might think that this isn't all that useful, since it isn't that often that you have a zip code without the rest of the address. But Jeff points out that if you have a program like *zipcode*, then when you're taking down addresses you can skip writing down the town and city—you can get that information later from just the zip code. This can turn into quite a time-saver for our order-entry department!

city

In addition, Jeff wrote us a simple shell script to search in reverse, called *city*. *city* just runs a *grep* on the same list that *zipcode* does. Instead of the zip code, *city* takes the name of a town and shows you what zip codes are used in that town.

```
% city Bronx
10400:Bronx, NY
10451-10475:Bronx, NY
% city Brooklyn
06234:Brooklyn, CT
11200-11226:Brooklyn, NY
11228-11244:Brooklyn, NY
11247-11249:Brooklyn, NY
11251-11252:Brooklyn, NY
11254-11256:Brooklyn, NY
18813:Brooklyn, PA
36429:Brooklyn, AL
39425:Brooklyn, MS
42209:Brooklyn, KY
46111:Brooklyn, IN
49230:Brooklyn, MI
52211:Brooklyn, IA
53521:Brooklyn, WI
61378:West Brooklyn, IL
```

—*TOR, LM*

50.05 Automatic Reminders and More: calendar

If you type the command calendar, you'll see lines with "to-do" items for today and tomorrow from a file named *calendar* in your current directory. If you put that file in your home directory, your system administrator can run the command calendar - to mail *(1.33)* everyones' "to-do" items to them. You can also automate your personal calendar setup by running *calendar* yourself—the calendar can be mailed to you, sent to the printer, and so on, first thing each morning. See below for an example *calendar* file and more information.

calendar builds a complicated *egrep (28.05)* expression to search your *calendar* file. You can see that expression yourself if you want to.

How calendar Works

Let's start by showing a few lines of a sample *calendar* file. (Yours can be much longer.) Then I'll run *calendar* to show what lines it picks:

```
% cat calendar
--- WORK ---
12/28    Project report due tomorrow!
--- PERSONAL ---
* 8         rub Lisa's feet
Take Lisa out to dinner on December 8
dec 9      buy Lisa lunch
On 12/10, Lisa will be hungry for ice cream
--- BIRTHDAYS ---
1/1 Mom's birthday -- make dinner reservations by 12/20!
% date
Tue Dec  8 08:43:40 PST 1992
% calendar
* 8         rub Lisa's feet
Take Lisa out to dinner on December 8
dec 9      buy Lisa lunch
```

Today is December 8. The *calendar* utility found lines in my *calendar* file for today and tomorrow. *calendar* understands lots of date formats. The date can be anywhere on a line. If you leave a line in your file for more than one year (like Mom's birthday) *calendar* will show it every year. If a line has more than one date, you'll see the line on both of those dates (I'll be reminded before Mom's birthday and also in time to make a dinner reservation). An asterisk (*) in place of a month means "all months."

Many versions of *calendar* utility run your *calendar* file through the C language preprocessor, *cpp*. Among other things, this lets you include several calendar files in your own calendar file. Lines that start with a hash mark (#) in column 1 are read by the preprocessor. For instance, this line in your *calendar* file would include all the contents of the file */usr/local/lib/office.calendar* just as if you'd typed them into your own file:

```
#include "/usr/local/lib/office.calendar"
```

Someone (the office secretary) can maintain the *office.calendar* file. People in the office who want reminders from it can put the #include line in their own *calendar* files.

By the way, if you start a line with # and it's not for the preprocessor, you'll get a mysterious error like calendar: 1: undefined control. That means line 1 of the file had something the preprocessor couldn't understand.

The egrep Expression calendar Uses

How can *calendar* find dates in all the formats it accepts—and only for today and tomorrow? It runs a system program, usually named */usr/lib/calendar*, that generates an expression for *egrep* −*f* *(28.07)*. The expression searches for the dates of today and tomorrow; if today is a Friday, the expression includes dates on Saturday, Sunday, and Monday. Here's the expression I got by running */usr/lib/calendar* on Tuesday, December 8. TAB characters are shown as T; spaces are shown as □.

```
% /usr/lib/calendar
(^|[□T(,;])((([Dd]ec[^□T]*|\*)[□T]*|(012|12|\*)/)0*8)([^0123456789]|$)
(^|[□T(,;])((([Dd]ec[^□T]*|\*)[□T]*|(012|12|\*)/)0*9)([^0123456789]|$)
```

I'll turn the first line of that into English. I'm not writing this just for *egrep* fanatics :-); this is also useful for understanding what kinds of dates *calendar* will recognize. I'm going to skip some not-so-subtle things like the nesting of the parentheses and just give an overview. If you haven't seen extended regular expressions before, see article 27.04. The expression finds lines in your *calendar* file that meet these conditions, in order from left to right across the line:

(^|[□T(,;])
This matches whatever comes before the date. Match at the beginning of a line (^) or (|) match a space, TAB, opening parenthesis, comma, or semicolon ([□T(,;]). This keeps *egrep* from matching other words that start with or contain the month abbreviation [Dd]ec.

((([Dd]ec[^□T]*|*)[□T]*|(012|12|*)/)0*8)
This matches the date. Match *Dec* or *dec* with zero or more spaces or TABs after that ([Dd]ec[^□T]*)—or (|) have a literal asterisk (*), which means "match this on any month of the year." Or (|) match a numeric month like *012* or *12* or a literal asterisk ((012|12|*))—followed by a slash (/). Finally, you need today's date: it starts with any number of zeros and ends with *8* (/)0*8)).

([^0123456789]|$)
The end of the expression matches lines anything except a digit—or matches the end of the line. This keeps *egrep* from matching non-dates like *8.75*.

Whew. That expression is repeated for every other day that needs to be matched. On Fridays, the output of */usr/lib/calendar* has four lines—one each for Friday, Saturday, Sunday, and Monday.

Automating Your Own Calendar

If you want a calendar every weekday, put a line like the one below into your personal *crontab* file *(42.12)*. We've split this onto two lines for printing, but you should type it all on one line:

$USER 7.03
&& 46.09
< 14.01

```
6 6 * * 1-5 tf=/tmp/cal.$USER; /bin/calendar > $tf;
    test -s $tf && mail -s 'Calendar for today' $USER < $tf; rm -f $tf
```

That runs *calendar* from my home directory at 6:06 a.m. *(42.05)* every weekday morning. It sets a Bourne shell variable *(7.08)* named *tf* with the name of a temporary file in the */tmp* directory *(22.03)*. Then it runs *calendar* and saves the output in the temporary file. If there's a calendar for today, the *mail* command sends the file to me. (The *−s* option on our *mail* command adds the Subject: line *Calendar for today* to the message. It isn't required.) Finally, the temporary file is removed.

If you don't have personal *crontab*s, you can use a self-restarting *at* job *(42.08)* and the *nextweekday* script *(42.10)* instead.

—JP

50.06 *leave: A Maddening Aid to Quitting on Time*

Time to leave! The message flashes across your screen, the terminal bell rings. You keep working.

You're going to be late! Another message, a minute later. Sheesh. Did your mother learn to use *write(1.33)*, or what?

No. It's the *leave* program that you started to remind you of a meeting. (A little while ago, it already told you that You have to leave in 5 minutes.) If your system has *leave*, you can start it in one of three ways:

- **leave 1300** sets the alarm for 1:00 p.m.

- **leave +30** sets the alarm for 30 minutes from now.

- With no arguments, **leave** prompts you When do you have to leave? You can type an answer like 1300 or +30 above. Or, if you just press RETURN, *leave* will leave you alone. That's handy to put in your *.login* or *.profile(2.01, 2.02)* file.

When will it stop nagging you? When you log out, *leave* stops automatically. Also, newer versions of *leave* will quit after ten minutes, saying That was the last time I'll tell you. Bye. Older versions keep on forever.

On some versions of *leave*, you can't set an alarm for any time tomorrow (past midnight). But you can use *sleep (42.02)* to start the *leave* past midnight. For example, maybe it's 10 p.m. now and you want to leave at 1 a.m. Midnight is two hours or 7200 seconds (60 x 60 x 2) from now. Add a fudge factor of 10 minutes (600 seconds) and type:

( ) *14.07*

```
$ (sleep 7800; leave 100) &
1234
```

You can also kill *leave*—though you have to use the "sure kill," signal 9 *(40.08)*. To see *leave* lurking in the background and get its PID *(40.03)*, you usually need the *ps (40.05)* –*x* option. Piping through *grep leave* will shorten the *ps* output:

```
% ps x | grep leave
 6914 p3 S     0:00 leave
19283 p3 R     0:01 grep leave
% kill -9 6914
```

—*JP*

50.07 Get Calendar for Any Month or Year: cal

What day were you born? If you were born on September 23, 1962, type this command to get a calendar for the month:

```
% cal 9 1962
   September 1962
Su Mo Tu We Th Fr Sa
                   1
 2  3  4  5  6  7  8
 9 10 11 12 13 14 15
16 17 18 19 20 21 22
23 24 25 26 27 28 29
30
```

You were born on a Sunday. Be sure to type all four digits of the year. If you don't, you'll get the calendar for 62 A.D.—almost 2000 years ago!

To get a calendar for the current month, just type *cal* (no arguments). You can also get the whole calendar for any year by giving a single argument: the year you want (use all four digits for any year in the last millennium).

There seems to be a bug in September 1752:

```
% cal 9 1752
   September 1752
Su Mo Tu We Th Fr Sa
       1  2 14 15 16
17 18 19 20 21 22 23
24 25 26 27 28 29 30
```

But there isn't really a bug. That's when Great Britain and the (then) American colonies adopted the Gregorian calendar; what would have been September 3 became September 14, and the beginning of the year changed from March 25 to January 1. Hmmmph. Bugs—in UNIX? :-)

—*JP*

50.08 cal that Marks Today's Date

If you're like me and you tend to forget what day it is :-), a calendar like the one that *cal (50.07)* prints doesn't help much. Here's a little shell script below that puts angle brackets around the current date. For example, if today is November 18, 1991:

```
% cal
     November 1991
 Su Mo Tu We Th Fr Sa
                 1  2
  3  4  5  6  7  8  9
 10 11 12 13 14 15 16
 17>18<19 20 21 22 23
 24 25 26 27 28 29 30
```

If you're sure that this script will never be called by another program that expects the system version, you can name this *cal*, too—just be sure to put it in a directory somewhere in your PATH before */usr/bin (9.05)*, the system location of most versions of *cal*. Otherwise, give the script another name, such as *cal_today*.

The script uses the version of *date* that accepts an argument starting with a plus sign (+) to control its output format. If you don't have that version of *date*, you can work around it with some trickery—but it's better to get the *date* on the Power Tools disk *(53.10)* instead.

cal_today
eval *9.08*

"$@" *46.14*

```
#! /bin/sh
# IF USER DIDN'T GIVE ARGUMENTS, PUT > < AROUND TODAY'S DATE:
case $# in
0) eval `date +d=%d`
   /usr/bin/cal |
   sed -e 's/^/ /' -e "s/^$d />$d</" -e "s/ $d$/>$d</" -e "s/ $d />$d</"
   ;;
*) /usr/bin/cal "$@" ;;
esac
```

If you give any arguments, the script assumes that you don't want the current month; it runs the system *cal* command. Otherwise, the script pipes the system *cal* output into *sed (35.24)*. The *sed* expression puts a space before every line to make room for any > at the start of a line. Then it uses three substitute commands—one each for the beginning, middle, and end of a line—one is guaranteed to match the current date.

—*JP*

50.09 *Calendar for 132-Column Terminals or Printers*

The *cal (50.07)* program is convenient, but it's fairly no-frills. If you have a 132-col-umn terminal, or (more importantly) if you have a 132-column line printer, try using the *calen* program instead.

calen

The *calen* program prints out calendars using 132 columns, and draws boxes for each date that are large enough to scribble notes in. The syntax for the *calen* program is:

    calen month year [length]

The *length* is the optional number of months you want shown, starting with the specified month (the default number of months is 1). For example:

    % calen 6 1965

shows you a calendar for the month of June, 1965.

To get the entire year of 1965 (all 12 months), do:

    % calen 1 1965 12

The only real reason for using *calen* is to print out the calendar so you can write on it. But if you have a PostScript printer, forget about *calen*, since *pcal (50.10)* is much more powerful.

—LM

50.10 *Postscript Calendars with pcal*

Sometimes you want a hardcopy calendar. You can generate one using *cal (50.07)* and an ASCII-to-PostScript filter like *pstext (45.24)*, but the resulting calendar is nothing to write home about.

pcal

A nifty alternative for printing calendars is *pcal*. *pcal* isn't just a pretty face: yes, it prints nice calendars, but you can also configure it to do quite a lot more. I just discovered *pcal*, and it already has potential for becoming one of my favorite utilities.

In its default form, *pcal* just creates a PostScript calendar for the current month. The PostScript commands are written to standard output, so you need to pipe it to *lpr* for BSD-based systems, or *lp* for System V-based systems. (Of course, your printer has to be able to print PostScript.) For example:

    % pcal | lpr

You'll get a full-page calendar of the current month. The dates for Saturdays and Sundays are printed in gray. To get a different month, you can specify it the same way you would using *cal*. For a calendar for November 1992, you could do:

    % pcal 11 1992 | lpr

For a calendar for the whole year, use the −*w* option to *pcal*.

```
% pcal -w | lpr
```

Once you get a chance to see the *pcal* output, you'll already see how big an improvement it is over just printing the output of the *cal* program. But *pcal* also gives you the opportunity to configure your calendars.

pcal looks for a file called *.calendar* in either your home directory or your current directory. (This is a hidden file *(17.12)* because the name starts with a dot.) You can use this file to mark days in the year. For example, you can use it to define particular days as holidays:

```
1/1                       New Year's Day
Feb 14                    Valentine's Day
```

But *pcal* also understands a limited set of relational words as well. For example:

```
Second Sunday in May      Mother's Day
4th thu of nov            Thanksgiving
```

For each of these examples, the given day will have the specified text written in. If you use an asterisk (*) to mark a certain day, the day is marked as a holiday.

```
1/1*                      New Year's Day
Feb 14                    Valentine's Day
Second Sunday in May      Mother's Day
4th thu of nov*           Thanksgiving
```

This means that the day appears in gray on the calendar, like Saturday and Sunday. But more importantly, it means that *pcal* will understand that the marked day isn't a working day.

In addition to holidays, you can use *pcal* to mark things like birthdays and anniversaries.

```
June 4                    My Birthday!!!
September 3               Peter's birthday
April 1                   Mom and Dad's anniversary
```

Now here's where *pcal* starts to get useful. You can use *pcal* to mark meetings you have scheduled:

```
april 14                  Meet with tax attorney at 4:45
last day of october       Dr. Jekyll's office, 5:30
```

Or for regular appointments:

```
Each Friday of July       Leave early for Cape
```

As you can probably tell by now, the syntax accepted by *pcal* is very flexible. It's actually much too complicated to be able to explain in full here, but *pcal* comes with a complete manual page, and *pcal −h* will give you a list of syntax and command-line options. And if you just wing it, you're likely to come up with syntax that works.

In place of the name of a month, you can use the `all` keyword to mean all months, i.e., the entire year. For example:

```
First day of all          Send monthly report to boss
Each Monday in all        Status meeting at 11:30
```

Now, just above we used `First day of all` to specify when we should send our monthly report. What about when the first of the month falls on a weekend or holiday? Well, *pcal* also understands phrases like `workday` and `holiday`. To make sure that your reminder to submit your report appears on the first workday of the month, you can write:

```
First workday of all      Send monthly report to boss
```

By default, *pcal* considers only Saturdays and Sundays to be non-workdays. You add days to this list when you define holidays with asterisks (*) as described previously.*

Another feature of *pcal* is that you can use the phases of the moon in your date specifications.

```
2nd full_moon in all      Blue moon!
```

pcal supplies format specifiers for writing more detailed descriptions. For example, suppose you want to be reminded at the beginning of each month to make your monthly schedule. You can make up an entry that reads:

```
First workday of all      Write schedule for %B
```

The special format specifier `%B` expands into the name of the current month. So the first workday of October will read, "Write schedule for October."

Some other modifiers defined by *pcal* are `%A` for the name of the weekday, `%d` for the day of the month, `%Y` for the year, `%j` for the day of the year, and `%l` for the number of days remaining in the year. There are also a few modifiers available. The most useful ones are `%+` and `%-` for using the following or previous month or year. For example, suppose you want a reminder on the last day of the month to pay the rent for the next month. You can write:

```
Last day of all           Pay rent for month of %+B
```

In our office, we're expected to turn in time sheets for each 2-week period, on the 1st and 16th of each month. We can write:

```
first workday of all      Time sheet due for end of %-B
workday on_or_after all 16 Time sheet due for beginning of %B
```

You can also specify command-line options to *pcal* in your *.calendar* file, using the `opt` keyword. For example:

```
opt    -n Times-Italic -m
```

The *-n Times-Italic* option tells *pcal* to use the Times Italic font to display the

---

*Note that *pcal* only knows about holidays that have already been declared in your specification file. So in general, you want to define your holidays early in your *.calendar* file so that later references to workdays will be up-to-date.

text within the dates. The *−m* option tells *pcal* to show the new, half, and full moons in the month.

—LM

50.11 Working with Names and Addresses

One of the simplest applications of *awk (38.18)* is building a name and address database. It is a good exercise for learning *awk* as well. It involves organizing the information as a record and then writing programs that extract information from the records for display in reports. The scripts in this article use *nawk (38.05)* instead of *awk*, but the principles are the same.

The first thing to decide is the structure of a record. At the very least we'd like to have the following fields:

> Name
> Street
> City
> State
> Zip

But we may wish to have a more complex record structure:

> Name
> Title
> Company
> Division
> Street
> City
> State
> Zip
> Phone
> Fax
> E-mail
> Directory
> Comments

It doesn't matter to our programming effort whether the record has five fields or thirteen. It does matter that the structure is decided upon before you begin programming.

The next decision we must make is how to distinguish one field from the next and how to distinguish one record from another. If your records are short, you could have one record per line and use an oddball character as a field delimiter:

```
Name~Street~City~State~Zip
Name1~Street1~City1~State1~Zip1
```

The downside of this solution is that it can be difficult to edit the records. (We are going to try to avoid writing programs for automating data entry. Instead, we will assume that you create the record with a text editor—*vi* or Emacs, for example.)

Another solution is to put each field on a line by itself and separate the records with a blank line:

```
Name
Street
City
State
Zip

Name1
Street1
City1
State1
Zip1
```

This is a good solution. You have to be careful that the data does not itself contain blank lines. For instance, if you wanted to add a field for Company name, and not all records have a value for Company, then you must use a placeholder character to indicate an empty value.

Another solution is to put each record in its own file and put each field on its own line. This is the record organization we will implement for our program. Two advantages of it are that it permits variable length records and it does not require the use of special delimiter characters. It is therefore pretty easy to create or edit a record. It is also very easy to select a subset of records for processing.

We will give each file a name that uniquely identifies it in the current directory. A list of records is the same as a list of files. Here is a sample record in a file named *pmui*:

```
Peter Mui
International Sales Manager
O'Reilly & Associates, Inc.
East Coast Division
90 Sherman Street
Cambridge
MA
01240
617-354-5800
617-661-1116
peter@ora.com
/home/peter
Any number of lines may appear as
a comment.
```

In this record, there are thirteen fields, any of which can be blank (but the blank line must be there to save the position), and the last field can have as many lines as needed.

Our record does not contain labels that identify what each field contains. While we could put that information in the record itself, it is better to maintain the labels separately so they can be changed in a single location. (You can create a record template that contains the labels to help you identify fields when adding a new record.)

We have put the labels for these fields in a separate file named *dict*. We won't show this file because its contents describe the record structure as shown above.

We are going to have three programs and they share the same syntax:

```
command record-list
```

The *record-list* is a list of one or more filenames. You can use wildcard characters, of course, on the command line to specify multiple records.

The first program, *read.base*, reads the *dict* file to get the labels and outputs a formatted record.

```
% read.base record
```

```
pmui:
1.  Name:      Peter Mui
2.  Title:     International Sales Manager
3.  Company:   O'Reilly & Associates, Inc.
4.  Division:  East Coast Division
5.  Street:    90 Sherman Street
6.  City:      Cambridge
7.  State:     MA
8.  Zip:       01240
9.  Phone:     617-354-5800
10. Fax:       617-661-1116
11. E-mail:    peter@ora.com
12. Directory: /home/peter
13. Comments:  Any number of lines may appear as
a comment.
```

read.base first outputs the record name and then lists each field. Let's look at *read.base*:

```
nawk 'BEGIN { FS=":"
# test to see that at least one record was specified
if (ARGC < 2) {
print "Please supply record list on command line"
exit
}

# name of local file containing field labels:
record_template = "dict"

# loop to read the record_template
# field_inc = the number of fields
# fields[] = an array of labels indexed by position

field_inc=0
while (getline < record_template > 0) {
++field_inc
fields[field_inc] = $1
}
```

```
field_tot=field_inc
}

# Now we are reading the records
# Print filename for each new record
FNR == 1 {
field_inc=0
print "\n" FILENAME ":"
}
{

# Print the field's position, label and value
# The last field can have any number of lines without a label.

if (++field_inc <= field_tot){
if (field_inc >= 10)
space = ". "
else
space = ".  "

print field_inc space fields[field_inc] ":\t" $NF
}
else
print $NF
}' $*
```

Note that the program is not doing any input validation. If the record is missing a Division name (and you didn't leave the fourth line blank), whatever is on line 4 will match up with Division, even if it is really a street address. One of the uses of *read.base* is simply to verify that what you entered in the file is correct.

If you specify more than one record, then you will get all of those records output in the order that you specified them on the command line.

The second program is *mail.base*. It extracts mailing label information.

```
% mail.base pmui

Peter Mui
International Sales Manager
O'Reilly & Associates, Inc.
East Coast Division
90 Sherman Street
Cambridge, MA 01240
```

If you supply a *record-list*, then you will get a list of mailing labels.

Here is the *mail.base* program:

```
nawk 'BEGIN { FS="\n";

# test that user supplies a record
if (ARGC < 2) {
    print "Please supply record list on command line"
    exit
    }
```

```
}

# ignore blank lines
/^$/{next}

# this is hard-coded to record format;
# print first 5 fields and then print
# city, state zip on one line.
{
if (FNR < 6)
     print $0
else
     if (FNR == 6)
          printf $0 ", "
     else if (FNR == 7)
          printf $0
     else if (FNR == 8)
          printf " " $0 "\n\n"
}' $*
```

Variations on this very simple program can be written to extract or compile other pieces of information. You could also output formatting codes used when printing the labels.

The last program is *list.base*. It prepares a tabular list of names and records and allows you to select a particular record.

```
% list.base lwalsh pmui jberlin

   # NAME & COMPANY                             FILE
  1. Linda Walsh, O'Reilly & Associates, Inc. lwalsh
  2. Peter Mui, O'Reilly & Associates, Inc.   pmui
  3. Jill Berlin, O'Reilly & Associates, Inc. jberlin
Select a record by number: 2
```

When you select the record number, that record is displayed by using *read.base*. I have not built in any paging capability, so the list will scroll continuously rather than pause after 24 lines or so as it might.

Here is the *list.base* program:

```
nawk 'BEGIN {
# Do everything as BEGIN procedure

# test that user supplied record-list

if (ARGC < 2) {
     print "Please supply record list on command line"
     exit
}

# Define report format string in one place.
FMTSTR = "%3s %-40s %-15s\n"

# print report header

printf(FMTSTR, "#","NAME & COMPANY", "FILE")
```

```
# For each record, get Name, Title and Company and print it.
inc=0
for (x=1; x < ARGC; x++){
    getline NAME < ARGV[x]
    getline TITLE < ARGV[x]
    getline COMPANY < ARGV[x]
    record_list[x] = ARGV[x]
    printf(FMTSTR, ++inc ".", NAME ", " COMPANY, ARGV[x])
    }

# Prompt user to select a record by number

printf "Select a record by number:"
getline answer < "-"

# Call read.base program to display the selected record

system("read.base " record_list[answer])
}

' $*
```

Different versions of this program can be written to examine individual pieces of information across a set of records.

Article 47.22 shows how to write a shell script that creates a prompt-driven front end to collect names and addresses.

—DD

50.12 *The index Database Program*

The *index* program is a flexible database management program. *index* is pretty neat: it works by keeping two files for each database, a field description file and a file of sorted data. It's also fairly intuitive to use, once you get started.

To use index, you should first set up a database directory. By default, *index* looks for the directory *$HOME/.index*.

~ 15.12   **% mkdir ~/.index**

index

Then when you start up *index* for the first time, you're asked to select a name for the database you want to use.

    Select a database:

If you specify the name of a database that doesn't exist yet, *index* assumes that you want to create it. *index* puts you in the editor specified in your *EDITOR (7.03)* environment variable so you can list the titles for each field in the new database. Up to 16 fields can be supported. For example, you can create a database called *addresses*, defined to have the following fields:

    NAME
    TITLE
    ORGANIZATION
    STREET ADDRESS

```
CITY
STATE
ZIP CODE
VOICE PHONE NUMBER
FAX PHONE NUMBER
EMAIL ADDRESS
```

After exiting the editor, you are put into the main menu:

```
Database: addresses   (0 entries)


          a - Add new entry to database
          f - Find entry in database
          r - Read database entry by entry
          s - Save modifications, do not exit
          q - Save modifications, exit
          x - Exit


   Command:
```

There are no entries in the new database. You can start adding entries now by pressing a.

When editing an entry in the database, you're prompted by each of the fields that were set up when the database was defined. After completing a field, press RETURN to get to the next field. There are also a limited number of escape sequences supported for editing and moving around—for example, CTRL-d to delete to the end of the line, or CTRL-p to move up a line. When you're done with the entire entry, press ESCAPE.

```
NAME:                 Stella Rosenzweig
TITLE:                Mom
ORGANIZATION:
STREET ADDRESS:       2456 Bronx Park East
CITY:                 Bronx
STATE:                NY
ZIP CODE:             10467
VOICE PHONE NUMBER:   718-231-2618
FAX PHONE NUMBER:
EMAIL ADDRESS:
```

Once you've saved the new entry, you'll be back to the main menu. You can now add more entries, look at existing entries, search for a string in one of the existing entries, or exit.

To search for an existing entry, press f at the main menu. You'll be asked for the search pattern:

```
Pattern to search for: Ben
```

The *index* program searches all fields matching the string. Regular expressions (27.04) are also accepted in the search string. Each entry with the matching string is shown, one-by-one:

```
NAME:           Benjamin Braddock
TITLE:          Sales Manager
ORGANIZATION:   Acme Plastics, Inc.
```

```
STREET ADDRESS:        103 Morris St., Suite A
CITY:                  Tucson
STATE:                 AZ
ZIP CODE:              85472
VOICE PHONE NUMBER:    800-998-9938
FAX PHONE NUMBER:      800-999-9999
EMAIL ADDRESS:         ben@acme.com
```

```
<RET> = next entry                  "d" = delete this entry
 "-" = previous entry               "e" = edit this entry
 "q" = return to main menu
```

Command:

You can also search for strings on the *index* command line. To do so, specify both the database name and the string. (Enclose the search string in single quotes *(9.10)* if you want to use a regular expression.)

```
% index addresses '[bB]en'
```

All matching entries will be printed to standard output.

The most common use for a database like this is to maintain information about people. But you can use *index* to maintain all sorts of information. For example, you might keep one for information about local restaurants:

```
NAME:                            Rooster BBQ & Grill
STREET ADDRESS:                  1122 Rooster Ave.
CITY:                            Cambridge
PHONE:                           555-1212
RESERVATIONS (y,n):              n
FOOD (1=poor, 10=excellent):     8
DECOR (1=poor, 10=excellent):    2
SERVICE (1=poor, 10=excellent):  6
RECOMMENDED DISHES:              Baby-back ribs, Elvis pizza
STAY AWAY FROM:                  Pulled turkey plate, mango pie
RECOMMENDED BY:                  Jerry, Boston Phoenix
```

For even more flexibility, *index* can run a filter program *(50.13)*.

—*LM*

50.13 *Using index with a Filter*

A particularly useful feature of the *index (50.12)* program is that you can use the –*f* option to filter the output. When a filter is used, the *index* program produces output in TAB-separated columns. Instead of listing each matching entry individually, the field titles are shown at the top, and each entry then appears underneath, displayed horizontally, with TABs between fields:

```
% index -f 'sed s/Mui/Mud/' addresses Peter
NAME    TITLE   ORGANIZATION      STREET ADDRESS CITY     STATE    ...
Henry K Smith             Peter Johnson & Associates       324 Bur ...
Peter Mud        International Sales Manager      O'Reilly and As ...
Peter L. Loos    President         Introspective Solutions, Inc.   ...
```

The TAB-separated fields don't line up properly on your screen, but they make it convenient to manipulate columns using *cut (36.12)*, *awk (38.18)*, or *perl (39.01)*. For example, you can use the *cut* command as your filter to limit the output to a few significant fields:

```
% index -f 'cut -f1,8,10' addresses '.'
NAME    VOICE PHONE NUMBER    EMAIL ADDRESS
Henry K Smith    617-555-1212    henry@pja
Paul S. Spencer        617-693-1111    paul@lotus.com
Peter Mui        800-998-9938    peter@ora.com
```

(We use '.' as the search string to match all entries.)

For your convenience, you can write up a shell script as a filter and place it in your *$HOME/.index* directory with a *.fmt* suffix. This feature comes in useful for particularly complicated filter programs. For example, if you want to be able to read the output of the previous example properly, you can try using *awk* as shown in article 36.20, or you can just use *tbl (45.17)* and *nroff (45.14)*. To do this in a single step, try writing a filter [Linda is a great typist; she uses cat >> *(26.02)* to write short shell scripts (and show the script at the same time). A text editor like Emacs or *vi* will do fine, too, of course.—*JP*]:

~ *15.12*

```
% cat >> ~/.index/printinfo.fmt
#! /bin/sh
cut -f1,8,10 | sed '
1i\
.TS\
1 1 1.
$a\
.TE' | tbl | nroff | col
CTRL-d
```

chmod +x *1.05*

```
% chmod +x ~/.index/printinfo.fmt
% index -f printinfo addresses '.'
NAME                 VOICE PHONE NUMBER    EMAIL ADDRESS
Henry K Smith        617-555-1212         henry@pja
Paul S. Spencer      617-693-1111         paul@lotus.com
Peter Mui            800-998-9938         peter@ora.com
```

—*LM*

51

Working with Numbers

51.01 bc: Simple Math at the Shell Prompt

Want to do a few simple calculations? Standard UNIX provides two simple calculators: *dc* (desk calculator) and *bc*. (Who knows what the *b* stands for? The manual page refers to it only as "an arbitrary precision arithmetic language.")

To a novice, *dc* sounds more promising. However, it's a reverse-polish calculator. You enter each operand on a separate line, followed by an operator. The operands are stored on a stack; the operator pops them from the stack, replacing them with the result. Unfortunately for the novice, the result isn't printed. You need to type *p* ("print") to get any output.

bc is actually much easier to use:

```
% bc
5*2
10
CTRL-d
%
```

Simply type an arithmetic expression, followed by a RETURN. The result will be printed to standard output. Type CTRL-d to exit.

The only thing you need to learn to find *bc* really useful is the *scale* command, which tells the calculator how many decimal places to use. The default is 0, so typing an expression like 10/4 yields the unfortunate answer 2. However:

```
% bc
scale=2
10/4
2.50
```

gives a more acceptable two decimal places. Scale can be set from 0 to 99 decimal places.

As an alternative, invoke *bc* with the *–l* option, which will automatically give you up to 20 decimal places worth of precision (but a lot of trailing zeros on simple division).

bc is really quite complete—you can even define your own functions. See the *bc* manual page for details. It's also useful for base conversion *(51.02)*.

expr can also be used to do simple math *(51.07)* on the command line, but it's really better suited for doing math in shell scripts *(47.28)*.

Of course, if you're running the X Window System *(1.31)*, you can just use *xcalc*, which draws a Texas Instruments or HP calculator right on the screen, and lets you punch keys with the mouse.

—TOR

51.02 bc: Hexadecimal or Binary Conversion

One thing that's really handy to know about *bc* is how to use it for base conversion.

By default, *bc* takes its input and prints its output in decimal. However, you can set either the input or the output to be some other base numbering system—for example, hexadecimal or binary—using the *ibase* and *obase* commands.

For example, to find the decimal equivalents to a hexadecimal number, set *ibase* to 16, and leave *obase* alone (i.e., as decimal). Simply type the number (or a series of numbers separated by semicolons) you want converted, and press RETURN. The decimal equivalent will be printed below. (Hexadecimal numbers from A to F must be typed in uppercase, or *bc* will report an error.) For example:

```
% bc
ibase=16
B6;7F;FFF
182
127
4095
```

Or if you wanted to convert *to* hexadecimal, you'd set *obase* to 16, and leave *ibase* at 10:

```
% bc
obase=16
142
8E
```

Or, to convert binary to hexadecimal, set `ibase=2` and `obase=16` (or `ibase=16` and `obase=2` for the reverse operation):

```
% bc
obase=16
ibase=2
11010001
D1
```

Type CTRL-d to exit *bc*. Be careful to set *obase* before *ibase*, or you will have problems *(51.03)*

—TOR

51.03 Gotchas in Base Conversion

Say you want to convert between octal and hex, and you type:

```
% bc
ibase=8
obase=16
12
A
```

It looks like something's gone haywire. 12 octal ought to be 9 hexadecimal, not A. What's wrong?

In fact, since you set *ibase* to octal before you set *obase*, what you really asked for was *obase* equal to 16 octal (7 decimal)!

In short, always set *obase* before *ibase*, or you're in for a surprise.

Similarly, suppose you'd set *ibase* to 16, and want to set it back to 10. You need to type:

```
ibase=A
```

not:

```
ibase=10
```

Another thing to look out for is typing a hex digit when *ibase* is set to something other than 16. *bc* isn't smart enough to reject the input, and gives you back garbage.

—TOR

51.04 bc's Sine and Cosine are in Radians

While using the *bc* utility the other day, I had the occasion to use the arbitrary precision math library, which is the option *–l* (lowercase letter "l") of this utility. I wanted to do a simple computation involving the sine of an angle.

I *assumed*, after reading the manual page, that all I had to do was put in the angle (in degrees) in the *sine* function. For example, the sine of 30 degrees would be given by:

```
s(30)
```

However, this didn't work. A little investigation revealed that the angle shouldn't be in degrees but in radians. For example, the sine of 30 degrees or 0.5263 radians,

```
s(.5263)
```

Working with Numbers

gives the correct answer of 0.5.

This is also true of the *cosine* function.

—*MS* in *comp.unix.questions* on Usenet, *19 April 1989*

51.05 *Base Conversion Using cvtbase*

cvtbase

The *bc* command can be used to convert between different bases *(51.02)*, but an easier tool to use is *cvtbase*. *cvtbase* is designed specifically to convert from one format to another. For example, to convert a decimal IP address into its hexadecimal equivalent:

```
% cvtbase d h
140.186.65.25
8c.ba.41.19
```

The first argument, d, means that our input will be in decimal form. The second argument, h, means that we want the input converted into hexadecimal. In general, the syntax for calling *cvtbase* is:

```
cvtbase input_base output_base
```

where *input_base* and *output_base* are any of:

d, D   Decimal; i.e., digits 0 through 9.

x, h   Hexadecimal (using lowercase); i.e., 0 through 9 and a through f.

X, H   Hexadecimal (using uppercase); i.e., 0 through 9 and A through F.

o, O   Octal; i.e., digits 0 through 7.

b, B   Binary; i.e., digits 0 and 1.

Any input characters that aren't in the specified set are sent through unchanged. In the example above, the dots (.) in the IP address are retained in the hexadecimal output.

—*LM*

51.06 *derange.num: a Faster Way to Increment Numbers*

In the Bourne shell, the usual way to loop through a list of numbers is:

```
num=0
while [ $num -lt 100 ]
do
        num="`expr $num + 1`"
        ...use $num
done
```

while *46.10*
[*46.19*

expr *47.28*

For each pass of the loop, the shell has to run one or two subprocesses (depending on your shell) to test and increment the number in $num. The script below, *derange.num*, calls *awk (38.18)* to do the same thing a lot more efficiently. The script "de-ranges" a range of numbers into separate numbers. For example:

```
% derange.num 1-5 12-18
1 2 3 4 5 12 13 14 15 16 17 18
```

It's probably most useful in making a loop, like this:

```
for num in `derange.num 1-100`
do
        ...use $num
done
```

The script doesn't check for errors such as a backwards range (100-1), though you can add that if you want to:

derange.num

```
#! /bin/sh
case $# in
0) echo "Usage: `basename $0` range [ranges...]" 1>&2; exit 1 ;;
esac

# MAKE awk INPUT FIELD SEPARATOR DASH AND INPUT RECORD SEPARATOR SPACE;
# UNFORTUNATELY, CHANGING OUTPUT RECORD SEPARATOR TO SPACE HAS PROBLEMS:
echo "$@" | awk '
BEGIN { FS = "-"; RS = " " }
{
    # IF PRINTING FIRST RANGE, NO LEADING BLANK.  OTHERWISE, DO:
    if (notfirst != "y") {
        printf "%d", $1
        notfirst="y"
    }
    else
        printf " %d", $1

    # PRINT NUMBERS WITH LEADING BLANK BUT NO NEWLINES:
    for (i = $1 + 1 ; i <= $2 ; i++)
        printf " %d", i
}
END { printf "\n" }'     # PRINT THE NEWLINE
```

The *jot (47.11)* command can output a range of numbers.

—*JP*

51.07 Quick Arithmetic with expr

The *expr* command does arithmetic. It's not just for incrementing a variable in a Bourne shell loop. It's handy for quick integer math on the command line. For instance, if *wc* tells me a file has 2545 lines and I want to know how many 66-line pages that is:

```
$ expr 2545 / 66
38
```

It's 38 pages—actually, 39, because *expr* rounds down.

Article 47.28 has a complete list of *expr* math operators.

—JP

51.08 Total a Column with addup

addup

Some programs output information in columns. The *addup* script totals the numbers in a column. For example, *ls −s* outputs file sizes in column 1.* The *lastcomm* command shows CPU time used in column 4, like this:

```
% lastcomm tcomm
sleep              tcomm    _        0.08 secs Thu Mar 27 10:23
date               tcomm    _        0.08 secs Thu Mar 27 10:23
tail               tcomm    _        0.09 secs Thu Mar 27 10:23
pwho               tcomm    _        0.30 secs Thu Mar 27 10:23
% lastcomm tcomm | addup 4
0.55
```

We don't show *addup* here; it's on the Power Tools disk. This one-line *awk* script does the adding:

```
awk "{sum += \$$colnum} END{print sum}" ${1+"$@"}
```

The `${1+"$@"}` passes filenames (if any) from the command line and works around a shell quoting problem *(48.07)*. The *awk* script is inside double quotes *(9.10)*; the shell replaces `\$` with a literal dollar sign, and `$colnum` with the column number. So, if the *colnum* shell variable has 4, *awk* would get this program to sum column 4:

```
{sum += $4} END{print sum} filenames-if-any
```

—JP

51.09 It's Great to Have a Spreadsheet

sc

Calculators are very good, but nothing beats a spreadsheet when you have complicated calculations and want to explore, save, and print alternate computational scenarios. After years of waiting to see mainline spreadsheet programs ported to UNIX, I discovered *sc*.

Try it; you'll like it. Well . . . maybe not at first, but eventually. It's quite full featured, but has a slightly helter-skelter user interface with only barebones documentation to help you figure it out. Fortunately, there are built-in quick reference screens available by typing a question mark (?), so (especially if you already know how to use a spreadsheet), you can learn the basics pretty quickly.

---

*A BSD-type *ls* that normally shows several columns of filenames will switch to single-column mode when you redirect its output away from a terminal.

A couple of pointers, though: pay attention to the prompts provided by some of the commands. For example, if they show an argument in quotes, that probably means you'd better type the quotes. (But not brackets—they indicate an optional argument.) Also, watch for the order of arguments. (For example, the range copy command takes the destination range first.)

One feature that may be helpful (or may make the interface even more obscure) is that cursor movement and cell editing commands are based on the *vi (31.02)* command set.

While you might wish for a point and click interface like Excel, or even the keystroke-based menus that make *1-2-3* so easy to use, *sc* has a lot to offer. It lets you do just about everything pricier spreadsheets do, including hiding rows or columns, symbolic range or cell names, and a full range of numeric, string, financial and date/time functions. It even lets you encrypt your spreadsheets for security.

Some functions are implemented by pipes *(1.03)* to UNIX commands. For example, there's no print command. Instead, you use one of the save commands (P to save the file in sc format; W to save an image of the screen), supplying a pipe to the printer as the "filename." Of course, this means that if you know the format of the output stream (which is fairly simple), you can use any available UNIX utilities to transform the data.

You can't pipe data into *sc*, but you can prepare data with other programs, and then use the supplied *psc* program to convert it to *sc* format.

—*TOR*

51.10 *Business Graphics with ipl*

ipl

One of the weaknesses of *sc (51.09)* is that it doesn't provide the graphics that people now expect from a spreadsheet. However, all is not lost. *ipl* produces business graphics using PostScript (or SunView) for output. It provides scatter-plots, line plots, bar graphs, pie charts, schedule charts, and maps of the U.S. and Canada.

There are a variety of formatting commands (best learned by studying the examples supplied with the *ipl* distribution). The data is expected to be field-oriented, with white space as a separator. With a little massaging, you can get this out of *sc* (and of course, from many other UNIX programs).

—*TOR*

52

Help—Online Documentation, etc.

52.01 *UNIX Online Documentation*

The UNIX operating system was one of the first to include online documentation. It's not the best in the world—most users who haven't internalized the manual set curse it once a week—but it has proven surprisingly resilient. What's particularly interesting about UNIX's online documentation is that, unlike other early help systems, it isn't an adjunct to another set of printed documentation that contains the "real" truth. The online manual is complete, authoritative, and usually more current than any printed documentation.

The basis for UNIX's online documentation is the *man* command. Most simply, you use it as follows:

    % **man** *topic*

where *topic* is usually the name of some command; but it can also be the name of a system call, a library routine, an I/O device, or an administrative file (or file type). The output from *man* is usually sent to a pager like *more (26.03)*, which allows you to page through.

The manual pages are grouped into a number of categories. Unfortunately, there are three slightly different groupings: one for Berkeley-based systems, one for System V, and one for systems derived for XENIX. Table 52-1 lists these categories.

Table 52-1. UNIX Manual Page Categories

Category	BSD	System V	Xenix
User commands	1	1	*u_man*
System calls	2	2	*p_man*
Library routines	3	3	*p_man*
I/O and special files	4	7	*p_man*
Administrative files	5	4	*a_man*
Games	6	6 or 1	*u_man*
Miscellaneous	7	5	anything goes
Administrative commands	8	8	*a_man*
Maintenance commands	8	1M	*u_man* or *a_man*
Local commands	1 *(letter)*	*	
Obsolete commands	o *(letter)*	*	

As you can see, System V makes a strange distinction between "administration" and "maintenance"; if you can figure out what they really mean, please let us know! To a poor Berkeley soul, this has never made sense. Some of these categories are subdivided further; for example, you may see section 3S (the standard I/O library), 3M (the mathematics library), 1G (Berkeley graphics), 1V (commands derived from system V), and so on.

If you want to refer to a manual entry in a specific section of the manual, you can give a command of the form:

```
% man section topic
```

For example, if you want to read documentation about the */etc/passwd* file (rather than the *passwd* command) on a System V machine, give the command:

```
% man 4 passwd
```

This is an easy way to distinguish between topics with the same name, but in different groups.

—ML

---

*System V and Xenix make no provision for "local" or "obsolete" commands in their *man* system.

52.02   The apropos Command

The biggest problem with the UNIX manual set is finding what you want, given that you don't already know what you're looking for. For example: you want to search for a string in a file. If you don't remember that the command you want is called *grep*, how will you ever find it?

The *apropos* command, which is equivalent to *man −k* (and sometimes just an alias for *man −k*) helps to solve this problem. It's not always successful, but it's better than nothing. It looks through headings of all the "man pages" and prints any that match a given keyword. For example, to figure out how to search for a string, try the command:

```
% apropos string
...
gets, fgets (3S)          - get a string from a stream
getsubopt (3)            - parse sub options from a string
gettext, textdomain (3) - retrieve a message string, get & set text domain
grep, egrep, fgrep (1V) - search a file for a string or regular expression
puts, fputs (3S)         - put a string on a stream
...
```

We've cut some of the output for convenience, but you can see what you want: to search for a string, you clearly want to use *grep* or one of its relatives.

All BSD and SVR4 systems support *apropos*. However, there are plenty of SVR3 (and earlier) systems kicking around that don't. If you're facing this problem, see article 52.03.

MILD FLAME: Over the years, the output from *apropos* has gotten quite cluttered. It's considerably less useful now than it was five years ago.

—ML

52.03   apropos on Systems Without apropos

I was just asked to write an article about how to simulate *apropos* on systems that don't have it. I have to confess that I've never faced this problem. But I was able to come up with a solution. Your mileage may vary—particularly since different UNIX implementations have different ways of storing their manual pages.

The solution has two parts. First, you need a script that builds an index; that's better than *grep*ping through every manual page in the world. Then you need an *apropos* alias that automatically searches your index file. Here's the script to build the index file:

manindex

```
#!/bin/sh
# manindex: Generate a list of topic lines that you can grep through.
# Then create 'apropos' and other aliases to search the list.
# Run this periodically--once a month should suffice
mandir=/usr/share/man     # where the manual pages are stored
manlist="cat1 cat2 cat3"  # list particular directories you care about
indexfile="/home/mike/manindex.txt"

rm -f $indexfile
```

```
for 10.10       for directory in $manlist
                do
                        cd $mandir/$directory
                        # the sed command turns filenames into "manual page" names
sed 35.24               # e.g., converts sed.1.z to sed.
                        # BUG: won't handle names like a.out.4.Z correctly
`..` 10.14              for manpage in `ls | sed -e 's/\..*$//g'`
                        do
                                # use man to unpack the manual page; it might be compressed
col 45.20                       # use col to strip garbage characters
egrep 28.05                     # egrep looks for spaces, manual page name, and dash
uniq 36.18                      man $manpage | col -b -x | egrep "^ +$manpage.* - " | uniq
                        done
done > 47.23    done > $indexfile
```

This script goes through every directory in which manual pages are stored. It strips all suffixes from the filenames, and then uses *man* to print the actual manual page. This is better than trying to look at the raw manual pages themselves because some vendors don't provide the raw manual pages. If you let *man* give you the page you want, you'll always find it.* The *col* command strips out boldfacing, underlining, and other monstrosities that will confuse *grep*. Finally, *egrep* looks for lines to put in the index. It's not as fussy as the BSD *catman* program (which *mkindex* is emulating), so it will find a fair number of lines that don't belong; but we think this is only a mild flaw.

Before you can use this script you'll have to substitute definitions for three variables:

mandir   The top-level directory in which manual pages are stored. Often */usr/man*, but it may be different on your system.

manlist   Subdirectories containing the manual pages you care about. You'll probably want the directory in which user-level commands are stored, as a minimum. This level of directory naming may be radically different on different systems. I think this script is flexible enough to handle all the variations I can remember; if it can't, you'll have to hack it up a bit.

indexfile The file in which you want to keep your index (the output of this script).

Expect *manindex* to run for a long time; several minutes or more, depending on how thorough you want to be. Fortunately, you don't need to do this very often: once to get started, and then once a month (or so) to pick up any "stray" manual pages that someone else may have added. If you want to speed the task up, remember that you can skip any sections of the manual that you're not interested in by defining **manlist** appropriately. For example, if you're not interested in section 2 of the manual, just leave *cat2* out of the list.

---

*If you have the source files for the manual page online, rather than pre-formatted files, you might want to rewrite the script to search them directly. It will be a lot faster.

Once you've created the index, the rest of the problem is easy. Just make yourself an *apropos* alias *(11.02)* and add it to your *.cshrc* file:

```
alias apropos "grep -i \!$ /home/mike/manindex.txt"
```

Here's what its output looks like:

```
% apropos search
acctcom - search and print process accounting file(s)
egrep - search a file for a pattern using full regular expressions
fgrep - search a file for a character string
fmlgrep - search a file for a pattern
grep - search a file for a pattern
pathconv - search FMLI criteria for filename
```

As I pointed out, this isn't perfect. But I think it's a reasonable substitute.

—ML

52.04 *whatis: One-line Command Summaries*

whatis is almost identical to *apropos (52.02)*, but it requires a command name as an argument—rather than an arbitrary string. Why is this useful? Well, let's say you forget what *cat* does. On a SunOS 4.1 system, *apropos cat* gives you several screenfulls of output. You may not want to read the entire manual page. But *whatis cat* gives you a nice one-line summary:

```
% whatis cat
cat (1V)- concatenate and display
```

If you're using the *apropos* fake-out we discussed in article 52.03, you can simulate *whatis* with this alias *(11.03)*:

```
alias whatis "grep '^ *'\!$ /home/mike/manindex.txt"
```

—ML

52.05 *whereis: Finding Where a Command is Located*

The *whereis* command helps you to locate the executable file, source code, and manual pages for a program. I use it primarily as a sanity check; if I type more useless.txt, and get the message "more: command not found," I immediately try whereis more. This gives me a lot of information about what went wrong: someone may have removed *more* from the system, or my *PATH (7.04)* environment variable may be set incorrectly, etc.

Output from *whereis* typically looks like this:

```
% whereis more
more: /usr/ucb/more /usr/lib/more.help /usr/man/man1/more.1
```

This says that the executable file is */usr/ucb/more*, the command's internal help file is */usr/lib/more.help*, and the manual page is */usr/man/man1/more.1*.

---

whereis has a few options worth mentioning. *−b* says "only report the executable name"; *−m* says "only report the location of the manual page"; *−s* means "only search for source files"; and *−u* says "only issue a report if any of the requested information (executable, manual page, source) is missing."

There are other options for modifying the list of directories through which *whereis* searches; if you need these, check your manual pages.

—ML

52.06 How UNIX Systems Remember Their Name

Each computer on a network needs a name. On many UNIX versions, the *hostname* command shows you this name. On systems whose only network connection is by UUCP, the command *uuname −l* (lowercase L) may be what you want. If you use more than one system, the hostname is great to use in a shell prompt—or any time you forget where you're logged in.

—JP

52.07 Which Version am I Using?

The *which* command is a real life saver. It has become increasingly important in the last few years. Many vendors (like Sun) are providing separate directories of BSD-compatible and System V-compatible commands. Which command you'll get depends on your *PATH (7.04)* environment variable. It's often essential to know which version you're using. For example:

```
% which sort
/bin/sort
```

tells me exactly which version of the *sort* program I'm using. (Under SunOS 4.1, this is the BSD-compatible version in */bin*, not the System V version in */usr/5bin*.)

You'll find that *which* comes in handy in lots of other situations. I find that I'm always using *which* inside of backquotes to get a precise path. For example, when I was writing these articles, I started wondering whether or not *man*, *apropos*, and *whatis* were really the same executable. It's a simple question, but one I had never bothered to think about. There's one good way to find out:

```
% ls -li `which man` `which apropos` `which whatis`
102352 -rwxr-xr-x  3 root      24576 Feb  8  1990 /usr/ucb/apropos
102352 -rwxr-xr-x  3 root      24576 Feb  8  1990 /usr/ucb/man
102352 -rwxr-xr-x  3 root      24576 Feb  8  1990 /usr/ucb/whatis
```

What does this tell us? First, the three commands have the same file size, which means that they're likely to be identical; furthermore, each file has three links, meaning that each file has three names. The *−i* option confirms it; all three files have the same i-number *(1.22)*. So, *apropos*, *man*, and *whatis* are just one executable file that has three hard links.

which

A few System V implementations don't have a *which* command. The version of *which* on the Power Tools disk is even better than the BSD *which*, anyway. By default, this new *which* works about the same as the BSD *which*. The new *which* has a big plus: it doesn't try to read your *.cshrc* file to see what aliases you've set there. Instead, you set it up with its *-i* option to read your shell's *current* list of aliases. This lets the new *which* show aliases that you've typed at a prompt and haven't stored in *.cshrc*. The new *which* also works in Bourne-like shells *(1.08)* that have a built-in alias command.

csh_init

To make the new *which* read your current aliases, you need a trick. Here's the trick: make an alias that runs *which*, passing the definition (if any) of the alias you name.

Let's look at the setup, then explain it. For the C shell, use the following line in your *.cshrc* file: (the manual page shows how to make *which* work with Bourne-type shells that have aliases and shell functions *(11.10)*):

!\$ *11.03*
!* *11.03*

```
alias which alias !\$ \| /usr/local/bin/which -i !\*
```

For this example, let's say you've also defined an alias for *sort* that looks like:

```
alias sort /usr/local/bin/quicksort
```

Okay. To run *which*, you type:

```
% which sort
sort    /usr/local/bin/quicksort
```

How did that work? The C shell runs the alias you defined for *which*. In this example, that executes the following command:

```
alias sort | /usr/local/bin/which -i sort
```

The first part of that command, `alias sort`, will pipe the definition of the *sort* alias to the standard input of `/usr/local/bin/which -i sort`. When */usr/local/bin/which –i sort* sees an alias definition on its standard input, it outputs that definition.

What if you ask *which* to find a command that you haven't aliased?

```
% which tr
/bin/tr
```

The shell runs this command:

```
alias tr | /usr/local/bin/which -i tr
```

Because there's no alias for *tr*, the shell command `alias tr` sends no output down the pipe. When `/usr/local/bin/which -i tr` doesn't read text on standard input, it looks through your search path for the first command named *tr*.

Nice trick, isn't it? Maarten Litmaath, the program's author, is a clever guy.

That's not all the new *which* can do. With the - option, it shows any alias you name and *also* searches your path for *all* commands with that name. This is useful when you want to know all available versions of the command. Let's end this article with an example from the manual page. The first command shows all aliases (in this case, that's just the alias for the new *which.*) Second, we run the new *which* to find which *which* we're running :-); it shows the alias for *which.* Third, the –*a* option shows all available *which*es:

```
% alias
which    alias !$ | /usr/local/bin/which -i !*
% which which
which    alias !$ | /usr/local/bin/which -i !*
% which -a which
which    alias !$ | /usr/local/bin/which -i !*
/usr/local/bin/which
/usr/ucb/which
%
```

—*ML, JP, MAL*

52.08 Reading a Permuted Index

The first time that people new to UNIX take a look at the front of the system's *UNIX Reference Manual*, they are likely to be surprised by the most unlikely looking document: the ubiquitous permuted index. The index looks something like the one shown below, which actually shows a complete permuted index based on the three commands *ar*, *at*, and *awk*. This miniature index is used as an example throughout this article.

```
              maintainer  ar: archive and library ............ ar(1)
                     ar:  archive and library maintainer ..... ar(1)
                    time  at: execute commands at a later .... at(1)
    processing language   awk: pattern scanning and .......... awk(1)
            at: execute   commands at a later time .......... at(1)
                     at:  execute commands at a later time ... at(1)
pattern scanning and processing  language awk: ...................... awk(1)
    at: execute commands at a    later time ......................... at(1)
          ar: archive and   library maintainer ................. ar(1)
    ar: archive and library   maintainer ......................... ar(1)
          language awk:    pattern scanning and processing .... awk(1)
    awk: pattern scanning and   processing language ............... awk(1)
              awk: pattern   scanning and processing language ... awk(1)
    at: execute commands at a later   time .............................. at(1)
```

Like the *UNIX Reference Manual* itself, the permuted index takes a little getting used to, but it is fairly useful once that hurdle has been crossed. To find the command you want, simply scan down the middle of the page, looking for a keyword of interest on the right side of the blank gutter. When you find the keyword you want, you can read (with contortions) the brief description of the command that makes up the entry. If things still look promising, you can look all the way over to the right for the name of the relevant command page.

The key to the *UNIX Reference Manual* is the fact that each command is treated on a separate page—there are no continuous page numbers. This makes it easy to add new pages whenever a new command is added to the system. At the same time, if you know the name of a command, information about it is always easy to find because pages are ordered alphabetically, just like they are in a dictionary.

But what if you don't know which command to look for in the first place? If you are at a terminal on a Berkeley UNIX system, you can use the *apropos (52.02)* command, like this:

```
% apropos scanning
awk(1) - pattern scanning and processing language
```

But if you're using another UNIX variant or you are not at a terminal, the permuted index is your best bet.

—TOR

52.09 Make Your Own Man Pages without Learning troff

We strongly suggest that you write a manual page for each command that you place in your *bin* directory. UNIX manual pages typically have the following format, which we suggest you follow:

NAME
        the program's name - one line summary of what it does

SYNOPSIS
        how to invoke the program, including all arguments and
        command-line options. (Optional arguments
        are placed in square brackets)

DESCRIPTION
        a description of what the program does--as long as is necessary

OPTIONS
        an explanation of each option

EXAMPLE
        One or more examples of how to use the program

ENVIRONMENT
        Any environment variables that control the program's behavior

BUGS
        Any known bugs. The standard manual pages don't take
        bug-recording seriously, but this can be very helpful.

AUTHOR
        Who wrote the program

To see how a "real" manual page looks, type man ls.

Feel free to add any other sections that you think are necessary. You can use the *nroff (45.14)* "man" macros if you want a nicely formatted manual page. However, *nroff* is fairly complicated and, for this purpose, not really necessary. Just create a text file that looks like the one we showed above. If you are using a BSD system and want your manual pages formatted with *nroff,* look at any of the files in */usr/man/man1* and copy it.

HINT: If you insist on formatting your manual page properly, using the *troff* "man" macros, you can use *nroff* to preview the file. The *man (52.01)* command is essentially the same as:

more *26.03*
–s *26.10*

```
% nroff -e -man filename | more -s
```

You can safely omit the *–e* option to *nroff* and the *–s* option to *more.* And remember that *nroff* may not be available on many versions of System V UNIX.

Now, you want to make this manual page "readable" by the standard *man* command. For BSD systems, there are a few ways to do this. Create the directory *man* in your home directory; create the directory *cat1* as a subdirectory of *man*; then copy your manual entry into *cat1*, with the name *program.1* (where *program* is the name of your special command). When you want to read the manual page, give the command:

~ *15.12*

```
% man -M ~/man program
```

SHORTCUT: We like to be more strict about naming things properly, but you can omit the *man* directory, and just put the *cat1* directory into your home directory. In this case, the command would be:

```
% man -M ~ program
```

Some systems have a *MANPATH* environment variable *(7.01)*, a colon-separated list of directories where the *man* command should look. For example, my *MANPATH* contains:

```
/home/mike/man:/usr/local/man:/usr/man
```

MANPATH can be more convenient than the *–M* option.

HINT: We are telling you to put the manual page into the *cat1* directory rather than the *man1* directory because the *man* program assumes that files in *cat1* are already formatted.

If you are sharing your program with other people on the system, you should put your manual entry in a public place. Become superuser and copy your documentation into */usr/local/man/cat1*, giving it the name *program.l* (the "l" stands for "local"). If you can't become superuser, get the system administrator to do it for you. Make sure that everyone can read the manual page; the permissions should be something like this:

```
% ls -l /usr/local/man/cat1
-r--r--r--  1 root         468 Aug  5 09:21 program.l
```

Then give the command man *program* to read your documentation.

If you are working on some System V variants, the rules are a little different. For one thing, you may not have *nroff* or *troff* on your system; these are often extra-cost options. For another thing, the organization of the manual pages and the *man* command itself are slightly different—and really, not as good. Write your manual entry and place it in your *doc* directory. Then create the following C shell alias *(11.03)*:

```
alias myman "(cd ~/doc; man -d \!$ | pg)"
```

Now the command *myman docfilename* will retrieve your manual page. Note that you have to give the entire filename (e.g., *program.1*), not just the program's name.

If you want to make your manual page publicly available, copy the file into the directory */usr/man/u_man/man1*; you may have to become superuser to do so. Make sure that anyone on the system can read your file. If the entry is extremely long and you want to save space in you filesystem, you can use *pack* (25.06) on your documentation file. The resulting file will have the name *program.1.z*; the *man* command will automatically unpack the file whenever anyone reads it.

—ML

52.10   *Writing a Simple Man Page with the –man Macros*

If you're not satisfied with the simple manual pages we discussed in article 52.09, here's how to go all the way and create a "real" manual page. As we said, the best way to create a manual page is to copy one that already exists. So here's a sample for you to copy. Rather than discuss it blow by blow, I'll include lots of comments (these start with . \ " or \ ").

1 *52.01*

apropos *52.02*

```
.\" Title: Program name, manual section, and date
.TH GRIND 1 "1992 October 12"
.\" Section heading: NAME, followed by command name and one line summary
.\" It's important to copy this exactly; the "whatis" database (used
.\" for apropos) looks for the summary line.
.SH NAME
grind \- create output from input
.\" Section heading: SYNOPSIS, followed by syntax summary
.SH SYNOPSIS
.B grind              \" .B: bold font; use it for the command name.
[ -b ] [ -c ] [ -d ] \" Put optional arguments in square brackets.
[ input [ output ]]  \" Arguments can be spread across several lines.
.br                  \" End the synopsis with an explicit line break (.br)
.\" A new section: DESCRIPTION, followed by what the command does
.SH DESCRIPTION
.I Grind        \" .I:  Italic font for the word "Grind"
performs lots of computations. Input to
.IR grind ,     \" .IR: One word italic, next word roman, no space between.
is taken from the file
.IR input ,
and output is sent to the file
.IR output ,
which default to standard input and standard output if not specified.
.\" Another section: now we're going to discuss the -b, -c, and -d options
.SH OPTIONS
.\" The .TP macro preceeds each option
.TP
.B \-b  \" print the -b option in bold.
Print output in binary.
.TP
.B \-c  \" \- requests a minus sign, which is preferable to a hyphen (-)
Eliminate ASCII characters from input before processing.
.TP
```

```
.B \-d
Cause daemons to overrun your computer.
.\" OK, we're done with the description and the options; now discuss
.\" what can go wrong. You can add any other sections you want.
.SH BUGS
In order to optimize computational speed, this program always produces
the same result, independent of the input.
.\" Use .LP between paragraphs
.LP
If the moon is full,
.I grind
may destroy your input file. To say nothing of your sex life.
.\" Good manual pages end by stating who wrote the program.
.SH AUTHOR
I wouldn't admit to this hack if my life depended on it.
```

After all that, you should have noticed that there are four important macros, listed in Table 52-2, to know about:

Table 52-2. Important –man Macros

Macro	Meaning
.TH	Title of the manual page.
.SH	Section heading; one for each section.
.TP	Formats options correctly (sets up the "hanging indent").
.LP	Used between paragraphs in a section.

For some arcane reason, all manual pages use the silly `.B`, `.BI`, etc., macros to make font changes. I've adhered to this style in the example, but it's much easier to use "in line" font changes: `\fI` for *italic*, `\fB` for **bold**, and `\fR` for roman. There may be some systems on which this doesn't work properly, but I've never seen any.

—ML

52.11 *Common UNIX Error Messages*

For new UNIX users, one common frustration is that error messages are often nonexistent, usually terse, and often extremely obscure. Something like `Command not found` is reasonably self-explanatory, most of the time; but what about `You don't exist. Go away.`?

In this article, I'll cover some of the more common, obscure, or amusing messages that are around. I'll try to keep it brief, which means that it will be far from comprehensive. A complete list of all the messages you might get could easily fill a book—and lots of the messages report situations that you'd have to try *very* hard to reconstruct.

`arguments too long`

> UNIX has an unfortunate limit to the maximum length (in characters) of all arguments you can put on the command line. This limit was

originally fairly small; in the past few years, it's become quite large (5120 characters on SVR4), but no one has yet to fix the basic problem. So if you give a command like ls /*/*/*/*, you're very likely to find out that your argument list is too long. Workarounds for this problem are discussed in articles 10.19 and 10.21.

awk: bailing out near line *n*

You're running an *awk (38.01)* script that has a syntax error. The standard *awk* is incredibly uninformative about syntax errors; this is all the help you're likely to get. Newer versions (like *nawk* and *gawk (38.05)*) have more intelligent error messages.

bad magic number

You're most likely to get this message when you give a UNIX command. You can also get this message from programs like *ld*, the link editor for programmers. A "magic number" is a special number in an executable file that tells the kernel what kind of file it's dealing with. If you get this message, the file you're trying to execute may have been corrupted; or it may be an executable for another kind of computer; or it may not be an executable file at all.

broken pipe

This message appears when you're running a pipeline, and one part of the pipeline terminates before the rest. For example, say you're running the command:

```
% ls *.* | sort
```

If the *sort* program quits (for any reason) before it has read all the data from *ls*, you have a "broken pipe."

bus error (core dumped)

This is similar in nature to a segmentation fault. There's a subtle difference in that a "bus error" means that the kernel didn't detect the problem on its own; the memory system (i.e., hardware) realized that there was a problem. On many UNIX systems, this message can mean that you're trying to do an I/O operation incorrectly—you may be trying to access a device that doesn't exist, or something of that nature. What does I/O have to do with memory? A lot, but that's beyond the bounds of this book.

cross-device link

You attempted to create a hard link to a file on another filesystem. Try a symbolic link *(19.04)* instead.

directory not empty

You tried to delete a directory that's not empty, and *rmdir* won't let you. The solution is simple enough; but often, when you try to list the directory, it will look empty. Did you check for "invisible" filenames *(17.12)* (most likely, filenames beginning with a dot)? There are probably a few "turds" left over from some editing session. If you're absolutely sure that none of these invisible files are meaningful, just use *rm* −*rf (24.09, 24.16)*.

intruder alert!

> Comes from *whoami*, and means that *whoami* can't look you up in the */etc/passwd (37.03)* file. This probably means that someone managed to delete or corrupt */etc/passwd*.

make: must be a separator on rules line 46

> The bane of everyone who uses *make (29.12)*. *make*'s "rules" lines must begin with a TAB character. Spaces are not acceptable. This means that you used spaces, rather than a tab. Some editors (and reportedly, even some networks) will change tabs to spaces automatically—so even if you've been careful to observe the rule, you may still run across this message.

not a typewriter

> As someone on the net said, "Damn right, this isn't a typewriter. That's a problem?" Seriously, though: this is an obsolete message that still crops up occasionally. It means that the program attempted to perform some I/O operation that would be legal on a terminal, except that it wasn't writing to a terminal: it was writing to a file, or to a pipe, etc.

not enough memory

> There isn't enough swap space *(55.01)* to run your program. Note that many modern UNIX systems allow the system administrator to create new "swapping files"; this may help you to work around the problem without reconfiguring a disk drive. Under SunOS, for example, you'd use the *mkfile* and *swapon* commands to solve this problem.

segmentation fault (core dumped)

> A segmentation fault means that the program you're running attempted to read or write some address in memory that wasn't assigned to it. If it's a program that you wrote, a segmentation fault probably means that a pointer is pointing to something strange. If it's a standard UNIX utility, well—it really means the same thing (not that it helps). Most likely, though, you've given the program strange input—the input may be illegal, there may be more than the program can handle, etc.

typesetter busy

> I've seen this when using *troff (45.13)*; it usually means that you haven't specified the output device correctly; i.e., that you haven't used the *–t* option, which sends the output to standard output, for post-processing by some translator. Actually, it's very rare for a user to invoke *troff* directly. *troff* is usually run through some kind of a shell script. If you see this message, the shell script is doing the wrong thing. What does the message really mean? Simple. *troff*, on its own, generates output for a C/A/T phototypesetter. These typesetters were obsolete 10 or 15 years ago, and are now probably all rusting in junk heaps. But nobody bothered to change *troff*. If you don't include the *–t* option, *troff* tries to send the output to the

> typesetter; when it fails (because the typesetter doesn't exist), *troff* decides that the typesetter must be "busy."

who are you?
> Comes from *lpr*, and means that *lpr* can't look you up in the */etc/passwd* file. This probably means that someone managed to delete or corrupt */etc/passwd*.

you don't exist. Go away.
> I've never actually seen this message, though it's part of the UNIX mythology. Reportedly, it can come from the *talk (1.33)* program when you try to talk from a *tty* or (usually) a *pty(43.08)* that isn't in the list of logged-in users, */etc/utmp*.

While a lot of the error messages are more-or-less standard, a lot of them vary from vendor to vendor; some vendors have tried to protect you from the worst abuse. We hope that all systems incorporating the legendary "Don't you hate obscure messages" error message long since disappeared.

—ML

53

Miscellaneous Useful Programs and Curiosities

53.01 We Finally are Getting to the Bottom of the Bucket

OK. This is it: the miscellaneous chapter in the miscellaneous section of a rather miscellaneous book!

This chapter contains the articles that we edited out of other chapters but didn't want to throw away, stuff that really didn't fit anywhere else, and even a few things that probably would have fit in quite well elsewhere...but were added so late that they would have given our production staff fits if we'd tried to shoehorn them into earlier chapters!

—TOR

53.02 How UNIX Keeps Time

Like all other operating systems, UNIX has a concept of the time. And virtually all UNIX systems, even the smallest, include a clock with some sort of battery backup built in.

All UNIX systems keep time by counting the number of microseconds since midnight, January 1, 1970, Greenwich Mean Time. This date is commonly called the *epoch*, and has folk-significance as the begining of the UNIX era. Although the first work on UNIX began in the late '60s, the first versions of UNIX were available (within Bell Laboratories) in the early '70s.

This count gets updated roughly 60 times per second. The exact rate depends on your particular UNIX system and is determined by the constant, HZ, defined in the header file */usr/include/sys/param.h*:

```
#define   HZ   60
```

This is the time's "resolution," and is often referred to as the clock's "tick." Note that it has nothing to do with your system's CPU clock rate. Time measurements are normally no more precise than your system's clock resolution, although some systems have added facilities for more precise timing.

If your UNIX system belongs to a network, it is important to keep all the clocks on the network "in sync." Strange things happen if you copy a file from one system to another and its date appears to be some time in the future. Many UNIX systems run a *time daemon* (one of those mysterious helper programs *(1.14)*), which takes care of this.

UNIX automatically keeps track of daylight savings time, leap years, and other chronological trivia. When the system is installed, you have to tell it your time zone and the style of daylight savings time you want to observe. As UNIX has become an international standard, the number of time zones (and obscure ways of handling daylight savings time) it can handle correctly has proliferated. In a few cases, you still have to handle these things by hand; for example, in Great Britain, the beginning and end of daylight savings time are set annually by Parliament, on advice from the Navy, and thus changes every year. Care for Libyan Standard Time?

UNIX's internal routines compute time in relation to the epoch, but there is no reason for you to worry about it unless you're a C programmer. A library of time routines can convert between this internal representation and more usable representations; see the UNIX manual page for *ctime*(3).

—*ML*

53.03 ASCII Characters: Listing and Getting Values

Many UNIX systems come with a file named *ascii*—in a directory named something like */usr/pub* or */usr/share/lib/pub*. It's a list of the ASCII character set with the octal and hexadecimal value of each character. Here are two lines from the octal section:

```
|030 can|031 em |032 sub|033 esc|034 fs |035 gs |036 rs |037 us |
|040 sp |041  ! |042  " |043  # |044  $ |045  % |046  & |047  ' |
```

It's saying, for instance, that an escape (`esc`) character has a value of 033 octal, and the percent sign (`%`) is 045 octal.

If your system doesn't have a file like that, you can type one in by hand in a few minutes; start with a printed ASCII chart. You might also want to make your own version and replace names like `sub` with the key you'd type to get that character (in this case, the two-character representation `^Z`). If your UNIX system doesn't use ASCII, you can make a similar file for it.

Once you have that file, the shell script below, named *ascii*, can search for the octal value of a character. For example:

```
% ascii esc
033
% ascii a
```

```
141
% ascii \&
046
```

Remember to escape special characters *(9.15)* as I did with that ampersand (&).
Here's the script:

ascii

case **46.06**

```
#!/bin/sh
file=/usr/pub/ascii
# Make pattern with spaces to match field in $file exactly:
case "$1" in
?)      pat=" $1 " ;;
??)     pat="$1 " ;;
???)    pat="$1" ;;
*)      echo "Usage: `basename $0` char
        (char must be single character like 'a' or name like 'soh')." 1>&2
        exit 1
        ;;
esac
```

\(..\)..\1 **35.10**
```
sed -n "1,/^\$/s/.*|\([0-9][0-9][0-9]\) $pat|.*/\1/p" $file
```

The script makes a *sed (35.24)* expression that exactly matches an entry in the first
section of the *ascii* file (before the blank line that starts the hexadecimal section). For example, the command ascii a stores □a□ in the *pat* shell variable;
the *sed* substitute command becomes:

s/|*nnn*□□a□|/*nnn*/p

where □ stands for a space and *nnn* stands for the octal value of the entry for a.

The *jot (47.11)* command also translates a numeric value to the character it represents. But *jot* doesn't show non-printable characters by name (like esc).

—*JP*

53.04 Who's On?

The *who* command lists the users logged on to the system now. Here's an
example of the output on my system:

```
% who
naylor   ttyZ1   Nov  6 08:25
hal      ttyp0   Oct 20 16:04   (zebra.ora.com:0.)
pmui     ttyp1   Nov  4 17:21   (dud.ora.com:0.0)
alan     ttyp2   Nov  5 23:08   (foobar.xyz.edu)
hal      ttyp3   Oct 28 15:43   (zebra.ora.com:0.)
    ...
```

Each line shows a different terminal or window. The columns show the username logged on, the *tty (3.08)* number, the login time, and, if the user is coming
in via a network *(1.33)*, you'll see (in parentheses) the location where they're
coming from. The user *hal* is logged on twice, for instance.

It's handy to search that list with *grep (28.01)*—especially on systems with a lot of users. For example:

−v 28.03

```
% who | grep "^hal "        ...where is hal logged on?
% who | grep "Nov  6"       ...who logged on today?
% who | grep -v "Nov  6"    ...who logged on before today?
  ...
```

—*JP*

53.05 *Copy What You Do with script*

Are you typing a complicated set of commands that you need to show someone else or keep "on file" for documentation? Are you debugging a program that goes wrong somewhere—but the error message flashes by so fast that you can't see it? Do you want to show a "pre-recorded" demonstration of an interactive program? The *script* program can do all of these.

Note: Versions of *script* on UNIX systems without *ptys (43.08)* aren't as flexible as the version I'm explaining here. For instance, those versions won't let you use job control *(13.01)* during the script.

To copy everything you do into a file, just type:

```
% script
Script started, file is typescript
%
```

Now you can type any UNIX command that you'd use at a shell prompt. Everything you do is copied into a file named *typescript* in the current directory. (To use a different filename, type its pathname *(1.21)* on the command line, like `script scriptfile.`) When you're done, type CTRL-d or *exit (40.04)* at a shell prompt.

One thing that surprises people is that *everything* will be copied into the script file. That includes escape sequences *(6.08)* that programs send to your terminal. This is both good and bad.

The good part is that you can "play back" whatever happened by *cat*ting *(26.02)* the script to your screen. When things get boring, you can run an interactive program like *vi* inside the script—then quit the script and play it back with *cat typescript.* The cursor will fly across the screen and your file will be re-edited before your eyes. (This is easier to see if the terminal is set to a slow data rate.)

The bad part is that errors you correct and other terminal-control sequences will be in the file, too. If you edit or print the script file, it may be full of "junk" like ^M (carriage return) and ^H (backspace) characters. (A command like *cat −v* or *od −c (26.07)* will show you these characters.) If the file has just a few of these characters, you can clean it up by hand with your text editor's global substitu-

tion commands. You can also automate your "script cleaning" with techniques
like the ones in articles 36.09 and 45.20.

—JP

53.06 *Cleaning script Files*

As article 53.05 explains, the files made by the *script* program can have stray
control characters in them. The shell script called *script.tidy* can clean them up.
Dan Bernstein wrote it and posted it to Usenet; I made a few changes. It reads
from files or standard input; it writes to standard output.

script.tidy uses the *sed* *(35.24)* substitute command to remove CTRL-m (RETURN)
characters from the ends of lines. It uses the *sed* test command *(35.20)* to repeat a
series of commands that delete a character followed by CTRL-h (BACKSPACE). If
you use DELETE as your erase character *(6.09)*, change the script to eat DELETE
instead of BACKSPACE. *script.tidy* uses a trick *(47.34)* with *echo* and *tr* to store the
control characters in shell variables. Because the *sed* script has doublequotes
(9.10) around it, the shell variables are substituted in the right places before the
shell starts *sed*.

script.tidy

eval 9.08

```
#!/bin/sh
# Public domain.

# Put CTRL-M in $m and CTRL-H in $b.
# Change \010 to \177 if you use DEL for erasing.
eval `echo m=M b=H | tr 'MH' '\015\010'`

exec sed "s/$m\$//
:x
s/[^$b]$b//
t x" $*
```

You can also hack the *sed* script in *script.tidy* to delete some of your terminal's
escape sequences *(6.08)*; article 43.11 explains how to find these sequences. (A
really automated *script.tidy* would read your *termcap* or *terminfo* entry and
look for all those escape sequences in the script file.)

—JP in *comp.unix.questions* on Usenet, *4 October 1989*

53.07 *When You Get Impatient*

vis

Sometimes you find yourself repeating the same command over and over
again—for example, *ps* *(40.05)* to monitor the progress of your background
processes, or *lpq* *(45.02)* to know when your printout is finished. Instead of typing
the same command repeatedly, or even using C shell history *(12.01)* to repeat it,
use the *vis* command. For example:

```
% vis ps
```

The *vis* command takes over your screen and shows the output of the initial *ps*
command. Every 15 seconds, the command is executed again and your screen is

updated with the new information. If this delay is too long for you, you can get *vis* to use a shorter delay using the –*d* option:

```
% vis -d 2 ps
```

The information will now be updated every 2 seconds. Your screen is cleared and you are shown the output of *ps*. On the top line, *vis* tells you the command being run, how long your delay is (if not the default), and how many times it has been executed. The Exec: line is incremented every time the command is repeated.

```
Command: ps                          Delay: 2              Exec:  1

    PID TT STAT   TIME COMMAND
   2971 p1 S      0:06 -sh (csh)
   6139 p1 S      0:00 vis -d 2 ps
   6145 p1 R      0:00 ps
   3401 q0 IW     0:13 -sh (csh)
   5954 q0 S      0:01 vi ch01
  14019 q5 IW     0:02 -sh (csh)
  29380 r7 IW     0:00 -bin/csh (csh)
  29401 rd IW     0:00 -bin/csh (csh)
```

vis provides a few other command-line options. The –*s* option is particularly neat—using –*s*, any lines that have changed since the last iteration are printed in standout mode.

Note that variations of this command have floated around in the public domain under several different names, such as *display*, *rep*, and *watch*. We found *vis* to be the most useful.

—LM

53.08 Type Bang Splat. Don't Forget the Rabbit Ears

You don't need to be smart and rich and powerful for people to *think* that you are. Just dress that way. The same goes for UNIX. If you talk like an expert, people will think that you are one. UNIX gurus have their own secret code for the special characters they're always typing. Because knowing how to speak correctly is a real Power Tool :-), here's a brief introduction to "hackerese":

What	Traditional Term	Enlightened Terms
!	Exclamation Point	Bang, Shriek, Ball-Bat
"	Quotation Mark	Double Quote, Rabbit Ears
*	Asterisk	Splat, Star
'	Apostrophe	Single Quote, Tick
.	Period	Dot, Point

If this isn't enough to disgust errr, satisfy your curiosity, get a copy of *The Hacker's Dictionary* by Eric S. Raymond (MIT Press, 1991). It's based on the Jargon File, an online collection of hackerspeak. The Jargon File started as a list of terms used by early Artificial Intelligence hackers at MIT, Stanford University and CMU. It has since grown to include many terms from the Internet and UNIX communities.

—JP

53.09 *Making a "Login" Shell*

When you log in to most UNIX systems, your shell is a *login shell*. When a shell is a login shell, it acts differently. For example, the shell reads a special setup file *(2.02)* like *.profile* or *.login*. UNIX "knows" how to tell the shells to be login shells. If you type the shell's name (like *sh* or */bin/csh*) at a prompt, that will not start a login shell.

Sometimes, when you're testing an account or using a window system, you want to start a login shell without logging in. UNIX shells act like login shells when they are executed with a name that starts with a dash (-). The easiest way to do this, which wastes a lot of disk space (and may not work on your system anyway if the shells are read-protected), is to make your own copy of the shell and name it starting with a dash:

bin *5.02*
./— *24.13*

```
$ cd $HOME/bin
$ cp /bin/csh ./-csh
```

It's better to make a symbolic link *(19.04)* to the shell:

```
$ cd $HOME/bin
$ ln -s /bin/csh ./-csh
```

(Or, if your own *bin* subdirectory is on the same filesystem as */bin*, you can use a hard link *(19.04)*.) A third way is to write a little C program *(54.08)* that runs the actual shell but tells the shell that its name starts with a dash. This is how the UNIX login process does it:

```
main()
{
    execl("/bin/csh", "-csh", 0);
}
```

No matter which way you chose, you can execute your new shell by typing its name:

```
$ -csh
        ...normal C shell login process...
% ...run whatever commands you want...
% logout
$ ...back to original shell
```

—JP

53.10 The date Command

All UNIX systems come with a program called *date*. It shows you the time from the system clock *(53.02)*. (So, the time is only as accurate as your system's clock.) For example:

```
% date
Tue Dec  8 08:06:39 PST 1992
```

shellutils

If you need parts of that date, you can split the line into pieces. There are examples in articles 17.19, 22.03, and 2.05. Most newer versions of *date* (including the one distributed with the GNU *shellutils* package on the Power Tools disk) will also let you set the format of the date. To do that, type a single argument that starts with a plus (+) and has format specification characters in it. Check your online manual page for a list of format specification characters. The argument has to be all one word, so you'll usually need to put quotes *(9.10)* around it. Here's a simple example:

```
% date +'Today is %d %h 19%y.'
Today is 08 Dec 1992.
```

You'll usually use this in a shell script or alias *(11.02)*. For some "real-life" examples, see articles 17.17, 19.03, and 22.14.

—JP

53.11 Making an Arbitrary-size File for Testing

The *yes* command *(24.04)* outputs text over and over. If you need a file of some size for testing, make it with *yes* and *head (26.21)*. For example, to make a file 100k (102,400) characters long, with 12800 8-character lines (7 digits and a newline), type:

```
% yes 1234567 | head -12800 > 100k-file
```

Note: On some UNIX systems, that command may "hang" and need to be killed with CTRL-c—because *head* keeps reading input from the pipe. If it hangs on your system, replace head -12800 with sed 12800q.

—JIK, JP in *comp.unix.questions* on Usenet, *11 November 1991*

53.12 The '70s with a Twist

Remember those awful smiley face buttons that were so common in the early 1970s? They are still around, everywhere, in electronic mail *(1.33)*, but with a new twist. The twist is literal: they're printed sideways, like this: :-)

(At first you have to turn your head sideways to see the face, but eventually you get used to reading them. Then you have trouble reading them only when you turn your head!)

You see, in electronic mail, it's sometimes hard to know just what someone means. There's no tone of voice to indicate whether someone is serious or joking. Enter the smiley.

The standard smiley printed above is used to mean "don't take this too seriously." Then there's the frowning face used to indicate that something makes you sad: :-(

How about this one? 8-O

That translates as "Omigod!" (done after `rm -rf *`).

smiley

Smileys range from the practical to the absurd. David Sanderson, whom the *Wall Street Journal* called "the Noah Webster of smileys," has collected hundreds of symbols from as many contributors, and put them all into a program called *smiley*.

Call *smiley* with no arguments, and it will give you a random smiley symbol, plus interpretation:

```
% smiley
7:^]    Ronald Reagan
```

Type *smiley* with a smiley face as an argument, and you'll get possible interpretations (and an attribution for the explanation, if available):

```
% smiley ";-)"
;-)     "If you touch my daughter again, they won't be blanks" [RICHH]
        beaten up
        could be pirate smiling face??
        crying with happiness
        getting fresh
        sardonic incredulity
        smiling face gets his lights punched out
        winking
```

[Most smileys have bizarre characters that need to be protected from the shell. If the *smiley* program doesn't give you the answer you expect, or if you get an error message from the shell, it's time to practice your shell quoting *(9.10, 9.11)* :^).—*JP*]

Type `smiley -l` to see a list of all known smileys. (And if you can't get enough smileys online, see the little book *Smileys*, by David W. Sanderson, from O'Reilly & Associates.)

—*TOR*

54

What's On the Disk

54.01 Introduction

This book comes with a companion CD-ROM that contains source code and binaries for the programs described in the book.

There are two groups of files on the CD-ROM:

- Freely-available programs that we tested, liked, and wrote about in the book. Most of these programs are written in C and are distributed in both source and binary form. The binaries have been compiled for each of the platforms listed in article 54.03.

- Scripts that we wrote or adapted ourselves, and wanted to share with our readers.

In selecting freely-available software to put on the disk, we've tried to emphasize quality over quantity. Too many free software archives load you up with anything and everything they can find, without evaluating whether or not it's worthwhile. You're faced with the job of wading through everything to figure out whether it's worth using or not.

like this

Every program or script on the Power Tools disk is at least mentioned somewhere in this book. Near the first or most important of those mentions, it's got a disk icon in the margin, with the name of the program underneath. Our idea was that as you read about a program you like, you could simply install it (as described in article 54.05) and have it added to your private stock of power tools. (You can also add them all at once, and just use them as you read about them!) This chapter is designed to give you some background information about the software:

- A quick summary of what's on the disk (article 54.04).

- What versions of UNIX the programs are already compiled for (article 54.03).

- A detailed description of the installation procedure (article 54.05).

- How to get a CD-ROM drive if you don't already have one (article 54.06).

- How to get the software on alternate media and from the online archive (article 54.07).

- How to build the software from the source code if you don't have one of the supported platforms (article 54.08).

- How to get software support or porting help (article 54.09).

—TOR

54.02 Where Does Free Software End and UNIX Begin?

You may find that some of the programs on the disk are already available at your site. After all, UNIX itself is already a collection of free software *(1.01)*. For example, here are just a few of the now-standard programs that were once contributed to UNIX (most through the University of California at Berkeley's BSD version):

- the C shell *(1.08)*

- *vi (31.02)*

- *termcap (6.02)*

- *tar (21.02)*

Here are some other programs that are nearly universally available (and perhaps even official parts of some versions of UNIX, but not all):

- RCS *(21.15)*

- *compress (25.06)*

- *patch (34.09)*

- Emacs *(33.01)*

We wanted to make sure that you had all the great programs in the second group, so we've included them just to be sure.

—TOR

54.03 *Shrink-Wrapped Software for UNIX*

One of the great advantages of UNIX has always been its portability. It runs on more hardware architectures than any other operating system—in fact, there is hardly a single architecture in common use that does not support some version of UNIX.

Unfortunately, that strength is also UNIX's greatest weakness. Because UNIX runs on so many competing hardware platforms, it isn't possible to go into a software store, buy a UNIX application, take it home, and load it onto your computer. The kind of "shrink-wrapped" software you find for DOS or Macintosh systems is hard to come by.

Free software for UNIX is typically distributed in source code form, which limits its use to programmers who know how to build the executable programs from source. Application software is sold on a platform-by-platform basis. You need to tell the software vendor what kind of machine you have, and they have to provide you with a tape loaded with the software compiled for that class of machine.

The vast storage capacity of CD-ROM changes all that. Because there's over 600 megabytes of storage on a single disk, we've been able to offer not just source code for each of the programs on the disk, but also pre-compiled binaries for seven of the most common UNIX platforms:

> Sun4 SunOS 4.1.1
> Sun3 SunOS 4.1.1
> Digital Equipment Corp. DECstation Ultrix 4.1
> IBM RS/6000 AIX 3.2
> HP 700 HP-UX 8.07
> SCO XENIX 2.3.2
> SCO UNIX 3.2.x

If you have one of these platforms, all you need to do is to mount the CD-ROM on your system, and run the installation program. The installation program is smart enough to figure out your platform and load the right version. See article 54.05 for details.

If you don't have one of the supported platforms, it should still be possible to build the software from the source code, using the build scripts that we supply. See article 54.08 for details.

—*TOR*

54.04 Quick Descriptions of What's On the Disk

All the packages included on the Power Tools disk are discussed somewhere in the book, complete with an icon in the margin to let you know it's there. But here's a quick listing of what each program does and where the book talks about it.

Many of the programs listed here are shell scripts. All shell scripts are theoretically portable from one platform to another; however, they might have dependencies on programs that either aren't installed on your system, or behave somewhat differently than the programmer expected. So beware that you might have to tweak the shell scripts a little to make them work correctly on your system.

Also beware that some scripts written in *awk*, *sed*, or *perl* use #! syntax on the first line of the script, to tell the shell what program to run. Not all shells support this feature. If your shell doesn't, you'll have to convert the script to a shell script. See articles 47.03 and 38.14 for more information.

.emacs_ml

The *.emacs_ml* file contains a listing of Mike's favorite Emacs commands. If you like them, put them in your own *$HOME/.emacs* file. Article 33.08.

.enter

.enter is an example of a shell script you might want to always run when you enter a directory. It is meant to be used with an alias (which can be found in the *csh_init* file) and with a *.exit* script. A sample *.exit* script is also included on the disk. Article 15.15.

.exit

.exit is an example of a shell script you might want to always run when you exit a directory. It is meant to be used with an alias (which can be found in the *csh_init* file) and with a *.enter* script. A sample *.enter* script is also included on the disk. Article 15.15.

.hushlogin

.hushlogin is a Makefile to be called by the *make* command from your *.login* file. It prints the message-of-the-day only if it's changed since the previous day. Article 2.16.

80cols

The *80cols* file simply contains 80 digits on a single line. You can use this file to determine whether your screen is 80 columns wide, with:

```
cat 80cols
```

Article 44.06.

Clear

The *Clear* shell script can be used to execute VT100 escape sequences. It is also linked to the names *NOG* (to cancel an alternate character set); *Graphics* (to enable graphics mode); *C132* (to enable 132-column mode); *C80* (to enable 80-column mode); *Revvid* (to enable reverse video); *Normal* (to re-enable normal video); *ToStatus* (to write a message to the terminal status line); and *ClrStatus* (to clear the status line). Article 43.09.

!

The *!* command (pronounced *bang*) creates temporary files to be used with programs that require filenames in their command lines. For example, to *diff* two files after sorting them, you might do:

```
diff `! sort file1` `! sort file2`
```

Article 10.16.

addup

addup is a shell script that uses *awk* to add up the values in a specfied column in its input. Article 51.08.

age_files

The *age_files* shell script reports the size of the files in a given directory by age. Article 17.26.

agrep, Version 2.04

agrep is a tool for fast text searching. *agrep* is similar to the other members of the *grep* family, but it is much more general (and usually faster). The enhancements over other *grep*s include the ability to search for approximate patterns. Article 28.08.

areacode

areacode is used to display the region and state that a given area code is assigned to. This program is very handy when someone leaves you a phone number, but no city or state reference. Article 50.03.

ascii

ascii is a shell script that searches a listing of the ASCII character set and returns the ASCII decimal value of a specified character. Article 53.03.

awf

awf (Amazingly Workable Formatter) is an *nroff −man* or *nroff −ms* clone written entirely in (old) *awk*. It is slow and has many restrictions, but does a decent job on most manual pages and simple −*ms* documents, and isn't subject to AT&T's licensing which denies many System V users any text formatter at all. It is also a text formatter that is simple enough to be tinkered with, for people who want to experiment. Article 45.19.

GNU bash, Version 1.12

bash is the GNU Project's Bourne Again SHell, an interactive shell with Bourne shell syntax. It also includes interactive command-line editing, job control on architectures that support it, *csh*-like history features and brace expansion, and a slew of other stuff. Article 1.08.

behead

The *behead* shell script removes all lines in a file up to the first blank line. This effectively removes the header from files saved from mail or news *(1.33)*. Article 36.03.

bitmaps

The Poskanzer Bitmap Collection is a collection of monochrome bitmaps, for use as background patterns, clip-art, etc. They are stored in X11 *(1.31)* bitmap format, and most of them are compressed. If you need them in some other format, use Poskanzer's *pbmplus* package, which is also included on the Power Tools disk. Article 45.28.

bkedit

bkedit is a shell script for making a backup copy of a file before starting the *vi* editor on it. Article 46.11.

bsdtar

bsdtar is very similar to *tar*, but can remap long filenames to unique 14-character filenames on systems that have a 14-character filename limit. *bsdtar* can only read archives, it cannot create archives.

bsplit

bsplit enables you to split binary files into manageable pieces. Users who are familiar with *split* will have no problem with *bsplit*, as the usage of *bsplit* is exactly like the *split* program. Article 36.07.

cal_today

cal_today is a simple shell script that runs *cal* and places angle brackets around the current date. Article 50.08.

calen

calen generates a calendar for a whole year or for a certain range of months within a year in 132 columns. Article 50.09.

catsaway

The *catsaway* shell script is included here as an example of using a loop to repeat a command until it fails. Article 46.10.

center

center is an *awk* script that centers each line of a file. Article 36.06.

cgrep

cgrep is a context-*grep* script for showing the given string with several lines of surrounding text. Article 28.13.

chmod_edit

The *chmod_edit* shell script adds write permission to a file, places you in your favorite editor, and then removes write permission again. Article 23.09.

chunksort

The *chunksort* program sorts multi-line records that are separated by blank lines. Article 37.07.

cleanup

cleanup is an example of a shell script to be run by *cron*. By combining multiple *find* conditions, the *find* command is run only once instead of multiple times. Article 24.21.

cleanup.sed

cleanup.sed is a *sed* script to be run on *troff* input files. It converts double quotes to "curly" quotes, two dashes to em-dashes, and places a no-space character before constant-width font changes. It should be called with *sed –f cleanup.sed*. Article 45.23.

cls

cls is a compressed directory lister that can list directories in nice columns and indicate "long" names that have been truncated. It is also linked to the names *clf, cls2,* and *clf2*. Article 17.07.

cols

The *cols* shell script displays output in columns. It is also linked to the *c2, c3, c4, c5, c6, c7,* and *c8* commands, to force it to display respective number of columns. Article 36.14.

compress, Version 4.0

compress allows compression/decompression of files. In addition to the *compress* program itself, the package includes *uncompress, zcat, zcmp, zdiff,* and *zmore*. Article 25.06.

concordance

concordance reports the number of times each word appears in a given file. Article 30.08.

count.it

count.it reports the difference in word length between two files. Article 30.06.

count_types

count_types is a shell script that reports the number of files of each type, as reported by the *file* command. Article 17.25.

cpmod

cpmod allows you to copy modes, ownerships, and times from one file to others, without affecting the data. Article 23.17.

crontab

The *crontab* shell script provides interactive editing of your *crontab* entries. This script is meant for systems that do not already provide interactive *crontab* file editing. Article 42.16.

crush

crush is a *sed* script that removes blank lines from text and sends the result to standard output. Article 26.11.

csh_init

The *csh_init* file is a collection of C shell commands and alias definitions that are shown throughout the book. Although we show C shell versions, most of these are easy to change into Bourne and Korn shell functions *(11.10)* and Korn shell aliases *(11.04)*.

In its distribution form, each set of commands is commented out and needs to be explicitly uncommented before you can use them; this is because many of the definitions override or conflict with one another. You can copy or source *(46.22)* the file into your shell setup file *(2.02)*, and then enable the definitions that you want. Articles 8.05, 8.06, 8.08, 8.11, 11.07, 11.09, 12.15, 12.16, 15.10, 15.14, 15.15, 16.06, 17.06, 17.16, 17.27, 18.24, 22.14, 23.02, 23.09, 26.18, 30.09, 31.20, 43.09, 45.08, 49.05, and 52.07.

csh_logout

The *csh_logout* file contains a set of commands for removing temporary files. C shell users can input these commands into their *$HOME/.logout* file. Article 22.03.

csplit

The *csplit* program splits a file according to context. Article 36.08.

cut+paste

cut+paste is a collection of three programs. *cut* and *paste* are public domain versions of AT&T's *cut* and *paste* commands. The third utility is *spaste*, which allows you to serially paste a file together. Articles 36.12 and 36.16.

cvtbase

cvtbase is a program for converting from one base to another. Supported bases are decimal, hexadecimal, octal, and binary. Article 51.05.

date-month

The *date-month* script expands a date such as 11/3/92 or 11-3-92 into November 3, 1992. Article 38.11.

del

del is a shell script that prompts you for the removal of the specified files. Unlike *rm −i*, *del* prompts you only once for all files when there are more than three to remove. Article 24.05.

delete, Version 1.26

The *delete* program is a replacement for *rm* that allows files to be recovered later on. Instead of actually deleting files, *delete* marks them for deletion by adding a `.#` prefix. To recover the file, use *undelete* (version 1.24). To delete the files for real, use *expunge* or *purge* (version 1.20). To list all the files in the current directory that are marked for deletion, use the *lsdel* command (version 1.19). Article 24.08.

derange.num

derange.num is a shell script that outputs a range of numbers. This can be useful on the command line and for constructing loops in shell scripts. Article 51.06.

GNU diff, diff3, sdiff, and cmp Utilities, Version 2.0

The GNU versions of *diff*, *diff3*, *sdiff*, and *cmp* provide all the features of BSD's *diff*, but with some additional features. Articles 29.01, 29.02, 29.03, and 29.10.

dir_path

dir_path is a shell script that shows all directories with the same name. Article 17.22.

dirtop

The *dirtop* shell script uses VT100 escape sequences to make an *ls* directory listing that stays at the top of the window while you work. Article 22.10.

doublespace

doublespace is a *sed* script that double-spaces text and sends the result to standard output. Article 26.12.

dtp

dtp is a program that tries to return the command line required to properly format a given *troff* document. It recognizes the *ms*, *man*, and *me* macro sets, as well as *tbl* and *eqn* commands. Article 45.16.

ediff

ediff is a program that translates *diff(29.01)* output into English. Article 29.07.

elookfor

The *elookfor* script is similar to the *lookfor* script, but faster. It finds all files in the given directory tree that contain the given string(s), using *egrep*. Article 18.22.

GNU emacs, Version 18.58

GNU *emacs* is the GNU incarnation of the advanced, self-documenting, customizable, extensible real-time display editor Emacs. Chapter 33.

exrc

The *exrc* file is a collection of *vi* and *ex* commands that are shown throughout the book. In its distribution form, each set of commands is commented out and needs to be explicitly uncommented before you can use them; this is because many of the definitions override or conflict with one another. You can copy this file into your *.exrc* file *(5.09)*, and then enable the definitions that you want. Articles 31.23, 31.32, 32.04, 32.08, 32.11, 32.12, and 32.15.

fgrep, Version 1.1

Although maligned for its slowness, *fgrep* has several features that make it worth installing. This is one of the fastest *fgreps* that we've been able to find. Article 28.06.

filesum

The *filesum* script counts the total size of files in the current directory. Article 38.10.

GNU File Management Utilities (fileutils), Version 3.3

The GNU file utilities have significant advantages over their standard UNIX counterparts, such as greater speed, additional options, and fewer arbitrary limits. Programs included are: *chmod, chgrp, chown, cp, dd, df, install, ln, mkdir, mkfifo, mknod, mv, rm, du, ls, mknod, rmdir,* and *touch*. Most of these programs are covered throughout the book.

GNU find, Version 3.7

GNU *find* has several enhancements over the standard *find* command found on most systems. Among other things, it has the option to measure times from the beginning of today rather than from 24 hours ago, and it has user-settable maximum search depth. *find* is also distributed with the GNU *xargs* program; as well as the *locate* program, which lists files in a database that matches a pattern (similar to *finder(18.20)*). Articles 18.01 and 18.24.

findcmd

findcmd searches your path and prints the name of all executables that contain the given substring. Article 17.11.

finder

The *finder* program prints the names of directories that match the given regular expression. You must first use the included *mkfindex* shell script to search the specified directories and create an index file of subdirectory names at the root of each directory. Article 18.20.

findtext

The *findtext* shell script prints the names of specified files that are text files (i.e., human-readable). Article 17.27.

flip

flip is a shell script that reverses the text in a given file line-by-line. That is, the first line in the file switches position with the last, the second line in the file switches with the next-to-last, and so on. Article 26.20.

fmt.sh

fmt.sh is a shell script that uses *sed* and *nroff* to simulate the behavior of the *fmt* command. It is meant for systems that are not distributed with *fmt* already installed. Article 31.38.

formprog

formprog is a shell script for filling in forms. It looks for a template file (argument 1) and prompts the user for information, placing the completed form into an output file (argument 2). Article 47.22.

ftpfile

ftpfile is a shell script for anonymously *ftp*'ing a file. It is included on the disk as an example of a Here document. Article 9.14.

GNU awk (gawk), Version 2.13.2

gawk is a version of *awk* that is faster and uses less memory. Article 38.05.

getmac

getmac is a shell script for printing a *troff* macro definition in the specified macro package. Article 45.22.

getmatch

The *getmatch* script returns the strings in a given file that match the given regular expression. Article 27.06.

getopt

getopt is a public-domain implementation of the System V *getopt* program. Not to be confused with the library routine, this program helps scripts parse their options/flags/arguments. Article 46.17.

grabchars, Version 1.9

grabchars gets one or more keystrokes from the user, without requiring them to press RETURN. It was written to make all types of shell scripts more interactive. Article 47.31.

GNU grep, Version 1.6

GNU *egrep* (also linked to *grep*) is about twice as fast as stock UNIX *egrep*. Article 28.09.

GNU groff, Version 1.06

groff is the GNU version of the *troff* text formatter. Included are implementations of *troff*, *pic*, *eqn*, *tbl*, *refer*, the *man* macros and the *ms* macros, and drivers for PostScript, TeX dvi format, and typewriter-like devices. Also included is a modified version of the Berkeley *me* macros, and an enhanced version of the X11R4 *(1.31)* *xditview*. Article 45.18.

---

head

The *head* shell script simulates the behavior of the *head* command distributed with many versions of UNIX. It is meant for systems that do not have the *head* program already installed. Article 26.21.

hgrep

hgrep is a trivial, but cute, front-end for *grep.* It takes the results of the *grep* and highlights the word that was searched for. Article 28.20.

index, Version 1.0

index allows you to maintain multiple databases of textual information, each with a different format. With each database, index allows you to add entries, delete entries, edit existing entries, search for entries using full regular expressions, and run all or part of the database through a user-configured filter. Articles 50.12 and 50.13.

ipl, Version 1.0

ipl is a two-dimensional graphic production system. It produces scatter plots, line plots, bar graphs, range displays, pie graphs, US/Canada maps, schedule charts, boxes, arrows, text, etc. *ipl* produces PostScript output, based on a user-supplied control file. It also includes a table beautifier that is useful for taking plain text tables, spreadsheet output, etc. and setting them in a nice font. Article 51.10.

ispell, Version 3.0

ispell is a fast screen-oriented spelling checker that shows your errors in the context of the original file, and suggests possible corrections when it can figure them out. Compared to UNIX *spell,* it is faster and much easier to use. *ispell* can also handle languages other than English. Article 30.02.

jot

jot is a simple tool that allows you to print sequential or random data. It can be very useful for constructing loops in shell scripts. Article 47.11.

lensort

lensort sorts lines from shortest to longest. Article 37.08.

less, Version 1.77

less is an extremely flexible pager and is preferred by many to *pg* or *more.* *less* has all of the functionality of *more,* in addition to backwards scrolling, bookmarks, searching (forward and backward, single, and multi-file), and many other useful features. Article 26.04.

lf

lf is actually five commands linked to the same script. Each command results in calling the *ls* command with a different set of command-line options. In addition to *lf,* there is also *ll, lg, lm,* and *lr.* Article 17.08.

lndir

lndir is a safe way to duplicate a directory structure elsewhere on the filesystem. It's necessary because a *cd* into a straight symbolic link actually changes to the directory pointed to by the link, which can be confusing or even dangerous if the link is in a sensitive area of the filesystem. *lndir* recursively re-creates a directory structure, making symbolic links to all the files in the directory. Article 19.07.

logerrs

The *logerrs* script sends errors to a log file as well as to standard error. Article 14.16.

longlines

The *longlines* file contains several lines with 200 columns of text. You can use this file to test whether line wrapping is working correctly, or to adjust windows to a particular size, with:

```
cat longlines
```

Article 44.06.

look

look is a fairly fast, fairly portable version of *look*. Article 28.18.

lookfor

The *lookfor* script finds all files in the given directory tree that contain the given string(s). Article 18.22.

ls_today

ls_today is a shell script to print the names of files that have been created or edited today. Article 17.19.

make_print

make_print is an example Makefile for printing a series of files that have changed. It is meant to be renamed *makefile* or *Makefile* and run with *make*. Article 22.09.

manindex

manindex simulates the behavior of the *apropos* command found on many systems. It generates an index that you can later search using the following alias:

```
alias apropos "grep -i \!$ indexfile"
```

Article 52.03.

mced

mced is a utility that allows you to browse, edit, and execute commands from your C shell history list. It is not a shell itself, but it executes the commands in your current shell as if you had typed them in. It is executed using an alias that appears in the *csh_init* file. As enhanced by Ready-to-Run Software, *mced* automatically selects which editor to use (Emacs or *vi*) depending on the value of your EDITOR environment variable. Article 12.16.

motd.diff

motd.diff is a shell script to be called from your *.login* file. It only displays lines in the message-of-the-day that have changed since the previous login. Article 2.15.

namesort

The *namesort* program sorts a list of names by the last name. Article 37.09.

nextday

The *nextday* shell script returns the name of the next day of the week, to supply to the *at* command. It can also be linked to the name *nextweekday*, in which case the next weekday is returned (for example, on Friday *nextweekday* will return Monday). Article 42.10.

no_run

The *no_run* file contains an example of a shell script that you can enter into your private *$HOME/bin* and link to the names of programs that you might not want to run on some systems. It's meant for use on a network where you have the same home directory on several machines of different architectures. After editing the script, you can link it to the names of the commands that are run differently (or not at all) on some systems. Of course, the directory that you install and link the scripts in (such as *$HOME/bin*) must be in your path before any systemwide executables. Article 9.06.

nom

nom supplies the names of the files in the current directory that *don't* match the given shell wildcards. For example, to edit all files in the current directory that don't end in *.o*, try:

```
vi `nom *.o`
```

Article 16.10.

offset

The *offset* shell script indents text for printing or other uses. Article 36.05.

oldlinks

oldlinks is a shell script that prints the names of "stale" symbolic links. Article 17.29.

opttest

opttest is a shell script for parsing *getopt* output. It's meant to demonstrate *getopt*'s behavior. Article 46.17.

paircheck

paircheck is an example script for making sure that strings in a file have matching counterparts. *paircheck* checks that each `.TS` in a given *troff* file has a corresponding `.TE`. Article 30.10.

patch, version 2.0.12u7

patch is Larry Wall's program for distributing source patches to files. By using *diff* files (generally "context" *diffs*), *patch* can intelligently apply patches to a file even if modifications have been made to the source in the meantime. *patch* is now used extensively to communicate source changes throughout the world. Article 34.09.

pbmplus

pbmplus is the Extended Portable Bitmap Toolkit, for converting various image formats to and from portable formats, and therefore to and from each other. In addition to the converters, the package includes some simple tools for manipulating the portable formats. Article 45.28.

pcal, Version 4.3

pcal generates PostScript to produce landscape or portrait calendars for any month and year. By default, *pcal* simply prints an empty calendar. Its real power is in its ability to place "events" in appropriate days on the calendar, thus allowing the user to create personalized calendars. Article 50.10.

perl, Version 4.035

perl (Practical Extraction and Report Language) is an interpreted language optimized for scanning arbitrary text files, extracting information from those text files, and printing reports based on that information. It has exceptionally powerful string, file, and system routines to quickly create almost any utility. An added debugger makes *perl* an attractive alternative to *awk* or *gawk*. Chapter 39 and Article 28.12.

phone

phone is a shell script that displays lines in a file called *phone*, matching the given string to standard output. It is also linked to the name *address*, in which case it returns matching lines in a file named *address* to *stdout*. Article 50.02.

phrase

phrase is a shell script that searches for a pattern across multiple lines. Articles 28.11 and 35.17.

pipegrep

pipegrep searches through the output of a series of commands, printing the command that produced each line of output. Article 28.13.

pstext

pstext is a utility for converting text files to PostScript files—usually for a PostScript printer. It includes options for printing "landscape" mode, for specifying a font, and for specifying a point size. Article 45.24.

psutils, Version 2.2

psutils is a collection of utilities for manipulating PostScript documents. It includes five programs:

* *psbook*, for rearranging pages into signatures;

- *psselect*, for selecting pages and page ranges;

- *pstops*, for performing general page rearrangement and selection;

- *psnup*, for merging multiple pages per sheet using *pstops*;

- *epsffit*, for fitting an EPSF file to a given bounding box.

In addition, it includes six scripts:

- *getafm*, a shell script for outputting PostScript commands to retrieve an AFM file from a printer;

- *showchar*, a shell script for outputting PostScript commands to draw a character with metric information;

- *fixfmps*, a *perl* filter to fix FrameMaker documents so that *psselect* and other programs will work properly;

- *fixwpps*, a *perl* filter to fix WordPerfect documents so that *psselect* and other programs will work properly;

- *fixmacps*, a *perl* filter to fix Macintosh documents with a "saner" version of *md*;

- *fixpspps*, a *perl* filter to fix PSPrint PostScript so that *psselect* and other programs will work properly.

Articles 45.25 and 45.26.

pushin

pushin is a *sed* script that removes any extra white space characters in a file and sends the result to standard output. Article 26.14.

qcsh

The *qcsh* file has a shell function that lets you use C shell features such as the curly brace ({ }) operators *(10.05)* from either the Bourne or Korn shell. Article 16.03.

qsubst

qsubst is designed for substituting strings in (large) files. It accepts a list of filenames and two strings. For each of the files, *qsubst* modifies it in-place to replace *string1* with *string2* wherever the user approves the change. Article 34.10.

qterm, Version 5.0

qterm is a program that queries terminals to find out what kind of terminal is responding. It is useful to "automagically" define your terminal type. It prints the name of the terminal (such as "vt100") to standard output. (This name is hopefully compatible with a *termcap/terminfo* name on your system.) Article 6.05.

rcs, Version 5.6

rcs (Revision Control System) is a set of commands for managing multiple revisions of files. *rcs* automates the storing, retrieval, logging, identification, and merging of revisions. *rcs* is useful for text that is revised frequently; for example programs, documentation, graphics, papers, and form letters. Article 21.15.

rcsgrep

rcsgrep is a shell script that searches for the most recent revision of a set of *rcs* files for a given string. Can also be called through links named *rcsegrep* and *rcsfgrep*. Article 28.10.

recomment

The *recomment* shell script runs *fmt (31.37)* on files with lines that are commented out, with wrapped lines recommented. Article 36.02.

redo

redo is a utility that allows you to browse through, edit, and execute commands on your C shell history list. It is a C shell script that is sourced in using an alias. This alias appears in the *csh_init* file. Article 12.16.

relink

relink is a *perl* script for relinking multiple files, similar to the *rename* script. Article 19.15.

ren

ren is a program that can rename many files according to search and replacement patterns, ala VMS (but better). *ren* checks for replacement name collisions and handles rename chains gracefully. Article 19.12.

rename

rename is a *perl* script for renaming multiple files. Article 19.11.

rename.sh

rename.sh is a shell script for renaming multiple files. Article 19.09.

rot, Version 1.2

rot rotates a file, so that lines become columns, and vice versa. Without any options, the file will be rotated clockwise. Article 36.21.

runsed

The *runsed* shell script runs the *sed* commands in a file called *sedscr* on the specified files, overwriting the original files. Article 35.03.

runtime

runtime repeatedly executes *time* on a given command and then reports the average time taken over those iterations. The actual output of the command is discarded. Article 41.04.

sc, Version 6.21

sc is a spreadsheet calculator based on rectangular tables, much like a financial spreadsheet. Article 51.09.

screen, Version 3.2b

screen is a window manager that allows you to handle several independent screens (UNIX *ptys* *(43.08)*) on a single physical terminal. *screen* is supplied for each of the platforms described in 54.03, except for SCO Xenix. Articles 13.09 and 3.07.

screensize

The *screensize* file contains 69 lines of text, starting at 69 and ending at 1. You can use this file to determine how many rows are displaying on your screen, with:

```
cat screensize
```

Article 44.06.

script.tidy

script.tidy uses *sed* to clean up files generated with the *script* program. Article 53.06.

search.el

The *search.el* file contains a set of Emacs search commands. To use these commands, use the *load-file* command in your *$HOME/.emacs* file to point to this file. Article 33.09.

sedman

sedman is a *sed* script for formatting simple manual pages. Article 45.21.

sh_prompt

The *sh_prompt* file contains lines of code meant to be copied into your *.profile* file, for Bourne or Korn shell users. They put the current date and time into your prompt. Article 8.12.

shar, Version 2.1

The *shar* package is a set of tools to create and unpack shell archives. This set of tools is designed to make it easier to ship sources around. Included are a program to find source files (*findsrc*, version 2.2); a program to partition them into reasonable sizes (*makekit*, version 2.2); a program to make shell archives out of them (*shar*, version 2.1); a program to strip mail, news, and notes headers from archives before feeding them to a shell (*unshar*, version 2.2); and a program that simulates enough Bourne shell syntax so that non-UNIX systems can unpack them (*shell*, version 2.0). Articles 20.02 and 20.03.

GNU Shell Utilities (shellutils), Version 1.7

GNU Shell Utilities is a package of small shell programming utilities. These utilities are generally more robust and have more features than the system-supplied alternatives. Programs included are: *basename, date, dirname, env, expr, false, groups, id, nice, nohup, pathchk, printenv, printf, sleep, stty, tee, test, true, tty, uname, who, whoami,* and *yes.* Most of these programs are covered throughout the book. Note that because *nice, stty,* and *uname* require facilities that are not available on all systems, they are only installed when appropriate.

showmatch

The *showmatch* shell script shows the strings in a given file that match the specified regular expression. Article 27.06.

sl

sl is a Perl script for showing the actual filenames for symbolic links. Article 19.08.

sls, Version 7

sls is a program designed to overcome the limitations of the standard UNIX *ls* program, providing a more consistent interface to file inode information. It is particularly designed for use by shell scripts to make obtaining information about files easier. It uses *printf*-style format strings to control the sorting and output of file information. Article 17.30.

smiley, Version 4

smiley is a "smiley server." It can explain any smiley it knows, or print one it knows at random. Article 53.12.

squoze

squoze is a utility for shrinking a huge directory. Article 25.16.

stat, Version 1.5

stat prints out the contents of an inode (as it appears to the *stat(2)* system call) in a human-readable format. Article 22.13.

stree

stree is a shell script that prints a simple directory tree. Article 17.20.

stripper

stripper is a simple shell script for stripping any binary files in *$HOME/bin* that aren't already stripped. Article 25.13.

su

The *su* shell script is a front-end to the system-wide *su,* for versions of *su* that don't set your home directory properly in the new shell. It must be installed in a directory that is earlier in your search path than */bin/su.* Article 23.23.

GNU tar, Version 1.11.1

GNU *tar* is upwards compatible with the standard *tar* supplied with your operating system. It adds many new features including remote devices, compression, multi-volume archives, the ability to extract to standard output, the ability to extract using wildcards, interactive confirmation, the ability to extract only "missing" files, and the ability to store only files newer than a given date. Article 20.06.

tcap, Version 1.4

tcap is a utility that gives shell scripts access to *termcap* escape sequences, similar to *tput*. It is generally distributed under the name *tc*. We have renamed it here to avoid confusion with the standard *tc* command that is distributed under many operating systems. Article 43.10.

tcsh, Version 6.03

tcsh is a version of the Berkeley C shell, with the addition of a command line editor; command and filename completion, listing, etc.; and several small additions to the shell itself. Article 1.08.

termtest

termtest is a shell script that quickly sends repeated characters to the screen. You can use it to test your terminal connection, by scanning for line noise or dropped characters. Article 44.07.

testsed

The *testsed* shell script runs the *sed* commands in a file called *sedscr* on the specified files, putting the output in a file called *tmp.filename*. Article 35.03.

tgrep

tgrep only searches through files that contain text. It is useful for searching through directories that contain both binary and text files. Article 28.13.

tpipe, Version 1.02

tpipe is a simple utility program that can be used to split a UNIX pipeline into two pipelines. Like *tee*, *tpipe* transcribes its standard input to its standard output. But where *tee* writes an additional copy of its input to a file, *tpipe* writes the additional copy to the input of another pipeline that is specified as the argument to *tpipe*. Article 14.11.

tputinit

tputinit is a shell script for simulating the terminal initialization commands generated by *tput init*. It can be used on systems with older versions of *tput* that don't support the *init* keyword. Article 6.13.

triplespace

triplespace is a *sed* script that triple-spaces text and sends the result to standard output. Article 26.13.

ttykind

ttykind searches */etc/ttytab* and returns the type of port that you are logged in on. You can use this in your *.login* file to set up your environment differently according to the type of connection. Article 6.10.

twin

twin is used to compare two similar files. They will be displayed side-by-side with any mismatched lines shown in reverse video. Article 29.04.

vgrep

The *vgrep* shell script supplies a list of filenames that don't contain the given string. It's sort of a *grep −v* for complete files instead of for individual lines. Article 16.09.

vis

vis is a program that repeatedly executes a specified command and refreshes the display of its output on the screen. Article 53.07.

vtree, Version 1.2

vtree gives a visual directory tree, designed to show the layout of a directory tree or filesystem. It has options to show the amount of storage being taken up in each directory, count the number of inodes, etc. Article 17.21.

watchq

watchq is a daemon *(1.14)* that monitors the queues for several printers and sends messages to users when errors occur. Article 40.11.

whereiz

whereiz lists all executables in your path that match the given name. Article 5.10.

which, Version 6

which is an improved version of the standard *which* utility. This version returns the the full expansion of the command argument, be it either an alias, a shell function, or the path to an executable file. Article 52.07.

whichweek

The *whichweek* script executes a given command from *cron (42.12)* only if the current day falls in the specified week of the month. Article 42.15.

wordfreq

wordfreq reports the number of times each word appears in a given file. Article 30.07.

xargs

The *xargs* utility is used to execute a command with many arguments. Articles 10.19 and 10.20.

xtail, Version 2

xtail watches the growth of files. It is similar to *tail −f*, but can be used to watch many files at once. Article 26.19.

zap

zap interactively allows you to kill processes by running *ps* and then querying you about killing each process reported by *ps*. Article 40.13.

zipcode, Version 1.0

zipcode is a *perl* script that examines a list of zip codes and returns the city and state that match the requested zip code. It also includes a shell script called *city*, which takes a city name and optional state abbreviation and returns a list of zip codes, and cities and states that match the requested city (and state if specified). Article 50.04.

zloop
> *zloop* is a shell script for running a command on a set of compressed files. Article 25.09.

zmore
> The *zmore* shell script runs *more* on compressed files. It is also linked to the names *zpg* and *zless*. (Note that the *compress* package also contains a script called *zmore*.) Article 26.05.

zvi
> *zvi* is a shell script for running the *vi* editor on compressed files. It is also linked to the programs *zex* and *zed* for running *ex* or *ed* on compressed files, respectively. Article 25.10.

zview
> *zview* runs *vi* in read-only mode on compressed files. Article 25.11.

—LM

54.05 *Using the Power Tools CD-ROM*

[In addition to this article, be sure to read the file called README *for any late-breaking news on using the CD-ROM.—LM]*

The CD-ROM that comes with this book can be used in two different ways. First, it can be mounted just long enough for software to be copied onto a local hard disk. In this respect, it is a distribution medium similar to magnetic tapes or floppy disks. Second, it can be mounted so that it is always present and available as a local read-only hard disk. It will appear as a filesystem and you can use familiar UNIX commands to peruse it.

CD-ROM Formats
The Power Tools CD conforms to the ISO standard 9660. This is sometimes called "High Sierra," but there are differences between the two formats. The 9660 standard is what most CD-ROM drivers will support from now on, even though they will read High Sierra disks.

For UNIX users, ISO 9660 may come as a shock. For example, a directory listing of an ISO 9660 disk might look like this:

```
% ls /cdrom
COMMON      INSTALL.PT;1    RISC      SUN3
HP700       INSTINFO        RS6000    SUN4C
I386        README.;1       SOURCES   XENIX
```

ISO 9660 specifies that the filenames are mono-case, and limited to 8 characters with 3-character extensions. If the filename doesn't contain a dot, one is added at the end of the filename. A "version number" is also appended, following a semicolon (version numbers are used in some non-UNIX filesystems such as VMS). Some systems do not use all these features, so there are several variations that you will encounter.

For example, a file called *install.pt* may appear as any of the following, depending on what system you mount the CD-ROM on:

```
INSTALL.PT;1 INSTALL.PT install.pt;1 install.pt
```

Directory names are simply 8 characters or less and mono-case. A directory called "SOURCES" can appear as *SOURCES* or *sources*.

ISO 9660 also limits directory depth to 8 levels.

Note that the semicolon character (;) in version numbers needs to be quoted *(9.10)* when you are specifying the filename in a UNIX shell. If you don't quote such a filename, you'll get a message like this:

```
INSTALL.PT: Command not found.
1: Command not found.
```

Luckily for you, we provide installation software that hides most of this ugliness.

Mounting the CD-ROM

For UNIX users, the CD-ROM should be made available as if it were a filesystem. In most cases, the standard *mount* command can be used. This usually has the form:

```
# mount CD-ROM_device mount_point
```

The CD-ROM device name varies depending on the type of system. If you do not know the device name, consult the documentation that comes with your system. On some systems, the SCSI ID of the CD-ROM device can vary. The SCSI ID will be part of the device name—for example, */dev/rz3c/* is the CD-ROM at SCSI ID 3 on a DECstation.

The mount point is simply a directory that will become the parent directory of the CD-ROM when it is mounted.

Most systems do not provide a way for unprivileged users to mount the CD. It is probably necessary to mount and use it as the superuser *(1.24)*. For this reason, the bulk of this article assumes some knowledge of system administration and superuser commands. You may need to have your system administrator install the power tools software for you.

As the CD is read-only, you may have to specify this fact to the *mount* program or it will generate an error if it tries to open the CD-ROM device for writing. Some systems also need to be told the type of filesystem being mounted if it is not the default (usually `ufs` or `nfs`). There may be options to the *mount* program that control whether all the ISO 9660 features (such as version numbers) are turned on.

For example, the CD can be mounted on a SunOS 4.1.1 system with the command:

```
# /etc/mount -r -t hsfs /dev/sr0 /cdrom
```

This command mounts the CD (*/dev/sr0*) on the mount point (*/cdrom*) in a read-only fashion (*–r*). If you omit the *–r* option, *mount* will give the following error:

```
mount_hsfs: must be mounted readonly
mount: giving up on:
    /cdrom
```

If you omit the filesystem type of hsfs (High Sierra Filesystem, which preceded the ISO 9660 format), you will get:

```
mount: /dev/sr0 on /cdrom: Invalid argument
mount: giving up on:
    /cdrom
```

The procedure for mounting a CD-ROM varies with each type of operating system. You should consult the manual pages for the *mount* command and look for a mention of CD-ROM, ISO 9660, or High Sierra:

```
% man mount
```

Some examples of *mount* commands for the supported systems are:

Sun4 and Sun3 SunOS 4.1.1

```
# /etc/mount -r -t hsfs /dev/sr0 /cdrom
```

IBM RS/6000 AIX 3.2

```
# /etc/mount -r -v cdrfs /dev/cd0 /cdrom
```

HP 700 HP-UX

```
# /etc/mount -r -s cdfs /dev/dsk/c201d2s0 /cdrom
```

DECstation Ultrix 4.X

```
# /etc/mount -t cdfs -o noversion /dev/rz3c /cdrom
```

(The *noversion* option will disable the version information on the filenames.)

SCO UNIX

```
# /etc/mount -r -fHS,lower,intr,soft,novers /dev/cd0 /cdrom
```

Some examples of *mount* commands for other systems are:

SGI IRIX 4.x

```
# /usr/etc/mount -o ro,notranslate -t iso9660 \
    /dev/scsi/sc0d510 /cdrom
```

You can also start up the *cdromd* process:

```
# cdromd -o ro,notranslate -d /dev/scsi/sc0d510 /cdrom
```

To mount the disk, just insert it in the drive. To unmount it, use the *eject* command.

OSF/1 for Alpha AXP

```
# /etc/mount -t cdfs -o noversion /dev/rz3c /cdrom
```

Once you have the CD-ROM mounted, you can run the installation program to copy pre-compiled binaries off the CD and onto your system's hard disk. The installation program is Ready-to-Run Software's "Smart Installation System."

Installing Pre-Compiled Binaries

There are two software installation programs provided on the CD. The first program "installs" pre-compiled binaries. The second program "builds" programs from source code. If you have one of the supported platforms, you can install software off the CD-ROM and use it immediately. If your platform is not one of the supported platforms or you wish to change the software in some way, you should be able to build it from source code (54.08).

Binaries for the following platforms are on this CD-ROM:

- Sun4 SunOS 4.1.1
- Sun3 SunOS 4.1.1
- DECstation Ultrix 4.1
- IBM RS/6000 AIX 3.2
- HP 700 HP-UX 8.07
- SCO XENIX 2.3.2
- SCO UNIX 3.2.x

The pre-compiled binaries may work on operating system versions slightly older or newer than the ones listed here. Some programs take advantage of features that are not supported on all the platforms. The install program will tell you if a program is not available for your platform.

If you are uncertain of your operating system version, the *uname* command may help:

```
% uname -a
SunOS ruby 4.1.2 1 sun4m
```

If your platform is not listed, you should try building the programs from source code as described in article 54.08.

Directory Structure

There is a standard installation structure for all packages on the CD-ROM. Using this structure (and some simple variations of it), you can tailor how and where your packages will be installed on your system.

The basic directory structure is shown in Figure 54-1.

Some packages may deviate from this structure by having extra directories at the *<install_dir>* level.

Shareable files are those files that are machine independent and can be shared across many machines in a network using a network filesystem (NFS) (1.33). These are typically text files, such as manual pages or "include files." Sharing

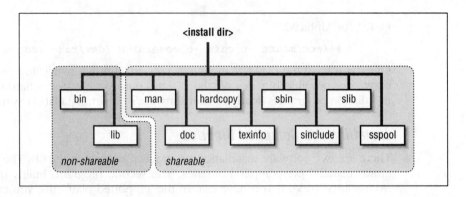

Figure 54-1. Basic Directory Structure

files reduces the amount of disk space required by allowing several different systems to use the same set of files, as opposed to having to duplicate them for each machine. It also simplifies administration of the files by having only a single copy to maintain.

Non-shareable files are machine/architecture specific and may not be shared (except with other hosts of the same architecture). These are typically binaries or data files that depend on a certain architecture or byte order.

The installation program gives you the ability to split the shareable and non-shareable files into separate directories. Using this scheme, you could put shareable files onto a partition or directory that is mounted by multiple machines.

If you want to store shareable and non-shareable files at the same directory level, the shareable directories will be preceded by a leading *s* to mark them as "shareable." For example, *sbin* is shareable, while *bin* is non-shareable.*

Figure 54-2 shows how the default installation directories are arranged.

You can modify this structure using the Smart Installation System and any necessary directories will be created (if you have permission to do so).

In order to run the software after installation, you will need to make sure that your shell path variable includes *<install_dir>/bin* (and possibly *<install_dir>/share/bin* if you choose to use this structure). For example, if *<install_dir>/bin* is set to */usr/local*, set your search path *(9.05)* as appropriate for your shell:

```
% set path=($path /usr/local/bin /usr/local/share/bin)          csh
$ PATH=$PATH:/usr/local/bin:/usr/local/share/bin ; export PATH   sh
```

---

*You may also remove the leading *s* from the the shareable directories *sinclude, sspool, sbin,* and *slib.* This way, you can merge *slib* into *lib,* and *sbin* into *bin* if your shareable and non-shareable files are stored in the same directory, or make names clearer if your shareable and non-shareable files are not stored together.

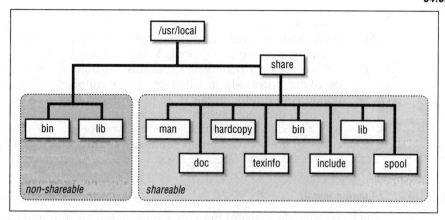

Figure 54-2. Default Installation Directory Structure

The installation software will automatically print out a suggested path when it finishes installing a program.

Starting the Installation

To begin the installation process, become the superuser and mount the CD-ROM. For example, on a Sun:

```
% su
Password:
# /etc/mount -r -t hsfs /dev/sr0 /cdrom
```

Then change directories to the mount point you specified for the CD-ROM and see what is there. In our case, we specified */cdrom* as our mount point:

```
# cd /cdrom
# ls
common          install.pt      risc            sun3
hp700           instinfo        rs6000          sun4c
i386            readme          sources         xenix
```

The output could look slightly different depending on the type of system:

```
COMMON          INSTALL.PT;1    RISC            SUN3
HP700           INSTINFO        RS6000          SUN4C
I386            README.;1       SOURCES         XENIX
```

One of the first things that the installation program will do when installing software is to copy the programs into a "staging" area. By default, this is the directory */tmp*. By setting the environment variable *TMPDIR* to another directory, you can alter this location.

For example, if you want to use the directory */mondo* for the staging area:

```
% setenv TMPDIR /mondo                          csh
$ TMPDIR=/mondo; export TMPDIR                   sh
```

Note: If you wish to install software in "system" areas, you will likely run into problems with file permissions. You can just become the superuser and not worry about permissions, but this is dangerous because you could overwrite previously installed or vendor-supplied software. The other option is to run the install as an unprivileged user. This should prevent you from damaging system areas, but you will have to use *chmod (23.07)* to make directories writable before you begin the installation process—or possibly use group permissions *(23.14)* to control access.

Running Install

Once you have the CD-ROM properly mounted, run the appropriate install command for your system. For example:

```
% ./install.pt
```

or:

```
% ./INSTALL.PT\;1
```

The installation program will display menus and prompt you for input from now on. It will also try to guess the type of machine you are running it on and the mount point of the CD-ROM:

```
Assuming CD-ROM   is mounted at /cdrom
Assuming MACHINE is sun4c

                    Welcome to Ready-to-Run Software's
                      * Smart Installation System *

This installation system requires write permission in the current working (or
$TMPDIR if it's set) directory (for staging the install) and write permission
in the installation directory for the actual install (these may be the same).
    ...
```

At this point, the installation program may ask if you want to use a different *umask (23.04)* value for the installation process:

```
Use umask of 022 instead of 002 for install [y]?
```

This will affect the permissions of the software when it is installed. The suggested value of 022 will allow anyone to execute or read the programs, but gives write permission only to you.

The install program will then present a list of the available software:

```
The Power Tools package contains:

agrep         areacode      awf           bash          bitmaps       bsdtar
bsplit        calen         cls           compress      cpmod         cut+paste
cvtbase       delete        diff          dtp           ediff         emacs
    ...
```

After the names of the software packages have been displayed, you are prompted for which ones to install:

```
Enter the name of a package to install or choose Search, Quit or All
<package>, S(earch), A(ll), Q(uit) [Search]?
```

You can now type the name of the package, search for packages, quit the installation program, or install all packages in one fell swoop.

Installing a Single Program

Some of you might prefer not to install the entire distribution, but just selected programs.

For this example, let's assume you are looking for programs that do something with terminals, but you don't know what they are called. You can use the "Search" function at the main menu to look for you. Just press RETURN at the prompt, as the "Search" is the default action in the square brackets ([ ]).

```
<package>, S(earch), A(ll), Q(uit) [Search]?
```

Then type in "terminal" for the search keyword:

```
Search package descriptions for [?]? terminal
```

All packages matching this description will be displayed:

```
The descriptions for the following packages mention "terminal":
    1.  qterm
    2.  screen
    3.  tcap

    A.  ALL
    N.  NONE
Choose one please:
```

For this example, the *qterm* program is selected, which is option 1:

```
Choose one please: 1
```

A description of the program is now displayed:

```
qterm - version 5.0

                    Version 5.0

Qterm is a program that queries terminals to find out what kind of
terminal is responding. It is useful to automagically define your
terminal type. It prints the name of the terminal (compatible,
hopefully, with a termcap/terminfo name) such as "vt100" to standard
output.
```

After information about *qterm* is printed, you are told how much space it will require and then asked whether you want it installed. Press RETURN to install it, or "n" for "no" (followed by RETURN) if you don't want it installed. For our example, we want *qterm* installed, so we just press RETURN.

```
The qterm package is approximately  56Kb
      24Kb - Required
      15Kb - Shared: Formatted Man pages
       3Kb - Shared: Other Shareable files
```

```
       13Kb - Shared: Unformatted Man pages
Install qterm [y]? RETURN
```

Any copyright information for the *qterm* package is printed out now:

```
qterm was compiled and made "Ready-to-Run" by
       Ready-to-Run Software, Inc.
/*
 * Copyright (c) 1990 Michael A. Cooper.
 * This software may be freely distributed provided it is not sold for
 * profit and the author is credited appropriately.
 */
                ************************
```

You are then prompted with installation questions, with the default answers printed within square brackets ([ ]).

The first question is where to install the software. The installation program assumes */usr/local* as the default installation directory. If you want to change the default, type the name of a different directory here. This directory will now be used when you are prompted for the same information in all subsequent packages.

```
Install package at dir [/usr/local]? /work/tools RETURN
```

The next question is where to install the shared files for the package. The default is to use a *share* subdirectory of whatever directory you specified in the previous question.

```
Install shared files at [/work/tools/share]? RETURN
```

Third, you're asked whether to remove the *s* prefix from the names of the directories in which you install the shared files. The default is "y" for "yes"—remove the *s* prefix.

```
Convert slib->lib, sbin->bin, sspool->spool, sinclude->include [y]? RETURN
```

The fourth question is whether to install all the shared files, some, or none of them. The default is to install just some selected shared files.

```
Install Shared files (All, Some, None) [s]? RETURN
```

Now you're asked whether to install the manpages. The default is to install them all. You might choose not to install unformatted manpages if you are low on disk space or if you don't have *nroff* on your system to format them with:

```
Install Unformatted Man pages (Approx  13Kb) [y]? RETURN
Install Formatted Man pages (Approx  15Kb) [y]? RETURN
```

Finally you're asked about any other sharable files.

```
Install Other Shareable files (Approx  3Kb) [y]? RETURN
```

(Other packages might have other questions, as appropriate. For example, the *gawk* installation asks whether to install Texinfo files, PostScript format documentation, and DVI format documentation.)

If you want the answer to any question to be used for all subsequent packages without further prompting, enter the answer in uppercase. You can enter a pathname in uppercase, and the installation script will convert it to lowercase before using it. For example:

```
Install package at dir [/usr/local]? /WORK/TOOLS RETURN
Install shared files at [/work/tools/share]? /WORK/TOOLS/SHARE RETURN
Convert slib->lib, sbin->bin, sspool->spool, sinclude->include [y]? Y RETURN
Install Shared files (All, Some, None) [s]? S RETURN
Install Unformatted Man pages (Approx  13Kb) [y]? Y RETURN
Install Formatted Man pages (Approx  15Kb) [y]? Y RETURN
Install Other Shareable files (Approx   3Kb) [y]? Y RETURN
```

After answering all the questions, the installation script sets up its installation information and asks you once more if it's correct. If you change your mind about the current configuration, press "n" to get another chance to change some of your installation parameters or to abort the installation of this package entirely. If the current configuration is acceptable, press RETURN a final time, and the package is installed.

```
Please wait....
    About To Install: qterm

        at /work/tools
        with shareable files at /work/tools/share
        slib->lib, sbin->bin, sspool->spool, sinclude->include

Are these correct [y]? RETURN
Proceeding with install...

0 directories added, 6 files installed, 0 symbolic links created.
Approximately  99Kb installed.
```

Once the *qterm* installation is completed, the installation script returns to the main menu if this is the only package you have selected.

After all programs are installed, you can quit the installation program. Upon quitting, the installation program suggests a new search path *(9.05)* for you.

```
You may want to change your path to include:
   /work/tools/bin
   /work/tools/share/bin

Suggested new path:
/work/tools/bin:/work/tools/share/bin:/bin:/usr/bin ...
```

A log file of the installation process is kept in */tmp/RTRinstall.log*. A typical entry looks like this:

```
Package: zipcode -- installed Mon Dec 14 14:55:25 EST 1992

   /usr/local/share/bin/city
   /usr/local/share/bin/zipcode
   /usr/local/share/lib/zipcode/zipcode.txt
   /usr/local/share/man/cat1/zipcode.1
   /usr/local/share/man/man1/zipcode.1

0 directories added, 5 files installed.
Approximately 653Kb installed.
```

Installing Everything Using the Defaults

If you don't want to be bothered with being questioned about every package in the installation, and the default values are fine with you, you can bypass the questions and install everything at once.

At the main menu, press "A" for "All" to install all packages:

```
agrep        areacode     awf          bash         bitmaps      bsdtar
bsplit       calen        cls          compress     cpmod        cut+paste
cvtbase      delete       diff         dtp          ediff        emacs
    ...
Enter the name of a package to install or choose Search, Quit or All
<package>, S(earch), A(ll), Q(uit) [Search]? A  RETURN
```

You are shown information about the first program, *agrep*. Then you are asked whether to install *agrep*:

```
agrep   - version 2.01

This is version 2.01 of agrep - a new tool for fast text searching allowing
errors.  agrep is similar to egrep (or grep or fgrep), but it is much more
general (and often faster).
    ...
The agrep package is approximately  99Kb
    72Kb - Required
    15Kb - Shared: Formatted Man pages
    12Kb - Shared: Unformatted Man pages

Install agrep [y]?
```

The default answer is "y", to install *agrep*. However, if you respond instead with the string ++, *agrep* will be installed and furthermore, all default values will be used from now on without prompting.

```
Install agrep [y]? ++  RETURN
agrep was compiled and made "Ready-to-Run" by
        Ready-to-Run Software, Inc.

AGREP material was developed by Sun Wu and Udi Manber at the
University of Arizona, Department of Computer Science.  Permission is
    ...
4. Redistribution for profit requires the express, written permission
of the authors.
                        ************************

Please wait.....

    About To Install: agrep

        at /usr/local
        with shareable files at /usr/local/share
        slib->lib, sbin->bin, sspool->spool, sinclude->include
Proceeding with install...

0 directories added, 6 files installed, 0 symbolic links created.
Approximately  99Kb installed.
areacode - not specified

AREACODE is used to display the region and state, specified
by the user...very handy when someone leaves you a phone
    ...
Please wait....
```

```
About To Install: areacode
        at /usr/local
        with shareable files at /usr/local/share
        slib->lib, sbin->bin, sspool->spool, sinclude->include
Proceeding with install...
```

At this point, you can go to lunch and come back to find everything installed in */usr/local.*

Another alternative is to call the installation script with the *–D* option to use the defaults. For example:

```
% install.pt -D
```

You'll still have to answer the question about your *umask*, and you'll have to answer "A" for "All" to the main menu, but then all packages will be installed without prompting.

Note that to run a default installation, you will need to have write permission to the default directory of */usr/local.*

Unmounting the CD-ROM

When you are finished with the installation, you can unmount the CD-ROM with the *umount* command with just the mount point as the argument:

```
# /etc/umount /cdrom
```

What to Do if You Have Problems

If you can't get the software to install and/or run, then you can call Ready-to-Run Software for support. Ready-to-Run will be glad to provide answers to simple questions, but will ask you to pay for extensive support or porting questions *(54.09)*

—EP

54.06 Don't Have a CD-ROM Drive?

If you don't have a CD-ROM drive, don't despair. You can always get the software on the disk on alternate media, as described in article 54.07.

But if you don't have a CD-ROM drive, we strongly suggest that you get one. And not just for this disk—CD-ROM is quickly becoming the distribution method of choice, and not just for software.

To get a CD-ROM drive, the first thing we recommend is to call your UNIX system's manufacturer. Since CD-ROM formats are still in flux, you need to be sure that the drive you get is compatible with both your hardware and your operating system. Be warned that if your vendor distributes their own CD-ROM drive, it's likely that they will only recommend theirs. (If the price isn't exorbitant, that may not be such a bad idea—support may be lot easier if the hardware and software vendors are the same.)

Another approach is to call CD-ROM manufacturers directly and ask them whether their drive will work on your platform. This would be helpful if you intended to use the same drive on several different systems, manufactured by different vendors.

On the low end, street prices for CD-ROM drives are as low as $275. On the high end ... well, the sky's the limit. As the price of the drive goes up, so does its speed or access time. If you want to use the same drive on several different machines, you need to spend more for an external drive. And if you ever want to use the CD-ROM to boot off, you'll need one that has switches for different block sizes.

Most CD-ROM drives on the market today are geared towards the PC-DOS market. You might be able to use a PC drive on your UNIX system, but only if they support standard SCSI (Small Computer Systems Interface).

—EP, LM

54.07 *Other Ways to Get the Software*

If you are unable to read the CD-ROM, here are two other sources for all or some of the software on it.

Alternate Media

Ready-to-Run Software can provide the Power Tools software on alternate media such as floppies, QIC, 8 mm, 4mm, or DEC TK50 tape cartridges. Obviously, some of these media are appropriate only for certain platforms.

Because of the large volume of data on the CD, each tape/floppy package is for a single platform. In addition, for the floppy distributions, source and binaries are treated as separate packages, as are the bitmaps for use with pbmplus *(45.28)*. For QIC-24 (60 megabyte tape) we've also had to separate the bitmaps from the source and executables for the Power Tools software.

For ordering instructions, please see the very last page of this book, immediately facing the envelope that contains the CD-ROM disk.

Online Archive

Scripts and other example files from the book are in a freely-available archive on the UUNET computer. (Other computers around the Internet have copies of UUNET's archives. If you aren't in the USA, ask your network administrator whether there's a UUNET "mirror" archive in your part of the world.)

The archive doesn't have everything from the CD-ROM. We didn't include the source code for programs that must be compiled *(54.08)* because you can get periodically-updated copies from online archives around the Internet. The executable binary files for those programs aren't in our online archive, either.

Ready-to-Run Software invested a lot of time and money to build and debug them. You'll need to get those binaries from this book's CD-ROM or alternate media.

Here are four ways to get this book's online archive electronically: by ftp, ftpmail, bitftp, and uucp. The cheapest, fastest, and easiest ways are listed first. If you read from the top down, the first one that works for you is probably the best. Use *ftp* if you are directly on the Internet. Use ftpmail if you are not on the Internet but can send and receive electronic mail to internet sites (this includes CompuServe users). Use BITFTP if you send electronic mail via BITNET. Use UUCP if none of the above works.

The file is a compressed *tar* archive. After you get the archive, read article 20.07 to find out how to extract the files.

FTP

To use FTP, you need a machine with direct access to the Internet. A sample session is shown, with what you should type in **boldface**.

```
% ftp ftp.uu.net
Connected to ftp.uu.net.
220 FTP server (Version 6.21 Tue Mar 10 22:09:55 EST 1992) ready.
Name (ftp.uu.net:janetv): anonymous
331 Guest login ok, send domain style e-mail address as password.
Password: janetv@foobar.com (use your user name and host here)
230 Guest login ok, access restrictions apply.
ftp> cd /published/oreilly/power_tools/unix
250 CWD command successful.
ftp> binary Very important! You must specify binary transfer for compressed files.)
200 Type set to I.
ftp> get upt.oct93.tar.Z
200 PORT command successful.
150 Opening BINARY mode data connection for upt.oct93.tar.Z.
226 Transfer complete.
ftp> quit
221 Goodbye.
%
```

FTPMAIL

FTPMAIL is a mail server available to anyone who can send and receive electronic mail to and from Internet sites. This includes most workstations that have an email connection to the outside world, and CompuServe users. You do not need to be directly on the Internet. Here's how to do it.

You send mail to *ftpmail@decwrl.dec.com*. In the message body, give the name of the anonymous ftp host and the ftp commands you want to run. The server will run anonymous ftp for you and mail the files back to you. To get a complete help file, send a message with no subject and the single word "help" in the body. The following is a sample mail session that should get you the examples. This command sends you a listing of the files in the selected directory, and the requested examples file. The listing is useful in case there's a later version of the examples you're interested in.

```
% mail ftpmail@decwrl.dec.com
Subject:
reply janetv@foobar.com        (where you want files mailed)
connect ftp.uu.net
chdir /published/oreilly/power_tools/unix
dir
binary
uuencode                       (or btoa if you have it)
get upt.oct93.tar.Z
quit
.                              (The dot is a command to send the message, not part of it)
```

A signature at the end of the message is acceptable as long as it appears after "quit."

All retrieved files will be split into 60KB chunks and mailed to you. You then remove the mail headers, concatenate them into one file, and run *uudecode* *(20.05)* or *atob* on it. Once you've decoded the file, follow the directions at the top of this section to extract the files from the archive.

VMS, DOS, and Mac versions of *uudecode, atob, uncompress,* and *tar* are available. VMS tar conversion tools are on *gatekeeper.dec.com* in */pub/VMS.*

BITFTP

BITFTP is a mail server for BITNET users. You send it electronic mail messages requesting files, and it sends you back the files by electronic mail. BITFTP currently serves only users who send it mail from nodes that are directly on BIT-NET, EARN, or NetNorth. BITFTP is a public service of Princeton University. Here's how it works.

To use BITFTP, send mail containing your ftp commands to *BITFTP@PUCC*. For a complete help file, send HELP as the message body.

The following is the message body you should send to BITFTP:

```
FTP  ftp.uu.net   NETDATA
USER  anonymous
PASS  myname@podunk.edu Type your Internet email address (not your BITNET address)
CD  /published/oreilly/power_tools/unix
DIR
BINARY
GET  upt.oct93.tar.Z
QUIT
```

If you aren't on a UNIX system, you may need to get versions of *uudecode (20.05)*, *uncompress (25.06)*, *atob*, and *tar* for your system. VMS, DOS, and Mac versions are available. The VMS versions are on *gatekeeper.dec.com* in */pub/VMS.*

Questions about BITFTP can be directed to Melinda Varian, *MAINT@PUCC* on BIT-NET.

UUCP

UUCP is standard on virtually all UNIX systems, and is available for IBM-compatible PCs and Apple Macintoshes. The examples are available by UUCP via modem from UUNET; UUNET's connect-time charges apply.

You can get the examples from UUNET whether you have an account there or not. If you or your company has an account with UUNET, you will have a system with a direct UUCP connection to UUNET. Find that system, and type the following command on one line (it's broken onto two lines here for publishing):

```
uucp uunet\!~/published/oreilly/power_tools/unix/upt.oct93.tar.Z
    yourhost\!~/yourname/
```

The backslashes can be omitted if you use the Bourne shell (*sh*) instead of *csh*. The file should appear some time later (up to a day or more) in the directory */usr/spool/uucppublic/***yourname**. If you don't have an account but would like one so that you can get electronic mail, contact UUNET at 703-204-8000.

If you don't have a UUNET account, you can set up a UUCP connection to UUNET using the phone number 1-900-468-7727. As of this writing, the cost is 50 cents per minute. The charges will appear on your next telephone bill. The login name is "uucp" with no password. For example, an *L.sys/Systems* entry might look like:

```
uunet Any ACU 19200 1-900-468-7727 ogin:--ogin: uucp
```

Your entry may vary depending on your UUCP configuration. If you have a PEP-capable modem, make sure `s50=255s111=30` is set before calling.

It's a good idea to get the file */published/oreilly/ls-lR.Z* as a short test file containing the filenames and sizes of all the files available.

—*TOR, JP*

54.08 Building Programs from Source Code

The programs on the disk are supplied in binary form for the most popular UNIX platforms, as listed in article 54.03. But we also supply C source code for those of you who are on unsupported platforms.

Now, don't run away. You don't have to be a C programmer to compile these sources. I've never written a C program in my life, and I compile public domain software all the time. The Power Tools disk provides build scripts for each of the packages, so many of you can just run the script and have everything installed automatically.

If the build scripts don't work, the Power Tools disk also has a script to copy the sources to your local hard disk. Although we can't promise that you'll be able to build the sources on your own without a hitch, this article includes some explanation of how to build sources without needing to learn how to program in C.

Running the Build Scripts

Before you do anything, try out the *build* scripts. You might be able to get away without knowing anything at all about the build process.

To build programs from source code, first mount the CD-ROM as described in article 54.05.

Each package on the CD-ROM that has source code can be compiled with the "build" script. The build script will copy the files off the CD into your current directory, compile, and install them.

As the CD-ROM is read-only, you must use a directory on some other disk for the build. For example, if you wanted to build the "compress" package, a directory called *compress* will be created in the current directory when the build script is run. The build script has default settings for the directory where the source code will be copied to, the directory where the package will be installed, the directory where the "shareable" portion of the package will be installed, and a "prefix" for the shareable directories. These settings can be overridden by the following environment variables *(7.01)*:

SOURCEDIR
> This is where the source code for the package resides on the CD-ROM. The build script tries to determine this automatically, so you should not have set *SOURCEDIR* unless you are using the build script somewhere other than the CD-ROM.

INSTALLDIR
> This is the directory where the package will be installed. It is set to */usr/local* by default. For example, to change *INSTALLDIR* to */opt*:

```
% setenv INSTALLDIR /opt                               csh
$ INSTALLDIR=/opt ; export INSTALLDIR                  sh
```

INSTALLSHAREDIR
> This is the directory where "shareable" portions of the package will be installed (*/usr/local/share* by default). You can set it to the same value as *INSTALLDIR* if you want them in the same location.

SHAREPREFIX
> This "prefix" will be prepended to the directory names for *lib*, *include*, *spool*, and *bin*. There is no default setting, but you could use *s* if you wanted to conform to the same scheme used by the "install" program to name shareable directories *slib*, *sinclude*, *sspool*, and *sbin*.

By default, the files generated by the build process will not be removed. If you set the *RM* variable before running the build, the entire build directory will be removed once the build finishes:

```
% setenv RM true                               csh
$ RM=true ; export RM                          sh
```

For a list of the available packages, run the *build.pt* script in the CD-ROM mount
directory. The actual name of the script depends on your operating system (as
described in article 54.05), but assuming that the CD-ROM is mounted on
/cdrom, it is likely to be one of the following commands:

```
% /cdrom/BUILD.PT\;1
% /cdrom/BUILD.PT
% /cdrom/build.pt\;1
% /cdrom/build.pt
```

The command will print a list similar to the following:

```
areacode    awf      bash       bitmaps    bsdtar      bsplit
calen       cls      compress   cpmod      cut+paste   cvtbase
delete      diff     dtp        ediff      emacs       fgrep
      . . .
```

To build one of these packages, run the same command followed by the package name. For example:

```
% /cdrom/build.pt areacode
```

The build script will copy the package to the current directory, compile, and
install the package according to the values of the environment variables. For
this example, the shareable and non-shareable portions of the package are combined.

```
% pwd
/usr/local/src
% setenv INSTALLDIR /opt
% setenv INSTALLSHAREDIR /opt
% /cdrom/BUILT.PT areacode
+ echo Ignore any errors about directories already existing
Ignore any errors about directories already existing
+ mkdir -p /opt
+ mkdir /opt/bin
mkdir: /opt/bin: File exists
+ mkdir /opt/lib
mkdir: /opt/lib: File exists
+ mkdir -p /opt
+ mkdir /opt/man
mkdir: /opt/man: File exists
+ mkdir /opt/man/man1
mkdir: /opt/man/man1: File exists
+ mkdir /opt/doc
mkdir: /opt/doc: File exists
+ mkdir /opt/bin
mkdir: /opt/bin: File exists
+ mkdir /opt/lib
mkdir: /opt/lib: File exists
+ cd /usr/local/src
+ mkdir areacode
+ cd areacode
+ unshar+ zcat
 ../areacode.Z
```

```
unshar:  Sending header to UNSHAR.HDR.
unshar:  Doing the standard input:
Extracting file README
Extracting file archie
Extracting file areacode.news
Extracting file areacode.q
Extracting file areacode.unl
Extracting file areacode.w
Done.
+ patch -s -p
+ sed -e s;<installsharedir>;/opt; -e s;<prefix>;; -e s;<installdir>;
/opt; ../rtrpatch.areacode
+ cp areacode.news areacode.c
+ cc -O -o areacode areacode.c
+ install -s areacode /opt/bin
+ cd ..
%
```

Missing Programs

Some of the build scripts expect non-standard programs to be installed. Some of these come on the CD-ROM:

patch   Several packages depend on the *patch (34.09)* program to apply "patches" or "diffs" to source code. This is the primary method of updating source code without replacing the entire file.

perl   Perl *(39.01)* is a scripting language used by several packages, including the install and build scripts.

unshar   The *unshar* program is needed to unpack shell archive files *(20.03)*.

uncompress   The *uncompress* program is needed to unpack files that have been compressed with the *compress (25.06)* command.

Some other utilities are not included:

gcc   The GNU *(55.01)* C compiler was used to compile most of the packages. You can try your system's default C compiler, but it may not work for every package.

GNU make   GNU *make (29.12)* was used to compile most of the packages. If you don't have it, try using your system's version.

Problems

Any number of things can go wrong with your build. You might not have the right libraries or include files installed. Your compiler may not work the way the program expects it to. You might not have the right permissions. You might run out of disk space.

These problems are so varied that there's no way we can list any generalized solutions. Try asking an administrator or programmer on your site, or try calling Ready-to-Run Software's technical support *(54.09)*. But we have a few tips that might help:

bsdtar

- If your system has problems with filenames longer than 14 characters, you may have to install *bsdtar* to be able to "untar" the source code. *bsdtar* creates unique 14-character filenames as it unpacks an archive.

- If your system lacks the *-p* option *(5.08)* to the *mkdir* command, you may need to install a new version from the GNU *fileutils* package. The *-p* option is used by the installation and build scripts.

And if all else fails, you can try to delve into the source code itself. That brings us to our next section ...

Compiling Source Code

Compiling programs from source doesn't require you to be a C programmer, just that you understand the general procedure and that you have some common sense and luck.

Almost all UNIX binary programs are written in the C language. These programs are written in text files—the text files are referred to as the *source code*—and then converted to binary files using a *compiler*. The typical compiler on a UNIX system is called *cc*.

Although most people call *cc* a "compiler," it's really a front-end program. Unless you tell it not to, *cc* first runs a *preprocessor*. Next it runs the compiler. Then it runs the *linker/loader* to make the actual executable file. We'll gloss over that in this article and just say that "*cc* does it."

On top of *cc*, there's usually another front-end: almost all programs are designed to be compiled using the *make* program.

Although we can't prepare you for everything you might need to know to compile programs from the CD-ROM for your platform, this section should at least give you an idea of how it's *supposed* to work.

Copying the Sources

Before you can actually compile the sources, you need to copy the sources to your local hard disk. You can't just compile the sources directly from the CD-ROM because the CD-ROM is read-only.

The first thing you need to do is to decide where you want to install the sources, and then *cd* to that directory. For example, I like to build sources in a subdirectory of my home directory. Let's suppose I want to install the *pcal* program. I create the new directory and then *cd* there:

15.12
```
% mkdir ~/pcal_src
% cd ~/pcal_src
```

For installing the sources onto your local hard disk, the CD-ROM has a script called *source.pt*. Assuming that the CD-ROM is mounted on */cdrom*, the script can be called using one of the following commands:

```
% /cdrom/SOURCE.PT\;1 package-name
% /cdrom/SOURCE.PT package-name
```

```
% /cdrom/source.pt\;1 package-name
% /cdrom/source.pt package-name
```

Where *package-name* is the name of the package that you want to install sources for. To get a listing of the files, call *source.pt* without any arguments:

```
% /cdrom/source.pt
SOURCE script provided by Ready-to-Run Software, Inc.
Copyright 1993 Ready-to-Run Software, Inc. All Rights Reserved.


Usage: /cdrom/source.pt <package>
Available packages are:
```

!	80cols	Clear	_emacs_ml	_enter
_exit	_hushlogin	addup	age_files	agrep
areacode	ascii	awf	bash	behead
bkedit	bsdtar	bsplit	cal_today	calen
catsaway	center	cgrep	chmod_edit	chunksort
cleanup	cleanup_sed	cls	cols	compress
concordance	count_it	count_types	cpmod	crontab
crush	csh_init	csh_logout	csplit	cut+paste
cvtbase	date-month	del	delete	derange_num
diff	dir_path	dirtop	doublespace	dtp
ediff	elookfor	emacs	exrc	fgrep
filesum	fileutils	find	findcmd	finder
findtext	flip	fmt_sh	formprog	ftpfile
gawk	getmac	getmatch	getopt	grabchars
grep	groff	head	hgrep	index
inserts	ipl	ispell	jot	lensort
less	lf	lndir	logerrs	longlines
look	lookfor	ls_today	make_print	manindex
mced	motd_diff	namesort	nextday	no_run
nom	offset	oldlinks	opttest	paircheck
patch	pbmplus	pcal	perl	phone
phrase	pipegrep	pstext	psutils	pushin
qcsh	qsubst	qterm	rcs	rcsgrep
rcsit2	recomment	redo	relink	ren
rename	rename_sh	rolodex	rot	runsed
runtime	sc	screen	screensize	script_tidy
search_el	sedman	sh_prompt	shar	shellutils
sherror	showmatch	sl	sls	smiley
squoze	stat	stree	stripper	su
tar	tcap	tcsh	termtest	testsed
tgrep	tpipe	tputinit	triplespace	ttykind
twin	vgrep	vis	vtree	watchq
whereiz	which	whichweek	wordfreq	xargs
xref	xtail	zap	zipcode	zloop
zmore	zvi	zview		

(Note that all the packages on the CD-ROM are listed here, shell scripts as well as C sources.)

In my case, I want to install *pcal*, so I run the following command:

```
% /cdrom/source.pt pcal
SOURCE script provided by Ready-to-Run Software, Inc.
Copyright 1993 Ready-to-Run Software, Inc. All Rights Reserved.

Copied /POWER_TOOLS/SOURCES/PCAL/PCAL_43.Z to pcal-4.3.tar.Z
```

```
Copied /POWER_TOOLS/SOURCES/PCAL/RS6000/PCAL to RS6000patch.pcal
Copied /POWER_TOOLS/SOURCES/PCAL/RTR/PCAL to rtrpatch.pcal
3 files copied successfully.
```

The *source.pt* script copies all the relevant files into your current directory.

Uncompressing the Sources

If you now list the directory, you'll find the files that were just copied there.

```
% ls
RS6000patch.pcal        pcal-4.3.tar.Z          rtrpatch.pcal
```

The file called *pcal-4.3.tar.Z* is the *pcal* source package, in a tarred and compressed form. The *.Z* suffix tells you that the file was compressed using the *compress*(25.06) command. You need to run *uncompress* first:

```
% uncompress pcal-4.3.tar.Z
```

If you don't have the *uncompress* command, you can get it from the CD-ROM.

Untarring the Sources

After you have uncompressed the file, you'll see the file without the *.Z* suffix.

```
% ls
RS6000patch.pcal        pcal-4.3.tar            rtrpatch.pcal
```

The *.tar* suffix to the *pcal-4.3.tar* file means that the file was packed using the *tar* command (20.05). Again, if you don't have *tar*, it's on the CD-ROM.

To unpack the file, use *tar* with the −*x* option for "extract" and the −*f* option to specify a filename. (I also like to use −*v* for verbose output.) My command line might read:

```
% tar xvf pcal-4.3.tar
x pcal-4.3/ReadMe, 7673 bytes, 15 tape blocks
x pcal-4.3/Descrip.mms, 3713 bytes, 8 tape blocks
x pcal-4.3/Make_Pcal.com, 3090 bytes, 7 tape blocks
x pcal-4.3/Makefile, 1159 bytes, 3 tape blocks
x pcal-4.3/Makefile.Amiga, 1010 bytes, 2 tape blocks
x pcal-4.3/Makefile.DOS, 1023 bytes, 2 tape blocks
x pcal-4.3/Makefile.VMS, 2505 bytes, 5 tape blocks
x pcal-4.3/Orig.ReadMe, 984 bytes, 2 tape blocks
x pcal-4.3/Pcal.TeX, 28199 bytes, 56 tape blocks
x pcal-4.3/Pcal.hlp, 29099 bytes, 57 tape blocks
x pcal-4.3/SetUp.com, 670 bytes, 2 tape blocks
x pcal-4.3/VaxCrtl.opt, 31 bytes, 1 tape blocks
x pcal-4.3/calendar, 12101 bytes, 24 tape blocks
x pcal-4.3/exprpars.c, 8538 bytes, 17 tape blocks
x pcal-4.3/moon91, 2828 bytes, 6 tape blocks
x pcal-4.3/moon92, 2887 bytes, 6 tape blocks
x pcal-4.3/pcal.c, 46440 bytes, 91 tape blocks
x pcal-4.3/noprotos.h, 2530 bytes, 5 tape blocks
x pcal-4.3/pcalglob.h, 4551 bytes, 9 tape blocks
x pcal-4.3/pcalinit.c, 4071 bytes, 8 tape blocks
x pcal-4.3/protos.h, 4341 bytes, 9 tape blocks
x pcal-4.3/moonphas.c, 17817 bytes, 35 tape blocks
```

```
x pcal-4.3/troffman.sty, 4894 bytes, 10 tape blocks
x pcal-4.3/writefil.c, 24597 bytes, 49 tape blocks
x pcal-4.3/pcal.man, 25296 bytes, 50 tape blocks
x pcal-4.3/pcaldefs.h, 17643 bytes, 35 tape blocks
x pcal-4.3/pcalinit.ps, 14297 bytes, 28 tape blocks
x pcal-4.3/pcalutil.c, 21238 bytes, 42 tape blocks
x pcal-4.3/pcallang.h, 35465 bytes, 70 tape blocks
x pcal-4.3/readfile.c, 32888 bytes, 65 tape blocks
```

tar creates a subdirectory called *pcal-4.3*. *cd* to this directory to continue your build.

```
% cd pcal-4.3
```

Note that if you have the *zcat* command, you might have combined the steps for uncompressing and untarring the files into a single command line, as shown in article 20.07:

```
% zcat pcal-4.3.tar.Z | tar xvf -
```

If you are on a System V-based system, you may have to use *tar* with the *−o* option (20.07) to make sure that you get ownership of the files.

Unsharring the Sources

Before we go on, let's back up a bit. Some packages aren't stored as *tar* archives, but as *shar* archives (20.02). *shar* archives are generally distributed in multiple files, under names such as *part01.Z, part02.Z,* etc. The *qterm* source package is an example of a package that is distributed as *shar* files.

```
% mkdir ~/qterm_src
% cd ~/qterm_src
% /cdrom/source.pt qterm
SOURCE script provided by Ready-to-Run Software, Inc.
Copyright 1993 Ready-to-Run Software, Inc. All Rights Reserved.

Copied /POWER_TOOLS/SOURCES/QTERM/PART01.Z to part01.Z
Copied /POWER_TOOLS/SOURCES/QTERM/PART02.Z to part02.Z
Copied /POWER_TOOLS/SOURCES/QTERM/RISC/QTERM to RISCpatch.qterm
Copied /POWER_TOOLS/SOURCES/QTERM/RS6000/QTERM to RS6000patch.qterm
Copied /POWER_TOOLS/SOURCES/QTERM/I386/QTERM to i386patch.qterm
Copied /POWER_TOOLS/SOURCES/QTERM/SUN3/QTERM to sun3patch.qterm
Copied /POWER_TOOLS/SOURCES/QTERM/SUN4C/QTERM to sun4cpatch.qterm
Copied /POWER_TOOLS/SOURCES/QTERM/HP700/QTERM to hp700patch.qterm
8 files copied successfully.
```

To extract the *qterm* sources, uncompress the "part" files and then use the *unshar* program to unpack them.

? 1.16
```
% uncompress part0?.Z
% unshar part0?
unshar:  Sending header to part01.hdr.
unshar:  Doing part01:
If this archive is complete, you will see the following message:
        "shar: End of archive 1 (of 2)."
shar: Extracting "README" (2200 characters)
shar: Extracting "options.3" (7383 characters)
shar: Extracting "options.c" (10901 characters)
```

```
shar: Extracting "options.h" (2592 characters)
shar: Extracting "qterm.c" (24777 characters)
shar: End of archive 1 (of 2).
You still must unpack the following archives:
        2
unshar:  Sending header to part02.hdr.
unshar:  Doing part02:
If this archive is complete, you will see the following message:
        "shar: End of archive 2 (of 2)."
shar: Extracting "Makefile" (1908 characters)
shar: Extracting "qterm.1" (5805 characters)
shar: Extracting "qterm.h" (3281 characters)
shar: Extracting "qtermtab" (3311 characters)
shar: End of archive 2 (of 2).
You have unpacked both archives.
```

If you don't have *shar* and *unshar*, it's on the CD-ROM; but the true beauty of *shar* archives is that you can always remove any headers and footers from the file and use the Bourne shell (*sh*) to unpack the files.

To edit out the header, remove any lines at the top of the file that don't resemble Bourne shell syntax. Since many *shar* archives are distributed in e-mail or in newsgroups, the files might include the header of a mail message or news posting. The author might also precede the actual *shar* archive with some explanation of what the program does. A good bet is to look for a line reading #!/bin/sh and remove all lines preceding it. Even better, most shell archives contain directions right in the file:

(text ....)

```
#! /bin/sh
# This is a shell archive.  Remove anything before this line,
# then feed it into a shell via "sh file" or similar.
# To overwrite existing files, type "sh file -c".
```

To remove the footer, look for anything resembling a user's mail signature. (*shar* archives usually have an *exit* message at the end, so editing out the footer isn't always needed ... but it doesn't hurt.)

After editing out the header and footer, just run the files through *sh* individually:

```
% vi part0?
    edit out headers
% sh part01; sh part02
    ...
```

Note that it's especially important to install and unpack *shar* archives in discrete, well-named directories (such as *qterm_src*, in this case). Since *shar* files are almost always given generic names of *part01*, *part02*, etc., it's easy to overwrite files or to get confused if you accidentally unpack more than one package in the same directory.

Applying Patches

When I copied the *pcal* sources using the *source.pt* shell script, I also got two
patch files *(34.09)*: *rtrpatch.pcal* and *RS6000patch.pcal*. These are patches prepared by Ready-to-Run Software for compiling the *pcal* package.

The *RS6000patch.pcal* file is a patch for compilng on IBM's RS6000 platform. If
you aren't on a RS6000, then you probably don't need this file. When building
other packages, you might see other platform-specific patch files, with prefixes
like *i386, xenix, hp700, sun3, sun4*, etc. Naturally, you shouldn't use these
packages if you aren't on one of these platforms.

The *rtrpatch.pcal* file is a general-purpose patch for all platforms. You should
apply this patch for all platforms.

Before you apply any of Ready-to-Run's patches, you should first make sure
that there aren't any patch files in the untarred source directory. If the sources
did come with patch files, they would have to be applied before
Ready-to-Run's. In the *pcal-4.3* directory, list the directory contents:

```
% ls -aF
./                 Makefile.VMS    calendar      pcal.man       protos.h
../                Orig.ReadMe     exprpars.c    pcaldefs.h     readfile.c
Descrip.mms        Pcal.TeX        moon91        pcalglob.h     troffman.sty
Make_Pcal.com      Pcal.hlp        moon92        pcalinit.c     writefil.c
Makefile           ReadMe          moonphas.c    pcalinit.ps
Makefile.Amiga     SetUp.com       noprotos.h    pcallang.h
Makefile.DOS       VaxCrtl.opt     pcal.c        pcalutil.c
```

A *patch* file generally has the string *patch* or *pch* in it. There are no patch files in
this directory.

Now that I'm sure that there aren't any other patches, I run the *patch* command.
(Naturally, if you don't already have *patch*, you can get its sources off the
CD-ROM.) To run *patch*, make sure you're in the source directory (in this case,
the *pcal-4.3* subdirectory created when I ran *tar*). Then run *patch*, taking input
from the patch file in the parent directory:

< 14.01
../ 1.21

```
% patch < ../rtrpatch.pcal
Hmm... Looks like a new-style context diff to me...
The text leading up to this was:
--------------------------
|*** Makefile.orig     Tue Dec 17 05:34:19 1991
|--- Makefile    Mon Nov 23 05:59:49 1992
--------------------------
Patching file Makefile using Plan A...
Hunk #1 succeeded at 5.
Hunk #2 succeeded at 46.
done
```

The patch is now applied.

An Easy Build

Up to now, all we've been doing is just getting the source tree together. Now
we're up to the part where we actually build the package.

First of all, if there's any universal rule about compiling sources, it's:

If there's a file called README, read it!

README files often contain esoteric details about the history of the program and what improvements could be made, etc. But they might also contain details about how to build the package. Reading a *README* can save you hours of frustration trying to figure out what to tweak to make the program build on your platform.

Another file to look for is one called *Configure. Configure* is a shell script that tries to figure out what sort of platform you're on and how to build the package for you, and it's remarkably effective. The sources for *perl* and *patch* both come with *Configure* scripts.

pcal doesn't come with a *README* or with a *Configure* script. But it does come with a file called *Makefile*. (Actually, it comes with several *Makefiles*, for different platforms—but the default *Makefile* is the one for UNIX systems, which is what you want.) The *Makefile* is used by the *make* program *(29.12)*. There have been entire books written about *make*, but if you're lucky, all you need to know about it is that if you see a *Makefile*, then all you need to compile a program is to type *make*.

First, though, scan through the *Makefile* to see if there are any comments there. You might have to make some changes in the *Makefile* to configure it for your system. For example, the *qterm Makefile* has the following very helpful lines:

```
#
# Add "-DUSG5" to DEFS below, if your system is Unix System V.
# Add "-DHAS_VARARGS" if your system supports varargs.
# Add "-DOPT_COMPAT" to support old command line options.
#
DEFS    = -DTABFILE=\"$(TABFILE)\" -DOPT_COMPAT
```

You probably know whether your system is System V-based or not. If you never used this program before, you probably don't care about old command line options. And if you don't know what *varargs* are or whether your system supports it ... try seeing if there's a manpage *(52.01)* for it. (You might even find out what it is!)

```
% man varargs

VARARGS(3)              C LIBRARY FUNCTIONS              VARARGS(3)
•
NAME
     varargs - handle variable argument list

SYNOPSIS
     #include <varargs.h>
     ...
```

What do you know, I have *varargs*. So I add the -DHAS_VARARGS command-line option to the DEFS= line:

```
DEFS    = -DTABFILE=\"$(TABFILE)\" -DOPT_COMPAT -DHAS_VARARGS
```

The *pcal Makefile*, on the other hand, only includes a single line of instruction towards the top:

```
# Set the configuration variables below to taste.
```

This isn't particularly helpful, but scan the *Makefile* anyway for anything obviously wrong. When you're satisfied, just cross your fingers and run *make*:

```
% make
/bin/cc    -c pcal.c
/bin/cc    -c exprpars.c
/bin/cc    -c moonphas.c
/bin/cc    -c pcalutil.c
/bin/cc    -c readfile.c
/bin/cc     -o pcalinit pcalinit.c
pcalinit pcalinit.ps pcalinit.h
/bin/cc    -c writefil.c
/bin/cc  -o pcal pcal.o exprpars.o moonphas.o pcalutil.o readfile.o
writefil.o -lm
```

There were no error or warning messages, so you're fine. Errors mean that the program package probably didn't build completely; you'll have to find the cause and fix them. If there were warnings, the programs may not work right or have a subtle flaw. For a program like a spreadsheet, where hidden flaws can be a disaster, you'd better find out what the warnings mean and fix them. Otherwise, just cross your fingers some more and see if the program works.

When you list the *pcal* source directory now, you should see several new files with a *.o* suffix, but the most important thing is that the *pcal* executable is now built and ready to be installed on your system.

```
% ls -aF
./             Orig.ReadMe    moon91         pcaldefs.h     protos.h
../            Pcal.TeX       moon92         pcalglob.h     readfile.c
Descrip.mms    Pcal.hlp       moonphas.c     pcalinit*      readfile.o
Make_Pcal.com  ReadMe         moonphas.o     pcalinit.c     troffman.sty
Makefile       SetUp.com      noprotos.h     pcalinit.h     writefil.c
Makefile.Amiga VaxCrtl.opt    pcal*          pcalinit.ps    writefil.o
Makefile.DOS   calendar       pcal.c         pcallang.h
Makefile.VMS   exprpars.c     pcal.man       pcalutil.c
Makefile.orig  exprpars.o     pcal.o         pcalutil.o
```

You can now try out the program, and once you're sure it works, install it. To install the program, many *Makefiles* provide an *install* target.

```
% make install
```

On many machines, you'll need to be logged in as *root* to be able to install the binary and manpage system-wide. If so, it might be a good idea to run *make* with the *−n* option first. The *−n* option says to just show what commands would be executed without actually executing them.

```
% make -n install
```

Or if you prefer to just install the program by hand, just move the executable and the manpage to the right directories (be sure to rename the manpage as appropriate):

```
% mv pcal /usr/local/bin
% mv pcal.man /usr/local/man/man1/pcal.1
```

Note, however, that some programs may have extra steps in installing the executable. If all this worked as advertised, you can bail out now. Otherwise, you might need to know more about what goes on behind the scenes before you can figure out what went wrong.

Functions, Libraries, and Header Files

To understand the compilation process, it helps to understand a little about libraries and header files.

C programs are written almost entirely using *functions*. Article 16.03 shows an example of a function defined in the Bourne shell programming language. C language functions are basically the same idea: group together a series of commands, give them a name, and then you can execute those commands using that name whenever you want and as many times as you want. Functions are also sometimes referred to as *subroutines*, *library functions*, or just *routines*.

Now, you can define C functions in the same source file. But the operating system also provides a vast collection of function definitions—which is very nice, because otherwise you'd be building every program from scratch. The function definitions are kept in *libraries*, which are generally installed on your system in */usr/lib/* with a *lib* prefix and a *.a* suffix (for example, */usr/lib/libc.a*).

Functions also have to be *declared* in the program. Function declarations are kept in *header* or *include* files, which are generally installed on your system in */usr/include/* with *.h* suffixes (for example, */usr/include/stdio.h*).

If you use functions that are defined in libraries (and you most definitely will), you need to make sure that when the program is compiled, it is *linked* to the libraries it needs. You also have to make sure that the proper header files are read by your program, since the program won't compile unless all functions have been declared.

For example, if you need to take the square root of a number in your program, you need to use the *sqrt()* function. This function resides in the Math library. This means that you need to link the program with *libm.a* and you need to read in the *math.h* header file (which declares *sqrt()*). So in the program, you need to have the following line near the top of the source file:

```
#include <math.h>
```

and when you compile the program, you need to use the *–l* command-line option to link with *libm*:

```
% cc -o file file.c -lm
```

Note the following facts:

- Unless you name the executable file with -o *file*, *cc* will name it *a.out*.

- The source filename must end with a *.c* suffix.

- Since *math.h* lives in */usr/include*, you don't need to give its full pathname on the #include line, just put the name of the header file between angle brackets as shown. Relative pathnames *(15.02)* starting at */usr/include* can be used in angle brackets. For instance, <sys/foo.h> means */usr/include/sys/foo.h*.

  By default, *cc* looks for header files in */usr/include*, and you can have it look automatically in other directories by specifying them with the *–I* command-line option. If you want to use a header file in directory that isn't searched by default, supply its absolute or relative pathname in double quotes instead.

- When linking with a library on the command line, you should put the *–l* options at the end. If you use more than one library, you'll need more than one *–l* option. The order of the *–l* options is important; check the documentation or look for a comment in the source code.

- The compiler found *libm.a* because it was in */usr/lib*, which it searches by default. If you want it to use a library in another directory, you may need to supply the directory using the *–L* command-line option.

As you can imagine, there's much more to know. But that's the general idea of compiling C programs on UNIX systems, and it's about as much as we can tell you without starting to teach you C.

The make Program

When you're writing a simple C program, you can simply compile the program using *cc*:

```
% cc test.c
```

But more complicated programs (like many of the programs on the Power Tools disk) require a bit more work. More complicated programs are easier to handle if you write them in *modules*. So, for example, the *pcal* source tree on the Power Tools disk contains several *.c* files: *exprpars.c, moonphas.c, pcalinit.c, pcalutil.c, readfile.c, writefil.c*, and, of course, *pcal.c*. Each of these source files needs to be compiled separately into *object files* (with *.o* suffixes). If you give the *–c* option, *cc* will compile ".*c* files" into ".*o* files" and stop without making the finished executable. When you run *cc* again—but give it the *.o* filenames (*exprpars.o, moonphas.o*, and so on) it will link all those object files with the libraries and make the executable file.

This makes compilation a bit harder to keep track of. There are a lot more steps. Furthermore, it means that whenever a file is changed, you have to remember not only to recompile it but also to relink the entire program.

This is a job for the *make* program. We showed uses for *make* in articles 2.16, 22.09, and 29.12, but this is what it was really meant for. The *pcal* source tree comes with a file called *Makefile*. (Actually, it comes with several different *Makefiles* for different platforms, but that's another issue.) The *Makefile* keeps track of each of the programs and each of their dependencies. It also keeps track of any command-line options you might want passed to *cc*, including libraries to link to. The result is that when you want to make the *pcal* program, all you need to do is type:

```
% make pcal
```

Or, even better, just:

```
% make
```

This is a lot easier than trying to keep track of all the modules and command-line options yourself.

So if you can't compile a program because the header file it needs is installed in a non-standard place, you'd specify that in the *Makefile*. You could add the appropriate *–I* option to the COPTS declaration line:

```
COPTS    = -I/usr/include/sys
```

Or if you want to use a different compiler than *cc*, you could redefine that variable:

```
CC       = /usr/local/bin/gcc
```

Again, this is only the tip of the iceberg. But a basic understanding of libraries, header files, and *make* has helped me build many programs that wouldn't compile the first time. For help with *make*, see the Nutshell Handbook *Managing Projects with make* by Andrew Oram and Steve Talbott.

—LM, EP

54.09 *Software Support from RTR*

Ready-to-Run Software (the company that prepared the executable programs, build scripts, and patches for the Power Tools software) also provides support for the software delivered on the CD-ROM (or alternate media).

RTR will provide support for the following:

- use of packages

- compiling/building packages

- installation

- porting to unsupported platforms

You might think that because the software is free, the support ought to be, too! However, software support is time-consuming—especially for such a wide-range of packages as we provide here.

Charges for telephone support are as follows (per call):

first two minutes .... no charge
next five minutes $10
each additional ten minutes $10

Ready-to-Run Software will *not* provide Power Tools support on its 800 number, so please call the Power Tools support number: 1-508-448-9897.

Please have a valid MasterCard or Visa available when placing your support call. If you prefer to use a company Purchase Order for support, RTR will require hard copy of the PO in advance of your call. Please mail or fax the PO to RTR before placing your call. Minimum support billing against a PO will be $50 in any month in which there are charges.

Fixed price support agreements are also available. Please call or write for a price quote. (The price will depend on the platforms and packages to be supported.)

Ready-to-Run Software, Inc.
Rustic Trail
Groton, MA 01450

508-448-9897 (9 a.m. to 5 p.m. EST)

508-448-2989 (fax)

—JM

55

Glossary

AIX
A version of UNIX from the IBM Corporation.

argument
Zero or more characters passed to a program as a single unit. The shell breaks a command line into arguments by cutting it at unquoted white space. *See also* article 9.03, **word**.

array
An ordered collection of data items. An array has a single overall name; each item in it is called an *element* or *member*. For instance, the C shell stores its command search path in an array *(49.05)* named *path (7.05)*. The first array member is named $path[1], the second is $path[2], and so on.

ASCII file
Formally, a file containing only ASCII *(53.03)* characters. More commonly (in the USA, at least) a file containing text that's printable, viewable, and has no "binary" (non-ASCII) characters. ASCII characters use only seven of the bits in a (8-bit) byte.

backquote
The character `. Not the same as a single quote ('). Does command substitution *(10.14)*.

backslash
The character \. In UNIX, it changes the interpretation of the next character in some way. *See also* article 9.16, **slash**.

batch queue
A mechanism for sequencing large jobs. A batch queue receives job requests from users. It then executes the jobs one at a time. Batch queues go back to the earliest days of data processing. They are an extremely effective, if uncomfortable, way to manage system load. *See also* article 42.06.

bin directory

A directory for storing executable programs. *See also* article 5.02.

binaries, binary file

A file with non-text characters. Often, a directly-executable file that can be run as a program. Binary characters use all the bits in a (8-bit) byte. *See also ASCII file*.

block size

The largest amount of data that a UNIX filesystem will always allocate contiguously. For example, if a filesystem's block size is 8 KB, files of size up to 8 KB are always physically contiguous (i.e., in one place), rather than spread across the disk. Files that are larger than the filesystem's block size may be fragmented: 8 KB pieces of the file are located in different places on the disk. Fragmentation limits filesystem performance. Note that the filesystem block size is different from a disk's physical block size, which is almost always 512 bytes.

brain damaged

A program with poor design or other errors can be called *brain-damaged*.

BSD UNIX

The versions of UNIX developed at the University of California, Berkeley. BSD UNIX has been dominant in academia and has historically had some more advanced features than System V: BSD introduced virtual memory, networking, and the "fast filesystem" to the UNIX community. It is also the system on which SunOS is based. System V Release 4 and some vendors' earlier System V versions also have Berkeley features.

buffer

A temporary storage place such as a file or an area of the computer's memory. Most text editors store the file you're editing in a buffer; when you're done editing, the edited buffer is copied over (i.e., replaces) the original file.

command line

The text you type at a shell prompt. A UNIX shell reads the command line, parses it to find the command name (which is the first word on the command line), and executes the command. A command line may have more than one command joined by operators like semicolons (;) *(9.03)*, pipes (|) *(1.04)*, or double ampersands (&&) *(46.09)*.

control character

A character you make by holding down the keyboard CTRL (Control) key while pressing a letter or another character key.

core file, core dump

When a program terminates abnormally, it may make a file named *core*. The *core* file can be used for debugging. *See also* article 25.05.

.cshrc file
See **dot files**.

CTRL-X
The character called "control *x*," where *x* is a key on the keyboard. *See also* **control character**.

daemon
A program that is invisible to users but provides important system services. Daemons manage everything from paging to networking to notification of incoming mail. BSD UNIX has many different daemons: without counting, I would guess that there are roughly two dozen. Daemons normally spend most of their time "sleeping" or waiting for something to do, so that they don't account for a lot of CPU load. *See also* article 1.14.

data switch
This hardware is something like a telephone switchboard. A data switch connects many terminals to two or more computers. The user, on a terminal or through a modem, tells the data switch which computer she wants a connection to. Also called a *terminal multiplexor*.

Computers without data switches usually have one terminal connected to each *tty* (3.08) port; characteristics like the terminal type (6.11) can be set in system files. Conversely, computers with data switches can't know in advance what sort of terminal is connected to each *tty* port.

default
In a program that gives you more than one choice, the default choice is the one you get by not choosing. The default is usually the most common choice.

As an example, the default file for many UNIX programs is the standard input. If you don't give a filename on the command line, a program will read its standard input.

dot (.) files (.cshrc, .login, .profile . . .)
Files that are read when you log in. These set up your environment and run any other UNIX commands (for instance, *tset*). If your account uses the C shell, it will read *.cshrc* and *.login*. Accounts that use the Bourne shell and shells like it read *.profile*. *See also* article 2.02.

double quote
The " character. This isn't the same as two single quotes (' ') together. The " is used around a part of a UNIX command line where the shell should do variable and command substitution (and, on the C shell, history substitution), but no other interpretation. *See also* articles 9.10 and 9.11, **single quote**.

escape

When you *escape* a character or a string of characters, you change the way it is interpreted. Escaping something can take away its special meaning, as in shell quoting *(9.10)*—or can add special meaning, as in terminal escape sequences *(6.08)*

flag

In programming, a *flag variable* is set to signal that some condition has been met or that something should be done. For example, a flag can be set ("raised") if the user has entered something wrong; the program can test for this flag and not continue until the problem has been fixed.

flame

A heated or irrational statement.

fragment

In the BSD filesystem, a fragment is a portion of a disk block—usually one-eighth of a block, but possibly one-quarter or one-half of a block. If the last portion of a file doesn't occupy a full disk block, the filesystem will allocate one or more fragments rather than an entire block. Don't confuse "fragments" with "fragmentation." Fragments allow the BSD filesystem to use larger block sizes without becoming inefficient.

Free Software Foundation, FSF

A group that develops the freely-available GNU software. Their address is: 675 Massachusetts Avenue, Cambridge, MA 02139 USA.

full-duplex

Communications between a terminal and a computer where data flows in both directions at the same time. *Half-duplex* communications, where data flows in only one direction at a time, are unusual these days. *See also* article 43.02.

GNU

Gnu's Not Unix, a system of software planned to eventually be a freely-available substitute for UNIX. *See also* **Free Software Foundation**

gotcha

A "catch," difficulty, or surprise in the way that a program works.

hardcoded

In general, a value that can't be changed. For example, in a shell script with the command `grep jane`, the value `jane` is hardcoded; *grep* will always search for *jane*. But in the command `grep $USER`, the text that *grep* searches for is not hardcoded; it's a variable value.

hash table

Hashing data into the format of a hash table lets specially-designed programs search for data quickly. A hash table assigns a special search code to each piece of data. For example, the C shell uses a hash table to locate commands more quickly; the *rehash* *(5.02)* command rebuilds the hash table after you add a new command.

I/O

Input/output of text from software or hardware.

inode

A data structure that describes a file. Within any filesystem, the number of inodes, and hence the maximum number of files, is set when the filesystem is created. *See also* article 1.22.

i-number

A UNIX file has a name (for people to identify it with) and an i-number (for UNIX to identify it with). Each file's i-number is stored in a directory, along with the filename, to let UNIX find the file that you name. *See also* article 1.22.

job

One UNIX command. It is easy to be sloppy and use the terms job, process, and program interchangeably. I do it and I'm sure you do, too. Within UNIX documentation, though, the word "job" is usually used to mean one, and only one, command line. Note that one command line can be complex. For example:

```
pic a.ms | tbl | eqn | troff -ms
```

is one command, and hence one job, that is formed from four processes.

job number

Shells with job control assign a job number to every command that is stopped or that is running in the background *(1.26)*. You can use job numbers to refer to your own commands or groups of commands. Job numbers are generally easier to use than process IDs; they are much smaller (typically between 1 and 10), and therefore easier to remember. The C shell *jobs* command displays job numbers. *See also* article 13.01.

kernel

The part of the UNIX operating system that provides memory management, I/O services, and all other low-level services. The kernel is the "core" or "heart" of the operating system.

kludge

A program or a solution to a problem that isn't written carefully, doesn't work as well as it should, doesn't use good programming style, and so on.

library function

Packages of system calls (and of other library functions) for programmers in C and other languages. In general (though not always), a library function is a "higher-level operation" than a system call. *See also* **system call**.

load average

A measure of how busy the CPU is. The load average is useful, though imprecise. It is defined as the average number of jobs in the run queue plus the average number of jobs that are blocked while waiting for disk I/O. The *uptime (41.07)* command shows the load average.

.login file
See **dot files**.

mode
In UNIX, an octal number that describes what access a file's owner, group, and others have to the file. *See also* article 1.23.

modulo
Think back to your fourth grade arithmetic. When you divide two numbers, you have a *dividend* (the number on top), a *divisor* (the number on the bottom), a *quotient* (the answer), and a *remainder* (what's left over). In computer science, this kind of division is very important. However, we're usually more interested in the remainder than in the quotient. When we're interested in the remainder, we call the operation a *modulus* (or *modulo*, or *mod*).

For example, one of the examples on your fourth grade arithmetic text might have been 13 ÷ 3 = 4 (with a remainder of 1). As computer users, we're more interested in 13 mod 3 = 1. It's really the same operation, though.

Modulo is also used in expressions like "modulo wildcards," which means "everything but wildcards."

NFS
*N*etwork *F*ile *S*ystem. NFS allows UNIX systems and many non-UNIX systems to share files via a TCP/IP network. Subject to certain security restrictions, systems are allowed complete access to another system's files. *See also* article 1.33.

newline
The character that marks the end of a line of text in most UNIX files. (This is a convention, not a requirement.)

null
Empty, zero-length, with no characters—for example, a *null string*. This is *not* the same as an ASCII NUL *(53.03)* character.

octal number
The base 8 numbering system. Octal numbers are made with the digits 0 through 7. For example, the decimal (base 10) number 12 is the same as the octal number 14. ASCII character codes *(53.03)* are often shown as octal numbers.

option switch
Typed on a command line to modify the way that a UNIX command works. Usually starts with a dash (–). The terms *option* and *switch* are more or less interchangeable. An option may have several settings, but a switch usually has two settings: on or off, enabled or disabled, yes or no, etc.

panic

UNIX jargon for a "crash." A panic is really a special kind of a crash. Panics occur when UNIX detects some irreconcilable inconsistency in one of its internal data structures. The kernel throws up its hands and shuts the system down before any damage can be done. As it is going down, it prints a "panic" message on the console.

parse

To split into pieces and interpret. Article 9.03 explains how the shell parses a command line.

partition

A portion of a disk drive. UNIX disk drives typically have eight partitions, although not all are in use.

path, search

See **search path**.

pipe

A UNIX mechanism for sending the output of one program directly to the input of another program, without using an intermediate file. All UNIX systems support pipes. *See also* article 1.04. System V and SunOS also provide "named pipes," which are FIFO (first-in/first-out) buffers that have names and can be accessed via the filesystem.

portable

A program that's *portable* can be used on more than one version of UNIX or with more than one version of a command.

POSIX

A developing standard for an "open" computer operating system that is similar to UNIX.

priority

A number that determines how often the kernel will run a process. A higher-priority process will run more often and, therefore, will finish faster, than a low-priority process.

process

A lot of the time, a process is nothing more than another name for a program that is running on the system. But there is a more formal definition: a process is a single execution thread, or a single stream of computer instructions. One job may be built from many different processes. For example, a command line with pipes *(1.04)* starts two or more processes. *See also* article 40.03.

process ID (PID)

UNIX assigns every process an ID number (called a PID) when it starts. *See also* article 40.03. This number allows you to refer to a process at a later time. If you need to kill *(40.10)* a runaway program, you refer to it by its process ID. The *ps (40.05)* command displays process IDs.

.profile file
> See **dot files**

prompt
> How a program asks you for information: by printing a short string like `Delete afile?` to the terminal and waiting for a response. *See also* **shell prompt**

pseudo-code
> A way to write out program text, structured like a program, without using the actual programming language. Pseudo-code is usually used to explain a program.

quote
> See **backquote, double quote, single quote**

read-only filesystem
> Filesystems are usually set up to allow write access to users who have the proper permissions *(1.23)*. The system administrator can mount a filesystem *read-only*; then no user will be able to make changes to files there.

recursive
> A program or routine that re-executes itself or repeats an action over and over. For example, the *find (18.01)* program moves through a directory tree recursively, doing something in each directory.

reverse video
> On a video display, reversed foreground and background colors or tones. Reverse video is used to highlight an area or to identify text to be used or modified.
>
> For instance, if text is usually shown with black letters on a white background, reverse video would have white letters on a black background. *See also* article 6.08.

SCSI
> Small Computer Systems Interface, a standard interface for disk and tape devices now used on many UNIX (and non-UNIX) systems.

search path
> A list of directories that the shell searches to find the program file you want to execute. *See also* articles 7.04 and 9.05.

shell
> A program that reads and interprets command lines and also runs those programs. *See also* articles 9.03 and 46.03.

shell prompt
> A signal from a shell (when it's used interactively) that the shell is ready to read a command line. By default, the percent sign (%) is the C shell prompt and the dollar sign ($) is the Bourne shell prompt.

slash

The character /. It separates elements in a pathname. *See also* article 1.21, **backslash**.

single quote

The ' character. This isn't the same as a backquote (`). The single quote is used around a part of a UNIX command line where the shell should do no interpretation (except history substitution in the C shell). *See also* articles 9.10 and 9.11, **double quote**.

special file

An entity in the filesystem that accesses I/O devices. There is a special file for every terminal, every network controller, every partition of every disk drive, and every possible way of accessing every tape drive. *See also* article 1.29.

string

A sequence of characters. *See also* **word**.

subdirectory

A directory within a directory. *See also* articles 1.21 and 5.07.

swapping

A technique that the UNIX kernel uses to clean up physical memory. The kernel moves entire processes from memory to disk and then reassigns the memory to some other function. Processes that have been idle for more than a certain period may be removed from memory to save space. Swapping is also used to satisfy extreme memory shortages. When the system is extremely short of memory, active processes may be "swapped out."

switch

See **option switch**.

system call

The lowest-level access to the UNIX operating system. Everything else in UNIX is built on system calls. *See also* **library function**.

System V UNIX

The version of UNIX that is under continuing development at AT&T. The most recent Release of System V is Release 4, known as V.4 or SVR4.

TCP/IP

A network protocol that is commonly used for communications via an Ethernet. TCP/IP is also called the "Internet protocol." It is also common to use TCP/IP over leased lines for long-distance communications.

termcap

Stands for *term*inal *cap*abilities, an early (and still common) way to describe terminals to UNIX. *See also* article 43.11, **terminfo**

---

terminal emulator

A program that makes a computer display emulate (act like) a terminal. For example, many terminal emulator programs emulate the Digital Equipment Corporation VT100 terminal.

terminfo

A newer way to describe terminal capabilities to UNIX. *See also* article 43.11, **termcap** .

the net

A term for two particular networks: Usenet and Internet *(1.33)* . For instance, "I read it on The Net" or "You can get that file on The Net."

timestamp

The UNIX filesystem stores the times that each file was last modified, accessed, or had a change to its inode. These times—especially the modification time—are often called *timestamps*.

truncate

To cut, to shorten—for example, "truncate a file after line 10" means to remove all lines after line 10.

uuencode, uudecode

Utilities that encode files with binary (8-bit) characters into an ASCII (7-bit) format—and decode them back into the original binary format. This is used for transferring data across communications links that can't transfer binary (8-bit) data. *See also* article 20.05.

VAX/VMS

A popular computer operating system from the Digital Equipment Corporation.

wedged

A terminal or program is *wedged* when it's "frozen" or "stuck." The normal activity stops and often can't be restarted without resetting the terminal or killing the program.

white space

A series of one or more space or TAB characters.

word

Similar to a word in a spoken language like English, a word is a unit made up of one or more characters. But unlike English, words in UNIX can contain white space; they can also have no characters (a *zero-length* word). *See also* **argument**

XENIX

One of the first versions of UNIX to run on IBM PCs, and one of the few that will run on 80286 systems. XENIX descends from Version 7 UNIX, a version developed by AT&T in the late-1970s. It has many resemblances to BSD UNIX. Over time, XENIX has been rewritten as a variant of System V.2.

zombies

Dead processes that have not yet been deleted from the process table. Zombies normally disappear almost immediately. However, at times it is impossible to delete a zombie from the process table, so it remains there (and in your *ps* output) until you reboot. Aside from their slot in the process table, zombies don't require any of the system's resources. *See also* article 40.16.

—JP, ML

Index

B

background output, stopping, 216
background processes, 31-32, 211-213
  and job control, 32
  and the Bourne shell, 33
  bringing into the foreground, 212
  getting report of, 212
  killing automatically, 755
  listing, 217
  notifying when done, 109
  preventing from continuing past logout, 751
  running, 212
  seeing which are running, 213
  terminating, 213
  testing exit status of, 878
backquotes, 128, 141
  and command substitution, 160
  and command-line priority, 128
  and putting command output on another
    command line, 166
  glossary definition, 1071
  in aliases, 954
  (see also quotation marks.)
backslashes, and quotes, 139
  disabling special characters, 137
  escaping, 661
  how many to use, 147
backspaces, 795
backup files, (see backups)
backups, 16, 363
  creating timestamp files for, 360
  devices and filenames, 354
  Emacs, 594-595
  extensions for backup files, 360
  finding tape drive name, 354
  making, 879
  making your own, 352-353
  RCS, 373;
    basics, 367-368;
    introduction to, 365;
    tutorial, 368-375;
    (see also RCS.)
  SCCS; basics, 366-367;
    introduction to, 365
  with local tape drive, 353
  (see also tar command.)
bad magic number, error message, 1005
bailing out near line, error message, 1005
ball-bat (slang), 1014
bang (slang), 1014
banner command, 843

bar graphs, 991
base conversion, 986-987
  cvtbase, 988
basename program, 113, 1036
  example of, 915
  introduction to, 914-915
bash (Bourne-again shell), 873, 1024
  introduction to, 10
batch command, and delayed job execution, 775
batch editing, 605-615
  avoiding errors when no match, 612
  introduction to, 605
  on large files, 613
batch queues, 778
  and system performance, 773
bc command, 986-988
  introduction to, 985
  –l option, 986-987
  precision math library, 987
  sine and cosine, 987
bdiff, 512
BEGIN rule (awk), 694, 703, 717
behead script, 655, 1024
bg command, 32, 212
  definition, 217
bin, glossary definition, 1072
bin directories, 74
binaries, glossary definition, 1072
binary conversion, with online calculators, 986
binary files, glossary definition, 1072
/bin, 247, 874
/bin/time, 757-758, 761
BITFTP, 1054
bitmap files, 1024
bitmaps, converting graphics formats to X bitmaps, 862
  creating out of pictures, 862
  manipulating, 864
bitwise operators (csh), 956
bkedit script, 881, 1024
blank lines, deleting, 462-463, 551
  replacing multiple with single, 462
blinking characters, in VT100s, 117
block input operations, and time comand, 759
bold text, 852-853
boolean capabilities, termcap/terminfo, 807
boot scripts, directory containing, 248
Bourne shell (sh), 873
  and background processing, 33
  arrays in, 935
  functions, 186

columns (cont'd)
   rotating, 674-675
   selecting from one or more files, 665-666
   straightening, 673
   totaling numbers in, 990
COLUMNS environment variable, 825
comm command, 288, 517-518
command binaries directory, 247
command history, saving, 202
command interpreter, testing #!, 874-875
command line, arguments;(see command-line
   arguments)
   doing calculations on, 985-986
   editing; C shell, 206-207;
     Korn shell, 204-205
   glossary definition, 1072
   grab previous command's arguments, 191
   grabbing previous command's arguments,
   191
   handling long, 167-169
   how shell interprets, 126-127, 135
   making global changes from, 615
   options; glossary definition, 1076
   parsing, 888-890
   priorities; bypassing, 134
   referring to last word in previous, 178
   reprinting, 150
   saving time on, 149-174
   syntax, awk, 716
   using shell scripts to execute, 160
command substitution, 160-162
command-line arguments, and quoting, 941-943
   finding last, 912
   grabbing previous command's, 191
   in shell scripts, 884;
     counting, 885;
     "$@", 884;
     for loops, 885-887;
     while loops, 885, 887-888
   moving through list of, 913
   quoting, 3
   resetting, 890
   unsetting, 912
   using as aliases, 178-180
commands, aliases for, 175
   answering automatically with yes, 417
   built-in, 11-12
   built-in shell, 950;
     and setting prompts, 113;
     testing, 943
   checking existence of, 893

creating custom, 175
custom, vi, 576
directory contained in, 74, 247
displaying aliases of, 998-1000
emacs, 204
ex editor, 608
executing; in place of current shell, 902;
   multiple on multiple variables, 913;
   on lists of files, 162;
   repeatedly, 173, 1013
exit status of, 877-878;
   (see also exit status.)
external, 11-12
give copy of previous, 200
history; (see history commands)
how interpreted by shell, 126-127
installing customized system commands, 131
internal, 11-12
keeping quiet, 779
locating on a system, 278
names in error messages, 893
naming, 893
online, 993;
   locating, 995, 997;
   one-line summaries of, 997
output; ignoring, 779;
   putting on another command line, 166;
   using as argument to another command,
   162
pathnames; displaying, 998-1000;
   finding complete, 78
redefining with aliases, 182
renaming, 175
repeating on several files, 155
running; a series on a file, 201;
   automatically at login, 42;
   from vi, 215, 560;
   on output of find, 305;
   one while using another, 560;
   selected, 132-133;
   with a previous set of arguments, 167-169
search path, 101
sed, summary of, 645
showing last executed, 764
staggering execution of, 776
storing for execution, 99
substituting; command-line priority, 127;
   disabling special characters, 141
testing how executed by system, 874-875
that don't return exit status, 944-945
timing, 757-758, 761

dd command, 357-359, 653, 656, 1028
   converting; between uppercase and lower-
      case, 665;
      byte order of byte pairs, 665
   reading tapes generated on non-UNIX sys-
      tems, 664
debugging, awk scripts, 711-716
   shell scripts, 937-938;
      quoting, 939;
      saving output in files, 938;
      showing variable values, 939;
      using echo command, 939
decimal places, in calculators, 985
default, glossary definition, 1073
del script, 418, 1026
Delete command (D), sed, 646
delayed execution, 775, 775-788
   (see also job execution, delayed.)
delete command, 421, 1027
   awk, 721
   ex, 608
   sed, 620, 646
deleting, files;(see files, removing)
   text, 545
delimiters, for regular expressions, 623
   sed, 936
   sort command, 680, 680-682
derange.num script, 988-989, 989, 1027
deroff, options;–w, 535
desk calculators, 985
/dev directory, 248
device directory, 248
device numbers, 318
/dev/null, and command output, 779
df command, 439, 1028
   options; –i, 440;
      –t, 440
dictionary attacks, 66
dictionary files, ispell, 528-529
dictionary order, sorting in, 684
diff command, 54, 1027
   and cmp, 516
   and tabstops, 516
   applying diff file to an original, 613-614
   comparing files side-by-side, 510-511
   for very long files, 512
   introduction to, 507-508
   making editing scripts with, 513-515, 611
   making ouput more readable, 512
   options; –e, 513-515;
      –h, 512;

–r, 287;
   –t, 516
diff3, 509, 511, 1027
   –e option, 509
diffmk, 522
DIR command, alias for, 282
dircmp, 287-288
   options; –d, 288;
      –s, 288
directories, 340
   about, 324-325
   access to, 31
   administrative, 249
   aliases for, 244
   archiving, 361
   automatic setup when entering/exiting,
      257-258
   bin, 74, 247
   changing, 24
   comparing, 287-288
   copying files to, 387
   creating, 77-78, 428
   current; about, 242;
      and relative pathnames, 242;
      how UNIX finds, 243;
      setting, 102
   decreasing size of, 320-321, 446-447
   definition of, 21
   determining size of all files in, 703
   device, 248
   finding, 316;
      all with same name, 286;
      how much disk space used for, 286;
      using variables, 253
   for include files, 249
   for local files, 249
   getting name from file pathname, 284
   home, 23-24, 73-79, 248
   introduction to, 73
   keeping list at top of screen, 385
   library, 249
   linking, 330-331
   listing, 277;
      in columns, 274;
      subdirectories, 272
   making; (see directories, creating)
   manual page, 249
   moving to and from, 245
   pathnames, 74
   personal, 75
   previous working, setting, 102

files, size (cont'd)
determining for all in a directory, 703;
limiting, 436;
setting maximum, 436
sparse, 449
splitting into smaller pieces, 653
at fixed points, 658-660;
by context, 660-663
stopping from overwriting, 109
stripping; all but text, 535;
while compiling, 445
temporary; automatically removing, 378;
cleaning up, 61;
removing, 61;
where to keep, 377-378
testing, 892
times; (see file times)
timestamp, 26
two or more names for, 325-326
type, 26, 460-462
uncompressing, 347;
paging through, 457-458
unprintable, paging through, 457-458
updating modification time, 381
using variables to find, 253
versions, 16
viewing contents of, 453-470
with control characters in name, 424
filesum script, 704, 1028
filesystems, current directories, 242
layout, 247-251
moving around in, 239
relative and absolute pathnames, 240-242
structure, 21-23
fileutils, 1028
filtering text, 555-557
filters, definition of, 35
for index program, 982-983
filter-throughs (vi), 555, 558
find command, 297-321, 1028
and multiple searches, 431
and NFS servers, 321
and xargs, 300
arguments, 300
combining searches in, 307
custom tests, 307
directory trees; grepping, 316;
navigating, 299-300
fast find, 312-314
find database, 314-316
operators, 297-299;

about, 302-303;
–atime, 298, 304;
–cpio, 430;
–ctime, 298, 301, 304, 381;
–exec, 298, 305, 307;
–group, 297, 311;
–inum, 298;
–links, 301;
–mtime, 298, 301, 304-305;
–name, 297, 301;
–newer, 298, 305, 433;
–nogroup, 311;
–nouser, 311;
–ok, 299, 306;
–perm, 297;
–print, 298-300;
–prune, 319-320, 426;
–size, 297, 309;
–type, 309;
–user, 297, 311
removing stale files, 429
running commands on output, 305
running on directory trees; skipping standard
directories, 320-321
searching current directory only, 319-320
speeding up, 314-316
summary of, 297-299
using, 302-303
findcmd script, 278, 1028
finder program, 316, 1028
finding, directories, 316
files, 269-295
(see also files, finding)
findsrc program, 1036
findtext script, 291-292, 1028
fixed strings, 482
fixfmps program, 1034
fixmacps program, 1034
fixpspps program, 1034
fixwpps program, 1034
flag, glossary definition, 1074
flame, glossary definition, 1074
flip script, 468-469, 1029
flow control, 796-797
Emacs, 601-602
ENQ/ACK, 797
hardware, 797
in C shell programming, 950
RTS/CTS, 797
XON/XOFF, 796
fmt command, 166, 571

graphics formats (cont'd)
ppm (portable pixmap), 862
Graphics script and alias, 1023
graphics utilities, pbmtoxbm, 863
pnm, 863
pnmflip, 863
pnmrotate, 863
pnmscale, 863
graymaps, manipulating, 864
grep, 3, 54, 172, 1029
and system performance, 773
directory trees, 316
in PostScript files, 861
options; –c, 265;
–h, 5;
–l, 160, 172, 265;
–s, 54
valid metacharacters for, 486
groff, 851, 1029
group access, 29
group IDs, 739
setting, 29
groups, 403
accessing files owned by another group, 403
denying access, 404
ownership, 403
permissions, 393;
and setgid, 394
user, 27
groups program, 1036
gsub function (nawk), 701, 722

H

hackerese, speaking, 1014
hard links, 327
and copying directories, 341
and files with two or more names, 325-326
creating, 328
versus symbolic links, 327
hardcoded, glossary definition, 1074
hardpaths variable (csh), 109, 256
hardware, loose connections, 819
flow control, 797
hash mark (#), in passwords, 70
hash table, glossary definition, 1074
head command, 469
viewing entire file, 841
head script, 1030
header files, about, 1067
header lines, mail, removing, 655

news, removing, 655
help, 993-1007
help command (lpc), 835
here documents, 143, 159, 344
hereis document terminators, 927
hex, converting to octal, 987
hexadecimal conversion, with online calculators, 986
.h filename extension, 19
hgrep, 1030
hidden files, showing, 279
hierarchical filesystems, 21
High Sierra standard, 1040
histchars variable (csh), 109, 209
history characters (csh), setting, 109
history command (csh), 189
!$ (grab previous command's argument), 191
^^ (replacing characters), 192
adding commands to history list, 203
characters, changing, 209
–h option, 202
list of, 194-198
listing in reverse, 193
passing commands to another shell, 203
setting number of commands to save, 193
history file, emacs, 205
history substitution (csh), 189-209, 190
!! (give copy of previous command), 200
: operator (editing substitutions), 198-200
changing characters, 209
definition, 149
in command-line priorities, 127
preventing, 127
testing, 202
history variable (csh), 107, 109
.history file, 202
Hold command (H), sed, 627-629, 634-636, 648
hold command (h), sed, 627-629, 634-636, 647
hold space (sed), 627, 634-636
home directories, 23-24, 248
organizing, 73-79
setting, 102
shortcut to, 255
symbolic links to, 255
HOME variable, 102, 255
/home, 24
hostname command, 998
hung terminals, fixing, 817
when logging in, 87
HUP signal, 746
ignoring, 756

L

M

mouse, versus vi, 540
moving, text (vi and ex), 549-550
ms macros, 855, 858
mtime, 381
multi-line, commands, 158
 prompts, 114, 119
 quoting, 139
 records, awk, 700
 sorts, 685-687
multiple, addresses, 620
 lines; deleting, 638-640;
  edits across, 631-634
multiplication operator (expr), 928
munchlist script, 529
mush, e-mail program, 37
mv command, 1028
 and file ownership, 393
 options; –f, 398;
  –i, 386
myprint script, 837

N

name and address database, 975-980
name lines, (termcap and terminfo), 807
names, command;checking existence of, 893;
  multiple, 893
 name and address database, 975-980
namesort script, 687, 1032
naming, files, 75
National Institute of Standards and Technology
  (NIST), 66
nawk, 692, 697
 command-line syntax, 716
 debugging, 711-716
 –f option, 708
 features of, 692
 functions, writing your own, 706
 system variables; ARGC, 718;
  ARGV, 718;
  FNR, 718;
  OFMT, 718;
  RLENGTH, 718;
  RSTART, 718;
  SUBSEP, 718
netstat, and I/O information, 772
network, and system performance, 773
 bandwidth, 772
 integrity, 772
 I/O problems, 772
 time, 763

Network Filesystem, 37
networking, 36
newgrp, 393, 403
newline characters, 34
 and quoting, 141
newlines, and echo command, 871
 and xargs, 169-170
 glossary definition, 1076
 in sed, 624
 stty, 794
next command, awk, 722
 sed, 648
Next command (N), sed, 631-634, 648
nextday script, 781, 1032
nextweekday script, 1032
NF variable (awk), 699, 704, 718
NFS, 37
 servers, keeping find command from searching, 321
nfsstat, and I/O information, 772
nice command, 766-770, 770, 1036
 and foreground jobs, 769
 BSD, 767
 nice numbers, 766
 prioritizing processes, 34
 standalone; C shell, 768;
  System V, 768-769
 (see also renice.)
nice number, 766
noautowrite option (vi and ex), 558
noclobber variable (csh), 107, 109, 418
NOG script and alias, 1023
noglob variable (csh), 85, 109, 262
nohup, 756, 1036
nom script, 267, 1032
nonomatch variable (csh), 109, 263
non-printable characters, 281-282
 displaying, 458
 making printable, 458-460
 using in scripts, 935-936
non-printable files, displaying, 458-460
Normal script and alias, 1023
no_run script, 133, 1032
not a typewriter, error message, 1006
not enough memory, error message, 1006
Not login shell, error message, 103
notify variable (csh), 109, 216
NR variable (awk), 699, 718
nroff, 847
 awk-based version of, 852
 macros, 848

Q

qcsh file, 1034
qcsh function, (on disk), 262
qsubst program, 615, 1034
   –noask option, 615
qterm, 52, 85,k 1034
qtermtab file, 86
question mark (?), wildcard, 17
queueing systems, 778
queues, printer, 780;
      checking if jobs are in, 833;
      (see also atq.)
   process, reporting jobs in, 780
quit command (q), ex, 609
   sed, 642-643, 649
QUIT signal, 746
quotation marks, and Bourne shell, 136-140
   and expanding wildcards, 20
   backquotes, glossary definition, 1071
   command-line priority, 127
   disabling special characters, 137, 141
   double quotes, glossary definition, 1073
   single quotes, glossary definition, 1079
quoting, and C shell programming, 951
   and command-line arguments, 891, 941-943
   and debugging shell scripts, 939
   and special characters in filenames, 142
   awk scripts, 711
   Bourne shell, 136-140
   Bourne versus C shell, 140-142
   definition, 149
   in aliases, 185
   in here documents, 143
   in shell scripts, 938
   multi-line, 139
   when to use, 144

R

rabbit ears (slang), 1014
rand function (nawk), 723
ranges, matching with wildcards, 17
raw input mode, 793
rcp, 37
RCS, 1035
   access lists, 375
   basics, 367-368
   changing version numbers, 374
   checking files in, 367, 369, 373
   checking files out, 367, 369
   ci command, 367, 373
   co command, 367
   directories, 371
   file management, 368-375
   files, 371
   identification strings, 372
   introduction, 365
   listing files currently checked out, 368
   options; –L, 373;
     –U, 368, 373
     –u, 371, 373
   rlog command, 368, 371
   states, 374
   strict-access mode, 373
   symbolic names, 374
   unlocking files, 368
   version log, 371
   version numbers, 369
rcsgrep script, 1035
read access, 29
   for directories, 31
read command, ex (r), 609
   ksh and sh, 884
   sed (r), 649
read permission, directory, 400
   introduction, 390
read-only filesystem, glossary definition, 1078
real time, reporting, 758
recomment script, 654-655, 1035
records, awk, 697
recursive, glossary definition, 1078
redirected I/O loops, 922, 925-926
   and debugging shell scripts, 938
redirecting, I/O, 35
redo script, 207, 207-208, 1035
reformatting paragraphs, 571
regular expressions, 471-490
   about, 471
   awk, 717
   beginning-of-line character, 475
   character sets, 476
   delimiters, 623
   end-of-line character, 475
   examples of, 479, 485
   excluding characters from search, 477
   extended, 475, 480
   how they work, 473-475
   limiting extent of matches, 484
   matching; any single character, 474;
     preceding characters, 474;
     range of characters, 477;
     specific number of sets, 478;

---

shell programming (cont'd)
  testing scripts from the command line, 879
  tips, 895
  (see also shell scripts.)
shell programs, and terminfo, 805-806
shell prompts, backspacing over, 800-801
  glossary definition, 1078
  (see prompts)
shell quoting, (see quoting)
shell scripts, about, 12
  accessing, 74
  and standard input, 926;
    on the fly, 926-927
  and subshells, 741
  command-line arguments in, 884;
    $#, 885;
    "$@", 884;
    for loops, 885-887;
    while loops, 885, 887-888
  control characters in, 935-936
  debugging, 937-938;
    missing braces, 938;
    missing parentheses, 938;
    quotes, 939;
    redirected loops, 938;
    saving output in files, 938;
    showing variable values, 939;
    unmatched code, 938;
    using echo command, 939
  deciding which commands to run next, 876
  definition of, 873
  ending, 881
  executing last command of, 902
  file permissions for, 409
  invisible screen output, 928
  limitations of, 180
  making sure they run with Bourne shell, 901
  multiple names for, 911-912
  passing arguments with multiple words,
    941-943
  putting sed and awk programs in, 710-711,
    711
  quotes in, 938
  setting exit status of, 881-882
  sourceable, 180
  testing from the command line, 879
  using for long commands, 160
  versus aliases, 180
  when not to use, 898
  writing simple, 871-872
shell sessions, running multiple, 218-219

shell variables, 99-110, 107
  ?, 110
  $ in front of, 108
  accomodating different, 53
  as aliases, 184
  cdpath, 108, 244
  changing values of in loops, 926
  complete, 109
  cshlevel, 117
  cwd, 109, 256
  displaying values of, 939
  echo, 109
  fignore, 109, 154
  filec, 109, 153
  hardpaths, 109, 256
  histchars, 109, 209
  history, 109
  IFS, 672
  ignoreeof, 109
  listing all, 107
  listing individual, 108
  mail, 109, 382
  MAIL, 383
  MAILCHECK, 384
  MAILPATH, 384
  nobeep, 153
  noclobber, 109
  noglob, 109, 262
  nonomatch, 109
  notify, 109, 216
  path, 105
  prompt, 109
  rmstar, 417
  savehist, 109, 202
  seeing which are set, 253
  setting, 107;
    operators for, 909;
    to hold pathnames, 244
  simulating Bourne shell functions, 186
  special C shell, 108
  status, 110
  testing (ksh and sh), 909;
    operators for, 909
  time, 110, 758, 758-760
  user, 109
  verbose, 109
  versus environment variables, 100, 107
shells, aliases, if-then-else, 183
  and wildcards, 20-21
  approved and unapproved, 55
  Bourne-again (bash), 10

striped filesystems, and system performance, 773

stripper script, 445, 1037

stty, 798, 1037
about, 792-798
canonicalized input lines, 794
carriage returns, 794
commands in .login files, 90
input parity checking, 794
introduction to, 791
keys to set with, 91
newline control, 794
options; –echo, 928;
–g, 822;
icanon, 794-795, 802;
inpchk, 794;
isig, 794;
ocrnl, 794;
opost, 794;
tabs, 800;
tostop, 216-217
output parity checking, 794
setting characters, 90
setting values for other serial ports, 801
signals, 794
size command, 825
system and terminal communication, 816

stuck login command, 87

su command, 410, 412, 1037
correcting HOME, 412
keeping current environment, 413
options; –, 414;
–e, 413;
–f, 413;
–username, 43
simulating full login to other accounts, 414
starting subshells, 742

su stucklogin command, 87

sub function (nawk), 701, 724

subdirectories, 76
and the find command, 299-300
glossary definition, 1079
listing, 272

subprocesses, 740
and size of parent environment, 765

SUBSEP variable (nawk), 718

subshells, 741-742
ending with exit command, 742
going back to parent shell, 741
setup information, 41
starting; from current shell, 741;

with shell escapes, 742;
with su command, 742

substitute command, 622
ex (s), 609
sed (s), 650

substitutions, awk, 701
history; (see history substitution)
in vi, 547
sed, 650
variable; (see variable substitutions)

substr function (awk), 724

subtraction operator (expr), 928

SUID bits, 29

SunOS, /etc directory, 249
storage of System V compatibility commands, 250

superuser, 30

susp character, setting, 91

suspend command, 411
stopping subprocesses, 741

suspend signal, 32

SVR4, glossary definition, 1079

swapping, 771
glossary definition, 1079

swaps, and csh time variable, 760
showing number of, 758

switch statement (csh), 959

switches, glossary definition, 1076

symbolic links, 327
and copying directories, 341
and current directories, 256
and directories on different filesystems, 258
and files with two or more names, 325-326
and shell variables, 109
creating, 328
directory, 330-331
finding unconnected, 293
invalid, 329
outdated, 329-330
relinking multiple, 337
showing actual filenames for, 331
to home directories, 255
versus hard links, 327

symbolic modes, chmod, 396

symlinks, 256
(see also symbolic links.)

sync, 15

synchronous transmission, 797

syntax, awk, 716
hackerese, 1014

syntax errors, in numeric tests, 940

The Power Tools Series

In addition to UNIX Power Tools, the following titles are in the Power Tools Series available:

- Clipper 5.2 Power Tools, ISBN 0-679-79307-3, 1300 pages, $39.95, 4x4 disks included, October 1993

- DOS Power Tools: Techniques, Tricks, and Utilities, ISBN 0-679-79274-3, 2nd ed., 1500 pages, 3½" disk included

- Norton Utilities Power Tools for Windows, ISBN 0-679-79000-7, 600 pages, 3½" disk included

- Pc Techniques C/C++ Power Tools: Tips, Techniques, and Hidden Knowledge, ISBN 0-679-79201-8, 600 pages, 3½" disk included

- Windows NT Power Tools, ISBN 0-679-79075-9, 1000 pages, 3½" disk included

- WordPerfect for Windows Power Tools, ISBN 0-679-79002-3, 900 pages, 3½" disk included

To order, call toll-free 1-800-733-3000.

RANDOM HOUSE ELECTRONIC PUBLISHING *The Power Tools® Series*

In addition to **UNIX Power Tools**,® the following titles in the Power Tools® Series are available:

- **Clipper® 5.2 Power Tools®** (ISBN 0-679-79072-1, 1200 pages, 1 3½" 1.44M diskette), available October 1993

- **DOS Power Tools**:® **Techniques, Tricks, and Utilities** (ISBN 0-679-79138-8, 768 pages, 2 5¼" 360K diskettes)

- **NetWare® Power Tools® for Windows** (ISBN 0-679-79099-3, 640 pages, 2 3½" 1.44M diskettes)

- *PC Techniques* **C/C++ Power Tools®: Hax, Techniques, and Hidden Knowledge** (ISBN 0-679-79126-4, 640 pages, 1 5¼" 1.2M diskette)

- **Windows™ 3.1 Power Tools®** (ISBN 0-679075-6, 1072 pages, 1 3½" 1.44M diskette)

- **WordPerfect® for Windows™ Power Tools®** (ISBN 0-679-79084-5, 992 pages, 2 5¼" 360K diskettes)

To order, call toll-free 1-800-733-3000.

About the Authors

Jerry Peek has used UNIX since the early 1980's. He has a B.S. in Electronic Engineering Technology from California Polytechnic State University, San Luis Obispo. At Syracuse University, Jerry was a user consultant for UNIX and VMS. At Tektronix, Inc., he was a UNIX course developer and trainer; a System Administrator of a VAX 11/780 running BSD UNIX; and a Bourne shell and C language job-shop programmer. Jerry is currently a writer for O'Reilly & Associates, Inc.

Tim O'Reilly is founder and president of O'Reilly & Associates, publisher of the X Window System series and the popular Nutshell Handbooks on UNIX. Tim has had a hand in writing or editing many of the books published by O'Reilly & Associates. He is also the author of a book about science-fiction writer Frank Herbert. Tim's long-term vision for the company is to create a vehicle where creative people can support themselves by exploring interesting ideas. Technical book publishing is just the first step. Tim graduated cum laude from Harvard in 1975 with a B.A. in Classics.

Mike Loukides is an editor for O'Reilly & Associates, with a focus on developing titles on UNIX utilities and system administration. He is the author of *System Performance Tuning* and *UNIX for FORTRAN Programmers*. Mike previously worked at Multiflow Computer, where he created all of Multiflow's documentation on programming languages. Mike's interests are system administration, networking, programming languages, and computer architecture. His academic background includes degrees in Electrical Engineering (B.S.) and English Literature (Ph.D.). He is also a passable pianist—in fact, one of the few amateur pianists who even tries to play music by Olivier Messiaen.

Colophon

Edie Freedman designed this cover, which was created using a Macintosh computer. The drill image was scanned from a photograph and retouched using Adobe PhotoShop software. The drill itself is a Miller's Falls "Dyno-Mite" Model A, circa 1950's.

Edie Freedman designed the page layout and the margin icons, which were created on a Macintosh computer and captured as encapsulated PostScript files. The icon graphics were bound to custom troff macros for formatting. Text was prepared using the SoftQuad sqtroff text formatter and the book was typeset from generated PostScript files in two passes to accomplish color separation. Lenny Muellner modified and developed the troff macros necessary to implement the book design, including cross-referencing and indexing.

The body text of the book is set in ITC Garamond typeface. The examples are set in Courier, Courier Bold, and Courier Italic typefaces. Headings and captions are set in Helvetica Bold Condensed Oblique typeface.

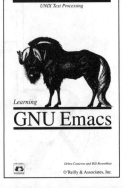

Volume 8: X Window System Administrator's Guide for X11 Release 4 and Release 5

By Linda Mui and Eric Pearce

As X moves out of the hacker's domain and into the "real world," users can't be expected to master all the ins and outs of setting up and administering their own X software. That will increasingly become the domain of system administrators. Even for experienced system administrators X raises many issues, both because of subtle changes in the standard UNIX way of doing things and because X blurs the boundaries between different platforms. Under X, users can run applications across the network, on systems with different resources (including fonts, colors, and screen size) than the applications were designed for originally. Many of these issues are poorly understood, and the technology for dealing with them is in rapid flux.

This book is the first and only book devoted to the issues of system administration for X and X-based networks, written not just for UNIX system administrators but for anyone faced with the job of administering X (including those running X on stand-alone workstations).

The book includes:

- An overview of X that focuses on issues that affect the system administrator's job.

- Information on obtaining, compiling, and installing the X software, including a discussion of the trade-offs between vendor-supplied and the free MIT versions of X.

- How to set up *xdm*, the X display manager, which takes the place of the login program under X and can be used to create a customized turnkey X session for each user.

- How to set up user accounts under X (includes a comparison of the familiar shell setup files and programs to the new mechanisms provided by X).

- Issues involved in making X more secure. X's security features are not strong, but an understanding of what features are available can be very important, since X makes it possible for users to intrude on each other in new and sometimes unexpected ways.

- How fonts are used by X, including a description of the font server.

- A discussion of the issues raised by running X on heterogenous networks.

- How colors are managed under X and how to get the same colors across multiple devices with different hardware characteristics.

- The administration issues involved in setting up and managing X terminals.

- How to use PC and Mac X servers to maximize reuse of existing hardware and convert outdated hardware into X terminals.

- How to obtain and install additional public domain software and patches for X.

- Features new in R5, including the font server and Xcms.

The *X Window System Administrator's Guide* is available either alone or packaged with the XCD.

The CD-ROM contains the source code for MIT's public domain X Window System. It contains pre-compiled binaries for popular platforms, and allows custom installation of the software from the CD-ROM. The CD includes:

- RockRidge CD-ROM drivers from Young Minds, so you can install the CD as a UNIX file system on several popular UNIX platforms.

- Complete MIT X11R5 "core" and "contrib" source code with fixes 1-21 applied to core.

- Complete MIT X11R4 "core" and "contrib" source code.

- Complete examples and source code for all the books in the O'Reilly X Window System Series.

- Programs and files that are discussed in Volume 8. These were previously available only to administrators with Internet access.

- Pre-compiled X11 Release 5 "core" binaries for Sun3, Sun4, DECstation and IBM RS6000 platforms.

372 pages
Without CD-ROM: ISBN 0-937175-83-8
With CD-ROM: ISBN 1-56592-052-X

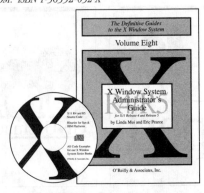

The Definitive Guides to the X Window System
Volume Eight

X Window System Administrator's Guide
for X11 Release 4 and Release 5
by Linda Mui and Eric Pearce

O'Reilly & Associates, Inc.

X11 R4 and R5 Source Code
Binaries for Sun & IBM Platforms
All Code Examples for our X Window System Series Books

HOW TO GET POWER TOOLS SOFTWARE ON ALTERNATE MEDIA

For those people unable to read the CD-ROM, Ready-to-Run Software can provide the Power Tools software on alternate media such as floppies, QIC, 8 mm, 4mm or DEC TK50 tape cartridges. Obviously, some of these media are appropriate only for certain platforms.

Because of the large volume of data on the CD, each tape/floppy package is for a single platform. In addition, for the floppy distributions, source and binaries are treated as separate packages, as are the bitmaps for use with For QIC-24 (60 megabyte tape). We've also had to separate the bitmaps from the source and executables for the Power Tools software.

Please specify your choice of the following:

SCO UNIX	SCO XENIX
Sun-4 Sparc	Sun-3
IBM RS/6000	DECstation
HP-9000 series 700	

Prices are as follows:

PACKAGE	PRICE
3.5" floppies executables (SCO UNIX or XENIX only)	$39.95
3.5" floppies SOURCE (SCO UNIX or XENIX only)	$39.95
3.5" floppies bitmaps (SCO UNIX or XENIX only)	$39.95
5.25" floppies executables (SCO UNIX or XENIX only)	$39.95
5.25" floppies SOURCE (SCO UNIX or XENIX only)	$39.95
5.25" floppies bitmaps (SCO UNIX or XENIX only)	$39.95
QIC-150	$39.95
QIC-24 source and executables	$39.95
QIC-24 bitmaps	$39.95
8MM	$39.95
4MM	$39.95
TK50	$54.95

Order tapes or floppies from:

READY-TO-RUN SOFTWARE, INC.

Rustic Trail • Groton, MA 01450

(508) 448.3959

Fax/modem (508) 448.2989 • e-mail: info@rtr.com

We also provide installation support. Please see article 54.09 for details.